EYEWITN...
CALIFORNIA

LONDON, NEW YORK,
MELBOURNE, MUNICH AND DELHI
www.dk.com

Produced by Duncan Baird Publishers, London, England

MANAGING ART EDITOR Clare Sullivan
EDITORS Slaney Begley, Joanne Levêque, Zoë Ross
EDITORIAL ASSISTANT Leo Hollis
DESIGNERS Christine Keilty, Susan Knight, Jill Mumford, Alison Verity

MAIN CONTRIBUTORS Jamie Jensen, Barry Parr,
Ellen Payne, J Kingston Pierce, Rebecca Poole Forée,
Nigel Tisdall, John Wilcock, Stanley Young

PHOTOGRAPHERS
Max Alexander, Peter Anderson, John Heseltine, Dave King,
Neil Lukas, Andrew McKinney, Neil Setchfield

PICTURE RESEARCH Lindsay Hunt

ILLUSTRATORS
Arcana Studios, Joanna Cameron, Stephen Conlin,
Dean Entwhistle, Nick Lipscombe, Lee Peters, Robbie Polley,
Kevin Robinson, John Woodcock

REPRODUCED BY Colourscan (Singapore)
PRINTED AND BOUND BY South China Printing Co., Ltd., China

First American Edition, 1997
06 07 08 09 10 9 8 7 6 5 4 3 2 1

Published in the United States by
DK Publishing, Inc., 375 Hudson Street,
New York, New York 10014

**Reprinted with revisions 1999, 2000, 2001, 2002,
2003, 2004, 2005, 2006**

Copyright © 1997, 2006 Dorling Kindersley Limited, London

Published in Great Britain by Dorling Kindersley Limited.

A CATALOGING IN PUBLICATION RECORD IS AVAILABLE FROM THE
LIBRARY OF CONGRESS.

ISSN 1542-1554
ISBN 0-75661-531-3
ISBN 978-0-75661-531-4

Front cover main image: Hollywood sign, Hollywood, California

**The information in this
DK Eyewitness Travel Guide is checked regularly.**

Every effort has been made to ensure that this book is as up-to-
date as possible at the time of going to press. Some details,
however, such as telephone numbers, opening hours, prices,
gallery hanging arrangements and travel information are liable to
change. The publishers cannot accept responsibility for any
consequences arising from the use of this book, nor for any material
on third party websites, and cannot guarantee that any website
address in this book will be a suitable source of travel information.
We value the views and suggestions of our readers very highly.
Please write to: Publisher, DK Eyewitness Travel Guides,
Dorling Kindersley, 80 Strand, London WC2R 0RL, Great Britain.

CONTENTS

Volleyball on Pismo Beach

LOS ANGELES

Half Dome in Yosemite National Park

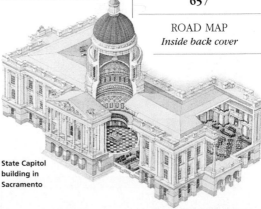

State Capitol
building in
Sacramento

HOW TO USE THIS GUIDE

This guide helps you to get the most from your stay in California. *Introducing California* maps the whole state and sets it in its historical and cultural context. The ten regional chapters, plus *Los Angeles* and *San Francisco and the Bay Area*, describe important sights with maps, pictures, and illustrations, as well as introductory features on subjects of regional interest.

Suggestions on restaurants, accommodations, shopping, and entertainment are in *Travelers' Needs*. The *Survival Guide* has tips on getting around the state. LA, San Francisco, and San Diego have their own *Practical Information* sections.

LOS ANGELES AND SAN FRANCISCO AND THE BAY AREA

The centers of the two major cities have been divided into a number of sightseeing areas. Each area has its own chapter that opens with a list of the sights described. All the sights are numbered and plotted on an *Area Map*. Information on each sight is easy to locate within the chapter as it follows the numerical order on the map.

Sights at a Glance lists the chapter's sights by category: Historic Streets and Buildings, Shops, Modern Architecture, etc.

A locator map shows where you are in relation to other areas of the city center.

All pages relating to Los Angeles have lilac thumb tabs. San Francisco pages have grass-green thumb tabs.

1 Area Map
For easy reference, the sights are numbered and located on a map. The sights are also shown on the Los Angeles Street Finder (see pp182–93) or the San Francisco Street Finder (see pp400–9).

2 Street-by-Street Map
This gives a bird's-eye view of the heart of each sightseeing area.

A suggested route for a walk covers the more interesting streets in the area.

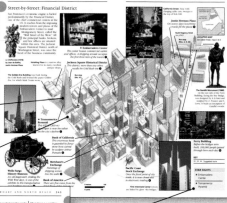

Stars indicate sights that no visitor should miss.

3 Detailed Information on Each Sight
All the sights in Los Angeles and in San Francisco and the Bay Area are described individually. Addresses and practical information are provided. The key to the symbols used in the information block is shown on the back flap.

Story boxes explore specific subjects in more detail.

SOUTH CENTRAL CALIFORNIA

1 Introduction
The landscape, history, and character of each region is described here, showing how the area has developed over the centuries and what it offers to the visitor today.

NORTHERN CALIFORNIA AND SOUTHERN CALIFORNIA
Apart from San Francisco and the Bay Area and Los Angeles, California has been divided into two regions (Northern and Southern California), each of which has five separate area chapters. The most interesting towns and places to visit are numbered on a *Regional Map* at the beginning of each chapter.

Exploring South Central California

Each area of California can be identified quickly by its own color coding, which is shown on the inside front cover.

2 Regional Map
This shows the main road network and gives an illustrated overview of the whole area. All entries are numbered, and there are also useful tips on getting around the region.

3 Detailed Information
All the important towns and other places to visit are described individually. They are listed in order, following the numbering on the Regional Map. Within each entry, information is given on the most important sights. A map reference refers the reader to the road map inside the back cover.

Santa Barbara Mission

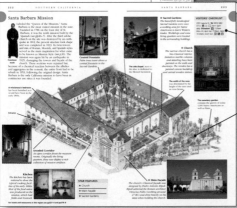

For all the top sights, a visitors' checklist provides the practical information you need to plan your visit.

4 California's Top Sights
These are given two or more full pages. Historic buildings are dissected to reveal their interiors; museums and galleries have color-coded floor plans to help you locate the most interesting exhibits; national parks and forests have maps showing facilities and trails.

INTRODUCING
CALIFORNIA

DISCOVERING CALIFORNIA

California is a land of breath-taking extremes. Its rugged, redwood-covered bluffs, idyllic sun-drenched sands, soaring granite cliffs, and snow-capped peaks have inspired generations of artists, athletes, and explorers. Since the 1840s Gold Rush, the state has exerted great cultural and political influence. A lifetime could be spent discovering every unique town and temperament, so the following pages give a taste of the 12 distinct regions to help you determine which aspects are of most interest.

Hollywood's Walk of fame

Mann's Chinese Theatre, one of Hollywood's most famous landmarks

LOS ANGELES

- Hollywood landmarks
- Fantastic art collections
- Vibrant Downtown

Los Angeles is a city of paradoxes. The same place that spawned the commercial Hollywood **Walk of Fame** *(see p111)* and **Sunset Strip** *(see pp102–104)* also accommodates **Griffith Park** *(see pp150–51)*, the largest urban wilderness in the US. An identity rooted in the film industry belies one of the greatest concentration of museums in the world, including the **J Paul Getty Museum at the Getty Center** *(see pp82–5)*, the **Los Angeles County Museum of Art** *(see pp114–7)*, and the **Huntington Library, Art Collections, and Botanical Gardens** *(see pp158–61)*. Visitors can experience the glamour of the movie industry by taking a tour of one of the major studios in **Burbank** *(see pp144–5)*, or

of **Universal Studios** *(see pp146–7)*. Downtown LA's resurgence is evident in the undulating forms of Frank Gehry's Disney Theatre at the **Music Center** *(see p125)* as much as in the bustling stands of the **Grand Central Market** *(see p124)*. Beach communities such as those in **Venice** *(see p80)*, **Santa Monica** *(see pp76–9)*, and **Malibu** *(see pp86–7)* delight with their distinctiveness.

Marine life abounds on the coast of South Central California

SOUTH CENTRAL CALIFORNIA

- Palatial Hearst Castle
- Whale watching
- Santa Ynez wineries

Massive hills define this rugged region, forming an imposing backdrop to the bohemian, handsome city of **Santa Barbara** *(see pp220–23)* to the south, and enhancing the jaw-dropping grandeur of fairytale **Hearst Castle** *(see pp212–5)* to the north. **Ojai** *(see p225)* is a favored getaway among the Hollywood elite for spa treatments and spiritual-wellness retreats. Marine biology buffs flock to **Channel Islands National Park** *(see p224)* for their remoteness and favorable odds for seeing gray whale pods, while at **Los Padres National Forest** *(see p225)* visitors may spot a condor patrolling the park's almost perennially cloudless skies.

Toward the coast, take a tour of one of the many wineries of the **Santa Ynez Valley** *(see p218)*. Winemakers in this region take advantage of the more temperate climate to produce famed and distinctive wines.

ORANGE COUNTY

- Wealthy seaside villages
- Legendary Disneyland
- Catalina Island

The profile of Los Angeles' sprawling southern neighbor has risen dramatically since Walt Disney's vision of a magic kingdom blossomed in 1955, and Orange County now counts some of the world's richest individuals among its handsome beach communities and rustic mountainside ranches. The world-famous, original **Disneyland® Resort** *(see pp232–5)* enchants children of all ages, and neighboring **Knott's Berry Farm and Soak City USA** *(see pp236–7)* pick up where Disney's more forgiving thrill rides leave off. Along the **Orange County Coastline** *(see pp230–31)*, places such as Laguna, Newport, and Huntington State Beach bear the distinctive Orange County hallmarks of surf, beach volleyball, stellar seafood, and stunning beachfront homes. Offshore, charming **Catalina Island** *(see pp242–3)* beckons weekenders from the bustle of Los Angeles with promises of pristine sands, fair breezes, and quaint harbors.

The enchanting façade of Mission San Luis Rey, San Diego County

Surfers riding waves along the Orange County coastline

SAN DIEGO COUNTY

- **Mission architecture**
- **San Diego Zoo and the Gaslamp Quarter**
- **La Jolla**

Located close to the busiest border crossing in the world at **Tijuana** *(see p265)*, **San Diego** *(see pp250–59)* offers an irresistible study in contrasts. In 1769, the first Franciscan mission of 21 in California, **Mission San Diego de Alacalà** *(see pp260–61)*, was founded here, marking

the city as a historic colonial center. **Mission San Luis Rey** *(see pp262–3)* is a striking example of Mission Architecture. In 1915, the Panama-Pacific Expo, held at **Balboa Park** *(see pp256–9)*, ushered in impressive public works such as the world-renowned **San Diego Zoo** *(see pp256–9)*, and Spanish-Colonial style pavilions. Next to the city's gleaming, modern Financial District, the **Gaslamp Quarter** *(see pp252–3)* preserves many Victorian-era buildings, housing excellent bars, cafés, and restaurants. On the city's outskirts, seaside hamlet **La Jolla** *(see p261)* ranks among the wealthiest, most exclusive communities in the US. Also, given the region's ideal climate, San Diego County is a sports enthusiast's paradise, with fantastic hiking trails in **Cuyamaca Rancho State Park** *(see p264)*, while **Mission Bay** *(see pp260–61)* offers every watersport conceivable.

INLAND EMPIRE & LOW DESERT

- **San Bernardino mountains**
- **Palm Springs and Riverside**
- **Joshua Tree National Park**

The Inland Empire and Low Desert offer city-weary Angelenos and San Diegans readily accessible outdoor recreation. With some of the most varied climates and topography in the state, one can remove tire chains from

a ski trip in the stunning **San Bernardino Mountains** *(see p272)* just one hour before tee time on the golf courses outside historic **Riverside** *(see p273)*. To the south in Coachella Valley, **Palm Springs** *(see pp274–6)* has a reputation as the state's de facto retirement community. It is far from dull, however, with first-rate luxury shopping on Palm Drive, renowned health spas, and, in neighboring Indio, an annual rock music festival with magnificent line-ups. Legendary **Joshua Tree National Park** *(see pp278–9)* presents a distinctive landscape, with undulating rock formations, palm-ringed oases, tumble-weeds, and groves of the contorted, ancient joshua trees that give the park its name.

Rugged desert dunes near Palm Springs

The unique and isolated beauty of Death Valley National Park

MOJAVE DESERT

- **Death Valley**
- **London Bridge and Las Vegas**
- **Edwards Air Force Base and Aeronautics Center**

Over 90 years have passed since the all-time highest temperature in US history was recorded in the Mojave Desert, yet today, in tourism terms, the expanse of arid land west of **Las Vegas** *(see p289)* is hotter than ever. **Death Valley National Park** *(see pp290–93)* earns its name with the hottest mean temperature on earth. Visitors can take in Stovepipe Wells' mesmerizing sand dunes, the sub-sea-level altitudes of Badwater, sweeping desert panoramas from Dante's View, or opt for the climate-controlled confines of the mirage-like Scotty's Castle. Other incongruous delights include the original London Bridge spanning manmade **Lake Havasu** *(see p288)*, and the unrepentant glitz of nearby Las Vegas, rising from the desert floor. **Edwards Air Force Base** *(see p284)* completes this otherworldly landscape, allowing visitors to learn about the country's space program.

SAN FRANCISCO & THE BAY AREA

- **Legendary Golden Gate Bridge**
- **Gay and Lesbian scene**
- **Marin Headlands**

The Bay Area is a dynamic, unpredictable environment where chilling fog yields to brilliant sunshine in a matter of minutes, architecture responds to landscape in creative, sometimes stubborn ways, and where an active seismic fault line is never far. Yet despite its occasionally volatile character, this region nurtures one of the world's great cities, San Francisco. Landmarks such as the **Golden Gate Bridge** *(see pp380–81)*, the junction of **Haight Ashbury** *(see p358)*, and the **Transamerica Pyramid** *(see p315)* are emblems of the city's myriad lifestyles. Vibrant enclaves include Italian North Beach, the Mexican-American Mission District, Chinatown, and the Castro, center of the thriving gay community. Off the peninsula, visit **Oakland** *(see pp422–5)*, windswept **Point Reyes National Seashore** *(see p414)*, and the **Marin Headlands** *(see pp416–7)*.

Steaming, sulfurous pools, Lassen Volcanic National Park

THE NORTH

- **Rugged Lost Coast**
- **Redwood National Park**
- **Towering Mount Shasta and Mount Lassen**

A realm of heavily wooded, desolate coastline, and primordial, volcanic mountain ranges, the North offers some of California's most varied, yet least visited, terrain. North of Cape Mendocino are the isolated rocky beaches and excellent hiking trails of the **Lost Coast** *(see p449)*. Further north, **Redwood National Park** *(see pp448–9)* protects one of the world's largest remaining old-growth redwood stands. The logging legacy of the North can be experienced in rural, personable towns such as **Weaverville** *(see p449)* and **Eureka** *(see p446)*. The imposing snow-covered peak of **Mount Shasta** *(see p452)*, and dramatic **Lassen Volcanic National Park** *(see p453)* are magnets for avid hikers. Glimpses of Lassen's fiery origins can be seen in the vast network of lava tubes and crystal-filled caves at **Lava Beds National Monument** *(see p453)*.

Dazzling views across San Francisco Bay

WINE COUNTRY

- **Napa Valley wine tastings**
- **Hot springs at Calistoga**
- **Delightful Mendocino**

Vineyards in the Napa Valley, famous for wineries

The soil, climate, and groundwater conditions of this rolling landscape provide for North America's premium winemaking region, founded in **Sonoma Valley** *(see pp464–5)*. The heart of the industry lies in the scenic and internationally renowned **Napa Valley** *(see pp462–3)*, home to more than 250 wineries; tastings and tours here are readily available. Stop nearby at the hot springs in **Calistoga** *(see p461)* for a relaxing volcanic mud bath or spa treatment.

The legacy of New England shipbuilders and fishermen who settled in California in the 19th century can be seen in the charming and quaint residences, galleries, and bed and breakfasts in **Mendocino** *(see p442)*. The coastline here is fantastic for bird- and whale-watching.

GOLD COUNTRY & THE CENTRAL VALLEY

- **Gold Rush-era towns**
- **Native American village re-creations**
- **Historic Sacramento**

In 1848, amid the heavily wooded Sierra foothills, James Marshall discovered gold flakes on his employer's land. The ensuing **Gold Rush** *(see pp48–9)* forever transformed California. Boom towns that survived after the Mother Lode had been completely depleted, include impeccably preserved and picturesque **Columbia State Historic Park** *(see pp480–81)*, and **Jackson** *(see p477)*, a thriving gateway town to the Sierras.

Northeast of Jackson, the fascinating **Chaw'se Indian Grinding Rock State Historic Park** *(see p477)* re-creates a pre-European-encounter Miwok village. To the west,

Sutter Creek *(see pp476–7)* is a delightful Gold Country town to stop at on the way to **Sacramento** *(see pp472–5)*, California's capital city. Highlights here include the grand State Capitol building with its striking rotunda, as well as a network of historic structures that line the waterfront of the well preserved old district.

Soaring granite peaks, Yosemite National Park

THE HIGH SIERRAS

- **Staggering natural wonders**
- **Yosemite and Lake Tahoe**
- **Lively Stateline casinos**

The High Sierras boast some of the country's most superlative natural wonders from **Mount Whitney** *(see p495)*, the highest peak on the US mainland, to the breathtaking **Sequoia and Kings Canyon National Parks** *(see pp496–7)*, whose giant sequoia trees are the world's largest living organisms

above sea level. The high camps of **Yosemite National Park** *(see pp488–91)* remain pristine, little-known gems. To the north, **Lake Tahoe** *(see pp486–7)*, the country's second deepest lake, sparkles year round, as do Stateline's gaudy casinos on its southern shore. Winter-sports enthusiasts flock here to ski and snowboard on the surrounding peaks, and watersports on the lake itself include fishing, kite surfing, canoeing, and scuba diving.

NORTH CENTRAL CALIFORNIA

- **Bohemian Santa Cruz**
- **Enchanting Monterey**
- **Magnificent Carmel Mission**

Rocky beachside bluffs, serene harbors, and hillside, Spanish missions define this unspoiled region. Visit inspiring seaside cliffs and secret waterfalls in **Big Sur** *(see pp514–5)*. Enjoy the bohemian café-bookstore culture in downtown **Santa Cruz** *(see pp506–7)*. The original capital of California, **Monterey** *(see pp508–11)* has the country's largest aquarium, and a fish-packing district made infamous by John Steinbeck's 1945 novel *Cannery Row*. Just south, in the hills surrounding Carmel, Father Junípero Serra founded the delightful **Carmel Mission** *(see pp512–3)*, one of California's most beautiful churches.

Putting California on the Map

California is the third largest state in the US (after Texas and Alaska) and, with over 30 million people, the most populous. Situated on the Pacific Coast, it is 800 miles (1,300 km) long and 250 miles (400 km) wide, covering an area of 158,710 sq miles (411,060 sq km). The state has two major cities: San Francisco and Los Angeles. Most visitors arrive via the airports in one of these cities; the main cities and towns are linked with each other and with other states by an extensive rail (Amtrak) and road system.

Downtown Los Angeles at dawn

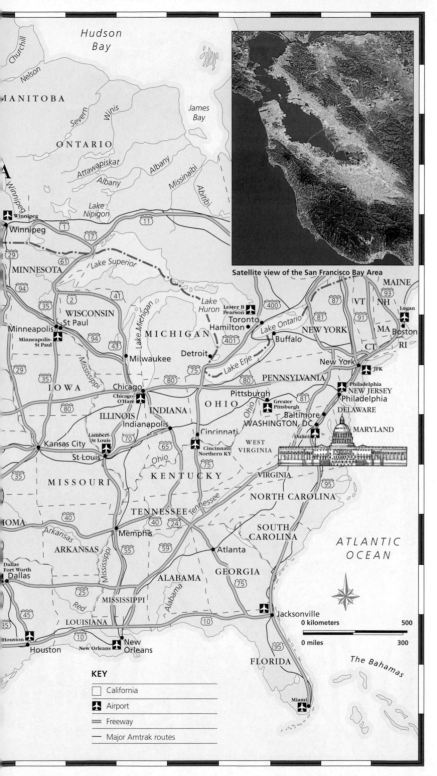

Satellite view of the San Francisco Bay Area

Hudson Bay

Churchill

Nelson

MANITOBA

Severn

Winis

Albany

James Bay

ONTARIO

Attawapiskat

Albany

Missinaibi

Abitibi

Winnipeg

Lake Nipigon

Winnipeg

MINNESOTA

Lake Superior

Lake Huron

Lester B Pearson

Toronto

Hamilton

Lake Ontario

NEW YORK

Buffalo

MAINE

Logan

VT   NH

MA   Boston

WISCONSIN

St Paul

MICHIGAN

Minneapolis

Minneapolis-St Paul

Milwaukee

Detroit

Lake Erie

CT   RI

New York

JFK

IOWA

Mississippi

Chicago

Chicago-O'Hare

INDIANA

Indianapolis

OHIO

Pittsburgh

Ohio

Greater Pittsburgh

PENNSYLVANIA

Philadelphia

NEW JERSEY

Philadelphia

DELAWARE

ILLINOIS

Lambert-St Louis

Cincinnati

Cincinnati Northern KY

WASHINGTON, DC

Baltimore

Dulles

MARYLAND

Kansas City

St Louis

Ohio

KENTUCKY

WEST VIRGINIA

VIRGINIA

MISSOURI

Tennessee

NORTH CAROLINA

OMA

Arkansas

TENNESSEE

Memphis

SOUTH CAROLINA

ATLANTIC OCEAN

ARKANSAS

Mississippi

Atlanta

Dallas Fort Worth

Dallas

ALABAMA

GEORGIA

Red

Alabama

MISSISSIPPI

Jacksonville

0 kilometers   500

LOUISIANA

Houston

Houston

New Orleans

New Orleans

0 miles   300

FLORIDA

The Bahamas

Miami

KEY

California

Airport

Freeway

Major Amtrak routes

A PORTRAIT OF CALIFORNIA

*I*mpressive for both its size and its sway over modern culture, California symbolizes the United States' diversity and sense of prosperity. Here can be found towering forests, deserts within half a day's drive of ocean beaches, and two of the world's foremost cities, San Francisco and Los Angeles.

Perceptions of California vary so greatly that some now joke that there are two states. The first is geographic: California is the third-largest state in the Union (after Alaska and Texas), con-taining its largest county, San Bernardino, which covers 20,155 sq miles (52,200 sq km) – larger than Vermont and New Hampshire combined. This California has 840 miles (1,350 km) of coastline and measures 365 miles (587 km) at its widest point. It claims the second highest peak in the coun-try (Mount Whitney) and its lowest expanse of dry land (Death Valley). More than 1,500 plant species grow here that cannot be found anywhere else on earth.

State seal

Roughly one in every eight Americans is a Californian, making this the most populous of the 50 states, represented by the largest congressional delegation.

And that other California? It is a realm of romance, formed by flickering celluloid images. Think "California" and pictures are imme-diately conjured up of bikini-clad beachcombers, middle-class subur-ban families in ranch houses, and film stars emerging from limousines into hordes of autograph-seekers. These stereotypes are perpetuated by the entertainment and tourism media.

Hollywood is only partly to blame for this blurring of fact and fiction. It goes back to Spanish legends of an exotic outpost called California, flung

Sun-worshipers on Manhattan Beach, Los Angeles

◁ Roller coaster at Knott's Berry Farm, Orange County

Joshua Tree National Park

out at the edge of the sea. Most of the world, though, knew nothing of this spot until the Gold Rush of 1849. Tales of the riches to be found encouraged thousands of would-be Croesuses to invade the region. Whether they found their fortunes or not, prospectors spread the same message: California was not as colorful or seductive as they had been told. It was even more so.

SOCIETY AND POLITICS

If the US as a whole is a melting pot of people, California is an ethnic microcosm. It receives the hig-hest number of immigrants (more than 200,000 annu-ally), and the racial make- up is the most diverse in the nation. The percentage of whites and African-Americans is lower than the national average, but the Asian residency is more than triple the national level. Hispanics account for more than a quarter of all Californians – three times the US average. Walk through any of the four most-populated cities

Surfer

(LA, San Diego, San Jose, and San Francisco), and you receive an immediate taste of this ethnic cocktail. It is still more potent during Mexican *Cinco de Mayo* (May 5) festivities, Chinese New Year bashes, and other multicultural events held around the state.

Racial prejudice has plagued the state since its early days. Abolitionists prevented California's 1849 constitutional convention from barring the entry of blacks into this land, but in the 1870s nativist orators such as Denis Kearney endorsed violence against Chinese immigrants, said to be "stealing" white jobs. Sadly, overcrowding is reigniting racial tensions today, with over-population having a negative effect on law enforcement and education. It is raising the already high student–teacher ratios in California's schools, which have been short of funding since property taxes, a source of revenue for state and local governments, were cut and capped in 1978.

But the most inevitable result of population growth has been an altered balance between rural and urban sectors. More people means that more land is needed for housing. The value of California's

Golden Gate Bridge, San Francisco

Red Rock Canyon in the Mojave Desert

agricultural goods still outranks that of all other states, but its farmland has declined steadily since the 1950s. Lumber workers have also had a hard time, because of con-servation measures and a continuing shrinkage of the state's forests. The fastest-expanding job markets now are in service industries and high technology, which suggest a more metropolitan than pastoral future. Visitors usually come to California to see one of two cities: San Francisco or Los Angeles. In the north and south of the state respectively, these cities define the opposing sides of its character: San Francisco is older and more compact. Although California in general is recognized for its eccentricities and is still the birthplace of new trends, San Francisco is particularly proud of its nonconformity and open-mindedness. It was here that the "Big Four" railroad barons built their millionaire's mansions, but the city has since evolved into a pro-labor hotbed, with a history of activism (the Bay Area was a hub of the anti-Vietnam War movement). It also

California oranges

has one of the world's largest concentrations of gays and lesbians, with a substantial gay vote.

In contrast to San Francisco, LA is a sprawling city without a real focal point. The car rules, demanding a network of freeways that have hemmed in some of the city's historical buildings and which grind to smoggy standstills during rush hours. The façades of wealth, fame, and glamour leave LA as a dimensionless creation of bright lights and conservative politics.

Wild poppies in Antelope Valley

This is not to say that the north is entirely Democrat (left wing) and the south, Republican (right wing). Hollywood is a chief sponsor of liberal causes, and there are pockets of antigovernment rebels in the northeast. But the conflicting power that the two cities exert on state government in Sacramento and the state's representatives in Washington, DC explains why California may appear a little schizophrenic.

Poster for *LA Story* (1991)

McLaughlin and Elmer Bischoff, and ceramists Peter Voulkos and Robert Arneson have all made international reputations. So have a few pioneers of photographic art, such as Imogen Cunningham and Ansel Adams. British artist David Hockney lived here for many years, capturing the state's sun-soaked image on canvas. California is also home to some of the world's finest art museums, including LACMA, the Oakland Museum, the San Francisco MOMA, and the two J Paul Getty Museums.

CULTURE AND LEISURE

High- and low-brow art enjoy comparable support here. For most people, the state's contributions to culture are the many blockbusters made by Hollywood movie studios or televised sitcoms shot on LA sound stages. This is art in unashamed pursuit of the almighty dollar, complete with tabloid scandals and giant movie billboards blotting out the Los Angeles sun. But another creativity reveals itself through the state's history of landscape painting, portraiture, and 20th-century avant-garde art. Modern artists John

Victorian architecture in the Bay Area has always been a major tourist attraction, as have the many historic buildings across the state designed by Californians such as Willis Polk and Bernard Maybeck. Visiting designers Frank Lloyd Wright and Daniel Burnham have left their

Al Pacino receiving an Academy Award in 1993

Napa Valley Train in Wine Country

El Capitán in Yosemite National Park

mark here, too. Recent influential architects include residents Frank Gehry and Joe Esherick.

The state has seen many writers over the years, including Nobel prize-winner John Steinbeck and Beat authors Jack Kerouac and Allen Ginsburg. The tradition continues with Armistead Maupin *(Tales of the City)*, detective novelist Sue Grafton, and Amy Tan *(The Joy Luck Club)*, among others. Music also plays a major role, whether the work of the cities' orchestras or rock musicians. This is where the Beach Boys, Janis Joplin, the Grateful Dead, and Red Hot Chili Peppers launched their careers.

Californians love to eat out, and chefs Wolfgang Puck and Alice Waters have made their name promoting "California cuisine" – a blend of local ingredients and Asian techniques. This, combined with a selection of local world-class wines, is proof that Californians take care of their palates. Yet residents are also body-conscious, aware that they live among the "beautiful people" who come here with dreams of film stardom. So they become slaves to the gym or take up a sport. On any weekend, in various parts of the state, you will see cyclists, surfers, in-line skaters, even white-water rafters. Californians are eager supporters of professional baseball and football, but they like to be active themselves. Luckily, surrounded by some of the nation's most beautiful countryside and the gentlest climate, they don't have to go far to enjoy a satisfying outdoor experience.

Padres baseball stadium in San Diego

California's Landscape and Geology

California's dramatic landscape includes the highest point in the US, Mount Whitney in the High Sierras, and the lowest, Death Valley in the southern deserts. Millions of years ago, subduction of the Pacific Ocean floor beneath the North American Plate created the Coastal Range, the Central Valley, and the granitic rocks of the Sierra Nevada Mountains. Later, the granites were uplifted and tilted westward. The meeting of tectonic plates, now a lateral movement along the San Andreas Fault, is still changing the shape of California.

The Coastal Range *along the Pacific Coast was created around 25 million years ago, when fragments of the ocean floor and oceanic islands were pushed up by plate movements.*

HOW THE WEST WAS MADE

Over a period of 150 million years, ending about 15 million years ago, the movement of the Pacific Plate and North American Plate formed the western margin of California.

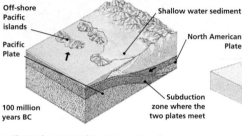

Off-shore Pacific islands

Shallow water sediment

Pacific Plate

North American Plate

Subduction zone where the two plates meet

100 million years BC

1 The North American Plate, moving westward, sweeps up any off-shore islands.

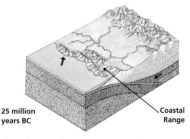

25 million years BC

Coastal Range

2 As the ocean floor moves north, the fragments of off-shore islands are scattered along the coast. They are then pushed up to form the Coastal Range.

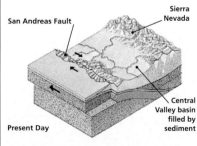

San Andreas Fault

Sierra Nevada

Central Valley basin filled by sediment

Present Day

3 The boundary between the North American Plate and the Pacific Plate is marked by the San Andreas Fault *(see pp24–5).*

MOUNT SHASTA 14,162 ft (4,317 m)

Mount Lassen (see p453) *and Mount Shasta (see p452) are part of the Cascades, a range of extinct and active volcanoes (including Mount St. Helens) created by a subduction zone beneath the northwestern corner of the North American Plate. Both Mount Lassen and Mount Shasta are still considered active. When young, the Sierra Nevada range must have resembled the Cascades.*

Lemon trees *flourish in central California. The highly fertile surface sediments of the flat Central Valley come from erosion of the surrounding mountains. The sediments have accumulated over the last few hundred thousand years.*

Mount Whitney (see p495) *in the High Sierras is the highest point in the continental United States, rising to 14,494 ft (4,418 m). The process that raised the Sierra Nevada Mountains began more than 50 million years ago, but peaked a few million years ago.*

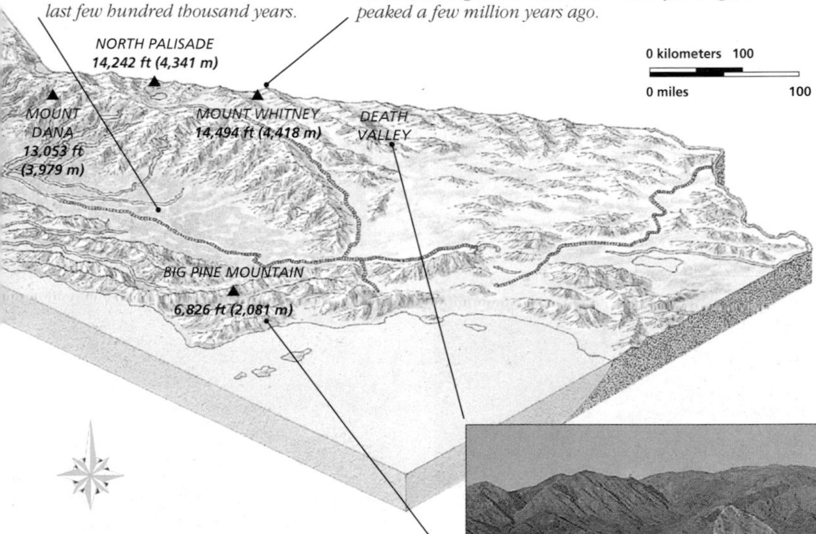

NORTH PALISADE
14,242 ft (4,341 m)

MOUNT
DANA
13,053 ft
(3,979 m)

MOUNT WHITNEY
14,494 ft (4,418 m)

DEATH
VALLEY

BIG PINE MOUNTAIN

6,826 ft (2,081 m)

0 kilometers   100

0 miles   100

Oil wells *sprang up at a frantic pace when oil was discovered in California. The drilling was so intense that the extraction of oil and gas deflated the land. Part of Los Angeles County subsided 28 ft (8.5 m) before oil companies were required to pump sea water down the wells to replace the extracted fuels.*

Death Valley (see pp290–3) *in the Mojave Desert has extreme height variations. Surrounded by some of the highest mountains on the continent, the valley floor lies 280 ft (85 m) below sea level. Death Valley was formed less than 15 million years ago when the North American Plate began to stretch due to the northwest drag created by the Pacific Plate.*

California's Earthquakes

The San Andreas Fault extends almost the full length of California, some 600 miles (965 km) from the Gulf of California northwest to Cape Mendocino. It is not the only fault in California but is the line of most activity. Each year, on average, the Pacific Plate moves 1–1.6 inches (2.5–4 cm) to the northwest. Earthquakes occur when this movement is resisted. Stresses build up and eventually they are released, causing an earthquake. Many of California's major earthquakes have occurred in the northern section of the fault. The terrible fire of 1906 that destroyed San Francisco was caused by an earthquake estimated at 7.8 on the Richter Scale. More recently, the earthquake of October 1989, south of San Francisco, killed 62 people and caused at least $6 billion worth of damage *(see p505)*. In 1994, the Northridge quake, magnitude R6.7, rocked Los Angeles and was felt in Las Vegas, Nevada. Scientists now predict that the next major earthquake, the "Big One," will hit Southern California.

The San Andreas Fault *is one of the few sites on earth where an active plate boundary occurs on land.*

Hayward Fault

1989 earthquake epicenter

1989 earthquake hypocenter

The 1906 earthquake *confounded contemporary geologists and led to the "elastic rebound" theory of earthquake formation, which is still in use today.*

The 1989 earthquake *struck the Santa Cruz Mountains in central California.*

TIMELINE

1769 Members of Portolá's expedition are first Europeans to experience an earthquake in California

1865 San Francisco hit by its first major earthquake on October 9 and another on October 23

1872 Town of Lone Pine is destroyed and Sierra Nevada Mountains rise 13 ft (4m)

1952 Kern County (R7.7)

1992 Yucca Valley outside LA (R7.4)

1940 Imperial Valley (R7.1)

1989 Loma Prieta (R7.1) strikes San Francisco area

1750	1800	1850	1900	1950

Don Gaspar de Portolá

1857 Fort Tejon (R8) is followed by smaller earth tremors in Bay Area

1906 San Francisco earthquake (R7.8) causes a devastating three-day fire that leaves 3,000 dead and 250,000 homeless

1994 Northridge (R6.7). At least 56 people killed, more than 7,000 injured, and 20,000 made homeless. Anaheim Stadium and several Los Angeles freeways are badly damaged

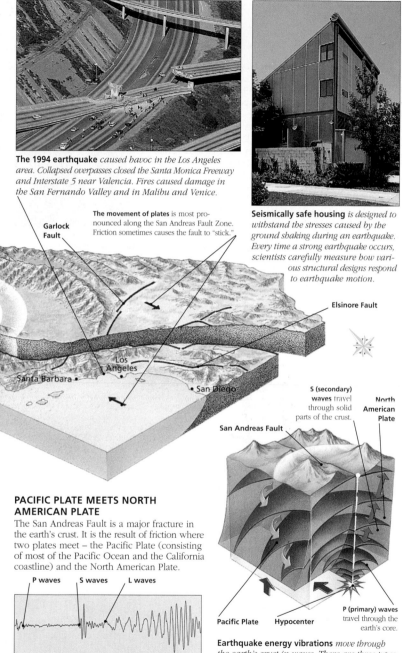

The 1994 earthquake *caused havoc in the Los Angeles area. Collapsed overpasses closed the Santa Monica Freeway and Interstate 5 near Valencia. Fires caused damage in the San Fernando Valley and in Malibu and Venice.*

Garlock Fault

The movement of plates is most pronounced along the San Andreas Fault Zone. Friction sometimes causes the fault to "stick."

Seismically safe housing *is designed to withstand the stresses caused by the ground shaking during an earthquake. Every time a strong earthquake occurs, scientists carefully measure how various structural designs respond to earthquake motion.*

Elsinore Fault

Santa Barbara •

Los Angeles

• San Diego

S (secondary) waves travel through solid parts of the crust.

North American Plate

San Andreas Fault

PACIFIC PLATE MEETS NORTH AMERICAN PLATE

The San Andreas Fault is a major fracture in the earth's crust. It is the result of friction where two plates meet – the Pacific Plate (consisting of most of the Pacific Ocean and the California coastline) and the North American Plate.

P waves   S waves   L waves

It is possible *to calculate the magnitude of an earthquake from a seismograph recording. Printouts show the intensity of earthquake vibrations graphically. The magnitude of the earthquake is registered on the Richter Scale (R).*

Pacific Plate   Hypocenter

P (primary) waves travel through the earth's core.

Earthquake energy vibrations *move through the earth's crust in waves. There are three types of wave: P or primary waves, S or secondary waves, and L or surface waves. The waves change as energy moves from the hypocenter to the earth's surface. Surface waves cause most of the damage associated with earthquakes.*

Literary California

Mask used in plays at Tao House

As journalist Carey McWilliams remarked in 1946, "What America is, California is, with accents, in italics." The chance to study the nation in microcosm has been especially appealing to authors. Many, such as Robert Louis Stevenson (1850–94), have simply passed through. He arrived in Monterey in 1879 and later based scenes in *Treasure Island* on the surrounding coastline. But California has not lacked for resident wordsmiths. This, after all, is where Henry Miller (1891–1980) blended erotic and verbal inventiveness and William Saroyan (1908–81) found his eccentric rural characters. Nobel prize-winning playwright Eugene O'Neill (1888–1953) produced some of his best work at Tao House in the Ramon Valley *(see p426)*. California is also where several successful contemporary writers, such as Amy Tan (born in 1952), now chase their muse.

Robert Louis Stevenson, author of *Treasure Island*

THE PIONEERS

Much of the very early writing about California was unsophisticated, satisfying readers who simply wanted a taste of the frontier environment. But the Gold Rush *(see pp48–9)* created a market for prose that captured the poignancy, romance, and raw humor of life in the West. Bay Area literary journals such as *The Golden Era* and *The Overland Monthly* nurtured many local fiction writers. These included Bret Harte (1836–1902), the author of *The Luck of Roaring Camp*, essayist Henry George (1839–97), and bards ranging from Joaquin Miller (1837–1913) to Ina Coolbrith (the nation's first poet laureate in 1915).

The literary journals also provided an apprenticeship for San Franciscan writer Samuel Clemens (1835–1910). His 1865 publication of the Gold Country yarn, "The Celebrated Jumping Frog of Calaveras County," introduced him to a national readership as Mark Twain.

Writer Samuel Clemens, alias Mark Twain

THE SOCIAL CRITICS

Ambrose Bierce (1842–1914) ranked among the first of many California writers who used their art to advocate wide-ranging political and social reforms. During the late 19th century, Bierce filled his *San Francisco Examiner* column with tirades against hypocrites and bureaucrats. His poisonous articles helped to trim the overweening influence of the vast Southern Pacific Railroad Company *(see pp50–51)*.

Frank Norris (1870–1902) attacked America's greed in his novel, *McTeague* (1899). In *The Octopus*, Norris also lashed out at the Southern Pacific, this time for its monopolistic mistreatment of ranchers in the San Joaquin Valley.

Back from the Klondike Gold Rush (setting for *The Call of the Wild*), working-class author Jack London alternated between writing adventure novels and stories – such as *The Iron Heel* – that showed his faith in Marxism.

Upton Sinclair (1878–1968) had already published *The Jungle*, his exposé of the Chicago stockyards, when he moved to California after World War I. But it was in Pasadena that he wrote most of his novels, campaigning against poverty and inequality.

Social injustice was a frequent theme for Salinas-born novelist John Steinbeck (1902–68). *Tortilla Flat* (1935), about a band of Mexican-American outcasts, was his first success. It was *The Grapes of Wrath* (1939), however, that brought him the prestigious Pulitzer Prize for

Jack London at his Sonoma Valley ranch

Steinbeck on the Californian coast

Literature. Steinbeck's book so powerfully portrayed the miseries endured by migratory laborers that it was banned from public libraries in some parts of the state.

THE CRIME WRITERS

Three California writers established the American school of private-eye fiction. The first of these was Dashiell Hammett (1884–1961), a tubercular former Pinkerton Agency detective and San Francisco resident. He began writing for *Black Mask* and other "pulp" crime-fiction magazines in the 1920s. He then went on to produce five novels, including *The Maltese Falcon* (1930). Hammett's work boasted a grim realism not found in either British whodunits or more venal tales by pulp writers lacking his investigative credentials.

Raymond Chandler (1888–1959) was less intimate with urban "mean streets," but was a more lyrical storyteller.

Poster for the film adaptation of Hammett's *The Maltese Falcon*

Chandler was an oil company executive in Los Angeles until he was sacked for drunkenness. He went on to create the quintessential American detective – Philip Marlowe, star of seven novels, the best being *Farewell, My Lovely* and *The Long Goodbye*. But it was Ross Macdonald (né Kenneth Millar) who finally rounded off his genre's rough edges and confirmed LA as its ideal setting. Macdonald was also the most prolific of this trio. He wrote 19 novels about sleuth Lew Archer, including *The Underground Man*.

Beat writers and friends, Jack Kerouac and Neal Cassady

THE BEATS

Protest against the political conservatism of President Eisenhower's America and against the conventions of society and art combined to produce San Francisco's "Beat Movement" of the 1950s. The Beats (or "Beatniks," as *San Francisco Chronicle* columnist Herb Caen labeled them) were led by the writers Allen Ginsberg (1926–97), Jack Kerouac (1922–69), and William Burroughs (1914–97). They extolled poetry made up of random word usages, produced stream-of-consciousness, drug-assisted narratives, and shunned social, literary, and sexual restraints.

The Beatniks' rebellion officially began in December, 1955, when Ginsberg gave a public reading of his poem "Howl," which was more like a shouting. Despite protests that "Howl" was obscene, it was subsequently published by San Franciscan Lawrence Ferlinghetti, poet and owner of City Lights *(see p340)*, the first paperbacks-only bookshop in the United States.

Two years later, Kerouac's novel *On the Road* spread the Beats' bohemian ethic nationwide. The most influential of the Beat writers, Kerouac also wrote *Desolation Angels* and *The Dharma Bums*, both novels set in California. By 1960 the Beat movement was waning, but not before it had paved the way for that decade's hippie movement.

THE MODERNS

Today, most best-seller lists feature at least one novel by a California author. The state has many distinctive young voices, such as Ethan Canin (*The Palace Thief*, 1988), Michael Chabon (*The Wonder Boys*, 1995), and Ron Hansen (*Mariette in Ecstasy*, 1991). More established authors, such as Joan Didion (*A Book of Common Prayer*, 1977), Amy Tan (*The Joy Luck Club*, 1989, *The Bonesetter's Daughter*, 2001), and Alice Walker (*The Color Purple*, 1985), are still shining as brightly as ever. There are also many genre writers in California, including James Ellroy (*LA Confidential*, 1990), Dean Koontz (*Sole Survivor*, 2000), and Sue Grafton (*P is for Peril*, 2001), all adding new depth to detective fiction.

Novelist Amy Tan

Art in California

In the wake of the Gold Rush *(see pp48–9)*, California became both a magnet and a breeding ground for artists. They generally eschewed native folk traditions, however, in favor of European aesthetics that, while making the most of this new land and its people, were not dramatically changed by it. Only after World War II did Californians – including painter Richard Diebenkorn and photographer Imogen Cunningham – shed subservience to Old World art movements in order to develop distinctive visual trends, which then spread internationally. Since the 1950s, Los Angeles has challenged San Francisco's cultural primacy, and California art has become a highly valued investment.

Figure on a Porch (1959) by Richard Diebenkorn

PAINTERS

California's mountain and desert landscapes and dramatic ocean shores dominated painters' attention here during the late 19th century. Thomas Hill (1829–1908) was born in England and trained in Paris. He moved to California in 1861 and began to produce epic natural panoramas, especially of the stunning Yosemite Valley *(see pp488–91)*. His work not only attracted new visitors to the West Coast but also helped win Yosemite its national park status in 1890. Even more popular was William Keith (1838–1911), a Scotsman who spent 50 years portraying the state's virgin wilderness. At that time, cities and people may have seemed comparatively pale inspirations. Yet Gilded Age California *(see pp50–51)* could not now be fully understood without such talents as William Hahn (1829–87), a German immigrant who captured life in nascent San Francisco; Grace Carpenter Hudson (1865–1937), renowned for her portraits of coastal natives; and William A Coulter (1849–1936), who recorded maritime scenes.

As early as 1900, the state's two halves displayed stylistically disparate growth. In the north, Xavier Martinez (1869–1943) and his fellow Tonalists filled canvases with the familiar hazy light and gray-brown hues of their environment. In the south, Guy Rose (1867–1925) led an Impressionist school that used the region's vibrant colors and brighter light to produce Monet-like effects.

Prohibition-era Los Angeles flirted with the Synchromist style of Stanton Macdonald-Wright (1890–1973). San Francisco was enchanted by Cubist Realists such as Otis Oldfield (1890–1969). Another popular artist there was the great Mexican muralist Diego Rivera, who in 1940 composed *Panamerican Mind*, an enormous fresco that can be seen at the City College.

Modernism flowered fully in California after World War II. It was at that time that David Park (1911–60), Richard Diebenkorn (born in 1922), and other members of the Bay Area Figurative School began to blend Expressionism with realistic imagery. In Southern California, Hard-Edge Abstractionists such as Helen Lundeberg and John McLaughlin (1898–1976) drew critical acclaim with their large-scale geometric shapes.

What is remarkable about contemporary California painters is not simply the worldwide recognition that they have earned, but their stylistic breadth. They range from Pop Artist Ed Ruscha (born in 1937) and urban landscapist Wayne Thiebaud (born in 1920), to cutting-edge British émigré David Hockney (born in 1937) and Arthur Carraway (born in 1927), whose work celebrates his African-American heritage.

Afternoon in Piedmont (Elsie at the Window) by Xavier Martinez

Two Callas by Imogen Cunningham

PHOTOGRAPHERS

Many early California photographs were either portraits or straightforward documentary scenes done by surveyors. Some photographers, however, such as Eadweard James Muybridge (1830–1904), found photography no less powerful than painting in depicting nature. Others preferred to focus on human subjects. Allegorical nudes and other images by Anne Brigman (1869–1950) found fans even in New York City. Arnold Genthe (1869–1942) studied the Bay Area's Asian community, producing (with writer Will Irwin) a 1913 volume called *Pictures of Old Chinatown.*

In 1932 an Oakland group called "f/64" mounted a major exhibition at the MH de Young Memorial Museum in San Francisco *(see pp372–3).* Members of f/64, among them Ansel Adams (1902–84), Imogen Cunningham (1883–1976), and Edward Weston (1886–1958), believed photography should emphasize realism. This approach was riveting when used in close-ups of plants, or as Dorothea Lange (1895–1965) applied it in her portraits of Californians during the Great Depression.

The range of approaches now includes the snapshot aesthetics of Judy Dater (born in 1941) and photographs of Weimaraner dogs by William Wegman (born in 1942).

SCULPTORS

German-born Rupert Schmid (1864–1932) arrived in San Francisco in the 1880s. He soon became famous for figurative works employing western themes, such as *California Venus* (1895), his life-size female nude adorned with California poppies. More important still was Douglas Tilden (1860–1935), a sculptor from Chico who created impressive civic monuments. Arthur Putnam (1873–1930) also won notoriety with his sensual representations of wild animals.

Schmid's *California Venus*

Californians have been expanding the parallel fields of sculpture and ceramics since the early part of this century. Peter Voulkos (born in 1924) experimented in large-scale fired clay sculptures. Robert Arneson (born in 1930) abandoned more traditional vessel aesthetics to pursue startling and amusing Pop Art ceramics, while Bruce Beasley (born in 1939) and Michael Heizer (born in 1944) have created pieces that take on different dimensions depending on the weather.

ART PATRONAGE IN CALIFORNIA

Private and public patronage have been essential to the vitality of California culture since the late 19th century. Had it not been for railroad baron Henry Huntington's money and interest in art treasures, there would be no Huntington Library, Art Galleries, and Botanical Gardens in Pasadena *(see pp158–9).* The public would not have access to that institution's collection of 18th-century British art, including Thomas Gainsborough's *The Blue Boy* (c.1770) and many other masterpieces. Multimillionaire J Paul Getty brought together the world-famous collection of Greek and Roman antiquities housed in the J Paul Getty Villa in Malibu *(see p88)* and the painting, sculpture, and decorative arts collection occupying the new J Paul Getty Center in Brentwood *(see pp82–3).* Another multimillionaire, Norton Simon, amassed the renowned selection of Goyas, Picassos, Rembrandts, and Van Goghs now on public display in the Norton Simon Museum *(see pp156–7).*

Public financing, too, has enriched the state's art offerings. In the 1930s, the New Deal paid artists to paint the frescoes in San Francisco's Coit Tower *(see p331)* and embellish public structures throughout the state. More recently, city funds have been used to make Los Angeles one of the most important centers of mural art in the world.

Henry Huntington

Architecture in California

California's architectural history began with the arrival of the Europeans in the 18th century (see pp46–7). Many of the Spanish missions of the late 18th and early 19th centuries were adaptations of Mexican baroque architecture, and the Spanish-Mexican influence continued to dominate California buildings until the middle of the 19th century. Later, the population influx caused by the Gold Rush led to this Hispanic vernacular merging with styles imported by settlers from the eastern United States and Europe. Architects such as Henry Cleaveland, S & J Newsom, and Bernard Maybeck were all influential in creating the state's unique Victorian style.

Hale House in Heritage Square, Los Angeles

MISSION

Franciscan missionaries, arriving in California from Mexico, established a chain of 21 missions from San Diego to Sonoma as centers from which to colonize the state. They were all designed to be within a day's journey of their nearest neighbors. These provincial versions of Mexican churches and their communal buildings were designed by friars and built of adobe bricks and wood by unskilled Native American laborers. Over the years their crude constructions decayed and were shaken by earthquakes, but many have been carefully restored in the 20th century. Distinctive features include massive walls covered with white lime cement, small window openings, rounded gables, and tiered bell towers.

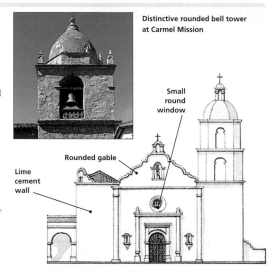

Distinctive rounded bell tower at Carmel Mission

Small round window

Rounded gable

Lime cement wall

Mission San Luis Rey (1811–51) was the 18th mission to be established and was so architecturally impressive that it was often referred to as a "palace."

MONTEREY

In the 1850s and 1860s, East Coast settlers flooded into the newly declared 31st state, bringing with them styles that were already going out of fashion on the East Coast, such as Greek Revival. Monterey, the state capital under Mexican rule, gave its name to an architecture that is, in essence, a wooden Greek temple wrapped around a Mexican adobe. Features include two-story wooden porticoes supported by slim square posts, wood shingle roofs, and a chaste symmetry of plan and elevation.

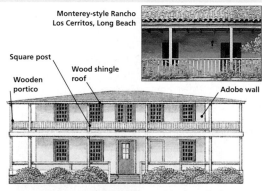

Monterey-style Rancho Los Cerritos, Long Beach

Square post

Wood shingle roof

Wooden portico

Adobe wall

Larkin House (1837), built by Thomas Larkin, was the first Monterey-style house, with its two stories of adobe brick.

VICTORIAN

Three major styles emerged in California during the Victorian era: Italianate, most popular in San Francisco *(see pp300–1)*, Queen Anne, and Eastlake. The two latter styles achieved a pinnacle of exuberance in California during the 19th century when they were brought to the state by migrants from the East Coast. The restrained Eastlake style, with its geometrically patterned façades and ornamentation, was often combined with the more extravagant Queen Anne style, notable for its gables, turrets, wraparound porches, and splendidly confused anthology of classical details.

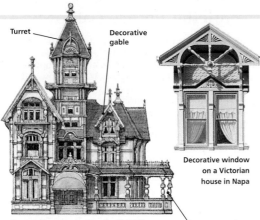

Turret

Decorative gable

Decorative window on a Victorian house in Napa

Wraparound porch

Carson Mansion *in Eureka (1886) was built by S & J Newsom, who were masters of the Queen Anne style. Now a private club, the house may be California's ultimate Victorian folly.*

ARTS AND CRAFTS

Pioneered by William Morris and Charles Voysey in England, the Arts and Crafts movement flourished briefly in California in the early 20th century. Also known as Craftsman style, its leading proponents included Bernard Maybeck and Charles and Henry Greene. Its emphasis is on simplicity and refinement on the outside and in the handcrafted interiors.

Characteristic beamed roof at Gamble House, Pasadena

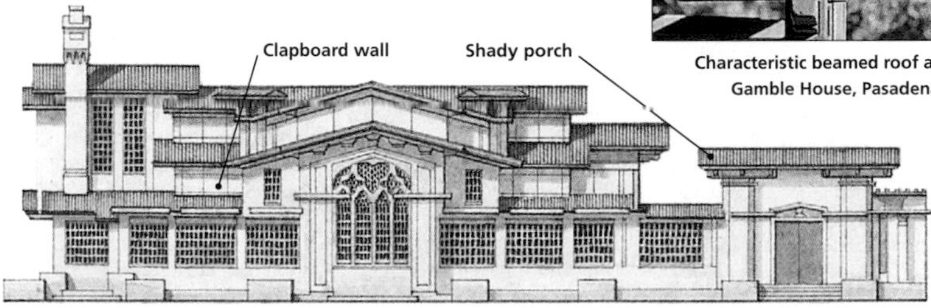

Clapboard wall

Shady porch

The First Church of Christ Science *in Berkeley (1907) is the finest example of Bernard Maybeck's Arts and Crafts designs.*

MISSION REVIVAL

The Spanish-Mexican style was dormant during the second half of the 19th century. Decorative or pared-down versions were then enthusiastically revived in the early 20th century. The style is distinguishable by its rounded arches, harmonious proportions, and absence of ornamentation.

Red-tiled roof at the Beverly Hills Hotel

White stucco wall

Red-tiled roof

Rounded arch

The Women's Club *(1913) in La Jolla was designed by Irving Gill, a pioneer of modernism who used poured concrete and stucco to create elegant versions of the Mission style.*

Twentieth-Century California Architecture

In the early 20th century an architecture distinctive to California emerged, after a brief return to the state's Hispanic roots and an Art Deco style imported from Europe. This California style borrowed post-and-beam construction and wide porches from traditional Japanese buildings. Later, during the postwar building boom of the 1950s, the whole country was influenced by Cliff May's California ranch house, with its fusion of indoor and outdoor living. In more recent years, many architects, such as Craig Ellwood and Frank Gehry, have helped to make LA a center of modern architectural innovation *(see pp 72–3)*.

San Francisco Museum of Modern Art (1995)

SPANISH COLONIAL

Ornate versions of traditional Spanish architecture were first given wide currency by the Panama-California Exposition in San Diego in 1915 *(see pp256–7)*, where many buildings were decorated in this style. Simplified versions became the popular style for houses and public buildings throughout the 1920s. Distinguishing features included ornamental wood, stone, and ironwork, used to set off expanses of white stucco, red pantiled roofs, and lush gardens.

George Washington Smith, the Montecito-based architect, was a master of the style, creating abstracted Andalusian-style villages, such as **Ostoff House** (1924) in San Marino and Casa del Herrero (1925), a private house in Montecito. Another striking example of this style is William Mooser's **Santa Barbara County Courthouse** (1929), with its hand-painted ceilings, murals, and sunken gardens.

STREAMLINE MODERNE

Art Deco made a brief appearance in California at the end of the 1920s, with jazzy reliefs and tile façades. It was superseded by Streamline Moderne, where sleek, rounded forms are animated by ribs, canopies, and reliefs. Its inspirations were machine-age imagery. The style is best seen in movie theaters, such as the **Academy Cathedral** (1939) in Inglewood and the **Paramount Theater** in Oakland (Miller & Pflueger, 1931).

PWA MODERNE

This movement was named after the Public Works Administration, established in the 1930s to fund public buildings. It is a marriage of Beaux-Arts formality and the simplicity of Modernism. It is notable for its stone façades, pilasters, and carved ornamentation. A good example is the **Monterey County Courthouse** (1937) in Salinas.

CONTEMPORARY

A diversity of approaches by leading architects has resulted in some striking contemporary buildings. Among the notable achievements of recent years are the ground-hugging, barnlike structures of **Sea Ranch.** This ecologically friendly vacation-home community on the Northern California coast began as a cluster of condominiums by Moore Lyndon Turnbull Whittaker in 1965. In sharp contrast is the **Salk Institute,** in La Jolla (Louis Kahn, 1959–65). State-of-the-art laboratories of poured concrete flank a bare travertine-paved plaza; a symbolic meeting place that links the continent and the ocean.

The **San Francisco Museum of Modern Art** (1995) by Swiss architect Mario Botta is both a civic symbol and an indoor plaza. A cylindrical skylight reaches up from stacked, top-lit galleries clad in precast panels of plain and angled bricks, to light an expansive foyer.

POST-MODERNISM

Reacting to the impersonality of corporate towers, architects such as Michael Graves, Venturi Scott-Brown,

George Washington Smith's Casa del Herrero in Montecito (1925)

and Robert Stern popularized a more decorative approach to Modernism in the 1970s. Buildings such as **The Library** (1984) by Robert Stern in San Juan Capistrano make playful use of historical elements (columns, pediments, and pergolas) while employing colorful palettes.

Jon Jerde scrambles colors and architectural references with even greater abandon in his popular shopping centers, most notably **Horton Plaza** (1989) in San Diego. This multilevel outdoor shopping mall with domes and tilework echoes local Spanish-style buildings.

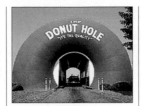

Programmatic Donut Hole in La Puente, east of Los Angeles

Post-Modern Horton Plaza

PROGRAMMATIC BUILDINGS

The automobile began to reshape California as early as the 1920s, and there was fierce competition to attract the attention of passing motorists on the commercial strips that linked scattered communities. An exuberant roadside architecture developed, in which travelers were invited to sleep in wigwam motels or have their shoes repaired inside a huge shoe (Doschander's Shoe Repair Shop, Bakersfield, 1947). Most of these fantasies have been demolished, but a few remain in outlying areas, notably the drive-thru **Donut Hole** (1958) in La Puente and the **Tail o' the Pup** hot dog stand (1946) in West Hollywood.

WHERE TO FIND THE BUILDINGS

FRANK LLOYD WRIGHT

Born in Wisconsin, Frank Lloyd Wright (1867–1959) lived in California in the 1920s and designed buildings in the state throughout his career. He began with **Hollyhock House** (1917–20) in Hollywood, and ended with the **Marin County Civic Center** in San Rafael, north of San Francisco, completed in 1972. Other notable buildings are the old VC Morris store (1949), now the **Union Square Frank Lloyd Wright Building** in San Francisco, and several LA "textile block" houses, inspired by Mayan temples.

Frank Lloyd Wright's Hollyhock House in Hollywood

Multicultural California

Japanese sign

California is the most ethnically diverse state in the Union. In the 19th century, the discovery of gold, silver, and oil each brought an influx of migrants of many nationalities to California; the landscape and climate still attract farmers, fishermen, and vintners from all over the world. By the mid-21st century, many believe California will be a hybrid of cultures, with no clear ethnic majority. The concentration of races varies state-wide: a greater number of Hispanics reside in the south, while the Silicon Valley and northern farmlands have attracted Asians and Europeans. Most ethnic communities still cele-brate their cultures with festivals *(see pp36–9)*.

San Francisco's Chinatown

entire areas of cities. Although many of the younger Chinese have now moved to middle-class areas, the Chinatowns of LA and San Francisco still attract tourists to their tradi-tional shops and restaurants.

THE NATIVE AMERICANS

California has more resident Native Americans than any other state. The indigenous population grew in the 1960s when they gained more political rights. A few Native Americans still live on reservations, but the majority have opted for integration throughout the state.

Mexican street musicians in Los Angeles

Girl in Native American dress

THE HISPANIC-AMERICANS

You cannot go far in California without becoming aware of the state's Hispanic heritage. Spanish explorers who arrived in the 17th and 18th centuries *(see pp46–7)* established many of today's cities. As early as the 1940s the state was home to the largest population of Mexicans outside their own country. Political and econ-omic troubles in Central and South America have contin-ued to fuel Hispanic immi-gration. Today, almost every city has Mexican influences in its architecture, cuisine, and art. The Hispanics are also responsible for some of the brightest fiestas, including the extravagant *Cinco de Mayo* (May 5) *(see p36)*.

THE CHINESE

Chinese immigrants first arrived in California during the Gold Rush *(see pp48–9)*. A further influx escaped the economic problems of their homeland in the 1860s to work as cheap labor building the transcontinental railroad *(see pp50–51)*. Following its completion, they remained in California, setting up laundries and other businesses, but were met with racial violence by activists claiming they were stealing "white jobs." In the 1880s Congress severely lim-ited Chinese immigration, a law that was not repealed until 1943.

Such antipathy resulted in ghettolike Chinese commu-nities, which dominated

THE AFRICAN-AMERICANS

African-Americans have been present in California since the days of Mexican rule. It was the increase in heavy industry during World War II, however, that led to the largest influx from the poorer southern states.

Rotchev House at Fort Ross

In the years that followed, low social standing and racism resulted in the growth of urban ghettos. Racial problems still persist, but many African-Americans are beginning to make their mark in government, entertainment, and business. Cities like Oakland *(see pp422–5)* continue to celebrate traditional festivals.

THE JAPANESE

The Japanese arrived in California in the early 20th century. The majority of them were farmers who literally sowed the seeds of the state's agricultural industry. During World War II, however, Japanese-Americans were considered a risk to national security and were interned for the duration of the war. The succeeding generation has overridden these events, and Japanese businesses have continued to grow since the 1980s property boom.

THE ITALIANS

Italians, predominantly fishermen, arrived in California in the late 19th century. and settled in North Beach, San Francisco *(see pp340–43)*. The climate and soil also tempted Italian vintners, who founded what is now a highly respected wine industry.

THE RUSSIANS

Fur trappers from Russia and Alaska were among the first European settlers in California, arriving in the early 1800s. For a short time, they established a successful settlement at Fort Ross *(see p460)*, and today there is a Russian population of some 25,000 in and around San Francisco.

THE IRISH

Fewer people of Irish descent reside on the West Coast than on the East Coast, and there are no distinct Irish districts in California. The Irish have largely integrated into a multicultural way of life, but their presence is still felt in the many Irish city bars, and particularly during the statewide parades on St. Patrick's Day *(see p36)*.

Santa Monica English pub sign

THE MELTING POT

Over the last few decades there has been a steady rise in immigrants from Asia. Long Beach has the largest population of Cambodians outside Cambodia, and the district is known as "Little Phnom Penh." Wars in Korea and Vietnam brought natives of these countries to the liberal atmosphere of California in the 1950s and 1970s. Made to settle in the poorer areas of inner cities, they have now turned many of these into thriving communities. Fresno *(see p516)* has the second largest Hmong population outside Laos in the world.

The technological opportunities of Silicon Valley *(see p428)* have continued to attract Indians and Pakistanis to the region since the 1970s. Santa Monica is home to a large British contingent, complete with "authentic" pubs *(see pp76–7)*. The town of Solvang *(see p219)* was founded by immigrants from Denmark in 1911 and retains its Danish heritage. California also has the second largest Jewish community in the US, two-thirds of whom live in LA.

Danish windmill in Solvang

CALIFORNIA
THROUGH THE YEAR

California generally enjoys a moderate climate (see pp40–41), which explains how residents can schedule annual events without concern for the weather. The size of the state, however, means that a range of activities can be pursued in different locations: winter can be spent skiing in the north or soaking up the sun in the warmer south. Californians love to celebrate, and the calendar is full of parades and festivals. Many are related to the state's agricultural heritage; others have been inspired by its social history, such as the Gold Rush, or its ethnic diversity. There are also cultural events, including jazz and film festivals, and national sports fixtures.

Runners in the Los Angeles Marathon

SPRING

There's a clear sense of re-emergence in spring, when wildflowers carpet California's coastal headlands, gray whales swim north with their newborn offspring, and people start searching frantically for the sunglasses they tucked away the previous October. *Cinco de Mayo* (May 5) celebrations in Los Angeles and San Francisco, Hollywood's glamorous Academy Awards ceremony, baseball games, and San Francisco's Bay-to-Breakers run are all familiar elements of the season.

MARCH

Return of the Swallows *(Mar 19)*, San Juan Capistrano. Crowds gather to see the birds fly back to the mission gardens from their winter homes in Argentina *(see pp240–41)*.

Los Angeles Marathon *(first Sun)*.
Snowfest *(first two weeks)*, Tahoe City. The winter carnival features ski competitions, a "polar bear" (cold water) swim and live music.
St. Patrick's Day Parade *(Sun nearest Mar 17)*, San Francisco. A parade down Market Street is usually followed by Irish coffee in the city's Irish bars.

St. Patrick's Day shamrock

Swallows returning to Mission San Juan Capistrano

Redwood Coast Dixieland Jazz Festival *(end Mar)*, Eureka. Some of the world's finest Dixieland bands gather for this annual event.

APRIL

Academy Awards Ceremony *(Mar)*, Los Angeles. Hollywood's finest gather to honor the year's top films and actors.
Major League Baseball *(Apr–Sep)*. The San Francisco Giants, LA Dodgers, Anaheim Angels, Oakland Athletics, and San Diego Padres compete.
Toyota Grand Prix *(mid-Apr)*, Long Beach. The biggest street race in the US.
Agua Cahuilla Indian Heritage Festival *(mid-Apr)*, Palm Springs. Festivities honor the Native Americans who discovered the local hot springs.
Cherry Blossom Festival *(mid-Apr)*, San Francisco. Japanese dancing and martial arts displays are all part of this traditional annual event *(see p352)*.
Anniversary of the 1906 Earthquake *(Apr 18)*, San Francisco. Survivors and history buffs gather around Lotta's Fountain, at Kearny and Market Streets, to remember the earthquake.
San Francisco International Film Festival *(mid-Apr–early May)*. Independent films from around the world.
Red Bluff Round-Up Rodeo *(third weekend)*. The largest two-day rodeo in the US.

MAY

Raisin Festival *(early May)*, Selma. A parade, art competitions and the Raisin Queen.
Cinco de Mayo *(May 5)*, LA and San Francisco. The state's largest Mexican celebrations feature folk dancing and mariachi music.
Bay-to-Breakers *(third weekend)*, San Francisco. The world's largest fun run is 7.5-miles (12.5-km) from the Embarcadero to Ocean Beach.
Calaveras County Fair *(mid-May)*, Angels Camp. The famous frog jumping contest *(see p479)* and a rodeo.
Mainly Mozart Festival *(end May–early Jun)*, San Diego. Leading orchestras perform Mozart masterpieces.
Carnaval *(last weekend)*, San Francisco. The Mission District turns Latin American, with salsa and reggae bands.
Sacramento Jazz Jubilee *(last weekend)*.

Mexican dancer at the *Cinco de Mayo* festival in Los Angeles

SUMMER

At no other time of year are the clichés of California so evident. Beaches are crowded with tanned, muscled bodies and daredevil surfers, and colorfully dressed gays and lesbians parade through San Francisco streets in June. Tourists flood into the state, attending its many outdoor music events, Wild West celebrations (such as Old Miners' Days in Big Bear Lake), and the renowned annual Gilroy Garlic Festival.

Lesbian and Gay Pride parade in San Francisco

JUNE

Lesbian and Gay Pride Day *(Sun in late Jun)*, San Francisco. The largest gay parade proceeds down Market Street.
Lumber Jubilee *(end Jun)*, Tuolumne. Logging competitions recall the history of California's lumber industry.
Monterey Blues Festival *(end Jun)*. Star blues performers draw crowds annually.
Juneteenth *(end Jun)*, Oakland. An African-American cultural celebration, featuring jazz and gospel music.

JULY

International Surf Festival *(whole month)*. Body boarding and surfing events take place at various beaches.
Fourth of July Fireworks Particularly good displays are at Disneyland and on Santa Monica Pier.
Mammoth Lakes Jazz Jubilee *(first weekend after Jul 4)*. Some dozen world-class jazz bands perform.
Obon Festival *(mid-Jul)*, San Jose. Taiko drummers and dancers join in this Japanese-American party.
Carmel Bach Festival *(mid-Jul–early Aug)*. Bach concerts and classes.
Gilroy Garlic Festival *(end Jul)*. This food festival serves garlic in all kinds of dishes.
San Francisco Marathon *(mid-Jul)*.
Old Miners' Days *(end Jul–mid-Aug)*, Big Bear Lake. The Gold Rush is recalled

with a chili cook-off and a liars' contest.
Festival of the Arts *(Jul–Aug)*, Laguna Beach.

AUGUST

Native American Powwow *(early Aug)*, Costa Mesa. A celebration of Native American food and culture.
Old Spanish Days Fiesta *(early Aug)*, Santa Barbara. Spanish markets, a carnival, and dancing.
Nisei Week *(early Aug)*, Japanese festival in LA's Little Tokyo.
Pebble Beach Concours d'Elegance *(mid-Aug)*. Classic automobile show.
California State Fair *(mid-Aug–early Sep)*, Sacramento. Everything from star-studded entertainment to pig races.
Bigfoot Days *(end Aug)*, Willow Creek. A parade and an ice cream social at this homage to Northern California's legendary hermit.

Native American dancers at the Costa Mesa Powwow

Mexican Independence Day
parade in Santa Monica

AUTUMN

In the High Sierras, leaves
of deciduous trees turn
stunning shades of red and
yellow. The Napa Valley
wineries *(see pp462–3)* invite
visitors to help celebrate
their grape harvests with wine
tastings and live music. All
over the state, Oktoberfests
serve up foamy mugs of
beer and the "oom-pah-pah"
of German bands, while
rodeos dramatize California's
frontier past.

SEPTEMBER

Pro Football *(Sep–Dec)*. The
San Francisco '49ers,
Oakland Raiders,
and San Diego
Chargers take
to the field.
**Los Angeles
County Fair** *(whole
month)*, Pomona.
This vast county fair
includes horse races.
Oktoberfest *(early Sep–end
Oct)*, Torrance. The largest
German beer festival in
Southern California.
Mexican Independence Day
(Sep 16). Mexican dancing,
music and food in Santa
Monica, Calexico, and
Santa Maria.
Monterey Jazz Festival
(third weekend). The
world's oldest continuously
held annual jazz festival.
Danish Days *(end Sep)*,
Solvang. Danish food stands
and parades *(see p219)*.
San Francisco Blues Festival
(last weekend). Popular
two-day jazz and blues
event at Fort Mason.

Football

OCTOBER

**Sonoma County Harvest
Fair** *(early Oct)*, Santa Rosa.
A grape stomp and a 6-mile
(10-km) run are highlights
of this annual fair.
**US National Gold Panning
Championship** *(early Oct)*,
Coloma. The 1849 Gold Rush
is remembered with a gold
panning competition.
Mountain Man Rendezvous
(early Oct), Bridgeport.
Shooting contests and a bar-
becue re-create an 1840s
get-together of mountain
guides and trappers.
**Black Cowboy Heritage
Invitational Parade and
Festival** *(early Oct)*, Oakland.
Commemorating the part
African-Americans played in
settling the American West.
Columbus Day Parade
(Sun nearest Oct 12), San
Francisco. Bands and floats
proceed down Columbus
Avenue to Fisherman's Wharf.
San Francisco Jazz Festival
(end Oct–early Nov).
All-star jazz performances
throughout the city.
Pumpkin Festival *(mid-Oct)*,
Half Moon Bay. The World
Heavyweight Pumpkin
Championship,
pumpkin carving,
and pumpkin
dishes are
served in every
edible variety.
**International
Festival of Masks** *(last
Sun)*, Los Angeles.
Originally part of Halloween,
this mask parade now cele-
brates LA's ethnic diversity.

Halloween *(Oct 31)*, San
Francisco. Costumed
residents parade through
the city streets.
Grand National Rodeo *(end
Oct–early Nov)*, Daly City.
Lassoing mustangs and a
livestock exposition are part
of this traditional event.
Butterflies *(end Oct–mid
Mar)*, Pacific Grove.
Thousands of monarch
butterflies migrate here
annually *(see p510)*.

Costumed participants in
Pasadena's Doo Dah Parade

NOVEMBER

Dia de los Muertos/Day of
the Dead *(Nov 1)*. Festivities
in LA's El Pueblo and San
Francisco's Mission District
highlight this Mexican
religious festival, when the
souls of the dead are said
to visit their surviving
relatives *(see p126)*.
**Death Valley '49ers
Encampment** *(mid-Nov)*.
Fiddlers' competitions,
cowboy poetry, and gold
panning are all featured.
Doo Dah Parade *(mid-Nov)*,
Pasadena. Costumed
merchants parody the
approaching holiday and
current events.

Mexican musicians at the *Dia de los Muertos* festival

Gray whale approaching a boat off Baja California

WINTER

Californians love bright lights, and this is most apparent at Christmas, when every building and public square seems to be draped in twinkling bulbs. Churches resound with carols, and film stars take part in seasonal parades. As Lake Tahoe's ski season gets under way, highways jam up with avid skiers traveling north.

DECEMBER

Hollywood Christmas Parade (*first Thu after Thanksgiving*), Los Angeles. Hollywood and Sunset Boulevards are crowded with this celebrity-heavy extravaganza, held since 1931.
Russian Heritage Christmas Celebration (*weekends, whole month*), Guerneville. Costumes, food, and music recall the area's early 19th-century Russian influences.

Christmas decorations in Carmel Plaza

International Tamale Festival (*early Dec*), Indio. Mexican dancing accompanies the *tamale* (spicy corn husk rolls) gluttony.
Whale-watching (*end Dec–Apr*). California gray whales, migrating south annually from the Bering Strait to Baja, can be sighted along the coast or from whale-watching boats out of many coastal cities (*see p614*).

Float at the Tournament of Roses Parade in Pasadena

JANUARY

Bald Eagles (*Jan–Feb*), Mount Shasta. Bird-watchers come to see bald eagles that nest here (*see pp436–7*).
Tournament of Roses Parade (*Jan 1*), Pasadena. A pageant, followed by the Rose Bowl intercollegiate football game (*see p154*).
Palm Springs International Film Festival (*early–mid Jan*). Screenings and awards.
Gold Discovery Day (*Jan 24*), Coloma. Gold-panning demonstrations take place on the anniversary of the first gold discovery (*see p475*).

AT&T Pebble Beach Pro-Am Golf Tournament (*end Jan–early Feb*). Pros and celebrities play golf together.

FEBRUARY

Dickens Festival (*early Feb*), Riverside. Writer Charles Dickens' life is celebrated in a re-creation of a mid-19th-century London marketplace.
Napa Valley International Mustard Festival (*mid-Feb*), Calistoga. Hundreds of mustards are available for tasting.
Riverside County Fair and National Date Festival (*mid–late Feb*), Indio. Date dishes and camel and ostrich races (*see p259*).
Chinese New Year Festival (*mid-Feb–early Mar*), San Francisco. The nation's largest Chinese New Year festival includes a Golden Dragon parade through the Financial District and Chinatown.

Chinese New Year celebrations in San Francisco

The Climate of California

Apart from the extremes of the North and the deserts, the state's climate is neither oppressive in summer nor too cold in winter. The Northern Coastal Range is temperate, although wet in the winter. To the east, rain turns to snow on the Sierra Nevada Mountains. Central California and the Central Valley have a Mediterranean climate. The weather becomes drier and warmer toward the south with soaring temperatures in the desert during the summer.

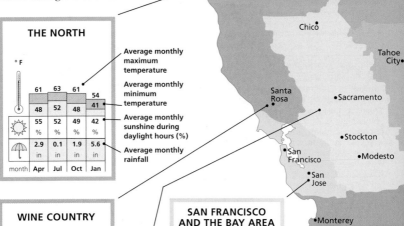

THE NORTH

°F				
	61	63	61	54
	48	52	48	41
☀	55 %	52 %	49 %	42 %
☂	2.9 in	0.1 in	1.9 in	5.6 in
month	Apr	Jul	Oct	Jan

Average monthly maximum temperature

Average monthly minimum temperature

Average monthly sunshine during daylight hours (%)

Average monthly rainfall

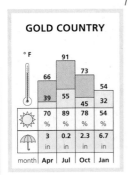

WINE COUNTRY

°F				
	70	82	77	57
	43	54	48	37
☀	75 %	85 %	80 %	52 %
☂	1.6 in	0 in	1.7 in	5.4 in
month	Apr	Jul	Oct	Jan

SAN FRANCISCO AND THE BAY AREA

°F				
	63	68	72	57
	50	54	55	46
☀	73 %	66 %	70 %	56 %
☂	1.3 in	0 in	1.3 in	4 in
month	Apr	Jul	Oct	Jan

GOLD COUNTRY

°F				
	66	91	73	54
	39	55	45	32
☀	70 %	89 %	78 %	54 %
☂	3 in	0.2 in	2.3 in	6.7 in
month	Apr	Jul	Oct	Jan

NORTH CENTRAL CALIFORNIA

°F				
	75	99	81	54
	48	64	50	37
☀	85 %	96 %	88 %	51 %
☂	0.9 in	0 in	0.5 in	1.9 in
month	Apr	Jul	Oct	Jan

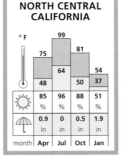

SOUTH CENTRAL CALIFORNIA

°F				
	70	82	77	61
	45	54	48	36
☀	83 %	97 %	87 %	46 %
☂	1.1 in	0.7 in	0.3 in	2.9 in
month	Apr	Jul	Oct	Jan

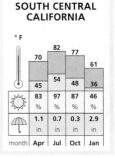

•Eureka

•Redding

Chico•

Tahoe City•

Santa Rosa•

•Sacramento

•Stockton

•San Francisco

•Modesto

•San Jose

•Monterey

•San Luis Obispo

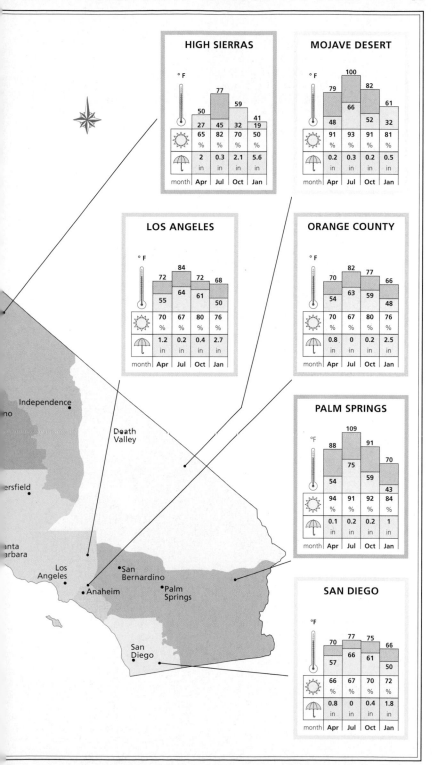

HIGH SIERRAS

°F				
	50	77	59	41
	27	45	32	19
☀	65 %	82 %	70 %	50 %
☂	2 in	0.3 in	2.1 in	5.6 in
month	Apr	Jul	Oct	Jan

MOJAVE DESERT

°F				
	79	100	82	61
	48	66	52	32
☀	91 %	93 %	91 %	81 %
☂	0.2 in	0.3 in	0.2 in	0.5 in
month	Apr	Jul	Oct	Jan

LOS ANGELES

°F				
	72	84	72	68
	55	64	61	50
☀	70 %	67 %	80 %	76 %
☂	1.2 in	0.2 in	0.4 in	2.7 in
month	Apr	Jul	Oct	Jan

ORANGE COUNTY

°F				
	70	82	77	66
	54	63	59	48
☀	70 %	67 %	80 %	76 %
☂	0.8 in	0 in	0.2 in	2.5 in
month	Apr	Jul	Oct	Jan

PALM SPRINGS

°F				
	88	109	91	70
	54	75	59	43
☀	94 %	91 %	92 %	84 %
☂	0.1 in	0.2 in	0.2 in	1 in
month	Apr	Jul	Oct	Jan

SAN DIEGO

°F				
	70	77	75	66
	57	66	61	50
☀	66 %	67 %	70 %	72 %
☂	0.8 in	0 in	0.4 in	1.8 in
month	Apr	Jul	Oct	Jan

Independence

Death
Valley

ersfield

anta
arbara

Los
Angeles

San
Bernardino

Anaheim

Palm
Springs

San
Diego

THE HISTORY OF CALIFORNIA

An early 16th-century chivalric Spanish novel, *Las Sergas de Esplanadían (The Exploits of Esplanadían)*, first gave the name *California* to a mythical island, plump with natural wealth and ruled by Calafía, a pagan queen. By 1542, when the Portuguese navigator Juan Rodríguez Cabrillo (João Rodrigues Cabrilho) sailed north from Mexico on Spain's behalf and discovered what he believed to be an island, the name California was already familiar enough for him to use it in his journal. Two centuries would pass, however, before Spain made a real claim on the land, sending Father Junípero Serra in 1769 to establish Franciscan missions along the length of California.

State seal

THE GOLD RUSH
Still, the territory remained remote until 1848; the same year that Mexico ceded California to the US, gold was found in the Sierra Nevada foothills. By 1849, hordes of fortune seekers had arrived in Northern California.

The Gold Rush, followed by silver finds in the western Sierras and the completion of the transcontinental railroad in 1869, brought prosperity to the whole state. But the changes caused social rifts: whites charged Chinese immigrants with "stealing" their jobs, and by the beginning of the 20th century, economic divisions left over from the time of plenty had helped to create powerful labor unions.

20TH-CENTURY CALIFORNIA
San Francisco's earthquake in 1906 convinced many that California's heyday was over. However, during the next 90 years, Hollywood drew international attention with its movie-making. Oil wells serviced the needs of increasingly car-dependent residents, and by 1937 orange groves had become a symbol of the state's fertile future. When the UN charter was signed in San Francisco in 1945, it was clear that California, once considered at the edge of civilization, was finally a player at center stage.

Early map of the United States, showing California as an island

◁ Mural at the Santa Barbara County Courthouse showing Cabrillo's landing in California

Early California

It is estimated that, at the time of European discovery, between 100,000 and 275,000 natives lived in California. They were not warlike, nor did they have much in the way of government. Only on the Colorado River did they practice agriculture; most relied on hunting, fishing, or the gathering of staples such as acorns for food. Their religion and medical beliefs were bound together in the person of a shaman, said to be in direct communication with the spirit world. They congregated in villages of 100 to 150 inhabitants generally living in conical or dome-shaped dwellings. Social classes were almost nonexistent, but there were great language divisions between different tribes.

Early basketry

Tcholovoni People
Various tribes, including these Tcholovoni people, settled in small villages on the shores of San Francisco Bay.

Money Box
Natives of Northern California used dentalium shells for money, held in ornately carved boxes.

Jewelry
This necklace, made of abalone and clamshells, is thought to be one of the earliest artifacts of Native California life.

Gift baskets, such as this Miwok example, were often decorated with beads.

Quail feathers and geometric dancers decorate this basket of the Yokut people.

Eel trapper

BASKETRY

Basket-weaving was the primary native activity. They used a wide range of materials, which were twined or coiled into imaginative or symbolic designs. Baskets were used in all walks of life, including hunting, storage, cooking, and eating.

Headdresses
This headpiece, made out of black and white magpie feathers, derives from the native Miwok people.

TIMELINE

3,400,000 BC Volcanic ash from Mount St. Helens creates the Petrified Forest at Calistoga *(see p461)*		**200,000 BC** Early inhabitants, possibly predecessors of *Homo sapiens*, live near what is now Calico *(see p285)* *Early flint stone tool*
3,400,000 BC	**2,000,000 BC**	**200,000 BC**

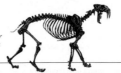

3,000,000 BC Plate movements form Redrock Canyon in Death Valley *(see pp290–93)*

Sabre-toothed tiger skeleton from La Brea Tar Pits

40,000 BC Mammoths, tigers, and other Pleistocene epoch creatures are trapped in Los Angeles' La Brea Tar Pits

Kule Loklo People
These early Bay Area inhabitants were depicted by Anton Refregier in his mural in the foyer of the Rincon Center (see p317).

WHERE TO SEE EARLY CALIFORNIA

The George C Page Museum of La Brea Discoveries *(see p118)* includes fossil reconstructions of creatures recovered from the nearby tar pits. The Chumash Painted Cave State Historic Park *(p219)* has rare pictographs executed by the Chumash people. LA's Southwest Museum *(p153)* and the California Academy of Sciences in San Francisco *(pp370–71)* both feature Native American artifacts.

Painted caves *dating back thousands of years have been carefully preserved in the Chumash Painted Cave State Historic Park in Southern California.*

Storage baskets were made in a variety of shapes, designs, and materials.

Water basket

Ladles were tightly woven to hold a large amount of water.

Woodpecker traps were made out of willow branches.

Ceremonial Costumes
Aprons made of animal skins and tails were worn by participants in the traditional White Deerskin Dance.

	8,000 BC Climate is warm enough to support cone-bearing trees	1,000 BC Ubehebe Crater formed in Death Valley *(see pp290–91)*	*Native American dwelling*	
10,000 BC	**6,000 BC**	**1,000 BC**		**AD 100**
10,000–8,000 BC Pleistocene epoch (Ice Age) ends. First Indians settle in California area	**6,000 BC** Climate is warm enough to support deciduous trees		**AD 100** Devil's Golf Course in Death Valley formed by an evaporated lake *(see pp290–91)*	

The Colonial Period

Although the Spanish "discovered" California in 1542, they did not colonize the area until the 18th century. Their rule was enforced through a trio of institutions – the mission (church), the *presidio* (fort), and the *pueblo* (town). Of these, the mission was the most influential. Beginning at San Diego in 1769, Franciscan friars founded 21 missions at **Mission** approximately 30-mile (48-km) intervals **statue** along *El Camino Real* ("the Royal Road"). Missionaries wanted to bring religion to the "benighted Indian," but they also used natives as cheap labor. European colonists committed a more serious crime by spreading diseases that would reduce the native population to about 16,000 by 1900.

• San Francisco de Solano *(1823)*
• San Rafael Arcangel *(1817)*

• San Francisco de Asis *(1776)*
   • San Jose *(1797)*
   • Santa Clara de Asis *(1777)*

Santa Cruz *(1791)*
•
   • San Juan Bautista *(1797)*

• Nuestra Señora de la Soledad *(1791)*
San Carlos Borromeo de Carmelo *(1770)*
• San Antonio de Padua *(1771)*

Sir Francis Drake
The English navigator landed in California in 1579 to make repairs to his ship, the Golden Hind. *He named the land "Nova Albion" and claimed it for Queen Elizabeth I.*

El Camino Real

San Miguel Arcangel
(1797)

San Luis Obispo de Tolosa
(1772)

La Purisma Concepcion
(1787)

• Santa Ines *(1804)*

Santa Barbara *(1786)*

San Buenaventura *(1782)* •

Father Junípero Serra
Originally from the Spanish island of Majorca, Father Junípero Serra led the Franciscan expedition to establish a chain of missions in California.

Jedediah Smith
In 1828, a fur-trapper, Jedediah "Strong" Smith, was the first white man to reach California overland across the Sierra Nevada Mountains, from the eastern United States.

TIMELINE

1524 Hernán Cortés, Spanish conqueror of Mexico, encourages King Charles V to seize control of the "California Islands"

1579 English privateer Francis Drake anchors his *Golden Hind* near Point Reyes *(see pp412–13)*

1500		1600	1650

1542 Juan Rodríguez Cabrillo (João Rodrigues Cabrilho) sails north from Mexico to San Diego harbor, making him the official discoverer of California

1595 Portuguese navigator Sebastián Rodríguez Cermeño discovers Monterey Bay

1602 Spanish merchant-adventurer Sebastián Vizcaíno sails up the California coast, naming landmarks as he goes – including San Diego, Santa Barbara, Point Concepcion, and Carmel

Juan Rodríguez Cabrillo

Mission San Gabriel Arcángel
Ferdinand Deppe's 1832 work is thought to be the first painting of a mission. It depicts the central role of the mission in the community, surrounded by Native American dwellings.

WHERE TO SEE COLONIAL CALIFORNIA

Restored living quarters *are displayed at the Santa Barbara Mission Museum.*

Mission-era artifacts can be found at San Francisco's Mission Dolores *(see p361)*, the Oakland Museum of California *(pp424–5)*, the Mission San Carlos Borromeo in Carmel *(pp512–13)*, and the Mission Santa Barbara *(pp222–3)*. Most of the 21 missions offer public tours.

US Victory
On July 9, 1846, 70 US sailors and marines marched ashore at San Francisco (then Yerba Buena) and claimed it for the US.

• San Fernando Rey de España *(1797)*

• San Gabriel Arcangel *(1771)*

• San Juan Capistranol *(1776)*

Mission Artifacts
The Franciscan friars brought many items from Spain and Mexico to California. As well as decorative objects, some, such as these prayer bells, had practical purposes.

• San Luis rey de Francia *(1798)*

• San Diego de Alcalá *(1769)*

EL CAMINO REAL
The 21 missions along El Camino Real, from San Diego to Sonoma, were planned so that each was one day's journey on horseback from the next.

1701 Father Eusebio Francesco Kino proves that Baja California is a peninsula, not an island

1781 Pueblo of Los Angeles founded

1776 Captain Juan Bautista de Anza reaches San Francisco and sites a new presidio *(see pp376–7)*

1835 William Richardson founds Yerba Buena, later renamed San Francisco

1822 Mexican Revolution ends Spanish rule of California

1700	1750	1800

18th-century presidio cannon

1769 Gaspar de Portolá discovers San Francisco Bay. California's first mission is founded at San Diego *(see p260)*

1777 Monterey becomes capital of Mexican California

1804 California's first orange grove is planted at San Gabriel Mission

John C Frémont

1846 John C Frémont leads Bear Flag Revolt *(see p464)*. US troops claim California from Mexico

The Rush For Riches

In 1848 newspaperman Sam Brannan brandished nuggets that had been found in the Sacramento Valley, shouting "Gold! Gold! Gold from the American River!" Most of the prospectors who thereafter stampeded California's Mother Lode did not find fortune. But the gold-seeking hordes changed the area forever – especially San Francisco. Between 1848 and 1850, the town's population shot from 812 to 25,000. Food and property prices skyrocketed and crime thrived. In 1859, after the Gold Rush had ended, silver ore (the Comstock Lode) was exposed on the eastern Sierras, and Northern California boomed again.

Nugget of Californian gold

Forty-Niners
Gold prospectors from all over the US traveled to California in 1849, hence their name. They carried tools, weapons, and food provisions on their journey.

Pickaxes were used to loosen hard rock ready for the sluice.

Barbary Coast Saloon
Gambling and prostitution were rife in San Francisco's Barbary Coast region, and men were often pressed into naval service.

State Capital
Once little more than farmland, Sacramento grew into a bustling city within two years of the Gold Rush. It became the state capital in 1854.

The sluice was a long trough with wooden bars. As water was flushed along, gold particles were trapped behind the bars.

TIMELINE

1848 California is annexed by the US. Gold discovered at Sutter's Mill *(see p475)*

1849 Almost 800 ships leave New York, full of men bound for the gold fields

Sign from the Flying Cloud clipper ship

1854 Sacramento becomes California state capital

1848	1850	1852	1854

John Sutter (1802–1880)

1850 California becomes 31st state in the Union

1851 San Francisco vigilante movement hangs several lawbreakers. Clipper ship *Flying Cloud* sails from New York to San Francisco in a record 89 days

1853 Levi Strauss lands in the Bay Area and begins selling his canvas trousers *(see p343)*

Count Agoston Haraszthy
The Hungarian was the first vintner to plant European grapevine cuttings in California.

Hydraulic mining blasted away rock with water to uncover gold underneath.

WHERE TO SEE THE ERA OF RICHES

Many of the settlements that were once thronged with gold miners have since disintegrated into ghost towns, such as Bodie *(p494)* and Calico *(p285)*. But you can still get a feel for the times at Columbia State Historic Park *(pp480–81)*, a restored Mother Lode town. The Wells Fargo History Museum in San Francisco *(p314)* has mementos of the Gold Rush. The Jackson Square Historical District *(p314)* was once part of the Barbary Coast.

Old schoolhouse at Calico ghost town

Comstock Lode Silver
Between 1859 and the mid-1880s, 400 million dollars worth of silver was extracted from mines in the High Sierras.

Gold panning involved swirling dirt and water around a flat-bottomed pan until only gold residue remained.

Emperor Norton
Self-proclaimed Emperor of the United States and Protector of Mexico, the eccentric Joshua Norton printed his own currency and gave advice to Sacramento legislators.

GOLD MINING TECHNIQUES

As the rush for gold increased, ways of extracting the ore became more sophisticated. What began as an adventure became a highly developed industry.

1855 Vigilante justice is enforced in Los Angeles	**1856** Street-murder of newspaper publisher James King of William sparks San Francisco's second vigilante uprising; William T Sherman leads militia campaign to restrain them		**1859** Prospector James Finney discovers silver deposits, the Comstock Lode	**1860** Bankrupt grain merchant Joshua Norton declares himself Norton I, Emperor of the United States until his death in 1880

1856	**1858**	**1860**

San Francisco vigilante medal

1857 Agoston Haraszthy, father of California's wine industry, founds the Buena Vista estate in the Sonoma Valley *(see p465)*

1861 California swears allegiance to the Union. The first oil well is drilled

Humboldt County oil well

The Gilded Age

For California's *nouveaux riches*, the smartest address during the late 19th century was on Nob Hill in San Francisco *(see p330)*, where grand mansions were built. This was a time of ostentation but also of expansion, thanks to train connections with the East and South. California oranges could now be exported easily to New York markets; taking the return trip were European immigrants and others hoping for a better life on the West Coast. Land prices increased in LA County, and by 1900 San Francisco's population exceeded 300,000.

Gold pocket watch

Victorian Décor
Windows in the Winchester Mystery House (see pp430–31) are typically ornate.

Bathroom, with original bath tub and tiles

Front parlor

Transcontinental Railroad
On May 12, 1869, the final spike was driven for the new railroad, linking the East and West Coasts.

Dining room

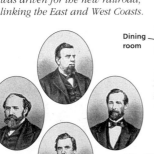

The "Big Four"
Charles Crocker, Leland Stanford, Collis Huntington, and Mark Hopkins made millions investing in the transcontinental railroad.

TIMELINE

1863 Construction begins on the Central Pacific Railroad

1871 Racial violence in LA leaves about 20 Chinese dead

1873–5 Orange planting begins in Riverside

1876 Southern Pacific Railroad reaches Los Angeles

California oranges

1884 Sarah Winchester embarks on her 38-year house-building project in San Jose *(see pp430–31)*

1870   **1875**   **1880**

1869 Transcontinental railroad is completed

1873 Andrew Hallidie tests San Francisco's first cable car

San Francisco's first cable car

1877 San Franciscans torch Chinese stores and laundries to protest against cheap labor

1882 US Congress passes the Chinese Exclusion Act, limiting Chinese immigration

Sutro Baths
The largest swimming pool in San Francisco stood from 1896 until the 1960s.

WHERE TO SEE GILDED AGE CALIFORNIA

Public tours are held at the Haas-Lilienthal House *(see p348)* and the first cable car is on display at the Cable Car Barn *(p331)*, both in San Francisco. The "golden spike" from the transcontinental railroad is displayed, along with Big Four mementos, at the Stanford University Art Museum *(p427)*. Train buffs will also enjoy the California State Railroad Museum in Sacramento *(p473)*.

Yosemite National Park
Made a national park in 1890, Yosemite also became California's first tourist attraction and a popular image for advertisers.

The California State Railroad Museum *is a celebration of rail travel on the West Coast.*

The living room was originally the master bedroom.

Porch

Hall, with Victorian corner sofa

Chinese Immigrants
The "coolies" who helped build the transcontinental railroad stayed and set up businesses, such as laundries and restaurants, but were met with racism.

HAAS-LILIENTHAL HOUSE

Grocer William Haas built this elaborate Queen Anne-style house in 1886, one of many in San Francisco. Today it is a museum, and shows how a wealthy family would have lived at the end of the 19th century *(see p348)*.

1890 Yosemite wins national park status *(see pp488–91)*

1893 San Andreas Fault discovered by University of California geologist Andrew Lawson

1896 Comstock tunnel builder Adolph Sutro opens the world's largest indoor saltwater swimming center in San Francisco

Stanford University seal

1885	1890	1895

1888 Hotel del Coronado opens in San Diego *(see p255)*

1891 Stanford University opens *(see p427)*; future president Herbert Hoover is in the first graduating class

1894 West Coast's first world's fair is held in San Francisco's Golden Gate Park

1897 San Francisco merchants prosper by outfitting gold miners traveling to Canada's Klondike River

The Rise of Hollywood

In 1887, Kansas prohibitionist Harvey Henderson Wilcox wanted to call his farm and the LA suburb surrounding it "Figwood," after his chief crop. His wife chose instead a name she had overheard on a train: "Hollywood." By the 1920s, the film industry was making the town famous and offering Americans entertainment to help them escape the reality of World War I, Prohibition, and later, the Great Depression. Silent film stars such as Mary Pickford and Charlie Chaplin were succeeded by icons of a more glamorous Hollywood, such as Mae West and Errol Flynn. Wall Street bankers were quick to realize their potential and invested heavily in the film industry.

Oscar statuette

Panama Canal
Two world fairs celebrated the completion of the canal in 1915.

San Francisco Earthquake and Fire
After the 1906 disaster, many buildings had to be demolished.

Clara Bow, dubbed the "It" girl, was one of Hollywood's first sex symbols.

Actors were chosen for their looks and often had little stage experience.

Los Angeles Aqueduct
The vast aqueduct was built at a cost of $24.5 million to irrigate the arid south with melted snow from the High Sierras.

HOLLYWOOD'S SILENT ERA
The movie industry grew rapidly and soon large corporate studios emerged. *Mantrap* (1927) was one of hundreds of silent movies made each month.

TIMELINE

1905 Tobacco magnate Abbot Kinney opens his many-canaled resort of Venice (see p80), west of LA. Excavations begin on La Brea Tar Pits (see p119)

1907 San Francisco political "boss" Abraham Ruef pleads guilty to extortion and brings down Mayor Eugene Schmitz

1913 Opening of Owens Valley–Los Angeles aqueduct improves LA's access to water

1900	1905	1910

1901 A three-month waterfront labor strike affects San Francisco business; four men die and 300 are injured in hostilities

1906 San Francisco is struck on April 18 by the worst ever US earthquake, at an estimated 8.3 on the Richter scale: 3,000 die and 25,000 are left homeless

Early Hollywood film camera

1911 *The Law of the Range*, shot by William and David Horsley, is the first film made in Hollywood

Prohibition *(1920–33)*
*Los Angeles became a popular port of entry for
smugglers bringing illegal alcohol into the United
States from Mexico during the nationwide ban.*

WHERE TO SEE CLASSIC HOLLYWOOD

The likenesses of numerous movie
stars are displayed at the Hollywood
Wax Museum *(p109)*. The Hollywood
Studio Museum *(p112)*, once Cecil B
De Mille's offices, now exhibits movie
mementos. Some 200 stars have
cemented their fame in front of
Mann's Chinese Theatre *(p110)*.

Mann's Chinese Theatre *has handprints, footprints, and autographs of
film stars cemented in its forecourt.*

Paramount Studios *are the only
studios now located in Hollywood
and still attract would-be stars* (p113).

Studios operated like
factories, filming different
movies on adjacent sets.

Cameramen
used 35 mm
cameras,
operating at
24 frames per
second.

Directors also
found fame and
fortune in the
new industry.

Orchestras were often hired to
play in the background of a
scene during filming to create
the right mood for the actors.

**Aimee Semple
McPherson**
*In 1923 the
controversial
evangelist and
spiritualist opened
her Angelus Temple
in LA where she held
regular spiritual
revivalist meetings.*

1916 The Lockheed
brothers start
building airplanes in
Santa Barbara

WR Hearst

1924 LA
eclipses San
Francisco as the
most important
port on the
West Coast

1929 Stock exchange
crash causes national
Depression. Actor
Douglas Fairbanks, Sr.
hosts the first Academy
Awards presentation

1915

1920

1925

1915 San
Francisco and
San Diego
both hold
Panama-
Pacific
Expositions

1917 The US
enters World
War I

Norma Talmadge

1919 WR Hearst
begins construction
of his magnificent
castle at San Simeon
(see pp212–15)

1927 Actress
Norma Talmadge
is the first star to
cement her foot-
prints at Mann's
Chinese Theatre
(see p110)

1928
Cartoonist
Walt Disney
creates
character
of Mickey
Mouse

The California Dream

Movies and the new medium of television made California *the* symbol of America's postwar resurgence – suddenly everybody wanted the prosperous middle-class existence they believed was common here. The airplane industry, ship-yards, and agriculture had burgeoned during the war, and a sense of prosperity lasted through the 1950s. Suburbs sprang up to meet the needs of returning soldiers, while new highways were laid to make them accessible. Yet at the same time, state schools lacked funds, African- and Mexican-Americans faced discrimination and violence, and Hollywood found itself attacked by politicians as a hotbed of Marxist Communism.

Olympic Games 1932
Los Angeles won the bid to hold the 1932 games and built Exposition Park for the event (see pp164–5).

Longshoreman's Strike
On July 5, 1934, police opened fire on dockers striking for better conditions, killing two.

Kitchen units became more practical, with Formica counters.

Household appliances became more widely available, easing domestic duties.

Hoover Dam
In 1936 Hoover Dam was built on the Colorado River to supply electricity.

TIMELINE

1932 LA hosts its first Olympic Games	**1934** Alcatraz Island becomes a maximum security penitentiary *(see pp32–3)*	**1936** Hoover Dam begins supplying Southern California with much-needed electricity	**1940** Los Angeles opens its first freeway – Arroyo Seco Parkway	**1942** Japanese-Americans sent to relocation camps for "war security reasons" *(see p495)*

1930   **1935**   **1940**

1933 Prohibition ends. "Sunny Jim" Rolph, a popular San Francisco mayor turned California governor, shocks supporters by praising a lynch mob in San Jose

"Sunny Jim" Rolph

1937 The Golden Gate Bridge opens

1939 San Francisco's third world's fair, the Golden Gate Exposition, is held on Treasure Island

1941 Japan attacks US fleet at Pearl Harbor

1943 California becomes nation's leading agricultural state

Golden Gate Bridge
On May 28, 1937, an official convoy of black limousines were the first vehicles to cross the bridge, which links San Francisco with Marin County.

WHERE TO SEE THE CALIFORNIA DREAM

LA's Petersen Automotive Museum celebrates California's love affair with the car *(see p118)*. At the Treasure Island Museum in San Francisco, memorabilia from the Golden Gate International Exposition is displayed *(p412)*. A trip to the Sleeping Beauty Castle in Disneyland is the ultimate California Dream experience *(p233)*.

The Petersen Automotive Museum *displays many classic models. This 1959 Cadillac epitomizes California cars.*

Land of Plenty
California's agricultural industry boomed in the 1940s, and its farmland was the most productive in the US.

Large refrigerators, stocked with food, were a symbol of the California "good life."

THE CALIFORNIA HOME

Eduardo Paolozzi's image is a pastiche of California's white, middle- class lifestyle in the 1950s. Nuclear families, ranch houses, and outdoor living were all part of the "dream."

San Francisco Giant
Willie Mays was part of the first team to bring professional baseball to California in 1958.

1945 End of World War II. International delegates meet at San Francisco April 25–June 25 to found the United Nations

1955 Disneyland opens in Anaheim. Actor James Dean, 24, dies in a car accident near Paso Robles

James Dean

| 1945 | 1950 | 1955 |

United Nations flag

1953 Beginning of Cold War is a boost to California defense industry

1958 New York Giants baseball team moves to San Francisco, finally bringing Major League baseball to the West Coast

California Today

Since 1962, when California surpassed New York as the most populous state in the Union, it has become the focus of many of the country's most significant issues. UC Berkeley was home to America's Free Speech Movement during the 1960s, and Haight Ashbury in San Francisco was the mecca for the "hippie" movement. Silicon Valley leads high-tech development in the US, and California benefits commercially from its proximity to the Far East. However, the state is still at risk from earthquakes; San Francisco has a high proportion of the country's AIDS cases; and racial tension, especially in LA, has led to riots.

1978 Apple Computer produces its first personal computer

1976 French judges award California the top two prizes for wine at a blind tasting

1968 Democratic presidential candidate Robert Kennedy is assassinated at LA's Ambassador Hotel on June 5 after announcing his victory in the California primary

1962 Actress Marilyn Monroe dies in Hollywood, at age 36, from an overdose of sleeping pills

1967 Haight Ashbury is swamped by half a million young people celebrating the "Summer of Love" *(see p359)*

1970s Huey Newton, a founder of Oakland's Black Panther Party, is arrested in 1967 and becomes a symbol of resistance during the 1970s

1960	1970	1980

1960	1970	1980

1960 Winter Olympic Games are held at Squaw Valley near Lake Tahoe

1966 LA becomes the most populous county in the nation, with more than 7 million inhabitants

INDIANS WELCOME

InDIAN LAND

1978 San Francisco Mayor George Moscone and his deputy Harvey Milk are assassinated at City Hall on November 27 by former policeman Dan White

1969 American Indian Movement occupies Alcatraz Island *(see pp338–9)* to publicize its differences with the Bureau of Indian Affairs

1963 Surfing becomes a popular sport in California

1968 Richard Nixon becomes the first native-born Californian to be elected President of the United States. Discredited, Nixon retired to San Clemente in 1974 *(see p238)*

NIXON'S THE ONE!

1984 LA hosts its second Olympic Games

1992 Riots in LA follow the acquittal of four white police officers who were videotaped beating a black motorist, Rodney King

2004 Iconic movie star Arnold Schwarzenegger, married to news journalist Maria Shriver, is elected as governor of California

1991 AIDS becomes San Francisco's number one killer of men

1996 After 15 years as the speaker of the California Assembly, Democrat Willie Brown is sworn in as San Francisco's first black mayor

1990	2000

1990	2000

1994 An earthquake measuring 6.8 on the Richter scale strikes LA, killing more than 60 people, injuring 9,000, and destroying freeways

2001 An energy crisis grips the state, with rolling blackouts affecting all major cities

1987 Film director Steven Spielberg starts his own studio, Dreamworks

1995 The America's Cup yacht race, in which five countries compete, is held in San Diego from January to May

1989 The Bay Area endures its second worst earthquake, measuring 7.1 on the Richter Scale; 67 people die, another 1,800 are left homeless

LOS ANGELES

Los Angeles at a Glance

Greater Los Angeles is made up of 80 different towns, with a total population of more than 8.5 million and covering more than 460 sq miles (1,200 sq km). In this book, LA has been divided into six areas. Downtown is a cultural melting pot, juxtaposing Hispanic El Pueblo, Chinatown, Little Tokyo, and the Business District. The glamour of the movies is just one aspect of Hollywood and West Hollywood, which today is a vibrant area of museums and galleries. Beverly Hills, Bel Air, and Westwood are still the playgrounds of the stars. Beaches and ports in the coastal regions of Santa Monica Bay, Palos Verdes, and Long Beach show the importance of the sea to Angelenos. Around Downtown covers some of the outlying districts of the city, including Pasadena.

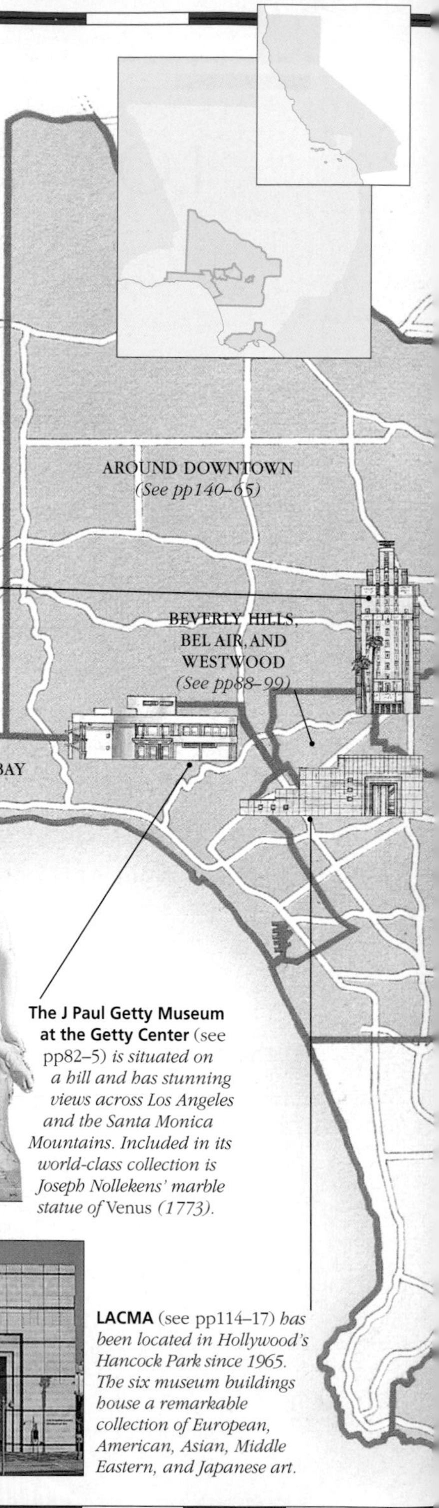

AROUND DOWNTOWN
(See pp140–65)

BEVERLY HILLS, BEL AIR, AND WESTWOOD
(See pp88–99)

SANTA MONICA BAY
(See pp74–87)

Sunset Boulevard (see pp102–7) *is one of the most famous roads in the world. Lined with clubs and hotels, the section known as Sunset Strip is the center of LA's nightlife.*

0 kilometers　5

0 miles　　　　5

The J Paul Getty Museum at the Getty Center (see pp82–5) *is situated on a hill and has stunning views across Los Angeles and the Santa Monica Mountains. Included in its world-class collection is Joseph Nollekens' marble statue of* Venus *(1773).*

LACMA (see pp114–17) *has been located in Hollywood's Hancock Park since 1965. The six museum buildings house a remarkable collection of European, American, Asian, Middle Eastern, and Japanese art.*

At Universal Studios (see pp146–9), *just north of Hollywood, visitors can see working film sets on the Studio Tour. A series of thrilling rides, based on the studios' movies, includes Jurassic Park – The Ride.*

The Huntington Library, Art Collections, and Botanical Gardens (see pp158–61) *in Pasadena have a wealth of treasures. The North Vista is one of the gardens' loveliest views.*

HOLLYWOOD AND WEST HOLLYWOOD
(See pp100–19)

DOWNTOWN LOS ANGELES
(See pp120–29)

AROUND DOWNTOWN
(See pp140–65)

El Pueblo (see pp124–5), *in the heart of Downtown Los Angeles, is the site of the city's first settlement. The area's Mexican population throngs its churches, plaza, and colorful markets, especially at festival time.*

The Queen Mary (see pp134–5), *one of the most famous liners in the world, is now permanently docked in Long Beach. The ship is still in use as a tourist attraction and luxury hotel. Many of its Art Deco features remain intact.*

LONG BEACH AND PALOS VERDES
(See pp130–39)

The Shape of Los Angeles

The city of Los Angeles sits in a broad, flat basin, facing the Pacific Ocean and enclosed by mountains. The San Gabriel Mountains and the Traverse Range come from the north, meeting the Santa Ana Mountains east of the city. The Santa Monica Mountains and the Hollywood Hills in the northwest split the basin, dividing the city center from the San Fernando Valley in the north. The shoreline varies from the rocky cliffs of Palos Verdes to the sands of Santa Monica Bay. Downtown, with the impressive skyscrapers of the Business District, sits in the center of the basin. Hollywood, Beverly Hills, and Santa Monica lie to the west.

Hollywood (see pp100–19) is the birthplace of the modern film industry. Its famous sign (see p145) stands out like a beacon above Tinseltown.

The San Fernando Valley (see p144), the city's great suburban sprawl, is home to the Mission San Fernando Rey de España.

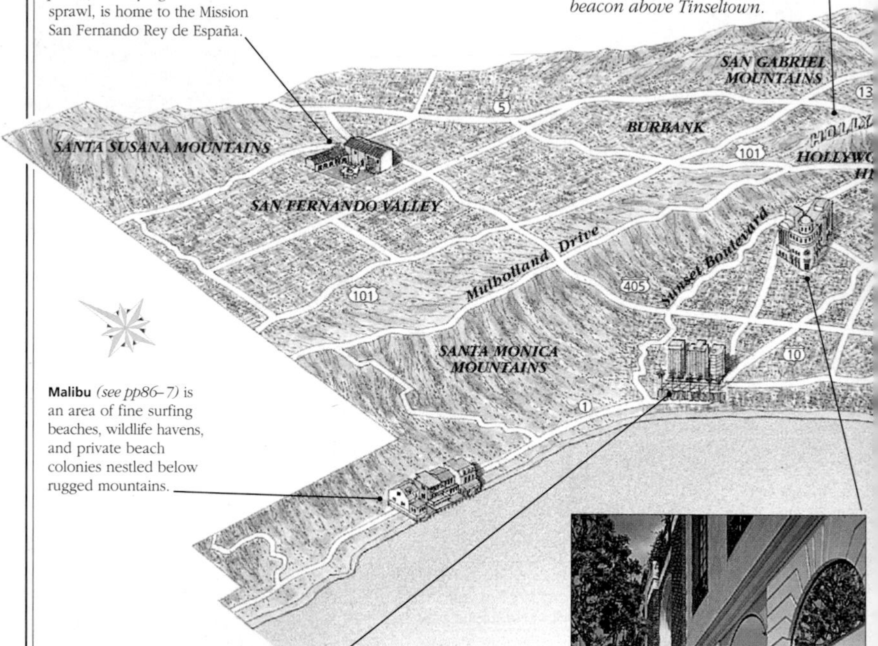

SAN GABRIEL MOUNTAINS

BURBANK

SANTA SUSANA MOUNTAINS

SAN FERNANDO VALLEY

HOLLYWOOD HI

Mulholland Drive

Sunset Boulevard

SANTA MONICA MOUNTAINS

Malibu (see pp86–7) is an area of fine surfing beaches, wildlife havens, and private beach colonies nestled below rugged mountains.

Santa Monica (see pp76–9), perched on palm-lined bluffs overlooking beautiful beaches, boasts stunning views. It is LA's oldest, largest beach resort, with all the traditional seaside attractions, such as a pier and amusement park. Santa Monica is also known for its excellent restaurants, boutiques, exciting nightlife, and vibrant arts scene.

Beverly Hills (see pp88–97) is home to the rich and famous of Los Angeles. Their lifestyle is epitomized by the exclusive shops that line Rodeo Drive.

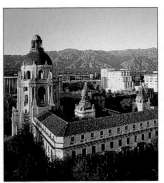

Pasadena (see pp154–61) *is an affluent community, with an ornate city hall. It grew up as a winter retreat for wealthy Easterners in the 19th century. Site of the Rose Bowl stadium, it has fine museums as well as excellent shopping and dining.*

Downtown Los Angeles *is a diverse area* (see pp120–29). *Attractions range from the skyscrapers of the Business District to the ethnic delights of Little Tokyo and Chinatown.*

Watts has the Watts Towers (see p163).

The City of Long Beach has a strong nautical tradition (see pp132–5).

VERDUGO MOUNTAINS

SAN RAFAEL HILLS

MONTEREY PARK

PUENTE HILLS

DOWNEY

BALDWIN HILLS

INGLEWOOD

COMPTON

DOMINGUEZ HILLS

SIGNAL HILL

TORRANCE

SANTA MONICA BAY

SAN PEDRO

PALOS VERDES HILLS

SAN PEDRO BAY

Los Angeles International Airport, *known simply as LAX, lies along the coast. It is well placed for easy access to most areas of the city and near major freeways leading out of town.*

Point Fermin lighthouse *is a Victorian landmark among the rocky cliffs of Palos Verdes* (see pp138–9).

North Los Angeles Coastline

Each year more than 30 million people visit the beaches around Los Angeles, making them the most popular destination on the West Coast. The Malibu headland, from Point Dume to Malibu Lagoon, alternates between rocky shorelines and beaches. Farther along, the shoreline becomes a long sandy strand leading to the renowned beaches at Santa Monica and Venice. Inland, the terrain of the Santa Monica Mountains is rugged and largely unspoiled, with plenty of hiking trails leading to panoramic views of the Pacific Ocean. The waters off the Malibu Pier, Leo Carillo, and Topanga state beaches are considered to be the best for surfing.

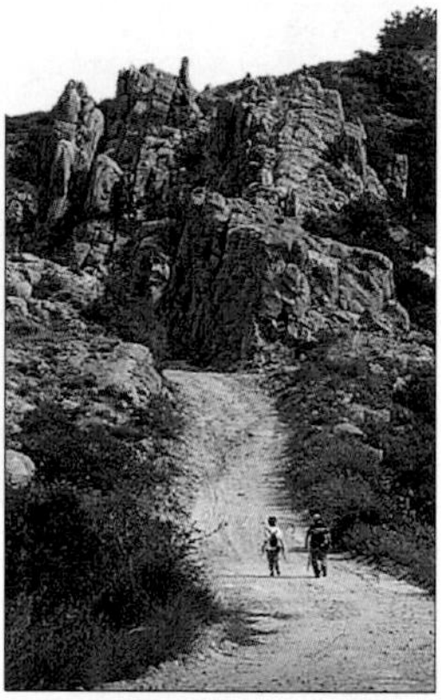

Castro Crest *is characterized by large areas of exposed reddish purple sandstone and oak woodland. The park's hiking trails offer magnificent views inland of the Santa Susana mountains and, offshore, the Channel Islands.*

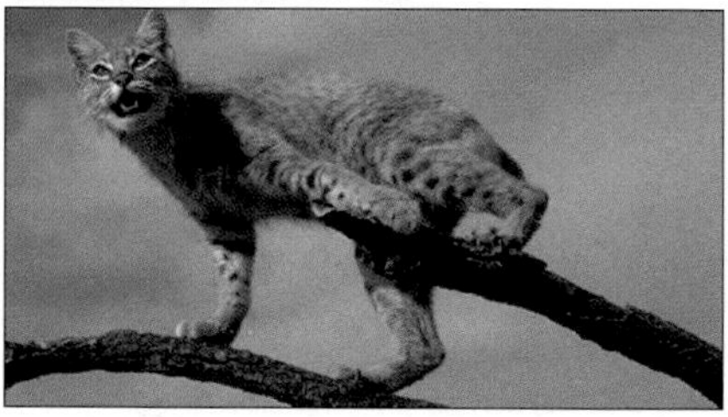

Cold Creek Canyon Preserve *was set up in 1970 to protect the rich diversity of fauna and flora found in the Santa Monica Mountains, including the bobcat, the Pacific tree frog, and the stream orchid.*

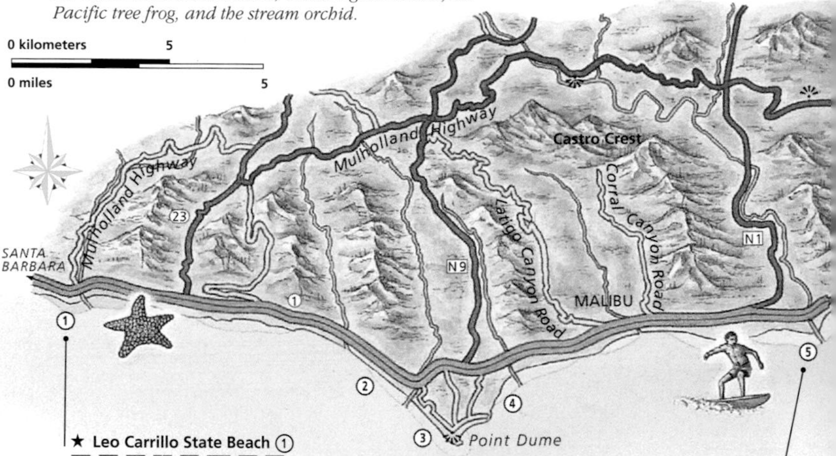
0 kilometers 5
0 miles 5
SANTA BARBARA
Mulholland Highway
Mulholland Highway
23
N9
N1
Castro Crest
Latigo Canyon Road
Corral Canyon Road
MALIBU
Point Dume
1
1
2
3
4
5

★ **Leo Carrillo State Beach** (1)

🏄 🌊 🏊 ⛑ ♿ 🚻 🤿 🎣

At low tide it is possible to explore the wide variety of life in the rock pools around Sequit Point.

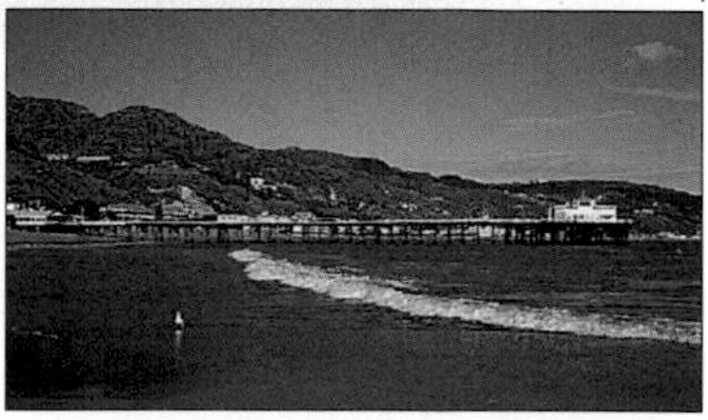

★ **Surfrider County Beach** (5)

🏄 🏊 ⛑ ♿ 🚻

One of California's finest surfing beaches, Surfrider has featured in many surfing films. Malibu Pier is a good place from which to watch the action.

Zuma County Beach ②
The white sands of Malibu's largest beach are very popular during the summer. There is good surfing and swimming, but be careful of the hazardous rip tides.

Point Dume County Beach ③
Surf fishing, diving, sunbathing, and exploring the rock pools beneath Point Dume are all popular activities on this sandy sheltered beach.

Paradise Cove ④
This privately owned cove was featured in the TV series *The Rockford Files*. The pier is a good place for surf fishing, and the beach is ideal for sunbathing and swimming.

Topanga State Beach ⑥
This narrow sandy beach is popular with windsurfers. It is divided in two by the mouth of Topanga Creek.

Marina del Rey Harbor ⑩
This is one of the world's largest artificial harbors *(see p80)*. The quaint Fisherman's Village, next to Basin H, has shops, cafés, and restaurants.

LOCATOR MAP

KEY

〰	Freeway
▬	Major road
▭	Minor road
⌇	River
⁂	Viewpoint

★ Venice City Beach ⑨
Backed by picturesque Venice *(see p80)*, Venice City Beach offers an eclectic mix of street performers, skaters, and body builders, working out on Muscle Beach.

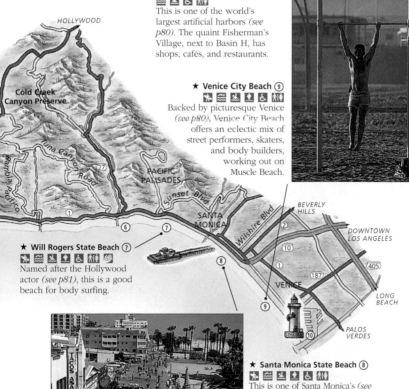

★ Will Rogers State Beach ⑦
Named after the Hollywood actor *(see p81)*, this is a good beach for body surfing.

★ Santa Monica State Beach ⑧
This is one of Santa Monica's *(see pp76–9)* most popular beaches. The group of houses at the western end of the beach are known collectively as "the Gold Coast."

South Los Angeles Coastline

The coast between Dockweiler State Beach and Torrance County Beach boasts shallow waters and wide stretches of sand, which are ideal for families. The two main communities, Manhattan Beach and Redondo Beach, have some of the cleanest waters off LA. Farther down the coast, the rocky bluffs of the Palos Verdes Peninsula shelter coves with rock pools teeming with marine life. Beyond Worldport LA, the coastline turns into a vista of white sand and rolling waves bordering Long Beach, the second largest city in LA County. Belmont Shores is popular with anglers. Windsurfers, sea kayakers, and jet-skiers frequent Alamitos Bay, home to the man-made canals and islands of Naples.

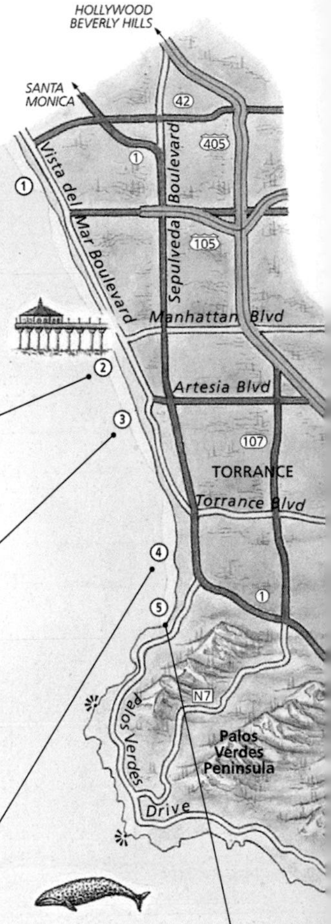

★ **Manhattan State Beach** ②
🏄 🌊 🏊 ⛑ ♿ 🚻
Backed by the coastal cycle path, this long wide beach is good for swimming, surfing, and fishing.

★ **Hermosa City Beach** ③
🏄 🌊 🏊 ⛑ ♿ 🚻
This family beach is ideal for all types of beach sports, as well as being popular with anglers who fish the surf for perch.

Worldport LA, *with its 28 miles (45 km) of waterfront, includes an oil terminal and cargo port. It is also home to the country's second largest fishing fleet.*

★ **Torrance County Beach** ⑤
🏄 🌊 🏊 ⛑ ♿ 🚻
Popular with surfers, swimmers, anglers, and divers alike, this beach marks the end of the Santa Monica Bay coastal cycle path *(see p178)*.

★ **Redondo State Beach** ④
🏄 🌊 🏊 ⛑ ♿ 🚻
A bronze bust commemorates George Freeth, who introduced surfing to California in 1907 at Redondo Beach.

Dockweiler State Beach ①
🚶 🏊 ⛵ 🎣 🚻

The north end of Dockweiler, beyond the harbor entrance, includes a nesting area for the rare California least tern.

Cabrillo Beach ⑥
🚶 🏊 ⛵ 🎣 ♿ 🚻

Split in two by the breakwater, Cabrillo has a fishing pier on the ocean side and a protected stretch of sand within San Pedro Bay.

Long Beach City Beach ⑦
🚶 🏊 ⛵ 🎣 ♿ 🚻

At the western end of Long Beach Strand, as it is also known, stands the old clap-board lifeguard headquarters, now a lifeguard museum.

Belmont Shores ⑧
🚶 🏊 ⛵ 🎣 ♿ 🚻

Belmont Pier, situated at the northern end of the beach, is used by anglers fishing for halibut, bonito, and perch. It is also a roosting site for the endangered California brown pelican. The beach stretches south as far as the mouth of the San Gabriel River.

LOCATOR MAP

Alamitos Bay ⑨
🏊 ⛵ ♿ 🚻

Windsurfing, waterskiing, and swimming are all popular activities in the protected waters of the bay.

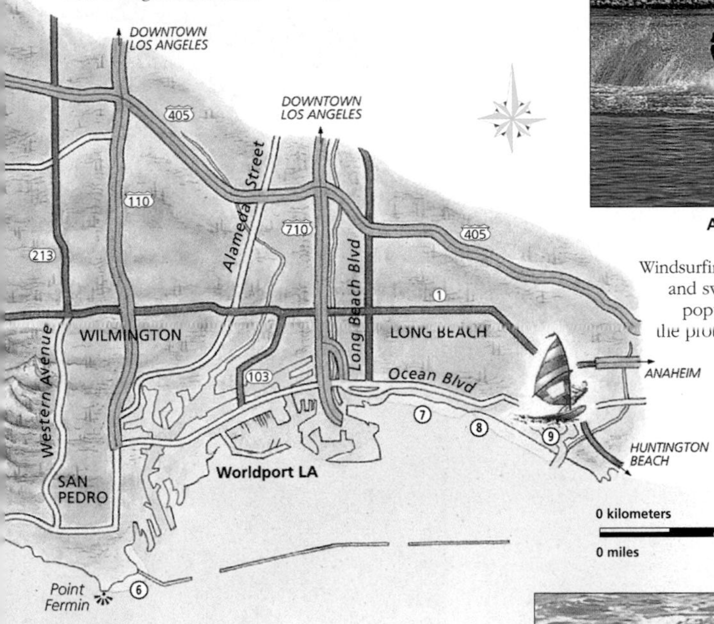

(Map of Long Beach area showing Downtown Los Angeles, freeways 405, 110, 213, 710, 103, Alameda Street, Long Beach Blvd, Western Avenue, Wilmington, Long Beach, Ocean Blvd, San Pedro, Worldport LA, Anaheim, Huntington Beach, Point Fermin ⑥, beaches ①⑦⑧⑨)

0 kilometers   5

0 miles   5

KEY

▬	Freeway
▬	Major road
▬	Minor road
～	River
☙	Viewpoint

Palos Verdes Peninsula *rises 1,300 ft (400 m) above the rocky shoreline, which is home to many wading birds. Steep trails connect the shore to the clifftop with its panoramic views.*

The Movies in Los Angeles

Hollywood street sign

When people refer to Los Angeles as an "industry town," they invariably mean the movie industry. Its great fantasy factories employ more than 60,000 people and pump about $4 billion into the LA economy every year. Hollywood Boulevard has sadly lost much of its glamour over the years; some film companies have decamped to cheaper movie-making places. But the air of Hollywood as a dream-maker, a place where a secretary named Ava Gardner or college football player John Wayne could be "discovered" and go on to earn million-dollar salaries, still persists.

Film crews *shooting location scenes for various Hollywood movies are a regular sight on Los Angeles' streets.*

The Griffith Observatory (see p150) was the setting for the teenage school trip and dramatic car race at the climax of the legendary film Rebel Without A Cause (1955). The film catapulted James Dean to stardom, but he was to die in a car crash later the same year.

WRITERS IN HOLLYWOOD

Hollywood novels have been a literary feature since the 1930s. Some writers, such as Nathaneal West and F Scott Fitzgerald, worked in Hollywood, only to turn against the town and publish novels that exposed its shallow and often cruel sides. West's *The Day of the Locust* (1939) is still considered the classic literary put-down of the film industry. Fitzgerald's posthumous *The Last Tycoon* (1941) sentimentalizes the career of Irving Thalberg, one of the most influential producers during Hollywood's "Golden Age." More recent is James Ellroy's *LA Confidential* (1997), a retro, atmospheric story of corruption and redemption in 1950s Los Angeles.

F Scott Fitzgerald

The Last Action Hero, *Arnold Schwarzenegger's 1993 blockbuster, filled this LA street with the excitement of controlled explosions, car chases, and stuntmen flying through the air.*

LA LOCATIONS

As well as utilizing the man-made sets erected on the backlots of the major studios in the 1940s and 1950s, film directors now regularly turn to the local landmarks of Los Angeles as locations for their films, often disguising them as other towns and cities. As a consequence, many of these places have become familiar to moviegoers all over the world.

Million-dollar contracts *have been a feature of Hollywood since Charlie Chaplin's eight-picture deal in 1917. Two-time Oscar winner Tom Hanks now demands as much as $20 million a picture – 100 times as much as the salary of the US President. Also in the eight-figure category are Robin Williams, Julia Roberts, and Harrison Ford. Studio executives justify these salaries by saying that big stars bring in a large enough audience to recoup the high production costs.*

Julia Roberts

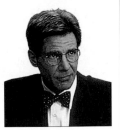
Harrison Ford

The Venice district *(see p80) saw actress Sarah Jessica Parker dancing around Steve Martin, in his 1991 hit film LA Story. The colorful buildings and characters of the area make it a popular film location.*

TOP GROSSING FILMS

Critics gush over *Citizen Kane* (1941) and *Casablanca* (1943) is the most popular Hollywood love story ever made. Yet neither of these films is on trade paper *Variety*'s list of the U.S. film industry's top ten moneymakers:

1. *Titanic* (1997)
2. *Star Wars* (1977)
3. *Shrek 2* (2004)
4. *E.T., the Extra Terrestrial* (1982)
5. *Star Wars: Episode I – The Phantom Menace* (1999)
6. *Spider-Man* (2002)
7. *The Lord of the Rings: The Return of the King* (2003)
8. *Spider-Man 2* (2004)
9. *The Passion of the Christ* (2004)
10. *Jurassic Park* (1993)

The only films made before 1960 on the top 50 list are *Gone With the Wind* (1939), at No. 40, and *Snow White and the Seven Dwarfs* (1937), at No. 45.

Santa Monica Pier *(see p78) should be familiar to fans of the gangster film The Sting (1973), starring actors Robert Redford and Paul Newman.*

Stargazing *is enjoyed by both visitors and locals in LA's many glamorous venues. Good opportunities to spot actors, directors, and film executives can be found at Wolfgang Puck's trendy Spagos (see p569) and the Polo Lounge at the Beverly Hills Hotel (see p525).*

Film poster for *E.T., the Extra Terrestrial*

Los Angeles's Best: Museums and Galleries

The museums of LA reflect the great diversity of the city. Collections ranging from natural history to Native American artifacts and from cowboy heritage to the history of the Holocaust educate and inspire the visitor. The city also contains many museums of art. Some of these display the private collections of the wealthy, such as Norton Simon, J Paul Getty, and Henry and Arabella Huntington, and feature internationally acclaimed Old Masters, Impressionist paintings, and European and Asian works of art. "Museum Row" on Wilshire Boulevard is home to five museums, including the renowned LACMA.

LACMA *is one of the top US art museums. Its collection includes La Trahison des Images (Ceci n'est pas une Pipe), painted by René Magritte in around 1928. (See pp114–17.)*

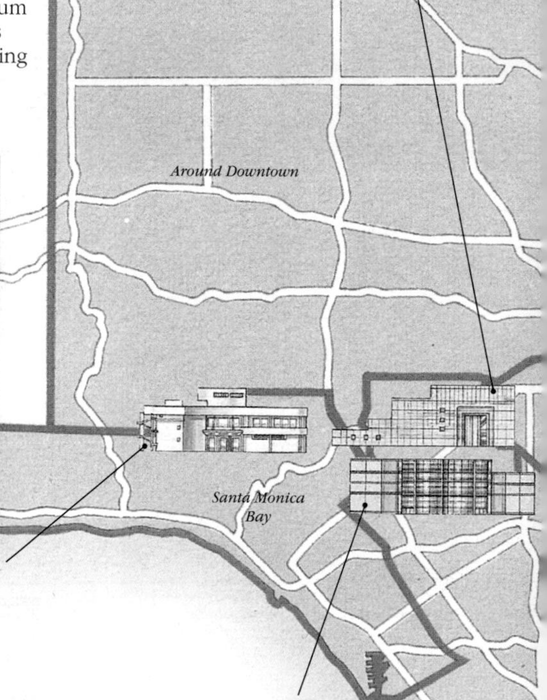

Around Downtown

Santa Monica Bay

J Paul Getty Museum *has recently relocated most of its holdings to the Getty Center in the Santa Monica Mountains. La Promenade (1870) by Pierre-Auguste Renoir is just one of the extraordinary paintings in this collection. (See pp82–5.)*

The Museum of Tolerance *aims to promote understanding between peoples. This sculpture of President Sadat of Egypt, with President Carter of the United States and Prime Minister Begin of Israel, illustrates that aim. (See p93.)*

0 kilometers   5

0 miles   5

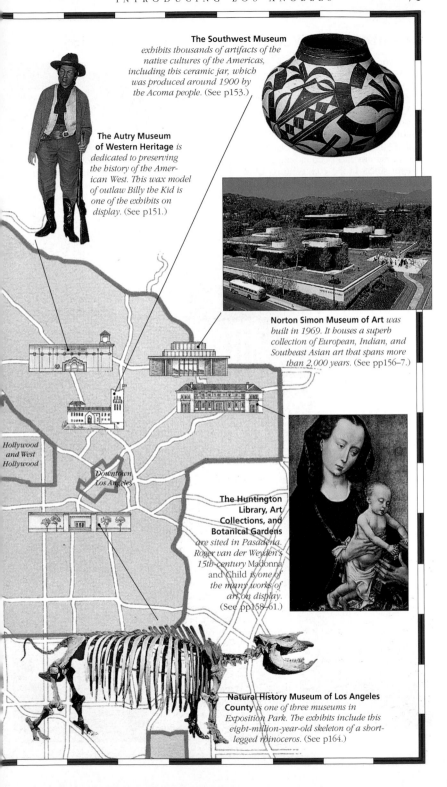

The Southwest Museum *exhibits thousands of artifacts of the native cultures of the Americas, including this ceramic jar, which was produced around 1900 by the Acoma people.* (See p153.)

The Autry Museum of Western Heritage *is dedicated to preserving the history of the American West. This wax model of outlaw Billy the Kid is one of the exhibits on display.* (See p151.)

Hollywood and West Hollywood

Downtown Los Angeles

Norton Simon Museum of Art *was built in 1969. It houses a superb collection of European, Indian, and Southeast Asian art that spans more than 2,000 years.* (See pp156–7.)

The Huntington Library, Art Collections, and Botanical Gardens *are sited in Pasadena. Roger van der Weyden's 15th-century Madonna and Child is one of the many works of art on display.* (See pp158–61.)

Natural History Museum of Los Angeles County *is one of three museums in Exposition Park. The exhibits include this eight-million-year-old skeleton of a short-legged rhinoceros.* (See p164.)

Contemporary Architecture in Los Angeles

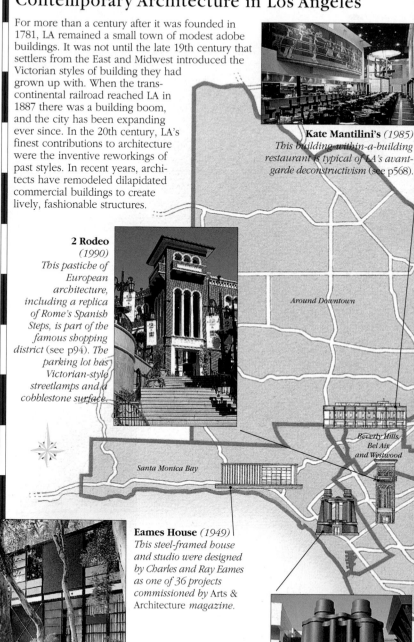

For more than a century after it was founded in 1781, LA remained a small town of modest adobe buildings. It was not until the late 19th century that settlers from the East and Midwest introduced the Victorian styles of building they had grown up with. When the transcontinental railroad reached LA in 1887 there was a building boom, and the city has been expanding ever since. In the 20th century, LA's finest contributions to architecture were the inventive reworkings of past styles. In recent years, architects have remodeled dilapidated commercial buildings to create lively, fashionable structures.

Kate Mantilini's *(1985)*
This building-within-a-building restaurant is typical of LA's avant-garde deconstructivism (see p568).

2 Rodeo
(1990)
This pastiche of European architecture, including a replica of Rome's Spanish Steps, is part of the famous shopping district (see p94). The parking lot has Victorian-style streetlamps and a cobblestone surface.

Around Downtown

Beverly Hills, Bel Air and Westwood

Santa Monica Bay

Eames House *(1949)*
This steel-framed house and studio were designed by Charles and Ray Eames as one of 36 projects commissioned by Arts & Architecture *magazine.*

TBWA Chiat/Day Advertising Agency *(1991)*
Frank Gehry, the leading LA architect, designed this striking building (see p78).

Disney Studio Office Building (1991)
Michael Graves' Post-Modern Disney building in Burbank includes a classically inspired pediment supported by 19-ft (5.7-m) statues of the Seven Dwarfs. Inside, chairs incorporate Mickey Mouse in their design (see pp144–5).

Ennis House (1924)
The base, plan, and textured interiors of this house are typical of Frank Lloyd Wright's "textile block" houses.

Gamble House (1908)
This is the finest example of Charles and Henry Greene's turn-of-the-century Arts and Crafts bungalows. Its expansive eaves, outdoor sleeping porches, and elegant interior are characteristic of the brothers' style (see p154).

Hollywood and West Hollywood

Downtown Los Angeles

Union Station (1939)
The last of the great American railroad terminals, the vaulted concourse, arches, waiting room, and patios combine Mission Revival and Streamline Moderne styles (see p128).

Eastern Columbia Building (1930)
This Art Deco building, designed by Claude Beelman, is one of the most impressive of its kind in LA.

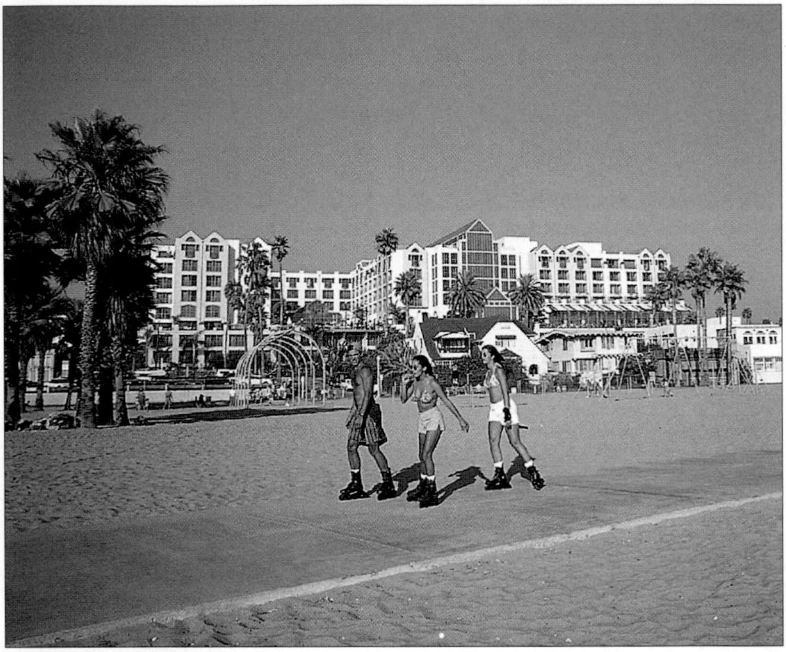

In-line skaters on Venice Beach boardwalk

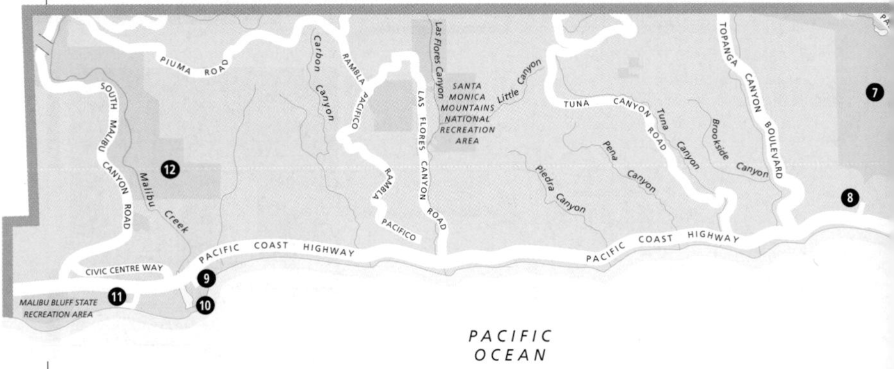
PIUMA ROAD
SOUTH MALIBU CANYON ROAD
Malibu Creek
Carbon Canyon
RAMBLA PACIFICO
Las Flores Canyon
LAS FLORES CANYON ROAD
SANTA MONICA MOUNTAINS NATIONAL RECREATION AREA
Little Canyon
TUNA CANYON ROAD
Tuna Canyon
Pena Canyon
Piedra Canyon
Brookside Canyon
TOPANGA CANYON BOULEVARD
PACIFIC COAST HIGHWAY
CIVIC CENTRE WAY
MALIBU BLUFF STATE RECREATION AREA
PACIFIC OCEAN

SIGHTS AT A GLANCE

Districts

Malibu Colony 11
Marina del Rey 3
Santa Monica pp76–9 1
Venice 2

Museums

Adamson House and Malibu Lagoon Museum 9
J Paul Getty Museum at the Getty Center pp82–5 5
The Getty Villa 8
Museum of Flying 4

Parks and Beaches

Malibu Creek State Park 12
Malibu Lagoon State Beach 10
Topanga State Park 7
Will Rogers State Historic Park 6

KEY

Street-by-Street map
See pp76–7

0 kilometers 2

0 miles 2

SANTA MONICA BAY

With its warm sun, cool sea breezes, miles of sandy beaches, excellent surf, and world-class museums, Santa Monica Bay epitomizes the best of California. The area was inhabited by the Chumash and Tongva/Gabrielino peoples for 2,500 years before the arrival in 1542 of the Spanish explorer Juan Cabrillo *(see p46)*. In the early 19th century, Santa Monica Bay was divided into several land grants, including Rancho San Vicente y Santa Monica and Rancho Topanga Malibu Sequit. In 1875, Nevada senator John Percival Jones bought control of the former, hoping the port of Los Angeles would be built there. Thankfully, that honor went to

San Pedro *(see pp138–9)* and the beach resorts of Santa Monica and Venice were developed in its place. These areas have remained two of the most attractive and lively parts of Los Angeles.

Farther along the coast, the Rancho Topanga Malibu Sequit was bought in 1887 by Frederick and May Rindge. The Rindge family fought with the state for many years to keep their property secluded. Eventually failing, they sold much of Malibu to the rich and famous. Large areas of Santa Monica Bay have remained undeveloped, however. The vast Topanga and Malibu Creek state parks help to improve Los Angeles's air quality and offer miles of hiking trails.

Swimmer in Venice Beach

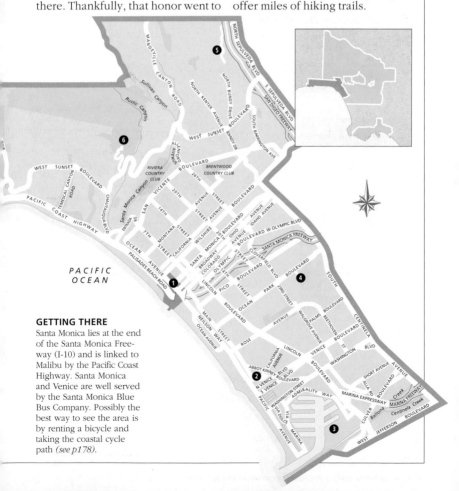

GETTING THERE

Santa Monica lies at the end of the Santa Monica Freeway (I-10) and is linked to Malibu by the Pacific Coast Highway. Santa Monica and Venice are well served by the Santa Monica Blue Bus Company. Possibly the best way to see the area is by renting a bicycle and taking the coastal cycle path *(see p178)*.

PACIFIC OCEAN

Street-by-Street: Santa Monica ❶

Street entertainer

Santa Monica's fresh sea breezes, mild climate (on average, the sun shines here 328 days a year), and pedestrian-friendly streets make it one of the best places in LA to go for a stroll. The city is perched on a high yellow cliff over-looking Santa Monica Bay and miles of broad, sandy beach. Running along the cliff edge is palm-shaded Palisades Park, a narrow, 26-acre (10-ha) garden offering spectacular views, especially at sunset. A stairway leads down to Santa Monica's famous beach and pier. A few blocks inland from the hotel-lined seafront is Third Street Promenade – a great place to sit outside a café or restaurant and people-watch.

View from Palisades Park
The cliff top park offers pano-ramic views of Santa Monica Bay. Looking northward, you can see all the way to Malibu.

★ Third Street Promenade
Metal and topiary fountains, shaped like dinosaurs, decor-ate these three lively blocks. This is one of the best outdoor shopping areas in LA.

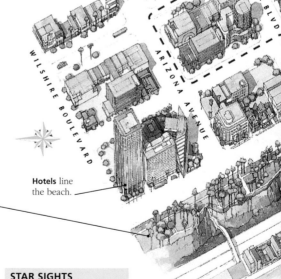

Hotels line the beach.

★ Palisades Park
This narrow strip of park-land, planted with mature palm trees, is a good place to walk, jog, or sit on a bench and admire the view. In the evening, many people come here to watch the sun go down.

STAR SIGHTS

★ Palisades Park

★ Santa Monica Pier

★ Third Street Promenade

KEY

– – – Suggested route

0 meters 200
0 yards 200

Santa Monica Place

This lively shopping mall was designed by architect Frank Gehry in 1979. The first-floor food hall offers a variety of reasonably priced meals. The stores on the upper two levels range from chain stores to individual boutiques.

LOCATOR MAP

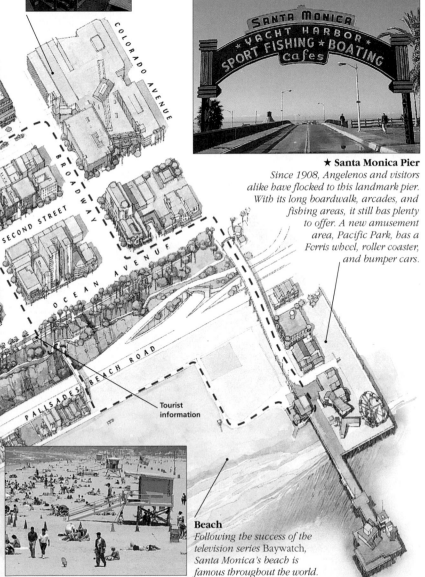

★ Santa Monica Pier
Since 1908, Angelenos and visitors alike have flocked to this landmark pier. With its long boardwalk, arcades, and fishing areas, it still has plenty to offer. A new amusement area, Pacific Park, has a Ferris wheel, roller coaster, and bumper cars.

Tourist information

Beach
Following the success of the television series Baywatch, *Santa Monica's beach is famous throughout the world.*

Exploring Santa Monica

Statue in Bergamot Station gallery

Santa Monica has been the star of LA's coastline since the 1890s, when trolleys linked it to the city, and beach parties became the rage. In the early days, it lived a dual life as a sleepy coast town and the headquarters for offshore gambling ships. In the 1920s and 1930s, movie stars such as Cary Grant and Mary Pickford bought land here, creating "the Gold Coast." The beach and pier are still major attractions, but the city is now also famous for its restaurants *(see p573)*. With the cleanest air in LA, Santa Monica offers many outdoor shopping areas and an active arts scene. Bergamot Station and the Edgemar complex on Main Street have a range of galleries.

Frank Gehry's innovative design for the TBWA Chiat/Day Advertising Agency

Around Santa Monica

Grassy parks dot the city's landscape, with none quite as beautiful or revered as **Palisades Park** on the bluff overlooking the ocean. Stretching 1.5 miles (2.5 km) along the cliff's edge, this narrow, well-manicured park is one of the best spots to watch the sun go down. For the quintessential California experience, take a walk or jog along the paths, with the ocean as a backdrop and the towering palms overhead. The landscaping is beautiful, with semitropical trees and plants. At the northern end, the aptly named Inspiration Point has great views of the bay, stretching from Malibu to Palos Verdes.

Inland, between Wilshire Boulevard and Broadway, is **Third Street Promenade**. Once a decaying shopping street, this boulevard has undergone a major face-lift and is now one of the liveliest places in Los Angeles. Its three pedestrian blocks are lined with shops, coffee houses, restaurants, bookstores,

and theaters. At night the mood is especially festive. Street performers entertain passersby with music, dance, puppet shows, and magic tricks. Nearby, on Arizona Avenue, a farmers' market on Saturdays and Wednesdays is one of the best in the city.

Santa Monica's other important shopping area is **Main Street**, which runs south toward Venice *(see p80)*. At the turn of the 20th century, Main Street was the commercial district for Pacific Ocean Park, an amusement park, baths, and pier. By the early 1970s, however, the majority of the neighborhood's attractions had been demolished, and Main Street itself had become a slum.

Today, this revitalized street abounds with a wide range of

shops, superb restaurants, and first-rate art galleries.

There are many examples of public art displayed along Main Street. Sculptor Paul Conrad's *Chain Reaction* (1991) is a stainless-steel and copper-link chain statement against nuclear war. It stands next to the Civic Auditorium. *Ocean Park Pier* (1976), a mural by Jane Golden and Barbara Stoll, is situated at the junction with Ocean Park Boulevard and depicts the Pacific Ocean Park in the early 1900s.

A lovely example of Spanish Colonial architecture remains at the northwest corner of Main Street and Pier Avenue. Nearby, the TWBA Chiat/Day Advertising Agency building, designed in 1991 by Frank Gehry and shaped like a giant pair of binoculars, dominates the street *(see p72)*.

🚋 Santa Monica Pier

Colorado & Ocean aves. *Tel* (310) 458-8900 (260-8744 Pacific Park). ◻ daily. **Carousel** *Tel* (310) 395-4248. ◻ May–Sep: 10am–5pm Tue –Sun; Oct – Apr: 10am–5pm Sat & Sun. 📷 **www**.santamonicapier.org

This popular 1908 landmark is the West Coast's oldest amusement pier, with popcorn, cottoncandy, bumper cars, and an amusement arcade. At the western end, Pacific Park has a roller coaster and a Ferris wheel rising 11 stories high. Nearby, the 1922 Looff Carousel, similar to that in Santa Cruz *(see p506)*, with 44 handcrafted horses, was featured in George Roy Hill's

Chain Reaction by Paul Conrad

Beach apartments along the front of Palisades Park

1973 film *The Sting (see p69)*. You can fish without a permit from the balconies on the pier's lower deck. On Thursday evenings during the summer, there is free dancing and live music *(see p173)*.

🏛 **Bergamot Station**
2525 Michigan Ave. **Tel** *(310) 829-5854.* ⬜ *10am–5:00pm Tue–Fri, 11am–5pm Sat.* ⚫ *Sun, public hols.*
Bergamot Station is a 5.5-acre (2-ha) arts complex that stands on the site of an abandoned Red Line trolley station. The crude buildings are constructed from aluminum siding, with an added touch of high-tech styling. More than 20 galleries showcase the latest works in contemporary and radical art, including painting, sculpture, photography, furniture, and glass, as well as collectibles and African art. Bergamot Station also houses a number of artists' studios.

Victorian façade of the California Heritage Museum

there are changing exhibitions on topics such as surfing *(see pp198–9)*, the Hollywood Western, quilts, and Monterey Rancho-style furniture.

🏛 **Santa Monica Museum of Art**
Building G-1, Bergamot Station. **Tel** *(310) 586-6488.* ⬜ *11am–6pm Tue–Sat.* ⚫ *Jan 1, Jul 4, Thanksgiving, Dec 25.* **www**.smmoa.org
The Santa Monica Museum of Art is dedicated to both contemporary and modern art. Its main aim is to publicize the work of living artists, particularly those involved in performance and multimedia art. In May 1998 the museum re-opened after moving to its exciting new, 930 sq m (10,000 sq ft) home. It is located in the large arts complex, Bergamot Station, along with over 20 other galleries. Although the museum does not have any permanent collections, a wide range of artists' work is represented in the individual exhibitions. The new site also houses a museum book shop.

VISITORS' CHECKLIST

Road map inset A. 🏠 *90,000.*
✈ *LAX 8 miles (13 km) SE of Santa Monica.* 🚌 *4th St & Colorado Blvd.* ℹ *Palisades Park, 1400 Ocean Ave (310-393-7593).* 🎪 *Santa Monica Festival (Apr).*

Cuban political poster on display in Bergamot Station

🏛 **California Heritage Museum**
2612 Main St. **Tel** *(310) 392-8537.* ⬜ *11am–4pm Wed–Sun.* ⚫ *Jan 1, Jul 4, Thanksgiving, Dec 25.* 🎟 ♿ **www**.californiaheritagemuseum.org
The Queen Anne museum building was built in 1894 by architect Sumner P Hunt as the home of Roy Jones, son of the founder of Santa Monica *(see p75)*. On the first floor, the rooms depict the lifestyle of various periods in Southern California history: a Victorian dining room, an Arts and Crafts living room, and a 1930s kitchen. Upstairs,

RAYMOND CHANDLER

Novelist and screenwriter Raymond Chandler (1888–1959) set several of his works wholly or partly in Santa Monica, a city that he loathed and that he thinly disguised as sleazy Bay City in *Farewell, My Lovely*. There was some truth in Chandler's portrayal of Santa Monica. Corruption and vice in the 1920s and 1930s are well documented. Illegal gambling ships were anchored offshore, including the *Rex*, 5 miles (8 km) out in Santa Monica Bay, called the *Royal Crown* in *Farewell, My Lovely*.
Chandler's novels *Farewell, My Lovely*, *The Big Sleep*, *The High Window*, *The Little Sister*, and *The Long Goodbye* were made into films that portrayed the shadowy side of LA. With an elegant, dark style, he wrote vivid dialogue in the voice of the common man. His character Philip Marlowe was the definitive detective. A loner with a hard-boiled veneer often hiding a soft heart, Marlowe uttered tough one-liners, played by the rules, and usually didn't get the girl.

Film poster for *The Big Sleep* (1946)

Venice ❷

Road map inset A. ▮ *2904 Washington Blvd, Suite 100 (310 396-7016).*
www.venice.net

Since its inception, Venice
has attracted a bohemian
society, from the rowdy crowd
who frequented its dance hall
and bathhouse in the 1910s to
beatniks in the 1950s. Today,
the town has a large population of artists, whose studios
line the streets.

The community was founded
in 1900 by tobacco magnate
Abbot Kinney as a US version
of Venice, Italy. Hoping to
spark a cultural renaissance in
southern California, he built a
system of canals and imported
gondolas and gondoliers to
punt along the waterways.
Unfortunately, Kinney did not
take the tides into considera-
tion when designing Venice,
and the area was constantly
dogged by sewage problems.

Today, only a few of the
original 7 miles (11 km) of
canals remain, the rest having
been filled in during 1927. The
traffic circle at Windward
Avenue was the main lagoon,
and Grand Boulevard, which
runs southeast from there, was
the Grand Canal. The best
place to see the remaining
canals is on Dell Avenue,
where old bridges, boats, and
ducks grace the waterways.

Over the years, the circus
atmosphere of Venice Beach

has never faltered. On the
boardwalk during weekends,
semiclad men and women
whiz past on bicycles and
skates, while a zany array of
street performers, like chain-
saw jugglers and one-man
bands, captivates the crowds. .
Muscle Beach, where Arnold
Schwarzenegger used to work
out, still attracts body builders.

While Venice Beach is safe
to explore on foot by day, it
is best avoided at night.

**Yachts moored in the harbor at
Marina del Rey**

Marina del Rey ❸

Road map inset A. ▮ *4111 Via
Marina (310 821-0555).*

Covering an area of just
1.3 sq miles (3.4 sq km),
approximately half of which
is water, Marina del Rey has

the world's largest artificial
small-craft harbor. Those
attracted to this town tend to
be young and single or with
families, and enjoy outdoor
activities such as skating,
cycling, and water sports.
Everything from paddle boats
to yachts can be rented, or you
can charter boats for deep-sea
fishing or a luxury cruise.

Fisherman's Village, on Fiji
Way, resembles a New England
fishing town. It has a variety of
shops, restaurants, and cafés,
many of which offer beautiful
views of the harbor.

Museum of Flying ❹

2772 Donald Douglas Loop North.
Tel *(310) 392-8822.* ⬤ Closed until
mid-2006; call or check website for details.
⬛ Wed–Sun, by advance reservation.
www.museumofflying.com

The first airplane to fly
around the world, the 1924
New Orleans, is on display at
this fascinating museum of
aviation history. Other highlights of the collection of 40
aircraft are P-51 Mustangs and
Spitfires, the victorious fighter
planes of World War II. Interactive exhibits explain the
complexities of aircraft design,
and there are workshops for
children, who can take part in
a variety of related activities.
Some of the vintage aircraft
remain airworthy, and visitors

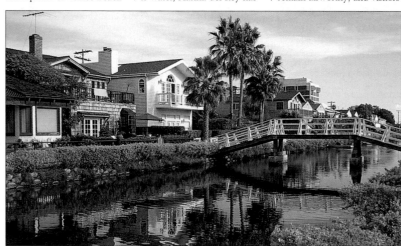

Man-made canal in Venice

can watch them take off from and land at the adjacent Santa Monica Airport. Classic aviation films are also shown.

Yellow Peril Boeing Stearman at the Museum of Flying

THE WILDLIFE OF SANTA MONICA BAY

Among the marine mammals that inhabit the waters of Santa Monica Bay are harbor seals, California sea lions, and bottle-nosed dolphins. From December to February gray whales can be seen migrating from Alaska to Baja California to calve. One of the best places in Los Angeles for whale-spotting is Point Dume. In the mountains, the range of wildlife is exceptional. The rare mountain lion can reach a size of 7 ft (2 m) in length and tends to live in the rockier, more remote areas. Its cousin the bobcat is smaller, with tufts of hair on the ends of its ears. Coyotes come out at dusk, often preying on the pets of people living in the hills. The bold, intelligent raccoon raids camp sites even when people are present. Mule deer, desert cottontail, and striped skunk also abound. Birds seen here include golden eagles and red-tailed hawks.

Raccoon *(Procyon lotor)*

J Paul Getty Center ❺

See pp82–5.

Will Rogers State Historic Park ❻

1501 Will Rogers State Park Blvd, Pacific Palisades. **Road map** inset A. **Tel** *(310) 454-8212.* ☐ *8am–sunset daily.* ● *Jan 1, Thanksgiving, Dec 25.* ☑ ♿ *lawn area.* ☑

Will Rogers (1879–1935) started life as a cowboy and went on to become a film star, radio commentator, and newspaper columnist. Called the "Cowboy Philosopher," he was famous for his homespun humor and shrewd comments on current events, usually made while performing rope tricks. His show business career lasted from 1905 until his death. When his widow, Betty, died in 1944, she deeded the house and the surrounding 186 acres (75 ha) of land to the state. Her will stipulated that nothing in the house be changed and that polo matches be held on weekends (Rogers was an avid polo player).

Hiking trails lead up from the ranch, many of them originally cut by Rogers. The lawn just east of the house is an ideal setting for a picnic. Tours of the house include the living room, where Rogers used to practice his roping skills.

Topanga State Park ❼

20825 Entrada Rd, Topanga. **Road map** inset A. **Tel** *(310) 455-2465 & (805) 488-8147 for fire conditions in summer & autumn.* ☐ *8am–sunset daily.* ☑ ♿

Topanga State Park stretches from the Pacific Palisades to the San Fernando Valley *(see p144).* Topanga is thought to be an Indian term meaning "the place where the mountains meet the sea." The area was inhabited by the Tongva/ Gabrielino and Chumash Indians 5,000 years ago. Today, its groves of sycamore and oak trees attract people seeking an alternative way of life.

The marked entrance to the 13,000-acre (5,300-ha) park lies just north of Topanga village, off Hwy 27 on Entrada Road. Most of the land falls within the LA city boundary, making it the largest city park in the US. As such, it vastly improves the region's air quality and provides ample space for hiking and riding.

As you ascend the Santa Monica Mountains, canyons, cliffs, and meadows give way to vistas of the ocean and the San Fernando Valley. Four trails begin from the park's headquarters at Trippet Ranch: a 1-mile (1.6-km) self-guided nature trail; the Dead Horse Trail; Musch Ranch Trail (which leads to a camp site); and East Topanga Fire Road, which connects with Eagle Junction. The 2.5-mile (4-km) Eagle Rock/Eagle Spring Trail from Eagle Junction is one of the most popular.

Bicycles are allowed on the park's dirt fire roads, and horses on all but one of the trails.

Hiking trails crossing the Santa Monica Mountains in Topanga State Park

J Paul Getty Museum at the Getty Center ❺

The Getty Center, which opened in December 1997, holds a commanding physical and cultural position in the city. It is situated amid the wild beauty of the Santa Monica Mountains, in the Sepulveda Pass, next to the San Diego Freeway (I-405). The complex houses not only the museum but also the Getty's research, conservation, and grant programs, dedicated to art and cultural heritage. Getty made his fortune in the oil business and became an ardent collector of art. He wanted his collection, which focuses on European art from the Renaissance to Post-Impressionism, to be open to the public without charge. Greek and Roman antiquities are displayed at the Getty Villa in Malibu *(see p86).*

LOCATOR MAP

▨	Illustrated area
▨	Research, conservation, education, administration, restaurant, café, and auditorium buildings
▨	Tram station

★ Irises *(1889)*
This work was painted by Vincent Van Gogh while he was in the asylum at St-Rémy. Its graphic style reveals the influence of artists such as Paul Gauguin (1848–1903) and the Japanese print-maker Hokusai (1760–1849).

East Pavilion

Hispano-Moresque Deep Dish
This elaborately decorated earthenware dish was made in Valencia, Spain, in the mid-15th century. The use of lustrous colors was a specialty of Moorish potters at that time.

North Pavilion

Courtyard

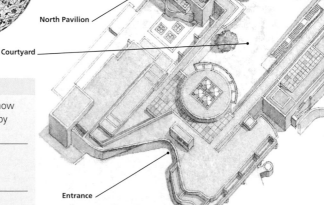

STAR PAINTINGS

★ Wheatstacks, Snow Effect, Morning by Claude Monet

★ The Abduction of Europa by Rembrandt

★ Irises by Vincent Van Gogh

Entrance

For hotels and restaurants in this region see pp524–31 and pp568–76

Cabinet on Stand
Attributed to the French master craftsman André-Charles Boulle, this 17th-century cabinet was made to celebrate the victories of Louis XIV.

VISITORS' CHECKLIST

1200 Getty Center Drive.
Road map inset A.
Tel (310) 440-7300. ◯
10am–6pm Tue–Thu, Sun;
10am–9pm Fri–Sat.
⬤ *public hols.* ♿ 📷 ⅰⅰ
💻 www.getty.edu

South Pavilion

West Pavilion

South Promontory

Korean Man
(c.1617)
This drawing in black and red chalk is by the Flemish artist Peter Paul Rubens. He used the red chalk to highlight the fine detail of the subject's face.

★ Wheatstacks, Snow Effect, Morning *(1891)*
This is one in a series of works by Monet that shows the same landscape at different times of the day and year.

Temporary exhibitions
and the museum café are
housed in this building.

★ The Abduction of Europa *(1632)*
One of Rembrandt's few landscapes, this depicts the Roman god Jupiter, disguised as a bull, kidnapping Europa, princess of Tyre.

GUIDE TO THE GETTY CENTER
From below, the Getty Center may look like a fortress, but once on top, the scale is intimate, with fountains, walkways, courtyards, and niches. An electric tram brings visitors from the parking lot to the complex. The museum has a tall, airy foyer that opens onto a central courtyard. From here radiate five two-story pavilions, which contain the art collections. The Conceptualist artist Robert Irwin has created a central garden to the west of the museum. Across the main plaza from the tram station there is a café and restaurant. Another café and a bookstore are located within the museum.

Exploring the Getty Museum

J Paul Getty (1892–1976) amassed a remarkable collection of European painting, sculpture, and decorative arts, focusing on pre-20th-century artistic movements. Getty was a bold collector who enjoyed the pursuit of an object almost more than the possession of it. Since his death, the Getty Trust has strengthened the museum's holdings by purchasing works of the highest quality to complement the existing collection. New departments in related areas such as drawings and manuscripts have also been added. Since the move to the Getty Center in 1997, the museum can now display twice as much of its collection as at the Getty Villa *(see p86).*

Man with a Hoe, painted between 1860 and 1862 by Jean-François Millet

EUROPEAN PAINTINGS AND SCULPTURE

The museum boasts a superb collection of European paintings, dating from the 13th century to the late 19th century. Italian works from the Renaissance and Baroque periods include *The Adoration of the Magi* (c.1495–1505) by Andrea Mantegna and *View of the Arch of Constantine with Colosseum* (1742–5) by Canaletto. Rembrandt's *The Abduction of Europa* (1632) is a highlight from the Flemish and Dutch collections, which also include an oil sketch by Peter Paul Rubens (1577–1640) and a portrait by Anthony Van Dyck (1599–1641).

Of the French artworks on display, *The Race of the Riderless Horses* (1817) is an important painting by the Romantic painter Théodore Géricault. In *Still Life with Apples* (1894) by Paul Cézanne, the artist's preoccupation with gradations of light and color reveals the progression in the late 19th century from the old, realistic, style of painting, to a more modern, abstract approach.

This painting, along with Claude Monet's *Wheatstacks, Snow Effect, Morning (see p83),* and Vincent Van Gogh's *Irises (see p82),* has helped elevate the museum's collection of Impressionists and Post-Impressionists.

European sculptures in the Getty date from the 16th century to the end of the 19th century. Pier Jacopo Antico's *Bust of a Young Man* (1520) was created at the end of the High Renaissance in Italy. The elongated body favored by the Mannerists can be seen in Benvenuto Cellini's *Satyr* (c.1542). Fine examples of Baroque sculpture are *Pluto Abducting Proserpine* (c.1693–1710) by François Girardon and Gian Lorenzo Bernini's *Boy with a Dragon* (c.1614). Neo-Classical works include three statues by Joseph Nollekens: *Venus, Juno,* and *Minerva* (1773–6).

DRAWINGS

The purchase in 1981 of Rembrandt's red chalk study of *Nude Woman with a Snake* (c.1637) marked the beginning of the museum's drawings collection. Today, the collection contains more than 400 works in a wide range of media, spanning the 15th to the late 19th century. *The Stag Beetle* (1505) by Albrecht Dürer is an exquisitely detailed illustration in watercolor and gouache. By contrast, Leonardo da Vinci's *Studies for the Christ Child with a Lamb* (c.1503–6) is a looser pen-and-ink study.

Peter Paul Rubens' *Korean Man (see p83)* is one of several portrait drawings. The *Self-Portrait* (c.1857–8) by Edgar Degas, executed in oil on paper and showing the young artist on the threshold of his extraordinary career, is another.

PHOTOGRAPHS

The museum launched its photographic department in 1984 with the purchase of several major private collections, including those of Bruno Bischofberger, Arnold Crane, and Samuel Wagstaff. The holdings focus on European and American photography up to the 1950s. Exceptionally rich in works from the early 1840s, the collection features

Columbia River, Oregon (1867) by Carleton E Watkins

many of the pioneers of photography. In daguerreotypes, the identity of the sitter was often more important than that of the maker. The museum has one portrait of Louis-Jacques-Mande Daguerre himself, taken in 1848 by Charles R Meade.

Englishman William Henry Fox Talbot (1800–1877) was the first to make prints from negatives. A lovely example of his work is *Oak Tree in Winter* (1841). Other early practitioners on exhibition include Hyppolyte Bayard (1801–87), portraitist Julia Margaret Cameron (1815–79), war photographer Roger Fenton (1819–69), Gustave Le Gray (1820–82), and Nadar (1820–1910).

Among the important early 20th-century artists represented are Edward Weston (1886–1958), who created beautiful still lifes, and Walker Evans (1903–75), who was a pivotal influence in American documentary photography.

Renaissance chalcedony, or agate, glass bowl, made in Venice, Italy, in around 1500

APPLIED ARTS

Applied arts in the museum encompass pre-1650 European pieces and works from southern Europe from 1650 to 1900. They have been chosen to complement the Getty's extensive holdings of French decorative arts.

Highlights include glass and earthenware from Italy and Spain; metalwork from France, Germany, and Italy; and highly decorated furniture. An extravagantly inlaid display cabinet from Augsburg in Germany (c.1620–30) falls into this last category. All four of the piece's sides open to reveal numerous drawers and compartments for collectibles.

Sèvres porcelain basket, dating from the mid-18th century

DECORATIVE ARTS

Decorative arts were Getty's first love as a collector, after he rented a New York penthouse furnished with 18th-century French and English antiques. Originally, his collection focused on furnishings from the reign of Louis XIV to the Napoleonic era (1643–1815), encompassing the Regency, Rococo, and Empire periods.

The age of Louis XIV saw the development of French furniture reach great artistic heights, where appearances mattered more than function. The premier craftsman during that time was André-Charles Boulle (1642–1732), who was noted for his complex veneers and marquetry. The museum has several pieces attributed to Boulle from the French royal household. Two coffers on stands (c.1680–85), made for the Grand Dauphin, son of Louis XIV, probably held jewelry and valuable objects.

Several of the tapestries in the collection have remained in excellent condition, with their colors still vibrant. They include one woven by Jean de la Croix (active 1662–1712) for Louis XIV. The holdings also include ceramics, silver and gilded objects such as chandeliers and wall lights.

In recent years, pieces from Germany, Italy, and northern Europe have been added. A Neo-Classical rolltop desk (c.1785), made by the German David Roentgen, has a weight-operated, concealed writing stand. This type of elaborate mechanical feature was Roentgen's trademark.

MANUSCRIPTS

The museum began collecting illuminated manuscripts in 1983 with the purchase of the Ludwig Collection of 144 works, which emphasized German and Central European texts. Tracing the development of illumination from the 6th to the 16th century, the collection today has masterpieces from the Byzantine, Ottoman, Romanesque, Gothic, and Renaissance periods.

Illuminated manuscripts were written and decorated entirely by hand. Initially, most were produced in monasteries, which were then the center of European intellectual life. Later, in the 12th century, they were also produced in the growing number of universities. Most books contained religious material, but some also preserved the philosophy, history, literature, law, and science of Western civilization. Kings, nobles, and church leaders commissioned these richly painted books, some of which were decorated with jewels and precious metals.

The manuscripts, as well as drawings and photos, are all rotated. Highlights include an Ottoman Gospel lectionary from either Reichenau or St. Gall (950–75); an English Gothic Apocalypse (1255–60); two Byzantine Gospel books; *The Visions of Tondal* (1475), in the Flemish holdings; and the *Hours of Simon de Varie*, illuminated by French artist Jean Fouquet in 1455.

Portrait of St. John (c.1120–40) from the German Abbey of Helmarshausen's Gospel book

The Getty Villa ❽

17985 Pacific Coast Hwy. **Tel** *(310)*
440-7300. ◯ *until late 2006.*

The J Paul Getty Villa, due to
re-open in 2006 after its
renovations, will be the new
home of the Antiquities
collection of the Getty Center
(see pp82-5). Getty's vision –
of a museum where his
collection of antiquities could
be displayed in a place
where such art might
originally have been seen –
will finally come to fruition.
The museum will display
ancient art on both floors of
the building.
    The Villa is a re-creation of
the Villa dei Papiri, the country
estate of a Roman consul.
The gardens of the villa are
planted with seeds and bulbs
imported from Italy. The Main
Peristyle Garden is spec-
tacular, with its large pool
bordered by bronze statuary.
The buildings combine
authentic Roman
detailing with
modern
technology.
    Getty's original
home on this
property, and the
site of the first
Getty Museum,
holds a library,
seminar rooms,
and offices for
scholars. The
Ranch House, as Getty called
it, will house the Antiquities
Conservation Department of
the Getty Museum.

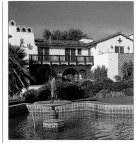

**Decorative façade and grounds of
Adamson House**

Adamson House and Malibu Lagoon Museum ❾

23200 Pacific Coast Hwy. **Road
map** inset A. **Tel** *(310) 456-8432.*
◯ *11am–3pm Wed–Sat.* ◯ *Jan1,
Jul 4, Thanksgiving, Dec 25.*
▨ ⬧ ▢ ▨ *last tour 2pm.*
www.adamsonhouse.org

Adamson House was built in
1929 for husband and wife
Merritt and Rhoda
Adamson. Rhoda
was the daughter
of Frederick and
May Rindge, the
last owners of the
Rancho Malibu
Spanish land grant.
Until 1928, the
family owned 24
miles (39 km) of
Malibu coastline.
    Situated on the
beach, the idyllic house,
designed by Stiles Clements,
and its 6 acres (2.5 ha) of gardens overlook Malibu Pier

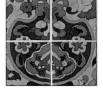

**Intricate tile detail in
Adamson House**

and Malibu Lagoon. The
Spanish Colonial style building is covered with vivid tiles
from the Malibu Potteries – a
ceramics firm that was started
by May Rindge and owned by
the family. These of these
individually designed tiles are
featured throughout the
house and grounds. The floors,
walls, doorways, and fountains
are all intricately decorated.
The house's original 1920s
furnishings are also on display.
    Located in the converted
garage of Adamson House is
the Malibu Lagoon Museum,
which is devoted to the history
of Malibu. Artifacts, documents,
and photographs tell the story
not only of the Rindge family
but also of the early Chumash
population and José Tapia,
who in 1802 became Malibu's
first Spanish landowner.

Malibu Lagoon State Beach ❿

Road map inset A. **Tel** *(818) 880-
0367.* ◯ *8am–sunset daily.* ▨ ⬧

The Chumash people built
Humaliwo, their largest
village, on the shores of this
lagoon. By the 16th century,
about 1,000 people had their
home here, making it one of
the most populated Native
American villages north of
what is now Mexico.
    The estuary supports a wide
range of marine life and is an
important feeding ground for
up to 200 species of migratory
and native birds. To the east of

The Getty Villa's Main Peristyle Garden

Exclusive beach houses in Malibu Colony

the lagoon, the 35-acre (14-ha) Surfrider County Beach is devoted to surfers; swimming is prohibited. With its rare point break, Malibu is one of the finest surfing spots in southern California. The area closest to the pier is thought to have the best waves for longboarding in the world. Volleyball courts are also located on the beach.

View across Malibu Lagoon to the Santa Monica Mountains

Malibu Colony ⓫

Road map inset A. 🚌 ℹ️ 23805 Stuart Ranch Rd, Suite 100 (310-456-5737).

In 1928, to raise money for an ongoing battle to keep Malibu in the family, May Rindge sold this section of shoreline to film stars such as Bing Crosby, Gary Cooper and Barbara Stanwyck. Today, the colony is a private, gated

compound, still favored by people working within the entertainment industry. There is no public access to the beach, but stars can often be spotted in the Malibu Colony Plaza, which is located near the entrance.

Malibu Creek State Park ⓬

Road map inset A. **Tel** (818) 880-0367, (818) 880-0350, or (800) 444-7275 for campsite reservations. 🚻 8am–sunset daily. 🅿️ ♿ 🎫

This 10,000-acre (4,000-ha) park was inhabited by the Chumash Indians until the mid-19th century. A varied landscape of forests, meadows, and rocky outcrops create the illusion of a vast wilderness, miles from civilization.

Some 2,000 acres (800 ha) of the park were once owned by 20th Century Fox, which made it a favorite location for movie-making *(see pp68–9)*.

M*A*S*H (1970), *Butch Cassidy and the Sundance Kid* (1969), and *Planet of the Apes* (1968) were all filmed here. The state bought the land back from the film company in 1974.

The information center is close to the parking lot and has exhibits on the area's history, flora, and fauna. The stunning Gorge Trail starts from the center of the park and leads to a rock pool, which was used as a pseudo-tropical location to film the movies *South Pacific* (1958) and *Tarzan* (1959).

Off Crags Road, the marshy Century Lake harbors catfish, bass, bluefish, red-winged blackbirds, buffleheads, coots, and mallards. In spring the meadows are a riot of colorful wildflowers. Groves of live and valley oaks, redwood, and dogwood trees are scattered throughout the park.

Within the park there are 20 trails for hiking, cycling, or horseback riding; a nature center; and many picnic areas.

Malibu Creek State Park, near Castro Crest *(see p64)*

BEVERLY HILLS, BEL AIR, AND WESTWOOD

Beverly Hills is a city, independent of Los Angeles and with its own laws and regulations. Since the early 1920s it has been the entertainment industry's favorite residential address. Beverly Hills' Golden Triangle is the West Coast's answer to New York's Madison Avenue, with its array of restaurants, shops, and coffee bars. South of Bel Air's shady canyons, youthful Westwood brims with UCLA students. In the business-minded Century City, high-rises crowd the skyline. Together, these areas are known as the Westside.

City limits sign

SIGHTS AT A GLANCE

Historic Buildings
Beverly Hills Civic Center ❶
Beverly Hills Hotel ❽
Hotel Bel-Air ⓫

Parks and Gardens
Greystone Park and Mansion ❼
Virginia Robinson Gardens ❾

Shopping Areas
Century City ❻
Rodeo Drive p94 ❸
2 Rodeo ❹

Tours
Tour of the Stars' Homes
pp96–7 ❿

Museums
Museum of Television and
  Radio ❷
Museum of Tolerance ❺

Universities
UCLA and Westwood
  Village ⓬

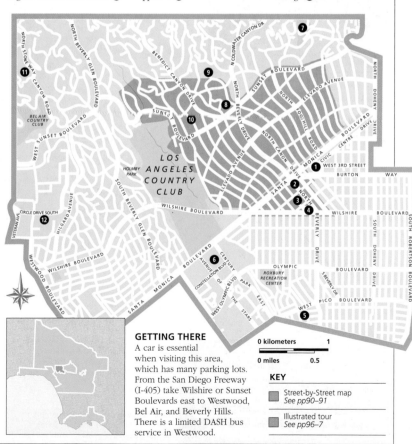

GETTING THERE
A car is essential when visiting this area, which has many parking lots. From the San Diego Freeway (I-405) take Wilshire or Sunset Boulevards east to Westwood, Bel Air, and Beverly Hills. There is a limited DASH bus service in Westwood.

0 kilometers 1
0 miles 0.5

KEY

| | Street-by-Street map See pp90–91 |
| | Illustrated tour See pp96–7 |

◁ Distinctive tower of Beverly Hills City Hall, part of the Civic Center

Street-by-Street: The Golden Triangle

The area bordered by Santa Monica Boulevard, Wilshire Boulevard, and North Crescent Drive, known as the "Golden Triangle," is the business district of Beverly Hills. The shops, restaurants, and art galleries lining the streets are some of the most luxurious in the world. Cutting through the middle is Rodeo Drive, where many international designer boutiques are to be found. On Wilshire Boulevard, the cream of American department stores offer a heady mix of style and opulence. To the north are the beautifully manicured Beverly Gardens, the elegant Civic Center with its landmark City Hall, and the recently opened Museum of Television and Radio.

★ **Museum of Television and Radio**
The latest addition to the Golden Triangle, this museum gives a comprehensive history of broadcasting **2**

The Electric Fountain was built in 1930. The statue on the top is of a Native American praying for rain. Scenes from California history are depicted on the base frieze.

Saks Fifth Avenue is one of the four major department stores along Wilshire Boulevard.

The Creative Artists Agency was built in 1989 by architect IM Pei. Its curving mirrored glass and marble walls anchor Santa Monica and Wilshire Boulevards.

★ **Beverly Hills Civic Center**
The 1932 Spanish Renaissance City Hall has recently been restored and a series of new administration and public buildings added ❶

LOCATOR MAP
See Street Finder, map 5

Anderson Court was designed by Frank Lloyd Wright in 1953.

2 Rodeo
When built in 1990, this center included the first new street in Beverly Hills since the city established independence from LA in 1914 ❹

The MGM Building was built in the 1920s by Louis B Mayer. The white and gold Art Deco structure was the headquarters of the newly formed Metro-Goldwyn-Mayer film studios.

The Beverly Theater, a Moorish-style building built in 1925, was the site of many film premieres in the 1920s and 1930s. It is now the Israeli Discount Bank.

| 0 meters | 100 |
| 0 yards | 100 |

KEY

– – – Suggested route

Rodeo Drive
The three blocks of Rodeo Drive are one of the most famous shopping areas in the world ❸

The Regent Beverly Wilshire Hotel first opened in 1928. In 1970 a second wing was added to the original Beaux-Arts building. A private, cobblestone street links the two wings *(see p525).*

STAR SIGHTS

★ Beverly Hills Civic Center

★ Museum of Television and Radio

Beverly Hills Civic Center with City Hall in the background

seminars, and screenings on specialized subjects and selected actors or directors.

The collection of more than 75,000 television and radio programs includes such timeless classics as *I Love Lucy (see p199)* and *The Honeymooners*. Favorite television and radio commercials, encompassing the industry's advertising history, are also available.

The holdings duplicate those of New York's highly successful Museum of Television and Radio, which was created in 1975 by the late William S. Paley, when he was the head of CBS Television.

Rodeo Drive ❸

See p94.

2 Rodeo ❹

Map 5 F3. 🏠 *268 N. Rodeo Drive* *(310-247-7040).* **www**.2rodeo.com

Developed in 1990 on the corner of Rodeo Drive *(see p94)* and Wilshire Boulevard, 2 Rodeo is one of the most expensive retail centers ever made. It looks like a film set of a European street, complete with a public square and Victorian-style streetlamps. Exclusive shops such as Cole Haan and Charles Jourdan line Via Rodeo, the cobbled

Beverly Hills Civic Center ❶

455 N Rexford Drive. **Map** 5 F3. **Tel** *(310) 285-1000.* ⭕ *7:30am–5:30pm Mon–Thu; 8am–5pm Fri.* 🌑 *public hols.* ♿

The Spanish Colonial City Hall, with its majestic tower capped by a tiled cupola, was designed in 1932 by local firm Koerner and Gage. Over the years it has become a symbol of the elegant, European-inspired city of Beverly Hills.

In 1990, architect Charles Moore linked the building to a new Civic Center by a series of diagonal landscaped and pedestrianized courtyards. On the upper levels, balconies and arcaded corridors continue the Spanish Colonial theme. The sympathetic modern addition houses a beautiful public library as well as the local fire and police stations.

Billboards are banned in the area, and a height restriction of three stories or 45 ft (14 m) is imposed on any new buildings, leaving City Hall to dominate the skyline.

Museum of Television and Radio ❷

465 N Beverly Drive. **Map** 5 F3. **Tel** *(310) 786-1000.* ⭕ *noon–5pm Wed–Sun (until 9pm Thu).* 🌑 *public hols.* 📷 ♿ 🎦 **www**.mfr.org

Visitors to the Museum of Television and Radio may watch and listen to news and a collection of entertainment and sports programs from the earliest days of radio and television to the present.

Pop music fans can see footage of the early Beatles or a young Elvis Presley making his television debut. Sports fans can relive classic Olympic competitions.

Visitors can select up to four extracts from the library's computerized catalogue at any one time. These are then played on small private consoles. The museum also has a 150-seat theater, which hosts major exhibitions,

Lucille Ball, the most popular television star during the 1950s

Spanish Steps leading to 2 Rodeo

lane that bisects the center. Via Rodeo meanders to the Spanish Steps, which descend to Wilshire Boulevard.

Museum of Tolerance ●

9786 W Pico Blvd. **Map** 5 F5. **Tel** (310) 553-8403. ◯ 11.30am–4pm Mon–Thu, 11.30am–1pm Fri, 11am–5pm Sun. ● Jan 1, Thanksgiving, Dec 25, and all major Jewish holidays. 🌆 🔓 🛈 www.museumoftolerance.com

This museum is dedicated to the promotion of respect and understanding among all people. Its two primary areas of focus are the history of racism and prejudice in the United States and the European Holocaust experience, examined in both historical and contemporary contexts.

The museum tour begins in the Tolerancenter, where visitors are challenged to confront racism and bigotry through interactive exhibits. "The Other America" is a computerized wall map that locates and gives information on more than 250 known racist groups in the US. A 16-screen video wall depicts the 1960s civil rights struggle in America. Interactive video monitors ask visitors for their personal profiles and then challenge them on questions of responsible citizenship and

social justice. They also offer footage of the LA riots of 1992 (*see p57*), with follow-up interviews. One of the most hard-hitting exhibits is the 15-ft (4.5-m) "Whisper Gallery," in which visitors hear racial and sexual taunts.

At the beginning of the Holocaust section, each visitor is given the details and photograph of a child whose life was in some way altered by that period.

Throughout the tour, the child's history is updated and, at the end, his or her fate is revealed. During the tour, visitors become a witness to events in Nazi Germany. Wax models in an outdoor café scene, set in prewar Berlin, seem to discuss the impending Nazi takeover of Germany. In a re-creation of the Wannsee Conference, the Third Reich leaders decide on the "The Final Solution of the Jewish Question." Videotaped interviews with concentration camp survivors shown in the "Hall of Testimony" tell of their harrowing experiences. Artifacts on display include Anne Frank's original letters and memorabilia from the camps.

The upper floors of the museum house special exhibits, films, and lectures. There is also a multimedia learning center with interactive computers containing additional information on World War II topics. Some of the exhibits may not be suitable for children under the age of ten.

History of racial prejudice at the Museum of Tolerance

Century City ●

Map 5 D5. 🛈 2049 Century Park E, Suite 2600, Century City, 90067 (310-553-2222).

This site used to be part of 20th Century Fox's backlot. It was sold in 1961 to the developers of Century City, who designed a high-rise complex of offices, stores, and homes on the 180 acres (73 ha).

Today lawyers, agents, and production companies fill the office blocks. Despite this, the area has never developed a community feel and at night the streets are empty.

The Century City Shopping Center, however, is a notable success. This outdoor complex has more than 120 stores, some 20 restaurants, and a 14-screen theater.

Century City Shopping Center

Greystone Park and Mansion ●

905 Loma Vista Drive. **Map** 5 F1. **Tel** (310) 550-4654. **Park** ◯ 10am–5pm daily. ● Jan 1, Dec 25. 🔓 terrace & lower grounds.

In 1928 Edward L Doheny, an oil millionaire, built this 55-room mock-Tudor manor house for his son. Just three weeks after moving in with his family, Doheny's son was found dead in his bedroom with a male secretary, an apparent murder-suicide. His wife and children soon moved out, and since then the mansion has often been vacant.

Now owned by the city of Beverly Hills, Greystone is used in films, music videos, and commercials. The house is closed to the public, but visitors can walk or picnic in the beautiful 18-acre (7-ha) terraced gardens, which offer views across Los Angeles.

Rodeo Drive ❸

The name Rodeo Drive is derived from *El Rancho Rodeo de las Aguas* ("the ranch of the gathering of waters"), the name of an early Spanish land grant that included Beverly Hills. Today, Rodeo Drive is one of the most celebrated and exclusive shopping streets in the world, with Italian designer boutiques, the best of French fashion, world-class jewelers, and some of the leading LA retailers. For those who enjoy celebrity-spotting, Rodeo Drive is a prime area.

Cartier, *at No.370, is well-known for its classic-style watches and diamond rings.*

Gucci, *at No. 347, is a leading Italian boutique. Best known for its leather accessories and colorful scarves, it also produces furnishings, such as this cushion.*

• 421

BRIGHTON WAY

• 370

• 347

• 317

RODEO DRIVE

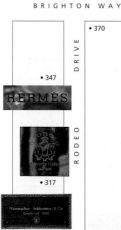

VAN CLEEF & ARPELS

DAYTON WAY

• 273

• 230

Barakat *sells fine jewelry and also has an impressive collection of pre-Columbian and ancient Greek artifacts. Barakat is located in the group of shops known as the Rodeo Collection, under an atrium, at No. 421.*

Lalique, *at No. 317, is famous for its Art Deco and Art Nouveau glassware. The shop's frosted lamps are typical of Lalique's style.*

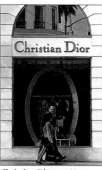

Christian Dior, *at No. 230, is one of the leading names in French haute couture. The founder of the house was responsible for the 1950s "New Look."*

Rodeo Drive's *wide sidewalks, bordered by trees, help create a pleasant shopping environment.*

0 meters   50

0 yards   50

The landmark Beverly Hills Hotel

Beverly Hills Hotel ❽

9641 Sunset Blvd. **Map** 5 D2. *Tel (310) 276-2251, (800) 283-8885.* ⬭ *daily.* ♿ www.thebeverlyhillshotel.com
See *Where to Stay* p525.

Dubbed "the Pink Palace," this extravagant Mission Revival-style hotel was built in 1912 by developer Burton E Green. The hotel's 21 secluded bungalows, set in 12 acres (5 ha) of landscaped gardens, have been romantic hideaways for film stars such as Marilyn Monroe, Clark Gable, Richard Burton, and Elizabeth Taylor.

Recently, the Beverly Hills Hotel has undergone a $100 million program of renovations, reviving the style of Hollywood's heyday. Its legendary pool and cabanas have remained one of the places to be seen and heard in Los Angeles, and its famous restaurants, The Polo Lounge and Polo Grill, are once more at the center of the movie industry's deal-making.

Virginia Robinson Gardens ❾

1008 Elden Way. **Map** 5 D1. *Tel (310) 276-5367.* ⬭ *Tue–Fri.* ⬤ *public hols.* 🎥 ♿ 🚻 *obligatory 10am & 1pm Tue–Thu, 10am Fri. Advance reservations required.*

In 1908 department-store heir Harry Robinson and his wife, Virginia, bought a plot of land in Beverly Hills. Three years later they completed the city's first house here and planted 6 acres (2.5 ha) of landscaped gardens set amid terraces, ponds, and fountains.

Bequeathed to LA County, the gardens were opened to the public in 1982. One of the most impressive sights is the 2.5-acre (1-ha) palm forest, where you can see the largest king palms outside Australia. The organized tour includes part of the house, which still has its original furnishings.

Tour of the Stars' Homes ❿

See pp96–7.

Hotel Bel-Air ⓫

701 Stone Canyon Rd. **Map** 4 A1. *Tel (310) 472-1211.* ⬭ *daily.* ♿ See *Where to Stay* p525 www.hotelbelair.com

Considered one of the best hotels in the US, Hotel Bel-Air is located in a heavily wooded canyon, giving it an air of privacy and tranquillity. The 1920s Mission Revival-style buildings are set in 11 acres (4.5 ha) of beautiful gardens, interspersed with fountains and intimate courtyards.

Among the trees and shrubs rarely seen in Southern California are coastal redwoods, white-flowering bird of paradise trees, and a floss silk tree – the largest of its kind outside its native South America. The gardens are fragrant with roses, gardenias, jasmine, and orange blossoms. In fact, the Bel-Air is so perfect that one guest stayed for 40 years.

Pool at Hotel Bel-Air, surrounded by attractive gardens

Tour of the Stars' Homes 🔟

BEL-AIR PATROL
PROTECTED BY
BEL-AIR PATROL
ELECTRONIC SYSTEMS
(310) 479-4646

ARMED PATROL

**Security
guard sign**

In Los Angeles image is everything, and Beverly Hills has long been the symbol of success for those in the entertainment industry. When, in 1920, Mary Pickford and Douglas Fairbanks built their mansion, Pickfair, at the top of Summit Drive, everyone else followed – and stayed. Sunset Boulevard divides the haves from the have-nots: people who live south of it may be rich, but it is those who live to the north of the road who are considered to be the super-rich. Houses come in almost every architectural style. Some are ostentatious, others are surprisingly modest.

**Jimmy Stewart's former home at
No. 918 Roxbury Drive ⑬**

South of Sunset

Start at No. 714 Palm Drive, the elegant home of Faye Dunaway ①, who starred with Warren Beatty in *Bonnie and Clyde* (1967). Continue south and turn right on Elevado Avenue. The former home of Rita Hayworth ② is situated on the corner at No. 512 Palm Drive.

At Maple Drive, turn right. No. 720 is the white and green New England-style home of the late George Burns and Gracie Allen ③. Continue north and just before Sunset Boulevard make a sharp left onto Lomitas Avenue. Go two blocks and turn left onto Foothill Road. On the corner, at No. 701, is the unassuming house of Carroll Baker ④. This blonde-haired beauty made her debut in *Giant* (1956) with James Dean. At one time she was being groomed to be the next Marilyn Monroe.

Turn right onto Elevado Avenue, take the next right onto Alpine Drive, left onto Lomitas Avenue, and left at Crescent Drive. Doris Day's modest house ⑤ is barely

visible at No. 713, hidden behind a tall hedge and gate.

Turn right on Carmelita Avenue and right again at Cañon Drive. The pretty house ⑥ where Robert

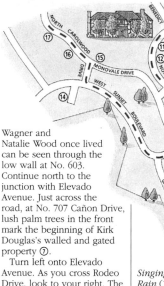

Wagner and Natalie Wood once lived can be seen through the low wall at No. 603. Continue north to the junction with Elevado Avenue. Just across the road, at No. 707 Cañon Drive, lush palm trees in the front mark the beginning of Kirk Douglas's walled and gated property ⑦.

Turn left onto Elevado Avenue. As you cross Rodeo Drive, look to your right. The lovely home of the late Gene

Kelly ⑧ is at No. 725 Rodeo Drive. This renowned Hollywood icon performed in such classics as *An American in Paris* (1951) and

Singing in the Rain (1952).

Continue along Elevado Avenue, then turn right on Bedford Drive. The comedian and actor Steve Martin ⑨ has a home at No. 721. A modern block structure, it has no front windows and can be only partially glimpsed behind a bougainvillea hedge. Lana Turner's scandal-ridden house ⑩ at No. 730, on the

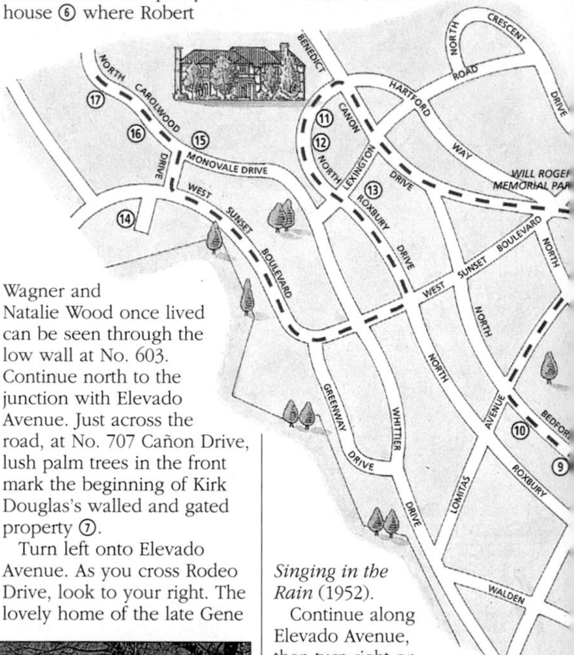

KEY

– – – Tour route

Faye Dunaway's house at No. 714 Palm Drive ①

For hotels and restaurants in this region see pp524–31 and pp568–76

Jayne Mansfield's Pink Palace at No. 10100 Sunset Boulevard ⑭

LOCATOR MAP

See Street Finder, map 5

His former neighbors at No. 1000 Roxbury Drive were Lucille Ball and Desi Arnaz ⑫. Their successful show *I Love Lucy (see pp92 and 149)* reruns daily on television. Nearby, at No. 918, is the mock-Tudor former home of the much-respected Jimmy Stewart ⑬.

At Sunset Boulevard, turn right. Jayne Mansfield's Pink Palace ⑭ is at No. 10100, on the southwest corner of Sunset Boulevard and Carolwood Drive. When Mansfield moved in, she put in a heart-shaped pool with the inscription "I love you Jaynie" written on the bottom.

Turn right onto North Carolwood Drive. Just to the right, at No. 144 Monovale Drive ⑮, is one of rock-and-roll king Elvis Presley's former homes. Only the tennis courts can be seen from the street.

Continue along Carolwood Drive. Barbra Streisand ⑯ lives at No. 301 on a heavily guarded estate. The actress won an academy award in 1969 for her role as Fanny Brice in the musical *Funny Girl.* The late Walt Disney, who captured the imagination of the world with his cartoon characters, used to live just north of here at No. 355 Carolwood Drive ⑰. His house is on a bend, behind a gate.

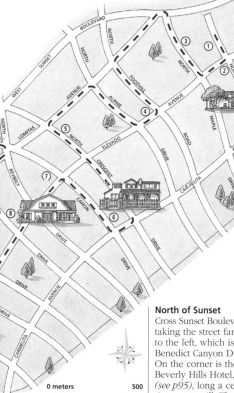

Walt Disney's mailbox ⑰

North of Sunset

Cross Sunset Boulevard, taking the street farthest to the left, which is now Benedict Canyon Drive. On the corner is the Beverly Hills Hotel, *(see p95),* long a celebrity rumor mill. The private bungalows behind its pink façade saw many a romantic tryst, including, it is said, those between Marilyn Monroe and John and Robert Kennedy.

At Roxbury Drive, turn left and curve south with the road. At No. 1002 is the late Jack Benny's traditional-looking brick house ⑪, which he occasionally used in his shows.

corner of Bedford Drive and Lomitas Avenue, was where her gangster-lover Johnny Stompanato was stabbed to death with a kitchen knife by her daughter, Cheryl Crane.

Turn right onto Lomitas Avenue, then make a sharp left on Cañon Drive.

TIPS FOR DRIVERS

Tour length: 5 miles (8 km).
Warning: Film stars' homes or former homes are private residences. Do not attempt to trespass or you may be arrested.

0 meters 500
0 yards 500

University of California Los Angeles, Westwood Village ⑫

A large university with a first-rate reputation, UCLA has a wide range of academic departments and professional schools, including the respected UCLA Hospital. Sited on 419 acres (170 ha), with more than 35,000 students, it is a city within a city. The original campus was designed in 1925 to resemble the Romanesque towns of southern Europe. The first four buildings followed this theme, but as the university expanded more modern architecture was favored. The disappointing mix of bland structures that resulted is redeemed by the beautiful landscaped grounds.

Romanesque-style façade of UCLA's Royce Hall

Exploring UCLA and Westwood Village

Since it was first developed in 1928, Westwood Village has been one of the most successful shopping districts in Southern California. For years, the pleasant streets south of UCLA were the most popular weekend destination in the city. People still enjoy the pedestrian-friendly avenues, the productions at the Geffen Playhouse *(see p174)*, and the large number of theaters that often preview the latest films. However, cheap modernization of some of the storefronts has disrupted the overall cohesiveness of the village's Spanish Colonial design.

Detail of ceiling in Royce Hall

🏛 Royce Quadrangle

Dickson Plaza. *Tel (310) 825-2101.* ⬜ *daily.*
The four buildings that make up the Royce Quadrangle are the oldest on UCLA's campus in Westwood. Built of red brick in the Italian Romanesque style, Royce, Kinsey, and Haines halls, and Powell

Library far surpass the other buildings at UCLA in beauty. The best of them all is Royce Hall, which is based on the basilica of San Ambrogio in Milan, Italy. Its auditorium hosts professional music, dance, and theater shows throughout the year. Next door, Powell Library's grand rotunda was modeled on San Sepolcro in Bologna, Italy.

🏛 UCLA at the Armand Hammer Museum of Art and Cultural Center

10899 Wilshire Blvd. *Tel (310) 443-7000.* ⬜ *11am–7pm Tue, Wed, Fri, Sat; 11am–9pm Thu; 11am–5pm Sun.* ⬤ *Jul 4, Thanksgiving, Dec 25.* 📷 *free 11am–9pm Thu.* 🦽 📷 ⬜ **www**.hammer.ucla.edu
The museum presents selections from the collection of businessman Armand Hammer (1899–1990). Works are largely Impressionist or Post-Impressionist by artists such as Mary Cassatt (1845–1926), Claude Monet (1840–1926), Camille Pissarro (1830–1903), John Singer Sargent (1856–1925), and

Vincent Van Gogh (1853–90). Exhibits from the Armand Hammer Daumier and Contemporaries Collection are also shown on a rotating basis and include paintings, sculptures, and lithographs by Daumier and his contemporaries. Displays are also drawn from the UCLA Grunwald Center for the Graphic Arts, which holds more than 35,000 works on paper dating from the Renaissance to the present day.

🦽 Franklin D Murphy Sculpture Garden

Tel (310) 443-7041. ⬜ *daily.*
This is the largest sculpture garden on the West Coast with more than 70 20th-century sculptures. The highlights

UCLA AND WESTWOOD VILLAGE

Entrance to UCLA at the Armand Hammer Museum of Art

Automne (*Autumn*, 1948) by Henri Laurens

BEVERLY HILLS
HOLLYWOOD
New Wight Art Gallery
STONE CANYON DRIVE
CIRCLE
Franklin D Murphy Sculpture Garden
PORTOLA
DRIVE
PLACE
NORTH
Royce Hall
PORTOLA
PLAZA
EAST
Royce Quadrangle
DICKSON COURT
AVENUE
Powell Library
Fowler Museum
WESTWOOD
BRUIN WALK
Hilgard Bus Terminal
PLAZA
HILGARD
UCLA
DRIVE
SOUTH
Mildred E Mathias Botanical Garden
DRIVE
LE CONTE PLACE
TIVERTON
AVENUE
AVENUE
WEYBURN
AVENUE
AVENUE
GLENDON AVENUE
HILGARD
Westwood Village
TIVERTON
WESTWOOD
AVENUE
DRIVE
BEVERLY HILLS
LINDBROOK
UCLA at the Armand Hammer Museum
BLVD
Westwood Memorial Park
WILSHIRE
BOULEVARD
SANTA MONICA
ASHTON AVE
AVENUE
WELLWORTH
AVENUE
ROCHESTER
0 meters 500
0 yards 500

include Henry Moore's *Two-Piece Reclining Figure, No. 3* (1961) and Jacques Lipchitz's *Baigneuse* (*Bather*, 1923–5).

Mildred E Mathias Botanical Garden

Tel *(310) 825-1260.* ◯ *8am–5pm Mon–Fri, 8am–4pm Sat & Sun.* ● *public hols.* ♿

Tucked away in a small shady canyon, this serene garden contains almost 4,000 rare and native species. Divided into 13 thematic sections, the gardens feature both subtropical and tropical plants. The trees are spectacular and include some outstanding Australian eucalyptus and some large specimens of dawn redwoods.

Fowler Museum of Cultural History

Tel *(310) 825-4361.* ◯ *noon–5pm Wed–Sun (until 8pm Thu).* ● *public hols.* 🎟 *free Thu.* 🔒

This university museum is committed to enriching the community's understanding of other cultures. Its exhibitions focus on the prehistoric, historic, and contemporary societies of Africa, Asia, the Americas, and Oceania. The collection of 750,000 artifacts makes it one of the nation's leading university museums.

VISITORS' CHECKLIST

Map 4 A3. 🚌 *20, 21, 22.*
UCLA Campus ℹ *Visitor Information (310 825-4321).*
Westwood Village
ℹ *10779 W Pico Blvd, Westside (310 475-8806).*

Westwood Memorial Park

1218 Glendon Ave. ***Tel*** *(310) 474-1579.* ◯ *8am–5pm daily.* ♿

Off the beaten track, this small cemetery is located behind the Avco Center theaters and parking lot. The tranquil grounds are now the final resting place for celebrities such as Dean Martin, Peter Lorre, Buddy Rich, Natalie Wood, and Marilyn Monroe. For several decades after her death, Monroe's second husband, Joe DiMaggio, used to have six red roses placed on her tomb every week.

Tranquil Westwood Memorial Park, shaded by trees

MARILYN MONROE

Born Norma Jean Baker in the charity ward of Los Angeles General Hospital, Marilyn Monroe (1926–62) was placed in foster care by her mother when she was two weeks old. Her first marriage, at the age of 16, lasted four years, before she gave it up to pursue her dream of being an actress. In 1950, her career took off with *The Asphalt Jungle* and *All About Eve*. With films such as *The Seven-Year Itch* (1955) and *Some Like It Hot* (1959), she became the biggest sex symbol Hollywood has ever seen. In the latter part of her life, she struggled to escape the narrow confines of her on-screen persona.

MARILYN MONROE
1926 - 1962

Marilyn Monroe's memorial plaque

Key to Symbols *see back flap*

HOLLYWOOD AND WEST HOLLYWOOD

In 1887, Harvey Henderson Wilcox and his wife, Daeida, set up a Christian community, free of saloons and gambling, in a Los Angeles suburb and called it Hollywood. It is ironic that the movie business with all its decadence came to replace their Utopia. The takeover started in 1913, when Cecil B De Mille filmed *The Squaw Man* in a rented barn at the corner of Vine and Selma.

For the next several decades the studios were based here, generating wealth and glamour. In recent years the area fell into decline, and today only a handful of landmarks recall its Golden Age. Sunset Boulevard has now become the focal point for nightlife in Los Angeles. West Hollywood, with its large gay community, is also a lively area for dining and shopping.

Hollywood's Walk of Fame

SIGHTS AT A GLANCE

Museums
Craft and Folk Art Museum **18**
George C Page Museum of La Brea Discoveries **17**
Hollywood Studio Museum **8**
Los Angeles County Museum of Art pp114–17 **13**
Petersen Automotive Museum **15**

Historic Streets and Buildings
Hollywood Bowl **7**
Hollywood Roosevelt Hotel **1**
Miracle Mile **14**
Paramount Studios **11**
Walk of Fame **5**

Cemeteries
Hollywood Memorial Park **10**

Cinemas and Theaters
El Capitan Theater **4**
Hollywood and Highland **3**
Mann's Chinese Theatre **2**
Pantages Theater **9**
The Improv **16**
Wiltern Theater **19**

Shops and Markets
Farmers Market **12**
Frederick's of Hollywood **6**

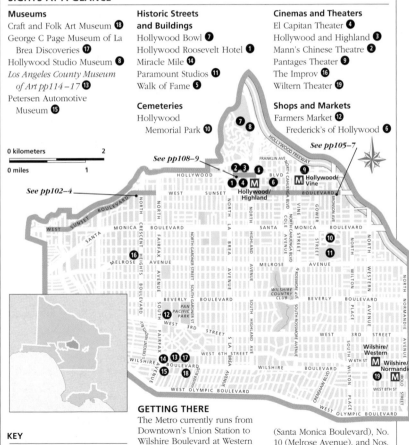

See pp105–7
See pp108–9
See pp102–4

0 kilometers 2
0 miles 1

GETTING THERE
The Metro currently runs from Downtown's Union Station to Wilshire Boulevard at Western Avenue. Bus services from Downtown include: No. 1 (along Hollywood Boulevard), No. 2 (Sunset Boulevard), No. 4 (Santa Monica Boulevard), No. 10 (Melrose Avenue), and Nos. 20, 21, and 22 (Wilshire Boulevard). Freeway 101 runs through Hollywood from Downtown and on to Ventura.

KEY
■ Illustrated areas
Ⓜ Metro station

◁ Mann's Chinese Theatre, a lavish remnant of Hollywood's Golden Age

A View of Sunset Boulevard: Sunset Strip

Sunset Boulevard curves west for 26 miles
(42 km) from downtown LA to the Pacific Coast
Highway. Sunset has been associated with the movies
since the 1920s, when it was a dirt track linking the
burgeoning film studios in Hollywood with the hillside homes of the screen stars. Today, much of the
boulevard is still lined with the mansions of the rich
and famous *(see pp96–7)*. Sunset Strip is the liveliest
and most historically rich stretch, filled with
restaurants, luxury hotels, and nightclubs. The 1.5-mile
(2.4-km) section was first paved in the mid-1930s. Its
lack of local government made it a magnet for gambling and bootlegging. Famous nightclubs included
the Trocadero, Ciro's, and the Mocambo – where
young Margarita Cansino met studio
boss Harry Cohen, who renamed her
Rita Hayworth. Sunset Strip is still
the center of LA's nightlife today.

**Sunset Strip and the Santa Monica
Mountains from Crescent Heights**

Rainbow Bar & Grill
*The walls of this restaurant, at No.
9015, are lined with wine casks and
gold records. Formerly the Villa
Nova, Vincente Minnelli
proposed to Judy Garland
here and, eight years later
in 1953, Marilyn Monroe
met Joe DiMaggio here
on a blind date.*

The Original Spago
*Wolfgang Puck,
who is regarded
by many as the
founder of Cali-
fornian cuisine,
had his first LA rest-
aurant at No. 8795.
During the 1970s
and 1980s Oscar
night parties were
held here, hosted
by the legendary
Hollywood
agent Irving
"Swifty"
Lazar.*

The Roxy
*This trendy nightclub, at
No. 9009, occupies the site
of the old Club Largo.*

The Viper Room, at No.
8852, is a popular live
music club *(see
p174)*, part-owned
by the actor Johnny
Depp. In October 1993
young film star River
Phoenix, having taken
a lethal cocktail of
drugs, collapsed and
died on the sidewalk
outside.

CLARK ST

LARRABEE ST

HORN AVE

HOLLOWAY DRI

HAMMOND ST

HILLDALE AVE

SAN VICENTE BLVD

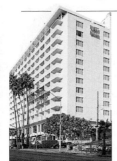

Hyatt Hotel
Visiting rock stars regularly stay at this hotel, at No. 8401 (see p531). *Jim Morrison stayed here when he played with The Doors at the nearby Whisky A Go Go.*

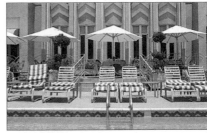

Argyle Hotel
This hotel is an Art Deco high-rise. In Hollywood's heyday it was an apartment complex and home to Jean Harlow, Clark Gable, and other luminaries. (See p530.)

THE COMEDY STORE

The Comedy Store
This is a world-famous spot for stand-up comedy, often enjoying television coverage. It stands on the site of the 1940s nightclub, Ciro's.

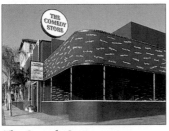

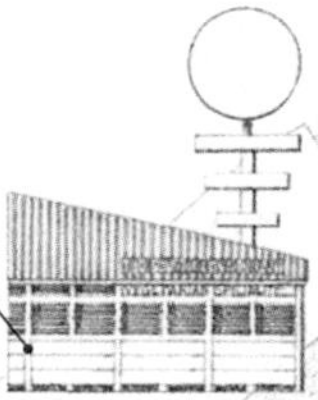

Carbo Cantina (The Source) at No. 8301 is where Woody Allen rants about LA in his film *Annie Hall* (1977).

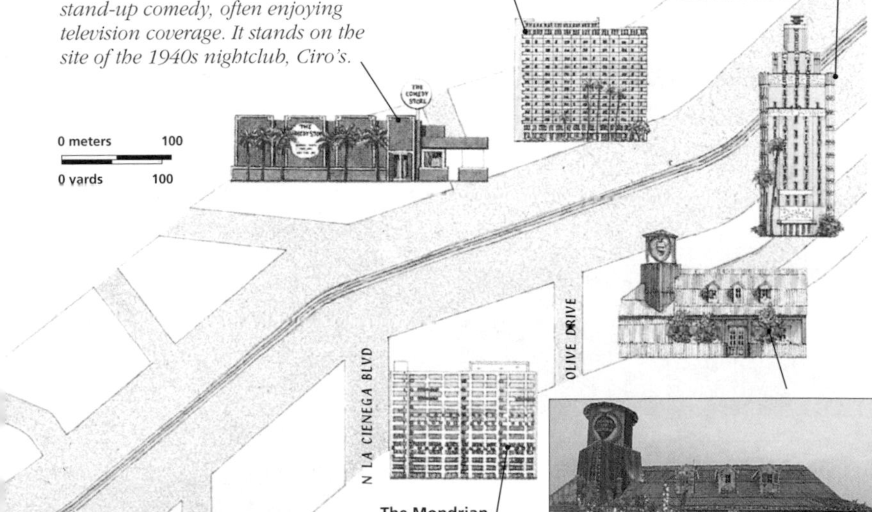

0 meters 100
0 yards 100
OLIVE DRIVE
N LA CIENEGA BLVD

The Mondrian Hotel, at No. 8440, is decorated with stripes in primary colors, as a tribute to artist Piet Mondrian. *(See p531.)*

The House of Blues
This tin-roofed blues bar, at No. 8430, has been transported from Clarksdale, Mississippi. It is part-owned by the actor Dan Ackroyd, who co-starred with John Belushi in the 1980 cult movie The Blues Brothers (see p174).

The Coffee Bean

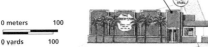

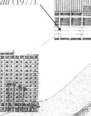

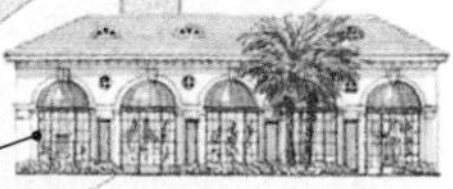

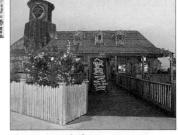

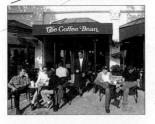

Sunset Plaza
This area is lined with chic stores and cafés. It is a good section to explore on foot.

Sunset Strip continued

Miyagi's, behind the big billboard to the west of the Chateau Marmont hotel, is currently popular with college crowds. It stands on the site of the Players Club, which was owned in the 1940s by movie director Preston Sturges.

Chateau Marmont
The hotel at No. 8221 (see p531) was modeled on a Loire Valley château. When it opened in 1929, it attracted actors such as Errol Flynn and Greta Garbo. Today's regulars include Christopher Walken and Winona Ryder.

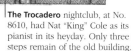

N LAUREL AVE

N FAIRFAX AVE

N LAUREL AVE

TO OLD
STUDIO
DISTRICT
(2KM)

**Directors' Guild
of America**
This is one of the many offices on Sunset Boulevard connected with the entertainment industry.

The Trocadero nightclub, at No. 8610, had Nat "King" Cole as its pianist in its heyday. Only three steps remain of the old building.

Schwab's
The former drugstore was a popular meeting place for film stars and columnists. A Virgin Megastore now occupies the site. Across Crescent Heights was the legendary Garden of Allah apartment complex whose residents included Scott Fitzgerald and Dorothy Parker.

BILLBOARDS

The most visible pieces of art along Sunset Strip are the huge, hand-painted billboards, produced by some of Hollywood's finest artists and designers to advertise new films, records, and personalities. They are often three-dimensional, a technique introduced in 1953 when Las Vegas's Sahara Hotel rented a billboard, erected a real swimming pool, and filled it with swimsuited models. During the 1960s the billboards were dominated by the music industry, with advertising space along Sunset Strip even being written into some rock stars' contracts. LA's well-known antipathy toward smoking now shows up in anti-smoking ads, which mimic the Marlboro cowboy style, on the massive boards outside the Chateau Marmont.

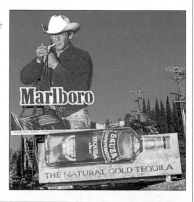

Famous Marlboro billboard, now gone from Sunset Strip

For hotels and restaurants in this region see pp524–31 and pp568–76

A View of Sunset Boulevard: Old Studio District

During the first half of the 20th century, this 2-mile (3-km) stretch of Sunset Boulevard, was the center of Hollywood's film industry. This historic district is located 1.2 miles (2 km) to the east of the fashionable nightlife and boutiques of Sunset Strip *(see pp102–4)*. Major studios, including 20th Century Fox, RKO, Warner Bros., Paramount, and United Artists, were all in the vicinity, and the streets were filled with directors, actors, and would-be film stars. In the area known as Gower Gulch, low-budget outfits churned out Westerns by the score.

Sunset Boulevard during its heyday in the 1940s

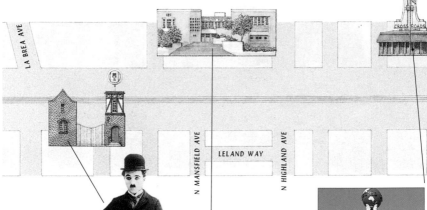

LA BREA AVE

N MANSFIELD AVE

LELAND WAY

N HIGHLAND AVE

A & M Records
These mock-Tudor buildings, stretching from the southeast corner of Sunset Boulevard down La Brea Avenue, were constructed by Charlie Chaplin as homes for workers at his studio.

Crossroads of the World
Hollywood's first shopping mall, built in 1936, is located at No. 6621. Designed to resemble an ocean liner, with a globe-topped tower on its prow, it has now been converted into offices.

Hollywood High School
A long list of famous alumni have attended Hollywood High School, at No. 6800, including Lana Turner. The actress was first discovered in 1936 by director Mervyn LeRoy, sipping a soda in the now-defunct Top Hat Malt Shop. Its site, opposite the school, is now occupied by a garage.

For hotels and restaurants in this region see pp524–31 and pp568–76

Old Studio District continued

ArcLight Cinerama Dome
The distinctive dome of No. 6360 was the first wide-screen movie theater on the West Coast.

Hollywood Athletic Club
Stars of the 1930s and 1940s exercised here. Flash Gordon star Buster Crabbe trained here before winning a gold medal at the 1932 Olympics.

CASSIL PLACE | N HUDSON AVE | N CAHUENGA BLVD | IVAR AVE | MORNINGSIDE CT

SEWARD ST | WILCOX AVE | COLE PLACE | VINE ST

The Cat and Fiddle
This British-style pub, at No. 6530, is built around an attractive Mediterranean-style patio. British beers are served along with pub food, such as bangers and mash. There is a dartboard inside.

TIME CAPSULE
In 1954 the Los Angeles Chamber of Commerce decided to preserve the history of Hollywood with a time capsule. A copy of Bing Crosby's hit record "White Christmas," released that year, a script of the most successful film made to date, *Gone With the Wind,* and various contemporary radio and television tapes were deposited under the sidewalk at the famous intersection between Sunset Boulevard and Vine Street. The time capsule is planned for retrieval 50 years after it was planted, in 2004.

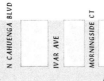

Singer Bing Crosby

A sidewalk plaque marking the site notes that the legend of Hollywood was born here in 1913 with the making of the first feature-length film, *The Squaw Man*, by Cecil B De Mille and Jesse Lasky. The actual location of their barn studio, now preserved on North Highland Avenue (*see p112*), was farther up the block at No. 1521 Vine Street. Hollywood had also been incorporated as a town ten years earlier and numerous short films had been made here during that decade.

Poster of *Gone With the Wind* (1939)

Hollywood Palladium
Norman Chandler, of the Los Angeles Times *dynasty, built this theater at No. 6215. It was opened by Lana Turner in 1940, when Frank Sinatra gave a concert. Big bands and musical stars still perform here.*

CBS Studios
No. 6121 was inherited from Columbia Pictures. It in turn succeeded the Nestor Film Co., which rented the site in 1911 for $40 a month.

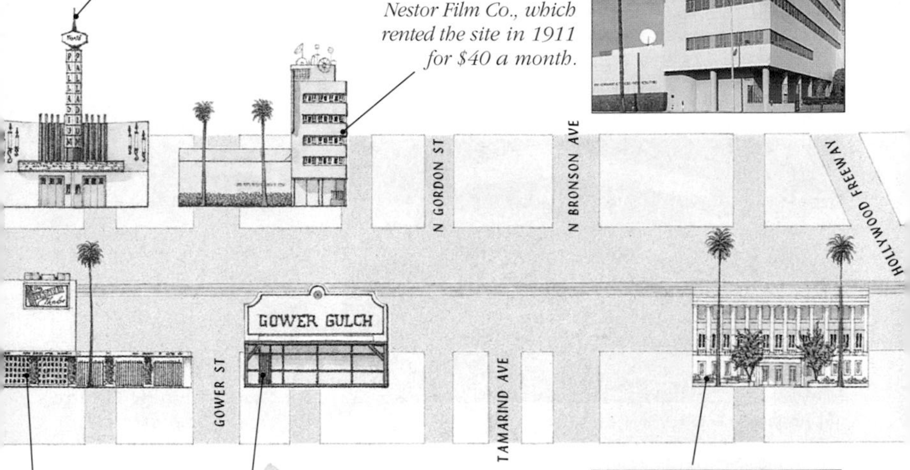

Gower Gulch
Now a shopping mall, in the 1930s and 1940s would-be actors gathered here each morning hoping for $10-a-day jobs at the small studios shooting low-budget Westerns.

Warner Bros. Studio
The first talkie, Al Jolson's The Jazz Singer *(1927), was made here at No. 5858. The following year the studio moved to Burbank (see p145). The building now houses local radio stations.*

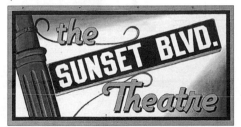

Sunset Boulevard Theater
Showman Earl Carroll's Vanities Theater originally occupied this site at No. 6220 in the 1940s. It had the world's largest revolving stage, which held 60 dancers.

WARNING

Unfortunately this section of Sunset Boulevard is run down and frequented by drug dealers and prostitutes. It is advisable to stay in your car, with the doors locked and valuables out of sight. If you decide to walk around, try to look as if you know where you are going. Keep your wallet in an inconspicuous place and do not wear valuable jewelry.

N GORDON ST

N BRONSON AVE

HOLLYWOOD FREEWAY

GOWER ST

GOWER GULCH

TAMARIND AVE

0 meters 100

0 yards 100

A View of Hollywood Boulevard

Hollywood Boulevard is one of the most famous streets in the world, and its name is still redolent with glamour. Visitors wishing to recapture a Golden Age of film should visit the Mann's Chinese Theatre and its autograph patio, the Walk of Fame, and the Hollywood Motion Picture museum situated on the top floor of the Hollywood and Highland shopping and entertainment complex. World premieres of Disney films at the El Capitan Theater often feature a live revue by the Magic Kingdom's favorite characters. Other attractions include the Hollywood Wax Museum, the Hollywood Guinness World of Records, and Ripley's Believe It or Not!®

First National Bank detail

LOCATOR MAP
See Street Finder map 2

★ **Mann's Chinese Theatre**
Stars' autographs are set in the concrete courtyard ❷

The Hollywood Entertainment Museum has film, television, radio, and recording memorabilia. It houses several real sets, including the original *Cheers* bar.

HOLLYWOOD BOULEVARD NORTH SIDE ▸▸▸▸▸▸▸▸▸▸▸▸▸▸▸▸▸▸▸▸▸▸▸▸▸▸▸▸▸▸▸▸▸▸

★ **Walk of Fame**
Marilyn Monroe's star is embedded in the sidewalk at No. 6776 Hollywood Boulevard. The camera symbol below her name indicates her career as a film actress ❺

MARILYN MONROE

Hollywood Guinness World of Records uses models, videos, and special effects to bring record-breaking achievements alive. It is housed in the area's first movie theater.

Ripley's Believe It or Not!® is a museum devoted to the bizarre. The building, topped by a model *Tyrannosaurus rex*, contains more than 300 exhibits, such as shrunken heads and two-headed calves.

HOLLYWOOD BOULEVARD SOUTH SIDE ▸▸▸▸▸▸▸▸▸▸▸▸▸▸▸▸▸▸▸▸▸▸▸▸▸▸▸▸▸▸▸▸▸▸

KEY

▶▶▶▶▶   North Side walking east

◀◀◀◀◀   South Side walking west

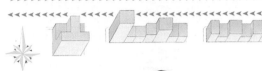

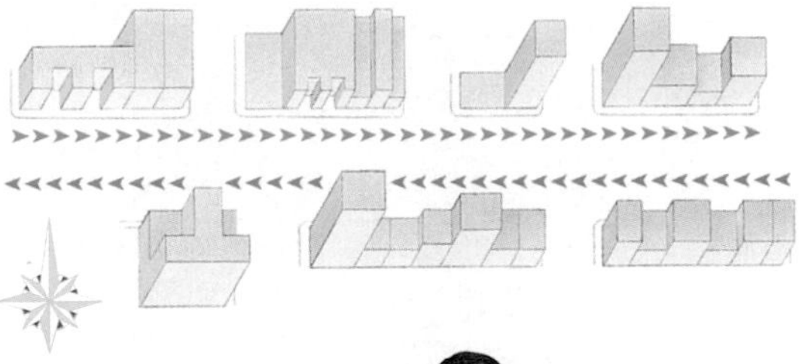

STAR SIGHTS

★ Mann's Chinese Theatre

★ Walk of Fame

The Hollywood Wax Museum has life-size models of film stars, musicians, and public figures. Clint Eastwood, Marilyn Monroe, Madonna, Michael Jackson, Dolly Parton, and Ronald Reagan are among those on display. There is also a wax tableau based on Leonardo da Vinci's painting *The Last Supper* (1497).

First National Bank marks the junction with Highland Avenue. Its tiered façade is decorated with stone reliefs of historical figures such as Christopher Columbus and Nicolaus Copernicus.

Hollywood and Highland *is great for retail shops and entertainment* ❸

0 meters   200

0 yards   200

Hollywood Roosevelt Hotel
An image of the actor Charlie Chaplin (1889–1977) decorates the wall of this 1920s hotel ❶

El Capitan Theater
Neon lights welcome filmgoers to this beautifully restored Art Deco theater. Movies can be seen in old-fashioned comfort, but with state-of-the art sound ❹

The Masonic Hall now displays interactive exhibitions of Disney shows.

Sid Grauman's famous Chinese Theatre (now Mann's)

Hollywood Roosevelt Hotel ➊

7000 Hollywood Blvd. **Map** 2 B4.
Tel (323) 466-7000.   *see* **Where to Stay** *p510*. www.hollywood roosevelt.com

Named after US president Theodore Roosevelt, this hotel was opened in 1927 by joint owners Louis B Mayer, Mary Pickford, Marcus Loewe, Douglas Fairbanks, Sr., and Joseph Schenk. Marilyn Monroe, Ernest Hemingway, and Clark Gable were all visitors and, on May 16, 1929, the first Academy Awards banquet was held in the Roosevelt's Blossom Room.
Renovations in 1986 revealed a Spanish Colonial design. The following year the pool was decorated by David Hockney *(see p28)*. The Hollywood Historical Review exhibition, documents the area's history.

Hollywood Roosevelt Hotel, locale for the first Academy Awards

Mann's Chinese Theatre ➋

6925 Hollywood Blvd. **Map** 2 B4.
Tel (323) 461-3331.   (323) 464-8111.   *daily.*   www.mann moviefone.com

One of the most famous sights in Hollywood has not changed much since it opened in 1927 with the gala premiere of Cecil B De Mille's *King of Kings*. The exterior is an ornate medley of Chinese temples, pagodas, lions, and dragons, reflecting the keen sense of showmanship of the theater's creator, Sid Grauman.
Grauman also thought up one of the longest-running publicity stunts in Hollywood history: inviting movie stars to impress their handprints, footprints, and autographs in the cement courtyard of his theater. There are many versions of how this custom began. One tells of silent screen star Norma Talmadge accidentally stepping in the wet cement at the gala opening *(see p53)*. Another is that the French stonemason, Jean Klossner, put his hand in the wet cement for posterity. Whatever the precedent, Sid Grauman liked the idea and invited Norma Talmadge, Mary Pickford, and Douglas Fairbanks, Sr. to legitimately leave their mark in the cement on May 17, 1927.
Anyone can visit the courtyard, but only filmgoers can see the extravagant interior of the various theaters.

Hollywood and Highland ➌

6801 Hollywood Boulevard. **Map** 2 B4.
Tel (323) 467 6412.   *10am -10pm Mon-Sat, 10am-7pm Sun.*   www.hollywoodandhighland.com

Opened in 2001 after a major refurbishment of this once neglected area, this shopping and entertainment complex features restaurants, clubs, retail shops, hotel, multiplex cinema and a costume museum. Visitors can also see a play or concert and take a tour of the new **Kodak Theatre**, the home of the Academy Awards ceremonies.

El Capitan Theater ➍

6838 Hollywood Blvd. **Map** 2 B4.
Tel (323) 467-7674.   *daily.*
www.elcapitan.com

Built in 1926 as a theater, El Capitan was later converted to a movie house. It was the venue for many premieres, such as Orson Welles's *Citizen Kane* (1941). In 1942 El Capitan was refurbished, and its interior was covered up. It was renamed the Hollywood Paramount.
Disney and Pacific Theaters bought El Capitan in 1991 and restored it to its former glory. Luckily, the original Art Deco interior was found virtually intact. Today, many Disney feature animations open here, such as *The Lion King* (1994) and *A Bug's Life* (1999).

For hotels and restaurants in this region see pp524–31 and pp568–76

Walk of Fame ❺

Map 2 B4. ℹ️ *6541 Hollywood Blvd (323) 461-2804.* 📠 *(323) 469-8311.*

Perhaps the only pavement in the city to be cleaned six times a week, the Walk of Fame is set with more than 2,000 polished marble stars. Since February 1960, celebrities from the worlds of film, radio, television, theater, and music have been immortalized on Hollywood Boulevard and Vine Street. Stardom does not come easily, however: each personality has to be sponsored and approved by the Chamber of Commerce, and pay a $7,500 installation fee. Among the most famous are Charlie Chaplin (No. 6751), and Alfred Hitchcock (No. 6506).

Frederick's of Hollywood ❻

6608 Hollywood Blvd.
Map 2 C4. **Tel** *(323) 957-5953.* 🕐 *10am–9pm Mon–Sat, 11am–7pm Sun.* ⬤ *Jan 1, Thanksgiving, Dec 25.* ♿ **www**.fredericksof hollywood.com

Frederick Mellinger launched his now world-famous mail-order business in 1946, selling provocative lingerie. He believed that "fashions may change, but sex appeal is always in style." This purple and pink Art Deco building is Frederick's flag-

Garish exterior of Frederick's of Hollywood

ship store. As well as selling underwear, it houses a Celebrity Lingerie Hall of Fame, which includes the bra worn by Marilyn Monroe in *Let's Make Love* (1960), Tony Curtis's black lace bra from the classic *Some Like It Hot* (1959), and Madonna's infamous black bustier.

Hollywood Bowl ❼

2301 N Highland Ave. **Map** 2 B3.
Tel *(323) 850-2000.* 🕐 *late Jun– late Sep.* 🅿️ ♿ **Box office** 🕐 *10am– 6pm Tue–Sun* **Edmund D Edelman Hollywood Bowl Museum
Tel** *(323) 850-2058.* 🕐 *late Jun– mid-Sep: 10am–0:30pm Tue–Sat; mid-Sep–late Jun: 10am–4:30pm Tue– Sat.* **www**.hollywoodbowl.com

Situated in a natural amphitheater, once revered by the Cahuenga Pass Gabrielino Indians, the Bowl is now

sacred to Angelenos. Since 1922 it has been the summer home of the LA Philharmonic *(see p125)*. Even though the acoustics are not perfect, the atmosphere cannot be beaten.

Thousands gather on warm evenings to picnic – often in high style – under the stars and listen to the orchestra. There are 13 picnic areas on the 60-acre (24-ha) site. Jazz, country, folk, and pop concerts are also performed during the season.

The most popular events at the Bowl are the concert with fireworks on the Fourth of July, the Easter Sunrise Service, and a Tchaikovsky Spectacular with cannons, fireworks, and a military band.

Much altered over the years, the shell-shaped stage was originally designed in 1929 by Lloyd Wright, son of architect Frank Lloyd Wright. Rumor has it that the materials for the building were taken from the set of Douglas Fairbanks, Sr.'s movie *Robin Hood* (1922). There is seating for 18,000 people at the Bowl, including the privately owned and much sought-after boxes at the front.

The Edmund D. Edelman Hollywood Bowl Museum explores the rich history of the Bowl, through videos, old programs and posters, and memorabilia of the artists who have come here, from violinist Jascha Heifetz to The Beatles. Film excerpts shot at the Bowl include William Wellman's *A Star is Born* (1937).

Hollywood Bowl, nestling in the Hollywood Hills

Mausoleum of William A Clark, Jr. in Hollywood Memorial Park

Hollywood Studio Museum ❽

2100 N Highland Ave. **Map** 2 B3.
Tel *(323) 874-2276.* ⬜
*11am–4pm Sat; noon–4pm Sun.
Weekdays by appt.* 📷 ♿ 📹

In 1913, Cecil B De Mille and the Jesse L Lasky Feature Play Company rented this barn, then located on Vine Street, just north of Sunset Boulevard. That year De Mille used the building to make *The Squaw Man*, the first feature-length movie produced in Hollywood. In 1935 the company was renamed Paramount Pictures.

The barn was moved to its present site, in the Hollywood Bowl parking lot *(see p111)*, in 1983. Thirteen years later a fire prompted a major renovation. Today the barn is a museum, displaying props, costumes, photographs, and other memorabilia from the early days of filmmaking.

Pantages Theater ❾

6233 Hollywood Blvd. **Map** 2 C4.
Tel *(323) 468-1770.* ⬜ *daily.* 📷 ♿

To attend a show at the Pantages is to experience the glory days of the 1930s movie palaces. Built in 1929, the marble and bronze Art Deco

theater catered to the comfort of its audience, with a spacious foyer and luxurious lounges. It opened in 1930 with *The Floradora Girl*, starring Marion Davies, the mistress of WR Hearst *(see p214)*. Between 1949 and 1959 the Academy Awards Ceremony was also held here.

Splendidly renovated in the 1980s, today Pantages is used to stage Broadway musicals. Only show ticket holders are allowed into the breathtaking interior, with its magnificent chandeliers, vaulted ceilings, and columns decorated with geometric patterns.

Elegant Art Deco façade of the Pantages Theater

Hollywood Memorial Park ❿

6000 Santa Monica Blvd. **Map** 8 C1.
Tel *(323) 469-1181.* ⬜ *8am–5pm Mon–Fri; 8:30am–4:30pm Sat–Sun.* ⬤ *public hols.* ♿
www.forevernetwork.com

The map of this cemetery (available at the front office) reads like a history of film. Tyrone Power has a white memorial overlooking a pond on the eastern side. Next to him, the mausoleum of Marion Davies bears her family name of Douras. Cecil B De Mille, Nelson Eddy, and many others from Hollywood's heyday are buried here. Douglas Fairbanks Sr.'s grave has a reflecting pool and monument, reputed to have been paid for by his ex-wife, the silent film star Mary Pickford. Inside the gloomy Cathedral Mausoleum is the tomb of Rudolph Valentino, still the cemetery's biggest attraction. Every year, on August 23, a "Lady in Black" pays her respects to the actor on the anniversary of his death.

The back of Paramount Studios forms the southern wall of the cemetery, and Columbia used to be to the north. Columbia boss Harry Cohn is said to have picked his plot so that he could keep an eye on his studio.

Paramount Studios ⓫

5555 Melrose Ave. **Map** 8 C1.
Tel (323) 956-5000. ◐ *Closed to the public since September 11, 2001.*
Visitors' Center and Ticket Window 860 N Gower St.
Tel (323) 956-1777. ☐ *9am–6pm Mon–Fri.* ◐ *Jan 1, Easter Sun, Thanksgiving, Dec 25.*

The last major studio still located in Hollywood, Paramount was also the first in operation. Cecil B. De Mille, Jesse Lasky, and Samuel Goldwyn joined forces with Adolph Zukor in 1914 to form what became known as the directors' studio. The roster of stars was equally impressive: Gloria Swanson, Rudolph Valentino, Mae West, Marlene Dietrich, Gary Cooper, and Bing Crosby all signed with Paramount.

Aspiring actors still hug the wrought-iron gates at Bronson Avenue and Marathon Street. Seeking luck, they quote Norma Desmond's final line in *Sunset Boulevard*: "I'm ready for my close-up, Mr. De Mille."

Classics such as *The Ten Commandments*, *The War of the Worlds*, *The Greatest Show on Earth*, and the *Godfather Parts I, II,* and *III* were all made in Paramount's 63 acres (25 ha) of backlot and sound stages. A two-hour tour of the studio provides details of its history and gives visitors a behind-the-scenes view of films and television shows currently in production *(see p175)*.

MELROSE AVENUE

Once a bland avenue, Melrose burst onto the Los Angeles street scene in the mid-1980s with quirky shops and good restaurants. The prime area stretches for 16 blocks between La Brea and Fairfax avenues, providing a rare opportunity to walk and shop outdoors in the city. From Fifties to punk to classic, the clothing, shoe, and accessory boutiques offer a wide range of styles and goods and stay open until late *(see pp176–7)*. The same can also be said of the avenue's many restaurants, which represent the diverse ethnic flavors of Los Angeles. Mexican and Thai are two of the favorite cuisines, but pasta and pizza dominate the street, as they do the rest of the city.

Colorful shop window on Melrose Avenue

At the western end of Melrose, at San Vincente Boulevard, is the huge 600-ft (183-m) high blue-glass Pacific Design Center, known to the locals as the Blue Whale. Designed by César Pelli in 1975, this showcase for interior designers and architects is the largest on the West Coast. Although it caters mainly to trade, the center also welcomes the general public. Admission charges and purchasing policies may vary between individual showrooms.

Farmers Market ⓬

6333 W 3rd St. **Map** 7 D3. *Tel (323) 933-9211.* ☐ *9am–9pm Mon–Fri, 9am–8pm Sat, 10am–7pm Sun.* ◐ *Jan 1, Easter Sun, Memorial Day, Jul 4, Labor Day, Thanksgiving, Dec 25.* ♿
www.farmersmarketla.com

In 1934, during the Great Depression *(see p53)*, a group of farmers began selling their produce directly to the public in a field then at the edge of town. Since then, Farmers Market has been a favorite meeting place for Angelenos. There are stalls selling fresh

Clock tower at entrance to Farmers Market

flowers, meats, cheeses, fruit, vegetables, and breads. There are also more than 100 shops that sell everything from antiques to T-shirts and garden supplies. Among the best of the numerous cafés and restaurants are Bob's Donuts, the Kokomo Café – try the strawberry pancakes or black bean-filled omelettes *(see p570)*; and The Gumbo Pot, with sweet *beignets* (dough fritters) and traditional Cajun food *(see p570)*.
Next to the market is The Grove, a huge retail complex filled with shops, restaurants and cinemas.

Poster for Paramount's *The War of the Worlds* (1953)

Los Angeles County Museum of Art ⑬

The largest encyclopedic art museum west of Chicago, the Los Angeles County Museum of Art (LACMA) has one of the finest collections in the country. Founded in 1910, the museum moved to its present site in prestigious Hancock Park in 1965. The six-building complex offers a wide selection of European and American art. LACMA West, across the street, holds Latin American art and a Children's Gallery. Also impressive are the museum's Asian and Middle Eastern works and its group of pre-Columbian artifacts. To display its Japanese art, including the Shin'enkan and Bushell collections, LACMA added the spectacular Pavilion for Japanese Art in 1988.

★ In the Woods at Giverny
This work of 1887, subtitled "Blanche Hoschedé at her easel with Suzanne Hoschedé reading," depicts the daughters of Monet's mistress.

★ Mother about to Wash her Sleepy Child *(1880)*
Mary Cassatt was a leading American Impressionist artist, who promoted that movement avidly in the United States. Nearly one third of the works that she produced are domestic scenes, such as this intimate portrait.

Third level

Second level

Flower Day *(1925)*
Diego Rivera depicts various religious influences in Mexico. This and other Latin American artworks are displayed in the new LACMA West.

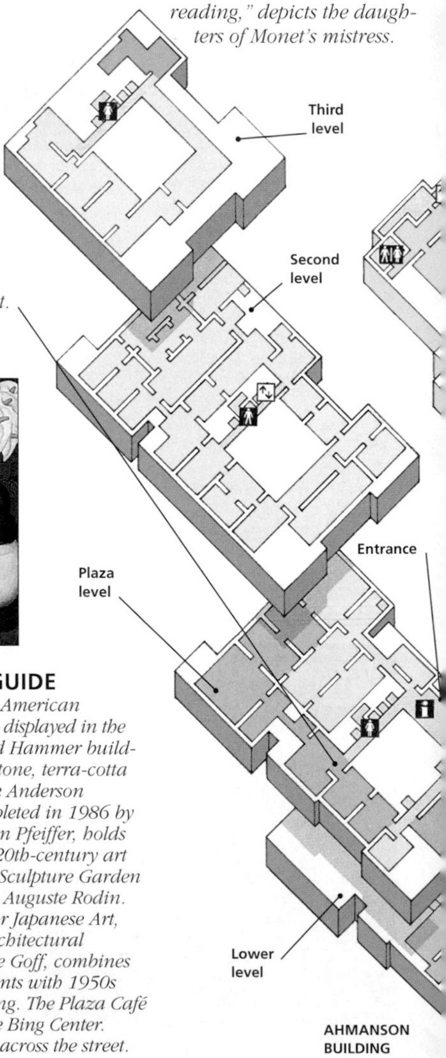

Plaza level

Entrance

MUSEUM GUIDE
European and American works of art are displayed in the Ahmanson and Hammer buildings. The limestone, terra-cotta and glass-brick Anderson Building, completed in 1986 by Hardy Holzman Pfeiffer, holds the museum's 20th-century art collection. The Sculpture Garden has bronzes by Auguste Rodin. The Pavilion for Japanese Art, designed by architectural maverick Bruce Goff, combines Japanese elements with 1950s American styling. The Plaza Café is located in the Bing Center. LACMA West is across the street.

STAR PAINTINGS

★ In the Woods at Giverny by Claude Monet

★ Mother about to Wash her Sleepy Child by Mary Cassatt

★ Mulholland Drive by David Hockney

Lower level

AHMANSON BUILDING

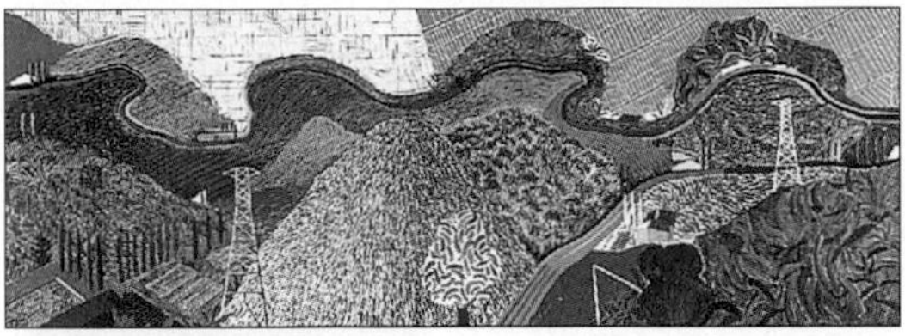

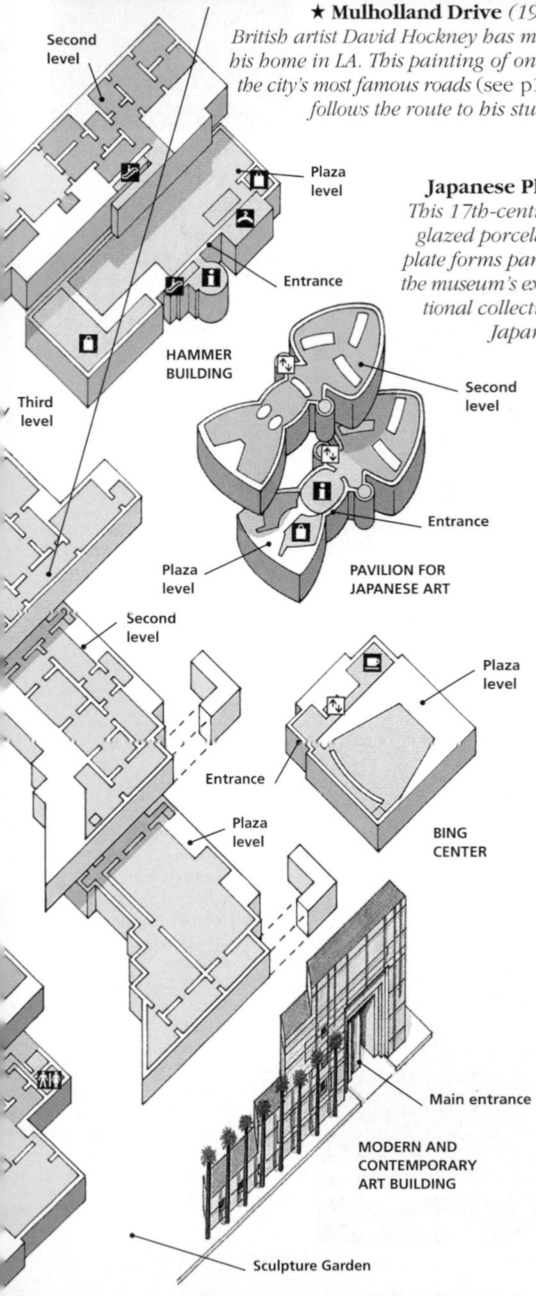

VISITORS' CHECKLIST

5905 Wilshire Blvd. **Map** 7 E4.
Tel (323) 857-6000. 20.
noon–8pm Mon, Tue, Thu
(until 9pm Fri), 11am– 8pm Sat &
Sun. Wed, Thnksg., Dec 25.
(free 2nd Tue of month).
www.lacma.org

★ **Mulholland Drive** (1980)
*British artist David Hockney has made
his home in LA. This painting of one of
the city's most famous roads (see p144)
follows the route to his studio.*

Second
level

Plaza
level

Entrance

**HAMMER
BUILDING**

Third
level

Second
level

Plaza
level

**PAVILION FOR
JAPANESE ART**

Second
level

Entrance

Plaza
level

Japanese Plate
*This 17th-century
glazed porcelain
plate forms part of
the museum's excep-
tional collection of
Japanese art.*

Plaza
level

Entrance

Plaza
level

**BING
CENTER**

Second
level

Main entrance

**MODERN AND
CONTEMPORARY
ART BUILDING**

Sculpture Garden

KEY TO FLOOR PLAN

	American art
	European painting, sculpture, and decorative art
	Modern and Contemporary art
	Photography, prints, and drawings
	Ancient and Islamic art
	Indian and Southeast Asian art
	Far Eastern art
	Costumes and textiles
	Temporary exhibitions
	Nonexhibition space

MUSEUM PLAN

	Ahmanson Building
	Modern and Contemporary Art Building
	Hammer Building
	Bing Center
	Pavilion for Japanese Art

Exploring LACMA

A tour of LACMA offers a comprehensive survey of the history of art throughout the world. The museum has more than 100,000 objects that represent many cultures, dating from prehistoric to modern and contemporary periods. Ancient art treasures encompass pre-Columbian finds as well as the largest Islamic art collection in the western United States. Decorative arts, which include European and American pieces from medieval times to the present, are exhibited alongside paintings and sculpture from the same period. The museum also has a superb collection of costumes and textiles. A program of world-class traveling exhibitions complements the permanent collection.

Standing Warrior

Magdalen with the Smoking Flame (c.1640) by Georges de la Tour

AMERICAN ART

The collection of paintings traces the history of American art from the 1700s to the 1940s. Dating from the Colonial period are John Singleton Copley's *Portrait of a Lady* (1771) and Benjamin West's *Cymon and Iphigenia* (1773).

In the mid-1800s American artists such as Edwin Church (1826–1900), Winslow Homer (1836–1910), and Thomas Moran (1837–1926) turned from portrait painting and Classical subjects to landscapes of the New World. Notable Impressionist works include Mary Cassatt's *Mother about to Wash Her Sleepy Child (see p110)* and Childe Hassam's *Avenue of the Allies* (1918). *Flower Day (see p114)* by Diego Rivera forms part of the Latin American collection.

Decorative arts range from Chippendale and Federal-style furniture to lamps by Louis Comfort Tiffany (1848–1933).

Monument to Balzac, sculpted in the 1890s by Auguste Rodin

EUROPEAN PAINTING, SCULPTURE, AND DECORATIVE ARTS

The collection of European works of art spans the 12th to early 20th centuries, beginning with medieval religious objects. Fine portraits by Lucas Cranach (1472–1553) and Hans Holbein (1497–1543) represent the Northern Renaissance.

Religious paintings by Fra Bartolommeo (1472–1517) and Titian (c.1490–1576) date from the Italian Renaissance.

One of the European collection's strengths is its 17th-century Dutch and Flemish canvases. Rembrandt's *The Raising of Lazarus* (c.1630) and Anthony Van Dyck's *Andromeda Chained to the Rock* (1637–8) are among the highlights. Works displayed from the French and Italian schools include Georges de la Tour's *Magdalen with the Smoking Flame,* painted around 1640, and Guido Reni's *Portrait of Cardinal Roberto Ubaldino,* which dates from before 1625. The French collections from the 18th and 19th centuries are also impressive, with works by Eugène Delacroix (1798–1863) and Camille Corot (1796–1875). The sculpture collection concentrates mostly on 19th-century French artists, with more than 40 works by Auguste Rodin (1840–1917).

Impressionist and Post-Impressionist works are hung in the Hammer Building. Two of the highlights are *In the Woods at Giverny* by Claude Monet *(see p114)* and Edgar Degas' *The Bellelli Sisters* (1862–4). Others include paintings by Pierre Auguste Renoir (1841–1919), Vincent Van Gogh (1853–90), and Paul Cézanne (1839–1906).

Among the finest decorative arts pieces are a Venetian enameled and gilded blue glass ewer, dating from about 1500, and a mid-16th-century Limoges plaque that depicts Psyche and Cupid.

The Cotton Pickers (1876) by Winslow Homer

MODERN AND CONTEMPORARY ART

Housed in the Anderson Building, the 20th-century collection has examples of every significant movement of modern art. The third level presents works dating from 1900 to 1970, including Pablo Picasso's *Portrait of Sebastian Juñer Vidal* (1903) and René Magritte's *La Trahison des Images (see p70)*. *Mulholland Drive* by David Hockney *(see p115)* is also hung here, due to its size. German Expressionists are well represented, with works from both *Die Brücke* (The Bridge) and *Der Blaue Reiter* (The Blue Rider) groups.

Post-1970 paintings, sculptures, and installations are displayed on the second level.

PHOTOGRAPHY, PRINTS, AND DRAWINGS

The museum's outstanding photography holdings give a rare overview of the medium. Exhibits range from early 19th-century daguerreotypes and albumen prints to abstract mixed media images. A large group of works by Edward Weston (1886–1958) is filled with texture and sensuality.

LACMA's holdings of prints and drawings includes the Robert Gore Rifkind Collection of German Expressionist works. Erich Heckel's woodcut, *Standing Child* (1910), is just one of its outstanding prints.

ANCIENT AND ISLAMIC ART

The ancient art of Egypt, western Asia, Iran, Greece, and Rome is displayed on the second level of the Ahmanson Galley. There are massive carved stone panels from a 9th-century BC Assyrian palace; a rare Egyptian bronze from the 25th Dynasty; and delicate Iranian figures, some dating from 3,000 BC. The Islamic art collection spans almost 1,400 years. Its Iranian and Turkish holdings are particularly strong.

Carved stone objects and ceramic vessels and statues from Central America and Peru comprise the pre-Columbian holdings. *Standing Warrior* (100 BC–AD 300), a Mexican effigy, is the largest known work of its kind.

INDIAN AND SOUTHEAST ASIAN ART

With more than 5,000 works dating from the 3rd century BC, the museum has one of the most comprehensive collections outside Asia. It is especially strong in Indian arts, from splendid sculpture to intricate watercolors on cloth and paper. There are manuscripts and *thankas* (paintings on cloth) from Tibet and Nepal, and stone and bronze sculptures from Indonesia, Thailand, Sri Lanka, Cambodia, and Burma.

Pair of Officials (618–907), from the Tang dynasty, China

FAR EASTERN ART

This section includes ceramics, sculpture, screens, and scrolls from China, Japan, and Korea. The highlight, however, is the Shin'enkan Collection in the Pavilion for Japanese Art. The collection's 200 screens and scroll paintings from the Edo period (1615–1868) are considered the most outstanding in the Western world. Masterpieces include Ito Jakuchu's 18th-century hanging scroll, *Rooster, Hen and Hydrangea,* and Suzuki Kiitsu's 19th-century *Seashells and Plums.* The Bushell Collection of *netsukes* (carved toggles used to secure a small container), ceramics, sculpture, and woodblock prints is also impressive.

COSTUMES AND TEXTILES

An encyclopedia of clothing and textiles, the collection boasts some 55,000 artifacts that represent more than 300 of the world's cultures. The oldest pieces are embroidered Peruvian burial shrouds that date from 100 BC and an Egyptian Coptic tunic from the 5th century AD. One of the most important pieces is the early 16th-century Iranian "Ardebil" carpet, named after a shrine in northwest Iran for which it was commissioned. A French noblewoman's gown, made from silk, gold, and silver, is one of only two complete 17th-century dresses in the US.

Dunes, Oceano (1936) by Edward Weston

Miracle Mile ⑭

Wilshire Blvd between La Brea & Fairfax Aves. **Map** 7 D4. ⓘ *685 S Figueroa St (213) 689-8822; 6801 Hollywood Blvd (323) 467-6412.*

In 1920, developer AW Ross bought 18 acres (7.2 ha) of land along Wilshire Boulevard and built a shopping district aimed at the wealthy families living in nearby Hancock Park. With its Art Deco and Streamline Moderne buildings, wide sidewalks and streets built for cars rather than carriages, it earned the nickname "Miracle Mile." The suburban department stores were designed with parking lots, a convenience that attracted hordes of shoppers from the city. It was the start of LA's decentralization.

Today, this stretch of boulevard is a shadow of its former self, dotted with grocery stores catering to various ethnic communities. At the eastern end, a few Streamline Moderne relics survive, such as the small gold-and-black building at No. 5209, a smaller version of the razed Richfield Tower in Downtown.

Fortunately, the western end of the Miracle Mile has fared somewhat better. Anchoring the corner of Fairfax Avenue, the May Company building has a gold and mosaic cylinder that resembles a large perfume bottle. With its five museums, including LACMA *(see pp114–17)*, the area has now become Museum Row.

Gold tower of the May Company building on Wilshire Boulevard

1932 Duesenberg Model J roadster at the Petersen Automotive Museum

Petersen Automotive Museum ⑮

6060 Wilshire Blvd. **Map** 7 D4. *Tel (323) 930-2277.* ◯ *10am–6pm Tue–Sun.* ● *Jan 1, Thanksgiving, Dec 25.* 🅿 ♿ 🎞 🅱 **www**.petersen.org

Dioramas and temporary exhibitions illustrate the evolution of the United States' car culture *(see pp200–1)*. On the first floor there are highly detailed displays featuring cars such as the 1911 American Underslung "Stuck in the Mud" and Earl Cooper's 1915 "White Squadron" Stutz Racer. A 1922 Ford Model-T is shown in a scene from a Laurel and Hardy film, and a trio of beautiful vintage cars appear in a 1920s street setting.

Other displays include a 1920s garage; a 1930s car showroom, whose opulence defied the Depression; and a 1950s drive-in restaurant. A 1930s billboard shows how advertising was used to boost the popularity of the car.

Upstairs, five galleries showcase everything from hot rods and motorcycles to vintage classics and cars of the stars. Vehicles that fall into the last category are Rita Hayworth's 1953 Cadillac and Clark Gable's Mercedes Benz.

The Improv ⑯

8162 Melrose Ave. **Map** 8 B2. *Tel (323) 651-2583.* ◯ *8pm Mon–Thu; 8.30pm & 10.30pm Sat & Sun.* 🅿 ♿ **www**.improv.com

When it opened in 1975, the Improv immediately became one of the finest comedy clubs in town, and today it is known throughout the world. Famous names such as Jay Leno, Richard Lewis, and Damon Wayans appear regularly, and Drew Carey performs most Thursdays with costars from the Drew Carey Show. The club is also a great place to see talented newcomers, many of whom have glittering careers ahead.

Food can be bought in the showroom itself or in the restaurant, Hell's Kitchen, which specialises in Italian food, and a minimum of two drinks per head can be ordered at the bar.

Given the club's popularity, it is best to book a table a day or two in advance.

Popular comedian Drew Carey performing at the Improv club

George C Page Museum of La Brea Discoveries ⑰

5801 Wilshire Blvd. **Map** 7 E4. *Tel (323) 934-7243.* ◯ *9.30am–5pm daily.* ● *Jan 1, Thanksgiving, July 4, Dec 25.* 🅿 *free first Tue of month.* ♿ 🎞 🅱

Opened in 1976, the George C Page Museum has a collection of over one million fossils that were discovered at the La Brea Tar Pits. These include more than 200 types of mammals, birds, reptiles,

LA BREA TAR PITS

The tar in the La Brea Pits was formed some 42,000 years ago by oil rising to the earth's surface and gelling. Animals entering the pits to drink the water became stuck in the tar and died. Their bones were then fossilized.

For centuries the tar was used by Gabrielino Indians to waterproof baskets and boats. Later, Mexican and Spanish settlers tarred their roofs with it. In 1906 geologists discovered the largest collection of fossils from the Pleistocene Epoch ever found in one place, and the pits began to attract greater attention. The land was deeded to the county in 1916.

Models at the La Brea Tar Pits depicting how animals were trapped

plants, and insects. Some of the pieces date back nearly 42,000 years. Among the highlights are mastodons, saber-toothed tigers, American lions, and an imperial mammoth. The display of more than 400 wolf skulls shows just how much variation can occur within a single species.

The only human skeleton to have been found in the pits is that of "La Brea Woman." A hologram changes her from a skeleton to a fully fleshed person and back again.

Pit 91 has produced most of the fossils. During the summer, visitors on the viewing station can watch paleontologists at work. Inside the museum, a glass-walled laboratory allows observation of the ongoing cleaning, identification, and cataloging of the fossils.

Mammoth skeleton at the George C Page Museum

Craft and Folk Art Museum ⑱

5814 Wilshire Blvd. **Map** 7 E4. *Tel* (323) 937-4230. ☐ 11am–5pm Wed–Sun. ⬤ Jan 1, Thanksgiving, Dec 25. 🖼 🗗 (Wed). 🖥 www.cafam.org

The museum's collection has more than 3,000 folk art and craft objects from around the world, ranging from 19th-century American quilts to contemporary furniture, to African masks. Those interested in design will enjoy the regular exhibitions on subjects such as toys, glassware, and textiles.

The extensive collection of Mexican artworks includes a fine selection of the Linares family's papier-mâché pieces.

A series of exhibitions is held throughout the year, and every October the museum runs the International Festival of Masks in nearby Hancock Park.

African mask at the Craft Museum

Wiltern Theater ⑲

3790 Wilshire Blvd. **Map** 9 D4. *Tel* (213) 380-5005. ☐ performances only. 🖼 🕭 🗗

Built as a movie theater in 1931, the Wiltern Theater was restored in 1985 and is a center for the performing arts. Its Art Deco tower and wings are faced with turquoise-glazed terra-cotta, and its main entrance is marked by a sun-burst canopy. The sun motif continues in the auditorium, where rays of low-relief skyscrapers decorate the interior ceiling.

To see inside the Wiltern Theater visitors must buy a ticket to a show.

DOWNTOWN LOS ANGELES

Considered a backwater a little over a hundred years ago, Los Angeles has confounded its critics by becoming a powerful worldwide influence. The city's Spanish roots are here, at El Pueblo, where the Avila Adobe and Old Plaza Church stand as reminders of Mexican frontier days, when *rancheros* and their *señoras* strolled through the streets. To the north of El Pueblo is Chinatown, with its numerous Asian shops and restaurants. To the south, Little Tokyo is the heart of the largest Japanese-American community in North America. Downtown's business district is centered on Bunker Hill, once a wealthy neighborhood where the city's Victorian elite lived. Today, confident office towers such as the First Interstate World Center and the Wells Fargo Center dominate the Downtown landscape. The district is also home to the Museum of Contemporary Art (MOCA) and the Music Center for the performing arts.

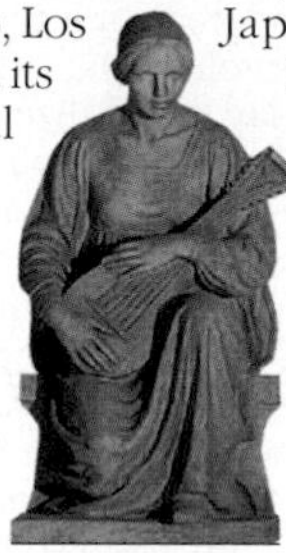

Detail from the Fine Arts Building on West 7th Street

SIGHTS AT A GLANCE

Historic Districts and Buildings
Angels Flight 2
Bradbury Building 4
Chinatown 8
El Pueblo pp126–7 7
Grand Central Market 3
Little Tokyo 13
Los Angeles Central Library 1
Los Angeles City Hall 11
Union Station 9

Museums and Galleries
Geffen Contemporary at MOCA 12
Japanese American National Museum 14
Los Angeles Children's Museum 10
Museum of Contemporary Art 5

Arts Complex
Music Center 6

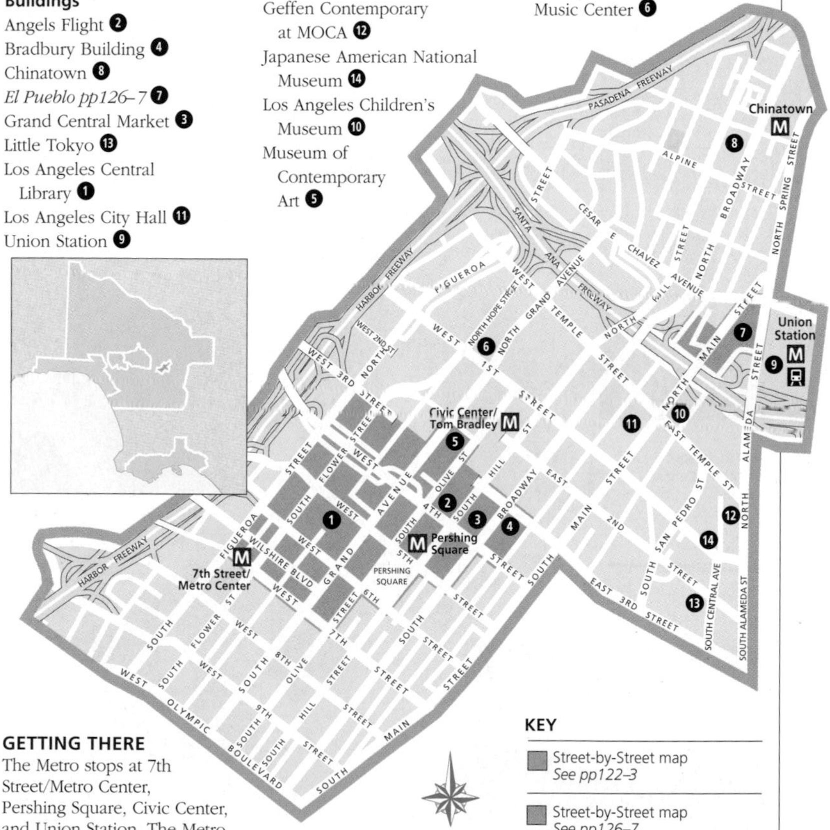

GETTING THERE

The Metro stops at 7th Street/Metro Center, Pershing Square, Civic Center, and Union Station. The Metro Blue Line runs between Long Beach and 7th Street/ Metro Center. DASH buses also serve the district.

0 meters 500

0 yards 500

KEY

Street-by-Street map *See pp122–3*

Street-by-Street map *See pp126–7*

Amtrak station

[M] Metro station

◁ **Wells Fargo Center, slicing the Downtown skyline**

Street-by-Street: Business District

Stone carving on Biltmore Hotel

The 20th century saw LA expand west toward the ocean, temporarily relegating Downtown to a minor role in the city. All that has changed. Today a revitalized business district has developed around Flower Street, and the sidewalk are once more filled with tourists and Angelenos alike. California's banking industry has its headquarters here, housed in striking skyscrapers such as the Wells Fargo Center. The revival has continued eastward across Downtown, where the jewelry, toy, food, and garment wholesale industries are flourishing. A commitment to the arts has also borne fruit. The Museum of Contemporary Art (MOCA), Music Center, and Los Angeles Central Library have together encouraged a thriving cultural environment that has drawn people back to the city's center.

The Westin Bonaventure Hotel has external elevators with views of the business district for guests ascending to the cocktail lounge *(see p527)*.

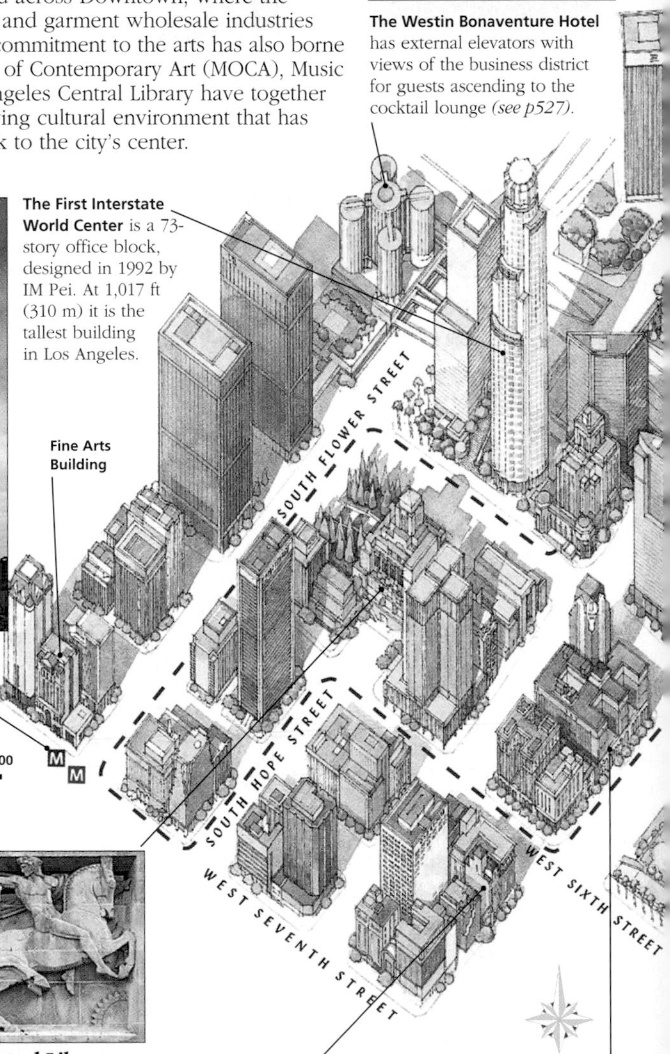

The First Interstate World Center is a 73-story office block, designed in 1992 by IM Pei. At 1,017 ft (310 m) it is the tallest building in Los Angeles.

Fine Arts Building

7th Street/ Metro Center

0 meters   500

0 yards   500

SOUTH FLOWER STREET

SOUTH HOPE STREET

WEST SIXTH STREET

WEST SEVENTH STREET

★ **Los Angeles Central Library**
The newly expanded Beaux-Arts library is decorated with carvings and inscriptions on the theme "the Light of Learning" ❶

The Oviatt Building (1925) is a marvelous example of Art Deco styling. René Lalique made some of the glass.

The Millennium Biltmore Hotel has been one of LA's most luxurious hotels since 1923 *(see p526)*.

★ **Museum of Contemporary Art**
Located off California Plaza, MOCA's sandstone building was greeted with acclaim when it opened in 1986. The collection gives an exciting overview of post-1940 art ❺

LOCATOR MAP
See Street Finder, map 11

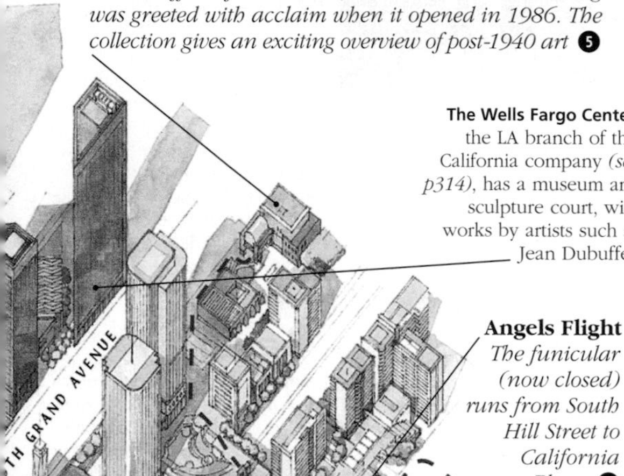

The Wells Fargo Center, the LA branch of this California company *(see p314)*, has a museum and sculpture court, with works by artists such as Jean Dubuffet.

Angels Flight
The funicular (now closed) runs from South Hill Street to California Plaza ❷

★ **Bradbury Building**
The atrium of this unassuming Victorian office block is one of the finest of its kind in the US ❹

Pershing Square Metro station

Grand Central Market
This indoor market lies at the heart of the old theater district ❸

KEY
— — —　Suggested route

STAR SIGHTS

★ Bradbury Building

★ Los Angeles Central Library

★ Museum of Contemporary Art

Pershing Square was designated the city's first public park in 1866. The now-concreted square is still a popular meeting place and has been landscaped with trees, benches, and statuary.

Façade of the Los Angeles Central Library

Los Angeles Central Library **❶**

630 W 5th St. **Map** 11 D4. **Tel** *(213) 228-7000.* ☐ *10am–8pm Mon–Thu; 10am–6pm Fri, Sat; 1–5pm Sun.* ● *public hols.* ♿ **www**.lapl.org

Built in 1926, this civic treasure was struck by an arson attack in 1986. It was closed for seven years while a $213.9 million renovation program was carried out. Sympathetic to the original architecture, the improvements have doubled the library's capacity to more than 2.1 million books.

The original building combines Beaux-Arts grandeur with Byzantine, Egyptian, and Roman architectural elements, inscriptions, and sculpture on the theme "the Light of Learning." The murals in the rotunda, painted by Dean Cornwell (1892–1960), depict the history of California and are well worth seeing.

The attention given to detail in the new Tom Bradley wing is impressive. One example is the three atrium chandeliers, created by Therman Statom to represent the natural, ethereal, and technological worlds.

The Central Library's garden is situated by the Flower Street entrance. Weary sightseers will appreciate its fountains, sculptures, shaded benches, and restaurant.

Statue on the library wall

A varied program of arts events takes place within the library, including prose and poetry readings, lectures, concerts, and plays.

Angels Flight **❷**

Between Grand, Hill, 3rd & 4th Sts. **Map** 11 D4. **Tel** *(213) 626-1901. Closed for the foreseeable future.*

Billed as the "shortest railway in the world," Angels Flight transported riders the 315 ft (96 m) between Hill Street and Bunker Hill for almost 70 years. Built in 1901, the funicular quickly became a familiar and much-loved method of travel. But, by 1969, Bunker Hill had sadly degenerated and was considered an eyesore. The city dismantled Angels Flight, but promised to reinstall the funicular once the area had been redeveloped. In 1996, some 27 years later, the city finally fulfilled that vow.

Grand Central Market **❸**

317 S Broadway. **Map** 11 E4. **Tel** *(213) 624-2378.* ☐ *9am–6pm daily.* ● *Jan 1, Thanksgiving, Dec 25.* ♿

Angelenos have been coming to this vibrant indoor bazaar since 1917. Today, more than 40 stallholders

operate inside the marketplace. Neatly arranged mounds of bargain-priced fresh fruits and vegetables line the many produce stands, and friendly stallholders frequently offer free samples of fruit.

Almost all the signs are in English and Spanish. The market's predominantly Latin American clientele come here to buy exotic products from their home countries, such as fresh Nogales cacti and beans from El Salvador. The seafood stands are filled with an array of fish caught in the waters off Southern California. Goat heads and tripe are offered alongside the more familiar cuts of meat at the butcher stalls. Herb stands offer a range of homeopathic alternatives for minor ills. Amid all this bustle, fragrant aromas of powdered chilies, herbs, and spicy foods waft through the air.

Among the many cafés and food stands in the market is China Café, which has been serving its popular chow mein since the 1930s. At Chapalita Tortilleria, visitors can enjoy watching the rickety assembly-line machine turn *masa* (corn flour dough) into tortillas and then partake of the free samples on the counter. Mexican stalls, such as Ana Maria, sell tacos and burritos, which are filled with all kinds of meat and seafood.

Venturing from the market onto Broadway, you will find yourself on the main shopping street of Los Angeles' Hispanic community. Before World War II, this was the movie district, with extravagant theaters and fashionable shops. Today, most of the theaters have either closed down or are being used for religious meetings conducted in Spanish. The street has a great deal of energy – the feel is that of Mexico City or Lima, Peru – but tourists should be wary of pickpockets.

China Café in the market

Atrium of the Bradbury Building

Bradbury Building ❹

304 S Broadway. **Map** 11 E4. **Tel** (213) 626-1893. ☐ 9am–6pm Mon–Fri, 9am–5pm Sat & Sun. ♿ from 3rd St.

The Bradbury Building was designed by architectural draftsman George Herbert Wyman in 1893. It is one of the few surviving Victorian structures in LA. Although the red façade is simple, the atrium is outstanding, with its lace-work of wrought-iron railings, oak paneling, glazed brick walls, two open-cage elevators, and a glass roof. It is the only office building in LA to be designated a National Historic Landmark. Visitors may get a feeling of *déjà vu* – the building is a popular film location, with Ridley Scott's *Blade Runner* (1982) just one of the movies shot here.

Museum of Contemporary Art ❺

250 S Grand Ave.
Map 11 D4. **Tel** (213) 621-2766. ☐ 11am–5pm Tue–Sun (until 8pm Thu). ☐ Jan 1, July 4, Thanksgiving, Dec 25. 🎫 free 5– 8pm Thu. ♿
www.moca.org

Rated by the American Institute of Architects as one of the best works of architecture in the US, this museum's building is as

interesting as its collection. It is an intriguing combination of pyramids, cylinders, and cubes, designed in 1986 by Japanese architect Arata Isozaki. Its warm native sandstone walls, which sit on a red granite foundation, are in pleasing contrast to the cool tones of the district's surrounding skyscrapers.

The gallery area lies off the sunken entrance courtyard and is reached via a sweeping staircase. Four of the seven galleries are naturally lit from pyramid-shaped skylights that punctuate the roofline.

Founded in 1979, the Museum of Contemporary Art has quickly amassed a respected selection of post-1940 work from artists such as Piet Mondrian, Jackson Pollock, Louise Nevelson, and Julian Schnabel. Added weight is given by the Panza Collection of 80 works of Pop Art and Abstract Expressionism by artists such as Robert Rauschen-berg, Mark Rothko, and Claes Oldenburg.

In 1995, MOCA acquired the 2,100-print Freidus Collection of photographs, which traces the development of documentary photo-graphy in the United States from the 1940s through the 1980s. The collection includes works by Diane Arbus and Robert Frank.

MOCA stands at the northern end of the 11-acre (4.5-ha)

Coca-Cola Plan (1958) by Robert Rauschenberg

California Plaza. This vast development funded the creation of MOCA, donating 1.5 percent of its budget, as stipulated by LA law, to public art. The spectacular fountain at the center of the plaza repeats its synchronized program every 20 minutes. The finale drops a 10,000-gal (45,500-litre) wave that washes over the fountain edge.

Music Center ❻

135 N Grand Ave. **Map** 11 E3. **Tel** (213) 972-7211. 🎫 ♿ **Dorothy Chandler Pavilion box office** ☐ 10am–6pm Mon–Sat. **Mark Taper Forum & Ahmanson Theater box offices** ☐ noon–8pm Tue–Sun. **Walt Disney Concert Hall box office** ☐ noon–6pm Tue–Sun. **www**.musiccenter.org

This complex is one of the three largest performing arts venues in the US. The Walt Disney Concert Hall, designed by architect Frank Gehry, opened in 2003. This striking 2265-seat venue is the new home of the Los Angeles Philharmonic Master Chorale. The Dorothy Chandler Pavilion is the venue for the LA Music Center Opera, LA Master Chorale, and LA Philharmonic. The Ahmanson Theater stages Broadway plays, while the Mark Taper Forum presents first-class plays.

The Walt Disney Concert Hall designed by architect Frank Gehry

Street-by-Street: El Pueblo ❼

El Pueblo de la Reina de Los Angeles, the oldest part of the city, was founded in 1781 by Felipe de Neve, the Spanish governor of California. Today, El Pueblo is a State Historic Monument. The shops along Olvera Street sell colorful Mexican dresses, leather *baraches* (sandals), *piñatas* (clay or paper-mâché animals), and snacks like *churros*, a Spanish-Mexican fried bread. During its festivals El Pueblo is ablaze with color and sound. The Blessing of the Animals, *Cinco de Mayo* (May 5), the Mexican Independence Day fiesta (September 13–15), and the candlelight procession of *Las Posadas* (December 16–24) are celebrated with passion *(see pp36–9)*.

Statue of LA's founder, Felipe de Neve

★ **Old Plaza Church**
The Annunciation *(1981)*, a mosaic by Isabel Piczek, is on the façade of the city's oldest church.

Site of the first cemetery in Los Angeles.

Pico House
California's last Mexican governor, Pío Pico, constructed the three-story Pico House in 1870. The Italianate building was for many years the area's finest hotel.

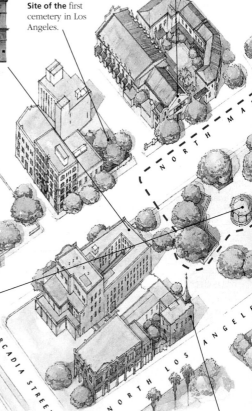

Plaza
A wrought-iron bandstand is set in the middle of the plaza. Nearby is a list of the first 44 settlers and a statue of Felipe de Neve.

ARCADIA STREET

NORTH MAI

NORTH LOS ANGELE

NORTH ANGELE

Firehouse

STAR SIGHTS

★ Avila Adobe

★ Old Plaza Church

KEY
– – – Suggested route

Chinatown ❽

Map 11 F2. ℹ️ *977 N Broadway, Suite E (213 617-0396).*

The Chinese first came to California during the Gold Rush *(see pp48–9)* to work in the mines and build the railroads. Confronted by prejudice, they developed tightknit communities. LA's first Chinatown was established in 1870 on the present-day site of Union Station *(see p128)*. It was relocated about 900 yds (820 m) northward in the mid-1930s. Today it is the home of over 12,000 people, who live and work in this colorful district.

The ornate East Gate on North Broadway leads into Gin Ling Way and the New Chinatown Central Plaza. This pedestrian precinct is lined with brightly painted buildings that have exaggerated pagoda-style roofs. Here, import shops sell everything from exquisite jade jewelry and antiques to inexpensive trinkets.

In the surrounding streets, the buildings are more bland, but tantalizing restaurants offer all manner of Chinese food, from dim sum (filled, steamed, or grilled dumplings, *see p564*) to spicy Szechuan dishes.

Although on a smaller scale than the celebrations in San Francisco *(see p39)*, LA has its own Chinese New Year Parade in early February. The festivities include dragon and lion dancers, who snake through the district's streets accompanied by drums, cymbals, floats, and firecrackers.

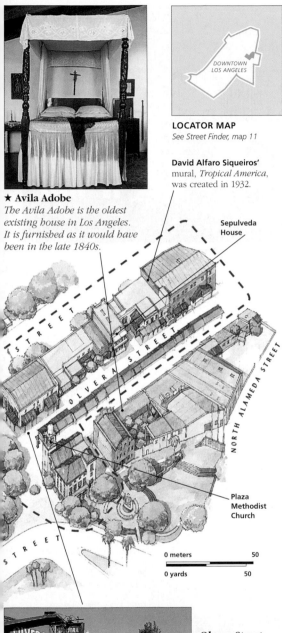

LOCATOR MAP
See Street Finder, map 11

David Alfaro Siqueiros' mural, *Tropical America*, was created in 1932.

★ **Avila Adobe**
The Avila Adobe is the oldest existing house in Los Angeles. It is furnished as it would have been in the late 1840s.

Sepulveda House

Plaza Methodist Church

0 meters   50
0 yards   50

Olvera Street
This pedestrian street was preserved in the 1930s as a Mexican marketplace following a campaign by local civic leader Christine Sterling.

Restaurant in Chinatown, topped by a pagoda

Unique blending of architectural styles on Union Station's façade

Union Station **9**

800 N Alameda St. **Map** 11 F3.
Tel (213) 683-6979; (800) 872-7245.
☐ *24 hours daily.* ♿

Dating from 1939, this grand railroad passenger terminal was the last of its kind to be built in the United States. The exterior is a successful merging of Spanish Mission, Moorish, and Streamline Moderne styles *(see pp30–3).* The tiles edging the interior walls, the inlaid marble designs of the floors, and the filigree work over the windows and doorways all use Spanish motifs.

The vast concourse, with its 52-ft (15.8-m) high roof, will be familiar to any fan of 1940s films – stars were frequently photographed here arriving in Los Angeles. In recent years it has been the location for several movies, including Sydney Pollack's *The Way We Were* (1973) and Barry Levinson's

Bugsy (1991). Today the station is quieter, but there are still daily departures to Chicago, Seattle, and San Diego.

Los Angeles Children's Museum **10**

Currently closed for renovation and relocation. Will open near Hansen Dam in the San Fernando Valley in 2007. **www**.childrensmuseumla.org

This imaginative and stimulating museum is guided by the principle that children learn best by doing. Opened in 1979, it quickly became a popular family destination.

Some 20 hands-on activities are linked by a series of ramps. Called the "discovery maze," the system was designed by architect Frank Gehry. One of the favorite exhibits is the Videozone.

This brings out the performer in children as they sing, dance, and tell stories on video. In Sticky City, large, brightly colored foam-and-Velcro blocks cling to each other, the walls, and even the participants as they build skyscrapers, mountains, and tunnels.

Children between 2 and 12 years old enjoy role-playing as the driver of a bus in the City Streets exhibit. In the Cave of the Dinosaurs, young visitors can experience primitive life in their own cave, complete with realistic dinosaur sounds.

All children must be accompanied by an adult.

Los Angeles City Hall **11**

200 N Spring St. **Map** 11 E4. **Tel** *(213) 485-2121.* ☐ *8am–5pm Mon–Fri.* ● *public hols.* ♿ *from Main St.* 🎫 *advance reservations required.*

Until 1957, this 28-story structure was the tallest in Downtown – all others were limited to 12 floors. When it was built in 1928, sand from every California county and water from each of the state's 21 missions was added to the City Hall's mortar.

Today City Hall is dwarfed by surrounding skyscrapers, but its distinctive tower is still one of Los Angeles's most

Entrance to Los Angeles Children's Museum

For hotels and restaurants in this region see pp524–31 and pp568–76

familiar landmarks. Among its many film and television roles it has been the location for the *Daily Planet*, Clark Kent's place of work in the television series *Superman*.

Inside, the rotunda has a beautiful inlaid-tile dome and excellent acoustics. The dome is decorated with eight figures showing the building's major concerns: education, health, law, art, service, government, protection, and trust.

Organized groups who take the 45-minute tour of the City Hall can ascend to an observation area in the tower, which has been restored after damage by the 1994 Northridge earthquake *(see p57)*. From here there are panoramic views across the city.

Rotunda of LA City Hall

Geffen Contemporary at MOCA ⑫

152 N Central Ave. **Map** 11 F4. *Tel (213) 621-2766.* ◯ *11am–5pm Tue–Sun (until 8pm Thu).* ● *Jan 1, Jul 4, Thanksgiving, Dec 25.* 🎫 *(free 5–8pm Thu).* ♿ 📷 www.atmoca.org

In 1983, this old police garage was used as a temporary exhibition space until MOCA's

California Plaza facilities were completed *(see p125)*. Frank Gehry's renovations were so successful that the warehouse became a permanent fixture. Exhibitions change regularly and often include highlights from MOCA's collection.

Little Tokyo ⑬

Map 11 E4. 🏠 *244 S San Pedro St. (213 628-2725).*

Lying between First, Third, Los Angeles, and Alameda streets, Little Tokyo has more than 200,000 visitors who throng its Japanese markets, shops, restaurants, and temples.

The first Japanese settled here in 1884. Today, the heart of the area is the Japanese American Cultural and Community Center at No. 244 South San Pedro Street, from which cultural activities and festivals such as Nisei Week *(see p37)* are organized. The center's fan-shaped Japan America Theater is often a venue for performers from Japan, such as the Grand Kabuki.

The Japanese Village Plaza at No. 335 East Second Street has been built in the style of a rural Japanese village, with blue roof tiles, exposed wood frames, and paths landscaped with pools and rocks. A traditional fire watchtower marks the plaza's First Street entrance. Stores include Enbun Market, one of Little Tokyo's oldest businesses, and the Mikawaya Candy Store. Off San Pedro Street, Onizuka Street offers more upscale shops.

Central Avenue entrance to the Japanese American Museum

Japanese American National Museum ⑭

369 E 1st St. **Map** 11 F4. *Tel (213) 625-0414.* ◯ *10am–5pm Tue–Sun (until 8pm Thu).* ● *Jan 1, Thanksgiving, Dec 25.* 🎫 ♿ 📷 www.janm.org

The former Nishi Hongwanji Buddhist Temple is now a museum. In 1925, architect Edgar Cline designed a building with a dual personality. The First Street entrance has an unremarkable brick façade, but the ceremonial entrance, on Central Avenue, mixes oriental and Egyptian motifs. The concrete canopy is modeled after the gateway to a Kyoto temple, and the brick pilasters have Egyptian-style capitals made of terra-cotta.

The museum is committed to preserving the history of Japanese-Americans in the US and has the largest collection of Japanese-American memorabilia in the world. Because most Japanese-Americans' property was lost when they were interned during World War II, the collection has simple, everyday items, such as newspapers, luggage, and clothing. An archive of camp records is available alongside camp mementos that include crafts and furniture.

Temporary exhibitions cover subjects such as the "Issei Pioneers," "America's Concentration Camps," and "Japanese-American Soldiers." A series of workshops is also offered.

Onizuka Street in Little Tokyo, looking toward Los Angeles City Hall

The *Queen Mary,* Long Beach's most famous hotel

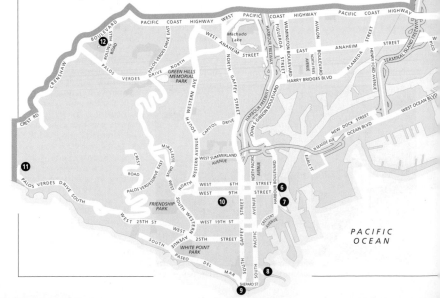

LONG BEACH AND PALOS VERDES

The ocean is the unifying force of this disparate region, where waves crash against the cliffs of the Palos Verdes Peninsula and tankers head for the busy ports of Los Angeles and Long Beach. The peninsula, a magnificent stretch of coastline, is an affluent area, with mansions and stables set amid the rolling

Statue in Ports O'Call Village

hills. On its southeastern side, working-class San Pedro is home to the Port of Los Angeles as well as generations of fishermen. The big city in the area – the fifth-largest in the state – is Long Beach. Aptly named for its 5.5-mile (9-km) expanse of white sand, this community has long attracted those who love the ocean. Its most famous landmark is the ocean liner *Queen Mary*.

SIGHTS AT A GLANCE

Historic Ships
Queen Mary pp134–5 **5**

Districts
Long Beach **1**
Naples **4**
Ports O'Call Village **7**
San Pedro **10**

Historic Buildings
Rancho Los Alamitos **3**
Rancho Los Cerritos **2**

Modern Architecture
Wayfarers Chapel **11**

Parks and Gardens
Point Fermin Park **9**
South Coast Botanic
  Garden **12**

Museums
Cabrillo Marine Aquarium **8**
Los Angeles Maritime
  Museum **6**

GETTING THERE
The Metro Blue Line connects Long Beach to downtown Los Angeles. The busy port is well served by freeways that link it to the rest of the city. A free shuttle bus, the Runabout, makes frequent trips between downtown Long Beach, Shoreline Village, the *Queen Mary,* and the Catalina Island terminal *(see pp242–3).* Cyclists can take the Oceanside Bike Path *(see p178)* from Long Beach to Naples.

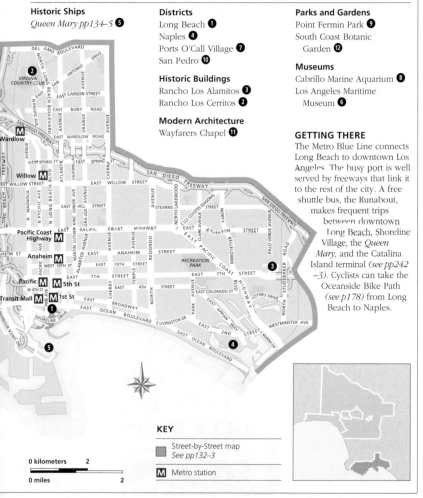

KEY

	Street-by-Street map See pp132–3
M	Metro station

0 kilometers 2

0 miles 2

Street-by-Street: Long Beach ❶

Shoreline Village sign

With palm trees and the ocean as a backdrop, downtown Long Beach is a mixture of carefully restored buildings and modern glass high-rises. At its heart, Pine Avenue still retains the early mid-western charm that gave the city its nickname of "Iowa by the Sea." The trendy atmosphere attracts locals, who come to relax, enjoy a cup of espresso, and sample some of the best food in the area. Nearby, Long Beach Convention and Entertainment Center was once the site of the Pike Amusement Park, famous for its roller coaster. Now the Terrace Theater's respected music and dance programs draw the crowds. Along the ocean, the shops and restaurants in Shoreline Village offer views of the *Queen Mary*.

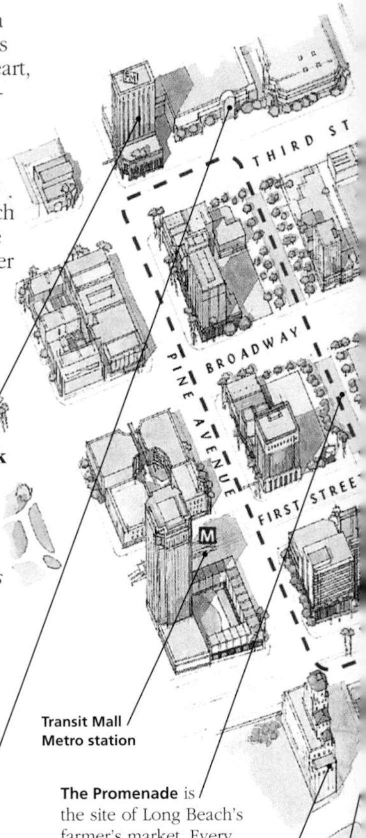

Farmers and Merchants Bank Tower
When erected in 1922, this terra-cotta building was Long Beach's first skyscraper. Its hall is a fine example of period styling.

Transit Mall Metro station

The Promenade is the site of Long Beach's farmer's market. Every Friday the street is filled with stands selling fruit, vegetables, and crafts.

Long Beach Municipal Auditorium Mural
This 1938 mural of a day at the beach was originally housed in the Municipal Auditorium. It was moved in 1979 when that building was demolished to make way for the Terrace Theater.

The 1929 Mediterranean-style Ocean Center Building was the start of the Pike Amusement Park's Walk of a Thousand Lights.

★ Pine Avenue
The center of down-town Long Beach, Pine Avenue is lined with stores, cafés, and restaurants. Some of these businesses are housed in historic buildings, such as the 1903 Masonic Temple at No. 230.

KEY

— — — Suggested route

STAR SIGHTS

★ Pine Avenue

★ Shoreline Village

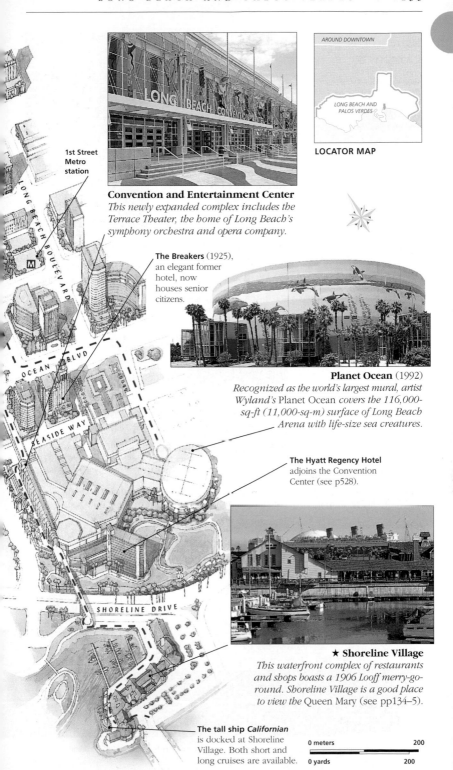

AROUND DOWNTOWN

LONG BEACH AND
PALOS VERDES

LOCATOR MAP

1st Street
Metro
station

Convention and Entertainment Center
*This newly expanded complex includes the
Terrace Theater, the home of Long Beach's
symphony orchestra and opera company.*

The Breakers (1925),
an elegant former
hotel, now houses senior
citizens.

Planet Ocean (1992)
*Recognized as the world's largest mural, artist
Wyland's* Planet Ocean *covers the 116,000-
sq-ft (11,000-sq-m) surface of Long Beach
Arena with life-size sea creatures.*

The Hyatt Regency Hotel
adjoins the Convention
Center (see p528).

★ **Shoreline Village**
*This waterfront complex of restaurants
and shops boasts a 1906 Looff merry-go-
round. Shoreline Village is a good place
to view the* Queen Mary *(see pp134–5).*

The tall ship *Californian*
is docked at Shoreline
Village. Both short and
long cruises are available.

0 meters   200

0 yards   200

Rancho Los Cerritos ❷

4600 Virginia Rd. **Tel** (562) 570-1755. 🔲 1–5pm Wed–Sun. 🔘 Jan 1, Easter Sun, Thanksgiving, Dec 25. 🔥 📷 1pm, 2pm, 3pm, 4pm Sat & Sun only.

Rancho Los Cerritos was once part of a 300,000-acre (121,400-ha) land grant, given between 1784 and 1790 to Spanish soldier Manuel Nieto. Mission San Gabriel reclaimed nearly half of the property. The rest was left to Nieto's children on his death in 1804. In 1834 it was split into five ranches.

In 1844 Los Cerritos was bought by John Temple, who built the adobe ranch house. Following droughts in the early 1860s he decided to sell to the firm Flint, Bixby & Co.

Over the years, most of the ranch was sold, but the house and surrounding 5 acres (2 ha) of land remained in the Bixby family until it was bought by the City of Long Beach in 1955.

Today, Rancho Los Cerritos is run as a museum, focusing on those who lived here from 1840 to 1940. The Monterey-style house (see p30) is furnished to reflect the late 1870s.

Rancho Los Alamitos ❸

6400 Bixby Hill Rd. **Tel** (562) 431-3541. 🔲 1–5pm Wed–Sun. 🔘 Jan 1, Easter Sun, Thanksgiving, Dec 25. **Donation**. 🔥 📷

Rancho Los Alamitos stands on a mesa inhabited since AD 500. In 1790 it formed part of the Manuel Nieto land grant.

Cactus Garden on the grounds of Rancho Los Alamitos

The house was built in 1806, making it one of Southern California's oldest dwellings. It changed hands frequently during the 19th century, until

Queen Mary ❺

Pier J, 1126 Queens Hwy. **Road map** inset A. **Tel** (562) 435-3511. 🔲 10am–4:30pm Mon–Thu, 10am–5pm Fri–Sat. 📷 🔥 📷 See **Where to Stay** p511 and **Where to Eat** p547. **www**.queenmary.com

Named after the wife of British King George V, this liner set new standards in ocean travel with its maiden voyage of May 27, 1936. The jewel in the crown of the Cunard White Star Line, the Queen Mary sailed weekly from Southampton, England, to New York City. Although the second- and third-class quarters may look small next

Royal Jubilee Week, 1935 by AR Thomson, above the bar in the Observation Lounge

to the grandeur of the first-class rooms, they were considered chic and spacious

for their time. On its five-day trips, the liner carried an average of 3,000 passengers and crew. There were two swimming pools, two chapels, a synagogue, gym, ballroom, and childrens' playrooms. Anyone who was anyone sailed on the Queen Mary, from royalty to Hollywood stars.

From 1939 to 1946, the liner was converted into a troopship

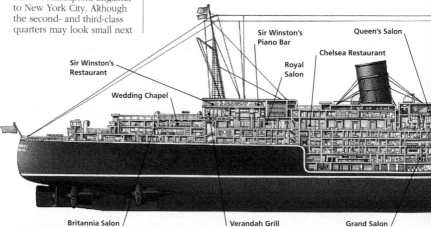

Sir Winston's Piano Bar

Queen's Salon

Chelsea Restaurant

Sir Winston's Restaurant

Royal Salon

Wedding Chapel

Britannia Salon

Verandah Grill

Grand Salon

it was bought by the Bixby family in 1881. In 1906 Fred and Florence Bixby moved into the property and began to shape the house and garden.

The ranch was given to the City of Long Beach in 1968, to be developed as a historic and educational facility. Inside, the house is furnished as it was in the 1920s and 1930s. The elegant grounds are a rare example of a pioneer garden.

Naples ❹

Road map inset A. ▦ *Long Beach.* 🛈 *One World Trade Center, Suite 300 (562 436-3645).* **Gondola Getaway** *5437 E Ocean Blvd (562 433-9595).* **www**.gondo.net

In 1903, developer Arthur Parson began creating his own version of the city of Naples in Italy, complete with winding streets and waterways spanned by small bridges (even though the real Naples does not have canals and gondolas).

Taking heed of the mistakes made by Abbot Kinney in Venice *(see p80)*, Arthur Parson designed his canals so that the Pacific Ocean's tidal flows would keep them clean.

Finished in the late 1920s, this most charming of Long Beach neighborhoods is actually three islands in the middle of Alamitos Bay. An eclectic architectural mix of shingled, Mission Revival, Victorian, and Arts and Crafts

Canal in residential Naples, with boats moored alongside the private jettys

houses *(see pp30–33)* line the Italian-named streets. The Rivo Alto Canal, the largest in the network, surrounds the Colonnade Park, which is in the center of Naples. You can explore by meandering the streets on foot, or book a Gondola Getaway two weeks in advance for a cruise on an authentic Venetian gondola.

called the *Grey Ghost*, carrying more than 800,000 soldiers during its wartime career. At the end of the war, it transported more than 22,000 war brides and children to the US during "Operation Diaper."

In 1967, after 1,001 transatlantic crossings, the liner was bought by the City of Long Beach. It was permanently docked for use as a hotel and tourist attraction.

Detail inside the ship's **Grand Salon**

Today, visitors can view part of the original Engine Room, examples of the different travel accommodations, and an exhibition on the war years. Many of the original Art Deco features, created by more than 30 artists, still decorate the interior. Open to the public for dining, the Grand Salon and Observation Lounge are fine examples of period styling.

Dual set of brass steering wheels in the *Queen Mary's* wheelhouse

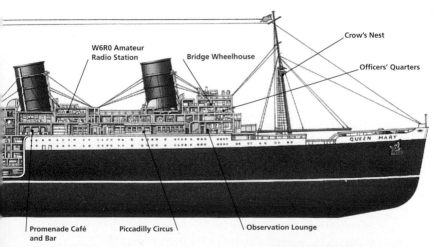

W6R0 Amateur Radio Station
Bridge Wheelhouse
Crow's Nest
Officers' Quarters
QUEEN MARY
Promenade Café and Bar
Piccadilly Circus
Observation Lounge

Relaxing on Redondo Beach, LA *(see p66)* ▷

Los Angeles Maritime Museum ❻

Berth 84, 6th St, San Pedro. **Road map** inset A. **Tel** *(310) 548-7618.* ◻ *10am –5pm Tue–Sat, noon–5pm Sun.* ● *Easter Sun, Thnksg, Dec 25.* **Donation.** ♿ www.lamaritimemuseum.org

Housed in a restored ferry terminal building, the Los Angeles Maritime Museum contains an array of nautical paintings and memorabilia, including a wooden figurehead of British Queen Victoria. An extensive model ship collection includes an 18-ft (5.5-m) scale model of the *Titanic.* Begun in 1971 by a 14-year-old boy, it took five years to complete. Also on display is the bow and bridge of US Navy cruiser USS *Los Angeles.* Early 20th-century Monterey fishing boats *(see p509)* can be seen in the museum's dock.

Figurehead of Queen Victoria

Ports O'Call Village ❼

Berth 77, San Pedro. **Road map** inset A. **Tel** *(310) 732-7696.* ◻ *11am–7pm Sun–Thu; 11am–8pm Fri & Sat.*

Ports O'Call Village is a pastiche of many different seaports from all around the world. Building styles range from a 19th-century New England fishing village, to a Mediterranean harbor, to a Mexican town.

The village's 75 shops and 15 restaurants are linked by cobblestone walkways. Street entertainers frequent this popular area during the summer. A number of fisheries supply freshly caught fish, which can be cooked and served to you on the premises. From the dockside boardwalk visitors can watch the huge cargo ships and cruise liners sail by. Daily harbor cruises tour the inner harbor, coastguard station, marina, freighter operations, and scrap yards. Tours to Catalina Island *(see pp242–3)* and winter whale-watching tours are also available.

Cabrillo Marine Aquarium ❽

3720 Stephen White Drive, San Pedro. **Road map** inset A. **Tel** *(310) 548 -7562.* ◻ *noon–5pm Tue–Fri; 10am –5pm Sat & Sun.* ● *Thanksgiving, Dec 25.* 🅿 *for parking only.* ♿ 🅿 www.cabrilloaq.org

Designed by architect Frank Gehry and surrounded by a geometric chain-link fence, the Cabrillo Marine Aquarium houses one of the largest collections of Southern California marine life. Sharks, moray eels, and rays thrill thousands of visitors each year. The exhibition hall includes interpretive displays that explain the typical plants and animals of the region. It is divided into three environments – rocky shores, beaches and mudflats, and open ocean.

An outdoor rock pool tank contains sea cucumbers, sea anemones, starfish, and sea urchins that visitors are permitted to touch. This small museum also boasts 14,150 gallons (64,400 liters) of circulating sea water, as well as a tidal tank that allows viewers to see below a wave. Another exhibit shows how human activities have altered Los Angeles Harbor.

The beautifully maintained clapboard Point Fermin Lighthouse

Point Fermin Park ❾

Gaffey St & Paseo del Mar, San Pedro. **Road map** inset A. **Tel** *(310) 548-7756 (310 832-4444 for whale-watching tours Dec– Apr).* ◻ *daily.*

This tranquil 37-acre (15-ha) park sits on a bluff overlooking the Pacific Ocean. Between January and March, migrating gray whales can be spotted offshore and, on a clear day, there are views of Catalina Island. The charming Eastlake-style lighthouse dates from 1874. Its bricks and lumber were shipped around Cape Horn. The lighthouse originally used oil lamps that emitted approximately 2,100 candlepower. They were replaced by an electric lamp in 1925.

San Pedro ❿

Road map inset A. ✈ *LAX, 15 miles (24 km) NW of San Pedro.* 🚌 *MTA.* ℹ *390 W 7th St (310 832-7272).*

Famous for the Worldport LA, blue-collar pride, and a tradition of family fishermen, San Pedro ("San Peedro" to the locals) has a strong Eastern European and Mediterranean flavor. The harbor is the nation's busiest import-export site and an important link with the Pacific Rim. The houses are tiny compared to those in Palos Verdes, but this is a very important center of industry.

Street scene in the picturesque Ports O'Call Village

For hotels and restaurants in this region see pp524–31 and pp568–76

Korean Friendship Bell in Angels Gate Park, San Pedro

In Angels Gate Park, at the end of Gaffey Street, there is a Korean Friendship Bell, given to the United States in 1976 by South Korea.

Steps leading to the hilltop Wayfarers Chapel

Wayfarers Chapel ⓫

5755 Palos Verdes Drive S, Rancho Palos Verdes. **Road map** inset A. **Tel** (310) 377-1650. ☐ call ahead (frequently booked for weddings). **Gardens** ☐ daily. ⓰ www.wayfarerschapel.org

This glass and redwood-framed chapel sits on a hilltop above the ocean. From the street below, all that can be seen is a thin stone and concrete tower rising from the greenery.

When the architect Lloyd Wright (son of Frank Lloyd

Wright) designed the chapel in 1949, he tried to create a natural place of worship, surrounding it by trees. Today, its charm makes it a popular site for weddings.

The chapel is sponsored by the Swedenborgian church, which follows the teaching of Emanuel Swedenborg, the 18th-century Swedish theologian and mystic.

South Coast Botanic Garden ⓬

26300 S Crenshaw Blvd, Palos Verdes. **Road map** inset A. **Tel** (310) 544-6815. ☐ 9am–5pm daily. ⓰ Dec 25 . ⓰ ⓰ ⓰

This 87-acre (35-ha) garden was created on top of some 3,175,000 tons of waste that were dumped here from 1956 to 1960. Prior to that, the area

was the location of a mine for algae-rich diatomaceous earth. Today, gas formed underground as a result of the waste decomposing is collected and used to generate electricity.

The garden is a study in land reclamation, with an emphasis on drought-resistant landscaping. Specimens from all the continents except Antarctica are planted within the grounds.

In the Herb Garden plants are divided into three main categories: fragrant, medicinal, and culinary. The Rose Garden has more than 1,600 roses, including old-fashioned and miniature roses, floribundas, hybrid teas, and grandifloras.

One of the most innovative areas is the Garden for the Senses. Here, plants are chosen for their extraordinary qualities of color, smell, or touch. Some of the flowerbeds are raised, making them more accessible.

Children's Garden in the South Coast Botanic Garden

AROUND DOWNTOWN

*F*rom the freeways, it is hard to appreciate the many treasures that lie within Los Angeles's sprawl. But a short drive beyond the central sights to nearby areas can be surprisingly rewarding. Up-scale Pasadena, with its delightful Old Town, also has the excellent Norton Simon Museum as well as the Huntington Library, Art Collections, and Botanical Gardens.

Northeast of Downtown are the Heritage Square Museum with its historic buildings, Lummis House, and the Southwest Museum, one of the finest collections of Native American artifacts in the country. Just north of Hollywood, hilly Griffith Park offers precious open spaces for picnicking, hiking, and horseback riding as well as the Los Angeles Zoo, Griffith Observatory and Autry Museum of Western Heritage.

Nearby, Universal Studios offers tours of its backlots as well as theme park rides. Universal is one of four major studios based in Burbank, which has replaced Hollywood as the head-quarters for the film and television industries. Farther north in the broad, flat San Fernando Valley, Mission San Fernando Rey de España provides a historical insight into California's origins.

South of Downtown, the Natural History Museum of Los Angeles County and the California Museum of Science and Industry are among the top attractions at Exposition Park, along with the stately buildings of the University of Southern California.

For sheer scenic delight and outstanding views over the city and San Fernando Valley, twisting mountainous Mulholland Drive is hard to beat.

Tranquil Japanese Garden at the Huntington Botanical Gardens

◁ Monument to astronomers outside the Griffith Observatory

Exploring Around Downtown

The outlying areas of Los
Angeles contain a vast range
of museums, galleries, historic
buildings, and parks. A little
forward planning is necessary,
however, to make the best use
of time. The Heritage Square and
Southwest museums are easily
visited on the way to Pasadena.
While Universal Studios needs a
day to itself, other studio tours in
Burbank can be combined with
a trip to Griffith Park (a good
spot to see the Hollywood sign)
or to Mission San Fernando Rey
de España. Get an early morning
start at the Flower Market before
tackling the three museums at
Exposition Park, or take a trip
east to see the Watts Towers in
between museum visits.

SIGHTS AT A GLANCE

Districts

**Historic Streets
and Buildings**

Museums and Galleries

Parks and Gardens

Shopping Areas

Sports Venues

Film Studios

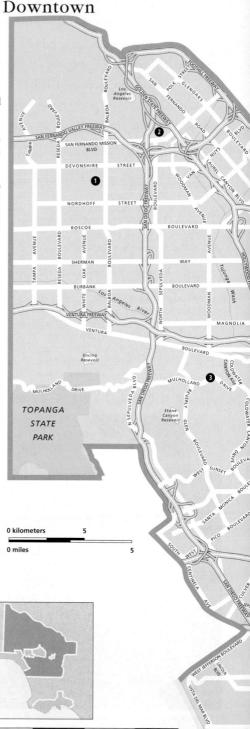

0 kilometers 5

0 miles 5

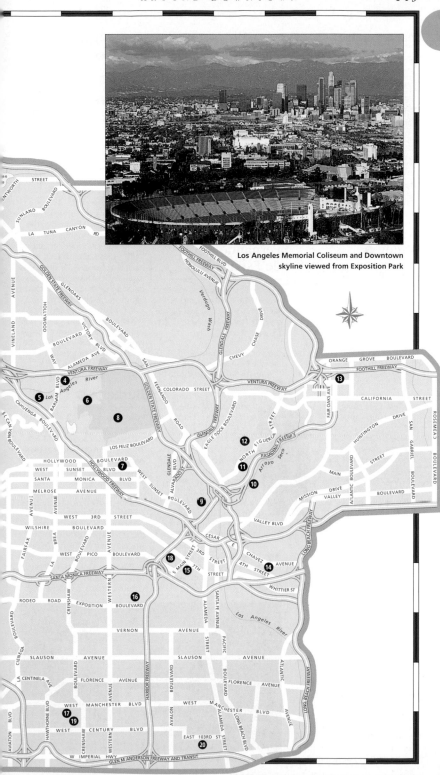

Los Angeles Memorial Coliseum and Downtown
skyline viewed from Exposition Park

View of San Fernando Valley from Mulholland Drive

San Fernando Valley ❶

Road map inset A. ✈ *Burbank-Glendale-Pasadena, 20 miles (32 km) SE of San Fernando.* 🚌 *MTA.* ℹ *519 S Brand Blvd, San Fernando (818 361-1184).*

The city of Los Angeles is split into two distinct halves by the Santa Monica Mountains *(see pp62–3).* To the north, the San Fernando Valley spreads out in a seemingly endless vista of neat houses, freeways, and shopping malls, such as the Sherman Oaks Galleria *(see p166).* Residents south of the mountains tend to dismiss "the Valley," as they call it, as it is more smoggy and noticeably hotter in the summer.

In the 19th century, the San Fernando Valley was made up of ranches, orange groves, and nonirrigated farms. With the completion of the LA Aqueduct in 1913 *(see pp202–3),* the city was insured a plentiful water supply. As a result, the Valley quickly developed into a mass of suburbs. Today, more than a million people live in this area of Los Angeles, which encompasses only 177 sq miles (460 sq km).

On January 17, 1994, San Fernando Valley was at the epicenter of a devastating earthquake, which measured 6.8 on the Richter Scale *(see pp24–5).* The area had also been badly damaged by the February 1971 earthquake.

Mission San Fernando Rey de España ❷

15151 San Fernando Mission Blvd, Mission Hills. **Road map** inset A. **Tel** *(818) 361- 0186.* ⏰ *9am–4:30pm daily.* ⬤ *Thanksgiving, Dec 25.* 💵 ♿ *grounds only.* 📷

One of the 21 Franciscan missions in California *(see pp46– 7),* San Fernando Rey de España was founded in 1797 and named after King Ferdinand III of Spain. The present church is an exact replica of the original, which was completely destroyed in the 1971 earthquake. The *convento* (living quarters) has a 21-arch portico, and is the largest mission building still standing in California. A tour of the complex offers an insight into the early days of Spanish rule, when the monks and Native Americans worked together to make the mission self-sufficent.

Mission altar detail

Mulholland Drive ❸

Off Hwys 1 & 27, from Hollywood Fwy to Leo Carrillo State Beach. **Map** 1 C2. ℹ *Malibu Chamber of Commerce, 23805 Stuart Ranch Rd, Ste 100 (310 456-9025).*

Mulholland Drive, one of the most famous roads in Los Angeles, runs for nearly 50 miles (80 km) from north Hollywood to the Malibu coast *(see pp64– 5).* As it winds along the ridge of the Santa Monica Mountains, the route has spectacular views across the city, San Fernando Valley, and some of LA's most exclusive houses. Its spirit was captured in David Hockney's painting of the area, which hangs in LACMA *(see p115).*

The road was named after William Mulholland *(see p202).* Although better known for his work on the LA Aqueduct, he oversaw the completion of Mulholland Drive in 1924.

Burbank ❹

Road map inset A. ✈ *Burbank-Glendale-Pasadena.* 🚌 *MTA.* ℹ *200 W Magnolia Burbank (818 846-3111). See **Entertainment in Los Angeles** pp174–5.* www.burbankchamber.com

Since 1915, when Universal Studios moved near here *(see pp146–9),* Burbank has been competing with Hollywood as the true center of the Los Angeles film industry. Today there are four major studios in the area: Universal, Disney, NBC, and Warner Bros. The Disney studios are closed to

Mission San Fernando Rey de España in the Mission Hills

Warner Bros Studios in Burbank

the public, but the building, designed by Michael Graves, can be seen from Alameda Avenue. Its fanciful façade incorporates the Seven Dwarfs as pillars supporting the pediment *(see p73)*.

Next door, at NBC, *The Tonight Show* and many other television programs are recorded before a live studio audience. Visitors are offered a 70-minute tour of the wardrobe area, production studios, and *The Tonight Show* set.

Nearby, at the Warner Bros lot, a 2-hour-plus VIP Tour includes the backlot, sound stages, craft, and technical areas. Visitors may view the sets of *The West Wing* and other television series, subject to availability.

Universal Studios **5**

See pp146–9.

Hollywood Sign **6**

Mt Cahuenga, above Hollywood. 🏢 *Hollywood Visitors Information Center, 6801 Hollywood Blvd (323) 467-6412.*

The Hollywood Sign is an internationally recognized symbol of the movie business. Set high up in the Hollywood Hills, it is now a protected historic site. It is visible for miles from many parts of Los Angeles, but it is not possible for the public to reach the sign itself as there is no legitimate trail leading up to the 45-ft (13-m) tall letters.

Erected in 1923, it originally advertised the Hollywoodland housing development of the former *LA Times* publisher Harry Chandler *(see p125)*. The "land" was removed in 1949. Nearly 30 years later, donors pledged $27,000 per letter for a new sign. It has been the scene of one suicide – that of

disappointed would-be actress Peg Entwhistle, who jumped off the "H" in 1932 – and numerous prank spellings, such as "Hollyweed," acknowledging the more lenient marijuana laws of the 1970s, "UCLA" during a football game, and "Perotwood" for the 1992 presidential election.

Hollyhock House **7**

4808 Hollywood Blvd. **Tel** *(323) 644-6269.* ◻ *call for details.* ✓ *Sat, Sun (Wed–Fri: by appointment only).* **www**.hollyhockhouse.net

American architect Frank Lloyd Wright *(see p33)* designed a number of houses in LA. Hollyhock House was the first and remains one of the best known. An excellent example of Wright's infatuation with pre-Columbian styles, the hilltop house resembles a Mayan temple. The house is undergoing renovation, but there are tours of the exterior.

It was completed in 1921 for oil heiress Aline Barnsdall, who asked that her favorite flower, the hollyhock, be used as a decorative motif throughout the building. A band of stylized hollyhocks, fashioned in concrete, therefore adorns the exterior of the house. The flowers also feature as ornamentation inside, such as on the dining room chairs and other Wright-designed furnishings. The adjacent 11-acre Barnsdall Park, donated by Aline Barnsdall, is now a public art park with galleries.

Hollywood Sign, high above Los Angeles in the Hollywood Hills

Universal Studios

Universal Studios Logo

Carl Laemmle bought a chicken ranch on this site in 1915 and moved his film studio here from Hollywood. He charged visitors 25 cents to see films being made, and guests could also buy fresh eggs. With the advent of the "talkies" in 1927, the sets needed quiet and the visits stopped. In 1964, Universal Studios Hollywood was launched as a behind-the-scenes tram ride. The Studio Tour through Universal's 415 acres brings visitors face-to-face with soundstages and movie sets. Here, everything is, or looks like, a film set. The attractions, from Shrek to the latest virtual-reality thrill ride, create a world of magic and Hollywood glamor.

LOCATOR MAP

- ▨ Universal City
- ☐ Universal Studios

The Studio Tour takes in over 500 sets and façades on the backlot

TACKLING THE PARK

Spread over 415 acres (168 ha) Universal Studios Hollywood is the world's largest working movie and television studio and theme park. The complex is divided into three areas: the Entertainment Center, Studio Center, and the studio lots.

As soon as you walk through the gate, visitors stroll through the Streets of the World, which are actual working sets depicting anything from a 1950s America to a European village. The Studio Tour, boarded from the Entertainment Center, is the only way of seeing Universal's main television and movie stages, sets, and movie stars. The Entertainment Center is also the place to catch such shows as Spiderman Rocks and Animal Planet

Live! and other spectacular shows. A futuristic escalator, the Starway, links the upper and lower portions of the studio lots. The lower level is where the major thrill rides, such as Revenge of the Mummy – The Ride can be found. Universal CityWalk connects the working studios, the theme park, and 18-theater cinemas. There are also more than 65 different retail and entertainment venues.

STUDIO TOUR

The original Universal Studios attraction, this classic Studio Tour gives visitors an up-close and personal view of the past, present, and future of Hollywood moviemaking. Guests ride through Universal's soundstages and

sets in trams, each outfitted with state-of-the-art audio and video systems. Celebrity hosts, such as actor Jason Alexander and director Ron Howard, narrate and explain the inner workings of the real Hollywood. If they are lucky, visitors may also see a film being made on one of the working soundstages. Passengers experience an earthquake, see King Kong and Jaws, and survive a collapsing bridge, flash flood, and avalanche. The tour also passes the Bates Motel, from *Psycho* (1960), and Who-ville from *Dr Seuss' How the Grinch Stole Christmas*.

A favorite part of the tour is the "Before They Were Stars" montage and the special weather-effects demonstrations. The 35 different soundstages, various movie and TV sets, props, cameras, lights, and lots of action give guests a first-hand look into filmland's realities and illusions. Special installations of 'The Mummy," "Earthquake – The

SET LOCATIONS ON THE BACKLOT

Guests on the Studio Tour will see these working sets for hundreds of movies and TV productions, many of which are instantly recognizable. Each tram has an LCD flat screen, audio system, and DVD player to put a frame of reference to every set visited.

1. Courthouse Square: most frequently used set (***Back to the Future*** film series, ***To Kill a Mockingbird, Batman & Robin, Bruce Almighty, Dr Seuss' The Cat in The Hat***).
2. Psycho House/Bates Motel: most famous set (***Psycho*** original and the remake of the same movie).
3. Who-ville: main town scenes from ***Dr Seuss' How the Grinch Stole Christmas***.
4. Denver Street: 7/8 scale to make actors in Westerns look larger than life (***Winchester '73, Babe***).
5. Falls Lake with Backdrop: most flexible set (***Apollo 13, Charlie's Angels, O Brother Where Art Thou, Van Helsing***).

UNIVERSAL STUDIOS HOLLYWOOD TICKETS AND PASSES

General Admission: Tickets are either Adult or Child (3-9).
Parking is extra.
1. Hollywood CityPass: Admission to Universal Studios and
six other themed Hollywood sights. Valid for 30 days.
2. Front of Line Pass: All day admission with priority entry
to all attractions and reserved seating at all shows.
3. Celebrity Annual Pass: Unlimited park access for one
year (contains 30 blackout days).
4. VIP: Admission, private tram, personalized tours, front-
of-line privileges, and reserved seats for all shows.
5. Southern California Value Pass: Admission to Universal
Studios and Sea World San Diego. Valid for 14 days.
For more information, call 1-800-UNIVERSAL (1-800-
864-8377) or visit the website.

Big One," "King Kong," and
"Jaws Lake" let visitors
experience the live action
of each working set.
The Tour brings a pleasant
sense of deja-vu to every
guest because they have
vicariously visited many of
the film locations through the
magic of movies. In spite of
all the virtual-reality, thrill-
action rides and state-of-the-
art attractions, the Studio Tour
is really what Universal Studios
Hollywood is all about.

UNIVERSAL CITYWALK

In 1993, American architect
Jon Jerde designed a festive
assortment of façades for the
shops and restaurants that
make up CityWalk's
promenade. Now, with the
addition of more than 30
new attractions, including
bars, nightclubs, and theaters
Universal's CityWalk is being
hailed as the entertainment

mecca of Southern California.
Designed to appeal to guests'
sense of whimsy, a giant
neon-lit baseball player swings
his bat above a sports store.
To enter an ice-cream store,
visitors must walk under an
upside-down pink convertible
that has crashed through a
Hollywood Freeway sign.
Jillian's Hi-Life Lanes, a
multimedia rock 'n' roll
bowling alley gives guests a
chance to work off some
extra energy; Howl at the
Moon, a duelling piano bar,
encourages audience participation; and the festive Cafe
TuTu Tango offers tapas and
a decor that mimics an artist's
loft, complete with paint-
brushes on the tables,

**An upside-down car hangs above
the entrance to a CityWalk store**

artworks in progress, and
spontaneous performances
by dancers and musicians.
The three-storey IMAX 3D
theater shows the latest
venture into knock-your-
socks-off film, and the
NASCAR virtual racecar
experience can be an antidote
to the newest retail shops,
name-brand outlets, and
restaurants. This spectacular
venture into California fantasy
and entertainment is still one
of the prime areas where you
can buy Hollywood souvenirs
and memorabilia.

TOP 5 ATTRACTIONS

★ Animal Planet Live!

★ Studio Tour

★ Universal CityWalk

★ Terminator 2 3-D

★ Jurassic Park

Bright lights, big buildings, and prime entertainment in CityWalk

Rides and Special Effects

Thrill rides are what theme parks do best. Not only does Universal offer some of the most spectacular rides but, coupled with the special effects at this working studio, some of the best in the business. The newest is Revenge of the Mummy – The Ride, which is a mix of high-speed roller coaster and space age robotics, while an updated ride, complete with more horrifying monsters, is the Terminator 2: 3D. Visitors can also see King Kong on the world's largest soundstage and may get the rare chance to get a sneak peek at dozens of the films currently in production. Each attraction here is a thrill ride in itself, where the excitement of movies literally comes alive.

Filming at the Studios

A star of Animal Planet Live! shows a talented paw

ENTERTAINMENT CENTER

The entertainment center has dozens of themed souvenir shops and restaurants. The spectacular shows in this area of the park give visitors an insight into the stunts and special effects used to make a film.

Animal Planet Live!
Animal stars, multi-media effects, human co-stars, and unique sketches from TV's Animal Planet Network offer warm, family entertainment.

Terminator 2: 3D
This new show has been hailed as the world's most advanced film-based attraction. Arnold Schwarzenegger and the rest of the original cast from *Terminator 2: Judgment Day* (1991) star in this sequel and continues the science-fiction epic in startling 3D. Interactive virtual

adventures and spectacular stunts are projected onto the world's largest 3D screen.

WaterWorld – A Live Sea War Spectacular
The audience is part of the action and right in the middle of this thrilling, high-tech show, which packs dazzling pyrotechnics – a giant fireball that rises 50 feet (15 m) in the air – battle scenes, extraordinary stunts, and some wild jet-skiing into 16 minutes of daredevil action.

Shrek 4D
This all-new "multi-sensory" attraction continues Shrek's adventures in the "greatest fairytale never told". Picking up where the DreamWorks movie left off, the second comic installment features ground-breaking "OgreVision" animation.

Back to the Future – The Ride
Housed in the world's tallest Omnimax theater, guests accompany Doc Brown in eight-seat DeLorean time-travel simulator cars. They pursue the diabolical Biff from the 1980s movie trilogy as they try to save the Universe. Hurtling through the space-time continuum, from the Ice Age to the year 2015, the car free-falls through a volcanic tunnel, cascades down glacial cliffs, and almost ends up as dinner for some prehistoric monsters. This ambitious ride uses sophisticated sound, film outtakes, and hydraulics to simulate the wild chase.

Fun and games at the Blast Zone

Nickelodeon Blast Zone:
This huge interactive playground brings Nickelodeon's most popular animated children's TV shows to life. Highlights include the "Nickelodeon Splash!," an elaborate water play area, "Wild Thornberry's Adventure Temple," a rough and tumble

Terrifying the audience at the Terminator 2: 3D show

arena, which comprises more than 25,000 molten lava-colored foam balls, and the "Nick Jr. Backyard," a fun and safe attraction for kids under the age of six.

Blues Brothers Show
This 20-minute live music stage show celebrates the antics and blues songs of the Blues Brothers. There's plenty of audience participation, with dancing, sing-alongs, and some outrageous humor.

Spider-Man Rocks! A Rock-n-Rock Stunt Show
This superhero comes to the stage in an elaborate production packed with pyrotechnics, stunts, music, and dance. The show pits Peter Parker against his arch-enemy, Green Goblin, testing his "spider-sense" to the limit. The action includes stunts that propel Spider-Man more than 30 feet into the air above the audience.

Van Helsing: Fortress Dracula
Experience hundreds of special effects from the movie as you are drawn into the supernatural world of 19th century Transylvania. Highlights include original movie props and set pieces, Dracula's crypt, and a werewolf transformation.

STUDIO CENTER

The Starway, which links the upper and lower portions of Universal's working lots, offers some spectacular

King Kong, beloved of filmgoers, on Universal's Studio Tour

views. The Studio Center on the lower lot has three super-thrilling rides and several other attractions that reveal the secrets of some of the studio's most successful films and television series. There are, of course, lots of photo opportunities around each corner, from the giant 24-ft (7-m) hanging shark to Universal's mascot Woody Woodpecker. Or you might bump into a host of characters, including Charlie Chaplin, Frankenstein, the Mummy, Dracula, or Marilyn Monroe.

Backdraft
In a re-creation of the final scene from the fire-fighting film *Backdraft* (1992), the audience can literally feel the heat of the film's blazing warehouse inferno. Beforehand, a technician explains how the scenes were created and controlled. The temperature rises when the firestorm explodes, causing red-hot ashes to rain down and overhead pipes to burst, leaving the audience scared and thrilled. The experience may be too frightening for young children.

Revenge of the Mummy – The Ride
This is California's fastest indoor roller coaster, and uses some of the most advanced animatronics ever engineered, together with space age robotics and technology to create a thrilling, scream-worthy ride. Light levels change from daylight to total darkness and don't forget to watch out for the skeleton warriors.

Jurassic Park – The Ride roars to life

Jurassic Park sign

Lucy – A Tribute
This exhibit displays memorabilia of the Queen of Comedy, Lucille Ball, one of the world's favorite stage and television stars. This tribute includes the "I Love Lucy" set and the den of her Beverly Hills home, which have been meticulously re-created. There's even an interactive game for trivia buffs to test their Lucy knowledge.

Jurassic Park – The Ride
Based on one of the most successful films of all time, Jurassic Park – The Ride takes visitors on a 5.5-minute trip through 6 acres (2.5 ha) of exotic prehistsoric wilderness. Steven Spielberg's epic movie leaps and roars to life with the most sophisticated state-of-the-art computer and robotic technology ever designed. Guests are hurled into the steamy world of Jurassic Park, where huge five-storey dinosaurs swoop to within inches of riders' faces, and a terrifying *Tyrannosaurus rex* with a mouthful of razorsharp teeth considers each rider part of his dinner. The ride ends with an 84-ft (25-m) drop into complete darkness.

Griffith Park

Merry-go-round horse

Griffith Park is a 4,000-acre (1,600-ha) wilderness of rugged hills, forested valleys, and green meadows in the center of LA. The land was donated to the city in 1896 by Colonel Griffith J Griffith, a Welshman who emigrated to the United States in 1865 and made his money speculating in mining and property. Today, people come to Griffith Park to escape from the city crowds, visit the sights, picnic, hike, or go horseback riding. The park is safe during the day, but it should be avoided at night.

Griffith Observatory on Mount Hollywood

Exploring Griffith Park

The ranger station, located on Crystal Springs Drive, has maps of the park showing its numerous picnic areas and miles of hiking trails and bridle paths. There are two public 18-hole golf courses on the eastern side of the park and tennis courts on Riverside Drive and in Vermont Canyon.

In the hills just off Griffith Park Drive is a 1926 merry-go-round. Adults and children can still ride on its 66 carved horses and listen to its giant band organ. Across the street, an informal Sunday gathering of drummers has been meeting since the 1960s.

Fern Dell, at the Western Avenue entrance, is a beautiful shady glen with a flowing stream and small waterfalls.

🔭 Griffith Observatory

2800 Observatory Rd.
Tel (323) 664-1181. 🎞 Planetarium.
Closed for renovation until June 2006.
www.griffithobs.org
Situated on Mount Hollywood, Griffith Observatory commands stunning views of the Los Angeles basin below. The Art Deco observatory is divided into three main areas: the Hall of Science museum, the Planetarium theater, and the telescopes.

In the Main Rotunda of the Hall of Science, the Foucault Pendulum demonstrates the speed of the earth's rotation. Above the pendulum are murals on a scientific theme, painted by Hugo Ballin in 1934. Characters from Classical mythology are depicted on the domed ceiling. Below this, eight rectangular panels show important scientific concepts and figures through the ages.

Visitors are taken on a journey through space and time, as some 9,000 stars, moons, and planets are projected onto the ceiling. On the roof, the 12-in (30-cm) Zeiss Telescope is open to the public on clear nights.

🏛 Travel Town

5200 W Zoo Drive.
Tel (323) 662-5874 for train ride. ☐ 10am–4pm Mon–Fri; Sat & Sun 10am–5pm. ● Dec 25.
The spirit of the rails comes alive at this outdoor collection of vintage trains and cars. Children and adults can climb aboard freight cars and railroad carriages, or ride on a small train.

East of Travel Town, on Zoo Drive, miniature steam trains take people on rides during weekends.

Steam locomotive from 1922 , one of 16 steam trains in Travel Town

🎭 Greek Theatre

2700 N Vermont Ave. **Tel** (323) 665-1927. ☐ Open for engagements only. 🎟 for concerts.
www.greektheatrela.com
Styled after an ancient Greek amphitheater, this open-air music venue has excellent acoustics. On summer nights, over 6,000 people can sit under the stars and enjoy performances by leading popular and classical musicians. Bring a sweater as evenings can be chilly.

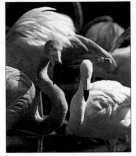

Flamingos at Los Angeles Zoo

Los Angeles Zoo

5333 Zoo Drive. ***Tel*** *(323) 644-4200.* *10am–5pm daily.* *Dec 25.* **www**.lazoo.org

This 113-acre (46-ha) hilly compound has more than 1,200 mammals, reptiles, and birds living in simulations of their natural habitats. All the favorite animals are here, from lions and gorillas to sharks and snakes.

Many newborn creatures can be seen in the Animal Nursery, including some from the zoo's respected breeding program for rare and endangered species. The Koala House is dimly lit to encourage the nocturnal creatures to be active. Adventure Island focuses on southwestern animals and habitats. There are several animal shows that are aimed toward a young audience. Be prepared to walk long distances, or use the Safari Shuttle bus.

VISITORS' CHECKLIST

Map 3 F2. *96.* *6am–10pm daily.* *4730 Crystal Springs Drive.* ***Tel*** *(323) 913-4688.*

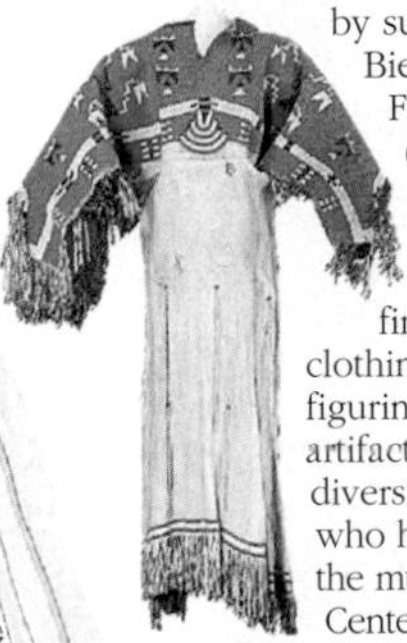

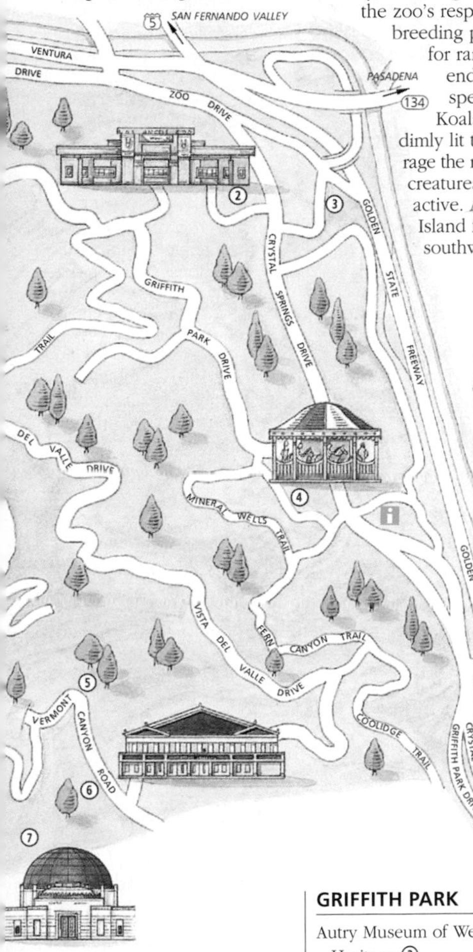

0 kilometers 1

0 miles 0.5

KEY

Tourist information

GRIFFITH PARK

Autry Museum of Western Heritage ③
Bird Sanctuary ⑤
Fern Dell ⑧
Greek Theater ⑥
Griffith Observatory ⑦
Los Angeles Zoo ②
Merry-go-round ④
Travel Town ①

Autry Museum of Western Heritage

4700 Western Heritage Way (opposite the zoo). ***Tel*** *(323) 667-2000.* *10am–5pm Tue–Sun (until 8pm Thu).* *Thanksgiving, Dec 25.* *(free Thu pm; second Tue of month).* **www**.autry-museum.org

The Autry Museum of Western Heritage explores the many cultures that have shaped the American West. Artworks by such artists as Albert Bierstadt and Frederic Remington *(see pp28–9)* depict a romantic view of life in the region. Tools, firearms, tribal clothing, and religious figurines are some of the artifacts that show the diversity of the people who have lived here. In the museum's Discovery Center, children can play in a replica of a 19th century Mexican-American ranch from Arizona. Founded by the film star Gene Autry, "the singing cowboy," the museum also houses a superb collection of movie and television memorabilia.

Deerskin Sioux dress

Bird Sanctuary

Vermont Canyon Rd (just N of Greek Theater). ***Tel*** *(323) 913-4688.* *10am–5pm daily.*

Many trees and bushes have been planted in this secluded canyon to encourage local birds to nest here. Although you may not see too many birds, you will definitely hear their song. Depending on the season, water may be running in the stream, adding to the serenity of the area.

Dodger Stadium ❾

1000 Elysian Park Ave (at Stadium Way). **Map** 11 F1. **Tel** *(323) 224-1400*. **Tickets Tel** *(323) 224-1471.* ◯ *for special events only.* 🖼️ ♿

This baseball stadium seats 56,000 spectators. Built in 1962 for the Brooklyn team, which had moved to LA in 1958, the stadium has a canti-levered design that guarantees every seat an unobstructed view of the field.

From the stadium there are equally impressive panoramas of the city. To the south is Downtown LA, to the north and east are the San Gabriel Mountains. Around the arena are 300 acres (120 ha) of land-scaped grounds, planted with more than 3,000 trees such as California rosewood, acacia, and eucalyptus.

Queen Anne-style Hale House at Heritage Square Museum

Heritage Square Museum ❿

3800 Homer St, Los Angeles. **Tel** *(626) 449-0193.* ◯ *12–4pm Fri–Sun.* 🖼️ ♿ 🎫 **www.**heritagesquaremuseum.com

Most Victorian buildings in Los Angeles were demolished during redevelopments, but some were saved by the Cultural Heritage Board and moved to this location. Dating from 1865 to 1914, they include a train depot, a church, and a carriage barn. Hale House, a Queen Anne-style building *(see p31)*, has been restored in authentic colors.

Restored interior of the 19th-century Lummis House

Lummis House ⓫

200 East Ave 43, Los Angeles. **Tel** *(323) 222-0546.* ◯ *8:30am–5pm Mon–Fri.* **Donation.** ♿ 🎫

Also known as "El Alisal," Spanish for "Place of the Sycamore," this house was the home of Charles Fletcher Lummis (1859–1928), who built it out of concrete and rocks from the local riverbed. The structure's various design elements – Native American, Mission Revival, and Arts and Crafts – reveal the dominant influences of Lummis's life. Constructed between 1898 and 1910, mostly by his own hands, the design reveals a creative, independent thinker.

Lummis was a newspaper editor, writer, photographer, artist, and historian. In 1885 he walked across the United States, from Ohio to LA, where he settled. He played a central role in the city's cultural life, editing the *LA Times.* As a co-founder of the California Land-mark Club, he campaigned successfully for the preser-vation of the state's missions *(see pp46–7).* His collection of Native American artifacts was the basis of the holdings at the Southwest Museum.

Today, Lummis House is the headquarters of the Historical Society of Southern California. Although few of Lummis's be-longings remain in the house, there are some Native Ameri-can artifacts. The built-in furn-ishings include a splendid Art Nouveau fireplace.

The garden was originally planted with vegetables and fruit trees. It was redesigned in 1985 and now grows drought-tolerant and native Southern California plant species.

THE DODGERS

The Dodgers came originally from Brooklyn, New York. They used to train by dodging the streetcars that traveled down that borough's streets, thus earning their name. Since moving to Los Angeles in 1958, they have become one of the most successful baseball teams in the United States. In 1955, they won the first of five world championships. Today, going to the Dodger Stadium is a rite of spring for Los Angeles fans.

Over the years the team has had a number of outstanding players, such as Sandy Koufax and Roy Campanella. In 1947, the Dodgers made headlines when they signed Pasadena-born Jackie Robinson, the first African-American to play in the major leagues.

Japanese star pitcher Hideo Nomo joined the Dodgers team in 1995, and created a sensation in his first season. During the playoffs, crowds brought Tokyo to a standstill as Nomo prepared to pitch on the other side of the Pacific Ocean.

Part of the victorious 1959 world championship team

Mission Revival-style Southwest Museum

Southwest Museum ⑫

234 Museum Drive, Los Angeles.
Tel *(323) 221-2164.* ☐ *10am–5pm Tue–Sun.* ● *Jan 1, Easter Sun, Thanksgiving, Dec 25.* 📷 📹
www.*southwestmuseum.org*

With one of the nation's leading collections of Native American art and artifacts, the Southwest Museum was the brainchild of Charles Fletcher Lummis. During his cross-country trek in the late 19th century, Lummis spent a long time in the Southwest and became one of the first whites to appreciate the history and culture of Native Americans. Lummis donated many of his personal holdings to start the collection.

The museum displays tribal objects from prehistoric times to the present day. Exhibits come from South America to Alaska. They are organized by their place of origin: the Plains, the Northwest Coast, the Southwest, and California. The last two regions are the most strongly represented, but there is an excellent overview of Native American heritage. The 11,000 baskets in the collection are particularly

Sequoyah Indian relief

impressive. Tepees, workshops, and storytelling help to involve children at the museum. The Mission Revival building *(see p31)* is set on top of Mount Washington, with views of Downtown Los Angeles to the south. It has a seven-story tower and is surrounded by a garden planted with indigenous species.

GALLERY GUIDE

The galleries are situated on two floors, with the main entrance on the upper level. Artifacts from the Northwest Coast, California, and the Plains are displayed on this level, as are temporary exhibitions. The downstairs galleries are dedicated to the museum's collection of baskets and its holdings from the Southwest. The shop is also located here. Adjacent to the museum is the Braun Research Library, dedicated to the Native and Hispanic peoples of the Americas.

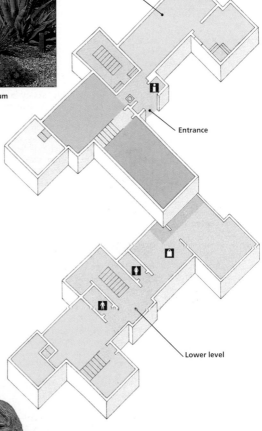

Upper level

Entrance

Lower level

KEY

☐	The Northwest Coast
☐	The Southwest
☐	The Plains
■	California
☐	Basketry study
☐	Temporary exhibitions
☐	Nonexhibition space

Pasadena ⓭

With the completion of the Santa Fe Railroad in 1887, wealthy people from the East Coast began to spend the winter in the warmth and sunshine of Southern California. Many settled in Pasadena and were soon joined by artists and bohemians, who were also seeking the sun. This mix of creativity and wealth has resulted in a city with a splendid cultural legacy. The highlights of the area include the Huntington Library, Art Collections, and Botanical Gardens *(see pp158–61)*, and the outstanding collection of Old Masters and Impressionist paintings at the Norton Simon Museum *(see pp156–7)*.

Rose Bowl statue

Exploring Pasadena

Just east of the Norton Simon Museum is **Old Pasadena**, once a decaying section of town. A dozen blocks of commercial buildings dating from the 1880s and 1890s have been restored and are now filled with stores, restaurants, and movie theaters. The mixture of Victorian, Spanish Colonial, and Art Deco architecture adds to the area's pleasant environment. The stately Beaux-Arts **Civic Center**, on Union Street at Garfield Avenue, was designed by Edward Bennett in the early 1920s. It includes the city hall, police station, post office, library, and civic auditorium. The neighborhood northeast of Gamble House has many examples of Arts and Crafts architecture *(see p31)*, most notably along tree-lined **Prospect Boulevard**.

Tiffany lamp in the Gamble House

🏟 Rose Bowl

1001 Rose Bowl Drive. *Tel* (626) 577-3100. ⏰ 7:30am–5:30pm Mon–Fri. ● public hols (except Jan 1). 🅿 www.rosebowlstadium.com

Sited in a wealthy neighborhood, the stadium seats more than 100,000 people. It was built in 1922 for the annual Rose Bowl football game, which matches college teams from the Midwest and the West Coast.

The first collegiate game played here was delayed for more than an hour when the visiting team was stuck in traffic, a fate that befalls many visitors today.

This is the home of UCLA's football team, the Bruins. Numerous Super Bowl games have also been played here as well as the World Cup Championships in 1994 and the 1984 Summer Olympics soccer competitions. There is also a flea market here every month.

Pasadena's city hall in the Beaux-Arts Civic Center

🏟 Gamble House

4 Westmoreland Place. *Tel* (626) 793-3334. ⏰ noon–3pm Thu–Sun. ● public hols. 🅿 ✔ obligatory. www.gamblehouse.org

A masterpiece of the era, this wooden house epitomizes the Arts and Crafts movement, which stressed simplicity of design with superior craftsmanship. The dwelling was built in 1908 for David Gamble, of the Procter and Gamble Company. It is considered the crowning achievement of brothers Charles and Henry Greene, Boston-trained architects who visited Pasadena in 1893 and never left *(see p31)*.

Gamble House was tailor-made for LA's climate. Its terraces and open porches facilitate indoor-outdoor living, and broad overhanging eaves shade the house. At certain times of day, the sun illuminates the stained-glass front door, a dazzling sight.

🏛 Pacific-Asia Museum

46 N Los Robles Ave. *Tel* (626) 449-2742. ⏰ 10am–5pm Wed–Sun (8pm Fri). ● public hols. 🅿 🚻 www.pacificasiamuseum.org

Built in 1924 to a traditional northern Chinese design, the Pacific-Asia Museum houses a collection of Far Eastern art founded by Grace Nicholson. Changing exhibitions on the arts of Asia and the Pacific Basin supplement the permanent collection. The museum's lovely courtyard garden is one of only two authentic Chinese gardens in the United States.

A packed Rose Bowl during a football game

For hotels and restaurants in this region see pp524–31 and pp568–76

🌲 LA State and County Arboretum

301 N Baldwin Ave, Arcadia. ***Tel*** *(626) 821-3222.* 🕒 *9am–4:30pm daily.* ⛔ *Dec 25.* 🎟 ♿ 🎟 *free third Tue every month.* **www**.arboretum.org

Situated on 127 acres (51 ha) east of Pasadena, the arboretum has more than 30,000 plant species displayed according to their geographical origin. The park includes a herb garden, a waterfall, lily ponds, and a tropical jungle. It was used as the backdrop for all of Johnny Weissmuller's *Tarzan* films (1932–48) and for some parts of Humphrey Bogart's *African Queen* (1951). Among the historical buildings in the grounds are Gabrielino Native American *wickiups* (huts) and the reconstructed 1839 Hugo Reid adobe.

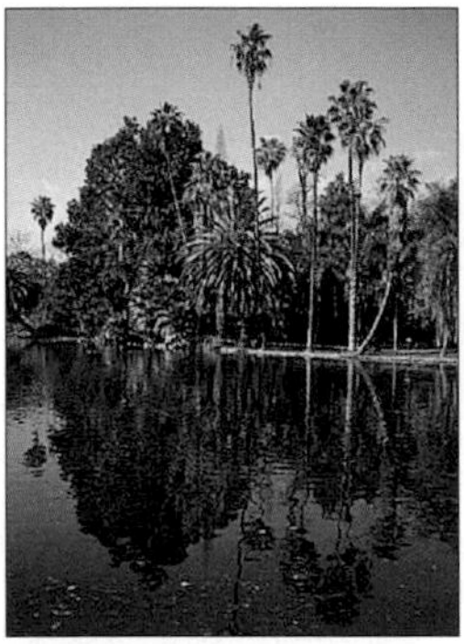

Tropical landscaping in the LA State and County Arboretum

🏛 Kidspace Museum

480 North Arroyo Blvd, Brookside Park. ***Tel*** *(626) 449-9144.* 🕒 *9:30am–5pm daily.* ⛔ *public hols.* 🎟 ♿ **www**.kidspacemuseum.org

The Kidspace Children's Museum engages children and families by sparking creativity and imagination through the 17 different indoor exhibits and 10 outdoor learing environments in the museum's new location in Brookside Park. There are also continually changing educational programs as well as a café and a learning store.

VISITORS' CHECKLIST

Road map inset A. 👥 *135,000.* 🚌 *79 from Downtown LA.* ℹ *171 S Los Robles Ave (626 795-9311).* 🎉 *Tournament of Roses Parade (Jan 1).* **www**.pasadenacal.com

THE ROSE PARADE

In 1890 the Pasadena Valley Hunt Club decided to hold the first Tournament of Roses to celebrate – and advertise – the region's balmy winters. Little did they know that their quaint parade of horse-drawn carriages draped with rose garlands would turn into a world-famous extravaganza. Today, many of the floats have moving parts and sometimes feature people doing stunts.

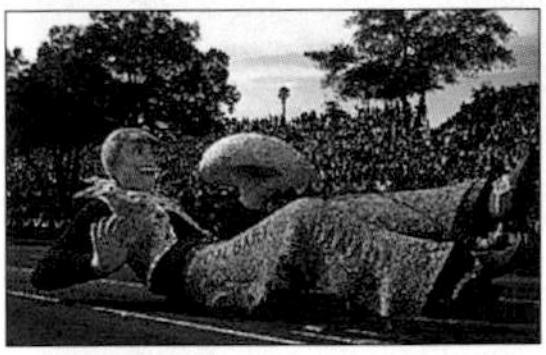

Rose Parade float

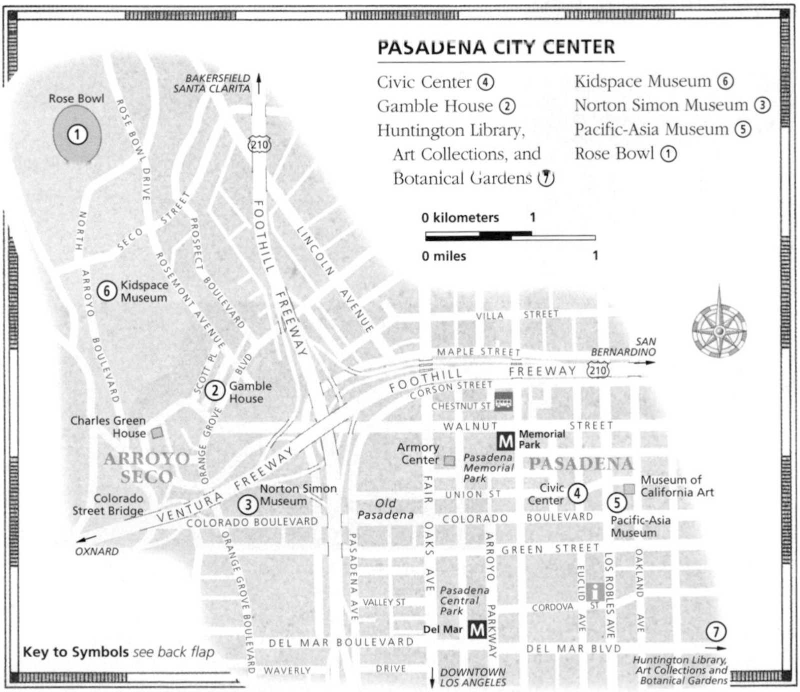

PASADENA CITY CENTER
Civic Center 4
Gamble House 2
Huntington Library, Art Collections, and Botanical Gardens 7
Kidspace Museum 6
Norton Simon Museum 3
Pacific-Asia Museum 5
Rose Bowl 1
0 kilometers 1
0 miles 1
Rose Bowl
BAKERSFIELD SANTA CLARITA
210
ROSE BOWL DRIVE
NORTH ARROYO BOULEVARD
SECO STREET
PROSPECT BOULEVARD
ROSEMONT AVENUE
FOOTHILL FREEWAY
LINCOLN AVENUE
Kidspace Museum
SCOTT PL
BLVD
Gamble House
Charles Green House
ARROYO SECO
ORANGE GROVE
Colorado Street Bridge
VENTURA FREEWAY
Norton Simon Museum
COLORADO BOULEVARD
OXNARD
ORANGE GROVE BOULEVARD
VILLA STREET
MAPLE STREET
SAN BERNARDINO
FOOTHILL FREEWAY 210
CORSON STREET
CHESTNUT ST
WALNUT STREET
Memorial Park
Armory Center
Pasadena Memorial Park
PASADENA
Museum of California Art
UNION ST
Civic Center
Old Pasadena
FAIR OAKS AVE
COLORADO BOULEVARD
Pacific-Asia Museum
ARROYO PARKWAY
GREEN STREET
PASADENA AVE
VALLEY ST
Pasadena Central Park
CORDOVA ST
EUCLID AVE
LOS ROBLES AVE
OAKLAND AVE
Del Mar
DEL MAR BOULEVARD
DEL MAR BLVD
Huntington Library, Art Collections and Botanical Gardens
WAVERLY DRIVE
DOWNTOWN LOS ANGELES
Key to Symbols see back flap

Norton Simon Museum

Norton Simon (1907–93) was a businessman who combined running his multinational corporation with forming an internationally acclaimed collection of works of art. From the 1950s to the 1970s, he amassed, with the genius of a connoisseur, masterpieces spanning more than 2,000 years of Western and Asian art. Within the European holdings, the Old Masters and Impressionist paintings are especially strong. Renaissance, Post-Impressionism, German Expressionism, and the modern period are also well represented. Sculptures from India and Southeast Asia are among the finest outside the region and offer an insight into the complex roles art and religion play in these cultures.'

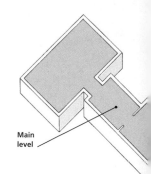

Main level

Sculpture Garden

★ **Woman with a Book** *(1932)*
Pablo Picasso, one of the great artistic forces of the 20th century, was a major influence on both the Cubist and Surrealist movements. His mistress Marie-Thérèse Walter, was the subject of a number of his paintings in the 1930s.

Self-Portrait *(c.1636–8)*
Rembrandt painted nearly 100 self-portraits during his lifetime. This one shows the artist in his early thirties.

Lower level

★ **Still Life with Lemons, Oranges and a Rose** *(1633)*
The Spanish painter Francisco Zurbarán excelled at contemplative still lifes. Many of his works were exported to the Spanish Americas, where they influenced colonial painters.

STAR PAINTINGS

- ★ Still Life with Lemons, Oranges and a Rose by Francisco Zurbarán

- ★ Woman with a Book by Pablo Picasso

GALLERY GUIDE

The museum's galleries are on two floors. European paintings, prints, sculpture, and tapestries, dating from the Renaissance to the 20th century, are on the main level. The lower galleries showcase the Norton Simon's impressive collection of Indian and Southeast Asian works, as well as special exhibitions. The buildings and gardens underwent an extensive renovation program in 1999. The outdoor space was transformed into a huge sculpture garden with a natural pond in the center, inspired by the artworks of Claude Monet.

Theatre

Spiral staircase

Main entrance

Spiral staircase

VISITORS' CHECKLIST

411 W Colorado Blvd. **Tel** (626) 449-6840. ▥ 181, 182. ◻ noon–6pm (9pm Fri) Wed–Mon. ◼ Jan 1, Jul 4, Thanksgiving, Dec 25. ▨ ▧ ▦ ◻ ▥ ▤ ▢ **www**.nortonsimon.org

Saints Paul and Frediano (c.1483)
This is one of a pair of religious panels executed by Florentine artist Filippino Lippi. It shows the influence of Lippi's more famous father, Fra Filippo Lippi, and his other mentor, Botticelli.

KEY

▨	14th-17th centuries
▨	17th-18th centuries
▨	19th century
▨	20th century
▨	South Asian
▨	Special exhibitions
▨	Non-exhibition space

The Little Fourteen-Year-Old Dancer
(1878–81)
This bronze is one of more than 100 works by Edgar Degas in the museum. It features one of the artist's favorite subjects, the ballet.

Buddha Enthroned
This bronze was made in Kashmir in India in the 8th century. It is inlaid with silver and copper.

Huntington Library, Art Collections, and Botanical Gardens

Detail from garden urn

Visitors and scholars alike are united in their love of the Huntington. The Beaux-Arts mansion was built between 1909 and 1911 for Henry Huntington (1850–1927), who made his fortune building a network of interurban trams in Los Angeles. In 1913 he married his uncle's widow, Arabella. Together they amassed one of the most important libraries and collections of 18th-century British art in the world. The key elements of the gardens were planted during Huntington's lifetime.

Mausoleum
Designed by the architect John Russell Pope, this building in the form of a Greek temple is made of Colorado yule marble.

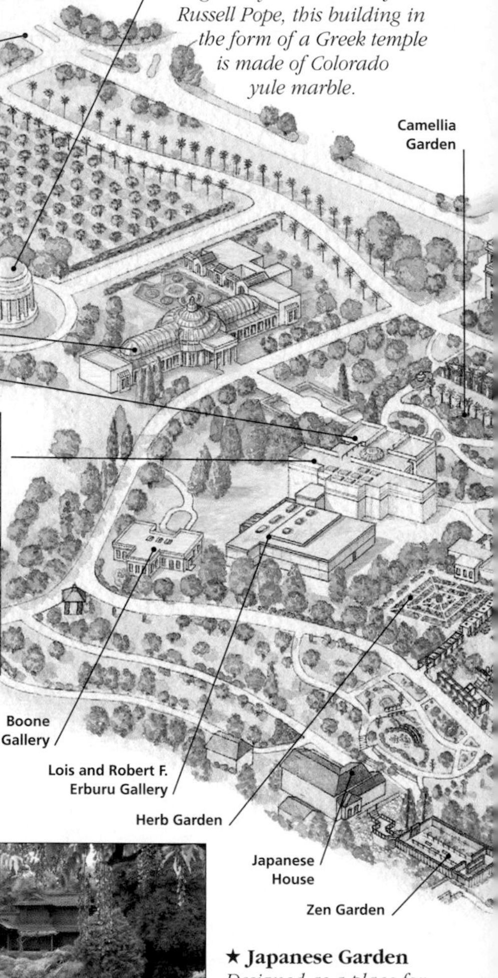

Main entrance

Orange Grove

Rose Hills Foundation Conservatory for Botanical Science

Virginia Steele Scott Gallery

Camellia Garden

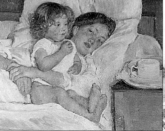

Breakfast in Bed *(1897)*
The Virginia Steele Scott Gallery is devoted to American art, including one of Mary Cassatt's most successful Impressionist paintings of a mother and child. The artist used this theme many times in her work (see p114).

Boone Gallery

Lois and Robert F. Erburu Gallery

Herb Garden

Japanese House

Zen Garden

STAR EXHIBITS

★ The Blue Boy by Thomas Gainsborough

★ Gutenberg Bible

★ Japanese Garden

★ Japanese Garden
Designed as a place for quiet contemplation, this typical Japanese garden includes a small lake, crossed by a curved moon bridge, and a traditional Japanese house.

★ Gutenberg Bible
This Bible was printed on vellum around 1450–55 by Johannes Gutenberg in Mainz, Germany. It is the oldest printed book in the Huntington Library.

Jungle Garden
The palms, ferns, gingers, and other plants in this garden are all typical of a tropical rainforest. The waterfalls add to the lush beauty of the garden.

Arabella D Huntington Memorial Collection

The Munger Research Center

Shakespeare Garden

Huntington Library

Palm Garden

Desert Garden

Lily Ponds

Huntington Art Gallery

Subtropical Garden

Australian Garden

Rose Garden

North Vista
Backed by the San Gabriel Mountains, the vista re-creates the feel of a 17th-century European garden, complete with an Italian Baroque fountain at one end.

★ The Blue Boy *(c.1770)*
Thomas Gainsborough's portrait of Jonathan Buttall, a merchant's son, is one of the most famous paintings in the Huntington Art Gallery.

Exploring the Huntington

In 1919 Henry and Arabella Huntington put their home and gardens into a trust, creating a nonprofit research institution. Today, the Huntington plays a dual role as an educational facility and cultural center, serving scholars and the general public. The institution comprises one of the world's great research libraries, an outstanding art collection, and more than 130 acres (50 ha) of botanical gardens. The Huntington is only open to the public for a few hours each day, so plan your visit in advance.

Diana Huntress (1782) by Jean-Antoine Houdon

HUNTINGTON LIBRARY

Built in 1920, the library specializes in British and American history and literature. It attracts nearly 2,000 scholars every year. The public can view key items and exhibits in the Library Exhibition Hall.

Among the 600,000 books and three million manuscripts are a copy of the *Magna Carta* and the Ellesmere manuscript of Chaucer's *Canterbury Tales* (c.1410). The collection includes a Gutenberg Bible (c.1455) – one of only 12 surviving copies printed on vellum in the world.

There are first editions and manuscripts by noted authors, including Mark Twain, Charles Dickens, and Lord Tennyson, and early editions of Shakespeare's plays. Letters written by George Washington, Benjamin Franklin, and Abraham Lincoln are also part of the collection.

Pilgrim from *The Canterbury Tales*

ARABELLA D HUNTINGTON MEMORIAL COLLECTION

The west wing of the library houses a small group of Renaissance paintings, including *Madonna and Child (see p71)* by Flemish artist Roger van der Weyden (c.1400–1464). The wing displays French furniture, Sèvres porcelain, and a large collection of French sculpture. *Portrait of a Lady* (1777) by Jean-Antoine Houdon is considered one of the sculptor's finest busts.

HUNTINGTON ART GALLERY

The Huntingtons' mansion houses the majority of the art collection, including British and French art from the 18th and early 19th centuries. The most famous works are the portraits in the Main Gallery, which include Thomas Gainsborough's *The Blue Boy* (c.1770). Also on display are paintings by John Constable, Thomas Lawrence, and Joshua Reynolds.

The Large Library Room contains some outstanding 18th-century furnishings, which include two Savonnerie carpets made for Louis XIV, and five Beauvais tapestries. The Small Library houses a collection of Renaissance bronzes. *Nessus and Deianira* by Italian sculptor Giovanni da Bologna (1529–1608) is a fine example of his work. *Anne Killigrew, Mrs Kirke* (c.1638) by Flemish artist Anthony Van Dyck (1559–1642), hangs at the head of the stairs. There are also works by Canaletto, who had a profound effect on British landscape painting.

BOONE GALLERY

The newest venue to open at the Huntington site, the Boone Gallery displays temporary exhibitions of American and English art, rare books, and manuscripts, as well as highlights of the Huntington's permanent collection.

Built in 1911 as a garage for Mr Huntington's fleet of automobiles, the Neoclassical building later fell into disrepair and was used only for storing garden equipment. Its recent restoration, funded by MaryLou and George Boone, provides 4,000 sq ft of additional exhibition space.

French furniture in the Large Library Room

VIRGINIA STEELE SCOTT GALLERY OF AMERICAN ART

Opened in 1984, this collection displays American art from the 1740s to the 1930s.

During the colonial period, artists such as Benjamin West (1738–1820) and Gilbert Stuart (1755–1828) were admirers of British portraitists. It was only prior to the Civil War that an American style of painting emerged. Following two visits to Ecuador, Frederic Edwin Church captured the vastness of that country in *Chimborazo* (1864). Another 19th-century highlight is Mary Cassatt's *Breakfast in Bed* (1897).

The Dorothy Collins Brown Wing houses furniture designed by the American architects, brothers Charles and Henry Greene *(see p31)*.

Desert Garden

BOTANICAL GARDENS

In 1904, Henry Huntington hired landscape gardener William Hertrich to develop the grounds, which now contain 15 principal gardens.

The 12-acre (5-ha) Desert Garden has more than 4,000 drought-tolerant species from around the world. In the Rose Garden, a walkway traces the history of the species over 1,000 years, with 2,000 varieties. The oldest are found in the Shakespeare Garden.

One of the most popular areas is the Japanese Garden, with a moon bridge, Zen Garden, and Japanese plants.

HUNTINGTON ART GALLERY

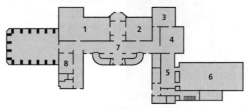

First floor

Second floor

1 Large Library Room
2 Large Drawing Room
3 Small Drawing Room
4 Dining Room
5 North Passage
6 Main Gallery
7 Hall
8 Small Library

9 Quinn Room
10 Southeast Room
11 Wedgwood Room
12 The Adele S Browning Memorial Collection
13 The Moseley Collection
14 Southwest Room
15 Temporary exhibitions

ARABELLA D HUNTINGTON MEMORIAL COLLECTION

HUNTINGTON LIBRARY

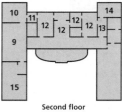

First floor

1 Sèvres Porcelain Room
2 French Furniture Room
3 French Sculpture Room
4 Renaissance Paintings Room
5 Temporary exhibitions

1 Medieval Manuscripts and Early Printing
2 English and American Literature
3 American History

VIRGINIA STEELE SCOTT GALLERY OF AMERICAN ART

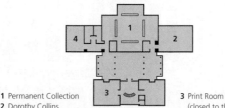

First floor

1 Permanent Collection
2 Dorothy Collins Brown Wing

3 Print Room (closed to the public)
4 Permanent Collection

Cowboy boot stand at El Mercado

El Mercado ⑭

3425 E 1st St. **Tel** *(323) 268-3451.*
☐ *10am–8pm Mon–Fri; 9am–9pm
Sat & Sun.* ♿

East Los Angeles is the heart
of the Mexican-American
community *(see p34)*, and this
marketplace caters to the
locals. Its three levels bustle
with taco vendors, *mariachis*
(Mexican street musicians),
and families out for a good
meal. Unlike Olvera Street
(see p127), El Mercado is not
designed as a tourist spot.
The greatest attraction here is
the authentic Mexican food
and regional music.

On the main floor stands
offer everything from chilies to
snack food. A *tortillaria* sells
fresh, hot tortillas; bakeries
display traditional Mexican
breads and pastries, and delicatessens have meats you may
never have seen before. To
hear the *mariachis*, go to the
mezzanine level, which is also
where the cafeteria-style restaurants are located.

Brightly colored Mexican
clothing, furniture, and crafts
fill the shops in the basement,
along with the sounds of
Latin American salsa music.

THE LAKERS AND BASKETBALL

Basketball originated in Springfield, Massachusetts in 1891
as a team sport that could be played indoors during the
harsh winters. LA's winter may be warm, but people still
love the fast-paced, high-scoring game. The city's team, the
Lakers, has a huge following.
Such illustrious players as
Magic Johnson, Wilt Cham-
berlain, Kareem Abdul-
Jabbar, Shaquile O'Neal, and
Kobe Bryant have helped
make the team one of the
most successful in the
National Basketball Association (NBA). The Lakers
started out in Minnesota; in
1960 they came to LA; they
won the NBA Championship
four times in the 1980s, and
now play in the new state-of-
the-art Staples Center.

Magic Johnson

Flower Market ⑮

752 Maple Ave. **Tel** *(213) 627-2482.*
☐ *8am–noon Mon, Wed, Fri;
6am–noon Tue, Thu, Sat.* ♿

In the early hours before
sunrise the city's florists flock
to this two-block long area to
buy wholesale flowers and
plants. Warehouses lined with
tables and stands are laden
with brightly colored
blossoms that contrast sharply
with the gray surrounding
buildings. An enormous
range of flowers is offered, so
that California varieties
compete with plants from
Columbia, New Zealand,
France, and Holland.

Anyone can take advantage
of the low prices (bargains
are available after 8 am).
However, it is best to arrive
early because supplies sell
out quickly.

Exposition Park and University of Southern California ⑯

See pp164–5.

Great Western Forum ⑰

3900 Manchester Blvd, Inglewood.
Road map inset A. **Tel** *(310)
419-3100.* ☐ *for events only.*
🎫 *for events.* ♿ **Box Office**
☐ *10am–6pm daily.*

The Great Western Forum is
one of LA's most famous
concert and sports arenas.
Seating 17,000, the Forum
also hosts local sports
contests, graduation
ceremonies, Hollywood
parties, and media events.

Great Western Forum in Inglewood

For hotels and restaurants in this region see pp524–31 and pp568–76

Staples Center ⑱

1111 S Figueroa St. **Map** 9 C5.
Tel (877) 305-1111.
⬛ for events. 🏟 for events.
www.staplescenter.com

Home to three professional
ball clubs, the LA Lakers, the
LA Clippers (basketball), and
the LA Kings (ice hockey),
this stadium has revitalized
downtown LA for sports fans.
It also hosts the US Figure
Skating Championships, major
rock and pop concerts, WWF
wrestling, and Hollywood
awards events, as well as
graduation ceremonies.

Hollywood Park Racetrack ⑲

1050 S Prairie Ave, Inglewood.
Road map inset A.
Tel (310) 419-1500.
⬛ 1–5pm Wed–Fri; 12:30–5pm
Sat & Sun. 🏟 ♿
www.hollywoodpark.com

From April to July racing
enthusiasts, Hollywood stars,
and tourists come to
Hollywood Park to bet on the
thoroughbreds. This is an
elegant, nostalgic racetrack,
beautifully landscaped with
lagoons and lush trees. A
large computer-operated
screen relays the action from
the obscured back straight, as
well as showing instant
replays, photo finishes, and
race statistics. In the North
Park, the children's play area
includes a merry-go-round.

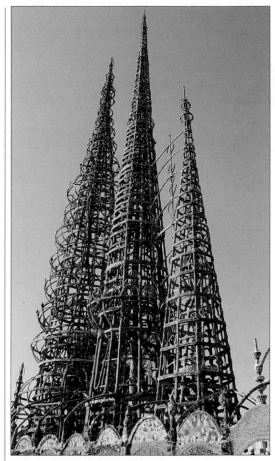

Watts Towers, covered in shells, china, and glass

**Landscaped racetrack at
Hollywood Park in Inglewood**

Watts Towers ⑳

1727 E 107th St, Watts. **Road
map** inset A. **Tel** (213) 847-4646.
⬛ 10am–4pm Tue–Sat; noon–4pm
Sun. 🏟 Towers only. ♿ Arts Center
only. 📷 **www**.wattstower.net

Watts Towers is a masterpiece
of folk art that embodies the
perseverance and vision of
Simon Rodia, an immigrant
from Naples, Italy. Between
1921 and 1954, the tile-worker
sculpted steel rods, pipes, and
whatever else he could find
into a huge skeletal frame-
work. The highest tower
reaches 100 ft (30 m). Rodia
adorned the cemented surface
with fragments of seashell,
tile, china, and glass. He never
gave a reason for building the
towers and, upon finishing, he
deeded the land to a neighbor and left Los Angeles.
   Despite several attempts to
have Watts Towers razed, it is
now a State Historic Site and
has undergone extensive
renovation. It stands as a
symbol of hope in this area
that, in 1965, was the site of
the worst riots in Los Angeles.
   Adjacent to the monument is
the Watts Towers Arts Center.
This complex displays temporary exhibitions of work by
African-American artists in the
community and hosts work-
shops for artists of all ages.
   South Central LA, which
includes Watts, is a high-crime
neighborhood. Visitors should
not stay in the area after dark.
Take common-sense pre-
cautions, and do not stray
from the towers or the Center.

Exposition Park and University of Southern California ⑯

Tommy Trojan statue

Exposition Park began life in the 1880s as an area of open-air markets, carnivals, and horse-racing. By the end of the century, the district was rife with drinking, gambling, and prostitution. When Judge William Miller Bowen's nearby Sunday school pupils began skipping church to enjoy local temptations, he pushed for the transformation of the area into a cultural landmark that today includes three museums. The Exposition Park Rose Garden in their midst contains more than 19,000 rose bushes. Across the street, the University of Southern California (USC) covers 152 acres (62 ha) and is attended by almost 28,000 students. Founded in 1880, it is the oldest and largest private university in the western United States.

🏛 Doheny Memorial Library

Corner of Hoover Blvd and Childs Way. ***Tel** (213) 740-4039.* 🕐 *daily.*

A majestic building with Italian Romanesque, Egyptian, and Moorish design influences, USC's main reference library was built in 1932 in memory of Edward L Doheny Jr, a trustee of the university. The building benefits from a monumental marble staircase at the entrance, and ornate stone and woodwork throughout. The main hall is illuminated by stained-glass windows.

🏛 Natural History Museum of Los Angeles County

900 Exposition Blvd. ***Tel** (213) 763-3466.* 🕐 *9:30am–5pm daily.* ● *Jan 1, Thanksgiving, Dec 25.* $ *free first Tue of every month.*

This is the third largest natural history and cultural museum in the US. From dinosaur fossils to gems, a wide variety of specimens and artifacts are on display. The Schreiber Hall of Birds, a Pueblo cliff dwelling, the Insect Zoo, and a hands-on Discovery Center are other attractions. The Page Museum *(see pp118–19)* at the La Brea Tar Pits is also part of the Natural History Museum.

Natural History Museum in Exposition Park

🏛 Bovard Administration Building

Hahn Plaza. 🕐 *daily.*

This Italian Romanesque structure was named after USC's fourth president, George Bovard. The former bell tower has eight sculpted figures of great men, including John Wesley, Abraham Lincoln, Theodore Roosevelt, Cicero, and Plato. The restored Gothic Norris Auditorium seats 1,600 people. *Tommy Trojan,* a statue of a Trojan warrior and the university's symbol, stands outside the main entrance. It was sculpted in 1930 by Roger Nobel Burnham.

SIGHTS AT A GLANCE

Aerospace Museum ⑦
Bovard Administration Building ①
California Afro-American Museum ⑧
California Science Center ⑨
Doheny Memorial Library ③
Fisher Gallery ⑤
Los Angeles Memorial Coliseum ⑩
Mudd Memorial Hall ④
Natural History Museum of Los Angeles County ⑥
Tommy Trojan ②

Bovard Administration Building

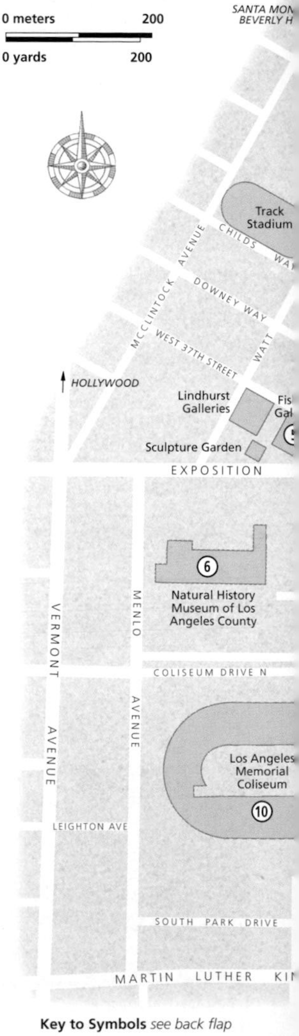

Key to Symbols see back flap

Los Angeles Memorial Coliseum

🏟 Los Angeles Memorial Coliseum

3939 S Figueroa St. **Tel** (213) 748-6136. ◯ for events and tours. 🚼 🎥 10:30am, noon, 1:30pm Tue, Thu & Sat; times may vary, so call ahead.

Host to the 1932 and 1984 Olympic Games, the Coliseum has also been the site of professional and USC football games, rock concerts, Pope John Paul II's Mass in 1987 and John F Kennedy's acceptance speech as the Democratic candidate at the Democratic National Convention in 1960. A 40-minute walking tour of the press conference room, locker rooms, and press boxes gives a history of the stadium.

🏛 California Science Center

700 State Drive. **Tel** (323) 724-3623. ◯ 10am–5pm daily. ● Jan 1, Thanksgiving, Dec 25. 🎥 www.casciencectr.org

One of the largest of its kind in the United States, the California Museum of Science and Industry aims to make science accessible to people of all ages. The World of Life exhibit in the Kinsey Hall of Health explores how living things function, with Body Works, a 50-ft (15-m) long trans-parent human figure with illuminated organs, as its centerpiece. The Creative World area shows how people create what they need, follow-ing an idea from inception to production. The IMAX Theater, also at the museum has a five-story-high screen with Surround Sound. It presents nature-related movies on such subjects as volcanoes, Africa, and outer space. Aerospace Museum, designed by Frank Gehry, has an F-104 Starfighter jet bolted to its façade. The building features all kinds of winged craft, from a Wright Brothers' glider to a Gemini 11 space capsule.

🏛 Fisher Gallery

Bloom Walk. **Tel** (213) 740-4561. ◯ noon–5pm Tue–Sat. ● public hols.

Named after the gallery's benefactor, Mrs. Walter Harrison Fisher, the collection includes 19th-century French and American landscapes as well as works by the Dutch artist Peter Paul Rubens.

DOWNTOWN LOS ANGELES ↗

🏛 California Afro-American Museum

600 State Drive. **Tel** (213) 744-7432. ◯ 10am–5pm Tue–Sun. ● Jan 1, Thanksgiving, Dec 25.

This museum is a record of Afro-American achievements in the arts, sciences, politics, religion, and sports. The permanent art collection includes works by artists such as Martin Pierré, Betye Saar, Noah Purifoy, and the 19th-century landscape painter Robert Duncanson. Frequent temporary exhibitions are held in the sculpture court at the entrance to the building.

🏟 Mudd Memorial Hall

Corner of Trousdale Parkway and Exposition Blvd. ◯ daily.

The philosophy department's hall was modeled after a medieval monastery in Tuscany. Its bell tower is 146 ft (44 m) high and was used in the 1939 film The Hunchback of Notre Dame. Statues of great philosophers are detailed on the exterior, with the Cynic Diogenes placed over the entrance. The Hoose Library of Philosophy has more than 60,000 volumes and is considered to be one of the best in the country.

Italianate façade of the Mudd Memorial Hall

SHOPPING IN LOS ANGELES

Whatever money can buy can be found in Los Angeles, from Cartier necklaces to organic farm produce. LA's temperate climate also allows for many pleasant outdoor alternatives to the ubiquitous malls. Melrose Avenue *(see p113)* and Santa Monica's Third Street Promenade *(see p78)* are both vibrant areas. Upscale Rodeo Drive *(see p94)* and Golden Triangle *(see p90)* are

LA shopper

famous for high couture houses and jewelers. Santa Monica's chic Montana Avenue is favored by both Hollywood wives and movie stars. The best areas for the latest in fashion and home decor are Robertson Boulevard near Burton Way, and Beverly Boulevard at Martel Avenue. Shopping is a pleasure in Old Pasadena *(see p154)*, which has many unique shops in restored, late 19th-century buildings.

Interior of the Westside Pavilion, just south of Westwood Village

SHOPPING CENTERS AND MALLS

Shopping centers in LA tend to outclass most other American malls. One of the newest outdoor malls in the city, **The Grove** offers a blend of shopping and entertainment venues. The street is popular with families and teens who, between all the stores, cinemas, and restaurants, find plenty to keep themselves busy. Also check out the adjacent Farmers Market *(see p113)*, where you will find many quaint souvenir shops, and inexpensive, yet excellent dining spots.

For a smooth indoor mall experience, try the trendy **Beverly Center**, which boasts a selection of more than 160 stores. Surrounded by Century City's office towers and set in an open-air setting, **Westfield Century City** shopping center has more than 120 shops. The newly built stadium-style cinemas and posh outdoor

dining terrace make this mall a popular weekend hangout. Nearby, **Westside Pavilion** has an excellent array of clothing stores for children. A small arthouse cinema adds to its appeal. A more intimate space, **Santa Monica Place** *(see p77)* is a short walk from the beach, and has several outlets for sportswear and sunglasses. In the suburban San Fernando Valley, **Westfield Fashion Square** offers an eclectic shopping mix, with special appeal to families. One of the smaller malls, **Sherman Oaks Galleria** also boasts a fitness center and spa, in addition to its film halls, shops, and restaurants.

DEPARTMENT STORES

Shop logo on Melrose Avenue

Every shopping mall has at least one department store, all of which stock a wide variety of goods, from cosmetics and clothes to cutlery and crockery. The old favorites are **Bloomingdale's**, best known for its shop-within-a-shop boutiques, and **Macy's**, with its in-house clothing lines that offer reasonably-priced designer fashion. The glamorous Wilshire Boulevard *(see pp90–91)* has come to be known as Department Store Row. Among

its four big-name retailers are **Barneys New York** and **Saks Fifth Avenue**. Barneys' rooftop deli is packed at lunchtime with shoppers and crowds from the film industry.

The shoe department at the high-end **Nordstrom** is legendary, as are its January and June half-price sales.

DISCOUNT STORES

Many of LA's discount stores are part of national chains. A dollar goes a long way at such outlets, but it's strictly no-frills shopping so do not expect gift wrapping or much customer service. These stores are usually very busy at weekends and before holidays. **Target** is popular for household items, toys, camping gear, and casual clothes, while **Costco** vends everything from bulk food items to computers. Wine and liquor are especially well

Upscale shops on Rodeo Drive *(see p94)*

priced here. Some stores even sell gas, though a nominal membership fee is required.

Bargain hunters will delight in **99 Cents Only** stores. It is hard to predict what will be in stock, but items range from food to flower pots. **Nordstrom Rack** has top quality clothes, cosmetics, and lingerie. Again, the products in stock here vary by day and season.

FOOD AND WINE

Food markets in LA reflect the region's ethnic diversity and obsession with a healthy lifestyle. Downtown, Grand Central Market *(see p124)* sells produce and also has plenty of inexpensive food stalls. Farmers Market *(see p113)* offers fresh fruit, vegetables, and specialties such as freshly ground peanut butter. Dining alfresco here at vintage tables is a popular pastime. The market is also home to **Monsieur Marcel**, a gourmet French mini-market and deli, which specializes in cheeses, wines, and several other delicacies.

LA's homegrown food emporium, **Trader Joe's** sells an array of healthy foods, ready-to-eat meals, and wines. You can find everything from vitamins to fresh seafood here. **Whole Foods Market** also services the health-conscious, discerning customers. Prepared delights, from soups and salads to sushi, can be consumed on the spot at tables here, making it a great choice for a quick bite. **Bristol Farms** is the city's most upscale grocer and wine merchant. The Beverly West branch is truly spectacular, with an in-store sushi bar.

A paradise for cheese lovers, **The Cheese Store of Beverly Hills** has the widest selection of domestic and imported cheeses in LA. It also stocks luxuries such as truffles and truffle oils.

In Beverly Hills, **The Wine Merchant** keeps one of the most superb cellars in town. Specializing in California-grown estate wines, **Silverlake Wine** offers weekly tastings and friendly service.

There is no dearth of ethnic food and spices in LA, and you will find Mexican, Chinese, and Thai markets dotted along the city's eastside. A must-try among ethnic stores is **India's Sweets and Spices**, which stocks all things Indian, and also serves vegetarian delicacies in its small cafeteria.

CLOTHES

Casual, of-the-moment styles dominate LA's fashion scene. The influence of Hollywood and its legion of slim actresses means that most trendy outlets store breathtakingly small sizes. Unsurprisingly, custom-made haute couture is best in Beverly Hills, where you will find glitzy, red-carpet outfits throughout the shopping district. Rodeo Drive's tenants are among the who's who of the fashion world, from **Armani** to **Chanel** and **Versace**, all the most important fashion labels are within walking distance. These stores also offer sophisticated leather goods and signature fragrances. Prepare to be put on a waiting list for in-demand items. Also on Rodeo Drive is the architecturally magnificent **Prada Epicenter**, which looks more like a museum than a retail store, with shoes and purses that are must-haves for the upwardly mobile.

For unusual and trendsetting women's fashions at relatively affordable rates, **Anthropologie** is a fashionista's dream come true. **Eduardo Lucero** and

Colorful stalls of produce in Grand Central Market *(see p124)*

Trina Turk are two of the city's most popular designers, and both sell distinctive designs in their eponymous boutiques. **American Rag** features both new and second-hand clothes and shoes for men, women, and children.

In West Hollywood, **Fred Segal** is more a collection of boutiques than a single store, and is frequented by many celebrities and movie stars. **Maxfield** also attracts fashionable and well-heeled clients, who love the exciting and stylish range of labels available. A companion to Fred Segal and Maxfield on Melrose Avenue, **Betsey Johnson** is known for her fun, colorful, and sometimes outrageous fashions for women.

For men, **Bernini** and **John Varvatos** have some of the finest fashions in stock, while for the ultimate hip LA look, visit **Urban Outfitters**, the favorite of the college-aged crowd. If you've left home without your bikini, try the trendy **Everything But Water**.

A Gucci cushion

A Hollywood classic, Fred Segal boutique on Melrose Avenue

CHILDREN'S CLOTHES

Seasonal styles sell quickly at big box retailer Target *(see p166)*, which offers good value for children's clothing. **Old Navy** has low-priced, trendy styles, and popular end-of-season sales, while **GapKids** can be found at most malls, selling the popular casual jeans and T-shirt look. Kids with a high-end brand sensibility can visit Bloomingdale's *(see p166)* for labels such as Guess and Juicy Couture.

For designer kids' clothes, be prepared to spend at speciality boutiques such as **Flicka** on Larchmont Avenue. **Babystyle** on Montana Avenue offers durable and stylish outfits, plus some kid-sized furniture. For the baby who has everything, **James Perse** is the store for sophisticated all-cotton clothing that has won over many Hollywood moms.

VINTAGE CLOTHES

Vintage clothes in LA can be anything from hardly worn designer styles, clothes from decades past, or yesterday's cast-offs. Sifting through the racks takes time at charity-run thrift stores such as **Out of the Closet** and **Goodwill**. You may well find treasures among the donated goods, but it's all hit-and-miss. Hipsters and teens

favor shops trading in funky recycled fashions. **Squaresville** on Vermont Avenue and **Wasteland** on Melrose Avenue have some of the most popular retro looks in stock. Don't be surprised by some of the high prices, as some vintage clothes are quite valuable.

Aaardvark's is known for its seemingly endless supply of used jeans and is a must-stop at Halloween. For slightly more contemporary styles, try **Buffalo Exchange**.

Clothes that come straight from film and TV show wardrobe departments can be found in the Valley at both **It's A Wrap** and **Reel Clothes & Props**. Those that were worn by celebrities have higher price tags to match.

SPECIALTY SHOPS

Hollywood memorabilia is on sale throughout LA. **Fantasies Come True** sells only Disney-related items. Located in the heart of Hollywood, **Larry Edmund's Cinema Bookshop** is a cinephile's dream. It has new and used books, plus vintage posters. **Dark Delicacies** has everything for the horror fan, with some truly creepy items on sale. **Every Picture Tells A Story** sells original art from children's books and has a comfortable reading room for youngsters. For unique,

handmade items, **The Folk Tree** in Pasadena has a superb selection of Latin American arts and crafts, while **New Stone Age** sells unusual artisan ceramics and jewelry.

ART & ANTIQUES

Fine antiques shops are found everywhere in the city. Those in Beverly Hills and West Hollywood cater to buyers with deep pockets. **Richard Shapiro** is filled with wonderful museum-quality pieces. His vine-covered building is close to more than 25 other dealers such as **Rose Tarlow**, also known for fabrics and candles, and **Licorne Antiques**, which offers 19th-century French artwork and furniture. Window shopping in this neighborhood is a rarefied pleasure. On Sunset Boulevard, **Wells Antiques** has the city's best collection of vintage tiles and California pottery.

In addition to LA's diverse antiques shops, its art galleries also span the gamut from the edgy grad-student work of Chung King Road, to the renowned contemporary artists at **Gagosian Gallery**. Bergamot Station *(see p79)* is home to several galleries, including top photograph dealer **Peter Fetterman**. Check listings for weekend gallery openings that bring out LA's art crowd.

DIRECTORY

SHOPPING CENTERS AND MALLS

Beverly Center
8500 Beverly Blvd.
Map 6 C2.
Tel *(310) 854-0070.*

The Grove
189 The Grove Drive.
Map 7 D3.
Tel *(323) 900-8080.*

Santa Monica Place
395 Santa Monica Place, Santa Monica.
Tel *(310) 394-5451.*

Sherman Oaks Galleria
15301 Ventura Blvd, Sherman Oaks.
Tel *(818) 382-4100.*

Westfield Century City
10250 Santa Monica Blvd, Century City.
Tel *(310) 277-3898.*

Westfield Fashion Square
14006 Riverside Drive.
Tel *(818) 783-0550.*

Westside Pavilion
10800 W Pico Blvd.
Tel *(310) 474-6255.*

DEPARTMENT STORES

Barneys New York
9570 Wilshire Blvd. **Map** F4. **Tel** *(310) 276-4400.*

Bloomingdale's
Beverly Center, 8500 Beverly Blvd. **Map** 6 C2.
Tel *(310) 360-2700.*
One of two locations.

Macy's
Beverly Center, 8500 Beverly Blvd. **Map** 6 C2.
Tel *(310) 854-6655.*
One of three locations.

Nordstrom
Westside Pavilion, 10830 W Pico Blvd.
Tel *(310) 470-6155.*
One of four locations.

Saks Fifth Avenue
9600 Wilshire Blvd.
Map 5 E4.
Tel *(310) 275-4211.*

DISCOUNT STORES

99 Cents Only
601 S Fairfax Ave.
Map 7 D4.
Tel (323) 936-3972.
One of several locations.

Costco
2901 Los Feliz Blvd.
Tel *(323) 644-5201.*
One of several locations.

Nordstrom Rack
227 N Glendale Ave, Glendale.
Tel *(818) 240-2404.*

Target
7100 Santa Monica Blvd, W Hollywood. **Map** 7 F1.
Tel *(323) 603-0004.*
One of several locations.

DIRECTORY

FOOD AND WINE

Bristol Farms
9039 Beverly Blvd.
Map 6 A2.
Tel (310) 248-2804.
www.bristolfarms.com

**The Cheese Store
of Beverly Hills**
419 N Beverly Drive,
Beverly Hills. **Map** 5 F3.
Tel (310) 278-2855.
www.cheesestorebh.com

**India's Sweets
and Spices**
3126 Los Feliz Blvd.
Tel (323) 345-0360.

Monsieur Marcel
Farmers Market, 6333 W
3rd St. **Map** 7 D3.
Tel (323) 939-7792.
www.mrmarcel.com

Silverlake Wine
2395 Glendale Blvd.
Tel (323) 662-9024.
www.silverlakewine.com

Trader Joe's
7304 Santa Monica Blvd.
Map 7 F1.
Tel (323) 851-9772.
www.traderjoes.com

**Whole Foods
Market**
6350 W 3rd St. **Map** 7 D3.
Tel (323) 964-6800.
www.wholefoods.com

The Wine Merchant
9467 Little Santa Monica
Blvd. **Map** 5 E4.
Tel (310) 278-7322.

CLOTHES

American Rag
150 S La Brea Ave. **Map** 7
F2. *Tel (323) 935-3154.*

Anthropologie
320 N Beverly Drive,
Beverly Hills. **Map** 5 F3.
Tel (310) 385-7390.
www.anthropologie.com

Bernini
8500 Beverly Blvd.
Map 6 C2.
Tel (310) 855-1786.
www.bernini.com

Betsey Johnson
8050 Melrose Ave.
Map 7 D2.
Tel (323) 852-1534.
www.betseyjohnson.com

Chanel
400 N Rodeo Drive,
Beverly Hills. **Map** 5 F3.
Tel (310) 278-5500.
www.chanel.com

Eduardo Lucero
7378 Beverly Blvd.
Map 7 E2.
Tel (323) 933-2778.

**Everything But
Water**
Beverly Center, 8500
Beverly Blvd. **Map** 6 C2.
Tel (310) 289-1550.

Fred Segal
8118 Melrose Ave.
Map 7 D1.
*Tel (323) 651-1935.
One of two locations.*

**Giorgio Armani
Boutique**
436 N Rodeo Drive,
Beverly Hills. **Map** 5 F3.
Tel (310) 271-5555.
www.armani.com

John Varvatos
8800 Melrose Ave.
Map 6 B2.
Tel (310) 859-2970.

Maxfield
8825 Melrose Ave.
Map 6 B2.
Tel (310) 274-8800.

Prada Epicenter
343 N Rodeo Drive,
Beverly Hills. **Map** 5 F3.
Tel (310) 278-8661.

Trina Turk
8008 W 3rd St. **Map** 6 C3.
Tel (323) 651-1382.

Urban Outfitters
1440 Third St Promenade,
Santa Monica.
Tel (310) 394-1404.

Versace
248 N Rodeo Drive,
Beverly Hills. **Map** 5 F3.
Tel (310) 205-3921.
www.versace.com

CHILDREN'S
CLOTHES

Babystyle
1324 Montana Ave,
Santa Monica.
Tel (310) 434-9590.

Flicka
204 N Larchmont Ave.
Map 8 B3.
Tel (323) 466-5822.

GapKids
6834 Hollywood Blvd.
Map 2 B4.
Tel (323) 462-6124.

James Perse
8914 Melrose Ave.
Map 6 A2.
Tel (323) 276-7277.

Old Navy
8487 W 3rd St. **Map** 6 C3.
Tel (323) 658-5292.

VINTAGE CLOTHES

Aardvark's
7579 Melrose Ave.
Map 7 E1.
Tel (323) 655-6769.

Buffalo Exchange
131 N La Brea Ave.
Map 7 F3.
Tel (323) 938-8604.

Goodwill
4575 Hollywood Blvd,
Hollywood.
Tel (323) 644-1517.

It's A Wrap
3315 N Magnolia Ave,
Burbank.
Tel (818) 567-7366.

Out of the Closet
360 N Fairfax Ave.
Map 7 D2.
Tel (323) 934-1956.

**Reel Clothes &
Props**
5025 Cahuenga Blvd.
Tel (818) 508-7762.

Squaresville
1800 N Vermont Ave.
Tel (323) 669-8473.

Wasteland
7428 Melrose Ave.
Map 7 E2.
Tel (323) 653-3028.

SPECIALTY SHOPS

Dark Delicacies
4213 Burbank Blvd,
Burbank.
Tel (818) 556-6660.
www.darkdel.com

**Every Picture Tells
A Story**
1311-C Montana Ave,
Santa Monica.
Tel (310) 451-2700.
www.everypicture.com

**Fantasies Come
True**
8012 Melrose Ave,
W Hollywood.
Map 7 D1.
Tel (323) 655-2636.
www.
fantasiescometrue.com

The Folk Tree
199 S Fair Oaks Ave,
Pasadena.
Tel (626) 793-4828.
www.folktree.com

**Larry Edmund's
Cinema Bookshop**
6644 Hollywood Blvd.
Map 2 B4.
Tel (323) 463-3273.
www.larryedmunds.com

New Stone Age
8407 W 3rd St.
Map 6 C3.
Tel (323) 658-5969.

ART AND
ANTIQUES

Gagosian Gallery
456 N Camden Drive,
Beverly Hills.
Map 6 A2.
Tel (310) 271-9400.

Licorne Antiques
8432 Melrose Place,
W Hollywood. **Map** 6 C1.
Tel (323) 852-4765.
www.licorneantiques.com

**Peter Fetterman
Gallery**
Bergamot Station
2525 Michigan Ave,
Santa Monica.
Tel (310) 453-6463.
www.peterfetterman.com

Richard Shapiro
8905 Melrose Ave,
W Hollywood.
Map 6 A2.
Tel (310) 275-6700.

Rose Tarlow
8454 Melrose Place,
W Hollywood. **Map** 6 C1.
Tel (323) 653-2122.
www.rosetarlow.com

Wells Antiques
2162 Sunset Blvd.
Tel (213) 413-0558.

BOOKS & MUSIC

Residents of LA buy more books than in any other city in the country. Some of the most popular independent bookshops are **Book Soup**, **Skylight Books**, and **Dutton's**. Each of these old favorites host readings by major writers each week. Also, the staff at these shops tend to be more knowledgeable about their merchandise than chain outlets. Book Soup has a great selection of art books and guidebooks devoted to California and LA, while **Hennessey & Ingalls** has one of the largest collections of art and architecture books on the west coast.

Many large chains, such as **Barnes & Noble** and **Borders**, also have coffee bars. Borders stocks music CDs as well. **Amoeba Music**, located in Hollywood, is the city's largest independent music store with two floors of new and used records and CDs. The weekly in-store performances are free and fun.

Music retail giants, **Tower Records** and **Virgin Megastore** both have branches on Sunset Boulevard, with wide-ranging collections and listening posts. Tower Records also has a store-within-a-store dedicated to classical recordings.

FARMERS' MARKETS

With 80 certified Farmers' Markets held in the city each week, there is no shortage of opportunities to see and taste Southern California's seasonal, newly-harvested bounty. Each outdoor farmers' market has vendors selling a range of fresh produce, including organically grown fruits and vegetables straight from the fields. Many markets also feature stalls, which offer prepared food as well as arts and crafts. Check out the **Farmernet** website for exact times and locations of the various markets.

The popular **Santa Monica's Wednesday Farmers' Market** at Arizona and Third Streets is the largest. The high quality of the produce on sale is attested to by the well-known chefs who frequent the stalls. Savvy buyers prefer to start their shopping early. On Sunday mornings, visit Ivar Avenue's **Hollywood Farmers' Market**, which attracts a very hip crowd. Famous faces can often be spotted browsing amidst the crowd. **Santa Monica Sunday Farmers' Market** on Main Street is a favorite with families who line up for delicious, freshly-made crêpes and omelets to picnic on in the busy streetside green.

FLEA MARKETS

Most of LA's best-known flea markets take place on Sundays at varying locations. All are in the open, with hundreds, and sometimes thousands of vendors spreading out their wares over massive parking lots. Be prepared to spend more than a couple of hours browsing, bargaining, and walking. Comfortable shoes and a discriminating eye are a must. It is possible to find outstanding bargains for antiques, jewelry, vintage clothes, and assorted knick-knacks.

On the first Sunday of the month, the **Pasadena City College Flea Market** adds huge numbers of used records to the mix, while on second Sundays, the **Rose Bowl Flea Market**, one of the largest and best-loved markets in LA, sells hard-to-find collectibles. However, those who arrive early have to pay an extra entry fee. The **Long Beach Outdoor Antique & Collectible Market** runs on the third Sunday of every month and offers bargains galore.

HOME ACCESSORIES

There's an entire universe of stores dedicated to outfitting LA's sprawl of homes and apartments. **IKEA** does basic home furnishings stylishly, and at extremely affordable prices. These items are generally home assembly and emphasis is more on looks than longlasting quality. **Pottery Barn** and **Crate & Barrel** serve those who do not mind spending more for durability and good design. Both have several outlets, as does the home accessory superstore, **Bed, Bath & Beyond**. Look here for items such as kitchen gadgets, picture frames, towels, and clever decorative accessories.

Anthropologie *(see p169)* offers endearingly whimsical, flea market-style goods for the home. Glassware and crockery change palettes and styles with each season. **Shabby Chic** on Montana Avenue helped popularize the casual Southern California look, as is evident from its oversized, comfortable, and slip-covered sofas and chairs.

For both vintage as well as modern reproduction furnishings, survey the stores along Beverly Boulevard from La Brea West, to Crescent Heights. Shops such as **Modern One**, **Twentieth Design**, and **Modernica** feature the best of sleek, mid-20th-century design. **Thai Teak** specializes in modern Asian-style furnishings, while **California Living** is best known for its stylish, designer, outdoor furniture. Chic and tasteful, **Bountiful** sells period furniture along with luxurious bath and home products on Venice's charming Abbot Kinney Boulevard.

GIFTS AND TOYS

Some of the best luxury gift products, ranging from picture frames to fine jewelry, can be found in Beverly Hills' **Gearys**, a shop also known for its opulent bridal and gift registry. At the other end of the price spectrum, **Wing Hop Fung** in Chinatown stocks all sorts of imported goods, from cheap toys to tea sets. Other smaller gift shops in the area are also within easy walking distance and are good for inexpensive shopping.

Very popular with trendy shoppers, **Uncle Jer's** in Silver Lake offers scented candles, plus Indian and Mexican handicrafts. **Boule** has the finest handmade chocolates packaged in beautifully wrapped boxes.

For toys, Target *(see p166)* has several branches selling many brands, games, and smaller sporting goods. **PuzzleZoo** has puzzles, games, and the most in-demand action figures. **The Last Wound-Up** is one of the many toy and gift shops at Universal CityWalk that sell items for both children and adults.

HAIR AND BEAUTY

LA is no less than the world's beauty capital. Credit goes to the youth-obsessed film and television business for the proliferation of high-quality soap-and-salve emporiums.

Glossy skin care and make-up superstore, **Sephora**, displays dozens of product lines. Sales clerks here are helpful and offer many samples. **Aveda** adheres to organic principles in its fragrant, natural skin and hair care lines. Shoppers can ask for a brief, relaxing chair massage and tea. **Palmetto** has two branches, both of which stock unusual, aromatic products from almost every continent. **Studio** at Fred Segal's Santa Monica branch specializes in what can be termed beauty couture. Fragrances can be made to order and make-up artists stand by for quick makeovers, using boutique brands such as Stilla. **Cost Plus** has bath products and candles at reasonable prices. Trader Joe's (*see p167*) has its own economical line of organic hair and skin care products, such as salt scrubs and lavender-scented shampoo. Many spas such as **Spa Mystique** sell higher-end skin care lines and anti-aging regimes. Notable hair salons, including **Privé Salon** also sell their own line of elegant hair care products. **MAC** is known for its seasonally changing color palette and alliances with top Hollywood make-up artists and stars.

DIRECTORY

BOOKS & MUSIC

Amoeba Music
6400 Sunset Blvd. **Map** 2 C5. **Tel** (323) 245-6400.

Barnes & Noble
1201 3rd St Promenade, Santa Monica.
Tel (310) 260-9110.

Book Soup
8818 W Sunset Blvd.
Map 1 A5.
Tel (310) 659-3110.

Borders
1360 Westwood Blvd.
Map 4 A5.
Tel (310) 475-3444.

Dutton's
11975 San Vicente Blvd, Brentwood.
Tel (310) 476-6263.

Hennessey & Ingalls
214 Wilshire Blvd, Santa Monica.
Tel (310) 458-9074.

Skylight Books
1818 N Vermont Ave.
Tel (323) 666-2202.

Tower Records
8844 W Sunset Blvd.
Map 1 A5.
Tel (310) 657-7300.

Virgin Megastore
8000 W Sunset Blvd.
Map 1 B5.
Tel (323) 650-8666.

FARMERS' MARKETS

Farmernet
www.farmernet.com

Hollywood Farmers' Market
Ivar and Selma Aves.
Map 2 C4.
Tel (323) 463-3171.

Santa Monica Sunday Farmers' Market
Ocean Park & Main St, Santa Monica.
Tel (310) 458-8712.

Santa Monica Wednesday Farmers' Market
Arizona & 3rd Sts, Santa Monica. **Tel** (310) 458-8712.

FLEA MARKETS

Long Beach Outdoor Antique & Collectible Market
Veterans Stadium, Faculty Ave & Conant St, Long Beach. **Tel** (323) 655-5703.

Pasadena City College Flea Market
1570 E Colorado Blvd, Pasadena.
Tel (626) 585-7906.

Rose Bowl Flea Market
1001 Rosebowl Drive, Pasadena.
Tel (323) 560-7469.

HOME ACCESSORIES

Bed, Bath & Beyond
1557 Vine St. **Map** 2 C5.
Tel (323) 460-4500.

Bountiful
1335 Abbot Kinney Blvd, Venice. **Tel** (310) 450-3620.

California Living
601 N La Brea Ave. **Map** 7 F2. **Tel** (323) 930-2601.

Crate & Barrel
189 The Grove Drive. **Map** 7 D3. **Tel** (323) 297-0370.

IKEA
600 N San Fernando Blvd, Burbank.
Tel (818) 842-4532.

Modernica
7366 Beverly Blvd. **Map** 7 E2. **Tel** (323) 933-0383.

Modern One
7956 Beverly Blvd. **Map** 7 D2. **Tel** (323) 651-5082.

Pottery Barn
131 N La Cienega Blvd.
Map 6 B3.
Tel (310) 360-1301.

Shabby Chic
1013 Montana Ave, Santa Monica.
Tel (310) 394-1975.

Thai Teak
2400 Main St, Santa Monica. **Tel** (310) 581-4255.

Twentieth Design
8057 Beverly Blvd.
Map 7 D2.
Tel (323) 904-1200.

GIFTS AND TOYS

Boule
420 N La Cienega Blvd.
Map 6 C2.
Tel (310) 289-9977.

Gearys
351 N Beverly Drive, Beverly Hills. **Map** 5 F3.
Tel (310) 273-4741.

The Last Wound-Up
100 Universal City Plaza.
Tel (818) 509-8129.

PuzzleZoo
1413 3rd St Promenade, Santa Monica.
Tel (310) 392-9201.

Uncle Jer's
4459 W Sunset Blvd.
Tel (323) 662-6710.

Wing Hop Fung
727 N Broadway. **Map** 11 F3. **Tel** (213) 626-7200.

HAIR AND BEAUTY

Aveda
6801 Hollywood Blvd.
Map 2 B4.
Tel (323) 962-1596.

Cost Plus
6333 W 3rd St. **Map** 7 D3.
Tel (323) 935-5530.

MAC
133 N Robertson Blvd.
Map 6 B2.
Tel (310) 854-0860.

Palmetto
8321 W 3rd St. **Map** 6 B2.
Tel (323) 653-2470.

Privé Salon
7373 Beverly Blvd. **Map** 7 E2. **Tel** (323) 931-5559.

Sephora
6801 Hollywood Blvd.
Map 2 B4.
Tel (323) 462-6898.

Spa Mystique
2025 Ave of the Stars. **Map** 5 D5. **Tel** (310) 556-2256.

Studio
500 Broadway, Santa Monica.
Tel (310) 394-8509.

ENTERTAINMENT IN LOS ANGELES

As the center of the film indus-try, Los Angeles has dominated the world stage during much of the 20th century. It is therefore not sur-prising that the city sees itself as the Entertainment Capital of the World. LA's large and suc-cessful artistic community ensures that there is always plenty to do in the city, although only small areas tend to be lively after dark.

Hollywood movie sign

LA also has a huge number of theaters, which range from 1930s movie palaces to state-of-the-art multiplexes. Stage productions are also plentiful and diverse. The city has a well-respected symphony orchestra and opera company, which in the summer give outdoor concerts in places such as the Hollywood Bowl *(see p111)*. Jazz and blues bars and clubs are centered on Sunset Boulevard.

LA listings publications

INFORMATION

Various publications can help sift through the city's embarrassment of entertain-ment riches. The *LA Weekly* – a free paper available at bars, clubs, and corner markets across the city – has the most comprehensive entertainment and arts listings. It is aimed at the younger generation and outshines the *Los Angeles View*. The *New Times* is a well-produced magazine and the *Sunday Los Angeles Times* "Calendar" section is another reliable source for information.

The monthly publications include *Los Angeles Magazine*, which lists all the main events in the city and also has reliable restaurant reviews. *Buzz* magazine's recommendations, "Buzz Bets," may appeal to a younger readership. More general information, aimed at tourists, is provided in the monthly *Where Magazine*.

Listings for gay and lesbian readers include *Planet Homo, The Edge,* and *LA Girl Guide*.

The main branch of the **Los Angeles Convention and Visitors' Bureau** is in Down-town, and it offers multilingual assistance. Their visitors' guide, *Destination Los Angeles*, gives list-ings of restaurants, hotels, shops, and attractions. There is also a 24-hour events hotline. The city's two other main information centers are the **Hollywood Conventions & Visit-ors' Bureau** and the **Beverly Hills Visitors' Bureau**.

BUYING TICKETS

The simplest source of tickets to concerts, plays, and sports events in LA is **Ticketmaster**. You can order the tickets by telephone using a credit card, or visit one of their centers in Music Plus or Tower Records stores, or Robinsons-May department stores. If you want to avoid their service charges, try calling the venues direct. Other agencies include **Tickets LA, Telecharge,** and **Good Time Tickets**. Theater productions and times are available by calling **Theater LA**'s information line.

DISCOUNT TICKETS

A good source of discount tickets is **Theater LA**. It supplies information on, and sells, cheap tickets only on the day of performance. **Tickets LA** also offers half-price tickets to some events. Bookings must be made by credit card, and tickets can be collected at the venue.

If you are willing to gamble on availability a few hours before the show starts, then you can try telephoning the box office direct. Many places offer last minute "rush" discounts on unsold seats for performances.

Students who hold a valid ISIC card *(see p620)* may be able to get discounts to some concerts and plays. The best spots to try are those affiliated with Los Angeles's universi-ties, such as UCLA's Geffen Playhouse *(see p174)*.

LACMA *(see pp114–17)*, a venue for free concerts

Hollywood Bowl, one of LA's premier concert venues (see p111)

FREE EVENTS

Most of the areas within Los Angeles have local festivals, particularly in the summer, which feature food, live music, arts, and crafts. Contact the **LA Cultural Affairs Department** for details. On Thursday nights in the summer, Santa Monica Pier has concerts featuring a variety of music styles (see pp78–9).

Also in the summer, the LA Philharmonic allows visitors to listen to its midday concert rehearsals at the Hollywood Bowl (see p111).

Some of Los Angeles's museums do not charge entrance fees. They include the California Museum of Science and Industry (see p165), Travel Town in Griffith Park (see p150), and the J Paul Getty Museum (see pp82–5). Los Angeles County Museum of Art (see pp114–17) hosts concerts of jazz and chamber music on Fridays and Sundays in the museum plaza.

Detail on a LA theater

FACILITIES FOR THE DISABLED

As elsewhere in California (see p620), almost all clubs, movies, and theaters in LA are wheelchair accessible and will provide special seating. Most establishments also have parking and toilets designed to facilitate the needs of people with disabilities.

A brochure published by the **Los Angeles County Commission on Disabilities** lists the services provided by both public- and private-sector agencies. It also includes information on transportation and recreational facilities as well as equipment for sale or rent.

A few local organizations provide services for persons with disabilities, such as the **Westside Center for Independent Living**.

Los Angeles's public transportation organization, the Metropolitan Transit Authority (see pp178–9), operates a fleet of buses equipped with automatic wheelchair lifts. The **800** number (for LA only) can help arrange local transportation for those with special needs.

Art Deco façade of Hollywood's Pantages Theater (see p108)

DIRECTORY

USEFUL NUMBERS

Beverly Hills Visitors' Bureau
239 S Beverly Dr, Beverly Hills, CA 90212. *Tel (310) 248-1015.*

Hollywood Conventions & Visitors' Bureau
6801 Hollywood Blvd, Hollywood, CA 90028.
Tel (323) 467-6412.
www.lacvb.com

LA Cultural Affairs Department
433 S Spring St, 10th Fl, Los Angeles, CA 90013.
Tel (213) 473-7700.
www.culturela.org

Los Angeles Convention and Visitors' Bureau
685 S Figueroa St, Los Angeles, CA 90017. *Tel (213) 689-8822.*
www.lacvb.com

TICKET AGENCIES

Good Time Tickets
Tel (323) 464-7383.
www.gtt.org

Telecharge
Tel (800) 432-7250.
www.telecharge.com

Theatre LA
Tel (213) 614-0556.
www.theatrela.org

Ticketmaster
Tel (213) 381-2000.
www.ticketmaster.com

Tickets LA
Tel (323) 655-8587.

FACILITIES FOR THE DISABLED

MTA
Tel (800) 266-6883 or (213) 922-2000. www.mta.net

Los Angeles County Commission on Disabilities
500 W Temple St, Room 383, Los Angeles, CA 90012.
Tel (213) 974-1053
or *(213) 974-1707 TDD.*

Westside Center for Independent Living
12901 Venice Blvd, Los Angeles, CA 90066. *Tel (310) 390-3611.*
www.wcil.org

Entertainment Venues

As befits a city of its size and reputation, LA has a vast range of entertainment spots. Sophisticated restaurants, concert venues, and lounges are found throughout the city. Downtown's Grand Avenue is the main cultural corridor, and is graced by the prestigious Museum of Contemporary Art and by the Music Center (*see p125*). Hollywood and West Hollywood abound with historic movie houses, theaters, and celebrity-owned nightclubs such as The Viper Room (*see p102*). By day, visitors can join a TV studio audience or watch a game at one of the major sports arenas. Almost every weekend, a vibrant themed festival takes place somewhere in the city.

The famous Rooftop Bar at the Standard Downtown Hotel

BARS

From traditional, old-school watering holes to the latest and trendiest hot spots, LA's diverse bar scene is always expanding. Enjoy yourself, but be aware of rigorously enforced anti drinking-and-driving laws when planning your itinerary for the evening.

At **Musso & Frank Grill**, a historic Hollywood corner-stone, the cocktails and decor remain almost unchanged since the time when renowned author William Faulkner drank here. **Beauty Bar**, with its faux

Hotel Casa del Mar's luxurious and popular lobby lounge, Veranda.

beauty salon look, attracts those who like a martini with their manicure. Top DJs spin here weekly. Specialty bars also abound. The kitschy yet hip **El Carmen** serves more than 270 kinds of tequila along with authentic Mexican bar fare. European-style gastro-pub **Father's Office** in Santa Monica has 36 artisan beers on tap and a wonderful choice of estate wines. It serves some of the most outstanding bar snacks in town. **Tom Bergin's Tavern** is a traditional Irish pub, with veteran bartenders who prepare the best Irish coffee in town. For star sightings, try **Polo Lounge** at Beverly Hills Hotel, or **Windows Lounge** at Four Seasons Hotel. Both venues cater to tycoons, the very well-heeled, and celebrities. **Rooftop Bar** at Standard Downtown combines panoramic skyscraper views, with alfresco lounging all year long. The bar is gently lit by lights from

THE COMEDY STORE

Club sign on Sunset Boulevard

the office towers nearby, while an outdoor fireplace keeps the rooftop warm. Another intimate and elegant bar is Hotel Casa del Mar's lobby lounge, **Veranda**, which is cosily furnished with plush leather couches, and offers picturesque ocean views.

CLUBS

Trends change rapidly in LA's dynamic club scene, so check local listings to stay up-to-date. Also, be prepared to show ID, since the 21-and-over drinking law is strictly enforced.

For the best clubbing action in LA, head to Hollywood. **The Avalon** is one of the oldest and most beloved clubs in the area, often attracting world-famous DJs and performers. It also houses the stylish Spider Club, an intimate VIP lounge. Both **White Lotus** and **Geisha House** are Oriental-themed clubs that offer full restaurant service along with a thriving party scene. Be ready to pay a hefty cover charge. For a new twist to clubbing, try **CineSpace**, which shows films on screens placed throughout the lounge.

In Santa Monica, **Zanzibar** has the hippest DJs and decor. For rock and indie music, **Spaceland** and **Temple Bar** are best, often featuring live gigs by up-and-coming bands. West Hollywood, with its sizable gay population, has many discos such as **The Factory** for a fun night out. **The Derby** offers a hint of nostalgia with its swing nights, while salsa and Latin beats energize **Conga Room**. For ample laughs, visit one of LA's many comedy clubs. Talented unknowns as well as major names perform at **The Comedy Store**, **Hollywood Improv**, and **Laugh Factory**.

MOVIE THEATERS

Most visitors do not spend a lot of time watching movies in LA, even though current releases and countless classics are always being shown. The movie palaces themselves, however, draw huge crowds, with Mann's Chinese and El Capitan theatres *(see p110)* being the best known.

Multiplexes, such as **The Grove**, **ArcLight Cinemas**, and **Loews Universal CityWalk Cinemas** offer state-of-the-art entertainment. Built as a silent film palace in 1922, **The Egyptian Theatre** is old Hollywood at its best, run by American Cinematheque, it now shows a mix of cult and international films. For a nostalgia trip, visit **Silent Movie Theater**, which shows classics from the 1920s. Screenings here are frequently accompanied by charming musical performances.

STUDIO TOURS AND TV SHOWS

Several of LA's television and film studios offer behind-the-scenes tours as well as tickets to tapings of popular shows. In the high-tech studios of **CBS-TV**, sitcoms and game shows are taped before live audiences. For tickets, write about six weeks before your trip, specifying the date and show you want to see. Audience members must understand and speak English. During production season, July through March, check the **TV Tickets** website for entrance to dozens of shows.

In Burbank *(see pp144–5)*, **NBC-TV** offers tickets to *The Tonight Show* and a tour of the studios. Next door, the **Warner Bros** tour is probably the truest look at modern-day filmmaking – the deluxe tour includes lunch at the studio commissary. Visitors on the Paramount Studios *(see p113)* tour must be at least 12 years old. Show tickets are also available.

THEATER

With hundreds of professional plays staged each year, there is something for everyone in Los Angeles. Downtown's Music Center *(see p125)* is home to two of the city's leading theaters – **Mark Taper Forum** and **Ahmanson Theatre**. Ahmanson and Pantages *(see p118)* are leading destinations

for touring Broadway musicals, while the Mark Taper Forum is known for its cutting-edge dramas. Also in Hollywood, **Kodak Theater** is where the annual Academy Awards are telecast. It hosts numerous other award shows, musical acts, and dance performances throughout the year, too. Housed in striking Mediterranean-style theaters, **Geffen Playhouse** and **Pasadena Playhouse** both put on new works as well as old favorites. More alternative productions are usually performed at the city's smaller spaces, such as **The Actors' Gang**, **Evidence Room**, or the innovative **REDCAT Theatre**. In summer, the popular **Theatricum Botanicum** stages Shakespeare's classics in its outdoor amphitheater.

ROCK, JAZZ, AND BLUES

Still rocking the world, Sunset Strip *(see pp102–104)* boasts the venerable **Whisky A Go-Go**. A rock'n'roll legend since the time it hosted performances by The Doors, it carries on the tradition by featuring gigs by many established artists. Nearby, perennial favorite **The Roxy** may be somewhat cramped, but that does not deter the big names in rock from performing there. **The Viper Room**, with its line-up of promising new bands, also remains hugely popular with the young Hollywood crowd.

LA's jazz scene is lively and characterized by cozy joints such as **The Baked Potato**, where there are weekly jam sessions, performances by

Music Center plaza and fountain leading to Mark Taper Forum

well-known studio artists, and gourmet baked potatoes on the menu. A refined, classic atmosphere defines the well-respected **Catalina Bar & Grill**, while **Jazz Bakery** offers a rarefied listening experience – there is no club scene, just a focus on the music.

Look for top soul and blues acts in **House of Blues**, and try its "Gospel brunch". The grungy **Troubador** often hosts promising newcomers, while **McCabe's Guitar Shop** is frequented by musicians for its emphasis on music and performances. The acoustically perfect rooms at **Knitting Factory** present the latest folk and rock acts.

The biggest names perform at LA's arenas, including Staples Center *(see p163)*, Greek Theater *(see p150)*, and Universal Amphitheater *(see p147)*. Expect stratospheric ticket prices plus parking charges at these top venues.

Roxy sign on Sunset Boulevard

Paramount Studios' famous gates *(see p113)*

OPERA, DANCE, AND CLASSICAL MUSIC

The **LA Philharmonic**, which winters at the Walt Disney Concert Hall *(see p125)* is a world-class orchestra. During the season, performances range from classical favorites to avant garde, modern works. The Philharmonic's summer home, the recently renovated Hollywood Bowl *(see p111)*, is famous for its magical musical moments, and is a perfect spot for relaxed alfresco picnicking.

The **LA Opera**, under the direction of Plácido Domingo, performs at the Dorothy Chandler Pavilion *(see p125)* between September and June. Chamber groups perform at various places, such as the **Colburn School of Performing Arts**, throughout the city. Colburn also offers a season of free performances, including music, dance, and drama.

Media City Ballet and other dance companies enliven Glendale's historic **Alex Theater**. The acoustically outstanding Royce Hall is the main venue at the **UCLA Center for the Performing Arts**. More than 200 performances are featured annually,

and offer an eclectic mix of vanguard theater, spoken word, music, and dance, with appearances by many prominent international artists. At the **Ford Amphitheatre**, you can enjoy music, dance, and outdoor film screenings as you feast on a picnic under the stars.

OUTDOOR ACTIVITIES

Los Angeles's beaches are a great natural resource and offer surfing, swimming, and volleyball. The 27-mile (43-km) long beach, with its adjacent bike and skate paths, makes for delightful and invigorating rides. Beachside bike and skate rental outlets are plentiful.

Griffith Park *(see pp150–51)* and Topanga State Park *(see p81)* offer miles of hiking trails. Griffith Park also has horse trails, two golf courses, and two tennis centers. Many city parks have free tennis courts.

Spectator sports include baseball at Dodger Stadium *(see p152)*, professional soccer at the Galaxy's deluxe **Home Depot Center**, and ice hockey and basketball at the Staples Center *(see p163)*.

Besides these, you can watch horse racing at the historic **Santa Anita Racetrack**, and polo at Will Rogers State Historic Park *(see p81)*.

CHILDREN'S ENTERTAINMENT

A variety of family-friendly diversions are available in Los Angeles, ranging from the free seaside street theater of the Venice Beach boardwalk to IMAX movies at the **California Science Center**. During the warmer months, splash out at **Raging Waters**, a waterpark that guarantees a full day of water-soaked activities. Children can romp at the expanded **Kidspace Children's Museum**, which blends science and fun in hands-on exhibits. An outdoor garden and waterway add much to the visit. Since 1963, **Bob Baker Marionette Theatre** has kept kids spellbound with its traditional puppet theater. Musical theater at **Santa Monica Playhouse** is especially tailored for young audiences.

You can also check for upcoming seasonal festivals, or have fun ice-skating downtown in Pershing Square.

DIRECTORY

BARS

Beauty Bar
1638 N Cahuenga Blvd.
Map 2 C4.
Tel (323) 469-9440.
www.beautybar.com

El Carmen
8138 W 3rd St.
Map 6 C3.
Tel (323) 852-1552.

Father's Office
1018 Montana Ave,
Santa Monica.
Tel (310) 393-2337.
www.fathersoffice.com

Musso & Frank Grill
6667 Hollywood Blvd.
Tel (323) 467-7788.

Polo Lounge
Beverly Hills Hotel,
9641 Sunset Blvd.
Map 5 D2.
Tel (310) 276-2251.

Rooftop Bar
Standard Downtown Hotel, 550 S Flower St.
Map 11 D4.
Tel (213) 892-8080.

Tom Bergin's Tavern
840 S Fairfax Ave.
Map 7 D4.
Tel (323) 936-7151.
www.tombergins.com

Veranda
Hotel Casa del Mar,
1910 Ocean Way,
Santa Monica.
Tel (310) 581-5533.

Windows Lounge
Four Seasons Hotel, 300 S Doheny Drive. **Map** 6 A3.
Tel (310) 273-2222.

CLUBS

The Avalon
1735 Vine St. **Map** 2 C4.
Tel (323) 462-3000.

The Comedy Store
8433 W Sunset Blvd.
Tel (323) 656-6225.
www.thecomedy
store.com

Conga Room
5364 Wilshire Blvd.
Tel (323) 938-1696.
www.congaroom.com

CineSpace
6356 Hollywood Blvd.
Tel (323) 817-3456.
www.cine-space.com

The Derby
4500 Los Feliz Blvd.
Tel (323) 663-8979.
www.the-derby.com

The Factory
652 N La Peer Drive.
Map 6 A2.
Tel (310) 659-4551.
www.thefactorynight
club.com

Geisha House
6633 Hollywood Blvd.
Tel (323) 460-6300.
www.geishahouse
hollywood.com

Hollywood Improv
8162 Melrose Ave,
W Hollywood.
Tel (323) 651-2583.
www.improv.com

Laugh Factory
8001 W Sunset Blvd.
Tel (323) 656-1336.
www.laughfactory.com

Spaceland
1717 Silver Lake Blvd.
Tel (323) 661-4380.
www.clubspaceland.com

Temple Bar
1026 Wilshire Blvd,
Santa Monica.
Tel (310) 392-6611.
www.templebarlive.com

DIRECTORY

White Lotus
1743 N Cahuenga Blvd.
Map 2 C4.
Tel (323)463-0060.
www.whitelotus
hollywood.com

Zanzibar
1301 Fifth St,
Santa Monica.
Tel (310) 451-2221.
www.zanzibarlive.com

MOVIE THEATERS

ArcLight Cinemas
6360 W Sunset Blvd.
Map 2 C5.
Tel (323) 464-4226.
www.arclightcinemas.com

The Egyptian Theatre
6712 Hollywood Blvd.
Map 2 B4.
Tel (323) 466-3456.
www.american
cinematheque.com

The Grove
189 Grove Drive.
Map 7 D3.
Tel (323) 692-0829.
www.thegrovela.com

Loews Universal CityWalk Cinemas
100 Universal City Plaza,
Universal City
Tel (818) 508-0711.
www.citywalk
hollywood.com

Silent Movie Theater
611 N Fairfax Ave.
Map 7 D1.
Tel (323) 655-2520.
www.silentmovie
theatre.com

STUDIO TOURS AND TV SHOWS

CBS-TV
7800 Beverly Blvd.
Map 7 D2.
Tel (323) 575-2624.

NBC-TV
3000 W Alameda Ave,
Burbank.
Tel (818) 840-3538.

TV Tickets
www.tvtickets.com

Warner Bros
4000 Warner Blvd, Burbank.
Tel (818) 977-1744.

THEATERS

The Actors' Gang
9070 Venice Blvd,
Culver City.
Tel (310) 838-4264.
www.theactorsgang.com

Ahmanson Theater
The Music Center, 135 N
Grand Ave. **Map** 1 E3.
Tel (213) 628-2772.
www.taperahmanson.com

Evidence Room
2220 Beverly Blvd.
Map 10 B2.
Tel (213) 381-7118.
www.evidenceroom.com

Geffen Playhouse
10886 Le Conte Ave.
Map 4 A4.
Tel (310) 208-5454.
www.geffenplayhouse.com

Kodak Theater
6801 Hollywood Blvd.
Map 2 B4.
Tel (323) 308-6300.
www.kodaktheatre.com

Mark Taper Forum
(see Ahmanson Theatre)

Pasadena Playhouse
39 S El Molino Ave,
Pasadena.
Tel (626) 356-7529.
www.pasadenaplay
house.com

REDCAT Theater
631 W 2nd St.
Map 11 D3.
Tel (213) 237-2800.
www.redcat.org

Theatricum Botanicum
1419 Topanga Canyon
Blvd, Topanga.
Tel (310) 455-2322.
www.theatricum.com

ROCK, JAZZ, AND BLUES

The Baked Potato
3787 Cahuenga Blvd W,
Studio City.
Tel (818) 980-1615.
www.thebakedpotato.com

Catalina Bar & Grill
6725 Sunset Blvd.
Map 2 B5.
Tel (323) 466-2210.
www.catalinajazzclubs.com

House of Blues
8430 W Sunset Blvd.
Map 1 A5.
Tel (323) 848-5100.
www.hob.com

Jazz Bakery
3233 Helms Blvd,
Culver City.
Tel (310) 271-9039.
www.jazzbakery.com

Knitting Factory
7021 Hollywood Blvd.
Tel (323) 463-0204.
www.knittingfactory.com

McCabe's Guitar Shop
3101 Pico Blvd,
Santa Monica.
Tel (310) 828-4497.
www.mccabes.com

The Roxy
9009 W Sunset Blvd.
Map 6 A1.
Tel (310) 276-2222.
www.theroxyonsunset.com

Troubadour
9081 Santa Monica Blvd.
Tel (310) 276-6168.
www.troubador.com

The Viper Room
8852 W Sunset Blvd.
Map 6 B1.
Tel (310) 358-1880.
www.viperroom.com

Whisky A Go-Go
8901 W Sunset Blvd.
Map 6 B1.
Tel (310) 652-4202.
www.whiskyagogo.com

OPERA, DANCE, AND CLASSICAL MUSIC

Alex Theater
216 N Brand Blvd,
Glendale.
Tel (818) 243-2539.
www.alextheater.com

City Ballet of Los Angeles
1532 W 11th St.
Tel (323) 292-1932.
www.cityballetofla.com

Colburn School of Performing Arts
200 S Grand Ave.
Map 11 D4.
Tel (323) 621-2200.
www.colburnschool.edu

Ford Amphitheatre
2580 E Cahuenga Blvd.
Map 2 B3.
Tel (323) 461-3673.
www.fordamphi
theatre.org

LA Opera
www.losangeles
opera.com

LA Philharmonic
www.laphil.org

UCLA Center for the Performing Arts
405 Hilgard Ave. **Map** 4
A4. *Tel (310) 825-2101.*
www.uclalive.org

OUTDOOR ACTIVITIES

Home Depot Center
18400 Avalon Blvd, Carson.
Tel (310) 630-2200.

Santa Anita Racetrack
285 W Huntington Drive,
Arcadia.
Tel (800) 574-6401.

CHILDREN'S ENTERTAINMENT

Bob Baker Marionette Theater
1345 W 1st St.
Tel (213) 250-9995.
www.bobbaker
marionettes.com

California Science Center
700 State Drive.
Tel (213) 744-7400.
www.californiascience
center.org

Kidspace Children's Museum
480 N. Arroyo Blvd,
Pasadena.
Tel (626) 449-9144.
www.kidspace
museum.com

Raging Waters
111 Raging Waters Drive,
San Dimas.
Tel (909) 802-2200.
www.ragingwaters.com

Santa Monica Playhouse
1211 4th St, Santa Monica.
Tel (310) 394-9779.

GETTING AROUND LOS ANGELES

The sheer size of Los Angeles – a sprawling 467 sq miles (1,200 sq km) – may seem daunting to navigate. A vast network of freeways *(see pp180–81)* provides an accessible, if sometimes crowded, means of traveling in the area. The fastest method of touring the city is by car, although the public transportation system works well in Downtown

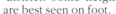

Los Angeles and Hollywood. Taxis must be ordered by telephone usually. They run from the airport, but can be expensive. Buses are often very crowded and slow, but they run on most of the main streets in the city. LA's growing rail system, the Metro, is useful when exploring the business district. Some neighborhoods are best seen on foot.

Taxi in Beverly Hills

Driving toward downtown Los Angeles on the freeway

DRIVING

Planning is the key to making driving in Los Angeles less overwhelming. First, refer to the map on pages 180–81 to see which freeway changes or exit you will need. Second, avoid rush hour on the freeways. The peak times are from Monday to Friday, 8am to 9:30am and 4pm to 6:30pm. Some freeways are busy regardless of the hour, and it can be less stressful to take one of the city's major streets. When parking, read the posted signs for limitations and carry plenty of quarters for the parking meters. At night it is safer to valet park.

WALKING

Even though the city is very spread out, some districts are pedestrian-friendly. Third Street Promenade and the beach and Main Street in Santa Monica *(see pp76–9)* are all nice areas for walking. Other areas include: the business district in Downtown Los Angeles *(see pp122–3)*, Old Pasadena *(see p154)*, Melrose Avenue *(see p113)*, the Golden Triangle in Beverly Hills *(see pp890–91)*, and Long Beach's Pine Avenue *(see p132)*. Do not walk at night unless the street is well lit and populated.

CYCLING

The coastal bike path that runs for 25 miles (40 km) beside Santa Monica Bay is the best place to cycle. Other popular areas are Griffith Park and the Oceanside Bike Path in Long Beach. Bicycles are not allowed on the freeways. The **LA Department of Transportation** provides detailed route maps. Bikes are available from **Sea Mist Skate Rentals** (Santa Monica Pier), the pizza stands (Santa Monica Beach, and **Marina Bikes** (Redondo Beach).

BUSES AND SUBWAY

Greater LA is served by the **Metropolitan Transportation Authority (MTA)**. Bus stops display an MTA sign. Buses run on main thoroughfares: Wilshire Boulevard to Santa Monica Beach, Nos. 20 and 720; to Westwood and UCLA, No. 21; Santa Monica Boulevard to the beach, No. 4; Sunset Boulevard to Pacific Palisades, No. 2.

The **DASH** shuttle provides travel within small areas, such as Downtown LA and Hollywood, for a quarter. The **Santa Monica Blue Bus Co.** and **Long Beach Transit** service those communities.

The new Metro Gold Line runs between Union Station in Downtown LA and Pasadena. The Metro Red Line also starts at Union Station and runs to Universal City and North Hollywood. The Blue Line operates between Downtown Los Angeles and Long Beach. The Green Line is useful for the airport.

Cycling through Venice on the coastal bike path

Train at Pershing Square station on the Metro Red Line

The subway runs between approximately 5am and 12:30am on all lines. A weekend service operates on public holidays.

Single bus rides cost $1.25 and you need to have the exact fare. Metro tickets are available at the stations from self-service machines.

OTHER WAYS TO GET AROUND

Someone else can always do the driving. Two reliable taxi companies are **Yellow Cab** and the **Independent Cab Co**. Rent a limousine for a luxurious alternative from **Limousine Connection** and **Pioneer Limousine**.

Private bus lines such as **Guideline Tours** offer package tours. **Hollywood Tours** and **Starline Tours** offer the chance to view the homes of movie stars and other local celebrities. **Beverly Hills Tours** offer tours of Beverly Hills and Hollywood in Japanese. **LA Nighthawks** arranges a luxurious night out.

DIRECTORY

CYCLING

Marina Bike Rentals
505 N Harbor Dr, Redondo Beach, CA 90277 *Tel* (310) 318-2453.

LA Department of Transportation (LADOT)
221 N Figueroa St, Los Angeles, CA 90012. **Map** 11 D3.
Tel (213-310-323-818) 808-2273.

Sea Mist Skate Rentals
1619 Ocean Front Walk, Santa Monica, CA 90401.
Tel (310) 395- 7076.

PUBLIC TRANSPORTATION

DASH
Tel (213-310-323-818) 808-2273.

Long Beach Transit
Tel (562) 591-2301.

Metropolitan Transportation Authority (MTA)
Tel (800) 266-6883.

Santa Monica Blue Bus Co.
Tel (310) 451-5444.

TAXIS

Independent Cab Co.
Tel (800) 521-8294.

Yellow Cab
Tel (800) 200-1085.

LIMOUSINES

Limousine Connection
Tel (800) 266-5466.

Pioneer Limousine
Tel (800) 640-0700.

TOURS

Beverly Hills Tours
Tel (213) 617-0818.

Guideline Tours
Tel (323) 461-0156;
(800) 604-8433.

Hollywood Tours
Tel (800) 789-9575.

LA Nighthawks
Tel (310) 392 - 1500.

LA Tours
Tel (323) 460 -6490.

Starline Tours
Tel (323) 463-3333;
(800) 959-3131.

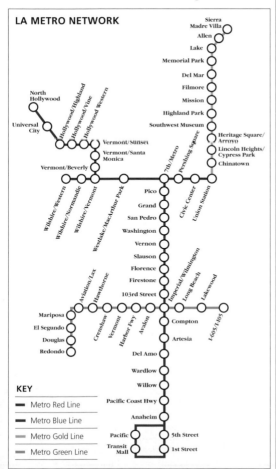

LA METRO NETWORK

KEY
- Metro Red Line
- Metro Blue Line
- Metro Gold Line
- Metro Green Line

Los Angeles Freeway Route Planner

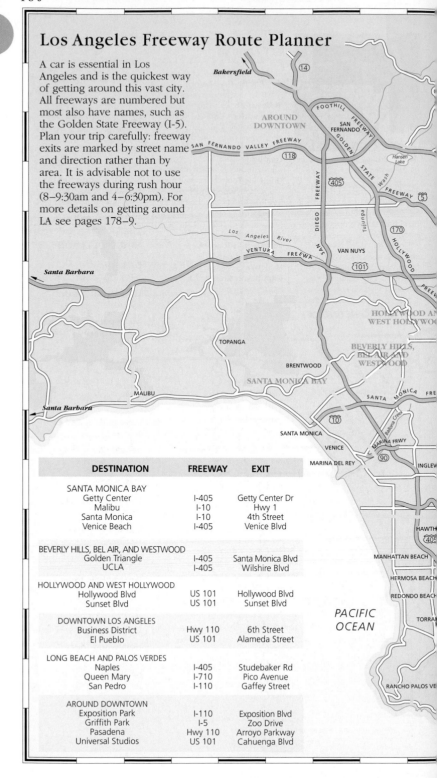

A car is essential in Los Angeles and is the quickest way of getting around this vast city. All freeways are numbered but most also have names, such as the Golden State Freeway (I-5). Plan your trip carefully: freeway exits are marked by street name and direction rather than by area. It is advisable not to use the freeways during rush hour (8–9:30am and 4–6:30pm). For more details on getting around LA see pages 178–9.

DESTINATION	FREEWAY	EXIT
SANTA MONICA BAY		
Getty Center	I-405	Getty Center Dr
Malibu	I-10	Hwy 1
Santa Monica	I-10	4th Street
Venice Beach	I-405	Venice Blvd
BEVERLY HILLS, BEL AIR, AND WESTWOOD		
Golden Triangle	I-405	Santa Monica Blvd
UCLA	I-405	Wilshire Blvd
HOLLYWOOD AND WEST HOLLYWOOD		
Hollywood Blvd	US 101	Hollywood Blvd
Sunset Blvd	US 101	Sunset Blvd
DOWNTOWN LOS ANGELES		
Business District	Hwy 110	6th Street
El Pueblo	US 101	Alameda Street
LONG BEACH AND PALOS VERDES		
Naples	I-405	Studebaker Rd
Queen Mary	I-710	Pico Avenue
San Pedro	I-110	Gaffey Street
AROUND DOWNTOWN		
Exposition Park	I-110	Exposition Blvd
Griffith Park	I-5	Zoo Drive
Pasadena	Hwy 110	Arroyo Parkway
Universal Studios	US 101	Cahuenga Blvd

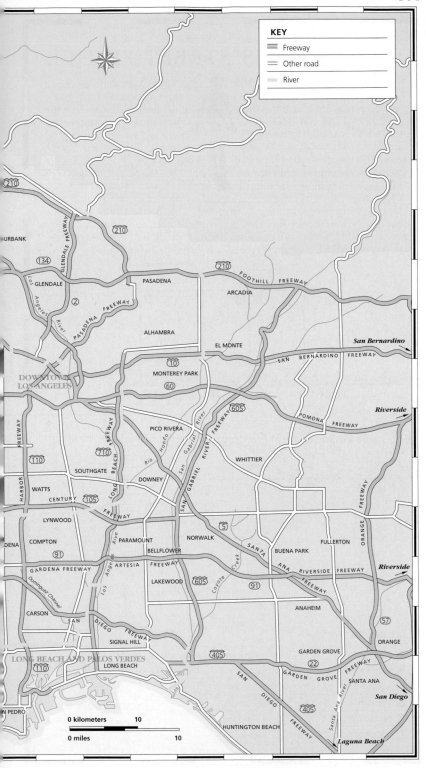

LOS ANGELES STREET FINDER

The key map below shows the areas of LA covered in the *Street Finder*. It includes the city districts of Beverly Hills, Bel Air and Westwood, Hollywood and West Hollywood, and Downtown Los Angeles. All places of interest in these areas are marked on the maps in addition to useful information, such as railroad stations, metro stops, bus terminals, and emergency services. A *Freeway Route Planner* can be found on pages 180–81. The map refer-

In-line skater at Venice Beach

ences given with sights described in the LA section of the guide refer to the maps on the following pages. Map references are also given for entertainment venues *(see p176–7)*, shops *(see p168–9)*, hotels *(see pp524–31)* and restaurants *(see pp568–76)* in LA. Road map references refer to the map inside the back cover. The symbols used for sights and other features on the *Street Finder* maps are listed in the key below.

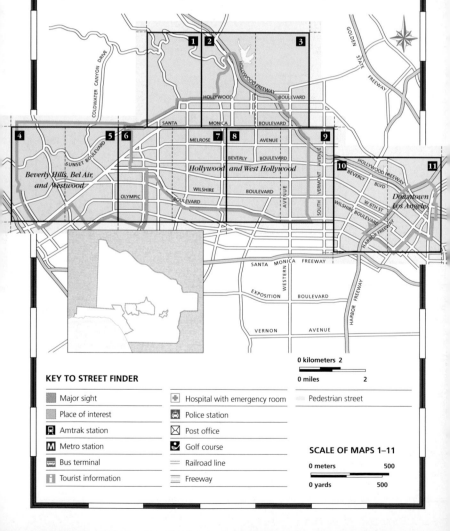

KEY TO STREET FINDER

Major sight	Hospital with emergency room	Pedestrian street
Place of interest	Police station	
Amtrak station	Post office	
Metro station	Golf course	
Bus terminal	Railroad line	**SCALE OF MAPS 1–11**
Tourist information	Freeway	0 meters 500
		0 yards 500

0 kilometers 2
0 miles   2

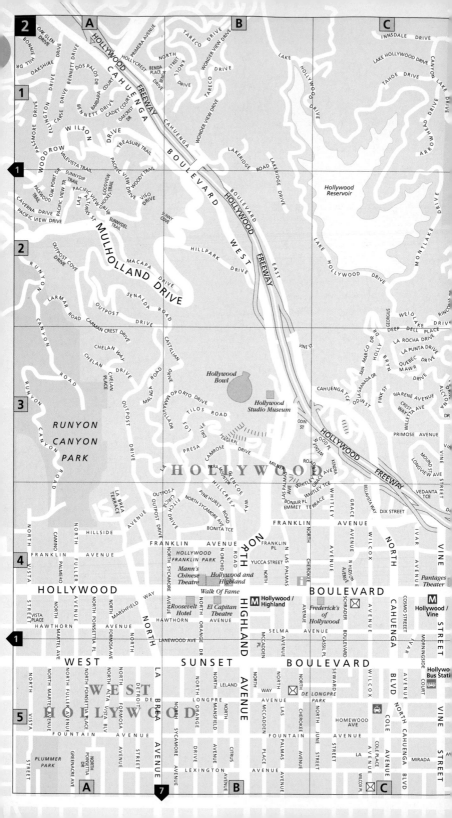

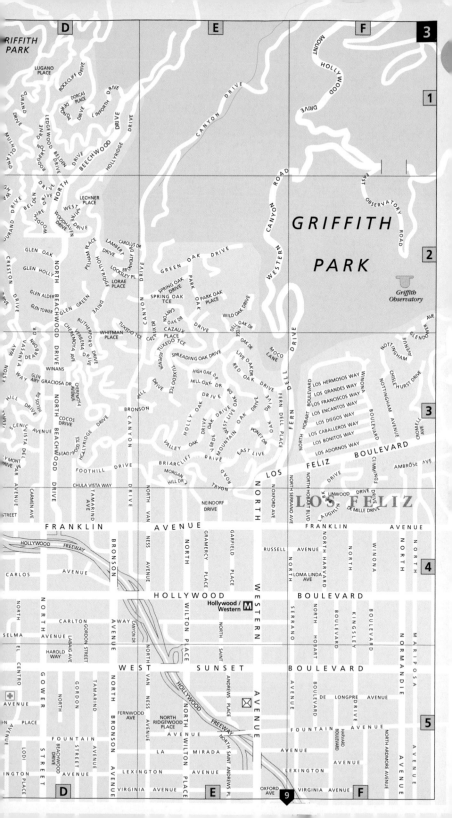

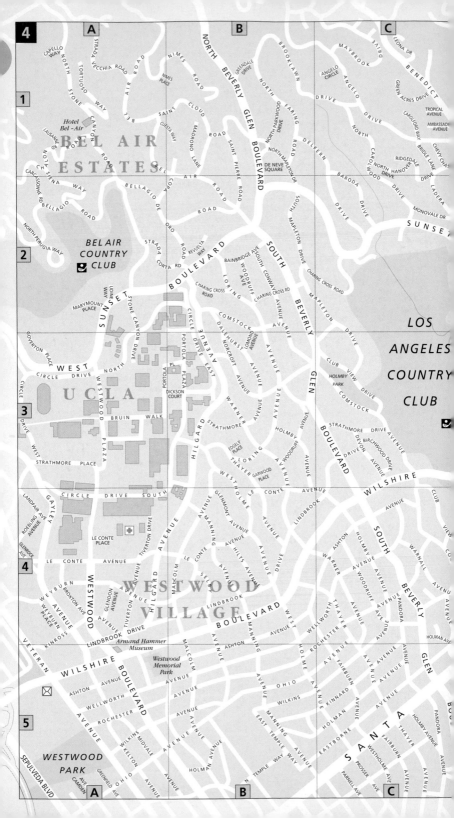

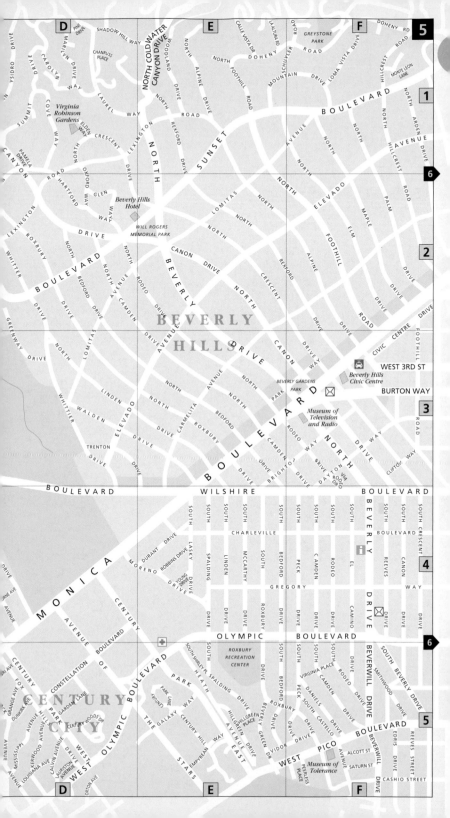

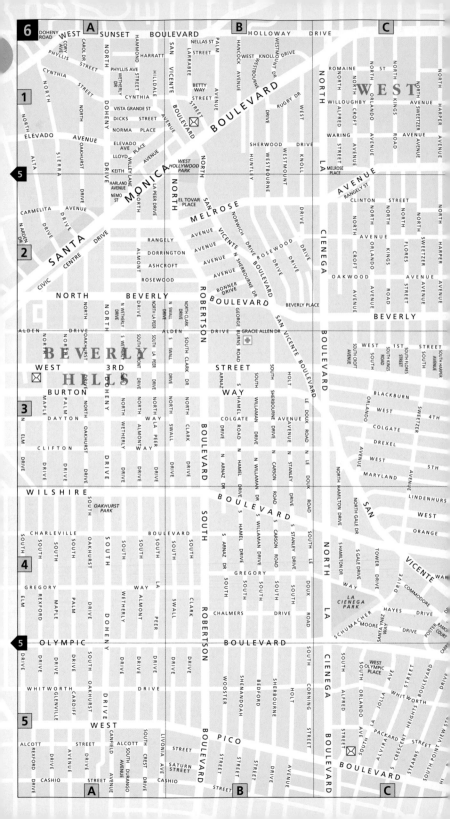

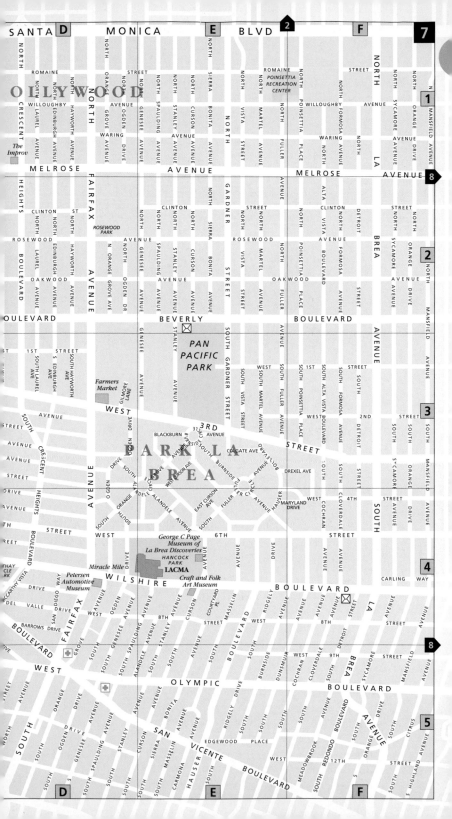

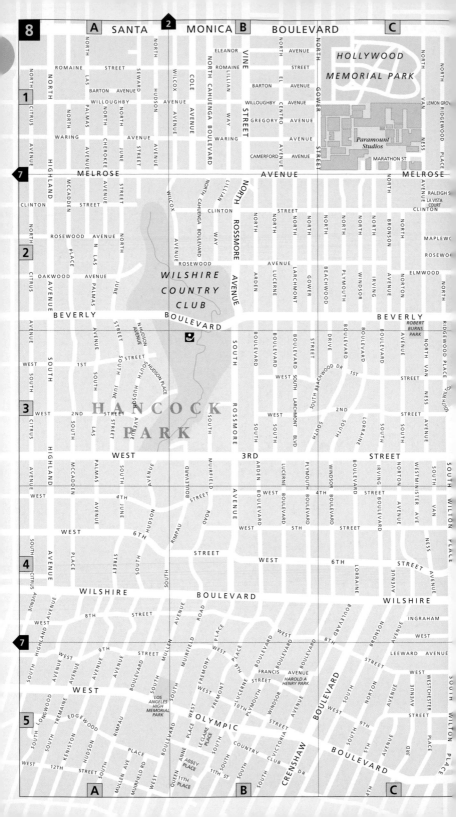

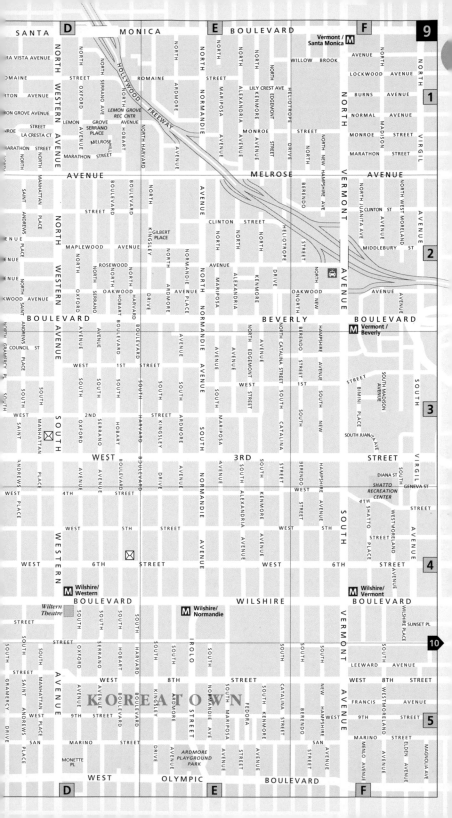

SOUTHERN CALIFORNIA

Southern California at a Glance

Southern California is a region of startling contrasts.
Scorching deserts give way to snowcapped mountains, with views of the coast. It is possible to surf in
the morning, ski in the afternoon, and play golf in the
evening. From San Simeon to San Diego, the coast is
lined with resorts, reflecting a shoreline that ranges
from rugged bluffs to golden sands. Attractions along
the way include historic missions, the charming cities
of Santa Barbara and San Diego, and the theme parks
of Orange County. Farther inland are two of the most
startling desert areas in the United States: Death Valley
National Park and the Joshua Tree National Park.

Santa Barbara Mission (see
pp222–3) *is the most visited mission in
the state and is the only one in the
chain of missions to have remained in
continuous use since it was founded
in 1786. The church façade is in
Classical style, a theme continued
inside the building.*

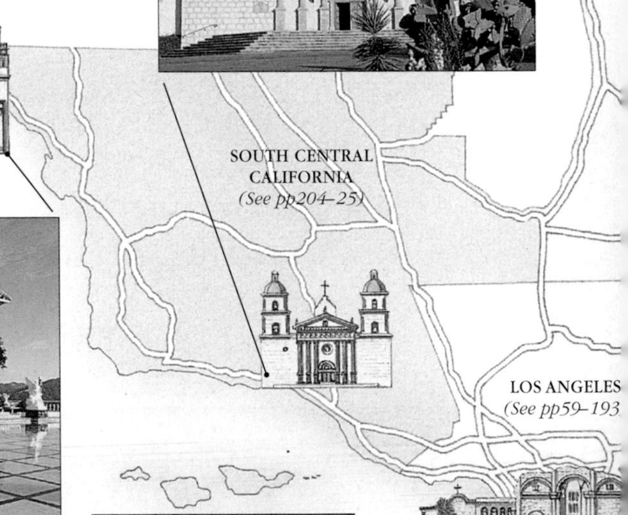

SOUTH CENTRAL
CALIFORNIA
(See pp204–25)

LOS ANGELES
(See pp59–193)

Hearst Castle™ (see pp212–
15), *on the south central
coast, was built by publishing
tycoon William R Hearst.
In the 1930s and '40s he
invited Hollywood stars and
royalty here and entertained
them lavishly. The Neptune
Pool is particularly stunning.*

0 kilometers   50

0 miles   50

ORANGE COUNTY
(See pp226–43)

Mission San Juan Capistrano
(see pp240–41) *in southern
Orange County is known as
the "Jewel of the Missions."
Founded in 1776, its main
buildings have been beautifully restored and feature historical exhibits.*

Death Valley National Park (see pp290–93) *in the Mojave Desert encompasses one of the hottest places on earth and the lowest point in the Western Hemisphere. Within Death Valley, which is 140 miles (225 km) long, lie dry lake beds, sand dunes, and small outposts built around springs. Despite the harsh conditions, the area is rich in flora and fauna. Sights of historical interest in the park include Scotty's Castle.*

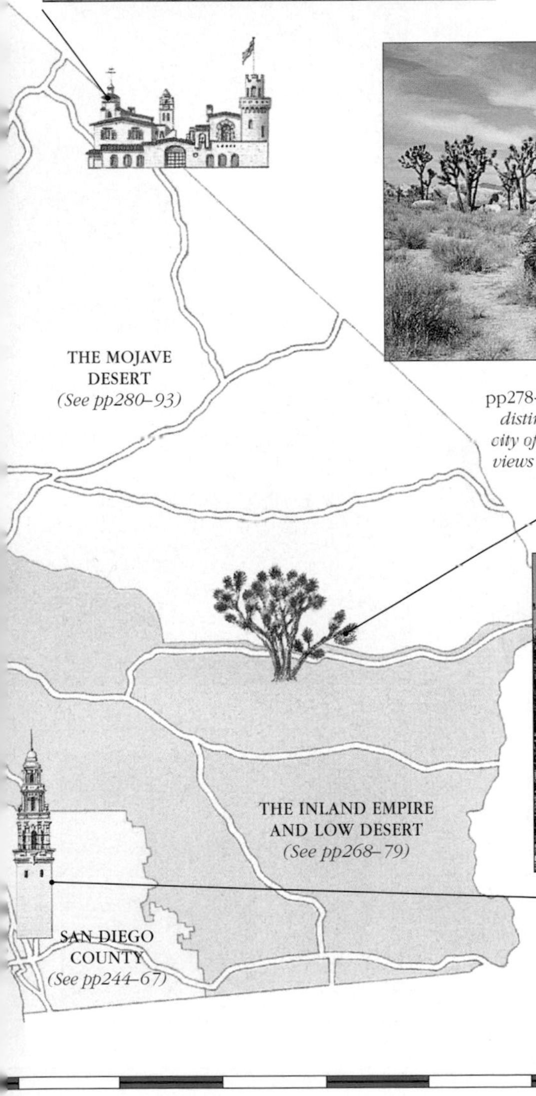

THE MOJAVE
DESERT
(See pp280–93)

Joshua Tree National Park (see pp278–9) *in the Low Desert is famed for its distinctive trees. Within easy reach of the city of Palm Springs, it offers breathtaking views of the stark desert landscape with its remarkable rock formations.*

THE INLAND EMPIRE
AND LOW DESERT
(See pp268–79)

SAN DIEGO
COUNTY
(See pp244–67)

Balboa Park (see pp256–9) *in San Diego was the site of the Panama–Pacific Exposition of 1915. The park is now home to many museums, such as the San Diego Museum of Man, housed in the landmark California Building. The famous San Diego Zoo lies just to the north of Balboa Park.*

Surfing and Beach Culture

Bust of Duke Kahanamoku

If Southern Californians worship at the altars of youth, health, and beauty, then their churches are the beaches. Here, unbelievably beautiful men and women parade their surgically enhanced bodies beneath the ever-present sun. Favorite sports include skating and volleyball, but the ability to look good on a surfboard is the ultimate cool. Surfing was originally practiced by the Hawaiian nobility as a religious ceremony. It was introduced to California by Hawaiian George Freeth in 1907 *(see p66)* and popularized in the 1920s in Waikiki by Olympic swimmer Duke Kahanamoku. In 1961 the Beach Boys released "Surfin'," and the sport took off around the world. Today surf culture is part of the mainstream consciousness. The loose-fitting clothes favored by surfers are reproduced on the catwalk, and surfing slang is used by many who have never been near the beach.

The Beach Boys *sang of the joys of surfing despite the fact that none of the group could surf.*

Films such as *Gidget (1959),* Ride the Wild Surf *(1964), and* Beach Blanket Bingo *(1965), as well as the documentary* Endless Summer, *helped to establish the cultural allure of surfing. Lengthy beach parties in the style of these films were highly popular during the 1960s.*

WHERE TO LEARN TO SURF

Beginners are advised to start by body surfing without a board. Boogie boarding, with a half-length board, is also far easier to master than surfing. Beaches with waves that break parallel to the beach (a surf break) are the most suitable. The best beaches on which to learn to boogie board include Santa Monica *(see p65)*, Carpinteria *(p209)*, and Del Mar *(p249)*. Beginners should avoid famous surfing beaches, such as Surfrider *(p64)*, San Clemente *(p230)*, and Huntington *(p230)*, as conditions can overwhelm the inexperienced.

Boys with boogie boards weighing up the surf

Lifeguards are stationed on most county and state beaches in California during the summer. Their distinctive gray huts have been made famous throughout the world by the television series Baywatch. *Always follow their instructions on the beach, and ask if you are in doubt about the tidal conditions.*

A "tube" is a cylindrical passage formed when a wave breaks and the crest curls over.

SURFING HIGHLIGHTS

One exhilarating surfing experience is to "beat the tube." The surfer rides beneath the crest, regulating his speed and position to stay just ahead of the falling wave. If he goes too fast he comes out of the wave; too slowly and he gets knocked off. The wave loses momentum as it nears the shore. At this point the surfer will shoot out of the tube, remaining upright.

By changing position a surfer can alter the speed and direction in which he or she is traveling. Crouching lowers the center of gravity and increases stability.

OTHER BEACH ACTIVITIES

Southern California's spectacular beaches are used by a wide variety of sports enthusiasts. Although the beaches are most popular in summer, activities are enjoyed year-round by hardy souls. Sailing is popular, with thousands of yachts of all sizes harbored in a string of marinas along the coast. Windsurfing and kite flying also take advantage of the prevailing onshore winds. Sea kayakers often explore the rocky coasts of the Channel Islands (see p224) and the mainland. Volleyball, once limited to friendly matches, is now a major professional sport with competitions held along the Southern California coast each summer.

Modern surfboards are made out of light, man-made materials, such as fiberglass, allowing surfers to reach much higher speeds. Their bright colors make them easy to see in the water.

The first boards *came from Hawaii and were called coffin lids because of their distinctive shape. Made out of wood, they were heavy and unwieldy. Early surfboards can be seen at the Lighthouse Surfing Museum in Santa Cruz (see p507).*

Friendly volleyball game in Santa Monica

California Car Culture

California license plate

It is difficult to understand Southern California without considering the influence of the car. The introduction of the freeway system in LA in 1940 *(see p54)* spawned an entirely new culture centered around the automobile. Owning a car became integral to the California identity, and the open desert road came to symbolize the freedom of the state. Customizing automobiles also made the car an art object. Drive-in movies led to the convenience of drive-in banks and fast-food restaurants. But there was a price to pay: smog, the result of car exhaust and sunlight, has become a fact of life in LA. Today, cars have cleaner exhausts, but LA has to cope with some 8 million cars on its increasingly "gridlocked" streets.

Los Angeles' freeways, *begun in the 1950s, have expanded into a complex network, linking the city with the rest of the state.*

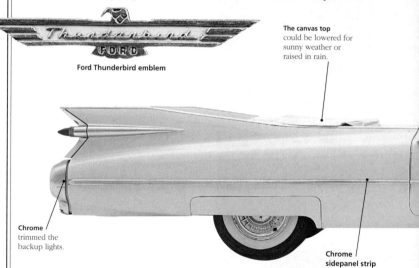

Ford Thunderbird emblem

The canvas top could be lowered for sunny weather or raised in rain.

Chrome trimmed the backup lights.

Chrome sidepanel strip

BIRTHPLACE OF THE MOTORCYCLE GANG

In the 1950s especially, California was home to rival gangs of "outlaw bikers." The most famous, the Hell's Angels, began with a group of World War II veterans in San Bernardino in 1948. Their notorious reputation was immortalized in the 1953 film *The Wild One* with Marlon Brando. Today, the Hell's Angels have around 1,000 members worldwide, who continue to symbolize defiance of authority.

Marlon Brando

Japanese cars, *such as those imported through Worldport LA (see p66), continue to be hot competition for American-made automobiles.*

This car advertisement *for Pontiac dates from 1950. As automobiles became more of a status symbol, manufacturers competed for customers with increasingly bright ads.*

WHERE TO SEE CALIFORNIA CAR CULTURE

Californians are very proud of their car culture and history; most towns have a parade or car show featuring vintage, classic, and customized automobiles. For information, inquire at the local visitors' center *(see p619)*. One of the largest automobile shows is held in early April at the LA County Fairgrounds in Pomona. Other meetings include the Muscle Car Show in Bakersfield *(see p225)*, West Coast Kustom Cars in Paso Robles *(see pp210–11)*, and the Graffiti USA Festival and Cruise in Modesto. California also hosts several famous motor races, such as the Long Beach Toyota Grand Prix in April *(p36)* and the Savemart 300 Nascar Winston Cup Race in Sonoma *(pp464–5)*. There are several world-class automobile museums in the state, including the Petersen Automotive Museum *(p119)* in Los Angeles and the Behring Auto Museum near San Jose *(pp428–9)*.

Tucker Torpedo, one of the cars on display at the Petersen Automotive Museum in LA

Chrome door lights were turned on from inside.

The wraparound windshield imitated aircraft designs.

PINK CADILLAC

With its glamorous design and convertible roof, the 1959 pink Cadillac suited California's image and climate perfectly. However, the car's two-ton weight meant that its steering was heavy, and it soon gave way to more efficient designs.

Chrome bumpers protected the front of the car.

White sidewall tires were a popular option because of their expensive look.

The Model T Ford *(affectionately known as the Tin Lizzie) first appeared in 1908. In 1913, Henry Ford introduced the assembly line and cars could be bought for as little as $500. This photograph of a 1924 beachside traffic jam shows that it took only a few years for Californians to become dependent on the car.*

Recreational vehicles *(RVs) became popular in the 1960s. Californians could now take to the open road and explore the state's wilderness without leaving any home comforts behind.*

Deserts and Water Networks

Much of Southern California is desert, and before
1913, migrants to this area depended on wells for their
water. The population grew extremely quickly and it
soon became necessary to engineer what is now one
of the most elaborate water networks on earth. This
network has turned parts of what was once inhospitable
desert into productive land, and made possible the
desert resort of Palm Springs and the huge populations
of the Southern Californian cities. However, the South's
high rate of water consumption places a great demand
on the region's major sources of water: the Colorado
River and the Sierra Nevada Mountains.

**The Sacramento/San Joaquin
River Delta** supplies water to
the farms of the south. At peak
times, pumping causes the river
to flow in reverse, bringing salt
water from San Francisco Bay.

Owens Lake (see p495) lies between the Sierra
Nevada Mountains and the Mojave Desert, in
Owens Valley. The Los Angeles Aqueduct divert-
ed water from Owens River to LA and the 100-sq
mile (260-sq km) lake gradually dried up.

The Los Angeles Aqueduct
made the San Fernando Valley
fertile (see p144). Land speculators
made their fortunes when the
aqueduct was completed in 1914.

WILLIAM MULHOLLAND

As head of the Los Angeles
city water department, William
Mulholland (1855–1935) (see
p144) and his colleague Fred
Eaton designed an aqueduct
and a series of tunnels to
lead from Owens Valley to LA.
Completed in 1914, it cost
more than $24 million. By
1929 the supplies were no
longer sufficient, and they had
to divert water from Mono
Basin and the Colorado River,
400 miles (645 km) away.

0 kilometers   75

0 miles   75

KEY

▨	Populated areas
〜	Rivers
═	Dry rivers
▬	Canals
▭	Aqueducts

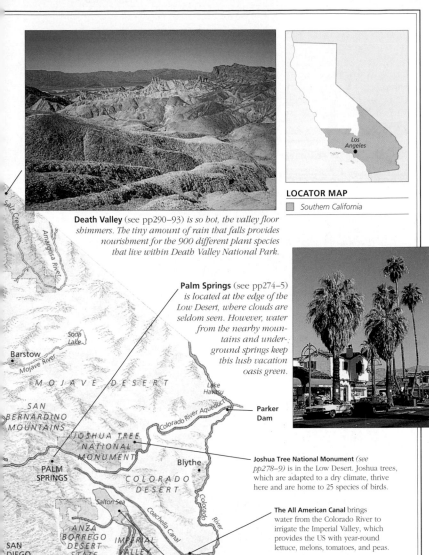

Death Valley (see pp290–93) *is so hot, the valley floor shimmers. The tiny amount of rain that falls provides nourishment for the 900 different plant species that live within Death Valley National Park.*

LOCATOR MAP

☐ Southern California

Palm Springs (see pp274–5) *is located at the edge of the Low Desert, where clouds are seldom seen. However, water from the nearby mountains and underground springs keep this lush vacation oasis green.*

Parker Dam

Joshua Tree National Monument *(see pp278–9) is in the Low Desert. Joshua trees, which are adapted to a dry climate, thrive here and are home to 25 species of birds.*

The All American Canal brings water from the Colorado River to irrigate the Imperial Valley, which provides the US with year-round lettuce, melons, tomatoes, and peas.

SOUTHERN CALIFORNIA'S WATER NETWORK

Southern California has two main sources of water: ice-melt from the Sierra Nevada Mountains in the north, brought to LA via the LA Aqueduct, and the Colorado River to the southeast. The Colorado River Aqueduct system carries water 672 miles (1,080 km) from the Parker Dam via 395 miles (635 km) of pipes. Imperial Valley has a network of canals, making it fertile. The same canals irrigate the desert resort of Palm Springs.

The Salton Sea *was formed in 1905 when a break in the Imperial Valley's irrigation system allowed flood waters into the Salton Basin.*

SOUTH CENTRAL CALIFORNIA

*S*outh Central California is a land of lonely passes and wooded streams. Broad sandy beaches stretch for miles along the gentle coast with empty, tawny hills as their only backdrop. It is a region of small and friendly towns, scattered farms and vineyards nestled in scenic valleys. Farther inland is Los Padres National Forest, where mountain lions roam freely, and eagles and condors soar overhead.

The region's Spanish heritage is highly visible, and no more so than in Santa Barbara. Here the area's most important garrison and the legendary structure that came to be known as "Queen of the Missions" *(see pp222–3)* can be found. The city's red tile Mission Revival-style architecture *(see p31)* has been imitated throughout the State.

Following the breakup of the wealthy missions during the 1830s, the land was divided into a handful of sprawling ranches, then the 1849 Gold Rush brought an influx of Easterners to California. The newcomers subdivided the large estates and set up small farming communities. They touted the land throughout the world as a "semitropical paradise," where the first season's crops would pay for the cost of the land.

In the early part of the 20th century the Central Coast was a popular vacation destination, drawing thousands of people each summer to seaside towns such as Pismo and Avila Beach. Farther north, at San Simeon, millionaire William Randolph Hearst built his own personal playground, the fabulous private museum now known as Hearst Castle™.

Today, South Central California provides a wealth of activities, from horse-drawn wine-tasting tours in the scenic Santa Ynez valley to relaxation on empty beaches. The more active can try kayaking on the Kern River near Bakersfield. Offshore, the Channel Islands offer a unique view of the area's ecosystems and an opportunity to see the annual passage of the magnificent gray whales. The east of the region is dominated by the Los Padres National Forest, an area of breathtaking beauty with miles of hiking trails and drives through mountain scenery. Here, too, are signs of the Chumash Indians who once lived in thriving communities along the coast. Their enigmatic petroglyphs remain as silent reminders of their presence throughout these hills.

Seasonal produce on display in Morro Bay

◁ Fishing off the pier at Pismo Beach

Exploring South Central California

South Central California's beaches and coastal plains
are backed by low rolling hills covered with groves of
oak. Beyond this, the Los Padres National Forest has
hundreds of miles of mountainous hiking trails. Just
north of Santa Barbara, the gentle countryside around
Santa Ynez has proved perfect for growing vines. Along
the coast of San Luis Obispo County, the seaside towns of
Morro Bay and Pismo Beach are known for their fishing
and clamming. In the northwest, Hearst Castle is one of
California's most
popular tourist
attractions.

**Mission San Miguel Arcángel's
campanario**

SIGHTS AT A GLANCE

KEY

▬▬	Freeway
▬▬	Major road
═══	Secondary road
═══	Minor road
▬▬	Scenic route
▬▬	Main railway
───	Minor railway
△	Summit

For additional map symbols *see back flap*

Rugged mountains in the vast Los Padres National Forest

GETTING AROUND
I-101 and Hwy 1 follow the coast, passing through all the major sights. Amtrak runs a daily service, the Coast Starlight, from Los Angeles to San Francisco, stopping at Santa Barbara and San Luis Obispo. Greyhound buses also stop at these cities. There are roads through the Los Padres National Forest to Bakersfield, but the most common route to that city is I-5 from Los Angeles. Trips to the Channel Islands National Park leave from Ventura.

San Francisco
Fresno
Delano
Glennville
Woody
43
McFarland
ost Hills
46
Wasco
5
99
Shafter
Kern River
178
Buttonwillow
Oildale
20 BAKERSFIELD
Rosedale
Edison
Caliente
Loraine
58
McKittrick
43
Greenfield
Lamont
Keene
Lake
Derby Acres
Old River
99
58
Fellows
Valley Acres
Monolith
Taft
Buena Vista
Lake Bed
Tehachapi
e Range
166
Mettler
Maricopa
6
33
Tehachapi
Cuyama
Los Angeles Aqueduct
Mountains
Cuyama
Frazier
Park
Lebec
Ventucopa
Mount Pinos
2692m
Gorman
Mountains
Big Pine
Mountain
2081m
Frazier
Mountain
2443m
Los
Angeles
33
LOS PADRES
NATIONAL FOREST
ma
Pine Mountains
19
CHUMASH PAINTED CAVE
STATE HISTORIC PARK
Topatopa Mountains
a
14
Mira Monte
18 OJAI
150
Fillmore
126
SANTA
BARBARA
Carpinteria
150
Casitas
Springs
Santa
Paula
126
RONALD REAGAN
PRESIDENTIAL LIBRARY
101
ara
33
Saticoy
17
VENTURA
15
118
Simi
Valley
Channel
Camarillo
Oxnard
101
Los Angeles
1
Thousand
Oaks
Port Hueneme
nta Cruz Island
IONAL PARK
Anacapa
Islands

| 0 kilometers | 25 |
| 0 miles | 25 |

Stearns Wharf, the fishing pier at Santa Barbara

California Coastline: South Central

The South Central coast offers miles of accessible, broad, sandy beaches and some of the best surfing in the state. The water here is cooler than the ocean off the Los Angeles to San Diego coast, but these beaches offer privacy and solitude for swimming, sunbathing, and picnicking. The rugged mountain backdrop appears so close you can almost smell the pine and chaparral. Several South Central beaches are within state parks and have hiking and nature trails that climb upward, offering spectacular views of the unspoiled coast below.

★ **Avila State Beach** ③

This white, sandy beach, near a quiet seaside town, has a wooden fishing pier. It is popular in the summer for surfing and swimming.

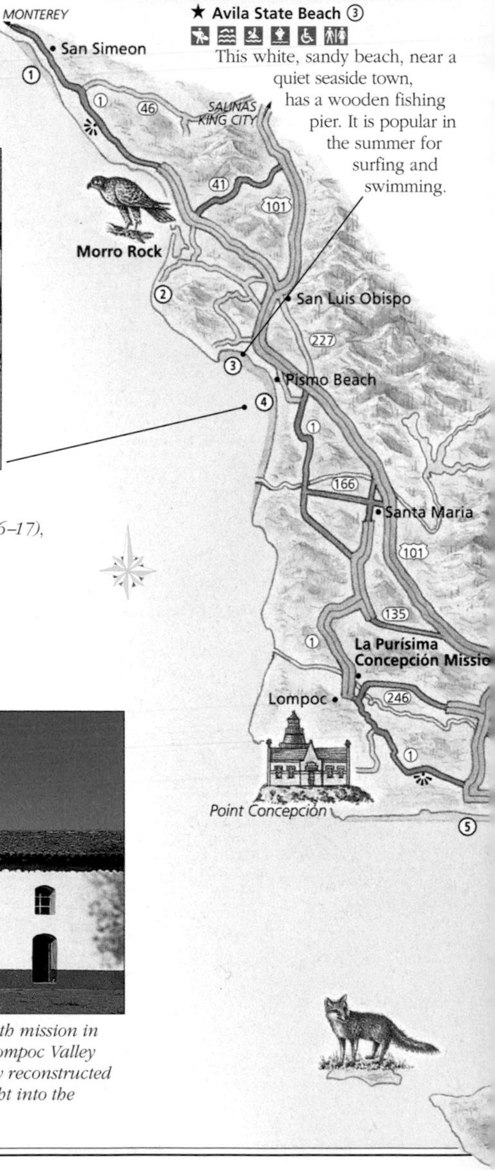

MONTEREY

• San Simeon

SALINAS
KING CITY

Morro Rock

• San Luis Obispo

• Pismo Beach

• Santa Maria

La Purísima Concepción Missio

Lompoc •

Point Concepción

★ **Pismo State Beach** ④

Known primarily for its clams *(see pp216–17),* the beach's compact sand also makes a perfect surface for volleyball.

0 kilometers   20

0 miles   20

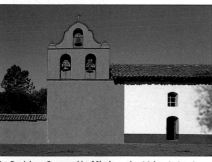

La Purísima Concepción Mission, *the 11th mission in the chain (see pp46–7), is situated in Lompoc Valley (see p217). La Purísima is the most fully reconstructed of the missions. A visit gives a real insight into the Franciscans' living conditions.*

Morro Rock *is one of South Central California's most endearing landmarks. Used as a navigation point by the first Spanish explorers, it is best seen at sunrise or sunset* (see p216).

LOCATOR MAP

William R Hearst Memorial State Beach ①
🏄 🌊 🛟 ♿ 🚻 🐚
Situated below Hearst Castle™ *(see pp212–15)*, this sheltered, crescent-shaped beach is a good spot for a picnic. Boats can be chartered from the pier for deep-sea fishing trips.

Montana de Oro State Park ②
🏄 🌊 🛟 🚻 ⛺
The rocky beach is backed by 8,000 acres (3,250 ha) of park. Hiking trails wind through the hills and, in winter, monarch butterflies can be seen in the eucalyptus trees *(see p209)*.

★ East Beach ⑦
🏄 🌊 🧍 🛟 ♿ 🚻
This sandy beach stretches for 1.5 miles (2.5 km) from Stearns Wharf, Santa Barbara's fishing pier. Children will enjoy the playground and paddling pool.

Gaviota State Park ⑤
🏄 🌊 🤿 🛟 🚻 ⛺ 🐚
This 5.5-mile (9-km) beach, in a sheltered cove, has a playground and fishing pier. It adjoins 2,800 acres (1,100 ha) of parkland with hiking trails.

El Capitan State Beach ⑥
🏄 🌊 🤿 🛟 🚻 ⛺ 🐚
El Capitan is a good place for spotting wildlife, both in the rock pools along the beach and in the woods behind. Gray whales pass close to the shore during the winter *(see p614)*.

Carpinteria State Beach ⑧
🏄 🌊 🤿 🛟 ♿ 🚻 ⛺ 🐚
Backed by the Santa Ynez Mountains, this sheltered beach is one of the safest and most pleasant places to swim in Southern California.

Point Mugu State Park ⑩
🌊 🤿 🛟 ♿ 🚻 ⛺ 🐚
At the western end of the Santa Monica Mountains, the park is crisscrossed with hiking trails. Dolphins and California sea lions are often seen offshore.

Leo Carrillo State Beach North ⑪
🏄 🌊 🤿 🛟 ♿ 🚻 ⛺ 🐚
This stretch of Leo Carrillo State Beach *(see p64)*, which extends across the LA County border, is one of the classic spots for surfing in California.

★ San Buenaventura State Beach ⑨
🏄 🌊 🤿 🛟 ♿ 🚻 🐚
Close to the center of Ventura *(see p224)*, this broad beach is sheltered by the harbor breakwater, making it a good area for swimming.

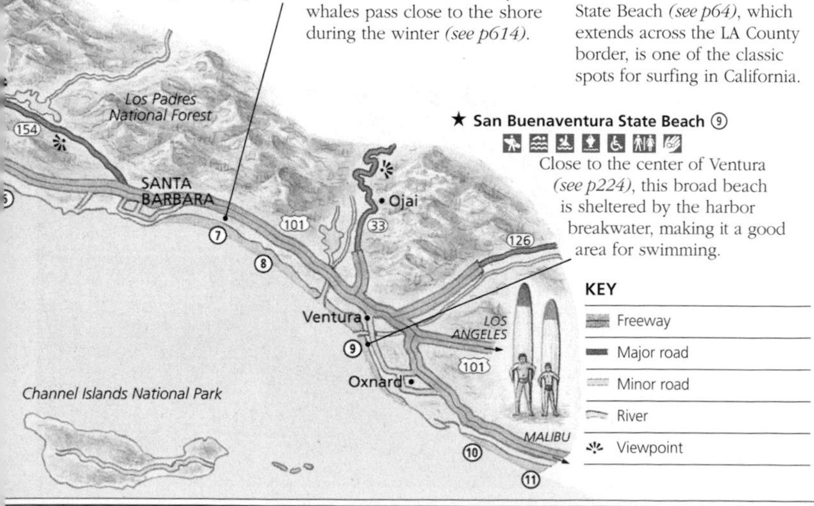

Arched colonnade at the Mission San Miguel Arcángel

Mission San Miguel Arcángel ❶

801 Mission St, San Miguel.
Road map B5. *Tel (805) 467-2131.*
🔵 *Closed to the public.*
www.missionsanmiguel.org

The mission is currently closed to the public, following earthquake damage in December 2003. The outside of the building can still be seen, and there are plans to open a temporary gift shop while the Mission complex is being preserved. This mission was the 16th in the Californian chain *(see pp46–7)*, and was founded in 1797 by Father Fermín de Lasuén, the successor to Father Junípero Serra *(see p46)*. Nine years later the original church was destroyed by fire and the present building, which was used as a parish church, was completed in 1819.

The six rooms in the mission's museum are furnished as they would have been in the early 19th century and the wall decorations in the church were painted in 1822–3.

In addition to growing grain and raising cattle, the padres made their own sacramental wine. Today the surrounding hills shelter over 30 wineries.

Following secularization in 1834, the mission was used as a warehouse and bar. In 1928 it was returned to the padres, and restoration was begun.

Hearst Castle™ ❷

See pp212–15.

Cambria ❸

Road map B5. 🏠 *5,000.* 🚏
🚉 *767 Main St. Tel (805) 927-3624.*
www.cambriachamber.org

Situated between rugged seashore and pine-clad hills, Cambria began as a mercury mining settlement in 1866. Later it became a center for dairy farming and lumber production, and today it is a popular location for artists and craftspeople.

The town is divided into two distinct districts: East Village, a charming colony of Arts and Crafts houses *(see p31)*, and West Village, which is more modern. Main Street, which joins the two, is lined with specialty shops, art galleries, and restaurants as well as Lull House, Cambria's oldest residence.

Among the houses on Hillcrest Drive, just north of Main Street, is Nit Wit Ridge. It was built by local contractor Art Beal, who was known as "Captain Nit Wit." This whimsical abode was fashioned over six decades, starting in the 1930s, out of salvaged material, from sea shells to old tires. To the

Statue of St. Michael the Archangel

north of the town, on Moonstone Drive, is the Leffingwell Landing, which offers excellent views of the surf and occasionally sea lions, whales, and otters out at sea. At low tide it is also possible to climb down to the rock pools at the bottom of the cliffs. The area is also well equipped for picnickers.

Paso Robles ❹

Road map B5. 🏠 *21,000.* 🚏 🚉
1225 Park St. Tel (805) 238-0506.
www.pasorobleschamber.com

Paso Robles, or "Pass of the Oaks," was once part of the 26,000-acre (10,500-ha) El Paso de Robles ranch. In 1857, a sulfurous hot spring, long used by Indians for its curative powers, was transformed into a health resort. With the arrival of the Southern Pacific railroad in 1886, the town quickly developed. Today, Paso Robles is ringed with horse ranches, vineyards, wineries, and more than 5,000 acres (2,000 ha) of almond orchards that bloom in early spring. The hot springs have now been capped – they were polluting the Salinas River – but the town still has much to offer. On Vine Street, between 12th and 20th streets, are several restored buildings from the 1890s, including **Call-Booth House Gallery**. Here works by mainly local artists are displayed in a Victorian setting.

Some of Paso Robles' many restaurants are also located in

Nit Wit Ridge in Cambria, made out of junk

For hotels and restaurants in this region see pp531–4 and pp576–8

Wine festival at the Arciero Winery in Paso Robles

19th-century buildings: Berardi & Sons was once the home of the town's daily newspaper; McLee's Steak House, with its huge stained-glass windows, was formerly a church; and Touch of Paso occupies a former post house on the Overland Stage Company route.

The Paso Robles Inn and Gardens, at 1003 Spring Street, stands on the site of the 1860 Hot Springs Hotel. The latter was replaced in 1891 with a three-story redbrick hotel designed by Stanford White. This building in turn was burned down in a fire in 1940. Visitors to the town may wander through the current hotel's landscaped gardens.

Two important events on Paso Robles' calendar are the California Mid-State Fair – a large agricultural and livestock fair in early August with a reputation for top entertainment – and the Wine Festival in May, during which visitors can sample wines from more than 20 vineyards in the surrounding area.

Environs
Situated 17 miles (27 km) northwest of Paso Robles, off County Road G14, **Lake Naciemento** is a local recreational spot. Set in a picturesque valley amid pine and oak trees, the lake offers fishing (bass and catfish are often caught here), camping, water sports, and picnicking.

At the second junction of Hwy 46 and Hwy 41, 24 miles (39 km) east of Paso Robles, is the **James Dean Monument**. Set around a tree of heaven, it is a memorial to the

film actor who died here, at the age of 24, when he crashed his silver Porsche 550 Spider on September 30, 1955. A metal plaque gives details of James Dean's short life.

🏛 **Call-Booth House Gallery**
1315 Vine St. **Tel** (805) 238-5473.
⭕ *11am–3pm Wed–Sun.*
⬤ *public hols.* 🈳

Atascadero ❺

Road map B5. 🏠 *25,300.*
🚉 *San Luis Obispo.* 🚌 *Dial-A-Ride (805 466-7433).* 🛒 ℹ *6550 El Camino Real (805 466 -2044).* **www**.atascaderochamber.org

Atascadero, which means "muddy place" in Spanish, was founded in 1913 by the publisher Edward G Lewis, who bought the 23,000-acre (9,300-ha) ranch to build his ideal town. Lewis's headquarters were in an attractive Italian Renaissance-style building, constructed in 1914 for almost half a million dollars. Since then it has been used as a boy's school and a veterans'

memorial. Today it houses the City Administration Building. The **Atascadero Historical Society Museum**, situated in the first floor rotunda, houses hundreds of photographs taken by Lewis's official photographer. The museum also contains artifacts that belonged to early settlers. The building is set in the lovely Sunken Gardens Park, surrounded by fountains and statuary.

Unfortunately, Lewis went bankrupt before Atascadero was finished. The town continued to grow steadily from the 1950s, however, as more people were attracted by its rural atmosphere. It was incorporated in 1979.

Today's visitors frequent the town's antique shops, stylish boutiques, and its weekly farmers' market. There is a week-long Colony Days celebration in October, when the town remembers its early history with a parade and other festivities.

Just south of the town, off Hwy 41, Atascadero Park and Lake has pleasant walks and offers fishing, picnic areas, and a children's playground. Next door, the 3-acre (1-ha) **Charles Paddock Zoo** houses more than 100 animal species, including monkeys, meerkats, grizzly bears, a pair of tigers, and a jaguar.

🏛 **Atascadero Historical Society Museum**
6500 Palma Ave. **Tel** (805) 466-8341. ⭕ *1–4pm Mon–Sat.* ⬤ *public hols.* **Donation**.

🦎 **Charles Paddock Zoo**
9100 Morro Rd, Atascadero.
Tel (805) 461-5080. ⭕ *daily.*
⬤ *Thanksgiving, Dec 25.* 🈳

Ducks swimming on Atascadero Lake

Hearst Castle™ ❷

Tile detail

Hearst Castle™ perches on a hill above the village of San Simeon. The private playground and museum of media tycoon William Randolph Hearst is today one of California's top tourist attractions. Its three guest houses are superb buildings in their own right, but the highlight of the tour is the twin-towered Casa Grande. Designed by the Paris-trained architect Julia Morgan and built in stages from 1922 to 1947, its 115 rooms hold many artworks and epitomize the glamour of the 1930s and 1940s.

Façade
Casa Grande's poured concrete façade is in the Mediterranean Revival style. It is embellished with ancient architectural fragments.

Theater
The walls of Hearst's private cinema are lined with damask. Lamps held by gilded caryatids light the 50 seats.

★ Billiard Room
This room features a French early 16th-century millefleurs tapestry.

TIMELINE

1865 George Hearst buys 48,000 acres (19,425 ha) of land near San Simeon	**1921** Casa del Mar completed		16th-century wooden chest, depicting Christ Meeting St. Peter *on the lid*	**1958** Hearst Castle™ opens to public
	1924 Casa del Sol completed		**1951** Hearst dies	
1920		**1930**	**1940**	**1950**
1919 WR Hearst inherits family fortune. Plans a house on "Camp Hill"	**1922** Work begins on Casa Grande	**1928** Hearst moves into Casa Grande	**1935** Neptune Pool completed	**1947** Hearst has heart attack and leaves San Simeon

Classical Greek amphora dating from 3rd century AD

★ Gothic Study
When in San Simeon, Hearst ran his empire from the Gothic Study. He kept his books behind grilles.

VISITORS' CHECKLIST

750 Hearst Castle Rd. **Road map** B5. **Tel** (805) 927-2020; 800-444-4445. 🚌 to San Simeon ⏰ 8am–4pm daily. ● Jan 1, Thanksgiving, Dec 25. 🎫 📷 ♿ call ahead. 🚻 🎟 obligatory. **www**.hearstcastle.org

Celestial Suite
The two Celestial Suite bedrooms are located high up in the north and south towers. They are linked by a spacious sitting room.

★ Assembly Room
A 16th-century French fireplace dominates the Assembly Room. Italian choir stalls line the walls, which are hung with Flemish tapestries.

Main entrance

★ Refectory
Tapestries, choir stalls, and colorful banners cover the walls of the massive dining hall. Its long tables are decorated with silver candlesticks and serving dishes.

STAR FEATURES

★ Assembly Room

★ Billiard Room

★ Gothic Study

★ Refectory

Exploring Hearst Castle™

Statue of Victory

Visitors to Hearst Castle™ must take one of four guided tours, all of which start from the Visitors' Center. Tour One is recommended for first-time visitors. It includes the ground floor of Casa Grande, one of the guest houses, both pools, and part of the gardens. Other tours cover the upper floors of the main house. During the spring and autumn, evening tours of the estate feature actors or "guests" in 1930s costume.

Hearst's private movie theater. Here, up to 50 guests would watch film premieres. The screen could be removed, revealing a small stage, where famous actors and actresses would sometimes put on plays.

The exquisite heated indoor Roman Pool, entirely covered in mosaics of hammered gold and Venetian glass, was a popular choice for romantic assignations, despite Hearst's disapproval of such activities.

The house was continually being renovated or rebuilt in accordance with Hearst's ever-changing ideas. One supporting wall was moved at great cost to make room for a bowling alley that was never built. With scores of bedrooms and bathrooms, two pools, and a theater, Casa Grande was a gilded playhouse for the many visitors who came here.

Gold and glass décor of the Roman Pool

CASA GRANDE: THE BIG HOUSE

La Casa Grande is built from reinforced concrete to withstand California's earthquakes. However, it has been designed to look like a masonry cathedral in the Mediterranean Revival style.

Houseguests stayed in one of 22 bedrooms, surrounded by works from the magnate's eclectic art collection. Hearst himself lived in the third-floor Gothic Suite. His bedroom was decorated with a 14th-century Spanish ceiling and a renowned *Madonna and Child* from the School of Duccio di Buoninsegna (c.1255–1318). A sitting room with ocean views linked it to Marion Davies' bedroom.

Across the hall, the Gothic Study housed Hearst's most prized books and manuscripts. It was from this room that he directed his media empire.

The Assembly Room, on the ground floor, was designed around a massive 16th-century French fireplace. It came from the d'Anglure family's Château

des Jours in Burgundy. The high-ceilinged Refectory Room, next door, features a medieval dining table, cathedral seats, and flagstones from Siena. Guests at Hearst Castle™ were required to attend their late evening meals here.

The Billiard Room, with its Spanish Gothic ceiling, showcases an early 16th-century millefleurs tapestry of a stag hunt. Adjoining this room is

THE GROUNDS AND NEPTUNE POOL

Hearst transformed the barren California hillside into a veritable Garden of Eden. Fan palms 15 ft (4.5 m) high, fully-grown Italian cypresses, and enormous 200-year-old oaks were hauled up the dirt road at great expense.

Massive loads of topsoil were brought up to create flower-beds for the 127 acres (51 ha) of gardens. Five greenhouses supplied colorful plants

WILLIAM RANDOLPH HEARST

The son of a multimillionaire, WR Hearst (1863–1951) was an ebullient personality who made his own fortune in magazine and newspaper publishing. He married Millicent Willson, an entertainer from New York, in 1903. On his mother's death in 1919, Hearst inherited the San Simeon property. He began to build the castle and grounds as a tribute to his mother. On moving in, he installed his mistress, actress Marion Davies. The couple entertained royally at San Simeon over the next 20 years. When Hearst suffered problems with his heart in 1947, he moved to a house in Beverly Hills, where he died in 1951.

Portrait of WR Hearst, age 31

throughout the year. To hide a water tank on the adjoining hill, 6,000 Monterey pines were planted in holes blasted out of the rock. An additional 4,000 fruit trees were planted on the estate, providing an abundance of fresh fruit.

Ancient and modern statues were collected to adorn the terraces. Among the finest are four statues of Sekhmet, the Egyptian goddess of war. The oldest works at San Simeon, they date from 1350–1200 BC.

The *pièce de résistance* of the grounds is the 104-ft (32-m) long Neptune Pool. Made in white marble, it is flanked by colonnades and the façade of a reproduction Greek temple. The latter is made from ancient columns and decorated with authentic friezes. The statues around the pool were carved in the 1920s by Charles-George Cassou, a Parisian sculptor.

A great lover of the outdoors, Hearst had a 1-mile (1.6-km) long covered bridlepath built, so that he could ride in all weathers. Two tennis courts were also constructed on top of the indoor Roman Pool.

Hearst had a private zoo on "Camp Hill." The remains of enclosures can still be seen where lions, bears, elephants, pumas, and leopards were once kept. Giraffes, ostriches, zebras, and even a baby elephant were free to wander the grounds.

JULIA MORGAN

Julia Morgan, the architect of San Simeon, was 47 when she began her 30-year collaboration with Hearst. One of the first women graduates of engineering at the University of California, Berkeley, Morgan was the first woman to receive a certificate in architecture from the Ecole Nationale et Spéciale des Beaux-Arts in Paris. She was a multitalented architect and artist – she designed almost every aspect of Hearst Castle™, from tiles and windows to swimming pools and fountains – and a rigorous supervisor of the project's many contractors and artisans. Her relationship with Hearst was based on mutual respect but was often tempestuous. After spending long hours together finalizing a plan, Hearst would often telegraph Morgan with changes.

Julia Morgan (1872–1957)

Tiered façade of Casa del Sol

THE GUEST HOUSES

Until the mid-1920s, when Casa Grande became ready for occupancy, Hearst lived in the 19-room Casa del Mar, the largest of the three guest houses. He enjoyed his years in the smaller house, but on viewing the completed Casa Grande admitted, "If I had known it would be so big, I would have made the little buildings bigger." The "little buildings," however, are mansions in their own right.

Casa del Sol is built on three levels and has 18 rooms. It features views of the sunset and has a broad terrace with a tall fountain topped with a cast bronze copy of *David* by Donatello. The smallest of the houses, Casa del Monte, faces the hills and has ten rooms.

Neptune Pool, flanked by colonnades and a reproduction Greek temple façade

Fishing boats encircling Morro Rock in Morro Bay

Morro Bay ❻

Road map B5. 🏃 10,000. 🚌 Dial-A-Ride (805 772-2744). 🚆 ℹ️ 880 Main St (805 772-4467).

This seaside port was founded in 1870 to ship produce from the area's cattle-ranching and dairy-farming businesses. Today, tourism has become the town's main industry, and the waterfront is lined with galleries, shops, an aquarium, and seafood restaurants. Whale-watching trips, bay cruises, and a commercial fishing fleet also operate from here. A redwood stairway, celebrating the town's 100th birthday, descends from a stone pelican at clifftop level down to the Embarcadero where a giant chessboard sports redwood pieces up to 33 inches (84 cm) tall. The view from Black Hill Lookout is worth the hike from the parking lot to the top of the mountain.

The bay's principal feature is Morro Rock, a dome-shaped 576-ft (175-m) high volcanic peak – one of nine in the area. Named "El Moro" by Juan Rodríguez Cabrillo (João Rodrigues Cabrilho) in 1542, who thought it resembled a Moor's turban, it was connected to the mainland by a causeway in 1933. Between 1880 and 1969 it was used as a quarry, and a million ton of rock were blasted away to construct breakwaters up and down the coast.

Today, Morro Rock is a wildlife preserve housing nests of peregrine falcons while Coleman Park, at the rock's base, is a highly popular fishing spot.

San Luis Obispo ❼

Road map B5. 🏃 43,000. ✈️ San Luis Obispo. 🚆 🚌 ℹ️ 1037 Mill St, (805 541-8000). www.sanluisobispo.com

This small city, situated in a valley in the Santa Lucia Mountains, developed around the **San Luis Obispo Mission de Tolosa**. The mission was founded on September 1, 1772, by Father Junípero Serra *(see p46)*. Fifth in the chain of 21 missions built by the Franciscan Order, and one of the wealthiest, it is still in use as a parish church. Beside the church, the mission's museum displays Chumash Indian artifacts, such as baskets, vessels, and jewelry; the padre's bed; and the mission's original altar.

In front of the church is Mission Plaza, a landscaped public square bisected by a tree-lined creek. During the 1860s, bullfights and bear-baiting took place in the park; today it is the site of many of the city's less bloody events. Just west of the plaza, at 800 Palm Street, is the Ah Louis Store. Founded in 1874 by a Chinese cook and railroad laborer *(see pp50–51)*, it became the center of a then thriving Chinatown, and was a post office, bank, and general store. It is still owned by the Louis family, but is now a gift shop.

🏠 **San Luis Obispo Mission de Tolosa**
751 Palm St. **Tel** (805) 781-8220. ⏰ 9am–5pm Mon–Fri. ⬤ Jan 1, Easter, Thanksgiving, Dec 25.

Pismo Beach ❽

Road map B5. 🏃 8,700. ✈️ San Luis Obispo. 🚆 San Luis Obispo. 🚌 ℹ️ 581 Dolliver St (805 773-4382). www.pismobeach.com

Pismo Beach is famous for the Pismo clam. At the turn of the century up to 40,000 clams were harvested per day. In 1911 harvesters were limited

Pismo Beach, backed by rolling hills

to 200 clams per person; now, with a license, they may pick only ten. A clam festival is held in Pismo Beach every autumn.

The town's beach *(see p208)* stretches south for 8 miles (13 km) to the Santa Maria River. It offers campsites, boating, fishing, and picnic facilities. The sand is firmly compacted, so cars can go onto the beach via ramps at Grand Avenue in Grover Beach and Pier Avenue in Oceano. Extensive sand dunes shelter birdlife, sagebrush, wildflowers, verbena, and other seashore plants along with the occasional foxes, rabbits and coyotes. Shell mounds in the dunes, especially near Arroyo Grande Creek, identify sites where Chumash Indians once lived.

During the 1930s and 1940s the dunes were the center of a cult of artists, nudists, and mystics. Filmmakers have also been drawn to these sands, which have been compared to the Sahara Desert. One of the many movies made here is *The Sheik* (1921) starring silent screen idol Rudolph Valentino *(see p112).*

Lompoc Valley ❾

Road map B5. ✈ *Santa Barbara.* 🚌 *Lompoc.* ℹ *111 S I St, Lompoc (805 736-4567).* **www**.lompoc.com

Lompoc Valley is one of the world's major producers of flower seed. The hills and flower fields surrounding the valley are a blaze of color between late spring and midsummer. Among the varieties grown are marigolds, sweet peas, asters, lobelia, larkspur,

---

DUNE ECOLOGY

Coastal dunes are the product of wind and, surprisingly, plants. Just above the high-tide line, dry sand is stabilized by sea lettuce. Behind it, beach grass and silver lupine trap more sand, creating small hummocks held in place by the plants' roots. Lupine compost mixes with the sand to produce soil, allowing other plants, such as dune buckwheat and haplopapus, to move in and overcome the lupine itself. Eventually, ice plant, verbena, and morning glory take root in the sandy soil. The plants provide food and protection for a broad range of insects and animals, from sand wasps and beetles to Jerusalem crickets and tiny mice. Most beach wildlife depends on the dew that drops from these plants into the sand below. If part of the fragile plant cover is destroyed by storms, high winds, or people, sand is dispersed farther inland, and a new dune is formed.

Ice plant growing among the coastal sand dunes

---

nasturtiums, and cornflowers. A map of the flower fields in the area is distributed by the town of Lompoc's Chamber of Commerce. The Civic Center Plaza, between Ocean Avenue and C Street, has a display garden in which all the many flowers are identified.

La Purísima Concepción Mission, 3 miles (5 km) northeast of the town, was the 11th mission to be founded in California. It was declared a State Historic Park during the 1930s. The early 19th-century buildings have now been sympathetically reconstructed, and the complex and grounds provide a real insight into the missionary way of life.

Visitors to the mission are able to view the priests' living quarters, furnished with authentic pieces, in the elegant residence building. The simple, narrow church is decorated with colorful stencilwork. In the adjacent workshops, cloth, candles, leather goods, and furniture were at one time produced for the mission.

La Purísima's gardens have been faithfully restored. The varieties of fruit, vegetables, and herbs that are grown here were all common in the 19th century. Visitors can also view the system that provided the mission with water.

🏛 **La Purísima Concepción Mission**
2295 Purísima Rd, Lompoc. **Tel** (805) 733-3713. 🕘 9am–5pm daily. 🚫 Jan 1, Thanksgiving, Dec 25. ♿

La Purísima Concepción Mission in Lompoc Valley

Tour of the Santa Ynez Valley Wineries ⑩

Local wine

Santa Ynez valley is one of the newest and most distinctive wine regions in the state. The area is prone to coastal fog, which produces microclimates according to shifts in altitude and distance from the sea. The area also has a longer growing season than Northern California. These unique conditions, coupled with varied soils, produce a selection of classic grape varieties.

TIPS FOR DRIVERS

Tour length: *30 miles (48 km).*
Stopping-off points: *Los Olivos Café* *(see p576)* *is a pleasant place to stop for lunch. You can buy picnic fare or a packed basket at the café's deli. The wineries all have picnic areas where you can enjoy a local wine with your meal.*

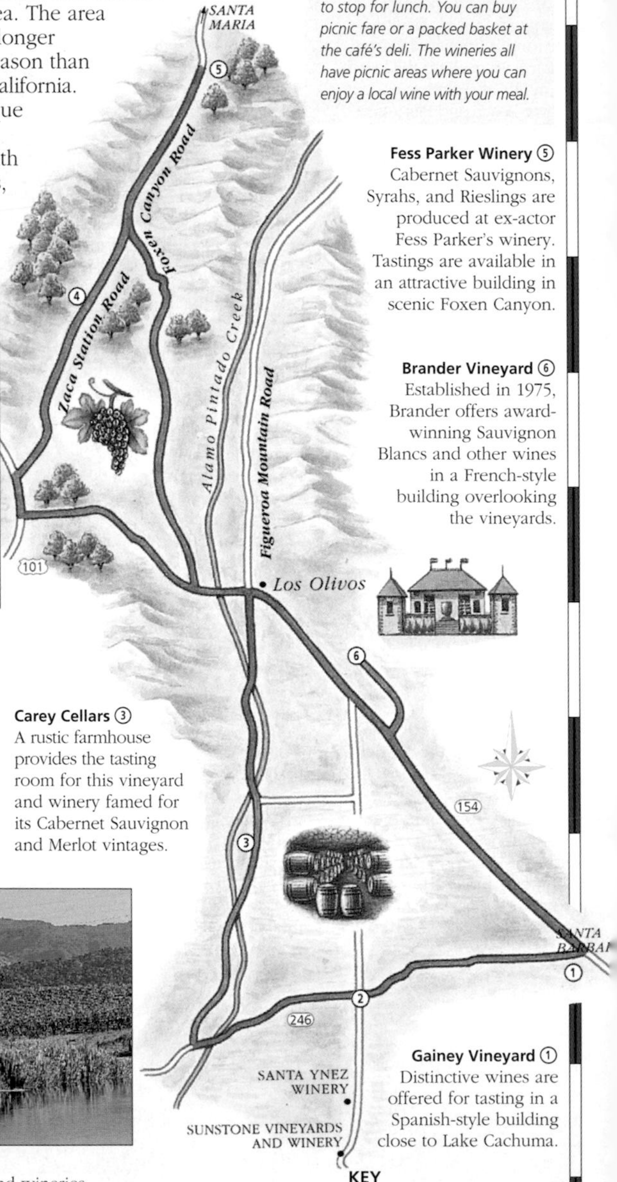

Fess Parker Winery ⑤
Cabernet Sauvignons, Syrahs, and Rieslings are produced at ex-actor Fess Parker's winery. Tastings are available in an attractive building in scenic Foxen Canyon.

Brander Vineyard ⑥
Established in 1975, Brander offers award-winning Sauvignon Blancs and other wines in a French-style building overlooking the vineyards.

Firestone Vineyard ④
The largest producer in the region presents distinctive Rieslings, Chardonnays, and Merlots in a large tasting room adjoining the winery.

Carey Cellars ③
A rustic farmhouse provides the tasting room for this vineyard and winery famed for its Cabernet Sauvignon and Merlot vintages.

Gainey Vineyard ①
Distinctive wines are offered for tasting in a Spanish-style building close to Lake Cachuma.

Santa Ynez ②
Among the vineyards and wineries surrounding this town are the Santa Ynez Winery and the Sunstone Vineyards and Winery.

0 kilometers 2
0 miles 2

KEY
Tour route
Other roads

Mission Santa Inés church façade and campanile

Solvang ⓫

Road map C5. 🏠 *5,000.* 🚌
ℹ️ *1511-A Mission Drive (805 688-6144).* www.solvangusa.com

This Scandinavian-style town was established in 1911 by a group of Danish educators. They paid $360,000 for 9,000 acres (3,650 ha) of land on which to build a Danish colony and school. The original schoolhouse, a two-story frame structure on Alisal Road, is no longer standing, having been replaced by the Bit o' Denmark Restaurant. Solvang's Bethnania Lutheran church, built in 1928 to a traditional Danish design, has a model sailing ship hanging from its ceiling. Visitors can tour the town in a horse-drawn streetcar, the *honen* (hen), and see windmills, chimneys with artificial storks, and gas streetlights. Beer gardens serve *aebleskiver* (a type of Danish pastry), during the town's Danish Days festival *(see p38).*

Statue of the Madonna

Mission Santa Inés ⓬

1760 Mission Dr, Solvang. **Road map** C5. **Tel** (805) 688-4815.
⭕ *9am–5:30pm daily.* ● *Easter, Thanksgiving, Dec 25.* & 🅿️
www.missionsantaines.org

Founded on September 17, 1804, Santa Inés was the 19th in the chain of California missions *(see pp46–7).* In 1812 an earthquake destroyed the larger part of the church. It was rebuilt with 5-ft (1.5-m) thick walls and rededicated five years later. Before secularization in 1834 the mission was prosperous, with a herd of 12,000 cattle; afterward, it fell into disrepair and most of the Native Americans left. In 1843, the mission became the site of the state's first seminary. Restoration work began after World War II, including the campanile (financed by WR Hearst, *see p214)* and the church sanctuary. The mission also has a small museum, with period furnishings, parchment books, the vestments worn by early priests, and original murals by Native Americans. There is a landscaped garden.

Chumash Painted Cave State Historic Park ⓭

Painted Cave Road. **Tel** (805) 968-1033. 🚌 *from Santa Barbara. Parking limited to 2 vehicles.*

In the Santa Ynez Mountains, 8 miles (13 km) to the northwest of Santa Barbara, are a number of remote and scattered caves with Chumash drawings or pictographs. The most famous example is a 20 by 40 ft (6 by 12 m) cave just off Hwy 154. Inside, an egg-shaped cavity, covered in small ocher scratchings, is protected by a metal screen.

Some caves have primitive drawings that resemble lizards, snakes, and scorpions, executed in red, black, or white paint. Tribes are known to have traded different pigments with each other. Some experts believe the drawings are symbolic of the Chumash religion; others think they are random, with no significant meaning.

Native American paintings in the Chumash caves

MONARCH BUTTERFLIES

Each year millions of monarch butterflies migrate from the western US and Canada to winter in Southern and Central California and Mexico. Starting their journey in October and November, the butterflies cover up to 80 miles (130 km) a day at speeds approaching 30 mph (50 km/h). Along the central coast, they usually settle in eucalyptus groves. After the mating season in January and February, the butterflies attempt the journey back to their summer habitat. In season they can often be seen around Montana de Oro State Park *(see p209)*, Pismo Beach, and Ventura.

Monarch butterfly

Street-by-Street: Santa Barbara 🄮

To Santa
Barbara
Mission

**Fountain outside the
County Courthouse**

Santa Barbara is a Southern Californian rarity: a city with a single architectural style. Following a devastating earthquake in 1925, the center was rebuilt according to strict rules that dictated Mediterranean-style architecture. The city was founded as a Spanish garrison in 1782 – four years before Santa Barbara Mission (*see pp222–3*). During the 19th century Santa Barbara was a quiet pueblo, home to only a few hundred families and a center for the nearby cattle ranches. Remarkably, about a dozen adobes from that era have survived. Today, Santa Barbara is a quiet administrative center with a large student population, which lends an informal feel to the city.

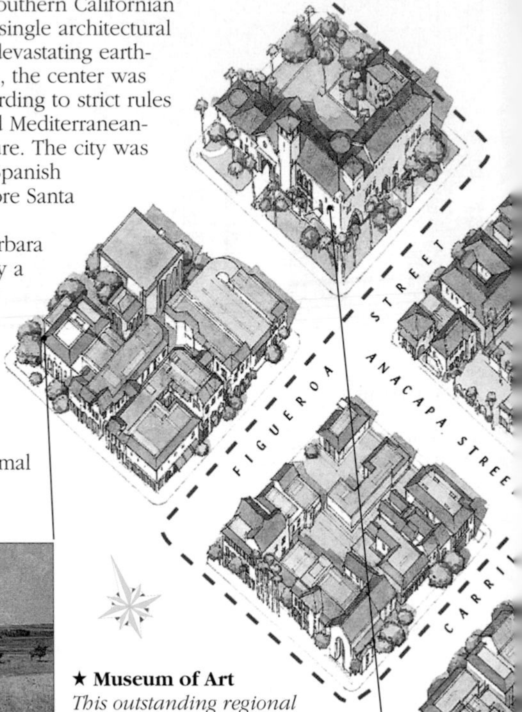

★ **Museum of Art**
This outstanding regional art collection includes Asian art, antiquities, American art, prints, drawings, and photography. In the 19th-century French section is Jules Bastien-Lepage's The Ripened Wheat *(1884).*

★ **County Courthouse**
The 1929 Spanish Colonial-style courthouse is still in use. It is decorated with Tunisian tiles and wrought-iron metalwork. Murals by DS Groesbeck in the Assembly Room depict California history (see p42). There are panoramic views from the clock tower.

KEY

━ ━ ━ Suggested route

STAR SIGHTS

★ County Courthouse

★ Museum of Art

★ Presidio

Paseo Nuevo
This colorful outdoor shopping and dining center complements an older arcade on the opposite side of State Street.

★ Presidio
Santa Barbara's Presidio was built in 1782 by the Spanish. It was the last in a chain of four fortresses erected along the California coast.

VISITORS' CHECKLIST

Road map C5. 90,200. Santa Barbara Airport, 8 miles (13 km) N of Santa Barbara. 209 State St. 1020 Chapala St. 34 W Carrillo. Stearns Wharf. 12 E Carrillo St (805 965-3023). www.santabarbaraca.com I Madonnari Italian St Painting Festival (late May); Fiesta (early Aug). **Museum of Art** *Tel* (805) 963-4364. 11am–5pm Tue–Sun. **County Courthouse** *Tel* (805) 962-6464. Mon–Fri. **Presidio** *Tel* (805) 965-0093. daily. **Santa Barbara Historical Museum** *Tel* (805) 966-1601. Tue–Sun. **Donation.** www.santabarbaramuseum.com

The Cañedo Adobe once housed soldiers and families from the Presidio.

El Cuartel is the Presidio's family living quarters.

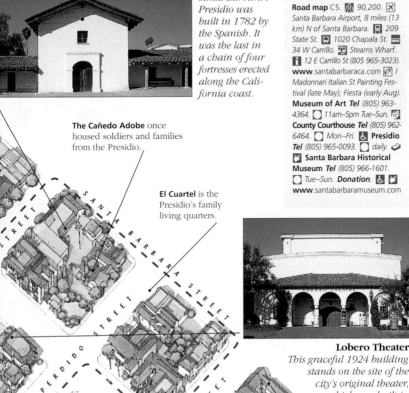

Lobero Theater
This graceful 1924 building stands on the site of the city's original theater, which was built in 1873 by Jose Lobero, an Italian musician.

Historical Museum
The Historical Society's collections are housed in two adobe buildings. Among the many artifacts is a statue of the 4th-century martyr St. Barbara.

To East Beach

| 0 meters | 100 |
| 0 yards | 100 |

Santa Barbara Mission

Labeled the "Queen of the Missions," Santa Barbara is the most visited mission in the state. Founded in 1786 on the feast day of St. Barbara, it was the tenth mission built by the Spanish *(see pp46–7)*. After the third adobe church on the site was destroyed by an earthquake in 1812, the present structure took shape and was completed in 1833. Its twin towers and mix of Roman, Moorish, and Spanish styles served as the main inspiration for what came to be known as Mission Style *(see p30)*. The mission was again hit by an earthquake in 1925, damaging the towers and façade of the church. These sections were repaired but, because of a chemical reaction between the alkalies and aggregates in the cement, the entire front had to be rebuilt in 1953, following the original design. Santa Barbara is the only California mission to have been in continuous use since it was founded.

Franciscan monk

Central Fountain
Palm trees tower above a central fountain in the Sacred Gardens.

A missionary's bedroom has been furnished as it would have been in the early 1800s.

Entrance

Arcaded Corridor
An open corridor fronts the museum rooms. Originally the living quarters, these now display a rich collection of mission artifacts.

Kitchen
The kitchen has been restored to show the typical cooking facilities of the early 1800s. Most of the food eaten was produced on the mission, which had fields and livestock.

STAR FEATURES

★ Church

★ Main Façade

★ Sacred Gardens

★ Sacred Gardens
*The beautifully landscaped
Sacred Gardens were once
a working area for Native
Americans to learn Western
trades. Workshops and some
living quarters were located
in the surrounding buildings.*

VISITORS' CHECKLIST

2201 Laguna St. **Tel** *(805) 682-
4713.* 🚌 *22.* 🕐 *9am–5pm
daily.* **Donation.** ✝ *7:30am
Mon–Fri; 4pm Sat; 7:30am, 9am,
10:30am, noon Sun.* 📷 ♿ 🛍

★ Church
*The narrow church has a
Neo-Classical interior.
Imitation marble columns
and detailing have been
painted on the walls and
doorways. The reredos has a
painted canvas backdrop
and carved wooden statues.*

The side chapel, next to
the altar, is dedicated to
the Blessed Sacrament.

The width of the nave
was determined by the
height of the trees used
as cross beams.

The cemetery garden
contains the graves of some
4,000 Native Americans as
well as friars.

★ Main Façade
*The church's Classical façade was
designed by Padre Antonio Ripoll.
Ripoll admired the Roman architect
Vitruvius Pollio (working around
27 BC) and drew heavily on his
ideas when building the church.*

San Buenaventura Mission's
church in Ventura

Ventura ⑮

Road map C5. 🏛 *102,000.* 🚌
🚏 *89C S California St.* **Tel** *(805) 648-2075.* **www**.ventura–usa.com

All that remains of the **San Buenaventura Mission**, founded in 1782 and completed in 1809, is a church with a courtyard garden and tiled fountain. A museum at the mission details the buildings of the original complex.

Two mid-19th-century adobe houses survive in the city. The tiny **Ortega Adobe** reveals the harsh living conditions many experienced at that time. In contrast, the Monterey-style *(see p30)* **Olivas Adobe** is a two-story ranch hacienda, furnished in period style, with rose and herb gardens.

Today Ventura is largely an agricultural center. Ventura Harbor Village has 30 stores, restaurants, a merry-go-round, and a community theater. Harbor and whale-watching cruises, as well as boats to the Channel Islands National Park depart from here. At the northern end of town, the **City Hall** (1913) has a copper-covered dome and marble exterior.

🏛 **San Buenaventura Mission**
211 E Main St. **Tel** *(805) 643-4318.* 🔲 *daily.* ● *Jan 1, Easter, Thanksgiving, Dec 25.*

🏛 **Ortega Adobe**
100 W Main St. **Tel** *(805) 658-4726.* 🔲 *daily.* ● *Jan 1, Easter Sun, Labor Day, Thanksgiving, Dec 25.*

🏛 **Olivas Adobe**
4200 Olivas Park Drive. **Tel** *(805) 648-5823.* **Grounds** 🔲 *daily.* **House** 🔲 *Sat & Sun.* ● *Jan 1, Easter, Thanksgiving, Dec 25.*

Channel Islands National Park ⑯

Road map C6. 🚉 *Ventura.* 🚌
Visitors' Center Tel *(805) 658-5730.* 🔲 *daily.* 🚢 *Island Packers, 1867 Spinnaker Drive (805 642-1393).*

The islands of Santa Barbara, Anacapa, San Miguel, Santa Cruz, and Santa Rosa together make up the Channel Islands National Park, a series of volcanic islands unpopulated by humans. Access to the islands is strictly monitored by park rangers, who issue landing permits from the Visitors' Center. Camping is allowed on all the islands, but visitors must make reservations at least two weeks in advance. They must also bring all their own food and water supplies, because there are none available on any of the five islands.

Depending on the island and the time of year, lucky visitors may spot dolphins, gray whales, and California brown pelicans on the passage across the Santa Barbara Channel. Wildlife on the small, picturesque islands is plentiful and includes cormorants, sea lions, elephant seals, and gulls.

Day trips to Anacapa, the nearest island to the mainland, offer an insight into this unique coastal ecosystem. Even more can be learned, however, by taking one of the various guided walks, conducted by park rangers, on all the islands. Visitors must stay on

California brown
pelican

the designated trails, and pets are not allowed.

The rock pools on all of the islands are rich in marine life, and the kelp forests surrounding the islands provide shelter for more than 1,000 plant and animal species.

The islands' many sea caves make sea-kayaking a unique and exciting experience. The snorkeling and scuba diving in this area are also considered to be among the best on the entire Pacific Coast.

Ronald Reagan Presidential Library ⑰

40 Presidential Drive, Simi Valley.
Road map C5. **Tel** *(800) 410-8354.* 🔲 *10am–5pm daily.* ● *Jan 1, Thanksgiving, Dec 25.* 📷 ♿
www.reagan.utexas.edu

President Reagan's papers are all archived in this Mission Revival-style structure. The library features a permanent exhibition documenting the life of Reagan and his wife, Nancy. There are also temporary exhibitions of gifts, costumes, works of art, and other objects related to his eight-year tenure in the White House. A full-size replica of the Oval Office is correct in every detail, and a large piece of the Berlin Wall, with its original graffiti, can be seen on the patio against the panoramic backdrop of the nearby Simi Hills and the Santa Susana Mountains.

Reconstruction of the Oval Office at the Reagan Presidential Library

Mission Revival arcade on Main Street, Ojai

Ojai ⓲

Road map C5. ⓶ 8,000. ▦ ▦
ℹ 150 W Ojai Ave. **Tel** (805) 646-
8126. **www**.ojaichamber.org

Founded in 1874, this town was originally called Nordhoff after the author Charles Nordhoff, who wrote a book promoting California in the 1870s. In 1917 the town was renamed Ojai, a Chumash Indian word for moon, a reference to the crescent-shaped valley where the town lies.

Ojai's Mission Revival arched arcade was funded by Edward J Libby, a glass-manufacturing millionaire, and was designed in 1917 by Richard Requa. Its tower was modeled on a campanile in Havana, Cuba. The arcade fronts two blocks of shops on the main street.

Barts Corner bookshop at No. 302 West Matilija Street has 25,000 volumes, many of which are displayed outdoors. Late-night readers can browse and then pay for their finds through a slot in the door. Spiritual groups have been going on retreats in the Ojai Valley since the 1920s. Today several New Age and religious organizations are based here.

Los Padres National Forest ⓳

Road map C5. ▦ Santa Barbara.
Visitors' Center ◯ 8:30am–4:30pm
Mon–Fri. **Tel** (805) 968-6640.

Los Padres National Forest covers almost 2 million acres (810,000 ha) of terrain that varies from desert to pine-clad mountains with peaks as high as 9,000 ft (2,700 m). Black bears, foxes, deer, and mountain lions are among the animals found here. Birds include golden eagles and giant condors. The latter are North America's largest birds with a wingspan of 9 ft (3 m).

Coastal redwood trees grow on the lower slopes, and the higher elevations are thick with firs, bristling with pine cones. Temperatures in the summer can be scorching, and there is very little, if any, rain here between May and October.

The forest is crisscrossed by hundreds of miles of hiking trails for experienced hikers, but there are few roads. Hwy 33 and Hwy 150 are two exceptions. Hwy 154 crosses one corner as it runs between Santa Ynez (see p218) and Santa Barbara (see pp220–23). On the way, it passes over the spectacular Cold Spring Arch Bridge.

Scattered within Los Padres National Forest are 88 camp sites. Activities include fishing, horseback riding, and, on Mount Pinos, skiing.

Bakersfield ⓴

Road map C5. ⓶ 384,000. ▦
ℹ 1325 P St. **Tel** (661) 325-5051.
www.bakersfieldcvb.org

Bakersfield was named after Colonel Thomas Baker, a settler who planted a field of alfalfa here. The shrub fed the animals of early travelers who rested here before crossing the Tehachapi Mountains, the "border" that divides Northern and Southern California.

The town can be reached on the I-5 from San Francisco, before the ascent up Grapevine Canyon to LA. It can also be reached from Santa Maria or Ojai through the Los Padres National Forest.

Bakersfield's modern history began with the discovery of gold in the 1850s and several oil strikes in the following decades. Many people from Mediterranean countries settled on the fertile land, bringing agriculture to the area.

Today it is among the fastest growing cities in California, but still manages to retain a rural feel and is a recognized center for country music. There are also fine antique shops and the **Kern County Museum**, a 16-acre (6.5-ha) outdoor museum. Bisecting Bakersfield, Kern River is renowned for its whitewater rafting and kayaking (see p612). Lake Isabella, 40 miles (65 km) east of the city, is a center for water sports.

🏛 **Kern County Museum**
3801 Chester Ave. **Tel** (661) 636-4000. ◯ daily. ● Jan 1, Thanksgiving, Dec 24, 25, 31. ⚑
www.kcmuseum.org

Cold Spring Arch Bridge, Los Padres National Forest

ORANGE COUNTY

A century ago Orange County lived up to its name. This dry, sunny land, which stretches from the Santa Ana Mountains to the beautiful Pacific coastline, was indeed scattered with orange orchards and farms. Today, the region is a mass of freeways and suburban housing. Visitors to the county can explore a wide range of museums, sites of historical interest, and entertainment complexes.

In the mid-1950s, the roads leading to the county's theme parks still passed through extensive orange groves. At that time, Disneyland was attracting its first enthusiastic crowds, and a local boy called Richard Nixon had become Vice President of the US. Today, orange groves have given way to urban development and fruit crate labels have become collectors' items. More than two million people live here, enjoying perennial sunshine and a high standard of living.

The coastline of Orange County is lined with wide, sandy beaches and a succession of legendary surfing haunts, marinas, and artists' enclaves. In the affluent coastal towns, few visitors can resist the temptation to seek out a clifftop bar and watch the sun set.

Inland lies a variety of cultural sights. Mission San Juan Capistrano, founded in 1776, is a reminder of the days of the Spanish Franciscan settlers. The Bowers Museum of Cultural Art in Santa Ana houses superb examples of the art of indigenous peoples from all around the world. At Yorba Linda, the impressive Richard Nixon Library and Birthplace commemorates the life of Orange County's most famous son.

Orange County is the entertainment capital of California. For visitors seeking family fun and roller-coaster thrills, there are the homey Knott's Berry Farm, America's oldest theme park, and the fantasy kingdom of Disneyland, which is, as the saying goes, "the most famous people-trap ever built by a mouse."

Reflecting Pool at the Richard Nixon Library and Birthplace

◁ **Log Ride at Knott's Berry Farm theme park**

Exploring Orange County

Much of Orange County's 798-sq mile (2,050-sq km)
area is covered with sprawling urban communities
linked by ever-busy freeways. Anaheim, home of
Disneyland, is its second largest city, after Santa Ana.
The popular Knott's Berry Farm theme park lies a few
miles northwest at Buena Park, and together these
cities form the tourist capital of the county. Most of
the coastline is built-up, but its communities have
more variety and character than those around the
theme parks. Inland, open spaces can be found
where the county's eastern region encompasses part of the vast Cleveland National
Forest and the Santa Ana Mountains.

Catalina Island's Two Harbors

SEE ALSO

La Habra

Los Angeles 90   Brea   York
                                         Lind
La Mirada

Long
Beach   **RICHARD NIXON LIBRARY
               AND BIRTHPLACE** ❸
               Fullerton

La Palma   91

**KNOTTS BERRY FARM
& SOAK CITY USA** ❷   Anaheim
               39   5   57   Vill
                                                   Parl
**DISNEYLAND
RESORT** ❶   **CRYSTAL
               ❹ CATHEDRAL**

               22 Garden Grove   Orange
Westminster   **BOWERS MUSEUM** ❺   Tusti
               405   **OF CULTURAL ART**
Seal Beach   Santa Ana

Bolsa Chica   Fountain   **DISCOVERY
State Beach   Valley   MUSEUM**
                                       ❻   Irvine
                                       55

               39
Huntington Beach   Costa Mesa
               Huntington
               State Beach
               Newport Beach   Balboa
                                       Island
               Corona del Mar
               State Beach
                              Crystal   La
                              Cove   B

Santa Catalina Island map

Silver Peak
550m
San Pedro Channel   Two Harbors

Black Jack Mountain
610m   Whitleys Peak
               648m
❽
**SANTA CATALINA
ISLAND**   Avalon

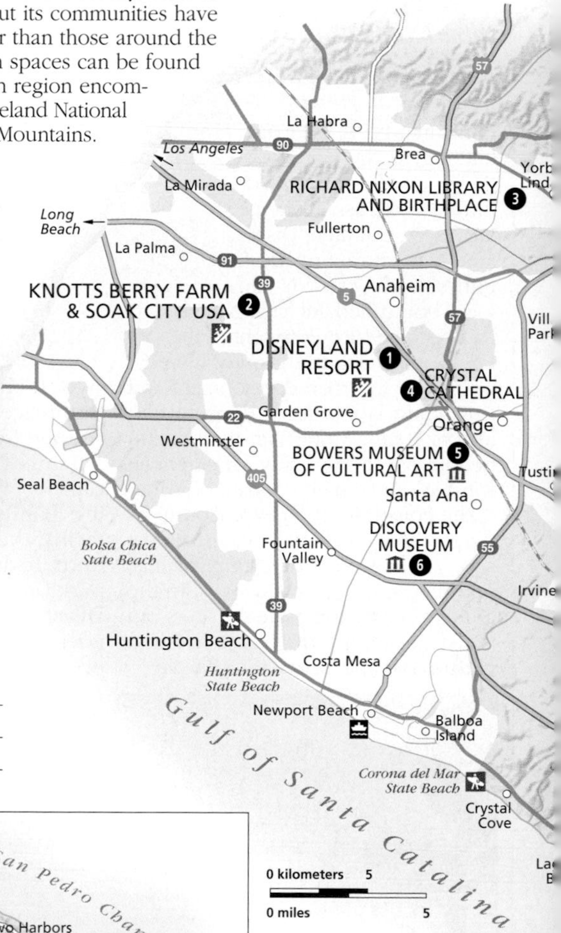

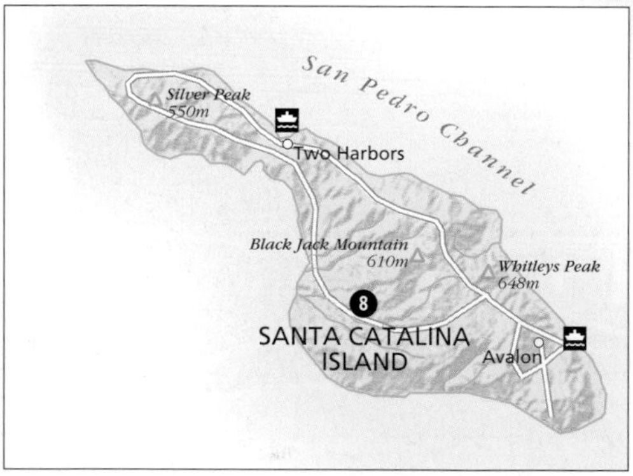

0 kilometers   5

0 miles   5

KEY

- Freeway
- Major road
- Secondary road
- Minor road
- Main railway
- Minor railway
- △ Summit

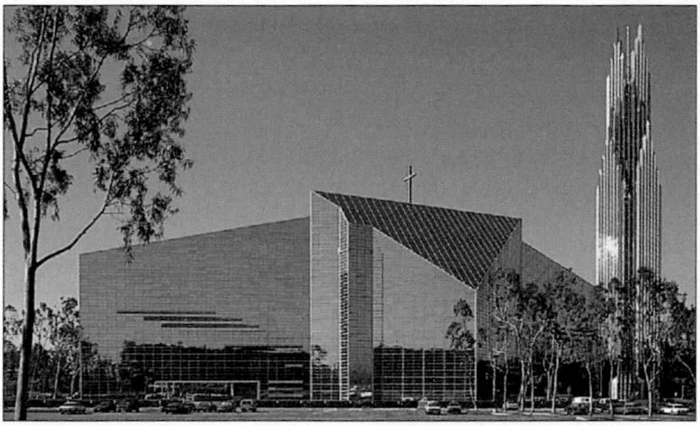

Enormous Crystal Cathedral at Garden Grove, south of Anaheim

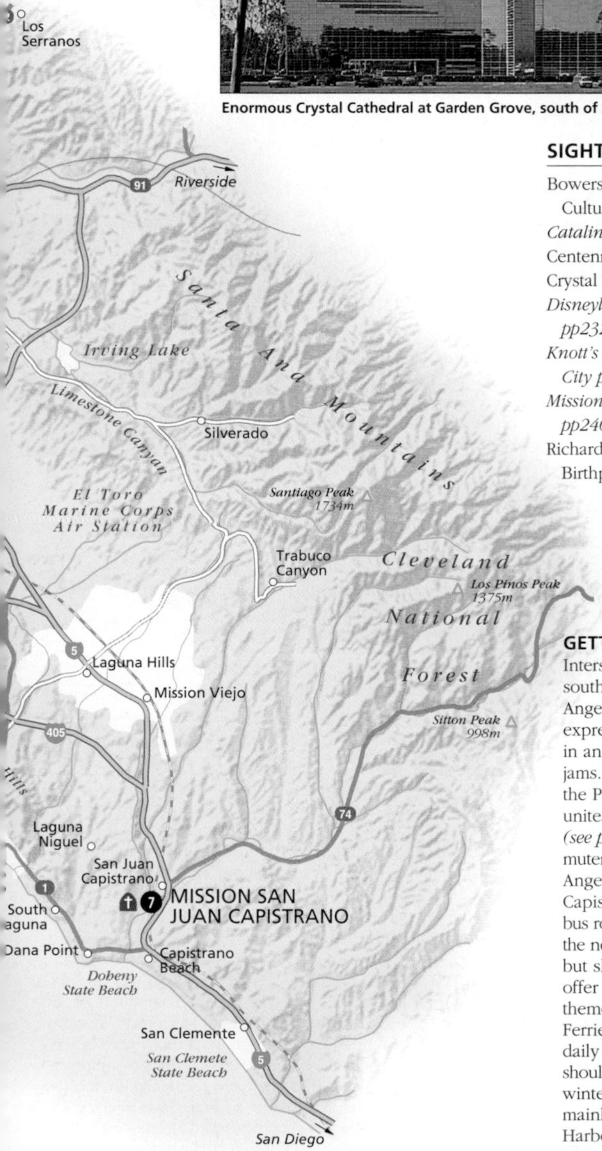

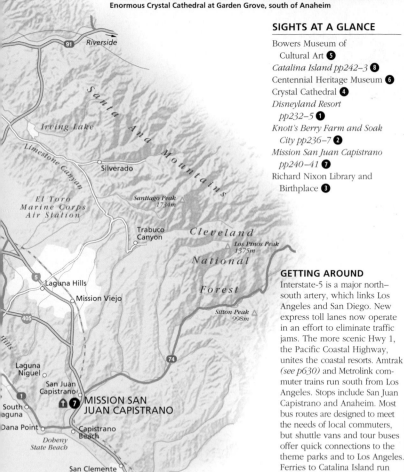

SIGHTS AT A GLANCE

Bowers Museum of Cultural Art [5]
Catalina Island pp242–3 [8]
Centennial Heritage Museum [6]
Crystal Cathedral [4]
Disneyland Resort pp232–5 [1]
Knott's Berry Farm and Soak City pp236–7 [2]
Mission San Juan Capistrano pp240–41 [7]
Richard Nixon Library and Birthplace [3]

GETTING AROUND

Interstate-5 is a major north–south artery, which links Los Angeles and San Diego. New express toll lanes now operate in an effort to eliminate traffic jams. The more scenic Hwy 1, the Pacific Coastal Highway, unites the coastal resorts. Amtrak *(see p630)* and Metrolink commuter trains run south from Los Angeles. Stops include San Juan Capistrano and Anaheim. Most bus routes are designed to meet the needs of local commuters, but shuttle vans and tour buses offer quick connections to the theme parks and to Los Angeles. Ferries to Catalina Island run daily in summer, but travelers should check schedules in winter. Crossings from the mainland to Avalon or Two Harbors take 1–2 hours.

Orange County Coastline

The beaches and resorts that make up Orange County's coast are Southern California at its most classic. The northern shoreline is flat and low-lying. South of the Balboa Peninsula, the coast features scenic cliffs and sheltered coves. Million-dollar homes, luxury marinas, constant sports activity, and a fashionable lifestyle reflect the wealth and vitality of its communities.

The Balboa Pavilion
opened in 1905 as a terminal for the Pacific Electric Red Car Line from LA. Stars of the Big Band era, such as Count Basie, played here in the 1930s and 1940s. Today the wooden pavilion is a restaurant and center for sightseeing cruises around Newport Harbor.

★ **Huntington State Beach** ③
🏃 ⛱ 🏊 🚻 ♿ 🚹 🅿️ 🚲
A premier Californian "surf city." Huntington Beach has a surfing museum, international competitions, and waters full of surfers whose exploits can be watched from the long pier.

Upper Newport Bay Ecological Preserve *is a 750-acre (300-ha) wedge of coastal wetland providing a refuge for wildlife and migratory birds. Facilities in the bay include a bike path, fishing, and guided tours on foot and by kayak.*

KEY

🚊	Freeway
━	Major road
═	Minor road
〰	River
🌿	Viewpoint

Seal Beach ①
🏃 ⛱ 🏊 🚻 ♿ 🚹
This is a quiet, 1-mile (1.6-km) long beach with level sand and some surfers. The wooden pier is popular with anglers. A walk along its 1,865-ft (570-m) length offers views northward to the high-rise buildings of Long Beach *(see pp132–3)*.

Bolsa Chica State Beach ②
🏃 ⛱ 🏊 🚻 ♿ 🚹 🚲
The name Bolsa Chica means "little pocket" in Spanish. Flat, wilderness sands, oil extractors, and the protected wetlands of the 300-acre (120-ha) Bolsa Chica Ecological Reserve give this beach a unique atmosphere.

Newport Beach ④
🏃 ⛱ 🏊 🚻 ♿ 🚹
Famous for its million-dollar homes and lifestyles to match, Newport Beach boasts a 3-mile (5-km) stretch of wide sand and two piers. Fresh fish, caught by the historic Dory fishing fleet, is sold beside Newport Pier at the northern end of the beach.

Aliso Beach ⑦
🏃 ⛱ 🏊 🚻 ♿ 🚹
At the mouth of Aliso Creek lies this small, sandy beach. The 620-ft (190-m) long concrete pier is used by anglers. At the southern end of the beach is a marine life refuge with beds of giant kelp offshore.

Doheny State Beach ⑧
🏃 ⛱ 🏊 🚻 ♿ 🚹 🅿️ 🚲
This sandy beach and marine life refuge is close to the mouth of San Juan Creek. The beach attracts a typically Southern Californian mix of swimmers, surfers, bird-watchers, anglers, cyclists, and campers.

San Clemente State Beach ⑨
🏃 ⛱ 🏊 🚻 ♿ 🚹 🅿️ 🚲
The hillside community of San Clemente has a narrow, sandy beach at its foot. Near the railroad station there is a municipal pier. Farther south, the 100-acre (40-ha) State Beach has landscaped facilities including picnic areas and a camp site.

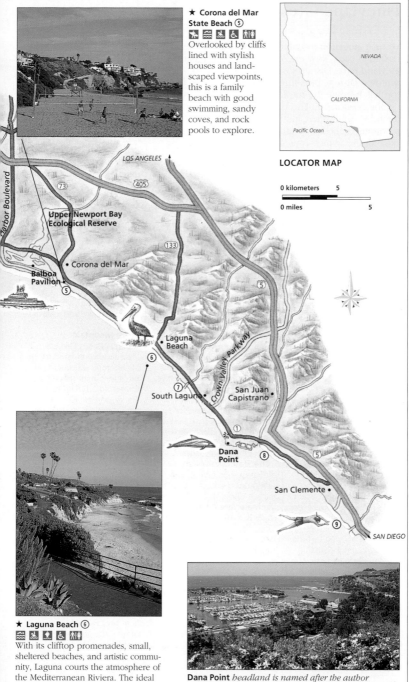

★ Corona del Mar State Beach [5]

🏄 🌊 🏊 ♿ 🚻

Overlooked by cliffs lined with stylish houses and landscaped viewpoints, this is a family beach with good swimming, sandy coves, and rock pools to explore.

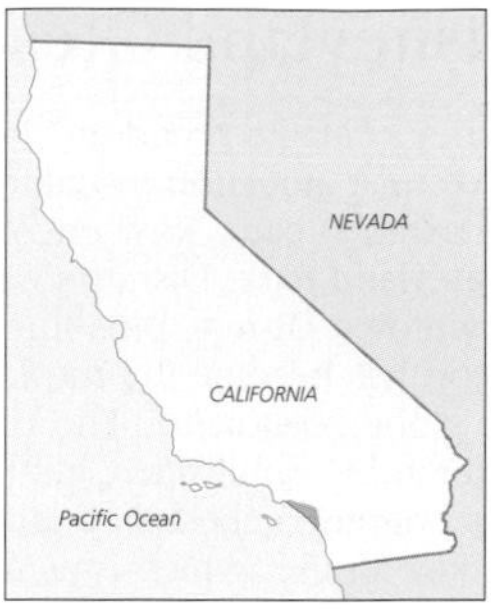
NEVADA
CALIFORNIA
Pacific Ocean

LOCATOR MAP

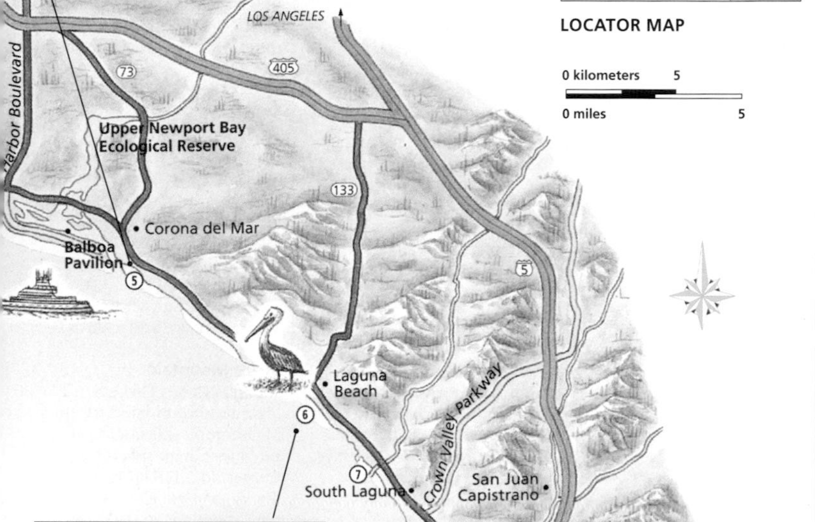
0 kilometers 5
0 miles 5
LOS ANGELES
Harbor Boulevard
73
405
Upper Newport Bay Ecological Reserve
133
Corona del Mar
Balboa Pavilion
5
5
Laguna Beach
6
Crown Valley Parkway
7
South Laguna
San Juan Capistrano

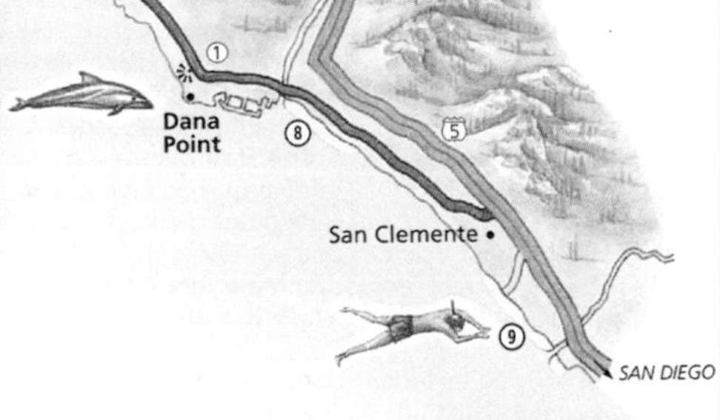
1
Dana Point
8
5
San Clemente
9
SAN DIEGO

★ Laguna Beach [6]

🌊 🏊 🐚 ♿ 🚻

With its clifftop promenades, small, sheltered beaches, and artistic community, Laguna courts the atmosphere of the Mediterranean Riviera. The ideal spot for a cocktail at sunset, Laguna is famous for its summer arts festival, the Pageant of the Masters *(see p37)*.

Dana Point *headland is named after the author Richard Dana, whose 1840 book* Two Years Before the Mast *chronicled the early days of California. A replica of the contemporary brig,* Pilgrim, *is moored in the harbor.*

Disneyland® Resort ❶

Disney's "Magic Kingdom" in Anaheim is not only the top tourist attraction in California, it is part of the American Dream. Now encompassing the original Disneyland Park, Disney's California Adventure, Downtown Disney, plus three enormous hotels, the Resort has become the model for theme parks around the globe. Visitors to "The Happiest Place on Earth" find fantasy, thrill rides, glittering shows, and shopping in a brightly orchestrated land of lines, fireworks, and Mickey Mouse, which is as American as apple pie.

Exploring the Resort

Spread over 85 acres (34 ha), the original Disneyland Park is divided into eight theme areas, known as "lands." Transportation around the park is provided by the Disneyland Railroad and monorail. Disney's California Adventure Park has three theme areas *(see p235)*. Smaller in area than Disneyland Park, Disney's California Adventure is easily covered by walking. This newest venture into nostalgia Disney-style is more suited to the interests and tastes of teenagers and young adults, as the rides and attractions may be too intense for toddlers. In the heart of the Resort, between the two theme parks, lies Downtown Disney. This lively area is full of restaurants, shops, and innovative entertainment venues.

It takes at least three days to make the best of a visit, now that the Resort has grown so large. A joint ticket *(see p233)* can be bought for all the theme parks; it provides access to all the rides and shows, and includes a park map, and a schedule of the day's events. Both parks stay open late in the evening during the peak seasons; and the **Fireworks Show** in Disneyland and in Downtown Disney are well worth losing a little sleep for.

MAIN STREET USA

This spotlessly clean, colorful street lined with turn-of-the-century buildings welcomes visitors to Disneyland. The circular **Central Plaza** is where the daily "Parade of the Stars," takes place, featuring cheerfully waving Disney characters and scenes from many of Disney's most famous movies. This is only one of the places where guests can meet and talk with many of the famous Disney cartoon characters. If you're lucky, you can find ample opportunities here for photographs and videos.

City Hall offers maps, dining and entertainment schedules, and general information about the park, while the **Main Street Cinema** screens early Disney silent films. Main Street itself has a large selection of attractions, shops, and places to eat.

TOMORROWLAND

Visions of the future inspire the attractions here, and sights change regularly to keep one step ahead of real-life technology and still retain a sense of fantasy. One of the first attractions in 1955 was **Autopia**, now completely redesigned and updated to take guests into a parallel universe from a car's point of view. The track winds through Tomorrowland and Fantasyland.

Star Tours

Designed in collaboration with the *Star Wars* genius George Lucas, the use of flight-simulator technology makes this one of the most realistic rides in the park. Visitors board a Star-Speeder space-ship and are taken on a wild ride through outer space strewn with star-ships, comets, and asteroids.

Space Mountain

A hands-down Disneyland favorite and updated for the Millennium, this attraction provides a high speed roller-coaster ride, 118 ft (36 m) above ground. Conducted almost entirely in darkness, the ride has sudden meteoric flashes, celestial showers, and space-age music. Not suitable for very young children.

MICKEY'S TOONTOWN

The colorful architecture of cartoons comes to life in this three-dimensional cartoon world, Mickey Mouse's hometown. All of

TOP 5 ATTRACTIONS

★ Pirates of the Caribbean

★ Haunted Mansion

★ Space Mountain

★ Matterhorn Bobsleds

★ Star Tours

SHOPPING

The Disneyland shops, particularly those along Main Street, USA, are often busy late in the day, especially at closing time. If you can, it is worth making your purchases earlier in the day and then collecting them later from the Redemption Center. Although many of the goods on sale in the theme park bear the faces of Disney characters, each of the eight lands adds its own variations to what is on offer to buy. In Adventureland, for example, you can buy Indiana Jones-style clothing and Native American Crafts are on sale in Frontierland. The Disney Gallery in New Orleans Square sells limited-edition lithographs by the Disney cartoonists. The largest of all the shops within the Magic Kingdom is the Emporium in Main Street.

For hotels and restaurants in this region see pp534–5 and pp579–81

Fairytale facade of Sleeping Beauty Castle in Fantasyland

VISITORS' CHECKLIST

1313 Harbor Blvd, Anaheim.
Tel *(714) 781-7290.* [cross] *(714) 781-4565.* [plane] *from LAX.* [bus] *435.* [clock] *Jun–Aug: 8am–midnight daily; Sep–May: 9am–6pm daily.* [icons]
[computer] **www**.disneyland.com

canal boats and the Mad Hatter's giant spinning teacups. There are almost twice as many attractions to enjoy here as in most of the other lands, and the constant crowds illustrate the enduring appeal of this area.

Matterhorn Bobsleds

This historic attraction and major park landmark has been providing "icy" roller-coaster rides since 1959. A copy of the famous peak near Zermatt in Switzerland, the Matterhorn Mountain towers 147 ft (45 m) above the park. Bobsleds carrying four passengers climb to the mountain's snow-capped summit, then drop into a steep, high-speed descent, zooming in and out of the hollow peak, passing glacier caves and waterfalls as they go. At the end of the trip, riders in the front seats are splashed as the sleds careen into a lake.

It's a Small World

This show offers a Utopian vision of global harmony and the famous song, repeated throughout the ride. Colorful boats transport passengers through the attraction, which features nearly 300 singing-and-dancing Audio-Animatronics dolls, all in intricate national costumes.

Disney's favorite animated characters reside here. This is the part of the park where visitors are most likely to find Mickey, Goofy, and other well-known cartoon characters strolling around, having their pictures taken with guests.

The most popular celebrity residences are Mickey's house and Minnie's cottage, where subtle touches typify Disney's legendary attention to detail.Most of the attractions in this area are geared toward kids from age three up. **Chip 'n Dale Treehouse**, a mini-roller coaster, **Goofy's Bounce House**, and a floating bumper-boat ride offer gentle excitement for this younger set.

Roger Rabbit's Car Toon Spin is Toontown's largest and most popular attraction. It's spinning cars provide a madcap taxi drive through a surreal cartoon world fraught with near misses.

FANTASYLAND

Dominated by the pink and gold towers of **Sleeping Beauty Castle** and a replica of the **Matterhorn**, Fantasyland is a shrine to children's dreams and adult nostalgia. Nursery heroes such as Peter Pan, Dumbo, and Snow White provide the themes for gentle fairytale rides in vehicles that range from flying galleons

TICKETS AND TIPS

A basic one-day ticket to Disneyland or Disney's California Adventure covers admission and most of the rides and attractions. Parking is extra, as are certain shows, food, and arcades. Multi-day tickets for three to four days and Annual Passports allow unlimited admission and access to rides and attractions. Fastpass lets guests obtain a voucher with a computer-assigned boarding time for specific attractions or rides. This eliminates waiting in long lines. You can also save time at the front gate by buying your tickets in advance.at any Disney store or online at www.disney.com. To help you plan your day, there is updated information on showtimes, waiting times and ride closures at the information board at the end of Main St, opposite the Plaza Pavilion.

Mark Twain Riverboat navigating the Rivers of America

FRONTIERLAND

This area is inspired by the adventurous days of the Wild West. Skirt-lifting song and dance take place on the **Golden Horseshoe Jamboree** stage. Every weekend at night the spectacular **Fantasmic!** show, complete with fireworks, sound effects, and live performers light up the

skies above Frontierland. The **Mark Twain River-boat** offers visitors a 15-minute cruise on a paddle-wheel boat. While it crosses the Rivers of America, look out for the plastic moose and deer inhabiting the forests along the shore and on Tom Sawyer Island.

Thrill-seekers love the **Big Mountain Thunder Railroad** roller-coaster ride. Open ore trucks set off from the 1880s mining town of Big Thunder without a driver. The runaway train then speeds through the cavernous interior of Big Thunder Mountain, narrowly escaping boulders and waterfalls. Remember that this ride has height and age restrictions.

CRITTER COUNTRY

Built in a rustic style, based on the rugged American Northwest, Critter Country is a 4-acre (1.6-ha) area next to Frontierland. Home of Splash Mountain, one of the most popular attractions in Disneyland, and a quiet restaurant, the Hungry Bear.

Splash Mountain
This is a winding, watery ride in hollowed-out logs. Brer Rabbit and Brer Fox are among the furry, singing characters from the 1946 film

Song of the South, who inhabit the mountain through which the ride passes. The ride culminates in a plummet down a steep waterfall. As on the Matterhorn ride, people in the front seats will get wet.

Davy Crockett's Explorer Canoes
Groups can take to the water and row downriver frontier-style. Guides provide lessons and ensure safety.

Teddi Barra's Swingin' Arcade
In keeping with the spirit of Critter Country, this is a frontier-style gallery of electronic games.

NEW ORLEANS SQUARE

This charming town square is modeled on the French Quarter in New Orleans, as it was in that city's heyday in the 19th century. The buildings have wrought-iron balconies and house interesting French-style shops.

Haunted Mansion
Some of the visitors to this attraction, which promises 999 "ghosts and ghouls," are now so familiar with its introductory commentary that they join in as they descend into its spooky world of mischievous spirits and grave-diggers. The ethereal

---

DOWNTOWN DISNEY

Located between the entrances to Disneyland park and Disney's California Adventure, Downtown Disney® is a garden paradise, offering guests some 300,000 sq.ft. of innovative restaurants, shops, and entertainment venues. The fact that this area has no admission fee makes Downtown Disney® one of the more popular – but crowded – spaces. A 12-screen AMC Theatre®, ESPN Zone™, and a LEGO Imagination Center® are the top attractions here. The snack shops, top-notch restaurants, plus a vast range of retail and specialty shops and a travel center, create a total Disney experience.

For hotels and restaurants in this region see pp534–5 and pp579–81

figures, including a talking woman's head in a crystal ball, are extremely realistic.

Pirates of the Caribbean
This show provides a floating ride through a yo-ho-ho world of ruffians and wenches who have been empowered with the gifts of song, dance, and heavy drinking by Audio-Animatronics. This technique, which brings models to life using electronic impulses to control their sounds and actions, was perfected at Disneyland.

The Disney Gallery
Visitors interested in the art behind the world of Disney should visit this gallery, located above the entrance to Pirates of the Caribbean. Some of the original artwork and designs for Disney's elaborate projects are on display here.

ADVENTURELAND

The exotic atmosphere in Adventureland offers dark, humid waterways lined with tropical plants. This is the smallest, but perhaps the most adventuresome, "land" in the park. **The Enchanted Tiki Room** showcases mechanical singing birds in a zany, musical romp through the tropics.

Indiana Jones™ Adventure
Inspired by the 1982 film trilogy, passengers set off on a jeep-style drive through the Temple of the Forbidden Eye.

Theatrical props and scenery, a realistic soundtrack, sensational film images, and the physical sensation of a roller coaster make this the ultimate experience created by Disneyland to date.

Jungle Cruise
This safari-style boat ride through a jungle forest full of rampant apes and bloodthirsty headhunter is narrated by a real-life captain, who tells his captive audience terrible but amusing jokes during the ride through steamy waterways.

Tarzan™'s Treehouse
A climb-up, climb-through experience, starring Tarzan and Jane, with an interactive and musical play area at the base of the tree.

Disney's California Adventure

The newest star in Anaheim is Disney's California Adventure, adjacent to Disneyland and built on 55 acres (22 ha) of the old parking lot. Disney's California Adventure is divided into three primary "lands," each offering themed experiences that celebrate the California dream. The emphasis here is on adults and older teens, but there are still plenty of rides and attractions that appeal to all ages. Together with the original Disneyland Park, Disney's California Adventure adds to the Disney legend.

HOLLYWOOD PICTURES BACKLOT

The Backlot offers a great tongue-in-cheek view of the motion picture industry. There are two blocks of facades and fakery, giving the visitor a Disney-eye view of the Hollywood. The **Hyperion Theater** features staged live musical shows, and at Jim Henson's **Muppet*Vision 3-D** you can see Miss Piggy and Kermit and all the lovable Muppet characters in a salute to movie making.

GOLDEN STATE

A tribute to the state's topography and agriculture, the rock-carved Grizzly Peak stands as the landmark icon of California Adventure. The centerpiece ride is **Soarin' Over California**, a simulated hang-glider ride that portrays the beauties of California's varied landscape on a huge wrap-around screen. There is no narrative, but guests can feel the wind currents and smell the scent of orange blossoms as they soar 40 feet (12 m) aloft. **Bountiful Valley** features healthy snacks and a 3-D film starring Flik from *A Bug's Life*. Smell-o-Vision and touchy-feelies make this a completely buggy experience for all.

PARADISE PIER

Considerably lower key than the thrill rides in the original park, Paradise Pier is the place where roller coasters, Ferris wheels, and parachute rides rule. **California Screamin'**, the giant Sun Wheel, **Boardwalk Games**, and **King Triton's Carousel** are reminiscent of seaside recreation parks of years ago.

Grizzly River Run is California Adventure's signature attraction

Knott's Berry Farm and Soak City USA ❷

Statues of cowboys on a Ghost Town bench

Knott's Berry Farm has grown from a 1920s boysenberry farm to a 21st-century multi-day entertainment complex. America's first theme park offers more than 165 different rides and attractions, but its main charm lies in its emphasis on authenticity. The Old West Ghost Town at the heart of the park has original ghost town buildings and artifacts. Located in Buena Vista in Orange County, a half-hour drive from LA, Knott's offers six themed areas, dozens of live-action stages, thrill rides, shopping and dining, and a full-fledged resort.

STAR FEATURES

★ Old West Ghost Town

★ Camp Snoopy

★ Soak City USA

GHOSTRIDER

Built in 1998, this mega-woodie has risen to the top of the "best coaster ride" list. The initial drop of 108 ft (33 m) at speeds approaching 60 mph (97km/h), the 2.5-minute ride is a must for every visitor to the Old Ghost Town.

OLD WEST GHOST TOWN

This 1880s Goldrush town has authentic century-old buildings lining its streets. An 1880 steam train, the **Ghost Town & Calico Railroad**, circles the park, and a genuine **Overland Trails stagecoach** takes passengers on a trip into the past.

The **Gold Trails Hotel and Mercantile**, a restored Kansas school-house, and the **Western Trails Museum** are chock full of Wild West memorabilia and artifacts. Visitors can pan for gold at the **Old Farm Mine** or join a line-dance at **Calico Square**. The **Ghost Rider Log Ride** floats visitors through a real 1880s sawmill before plunging down a 42-foot (13-m) waterfall. At the heart of Ghost Town, the spectacular 4533-ft- (1382-m)-long **GhostRider** wooden roller coaster towers over the park.

Largest wooden coaster in the United States at 118 ft (36 m) high

4,533-ft (1,382-m) long track

An 1880 steam engine transports visitors around the park

CAMP SNOOPY

Inspired by the majestic High Sierra, Camp Snoopy's six-acre (2.4-ha) wonderland is an interactive participatory children's paradise. There are 30 kid-tested attractions and pint-sized rides, hosted by the beloved Peanuts characters Snoopy, Lucy, and Charlie Brown. Children under 12 delight in the **Timberline Twister** roller coaster, the Red Baron's airplanes, and an old-fashioned Ferris wheel, where parents and kids can soar over the park for some wonderful views. The **Charlie Brown Speedway** appeals to little stock-car enthusiasts and their parents. There's a barnyard for petting baby animals, a swinging bridge competition, rushing waterfalls, and lively musical shows – all themed to the Peanuts comic strip.

Kids get behind the wheel at the Charlie Brown Speedway

FIESTA VILLAGE

Celebrating California's Spanish legacy, Fiesta Village offers a collection of south-of-the-border adventures and high-energy thrills. **Casa Arcada** challenges the whole family to the latest video technology, while a ride on the world's oldest **Dentzel Carousel** is a nostalgic treat. Two large roller coasters, the **Jaguar** and **Montezooma's Revenge** provide the thrills. End your day with a sizzling fireworks and laser display at **Reflection Lake.**

Replica of Philadelphia's Independence Hall

INDIAN TRAILS

Intricate arts and crafts of Native Americans from the Pacific Northwest, Great Plains, Southwest, and Far West are showcased in this area. Totem poles and tipis from the Blackfoot, Nez Perce, and Arapaho tribes seen throughout Indian Trails were built to convey the beauty and diversity of Native American culture. Through participatory learning adventures and exquisite artworks, visitors will understand how the people lived, and how their beliefs, climate, and environment influenced their daily lives.

THE BOARDWALK

A continuous beach party is the theme here, where everything centers around Southern California's seaside culture. Beachside concessions and the most radical thrill rides rule: **Supreme Scream** simulates a rocket launch while the **Perilous Plunge** is not for the faint of heart. Then, relax and take in a big-stage show at the **Charles M. Schultz Theater.**

WILD WATER WILDERNESS

Experience the magic of the 1900s river wilderness with a raging white-water river, soaring geysers, and a giant waterfall – **Bigfoot Rapids** will fulfill your wildest dreams. The multi-sensory **Mystery Lodge** celebrates Native American culture, complete with an Indian storyteller, music, and dance.

The **Ranger Station** has a resident naturalist who makes friends with Sasquatch, the California High Sierra creature also known as Bigfoot.

SOAK CITY USA

Southern California's newest water adventure park has 21 awesome water rides – all themed to the 1950s and 1960s surfing culture.

Adjacent to Knott's main park, and separately gated, Soak City USA serves up 13 water-logged acres (5.3 ha),

VISITORS' CHECKLIST

8039 Beach Blvd, Buena Park.
Tel (714) 827-1776.
(714) 220-5200. 29,
38, 42. daily. Opening
hours vary daily and seasonally.
Phone ahead for details.
Dec 25.
www.knotts.com

replete with tube and body slides, surfing pipelines, a six-lane super slide, and **Tidal Wave Bay**, a special pool with gentle to moderate wave action. **Gremmie Lagoon** is a wet kid's playground with hands-on fun.

All rides have age and height requirements. There are plenty of places to snack and buy souvenirs; men's and women's changing rooms and lockers are also available.

RADISSON RESORT, KNOTT'S BERRY FARM

Under this umbrella are Southern California's three finest entertainment venues: Knott's Berry Farm Theme Park, Soak City USA, and the Radisson Resort. Guests in the 321-room hotel can stay in Snoopy-themed suites and take advantage of the pools, sports facilities, fitness center, and children's activity area. First-rate restaurants, such as Cucina! Cucina! Italian Cafe add to the festive atmosphere. There are, of course, special rates for frequent guests, value-added packages.

Spectacular water rides at Soak City USA

House in which Richard Nixon was born

aspects of US presidential history, such as the visits paid to the White House by such pop stars as Elvis Presley.

Crystal Cathedral ❹

12141 Lewis St, Garden Grove. **Tel** (714) 971-4013. 🚌 45 N. ☐ Mon–Sat. ♿ 📷 ⛪ 9:30am, 11am, 6:00pm Sun. www.crystalcathedral.org

Constructed from an elaborate maze of white steel trusses covered with more than 10,000 panes of silvered glass, the Crystal Cathedral is a shimmering monument to the television-led evangelism that enthrals millions of Americans today. The cathedral, which can comfortably hold almost 3,000 worshipers, is the pulpit from which its founder, Dr. Robert H Schuller, broadcasts his famous "Hour of Power" service live on Sundays.

Everything about this unique cathedral is large – music is provided by one of the biggest pipe organs in the world, and there is a 15-ft (4.6-m) wide color video screen. A huge glass door opens during the

Richard Nixon Library and Birthplace ❸

Road map D6. 18001 Yorba Linda Blvd. **Tel** (714) 993-5075. 🚗 to Fullerton. ☐ 10am–5pm Mon–Sat; 11am–5pm Sun. ● Thanksgiving, Dec 25. 📷 ♿ 📷 www.nixonlibrary.org

The life and achievements of the Republican politician Richard Nixon, president of the United States from 1969 to 1974, are celebrated in this museum and archive. In the immaculately landscaped grounds is the simple wooden house where the former president was born in 1913. Nearby are a Reflecting Pool and the graves of Nixon and his wife, Pat, marked by matching black granite tombstones.

In the museum, a walk-through exhibit provides a chronological account of Nixon's rise and fall, emphasizing his role as a peacemaker and international statesman. The Foreign Affairs gallery has a reconstruction of a Chinese pavilion housing an exhibit on Nixon's 1972 state visit to China. There is also a replica of St. Basil's Cathedral in Moscow, with a display on Nixon's trip to the Soviet Union that same year.

Don't miss the World Leaders' Room, where statues of famous politicians are surrounded by some of the many gifts that Nixon received while in office, such as a 6th-century BC statue of the goddess Isis from Anwar Sadat of Egypt, a Sonia Delaunay painting from Georges Pompidou of France,

and a malachite jewelry box from Leonid Brezhnev of the Soviet Union.

Historic items exhibited in other galleries include a three-billion-year-old lump of rock from the moon, a 12-ft (3.5-m) section of the Berlin Wall, and dresses worn by the First Lady. Visitors are able to eavesdrop on the infamous "Watergate Tapes," which led to Nixon's resignation. In the Presidential Forum, a touch-screen exhibit using archive footage allows visitors to put questions to the late president. In additional galleries changing exhibitions are held. These cover popular

Vast interior of the Crystal Cathedral in Garden Grove

Sunday services, to enable the drive-in congregation outside to listen to the service without leaving their cars. The memorial cemetery has a capacity of 10,000.

Designed in 1980 by Philip Johnson, the star-shaped cathedral is both a spiritual shrine and an architectural wonder. Beside the building is a 236-ft (72-m) steeple, added in 1990 and adorned with polished stainless-steel prisms.

The cathedral represents the culmination of a lengthy evangelical crusade that began in 1955 when the indefatigable Dr. Schuller started preaching in a nearby drive-in theater. Today he has many followers in the US, Canada, and Australia.

Worshipers come from afar to attend pageants performed at Christmas and Easter, featuring people dressed as angels flying from the ceiling.

There are free tours of the cathedral and to the adjacent Southern California Community Church, the drive-in church that preceded it. The original drive-in theater where it all began is still standing nearby.

Bowers Museum of Cultural Art ❺

2002 N Main St, Santa Ana. **Road map** D6. *Tel* (714) 567-3600. 🚆 to Anaheim. 🚌 45 S. ◯ 11am–6pm Tue–Sun. ◯ Jan 1, Jul 4, Thanksgiving, Dec 25. 🎟️ ♿ 📷 (Sat–Sun).**www**.bowers.org

The Bowers has long been considered to be Orange County's leading art museum. Its serene Mission-style buildings house rich permanent collections and high-profile temporary exhibitions. There is a stylish California café and a shop packed with ethnic crafts and art books.

The museum was founded in 1932. Its display of African masks, collected by Paul and Ruth Tishman and now on long-term loan from the Disney Corporation, is reason enough for a pilgrimage. Other galleries, with exhibitions of treasures from the pre-colonial cultures of Southeast Asia, Oceania, Mexico, and Native

Entrance arch leading to the Bowers Museum of Cultural Art

America, reflect the museum's commitment to art of indigenous peoples. Fascinating examples of their crafts illustrate both the religious beliefs and the daily lives of these people. The upstairs galleries, decorated with 1930s murals and plaster work, cover the mission and rancho periods of California and Orange County history (*see pp46–7*). One block away, a former bank has been converted into the companion **Kidseum**, where kids can enjoy arts-related activities and can try on masks and costumes from all over the world.

Mayan statuette (AD 800–950), Bowers Museum

🏛️ Kidseum
1802 N Main St, Santa Ana. *Tel* (714) 480-1520. ◯ 10am–4pm Sat & Sun only. 🎟️ ♿ **www**.bowers.org

Centennial Heritage Museum ❻

3101 W Harvard St, Santa Ana. **Road map** D6. *Tel* (714) 540-0404. 🚆 to Anaheim. 🚌 45 S. ◯ 1–5pm Wed–Fri; 11am –3pm Sun. ◯ Jan 1, Easter Sun, Thanksgiving, Dec 25. 🎟️ ♿ 📷 www.centennialmuseum.org

Victorian times in Orange County are brought to life in this curious three-story mansion, built in 1898 by a civil engineer, Hiram Clay Kellogg.

Fascinated by ships, Kellogg incorporated several nautical design features into his Santa Ana residence. The oval, cabinlike dining room has an oak and walnut floor, laid in strips to resemble a ship's deck. Some of the drawers in the built-in wooden cabinets can also be opened from the kitchen, on the other side of the wall. Clusters of fruit are painted on the ceiling, and the room is overlooked by an elegant circular staircase with a mastlike central pillar.

The mansion now houses an exciting and child-friendly museum, which is also of historic and architectural interest to adults. Young visitors are given the opportunity to dress up in genuine antique clothing and experience life as it was at the turn of the century.

Upstairs, rooms are furnished with antique school desks, dolls' houses, and period games. In the master bedroom, now the textile room, a treadle sewing machine and spinning wheel are on display. Downstairs, you can investigate such instruments as a stereoscope and a hand-crank telephone, and see the old fashioned kitchen that has an icebox and butter churn. Next door is an 1899 ranch house, carriage barn, and water tower. There is also an orchard of orange trees – now a rare sight in the county.

Implements for orange cultivation at the Centennial Heritage Museum

Mission San Juan Capistrano ❼

Statue of St. John of Capistran

This beautiful "Jewel of the Missions" was founded in 1776, and its chapel is the only surviving building in California in which the famous Father Junípero Serra *(see p46)* preached. One of the largest and most prosperous in the whole chain, the mission was crowned by a Great Stone Church, completed in 1806. Six years later this was destroyed by an earthquake, leaving a ruined shell set amid a rambling complex of adobe and brick buildings. A restoration program, ornamental gardens, and many historical exhibits now enable visitors to imagine the mission's former glory.

★ Padres' Living Quarters
The fathers of Mission San Juan Capistrano lived in sparsely furnished rooms and slept on hard plank beds. Visitors enjoyed more comfortable accommodation.

The kitchens have corner ovens and displays of utensils.

A domed hut, built from wooden poles, resembles the traditional dwellings of Native American villages at the time of the mission.

Sacred Garden Bells
The original four bells from the Great Stone Church now hang in the wall of a small garden. The larger pair date from 1796.

Junípero Serra
A statue of Father Serra and a Native American boy stands in a corner of the gardens.

STAR FEATURES

★ Courtyard Gardens

★ Padres' Living Quarters

★ Serra's Chapel

VISITORS' CHECKLIST

Camino Capistrano & Ortega
Hwy. **Road map** D6. **Tel** (949)
234-1300. ☐ 8:30am–5pm
daily. ◯ Good Fri pm, Thanksgiving, Dec 25. ▣ ◎ ⬡ ▯
▰ ▨ Swallow Festival (March).

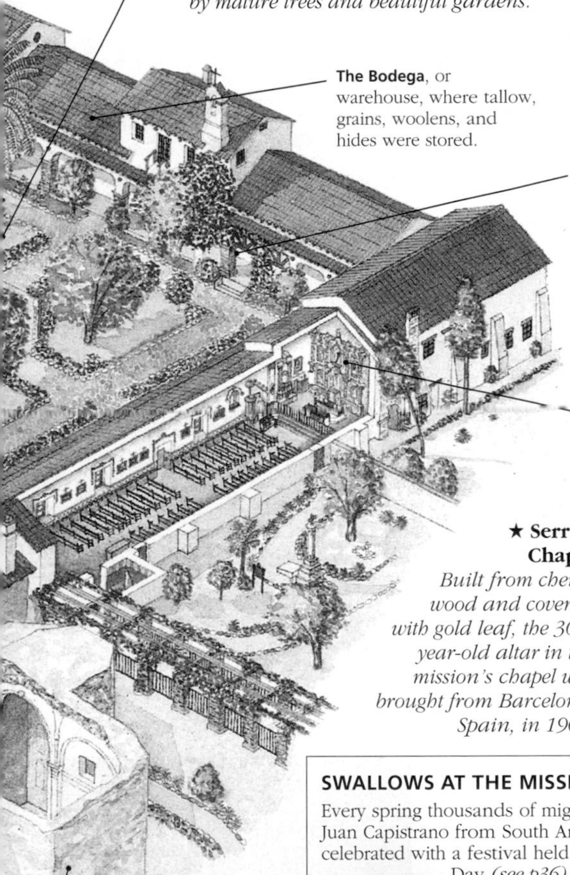

★ Courtyard Gardens
*This courtyard was at the heart of mission
life. Surrounded by cloisters, it still has a
fountain at its center and is today graced
by mature trees and beautiful gardens.*

The Bodega, or
warehouse, where tallow,
grains, woolens, and
hides were stored.

Cloisters
*Covered walkways with
arches frame the mission's
central courtyard. With their
tiled walls, the cloisters provide a cool, shaded place in
which to stroll or sit and
contemplate the gardens.*

**★ Serra's
Chapel**
*Built from cherry
wood and covered
with gold leaf, the 300-
year-old altar in the
mission's chapel was
brought from Barcelona,
Spain, in 1906.*

SWALLOWS AT THE MISSION
Every spring thousands of migrating swallows return to San
Juan Capistrano from South America. Their annual arrival is
celebrated with a festival held on March 19, St. Joseph's
Day *(see p36)*. The birds have been nesting
in the tiled roofs and adobe walls of the
mission for more than two centuries.
They use mud pellets to build enclosed
nests, in which four or five eggs are
incubated. When the autumn comes,
the swallows fly south again.

Migratory swallow at the mission

Ruins are all that remain of
the cruciform Great Stone
Church, which is currently
undergoing restoration.

Catalina Island ⑧

Just 21 miles (50 km) from the mainland, Catalina Island is the most accessible of California's Channel Islands. It was named Santa Catalina by the Spanish explorer Sebastián Vizcaíno when he landed here in 1602 on the feast day of St. Catherine of Alexandria. Much of the island's mountainous landscape remains unspoiled, and it has long been a favorite weekend and vacation destination.

Catalina's main town is the virtually traffic-free port of Avalon. The biggest buildings were constructed by the chewing-gum millionaire William Wrigley Jr., who bought the island in 1919. Today most of Catalina's 76 sq miles (200 sq km) are owned by the Santa Catalina Island Conservancy, which preserves the island's natural beauty.

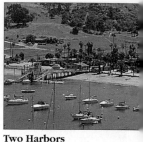

Two Harbors
This low-lying isthmus backed by two bays is a popular anchorage for yachts. Facilities include a camp site, diving center, and general store.

Airport-in-the-Sky and Nature Center

West End •

Two Harbors •

Catalina Harbor

El Rancho Escondido
is a ranch on which prize-winning horses are raised. It can be visited on guided tours of the island.

Little Harbor •

El Rancho Escondido

Little Harbor Road

Empire Landing Road

BLACK JACK MOUNTAIN

Middle Canyon Trail

BULLRUSH CANYON

Little Harbor
This out-of-the-way spot located on the island's west shore has a sheltered cove with a beach and a scenic harbor. There are also several hiking trails and a good camp site.

Black Jack Mountain,
which rises to 2,006 ft (610 m), is the second-highest mountain on Catalina Island and was mined in the 1920s for lead, zinc, and silver.

CATALINA WILDLIFE

Over the centuries, Catalina has become a sanctuary for plants and animals that have died out on the mainland. Rare ironwood and mahogany trees and the highly poisonous wild tomato are among eight endemic plants surviving on the island. Distinctive animal subspecies have also evolved, such as the small gray Catalina fox and the beechey ground squirrel. Some animals brought to the island by early settlers have now turned wild, including goats, pigs, and deer. Catalina even has a population of bison, ferried over in 1924 for a film shoot and never rounded up.

One of the island's wild bison

For hotels and restaurants in this region see pp534–5 and pp579–81

VISITORS' CHECKLIST

Road map C6. *3,000.* **Island Express Helicopter Service** *(310 510-2525) from San Pedro & Long Beach to Avalon.* **Catalina Express and Cruises** *(310 519-1212; 800 481-3470) from San Pedro to Avalon or Two Harbors & from Long Beach to Avalon;* **Catalina Passenger Service** *(949 673-5245) from Newport Beach to Avalon.* *1 Green Pleasure Pier (310 510-1520).* *Catalina Arts Festival (late Sep).* **www**.visitcatalina.org

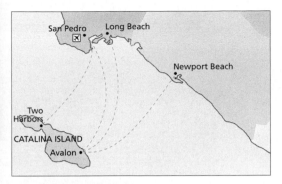

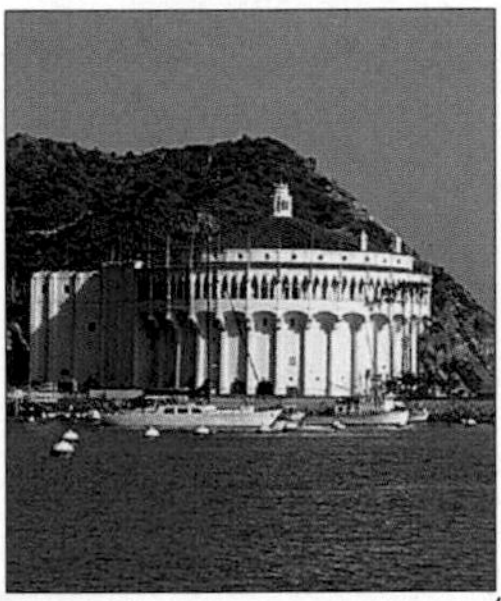

★ Avalon Casino
Guided tours can be taken of this 1929 Art Deco jewel, once a famous spot for big bands and now lovingly restored.

KEY

- Minor road
- Road in poor condition
- Trail
- River
- Airport
- Ferry service
- Tourist information
- Viewpoint

0 kilometers 5

0 miles 2

Avalon Museum is on the casino's lower floor. This historical museum shows how the island has been variously used for ranching, mining, tourism, and as a film location.

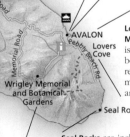

Lovers Cove Marine Reserve is visited by glass-bottomed boats that reveal the colorful marine life existing around Catalina.

Seal Rocks are included on sightseeing cruises, which visit this part of the island to admire colonies of migratory sea lions.

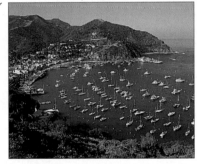

★ Avalon Bay
About 3,000 people live in Avalon, which has a pier and souvenir shops. Locals travel around in golf carts, which visitors can rent.

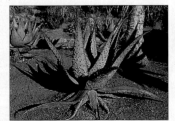

★ Wrigley Memorial & Botanical Gardens
This 38-acre (15-ha) park honoring William Wrigley, Jr. has an imposing memorial and a collection of plants endemic to Catalina.

STAR SIGHTS

- ★ Avalon Bay
- ★ Avalon Casino
- ★ Wrigley Memorial & Botanical Gardens

SAN DIEGO COUNTY

In San Diego in 1769, the Spanish friar Junípero Serra laid down the first link in the chain of 21 missions that underpins the modern state of California (see pp46–7). Blessed with a near-perfect climate and a magnificent natural harbor, his settlement has now become the sixth largest city in America. San Diego County has much to offer visitors, with its Pacific coastline, inland forests, and extensive state parks.

San Diego's character has always been determined by the sea. In the 19th century, gold prospectors, hide dealers, and whalers sailed into San Diego Bay. The United States Navy arrived in 1904, starting an enthusiastic courtship that has made San Diego the largest military establishment in the world. Aircraft carriers are a common sight in the bay, but so are cruise ships, fishing boats, yachts, and pleasure craft. San Diego is a city of sports and leisure – three times host to the Americas Cup, home of the Padres baseball team and the Chargers football team. There are plenty of opportunities for surfing, sailing, golf, and water sports.

First-time visitors are always surprised by the sense of space and how much there is to enjoy. Most have heard of San Diego Zoo and the Sea World marine park, but few realize that San Diego is a fast-growing city, with shimmering new skyscrapers soaring beside the waterfront. Culturally, San Diego is rapidly gaining prestige, as the many museums and arts venues of Balboa Park flourish.

North of the city the rugged Pacific Coast is lined with affluent beachside communities and wildlife preserves. Inland lie small towns, surrounded by peaceful countryside and fertile farmland. Deep forests and several state parks make the interior of San Diego County a paradise for hikers and campers escaping the frantic pace of city life. To the east, the region becomes increasingly mountainous, giving way to desert landscapes. And to the south, just a short trolley ride away from San Diego, is the bustling Mexican border town of Tijuana.

Bazaar del Mundo in San Diego Old Town

◁ Marina in San Diego Bay, with the skyscrapers of Downtown in the background

Exploring San Diego County

Covering more than 4,000 sq miles (10,350 sq km), San Diego County has a coastline of rocky cliffs, sandy beaches and wetlands, and a spacious, mountainous hinterland. The Anza-Borrego Desert *(see pp276–7)* forms a natural boundary to the east. San Diego city lies close to the border with Mexico, exploiting a large bay protected by two peninsulas. Stunning beaches and plentiful opportunities for leisure activities are the main attractions along the Pacific shoreline. A drive inland takes the visitor to the tranquillity of the Cleveland National Forest and the wilderness of state parks, such as Palomar Mountain and Cuyamaca Rancho.

Margarita Peak
972m
Riverside
Los Angeles
Rainbow
Fallbrook
5
15
Camp Pendleton
Bonsal
MISSION SAN
LUIS REY
8
76
Oceanside
Vista
LEGOLAND
14
78
San
Marcos
Carlsbad
Escondid
Leucadia
Encinitas
Cardiff-by-the-Sea
Rancho
Santa Fe
Solana Beach
Del Mar
Torrey Pines State Beach
805
52
LA JOLLA
5
Pacific Beach
MISSION BAY
4
SEA WORLD
3
Old Town
Ocean Beach
SAN DIEGO
1
Coronado
National
City
Point Loma
Silver Strand
Beach
75
13
CHULA VISTA
NATURE
CENTER
2

KEY

- Freeway
- Major road
- Secondary road
- Minor road
- Scenic route
- Main railway
- Minor railway
- International border
- △ Summit

Cuyamaca Rancho State Park landscape

SEE ALSO

- ***Where to Stay*** pp536–8
- ***Where to Eat*** pp581–4

Shelter Island yacht harbor in San Diego Bay

SIGHTS AT A GLANCE

Chula Vista Nature Center 13
Cuyamaca Rancho State Park 11
Julian 10
La Jolla 5
Lake Morena Park 12
Legoland 14
Mission Bay 4
Mission San Diego de Alcalá 2
Mission San Luis Rey 8
Palomar Mountain 9
San Diego pp250–59 1
San Diego Wild Animal Park 7
San Pasqual Battlefield 6
Sea World 3
Tijuana 15

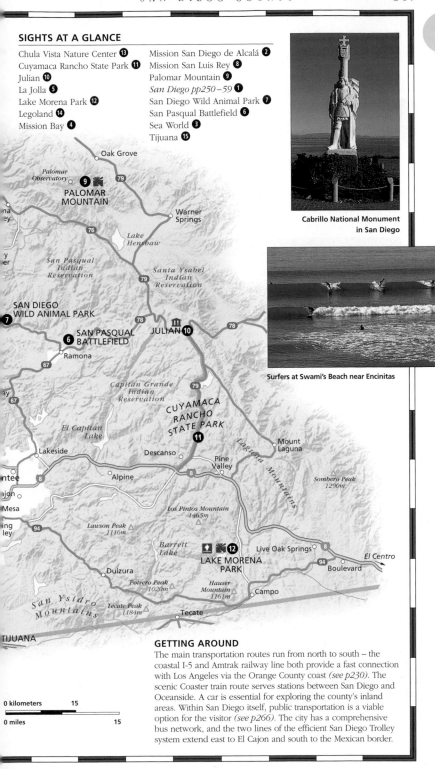

Cabrillo National Monument in San Diego

Surfers at Swami's Beach near Encinitas

Oak Grove
Palomar Observatory
9
PALOMAR MOUNTAIN
79
Warner Springs
76
Lake Henshaw
San Pasqual Indian Reservation
Santa Ysabel Indian Reservation
SAN DIEGO WILD ANIMAL PARK
7
78
JULIAN 10
6 SAN PASQUAL BATTLEFIELD
Ramona
67
Capitan Grande Indian Reservation
CUYAMACA RANCHO STATE PARK
11
El Capitan Lake
Lakeside
Descanso
Pine Valley
Mount Laguna
Laguna Mountains
Alpine
8
Sombero Peak 1290m
Los Pintos Mountain 1465m
Lawson Peak 1116m
94
Barrett Lake
12
LAKE MORENA PARK
Live Oak Springs
El Centro
Boulevard
Dulzura
Potrero Peak 1020m
Hauser Mountain 1161m
Campo
San Ysidro Mountains
Tecate Peak 1184m
Tecate
TIJUANA
0 kilometers 15
0 miles 15

GETTING AROUND

The main transportation routes run from north to south – the coastal I-5 and Amtrak railway line both provide a fast connection with Los Angeles via the Orange County coast *(see p230)*. The scenic Coaster train route serves stations between San Diego and Oceanside. A car is essential for exploring the county's inland areas. Within San Diego itself, public transportation is a viable option for the visitor *(see p266)*. The city has a comprehensive bus network, and the two lines of the efficient San Diego Trolley system extend east to El Cajon and south to the Mexican border.

San Diego County Coastline

Stretching from Orange County to the Mexican border, the coastline of San Diego County has 70 miles (112 km) of lovely sandy beaches, cliffs, coves, and seaside resorts. The beach culture is sophisticated, and the sports activity is frenzied. Peace can be found at Batiquitos Lagoon, Torrey Pines State Preserve, and the Chula Vista Nature Center (see p264), which are all sanctuaries for coastal wildlife. At Carlsbad, Legoland California is a 128-acre family theme park for youngsters aged 2–12, with a castle, miniature brick cities, and driving school.

Sign at entrance to Swami's Beach

Batiquitos Lagoon *lies between South Carlsbad and Leucadia State Beaches. A project is under way to clean up the lagoon and create a wildlife preserve with a nature trail and visitors' center. The lagoon has a large bird population and a rich variety of saltwater plants.*

The Del Mar Racetrack *was made famous in the 1930s by the singer Bing Crosby and other Hollywood stars. Its annual meetings remain a high point of the social calendar. San Diego's County Fair takes place at the adjacent fairground every June, and the racing season runs from late July to mid-September.*

Torrey Pines State Preserve *and Santa Rosa Island (see p224) are the only two places in the world where the Torrey Pine, or Pinus torreyana, survives. A remnant of pre-Ice Age forests, this tree is well adapted to this area's dry, sandy environment.*

KEY

▦	Freeway
▬	Major road
▭	Minor road
▭	River
❈	Viewpoint

0 kilometers 5

0 miles   5

★ **San Onofre State Beach ①**

Although close to the coastal San Onofre nuclear power plant and the vast Camp Pendleton military base, this beach is worth visiting to see serious California surfers in action.

Swami's ③

This surfing beach is named after the founder of the Self-Realization Fellowship Temple, which overlooks the shore.

Cardiff State Beach ④

On the south side of Encinitas, Cardiff offers swimming, surfing, and fine white sand, as well as oceanfront dining on Restaurant Row at its north end.

Torrey Pines State Beach ⑥

This beach is popular for picnics and swimming. Just to the south is the Torrey Pines State Preserve, where several cliff-top hiking trails among the pine trees offer views over the ocean.

Mission Beach ⑨

This is the liveliest beach in San Diego with plenty of opportunity for people-watching, plus the fairground attractions of Belmont Park (see p261).

Ocean Beach ⑩

Ocean Beach's T-shaped pier, popular with pelicans, has good views of the coastline.

Silver Strand Beach ⑫

This long, thin beach is sandwiched between areas of land reserved for naval training. It takes its name from the silvery shells in its sand.

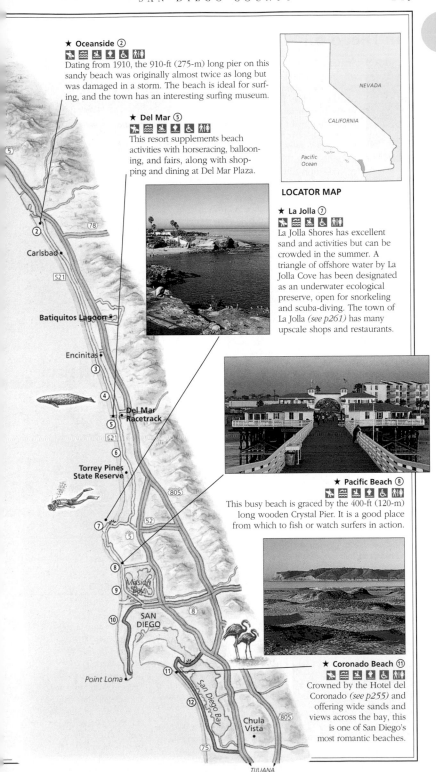

★ Oceanside (2)

🏄 🌊 🏊 🛟 ♿ 🚻

Dating from 1910, the 910-ft (275-m) long pier on this sandy beach was originally almost twice as long but was damaged in a storm. The beach is ideal for surfing, and the town has an interesting surfing museum.

★ Del Mar (5)

🏄 🌊 🏊 🛟 ♿ 🚻

This resort supplements beach activities with horseracing, ballooning, and fairs, along with shopping and dining at Del Mar Plaza.

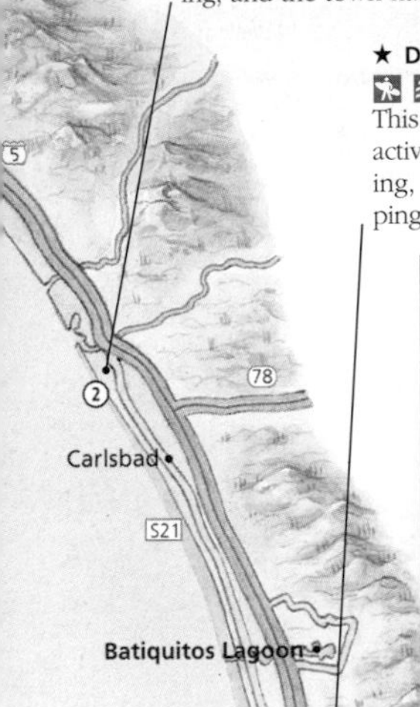
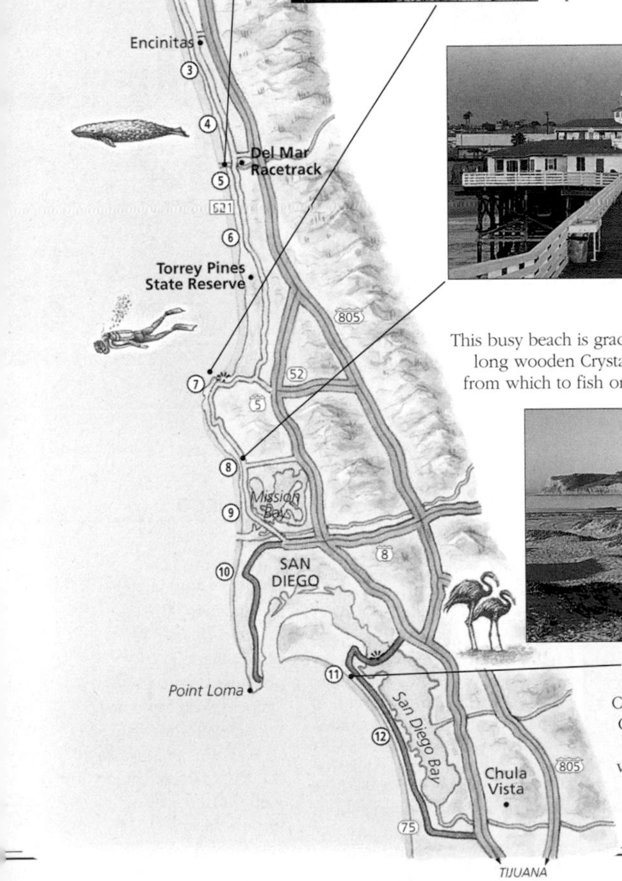
5
78
Carlsbad
S21
Batiquitos Lagoon
Encinitas
Del Mar Racetrack
S21
Torrey Pines State Reserve
805
52
5
Mission Bay
8
SAN DIEGO
Point Loma
San Diego Bay
Chula Vista
805
75
TIJUANA

NEVADA
CALIFORNIA
Pacific Ocean

LOCATOR MAP

★ La Jolla (7)

🏄 🌊 🏊 ♿ 🚻

La Jolla Shores has excellent sand and activities but can be crowded in the summer. A triangle of offshore water by La Jolla Cove has been designated as an underwater ecological preserve, open for snorkeling and scuba-diving. The town of La Jolla *(see p261)* has many upscale shops and restaurants.

★ Pacific Beach (8)

🏄 🌊 🏊 🛟 ♿ 🚻

This busy beach is graced by the 400-ft (120-m) long wooden Crystal Pier. It is a good place from which to fish or watch surfers in action.

★ Coronado Beach (11)

🏄 🌊 🏊 🛟 ♿ 🚻

Crowned by the Hotel del Coronado *(see p255)* and offering wide sands and views across the bay, this is one of San Diego's most romantic beaches.

San Diego ❶

Santa Fe

Tiles in Santa Fe Depot

Shaped like a hook and protected by the peninsula of Coronado *(see p255)*, the 22 sq miles (57 sq km) of San Diego Bay form a natural deep-water harbor around which the second largest city in California has grown. Discovered in 1542 by the Portuguese explorer Juan Rodríguez Cabrillo (João Rodrigues Cabrilho), colonization did not follow until 1769. In that year, the founding father of the mission chain, Junípero Serra, arrived in the region as part of a military expedition to secure Alta California (the part of California north of the Baja Peninsula) for Spain. Its commanders built a presidio and mission near the San Diego River, an area now known as Old Town *(see pp254–5)*.

Shops in Seaport Village

Exploring Downtown San Diego

The growth of modern San Diego began in the 1870s, when Alonzo Horton, a San Francisco businessman, began to develop the town's waterfront areas. He laid down the grid of streets of the Gaslamp Quarter *(see pp252–3)*, which, along with the Horton Plaza shopping center, has become the centerpiece of San Diego's rejuvenated Downtown district. Historically, the city's main street is Broadway, punctuated at its western end by the **Santa Fe Depot**. The towers and brightly tiled interior of this Spanish Colonial-style railroad station date from 1915. It was built to impress visitors to the Panama-Pacific Exposition in Balboa Park *(see pp256–7)*.

Since the 1980s, Downtown San Diego has become the site of an ongoing architectural competition. Close to the Santa Fe Depot, one of the city's tallest buildings, the **America Plaza**, is home to the Museum of Contemporary Art. On the waterfront, the galleon-like **San Diego Convention Center**, opened in 1989, overlooks San Diego Bay.

The promenades and piers of the **Embarcadero** waterfront pathway provide an introduction to San Diego's role as a major commercial and military port. At the northern end are the Maritime Museum's historic ships. A short stroll south is **Broadway Pier**, where visitors can join a harbor excursion. **Seaport Village**, a shopping and dining complex, has views across to the aircraft carriers of the **North Island United States Naval Air Station**.

Three of the colorful levels in the Horton Plaza shopping center

Horton Plaza

Broadway, G St, 1st & 4th Aves. **Tel** *(619) 239-8180.* ◯ *daily.* ● *Dec 25.* **www**.westfield.com

This innovatively designed shopping center, built in 1985, has acted as a catalyst in the regeneration of Downtown San Diego. The plaza is painted in a festive array of pastel shades and built on interlocking levels lined with 140 shops, department stores, and cafés. Visitors can enjoy some evening shopping, close to the restaurants of the Gaslamp Quarter.

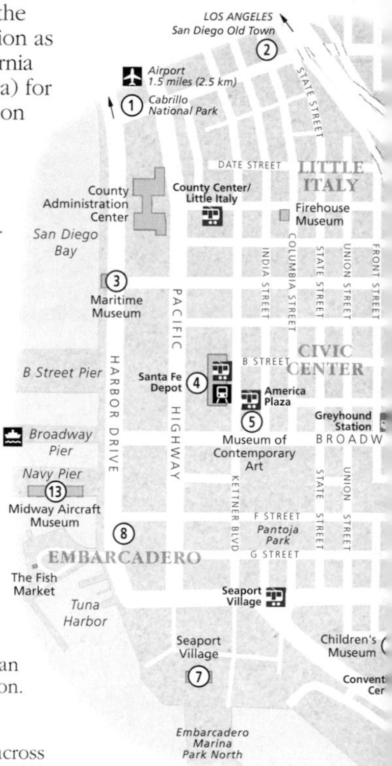
LOS ANGELES
San Diego Old Town
2
Airport
1.5 miles (2.5 km)
1
Cabrillo
National Park
STATE STREET
DATE STREET
LITTLE ITALY
County Administration Center
County Center/ Little Italy
Firehouse Museum
San Diego Bay
INDIA STREET
COLUMBIA STREET
STATE STREET
UNION STREET
FRONT STREET
3
Maritime Museum
PACIFIC HIGHWAY
HARBOR DRIVE
B STREET
CIVIC CENTER
B Street Pier
Santa Fe Depot
4
America Plaza
5
Greyhound Station
BROADW
Broadway Pier
Museum of Contemporary Art
Navy Pier
13
Midway Aircraft Museum
KETTNER BLVD
STATE STREET
UNION STREET
F STREET
Pantoja Park
G STREET
8
EMBARCADERO
The Fish Market
Tuna Harbor
Seaport Village
Seaport Village
7
Children's Museum
Convent Cer
Embarcadero Marina Park North

SAN DIEGO

Cabrillo National Monument ①
Children's Museum ⑨
Embarcadero ⑧
Gaslamp Quarter ⑩
Horton Plaza ⑥
Hotel del Coronado ⑫
Junípero Serra Museum ②
Maritime Museum ③
Midway Aircraft Museum ⑬
Museum of Contemporary Art ⑤
Santa Fe Depot ④
Seaport Village ⑦
Villa Montezuma ⑪

🏛 Maritime Museum

1492 North Harbor Drive. *Tel (619) 234-9153.* ◯ *9am–8pm daily, 9pm in summer.* 🌊
The lofty masts of the *Star of India*, an 1863 merchantman, dominate this museum of historic vessels. The beautiful San Francisco Bay passenger ferry, the *Berkeley* (dating from 1898), and the luxurious steam yacht *Medea* (built in 1904), are moored alongside.

🏛 Museum of Contemporary Art

1001 Kettner Blvd. *Tel (619) 234-1001.* ◯ *11am–5pm Thu–Tue.* ● *Jan 1, Dec 25.* **www.**mcasd.org
This two-story museum, which opened in 1993, is the Downtown counterpart of the museum of the same name in La Jolla *(see p261).* The four galleries display changing exhibitions of new work by living artists, as well as selections from the museum's large permanent collection. There is also a very well-stocked bookstore.

VISITORS' CHECKLIST

Road map D6. 👥 *1,500,000.* ✈ *Lindbergh Field Airport, 3707 N Harbor Drive.* 🚉 *1050 Kettner Blvd.* 🚌 *120 W Broadway.* ℹ *Bayside Embarcadero, cnr Harbor Dr & W Broadway (619 236-1212).* 🎭 *Street Scene Festival (Sep).* **www.**sandiego.org

🏠 Villa Montezuma

20 Ave and K St. *Tel (619) 239-2211.* ◯ *10am–4:30pm Fri, Sat & Sun.* ● *Jan 1, Dec 24 pm, Dec 25.* 🌊 🌊
This Victorian mansion was built in 1887 for Jesse Shepard, an author, musician, and spiritualist from England. The well-preserved Queen Anne-style interior gives an insight into life in old San Diego.

Stained-glass window in the Victorian Villa Montezuma

🏛 Children's Museum

200 W Island Ave. *Tel (619) 233-8792.* ● *Closed for renovation until 2006; call or check website for details.* 🌊 **www.**sdchildrensmuseum.org
The musuem is closed during the construction of its new premises in the Marina District. The new state-of-the art facility, designed by Rob Wellington Quigley, should prove to be a premier family attraction.

Taking part in one of the many activities at the Children's Museum

Key to Symbols *see back flap*

A Walk through the Gaslamp Quarter

During the boom years of the 1880s, the 16 blocks of the San Diego's Gaslamp Quarter became known as the "Stingaree." It was an area notorious for prostitution, gambling, and drinking, where naïve customers could easily be "stung" by confidence tricksters. In spite of police clampdowns in the following decades and the growth of a close-knit Asian community, its streets remained in decline until the 1970s, when moves were made to revive its fortunes and protect its wealth of historic buildings. In 1980, the area was designated a National Historic District. As a result, the Gaslamp Quarter has recently emerged as the new heart of San Diego. It is now renowned as a place to shop, dine, and dance. Visitors can also admire the period buildings, ranging from a pie bakery and a hardware store to ornate office blocks and grand Victorian hotels. The district is particularly attractive at night, when it is illuminated by graceful gaslamps that line its pavements.

One of the quarter's gaslamps

VISITORS' CHECKLIST

Broadway & 4th–6th Aves. **Road map** D6. ▣ 1. 🚃 Bayside. ℹ 410 Island Ave (619) 233-4692. **www**.gaslampquarter.org

Old City Hall
This 1874 Italianate office building once housed the entire city government.

The Lincoln Hotel at No. 536 was built in 1913. Its architecture is influenced by Chinese style.

The Backesto Building office block at No. 614 dates from 1873.

FIFTH AVENUE WEST SIDE ⪼⪼⪼⪼⪼⪼⪼⪼⪼⪼⪼⪼⪼⪼⪼⪼⪼⪼⪼⪼⪼⪼⪼⪼⪼⪼⪼⪼⪼

★ Louis Bank of Commerce
Constructed in 1888, this was the first granite building in the city and housed the Bank of Commerce for just five years. It has also served as an oyster bar and a brothel.

The Marston Building
This retail outlet on the corner of 5th Avenue and F Street dates from 1881. It was built by civic leader George Marston as a department store. The structure was remodeled in 1903 following fire damage.

FIFTH AVENUE EAST SIDE ⪼⪼⪼⪼⪼⪼⪼⪼⪼⪼⪼⪼⪼⪼⪼⪼⪼⪼⪼⪼⪼⪼⪼⪼⪼⪼⪼⪼⪼⪼

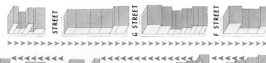

KEY

▷▷▷▷▷▷ West side walking north

◁◁◁◁◁◁ East side walking south

The Gaslamp Quarter at night
In the evening the streets of the Gaslamp Quarter bustle with people eating and drinking in its many restaurants and bars, or simply strolling around.

Llewelyn Building
Dating from 1877, this structure housed a shoe store until 1906 and then a succession of hotels.

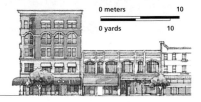

| 0 meters | 10 |
| 0 yards | 10 |

★ Yuma Building
Completed in 1882, this commercial property was one of the first brick buildings in Downtown. In 1915, the Yuma Building housed the first brothel to be closed down during a police raid of the red-light district.

STAR SIGHTS

★ Louis Bank

★ Yuma Building

Wyatt Earp
Lawman Wyatt Earp ran three gambling halls in the district during the 1880s. In order to distance themselves from the "Stingaree," the area's more respectable businesses moved north of Market Street.

Beyond Downtown

Four miles (6.5 km) north of the present Downtown lies the area now known as Old Town. Here, visitors can see San Diego's earliest buildings, many of which have been restored to their original state, and explore the fascinating Junípero Serra Museum. To the west of Old Town, the coast runs south to the end of the Point Loma Peninsula. From here, visitors have magnificent views of the Pacific Ocean and the city's waterfront across the bay. South of Point Loma, Coronado, with its numerous luxury hotels and popular sandy beaches, enjoys a privileged location at the end of a low-lying peninsula thrusting into San Diego Bay.

Victorian house in Heritage Park

Interior of Mason Street School in Old Town

Exploring Old Town

Until the 1870s the city of San Diego was centered around the presidio, the site of the original Spanish military outpost, in an area now known as Old Town. Today more than 20 historic buildings from this period have been restored or re-created to form the Old Town San Diego State Historic Park. At its center lies the grassy Plaza where parades and fiestas once took place. The **Robinson-Rose Building** at the western end of the Plaza now serves as the park's headquarters and visitors' center.

Other buildings of historical interest include the **Colorado House** and **Mason Street School**, which dates from 1866. Mexican themes are evoked in the vibrant **Bazaar del Mundo** shopping center (*see p266*) in the north corner of the Plaza.

Old Town San Diego spreads far beyond the official limits of the park. Constructed in 1856, **Whaley House** at No. 2482 San Diego Avenue was the first two-story brick building in California and once functioned as a courthouse.

🏛 Junípero Serra Museum

2727 Presidio Drive. *Tel (858) 297-3258.* ◯ 10am–4:30pm Fri–Sun. ◉ *Thanksgiving, Dec 25.* 🅿
Crowning Presidio Park, the whitewashed Junípero Serra Museum was built in 1929 in the Mission Revival style (*see p31*) and is named after the founder of California's mission chain. Overlooking the San Diego River, the park occupies the site of the presidio fort and mission, which were built by the Spanish in 1769. The ruins of the presidio are still being explored by a team of archaeologists, and some of their finds, from fine china to cannonballs, can be seen in the museum. Its displays cover San Diego's early days and the city's successive Native American, Spanish, Mexican, and American residents. Of particular interest is a didactic painting *La Madre Santissima de la Luz*, painted in Mexico by Luís Mena (c.1760), depicting Native Americans kneeling before the Virgin Mary. The painting is a rare surviving artifact from the time of the first mission, which moved to San Diego de Alcalá in 1774 (*see p260*). Exhibits upstairs describe the first Spanish expedition to California, daily life in the presidio, and the changing face of San Diego.

🏬 Heritage Park

2455 Heritage Park Row. *Tel (858) 565-3600.* ◯ *daily.* ◉ *Dec 25, Thanksgiving.* **www**.sdparks.org
On the east side of Old Town, Heritage Park is a collection of immaculately restored Victorian buildings, rescued from various corners of the city.

Junípero Serra Museum in Old Town San Diego

⚜ Casa de Estudillo

4001 Mason St. **Tel** *(619) 220-5422.*
⬜ *10am–5pm daily.* ● *Jan 1, Thanksgiving, Dec 25.* **Donation.** 🍴 📷 🔆
Of the original adobe and
wooden buildings that visitors
can now admire in Old Town
San Diego State Historic Park,
this is one of the oldest and
the most impressive. It was
constructed by the commander
of the presidio, José Mariá de
Estudillo, in 1829. The house
has 13 rooms built around an
internal courtyard and has
been refurnished in the style
of the late Spanish period.

⚜ Seeley Stable

Calhoun & Mason Sts. **Tel** *(619)
220-5427.* ⬜ *daily.* ● *Jan 1,
Thanksgiving, Dec 25.* **Donation.**
The museum housed in this
reconstructed stable displays
a collection of horse-drawn
carriages and stagecoaches,
as well as some interesting
Wild West memorabilia.

Exploring Point Loma

The 144-acre (58-ha) **Cabrillo
National Monument** park
straddles the southern part of
the Point Loma Peninsula. The
monument was named after
the Portuguese explorer Juan
Rodríguez Cabrillo (also
known as João Rodrigues
Cabrilho) *(see p46)*, the first
European to step ashore in
California in 1542. His statue
appropriately overlooks the
ships passing in and out of
San Diego Bay.
    Between late December and
the end of February the nearby
Whale Overlook is a popular
place from which to watch
enormous gray whales under-
taking their annual southward
migration. Visitors can also follow the 2-mile (3-km) Bayside
Trail around the Point, with the
aid of a highly informative
leaflet, and visit rock pools
on its western shore.

🏛 Cabrillo National Monument Visitor Center

1800 Cabrillo Memorial Drive.
Tel *(619) 557-5450.* ⬜ *daily.* 📷 📹
Close to the Cabrillo National
Monument park entrance, this
excellent visitors' center has a
small museum. A film recounts
Juan Rodríguez Cabrillo's 800-
mile (1,300-km) voyage along
the California coast.

Old Point Loma Lighthouse

⚜ Old Point Loma Lighthouse

1800 Cabrillo Memorial Drive.
Tel *(619) 557-5450.* ⬜
9am–5.15pm daily. 📷 ♿ 📹
The lighthouse, a short walk
south from the Cabrillo statue,
sent its first beams into the
night in 1855 and operated for
36 years. Although its tower is
usually closed to the public,
the lower rooms re-create the
lighthouse keepers' living
quarters as they were in 1890s.

Exploring Coronado

The city of Coronado, at the
head of a 4,100-acre (1,650-
ha) peninsula in the middle of
San Diego Bay, is moneyed
and self-confident. Businessman Elisha Babcock Jr. bought
the land in 1885 and set out to
develop a world-class resort.
Coronado now boasts San
Diego's most exclusive homes,
boutiques, hotels, and
restaurants. Its Pacific shore is
lined by a stunning beach *(see
p249)*, which is dominated at
its southern end by the landmark Hotel del Coronado.

🛥 Coronado Ferry

1050 N Harbor Drive. **Tel** *(619) 234-
4111.* ⬜ *daily.* 📷
Until the opening of the
spectacular San Diego–
Coronado Bay Bridge in 1969,
the ferry provided the area's
principal link with the mainland, a service that has now
been revived for the benefit
of both tourists and locals.
    The 15-minute trip between
the Broadway Pier on the
Embarcadero and the Ferry
Landing Marketplace is breathtaking at dusk when the setting
sun illuminates the skyscrapers
of Downtown. From the Ferry
Landing, visitors can take a bus
or walk along Orange Avenue
to the Pacific shore.

⚜ Hotel del Coronado

1500 Orange Ave, Coronado. **Tel**
(619) 435-6611; (800) 468-3533. ⬜
daily. 📷 ♿ 📹 www.hoteldel.com
Opened in 1888, the "Del" *(see
p536)* is a lovingly preserved
grand Victorian seaside hotel.
It was built using both architects and labor from the railroads – a heritage that is most
obvious in the domed ceiling
of the Crown Room, which is
built from sugar pine without
a single nail. The list of illustrious guests who have stayed
here reads like a Who's Who
of 20th-century United States
history – presidents from
Franklin D Roosevelt to Bill
Clinton, film stars from Marilyn
Monroe to the *Baywatch*
belles. The hotel has been the
setting for several films, including *Some Like It Hot*, the 1959
classic starring Marilyn Monroe,
Jack Lemmon, and Tony Curtis.
"Del" devotees can take a 35-
minute audio tour.

Impressive turrets and gables of the exclusive Hotel del Coronado

Balboa Park and San Diego Zoo

Statue of El Cid in Balboa Park

Named after the Spanish explorer who first set eyes on the Pacific Ocean in 1513, Balboa Park was founded in 1868. Its beauty owes much to the dedicated horticulturalist Kate Sessions who, in 1892, promised to plant trees throughout its 1,200 acres (485 ha) in exchange for renting space for a nursery. In 1915 the park was the site of the city's Panama-Pacific Exposition *(see p349)*, a world's fair celebrating the opening of the Panama Canal. Several of the Spanish Colonial-style pavilions built in that year survive along El Prado (the park's main street), and the animals gathered for the exhibition formed the nucleus from which San Diego Zoo has grown *(see p259)*. Twenty years later the organizers of the California-Pacific International Exposition added more exhibition spaces around Pan-American Plaza. All these buildings now form a rich concentration of museums and performance venues.

Plaza de Panama
This plaza in the center of the El Prado thoroughfare was at the heart of the Panama-Pacific Exposition.

Skyfari

★ San Diego Museum of Man
This historical museum is housed in the 1915 California Building. Designed in Spanish Colonial style, its façade is decorated with statues representing famous Californians.

Old Globe Theater

El Prado

San Diego Automotive Museum

Aerospace Museum
This A-12 Blackbird, built in 1962, stands beside a museum devoted to the history of flight.

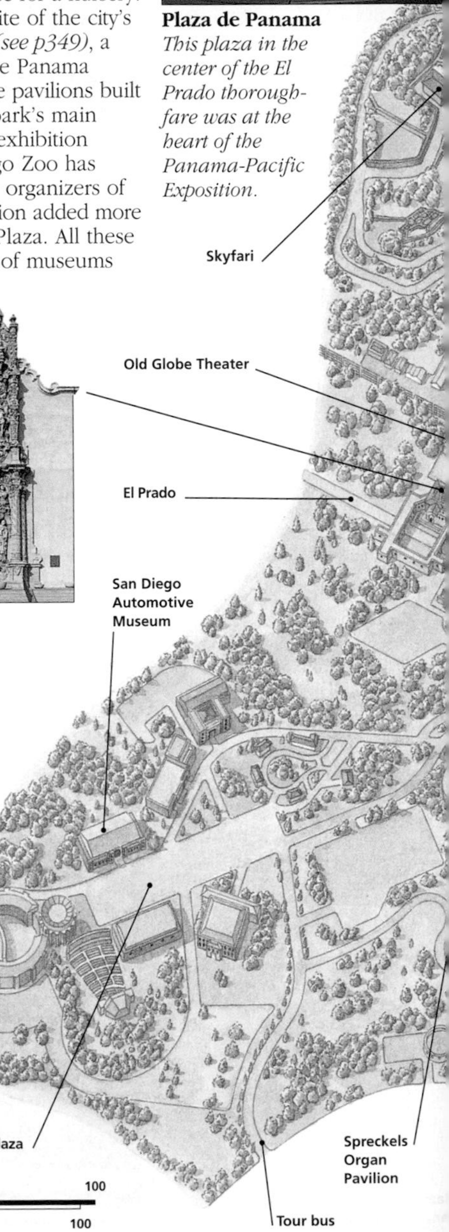

STAR SIGHTS

★ California Building/San Diego Museum of Man

★ San Diego Museum of Art

★ San Diego Zoo

Pan-American Plaza

Spreckels Organ Pavilion

Tour bus

0 meters   100

0 yards   100

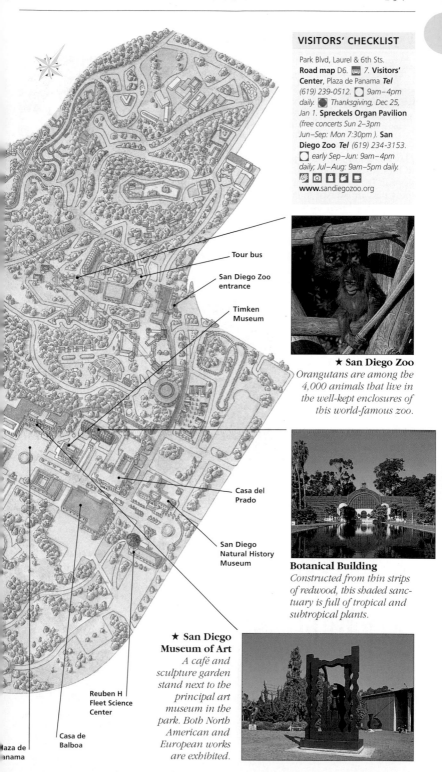

Tour bus

San Diego Zoo
entrance

Timken
Museum

★ **San Diego Zoo**
*Orangutans are among the
4,000 animals that live in
the well-kept enclosures of
this world-famous zoo.*

Casa del
Prado

San Diego
Natural History
Museum

Botanical Building
*Constructed from thin strips
of redwood, this shaded sanctuary is full of tropical and
subtropical plants.*

★ **San Diego
Museum of Art**
*A café and
sculpture garden
stand next to the
principal art
museum in the
park. Both North
American and
European works
are exhibited.*

Reuben H
Fleet Science
Center

Casa de
Balboa

Plaza de
Panama

Exploring Balboa Park and San Diego Zoo

Topiary elephant at zoo entrance

Balboa Park, located at the heart of San Diego, is one of the city's most popular attractions. On the weekend, its pleasant, lush grounds and traffic-free promenades are crowded with strollers, joggers, cyclists, and street artists. In between museum tours, visitors can picnic in one of the shady picnic groves or play ball games on the grassy lawns. Just to the north of the museums and recreation grounds of Balboa Park lies San Diego Zoo, where 800 species from all over the world are housed in enclosures designed to resemble as closely as possible their natural habitat.

Sunday afternoon street entertainers in Balboa Park

⌂ San Diego Museum of Man

1350 El Prado. *Tel (619) 239-2001.* ◯ *10am–5pm daily.* ● *Jan 1, Thanksgiving, Dec 25.*

The landmark pavilion of the Panama-Pacific Exposition of 1915 *(see p256)*, also known as the California Building, houses an anthropological museum about the early history of mankind. Exhibits arranged over two floors cover topics such as the cultures of ancient Egypt and the Mayans, and Native American crafts.

⌂ San Diego Museum of Art

1450 El Prado. *Tel (619) 232-7931.* ◯ *10am–6pm Tue–Sun (9pm Thu).* ● *Jan 1, Thanksgiving, Dec 25.*

This museum's large, varied art collection is boosted by a program of special exhibitions. European and American art from 1850 to the 20th century is shown in the first-floor galleries, along with exhibits

from southern Asia, Japan, and China. The displays on the second floor feature work from 1300 to 1850, including *Coronation of the Virgin* (1508), by Luca Signorelli.

Portrait of a Gentleman (1634) by Frans Hals in the Timken Museum

⌂ Timken Museum of Art

1500 El Prado. *Tel (619) 239-5548.* ◯ *Tue–Sun.* ● *Jan 1, Jul 4, Thanksgiving, Dec 25* www.timkenmuseum.org

Opened in 1965, the Timken exhibits a few exquisite works in an inviting space. On display are works by European masters such as Frans Hals (1581/5–1666), François Boucher (1703–70), and Paul Cézanne (1839–1906). The Timken also has works by 19th-century American artists, including *The Yosemite Fall* (1864) by Albert Bierstadt, and a collection of Russian icons.

Ornate Colonial-style façade of the San Diego Museum of Art

⌂ Museum of Photographic Arts

1649 El Prado. *Tel (619) 238-7559.* ◯ *daily.* ● *Dec 25.*

This museum is located on the main floor of the ornate Casa de Balboa. It specializes in high-quality traveling exhibitions that demonstrate the art and power of photography. There is also an interesting and well-stocked bookstore.

⌂ Museum of San Diego History

1649 El Prado. *Tel (619) 232-6203.* ◯ *10am–5pm Tue–Sun.* ● *Jan 1, Thanksgiving, Dec 24 & 25.*

As well as a large number of fascinating old photographs and books about the city, the museum has excellent exhibitions about cars, quilts, and the quest for a city water supply. "Out of Our Vaults" is an exhibition of new material taken from the museum's research archives, and never before seen by the public.

⌂ Reuben H Fleet Science Center

El Prado, Plaza de Panama & Park Blvd. *Tel (619) 238-1233.* ◯ *daily.* *call ahead for IMAX® show times.*

The big attraction here is the vast dome of the IMAX cinema in the Space Theater, where impressive films about the world around us are projected onto an enormous tilting screen. Laser and plane-tarium shows are also staged.

The complex is open in the evenings and has a Science Center with hands-on exhibits that demonstrate the laws of science. There is also a café, and a shop selling books and intriguing games and puzzles.

🏛 San Diego Natural History Museum

1788 El Prado, Balboa Park. ***Tel*** *(619) 232-3821.* ○ *daily.* ● *Jan 1, Thanksgiving, Dec 25.* ♿ *free first Tue of month.*
www.sdnhm.org

In the museum's new expansion, visitors can enjoy traveling exhibitions and regional displays of its 7.5 million specimen scientific collection. All areas are covered, including whales, minerals, dinosaurs and prehistoric life and insects. There is also a Hall of Mineralogy, which is built to resemble a mine.

🏛 San Diego Aerospace Museum

2001 Pan American Plaza. ***Tel*** *(619) 234-8291.* ○ *daily.* ● *Jan 1, Thanksgiving, Dec 25.* ♿
www.aerospacemuseum.org

San Diego has long been a city of pioneering aviation. The *Spirit of St. Louis*, in which pilot Charles Lindbergh made the first nonstop solo transatlantic flight in 1927, was built here. A model of the plane takes pride of place among a collection of more than 60 original and full- scale reconstructions of aircraft. Exhibits range from a batwing glider to a Vietnam War helicopter.

A 1948 Tucker Torpedo from the Automotive Museum's collection

🏛 San Diego Automotive Museum

2080 Pan American Plaza. ***Tel*** *(619) 231-2886.* ○ *daily.* ● *Jan 1, Thanksgiving, Dec 25.* ♿

Dream cars and motorcycles from both the United States and Europe shine on in this unashamedly nostalgic museum. Because most of the cars are privately owned, the collection is constantly changing, but gleaming paintwork, esthetic curves, and whitewall tires are guaranteed.

SAN DIEGO ZOO

San Diego Zoo is one of the best-known zoos in the world, famous both for its conservation programs and as a highly educational source of family entertainment. With some 4,000 animals dispersed over 100 acres (40 ha), the best introduction is to take the 35-minute narrated bus tour that covers most of the zoo. The aerial Skyfari ride, which offers a trip across the south of the park in gondola cars 180 ft (55 m) up, is also rewarding. After these, visitors can track down their favorites in the animal world by following the paths and moving walkways. There is also a Children's Zoo, and in summer the zoo is open for nocturnal exploration.

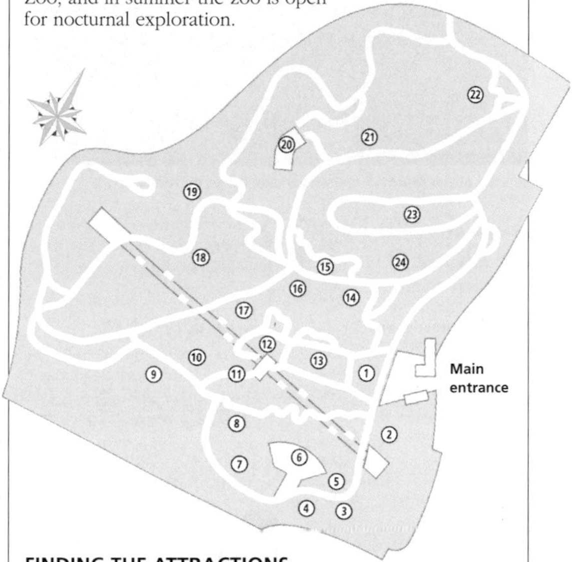
Main entrance

FINDING THE ATTRACTIONS

[1] Flamingo Lagoon
[2] Reptile House
[3] Petting Paddock
[4] Bromeliad Garden
[5] Hummingbird Aviary
[6] Wegeforth Bowl
[7] Reptile Mesa
[8] Tiger River
[9] Ituri Forest
[10] Pygmy Chimps
[11] Scripps Aviary
[12] Gorilla Tropics
[13] Bird and Primate Mesa
[14] Orchid Display
[15] Sun Bear Forest
[16] Rain Forest Aviary
[17] Wings of Australasia
[18] Horn and Hoof Mesa
[19] Birds of Paradise
[20] Hunte Amphitheater
[21] Dog and Cat Canyon
[22] African Rock Kopje Exhibit

Sichuan takin calf resting in San Diego Zoo

Interior of the church at the Mission San Diego de Alcalá

Mission San Diego de Alcalá ❷

10818 San Diego Mission Rd,
San Diego. **Road map** D6.
Tel (619) 283-7319. 🚌 20, 13.
⬜ daily. ● Jan 1, Thanksgiving,
Dec 25. Donation. ✝ daily. ♿
www.missionsandiego.com

Originally located at what is
now the Junípero Serra
Museum in Presidio Park *(see
p254)*, San Diego's mission
was moved to Mission
Valley in 1774. The land
surrounding the new
site was more fertile and
had a larger population
of potential Native
American converts. The
name Diego refers to St.
Didacus, born in Alcalá,
Spain, in 1400.

The first mission in
the California chain
(see pp46–7) is today
engulfed by freeways
and urban development, but
its harmonious buildings and
gardens retain an atmosphere
of peace. Early this century,
the complex was restored to
its appearance of 1813. The
church retains some original
materials, such as the timbers
over its doorways, the floor
tiles, and the adobe bricks in
the baptistry. In the garden
stands the Campanario (bell
tower), and a statue of St.
Francis. A small museum
honors the state's first
Christian martyr, Padre Luís
Jayme, who was murdered

**Statuette at San
Diego de Alcalá**

when a gang of 600 Native
Americans attacked the newly
established mission in 1775.

Sea World ❸

500 Sea World Drive. **Road map** D6.
Tel (619) 226-3901. 🚌 9. ⬜ daily.
🅿 ♿ 🎫 **www.**seaworld.com

In this state famous for its
theme parks, the great lure of
San Diego's Sea World is
the chance to get close to
many ocean creatures.
Opened in 1964, the
marine park now
covers 150 acres (60
ha) of Mission Bay and
provides its visitors
with entertainment for
a full day. A good
starting point is the five-
minute ride up the
Skytower, a 320-ft (98-
m) column with
panoramic views.

Another view is offered by
the 100-ft (30-m) high Bayside
Skyride in the park's northwest corner, where gondola
cars take you in a 0.5-mile
(1-km) loop over the waters
of Mission Bay.

The stars of Sea World are its
performing whales and dolphins. One show reveals the
intelligence of dolphins and
pilot whales, while another
demonstrates the virtuosity of
killer whales. Among the
other attractions in the park
are pools with sharks, otters,
and turtles, freshwater
aquariums, and opportunities
to feed killer whales and seals
and to touch rays and starfish.
Kids will particularly enjoy
Shamu's Happy Harbor, an
aquatic adventure park, and
its largest attraction, Journey
to Atlantis. It includes a wet
and wild thrill ride that ends
with a 60-ft (18-m) plunge
and a negative G-force drop.

There is also a more serious
side to Sea World – its staff are
devoted to animal rescue and
rehabilitation and take in an
average of one sick or abandoned animal per day. The
park also runs education and
conservation programs.

Mission Bay ❹

Road map D6. 🚌 from Downtown
San Diego. **Visitors' Center Tel**
(619) 276-8200. ⬜ daily.

Mission Bay park is an area
of 4,600 acres (1,850 ha)
entirely given over to public
recreational use. San Diegans
come here to keep fit and relax
in the well-tended parkland.

Killer whales performing acrobatic feats for the crowds at Sea World

Sailing on the peaceful waters of Mission Bay

The area was once a marsh, but systematic dredging and landscaping, begun in the 1930s, transformed it. The San Diego River has been corralled into a channel to the south, creating a pleasant world of beaches, water-sports centers, and islands. Although the main attraction in Mission Bay is Sea World, visitors can also enjoy kite-flying, volleyball, golf, and cycling. Along the 27-mile (43-km) shoreline, swimming, fishing, and sailing take place in designated areas.

In the southwest corner of the bay is Mission Beach (see p248), one of the most lively beaches in San Diego County. Lovers of traditional seaside amusements will enjoy the beachfront **Belmont Park.** Its restored wooden Giant Dipper dates from 1925.

▓ Belmont Park
3146 Mission Blvd. *Tel* (858) 488-0668. ◯ *daily.*

La Jolla ❺

Road map D6. 🖾 *32,000.*
🚌 *from San Diego.* ℹ *1055 Wall St, Suite 110 (858 454-1444).*
www.lajollabythesea.com

The origin of the name La Jolla (which is pronounced "La Hoya") is the subject of an ongoing debate – while some people believe it to come from the Spanish *la joya*, meaning "jewel," others claim it was inspired by a Native American word, with the same pronunciation, which means "cave." Located 4 miles (6 km) north of San Diego's Mission Bay, La Jolla is an elegant, upscale coastal resort set amid beautiful cliffs and coves (see p249). Its pretty streets are lined with gourmet chocolatiers, designer clothes shops, and top-name jewelers. San Diegans and tourists alike come to enjoy the many art galleries and the chic restaurants promising a

"Mediterranean" view. A companion to the gallery in Downtown San Diego (see p251), La Jolla's **Museum of Contemporary Art** occupies a prime oceanfront location. It displays works from its permanent collection of post-1950 art and houses a bookstore, café, and sculpture garden.

The town is also home to the University of California at San Diego and to the famous **Salk Institute for Biological Studies,** founded in 1960 by Dr. Jonas Salk, who developed the polio vaccine. Overlooking Scripps Beach is the Scripps Institution of Oceanography, with its magnificent **Birch Aquarium at Scripps.** The aquarium provides an insight into the fascinating world of oceanography, with exhibits, interactive displays, and even a simulated deep-sea dive. In the adjacent aquarium, visitors can observe sea life from the waters of the north Pacific as well as the tropics, including an Alaskan giant octopus.

🏛 Museum of Contemporary Art
700 Prospect St. *Tel* (858) 454-3541. ◯ *Mon–Tue, Thu–Sun.* ⬤ *Wed, Jan 1, Dec 25, Thanksgiving.* 🖾

⚱ Salk Institute for Biological Studies
10010 N Torrey Pines Rd. *Tel* (858) 453-4100. ◯ *daily.* ⬤ *public hols.* 🖾 *11am, noon.* **www**.salk.edu

🐟 Birch Aquarium at Scripps
2300 Expedition Way. *Tel* (858) 534-3474. ◯ *daily.* ⬤ *Thanksgiving, Dec 25.* 🖾
www.aquarium.ucsd.edu

Beautiful rocky shoreline of La Jolla Cove

Memorial plaque at the battlefield site in San Pasqual Valley

San Pasqual Battlefield ❻

Road map D6. **Tel** (760) 489-0076, 737-2201. ☐ 10am–5pm Sat & Sun. ● Jan 1, Thanksgiving, Dec 25.

In 1846, during the war between the United States and Mexico *(see p47)*, the San Pasqual Valley was the scene of a costly victory for the US Army over the rebel Californios (Mexican settlers in California). Handicapped by wet gunpowder, exhaustion, and cold, 22 of the 100 soldiers fighting under General Kearny were killed by the Californio lancers and 16 were wounded.

There is a **Visitors' Center**, run by volunteers, in which a film about the battle is shown.

Every December, local history enthusiasts in replica 19th-century military uniforms re-enact the events of the battle.

🛈 Visitors' Center
15808 San Pasqual Valley Rd. **Tel** (760) 737-2201. ☐ May–Sep: daily; Oct–Apr: Sat & Sun. ● public hols.

San Diego Wild Animal Park ❼

Hwy 78. **Tel** (760) 480-0100. 🚌 Escondido. ☐ daily. 🖼 ♿ 📷 **www.**wildanimalpark.org

A rural counterpart to San Diego Zoo *(see p259)*, this wildlife park displays an encyclopedic variety of birds and mammals in its 1,800 acres (730 ha) of carefully landscaped grounds. Opened in 1972, the park was conceived as a breeding sanctuary for the world's endangered species and has remained at the forefront of the conservation race. As well as caring for its 3,200 residents, the park exchanges animals with zoological institutions around the world, with the ultimate goal of releasing endangered species back into the wild. Among the program's success stories is that of the California condor, a species once close to extinction. Many condors successfully reared in the park have been returned to their natural habitat.

A good way to begin a visit is to take the Wgasa Bush Line Monorail. This 50-minute, five-mile guided ride around the

large park passes the principal animal enclosures and provides a useful orientation. Another fascinating journey is along the 2-mile (3-km) Kilimanjaro Safari Walk, offering superb views of re-created African and Asian landscapes.

For many visitors, the big animals, such as elephants, lions, and rhinos, are the stars. However, the park's various simulated natural environments, such as the Australian Rainforest and the Hidden Jungle, are also engrossing, and the Petting Kraal is very popular with children. Before visiting the Wild Animal Park, it is worth calling ahead to find out the times of daily events.

Anyone who likes to see wildlife in close-up can join a Photo Caravan, which takes small groups around the park in an open-topped truck. Call ahead for reservations.

Nairobi Village is a 17-acre (7-ha) area, where the park's amphitheaters and most of its facilities are to be found. Its many shops sell Africa-related books and souvenirs.

Mission San Luis Rey ❽

Hwy 76 (Mission Ave), Rancho del Oro Drive, San Luis Rey. **Tel** (760) 757-3651. 🚌 from San Diego. ☐ daily. **Donation**. **www.**sanluisrey.org

One of the largest and most prosperous estates in the California mission chain *(see p46)*, San Luis Rey de Francia

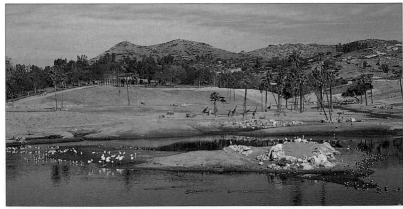

Animals roaming around freely in the San Diego Wild Animal Park

For hotels and restaurants in this region see pp536–8 and pp581–4

Façade of Mission San Luis Rey

was founded by the Spanish priest Padre Fermín Lasuén in 1798. The mission was named after the canonized 13th-century French king, Louis IX, and owed much of its success to the cooperation of the local Luiseño Indians. More than 3,000 Native Americans lived and worked in Mission San Luis Rey. They kept sheep and cattle and cultivated crops such as grain and fruit.

The majority of the mission's remaining buildings benefited from a long period of restoration in the early 20th century. Visitors are guided first into a **museum** outlining the history of

A statue in the church

the mission and the surrounding area. Of the vestments and religious artifacts on display, several have survived only because, after the church was secularized in 1833, some of its treasures were hidden by the Christian Native Americans. Their families returned the artifacts to the mission only when it was designated a Franciscan monastery in 1893.

The church at San Luis Rey has a cruciform shape as at San Juan Capistrano *(see p241),* but it was the only one in the chain with a domed wooden ceiling. The wooden pulpit is original, and the painted designs are based on surviving stencils. The mission still functions as a church and retreat, and in its grounds are

a partly restored laundry area, a large cemetery, and California's oldest pepper tree, brought from Peru in 1830.

🏛 Museum
Eastern Cloister. ⬜ *daily.* ⬤ *Jan 1, Thanksgiving, Dec 25.* 📷 ♿

Palomar Mountain ❾

Road map D6. 🚌 *from Julian.*

Rising to 6,200 ft (1,900 m) and thickly forested, Palomar Mountain offers visitors breathtaking views over north San Diego County from the long, winding road that climbs its slopes. The Palomar Mountain State Park encompasses 1,600 acres (645 ha) of the mountain's scenic landscape. It has good hiking trails and also provides facilities for activities, such as camping, hiking, and trout fishing.

At the summit of Palomar Mountain is the surreal-looking white dome of the **Palomar**

Observatory. Operated by the California Institute of Technology, this internationally renowned observatory first opened in 1948. It houses a computer-controlled Hale telescope with a 200-inch (510-cm) mirror capable of studying areas of the universe that are more than a billion light years away. From 1948 to 1956, the observatory's Oschin telescope was used to photograph the entire night sky. A second survey began in 1983 and is still in progress today. The images it produces will be compared to the earlier ones to reveal the changes that have taken place since the 1950s and thus provide vital data for researchers.

Visitors are not permitted to look through the 540-ton telescope, however, an exhibition area and photo gallery explain how it functions.

🏛 Palomar Observatory
35899 Canfield Rd, Palomar Mountain. **Tel** (760) 742-2119. ⬜ *9am–4pm daily.* ⬤ *Dec 24, Dec 25.* 📷

Dome of the Palomar Observatory at sunset

Julian

Road map D6. 🚶 2,000. 🚌 from San Diego. 🏛 2129 Main St (760 765-1857). **www**.julianca.com

When San Diegans want to go for a pleasant drive or spend a romantic weekend in the "back country," they often head for the mountain town of Julian. Gold was discovered here in 1870, and the restored 19th-century wooden buildings that line the main street help to re-create the atmosphere of those pioneer days.

Today tourists rather than gold-diggers flock here. In autumn, the "Apple Days" of October attract hundreds of visitors, who come to taste Julian's famous apple pie and buy rustic souvenirs in the quaint gift shops. The delightfully cluttered **Julian Pioneer Museum** is packed with curiosities and photographs evoking the town's history. Visitors can also venture inside an original gold mine at the **Eagle and High Peak Mines**.

For visitors wishing to stay overnight, there is plenty of homey bed-and-breakfast accommodation both in and around the town (see p536).

🏛 **Julian Pioneer Museum**
2811 Washington St. **Tel** (760) 765-0227. ☐ Apr–Nov: Fri–Sun; Dec–March: Sat–Sun. 📷

🎫 **Eagle and High Peak Mines**
C St. **Tel** (760) 765-0036. ☐ daily, but call ahead. ● Jan 1, Easter Sun, Thanksgiving, Dec 25. 📷

Cuyamaca Rancho State Park ⑪

Road map D6. 🚌 🏛 (760) 765-0755. ☐ daily. **www**.cuyamacaca.statepark.org

Only an hour's drive east of San Diego, Cuyamaca Rancho State Park is a place to get away from it all. Almost half of its 25,000 acres (10,100 ha) are an officially designated wilderness that is home to skunks, bobcats, coyotes, mule deer, and mountain lions.

As well as horseback riding, camping, and mountain biking facilities, there are 130 miles (210 km) of hiking trails in the park. The Cuyamaca Peak Trail is an arduous but rewarding ascent by paved fire road. From the summit, hikers can enjoy fine views of the forested hills of northern San Diego County as far as Palomar Mountain (see p263).

At the northern end of the park lies the Stonewall Gold Mine. Once a 500-strong prospectors' town, it yielded over two million dollars' worth of gold in the 1880s.

Apple pie store sign in Julian

🏛 **Park Headquarters and Museum**
12551 Hwy 79. **Tel** (760) 765-0755. ☐ daily. ● public hols.

Lake Morena Park ⑫

Road map D6. 🚌 from San Diego. **Tel** (619) 478-5473.

This lush, oak-shaded park surrounding a large fishing lake forms an oasis in the dry

Shores of Lake Morena

southeastern corner of San Diego County. The park covers 3,250 acres (1,300 ha) of land. For those who come to fish or simply enjoy a peaceful afternoon on the lake, rental boats are available.

Chula Vista Nature Center ⑬

Road map D6. **Tel** (619) 409-5900. 🚌 E St, Bay. ☐ 10am–5pm Tue–Sun. ● Jan 1, Easter Sun, Thanksgiving & next day, Dec 23–27, 31, Jan1. 📷 ♿ **www**.chulavistanaturecenter.org

This remarkable conservation project beside San Diego Bay was established in 1988 to provide refuge for the wildlife of California's coastal wetlands. A free bus takes visitors to the Nature Center from a parking lot located by I-5.

Here visitors can learn about the fragile environment of the 316 acres (130 ha) of protected land. Birds that can be seen all year round include herons, ospreys, and kestrels.

Legoland® ⑭

1 Legoland Drive, Carlsbad **Road map** D6. **Tel** (760) 918-5346. 🚌 S Carlsbad. ☐ check website. ♿ **www**.lego.com/legoland/california

This 128-acre (744-ha) park is aimed at kids of all ages, and offers over 50 family rides, attractions and shows.

See model fire trucks put out a "burning" building at Fun Town Fire Academy or race brick cars at the Daytona International Speedway.

Horseback riding in the Cuyamaca Rancho State Park

For hotels and restaurants in this region see pp536–8 and pp581–4

Tijuana ⑮

Few visitors to San Diego can resist a brief trip south into Baja California. The international border crossing at Tijuana is the busiest in the world, and the contrast between the American and Mexican ways of life is marked. Thousands of Americans, who come to Tijuana every year to enjoy its inexpensive shopping and exuberant nightlife, often affectionately refer to the city as "TJ."

Carved wooden Mexican bird

LOCATOR MAP

— International border

— San Diego Trolley line

▨ Mexico

Exploring Tijuana

The border city of Tijuana is hardly representative of the fabled Mexico of Mayan art and Spanish colonial architecture, but it is interesting as a hybrid frontier town devoted to extracting dollars from its wealthy neighbor.

The city's futuristic **Centro Cultural Tijuana** was built on the banks of the Tijuana River in 1982. This cultural center has an OMNIMAX theater, where films about Mexico are shown on an enormous tilting screen. Changing exhibitions on various Mexican themes are also held here. The open-air **Mexitlán** rooftop exhibition re-creates the country's architectural treasures in miniature.

Most visitors come to shop and party – Tijuana has long been popular with young Americans taking advantage of laws permitting anyone over 18 to drink alcohol.

The best shopping is in the quiet bazaars situated to the sides of the lively Avenida Revolución. Painted pottery,

Bottles of liqueur on sale in a street bazaar in Tijuana

leather boots, silver jewelry, and tequila are some favorite buys. Tourists are encouraged to barter with the merchants.

English-speaking staff at the **Tijuana Tourist Office** can provide maps and free advice on visiting the city.

🏛 **Centro Cultural Tijuana**
Paseo de los Héroes. **Tel** (011-52-66) 84-11-11. ◯ daily. ▨

🏛 **Mexitlán**
Ave Ocampo, Calles 2–3. **Tel** (011-52-66) 38-41-01. ◯ Wed– Sun. ▨

🛈 **Tijuana Tourist Office**
Ave Revolución y Calle. **Tel** (011-52-66) 88-05-55. ◯ daily.

TIPS FOR TRAVELERS

Getting there: *Since the San Diego Trolley (see p266) runs as far as the international border, the cheapest and simplest way to cross the border into Tijuana is on foot. Take a southbound trolley to San Ysidro and follow the crowds across the pedestrian bridges and walkways that lead to the city. You can also take a bus from San Ysidro across the border to downtown Tijuana, or book an excursion through a San Diego travel agent. Those taking a car or a motorbike will need Mexican vehicle insurance. This is inexpensive and is available at the border.*
Visas: *Citizens of the United States do not require a visa for a stay of less than six months and need only show their driver's license if they are staying for less than 72 hours. Immigration controls for returning to the US are strict, so you will need to take your passport or suitable personal identification documents and be sure that you meet the necessary US visa requirements. Citizens of Australia, Canada, and the United Kingdom require passports but not visas to enter Mexico, unless they are planning to remain in the country for longer than six months. When crossing the border, non-American nationals must present a completed Mexican Tourist Card, which may be obtained from the border guards. For further information, contact the Mexican consulate in your home country before departure.*
Currency: *Visitors on a short trip will rarely need to change money since US dollars and major credit cards are widely accepted.*

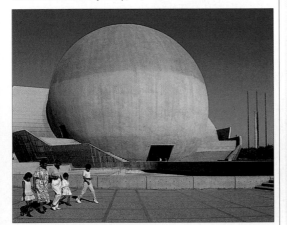

Façade of the Centro Cultural Tijuana

PRACTICAL INFORMATION

San Diego is an easy city to get to know, with a clean, efficient public transit system and a welcoming attitude toward visitors. The regeneration of the city's heart is evident in the growing number of shops, restaurants, and nightspots around Horton Plaza *(see p250)* and the Gaslamp Quarter *(see pp252–3)*. A variety of public transportation penetrates this Downtown area, where there are all the shops and entertainment spots you would expect in a vibrant California city. There are also regular connections to Old Town, Balboa Park, Coronado, and the Mexican border, while the best way to enjoy the waterfront of the Embarcadero *(see p250)* is on foot. Tourist information is available from excellent visitors' centers located in Horton Plaza, and Balboa Park, as well as in Coronado.

Jessop's Clock in Horton Plaza

Passengers boarding a San Diego bus

GETTING AROUND

The two lines of the **San Diego Trolley**, the city's streetcar system, link Old Town, El Cajon, and San Ysidro on the Mexican border with the city center. Trolleys run every 15 minutes during the day and operate until around 1am. A comprehensive bus network runs throughout the city. The **San Diego–Coronado Bay Ferry** offers a regular service to the Coronado Peninsula *(see p255)*. Maps, timetables, and special one- or four-day Day Tripper passes, valid for unlimited travel on any bus, trolley, or ferry, can be obtained from the **Transit Store**. **Old Town Trolley Tours** offer regular guided tours visiting all the principal sights.

The city's **Amtrak** station is housed in the beautiful Santa Fe Depot in Downtown. **San Diego International Airport** is located 3 miles (5 km) northwest of Downtown. Buses, taxis, and rental cars are all available from the airport.

The **Balboa Park Tram** provides free rides around the cultural park *(see pp256–7)*. In the vast Mission Bay aquatic playground *(see pp260–61)*, the **Water Taxi Service** takes visitors to points of interest around the shoreline.

San Diego is also a bicycle-friendly city, well served with bike paths and bike rental shops. There is a gentle route from Mission Beach to La Jolla *(see p261)*, offering fine ocean views. Bikes can be carried on trolleys and buses for a small fee. If you prefer to let someone else do the work, you can hail bicycle taxis in Downtown.

It is generally safe to walk around the areas to the north and west of Downtown, even at night. However, the areas to the south of Downtown and, particularly, to the east of the Gaslamp Quarter are best avoided after dark.

Mexican-style shopping in the Bazaar del Mundo

SHOPPING

If you intend to visit Tijuana *(see p265)*, avoid doing too much shopping before you go, since bargain goods are the main reason for crossing the border. The Bazaar del Mundo in Old Town San Diego *(see p254)* also has plenty of Mexican crafts and souvenirs.

Horton Plaza is the city's most colorful shopping center and can meet most tourists' needs, while the Paladion next door sells couture clothing. The oceanfront Seaport Village complex *(see p250)* is a good place to buy souvenirs and gifts to take home. Farther up the coast, Prospect Street in

A San Diego Trolley, offering a fast, frequent service to the Mexican border

Attractive shopping area of Seaport Village, on the waterfront

La Jolla has a selection of elegant stores. Del Mar and Carlsbad also have a good mix of boutiques, antique shops, and art galleries.

There are several factory outlet centers in San Diego County, where outlet stores sell well-known brand-name goods at considerably reduced prices *(see p607)*. The San Diego Factory Outlet Center, located just before the Mexican border crossing in San Ysidro, is one of the largest and best in the region, with more than 30 factory outlet stores. Ask at the information desk in the large parking lot for a sheet of discount tokens, which allow you to obtain further reductions of up to 15 percent in many of the shops.

Here, as throughout the state, major credit cards are accepted, and the hours of most shops are 10am–6pm Monday to Saturday, with some stores open on Sundays as well. A local sales tax of 8.5 percent applies to all purchases. This is automatically added to the advertised price of the goods when you pay for them.

ENTERTAINMENT

San Diego has a reputation for its cultural energy and has its own symphony orchestra, opera, and repertory theater companies. Listings of all the current cultural events can be found in the *San Diego Union-Tribune* and a range of complimentary tourist magazines. *The Reader*, available free in cafés, bars, and bookstores, is a good weekly source for finding out about poetry readings, live music, and the

alternative arts. Tickets for all these events can be bought from the **Times Arts Tix** office in Horton Plaza.

The Gaslamp Quarter *(see pp252–3)* is the best area to go to for good restaurants and nightclubs. The nearby Lyceum and Spreckels theaters have regular stage performances. In Balboa Park, the Old Globe Theater *(see p256)* stages award-winning shows and is one part of a three-stage performing arts complex.

Like most Californians, San Diegans are also avid sports fans – the Chargers football team and the Padres baseball team each has a stadium in Mission Valley. If, however, you prefer participating in sports to watching them, Mission Bay *(see pp260–61)* offers a wide range of water sports, as well as beach games such as volleyball. San Diego County also benefits from 83 excellent golf courses – ask at hotels or at local visitors' centers for more information.

San Diego's own baseball team, the Padres

DIRECTORY

GETTING AROUND

Amtrak
Santa Fe Depot, 1050 Kettner Blvd.
Tel (800) 872-7245.
www.amtrak.com

Balboa Park Tram
Tel (619) 298-8687.

Water Taxi Service
Tel (619) 235-8294.

Metropolitan Transit System (MTS)
1255 Imperial Ave, #1000.
Tel (619) 233-3004.

Old Town Trolley Tours
2115 Kurtz St.
Tel (619) 298-8687.

San Diego–Coronado Bay Ferry
1050 N Harbor Drive.
Tel (619) 234-4111.

San Diego International Airport
Lindbergh Field.
Tel (619) 231-2100.

San Diego Trolley
(619) 231-8549.

Transit Store
102 Broadway.
Tel (619) 234-1060.

SHOPPING

Horton Plaza
G St & 1st Ave.
Tel (619) 238-1596.

ENTERTAINMENT

Times Arts Tix
Broadway Circle, Horton Plaza.
Tel (619) 497-5000.
www.sandiegoperforms.com

TOURIST INFORMATION

Balboa Park
1549 El Prado.
Tel (619) 239-0512.

Bayside Embarcadero
Cnr Harbor Dr & West Broadway.
Tel (619) 232-1212.
www.sandiego.org

Coronado
1111 Orange Ave.
Tel (619) 437-8788.

THE INLAND EMPIRE AND LOW DESERT

*T*he Inland Empire and Low Desert landscape is one of the most varied in California. The countryside changes from pine forests, cooled by gentle breezes, to searing desert. The contrast can be startling: passengers taking the Palm Springs Aerial Tramway make the transition between these two ecosystems in 14 minutes.

The Anza-Borrego Desert State Park was the forbidding entry point to California for tens of thousands of hardy miners and settlers coming overland in the 1850s. Thirty years later communities in the northwest of the region, known as the Inland Empire, were transformed from a small collection of health resorts into the heart of a veritable economic empire based on the navel orange. The thick-skinned seedless Brazilian fruit, which traveled well, came to represent the sweet and healthy promise of California for millions of Americans. Many of the Victorian mansions built by citrus millionaires are still standing in the towns of Redlands and Riverside, but most of the fragrant orange groves have disappeared under asphalt and urban sprawl. Today Riverside is practically a suburb of Los Angeles.

At the heart of this region is Palm Springs, a favorite weekend retreat for Angelenos seeking relaxation and the desert sun. Just under two hours drive from LA, it has luxurious hotels, verdant golf courses, 600 tennis courts, and more than 10,000 swimming pools.

Lying to the east of Palm Springs is the Joshua Tree National Park. This is a land of hot, dry days, chilly nights, tumbleweed, and creosote bushes. The stark and silent beauty of the rocky landscape evokes images of desperados, hardy pioneers in covered wagons, and leather-clad high plains drifters – visions of the Wild West of so many novels and films.

When the desert becomes too hot, travelers can escape to one of the mountain resorts. The Rim of the World Tour is a spectacular drive in the heart of the San Bernardino Mountains.

Western film set in Pioneertown, near Yucca Valley

◁ Joshua tree silhouetted against the barren desert landscape

Exploring the Inland Empire and Low Desert

The Inland Empire is a region of vast scenic and climatic contrasts. In the northwest is the San Bernardino National Forest, with its cool mountain air and breathtaking views. Farther south lies the sun-baked Coachella Valley, ending in the steamy Salton Sea. Palm Springs, the largest of the desert resorts, is flanked by the stark Joshua Tree National Park and the alpine community of Idyllwild. The forbidding Anza-Borrego Desert State Park, in the southwest of the region, is the gateway to San Diego County.

A wild bighorn sheep in the Anza-Borrego Desert State Park

SEE ALSO

- **Where to Stay** pp538–40
- **Where to Eat** pp584–6

View across Desert Dunes golf course, near Palm Springs

KEY

===	Freeway
===	Major road
—	Secondary road
==	Minor road
—	Scenic route
—	Main railway
—	Minor railway
—	State border
===	International border
△	Summit

SIGHTS AT A GLANCE

Wind turbines in the Coachella Valley

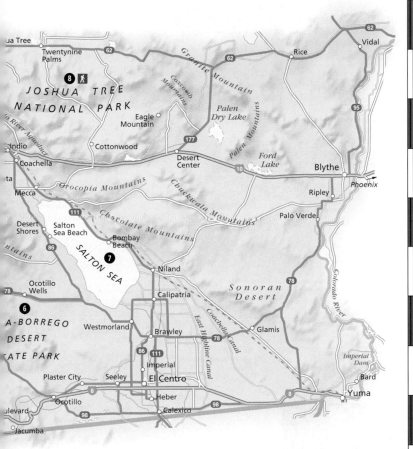

GETTING AROUND

The safest way to explore the desert areas is by car. The I-10 crosses the Inland Empire and Low Desert from east to west. Palm Springs, 107 miles (170 km) southeast of LA and 120 miles (190 km) northeast of San Diego, has a Greyhound bus terminal, an airport, and is a good base for exploring the region. Buses regularly go to and from the Amtrak station in nearby Indio.

0 kilometers   20

0 miles   20

Rim of the World Tour ❶

From San Bernardino this invigorating drive winds across the forested San Bernardino Mountains, offering spectacular views of the desert beyond. The altitude provides for distinct seasons, with warm, pine-scented air in the summer and brisk, cool days in the winter, when the snow-covered mountain trails are perfect for cross-country skiing. The tour passes through the resorts beside Lake Arrowhead and Big Bear Lake, both favorite destinations for those wanting to escape the heat and smog of LA. In Redlands visitors are offered a sense of the area's heady Victorian past, and yet another pleasure: the sweet smell of orange groves.

Elf at Santa's Village

San Bernardino Mountain landscape

Big Bear Lake ③
A popular resort area, Big Bear Lake offers a range of sports including fishing, sailing, swimming, and, in the winter, skiing. Its two commercial centers are Big Bear City, to the east, and Big Bear Village, to the south.

Heaps Park Arboretum ④
A 1,230-yd (1,130-m) nature trail winds through this wooded hillside, planted with native and other trees. Species include dogwoods, Jeffrey pine, ponderosa pine, black oaks, live oaks, and white fir.

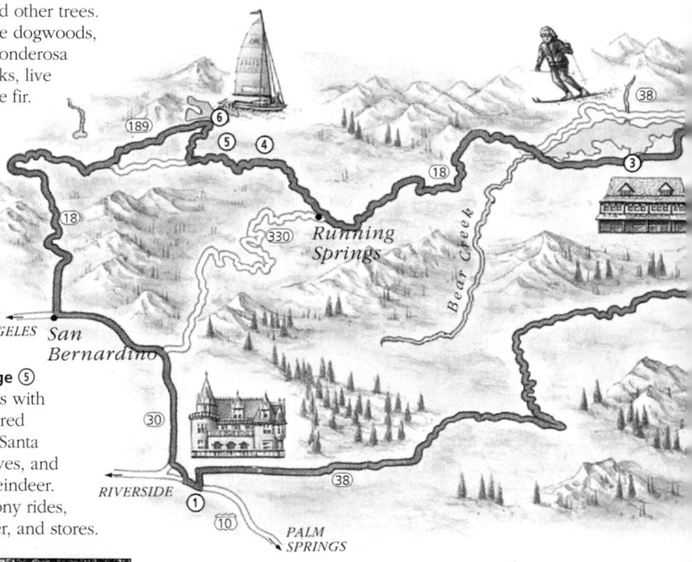

Santa's Village ⑤
Log buildings with brightly colored roofs house Santa Claus, his elves, and Rudolf the reindeer. There are pony rides, a pets' corner, and stores.

Lake Arrowhead ⑥
Lake Arrowhead Village, on the south shore, offers shops, restaurants and accommodations in both hotels and log cabins. Trips up the lake aboard the *Arrowhead Queen* also begin here. The north shore is almost exclusively residential.

Redlands ①
This town is famous for its Victorian mansions, built at the end of the 19th century by those who made their fortunes growing navel oranges *(see p50)*. Among the finest are Kimberly Crest House and Gardens, the Morey Mansion, and the Edwards Mansion.

Ornate Mission Inn in Riverside

Onyx Summit ②

At 8,443 ft (2,573 m), Onyx Summit is the highest point on the Rim of the World Tour. From a viewpoint near the top there are stunning views across the mountainous San Bernardino National Forest to the desert.

0 kilometers   10

0 miles   5

KEY

━━ Tour route

═══ Other roads

Riverside ②

Road map D6. 👥 250,000. 🚆 ℹ️
7920 Limonite Ave (951 681-9242).
www.riversideca.gov

Some of the most elegant architecture in Southern California is to be found in Riverside. During the late 19th century, the town was the center of California's citrus industry and by 1905 it had the highest per capita income in the U.S. One of the two original orange trees responsible for this great success was planted in 1875 by Eliza and Luther Tibbetts *(see p50)*. It is still thriving in a small park at the intersection of Magnolia and Arlington avenues.

Pot at Hi-Desert Nature Museum

Riverside's **Mission Inn**, built in 1880 as a 12-room adobe house, was expanded early in the 20th century into a 234-room hotel *(see p540)*. Architecturally, the hotel is a mixture of Mission Revival, Moorish, and oriental styles, with flying buttresses, spiral staircases, and gargoyles. The **Riverside Municipal Museum** has exhibits on the town's history and Native American culture. Riverside is also known for two major car races: the California 500 in early September, and the Winston Western 500 in January.

🏨 **Mission Inn**
3649 Mission Inn Ave. **Tel** (909) 784-0300. ℹ️ www.missioninn.com

🏛 **Riverside Municipal Museum**
3720 Orange St. **Tel** (951) 826-5273. ⬜ daily.

Yucca Valley ③

Road map D5. 👥 44,000. 🚆 ℹ️
56711 Twenty-nine Palms Hwy (760 365-6323). www.yuccavalley.org

Yucca Valley is a small town located just north of the Joshua Tree National Park *(see pp278–9)*. On a hillside, the **Desert Christ Park** has 30 statues depicting the life of Jesus, sculpted by Antone Martin in the 1950s. The town's **Hi-Desert Nature Museum** has various exhibits on the region's geology, crafts, flora, and fauna.
Pioneertown, 4 miles (6 km) northwest of Yucca Valley, is a hamlet built in 1947 as a Western film set.

🌵 **Desert Christ Park**
End of Mohawk Trail. **Tel** (760) 365-6323. ⬜ daily.

🏛 **Hi-Desert Museum**
58116 Twenty-nine Palms Hwy. **Tel** (760) 369-7212. ⬜ 10am–5pm Tue–Sun. ⬛ public hols.

Statue of Christ at the Antone Martin Memorial Park

Palm Springs ❹

Popcorn in Ruddy's

The Coachella Valley has been inhabited for 10,000 years, but it was only in 1853 that a government survey party came across a grove of palm trees surrounding a mineral pool bubbling up out of the desert sand. The area's first hotel was constructed in 1886, and by the turn of the century the city of Palm Springs was a thriving health spa. In the 1920s and 1930s the area become a fashionable winter resort, colonized by the rich and famous.

Exploring Palm Springs

The postwar building boom (*see p54*) brought rapid hotel and residential development to Palm Springs. Drawn by the city's growing popularity, developers later began opening up the empty desert lands eastward along the Coachella Valley. From 1967 to 1981, the resort cities of Cathedral City, Rancho Mirage, Palm Desert, Indian Wells, and La Quinta shot up between Palm Springs and the date-growing center of Indio, 22 miles (35 km) away. Desert Hot Springs, a spa just northeast of Palm Springs, also became a popular vacation destination. The extraordinary proliferation of luxury golf courses – there are more than 80 in the region – dates from this period (*see p277*).

Today Palm Springs remains the largest of the desert cities. Its population doubles each winter, when visitors come to enjoy its healthy, relaxing, outdoor lifestyle. First-class accommodations, such as the Givenchy and Marriot hotels, abound (*see p539*). Many celebrities still live here, and several companies offer guided tours that point out their houses.

The two main shopping streets in downtown Palm Springs are Palm Canyon and Indian Canyon drives. Each is lined with outdoor restaurants, exclusive boutiques, and art galleries. In the city center, the pedestrian Desert Fashion Plaza houses two department stores and several smaller luxury shops.

The city's unique sense of desert chic is maintained in discreet ways. Street lights, for example, are hidden within palm leaves and bushes to lend the area a subtle glow.

Old Shredded Wheat advertisement from Ruddy's in Village Green

🏛 Village Green Heritage Center

221 S Palm Canyon Drive. **Tel** (760) 323-8297. ⬤ Oct–May: Wed–Sun. ⬤ public hols. 📷

This quiet enclave, in the heart of Palm Springs' shopping district, contains four historical buildings. Palm Springs' first white resident, John Guthrie McCallum, built the McCallum Adobe in 1884. Originally it stood near the Indian village of Agua Caliente, the site of the natural hot springs that inspired the town's name. The house was moved to its present location during the 1950s.

The Cornelia White House (1893) is built partly out of railroad ties. It is furnished with antiques dating from Palm Springs' pioneer era.

The heritage of the area's Cahuilla people is related through artifacts and photographs in the Agua Caliente Cultural Museum. There is also a collection of antique baskets that were handcrafted by local Native American weavers.

Also in the Village Green Heritage Center is Ruddy's 1930s General Store Museum. Once the town's only druggist, Ruddy's is an immaculate and well-stocked replica of a Depression-era shop. Authentically packaged goods range from licorice and shoelaces to flour and patent medicines.

🏊 Knotts Soak City

1500 Gene Autry Trail. **Tel** (760) 327-0499. ⬤ Mar–early Sep: daily; Sep–Oct: Sat & Sun. ⬤ public hols. 📷 www.knotts.com

This state-of-the-art water park covers 21 acres (8.5 ha). It boasts 13 waterslides, including an exciting 70-ft (20-m) free-fall slide and a 600-ft (180-m) artificial "river" for riding inflated inner tubes. There are special slides and pools for young children. California's largest wave-action pool creates 4-ft (1.2-m) high artificial waves suitable for surfing and boogie boarding. Surfboards and inner tubes can be rented from the park on either an hourly or a daily basis.

The Oasis Water Resort has a hotel, a rock climbing center, heated spas, a health club, and many fine restaurants.

Children emerging from a Scorpion free-fall slide at Knotts Soak City

Palm Springs Aerial Tramway ascending to the Mountain Station

🚡 Palm Springs Aerial Tramway

Tramway Rd. **Tel** *(760) 325-1391.*
⬜ *daily.* 🏷️ **www.**pstramway.com
The Aerial Tramway's two Swiss-built cars, each holding 80 passengers, are one of Palm Springs' most popular attractions. The trams depart from Valley Station, situated 6 miles (10 km) northwest of Palm Springs. The 2.5-mile (4-km) trip at an angle of 50° takes 14 minutes and ascends 5,900 ft (1,790 m) over spectacular scenery to the Mountain Station in the Mount San Jacinto Wilderness State Park.

Passengers travel through five distinct ecosystems, ranging from desert to alpine forest, which is akin to traveling from Mexico to Alaska. The temperature changes dramatically during the journey. The heat of the valley floor sometimes differs as much as 50° F (10° C) from the icy temperature at the peak, so make sure you carry extra clothing.

At the top there are 54 miles (85 km) of hiking trails, one of which leads to Idyllwild *(see p276).* A Nordic ski center is open in the winter for cross-country skiing. There are also campsites, a ranger station, picnic areas, and 20-minute mule-pack rides on the slopes.

Observation decks perched on the edge of the 8,500-ft (2,600-m) high lookout offer views of the Coachella Valley, Palm Springs, and the San Bernardino Mountains. On a very clear day, it is possible to see for 50 miles (80 km) to the Salton Sea *(see p277).*

Both stations have gift shops, cocktail lounges, and snack bars. The Mountain Station also has a cafeteria.

🏛 Palm Springs Desert Museum

101 Museum Drive. **Tel** *(760) 325-7186.* ⬜ *Tue–Sun.* ⚫ *public hols.* 🏷️ *free first Fri of month.*
www.psmuseum.org
The Palm Springs Desert Museum focuses on art, natural science, and the performing arts. Paintings in the museum's galleries date from the 19th century to the present day. Native American artifacts and local natural history exhibits are also on display. A stunning array of modern sculpture adorns the patios and gardens.

The adjoining Annenberg Theater is a 450-seat center for the performing arts, which features both local and touring dance, drama, and orchestral companies. The lush gardens are enhanced by fountains and demonstrate that the desert need not be a barren place.

Two trails lead out from the museum and enable visitors to explore the flora and fauna of this desert region. The 2-mile (3-km) Museum Trail climbs 800 ft (244 m) up into the Mount San Jacinto State Park. It joins the Lykken Trail at Desert Riders Overlook (a viewpoint from which to look out across Palm Springs and the Coachella Valley). The

VISITORS' CHECKLIST

Road map D6. 🏘️ *42,000.* ✈️
Palm Springs Regional Airport,
1 mile (1.5 km) NE of Downtown.
🚉 *Indio.* 🚌 *3111 N Indian Ave.*
ℹ️ *2901 N Palm Canyon Dr;*
(800) 347-7746, (760) 778-8418.
🎬 *Palm Springs International*
Film Festival (early–mid-Jan).
www.palm-springs.org

Lykken Trail then continues for another 4 miles (6 km) to the mouth of the Tahquitz Canyon *(see p276).*

Sculpture garden in the Palm Springs Desert Museum

PALM TREES

Only one palm variety in Palm Springs is native to California, the desert fan palm *(Washingtonia filifera),* which crowds the secluded mountain oases. Unlike other palm varieties, the dead fronds do not drop off the trunk but droop down to form a "skirt" that provides a shelter for wildlife.

Date palms *(Phoenix dactylifera)* were introduced from Algeria in 1890 as an experiment. Today, the Coachella Valley supplies 90 percent of the dates consumed in the US. A mature date palm can produce up to 300 lb (135 kg) of dates a year. An annual ten-day National Date Festival in Indio features a cornucopia of dried and fresh dates *(see p39).*

Date palm grove in the Coachella Valley

🐾 Indian Canyons

S Palm Canyon Drive. **Tel** *(760) 325-3400.* ◯ *8am–4:30pm daily.* 📷 **www**.indian-canyons.com

Approximately 5 miles (8 km) south of Palm Springs are four spectacular natural palm oases, set in stark, rocky gorges and surrounded by barren hills. Clustered along small streams fed by mountain springs, Murray, Tahquitz, Andreas, and Palm canyons are located on the land of the Agua Caliente Cahuilla people. Rock art and other traces of the area's early inhabitants can still be seen.

The 15-mile (24-km) long Palm Canyon is the largest of the gorges and contains more wild palms in one place than anywhere else in the world. Refreshments are available near the parking lot and from here it is a short but steep walk down to the main trail. There are picnic tables beside a stream under the 82-ft (25-m) high fan palms *(see p275).*

Desert fan palm oasis in the Indian Canyons

🐾 Living Desert Wildlife and Botanical Park

47900 Portola Ave. **Tel** *(760) 346-5694.* ◯ *daily.* ⬤ *Dec 25.* 📷 **www**.livingdesert.org

The well-designed Living Desert Wildlife and Botanical Park offers a comprehensive view of North America's desert regions. The park covers 1,200 acres (485 ha), but most of its major attractions can be seen in half a day. Broad paths and paved walkways pass through interpretive botanical displays covering North America's 10 desert areas, which describe some of the 130 animal species that inhabit them.

Flowering ocotillo in the Living Desert Wildlife and Botanical Park

Of special interest are golden eagles, mountain lions, a large selection of nocturnal creatures, and the new cheetah exhibit. Roadrunners (desert birds that run rather than fly) roam free in their natural setting. On winter days, walking through the park is a pleasure. A guided tram tour is recommended in hotter weather.

Palms to Pines Highway ❺

Road map D6. ℹ️ *72–990 Hwy 111, Palm Desert (760 862-9984).*

One of the most interesting drives in Southern California begins at the junction of Hwy 111 and Hwy 74 in Palm Desert. As you climb Hwy 74, you gradually leave behind the desert ecosystem with its palms, creosote, and desert ironwood trees and move into mountain scenery, made up of pines, juniper, and

mountain mahogany. The view from Santa Rosa Summit, just under 5,000 ft (1,500 m) high, is spectacular. Continue northwest on Hwy 74 to Mountain Center and the lush meadows of Garner Valley.

At Mountain Center, take Hwy 243 to the picturesque alpine village of Idyllwild, with its many restaurants, lodges, and camp sites. The renowned Idyllwild School of Music and the Arts holds regular classical music concerts during the summer. More active visitors can follow one of the many surrounding hiking trails, for which maps are available at the Ranger Station. One 8-mile (13-km) trek leads to the Mountain Station of the Palm Springs Aerial Tramway *(see p275).* This provides the quickest way back to the desert floor. Mule-pack rides are available in the summer, and during the winter months there is cross-country skiing.

Anza-Borrego Desert State Park ❻

Road map D6. 🚌 *Escondido.* **Visitors' Center Tel** *(760) 767-4205.* ◯ *Jun–Sep: Sat, Sun and hols; Oct–May: daily.* **www**.anzaborregostatepark.org

Starting with the Gold Rush of 1849 *(see pp48–9),* the Southern Emigrant Trail, the only all-weather land route into California, brought tens of thousands of miners and early settlers through the Anza-Borrego Desert. Today, this former overland gateway is a

Picturesque mountain town of Idyllwild

For hotels and restaurants in this region see pp538–40 and pp584–6

Badlands in the Anza-Borrego Desert State Park

remote and pristine park, offering a rare insight into a unique desert environment.

The desert's well-equipped visitors' center is in Borrego Springs. This is the only significant town in the otherwise undeveloped park. Nearby, the leisurely 1.5-mile (2.5-km) Palm Canyon Nature Trail leads to an oasis where the endangered bighorn sheep can occasionally be seen.

The Box Canyon Historical Monument is 31 miles (50 km) southwest of the visitors' center on County Road S2. Here you can view the old road once used by those miners who braved the desert climate on their way to the goldfields, which lay 500 miles (800 km) to the north.

The Anza-Borrego Desert is inhospitable for most of the year. Between March and May, however, following the winter rains, the burning land bursts into life. Cacti and desert flowers such as brittle-bush, desert poppies, and dune primroses produce a riot of color.

The desert's geology is as fascinating as its ecosystem. Over the millennia, a network of earthquake faults lifted and tilted the ground. Winter rains then carved through the shattered landscape, leaving multicolored "layer-cake" bluffs, steep ravines, and jagged canyons such as the famous Borrego and Carizzo Badlands.

Much of the Anza-Borrego State Park, including its well-kept camp sites, is easily accessible via 100 miles (160 km) of surfaced and scenic highways. However, four-wheel drive vehicles are recommended for use on the park's 500 miles (800 km) of unsurfaced roads.

Drivers of standard vehicles should contact the visitors' center in advance to check on current road conditions.

Salton Sea ❼

Road map E6. 🚗 *Mecca*
🚌 *Indio.* **Visitors' Center**
Tel *(760) 393-3052.* ☐ *daily*

The Salton Sea was created by accident in 1905 when the Colorado River flooded and flowed into a newly dug irrigation canal leading to the Imperial Valley. It took a team of engineers two years to stem the flow. By then, however, a 35-mile (55-km) inland sea had formed in the Salton Sink, 230 ft (70 m) below sea level.

Despite rising salinity and selenium levels, and algae blooms that turn the water a brownish color during the summer, there are still saltwater game fish in this inland sea, with 10-lb (4.5-kg) orangemouth corvina being caught regularly.

Windsurfing, water-skiing, and boating are also popular activities here. The northeastern shore of the sea has the best spots for swimming, particularly the stretch of water off Mecca Beach.

The sea's adjoining marshlands are a refuge for a wide variety of migrating birds, such as geese, ducks, blue herons, and egrets. On the east side of the Salton Sea there are hiking trails and camp sites set within the State Recreation Area. There is also a visitors' center and a small playground.

DESERT GOLF

Thanks to irrigation with water supplied from underground sources, Palm Springs is now known as the golf capital of the United States. There are more than 80 courses in the region, most of which belong to private clubs or are attached to resorts or hotel complexes. Some courses are rugged, while others are more lush. Among the professional golf events held in the area each year are the Bob Hope Desert Classic in January and the Dinah Shore Tournament at the end of March. A few courses are open to the public, including the Desert Dunes course, noted for adding the desert terrain to its challenging layout. In the summer it is best to tee off early in the morning. November and December offer better value and cooler weather. Most courses are closed in October for reseeding.

Tahquitz Creek Palm Springs Golf Resort

Joshua Tree National Park ❽

National park sign

The Joshua Tree National Park was established in 1936 to preserve the groves of the unusual, spiny-leaved Joshua tree. The species was named in 1851 by early Mormon travelers, who saw in the twisted branches the upraised arms of the biblical Joshua. This large member of the yucca family is unique to the area and can grow up to 30 ft (9 m) tall, sometimes living for 1,000 years. The 630,800-acre (255,300-ha) park offers uncommon vistas of the stark Californian desert, with its astounding formations of pink and gray rocks and boulders. A climber's paradise, Joshua Tree is also a fascinating area for hikers, who can discover lost mines, palm oases, and in the spring, a wealth of desert flowers. The Visitors' Center provides the latest weather report.

Joshua Trees
Large groves of Joshua trees thrive in the higher, wetter, and somewhat cooler desert areas of the park's western half.

Hidden Valley
The gigantic boulders here formed natural corrals, making this a legendary hideout for cattle rustlers in the days of the Wild West.

Key's View gives a sweeping view of the stunning valley, desert, and mountain terrain from its summit.

KEY

━━	Freeway
━━	Major road
══	Minor road
═══	Unsurfaced road
- - -	Hiking trail
───	National Park boundary
🚶	Ranger station
📷	Fee station
⛺	Campsite
🏕	Picnic area
☀	Viewpoint

Lost Horse Mine
A 2-mile (3.2-km) trail leads to this historic gold mine, which was discovered by a cowboy searching for his lost horse. More than $270,000 in gold was extracted during the mine's first decade of operation.

DESERT WILDLIFE

Despite the harshness of the arid desert environment, a variety of animals thrives here. In many cases, they have adapted to cope with lack of water. The kangaroo rat gets both its food and water from seeds alone, while its very large hind feet enable it to travel over the hot sand. Powerful legs, rather than wings, also serve the roadrunner, which gets its moisture from insects and small prey. The jackrabbit is born with a full coat of muted fur to camouflage it from large predators such as the coyote, bobcat, and eagle.

Coyote, wily denizen of the desert

VISITORS' CHECKLIST

Road map D5. 🚌 *Desert Stage Lines from Palm Springs to Twentynine Palms.* 🏢 **Oasis Visitors' Center** *74485 National Park Drive, Twentynine Palms.* **Tel** *(760) 367- 5500.* ⬜ *daily.* ⚫ *Dec 25.* **www**.nps.gov/jotr

| 0 kilometers | 10 |
| 0 miles | 10 |

The arid wilderness of the Colorado Desert (*see p203*) occupies the park's eastern half. This inhospitable region is difficult to reach.

PINTO MOUNTAINS

COXCOMB MOUNTAINS

PINTO BASIN

Cholla Cactus Garden

HEXIE MOUNTAINS

Pinto Basin Road

Cottonwood 🚹 🏢
Cottonwood Spring △

COTTONWOOD MOUNTAINS

Lost Palms Oasis

EAGLE MOUNTAIN

PALM SPRINGS

(10) BLYTHE

Lost Palms Oasis
A 4-mile (6.4-km) trail leads through attractive desert scenery to the largest group of palms in the park. It is one of the few areas where water occurs naturally near the surface.

Cottonwood Spring is a man-made oasis of palms and cottonwood trees that attracts desert birds. There is a visitors' center nearby.

Cholla Cactus Garden
A dense concentration of cholla cacti are the focal point of a short nature trail featuring desert flora and fauna. But beware – the cactus's fluffy fingers are really sharp spines.

THE MOJAVE DESERT

The Mojave Desert is the state's greatest secret, all too often missed by travelers who zoom through it on the interstate highway. The desert is a harsh environment – Death Valley is one of the hottest places in the United States. But this dry region supports a surprising amount of plant life and for a few weeks each year, when the wildflowers appear amid the arid rocks, it becomes hauntingly beautiful.

The Mojave Desert was a year-round overland gateway to California for much of the 19th century. Trappers, traders, and early settlers traveled hundreds of miles along the Old Spanish Trail from Santa Fe in New Mexico to Los Angeles. Passing through the towns of Barstow and Tecopa, the journey across the vast desert was both demanding and dangerous.

In the 1870s, gold, silver, borax, and various other precious minerals were discovered in the region, attracting large numbers of miners. Instant cities such as Calico sprang up, but when the mines became exhausted, many of the settlements were abandoned. In 1883 commercial mining became more viable when the Santa Fe Railroad was completed. Towns located along the route prospered, and the human population of the Mojave Desert increased.

In the early 20th century a new breed of desert lovers emerged. Jack Mitchell settled in the empty expanses of the East Mojave Desert in the 1930s and turned the spectacular Mitchell Caverns into a popular tourist destination. Death Valley Scotty was another desert enthusiast. He spent much of his life in a castle built in the 1920s by his friend, Albert Johnson, near the hottest and lowest point in the western hemisphere. Death Valley National Park now attracts thousands of visitors each year, who come to explore the area's wealth of historical landmarks and impressive natural sights.

The main draw of the Mojave Desert region today, however, is Nevada's Las Vegas, a five-hour drive from Los Angeles. This center of entertainment and gambling is proof that people are still trying to strike it rich in the desert.

Death Valley's Moorish-style Scotty's Castle

◁ **Desert shrubs in Death Valley**

Exploring the Mojave Desert

Most of the Mojave Desert is at an altitude of
over 2,000 ft (600 m). It has cold winters and
baking hot summers. Many of the region's
rivers and lakes are seasonal and are dry during the summer. The desert is home to an
array of plant species and a range of animals,
from tortoises to foxes, which have evolved to
survive in this climate. Barstow, the largest town
in the Mojave region, caters to travelers to
and from Las Vegas. The northern Mojave is
dominated by the Death Valley National Park.
To the east lie the resorts of Lake Havasu.

**Premises of a 19th-century ore smelter
in Calico Ghost Town**

SIGHTS AT A GLANCE

Barstow ❸
Calico Ghost Town ❹
*Death Valley National
   Park pp290–93* ❾
Edwards Air Force Base ❷
Kelso Dunes ❺
Lake Havasu ❼
Las Vegas ❽
Mitchell Caverns ❻
Red Rock Canyon State Park ❶

KEY

 ══ Freeway

 ── Major road

 ── Secondary road

 ══ Minor road

 ── Scenic route

 ┄┄ Main railway

 ── Minor railway

 ══ State border

 △ Summit

SEE ALSO

• *Where to Stay* p540–41

• *Where to Eat* p586–7

0 kilometers 25

0 miles   25

Sand dunes north of Furnace Creek in the Death Valley National Park

GETTING AROUND

I-15 crosses the region. It links San Diego to Las Vegas, Nevada, via San Bernardino. This route follows the northern border of the East Mojave National Preserve, and I-40 skirts its southern border. The main south-north route across the desert is Hwy 127, from which Hwy 190 branches out, crossing the Death Valley National Park from southeast to southwest. In the west, US Hwy 395 leads south to LA. For safety reasons, it is vital that visitors to the desert obey posted signs and do not stray from main roads. Always carry water, a jack, a usable spare tire, a cell phone, and stay close to your vehicle if you break down. There is no public access to the area's clearly marked military zones *(see p284)*.

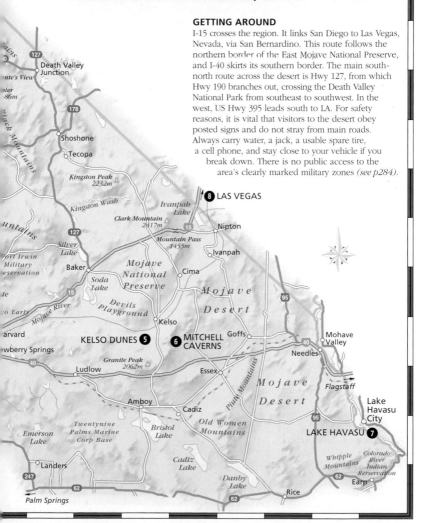

Stunning colors of Red Rock Canyon

Red Rock Canyon State Park ❶

Road map D5. 🚌 *from Mojave, Ridgecrest.* **Visitors' Center Tel** *(661) 942-0662.* ☐ *daily.* **www**.calparksmojave.com

Alternate layers of white clay, red sandstone, pink volcanic rocks, and brown lava are spectacularly combined in Red Rock Canyon. This beautiful state park is situated in the El Paso Mountains, which lie at the southern end of the Sierra Nevada Mountains. Like the High Sierras *(see p484),* Red Rock Canyon is the product of plate movements that pushed up the bedrock approximately 3 million years ago. The western side of the canyon slopes gently upward in stark contrast to the high, abrupt cliffs on its eastern side, which have been carved and crenellated by water and wind.

Three major desert ecozones overlap here, providing a wealth of plant and animal life. Eagles, hawks, and falcons nest in the cliffs. Coyotes, kit foxes, bobcats, and various reptiles, such as the desert iguana, are common. The landscape has been used as the backdrop for countless Westerns, advertisements, and science-fiction films, making it oddly familiar to many visitors.

Edwards Air Force Base ❷

Road map D5. **Tel** *(661) 276-3446.* 🚌 *from Mojave, Rosamond.* ☐ *Mon–Fri.* ● *public hols.* 📷 ♿ 📷 *by appointment only.*

While it is famous around the world as the site of the West Coast space shuttle landings, Edwards Air Force Base has been steeped in the history of America in flight since 1933. The 65-sq-mile (168-sq-km) flat expanse of Rogers Dry Lake provides an enormous natural runway that is perfect for emergency landings. The area's year-round fine and clear weather adds to its suitability for aircraft testing and the training of test pilots. It was here that the very first jet-propelled aircraft was tested in 1942. Here, too, Captain Chuck Yeager became the first to break the sound barrier on October 14, 1947, in a Bell XS-1 rocket

Space shuttle Atlantis landing at Edwards Air Force Base

plane. Fifty pilots still graduate each year from the Test Pilot School.

Edwards is also home to the NASA Dryden Flight Research Center. Free guided tours of the space Aeronautics Center are available by reservation. Tours include a video on the history of aeronautics research and a visit to a hangar housing current aircraft.

Barstow 3

Road map D5. 🏙 *22,000.* 🚌 ℹ️ *681 North First Ave (760 256-8617).*

During the 19th century, this was a small settlement that served farmers as well as emigrants and miners on the Old Spanish Trail *(see p281).* In 1886 the new Barstow–San Bernardino rail line opened, linking Kansas City with the Pacific Coast. Barstow's original railroad station, the Casa del Desierto, has recently been restored.

THE MILITARY IN THE MOJAVE

The United States government has set aside vast areas of the Mojave Desert for military use. All such areas are strictly off-limits to civilians. During World War II, the Desert Training Center covered 17,500 sq miles (45,300 sq km) and was used by General Patton to train his forces. Today, smaller military preserves include the China Lake Weapons Center, northeast of Mojave, which is used for live bombing and artillery testing. North of Barstow, the Fort Irwin National Training Center (NTC), which covers more than 1,000 sq miles (2,600 sq km), is an important US Army installation. The NTC has a population of 12,000, including civilian workers. Its desert terrain was used to prepare troops for the Gulf War in 1990 – 91, and is one of the main US training areas for tanks and weapons.

T-38 Talon high-altitude jet trainer at Edwards Air Force Base

Restored and reconstructed buildings in Calico Ghost Town

From 1937 to the late 1950s, Barstow was an important town along Route 66, the only surfaced road from Chicago to the West Coast. The town is best known today as being the midway point on I-15 between Los Angeles and Las Vegas. To the 41 million people who make this journey each year, it is a convenient stopping-off point. But many also come here in search of the precious minerals and gemstones to be found in the surrounding desert.

The **California Desert Information Center**, in Barstow, has informative indoor displays on the Mojave Desert's flora and fauna. Maps of the area and hotel and restaurant information are available, and the center has a bookstore.

California Desert Information Center
831 Barstow Rd, Barstow. **Tel** (760) 252- 6060. ☐ 11am–4pm Tue–Sat. ● Jan 1, Dec 25, public hols.

Calico Ghost Town ❹

Road map D5. **Tel** (760) 254-2122. 🚌 Barstow. ☐ 9am–5pm daily. ● Dec 25. 📷 ♿ www.calicotown.com

Calico Ghost Town, 11 miles (18 km) east of Barstow, is a late-19th-century mining town, which is part-authentic and part-reconstruction. Silver was found in the Calico Mountains on March 26, 1881, and soon hundreds of miners arrived. Some of the veins they struck were so rich that they produced 25 lb (11 kg) of silver per ton. Two years later, borax was discovered 3 miles (5 km) east of Calico, and the town's prosperity seemed assured. During the 1880s, Calico boasted a population of 1,200 – and 22 saloons – but after the price of silver fell

A flint tool from the Early Man Site

and the equally valuable borax gave out, the miners left. By 1907, Calico was a ghost town.

Walter Knott, founder of Knott's Berry Farm (see p236), began the restoration process in the 1950s. Calico's isolation and desert setting reinforce the sense of a rough old mining town. Many of the original buildings remain, and visitors can take a ride in a mine train or explore tunnels in Maggie Mine, one of the most famous silver mines on the West Coast. Shows and tours are also held, including mock "shoot-outs" staged on the main street, and walking tours given each day by the town's resident historian.

Environs

About 10 miles (16 km) west of Calico lies the **Calico Early Man Site**. At this archaeological site, thousands of 100,000-year-old stone tools have been discovered. They were made by North America's earliest-known inhabitants, who once lived in this area on the shores of a great lake. The renowned archaeologist and paleontologist Dr. Louis Leakey was director of the site from 1964 until his death in 1972.

Calico Early Man Site
Off I-15 & Minneola Rd. **Tel** (760) 254-2288. ☐ Mon–Fri. ● Jan 1, Jul 4, Dec 25. **Donation.** www.calicodig.com

Casa del Desierto, Barstow's historic railroad station

Mesquite mud flats in Death Valley National Park (see pp290–93) ▷

Kelso Dunes **❺**

Road map E5. 🚌 *Baker.* **Tel** *Mojave National Preserve (760) 733-4040.*

Kelso Dunes tower more than 700 ft (210 m) above the desert floor. Situated in the Mojave National Preserve, the dunes are formed from grains of golden rose quartz that have been blown from the Mojave River basin, 35 miles (56 km) to the west. Known as the "singing" dunes, they occasionally emit buzzing and rumbling sounds. These are thought to be caused by the upper layers of sand sliding down the face of the dune, producing vibrations that are then amplified by the underlying sand.

The desert floor with the Kelso Dunes in the background

Mitchell Caverns **❻**

Tel *(760) 928-2586.* 🚌 *from Barstow.* ◯ *Sep–Jun: daily.* 🏞 🎫 *(Sat & Sun summer only).* **www**.calparksmojave.com

Mitchell Caverns are a spectacular collection of caves along the eastern slope of the Providence Mountains.

The original London Bridge, now located in Lake Havasu City

The caverns were formed 12–15 million years ago, when acidic rainwater began to carve through layers of ancient limestone. Arrowheads and pottery shards have been found here, left behind by the Chemehuevi people. Until the 1860s, the Native Americans had stored food and held religious ceremonies in the caves for nearly 500 years. Opened as a tourist attraction in the 1930s by silver miner Jack Mitchell, the caverns are now owned and run by California State Parks.

Inside, the chambers feature three types of cave formation: flow stones (delicate curtain shapes); drip stones (stalagmites and stalactites); and erratics (ribbons, shields and "staghorn coral"). In one, there is a rare combination of a cave shield, flowstone column, and coral pipes. Sturdy shoes are advisable for the two-hour tour, which includes El Pakiva (The Sacred Pools), one of the most famous chambers. A nearby 1-mile (1.6-km) trail up Crystal Spring Canyon climbs into the Providence Mountains and offers views of the desert.

Lake Havasu **❼**

Road map E5. 🚌 *Las Vegas.* **Tel** *(928) 855- 4115.* **www**.lakehavasu.com

Lake Havasu is a 46-mile (74-km) long reservoir, which was created in 1938 when the Colorado River was blocked by the Parker Dam *(see p203).* Lake Havasu City, a resort town on the border between California and Arizona, was developed by the millionaire Robert McCulloch in the 1960s. McCulloch imported the historic London Bridge stone-by-stone to the newly created development. The bridge spans a channel dredged especially for it and overlooks English-style shops and restaurants on a nearby plot of land known as English Village.

The lake itself lies within a National Wildlife Refuge, which is frequented by bird-watchers and anglers. There are many camp sites and marinas that offer houseboats, boats, and water-sports equipment for rent. Several short boat tours around the lake are available. A daily three-hour excursion to Topock Gorge, at the northern end of Lake Havasu, offers a more leisurely introduction to this rugged desert setting.

Environs

Off Hwy 95, 20 miles (32 km) south of Lake Havasu City, lies the Colorado River Indian Reservation. Here, visitors can admire a collection of giant prehistoric figures, carved out of the rocks that form the desert floor. In both human and animal form, it is not known whether the figures were made for religious or artistic reasons.

Impressive cave formations in Mitchell Caverns

Las Vegas ⑧

Las Vegas is in Nevada, 37 miles (60 km) from the California border. With the construction of the Hoover Dam in the 1930s, it grew into a major city. Gambling was legalized in Nevada in 1931. In 1945 the Flamingo Hotel and Casino were built on the outskirts on what is known as "The Strip." Similar places soon sprang up, and Las Vegas became a 24-hour oasis of gambling and entertainment.

One of the city's many neon signs

Las Vegas "Strip" at dusk

Exploring Las Vegas

Today, Las Vegas is changing its image to appeal to families as well as gamblers. The city offers a wide variety of entertainment for all tastes and budgets in some of the most affordable and largest hotel and convention complexes in the world. Las Vegas is now a city of nearly one million permanent residents, with its own museums and other cultural institutions. But it is the 30 million tourists who visit Las Vegas each year who continue to fuel the amazing development of

this metropolis. Despite the neon lights, swimming pools, and hotels, the blazing sun and cloudless skies serve as a constant reminder that Las Vegas is surrounded by desert.

Hotels in Las Vegas provide more than just food and lodging. They are architectural marvels that offer some of the best sightseeing and entertainment in town. The Treasure Island Hotel and Casino stages mock sea battles between the British Navy and pirates. Next door is the Mirage Hotel and Casino with its massive aquariums, tropical rainforest, white tigers, and rumbling "volcano." The Luxor, built on the same scale as the pyramids of Egypt, houses the largest atrium in the world, complete with animatronic camels, Egyptian decor and high-tech laser shows. At night, the Luxor shoots the world's brightest beam of light into the sky from its pinnacle. The nearby MGM Grand offers a theme park called "The Emerald City of Oz," always a great favorite with children.

🏛 Stratosphere Tower

2000 Las Vegas Blvd S. *Tel (702) 380-7777.*
At 1,149 ft (350 m), Stratosphere Tower is the tallest freestanding observation tower in the United States. At the top there is an incomparable view of Las Vegas (best seen at night), a revolving restaurant and cocktail lounge, three wedding chapels, and two thrilling rides. The world's highest roller coaster leaves from 909 ft (275 m) up and runs for 865 ft (265 m) around the outside of the tower.

🏛 Fremont Street Experience

Bordered by Charles & Stewart Sts. *Tel (702) 678-5777.* ◯ daily.
Las Vegas's first gaming license was issued on Fremont Street in the 1930s. Over the years, this downtown area became known as "Glitter Gulch," due to its profusion of neon signs and lights. Now five blocks of Fremont, stretching from Main Street to Las Vegas Boulevard, have been transformed into the Fremont Street Experience – a covered pedestrian promenade. Casinos line the street. A spectacular light and sound show is held each night, using more than two million computer-controlled lights.

Environs

Lake Mead, which lies 25 miles (40 km) east of Las Vegas, was created by the construction of Hoover Dam, completed in 1931. The lake extends 110 miles (175 km) and has more than 500 miles (800 km) of shoreline. Scuba-diving, boating, water-skiing, and fishing facilities are all available. There are daily tours of the 726-ft (220-m) high dam and a visitors' center with exhibits on the region's natural history. The Valley of Fire State Park, 55 miles (88 km) northeast of Las Vegas, has stunning orange sandstone formations. Petroglyphs and other remains of an ancient Native American civilization can still be seen. Red Rock Canyon (not the same as the park on *page 284*), 15 miles (24 km) west of Las Vegas, has 3,000-ft (900-m) high escarpments, and ridges, and trails for all levels of hikers.

Stratosphere Tower

VISITORS' CHECKLIST

Road map E4. 🏛 *1,200,000.* ✈ *McCarran International Airport, 4 miles (6.5 km) S of Las Vegas.* 🚌 *200 S Main St.* 🚉 *1 Main St.* ℹ *3150 Paradise Rd (702 892-0711).* **www**.vegasfreedom.com **Treasure Island Hotel and Casino** 3300 Las Vegas Blvd. *Tel (702) 894-7111.* **Mirage Hotel and Casino** 3400 Las Vegas Blvd. *Tel (702) 791-7111.* **Luxor Las Vegas Hotel and Casino** 3900 Las Vegas Blvd. *Tel (702) 262-4000.* **MGM Grand Hotel, Casino and Theme Park** 3799 Las Vegas Blvd. *Tel (702) 891-7777.*

Death Valley National Park ❾

Throughout the summer months, Death Valley National Park has the highest mean temperature of anywhere on the planet. This is a land of wrenching extremes, a sunken trough in the earth's crust that reaches the lowest point in the Western Hemisphere. The valley is guarded on both sides by ranges of rugged mountains. The range on the western side soars 11,000 ft (3,350 m) to form razor-sharp peaks. Even though it is always inhospitable, Death Valley is also a place of subtle colors and polished canyons, of burning salt flats and delicate rock formations. It is now one of the most unique and popular tourist destinations in the state of California.

Central Death Valley

Furnace Creek, with its various provisions and accommodation centers, is located in the heart of Death Valley. Many of the most impressive sights in the park are within easy reach of this visitors' complex.

🐟 Salt Creek

Salt Creek supports the hardy pupfish. Endemic to Death Valley, the pupfish can live in water almost four times as salty as the sea and withstand temperatures of up to 111° F (44° C). The fish attract other wildlife, including great blue herons. Wooden walkways allow visitors to explore this unique site without disturbing the fragile habitat.

🏛 Borax Museum

Furnace Creek Ranch. *Tel* (760) 786-2345. ☐ *daily.*
Borax was discovered in Death Valley in 1873, but mining did not begin until the 1880s when crystallized borate compounds

Ruins of the Harmony Borax Works processing plant

were taken to the Harmony Borax Works to be purified. They were then loaded onto wagons and hauled by teams of 20 mules the 165 miles (265 km) to Mojave Station. Each team of mules pulled two wagons carrying up to 10 tons of borax each. The wagons carried their heavy mineral loads from 1883 to 1888.

Used for producing glass that is heat-resistant, borax is more commonly used today as an ingredient in washing powder.
  The Borax Museum has displays of mining tools and transport machinery used at the 19th-century refinery. On Hwy 190, 1 mile (1.5 km) north of the Death Valley Visitor Center, the eerie ruins of the Harmony Borax Works can still be seen.

🏛 Death Valley Museum and Visitor Center

Rte 190, Furnace Creek. *Tel* (760) 786-2331. ☐ *daily.* ● *Jan 1, Dec 25, Thanksgiving.* 🖳 www.nps.gov
Interesting exhibits and a slide show every 30 minutes explain the natural and human history of Death Valley. Evening park-ranger programs and guided walks are available in winter.

Furnace Creek

At Furnace Creek, millennia of winter floods have carved a natural gateway into Death Valley through the hills to the east. The springs here once drew Shoshone Indians each winter. Today, the same abundant springs make Furnace Creek a desert oasis and the de facto center of Death Valley. Shaded by date-bearing palms are a variety of restaurants and motels. The world's lowest golf course can also be found here, lying at 214 ft (65 m) below sea level. The Furnace Creek Inn (*see p541*), a four-star hotel built in the 1920s, sits above the valley on a small mesa.

Historic Furnace Creek Inn, set in lush surroundings

For hotels and restaurants in this region see pp540–41 and pp586–7

Salt formations at the Devil's Golf Course

Southern Death Valley
Some of the valley's most breathtaking natural features are to be found in this area south of Furnace Creek.

🏵 Golden Canyon
Just over 3 miles (5 km) south of Furnace Creek on Hwy 178, a one-mile (1500-m) hike leads into Golden Canyon. The mustard-colored walls, after which the canyon was named, are best seen in the afternoon sun. Native Americans used the red clay at the canyon mouth for face paint. These layers of rock were originally horizontal, but geological activity has now tilted them to an angle of 45°.

A paved road once led to the Golden Canyon, but it was washed out by a sudden storm in 1976. The battered state of the few remaining stretches of the road demonstrate the sheer power of fast-flowing water.

🏵 Devil's Golf Course
This expanse of salt pinnacles is located 12 miles (19 km) south of Furnace Creek, off Hwy 178. Until approximately 2,000 years ago, successive lakes covered this area. When the last lake evaporated, it left behind alternating layers of salt and gravel deposits, at least 1,000 ft (305 m) deep and covering 200 sq miles (520 sq km). As surface moisture continued to evaporate, ridges and spires of crystallized salt were formed. The ground is now 95 percent pure salt. Visitors can hear the salt expand and contract in the continual changes of temperature. New crystals (recognized by their whiter hue) are constantly forming.

🏵 Badwater
Temperature increases as elevation decreases, so the air at Badwater can reach 120° F (49° C). With the ground temperature 50 percent higher than the air temperature, it really is possible to fry an egg on the ground here. Rain is very rare, although flash flooding, caused by rainstorms, is common. In spite of its inhospitable environment, Badwater is home to several species of insect and to the endangered Death Valley snail.

Northern Death Valley
This area includes Ubehebe Crater *(see p292)*, where only a few tourists venture, despite the beauty of the landscape. Scotty's Castle, which has more visitors per year than any other sight in the park, is also here.

🏵 Scotty's Castle
Hwy 267. *Tel (760) 786-2392.*
Castle ☐ *daily.* 🎫 📷 **Grounds** ☐ *daily.*
Albert Johnson began work on his "Death Valley Ranch" in 1922 after rejecting an original design by Frank Lloyd Wright. Materials were hauled from a railroad line 20 miles (32 km) away. When work ended in 1931 the castle covered more than 30,000 sq ft (2,800 sq m). Johnson died in 1948. "Death Valley Scotty" *(see p292)*, who lent his name to Johnson's ranch, was allowed to remain there until his death in 1954.

Western Death Valley
Sand dunes cover 15 sq miles (39 sq km) on this side of the park, not far from the second-largest outpost in Death Valley, Stovepipe Wells *(see p292)*.

🏵 Sand Dunes
A walk along the 14 sq miles (36 sq km) of undulating sand dunes, north of Stovepipe Wells, is one of the greatest experiences of Death Valley. Shifting winds blow the sand into the classic crescent dune configuration. Mesquite trees dot the lower dunes. A variety of wildlife feeds on the seeds of these trees, such as kangaroo rats and lizards. Included among the region's other, mainly nocturnal, creatures are the rattlesnake, the chuckwalla lizard, and the coyote.

Impressive sand dunes north of Stovepipe Wells

A Tour of Death Valley

The Native Americans called the valley Tomesha, "the land where the ground is on fire" – an apt name for the site of the highest recorded temperature in the United States: 134° F (57° C) in the shade, in July 1913. Death Valley stretches for some 140 miles (225 km) north to south and was once an insurmountable barrier to miners and emigrants. The valley and surrounding area were declared a National Park (see pp290–91) in 1994. Death Valley is now accessible to visitors, who can discover this stark and unique landscape by car and by taking short walks from the main roads to spectacular viewpoints. However, this remains the California desert at its harshest and most awe-inspiring.

Scotty's Castle ⑧

This incongruous Moorish-style castle was commissioned by Albert Johnson at a cost of $2.4 million. However, the public believed it belonged to Walter Scott, an eccentric prospector. The house remained unfinished after Johnson lost his money in the Wall Street Crash of 1929. In 1970 the building was bought by the National Park Service, who now hold hourly guided tours of the interior (see p291).

Ubehebe Crater ⑦

This is one of a dozen volcanic craters in the Mojave area. The Ubehebe Crater is 3,000 years old. It is more than 900 yds (800 m) wide and 500 ft (150 m) deep.

DEATH VALLEY SCOTTY

Walter Scott, would-be miner, beloved charlatan, and sometime performer in Buffalo Bill's Wild West Show, liked to tell visitors to his home that his wealth lay in a secret gold mine. That "mine" was, in fact, his friend Albert Johnson, a Chicago insurance executive, who paid for the castle where Scott lived and received visitors. Built during the 1920s by European craftsmen and local Native American labor, the castle represents a mixture of architectural styles and has a Moorish feel. Scott never owned the land or the building, and Johnson paid all his bills. "He repays me in laughs," said Johnson. Although Scott died in 1954, the edifice is still known as Scotty's Castle.

Stovepipe Wells ⑥

Stovepipe Village, founded in 1926, was the valley's first tourist resort. According to legend, a lumberjack traveling west struck water here and stayed. An old stovepipe, similar to the ones that were then used to form the walls of wells, marks the site.

Grandiose Scotty's Castle

KEY

▬▬▬	Tour route
═══	Other roads
ℹ	Tourist information
🚶	Ranger station
⛽	Gas station

Zabriskie Point ②
Made famous by Antonioni's 1960s film of the same name, Zabriskie Point offers views of the multicolored mud hills of Golden Canyon *(see p291)*. The spot was named after a former general manager of the borax operations in Death Valley *(see p290)*.

Furnace Creek ①
The springs here are one of the few freshwater sources in the desert. They are thought to have saved the lives of hundreds of gold prospectors crossing the desert on their way to the Sierra foothills. The full-service visitors' complex here *(see p290)* is the valley's main population center.

Dante's View ③
At 5,475 ft (1,650 m), the view takes in the entire valley floor and is best seen in the morning. The name of the viewpoint was inspired by Dante's *Inferno*. In the distance is Telescope Peak in the Panamint Range.

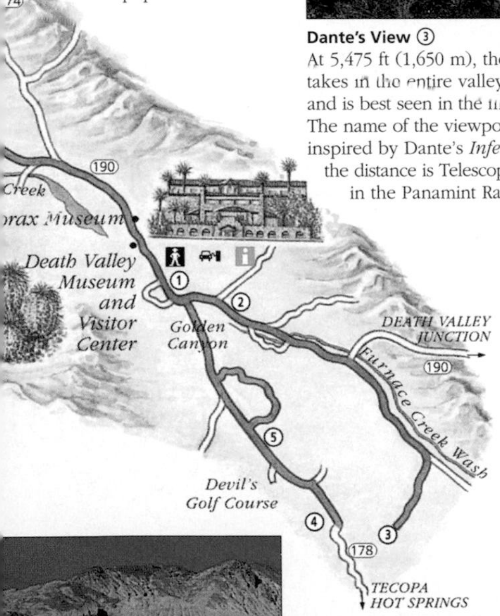
74
190
Creek
rax Museum
Death Valley Museum and Visitor Center
Golden Canyon
DEATH VALLEY JUNCTION
190
Furnace Creek Wash
Devil's Golf Course
178
TECOPA HOT SPRINGS

Artist's Palette ⑤
These multicolored hills of cemented gravels were created by mineral deposits and volcanic ash. The colors are at their most intense in the late afternoon sun.

TIPS FOR DRIVERS

Tour length: *236 miles (380 km).*
When to go: *The best time to visit is October to April, when temperatures average 65° F (18° C). May to September, when the ground temperature can be extremely hot, should be avoided. Try for an early start, especially if you are planning to take any hikes. Always wear a hat and use plenty of sunblock.*
Precautions: *Check the weather forecast before you leave and always carry water, a map, a first aid and snake-bite kit, a cell phone, a jack, and a spare tire. Remain near your vehicle if you break down. If you plan to travel in remote areas, inform someone of where you are going and when you plan to return. The area is not suitable for rock climbing. Do not feed wild animals or reach into burrows or holes.*
Stopping-off points: *Furnace Creek Ranch, Furnace Creek Inn, Stovepipe Wells Village (see p541), and Panamint Springs are the only lodging and eating places in the park. Shoshone, Amargosa, and Tecopa, outside the park, also have motels.*
Emergency: *Phone park rangers on 911 or (760) 786-2331.*
www.nps.gov/deva

Badwater

Badwater ④
Badwater *(see p291)* is the lowest point in the western hemisphere. It lies 282 ft (85 m) below sea level and is one of the world's hottest places. The water is not poisonous, but it is unpalatable, filled with sodium chloride and sulfates.

0 kilometers 10
0 miles 10

SAN FRANCISCO AND THE BAY AREA

San Francisco and the Bay Area at a Glance

San Francisco is a compact city and much of the central area can be explored on foot. The many hills give rise to some strenuous climbing, but are useful landmarks for orientation and offer superb views. A rich ethnic mix adds a distinctive character to the city's many neighborhoods. The smaller cities of Oakland and Berkeley on the East Bay are reached via the Bay Bridge, while to the north, Golden Gate Bridge links the peninsula to the Marin Headlands and the Point Reyes National Seashore. To the south are the colonial city of San Jose and rugged stretches of coastline inhabited by a variety of flora and fauna.

LOCATOR MAP

San Francisco & the Bay Area

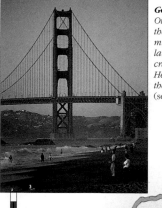

Golden Gate Bridge
Over 60 years old, the bridge is as much a part of the landscape as the craggy Marin Headlands and the idyllic bay (see pp380–81).

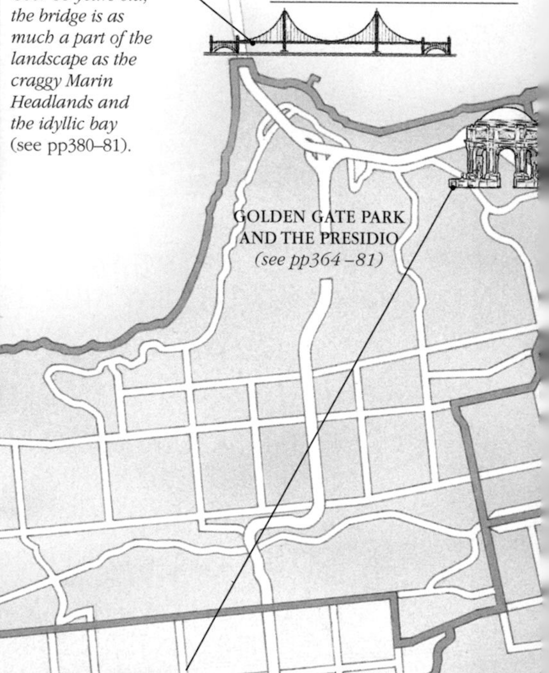

GOLDEN GATE PARK
AND THE PRESIDIO
(see pp364–81)

Palace of Fine Arts
Built for the Panama-Pacific Exposition of 1915, this Neo-Classical monument was fully restored in 1962 (see p349).

Coit Tower
The 1933 tower is floodlit at night (see p343).

BAY AREA
pp410–31

San Francisco

0 kilometers 25

0 miles 25

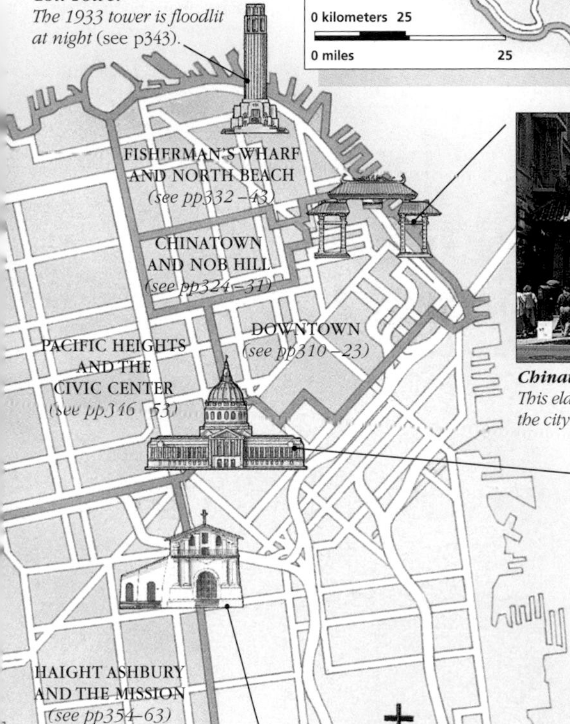

FISHERMAN'S WHARF
AND NORTH BEACH
(see pp332–43)

CHINATOWN
AND NOB HILL
(see pp324–31)

DOWNTOWN
(see pp310–23)

PACIFIC HEIGHTS
AND THE
CIVIC CENTER
(see pp346–53)

HAIGHT ASHBURY
AND THE MISSION
(see pp354–63)

Chinatown Gateway
This elaborate gate is the entrance to the city's historic Chinatown (see p328).

City Hall
The building is the city's most imposing structure, with a vast rotunda displaying a wealth of architectural detail (see p353).

Mission Dolores
The oldest building in San Francisco is one of the 21 Franciscan missions in California (see p361).

0 kilometers 2

0 miles 2

The Shape of San Francisco

San Francisco, with its estimated 43 hills, sits at the tip of a peninsula, surrounded by the Pacific Ocean to the west and San Francisco Bay to the east. To the north, linked by the Golden Gate Bridge, are the rugged Marin Headlands and the protected wildlife area of the Point Reyes Peninsula. The Diablo Coast Range, with the 3,850-ft (1,170-m) Mount Diablo at its heart, forms a mountainous backdrop to the heavily populated cities of Richmond, Oakland, and Berkeley in the East Bay, and divides the region from the flat plains of the Central Valley. To the south, the coastal mountains enclose the industrial Silicon Valley and run along the coastline toward Big Sur.

Vallejo
This town, in the north of the bay, is home to Marine World Africa wildlife park and oceanarium, which includes dolphin displays (see p415).

Red and White ferries

Sausalito
This former fishing community, across the Golden Gate Bridge, is lined with Victorian houses looking out toward the bay (see p414).

RICHMOND

RICHMOND BRIDGE

TIBURON

SONOMA MOUNTAINS

MOUNT TAMALPAIS

POINT REYES NATIONAL SEASHORE

PACIFIC OCEAN

The Marin Headlands are part of the Golden Gate National Recreation Area. These green hills and quiet beaches offer perfect relaxation away from the city, with hiking, fishing, and bird-watching opportunities (see pp416–17).

Point Reyes Peninsula
The rugged coastline of the peninsula, situated on the San Andreas Fault and only partly attached to the mainland, is abundant with wildlife and is a very productive dairy farming community (see p414).

Downtown
One of the major financial districts in the United States is located in San Francisco's Downtown area. Its skyline is dominated by the Transamerica Pyramid (see pp310–23).

Livermore
This rural community is home to the world's largest wind farm, making use of the area's strong winds to produce natural energy (see p426).

Berkeley includes the University of California at Berkeley campus, once known for its radicalism *(see pp418–21).*

The Diablo Coast Range separates the East Bay from the Central Valley. Mount Diablo is at the heart of the range *(see p426).*

BAY BRIDGE

SAN MATEO BRIDGE

Golden Gate Bridge

GOLDEN GATE NATIONAL RECREATION AREA

SAN BRUNO MOUNTAINS

Oakland
This busy city has a multicultural population and many historic landmarks. It is linked to San Francisco by the Bay Bridge (see pp422–5).

San Jose was originally a Spanish colonial city and preserves its history. It is still home to a large Mexican–American population *(see pp428–9).*

Palo Alto
This town was built up specifically to serve the Stanford University campus, which was created by railroad baron Leland Stanford in 1891 (see p427).

Victorian Houses in San Francisco

Italianate window

Despite earthquakes, fires, and the inroads of modern life, thousands of ornate, late-19th-century houses still line the streets of San Francisco. In fact, in many neighborhoods they are by far the most common type of houses. Victorian houses are broadly similar, in that they all have wooden frames, elaborately decorated with mass-produced ornamentation. Most were built on narrow plots to a similar floor plan, but they differ in the features of the façade. Four main styles prevail in the city, although in practice many houses, especially those constructed in the 1880s and 1890s, combine aspects of two or more styles.

Detail of Queen Anne-style gateway at Chateau Tivoli

GOTHIC REVIVAL (1850–80)

Gothic Revival houses are the easiest to identify, as they always have pointed arches over the windows and sometimes, over the doors. Other features are pitched gabled roofs, decorated verge-boards (again, with pointed arch motifs), and porches that run the width of the building. The smaller, simpler houses of this type are often painted white, rather than the vibrant colors of later styles.

No. 1111 Oak Street *is one of the city's oldest Gothic Revival buildings. Its front garden is unusually large.*

The pitched roof over the main façade often runs lengthwise, allowing the use of dormer windows.

A gabled roof with ornate verge-boards is the clearest mark of Gothic Revival.

Gothic porch with cross bracing at No. 1978 Filbert Street

Full-width porches are reached by a central stair.

Balustrades on the porch betray the Deep South origins of the style.

ITALIANATE (1850–85)

Italianate houses were more popular in San Francisco than elsewhere in the US, perhaps because their compact form was suited to the city's high building density. The most distinctive feature of the style is the tall cornice, usually with a decorative bracket, which adds a palatial air even to modest homes. Elaborate decoration around windows and doors is also typical of the style.

No. 1913 Sacramento Street *displays a typical formal Italianate façade, modeled on a Renaissance palazzo. The wood boarding is made to look like stone.*

Tall cornices, often with decorative brackets, conceal a pitched roof.

Imposing entrance with Italianate porch

Symmetrical windows are capped by decorative arches.

Neo-Classical doorways, sometimes with ornate pedimented porches, are a typical Italianate touch.

STICK (1860–90)

This architectural style, with its ungainly name, is perhaps the most prevalent among Victorian houses in the city. Sometimes also called "Stick–Eastlake" after London furniture designer Charles Eastlake, this style was intended to be more architecturally "honest." Vertical lines are emphasized, both in the wood-frame structure and in ornamentation. Bay windows, false-gabled cornices, and square corners are key identifying features.

Gabled roof with Eastlake windows at No. 2931 Pierce Street

Wide bands of trim often form a decorative truss, emphasizing the underlying structure of Stick houses.

Decorative gables filled with "sunburst" motifs are used on porches and window frames.

No. 1715–17 Capp Street *is a fine example of the Stick–Eastlake style, with a plain façade enlivened by decorative flourishes.*

Adjoining front doors can be protected by a single projecting porch.

QUEEN ANNE (1875–1905)

The name "Queen Anne" does not refer to a historical period; it was coined by the English architect Richard Shaw. Queen Anne houses combine elements from many decorative traditions but are marked by their towers, turrets, and large decorative panels on wall surfaces. Many of the houses display intricate spindle-work on balustrades, porches, and roof trusses *(see pp30–31).*

Palladian windows were used in gables to give the appearance of an extra floor.

Queen Anne gable filled with ornamental panels at No. 818 Steiner Street

Queen Anne turret topped by a finial at No. 1015 Steiner Street

Round, square, and polygonal turrets and towers are typical of Queen Anne-style houses.

Gable pediments hold ornamental windows and decorative panels.

The asymmetrical façade *of No. 850 Steiner Street, together with its eclectic ornament, is typical of a Queen Anne house. Such features are often painted in various bright colors.*

The curved window frame is not itself characteristic of Queen Anne style, but many houses include features borrowed from other styles.

WHERE TO FIND VICTORIAN HOUSES

1715–1717 Capp St. Map **10 F4.**
Chateau Tivoli, 1057 Steiner St. Map **4 D4.**
1978 Filbert St. Map **4 D2.**
1111 Oak St. Map **9 C1.**
2931 Pierce St. Map **4 D3.**
1913 Sacramento St. Map **4 E3.**
818 Steiner St. Map **4 D5.**
850 Steiner St. Map **4 D5.**
1015 Steiner St. Map **4 D5.**
2527–2531 Washington St. Map **4 D3.**
Alamo Square *p353.*
Clarke's Folly *p363.*
Haas-Lilienthal House *p348.*
Liberty Street. Map **10 E3.**
Masonic Avenue. Map **3 C4.**
Octagon House *p351.*
Spreckels Mansion *p348.*

San Francisco's Cable Cars

The cable car system was launched in 1873, and its inventor Andrew Hallidie rode in the first car. He was inspired to tackle the problem of transporting people up the city's steep slopes after witnessing a bad accident, when a horse-drawn tram slipped down a hill, dragging the horses with it. His system was a success, and by 1889 cars were running on eight lines. Before the 1906 earthquake *(see pp52–3)*, more than 600 cars were in use. With the advent of the internal combustion engine, cable cars became obsolete, and in 1947 attempts were made to replace them with buses. After a public outcry the present three lines, using 17 miles (25 km) of track, were retained.

Cable car traffic lights

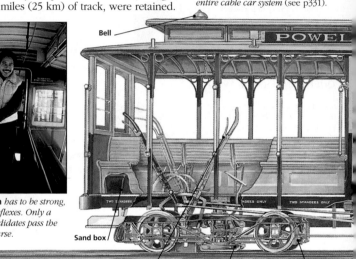

The Cable Car Barn *garages the cars at night, and is a repair shop, museum, and powerhouse for the entire cable car system (see p331).*

The gripman *has to be strong, with good reflexes. Only a third of candidates pass the training course.*

Bell

POWEL

Sand box

Grip handle

Center plate and jaws grip the cable

Emergency brake

Wheel brake

Cable

HOW CABLE CARS WORK

Engines in the central powerhouse wind a looped cable under the city streets, guided by a system of grooved pulleys. When the gripman in the cable car applies the grip handle, the grip reaches through a slot in the street and grabs the cable. This pulls the car along at a steady speed of 9.5 mph (15.5 km/h). To stop, the gripman releases the grip and applies the brake. Great skill is needed at corners where the cable passes over a pulley. The gripman must release the grip to allow the car to coast over the pulley.

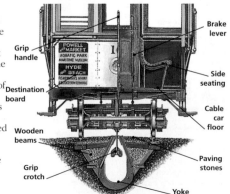

Cable car grip mechanism

Grip handle

Destination board

Wooden beams

Grip crotch

Brake lever

Side seating

Cable car floor

Paving stones

Yoke

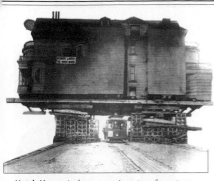

Hatch House *is the name given to a four-story house that needed to be moved in its entirety in 1913. Herbert Hatch used a system of jacks and hoists to maneuver the house across the cable car line without causing any cessation of the service.*

A cable car celebration *was held in 1984 after a two-year-long system refurbishment. Each car was refitted, and all lines were replaced with reinforced tracks. The system should now work safely for the next 100 years.*

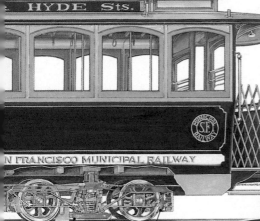

A cable car bell-ringing contest *is held at Union Square every July, when conductors ring out their most spirited rhythms. On the street, the bell signals a warning to other traffic.*

Brake block   Brake shoe

The original *San Francisco cable car, tested by Hallidie on Clay Street on August 2, 1873, is on display in the Cable Car Barn (see p331). The cable car system has remained essentially unchanged since its invention.*

Rebuilding the cable cars *has to be done with attention to historical detail, since they are designated historic monuments.*

ANDREW SMITH HALLIDIE

Andrew Smith was born in London in 1836 and later adopted his uncle's surname. He trained as a mechanic, moved to San Francisco in 1852, and formed a company that made wire rope. In 1873 he tested the first cable car, which soon became profitable by opening the hills of the city to development.

San Francisco's Best: Museums and Galleries

Museums and galleries in the city range from the encyclopedic de Young Museum and the Legion of Honor, to the contemporary art of the Museum of Modern Art and its neighbor, the Yerba Buena Center for the Arts. There are several excellent science museums, including the Exploratorium and the California Academy of Sciences. Other museums celebrate the city's heritage, including its ancestral Native American culture, and the people and events that made the city what it is today.

The Exploratorium *is one of the best science museums in the US. Here visitors experiment with* Sun Painting, *a feast of light and color.* (See p349.)

Legion of Honor *houses a collection of European art from the Middle Ages to the 19th century, including* Sailboat on the Seine *(c.1874) by Claude Monet.* (See pp374–5.)

Golden Gate Park and the Presidio

Pacific Her and the C Center

de Young Museum *has recently reopened after a multi-million dollar expansion. The museum has collections of American art, as well as art from Central and South America, the Pacific Islands, and Africa.*

0 kilometers   2

0 miles   1

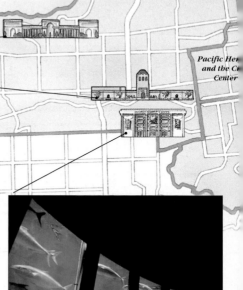

California Academy of Sciences *has temporarily relocated to Howard Street (see p311) until extensive renovations are completed in 2008.*

The Chinese Historical Society administers one of the city's smallest museums. Inside is a unique collection that details the history of California's Chinese communities and their participation in the development of the state. Included among the exhibits is this magnificent costume dragon's head. (See p330.)

Fort Mason Museums house ethnic culture artifacts. Muto by Mimo Paladino (1985) is one of the many exhibits. (See pp350–51.)

Wells Fargo History Museum is a small gallery that displays the colorful history of California, from the early days of the Gold Rush. This bronze stagecoach (1984) is by M Casper. (See p314.)

Fisherman's Wharf and North Beach

Chinatown and Nob Hill

Downtown

Haight Ashbury and the Mission

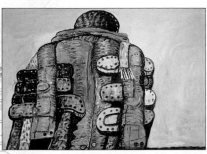

San Francisco Museum of Modern Art is a highly regarded showcase of 20th-century art. In 1994 the museum moved to new premises, designed by architect Mario Botta. Back View by Philip Guston (1977) is in the permanent collection. (See pp318–19.)

The Asian Art Museum, loacted in a beautiful 1917 Beaux Arts building, was once the Old San Francisco Main Library. (See p352.)

Yerba Buena Center for the Arts is a new gallery that displays diverse works of contemporary art. These change regularly, since there is no permanent collection here. (See pp322–3.)

San Francisco's Murals

San Francisco is proud of its reputation as a culturally rich and cosmopolitan city, and these qualities are evident in the bright murals that decorate walls and other public places in several areas of the city. Many were painted in the 1930s and many more in the 1970s, with some appearing spontaneously, while others were specially commissioned. One of the best is the *Carnaval Mural* on 24th Street in the Mission District *(see p362)*; other examples are shown here.

503 Law Office at Dolores and 18th streets

SCENES FROM HISTORY

Some of the best examples of San Francisco's historical mural art can be found inside Coit Tower *(see p343)*, where a series of panels, funded during the Great Depression of the 1930s by President Roosevelt's New Deal program, is typical of the period. Many local artists participated in creating the work, and themes include the struggles of the working class and the rich resources of California. The city also boasts three murals by Diego Rivera, the Mexican artist who revived fresco painting during the 1930s and 1940s.

The making of a mural depicted by Diego Rivera at San Francisco Art Institute

Detail from Coit Tower mural illustrating the rich resources of California

Architect Frank Lloyd Wright

Emmy Lou Packard, Rivera's assistant on the mural

Otto Diechman, architect

Mussolini, as portrayed by Jack Oakie in *The Great Dictator*

Coit Tower mural showing life during the Great Depression

The 1940 Diego Rivera mural *at City College has a theme of Pan-American unity, and features many important historical figures. The section illustrated here lays emphasis on creative endeavor in the United States and on the role played by artists in the fight against Fascism.*

Adolf Hitler

Benito Mussolini

Charlie Chaplin in *The Great Dictator*, a film made in 1940 that poked fun at Fascism. Chaplin had two parts, playing both a Jewish barber and Hitler.

Edward G Robinson

Joseph Stalin

MODERN LIFE

Life in the modern metropolis is one of the major themes of mural art in San Francisco, as much now as it was in the 1930s. In the Mission District particularly, every aspect of daily life is illustrated on the walls of banks, schools, and restaurants, with lively scenes of the family, community, political activity, and people at work and play. The Mission District contains about 200 murals, many painted in the 1970s, when the city government paid rebellious young people to create works of art in public places. The San Francisco Arts Commission continues to foster this art form.

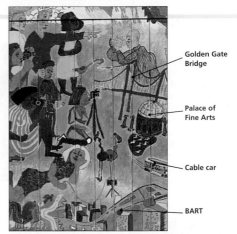

Golden Gate Bridge

Palace of Fine Arts

Cable car

BART

This Balmy Alley mural *is a view of the city as tourists see it. The alley, in the Mission District, is decorated with numerous vivid murals, first painted by local children, artists, and community workers in the 1970s. The works are now a major attraction.*

The Learning Wall, Franklin St, depicts education and art

Positively Fourth Street, a weathered mural at Fort Mason

THE MULTICULTURAL CITY

San Francisco's heritage of diversity and tolerance comes alive in the murals that enliven its ethnic neighborhoods. In Chinatown, Chinese-American artists evoke memories of the "old country." The Mission District is filled with art, some of it politically inspired, which celebrates the struggles and achievements of its Mexican and Latin American population.

Mexican-American dancer

Native American drummer

Caucasian bass player

African-American maracas player

Multicultural San Francisco *is celebrated at Park Branch Library in Haight Ashbury.*

Mural in Washington Street encapsulating life in China

WHERE TO FIND THE MURALS

Balmy Alley, 24th & 25th Sts.
City College of San Francisco
    50 Phelan Ave.
Coit Tower *p343*.
Dolores and 18th St. **Map 10 E3.**
Fort Mason *pp350–51*.
Franklin Street. **Map 4 E1.**
Park Branch Library
    1833 Page St. **Map 9 B1.**
San Francisco Art
    Institute *pp340–41*.
Washington Street. **Map 4 E3.**

The 49-Mile Scenic Drive

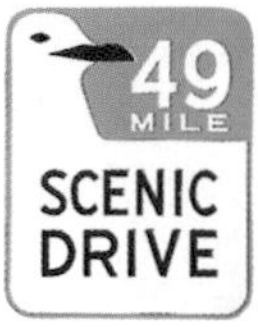

Official sign

Linking the city's most intriguing neighborhoods, fascinating sights and spectacular views, the 49-Mile Scenic Drive (79 km) provides a splendid overview of San Francisco. Keeping to the well-marked route is easy – just follow the blue-and-white seagull signs. Some of these are hidden by overhanging vegetation, so you need to be alert. Set aside a whole day for this trip; there are plenty of places to stop to take photographs or admire the views.

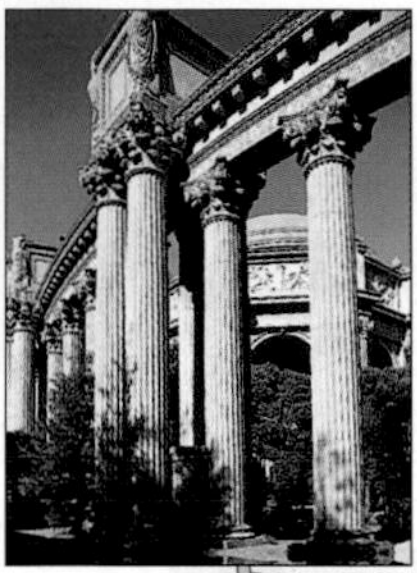

The Palace of Fine Arts and the Exploratorium (24)
The grand Neo-Classical building and its modern science museum stand near the entrance to the Presidio.

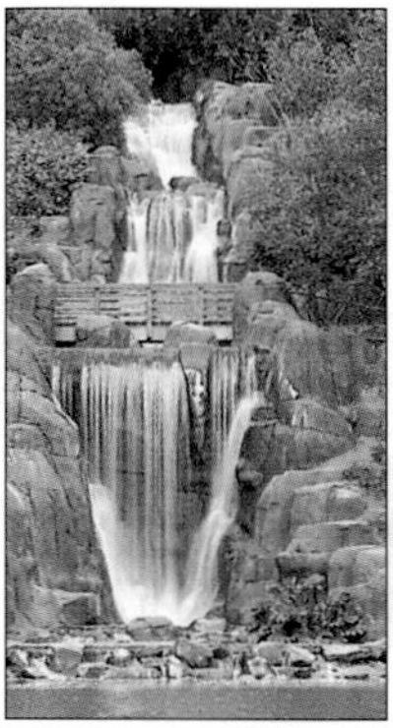

Stow Lake (5)
There is a waterfall and a Chinese pavilion on the island in this picturesque lake. Boats can be rented.

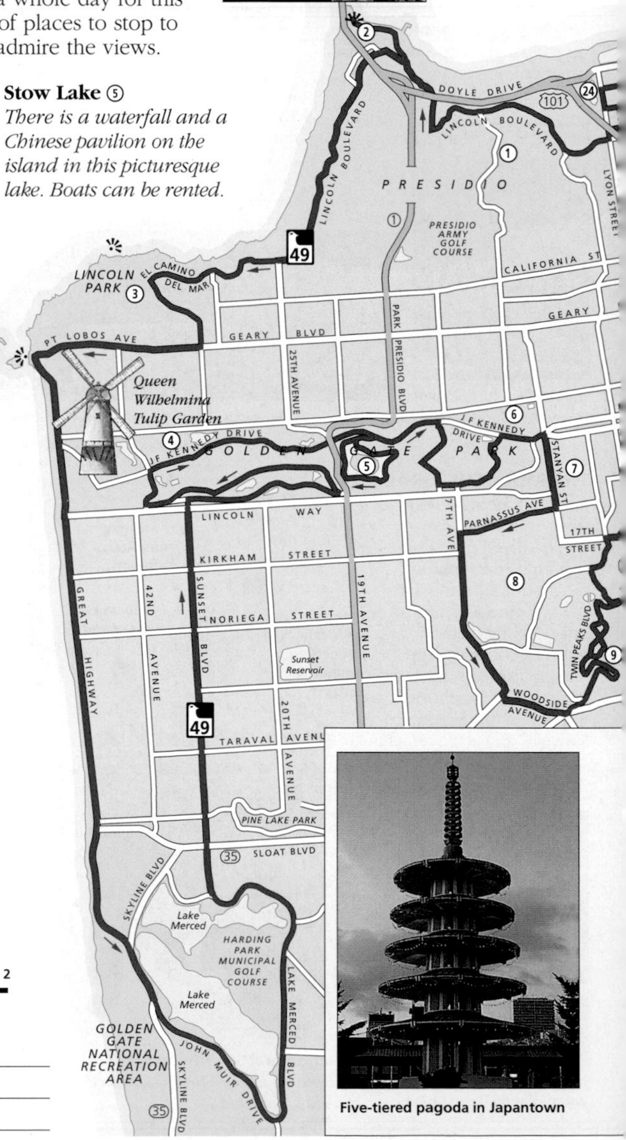

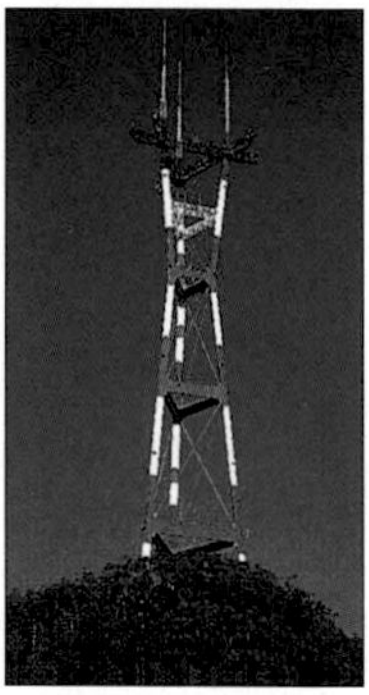

Sutro Tower (8)
This distinctive orange and white tower is visible from all over the city.

0 kilometers 2

0 miles 1

KEY

— 49-Mile Scenic Drive

✲ Viewpoint

Five-tiered pagoda in Japantown

Coit Tower ⑳
Overlooking North Beach, Telegraph Hill is topped by this tower, which has fine murals and an observation deck.

Marina Green ㉓
This is an excellent vantage point from which to view or photograph Golden Gate Bridge.

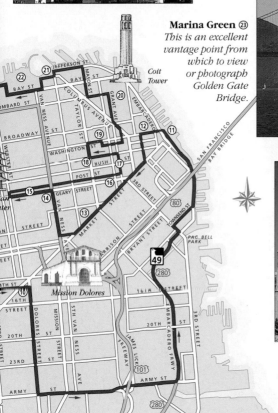

Grace Cathedral ⑱
This impressive cathedral, based on Notre Dame in Paris, dominates the summit of the city's steepest hill, Nob Hill.

TIPS FOR MOTORISTS

Starting point: *Anywhere. The circuit is designed to be followed in a counterclockwise direction starting and ending at any point.*
When to go: *Avoid driving during rush hours: 7–9am, 4–7pm. Most of the views are as spectacular by night as by day.*
Parking: *Use the parking lots that are situated around the Financial District, the Civic Center, Japantown, Nob Hill, Chinatown, North Beach, and Fisherman's Wharf. Elsewhere, street parking is usually easily available.*

FINDING THE SIGHTS

DOWNTOWN
SAN FRANCISCO

ontgomery Street, now right in the heart of the Financial District, was once a street of small shops, where miners came to weigh their gold dust. Wells Fargo built the city's first brick building on the street during the Gold Rush (*see pp48–9*). Today, old-fashioned

Motif on Union Bank

banks stand in the shadow of modern skyscrapers. Union Square is the city's main shopping district and has a wealth of fine department stores. SoMa (South of Market) has become the city's "artists' quarter," with its old warehouses converted into studios, bars, and avant-garde theaters.

SIGHTS AT A GLANCE

Historic Streets and Buildings
Bank of California **6**
California Historical Society **12**
Ferry Building **10**
Jackson Square Historical District **2**
Merchant's Exchange **7**
Old United States Mint **25**
Pacific Coast Stock Exchange **8**
Powell Street Cable Car Turntable **23**

Shops
Crocker Galleria **18**
Gump's **19**
San Francisco Center **24**
Union Square Shops **22**

Modern Architecture
Bank of America **4**
Embarcadero Center **1**
Rincon Center **11**
Transamerica Pyramid **5**
Yerba Buena Gardens pp322–3 **14**

Theaters
Theater District **21**

Hotels
Sheraton Palace Hotel **16**

Museums and Galleries
California Academy of Sciences **17**
Museum of Cartoon Art **15**
Museum of Modern Art pp318–9 **13**
Wells Fargo History Museum **3**

Parks and Squares
Justin Herman Plaza **9**
Union Square **20**

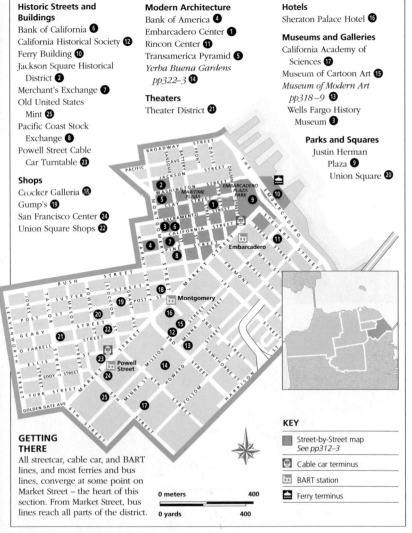

GETTING THERE
All streetcar, cable car, and BART lines, and most ferries and bus lines, converge at some point on Market Street – the heart of this section. From Market Street, bus lines reach all parts of the district.

0 meters   400
0 yards   400

KEY
| | Street-by-Street map *See pp312–3* |
| Cable car terminus |
| BART station |
| Ferry terminus |

◁ **A view of downtown San Francisco at night**

Street-by-Street: Financial District

San Francisco's economic engine is fueled predominantly by the Financial District, one of the chief commercial centers in the US. It reaches from the imposing modern towers and plazas of the Embarcadero Center to staid Montgomery Street, called the "Wall Street of the West." All the principal banks, brokers, and law offices are situated within this area. The Jackson Square Historical District, north of Washington Street, was once the heart of the business community.

La Chiffonière (1978)
by Jean de Buffet,
Justin Herman Plaza

★ **Embarcadero Center**
The center houses commercial outlets and offices. A shopping arcade occupies the first three tiers of the towers ❶

Hotaling Place is a narrow alley known for its many excellent antique shops.

Jackson Square Historical District
This district, more than any other, recalls the Gold Rush era ❷

The Golden Era Building was built during the Gold Rush and housed the paper *Golden Era*, for which Mark Twain wrote.

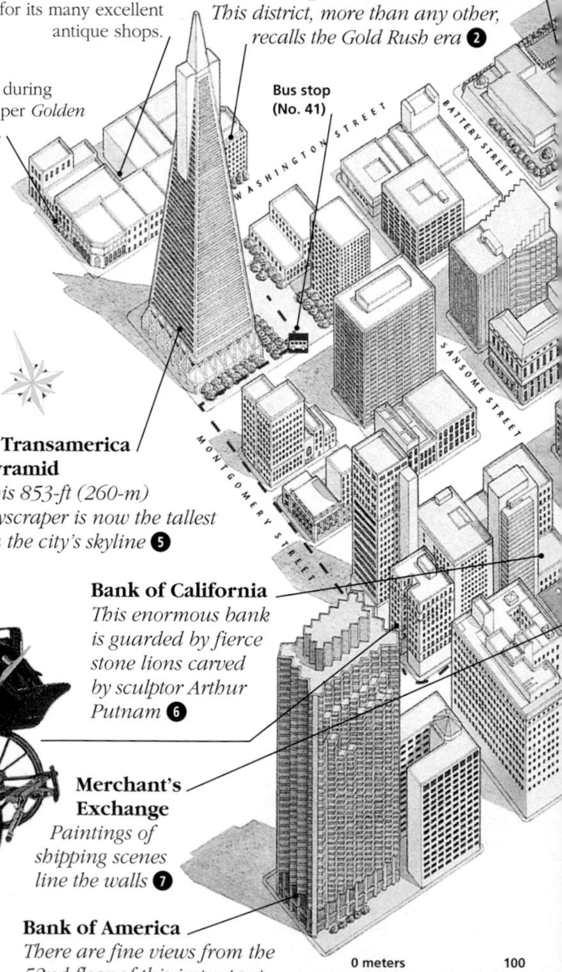

Bus stop (No. 41)

★ **Transamerica Pyramid**
This 853-ft (260-m) skyscraper is now the tallest on the city's skyline ❺

Bank of California
This enormous bank is guarded by fierce stone lions carved by sculptor Arthur Putnam ❻

Merchant's Exchange
Paintings of shipping scenes line the walls ❼

Wells Fargo History Museum
An old stagecoach, evoking the Wild West days, is one of the exhibits in this transportation and banking museum ❸

Bank of America
There are fine views from the 52nd floor of this important banking institution ❹

| 0 meters | | 100 |
| 0 yards | | 100 |

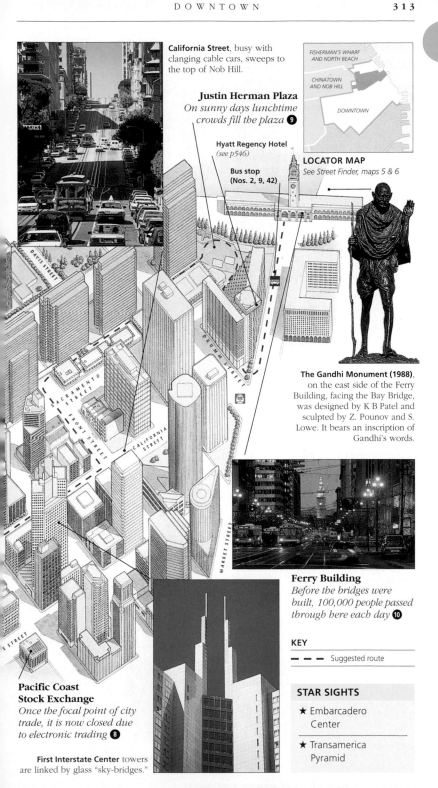

California Street, busy with clanging cable cars, sweeps to the top of Nob Hill.

Justin Herman Plaza
On sunny days lunchtime crowds fill the plaza ❾

Hyatt Regency Hotel
(see p546)

Bus stop
(Nos. 2, 9, 42)

LOCATOR MAP
See Street Finder, maps 5 & 6

FISHERMAN'S WHARF AND NORTH BEACH

CHINATOWN AND NOB HILL

DOWNTOWN

The Gandhi Monument (1988),
on the east side of the Ferry Building, facing the Bay Bridge, was designed by K B Patel and sculpted by Z. Pounov and S. Lowe. It bears an inscription of Gandhi's words.

Ferry Building
Before the bridges were built, 100,000 people passed through here each day ❿

KEY

— — — Suggested route

Pacific Coast Stock Exchange
Once the focal point of city trade, it is now closed due to electronic trading ❽

First Interstate Center towers are linked by glass "sky-bridges."

STAR SIGHTS

★ Embarcadero Center

★ Transamerica Pyramid

Embarcadero Center ❶

Map 6 D3. 🚌 *1, 32, 42.*
🚃 *J, K, L, M, N.* 🚋 *California St.*
See **Shopping** *p382–7* and **Where to Stay** *p546.*

Completed in 1981 after a decade of construction, San Francisco's largest redevelopment project stretches from Justin Herman Plaza to Battery Street. Office workers and shoppers use its open spaces to relax in the sun and eat their lunch. Four high-rise towers reach 35 to 45 stories above the landscaped plazas and elevated walkways.

The Embarcadero Center's most spectacular interior is the foyer of the Hyatt Regency Hotel *(see p546).* Its 17-story atrium contains an immense sculptured globe by Charles Perry entitled *Eclipse.* Glass elevators glide up and down one wall, carrying visitors to and from the Equinox, a revolving rooftop restaurant that completes a full circle every 40 minutes.

Lobby of the Hyatt Regency Hotel at the Embarcadero Center

Hotaling Place in Jackson Square

Jackson Square Historical District ❷

Map 5 C3. 🚌 *12, 15, 42, 83.*

Renovated in the early 1950s, this neighborhood contains many historic brick, cast-iron, and granite façades dating from Gold Rush days. From 1850 to 1910 it was known as the Barbary Coast, notorious for its squalor and the crudeness of its inhabitants. The old Hippodrome theater at No. 555 Pacific Street contains bawdy relief sculptures in the recessed front, which recall the risqué shows that were performed there. Today the buildings are used as showrooms, law offices, and fine antique shops; the best ones can be seen in Jackson Street, Gold Street, Hotaling Place, and Montgomery Street.

Wells Fargo History Museum ❸

420 Montgomery St. **Map** 5 C4.
Tel *(415) 396-2619.* 🚌 *1, 12, 15, 42.* 🚃 *Montgomery St.* 🕐 *9am–5pm Mon–Fri.* ● *public hols.* ♿ 📷
www.wellsfargohistory.com

Founded in 1852, Wells Fargo & Co. became the greatest banking and transportation company in the West and was influential in the development of the American frontier.

The company moved people and goods from the East to the West Coast, and between the mining camps and towns of California. It also transported gold from the West Coast to the East, and delivered mail, placing mailboxes in convenient locations to enable the messengers to sort letters en route. The Pony Express was another mail venture in which Wells Fargo & Co. played a major role.

The splendid stagecoaches on display are famous, particularly for the legendary stories of their heroic drivers and the bandits who robbed them. The best-known bandit was Black Bart, who left poems at the scene of his crimes. He stalked the many lonely roads from Calaveras County up to the Oregon border from 1875 to 1883. In one holdup he mistakenly left behind his handkerchief. Its distinctive laundry mark revealed him as mining engineer Charles Boles *(see p479).*

Museum visitors can experience how it felt to sit for days in a jostling stagecoach, and listen to the recorded diary of an immigrant called Francis Brocklehurst. Exhibits include Pony Express mail, photographs, early checks, gold nuggets, and the imperial currency of Emperor Norton *(see p51).*

Black Bart, the poet bandit

Bank of America ❹

555 California St. **Map** 5 C4.
Tel *(415) 433-7500 (Carnelian
Room).* 📷 *1, 15.* 🚃 *California St.*

The red granite-clad building
housing the headquarters of
the Bank of America opened
in 1972. Its 52 floors make it
the tallest skyscraper in San
Francisco, and incredible
views from the Carnelian
Room on the 52nd floor show
the fascinating workings of
city life. The Bank of America
was originally the Bank of
Italy, which was founded by
AP Giannini in San Jose *(see
pp428–9).* It built up a huge
clientele early in the 20th
century by catering to immigrants and investing in the
booming farmlands and small
towns. In the great fire of
1906 *(see pp52–3),* Giannini
personally rescued his bank's
deposits, carrying them to
safety by hiding them in fruit
crates, so there were sufficient
funds for the bank to invest
in the rebuilding of the city.

Transcendence by Masayuki Nagari
(1972) at the Bank of America

Transamerica Pyramid ❺

600 Montgomery St. **Map** 5 C3.
🚃 *1, 15, 42.* ⏰ *8:30am–4:30pm
Mon–Fri.* ⬤ *public hols.* ♿
www.tapyramid.com

Capped with a pointed
spire on top of its
48 stories, the pyramid
reaches 853 ft (260 m)
above sea level. It is the
tallest and most widely
recognized building in
the city, and although
San Franciscans disliked
it when it opened in
1972, they have since
accepted it as part of
their city's skyline.

Designed by William
Pereira & Associates, the
pyramid houses 1,500
office workers on a site
that is historically one of
the richest in the city.
The Montgomery Block,
which contained many
important offices and
was the largest building
west of the Mississippi,
was built here in 1853.
In the basement was
the Exchange Saloon,
which was frequented
by Mark Twain/
Samuel Clemens. The
Financial District was
extended south in the
1860s, and artists and
writers took up
residence in the
Montgomery Block.
The Pony Express
terminus, marked
by a plaque, was
at Merchant
Street, opposite
the pyramid.

The spire is hollow, rising 212 ft (64 m) above the
top floor. Lit from inside, it casts a warm, yellow
glow at night. Its purpose is purely decorative.

The vertical wings *of the
building rise from the middle of
the ground floor and extend
beyond the frame, which tapers
inward. The eastern wing houses
18 elevator shafts, and the
western wing houses a smoke
tower and emergency stairs.*

**The observation
deck** *is situated on the
ground floor. Here, a
bank of monitors
provides visitors with
stupendous views
beamed down from
four cameras that
revolve at the
apex of the spire.*

Earthquake protection *is
ensured by white precast
quartz aggregate, interlaced
with reinforcing rods at
four places on each floor,
that cover the exterior of the
pyramid. Clearance
between the panels allows
for lateral movement in
case of an earthquake.*

The shape *of the
building tapers so that it casts
a smaller shadow than a
conventional design.*

The 3,678 windows
take cleaners an entire
month to wash.

The foundations rest on a steel and
concrete block, sunk 52 ft (15.5 m)
into the ground and designed to
move with earth tremors.

Bank of California ❻

400 California St. **Map** 5 C4.
Tel *(415) 765-0400.* 🚌 *1, 42.* 🚋
California St. **Museum of American
Money** ⭘ *10am–4pm Mon–Thu,
10am–5pm Fri.* ⬤ *public hols.* ♿

William Ralston and Darius
Mills founded this bank in
1864. Ralston, known as "the
man who built San
Francisco," invested profitably
in the Comstock mines *(see
p49)*. He used the bank and
his personal fortune to
finance many civic projects in
San Francisco, including the
city's water company, a
theater, and the Palace Hotel
(see p547). When economic
depression struck in the 1870s,
Ralston's empire collapsed.
    The present colonnaded
building was completed in
1908. In the basement, the
Museum of American Money
displays gold, coins, old
banknotes, and diagrams of
the Comstock mines.

**Classical façade of the Bank of
California**

Merchant's Exchange ❼

465 California St. **Map** 5 C4. **Tel**
(415) 421-7730. 🚋 *Montgomery St.*
🚌 *1, 4, 10, 15.* ⭘ *8:30am–6pm
Mon–Fri, Sat–Sun by appt.* ⬤ *public
hols.* ♿ **www**.merchantsexchange
building.com

The exchange, designed by
Willis Polk in 1903 survived the
great fire of 1906 with little
damage *(see pp52–3)*. Inside,
William Coulter seascapes line
the walls, depicting epic maritime scenes from the age of
steam and sail. This was the
focal point of San Francisco's
commodities exchange in the
early 20th century, when look-

outs in the tower relayed news
of ships arriving from abroad.
Now dwarfed by skyscrapers,
it once dominated the skyline.

Pacific Coast Stock Exchange ❽

301 Pine St. **Map** 5 C4. **Tel** *(415)
393-4000.* 🚌 *3, 4, 15, 42.* ⬤ *to
the public, except by prearranged tour.*
www.pacificex.com

This was once America's
largest stock exchange
outside New York. Founded
in 1882 it occupied these
buildings, which were re-
modeled in 1930 by Miller
and Pflueger from the existing
US Treasury. The monumen-
tal granite statues that flank
the Pine Street entrance were
sculpted by Ralph Stackpole,
also in 1930. The building is
now closed, its once-frantic
trading floor silent due to the
emergence of electronic and
Internet trading.

Justin Herman Plaza ❾

Map 6 D3. 🚌 *many buses.* 🚋 *F, J,
K, L, M, N.* 🚋 *California St.*

Popular with lunchtime
crowds from the nearby
Embarcadero Center *(see
p314)*, this plaza is best
known for its avant-garde
Vaillancourt Fountain,
built in 1971 by the
Canadian artist Armand
Vaillancourt. The fountain
is modeled from huge
concrete blocks, and
some people find it
ugly, especially when
it is allowed to run
dry during times of
drought. However,
you are allowed to
climb on and through
it, and with its
splashing pools and
columns of falling
water, it is an
intriguing public work
of art when function-
ing as intended.
    The area is often
rented out to musicians
during the lunch hour –
the popular rock
band U2 performed a

**The Vaillancourt Fountain in
Justin Herman Plaza**

lunchtime concert here in
1987, after which they spray-
painted the fountain.

Ferry Building ❿

Embarcadero at Market St. **Map** 6 E3.
🚌 *many buses.* 🚋 *J, K, L, M, N.*
🚋 *California St.*

Constructed between 1896
and 1903, the Ferry Building
survived the great fire of 1906
through the intercession of
fireboats pumping water from
the bay. The clock tower
is 235 ft
(71 m) high and was
inspired by the Moorish
bell tower of Seville
Cathedral in Spain. In the
early 1930s more than 50
million passengers a year
passed through the build-
ing. Many of these were
travelers to and from
the transcontinental
railroad terminal in
Oakland, while others
were commuters
using the 170 daily
ferries between the
city and their homes
across the bay. With
the opening of the
Bay Bridge in 1936
(see pp422–3), the
Ferry Building ceased
to be the city's main
point of entry and
began to deteriorate.
A few ferries still
cross the bay, to
Tiburon and Sausa-
lito in Marin County
(see pp414–15) and
Oakland in the East
Bay *(see pp422–3)*.

**The clock tower on
the Ferry Building**

Rincon Annex mural depicting the Spanish discovery of San Francisco

and include the original artwork for such well-known cartoon characters as Popeye, Charlie Brown, L'il Abner, Little Orphan Annie, and Walt Disney's numerous creations. Exhibitions change every four months. The museum also includes a children's area and a CD-ROM gallery.

Rincon Center ⓫

Map 6 E4. 🚌 14. See *Shopping* pp382–5.

This shopping center, with its soaring atrium and its 90-ft (27-m) fountain, was added on to the old Rincon Annex Post Office Building in 1989. The Rincon Annex dates from 1940 and is well known for its murals by the Russian-born artist Anton Refregier, showing aspects of the history of San Francisco. Some of the works depict harsh images of important events and people of the city, which caused much controversy when first shown.

California Historical Society ⓬

678 Mission St. **Map** 6 D5. *Tel* (415) 357-1848. 🚇 Montgomery St. ◑ noon–4:30pm Wed–Sat (Library closed Sat). 🔲 www.calhist.org

The California Historical Society is dedicated to preserving and interpreting Californiana. The Society offers a reference and research library, museum galleries, and a well-stocked bookstore. There is also an impressive photographic collection, more than 900 oil paintings and watercolors by American artists, a decorative arts exhibit, and a unique costume collection.

Museum of Modern Art ⓭

See pp318–19.

Yerba Buena Gardens ⓮

See pp322–3.

Cartoon art on a US stamp

Museum of Cartoon Art ⓯

655 Mission St. *Tel* (415) 227-8666. ◑ 11am–5pm Tue–Sun. 🎦 🔲 www.cartoonart.org

Founded in 1984, this is the only museum of original cartoon art on the West Coast. The 10,000 pieces in the collection date from the 18th century to the present day

Sheraton Palace Hotel ⓰

2 New Montgomery St. **Map** 5 C4. *Tel* (415) 512-1111. 🚌 7, 8, 9, 21, 31, 66, 71. 🚋 J, K, L, M, N. See *Where to Stay* p526. www.sfpalace.com

The original Palace Hotel was opened by William Ralston, one of San Francisco's best-known financiers, in 1875. It was the most luxurious of San Francisco's early hotels, with 7 floors, 700 windows, an inner courtyard, and exotic international décor. It was regularly frequented by the rich and famous. Among its patrons were the actress Sarah Bernhardt and writers Oscar Wilde and Rudyard Kipling. The celebrated tenor Enrico Caruso was a guest at the hotel at the time of the earthquake of 1906 when the hotel, like much of the city, caught fire. It was rebuilt shortly after under the direction of the architect George Kelham, and reopened in 1909. The Garden Court dining room can hold a reception for 1,000 people and is lit by 20 crystal chandeliers. The building was completely refurbished in 2002.

The Garden Court at the Sheraton Palace Hotel

San Francisco Museum of Modern Art 🔞

This dramatic museum forms the nucleus of San Francisco's reputation as a leading center of modern art. Created in 1935 with the aim of displaying works from 20th-century artists, it moved into its new quarters in 1995. The focus of Swiss architect Mario Botta's modernist building is the 125-ft (38-m) cylindrical skylight, which channels light down to the first-floor atrium court. The museum has over 23,000 works of art in its collection and 50,000 sq ft (4,600 sq m) of gallery space on four floors. It offers a dynamic schedule of changing exhibits from around the world.

Zip Light (1990) by Sigmar Willnauer

Personal Values
Belgian Surrealist René Magritte created this late masterpiece in 1952. It features his use of everyday objects in strange and often unsettling surroundings, all painted in a realistic style.

MUSEUM GUIDE

The museum shop, auditorium, café and special events space are on the first floor. On the second floor is the Koret Visitor Education Center and galleries devoted to works from the museum's collection of painting, sculpture, architecture and design. Photography and special exhibitions are displayed on the third floor, with media arts, special exhibitions and a sculpture terrace on the fourth floor. The fifth floor galleries feature contemporary works of paintings and sculpture from the museum's collection.

★ No. 14, 1960
This oil on canvas was painted by Mark Rothko, a leading Abstract Impressionist. It is one of the most beautiful and hypnotic works from the artist's oeuvre.

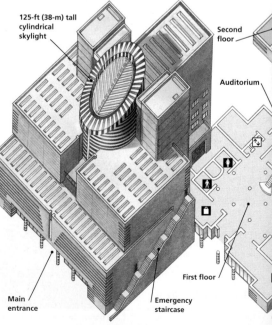

The Nest
Louise Bourgeois created this spidery sculpture in 1994, at the age of 83. The elongated forms are typical of her work.

125-ft (38-m) tall cylindrical skylight

Second floor

Auditorium

First floor

Main entrance

Emergency staircase

KEY TO FLOOR PLAN

- Painting and sculpture
- Architecture and design
- Photography and works on paper
- Media arts
- Koret Visitor Education Center
- Special exhibitions
- Non-exhibition space

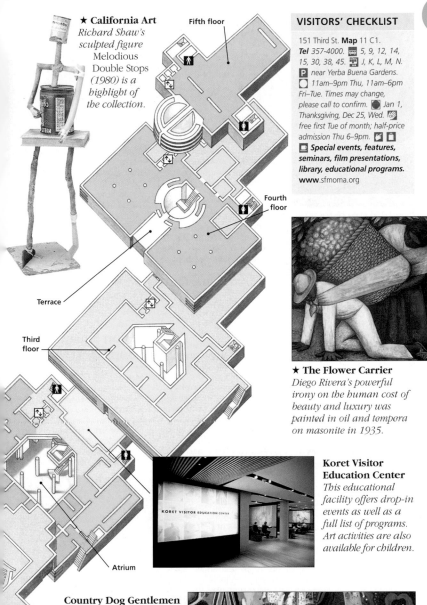

★ **California Art**
Richard Shaw's sculpted figure Melodious Double Stops *(1980) is a highlight of the collection.*

Fifth floor

Fourth floor

Terrace

Third floor

Atrium

VISITORS' CHECKLIST

151 Third St. **Map** 11 C1.
Tel 357-4000. 5, 9, 12, 14, 15, 30, 38, 45. J, K, L, M, N. near Yerba Buena Gardens. 11am–9pm Thu, 11am–6pm Fri–Tue. Times may change, please call to confirm. Jan 1, Thanksgiving, Dec 25, Wed. free first Tue of month; half-price admission Thu 6–9pm. Special events, features, seminars, film presentations, library, educational programs. www.sfmoma.org

★ **The Flower Carrier**
Diego Rivera's powerful irony on the human cost of beauty and luxury was painted in oil and tempora on masonite in 1935.

Koret Visitor Education Center
This educational facility offers drop-in events as well as a full list of programs. Art activities are also available for children.

Country Dog Gentlemen
Bay Area artist Roy De Forest painted this fantasy of a universe guarded by animals in 1972.

STAR EXHIBITS

★ The Flower Carrier

★ No. 14, 1960

★ California Art

Central plaza of the Crocker Galleria

California Academy of Sciences ⑰

875 Howard St. near Fifth St. ☎ *750 7145.* 🚌 *5, 9.* 🚊 *J, K, L.* ⬜ *phone for details.* **www**.*calacademy.org*

While its permanent home is undergoing renovation until 2008 *(see p370–1)*, the academy has moved to a temporary location on Howard Street, where it continues to showcase the natural sciences.

Crocker Galleria ⑱

Between Post, Kearny, Sutter, and Montgomery Sts. **Map** 5 C4. 🚌 *2, 3, 4.* 🚊 *J, K, L, M, N. See* ***Shopping*** *pp382–5.*

The Crocker Galleria was built in 1982. Inspired by Milan's Galleria Vittorio Emmanuelle, the building features a central plaza under an arched atrium. More than 50 shops and restaurants are housed here, with displays promoting the best of European and American designers.

Gump's ⑲

135 Post St. **Map** 5 C4. ***Tel*** *(415) 982-1616.* 🚌 *2, 3, 4, 30, 38, 45.* 🚊 *J, K, L,M, N.* 🚋 *Powell–Mason, Powell–Hyde.* ⬜ *10am–6pm Mon–Sat.* ♿ *See* ***Shopping*** *pp382–5.*

Founded in 1861 by German immigrants who were once mirror and frame merchants, this indigenous San Francisco

department store has now become a local institution.

Gump's houses the largest collection of fine china and crystal in the United States, by prestigious designers such as Baccarat, Steuben, and Lalique.

The store is also celebrated for its oriental treasures, furniture, and rare works of art. The Asian art is particularly fine, especially the jade collection, which enjoys an international reputation. In 1949 Gump's imported a great bronze Buddha and presented it to the Japanese Tea Garden *(see pp366–7)*. Gump's has a very refined atmosphere and is often frequented by the rich and famous. It is renowned for its extravagant window displays.

Union Square ⑳

Map 5 C5. 🚌 *2, 3, 4, 30, 38, 45.* 🚊 *J, K, L, M, N.* 🚋 *Powell–Mason, Powell–Hyde.*

Union Square was named after the big, pro-Union rallies held here during the Civil War of 1861–65. The rallies galvanized popular support for the Northern cause, which was instrumental in bringing California into the war on the side of the Union. The original churches, gentlemen's clubs, and the synagogue have been replaced by shops and offices. This green square, lined with palm trees, is at the heart of the shopping district and marks the edge of the Theater District. On the west side is the luxurious Westin St. Francis Hotel *(see p548)*. In the center, a bronze statue of the Goddess of Victory stands at the top of a 90-ft (27-m) Corinthian column. Sculpted by Robert Aitken in 1903, it commemorates Admiral Dewey's victory at Manila Bay during the Spanish–American War of 1898.

Theater District ㉑

Map 5 B5. 🚌 *2, 3, 4, 38.* 🚋 *Powell–Mason, Powell–Hyde. See* ***Entertainment*** *pp388–91.*

Several theaters are located near Union Square, all within a six-block area. The two largest are on Geary Boulevard: the Curran Theater, designed in 1922 by Alfred Henry D Jacobs, which imports Broadway shows, and the Geary Theater, with its Edwardian façade, now home to the American Conservatory Theater (ACT). The Theater on the Square mounts avant-garde, off-Broadway shows. The city has a fine reputation for the variety of performances it offers and has always attracted great actors. Isadora Duncan, the innovative 1920s dancer, was born nearby at No. 501 Taylor Street, which is now marked by a plaque.

Union Square Shops ㉒

Map 5 C5. 🚌 *2, 3, 4, 30, 38, 45.* 🚊 *J, K, L, M, N.* 🚋 *Powell–Mason, Powell–Hyde. See* ***Shopping*** *pp382–5.*

Many of San Francisco's largest department stores can be found here, including Macy's, Saks Fifth Avenue, and

Department stores overlooking Union Square

For hotels and restaurants in this region see pp542–9 and pp587–95

Rotating a cable car on the Powell Street Turntable

San Francisco Center

Market St and Powell St. **Map** 5 C5. **Tel** (415) 512-6776. 5, 7, 8, 9, 14, 21, 71. J, K, L, M, N. Powell–Mason, Powell–Hyde. 9:30am–8pm Mon–Sat, 11am–6pm Sun. See **Shopping** pp382–5.

Shoppers are carried upward on semispiral escalators through this vertical mall, with its nine floors of shops. It is topped by a retractable dome that is opened on fine days. The basement levels provide access to Powell Street Station. Nordstrom, a fashion store, occupies the top four levels. Entrances to Emporium, a department store famous for its Classical rotunda, are on the lower floors.

Old United States Mint

Fifth St and Mission St. **Map** 5 C5. 14, 14L, 26, 27. J, K, L, M, N. to the public.

San Francisco's Old Mint produced its last coins in 1937. It was built of granite in the Classical style by AB Mullet between 1869 and 1874, hence its nickname, the "Granite Lady." Its windows were fortified by iron shutters, and its basement vaults impregnable. The building was one of the few to survive the 1906 earthquake (see pp52–3). From 1973 to 1994 the building housed a museum, but today it is considered to be seismically unsafe. Closed for an indefinite period, its future is now uncertain.

Gump's. The Nieman Marcus store, at the request of San Franciscans, has preserved the 1900 rotunda and skylight from the City of Paris. The latter was the city's most elegant store at the end of the 19th century but was demolished in 1982. As well as the larger stores, the area houses many antiquarian bookshops and smaller boutiques. The Circle Gallery Building, at 140 Maiden Lane, is a contemporary art gallery. Designed by Frank Lloyd Wright in 1947, it was the precursor to his Guggenheim Museum in New York (see p33).

Powell Street Cable Car Turntable

Hallidie Plaza, Powell St at Market St. **Map** 5 C5. many buses. J, K, M, N. Powell–Mason, Powell–Hyde.

The Powell–Hyde and the Powell–Mason cable car lines are the most spectacular routes in San Francisco. They start and end their journeys to Nob Hill, Chinatown, and Fisherman's Wharf at the corner of Powell Street and Market Street. Unlike the double-ended cable cars that are found on the California Street line, the Powell Street cable cars were built to move in one direction only – hence the need for a turntable at the end of each line.

After the last passengers have disembarked, the car is pushed onto the turntable and rotated manually by the conductor and gripman. The next passengers for the return journey wait for the half-circle to be completed amid an ever-moving procession of street musicians, local shoppers, and office workers.

The impregnable "Granite Lady" Old Mint

Yerba Buena Center ⑭

The construction of the Moscone Center, San Francisco's largest venue for conventions, heralded the start of ambitious plans for Yerba Buena Gardens. New housing, hotels, museums, galleries, shops, restaurants, and gardens are being built, rejuvenating a once depressed area. Development is almost complete, with the exception of the New Moscone Convention facility at Fourth and Howard streets.

★ Yerba Buena Center for the Arts
The center is an arts forum, with galleries and regular screenings of contemporary films.

Esplanade Gardens
Visitors can wander along the paths or relax on benches.

The Martin Luther King Jr. Memorial has words of peace in several languages.

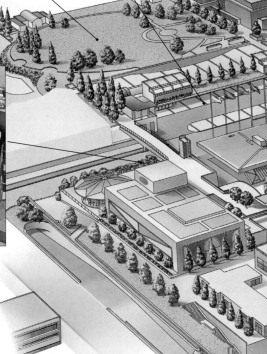

Zeum
Zeum is located at the Yerba Buena Rooftop. It has an ongoing program of events and provides opportunities for youngsters and artists to collaborate in the design and creation of anything from airplanes, robots, and futuristic buildings to mosaics and sculptures.

STAR SIGHTS

★ Yerba Buena Center for the Arts

★ SF Museum of Modern Art

MOSCONE CENTER

Engineer TY Lin found an ingenious way to support the rooftop garden above this huge underground hall without a single interior column. The bases of the eight steel arches are linked, like an archer's bow strings, by cables under the floor. By tightening the cables, the arches exert enormous upward thrust.

For hotels and restaurants in this region see pp542–9 and pp587–95

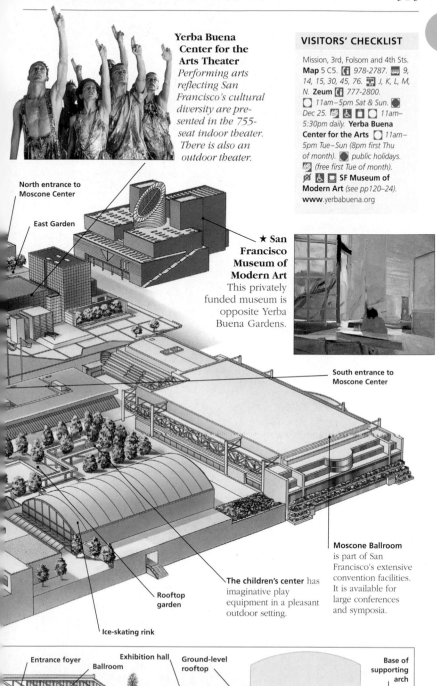

Yerba Buena Center for the Arts Theater
Performing arts reflecting San Francisco's cultural diversity are presented in the 755-seat indoor theater. There is also an outdoor theater.

North entrance to Moscone Center

East Garden

★ **San Francisco Museum of Modern Art**
This privately funded museum is opposite Yerba Buena Gardens.

South entrance to Moscone Center

Moscone Ballroom is part of San Francisco's extensive convention facilities. It is available for large conferences and symposia.

The children's center has imaginative play equipment in a pleasant outdoor setting.

Rooftop garden

Ice-skating rink

Entrance foyer
Ballroom
Exhibition hall
Ground-level rooftop
Base of supporting arch

CHINATOWN AND NOB HILL

The Chinese settled in the plaza on Stockton Street during the 1850s; the steep hills had made the area unpopular among wealthier San Franciscans. Today the district recalls the atmosphere of a typical southern Chinese town, although the architecture, customs, and public events are distinctly American hybrids on a Cantonese theme. This densely populated neighborhood has been called the "Gilded Ghetto," because its colorful façades and teeming markets screen a much harsher world of sweatshops, cramped living quarters, and poor inhabitants.

Chinese symbol outside the Bank of America

Nob Hill is San Francisco's most celebrated hilltop, famous for its cable cars, plush hotels, and views. In the late 19th century, the "Big Four," who built the first transcontinental railroad, were among its richest tenants in their large mansions on the hill. In 1906, the earthquake and fire *(see pp52–3)* leveled all but one of these houses, but today's luxury hotels still recall the opulence of the Victorian era *(see pp544)*.

SIGHTS AT A GLANCE

Historic Streets and Buildings
Chinatown Alleys ❺
Chinatown Gateway ❶
Grant Avenue ❻
Nob Hill ❿

Galleries and Museums
Cable Car Barn ⓫
Chinese Historical Society ❾
Pacific Heritage Museum ❽

Churches and Temples
Grace Cathedral ⓬
Kong Chow Temple ❸
Old St. Mary's Church ❷
Tin How Temple ❹

Parks and Squares
Portsmouth Plaza ❼

KEY

Street-by-Street map
See pp326–7

Cable car turntable

0 meters   500
0 yards   500

GETTING THERE
Visit on foot if possible. Car drivers can sometimes park in one of the Nob Hill hotel garages, under Portsmouth Plaza, or at St. Mary's Square in Chinatown. All cable car lines go to Nob Hill and Chinatown.

◁ **Colorful oriental architecture along Chinatown's streets**

Street-by-Street: Chinatown

Grant Avenue is the Chinatown for tourists, with dragon lampposts, up-turned roofs, and neighborhood hardware stores selling everything from kites to cooking utensils. Locals shop on Stockton Street, where boxes of the freshest vegetables, fish, and other produce spill over onto crowded sidewalks. In the alleys in between, look for temples, laundries, and family-run restaurants.

A street lamp in Chinatown

★ Chinatown Alleys
Authentic sights and sounds of the Orient echo in these busy alleys ❺

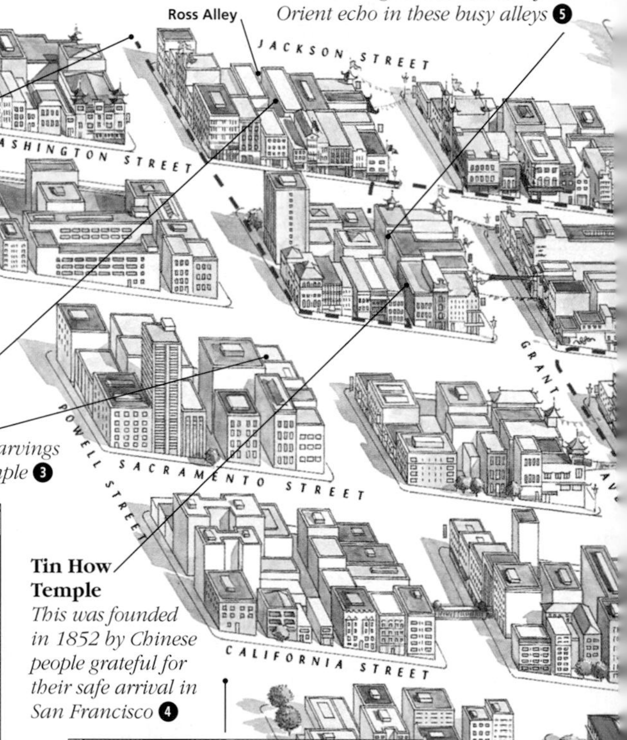

Ross Alley

To bus no. 83

The Fortune Cookie Factory welcomes visitors to its tiny premises, to see how the famous San Francisco creation, the fortune cookie, is made *(see pp384–5).*

Kong Chow Temple
Fine Cantonese wood carvings are a feature of this temple ❸

Tin How Temple
This was founded in 1852 by Chinese people grateful for their safe arrival in San Francisco ❹

The Bank of Canton was home to Chinatown's telephone exchange until 1946. The operators spoke five Chinese dialects.

STAR SIGHTS

- ★ Chinatown Alleys
- ★ Chinatown Gateway
- ★ Grant Avenue

Cable Cars run down two sides of Chinatown and are an essential part of the area's bustling atmosphere. Any of the three lines will take you there.

0 meters   100
0 yards   100

Portsmouth Plaza
Laid out in 1839, this was the social center for the village of Yerba Buena. Today it is a gathering place for players of cards and mahjong ⑦

★ Grant Avenue
In the 1830s and early 1840s this was the main thoroughfare of Yerba Buena. It is now the busy commercial center of Chinatown ⑥

LOCATOR MAP
See Street Finder, map 5

KEY

‒ ‒ ‒ Suggested route

The Chinese Cultural Center
contains an art gallery and a small crafts shop. It sponsors a lively program of lectures and seminars.

Chinese Historical Society
The society's collection of historical artifacts, documents, and photographs is exhibited here ⑨

Pacific Heritage Museum
Housed in an elegant building below the Bank of Canton, this small museum has fine exhibitions of Asian art, which are regularly changed ⑧

Old St. Mary's Church
The clock tower of this church, built while the city was still in its infancy, bears an arresting inscription ②

St. Mary's Square is a quiet haven in which to rest.

To bus nos. 31, 38

★ Chinatown Gateway
Also known as the "Dragons' Gate," this marks Chinatown's south entrance ①

Chinatown Gateway ❶

Grant Ave at Bush St. **Map** 5 C4.
🚌 *2, 3, 4, 15, 30, 45.*

This ornate portal, opened in 1970, was designed by Clayton Lee as an arch over the entrance to Chinatown's main tourist street, Grant Avenue. It was inspired by the ceremonial entrances of traditional Chinese villages. The three-arched gateway is capped with green roof tiles and a host of propitiatory animals, all of glazed ceramic. The gate was erected by an American institution, the Chinatown Cultural Development Committee. The materials were donated by Taiwan (Republic of China).

It is guarded by two stone lions that are suckling their cubs through their claws, in accordance with ancient lore. Once through the gate, visitors can buy antiques, embroidered silks, and gems, though prices are aimed at tourists.

Stone lions decorating the Chinatown gateway

Old St. Mary's Church ❷

660 California St. **Map** 5 C4. *Tel (415) 288-3800.* 🚌 *1, 15, 30, 45.* 🚋 *California St.* 🕐 *7:30am, noon daily; 5pm Sat; 8.30am, 11am Sun.*

San Francisco's first Catholic cathedral, Old St. Mary's, was consecrated on Christmas Day 1854 as the seat of the Roman Catholic bishop of the Pacific Coast. Until 1891 it

served a largely Irish congregation, when the new St. Mary's Cathedral was built on Van Ness Avenue. Because of the unavailability of the right building materials in California, the bricks and iron for the church were imported from the East Coast, while the granite foundation stones came from China. The clock tower of the church bears a large inscription, "Son, observe the time and fly from evil," said to have been directed at the brothels that stood across the street at the time it was built. It was one of the few buildings to remain unharmed by the 1906 earthquake and retains its original foundations and walls. The interior, with stained-glass windows and a balcony, was completed in 1909.

Entrance to Old St. Mary's Church below the clock tower and its inscription

Kong Chow Temple ❸

4th floor, 855 Stockton St. **Map** 5 B4. *Tel (415) 788-1339.* 🚌 *30, 45.* 🕐 *10am–4pm daily.* **Donation.** ♿

From the top floor above the district's post office, the Kong Chow Temple looks out over Chinatown and the Financial District. Although the building itself dates from only 1977, the temple altar and statuary are thought to form the oldest Chinese religious shrine in the United States. One altar was hand-carved in Guangzhou (Canton), and shipped to San Francisco in the 19th century. The main shrine is presided over by a carved wooden statue of Kuan Di, also dating from the 19th century. He is the deity most often found in shrines in Cantonese cities.

Kuan Di is also frequently seen in the city's Chinatown

Carved statue of Kuan Di inside the Kong Chow Temple

For hotels and restaurants in this region see pp542–9 and pp587–95

district: his highly distinctive face looks down from Taoist shrines in many of the area's restaurants. He is typically depicted holding a large sword in one hand and a book in the other. These are symbols of his unswerving dedication to both the martial and the literary arts.

Tin How Temple ●

Top floor, 125 Waverly Pl. **Map 5** C3. 🚌 1, 15, 30, 45. ◯ 10am–5pm daily. **Donation**.

This unusual temple is dedicated to Tin How (Tien Hau), the Queen of Heaven and protector of seafarers and visitors, and is the oldest operating Chinese temple in the United States. The sanctuary was originally founded in 1852 by a group of Chinese sailors, in gratitude for their safe voyage across the Pacific Ocean from their homeland to San Francisco. The temple is now situated at the top of three steep, wooden flights of stairs, which are considered to place it closer to heaven. The narrow space is filled with the smoke from both incense and burned paper offerings, and is brightly decorated with hundreds of gold and red lanterns. It is lit by red electric light bulbs and burning wicks floating in oil. Gifts of fruit lie on the carved altar in front of the wooden statue of the temple's namesake deity.

The impressive façade of the Tin How Temple on Waverly Place

A view along Chinatown's main street, Grant Avenue

Chinatown Alleys ●

Map 5 B3. 🚌 1, 30, 45.

Contained within a busy neighborhood, the Chinatown Alleys are situated between Grant Avenue and Stockton Street. These four narrow lanes intersect at Washington Street within half a block of each other. Of these, the largest is Waverly Place, known as the "Street of Painted Balconies" for reasons that are apparent to every passerby. Its other nickname, "15 Cents Street," derives from the cost of a haircut by the Chinese barbers trading here at the turn of the century. Nearby, Sun Yat-sen spent many years in exile at No. 36 Spofford Alley.

The alleys contain many old buildings, as well as traditional shops and restaurants. There are also atmospheric, old-fashioned herbalist shops, displaying elk antlers, sea horses, snake wine, and other exotic wares in their windows. Numerous small restaurants, above and below street level, serve cheap and delicious home-cooked food.

Grant Avenue ●

Map 5 C4. 🚌 1, 30, 45. 🚃 California St.

Grant Avenue is historically important for being the first street of Yerba Buena, the village that preceded San Francisco. A plaque at No. 823 marks the site of the first dwelling, a canvas tent that was erected on June 25, 1835. By 1836 the tent was replaced with a wooden structure and by 1837 with an adobe house. The street was then named Calle de la Fundacíon, the "Street of the Foundation."

An estimated 25,000 Chinese arrived in San Francisco during the Gold Rush era (see pp48–9). They settled in this area on the undesirable lower east slopes of Nob Hill, which were too steep for horse-drawn carriages. In 1885 the street was renamed Grant Avenue, in memory of Ulysses S Grant, the US president who died that year.

Most of the buildings on Grant Avenue were built after the 1906 earthquake in an Oriental Renaissance style. They now form the main tourist street in Chinatown.

Portsmouth Plaza, at the hub of Chinatown life

Portsmouth Plaza ❼

Map 5 C3. 🚌 *1, 15.*

San Francisco's original town square was laid out in 1839. It was once the social center for the village of Yerba Buena. On July 9, 1846, just after US rebels in Sonoma had declared California's independence from Mexico *(see pp464–5)*, marines raised the American flag above the plaza, officially seizing the port as part of the United States. Two years later, Sam Brannan announced the discovery of gold in the Sierra Nevada Mountains *(see pp48 –9)* here. In the 1850s the area was the hub of this new dynamic city, but in the 1860s the business district shifted to flatlands reclaimed from the bay and the plaza declined in civic importance.

Today Portsmouth Plaza is the social center of Chinatown. In the morning people practice *t'ai chi*, and from noon to evening gather to play cards.

Pacific Heritage Museum ❽

608 Commercial St. **Map** 5 C3. *Tel (415) 399-1124.* 🚌 *1, 15.* ⏰ *10am– 4pm Tue–Sat, except public hols.* ♿

The museum building is as elegant as the changing collections of Asian arts displayed inside. It is a synthesis of two buildings. The US Sub-Treasury was erected here in 1875–77 by William Appleton Potter, on the site of the city's first mint. Old coin vaults can still be seen in the basement.

In 1984 the 17-story Bank of Canton headquarters were built above the Treasury, incorporating the old façade and basement. The result is a building of great refinement.

Chinese Historical Society ❾

965 Clay St. **Map** 5 C3. *Tel (415) 391-1188.* 🚌 *1, 30, 45.* 🚃 *Powell St.* ⏰ *11am–4pm Tue–Fri & Sun.* ⏰ *public hols.* 🏠 📷 🎥 *free 1st Thu every month.* **www**.chsa.org

Among the exhibits in this museum are a ceremonial dragon costume and a "tiger fork." This triton was wielded in one of the battles during the reign of terror known as the Tong Wars. The tongs were rival Chinese clans who fought over the control of gambling and prostitution in the city in the late 19th century. Other objects, documents and photographs illuminate the daily life of Chinese immigrants in San Francisco. There is a yearbook of the neighborhood written in Chinese, and the original Chinatown telephone directory, written by hand.

The contribution of the Chinese to California's development was extensive despite the antagonism and poor treatment they were met with, as the many museum displays make clear. Chinese workers made the

Dragon's head in the Historical Society

perilous voyage to California in the thousands to find gold and escape the economic difficulties of their homeland. Rich merchants used them as cheap labor in the gold mines, and later they were used to build the western half of the transcontinental railroad *(see pp50–51)*. They also constructed dikes in the Sacramento River delta, were pioneers in the fishing industry, and planted the first vines in many of California's early vineyards.

Nob Hill ❿

Map 5 B4.

Nob Hill is the highest summit of the city center, rising 338 ft (103 m) above the bay. Its steep slopes kept prominent citizens away until the opening of the California Street cable car line in 1878. The rich then flocked to build homes here, including the "Big Four" railroad barons *(see pp472 –3)*. Its name is thought to come from the Hindi word *nabob*, meaning governor. Sadly, all the mansions were burned down in the fire of 1906 *(see pp52–3)*, except the home of James C Flood, now the Pacific Union Club.

Nob Hill still attracts the affluent to its splendid hotels, which benefit from spectacular views of the city.

A panoramic view of the city from a penthouse bar on Nob Hill

Cable Car Barn ⓫

1201 Mason St. **Map** 5 B3. *Tel* (415) 474-1887. ▦ 1, 12, 30, 45, 83. ▣ Powell–Mason, Powell–Hyde. ◻ 10am–6pm daily (10am–5pm in winter). ◖ Jan 1, Thanksgiving, Dec 25. ♿ mezzanine only. **Video show**. ◻ www.cablecarmuseum.com

This is both a museum and the powerhouse of the cable car system *(see pp302–3)*. Anchored to the floor are the wheels that wind the cables through the system of channels and pulleys beneath the city's streets. You can observe them from the mezzanine, then walk downstairs to see under the street. The museum also houses an early cable car and specimens of the mechanisms that control the movements of individual cars. The cable car system is the last of its kind in the world. The brick building was constructed in 1909.

The entrance to the Cable Car Barn Museum

Grace Cathedral ⓬

1100 California St. **Map** 5 B4. *Tel* (415) 749-6300. ▦ 1. ▣ California St. ✝ Choral evensong 5:15pm Thu, 3pm Sun; Choral Eucharist 7:30am, 8:15am, 6am, 11am Sun. ♿ ✦ 12:30–2pm Sun, 1–3pm Mon–Fri, 11:30am–1:30pm Sat. ◻

Grace Cathedral is the main Episcopal church in San Francisco. It was designed by Lewis P Hobart. Preparatory work began in February 1927, and building started in September 1928, but the cathedral was not completed until 1964. Despite its modern construction, the building is inspired by Notre Dame in Paris, using traditional materials. The interior is replete with marble, and the leaded windows were designed by Charles Connick, using the blue glass of Chartres as his inspiration. The rose window is made using 1-inch (2.5-cm) thick faceted glass, which is illuminated from inside the building at night. Other windows were executed by Henry Willet and Gabriel Loire. These include depictions of modern heroes such as Albert Einstein and astronaut John Glenn. Objects in the cathedral include a 13th-century Catalonian crucifix and a 16th-century Brussels tapestry. The entrance doors are cast from molds of Ghiberti's "Doors of Paradise," made for the Baptistry in Florence.

Cast figure from the main entrance

The New Testament Window, made in 1931 by Charles Connick, is placed on the south side of the church.

The Rose Window was made in Chartres by Gabriel Loire in 1964.

The Carillon Tower houses 44 bells made in England in 1938.

The Chapel of Grace, funded by the Crocker family, has a 15th-century French altarpiece.

The Doors of Paradise are decorated with scenes from the bible and portraits of Ghiberti and contemporaries.

Entrances

FISHERMAN'S WHARF AND NORTH BEACH

ishermen from Genoa and Sicily first arrived in the Fisherman's Wharf area in the late 19th century and founded the San Francisco fishing industry. The district has slowly given way to tourism since the 1950s, but brightly painted boats still set out from the harbor on fishing trips early each morning. To the south of

Fisherman's Wharf entrance sign

Fisherman's Wharf lies North Beach, sometimes known as "Little Italy." This lively part of the city has an abundance of delis, bakeries, and cafés, from which you can watch the crowds. It is home to many Italian and Chinese families, with a sprinkling of writers and bohemians; Jack Kerouac *(see pp26–7)*, among others, found inspiration here.

SIGHTS AT A GLANCE

Museums and Galleries
North Beach Museum **13**
Ripley's Believe It Or Not! Museum **5**
San Francisco Art Institute **10**
San Francisco National Maritime Museum **8**
USS *Pampanito* **3**
Wax Museum **4**

Historic Streets and Buildings
Alcatraz Island pp338–9 **1**
Lombard Street **9**
Pier 39 **2**
Vallejo Street Stairway **11**

Shopping Centers
The Cannery **6**
Ghirardelli Square **7**

Restaurants and Bars
Club Fugazi **12**

Parks and Gardens
Levi's Plaza **17**
Telegraph Hill **16**
Washington Square **14**

Churches
Saints Peter and Paul Church **15**

KEY

	Street-by-Street map See pp334–5
	Cable car turntable
	Ferry terminal
	Historical trolley line

| 0 meters | 500 |
| 0 yards | 500 |

GETTING THERE
The Powell–Hyde cable car line goes to Ghirardelli Square and Russian Hill. The Powell–Mason line passes through North Beach, to Fisherman's Wharf and Pier 39. Many buses run through the district.

◁ **View of Fisherman's Wharf and Alcatraz Island from the Powell–Hyde cable car**

Street-by-Street: Fisherman's Wharf

Italian seafood restaurants have now replaced fishing as the primary focus of the Fisherman's Wharf local economy. Both the expensive restaurants and the cheap outdoor crab pots serve San Francisco's celebrated Dungeness crab, in season from November to June. As well as sampling the seafood, visitors also enjoy taking in the many shops, museums, and other attractions for which Fisherman's Wharf is noted.

★ **USS *Pampanito***
A tour gives an idea of the hardships endured by sailors in this World War II submarine ❸

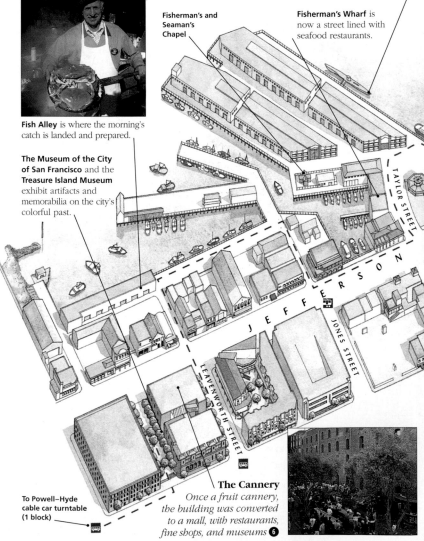

Fish Alley is where the morning's catch is landed and prepared.

The Museum of the City of San Francisco and the **Treasure Island Museum** exhibit artifacts and memorabilia on the city's colorful past.

Fisherman's and Seaman's Chapel

Fisherman's Wharf is now a street lined with seafood restaurants.

TAYLOR STREET

JEFFERSON

JONES STREET

LEAVENWORTH STREET

The Cannery
Once a fruit cannery, the building was converted to a mall, with restaurants, fine shops, and museums ❻

To Powell–Hyde cable car turntable (1 block)

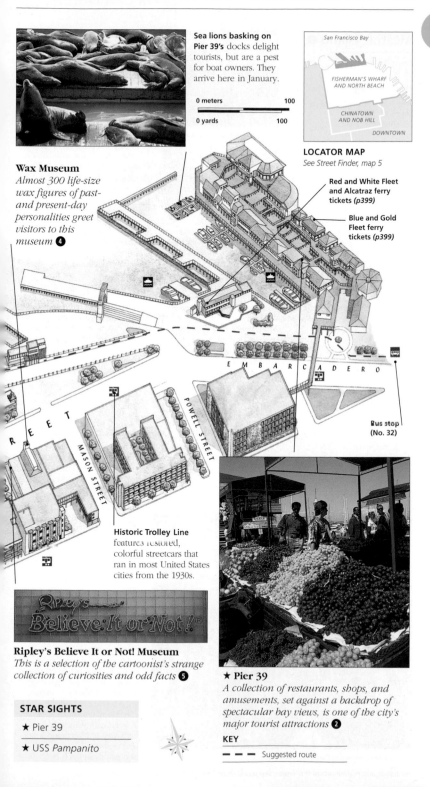

Sea lions basking on **Pier 39's** docks delight tourists, but are a pest for boat owners. They arrive here in January.

| 0 meters | 100 |
| 0 yards | 100 |

LOCATOR MAP
See Street Finder, map 5

San Francisco Bay

FISHERMAN'S WHARF AND NORTH BEACH

CHINATOWN AND NOB HILL

DOWNTOWN

Wax Museum
Almost 300 life-size wax figures of past-and present-day personalities greet visitors to this museum ❹

Red and White Fleet and Alcatraz ferry tickets (p399)

Blue and Gold Fleet ferry tickets (p399)

EMBARCADERO

POWELL STREET

MASON STREET

REET

Bus stop (No. 32)

Historic Trolley Line features restored, colorful streetcars that ran in most United States cities from the 1930s.

Ripley's Believe It or Not!®

Ripley's Believe It or Not! Museum
This is a selection of the cartoonist's strange collection of curiosities and odd facts ❺

★ **Pier 39**
A collection of restaurants, shops, and amusements, set against a backdrop of spectacular bay views, is one of the city's major tourist attractions ❷

STAR SIGHTS

★ Pier 39

★ USS *Pampanito*

KEY

- - - Suggested route

Alcatraz Island ❶

See pp338–9.

Pier 39 ❷

Map 5 B1. 🚌 25.
See **Shopping** *pp382–5.*

Refurbished in 1978 to resemble a quaint wooden fishing village, this 1905 cargo pier now houses many tourist shops and specialty stores spread over two levels.

The pier's street performers and amusements are popular and appealing, particularly to families with children. You can ride on the two-level carousel, or brave the Turbo Ride, a roller-coaster simulator where a film gives the illusion of speed and danger.

A sensational multimedia show called the San Francisco Experience takes visitors through a whirlwind historical tour of the city, complete with Chinese New Year celebrations and an earthquake.

USS *Pampanito's* torpedo room

USS *Pampanito* ❸

Pier 45. **Map** 4 F1. *Tel* (415) 775-1943. 🚌 47. ◯ *May–Oct: 9am–9pm; Sun–Thu: 9am–8pm Fri–Sat.* 🗐 🐾 www.maritime.org

This World War II submarine fought in, and survived, several bloody battles in the Pacific, sinking six enemy ships and severely damaging others. Tragically for the Allies, two of its fatal targets were carrying British and Australian prisoners of war. The *Pampanito* managed to rescue 73 men, however, and carry them to safety in the United States. A tour of the ship takes visitors from stern to bow and includes visits to the torpedo room, the claustrophobic galley, and officers' quarters. In the days when the USS *Pampanito* was in service, it had a crew of ten officers who were in command of 70 enlisted seamen.

Wax Museum ❹

145 Jefferson St. **Map** 5 B1. 🖪 (800) 439-4305. 🚌 32. 🚻 F. ◯ *10am–9pm Mon–Fri (6pm Wed); 9am–9pm Sat & Sun.* 🗐 📷 🐾 *limited.* www.waxmuseum.com

One of the world's largest and most absorbing collections of life-size wax figures is displayed here. All aspects of life and history are displayed here, from the gruesome Chamber of Horrors to the inspiring Hall of Religions and the Library of US Presidents. In the Palace of Living Art, world-famous portraits are rendered in wax. The entire Lower Lobby is dedicated to a *Titanic* exhibit.

A gallery of wax figures includes such diverse personages as members of the British Royal Family, Elvis Presley, Beethoven, Neil Armstrong, Marilyn Monroe, and Martin Luther King Jr. The building is also home to the Rainforest Cafe with its waterfall and theme shops.

Ripley's Believe It Or Not! Museum ❺

175 Jefferson St. **Map** 4 F1. *Tel* (415) 771-6188. 🚌 32. 🚻 F. ◯ *10am–10pm Sun–Thu, 10am–midnight Fri–Sat.* 🗐 🐾 www.ripleysf.com

Californian native Robert L Ripley was an illustrator who collected peculiar facts and artifacts and earned his fame from syndicating his celebrated US newspaper cartoon strip, called "Ripley's Believe It Or Not!" Among the 350 oddities on display are a cable car built of 275,000 matchsticks, a two-headed calf, tombstones with wry epithets, and a life-size replica of a man with two pupils in each eyeball.

The two-level Venetian Carousel on Pier 39

The Cannery ⑥

2801 Leavenworth St. **Map** 4 F1.
🚌 19, 30. 🚋 Powell–Hyde.
◻ 10am–4pm daily. ♿ See
Shopping pp382–5.

The interior of this 1909
fruit-canning plant was
redeveloped in the 1960s. It
now incorporates footbridges,
rambling passages, and sunny
courtyards, with restaurants
and shops selling clothing,
collector dolls, and Native
American arts and crafts.
  The Cannery also houses
the Treasure Island Museum.
Chief among its displays are
memorabilia from the 1939
World's Fair, which celebrated
the unity of Pacific cultures.
Other permanent displays
include the China Clippers –
the silver Pan American
Airways seaplanes which
flew between Treasure Island
and the Far East during
World War II – and a Fresnel
lens once used at the Farallon
Island lighthouse.

Ghirardelli Square

Ghirardelli Square ⑦

900 North Point St. **Map** 4 F1.
🚌 19, 30, 47, 49.
🚋 Powell–Hyde. See **Shopping**
pp382–5.

This former chocolate factory
and woolen mill is the most
attractive of the city's many
refurbished sites, with elegant
shops and restaurants. The
clock tower and roof sign
from the original building still
remain. The Ghirardelli Chocolate Manufactory on the
plaza houses old chocolate-
making machinery and sells
the confection, but the chocolate bars are now made in
San Leandro, across the bay.
  Fountain Plaza is a colorful
focal point for shoppers, at
any time of day and evening.

San Francisco National Maritime Museum ⑧

900 Beach St. **Map** 4 F1. **Museum**
Tel (415) 561-7100. ◻ 10am–5pm
daily. **Hyde Street Pier** **Tel** 447-5000.
🚌 19, 30, 32. 🚋 Powell–Hyde. ◻
mid-May–mid-Sep: 9am–5:30pm daily;
mid-Sep–mid-May: 9:30am–5pm daily.
🎟 pier. ♿ pier and museum. 📷
**Lectures, maritime demon-
strations, activities.** 📷
www.maritime.org

Resembling a beached
ocean liner, this 1939
building first housed
the Maritime
Museum in 1951.
On display is a
collection of ship
models, vintage
nautical instruments,

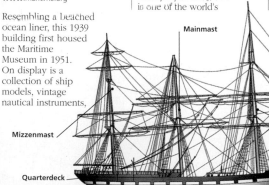
Hyde Street Pier

paintings, and photographs
illustrating local nautical
history. Moored at the
nearby Hyde Street Pier
is one of the world's
largest collections of old ships.
Among the most spectacular
is the *C.A. Thayer*, a three-
masted schooner built in 1895.
It carried lumber along the
northern California coast and
later was used as a fishing
boat in Alaska. Also at the pier
is the 2,320-ton side-wheel
ferryboat, *Eureka*, built in 1890
to ferry trains between Hyde
Street Pier and the counties
north of San Francisco Bay. It
carried 2,300 passengers and
120 cars and was the largest
passenger ferry of its day.

BALCLUTHA

*This ship is the star of Hyde
Street Pier. Launched in
1886, she sailed twice a
year between Britain
and California,
trading wheat
for coal.*

Mainmast

Mizzenmast

Foremast

Quarterdeck

Bowsprit

Alcatraz Island ❶

Alcatraz means "pelican" in Spanish and refers to the first inhabitants of this rocky, steep-sided island. Lying 3 miles (5 km) east of the Golden Gate, its location is both strategic and exposed to ocean winds. In 1859, the US army established a fort here that guarded San Francisco Bay until 1907, when it became a military prison. From 1934 to 1963, it served as a maximum-security Federal Penitentiary. In 1969 the island was seized by members of the Native American Movement (*see p56*) claiming it as their land. They were expelled in 1971, and Alcatraz is now part of the Golden Gate National Recreation Area.

Badge on entrance to cellhouse

★ Cell Block
The cell house contains four cell blocks. No cell has an outside wall or ceiling. The dungeonlike foundation of the prison block shares the original foundation of the old military fortress.

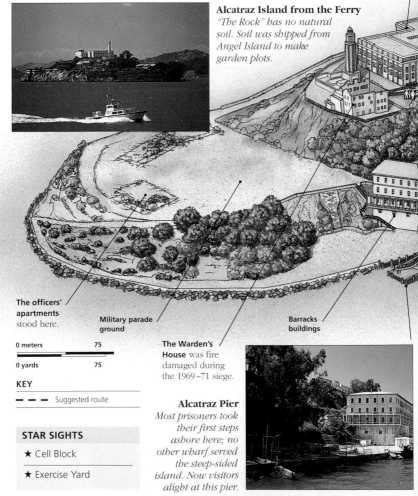

Alcatraz Island from the Ferry
"The Rock" has no natural soil. Soil was shipped from Angel Island to make garden plots.

The officers' apartments stood here.

Military parade ground

Barracks buildings

| 0 meters | 75 |
| 0 yards | 75 |

The Warden's House was fire damaged during the 1969–71 siege.

KEY

– – – Suggested route

Alcatraz Pier
Most prisoners took their first steps ashore here; no other wharf served the steep-sided island. Now visitors alight at this pier.

STAR SIGHTS

★ Cell Block

★ Exercise Yard

★ **Exercise Yard**
Meals and a walk around the exercise yard were the highlights of a prisoner's day. The walled yard featured in films made at the prison.

VISITORS' CHECKLIST

Map 6 F1. *Tel (415) 705-5555 for tickets and schedules.* **Night tours** *Tel (415) 561-4926.* 🚢 *from Pier 41.* ⭕ *daily.* 🌙 *Jan 1, Dec 25.* ♿ *in places, but difficult.* 📷 obligatory. *Advance reservations suggested.* **No restaurant or café.** www.nps.gov/goga

Metal detectors checked prisoners when they passed to and from the dining hall and exercise yards.

The Military Morgue is tiny and cramped, and is not open to the public.

Prison workshops

Water tower

The Visitors' Center is in the old barracks.

The Military Dorm was built in 1933.

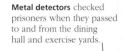

The officers' club, dating from the days of Fort Alcatraz, was a military store that also served as a recreation center.

FAMOUS INMATES

Al Capone
The Prohibition gangster, "Scarface" Capone was actually convicted in 1934 for income tax evasion! He spent much of his five-year sentence on Alcatraz in an isolation cell, and left the prison mentally unstable.

Robert Stroud
The original *"Birdman of Alcatraz"* spent the majority of his 17 years on The Rock in solitary confinement.

Carnes, Thompson, and Shockley
In May 1946, prisoners led by Clarence Carnes, Marion Thompson, and Sam Shockley overpowered guards and captured their guns. The prisoners failed to break out of the cell house, but three inmates and two officers were killed in what became known as the "Battle of Alcatraz." Carnes received

an additional life sentence, and Shockley and Thompson were executed at San Quentin prison for their part in the insurrection.

Anglin Brothers
John and Clarence Anglin, together with Frank Morris, chipped through the walls of their cells, and hid the holes with cardboard grates. Leaving dummy heads in their beds, they made a raft to enable their escape and were never caught. Their story was dramatized in the film *Escape from Alcatraz* (1979).

Cars negotiating the steep and crooked section of Lombard Street

Lombard Street ❾

Map 5 A2. 🚌 45. 🚋 Powell–Hyde.

Banked at a natural incline of 27°, this hill proved too steep for vehicles to climb. In the 1920s the section of Lombard Street close to the summit of Russian Hill was revamped, and the severity of its gradient was lessened by the addition of eight curves.

Today it is known as "the crookedest street in the world." Cars can travel downhill at a speed of only 5 miles per hour (8 km/h), while pedestrians use steps. There are spectacular views of San Francisco from the summit.

San Francisco Art Institute ❿

800 Chestnut St. **Map** 4 F2. **Tel** *(415) 771-7021.* 🚌 *30.* **Diego Rivera Gallery** ◐ *8am–9pm daily.* ● *public hols.* ♿ *partial.* 📷 🖥

San Francisco's Art Institute dates from 1871 and once occupied the immense

A 30-Minute Walk through North Beach

Settlers originally from Chile, and more recently Italy, have brought their enthusiasm for nightlife to North Beach, earning this quarter its vibrant reputation. Its café-oriented atmosphere has long appealed to bohemians, particularly the 1950s Beat Generation *(see pp26–7)*.

The Beat Neighborhood

Start the walk from the southwest corner of Broadway and Columbus Avenue at City Lights Bookstore ①. Owned by Beat poet Lawrence Ferlinghetti, City Lights was the first bookshop in the US to sell paperbacks exclusively. The author Jack Kerouac, a friend of Ferlinghetti, coined the word "Beat," later referred to as "Beatnik."

One of the most popular Beat bars was Vesuvio ②, south of City Lights, across Jack Kerouac Alley. Welsh poet Dylan Thomas was a patron here, and it is still a favorite with

Jack Kerouac

poets and artists. From here travel south to Pacific Avenue, cross to the opposite side of Columbus Avenue and walk back toward Broadway, stopping at Tosca ③. The walls of this bar and café display murals of Tuscany, and a jukebox plays selections from Italian opera. A few steps north bring you to Adler Alley. Specs ④, a lively bar filled with memorabilia of the Beat era, is at No. 12. Walking back to Columbus Avenue, turn right into Broadway and at the corner of Kearny Street cross over to Enrico's Sidewalk Café ⑤.

Columbus Café ⑪

The Strip

Enrico's celebrated outdoor café is the best place from which to watch the action on this stretch of Broadway, called The Strip ⑥, noted for its "adult entertainment." At the junction of Broadway and Grant Avenue is the former Condor Club ⑦, where the world's first topless stage show was performed in June 1964.

For hotels and restaurants in this region see pp542–9 and pp587–95

wooden mansion built for the family of railroad baron Mark Hopkins on Nob Hill *(see p330)*, which burned down in the fire of 1906 *(see pp52–3)*. Its students today are housed in a Spanish Colonial-style building that was constructed in 1926, complete with cloisters, a courtyard fountain, and bell tower. A modern extension was added at the rear of the building in 1969. The Diego Rivera Gallery, named after the famous Mexican muralist *(see pp306–7)*, can be found to the left of the main entrance.

The Institute holds temporary exhibitions of works by its young artists.

Diego Rivera's *Making of a Mural* (1931), San Francisco Art Institute

Vallejo Street Stairway ⓫

Mason St and Jones St. **Map** 5 B3.
🚌 30, 45. 🚋 Powell–Mason.

The steep climb from Little Italy to the summit of Russian Hill reveals some of the best views of Telegraph Hill, North Beach, and the bay. The street gives way to steps at Mason Street, which climb up through Ina Coolbrith Park.

Above Taylor Street, there are lanes, with several Victorian houses *(see pp300–1)*. At the crest of the hill is one of the rare parts of the city not destroyed in the earthquake of 1906 *(see pp52–3)*.

Club Fugazi ⓬

678 Green St. Map 5 B3. **Tel** (415) 421-4222. 🚌 15, 30, 45. ⏰ Wed–Sun. See **Entertainment** pp390–95.

Built in 1912 as a North Beach community hall, the Club Fugazi is the venue for the musical cabaret *Beach*

Blanket Babylon. This is a lively show that has been running for more than two decades and has become an institution among San Franciscans. It is popular with locals and tourists alike and is famous for its topical and outrageous songs, and for the bizarre hats often worn by the performers.

North Beach Museum ⓭

1435 Stockton St. Map 5 B3.
Tel (415) 566-4497. 🚌 15, 30, 45.
⏰ 9am–5pm Mon–Thu, 9am–6pm Fri, 9am–1pm Sat. 🔴 public hols.

This small museum, on the second floor of the Eureka Bank, documents the history of North Beach and Chinatown through exhibitions of old photographs. These celebrate the heritage of the Chilean, Irish, Italian, and Chinese immigrants who have arrived in the area since the 19th century. Other photographs illustrate the bohemian community of North Beach.

Upper Grant Avenue
Turn right into Grant Avenue where you will find The Saloon ⑧ with its original 1861 bar. On the corner of Vallejo Street is Caffè Trieste ⑨, the oldest coffee house in San Francisco, and a

genuine Beat rendezvous since 1956. Very much a part of Italian-American culture, it offers live opera on Saturday afternoons. Follow Grant Avenue north past the Lost and Found Saloon ⑩, now a blues club but formerly the Coffee Gallery, another of the Beat haunts. Turn left at Green Street and look for Columbus Café ⑪, whose exterior

Vesuvio, a popular Beat bar ②

walls are decorated with attractive murals. Turning left again at Columbus Avenue, follow this main street of North Beach south past many more Italian coffee houses, to return to your starting point.

TIPS FOR WALKERS

Starting point: *Corner of Broadway and Columbus Avenue.*
Length: *1 mile (1.6 km).*
Getting there: *Muni bus No. 15 runs along Columbus Avenue.*
Stopping-off points: *All the bars and cafés mentioned are worth visiting for a drink and the atmosphere. Children are not usually allowed in bars.*

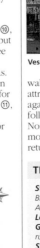

KEY

••• Walk route

0 meters 200
0 yards 200

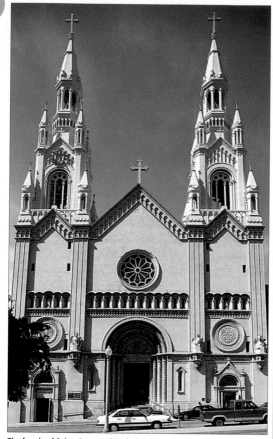

The façade of Saints Peter and Paul Church, Washington Square

notable for its many columns and ornate altar. There are also statues and mosaics illuminated by stained-glass windows. The concrete and steel structure of the church, with its twin spires rising over the surrounding rooftops, was completed in 1924.

Cecil B De Mille filmed the workers working on the foundations of Saints Peter and Paul, and used the scene to show the building of the Temple of Jerusalem in his film *The Ten Commandments*, made in 1923.

The church is sometimes referred to as the Fishermen's Church (many Italians once earned their living by fishing), and there is an annual mass and procession from Columbus Avenue to Fisherman's Wharf to celebrate the Blessing of the Fleet in October. Masses in the church can still be heard in Italian and Cantonese, as well as English.

Telegraph Hill ⑯

Map 5 C2. **Coit Tower** Telegraph Hill Blvd. **Tel** *(415) 362-0808.* 🚌 *39.* ⬜ *10am–6pm (7:30pm summer) daily.* 🎫 ♿ *murals only.* 📷

Originally called Alta Loma by the Mexicans, then Goat Hill after the animals that grazed on its slopes, Telegraph Hill was renamed in 1850 after the semaphore installed on its crest. This alerted the city's merchants to the arrival of ships through the Golden Gate. On the eastern side,

Washington Square ⑭

Map 5 B2. 🚌 *15, 30, 39, 45.*

The square consists of a simple expanse of lawn, surrounded by benches and trees, set against the twin towers of Saints Peter and Paul Church. It has an almost Mediterranean atmosphere, appropriate for the "town square" of Little Italy. Near the center of the square stands a statue of Benjamin Franklin. A time capsule was buried under the statue in 1979 and is scheduled to be reopened in 2079. It is said to contain some Levi's jeans, a bottle of wine, and a poem written by Lawrence Ferlinghetti, one of San Francisco's famous beat poets *(see pp26–7)*.

Saints Peter and Paul Church ⑮

666 Filbert St. **Map** 5 B2. **Tel** *(415) 421-0809.* 🚌 *15, 30, 39, 45.* ✝ *Italian mass and choir 11:45am Sun; phone for other masses.* ♿

Still known by many as the Italian Cathedral, this large church is situated at the heart of North Beach, and many Italians find it a welcome haven when they first arrive in San Francisco. It was here that the local baseball hero, Joe Di Maggio, was photographed after his marriage to the actress Marilyn Monroe in 1957, although the actual wedding ceremony was held elsewhere. The building, designed by Charles Fantoni, has an Italianesque façade, with a complex interior

Coit Tower mural showing Fisherman's Wharf in the 1930s

Steps at the bottom of Filbert Street leading up to Telegraph Hill

which, until 1914, was regularly dynamited to provide rocks for landfill and paving, the hill falls away abruptly to form steep paths, bordered by leafy gardens.

The western side slopes more gradually into the area known as "Little Italy," around Washington Square, although in recent years the city's Italian population has begun to settle in the Marina District. In the past the hill has been a neighborhood of immigrants living in wooden cabins, and of struggling artists, who appreciated the panoramic views. These days, however, the quaint pastel clapboard homes are much sought after, and this is one of the city's prime residential areas.

Coit Tower was built in 1933 at the top of 284-ft (86-m) high Telegraph Hill with funds left to the city by Lillie Hitchcock Coit, an eccentric San Franciscan pioneer and philanthropist. The 210-ft (64-m) reinforced concrete tower was designed as a fluted column by the architect Arthur Brown. When floodlit at night, its glow can be seen from most of the eastern half of the city. The encircling view around the North Bay Area from the observation platform (reached by an elevator) is quite spectacular.

In the lobby of the tower are absorbing murals *(see pp306–7)*. These were sponsored in 1934 by a government-funded program designed to keep artists in employment during the Great Depression. Twenty-five

artists worked together on the vivid portrait of life in modern California. Scenes range from the busy streets of the city's Financial District (with a robbery in progress) to factories, dockyards, and the Central Valley wheat fields. There are a number of fascinating details – a car crash, a family of immigrants encamped by a river, newspaper headlines, magazine covers, and book titles. There is a sense of frustration, satire, and whimsy in the pictures. Various political themes also feature. Many of the faces in the paintings are those of the artists and their friends, along with local figures such as Colonel William Brady, the caretaker of Coit Tower. The work's political subject matter caused some public controversy and delayed its official unveiling.

On the eastern side of Telegraph Hill the streets become steep steps. Descending from Telegraph Hill Boulevard,

Filbert Street is a rambling stairway, constructed of wood, brick, and concrete, where rhododendron, fuschia, bougainvillea, fennel, and blackberries thrive.

Levi's Plaza ⑰

Map 5 C2. 🚌 42.

This square is where the headquarters of Levi Strauss & Co., the manufacturers of blue jeans, can be found. The square was landscaped by Lawrence Halprin in 1982, with the intention of recalling the company's long history in the state. The plaza is studded with granite rocks and cut by flowing water, thus symbolizing the Sierra Nevada canyon scenery in which the miners who first wore the jeans worked. Telegraph Hill in the background adds a more natural mountainous element.

LEVI STRAUSS AND HIS JEANS

First manufactured in San Francisco in the days of the Gold Rush *(see pp48–9)*, denim jeans have had a great impact on popular culture, and they are just as fashionable today as they were when they first appeared. One of the leading producers of jeans is Levi Strauss & Co., founded in the city in the 1860s.

The company's story started in 1853, when Levi Strauss left New York to establish a dry goods business with his brother-in-law in San Francisco. In the 1860s, though still primarily a seller of dry goods, he pioneered the use of a durable, brown, canvaslike material to make work trousers, sold directly to miners. In the 1870s his company began to use metal rivets to strengthen the stress points in the garments, and demand increased. The company then expanded, and early in the 20th century it moved to 250 Valencia Street in the Mission District. Levi's jeans are now an institution, and are produced, sold, and worn all over the world. The company that was first founded by Levi Strauss is still owned and managed by his descendants.

Levi Strauss

Two miners sporting their Levis at the Last Chance Mine in 1882

PACIFIC HEIGHTS AND THE CIVIC CENTER

Pacific Heights is an exclusive neighborhood, rising 300 ft (90 m) above the city. After cable cars linked it with the city center in the 1880s, it quickly became a desirable place to live, and many fine Victorian houses now line its streets. To the north of Broadway, the streets drop steeply down to the Marina District, with its smart shops, fashionable cafés, and two prestigious yacht clubs.

To the south of Pacific Heights is the Civic Center, which was built after the earthquake of 1906. It includes some of the best Beaux-Arts architecture in the city, and in 1987 the area was declared a historic site. The Civic Center is perhaps the most elegant city complex in the US.

Fort Mason logo

SIGHTS AT A GLANCE

Historic Streets and Buildings
Alamo Square ⑱
Asian Art Museum ⑭
Bill Graham Civic Auditorium ⑮
City Hall ⑯
Cow Hollow ⑨
Fort Mason ⑦
Haas-Lilienthal House ❶
Octagon House ⑩
Palace of Fine Arts and the Exploratorium ❺
Spreckels Mansion ❷
University of San Francisco ⑲

Shopping Areas
Chestnut Street ❽
Fillmore Street ⑪
Hayes Valley ⑰

Modern Architecture
Japan Center ⑫

Churches
St. Mary's Cathedral ⑬

Parks and Gardens
Alta Plaza ❹
Lafayette Park ❸
Marina Green ❻

GETTING THERE
Muni buses 1 and 12, and the California Street cable car serve the Pacific Heights area. The Civic Center BART/Muni station on Market Street is two blocks east of City Hall. Buses 5, 8, and 19 all travel into the Civic Center.

KEY
▓ Street-by-Street map
  See pp346–7
🚡 Cable car terminus
🚇 BART station
🚋 Streetcar terminus

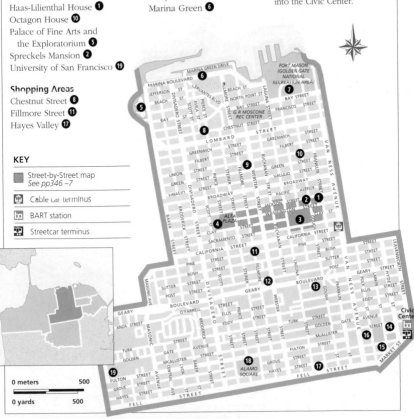

0 meters   500
0 yards   500

◁ **View from Alamo Square across the Civic Center toward the Financial District**

Street-by-Street: Pacific Heights

The steep blocks between Alta Plaza and Lafayette Park are set in the heart of the exclusive Pacific Heights district. The streets here are quiet and tidy, lined with stylish apartment blocks and palatial Victorian houses. Some of these date from the late 19th century, while others were built after the great earthquake and fire of 1906 *(see pp52–3)*. To the north of this area, the streets drop steeply down toward the residential Marina District and offer outstanding views of San Francisco Bay. Wander through the two large landscaped parks and past the luxurious gardens of the private mansions in between, then visit one of the many fashionable bars, cafés, and restaurants along Fillmore Street.

The Webster Street Row houses have been declared a historic landmark. They were built for a middle-class clientele in 1878 and have since been restored to their original splendor.

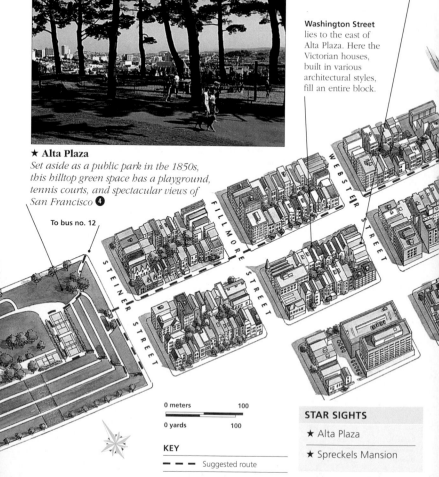

Washington Street lies to the east of Alta Plaza. Here the Victorian houses, built in various architectural styles, fill an entire block.

★ Alta Plaza
Set aside as a public park in the 1850s, this hilltop green space has a playground, tennis courts, and spectacular views of San Francisco ❹

To bus no. 12

WEBSTER STREET

FILLMORE STREET

STEINER STREET

0 meters   100

0 yards   100

KEY

– – – Suggested route

STAR SIGHTS

★ Alta Plaza

★ Spreckels Mansion

Haas-Lilienthal House

Furnished in Victorian style, this mansion is the head-quarters of the Architectural Heritage Foundation **1**

LOCATOR MAP
See Street Finder maps 3, 4

To bus nos. 47, 76

No. 2151 Sacramento Street is an ornate French-style mansion. A plaque commemorates a visit by the author Sir Arthur Conan Doyle in 1923.

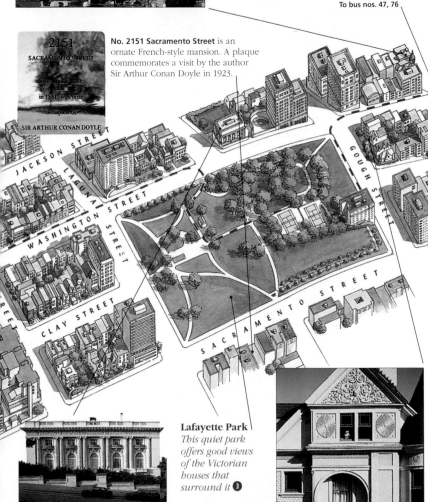

Lafayette Park
This quiet park offers good views of the Victorian houses that surround it **3**

★ Spreckels Mansion

This impressive limestone building, constructed on the lines of a French Baroque palace, has been home to best-selling novelist Danielle Steele since 1990 **2**

No. 2004 Gough Street, one of the more elaborate Victorian houses in Pacific Heights, was built in 1889.

The Haas-Lilienthal House, a Queen Anne mansion from 1886

Haas-Lilienthal House ●

2007 Franklin St. **Map** 4 E3. **Tel** (415) 441-3004. *1, 19, 27, 47, 49, 83.* ○ *noon–3pm Wed & Sat, 11am–4pm Sun.* ◩ ⬛ **www.sfheritage.org**

This attractive Queen Anne-style mansion *(see pp300–1)* was built in 1886 for the rich merchant William Haas. Alice Lilienthal, his daughter, lived here until 1972, when it was given to the Foundation for San Francisco's Architectural Heritage. It is the only intact private home of the period in San Francisco, now open as a museum, and it is complete with authentic furniture. A fine example of an upper-middle-class Victorian home, Haas-Lilienthal House has elaborate wooden gables, a circular corner tower, and luxurious ornamentation.

A display of photographs in the basement describes the history of the building and reveals that this grandiose house was modest in comparison with some of the mansions destroyed in the great fire of 1906 *(see pp52–3)*.

Spreckels Mansion ●

2080 Washington St. **Map** 4 E3. *1, 47, 49.* ● *to the public.*

Dominating the north side of Lafayette Park, this imposing Beaux-Arts mansion is sometimes known as the "Parthenon of the West." It was built in 1912 for the flamboyant Alma de Bretteville Spreckels and her husband, Adolph, heir to the sugar fortune of Claus Spreckels *(see p348)*. The house contains 26 bathrooms, and a large swimming pool in which Alma Spreckels swam daily until the age of 80. Her love of French architecture inspired the design. The architect of Spreckels mansion was George Applegarth, who in 1916 also designed the California Palace of the Legion of Honor in Lincoln Park *(see pp374–5)*. The Palace was donated to the city by the Spreckelses in 1924.

Today Spreckels Mansion is privately owned. It occupies a block of Octavia Street, which is paved and landscaped in a similar style to curvy Lombard Street *(see p340)*.

Façade of the impressive Spreckels Mansion

Lafayette Park ●

Map 4 E3. ▦ *1, 12.*

One of San Francisco's prettiest hilltop gardens, Lafayette Park is a leafy green haven of pine and eucalyptus trees, although its present tranquillity belies its turbulent history. Along with Alta Plaza and Alamo Square *(see p353)* the land was set aside in 1855 as a city-owned open space. Then squatters and others, including a former City Attorney, laid claim to the land and began to build their houses on it. The largest of these houses remained standing at the center of the hilltop park until 1936, the squatter who had built it refusing to move. It was finally demolished after the city authorities agreed to swap it for other land on nearby Gough Street. Steep stairways now lead to the summit of the park and its delightful views.

In the streets surrounding Lafayette Park there are a number of other palatial Victorian buildings. Particularly ornate examples are situated along Broadway, Jackson Street, and Pacific Avenue going east-west, and Gough, Octavia, and Laguna streets going north-south.

Alta Plaza ●

Map 4 D3. ▦ *1, 3, 12, 22, 24.*

Situated in the center of Pacific Heights, Alta Plaza is a landscaped urban park, where the San Franciscan elite come to relax. The stone steps rising up from Clay Street on the south side of the park offer good views of Haight Ashbury *(see pp354–63)*, the Fillmore district, and Twin Peaks *(see p363)*. The steps may be familiar to film buffs – Barbra Streisand drove down them in *What's Up Doc?* There are also tennis courts and a playground.

From the north side of the park some splendid views of Victorian mansions are visible, including Gibbs House, at No. 2622 Jackson Street, built by Willis Polk in 1894. Smith House, at No. 2600 Jackson Street, was

Relaxing in the peaceful Alta Plaza park

one of the first houses in San Francisco to be supplied with electricity in the 1890s.

Palace of Fine Arts and the Exploratorium 5

3601 Lyon St. **Map** 3 C2. ***Tel*** *(415) 561 0360.* 🚌 *22, 28, 29, 30, 43, 45, 47, 49.* 🕐 *10am–5pm Tue–Sun.* ⛔ *Mon, public hols.* 📷 ♿ **Tactile Dome** ***Tel*** *(415) 561-0362 (reservations).* **www**.exploratorium.com

Sole survivor of the many grandiose monuments built as part of the 1915 Panama-Pacific Exposition, the Palace of Fine Arts is a Neo-Classical folly. It was designed by the architect Bernard R Maybeck, who was inspired by the drawings of the Italian architect Piranesi and by the painting *L'Isle des Morts* by Swiss artist, Arnold Böcklin. Originally built of wood and plaster, the Palace eventually began to crumble, until one concerned citizen raised funds for its reconstruction in 1959. It was restored to its original splendor between 1962 and 1975 using reinforced concrete.

The central feature is the rotunda, perched on the edge of a landscaped, swan-filled lagoon. Its dome is decorated with allegorical paintings, all depicting the defense of art against materialism. On top of the many Corinthian columns, nymphs with bent heads are symbolic of the "melancholy of life without art."

The Palace's auditorium can hold up to 1,000 spectators, and its most important annual event is the May Film Festival, which highlights the work of new directors, particularly those from the Third World.

An elongated industrial shed inside the Palace houses the Exploratorium Museum, one of the most entertaining science museums in the United States. Established in 1969 by the physicist Frank Oppenheimer (whose brother Robert helped to develop the atom bomb), it is filled with more than 650 interactive exhibits, exploring the world of science and the senses. The exhibits, on two floors, are divided into 13 subject areas, each one color-coded by an overhead sign. These include a room for Electricity, where balls of lightning are produced in a tube; Vision, Color, and Light, where optical illusions are explained; and Motion, featuring the thrilling Momentum Machine. The Tactile Dome offers a sensory journey taken in total darkness.

The gardens form a relaxing and attractive backdrop to this imitation Roman ruin, which is a firm favorite with San Francisco residents.

The world of science explained in the Exploratorium Museum

Classical rotunda of the Palace of Fine Arts

PANAMA-PACIFIC EXPOSITION

In 1915 San Francisco celebrated its successful recovery from the 1906 earthquake and fire with a monumental fair. Officially, it was intended to celebrate the opening of the Panama Canal, and was designed to be the most splendid world's fair ever held. Its grand structures were indeed described by one highly enthusiastic visitor as "a miniature Constantinople."

The halls and pavilions of the fair were constructed on land reclaimed from San Francisco Bay, on the site of today's Marina District. They were donated by all the states and by 25 foreign countries, and lined a concourse 1 mile (1.6 km) long. Many of the buildings were based on such architectural gems as a Turkish mosque and a Buddhist temple from Kyoto. The brilliant Tower of Jewels, at the center of the concourse, was encrusted with glass beads and lit by spotlights. To the west stood the beautiful Palace of Fine Arts, which visitors reached by gondola across a landscaped lagoon.

Marina Green ❻

Map 4 D1. 🚌 22, 28, 30.

A long thin strip of lawn running the length of the Marina District, Marina Green is popular with kite-flyers and picnickers, especially on the Fourth of July, when the city's largest fireworks display can be seen from here. Paths along the waterfront are the city's prime spots for cyclists, joggers, and skaters. Golden Gate Promenade leads from the west end of the green to Fort Point, or you can turn east to the Wave Organ at the end of the harbor jetty.

Chestnut Street ❽

Map 4 D1. 🚌 22, 28, 30, 43.

The main shopping and nightlife center of the Marina District, Chestnut Street has a varied mix of movie theaters, markets, and restaurants, catering more to the local residents than to visitors. The strip stretches just a few blocks from Fillmore Street west to Divisadero Street, after which the neighborhood becomes residential in character.

Cow Hollow ❾

Map 4 D2. 🚌 22, 41, 45.

Cow Hollow is a shopping district along Union Street. It is so called because it was used as grazing land for the city's dairy cows up until the 1860s. It was then taken over

for development and turned into a residential neighborhood. In the 1950s the area became fashionable, and chic boutiques, antique shops, and art galleries took over the old neighborhood stores. Many of these are in restored 19th-century buildings, lending an old-fashioned air to the district, in stark contrast to the sophistication of the merchandise on display.

Union Street itself has more than 300 boutiques, and open-air arts, crafts, and food fairs are held regularly in the area.

View from Fillmore Street, overlooking Cow Hollow

Fort Mason ❼

Map 4 E1. 🛈 (415) 441-3400. **Events** 441-3400. 🚌 22, 28, 30, 42, 43. ♿ partial. **www**.fortmason.org

Fort Mason reflects the military history of San Francisco. The original buildings were private houses, built in the late 1850s, which were confiscated by the US Government when the site was taken over by the US army during the American Civil War (1861–65).

The Fort was an army command post until the 1890s. It later housed refugees whose homes had been destroyed in the 1906 earthquake *(see pp52–3)*. During World War II, it was the embarkation point for around 1.6 million soldiers.

The Fort was converted to peaceful use in 1972 although some of the white-painted mid-19th-century buildings still house military personnel. Other buildings, however, are open to the public. These include the original barracks, and the old hospital, which

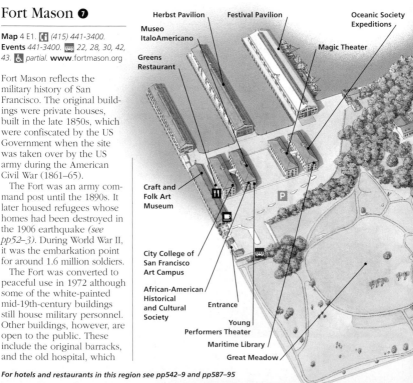

Herbst Pavilion

Museo ItaloAmericano

Greens Restaurant

Festival Pavilion

Oceanic Society Expeditions

Magic Theater

Craft and Folk Art Museum

City College of San Francisco Art Campus

African-American Historical and Cultural Society

Entrance

Young Performers Theater

Maritime Library

Great Meadow

Octagon House ⑩

2645 Gough St. **Map** 4 E2. **Tel** *(415) 441-7512.* 🚌 *41, 42, 45, 47, 49.* ◯ *noon–3pm on second Sun and second and fourth Thu of the month, except Jan.* **Donation.** 🚫 ♿ *limited.*

Built in 1861, the Octagon House, with its eight-sided cupola, is a well-preserved example of a house style that was once popular throughout the United States. The ground floor has now been opened up into one large room, and this and the first floor house a small but engaging collection of decorative arts as well as historic documents of the Colonial and Federal periods of the United States. Among the exhibits are furniture, paintings, porcelain, silver, pewter, samplers, playing cards from the American Revolution era, and signatures of 54 of the 56 signatories to the Declaration of Independence. The house now serves as the headquarters of the National Society of Colonial Dames of America.

Octagon House's cupola ensures sunlight in each room

Fillmore Street ⑪

Map 4 D4. 🚌 *1, 2, 3, 4, 22, 24.*

Fillmore Street managed to survive the 1906 earthquake and fire virtually intact, so for several years afterward it was forced to serve as the civic heart of the ruined city. Government departments, as well as several independent businesses, were housed in local shops, homes, and even churches. Today the main commercial district linking Pacific Heights and the Civic Center is located here, from Jackson Street to the outskirts of the Japan Center *(see p352)* around Bush Street. This area is filled with fine bookstores, fashionable restaurants, and exclusive boutiques.

International Youth Hostel

Fort Mason Officers' Club

Chapel

Visitors' Center

Golden Gate National Recreation Area headquarters

Meta III (1985) by Italo Scanga at Museo ItaloAmericano Chapel

serves both as a Visitors' Center and as the headquarters of the Golden Gate National Recreation Area (GGNRA). Besides being rich in history and culture, Fort Mason also offers some of the city's finest views, looking across the bay toward Golden Gate Bridge *(see pp380–81)* and Alcatraz Island *(see pp338–9)*. Starting from the west gate of the Fort, Golden Gate Promenade winds eastward to Aquatic Park and then to Fisherman's Wharf *(see pp334 – 5)*.

Fort Mason Center

Part of the Fort is now occupied by one of San Francisco's major art complexes. The Fort Mason Center houses about 50 cultural organizations, which include art galleries, museums, and theaters, such as the Cowell Dance Theater and the Bayfront Improv. Italian and Italian-

American artists display their works at the Museo Italo-Americano. The Magic Theater is an experimental theater, and the Young Performers Theater is a playhouse for children. The Maritime Library holds a wonderful collection of books, oral histories, and ships' plans. The Maritime Museum itself is located near Fishermans Wharf *(see p337)*.

The Fort Mason Center produces a monthly calendar of current events. Call the Events Line or visit their website for more information.

The SS *Balclutha*, at Hyde Street Pier, part of the Maritime Museum

The pagoda in the Japan Center's Peace Plaza

Japan Center 🔢

Post St & Buchanan St.
Map 4 E4. 🚌 *2, 3, 4, 22, 38.*
⏰ *10am–6pm daily.*

The Japan Center was built as part of an ambitious 1960s scheme to revitalize the Fillmore District. Many blocks of aging Victorian houses were demolished and replaced by the Geary Expressway and the large shopping complex of the Japan Center. The neighborhood has been the heart of the Japanese community for some 75 years.

At the heart of the complex, and centered upon a five-tiered, 75-ft (22-m) concrete pagoda, is the newly remodeled Peace Plaza. Taiko drummers and others perform here at the annual Cherry Blossom festival each April. Each side of the pagoda are malls lined with Japanese shops, sushi bars, bathhouses, and *Shiatsu* massage centers, all modeled on Tokyo's Ginza district. One of the city's best movie theaters, the eight-screen AMC Kabuki *(see pp390–91)*, is also found here. More Japanese shops line the open-air mall across Post Street, flanked by twin steel sculptures by Ruth Asawa.

St. Mary's Cathedral 🔢

1111 Gough St. **Map** 4 E4. **Tel** *(415) 567-2020.* 🚌 *38.* ⏰ *8:30am–4:30pm Mon–Fri, 9am–5:30pm Sat, 9am–6:30pm Sun.* 🔔 *6:45am, 8am, 10pm Mon–Sat, 7:30am, 9am, 11am, 1pm Sun.* 🚫 *during services.* ♿

Situated at the summit of Cathedral Hill, St. Mary's is one of San Francisco's most prominent architectural landmarks. Designed by Pietro Belluschi and Pier Luigi Nervi, it was completed in 1971.

The four-part arching paraboloid roof stands out like a white-sailed ship on the horizon. The 200-ft (60-m) high concrete structure, which seems to hover effortlessly above the nave, supports the cross-shaped stained-glass ceiling representing the four elements. A canopy of aluminium rods sparkles above the stone altar, from which the priest faces the congregation.

Asian Art Museum 🔢

Larkin at Grove St. **Map** 4 F5.
Tel *(415) 581-3500.* 🚌 *5, 8, 19, 21, 26, 47, 49.* 🚃 *F, J, K, L, M, N.*
⏰ *9am–5pm Tue–Sun (9pm Thu).*
🔵 *public hols.* 🆓 *free 1st Tue every month.*
♿ 📷 📱 💻
www.asianart.org

The Asian Art Museum is located in a building that was the crown jewel of the Beaux Arts movement. The former Main Library, built in 1917, underwent seismic strengthening and the original space has been reused to create the largest museum outside Asia devoted purely to Asian art. The new museum's exhibits include 12,000 art objects spanning 6,000 years of history and representing more than 40 Asian nations. In addition to increased gallery space, there are performance venues and a hands-on discovery center. The cafe overlooks the Civic Center and Fulton Street mall.

Bill Graham Civic Auditorium 🔢

99 Grove St. **Map** 4 F5. **Tel** *(415) 974-4060.* 🚌 *5, 8, 19, 21, 26, 47, 49.* 🚃 *J, K, L, M, N.*

Designed in Beaux-Arts style by architect John Galen Howard, the city's Civic Auditorium was opened in 1915 and has since become one of San Francisco's major performance venues. It was inaugurated by the French pianist and composer Camille Saint-Saëns. The building was completed along with City Hall, during the architectural renaissance that followed the great earthquake of 1906 *(see pp52–3)*. It was built, together with the adjoining Brooks Exhibit Hall, beneath the Civic Center Plaza.

The civic auditorium now serves as the city's main conference center, and seats 7,000 people. In 1964 its name was changed in honor of Bill Graham *(see p349)*, the local rock music impresario.

Grand staircase in the Asian Art Museum

The imposing façade of City Hall in San Francisco's Civic Center

City Hall ⑯

400 Van Ness Ave. **Map** 4 F5. **Tel**
(415) 554-4000. 5, 8, 19, 21, 26,
47, 49. J, K, L, M, N. 8am–
5pm Mon–Fri. phone (415)
554-6023. **www**.sfgov.org

City Hall, completed in 1915,
just in time for the Panama-
Pacific Exposition *(see p349)*,
was designed by the architect
Arthur Brown at the height of
his career. Its grand Baroque
dome was modeled after St.
Peter's in Rome and is higher
than that of the US Capitol in
Washington, DC.

The newly renovated building stands at the heart of the
Civic Center complex, and is a
magnificent example of the
Beaux-Arts style. Allegorical
figures evoking the city's
Gold Rush past fill the pediment above the Polk Street
entrance, which leads into the
rotunda, one of the city's
finest interior spaces.

Hayes Valley ⑰

Map 4 E5. 21, 22.

Situated west of City Hall,
these few blocks of Hayes
Street have become one of
San Francisco's trendier shopping districts. After US 101
highway was damaged in the
1989 Loma Prieta earthquake
(see p505) the road was
demolished. The former

highway had previously divided Hayes Valley from the
wealthy power-brokers and
theatergoers who frequented
the rest of the Civic Center. A
small number of adventurous
cafés and restaurants, such as
Ivy's and Mad Magda's Russian
Tea Room, had already established themselves alongside
Hayes Street's second-hand
furniture and reject shops.
Today a new influx of art galleries, interior design shops,
trendy cafés, and exclusive
boutiques has made the area
noticeably more stylish.

View from Alamo Square toward
the Downtown skyscrapers

Alamo Square ⑱

Map 4 D5. 21, 22.

The most photographed row
of Victorian houses in the city
lines the eastern side of this
sloping green square. It is set

225 ft (68 m) above the Civic
Center, offering great views
of City Hall and the
Downtown skyscrapers. The
square was laid out at the
same time as the beautiful
squares in Pacific Heights, but
it developed later, with speculators building nearly
identical houses.

The "Six Sisters" Queen
Anne-style houses built in
1895 at 710–20 Steiner Street
on the east side of the square
appear on numerous post-
cards of San Francisco. The
city has now declared the
area to be a historic district.

University of San Francisco ⑲

2130 Fulton St. **Map** 3 B5 **Tel** (415)
422-5555. 5, 31, 33, 38, 43.
8am–5pm Mon–Fri. **www**.usfca.edu

Originally founded in 1855
as St. Ignatius College, the
University of San Francisco
(USF) remains a Jesuit-run
institution, though classes are
now coeducational and non-
denominational. The land-
mark of the campus is the St.
Ignatius Church, completed in
1914. Its buff-colored twin
towers are visible from the
western half of San Francisco,
especially when lit up at night.
The campus and the surrounding residential area occupy
land that was once San Francisco's main cemetery district,
on and around Lone Mountain.

HAIGHT ASHBURY AND THE MISSION

To the north of Twin Peaks – two windswept hills rising 900 ft (274 m) above the city – lies Haight Ashbury. With its rows of Victorian houses *(see pp300–1)*, it is mostly inhabited by the wealthy middle classes, although this is where thousands of hippies lived in the late 1960s *(see p359)*. The Castro

Figure from Mission Dolores

District, to the east, is the center of the city's gay community. Well known for its hedonism in the 1970s, the area has become far quieter in recent years, although its cafés and shops are still lively. The Mission District, even farther east, was first founded by Spanish monks *(see pp46–7)* and is home to many Latin Americans.

SIGHTS AT A GLANCE

Historic Streets and Buildings
Castro Street **8**
Clarke's Folly **15**
Dolores Street **10**
Haight Ashbury **2**
Lower Haight Neighborhood **5**
Noe Valley **14**
(Richard) Spreckels Mansion **3**

Churches
Mission Dolores **9**

Landmarks
Sutro Tower **18**

Parks and Gardens
Buena Vista Park **4**
Corona Heights Park **6**
Dolores Park **11**
Golden Gate Park Panhandle **1**
Twin Peaks **16**
Vulcan Street Steps **17**

Museums and Galleries
Carnaval Mural **13**
Mission Cultural Center for the Latino Arts **12**

Theaters
Castro Theater **7**

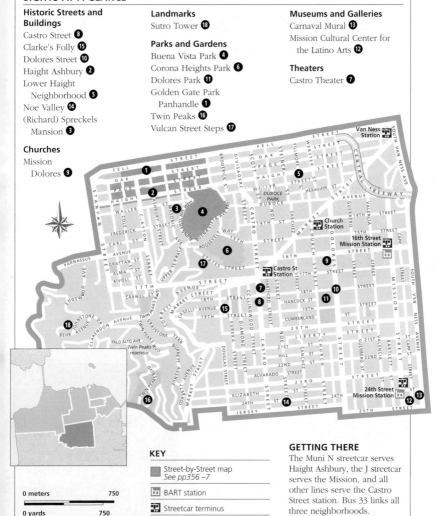

KEY
Street-by-Street map *See pp356–7*
BART station
Streetcar terminus

0 meters 750
0 yards 750

GETTING THERE
The Muni N streetcar serves Haight Ashbury, the J streetcar serves the Mission, and all other lines serve the Castro Street station. Bus 33 links all three neighborhoods.

◁ Street scene in Haight Ashbury

Street-by-Street: Haight Ashbury

Stretching from Buena Vista Park to
the flat expanses of Golden Gate Park,
Haight Ashbury was a place to escape to
from the city center in the 1880s. It then
developed into a residential area, but
between 1930 and 1960 it changed
dramatically from a middle-class suburb
to the center of the "Flower Power" world,
with a free clinic to treat hippies without
medical insurance. It has now settled
into being one of the liveliest and most
unconventional places in San Francisco,
with an eclectic mix of people, excellent
book and music shops, and good cafés.

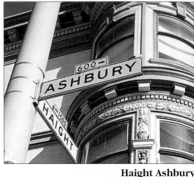

Haight Ashbury
*In the 1960s, hippies met at this crossroads,
which gives the area its name* ❷

Golden Gate Panhandle
*This thin green strip runs west
into the heart of Golden
Gate Park* ❶

Cha Cha Cha is one of the
liveliest places to eat in
San Francisco, serving
Latin American food in a
series of small dishes
(see p594).

To bus nos. 7, 33

STAR SIGHTS

★ Buena Vista Park

★ (Richard) Spreckels
    Mansion

**The Red Victorian Bed
& Breakfast**, a relic of
the 1960s hippie era,
caters to a New Age
clientele, with health
food and rooms with
transcendental themes
(see p548).

No. 1220 Masonic Avenue is one of many ornate Victorian mansions built on the steep hill that runs down from Golden Gate Park Panhandle to Haight Street.

LOCATOR MAP
See Street Finder, map 10

KEY

--- Suggested route

★ **(Richard) Spreckels Mansion**
This grand home at No.737 Buena Vista Avenue was built in 1897 ❸

★ **Buena Vista Park**
Through its mass of twisting, matted trees, this dramatic park offers magnificent views over the city ❹

| 0 meters | 100 |
| 0 yards | 100 |

To bus no. 37

Golden Gate Park Panhandle ❶

Map 9 C1. 🚌 6, 7, 21, 43, 66, 71.

This one-block-wide and eight-block-long stretch of parkland forms the narrow "Panhandle" to the giant rectangular pan that is Golden Gate Park *(see pp366–9)*. It was the first part of the park to be reclaimed from the sand dunes that rolled across west San Francisco, and its eucalyptus trees are among the oldest and largest in the city.

The Panhandle's winding carriage roads and bridle paths were first laid out in the 1870s, and the upper classes came here to walk and ride. They built large mansions on the outskirts of the park, many of which can still be seen today. In 1906 the Panhandle was used as a refuge for families made homeless by the earthquake *(see pp52–3)*. Today the old roads and paths are frequented regularly by large crowds of joggers and cyclists.

The Panhandle is still remembered for its "Flower Power" heyday of the 1960s. The era's young hippies flocked to the park to listen to impromptu free concerts held here by the new psychedelic bands from Haight Ashbury. The area is still a popular spot for the city's street musicians and hippie guitarists.

Haight Ashbury ❷

Map 9 C1. 🚌 6, 7, 33, 37, 43, 66, 71. 🚃 N.

Taking its name from the junction of two major streets, Haight and Ashbury, this district contains alternative bookshops, large Victorian houses, and numerous cafés. Following the reclamation of Golden Gate Park *(see pp366–9)* and then the opening of a large amusement park called The Chutes, the area was rapidly built up in the 1890s as a middle-class suburb – hence the dozens of elaborate Queen Anne-style houses *(see pp300–1)* lining its streets. The Haight district survived the 1906 earthquake and fire *(see pp52–3)*, and then experienced a brief boom, which was followed by a long period of decline.

After the tram tunnel underneath Buena Vista Park was completed in 1928, the middle classes began their exodus to the suburbs in the Sunset. The area reached its lowest ebb in the years after World War II. The big Victorian houses were divided into apartments and low rents attracted a disparate population. By the 1960s the Haight had become host to a bohemian community that was a hotbed of anarchy. A component of this "hippie scene" was the music of rock bands such as the Grateful Dead, but the area stayed fairly quiet until 1967. Then the "Summer of Love," fueled by the media, brought some 75,000 young people in search of free love, music, and drugs, and the area became the focus of a worldwide youth culture.

Haight retains its radical atmosphere, but now there are problems with crime, drugs, and homelessness. However, from the cafés to the second-hand clothing shops, there is still an "only in San Francisco" experience to be found here.

Junction of Haight and Ashbury streets

Late-Victorian mansion built for Richard Spreckels

(Richard) Spreckels Mansion ❸

737 Buena Vista West. **Map** 9 C2. 🚌 6, 7, 37, 43, 66, 71. ⬤ to the public.

This house should not be confused with the grander Spreckels Mansion situated on Washington Street *(see p348)*. It was, however, also built by the millionaire "Sugar King" Claus Spreckels, for his nephew Richard. The elaborate Queen Anne-style house *(see pp300–1)*, built in 1897, is a typical late-Victorian Haight Ashbury home. It was once a guesthouse, whose guests included the acerbic journalist and ghost-story writer Ambrose Bierce, and the adventure writer Jack London, who wrote *White Fang* here in 1906 *(see p26)*. The house is now in private hands.

Buena Vista Park ❹

Map 9 C1. 🚌 6, 7, 37, 43, 66, 71.

Buena Vista Park rises steeply 570 ft (174 m) above the geographical center of San Francisco with views over the Bay Area. First landscaped in 1894, it is a pocket of land left to nature. Numerous overgrown and eroded paths wind up from Haight Street to the crest, but there is a paved route from Buena Vista Avenue. It is best to avoid the park at night.

Lower Haight Neighborhood ❺

Map 10 D1. 🚌 6, 7, 22, 66, 71. 🚃 K, L, M.

Halfway between City Hall and Haight Ashbury, and marking the southern border of the predominantly African-American Fillmore District, the Lower Haight is an area in transition. Unusual art galleries and boutiques, including the Used Rubber USA shop, which sells clothes and accessories made entirely of recycled rubber, began to open here in the mid-1980s. These were in addition to the inexpensive cafés, bars, and restaurants serving a bohemian clientele already in business in the area. This combination has created one of the most lively districts in San Francisco.

As in nearby Alamo Square *(see p353)*, the Lower Haight has dozens of houses known as "Victorians" *(see pp300–1)* built from the 1850s to the early 1900s, including pictur-esque cottages such as the Nightingale House at No. 201 Buchanan Street, built in the 1880s. The 1950s public housing blocks have discour-aged wholesale gentrification. The area is safe during the day but, like Alamo Square, it can seem threatening after dark.

Sign from Cha Cha Cha restaurant on Haight Street *(see p564)*

Corona Heights Park ❻

Map 9 D2. **Tel** *(415) 554-9600.*
🚌 24, 37. Randall Museum Animal Room ⬭ 10am–5pm, Tue–Sat. ⬤ public hols. ♿ limited.
www.randallmuseum.org

Corona Heights Park is a dusty and undeveloped rocky peak. Clinging to its side is an unusual museum for kids.

View from Corona Heights across the Mission

The Randall Museum at No. 199 Museum Way has an extensive menagerie of raccoons, owls, snakes, and other animals, many of which the children can handle and stroke. The emphasis of the museum is on participation, with many hands-on exhibits and workshops. Children also enjoy climbing on the craggy outcrops in the park. Corona Heights was gouged out by brick-making operations in the 19th century. It was never planted with trees, so its red rock peak has great views over the city. There is a good view of the winding streets of Twin Peaks *(see p363)*.

THE SOUNDS OF 1960S SAN FRANCISCO

During the late 1960s, and most notably during the 1967 "Summer of Love," young people from all over the country flocked to the Haight Ashbury district. They came not just to "turn on, tune in, and drop out," but also to listen to bands such as Janis Joplin's Big Brother and the Holding Company, Jefferson Airplane, and the Grateful Dead, all of whom emerged out of a thriving music scene. They estab-lished themselves at the city's new music venues.

Premier music venues
The Avalon Ballroom, now the Regency II theater on Van Ness Avenue, was the first and most significant venue. Run by Chet Helms and the Family Dog collec-tive, the Avalon pioneered the use of colorful psyche-delic posters by designers such as Stanley Mouse and Alton Kelly *(see pp440–41)*.
Fillmore Auditorium, facing the Japan Center *(see p352)* and a former church hall, was taken over by impresario Bill Graham in 1965, after whom the Civic Auditorium *(see p352)* is named. He put unlikely pairs such as Miles Davis and the Grateful Dead on the same bill, and brought in big-name per-formers from Jimi Hendrix to The Who. The Fillmore Auditorium was damaged in the 1989 earthquake but has recently reopened.
By the time Bill Graham died in 1992 he had become the most successful rock music promoter in the US.

Janis Joplin (1943–70), hard-edged blues singer

Castro Theater ●

429 Castro St. **Map** 10 D2. *Tel 621-6120.* 🚌 *8, 24, 33, 35, 37.* 🚈 *F, K, L, M. See* **Entertainment** *pp390–91.*

Completed in 1922, this brightly lit neon marquee is a Castro Street landmark. It is the most sumptuous and best preserved of San Francisco's neighborhood film palaces, and one of the first commissions of the architect Timothy Pflueger. With its Arabian Nights interior, complete with a glorious Wurlitzer organ that rises from the floor between the screenings, it is well worth the price of admission. The ceiling of the auditorium is cast in plaster and resembles the interior of a large tent, with imitation swathes of fabric, rope, and tassels. The theater seats 1,500 and shows mainly revival classics. It also hosts the Gay and Lesbian Film Festival, held each June.

Historic and ornate Castro Theater

Castro Street ●

Map 10 D2. 🚌 *8, 24, 33, 35, 37.* 🚈 *F, K, L, M.*

The hilly neighborhood around Castro Street between Twin Peaks and the Mission District is the heart of San Francisco's high-profile gay and lesbian community. Focused on the intersection of Castro Street and 18th Street, the self-proclaimed "Gayest Four Corners of the World" emerged as a homosexual nexus during the 1970s. Gays of the Flower Power generation moved into this predominantly working-class district and began restoring Victorian houses and setting up businesses such as the bookshop, A Different Light, at No. 489 Castro Street. They also opened gay bars such as the Twin Peaks on the corner of Castro Street and 17th Street. Unlike earlier bars, where lesbians and gays hid in dark corners out of public view, the Twin Peaks installed large windows. Though the many shops and restaurants attract all kinds of people, the area's openly homosexual identity has made it a place of pilgrimage for gays and lesbians. It symbolizes for this minority group a freedom not often found in cities elsewhere.

The city's first openly gay politician, Harvey Milk, was known as the Mayor of Castro Street before his assassination on November 28, 1978. He and Mayor George Moscone were killed by an ex-policeman, whose lenient sentence caused rioting in the city. Milk is remembered with a plaque outside the Muni stop on Market Street and a candlelit procession from Castro Street to City Hall every year.

Over a quarter of a million people come to the area for the Castro Street Fair, which is held each October. Arts, crafts, beer, food, and music are all provided, and proceeds go towards helping the local community.

AIDS Memorial Quilt on display in Washington, DC in 1992

THE NAMES PROJECT

The NAMES Project's AIDS Memorial Quilt was conceived by San Francisco gay rights activist Cleve Jones, who organized the first candlelit procession on Castro Street for Harvey Milk in 1985. Jones and his fellow marchers wrote the names of all their friends who had died of AIDS on placards, which they then taped to the San Francisco Federal Building. The resulting "patchwork quilt" of names inspired Jones to create the first panel for the AIDS Memorial Quilt in 1987. Public response to the quilt was immediate – both in the US and across the world. It is now made up of over 60,000 panels, some sewn by individuals and others by "quilting bees" – friends and relatives who have come together to commemorate a person lost to AIDS. All panels are the same size – 3 by 6 ft (90 by 180 cm) – but each is different: the design, colors, and material reflect the life and personality of the person commemorated. In 2002 the Memorial Quilt moved from its base in San Francisco to permanent headquarters in Atlanta, Georgia.

Mission Dolores 🟒

16th St and Dolores St. **Map** 10 E3.
🎫 621-8203. 🚌 22. 🚃 J.
🕙 8:30am–noon,
1–5pm daily. 🌑
Thanksgiving, Dec
25. 📷 🎥 🅿 ♿ 🛈
www.mission
dolores.org

Preserved intact since
it was built in 1791,
Mission Dolores is the
oldest building in the
city and an embodiment
of San Francisco's
religious Spanish colonial
roots (see pp46–7). The
mission was founded by
Father Junípero Serra and
is formally known as the
Mission of San Francisco

**Figure of saint in
the mission**

de Asis. The name Dolores
reflects its proximity to *Laguna
de los Dolores* (Lake of Our
Lady of Sorrows), an ancient
insect-plagued swamp.
The building is modest
by mission standards,
but its 4-ft (1.2-m) thick
walls have survived
the years without
serious decay and
Native American
paintings adorn
the ceiling.
There is a fine
Baroque altar and
reredos, and a
display of histor-
ical documents in
the small museum.
Most services are
now held in the
basilica, built next

to the mission in 1918. The
cemetery contains graves of
San Franciscan pioneers. A
statue marking the mass grave
of 5,000 Native Americans,
most of whom died in measles
epidemics in 1804 and 1826,
was later stolen. All that now
remains is a pedestal, reading
"In Prayerful Memory of our
Faithful Indians."

**The painted and gilded
altarpiece** *was imported from
Mexico in 1780.*

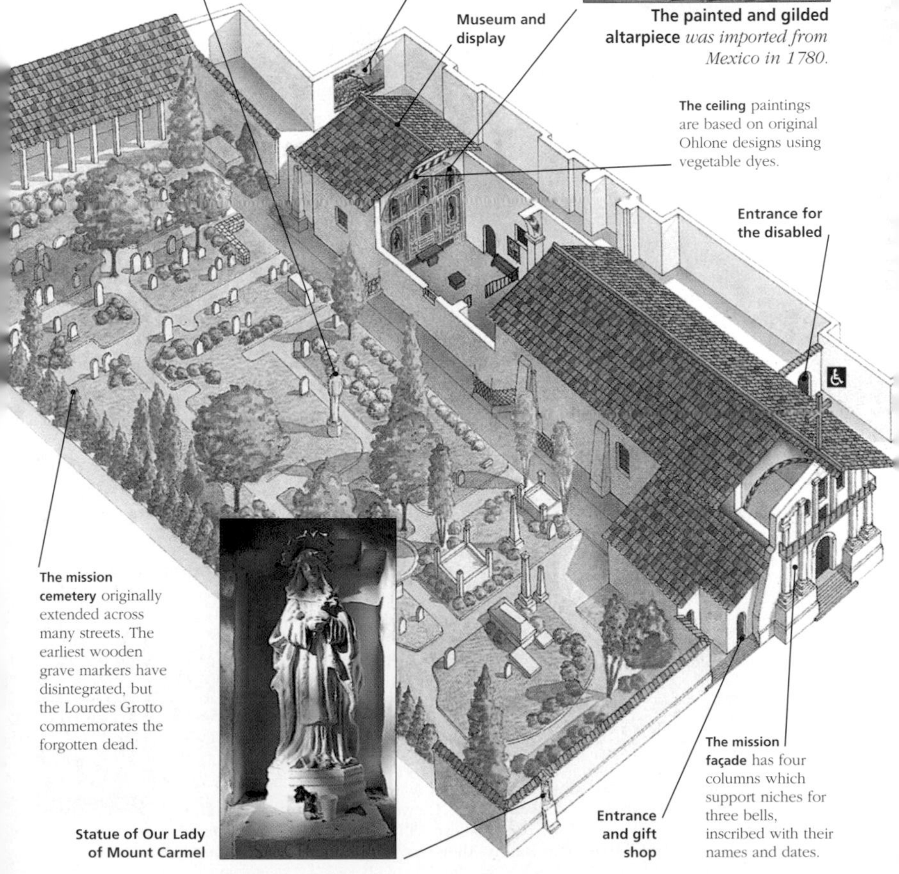

The statue of Father Junípero Serra is a copy of the work of local sculptor Arthur Putnam.

The ceramic mural was created by Guillermo Granizo, a native San Francisco artist.

Museum and display

The ceiling paintings are based on original Ohlone designs using vegetable dyes.

Entrance for the disabled

The mission cemetery originally extended across many streets. The earliest wooden grave markers have disintegrated, but the Lourdes Grotto commemorates the forgotten dead.

Statue of Our Lady of Mount Carmel

Entrance and gift shop

The mission façade has four columns which support niches for three bells, inscribed with their names and dates.

Spanish–American War memorial on Dolores Street

Dolores Street ⑩

Map 10 E2. 🚌 *8, 22, 33, 48.* 🚃 *J.*

Lined by lovingly maintained late-Victorian houses (see pp300–1) and an island of palm trees, this street is one of the city's most attractive public spaces. The broad street runs parallel to Mission Street, forming the western border of the Mission District. It starts at Market Street, where a statue honoring soldiers of the Spanish–American War is overwhelmed by the US Mint.

Mission High School, with the white walls and red tile roof typical of Mission-style architecture (see p30), and Mission Dolores (see p361) are both situated on Dolores Street. The street ends in the Noe Valley district.

Dolores Park ⑪

Map 10 E3. 🚌 *22, 33.* 🚃 *J.*

Originally the site of San Francisco's main Jewish cemetery, Dolores Park was transformed in 1905 into one of the Mission District's few large open spaces. Ringed by Dolores, Church, 18th, and 20th streets, it is situated high on a hill with an excellent view of the city center.

Dolores Park is very popular during the day with tennis players, sunbathers, and dog walkers, but after dark it is a haven for drug dealers. Above the park to the south and west, the streets rise so steeply that

many turn into pedestrian-only stairways. Some of the city's finest Victorian houses can also be seen here.

Mission Cultural Center for the Latino Arts ⑫

2868 Mission St. **Map** 10 F4. *Tel* (415) 821-1155. 🚌 *14, 26, 48, 49.* 🚃 *J. Gallery* ○ *10am–5pm Tue–Fri, 10am–6pm Sat.* ♿
www.missionculturalcenter.org

This dynamic arts center is partly funded by the city, and caters to the local, mainly Latino population. There are classes, workshops, theatrical events and exhibitions, as well as a festival to celebrate the Day of the Dead (see p38).

Detail from the *Carnaval Mural*

Carnaval Mural ⑬

24th St and South Van Ness Ave. **Map** 10 F4. 🚌 *12, 14, 48, 49, 67.* 🚃 *J.*

One of the many brightly painted murals on the walls of the Mission District, the *Carnaval Mural* celebrates the diverse people who come together for the Carnaval festival (see p36). This annual spring event is the highlight of the year.

Guided tours of the other murals, some with political themes, are given by civic organizations. There is also an outdoor gallery with murals in Balmy Alley (see pp306–7).

Noe Valley ⑭

🚌 *24, 35, 48.* 🚃 *J.*

Noe Valley is often referred to as "Noewhere Valley" by its residents, who remain determined to keep it off the tourist map. It is a pleasant, comfortable neighborhood, largely inhabited by young professionals. Its spotless streets and safe atmosphere seem at odds with the surrounding, densely populated Mission District.

The area was named after its original land-grant owner, José Noe, the last *alcalde* (mayor) of Yerba Buena, the Mexican village that eventually grew into San Francisco. The valley was first built up during the 1880s after a cable car line over the steep Castro Street hill was completed. The low rents attracted mostly working-class Irish families. Then, like so many other areas of San Francisco, this once blue-collar district underwent gentrification in the 1970s, raising the value of the properties and resulting in today's engaging mix of boutiques, bars, and restaurants. The Noe Valley Ministry, found at No. 1021 Sanchez Street, is a late 1880s Presbyterian church in the "Stick Style" (see pp300–1), the most prevalent architectural style in the city, with its emphasis on vertical lines. The ministry was converted into a community center in the 1970s.

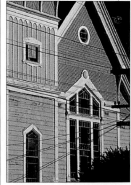

Victorian façade of the Noe Valley Ministry on Sanchez Street

Nobby Clarke's Folly

Clarke's Folly **⑮**

250 Douglas St. **Map** 10 D3. 🚌 *8, 33, 35, 37, 48.* ⬤ *to the public.*

This resplendent white manor house was at one time set in its own extensive grounds. It was built in 1892 by Alfred Clarke, known locally as Nobby. Clarke had worked for the San Francisco Police Department at the time of the Committee of Vigilance in 1851, when a group of local citizens attempted to control the city's growing lawlessness *(see pp48–9)*. The house is said to have cost $100,000 to build, a huge sum in the 1890s.

Although it is now surrounded by other buildings, the house is a fine example of Victorian domestic architecture. The turrets and the gabled roof are typical of the Queen Anne style, while the shingled walls and front porch adopt the elements of Eastlake architecture *(see pp300–1)*.

Today the house is divided into private apartments.

Twin Peaks **⑯**

Map 9 C4. 🚌 *33, 36, 37.*

These two hills were first known in Spanish as *El Pecho de la Chola,* the "Bosom of the Indian Girl." They lie at the heart of San Francisco, and reach a height of 900 ft (274 m) above sea level. At the top there is an area of parkland with steep, grassy slopes, from which incomparable views of the whole of San Francisco can be enjoyed.

Twin Peaks Boulevard circles both hills near their summits; there is a parking lot and viewing point that overlooks the city. Those who are prepared to climb up the steep path to the very top on foot can leave the crowds behind and get a breathtaking 360-degree view.

Twin Peaks are the only hills in the city left in their original state. The residential districts on the lower slopes have curving streets that wind around the contours of the hills, rather than the grid system that is more common in the rest of San Francisco.

Vulcan Street Steps **⑰**

Vulcan St. **Map** 9 C2. 🚌 *37.*

Apart from a tiny figure of Spock standing on a mailbox, there is no connection between the cult television program *Star Trek* and this block of houses climbing between Ord and Levant Streets. However, the Vulcan Steps do feel light years away from the busy Castro District below. The small, picturesque gardens of the houses spill out and soften the edges of the steps, and a canopy of pines muffles the city sounds. There are great views of the Mission District and the southern waterfront.

Sutro Tower **⑱**

Map 9 B3. 🚌 *36, 37.* ⬤ *to the public.*

Marking the skyline like an invading robot, Sutro Tower is 970 ft (295 m) high. It was named after the local philanthropist and landowner Adolph Sutro, and it carries antennae for the signals of most of San Francisco's TV and radio stations. Built in 1973, it is still much used, despite the rise of cable networks. The tower is visible from all over the Bay Area, and sometimes seems to float above the summer fogs that roll in from the sea. On the north side of the tower there are dense eucalyptus groves, first planted in the 1880s by Adolph Sutro.

View of the city and of Twin Peaks Boulevard from the top of Twin Peaks

GOLDEN GATE PARK AND THE PRESIDIO

T he spectacular Golden Gate Park is one of the world's largest urban parks, created in the 1890s out of sandy wasteland. It houses three museums and a range of sports facilities. Land's End, the city's wildest region and scene of many shipwrecks, is accessible from the park.

Cannon from the Presidio

To the north of Golden Gate Park, the Presidio, overlooking San Francisco Bay, was established as an outpost of Spain's New World empire in 1776, and for many years was a military base. In 1993 it became a National Park, and visitors can now stroll through its acres of woodland full of wildlife.

SIGHTS AT A GLANCE

Historic Streets and Buildings
Clement Street **12**
Golden Gate Bridge pp380–81 **17**
Presidio Officers' Club **14**

Parks and Gardens
Buffalo Paddock **8**
Conservatory of Flowers **5**
Japanese Tea Garden **3**
Queen Wilhelmina Tulip Garden **9**
Shakespeare Garden **2**
Stow Lake **7**
Strybing Arboretum **6**

Museums and Galleries
California Academy of Sciences (closed until 2008, see p320 for temporary location) **1**
de Young Museum **4**
Fort Point **16**
Legion of Honor pp374–5 **10**
Presidio Visitor Center **15**

0 kilometers   1

0 miles   0.5

Churches and Temples
Holy Virgin Cathedral **11**
Temple Emanu-El **13**

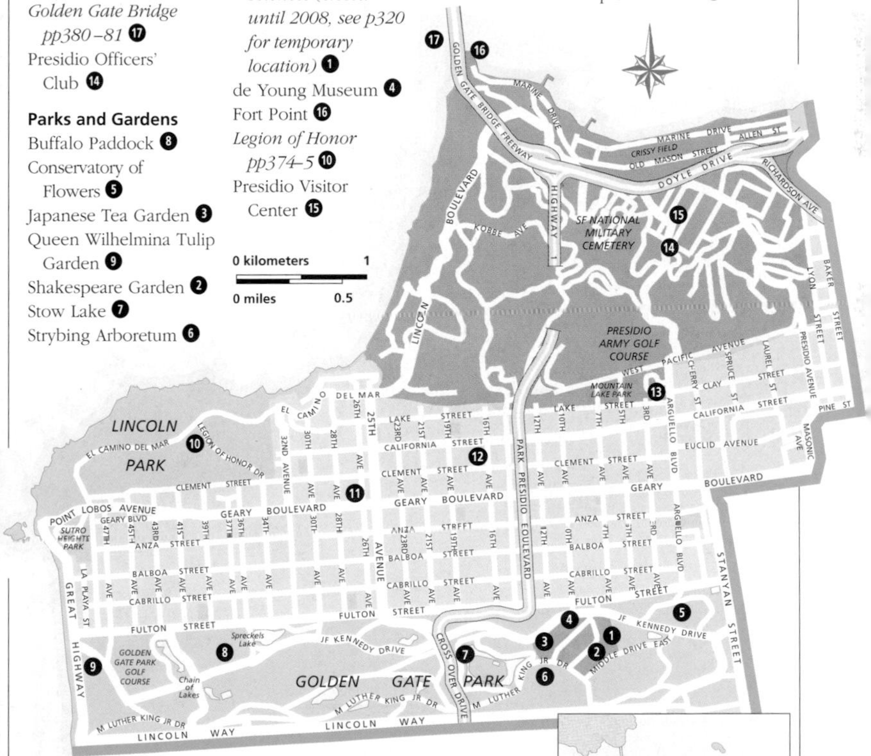

GETTING THERE

For Golden Gate Park, take buses 5, 7, 21, 71, or 73, or the N streetcar. The Presidio is best seen by car, but Muni bus 29 stops at the main sights, bus 43 serves the eastern end, and bus 28 the northern boundary.

KEY

Street-by-Street map
See pp366–7

The Presidio
See pp376–7

◁ **Golden Gate Bridge from Fort Point**

Street-by-Street: Golden Gate Park

Golden Gate Park is 3 miles (5 km) long and almost 1 mile (1.6 km) across. It stretches from the Pacific Ocean to the center of San Francisco, forming an oasis of greenery and calm in which to escape from the bustle of city life. Within the park an amazing number of activities are catered to, both sporting and cultural. The landscaped area around the Music Concourse, with its fountains,

Lamp in the Japanese Tea Garden

plane trees, and benches, is the most popular and developed section.

Here you can enjoy free Sunday concerts at the Spreckels Temple of Music. A total of three museums stand on either side of the Concourse, and the Japanese and Shakespeare gardens are within walking distance.

★ de Young Museum
Recently reopened after extensive renovations, this museum showcases collections from around the world. Exhibits include this mahogany chest, made in Philadelphia in 1780. ❹

The Great Buddha reaches almost 11 ft (3 m) in height.

HAGIWARA TE

★ Japanese Tea Garden
This exquisite garden, with its well-tended plants and pretty lake, is one of the most attractive parts of the park ❸

MARTIN LUTHER KING DRIV

KEY

— — — Suggested route

0 meters   80
0 yards   80

STAR SIGHTS

★ de Young Museum

★ Japanese Tea Garden

Shakespeare Garden
This tiny garden holds more than 150 species of plants, all mentioned in Shakespeare's poetry or plays ❷

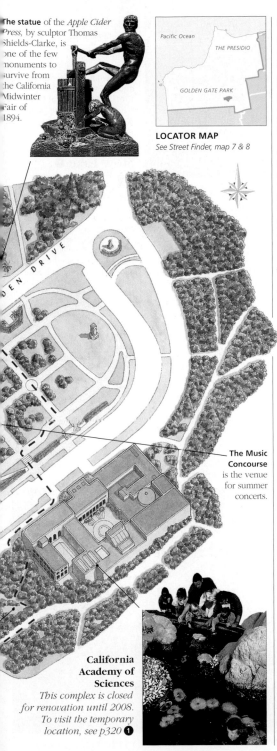

The statue of the *Apple Cider Press*, by sculptor Thomas Shields-Clarke, is one of the few monuments to survive from the California Midwinter Fair of 1894.

LOCATOR MAP
See Street Finder, map 7 & 8

The Music Concourse is the venue for summer concerts.

California Academy of Sciences
This complex is closed for renovation until 2008. To visit the temporary location, see p320 ❶

California Academy of Sciences ❶

See p320 & pp370–71.

Shakespeare Garden ❷

Music Concourse, Golden Gate Park. **Map** 8 F2. 🚌 *44.*

Gardeners here have tried to cultivate all the plants mentioned in Shakespeare's works. Relevant quotations are inscribed on plaques set in the wall at the back of the garden. A 19th-century bust of the playwright is kept in a box opened only occasionally.

Japanese Tea Garden ❸

Music Concourse, Golden Gate Park. **Map** 8 F2. 🚌 *44.* ☐ *Mar–Oct: 8:30am–6pm daily; Nov–Feb 8:30am–5pm daily.* 🖼 🔲 🔳

Established by the art-dealer George Turner Marsh for the 1894 California Midwinter Fair, this garden is very popular. A Japanese gardener, Makota Hagiwara, was later contracted to tend it. He and his family maintained and expanded the garden until 1942, when they were interned during World War II. The best time to visit is when the cherry trees blossom in April.

de Young Museum ❹

50 Tea Garden Drive, Golden Gate Park. **Map** 8 F2. *Tel 863-3330.* ☐ *9:30am–5:15pm daily (to 8:45pm Fri).* 🖼 *(free first Tue of month)* 🚻 **www**.thinker.org

Founded in 1895 the de Young Museum houses one of the city's finest art collections. In 1989 the building was too damaged by an earthquake to be saved. However, an exciting new state-of-the-art facility opened in 2005. The museum contains a broad range of American art, as well as extensive pre-Columbian-American, African, and Oceanic works.

Conservatory of Flowers ❺

John F Kennedy Drive, Golden Gate Park. **Map** 9 A1. *Tel (415) 666-7001.* 🚌 *33, 44.* ⏲ *9am–4:30pm Tue–Sun.* 🎫 *(free 1st Tue of the month.)* 🅿 📷 ♿ *limited.* 🏛

This ornate greenhouse, inspired by the one in London's Kew Gardens, is the oldest building in the park. A property developer, James Lick, imported the frame from Ireland, but he died before its erection in 1879. A jungle of ferns, palms, and orchids thrived here for over a century, but a hurricane hit the city in 1995 and largely destroyed the conservatory. San Franciscans campaigned for its repair and it reopened in 2003.

Strybing Arboretum ❻

9th Ave at Lincoln Way, Golden Gate Park. **Map** 8 F2. *Tel 661 1316.* 🚌 *44, 71.* ⏲ *8am–4:30pm Mon– Fri, 10am–5pm weekends and public hols.* 📷 ♿ 🅿 🏛 **www.**strybing.org

On display in the Strybing Arboretum are 7,500 species of plants, trees, and shrubs from around the world. There are Mexican, African, South American, and Australian

Garden of Fragrance in the Strybing Arboretum

gardens, and one that is devoted entirely to native California plants. Well worth a visit is the enchanting Moon-Viewing Garden. It exhibits Far Eastern plants in a setting that, unlike that of the Japanese Tea Garden *(see p367),* is naturalistic rather than formal. Both medicinal and culinary plants are grown in the Garden of Fragrance, which is designed for blind plant-lovers. Here the emphasis is on the senses of taste, touch, and smell, and all the plants are identified in Braille.

Another area, with a stream winding through it, is planted with indigenous California redwood trees. This re-creates the flora and the atmosphere of a northern Californian coastal forest. There is also a New World Cloud Forest,

with flora from the mountains of Central America. Surprisingly, all these gardens thrive in the Californian fogs.

The Arboretum has a small shop selling seeds and books, and it also houses the Helen Crocker Horticultural Library, which is open to the public. A colorful flower show is held in the summer.

Stow Lake ❼

Stow Lake Drive, Golden Gate Park. **Map** 8 E2. 🚌 *28, 29.* 📷 🚤

In 1895, the President of the Park Commission, WW Stow, ordered the construction of this artificial lake, the largest in the park. It was created encircling Strawberry Hill (named after the wild fruit that once grew here), so that the summit of the hill now forms an island in the lake. It is linked to the mainland by two stone-clad bridges. Stow Lake's circular stream makes an ideal course for rowing laps from the boathouse, although the tranquil atmosphere makes leisurely drifting seem more appropriate. A Chinese pavilion on the island's shore was a gift to San Francisco from its sister city in Taiwan, Taipei. The red and green pavilion arrived in San Francisco by ship in 6,000 pieces and then was reassembled on the island.

Chinese moon-watching pavilion on Stow Lake

The millionaire railway baron Collis Porter Huntington (*see pp50–51*) donated the money in 1894 to create the reservoir and the waterfall that cascades into Stow Lake. These are known as Huntington Falls. Damaged in the 1906 earthquake (*see pp52–3*), it was restored in the 1980s and is now one of the park's most attractive features.

Buffalo Paddock ❽

John F Kennedy Drive, Golden Gate Park. **Map** 7 C2. 🚌 *5, 29.*

The shaggy buffalo grazing in this specially designed paddock are the largest of all North American land animals. Immediately recognizable by their short horns and humped backs, buffaloes are the symbol of the American plains, and are more properly known as the American bison.

This paddock was opened in 1892, with the aim of protecting the species, then on the verge of extinction. The first herd, however, brought in from Wyoming, all died of a tuberculosis epidemic and had to be replaced. In 1902 William Cody, the American scout and showman "Buffalo Bill," traded one of his bulls for one from the Golden Gate Park herd. Both parties thought that they had rid themselves of an aggressive beast, but Cody's newly purchased bull jumped a high fence once it was back at his encampment and escaped. According to one newspaper, the *San Francisco Call*, it took 80 men to recapture it.

Queen Wilhelmina Tulip Garden and the Dutch Windmill

Queen Wilhelmina Tulip Garden ❾

Map 7 A2. 🚌 *5, 18.* **Windmill** ♿

This garden was named after the Dutch Queen Wilhelmina, and hundreds of tulip bulbs are donated each year by the Dutch Bulb Growers' Association. In the spring months, the area is carpeted with the flowers in full bloom. The Dutch Windmill, near the northwest corner of Golden Gate Park, was built in 1903. Its purpose, along with its companion, the Murphy Windmill, erected in the park's southwest corner in 1905, was to pump water from a source underground, in order to irrigate the park. The increasing volume of water required – about 5 million gallons, or 230 million liters per day – soon made the windmills obsolete, and they are no longer in use.

JOHN MCLAREN

Although Golden Gate Park was designed by William Hammond Hall, the park's current status owes the most to his successor, John McLaren.

McLaren was born in Scotland in 1846 and studied botany before emigrating to California in the 1870s. He succeeded Hall as administrator in 1887 and devoted the rest of his life to the park.

An expert landscape gardener and botanist, McLaren succeeded in importing exotic plants from all over the world and making them thrive, despite the poor soil and foggy climate. He planted thousands of trees and chose the right shrubs to make sure the park was in full bloom all year long.

John McLaren Lodge, a sandstone villa situated on the park's east side, was built in 1896 as a home for McLaren and his family. As McLaren lay dying in 1943, he requested that the cypress tree outside the lodge be lit with Christmas lights, and his request was granted, despite a wartime blackout being in force. The tree is still referred to as "Uncle John's Christmas Tree" and is lit every December in his honor. He is buried in a tomb in the San Francisco City Hall. Golden Gate Park still remains true to his vision – a place in which to escape from city life.

Buffalo in the Buffalo Paddock

California Academy of Sciences ●

This permanent complex is closed for renovation until 2008. In the meantime, exhibits are on display at a temporary location in Howard St *(see p320)*. The permanent site at Golden Gate Park was erected in several installments between 1916 and 1968, yet maintains a unified design around a central courtyard. The original science museum was located downtown but was severely damaged in the 1906 earthquake. The exhibits in two rooms were salvaged, and became the foundation of the museum's collection.

A penguin in the Steinhart Aquarium

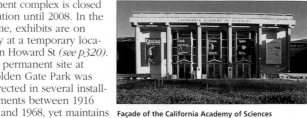

Façade of the California Academy of Sciences

MUSEUM GUIDE

The widely varied collections, arranged by subject, are housed in different halls on the first floor around the central courtyard. Several areas are allocated for the display of special exhibitions. The Academy Store, selling books and gifts, has a shop in Cowell Hall and another outside the Auditorium. The Academy library, which contains 70,000 volumes, is on the second floor.

Reptiles and Amphibians

Fish

Wattis Hall

Far Side of Science Gallery

Elkus Collection

Morrison Planetarium
One of the world's most precise star projectors transforms the ceiling here into a night sky.

Auditorium

KEY TO FLOOR PLAN

- [ ] African Hall
- [ ] Earth and Space
- [ ] Wattis Hall
- [ ] Life Through Time
- [ ] Steinhart Aquarium
- [ ] Gem and Mineral Hall
- [ ] Wild California
- [ ] Special exhibitions
- [ ] Non-exhibition space

★ Earthquake!
Experience the power and movement of great earth tremors, while learning of their destructive power.

★ Steinhart Aquarium
More than 8,000 specimens of tide-pool animals, sea mammals, and other aquatic animals dwell here in one of the world's most diverse aquariums.

VISITORS' CHECKLIST

The permanent home of the California Academy of Sciences is closed until 2008. The museum is temporarily located at 875 Howard St near Frith St *(see p320)*. For more information, visit **www**.calacademy.org

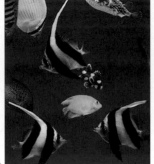

Sharks of the Tropics
Fish Roundabout
Wild California
Biodiversity Resource Center
Stairs
Insects
To café
Entrance

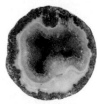

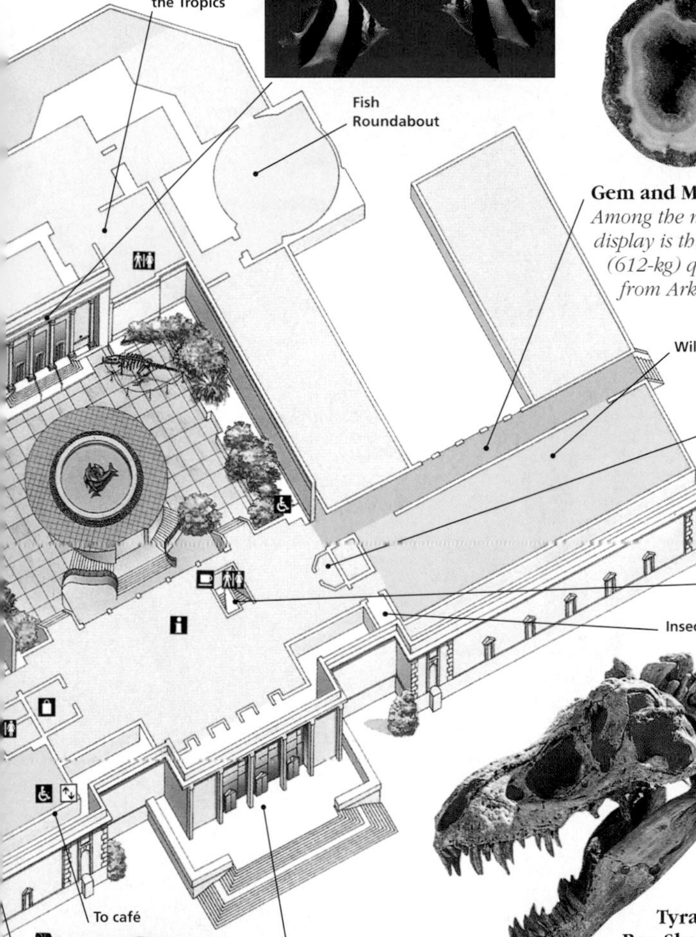

Gem and Mineral Hall
Among the minerals on display is this 1,350-lb (612-kg) quartz crystal from Arkansas.

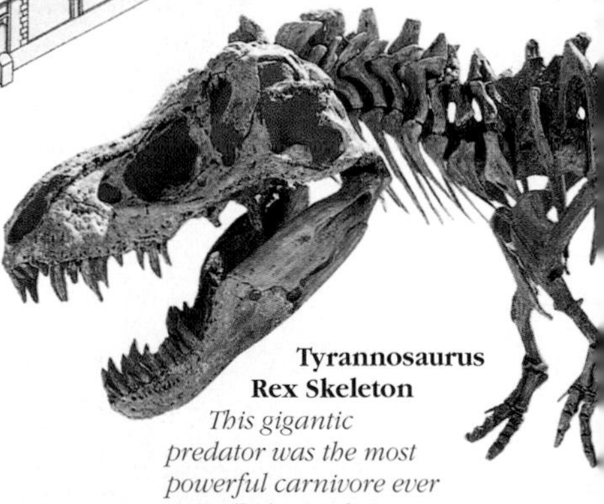

Tyrannosaurus Rex Skeleton
This gigantic predator was the most powerful carnivore ever to walk the earth.

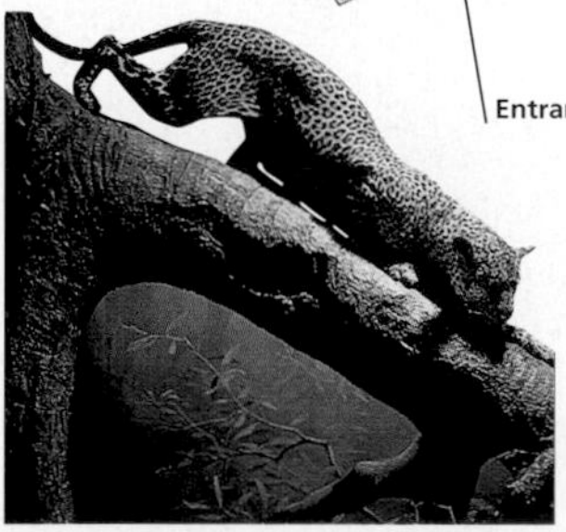

African Hall
Realistic models of animals from Africa's jungles and savannas are displayed here, in lifelike dioramas.

STAR EXHIBITS

- ★ Earthquake!
- ★ Steinhart Aquarium

Golden Gate Bridge from Lincoln Park golf course ▷

Legion of Honor ❿

Inspired by the Palais de la Légion d'Honneur in Paris, Alma de Bretteville Spreckels built this museum in the 1920s to promote French art in California. Designed by the architect George Applegarth, it contains works of European art from the last eight centuries, with paintings by Monet, Rubens, and Rembrandt, and more than 70 statues by Rodin. The Achenbach Foundation, a famous collection of graphic works, occupies part of the gallery.

Old Woman
French artist Georges de la Tour painted this female portrait in about 1618.

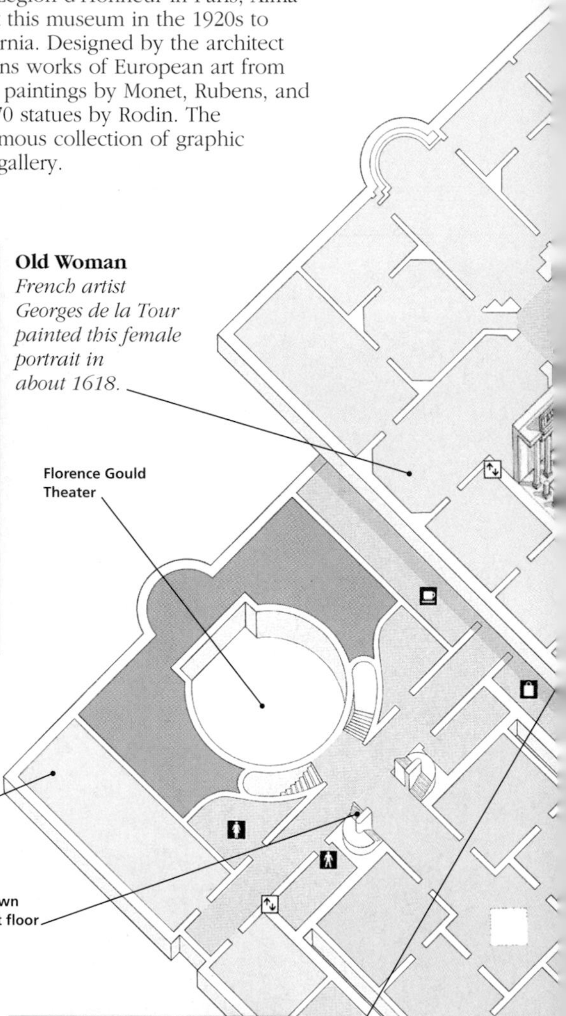

Florence Gould Theater

The Porcelain Gallery
contains figurines, china, and other pieces dating from the 18th century.

Stairs down
from first floor

Virgin and Child
This oil-on-panel by the Flemish artist Dieric Bouts dates from the 15th century. It forms part of a series of four panels titled Life of the Virgin.

STAR FEATURES

★ The Thinker by Auguste Rodin

★ Waterlilies by Claude Monet

For hotels and restaurants in this region see pp542–9 and pp587–95

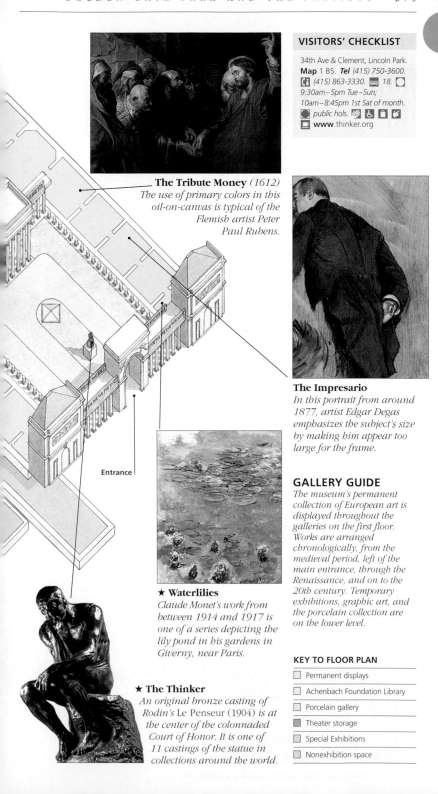

VISITORS' CHECKLIST

34th Ave & Clement, Lincoln Park.
Map 1 B5. **Tel** (415) 750-3600.
(415) 863-3330. 18.
9:30am–5pm Tue–Sun;
10am–8:45pm 1st Sat of month.
public hols.
www.thinker.org

The Tribute Money (1612)
The use of primary colors in this oil-on-canvas is typical of the Flemish artist Peter Paul Rubens.

The Impresario
In this portrait from around 1877, artist Edgar Degas emphasizes the subject's size by making him appear too large for the frame.

GALLERY GUIDE

The museum's permanent collection of European art is displayed throughout the galleries on the first floor. Works are arranged chronologically, from the medieval period, left of the main entrance, through the Renaissance, and on to the 20th century. Temporary exhibitions, graphic art, and the porcelain collection are on the lower level.

Entrance

★ Waterlilies
Claude Monet's work from between 1914 and 1917 is one of a series depicting the lily pond in his gardens in Giverny, near Paris.

★ The Thinker
An original bronze casting of Rodin's Le Penseur (1904) is at the center of the colonnaded Court of Honor. It is one of 11 castings of the statue in collections around the world.

KEY TO FLOOR PLAN

☐ Permanent displays
☐ Achenbach Foundation Library
☐ Porcelain gallery
☐ Theater storage
☐ Special Exhibitions
☐ Nonexhibition space

The Presidio

**Presidio
Park sign**

The winding roads and lush green landscaping of the Presidio belie its long military history. This prominent site has played a key role in San Francisco's growth, and it has been occupied longer than any other part of the city. Remnants of its military past, including the well-preserved barracks, artillery emplacements, and a museum, can be seen everywhere, and there are many hiking trails, bike paths, and beaches. The coastal path is one of the most popular walks and picnic areas in the city. The striking Golden Gate Bridge crosses the bay from the northwest corner of the Presidio to Marin County.

Fort Point
This impressive brick fortress, now a national historic site, guarded the Golden Gate during the Civil War of 1861–5 **16**

★ Golden Gate Bridge
Opened in 1937, the bridge has a single span of 4,200 ft (1,280 m) **17**

Mountain Lake is a large spring-fed lake and a popular picnic spot. The original Presidio was established nearby in 1776 to defend the bay area and Mission Dolores *(see p361)*.

Crissy Field was reclaimed from marshland for the 1915 Panama-Pacific Exposition *(see p351)*. It was used as an airfield from 1919 to 1936 and has been recently restored.

LOCATOR MAP
See Street Finder, map 2 & 3

The Military Cemetery holds the remains of almost 15,000 American soldiers killed during several wars.

The Tidal Marsh is part of the restoration of the Presidio area.

Arguello Gate
This decorative gate with its military symbols marks the entrance to the former army base, now open to the public.

★ **Presidio Visitor Center**
The visitor center on Montgomery Street is in the Main Post area of the Presidio.

STAR SIGHTS

★ Golden Gate Bridge

★ Presidio Visitor Center

0 meters	500
0 yards	500

Holy Virgin Cathedral ⓫

6210 Geary Blvd. **Map** 8 D1. ⓕ 221-3255. ⓦ 2, 29, 38. ⓣ 8am, 6pm daily, extra services 8am, 9:45am Sun.

Shining gold onion-shaped domes crown the Russian Orthodox Holy Virgin Cathedral of the Russian Church in Exile, a startling landmark in the suburban Richmond District. Built in the early 1960s, it is generally open to the public only during services. In contrast to those of many other Christian denominations, the services in this cathedral are conducted with the congregation standing, so there are no pews or seats.

The cathedral and the many Russian-owned businesses surrounding it, such as the lively Russian Renaissance restaurant, are situated at the heart of San Francisco's extensive Russian community (see p35). This has flourished since the 1820s, but it reached its highest population influx when a large number of new immigrants arrived after the Russian Revolution of 1917. It has since boomed twice more: in the late 1950s and late 1980s.

Clement Street ⓬

Map 1 C5. ⓦ 2, 28, 29, 44.

This is a bustling main thoroughfare of the otherwise sleepy Richmond District. Bookshops and small boutiques flourish here, and the inhabitants of the neighborhood meet together in a lively mix of bars, fast-food cafés, and ethnic restaurants. Most of these are patronized more by locals than by tourists.

Clement Street is surrounded by an area known as New Chinatown, home to more than one-third of the Chinese population of San Francisco. As a result, some of the city's best Chinese restaurants can be found here, and the emphasis in general is on Far Eastern cuisine (see p590-91).

The area is also known for the diversity of its restaurants, and Danish, Peruvian, and French establishments, among others, flourish here. The street stretches from Arguello Boulevard to the north/south cross-streets that are more commonly known as "The Avenues." It ends near the California Palace of the Legion of Honor (see pp374–5).

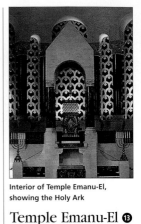

Interior of Temple Emanu-El, showing the Holy Ark

Temple Emanu-El ⓭

Lake St and Arguello Blvd. **Map** 3 A4. **Tel** 751-2535. ⓞ 8:30am–5:30pm Mon–Thu, 8:30am–5pm Fri (8:30am–7:30pm first Fri of month). ⓣ 5:30pm Fri, 10:30am Sat. ⓩ during services. ⓖ

After World War I hundreds of Jews from Russia and Eastern Europe moved into the Richmond District and built major religious centers. Among these is the Temple Emanu-El, its dome inspired by that of the 6th-century Hagia Sophia in Istanbul.

The temple stands out as a majestic piece of architecture. It was built in 1925 for the longest established congregation of Jews in the city, founded in 1850. The architect was Arthur Brown, who also designed City Hall (see p352). The temple is an architectural hybrid: Mission style (see pp30–31), Byzantine ornamentation, and Romanesque arcades. Its interior, which accommodates nearly 2,000 worshipers, is especially fine when sunlight shines through the stained-glass windows.

Presidio Officers' Club ⓮

50 Moraga Ave. **Map** 3 A2. **Tel** (415) 561-2582. ⓦ 29. ⓞ 9am–5pm daily. ⓞ some public hols.

Looking out across the original parade grounds of the Presidio and the 19th-century wooden barracks, the Officers' Club was built in

The Russian Orthodox Holy Virgin Cathedral

the Spanish Mission style *(see pp30–31)*. Although it dates from the 1930s, it was carefully built around the adobe (sun-dried brick) remains of the original 18th-century Spanish fort. Private events and public exhibitions are sometimes held here.

Presidio Visitor Center ⓯

Temporarily moved to the Presidio Officers' Club. **Map** 3 A2. *Tel (415) 561-4323*. **www**.presidiotrust.gov

The Presidio Museum, once housed in a white wooden building dating from the 1860s, that served as the Presidio hospital, is now part of the new Mott Visitor Center. Located in a brick barracks on Infantry Row, the Center houses exhibits and artifacts associated with the long history of the Presidio. The displays focus on eyewitness accounts of the evolution of the city of San Francisco, from the small frontier outpost in the 1770s to the major metropolis it is today. Other exhibits of uniforms, weapons, and newspaper accounts of the 1906 earthquake and fire are on display in other Presidio buildings.

Two small cabins stand behind the Old Post Hospital *(see p377)* and are representative of the hundreds of temporary shelters set up here following the great earthquake of 1906 *(see pp52–3)*.

Cannon near the Old Post Hospital on the grounds of the Presidio

Golden Gate Bridge, seen from Fort Point

Fort Point ⓰

Marine Drive. **Map** 2 E1.
📞 556-1693. 🕐 10am–5pm daily.
📷 ♿ *partial*.

Completed by the US Army in 1861, this fort was built partly to protect San Francisco Bay from military attack, and partly to defend ships carrying gold from the Californian mines *(see pp48–9)*. It is the most prominent of the many fortifications constructed along the Pacific coastline and is a classic example of a pre-Civil War brick and granite fortress. The building soon became obsolete, its 10-ft (3-m) thick brick walls not being strong enough to stand up to powerful modern weaponry. It was

closed in 1900, never having come under attack.

The fort's brickwork vaulting is extremely unusual for San Francisco, where the ready availability of good timber was an incentive to build wood-frame constructions. This may have saved the fort from collapse in the 1906 earthquake *(see pp52–3)*. It was nearly demolished in the 1930s to make way for the Golden Gate Bridge, but it survived and is now a good place from which to view the bridge. Restored in the 1970s, the fort now houses a museum displaying military uniforms and arms. Park Rangers dressed in Civil War costume conduct guided tours.

A HISTORY OF THE PRESIDIO

In 1776 José Joaquin Moraga, one of the first Spanish settlers, founded a presidio. His aim in erecting this camp of adobe buildings on the edge of San Francisco Bay was to defend the Mission

The Presidio in the 19th century

Dolores *(see p361)*. Following Mexican independence from Spain, the site remained the northernmost fort of the short-lived republic until the United States took it over in 1847. The Presidio was used for military purposes until 1990.

From the 1850s to the 1930s, the adobe buildings were replaced, first with wooden barracks, and later with concrete Mission- and Georgian-style cottages for the officers and their families. These buildings remain.

The site covers 1,400 acres (567 ha), and its landscaped forests of eucalyptus and cypress trees are not found on any other army base in the world. The Presidio has now been declared an historic site and is a protected member of the Golden Gate National Recreation Area (GGNRA).

Golden Gate Bridge ⑰

Named after that part of San Francisco Bay called "Golden Gate" by John Frémont in 1844, the bridge opened in 1937, connecting the city with Marin County. It took just over four years to build at a cost of $35 million. Breathtaking views are offered from this spectacular, world-famous landmark, which has six lanes for vehicles plus a free pedestrian walkway. It is the world's third largest single-span bridge and, when it was built, it was the world's longest and tallest suspension structure.

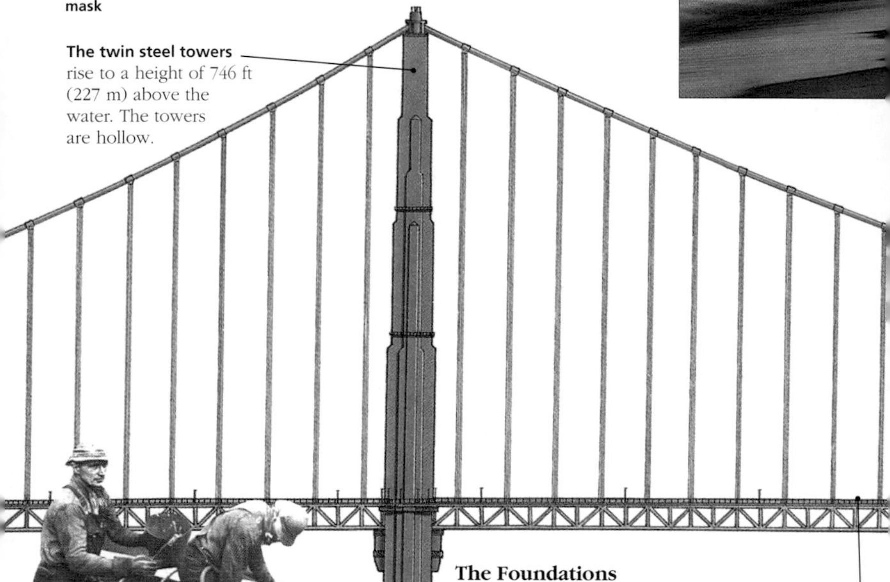

Bridge builder wearing protective mask

The twin steel towers rise to a height of 746 ft (227 m) above the water. The towers are hollow.

Catching the Hot Rivets
Working in gangs of four, one man heated the rivets and threw them to another, who caught them in a bucket. The other two fastened sections of steel with the hot rivets.

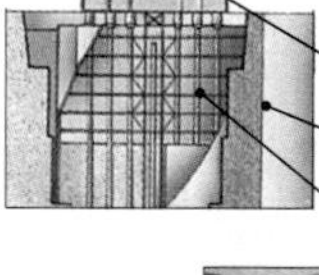

The Foundations
The foundations of the twin towers are a remarkable feat of engineering. The south pier, 1,125 ft (343 m) offshore, was sunk 100 ft (30 m) into the sea bed.

Pier base 65-ft (20-m) thick

Fender 155-ft (47-m) high

Reinforcing iron frame

The roadway is 220 ft (67 m) above water 318-ft (97-m) deep.

The Concrete Fender
During construction, the south pier base was protected from the force of the tides by a fender of concrete. Water was pumped out to create a vast watertight locker.

THE GOLDEN GATE BRIDGE
AT SAN FRANCISCO

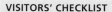

The Roadway
The original steel-supported concrete roadway was constructed from the towers in both directions, so that weight on the suspension cables was evenly distributed.

The length of the bridge is 1.7 miles (2.7 km), the span is 4,200 ft (1,280 m), and the roadway is 220 ft (67 m) above the water.

Joseph Strauss
Chicago engineer Joseph Strauss is officially credited as the bridge's designer, and he led the opening ceremony in April 1937. He was assisted by Leon Moisseiff and Charles Ellis. Irving F Morrow acted as consulting architect.

View from Vista Point
The best view of both the bridge and the San Francisco skyline is from the Marin County side.

THE BRIDGE IN FIGURES

• Every year more than 40 million vehicles cross the bridge; every day about 118,000 vehicles use it.
• The original coat of paint lasted for 27 years, needing only touch-ups. But since 1965, a crew has been stripping off the old paint and applying a more durable coating.
• The two great 7,650-ft (2,332-m) cables are more than 3 ft (1 m) thick, and contain 80,000 miles (128,744 km) of steel wire, enough to circle the earth at the equator three times.
• The volume of concrete poured into the piers and anchorages during the bridge's construction would be enough to lay a 5-ft (1.5 m) wide sidewalk from New York to San Francisco, a distance of more than 2,500 miles (4,000 km).
• The bridge can withstand 100 mph (160 km/h) winds.
• Each pier has to withstand a tidal flow of more than 60 mph (97 km/h), while supporting a 44,000-ton steel tower.

Painting the bridge

SHOPPING IN SAN FRANCISCO

Shopping in San Francisco is much more than simply making a purchase, it's a whole experience that allows a glimpse into the city's culture. It is the diversity of San Francisco that makes buying anything here an adventure. An enormous range of goods is available, from the practical to the more eccentric, but you can take your time in choosing, since browsers

Clock over entrance to Tiffany's

are generally made to feel welcome, particularly in the many small specialty shops and boutiques of the city. If you want convenience, the numerous shopping centers and department stores are excellent. For those in search of local color, every neighborhood shopping district has a charm and personality of its own, with each reflecting a different aspect of the city.

MALLS AND SHOPPING CENTERS

In contrast to a great many suburban shopping malls, those of San Francisco have character, and one or two of them are of considerable architectural interest. The Embarcadero Center (see p314) has more than 125 shops, in an area covering eight blocks. Ghirardelli Square (see p337) was a well-known chocolate factory from 1893 until early in the 1960s. It is now a mall that is very popular with visitors, and it houses more than 70 shops and several restaurants, overlooking San Francisco Bay.

The San Francisco Center (see p321) has nine levels and more than 100 shops. Pier 39 (see p336) is a marketplace on the waterfront, with restaurants, a double-decker Venetian merry-go-round, a marina, and many specialty boutiques. In the Cannery (see p337), located at Fisherman's Wharf, you will find a variety of charming small shops. The beautiful

Emporio Armani

Crocker Galleria (see p320) is one of the city's most spectacular malls, with three floors set under a high glass dome built around a central plaza.

The Japan Center (see p352), complete with pagoda, offers exotic foods, goods, and art from the East, as well as a Japanese-style hotel and traditional baths. The Rincon Center (see p317), with a 90-ft (27-m) water column at its center, is an Art Deco haven for shopping and eating.

DEPARTMENT STORES

Most of San Francisco's major department stores are in or near Union Square. They are huge retail stores that offer their customers an outstanding selection of goods and services.

Macy's department store spans two city blocks. It stocks an enormous range of goods, all beautifully presented and sold by enthusiastic sales people. It offers a wide range of extra facilities, including a currency exchange and an interpreting service. The men's department is particularly extensive.

Neiman Marcus is another stylish emporium. Its modern building caused a furor when it was opened in 1982, replacing a popular store built in the 1890s. The huge stained-glass dome in its Rotunda Restaurant was part of the original building and is well worth coming to see.

Nordstrom, known for its fashion and shoes, is often called the "store-in-the-sky"; it is located in the top five floors of the innovative San Francisco Shopping Center.

Flags flying in front of the pagoda at the Japan Center

SHOPPING AROUND UNION SQUARE

Serious shoppers should concentrate on the blocks bordered by Geary, Powell, and Post Streets, and on the surrounding blocks between Market and Sutter Streets. Here luxurious shops and inexpensive boutiques sell anything from designer bed linens to pedigree dogs to souvenirs. Exclusive hotels, chic restaurants, and colorful flower stalls all add to the fashionable atmosphere.

SHOPS FOR A GOOD CAUSE

San Franciscans take great pleasure in shopping for a good cause. The **Planetweavers Treasure Store** is the official UNICEF shop, where crafts and clothes made in developing countries are sold, as well as educational toys from around the world.

Flower stall on Union Square

UNICEF receives 25 percent of net profits. The **Golden Gate National Park Store** offers gifts and memorabilia; proceeds go to all national parks, including Golden Gate National Park. All the profits that are made at **Under One Roof** benefit the various groups set up to help combat AIDS. Those who want to protect the environment head for the **Greenpeace Store**, which sells jewelry, prints, and a variety of other gifts.

SOUVENIRS

Many souvenirs, such as T-shirts, keyrings, mugs, and Christmas ornaments, are decorated with motifs symbolizing San Francisco in **Only in San Francisco** and the **Cable Car Store**. Souvenir and novelty hats of every color, size, and shape are available at **Krazy Kaps**, while the store entrances on Grant Avenue (*see p329*) and Fisherman's Wharf (*see pp334–5*) are lined with baskets filled with inexpensive gifts.

BEST BUYS

Gourmet shoppers should look for seafood, one of the city's specialties. Wine from the Napa Valley (*see pp462–3*) is another good buy. You will find blue jeans at competitive prices, also vintage clothing, ethnic art, books, and records.

SHOPPING TOURS

Shoppers who want to be guided to the best shops for their own particular needs can go on a special tour, organized by companies such as **Shopper Stopper Shopping Tours**. A guide takes you from shop to shop to find unusual items.

MUSEUMS

Museum shopping offers exquisite gifts to suit all budgets. Among the city's best are the **Academy Store** in the California Academy of Sciences (*see p320*), the **Museum Store** at the Legion of Honor, (*see pp374–5*), the **San Francisco MOMA Museum Store** (*see pp318–19*) and the **Asian Art Museum** (*see p352*).

Grant Avenue, Chinatown

DIRECTORY

Academy Store
California Academy of Sciences, temporarily located at 875 Howard St. **Map** 6 D5.
Tel (415) 750-7330.

Asian Art Museum
200 Larkin St. **Map** 4 F5.
Tel (415) 379-8000.
www.asianart.org

Cable Car Store
Pier 39. **Map** 5 B1.
Tel (415) 989-2040.

Greenpeace Store
900 North Point. **Map** 4 F1.
Tel (415) 512-9025.

Golden Gate National Park Store
Embarcadero Center. **Map** 6 D3.
Tel (415) 984-0640.

Krazy Kaps
Pier 39. **Map** 5 B1.
Tel (415) 296-8930.

Macy's
Stockton & O'Farrell Sts.
Map 5 C5.
Tel (415) 397-3333.

Museum Store
Legion of Honor,
Golden Gate Park.
Map 1 B5.
Tel (415) 750-3600.

Neiman Marcus
150 Stockton St. **Map** 5 C5.
Tel (415) 362-3900.

Nordstrom
San Francisco Shopping Center, 865 Market St. **Map** 5 C5.
Tel (415) 243-8500.

Only in San Francisco
Pier 39. **Map** 5 B1.
Tel (415) 397-0122.

Planetweavers Treasure Store
1573 Haight St. **Map** 9 C1.
Tel (415) 864-4415.

San Francisco MOMA Museum Store
Museum of Modern Art.
Map 6 D5.
Tel (415) 357-4035.

Shopping Stopper Shopping Tours
Tel (707) 829-1597.

Under One Roof
549 Castro St. **Map** 10 D3.
Tel (415) 252-9430.

San Francisco Specials

Entrepreneurial spirit in San Francisco is strong and innovative, and the city's sophisticated image is very much deserved. Whether it is a small souvenir, a designer outfit, an antique, or a mouthwatering snack that is required, visitors will never be disappointed amid the shops and markets of San Francisco. The city is also home to many dedicated "foodies," gastronomes whose liking for fine wine and gourmet meals have resulted in unusual and delicious grocery stores. All this creates an environment that makes shopping in San Francisco an exciting experience.

SPECIALTY SHOPS

If you want to laugh, go to **Smile-A Gallery with Tongue in Chic**, where humorous art to wear or display is sold, including many objects made by Bay Area artists. Since Gold Rush days, **Malm Luggage**, a family-owned and operated shop for luggage, briefcases and small leather goods, has kept its reputation for excellence. You can describe the city's attractions on a designer card from **Flax Art and Design**, a sixty-year-old business offering a huge selection of hand-made papers and artists' tools.

The colorful exterior of Flax Art and Design on Market Street

Comix Experience sells a large selection of collector and special edition comics. Exquisite Italian ceramics (majolica) are on display at **Biordi Art Imports** in North Beach, where handpainted dishware, vases and platters are for sale. Those who would like to experience the authentic atmosphere of Chinatown will find it at **Ten Ren Tea Company** of San Francisco. At **Golden Gate Fortune Cookies** descendants of Chinese immigrants allow customers to taste samples before buying the San Francisco fortune cookies which were a Chinatown invention.

FOOD AND WINE

From abalone to zucchini, and from fresh California produce to imported specialty foods, the gourmet grocery **Whole Foods** carries a wide variety of items. **Williams-Sonoma** has jams, mustards, and gifts. **David's** is known for its lox (smoked salmon), bagels and New York cheesecake. The Italian **Molinari Delicatessen** is famous for its fresh ravioli and tortellini, ready to throw into a saucepan. **Lucca Ravioli** has a friendly staff, who make their pasta on the premises. **Pasta Gina** caters to the young, fashionable crowd with pasta, prepared pesto and other sauces.

It is well worth going to Chinatown (*see pp316–17*) for Far Eastern food products and produce. At **Casa Lucas Market** you will find a variety of Spanish and Latin American food specialties. A baguette of fresh sourdough bread from **Boudin Bakery** is a long-standing addiction

Ghirardelli Square, home to San Francisco's famous chocolate

with locals and a tradition with visitors. **Boulangerie** brings Paris to San Francisco, with some of the best bread in the city. **La Nouvelle Patisserie** sells tasty and colorful desserts. Chocoholics are catered to at San Francisco's own **Ghirardelli's**. San Franciscans are coffee connoisseurs, and there are many specialty houses. **Caffè Trieste** is the city's oldest coffee house and sells a range of custom-roasted and blended coffees, and a variety of brewing equipment. **Caffè Roma Coffee Roasting Company** and the **Graffeo Coffee Roasting Company** both sell excellent beans. The staff at the **California Wine Merchant** makes good

Fig jam, Williams-Sonoma

Caffè Trieste on Vallejo Street is a North Beach landmark

recommendations and are very knowledgeable about their affordable wines. The **Napa Valley Winery Exchange** features selections from the many Californian wineries, including the smaller local producers.

Locally grown fruit and vegetables arrive by the truckload at the regular farmers' markets in the center of the city. Stalls are erected for the day, and the farmers sell their goods directly to the public. The **Heart of the City** is open on Wednesdays and Sundays from 7am to 5pm, and **Ferry Plaza Farmers' Market** is held on Saturdays from 9am to 2pm. Chinatown's produce stores have the feel of an exotic farmers' market and are open every day.

BOOKS, MUSIC, ART, AND ANTIQUES

The largest independent bookshop in the city is **A Clean Well-Lighted Place for Books**, carrying the latest titles, plus classics and works by local authors. Beats once talked about the country's emerging 1960s social revolution at the **City Lights Bookstore** (see pp330–1), which stays open late and is a famous San Francisco institution. **Green Apple Books** has new and used books, and is open until 10pm, or midnight on Fridays and Saturdays. **The Booksmith**, located in Haight Ashbury, is notable for its stock of foreign and political periodicals. **The Complete Traveler** and **Rand McNally Map & Travel Store** stock a good selection of local and worldwide travel guides and maps.

A wide selection of music is offered at various branches of **Tower Records** and the **Virgin Megastore**. More obscure music can usually be found at **Recycled Records**. **Amoeba Music** has the largest selection of CDs and tapes in the country. It has 500,000 titles, both new and secondhand, including jazz, international blues and rock music. A

Pinot Noir, a popular wine of the region

music collector's paradise, this is the place to go if you are looking for hard-to-find music at low prices. All types of sheet music and books of collections can be found at the **Music Center of San Francisco**. Art lovers will find something to their liking in the city's hundreds of galleries. The **John Berggruen Gallery** has the city's largest collection of works by both emerging and more established artists. **The Simmons Gallery** sells limited edition prints by such modern masters as Picasso, Matisse, and Miró. **The Fraenkel Gallery** is known for its collection of 19th- and 20th-century photography. **Folk Art International, Xanadu, & Boretti** has masks, textiles, sculptures and jewelry.

Jackson Square is San Francisco's main area for antiques (see p304). **Ed Hardy San Francisco** offers English and French antiques and **Lang Antiques** has all kinds of items from the Victorian, Art Nouveau, Art Deco and Edwardian periods. **Dragon House** sells Oriental antiques and fine art, while antique books, prints and maps can be found at **Prints Old & Rare** – although you will need to make an appointment.

CLOTHING

San Francisco designer shops include **Diana Slavin** for classics, **Joanie Char's** for sportswear, and **Wilkes Bashford** for up-and-coming designs. **MAC** or Modern

Appealing Clothing, sources one-third of its menswear as well as womenswear from San Francisco designers. For discount designer clothes, head to the trendy SoMa district. Yerba Buena Square contains several kinds of outlets, including **Burlington Coat Factory**. Here you can find discounted lines from many local designers. **Georgiou Outlet** showcases classic styles made from natural fibers. **Jeremy's** in SoMa's swish South Park area, discounts formal clothing and designerwear for both men and women.

Wasteland on Haight Street, a treasure of vintage garments

Buffalo Exchange offers secondhand clothing with a history. **Wasteland** in the Haight-Ashbury District is known for its vintage clothes. **Guys and Dolls Vintage** stocks hip styles, while **Clothes Contact** sells vintage clothes by the pound.

Brooks Brothers is well known for its conservative men's suits and button-down shirts. Fashionable outdoor clothing is available from **Eddie Bauer**. For men's

City Lights Bookstore (see p330) on Columbus Avenue

designer brands, sportswear, shoes, and accessories with a European influence, try **Rolo**. Many of the world's famous names in fashion are in San Francisco, including **Chanel** and **Gucci**. **Gianni Versace** is in the Crocker Galleria. **Prada** is famous for its extra-fine merino wool and cashmere clothes. **Jorja** stocks various designers and specializes in Nicole Miller. **Banana Republic** and **Guess** are well known for stylish, wearable clothes. **Loehmann's** sells designer clothing from New York and Europe at a discount. **Urban Outfitters** has chic second-hand and new clothes, and **American Rag** has stylish new and used European and American clothing. **Original Levi's Store** has been in business since 1853, offering a broad range of clothes, all of which can be worn with their famous jeans *(see p343)*.

Small Frys is the locals' favorite for cotton children's clothes. Top-quality footwear is available at **Kenneth Cole**. Best names in comfort are at **Ria's**, including Clarks, Birkenstock, Timberland, Sebago and Rockport. **Nike Town** is a megastore for sneakers, and **DSW Shoe Warehouse** offers discounted shoes.

TOYS, GAMES, AND GADGETS

One of the city's main toy shops, **Toys R Us** sells everything a child desires. Inside you will find a vast range of toys, video games and collectible toys, as well as a department with equipment and gifts for babies.

At **Puppets on the Pier** new owners are given puppetry lessons in the shop. **Gamescape** sells a wide range of non-electronic games, such as traditional gameboards, collectible cards, and role-playing books. **The Chinatown Kite Shop** takes shopping to new heights, displaying an extraordinary assortment of flying objects. These range from traditional to World Champion stunt kites, all making attractive souvenirs. In the **Sharper Image** even the adult who has everything, is sure to be intrigued by the high-tech wizardry of the gadgets and electronic goods on sale.

DIRECTORY

SPECIALTY SHOPS

Biordi Art Imports
412 Columbus Ave.
Map 5 C3.
Tel 392-8096.

Comix Experience
305 Divisadero St.
Map 10 D1.
Tel (415) 863-9258.

Flax Art and Design
1699 Market St.
Map 10 F1.
Tel (415) 522-2355.

Golden Gate Fortune Cookies
56 Ross Alley.
Map 5 C3.
Tel 781-3956.

Malm Luggage
222 Grant Ave.
Map 5 C4.
Tel (415) 392-0417.

Smile-A Gallery with Tongue in Chic
500 Sutter St.
Map 5 B4.
Tel (415) 362-3437.

Ten Ren Tea Company of San Francisco
949 Grant Ave.
Map 5 C3.
Tel 362-0656.

FOOD AND WINE

Boudin Bakery
4 Embarcadero Center.
Map 6 D3.
Tel (415) 362-3330.

Boulangerie
2325 Pine St.
Map 4 D4.
Tel 440-0356.

Caffè Roma Coffee Roasting Company
526 Columbus Ave.
Map 5 B2.
Tel 296-7942.

Caffè Trieste
601 Vallejo St.
Map 5 C3.
Tel (415) 982-2605.

California Wine Merchant
3237 Pierce St.
Map 4 D2.
Tel 567-0646.

Casa Lucas Market
2934 24th St.
Map 9 C3.
Tel (415) 826-4334.

David's
474 Geary St.
Map 5 A5.
Tel 276-5950.

Ferry Plaza Farmers' Market
Market St at the Embarcadero.
Map 6 D3.
Tel (415) 291-3276.
www.ferryplaza
farmersmarket.com

Ghirardelli's
Ghirardelli Square.
Map 4 F1.
Tel (415) 474-3938.
44 Stockton St.
Map 5 C1.
Tel (415) 397-3030.

Graffeo Coffee Roasting Company
735 Columbus Ave.
Map 5 B2.
Tel 986-2420.

Heart of the City Farmers' Market
United Nations Plaza.
Map 10 A1.
Tel (415) 558-9455.

Lucca Ravioli
1100 Valencia St.
Map 10 F3.
Tel 647-5581.

Molinari Delicatessen
373 Columbus Ave.
Map 5 C3.
Tel (415) 421-2337.

Napa Valley Winery Exchange
415 Taylor St.
Map 5 B5.
Tel (415) 771-2887.
www.napavalley
wineryex.com

La Nouvelle Patisserie
2184 Union St.
Map 4 D2.
Tel 931-7655.

Pasta Gina
741 Diamond St.
Map 10 D4.
Tel 282-0738.

Whole Foods
1765 California St.
Map 4 F4.
Tel (415) 674-0500.

Williams-Sonoma
340 Post St.
Map 5 C4
Tel (415) 362-9450.

BOOKS, MUSIC, ART, AND ANTIQUES

Amoeba Music
1855 Haight St.
Map 9 B1.
Tel 831-1200.

The Booksmith
1644 Haight St.
Map 9 B1.
Tel 863-8688.

DIRECTORY

City Lights Bookstore
261 Columbus Ave.
Map 5 C3.
Tel (415) 362-8193.

A Clean Well-Lighted Place for Books
601 Van Ness Avenue.
Map 4 F5.
Tel (415) 441-6670.

The Complete Traveler
3207 Fillmore St.
Map 4 D2.
Tel 923-1511.

Dragon House
455 Grant Ave.
Map 6 C4.
Tel 421-3693.

Ed Hardy San Francisco
188 Henry Adams St.
Map 10 D2.
Tel 626-6300.

Folk Art International, Xanadu, & Boretti
Frank Lloyd Wright Bldg,
140 Maiden Lane.
Map 5 B5.
Tel 392-9999.

Fraenkel Gallery
49 Geary St.
Map 5 C5.
Tel 981-2661.

Green Apple Books
506 Clement St.
Map 3 A5.
Tel 387-2272.

John Berggruen Gallery
228 Grant Ave.
Map 5 C4.
Tel (415) 781-4629.

Lang Antiques
323 Sutter St. **Map** 5 C4.
Tel 982-2213.

Music Center of San Francisco
207 Powell St.
Map 5 B1.
Tel 781-6023.

Prints Old & Rare
580 Mount Crespi Drive,
Pacifica, California.
Tel (650) 355-6325.

Rand McNally Map & Travel Store
595 Market St.
Map 5 C4.
Tel 777-3131.

Recycled Records
1377 Haight St.
Map 9 C1.
Tel (415) 626-4075.

The Simmons Gallery
540 Sutter St.
Map 5 B4.
Tel (415) 986-2244.

Tower Records
Columbus Ave & Bay St.
Map 5 A2.
Tel (415) 885-0500.
One of several branches.

Virgin Megastore
Stockton St. & Market St.
Map 5 C5.
Tel (415) 397-4525.
One of several branches.

CLOTHING

American Rag
1305 Van Ness Ave.
Map 5 A5.
Tel 474-5214.

Banana Republic
256 Grant Ave.
Map 5 C4.
Tel 777-3087.

Brooks Brothers
201 Post St.
Map 5 C4.
Tel (415) 397-4500.

Buffalo Exchange
1555 Haight St.
Map 9 C1.
Tel 431-7733.
1210 Valencia St.
Map 10 F4.
Tel 647-8332.

Burlington Coat Factory
899 Howard St.
Tel 495-7234.

Chanel
155 Maiden Lane.
Map 5 C4.
Tel 981-1550.

Clothes Contact
473 Valencia St.
Map 10 F2.
Tel 621-3212.

Diana Slavin
3 Claude Lane.
Map 5 C4.
Tel (415) 677-9939.

DSW Shoe Warehouse
111 Powell St.
Map 5 B5.
Tel 445-9511.

Eddie Bauer
3251 20th Ave. **Map** 8 E2.
Tel (415) 664-9262.

Georgiou Outlet
925 Bryant St.
Tel 554-0150.

Gianni Versace
Crocker Galleria, 50
Post St. **Map** 5 C4.
Tel 616-0604.

Gucci
200 Stockton St.
Map 5 C5.
Tel 392-2808.

Guess
90 Grant Ave.
Map 5 C5.
Tel 781-1589.

Guys and Dolls Vintage
3789 24th St.
Map 10 E4.
Tel 285-7174.

Jeremy's
2 South Park St.
Tel 882-4929.

Joanie Char
285A Sutter St.
Map 5 C4.
Tel (415) 399-9867.

Jorja
2015 Chestnut St.
Map 4 D2.
Tel 674-1131.

Kenneth Cole
865 Market St.
Map 5 C5.
Tel 227-4536.

Loehmann's
222 Sutter St.
Map 5 C4.
Tel 982-3215.

MAC
387 Grove St.
Map 4 F5.
Tel 863-3011.

Nike Town
278 Post St.
Map 5 C4.
Tel (415) 392-6453.

Original Levi's Store
Union Square.
Map 5 C5.
Tel (415) 501-0100.

Prada
140 Geary St.
Map 5 C5.
Tel 391-8844.

Ria's
301 Grant Ave.
Map 5 C4.
Tel 834-1420.

Rolo
2351 Market St.
Map 10 D2.
Tel 431-4545.

Small Frys
4066 24th St.
Map 10 D4.
Tel (415) 648-3954.

Urban Outfitters
80 Powell St.
Map 5 B5.
Tel 989-1515.

Wasteland
1660 Haight St.
Map 9 B1.
Tel 863-3150.

Wilkes Bashford
375 Sutter St.
Map 5 C4.
Tel (415) 986-4380.

TOYS, GAMES, AND GADGETS

Chinatown Kite Shop
717 Grant Ave.
Map 5 C3.
Tel 391-8217.

Gamescape
333 Divisadero St.
Map 10 D1.
Tel 621-4263.

Puppets on the Pier
Pier 39. **Map** 5 B1.
Tel 781-4435.

Sharper Image
680 Davis St. **Map** 6 D3.
Tel 445-6100.

Toys R Us
2675 Geary Blvd.
Map 3 C5.
Tel 931-8896.

ENTERTAINMENT IN SAN FRANCISCO

San Francisco has prided itself on being the cultural capital of the West Coast since the city first began to prosper in the 1850s, and the entertainment offered is generally of high quality. The performing arts complex of the Civic Center, opposite the City Hall, is the principal venue for classical music, opera, and ballet. The latest addition to the city's cultural life is the highly rated Center for the Arts Theater at Yerba Buena Gardens. Many international touring shows can be seen

Beach Blanket Babylon
(see p341)

here. There are numerous repertory movie theaters offering filmgoers a wide range of programs, but theater, except for some of the "alternative" venues, is not the city's strongest suit. Popular music, in particular jazz and blues, is where San Francisco really excels, and you can hear good bands for the price of a drink or at the street fairs and music festivals that are held during the summer months. Facilities are also available for a wide variety of sports, from cycling to golf, tennis, and sailing.

INFORMATION SOURCES

Complete listings of what's on and where are given in the *San Francisco Chronicle* and *Examiner* newspapers. The *Chronicle*'s Sunday edition is very useful. Other good sources are the free weekly newspapers, such as the *San Francisco Weekly* (available in most cafés and bars) or the *San Francisco Bay Guardian*. These give both listings and reviews, especially of live music, films, and nightclubs.

Visitors planning farther in advance will find the *San Francisco Book* very helpful. This is published twice yearly by the **San Francisco Convention and Visitors' Bureau** and is available free at the **Visitors' Information Center** at Hallidie Plaza or for $2 if mailed out. You can also phone the visitors' bureau's Events Line for recorded information. Numerous free magazines for visitors are available, as well as calendars of events. Among these are *Key This Week San Francisco* and *Where San Francisco*.

BUYING TICKETS

The main source for tickets to concerts, theater, and sporting events is **Ticketmaster**, which has a virtual monopoly on ticket sales, running an extensive charge-by-phone operation with outlets in the Tower and Wherehouse record shops *(see pp608–9)* all over Northern California. There is

Storefront of San Francisco ticket agency

a "convenience charge" of about $4 per ticket. An alternative to Ticketmaster is to buy directly from the box offices, though many of these are only open just before the start of evening performances.

To see productions by the reputable San Francisco Symphony, Ballet, and Opera companies, advance planning is essential. All have subscription programs, which are useful if you are planning to stay in the city for a lengthy period of time.

There are only a few ticket agencies in San Francisco, and they mostly specialize in selling limited seats at marked-up prices. They are all listed in the Yellow Pages of the telephone directory, found in most public pay phones. Ticket scalpers are invariably found outside sold-out events, offering seats at extortionate prices. If you are willing to bargain (and risk missing the start of the game or the opening act) it is often possible to get a good deal this way.

Front entrance of the War Memorial Opera House

Outdoor chess, popular in Portsmouth Plaza, Chinatown

DISCOUNT TICKETS

Discount tickets for some selected events are available from **TIX Bay Area**, offering half-price seats from a booth on the east side of Union Square (see p320). Tickets are sold starting at 11am, on the day of the performance only. Occasionally, there are also some half-price tickets available on weekends for those events that are taking place on the following Sunday and Monday.

TIX Bay Area is also a full-service Ticketmaster outlet selling full-price tickets for advance sales. It is open on Tuesdays, Wednesdays, and Thursdays from 11am to 6pm, on Fridays and Saturdays from 11am to 7pm and from 11am to 3pm on Sundays.

FREE EVENTS

In addition to San Francisco's many ticket-only events, a number of free concerts and performances are regularly staged all over the city. Many of these take place during the day and outdoors in the summer; they can offer a welcome change of pace from the usual standard fare.

The San Francisco Symphony Orchestra (see pp390–91) gives a series of late-summer Sunday concerts at Stern Grove, south of the Sunset District. The same venue is also occasionally used for ballets.

Cobb's Comedy Club (see pp390–91) hosts the popular San Francisco International Comedy Competition in August and September.

Performers from the San Francisco Opera (see pp390–91) can be heard singing some favorite arias in the Financial District as part of the "Brown Bag Operas" series and in Golden Gate Park in "Opera in the Park" events. In the summer the park is also host to the Shakespeare Festival, Comedy Celebration Day, and the San Francisco Mime Troupe. A series of concerts called "Music in the Park" is held on summer Fridays at noon, in the redwood grove behind the Transamerica Pyramid (see p315). At Grace Cathedral (see p331) the fine cathedral choir sings choral music at Evensong, at 5:15pm on Thursdays.

FACILITIES FOR THE DISABLED

California is a national leader in providing facilities for the handicapped. Most theaters and concert halls in San Francisco are therefore fully accessible and have open areas set aside for wheelchair-users. Some smaller venues may require the use of special entrances, or elevators to reach the upper tiers. Many movies offer amplifying headphones. Contact the theaters to be sure of their facilities.

The Presidio Cinema

Pac Bell Park, home of the San Francisco Giants (see pp374–5)

Entertainment Venues

With a variety of entertainment options, San Francisco is one of the most enjoyable cities in the world. Whatever your cultural preferences, what you see here is sure to be good. Besides housing the West Coast's best opera and ballet companies, it has a highly regarded symphony orchestra. The city also offers a wide range of jazz and rock music, diverse theater companies, and specialty movie houses. For the sports fan there are also plenty of opportunities to both watch and take part.

The ultramodern Louise M Davies Symphony Hall

FILM AND THEATER

San Francisco has an avid film-going community. The city's newest multimedia experience is the **Sony Metreon**, a 15-screen complex plus IMAX with shops, restaurants, special programs, and other attractions.

The landmark Castro Theatre

One of the city's best movie houses is the **AMC Kabuki**, an eight-screen complex in the Japan Center *(see p352)*, which also hosts the **San Francisco International Film Festival** each May. Other popular venues for first-run films include the **Embarcadero**, the **UA Galaxy4**, and the **Metro** on Union Street. The Metro has recently been restored to its original splendor with new sound systems, seats, and film equipment. Main venues for first-run foreign films are the **Clay** in Pacific Heights, the Civic Center's **Lumiere**, and **Opera Plaza**. The **Castro Theatre** *(see p360)* shows Hollywood classics and other revivals, with a program that changes daily.

Many residents of San Francisco show apparent disdain for the international commercial successes, which explains why theater has a lower profile here than in other large cities. Mainstream theaters, which host a range of touring Broadway productions as well as those by local companies, are concentrated in the Theater District *(see p320)*. Three of the largest theaters are the **Golden Gate Theater**, the **Curran Theater**, and the **Orpheum Theater**, all part of the Best of Broadway performance series. The **Stage Door Theater** has a reputation for serious productions, while musicals and comedy are staged at **The Marsh**. The most respected major company is the **American Conservatory Theater (ACT)**. Its longtime home, the landmark Geary Theater, has now reopened after renovations following the 1989 earthquake *(see pp24–5)*. A variety of plays are performed during its October to May season.

OPERA, CLASSICAL MUSIC, AND DANCE

The main season of the **San Francisco Opera Association** runs from September to December; tickets can cost more than $100, but there is a summer season, with less expensive tickets.

The main venue for opera, classical music, and dance is the Civic Center performing arts complex on Van Ness Avenue. The **Louise M Davies Symphony Hall** located here is now San Francisco's principal location for fine classical music performances, and home to the highly regarded **San Francisco Symphony Orchestra**, which performs up to five concerts a week during its winter season. Guest conductors, performers, and touring orchestras perform additional special concerts. Next door to the Opera House, the **Herbst Theatre** also hosts recitals by prominent performers.

In addition to these big events, there are numerous less formal recitals and concerts in the Bay Area. The **Philharmonia Baroque Orchestra**, a period instrument ensemble, plays at various sites around the city, while the historic **Old First Presbyterian Church** has a series of chamber music and individual

The Geary Theater *(see p310)*

recitals on Friday nights and Sunday afternoons. The **Florence Gould Theater** in the Legion of Honor *(see pp374–5)* is often used for classical small group performances, including quartets, and there are also demonstrations of classical or pre-classical instruments, such as the clavichord. **Grace Cathedral** is a particularly striking setting for choral church music. The choir sings at Evensong on Thursdays at 5:15pm, while Choral Eucharist is celebrated on Sundays at 11am.

Founded in 1933, the **San Francisco Ballet** is the oldest professional ballet company in the US. Its season of classical and new works runs from February to April. There are performances by local talent which take place at the intimate **Theater Artaud** and the **ODC Performance Gallery**, both located in the Mission District. The new Yerba Buena Center for the Arts *(see pp322–3)* is home to the LINES Contemporary Ballet, while **Zellerbach Hall** across the Bay attracts the area's best touring productions.

Slim's, one of San Francisco's best rock venues

ROCK, JAZZ, AND BLUES

Two of the best rock clubs to hear live music are **Slim's** and **Bimbo's 365 Club**. Bimbo's hosts rock, jazz, country, and R&B – and attracts a similarly diverse crowd. Slim's is a bit more upscale, tending to feature established performers in its comfortable 436-seat room. Another popular place is the **Fillmore Auditorium**, which is the legendary birthplace of psychedelic rock during the 1960s *(see p359)*.

There are a number of excellent places to hear live jazz in the city. The entertainment is usually free, if you buy dinner or drinks. For traditional Dixieland in an informal (and free) setting,

visit the amiable **Gold Dust Lounge**, just off Union Square. If you prefer more modern sounds, head to **Jazz at Pearl's** in North Beach. Try also the piano bars located in downtown restaurants and hotels, the best of which is the beautiful **Carnelian Room** in the Bank of America. The restaurant **Enrico's** features live Dixieland jazz on Fridays and modern jazz on other nights. Patrons at **Moose's** can enjoy listening to first-rate jazz pianists over lunch and dinner. Many jazz fans plan trips to San Francisco to coincide with the world-famous **Monterey Jazz Festival**, which is held every September in Monterey *(see p38)*. Monterey is two hours south of San Francisco. Live blues is played somewhere in town every night of the week, in bars such as **The Saloon** and the **Boom Boom Room**. **Lou's Pier 47**, on Fisherman's Wharf, has one or more blues bands on the bill almost every day, with special shows on weekends. The award-winning **Biscuits and Blues** has local blues spotlights on weekdays and special shows on weekends. The annual **San Francisco Blues Festival** *(see p38)* attracts blues bands from all over the country.

Banner for the Jazz Festival *(see p34)*

CLUBS

Most of the larger clubs are located in the industrial South of Market (SoMa) area, and run from around 9pm until

2am. A few stay open all night, especially on weekends, but all places stop serving alcohol at 2am. Always bring valid ID to prove you are over 21 or you will not be admitted. San Francisco's largest and most popular disco is **DNA Lounge** on 11th Street, with its multiple dance floors, flashy decor, great sound system, and fashionably mainstream clientele. R&B, hip-hop and jazz are played at **Nickie's BBQ** in Haight Ashbury. To dance to tunes spun by some of the best DJs in San Francisco, head to the **Bambuddha Lounge**. There's great dining on offer, too.

Suede is also a great place to dance the night away, with different Indie music every night. Check out **330 Ritch Street** for house music, goth, Brit pop, mod, Indie, R&B, and hip-hop. Some of the most popular clubs are primarily, though rarely exclusively, gay. These include **Endup** and **Rawhide**, which has square dancing every night.

Piano bars all have nightly live music that you can enjoy for the price of a drink. One of the best is the beautiful Art Deco-style **Top of the Mark** at the top of the Mark Hopkins Inter-Continental Hotel. Another good rooftop piano bar is **Grand View** on the 36th floor of Union Square's Grand Hyatt Hotel.

The Saloon on Grant Avenue, North Beach

Julie's **Supper Club** serves up good live jazz and R&B along with tasty Cajun food. The **Tonga Room** in the Fairmont Hotel is an elaborate cocktail bar where you can dance or just listen to jazz with a simulated rainstorm every half-hour.

Check local newspapers for comedy club listings. Some of the best stand-up comedy shows take place at **Tommy T's Comedy House**, as well as at **Marsh's Mock Cafe-Theater**, and **Cobb's Comedy Club** in Fisherman's Wharf. **Kimo's** features drag, cabaret, and comedy shows every week.

SPORTS AND OUTDOOR ACTIVITIES

San Franciscans are sports enthusiasts, and there are plenty of activities to suit every taste. Popular spectator sports include football,

baseball, and basketball. The home ground of the **San Francisco 49ers** is 3 Com Park; the **Oakland Raiders** play at Network Associates Coliseum in Oakland. Local colleges, including the **University of California at Berkeley** (see p418) and **Stanford University** (see p427), also have good football teams. Two professional baseball teams play in the Bay Area: the National League **San Francisco Giants** play their home games at the new stadium at SBC Park; the American League **Oakland Athletics** play at the Network Associates Coliseum, just across the bay in Oakland. The Bay Area's only NBA basketball team is the **Golden State Warriors**, who play at the Oakland Coliseum Arena.

Large business hotels usually have health club facilities on the premises. Those that do not usually have an

agreement with a private club that gives short-term membership to hotel guests. If neither of these options is available, choose from the upscale **Bay Club**, near the Financial District, the **Pacific Heights Health Club**, or the **24-Hour Nautilus Fitness Center**.

Golfers have a range of courses to choose from, including the municipal links in **Lincoln Park** and **Golden Gate Park**, and the beautiful **Presidio Golf Club**. The Presidio and Golden Gate Park area is also ideal for cycling. Rental shops here include **Stow Lake Bike Rentals**. In North Beach, **Blazing Saddles** also rents bikes. Most of the public swimming pools are on the suburban fringes: contact the **City of San Francisco Recreation and Parks Department**. To swim in the chilly ocean, head out to China Beach, the only safe beach in the city.

DIRECTORY

FILM AND THEATER

AMC Kabuki
1881 Post St.
Map 4 E4.
Tel (415) 346-3243.

American Conservatory Theater (ACT)
Geary Theater,
415 Geary St.
Map 5 B5.
Tel (415) 749-2228.

Castro Theatre
429 Castro St.
Map 10 D2.
Tel (415) 621-6120.

Clay
2261 Fillmore St.
Map 4 D3.
Tel 267-4893.

Curran Theater
445 Geary St.
Map 5 B5.
Tel 551-2000.

Embarcadero
Embarcadero Center
Map 6 D3.
Tel 267-4893.

Golden Gate Theater
1 Taylor St.
Map 5 B5.
Tel 551-2000.

Lumiere
1572 California St.
Map 4 F3.
Tel 267-4893.

The Marsh
1062 Valencia St.
Map 10 F3.
Tel (415) 826-5750.

Metro
2055 Union St.
Map 4 D2.
Tel 931-1685.

Opera Plaza
601 Van Ness Ave.
Map 4 F5.
Tel (415) 267-4893.

Orpheum Theater
1192 Market St.
Map 4 F5
Tel 551-2000.

San Francisco Film Society International Film Festival
Tel (415) 561-5000.
Fax (415) 551-5099.
www.sffs.org

Sony Metreon
101 Fourth St.
Map 5 C5.
Tel 369-6000.

Stage Door Theater
420 Mason St.
Map 5 B5.
Tel 749-2228.

UA Galaxy4
1585 Sutter St.
Map 4 F4.
Tel 474-2849.

OPERA, CLASSICAL MUSIC, AND DANCE

Florence Gould Theater
Legion of Honor,
Lincoln Park.
Map 1 C5.
Tel 863-3330.

Grace Cathedral
1051 Taylor St. **Map** 5 B4.
Tel 749-6300.
www.gracecathedral.org

Herbst Theatre
401 Van Ness Ave.
Map 4 F5.
Tel 621-6600.

LINES Contemporary Ballet
Yerba Buena Center for the Arts, 700 Howard St.
Map 5 C5.
Tel (415) 978-2787.

Louise M Davies Symphony Hall Box Office
201 Van Ness Ave.
Map 4 F5.
Tel (415) 864-6000.

ODC Performance Gallery
3153 17th St.
Map 10 E3.
Tel 863-9834.

Old First Presbyterian Church
1751 Sacramento St.
Map 4 F3.
Tel 474-1608.

Philharmonia Baroque Orchestra Box Office
180 Redwood St,
Suite 100.
Map 4 F5.
Tel 392-4400.

San Francisco Ballet
455 Franklin St. **Map** 4 F4.
Tel (415) 861-5600.
www.sfballet.org

San Francisco Opera Association
301 Van Ness Ave.
Map 4 F5.
Tel (415) 861-4008.

DIRECTORY

San Francisco Symphony Orchestra
201 Van Ness Ave.
Map 4 F5.
Tel (415) 864-6000.

Theater Artaud
450 Florida St.
Tel 626-4370.

Zellerbach Hall
UC Berkeley.
Tel (510) 642-9988.

ROCK, JAZZ, AND BLUES

Bimbo's 365 Club
1025 Columbus Ave.
Map 5 A2.
Tel 474-0365.
www.bimbo365clubs.com

Biscuits and Blues
401 Mason St.
Map 5 B5.
Tel (415) 292-2583.

Boom Boom Room
1601 Fillmore St. **Map** 10 F2. **Tel** (415) 673-8000.

Carnelian Room
555 California St, 52nd Fl.
Map 5 C4.
Tel 433-7500.

Enrico's
504 Broadway.
Map 5 C3.
Tel 982-6223.

Fillmore Auditorium
1085 Geary at Fillmore St.
Map 4 D4.
Tel (415) 346-6000.
www.thefillmore.com

Gold Dust Lounge
247 Powell St.
Map 5 B5.
Tel 397-1695.

Jazz at Pearl's
256 Columbus Ave.
Map 5 C3.
Tel (415) 291-8255.

The Saloon
1232 Grant Ave.
Map 5 C3.
Tel (415) 989-7666.

Lou's Pier 47
300 Jefferson St.
Map 5 B1.
Tel 771-5687.

Monterey Jazz Festival
2000 Fairgrounds Rd at Casa Verde, Monterey.
Tel (831) 373-3366.
www.montereyjazz
festival.org

Moose's
1652 Stockton St.
Map 5 B2.
Tel 989-7800.

San Francisco Blues Festival
Fort Mason. **Map** 4 E1.
Tel (415) 826-6837.
www.sfblues.com

Slim's
333 11th St. **Map** 10 F1.
Tel (415) 255-0333.
www.slims-sf.com

CLUBS

330 Ritch St
330 Ritch St.
Tel 541-9574.

Bambuddha Lounge
601 Eddy St. **Map** 5 A5.
Tel (415) 885-5088.

Cobb's Comedy Club
The Cannery at Beach St, 915 Columbus Ave. **Map** 5 A1. **Tel** (415) 928-4320.

DNA Lounge
375 11th St.
Tel 626-1409.

Endup
401 6th St.
Tel (415) 357-0827.

Grand View
Grand Hyatt Hotel
24th floor
345 Stockton St.
Map 5 C4.
Tel 398-1234.

Julie's Supper Club
1123 Folsom St.
Tel (415) 861-0707.

Kimo's
1351 Polk St. **Map** 4 F4.
Tel 885-4535.

Marsh's Mock Cafe-Theater
1074 Valencia.
Map 10 F3.
Tel 826-5750.

Nickie's BBQ
460 Haight St.
Map 10 E1.
Tel 621-6508.

Rawhide
280 7th St.
Tel (415) 621-1197.

Suede
383 Bay St. **Map** 5 B2.
Tel (415) 399-9555.

Tommy T's Comedy House
1655 Willow Pass Rd.
Tel (925) 686-6809.
www.tommyts.com

Tonga Room
950 Mason St.
Map 5 B4.
Tel 772-5278.

Top of the Mark
Mark Hopkins
Inter-Continental Hotel.
1 Nob Hill. **Map** 5 B4.
Tel (415) 616-6916.

SPORTS AND OUTDOOR ACTIVITIES

Bay Club
150 Greenwich St.
Map 5 C2.
Tel 433-2550.

Blazing Saddles
1095 Columbus Ave.
Map 5 A2. **Tel** 202-8888.
One of two branches.
www.blazingsaddles.com

City of San Francisco Recreation and Parks Department
Tennis Information.
Tel (415) 831-6302.
www.parks.sf.gov.org
Swimming Information.
Tel (415) 831-2747.

Golden Gate Park
(Municipal 9 hole).
Map 7 B2.
Tel 751-8987.

Golden State Warriors
Oakland Coliseum Arena.
Tel (1) (888) 479-4667.

Lincoln Park
(Municipal 18 hole). **Map** 1 C5. **Tel** (415) 221-9911.

Oakland Athletics, Oakland Raiders
Network Associates.
Coliseum, Oakland
Tel (800) 949-2626.

Pacific Heights Health Club
2356 Pine St.
Map 4 D4. **Tel** 563-6694.
www.ph2c.com

Presidio Golf Club
300 Finley Rd. **Map** 3 A3.
Tel 561-4653.

San Francisco 49ers
3Com Park.
Tel (415) 656-4900.

San Francisco Giants
Pacific Bell Park.
Tel (800) 972-2000.
www.sfgiants.com

Stanford University Athletics
Stanford University.
Tel (1 800) 232-8225.

Stow Lake Bike Rentals
Golden Gate Park.
Map 8 E2.
Tel 752-0347.

24-Hour Nautilus Fitness Center
1200 Van Ness St.
Map 4 F4.
Tel 776-2200.
www.24hourfitness.com
One of several branches.

UC Berkeley Intercollegiate Athletics
UC Berkeley.
Tel (1 800) 462-3277.

San Francisco's Bars

San Francisco has been a drinkers' town ever since the heady days of the Gold Rush *(see pp48–9)*, when there was a saloon for every 50 residents. The bawdy public houses of the mid-19th century no longer exist. Instead, today, you can drink with a view; grab a local brew; sip an elegant, sweet cocktail in a chic lounge; sample a fine local country vintage wine; mingle with cheering local fans at a sports bar; see satellite-broadcast matches from Europe and soak up charm and an occasional concert at an Irish Bar. Alternatively, you can observe how a notable segment of San Francisco's population parties at a gay bar.

ROOFTOP BARS

Those with a head for heights and a craving to be above the hills can visit the bars at the top of the towers in the city center. Grand Hyatt's **Grand View Lounge**, the **View Lounge** at Marriott Hotel, and **Top of the Mark** at the Mark Hopkins *(see p544)*, all offer splendid views and evening jazz along with dance music. The highest of these rooftop bars is the ritzy, 52-story **Carnelian Room** (tie and reservations are required). The second in line, **Cityscape**, is on the 46th floor of the Hilton Hotel, with no pillars to obstruct the view.

BEER BARS

For a more down-to-earth experience, visit one of the city's many beer bars, popular gathering places for the after-work crowd and weekend revelers. The best of these specialize in beers brewed by West Coast breweries, including San Francisco's fine Anchor Steam and Liberty Ale.

One of the best, the English **Mad Dog in the Fog**, is situated on Haight Street. **Magnolia Pub & Brewery**, in a 1903 Haight Victorian, retains its original wooden bar and name from ex-dancer, Magnolia Thunderpussy. **The Thirsty Bear**, known for tapas; the **SF Brewing Company** with a bargain happy hour; and the upscale **Gordon Biersch Brewery**, all make their own excellent beer on the premises. At the Pacific Ocean edge of Golden Gate Park, **Beach Chalet**'s brews combine with fine views.

COCKTAILS BARS

Traditional cocktail bars, with a chatty bartender holding court in front of rows of gleaming bottles, are great fun in San Francisco, and there are plenty of venues to choose from.

Singles often drink at **Harry Denton's Starlight Room**, and those in the need-to-be-seen crowd are in the Clift Hotel **Redwood Room**, with a backlit bar and upper tier cocktail prices. A lively bohemian crowd can be found along Columbus Avenue at **Specs'**, **Tosca**, and **Vesuvio** – a one-time beatnik hangout where a poular house drink is the Jack Kerouac (rum, tequila, orange/cranberry juice and lime). Banquettes, cocktail tables and Rat Pack-era decor mix with a relaxed North Beach crowd at **Tony Niks**.

Across town in the Mission District, **Elixir** is a neighborhood bar with darts, and a wooden back-bar in a Victorian building that once had a bootblack on the premises. **Buena Vista Café** is the 1952 birthplace of Irish Coffee and serves 2,000 glasses per day. The **Red Room Bar** is as close as it gets to a classic, deep color cocktail lounge. Find a playful, imitation ethnic theme at Southeast Asian **Bambuddha Lounge**, or the Thai-style **Lingba Lounge** offers exotic drinks and music on Potrero Hill. In other bars, such as **Café du Nord,** in a former Prohibition speakeasy, and the award-winning **Biscuits and Blues**, live jazz is also available.

WINE BARS

With the proximity to Northern California Wine Country, the **Ferry Plaza Wine Merchant Bar**, surrounded by artisan cheesemakers and bakers, is a fine spot to sample wines.

Champagne and candlelight create the atmosphere of the **Bubble Lounge**. On weekdays, the **London Wine Bar** caters to Financial District workers, craving a British atmosphere with their California vintages. **Diablo Grande Wine Gallery** features its own estate-bottled wines in SoMa's museum area. Across the street at **Vino Venue**, the ounce-at-a-time self-serve dispensing from an automated wine bar is a way to taste the 100 wines on offer before buying. Closer to SBC Park in SoMa, **Bacar** caters to elegant drinkers as well as thirsty baseball fans with 1,400 wines each night.

THEMED BARS

One of the best spots to connect with local passion is **Knuckles Sports Bar**, with more than 24 televisions for live broadcasts. Bring your own food or snacks to the drinks-only **Greens Sports Bar**. **Pat O'Shea's Mad Hatter** combines the sports bar with another San Francisco tradition, the Irish Bar. Good Irish cheer and ample Guinness are quaffed at **The Irish Bank** and **The Chieftain**.

GAY BARS

Watering holes popular with the gay, lesbian, bisexual, and transgendered range from leather, biker, latex, and fetish-specialized to bars favored simply because the clientele is predominatly of one type. The Castro, SoMa and Mission Districts are magnet areas. **Daddy's**, in the Castro, draws a Levi's and leather crowd. **The Stud** and **EndUp** keep drinks flowing with the dancing. In a city where few lesbian bars have survived, **Cherry Bar** hosts live music-filled nights for ladies. **Divas** is a well-known transgendered spot.

DIRECTORY

ROOFTOP BARS

Carnelian Room
52nd floor,
555 California St.
Map 5 C4.
Tel 433-7500.

Cityscape
46th floor,
Hilton Hotel,
333 O'Farrell St.
Map 5 B5.
Tel 923-5002.

Grand View Lounge
36th floor,
Grand Hyatt Hotel,
345 Stockton St.
Map 5 C4.
Tel 398-1234.

Top of the Mark
19th floor,
Mark Hopkins
InterContinental Hotel,
999 California St.
Map 5 B4.
Tel 616-6916.

View Lounge
39th floor,
Marriott Hotel 55
4th St.
Map 5 C5.
Tel 896-1600.

BEER BARS

Beach Chalet
1000 Great Hwy.
Map 7 A2.
Tel 386-8439.

Gordon Biersch Brewery
2 Harrison St.
Map 6 E4.
Tel 243-8246.

Mad Dog in the Fog
530 Haight St.
Map 10 E1.
Tel 626-7279.

Magnolia Pub & Brewery
1398 Haight St.
Map 9 C1.
Tel 864-7468.

S F Brewing Company
155 Columbus Ave.
Map 5 C3.
Tel 434-3344.

The Thirsty Bear
661 Howard St.
Map 6 D5.
Tel 974-0905.

COCKTAIL BARS

Bambuddha Lounge
661 Eddy St.
Map 5 A5.
Tel 885-5088.

Biscuits and Blues
401 Mason St.
Map 5 B5.
Tel 292-2583.

Buena Vista Café
2765 Hyde St.
Map 4 F1.
Tel 747-5044.

Café du Nord
2170 Market St.
Map 10 D2.
Tel 861-5016.

Elixir
3200 16th St.
at Valencia St.
Map 10 F2.
Tel 552-1633.

Harry Denton's Starlight Room
450 Powell St.
Map 5 B4.
Tel 395-8595.

Lingba Lounge
1469 18th St.
Map 11 C3.
Tel 355-0001.

Red Room Bar
827 Sutter St.
Map 5 B4.
Tel 346-7666.

Redwood Room
495 Geary St.
Map 5 B5.
Tel 775-4700.

Specs'
12 Adler Place
(across Columbus Ave
from Vesuvio).
Map 5 C3.
Tel 421-4112.

Tony Niks
1534 Stockton St.
Map 5 B2.
Tel 693-0990.

Tosca
242 Columbus Ave.
Map 5 C3.
Tel 391-1244.

Vesuvio
255 Columbus Ave.
Map 5 C3.
Tel 362-3370.

WINE BARS

Bacar
448 Brannan St.
Map 11 C1.
Tel 904-4100.

Bubble Lounge
714 Montgomery St.
Map 5 C3.
Tel 434-4204.

Diablo Grande Wine Gallery
669 Mission St.
Map 5 C5.
Tel 543-4343.

Ferry Plaza Wine Merchant Bar
One Ferry Building,
Shop 23.
Map 6 E3.
Tel 391-9400.

London Wine Bar
415 Sansome St.
Map 5 C3.
Tel 788-4811.

Vino Venue
686 Mission St.
Map 5 C5.
Tel 341-1930.

THEMED BARS

Knuckles Sports Bar
555 North Point St.
Map 5 A1.
Tel 563-1234.

Greens Sports Bar
2339 Polk St.
Map 5 A3.
Tel 775-4287.

Pat O'Shea's Mad Hatter
3848 Geary Blvd.
Map 3 A5.
Tel 752-3148.

The Chieftain
195 5th St.
Map 11 B1.
Tel 615-0916.

The Irish Bank
10 Mark La
(off Bush St).
Map 5 B4.
Tel 788-7152.

GAY BARS

Cherry Bar
917 Folsom St.
Map 11 B1.
Tel 974-1585.

Daddy's
440 Castro St.
Map 10 D3.
Tel 621-8732.

Divas
1081 Post St.
Map 4 F4.
Tel 434-4204.

Endup
401 6th St.
Map 11 B2.
Tel 646-0999.

The Stud
399 9th St.
Map 11 A2.
Tel 252-7883.

GETTING AROUND
SAN FRANCISCO

San Francisco occupies a compact area, making it a sightseer's dream. Many of the sights featured on visitors' itineraries are only a short walk from each other. The public transportation system is also easy to use and efficient. Few visitors can resist a cable car ride. Bus routes crisscross town and pass many attractions. Muni Metro streetcars and BART lines serve the suburbs and the outlying neighborhoods. Taxis are affordable and recommended (but often hard to find) for trips after dark or during the day through certain areas. Passenger ferries and boat trips run regularly east and north across the bay. If driving in San Francisco see page 633 for details on the city's parking laws.

Do not cross the street

You may cross the street

WALKING IN SAN FRANCISCO

The best way to explore San Francisco is on foot. The main tourist areas are within 15 to 20 minutes of each other walking at average speed. The hills can be a struggle, but the views over the city and the bay make them well worth the strenuous climb.

Most road intersections are marked with a green and white sign bearing the name of the cross street, or names are imprinted in the concrete pavement at street corners.

Vehicles are driven on the right-hand side of the road and are allowed to turn right on a red light if the road is clear, so be careful when crossing at traffic lights. Never rely solely on a pedestrian "Walk" signal.

Jaywalking is common but illegal. Using a crossing when the "Don't Walk" signal is showing can result in a minimum $50 fine.

TAKING A TAXI

Taxis in San Francisco are licensed and operate 24 hours a day. To catch a cab, wait at a taxi stand, call for a pick-up, or hail a cab when its rooftop sign is illuminated.

There is a flat fee (about $2) for the first mile (1.6 km). This increases by about $2 for each additional mile or 35 cents a minute while waiting at an address or in heavy traffic. Pay with bills of $20 or smaller and add a 15 percent tip onto the fare.

BICYCLING

Cycling is very popular in San Francisco, and it is possible to find routes that avoid hills, especially along the waterfront. Bicycles can be rented for around $25 a day or $125 a week. There are cycle lanes in parts of the city, and some buses are equipped to carry bikes strapped to the outside. Details of scenic routes in the area are available from **Bay City Bike** and **Start to Finish**.

OTHER WAYS TO GET AROUND

Pedicabs and horse-drawn carriages can be found on The Embarcadero, especially near Fisherman's Wharf (see *pp334–5*). A fleet of motorized cable cars dashes around the city giving guided tours of all the sights. Passengers can get on or off where they choose. Sightseeing bus tours are offered as half- or full-day trips.

A pedicab – an increasingly popular way of sightseeing

DIRECTORY

TAXI COMPANIES

City Cab
Tel (415) 920-0700.

De Soto Cab
Tel (415) 970-1300.

Veteran's Cab
Tel (415) 552-1300.

Yellow Cab
Tel (415) 626-2345.

BICYCLE RENTAL

Bay City Bike
2661 Taylor St,
Fishermans Wharf
Map 4 F1.
Tel (415) 346-2453.
www.baycitybike.com

Start to Finish
2530 Lombard St.
Map 3 C2.
Tel (415) 202-9830.

Wait for the "Walk" signal before using a crosswalk

Traveling by Bus and Muni Metro Streetcar

San Francisco Municipal Railway (Muni) is the organization that runs the city's public transportation system. You can use one interchangeable pass – Muni Passport – to travel on Muni buses, Muni Metro streetcars (electric trams), the F Market & Wharves historic streetcar line, and the three cable car lines. Buses and streetcars serve most tourist attractions and all neighborhoods.

FARES AND TICKETS

Buses and streetcars both cost $1.25 per ride. When paying your fare, you can request a free transfer, which will allow you to change to another bus or streetcar without paying an additional fare. The transfer is valid for 90 minutes. Reduced fares are available for senior citizens over 65 and children aged five to 17 years. Kids under five travel free.

A Muni Passport, valid for one, three, or seven days, allows unlimited travel on buses, streetcars, and cable cars. Passports are available from information kiosks at San Francisco International airport, the **Visitors' Information Center** outside Powell Street BART/Metro station, and the cable car ticket booths at Powell & Market and Hyde & Beach streets.

USING BUSES AND STREETCARS

Buses stop only at their designated bus stops every two or three blocks. The route number and the destination are found on the front and side of each bus. Route numbers followed by a letter (L, EX, A, etc.) are limited-stop or express services.

Muni Metro streetcar with its distinctive red and silver cars

On boarding, put the exact change or tokens in the fare box or show your Muni Passport to the driver. To indicate that you want to get off at the next stop, pull the cord that runs along the windows or inform the driver. The "Stop Requested" sign above the front window will light up. Bus stops have signs displaying the Muni logo. The walls of the shelter list the route numbers of buses that stop there, and provide route maps and frequency guides.

Muni Passports

Muni Metro streetcars and BART trains *(see p398)* share four of the seven underground stations along Market Street, marked by orange, yellow, and white illuminated signs. Once inside, look for the separate "Muni" entrance.

To travel west of the city, choose "Outbound"; to travel east, choose "Downtown." Electronic signs indicate which streetcar is about to arrive. Doors open automatically on boarding; if they don't open when you're at a low-level or street-level station, push on the low bar beside the exit. Stops above ground level have an orange-and-brown flag or a yellow band around a pole, marked "Muni" or "Car Stop."

SIGHTSEEING BY BUS

Popular bus routes for visitors include numbers 15, 30, 39, 45, and 47. Route 38 runs to the hills above Ocean Beach; Golden Gate Park *(see pp366–9)* is on Routes 5, 21, 71, and N. For Chinatown *(see pp324–31)* take Routes 30 or 45; Nob Hill is on Route 1 or the California Street cable car line; for Haight Ashbury *(see pp354–63)* take Route 6, 7, or 71; Mission District is on Route 14. The Bay Area *(see pp410–31)* can be reached in about 30 to 45 minutes.

Muni bus shelter with glass walls and pay phones

DIRECTORY

MUNI INFORMATION

Tel *(415) 673-6864.*
www.sfmuni.com

MUNI PASSPORTS

Visitor Information Center
Hallidie Plaza. **Map** 5 C5.
Tel *(415) 391-2000.*
www.transitinfo.org

Route numbers shown on the front and side of the bus

Traveling by Cable Car, BART, and Ferry

San Francisco's cable cars are world famous (see pp302–3) and every visitor will want to ride one at least once. San Francisco peninsula and the East Bay are linked by BART (Bay Area Rapid Transit), a 71-mile (114-km) light rail system with a high speed, efficient fleet of trains, all wheelchair accessible. Boats and passenger ferries are also a favorite way to see the city's shoreline and get around.

Nob Hill, where the Powell and California lines cross

The thrilling descent down Hyde Street to the bay

USING THE CABLE CARS

The city's cable car service operates from 6:30am to 12:30am daily with special schedules at weekends. (For a complete timetable visit www.transitinfo.org.) There is a flat fare of $3 for a single trip with a discount for seniors and the disabled between 9pm and 7am. Cable cars run along three routes. The name of the line is displayed on the front, back, and sides of every cable car. The Powell–Hyde line is the most popular, starting at the Powell and Market turntable (see p321) and

ending on Hyde Street, near Aquatic Park. The Powell–Mason line also begins at Powell and Market streets and ends at Bay Street. Sit facing east on the Powell lines and you will see the best sights as you travel. The California line runs from the base of Market Street, then through part of the Financial District and Chinatown, ending at Van Ness Avenue. Cable cars run at 15-minute intervals.

To catch a cable car, you should be prepared to jump on board quickly. Stops are marked by maroon signs that display the outline of a cable car in white, or by a yellow line painted on the road at right angles to the track.

If you have not purchased a Muni Passport (see p397), you can buy a ticket or a one-day pass from the conductor. Tickets are collected once you board. Muni passes, souvenir tickets and maps are available at kiosks at Powell and Market streets and at Hyde and Beach streets, or at the city Visitor Information Center (see p397).

Commuters use cable cars too, so try to avoid traveling during rush hours if possible. Whenever you travel you are more likely to get a seat if you board the car at the start of the line you have chosen.

SIGHTSEEING BY CABLE CAR

The city's hills present no problem to the cable cars. They tackle precipitous slopes effortlessly, passing sights and areas popular with tourists. The most thrilling descent is the final stretch of the Powell–Hyde line as it dips down from Nob Hill to the bay.

TRAVELING SAFELY IN A CABLE CAR

If there is not a crowd, you can choose whether to sit or stand inside, sit outside on a bench, or stand on a side running board. If you choose the latter, ensure you hold on tightly to the "hang on" poles that are provided for your safety.

Try not to get in the way of the gripman; he needs a lot of room to operate the grip lever. This off-limits area is marked by yellow lines on the floor. Use caution while on board. Passing other cable cars is exciting, but be careful not to lean out too far because they get very close to one another. Be careful when boarding or getting off. Often cable cars stop at an intersection, and you have to get on or off between the car and other vehicles. All passengers must get off at the end of the line.

USEFUL NUMBERS

Cable Car Barn
1201 Mason St. **Map** 5 B3.
Museum Tel (415) 474-1887.

Muni Information
Tel (415) 673-6864. Cable car information, fares, Muni Passports.

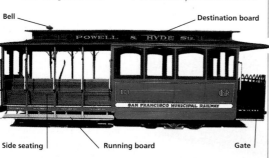

Bell — — Destination board

POWELL & HYDE Sts.

SAN FRANCISCO MUNICIPAL RAILWAY

Side seating — Running board — Gate

A San Francisco cable car

MAKING A JOURNEY BY BART

The BART logo

BART trains operate daily from early morning until midnight. During rush hours, 7am to 9am and 4pm to 7pm, they run at full capacity. The trains are clean and well kept, and the service is highly efficient.

BART trains stop at five central stations, all underneath Market Street – Van Ness, Civic Center, Powell, Montgomery, and Embarcadero. From here you can catch the train straight to the San Francisco International Airport.

All trains from Daly City stop at city center stations before heading for the East Bay through a dark, 4-mile (6-km) underwater tunnel.

BART ROUTE MAP

Transfers in the East Bay are best done at two stations: MacArthur and Oakland City. To explore the BART system without buying a new ticket each time you travel, you can purchase an excursion fare. All BART stations ensure that personnel are on hand to assist passengers.

KEY

— Richmond–Daly City

— Millbrae–Bay Point

— Fremont–Daly City

— Fremont–Richmond

— Pleasanton–SF Airport

— Millbrae–SF Airport

FERRY SERVICES AND DAY TRIPS

Residents of the Bay Area adore their ferries, and they are used as much by local commuters to and from the city as they are by tourists. Although these ferries do not provide audio tours to point out and describe the sights, they are less expensive than sightseeing cruises.
The Ferry Building (see p316) is the terminal for **Golden Gate Ferries**.

Bay sightseeing cruises from Fisherman's Wharf are operated by **Blue & Gold Fleet** and **Red & White Fleet**. Excursions offered include Angel Island, Alcatraz (see pp338–9), and towns that lie on the north shore of the bay (see pp414–15). There are also combined boat and bus tours to Six Flags Marine World and Muir Woods (see p414).

You can dine and dance aboard one of several cruisers that ply the bay's waters.
Hornblower Dining Yachts

offer lunch on Friday, brunch on weekends, and dinner daily on their cruises. Meals are also served at bayside tables that offer diners spectacular views of the waterfront. The **Oceanic Society** offers trips with an onboard naturalist around the Farallon Islands, which lie 25 miles (40 km) off the coast of San Francisco (see pp412–13). Whale-watching expeditions off the city's west coast (see p614) are also available, but you

should check with individual operators for seasonal details.

DIRECTORY

FERRIES

Blue & Gold Fleet
Pier 39 & 41. **Map** 5 B1.
Tel 773-1188. 75-minute tour.
www.blueandgoldfleet.com

Golden Gate Ferries
Tel 923-2000.

BAY TRIPS

Hornblower Dining Yachts
Pier 33. **Map** 5 C1.
Tel 394-8900, ext. 7.
Dinner and dancing cruises.

Oceanic Society Expeditions
Tel 441-1104.
www.oceanicsociety.org

Red & White Fleet
Pier 43½. **Map** 5 B1.
Tel 447-0597.
www.redandwhite.com

Red & White Fleet ferry

SAN FRANCISCO STREET FINDER

Map references given with sights, entertainment venues, shops and Practical Information addresses described in the San Francisco section refer to the maps on the following pages. Map references for hotels and restaurants in the city (see pp542–9 and pp587–95) also apply to these pages.

The key map below shows the area covered by the Streetfinder, including the sightseeing areas and other districts important for restaurants, hotels, and entertainment venues. A large scale map of the city center appears on pages 5 and 6. The symbols used on the Street Finder maps are listed in the key below.

KEY TO STREET FINDER

- ▮ Major sight
- ▮ Places of interest
- 🚊 CalTrain station
- 🚇 BART station
- 🚌 Long distance bus terminus
- 🚋 Streetcar station
- 🚌 Bus terminus
- 🚠 Cable car terminus
- ⛴ Ferry boarding point
- ℹ Tourist information office
- ✚ Hospital with emergency unit
- 🚓 Police station
- ✝ Church
- ✡ Synagogue
- ☪ Mosque
- 卍 Buddhist temple
- 🛕 Hindu temple
- ⊠ Post Office
- ⛳ Golf course
- ═ Railroad line
- ▬ Freeway
- <<665 House number (main street)

SCALE OF MAPS 1–4 AND 7–10

| 0 meters | 500 |
| 0 yards | 500 |

SCALE OF MAPS 5 & 6

| 0 meters | 500 |
| 0 yards | 500 |

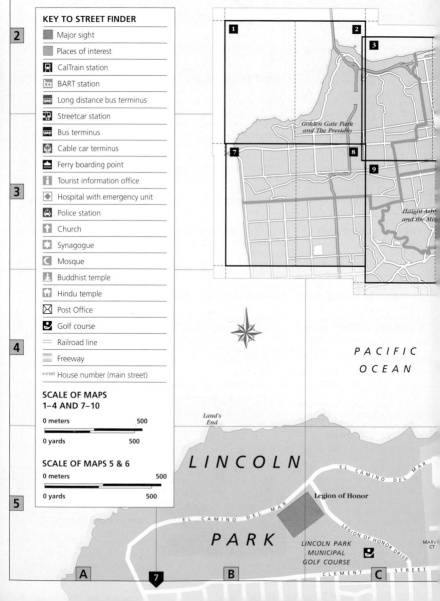

PACIFIC OCEAN

Golden Gate Park and The Presidio

Haight Ashbury and the Mission

Land's End

LINCOLN

PARK

Legion of Honor

EL CAMINO DEL MAR

LINCOLN PARK MUNICIPAL GOLF COURSE

CLEMENT STREET

LEGION OF HONOR DRIVE

MARVE CT

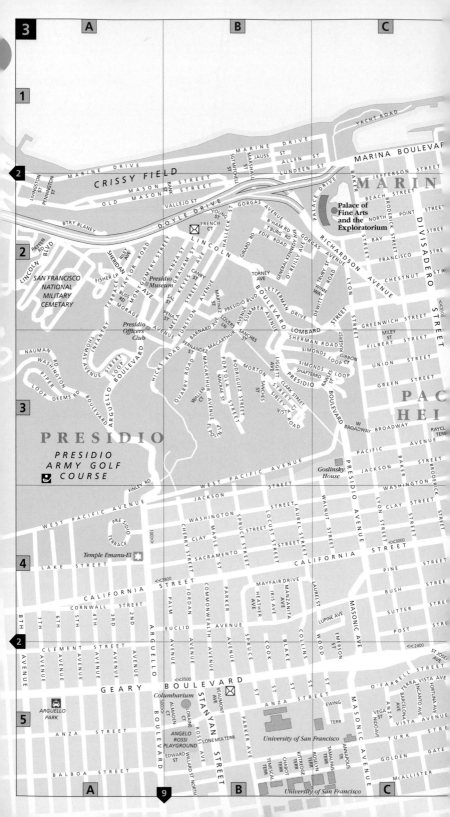

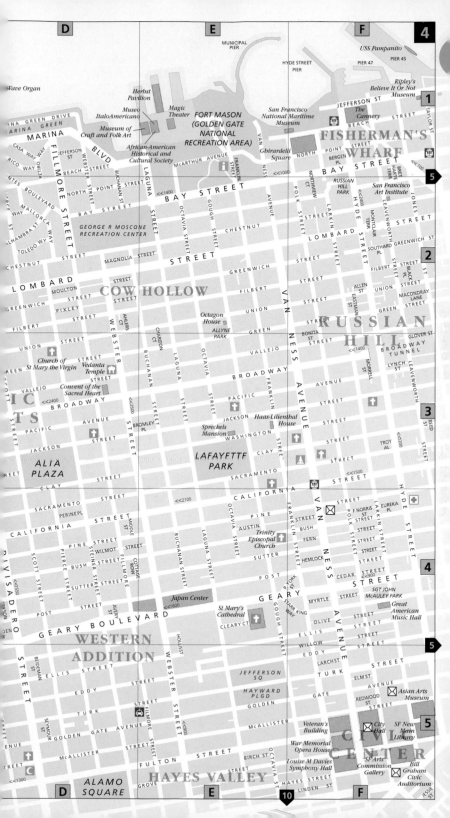

D   E   F   **6**

1

Alcatraz
Island

27

PIER 23

2

PIER 19

PIER 17

PIER 15

PIER 9

San Francisco

*Pier
7*

Bay

PIER 5

STREET

DAVIS STREET

PIER 3

THE EMBARCADERO

PIER 1

3

CKSON STREET

DRUMM STREET

World Trade Center

ASHINGTON STREET

PIER 2

MARITIME
PLAZA

EMBARCADERO
PLAZA PARK

JUSTIN
HERMAN
PLAZA

Ferry Building

Embarcadero Center

Hyatt Regency
Hotel

RAMENTO

FRONT ST

DAVIS ST

<< 200 STREET

STEUART STREET

Embarcadero
Station

STREET

STREET

SPEAR STREET

Rincon
Center

ic Coast
e Exchange

Amtrak
Terminal
Ticket Office

MISSION STREET

MAIN STREET

PIER 24

4

BEALE STREET

Folsom
Station

STEVENSON
ST

Greyhound
Bus Depot

FREMONT STREET

HOWARD STREET

STREET

gomery
ation

MINNA STREET

1ST

Transbay
Terminal

100>>

PIER 26

2ND

MALDEN

TEHAMA STREET

CLEMENTINA ST

FOLSOM STREET

ELKHART ST

2ZERO PL

350>>

PIER 28

oon
Museum

STREET

ALLY

GUY PL

GROTE
STREET

STREET

THE EMBARCADERO

PIER 30

Pacific
Telephone
Building

HAWTHORNE STREET

LANSING ST

<<460

Museum of
Modern Art

ESSEX STREET

PIER 32

DOW PL

STREET

oscone
vention
enter

HAMPTON
PL

VERONICA PL

HARRISON STREET

BRYANT
STREET

RINCON
ST

1ST

Brannan
Station

340>>

PIER 34

BRANNAN STREET

PIER 36

350>>

STILLMAN ST

DE BOOM
ST

PIER 38

D   E   F

SAN FRANCISCO OAKLAND BAY BRIDGE

5

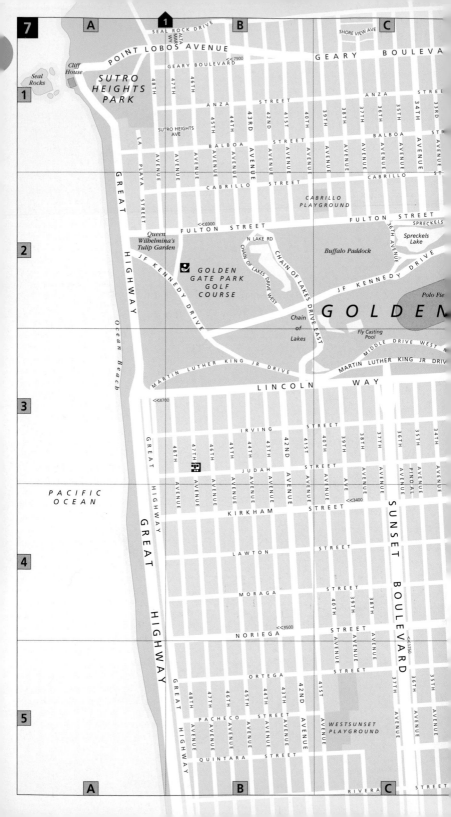

THE BAY AREA

Many of the settlements encircling San Francisco Bay were once summer retreats for the city's residents, but today they are sprawling suburbs or cities in their own right. Two of the most popular destinations in the East Bay are Oakland's museum and harbor and Berkeley's gardens and famous university. Farther south, San Jose has emerged as the region's newest commercial and cultural center, combining the technology of Silicon Valley with fine museums and preserved architecture of its Spanish Colonial past. Smaller towns such as Tiburon, Pescadero, and Sausalito, however, have managed to retain their village atmosphere, despite their closeness to the city. The area also has the advantage of its coastal landscapes: the cliffs of Point Reyes and the Marin Headlands, with their abundance of wildlife, offer perfect afternoon retreats away from the metropolis.

**Detail from
Sather Gate, Berkeley**

SIGHTS AT A GLANCE

Historic Towns
Benicia **8**
Berkeley **9**
Livermore **13**
Oakland **10**
Pescadero **16**
San Jose **17**
Sausalito **5**
Tiburon **6**

Theme Parks
Six Flags
  Marine World **7**

Historic Buildings
Filoli **15**
Stanford University **14**
Tao House **11**

Parks and Beaches
John Muir National Historic
  Site **2**
Marin Headlands **4**
Mount Diablo State Park **12**
Muir Woods and Beach **3**
Point Reyes National
  Seashore **1**

0 kilometers   25

0 miles   25

KEY

	Central San Francisco
	Urban areas
✈	Airport
	Amtrak station
	Major road
	Minor road

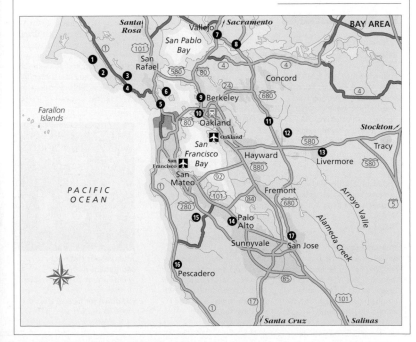

◁ Houseboats in the picturesque town of Sausalito

The Bay Area Coastline

The coastline around San Francisco varies a great deal, its rugged cliffs alternating with sandy beaches. Since the ocean water hovers around 60° F (15° C) all year, nobody swims or surfs without a wet suit, but for sunbathing or aimless beachcombing strolls, the Bay Area beaches are hard to beat. Much of the coast is protected by a series of state and federal parks, such as the Point Reyes National Seashore *(see p406)*, the Marin Headlands section of the Golden Gate National Recreation Area *(pp416–17)*, and the many state beaches that line the southern coast.

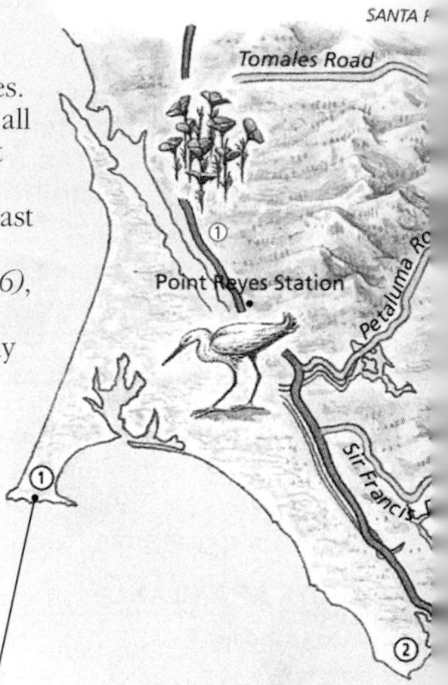

Pacifica *was once the agricultural outpost of Mission Dolores* (see p361). *The two-story Sanchez Adobe in the town now houses a museum of 19th-century farming equipment.*

★ **Point Reyes National Seashore** ①

This protected stretch of land is noted for its diverse eco-systems and its 360 species of birds *(see p414)*.

Bolinas ②

Following the Gold Rush *(see pp48–9)*, Bolinas became a summer haven for San Franciscans, and some Victorian buildings still survive. The town is also a winter home to monarch butterflies.

Marin Headlands ④

The Marin Headlands benefit from stunning views of San Francisco as well as a wilderness rife with diverse birdlife *(see pp416–17)*.

Treasure Island ⑥

At the center of the Bay Bridge *(see pp416–17)*, the island was the site of the 1939 World's Fair. Connected to Yerba Buena Island, Treasure Island is now an upscale community.

Fort Funston ⑦

The bluff overlooking this beach, which is also used as an observation site, is a favorite launch site for professional and amateur hang gliders.

Colma ⑧

This unusual town consists almost entirely of cemeteries, containing the graves of former San Franciscans and Bay Area residents. Cemeteries are prohibited within the city of San Francisco.

Pillar Point Harbor ⑨

This is the only naturally protected harbor located between San Francisco and Santa Cruz. In the late 19th century it was used as a whaling station.

★ **Farallon Islands** ⑫

Twenty-seven miles (44 km) west of Point Bonita, the islands are the most important nesting site for sea birds and stopover point for migratory birds in California. They are also a breeding ground for elephant seals. There is no public access.

Muir Woods National Monument *is the last remaining redwood forest in the Bay Area. The others were cut down for lumber during the 19th century* (see p414).

SANTA R

Tomales Road

①

Point Reyes Station

②

⑫

Peṭaluma Rd

Sir Francis

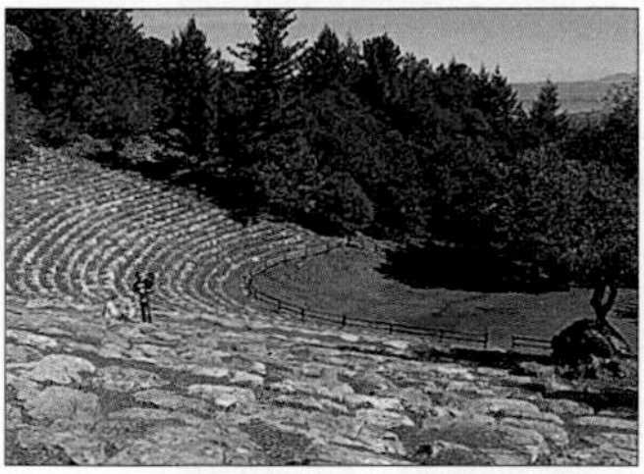

Mount Tamalpais, *reaching a height of 2,604 ft (794 m), is the habitat of various flora and fauna, including the rarely sighted mountain lion. The Mountain Theater is set in a natural bowl overlooking the bay.*

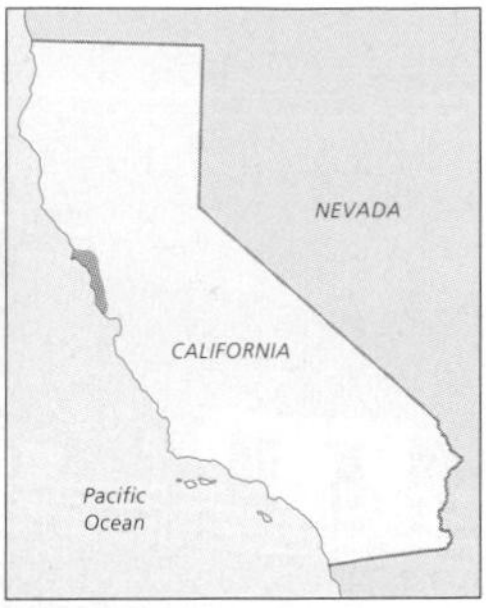
NEVADA
CALIFORNIA
Pacific Ocean

LOCATOR MAP

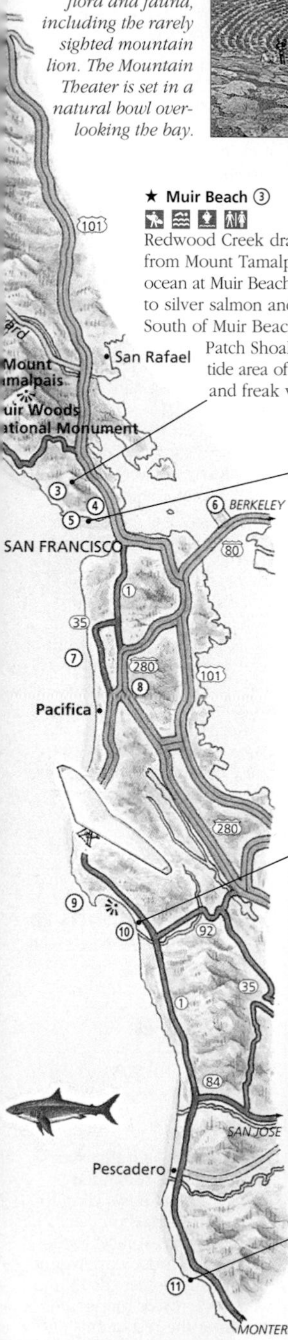
101
San Rafael
Mount
BERKELEY
80
SAN FRANCISCO
1
35
280
101
Pacifica
280
92
35
1
84
SAN JOSE
Pescadero
MONTEREY
0 kilometers 10
0 miles 10

★ Muir Beach ③

🚶 🌊 ⛱ 🚻

Redwood Creek drains down from Mount Tamalpais to the ocean at Muir Beach. It is home to silver salmon and crayfish. South of Muir Beach, Potato Patch Shoal is a low-tide area of turbulence and freak waves.

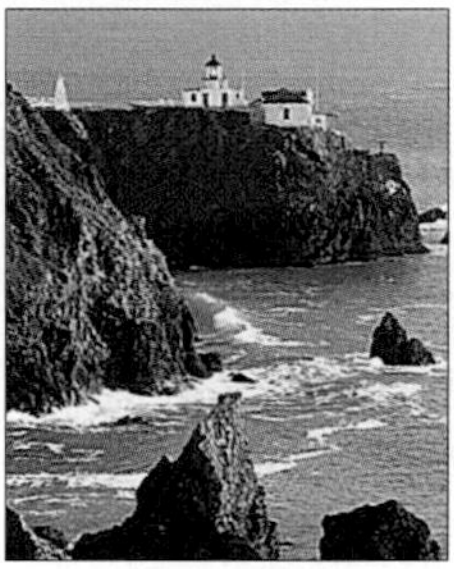

★ Point Bonita ⑤

Point Bonita's lighthouse on this rugged clifftop was the last manually operated lighthouse in the state, only changing to automation in 1980. The lighthouse is reached via a tunnel carved through solid rock or over a surf-lashed bridge.

★ Half Moon Bay ⑩

🚶 🌊 ⛱ ♿ 🚻 🐚

The oldest town in San Mateo County, the area's soil is ideal for growing artichokes, broccoli, and pumpkins. The town holds a pumpkin festival each October in celebration of its prime crop.

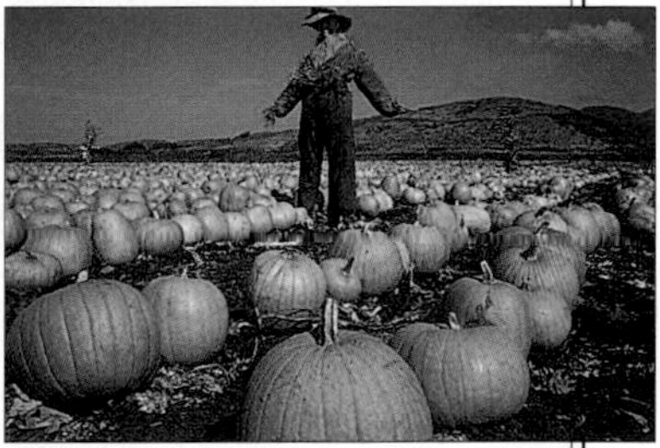

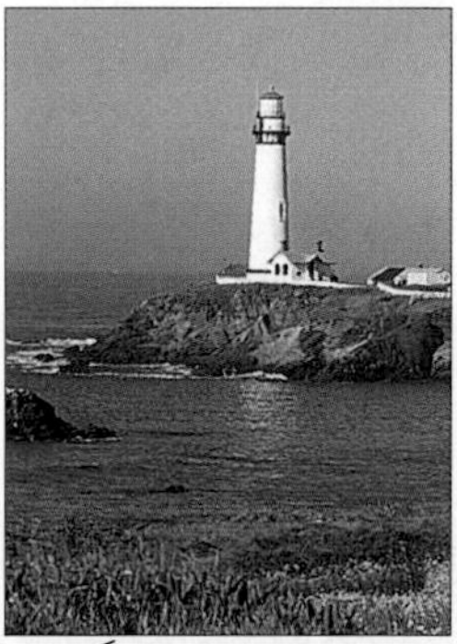

★ Pigeon Point ⑪

🚶 🌊 ⛱

Following numerous shipwrecks in the area, including the *Carrier Pigeon,* which gave the area its name, a 115-ft (35-m) lighthouse was erected in 1872. Sea lions can often be spotted offshore.

KEY

- Freeway
- Major road
- Minor road
- River
- Viewpoint

Dairy farm at picturesque Point Reyes

Point Reyes National Seashore ❶

Road map A3. 🚌 *from San Rafael Center (weekends only).* **Bear Valley Visitors' Center** *Bear Valley Rd, main entrance to National Seashore, Point Reyes.* **Tel** *(415) 464-5100.* ⏷ *9am–5pm daily.*

This triangular-shaped area of land, only half attached to the San Franciscan coastline, has been gradually drifting north-ward along the California coast for more than six million years. Situated due west of the San Andreas Fault, the peninsula moved a full 20 ft (6 m) north of the mainland during the 1906 earthquake *(see pp52–3).* A displaced fence on the Earthquake Trail near Bear Valley Visitor Center is evidence of this overnight movement. The visitors' center itself contains interesting displays on local geology and geography and supplies and trail maps for hikers.

Signpost to Point Reyes

A notable feature of this stretch of coastline is its abundance of wildlife, including a herd of tule elk. The area has cattle and dairy ranches, and three small towns: Point Reyes Station, Olema, and Inverness.

Drake's Bay is named after the English explorer Sir Francis Drake, who is thought to have anchored here in 1579. He named the land Nova Albion and briefly claimed it for England *(see pp46–7).*

John Muir National Historic Site ❷

4202 Alhambra Ave, Martinez. **Tel** *(925) 228-8860.* ⏷ *10am–5pm Wed–Sun.* ⬤ *Jan 1, Thanksgiving, Dec 25.* 🎟️ 🚻 *1st floor & grounds only.* **www**.nps.gov/jomu

Set amid the suburban neighborhood of Martinez, the John Muir National Historic Site preserves the home where the naturalist and writer lived from 1890 until his death in 1914. The 17-room Italianate house is typical of a late Victorian upper-middle-class dwelling, conveying little of Muir's simple tastes and back-to-nature inclinations. Only the library, which Muir called his "scribble den," gives a real sense of the man. The house was once surrounded by 2,600 acres (1,052 ha) of fruit trees, only one of which survives. In season, rangers pick fruit for visitors to sample.

John Muir (1838–1914)

Muir Woods and Beach ❸

📷 *Mill Valley.* **Visitors' Center** *Hwy 1, Mill Valley.* **Tel** *(415) 388-2595.* ⏷ *8am–5pm daily.*

Nestling at the foot of Mount Tamalpais *(see pp413)* is Muir Woods National Monument, one of the few remaining stands of old-growth coastal redwoods. Before the 19th-century lumber industry flourished, these tall trees (the oldest is at least 1,000 years old) once completely covered the coastal area of California. The woods were named in honor of John Muir, the 19th-century naturalist responsible for turning Yosemite into a national park *(see pp488–91).*

Redwood Creek bubbles out of Muir Woods and makes its way down to the ocean at Muir Beach, a wide expanse of sand popular with beachcombers and picnickers *(see pp412–13).* Along the road to the beach is the incongruous Pelican Inn, a 16th-century-style English inn – proud of its traditional English menu, with items such as roast beef, and offering visitors a warm welcome.

Muir Beach is likely to be crowded at weekends, especially during the summer, but visitors who are prepared to walk for 15 minutes or more along the sand are rewarded with peace and quiet.

Marin Headlands ❹

See pp416–17.

Sausalito ❺

Road map inset B. 🏠 *7,300.* 🚗 🚌 ⛴️ ℹ️ *777 Bridgeway Ave, 4th flr (415 332-0505).*

In this small town that was once a fishing community, Victorian bungalows cling to steep hills rising from San Francisco Bay. Parallel to the waterfront, Bridgeway Avenue serves as a promenade for the weekend crowds that come to patronize the restaurants and shops and enjoy the views.

Harbor scene in Sausalito

These unique buildings are in fact houseboats from the early 20th century that have been pulled ashore and innovatively refurbished. They now stand in what is called "Ark Row."

Less hectic than nearby Sausalito, Tiburon is a good town for walking. Parks are situated along the waterfront from which you can contemplate the bay. At night, the harbor shines with fairy lights.

The **Bay Model Visitor Center** is a unique and fascinating hydraulic model that simulates the movement of the tides and currents in San Francisco Bay, and in the bay-delta system.

Bay Model Visitor Center
2100 Bridgeway Ave. **Tel** (415) 332-3871. ☐ Sep–May: Tue–Fri; Jun–Aug: Tue–Sun. ☐ public hols. **www**.spn.usace.army.mil/bmvc

Tiburon ❻

Road map inset B. 🏠 8,200. 🚇 🚢 ℹ 96B Main St (415 435-5633).

The main street of this elegant waterfront town is lined with fashionable shops and restaurants housed in "arks."

Six Flags Marine World ❼

Road map inset B. **Tel** (707) 643-6722. 🚇 🚌 🚢 from San Francisco. ☐ Jun–Aug: 10am–8pm Sun–Fri, 10am–7pm Sat; Mar–May: 10am–7pm Wed–Sun. ☐ Dec 25, Thanksgiving. 🎫 ♿ 🎥 **www**.sixflags.com

The most unique wildlife park and oceanarium in Northern California, Six Flags Marine World attracts 1.6 million visitors each year. Its lush 160-acre (65-ha) site is located along I-80 at Hwy 37 on the outskirts of Vallejo. There is equal emphasis on education and

Sign for Marine World

entertainment in the park, but the primary attractions are the shows featuring marine mammals. Arenas housing large pools showcase killer whales, sea lions, and dolphins. In the Shark Experience, visitors walk by way of a transparent tunnel through a tank filled with large sharks and tropical fish swimming overhead.

Land animal attractions include shows featuring Bengal tigers and baboons, an aviary of exotic birds and colorful tropical butterflies.

Benicia ❽

Road map inset B. 🏠 24,400. 🚌 🚇 🚢 ℹ Benicia Chamber of Commerce, 601 1st St (707 745-2120).

Set on the north side of the Carquinez Straits, the narrow waterway through which the Sacramento and the San Joaquin rivers flow from the Sierra Nevada to San Francisco Bay, Benicia is one of California's most historic small towns.

From February 1853 until February 1854, Benicia served as an early state capital. The Greek Revival building that once housed the government has been preserved as a state historic park, complete with many original fixtures and furnishings. Next door to the former capitol, the Fisher-Hanlon House, a former Gold Rush hotel, has also been restored to its original condition as part of **Benicia State Historic Park**.

At the other end of Main Street from the capitol complex is the Benicia waterfront where ferries shuttled to Port Costa during the 1850s. The former Benicia Arsenal, which stored army weapons from the 1850s to the 1950s, has now been converted into studio space for local artists and craftspeople.

Benicia State Historic Park
1st & G Sts. **Tel** (707) 745-3385. ☐ 10am–5pm Wed–Sun . ☐ Jan 1, Thanksgiving, Dec 25. 🎫

Attractive main street of Tiburon

A 90-Minute Walk through the Marin Headlands [4]

At its northern end, the Golden Gate Bridge is anchored in the rolling green hills of the Marin Headlands. This is an unspoiled wild area of windswept ridges, sheltered valleys, and deserted beaches, once used as a military defense post and now part of the vast Golden Gate National Recreation Area. From several vantage points there are spectacular views of San Francisco and vast panoramas of the sea, and, on autumn days you can see migrating eagles and ospreys gliding past Hawk Hill.

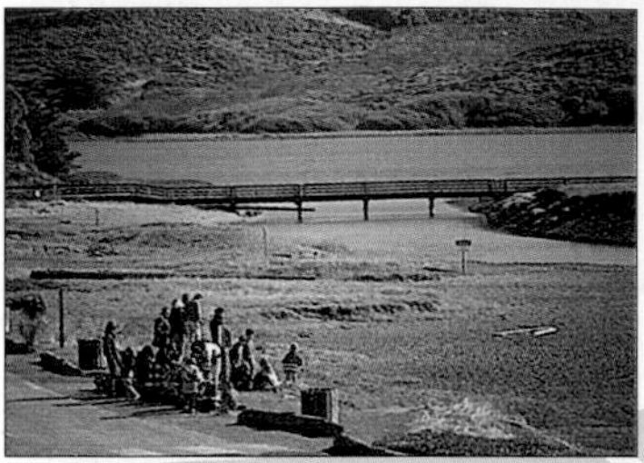

Schoolchildren on a trip to the Marin Headlands

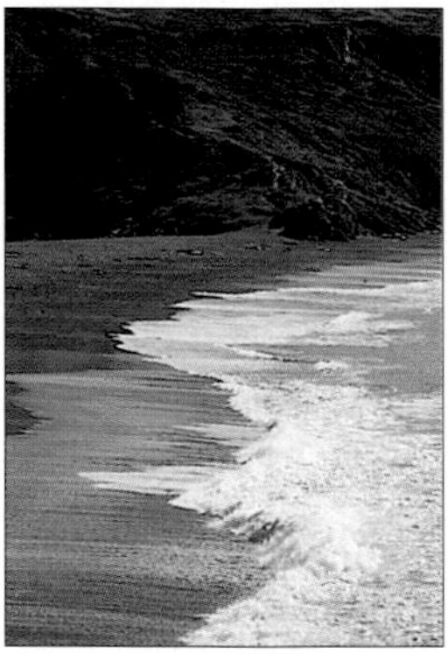

Rodeo Beach ③

Visitors' Center to Rodeo Beach

Before starting this walk, pause a while at the steepled Visitors' Center ①, which was once the interdenominational chapel for Fort Cronkhite. It has since been refurbished and is now a museum and information center, with a natural history bookshop that specializes in books on birds. Here you can discover the history of the Marin Headlands and see a Coast Miwok Indian shelter. The walk, which will take you around Rodeo Lagoon ②, begins at the gate on the west, ocean side, of the parking lot. Take the path to the left that leads to the sea. This part of the trail is thick with trees and shrubs, including poison oak, of which visitors should be aware. The songs of birds fill the air and around the edges of the lagoon you will see brown pelicans, snowy egrets, and mallards.

A 15-minute walk will bring you to the sandy, wind-blown Rodeo Beach ③, and from here you can see Bird Island ④ lying offshore

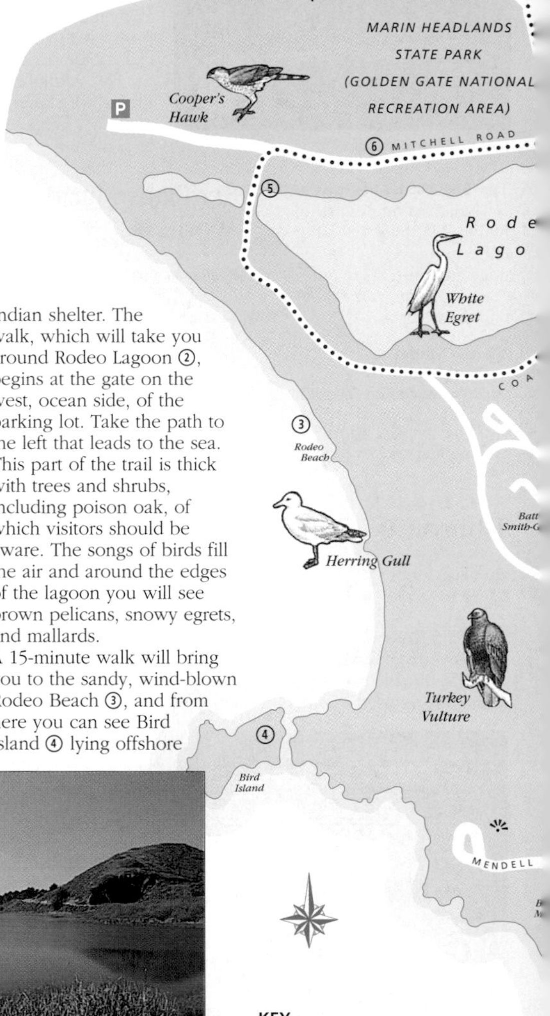
MARIN HEADLANDS STATE PARK (GOLDEN GATE NATIONAL RECREATION AREA)
Cooper's Hawk
⑥ MITCHELL ROAD
⑤
White Egret
③ Rodeo Beach
Herring Gull
Turkey Vulture
④ Bird Island
MENDELL

KEY

- ••• Walk route
- ✲ Viewpoint
- [P] Parking

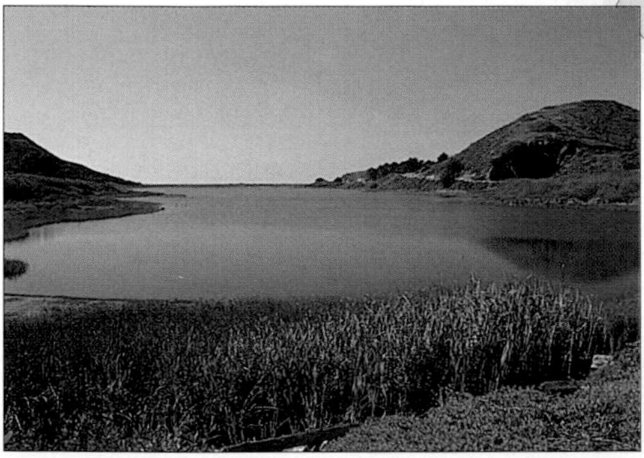

Rodeo Lagoon ②

For hotels and restaurants in this region see pp549–51 and pp595–7

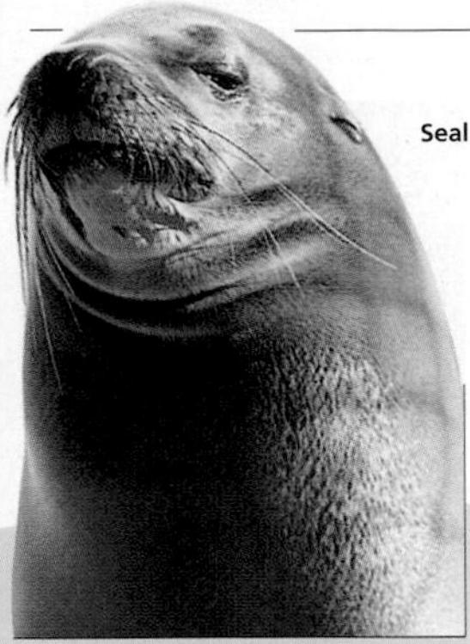
Seal at the Marine Mammal Center [7]

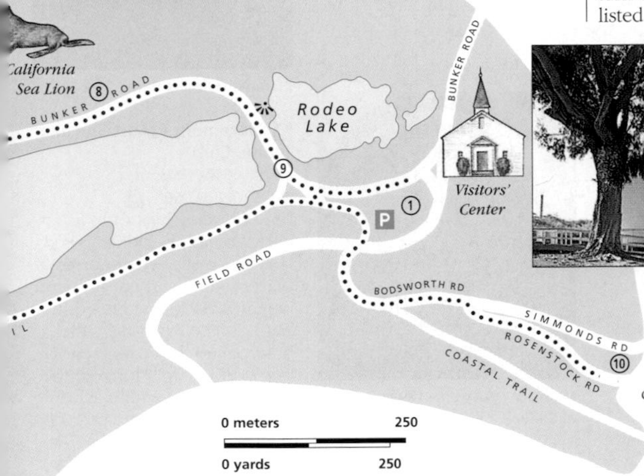

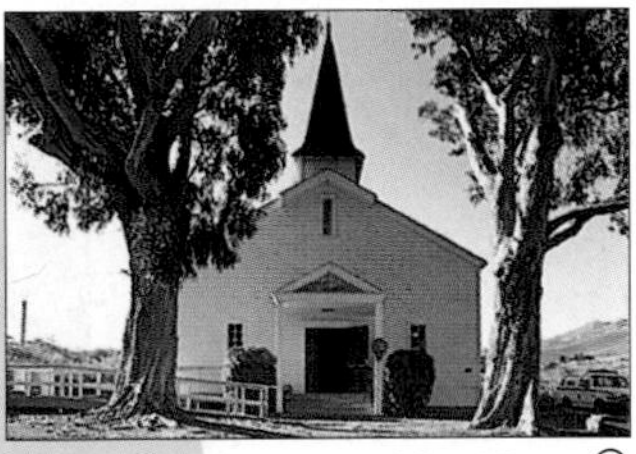
Visitors' Center [1]

to the south. Fishing boats may be seen bobbing out at sea, but the beach is mostly empty of people, although sometimes you might see groups of children working on coastal ecology programs. These are run by the Headlands Institute, which is based in the nearby clutch of former army barracks.

Barracks to the California Marine Mammal Center

From the beach, turn inland again as you approach the tip of the lagoon, crossing a wooden footbridge [5]. Here there are lavatories, and barracks [6] housing various offices, among them the Headlands District Office, the Raptor Observatory, and an energy and resources center. Walking past the barracks, continue along the path, then turn left at the road that climbs a steep hill to the California Marine Mammal Center [7]. This was used as a missile defense site during the Cold War, but is now run by volunteers who rescue and care for sick or injured marine mammals. Sea lions and seals, including the rare elephant seals are examined and treated here, in specially designed pens. They are then returned to the sea when they have recovered. You can watch the vets at work and get a close view of the mammals, many of which are orphaned pups. There are also some displays of the marine ecosystem.

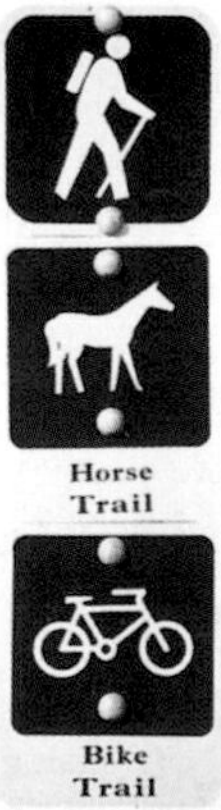

Sign marking a trail

Lagoon to the Golden Gate Hostel

Make your way back down the hill and return to the paved road that runs past Rodeo Lagoon [8]. There is a separate pathway beside the road for hikers, but you have to climb over a guard rail to get to it. Just before the road crosses a bridge, there is a large bench where you can view the water birds. There are plenty of birds to be seen in this brackish lagoon with its tall grasses.

Cross the bridge, not on the roadway but on the separate footpath at the side. Before the guard rail ends, a path [9] plunges down to the right into the dense shrubbery. From here, continue up the hill again, via a series of steps that will return you to the path at the end of the Visitors' Center parking lot. Walk across the lot and up the hill to a three-story wooden building, constructed at the turn of the century. This is listed on the National Historic Registry and has been officers' headquarters, a hospital, and a missile command center. It is now the Golden Gate Hostel [10] for travelers. The Marin Headlands also offer a wide range of longer, more challenging walks. Wolf Ridge and Bobcat Trail are two popular routes you may want to try.

TIPS FOR WALKERS

***Starting point**: The Visitors' Center at Fort Cronkhite.*
***Length**: 2 miles (3 km).*
***Getting there**: San Francisco Muni bus 76 leaves from the intersection of Fourth Street and Townsend Street on Sundays and some holidays, **Tel** (415) 673-6864. By car, drive across the Golden Gate Bridge, taking the Alexander Avenue exit. Turn under the freeway, following signs for the Headlands, Fort Cronkhite and Fort Barry.*
***Stopping-off points**: Water is available, but there are no refreshment facilities or restaurants in the Marin Headlands. You will need to bring your own picnic lunch, which can be enjoyed at any number of tables dotted along the trails and along the beaches.*

Berkeley ⑨

Berkeley began to boom following the earthquake of 1906 *(see pp52–3)*, when many San Franciscans fled their ruined city and settled on the east side of the bay. Berkeley did not really find its own voice, however, until the birth of the Free Speech Movement and the student uprisings against the Vietnam War during the 1960s, earning itself the nickname "Beserkeley." Many stores and market stalls still hark back to the hippie era with their psychedelic merchandise, but in recent years Berkeley has begun to raise its profile. Stylish restaurants and cafés have emerged, as well as a reputation for fine food – it was here that the popular California cuisine was born. Today the city blends idealism and style in unique harmony.

Claremont Resort Hotel

🏛 University of California at Berkeley

Tel (510) 642-6000. **Hearst Museum of Anthropology** *Tel (510) 643-7648.* ☐ *10am–4:30pm Wed–Sat, noon–4:30pm Sun.* ● *public hols.* **Berkeley Art Museum and Pacific Film Archive** *Tel (510) 642-0808.* ☐ *11am–7pm Wed–Sun.* ● *public hols.* ▦ 🕭 www.berkeley.org

The reputation of UC Berkeley for counter-cultural movements sometimes eclipses its academic reputation, yet it is one of the largest and most prestigious universities in the world. Founded in 1868, Berkeley numbers at least ten Nobel laureates among its professors. The campus *(see pp420–21)* was laid out by the architect Frederick Law Olmsted. There are more than 30,000 students and a wide range of museums, cultural amenities, and buildings of note to visit. These include the University Art Museum *(see p421)*, Sather Tower, (the Campanile), and the Hearst Museum of Anthropology.

Model of DNA at the Lawrence Hall of Science

🏛 Lawrence Hall of Science

Centennial Dr, UC Berkeley. *Tel (510) 642-5132.* ☐ *10am–5pm daily.* 🕭 ▨ www.lawrencehallofscience.org

Science is fun here. Hands-on exhibits tempt visitors to manipulate a hologram, track earthquakes, or plot stars in the planetarium. There are also changing exhibitions.

At night, the view of the lights around the northern Bay Area from the Hall's plaza is an extraordinary sight.

🏛 Claremont Resort Spa and Tennis Club

41 Tunnel Rd, Oakland. *Tel (510) 843-3000.* 🕭

The Berkeley hills form a backdrop to this half-timbered, fairytale castle. The enormous Claremont Resort construction began in 1906 and ended in 1915. In the early years the hotel failed to prosper, partly due to a law that forbade the sale of alcohol within a 1-mile (1.6-km) radius of the UC Berkeley campus. In 1937 an enterprising student actually measured the distance and discovered that the radius line passed through the *center* of the building. The Terrace Bar was opened beyond the line, in the same corner of the hotel that it occupies today.

The Bay Area's plushest hotel is a good place to have a drink and enjoy the views.

❧ University of California Botanical Garden

Centennial Dr, Berkeley Hills. 🎬 *(510) 643-2755.* ☐ *9am–5pm daily.* ● *1st Tue of month, Dec 25.* 🕭 *limited.*

More than 12,000 species from all over the world thrive in the Mediterranean-style climate of Berkeley's Strawberry Canyon. Although primarily used for research, the collections are arranged in thematic gardens linked by paths. Particularly noteworthy are the Asian, African, South American, European, and California sections. The Chinese medicinal herb garden, the orchid houses, cactus garden, and the carnivorous plants are also well worth a visit.

Wellman Hall on the University of California campus

For hotels and restaurants in this region see pp549–51 and pp595–7

Tilden Park

Tel *(510) 843-2137.* **Steam trains** *run 11am–5pm Sat & Sun, and daily during summer.* 🎫 **Carousel** ○ *10am–5pm Sat & Sun, 11am–5pm daily during summer.* 🎫 **Botanical Garden** *open 8:30am–5pm daily.* ♿ *limited.* **www**.ebparks.org

Though preserved for the most part in a natural wild condition, Tilden Park offers a variety of attractions. It is noted for the enchantingly landscaped Botanical Garden, specializing in California plants. Visitors can stroll from alpine meadows to desert cactus gardens by way of a redwood glen, and there are guided nature walks. If you have children, don't miss the carousel, the miniature farmyard, and the model steam train.

Judah L. Magnes Museum

2911 Russell St, Berkeley.
Tel *(510) 549-6950.* ○ *phone for details.* ● *Fri, Sat, Jewish and federal hols.* 📷 ♿ *in advance.*
www.magnes.org

Located in a rambling old mansion, this is California's largest collection of art and historical artifacts pertaining to Jewish culture from ancient times to the present day. Among the exhibits are art treasures from Europe, Turkey, and India, and graphic works and paintings by Marc Chagall, Max Liebermann, and others. There are also mementos of the experience of Jews during the Holocaust, such as a burned Torah scroll rescued from a German synagogue.

Lectures, videos, and temporary exhibitions often enliven the museum's halls.

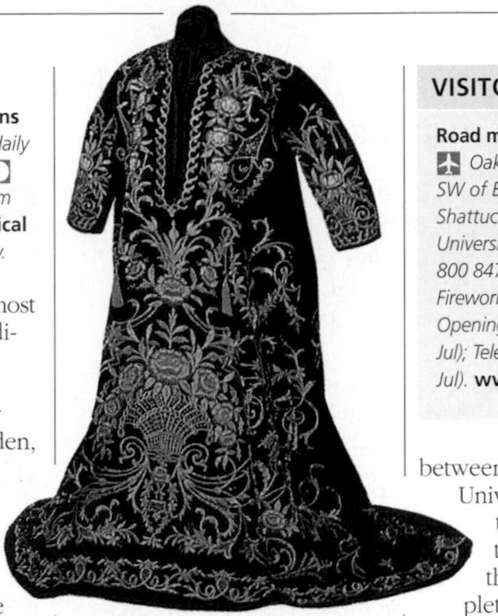

19th-century Jewish ceremonial dress, Judah L Magnes Museum

Telegraph Avenue

Berkeley's most fascinating street is Telegraph Avenue, especially the blocks between Dwight Way and the University. It has one of the highest concentrations of bookstores in the country, and a plethora of coffee houses and cheap eateries. The district was the center of student protest during the 1960s. It still swarms with students from dawn to dark, along with street vendors, musicians, protesters, and eccentrics.

Fourth Street

This gentrified enclave north of University Avenue is characteristic of Berkeley's fine craftsmanship and taste. Here you can buy everything from stained-glass windows and furniture, to organically grown lettuce and designer garden tools. There is also a handful of good restaurants *(see p595)*.

VISITORS' CHECKLIST

Road map inset B. 👥 *104,900.* ✈ *Oakland, 12 miles (19 km) SW of Berkeley.* 🚌 🚆 *2160 Shattuck Ave.* ℹ *1834 University Ave (510 549-7040, 800 847-4823).* 🎉 *Fourth of July Fireworks; Farmers' Market Grand Opening & Parade (2nd Sun in Jul); Telegraph Ave Book Fair (late Jul).* **www**.visitberkeley.com

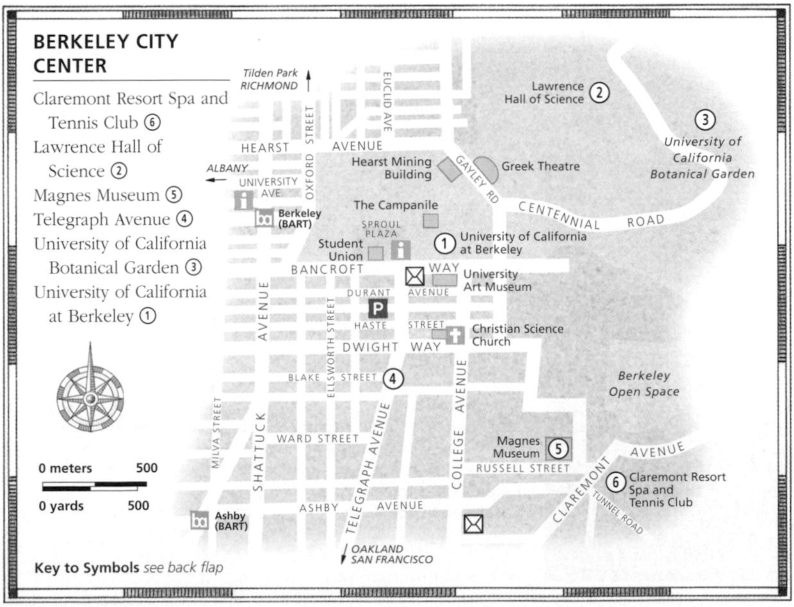
BERKELEY CITY CENTER
Claremont Resort Spa and Tennis Club 6
Lawrence Hall of Science 2
Magnes Museum 5
Telegraph Avenue 4
University of California Botanical Garden 3
University of California at Berkeley 1
0 meters 500
0 yards 500
Key to Symbols see back flap
Tilden Park RICHMOND
EUCLID AVE
HEARST AVENUE
OXFORD STREET
ALBANY
UNIVERSITY AVE.
Berkeley (BART)
Hearst Mining Building
GAYLEY RD
Greek Theatre
Lawrence Hall of Science 2
3 University of California Botanical Garden
CENTENNIAL ROAD
The Campanile
SPROUL PLAZA
Student Union
1 University of California at Berkeley
BANCROFT WAY
University Art Museum
DURANT AVENUE
HASTE STREET
DWIGHT WAY
Christian Science Church
ELLSWORTH STREET
BLAKE STREET 4
SHATTUCK AVENUE
MILVIA STREET
WARD STREET
TELEGRAPH AVENUE
COLLEGE AVENUE
Magnes Museum 5
RUSSELL STREET
Berkeley Open Space
ASHBY AVENUE
CLAREMONT AVENUE
TUNNEL ROAD
6 Claremont Resort Spa and Tennis Club
Ashby (BART)
OAKLAND SAN FRANCISCO

A 90-Minute Walk around the University of California Campus in Berkeley

This walk concentrates on a distinct area of Berkeley, the famous main campus of the University of California. It allows a stimulating glimpse into the intellectual, cultural, and social life of this vibrant university town *(see pp418–19)*.

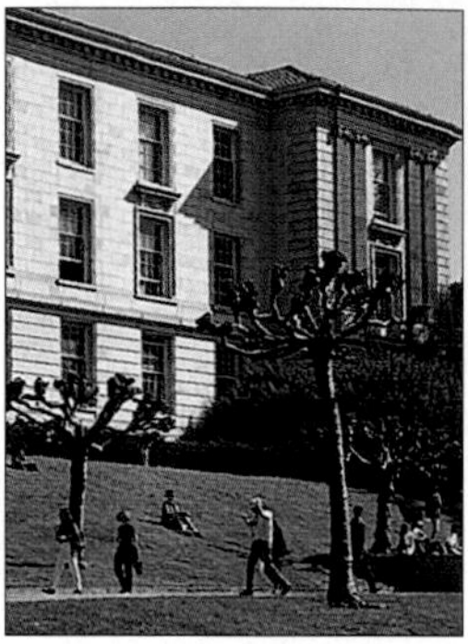

Students outside Wheeler Hall on Cross Campus Road ④

West Entrance to Sather Tower

From University Avenue ①, cross Oxford Street and walk along University Drive past the Valley Life Sciences Building ②. Wellman Hall can be seen on the north fork of Strawberry Creek as you follow the road to the right, keeping California Hall ③ on your right. Take a left turn on Cross Campus Road ④. Wheeler Hall lies to the right, and ahead is the main campus landmark, the 307-ft (94-m) tall Sather Tower ⑤. Built by John Galen Howard in 1914, it was based on the campanile in the Piazza San Marco in Venice.

Before visiting the bell tower, go to the Doe Library ⑥ then the AF Morrison Memorial Library ⑦ in the north wing. The adjacent Bancroft Library houses the plate supposedly left by Sir Francis Drake in 1579, when he claimed California for England *(see pp46–7)*.

Return to Sather Tower, open 10am–3:30pm Monday to Saturday. There are fine views of the bay from the top of the tower. Across the way lies South Hall ⑧, the oldest building on campus.

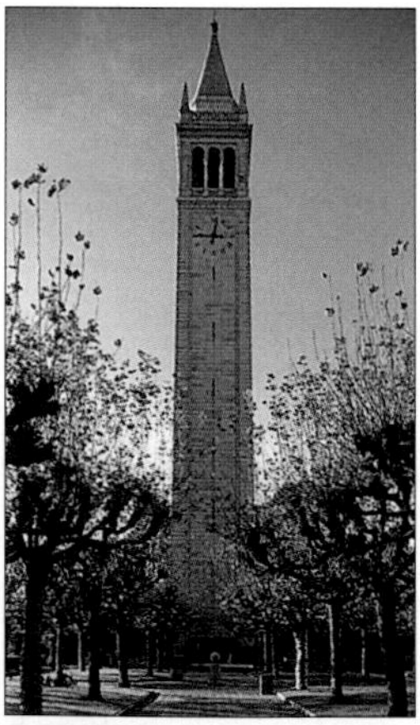

Esplanade near Sather Tower ⑤

Hearst Mining Building to the Greek Theater

Continuing north, walk past LeConte Hall then cross over University Drive to the Mining Circle. Here is the Hearst Mining Building ⑨, built by Howard in 1907. Inside are ore samples and pictures of old mining operations. Return to University Drive, turn left out of East Gate to the Hearst Greek Theater ⑩.

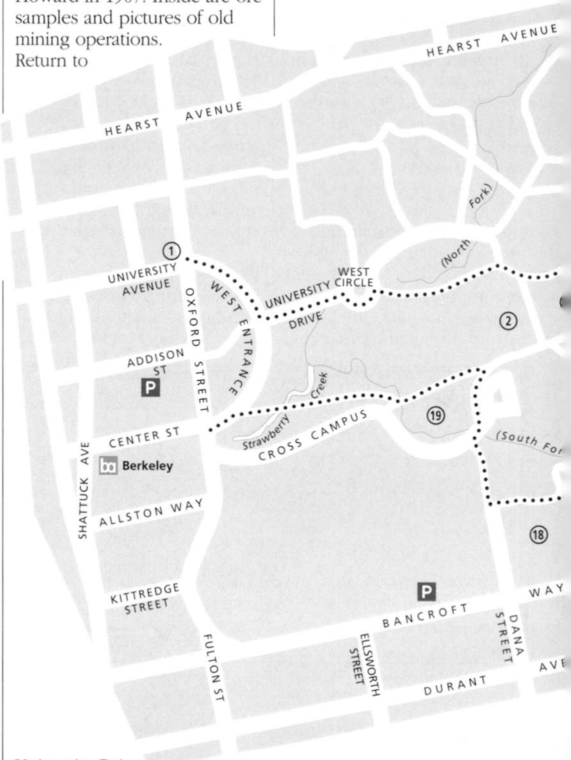

0 meters 250

0 yards 250

KEY

••• Walk route

[bart] BART station

[P] Parking

Faculty Club to the Eucalyptus Grove

Follow Gayley Road, which straddles a major earthquake fault, and turn right down the first path past Lewis Hall and

Hildebrand Hall, then left over a footbridge. The path winds between a log house and the Faculty Club ⑪. This rambling, rustic building was partly designed by Bernard Maybeck and dates from 1903. Faculty Glade ⑫ in front of the club is a favorite picnic and resting place with students and visitors alike.

The path now swings to the right, then sharp left. Take a look at Hertz Hall ⑬, then go down the diagonal walk that passes Wurster Hall to Kroeber Hall. Here you can visit the Hearst Museum of Anthropology *(see p418)*.

Included in the museum are artifacts made by Ishi, the last surviving Yahi Indian who was brought by scientists to live on the campus from 1911 until his death in 1916. Cross Bancroft Way to the Caffè Strada ⑭ and then proceed to the University Art Museum ⑮, which includes Picassos and Cézannes among its exhibits *(see p418)*. Continue along Bancroft Way to Telegraph Avenue ⑯, famous for the student riots of the 1960s and '70s *(see p419)*.

The entrance to the university opposite Telegraph Avenue opens on to Sproul Plaza ⑰, which is often

Within (1969) by A Lieberman at UCB Art Museum ⑮

enlivened by street musicians. Step into the lower courtyard with its modern Zellerbach Hall ⑱, then, noting the state-of-the-art Harmon Gym, pass Alumni House and turn right. Cross over the south fork of Strawberry Creek at Bay Tree Bridge and bear left for the nature area, with some of the world's tallest eucalyptus trees ⑲. The path ends at Oxford Street, near the start of the walk.

TIPS FOR WALKERS

Starting point: The West Gate at University Avenue and Oxford Street.
Length: 2.5 miles (4 km).
Getting there: San Francisco–Oakland Bay Bridge, Hwy 80 north, University Avenue exit. By BART, Berkeley stop.
Stopping-off points: The upscale Caffè Strada, on Bancroft Way, is always crowded with students sipping cappuccinos or eating bagels and cakes. A few steps down the street, in the University Art Museum, is the Café Grace, which looks out on to the sculpture garden. You may want to browse in the bookstores on Telegraph Avenue that also have coffee shops, or try one of the food carts that crowd the entrance to Sproul Plaza. Here you could sample a "smoothie" (blended fruit and ice) or a wide selection of Mexican food. In the lower Sproul Plaza of the University, amid a phalanx of bongo drummers, there are several other inexpensive cafés.

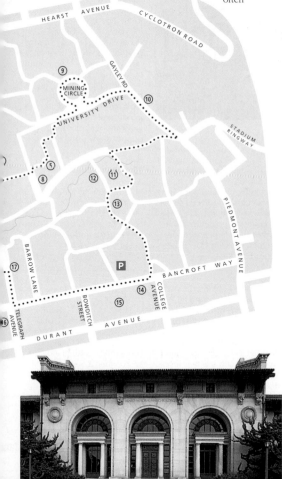

The Hearst Mining Building around the Mining Circle ⑨

Oakland ❿

At one time a small, working-class suburb of San Francisco, Oakland grew into a city in its own right when it became the West Coast terminus of the transcontinental railroad. With access to the town, businesses inevitably boomed, and it soon became one of the largest container ports in the United States. Many of the African-Americans who worked on the railroad then settled in Oakland, later followed by a Hispanic population, giving the city a multicultural atmosphere that continues to this day. Oakland's literary associations, including Jack London and Gertrude Stein, have also enhanced the area as a cultural center.

VISITORS' CHECKLIST

Road map inset B.
🏛 387,000. ✈ Oakland, 5 miles (8 km) SW of Oakland.
🚉 1245 Broadway St. 🛈 475 14th St (510 874-4800). 🎭 Festival at the Lake (early Jun).
www.oaklandchamber.com

Façade and gardens of the Mormon Temple

🏛 Mormon Temple
4770 Lincoln Ave.
Tel (510) 531-1475. 🚉 Fruitvale, then AC Transit 46 bus. **Visitors' Center** ⭕ 9am–9pm daily. **Temple** ♿ 📷 ⦰

Designed in 1963 and built on a hilltop, this is Northern California's only Mormon temple. Its full name is the Oakland Temple of the Church of Jesus Christ of Latter Day Saints. Floodlit at night, it can be seen from Oakland and San Francisco. The central ziggurat is surrounded by four shorter terraced towers, all clad with white granite and capped by glistening golden pyramids.

From the temple there are magnificent views over the entire Bay Area.

🏛 Lake Merritt
Formed when a saltwater tidal estuary was dredged, embanked, and partly dammed, Lake Merritt and its surrounding park form an oasis of rich blue and green in the urban heart of Oakland. Designated in 1870 as the first state game refuge in the US, the lake still attracts migrating flocks of birds. Boats can be rented from two boathouses on the west and north shores, and joggers and cyclists can circle the lake on a 3-mile (5-km) path. The north shore at Lakeside Park has flower gardens, an aviary, and a Children's Fairyland with pony rides, puppet shows, and nursery rhyme scenes.

🏛 Jack London Square
Author Jack London, who became famous for his adventure novels *The Call of the Wild* and *White Fang (see pp26–7)*, grew up in Oakland in the 1880s and was a frequent visitor to the Oakland waterfront. Today the area

🏛 Bay Bridge
Map 6 E4

The compound, high-level San Francisco–Oakland Bay Bridge was designed by Charles H Purcell. It has two distinct structures, joining at Yerba Buena Island in the middle of the Bay, and reaches 4.5 miles (7.2 km) from shore to shore. Its completion in 1936 heralded the end of the age of ferry boats on San Francisco Bay by linking the peninsular city at Rincon Hill to the Oakland "mainland." Train tracks were removed in the 1950s, leaving the bridge for use by more than 250,000 vehicles a day. It is five traffic lanes wide and has two levels. The westbound traffic uses the top deck, eastbound the lower. The eastern cantilever is raised on more than 20 piers, climbing up from the toll plaza causeway in Oakland to 191 ft (58 m) above Yerba Buena Island.

In 1989 the bridge was closed for a month after the Loma Prieta earthquake *(see p505)* when a 50-ft (15-m) segment disconnected where the cantilever span meets the approach ramp from Oakland. Two suspension spans join at

10 miles (16 km) of cable holding up the bridge

2,310 ft (704 m)

The West Bay Crossing section of Bay Bridge

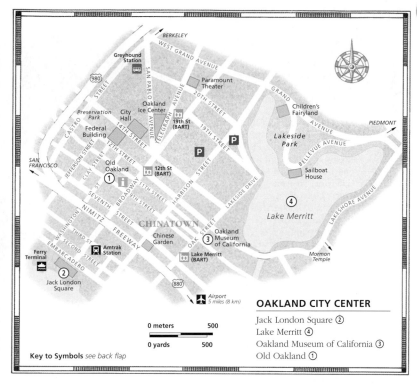

OAKLAND CITY CENTER

Jack London Square ②
Lake Merritt ④
Oakland Museum of California ③
Old Oakland ①

Key to Symbols *see back flap*

---

named after him is a bright promenade of shops, restaurants with outdoor tables, and pleasure boats. London's footsteps can be traced to the First and Last Chance Saloon, now sunken with age into the street, and the Yukon cabin occupied by London in 1898.

🏛 Old Oakland

Farmers' Market *Tel* (510) 745-7100. 🕐 8am–2pm Fri.
Also known as Victorian Row, these two blocks were erected between the 1860s and 1880s and renovated in the 1980s. Crowds of shoppers visit the Farmers' Market on Fridays at Clay and 9th streets, where

stalls sell fresh produce as well as prepared foods
At night, try 103-year-old Rattos, at No. 827 Washington Street. It is an Italian delicatessen famed for its Friday and Saturday night "Pasta Operas," when the management and visiting singers serenade the clientèle.

---

the central anchorage, which is sunk deeper in the water than that of any other bridge. Now there are plans to completely rebuild the East Bay crossing. Treasure Island, the larger part of Yerba Buena Island, hosted the 1939–40 World's Fair to celebrate the bridge's completion. This small island is now home to small parks and an upscale community.

East Bay Crossing

Central anchorage

5-lane double-level roadway

Pylons supporting both road decks

400 ft (122 m)   2,310 ft (704 m)

Oakland Museum of California

California's only museum exclusively dedicated to documenting the state's art, history, and ecology first opened in 1969. The building, handsomely terraced and landscaped with courtyards and gardens, was designed by architect Kevin Roche and encompasses three disciplines: the art, social, and natural history of California. The natural history dioramas in the Hall of California Ecology are among the most impressive in the entire country. The Cowell Hall of California History has one of the largest collections of California artifacts in the state, and the Gallery of California Art is famous for its early oil paintings of Yosemite and San Francisco.

California gold miner's banjo

Welcome to California
This display celebrates past and present-day life in California.

Roof and gardens

The Great Hall is used for special exhibitions and functions.

Gallery of California Art
The modern art in this collection includes Ocean Park No: 107 (1978) by Richard Diebenkorn.

Level 3

Level 2

10th Street entrance

★ **Dream on Wheels**
A drive-in restaurant sign and jukebox in the 1951 diorama capture the atmosphere of postwar California.

KEY TO THE OAKLAND MUSEUM LEVELS

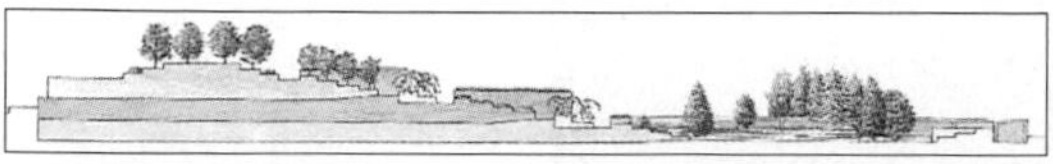

☐ Art Gallery   ☐ History   ☐ Natural Sciences

VISITORS' CHECKLIST

Oak & 10th Sts. **Road map** inset B.
🚔 (510) 238-2200. 🚌 from Lake
Merritt. ⬤ 10am–5pm Wed–Sat
(to 9pm 1st Fri of month), noon–
5pm Sun. ⬤ Jan 1, Thnksg, Dec
25. 🎫 free 2nd Sun. 📷 ♿ 🎁
📧 🖥 www.museumca.org

California Mud Wagon
Developed for rural life during the mid-19th century, this multipurpose vehicle could be converted easily from a field wagon to a stylish carriage.

Food Chain Diorama
This diorama features a mountain lion and its prey, to show how wildlife competes to survive.

Level 1

MUSEUM GUIDE
Level 1 contains the shop and the Hall of Ecology, where the exhibits show the changes in the state's ecology from west to east. Artifacts in the Cowell Hall on level 2 are arranged chronologically. Level 2 has the cafeteria, level 3 the Art Gallery.

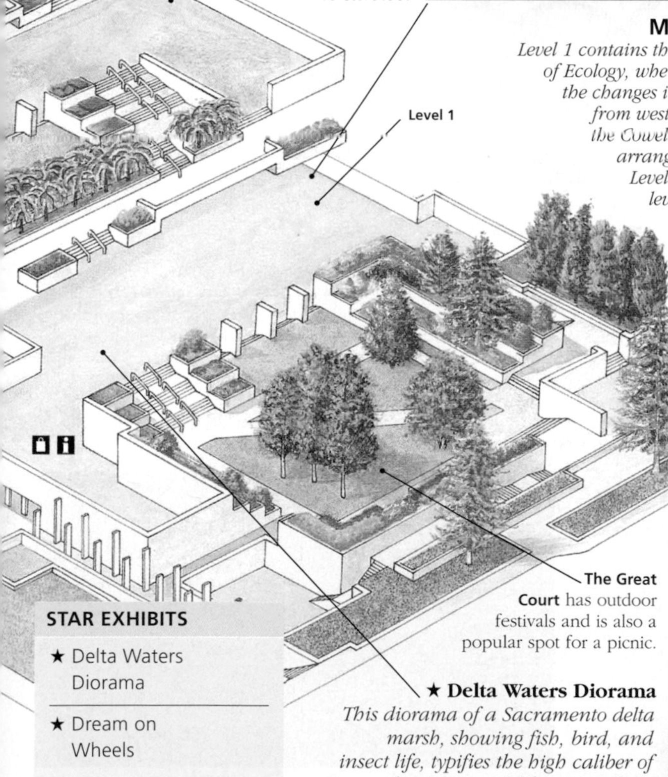

The Great Court has outdoor festivals and is also a popular spot for a picnic.

STAR EXHIBITS

★ Delta Waters Diorama

★ Dream on Wheels

★ Delta Waters Diorama
This diorama of a Sacramento delta marsh, showing fish, bird, and insect life, typifies the high caliber of the Aquatic California Gallery.

Eugene O'Neill's beautiful Tao House, in Danville

Tao House ⑪

Road map inset B. **Tel** (925) 838-0249. ◯ 8am–4:30pm daily, by reservation only. ♿ 🎥 obligatory: 10am & 12:30pm. **www**.nps.gov/evon

When the American playwright Eugene O'Neill (1888–1953) won the Nobel Prize for Literature in 1936, he used the stipend to build a home for himself and his wife in the then-rural San Ramon Valley at the foot of Mount Diablo. Tao House, a hybrid of Spanish Colonial and oriental styles, was completed in 1937. Over the next six years O'Neill worked in this house on what is now considered his best work, the semi-autobiographical series of tragic plays, including *The Iceman Cometh, A Moon for the Misbegotten,* and *Long Day's Journey Into Night.* In 1944, however, O'Neill was struck down with Parkinson's disease. The remote location of the house and the lack of available nursing staff due to the war forced the disabled O'Neill to abandon his beloved home. He died in a Boston hotel in 1953.

Although the surrounding valleys have now been developed into suburbs of San Francisco, Tao House and its beautiful landscaped grounds have been turned into a National Historic Site, operated by the National Park Service. Both have been preserved in the condition the playwright left them.

Mask used in O'Neill's stage plays

Mount Diablo State Park ⑫

Road map inset B. 🚌 🚆 Walnut Creek. 🛈 Walnut Creek (925 837-2525). **Tel** (925) 837-6119. ◯ 11am–5pm Wed–Sun (10am–4pm Winter).

Rising voluminously over the inland suburbs, the 3,849-ft (1,173-m) high Mount Diablo dominates the East Bay region. Its summit offers one of the most impressive panoramas in North America. On a fine and clear day it is possible to see for more than 200 miles (320 km) in each direction, stretching from Mount Lassen *(see p453)* and the Cascade Mountains in the north to Mount Hamilton in the south, and from the Sierra Nevada mountains in the east to the Farallon Islands *(see pp412–13)* in the Pacific Ocean to the west.

Almost 20,000 acres (8,000 ha) of land surrounding the summit have now been set aside as a state park, and there is a wide range of hiking trails. A twisting road takes car drivers within 50 ft (15 m) of the summit, which is a popular picnic spot. The park's Visitors' Center at the summit offers information on the mountain's fauna and flora, including the wildflowers that cover the mountainside in spring and the abundant oak trees.

Livermore ⑬

Road map inset B. 🏠 67,000. 🚌 🚆 🛈 2157 First St (925 447-1606). **www**.livermorechamber.org

Founded in the 1870s as a cattle-ranching and grape-producing community, Livermore in recent years has grown into an outlying suburb of San Francisco. Still rural in feel and retaining a few ranches and vineyards, the town is now best known as the home of the Lawrence Livermore National Laboratory. This state-of-the-art technology research center is operated by the University of California on behalf of the United States Department of Energy. During the Cold War era the laboratory had primary responsibility for the design of the nation's nuclear weapons arsenal, but today it has diversified into civilian applications.

To the east of Livermore, along I-580 as it climbs over hilly Altamont Pass, are hundreds of shining high-tech windmills. This is the world's largest wind farm, producing natural, nonpolluting energy from the area's constant winds. The windmills are all privately owned and operated, with no

Windmills producing natural energy at Livermore's wind farm

For hotels and restaurants in this region see pp549–51 and pp595–7

government funding. They consist of two main types: the traditional propeller type, and the more unusual vertical axis windmills, which resemble giant egg-whisks.

Stanford University ⓮

Junípero Serra St. **Road map** inset B. **Tel** *(650) 723-2053.* **Visitors' Center** ● *university hols; call ahead.* ● *phone (650) 723-2560 for details.* **www**.stanford.edu

Among the most pleasant of the Bay Area suburbs, the town of Palo Alto grew up specifically to serve Stanford University, one of the most reputed centers of higher education in the country.

Founded by the railroad tycoon Leland Stanford *(see pp50–51)* in honor of his son who died in 1885 at the age of 16, Stanford University opened in 1891. The campus occupies the former Stanford family farm, covering 8,200 acres (3,320 ha) at the foot of the coastal mountains – larger than the entire downtown district of San Francisco. It was designed in a mixture of Romanesque and Mission styles *(see pp30–31)* by the architect Frederick Law Olmsted, and its sandstone buildings and numerous arcades are capped by

red-tiled roofs. At the heart of the university campus is the Main Quadrangle, where the Memorial Church is decorated with a gold-leaf and tile mosaic. Also on the campus is the Stanford Museum of Art. This small but intriguing museum holds one of the largest collections of sculptures by Auguste Rodin, including the impressive *Gates of Hell*.

Filoli ⓯

Canada Rd. **Road map** inset B. **Tel** *(650) 364-2880, ext 507.* ● *9am–4pm Mon–Fri.* ● *Federal and public hols.* ● ● ●

One of the most impressive mansions in Northern California open to the public, the Filoli estate was the home of gold mining millionaire William Bourn, owner of the Empire Gold Mine *(see p470)*. It was designed in Palladian style by Willis Polk in 1916. The redbrick exterior resembles a Georgian terrace and encloses more than 18,000 sq ft (1,672 sq m) of living space on two fully furnished floors.

The house is surrounded by 16 acres (6.5 ha) of formal gardens, landscaped to provide blooms of varying colors through the year – 25,000 tulips and daffodils in spring, roses in summer, and the brilliant russet maple leaves

in the autumn. The estate's name, Filoli, is an acronym for the motto "Fight for a just cause, Love your fellow man, Live a good life," which commemorates William Bourn's love for the Irish.

Picturesque church in the tiny village of Pescadero

Pescadero ⓰

Road map inset B. ● *360.* ● *520 Kelley Ave, Half Moon Bay (650 726-5202).* **www**.halfmoonchamber.org

Only half an hour's drive from San Francisco to the north and the Silicon Valley *(see p428)* to the south, the tiny town of Pescadero seems light years away from the surrounding modern world.

Pescadero is a sleepy little farming community that produces an abundance of vegetables such as asparagus, pumpkins, and Brussels sprouts. It contains little more than a whitewashed church (the oldest in the county), a general store, a post office, and the popular Duarte's Tavern *(see p597)* along its two main streets. Its many whitewashed buildings follow a tradition that goes back to the 19th century, when a cargo of white paint was rescued from a nearby shipwreck.

Eight miles (13 km) south of town, the Pigeon Point Lighthouse is well worth a visit. The lighthouse also operates as a hostel *(see pp412–13)*.

Façade of the Memorial Church at Stanford University

San Jose ⑰

The only other original Spanish Colonial town in California after Los Angeles (see pp58–193), San Jose was founded in 1777 by Felipe de Neve and has grown to become the state's third largest city, its population exceeding that of San Francisco. Now the commercial and cultural center of the South Bay and civic heart of the Silicon Valley region, San Jose is a bustling and modern city that has only recently taken action to preserve its history. High-rise offices and high-tech factories now stand on what was only farmland in the 1950s, yet the city's fine museums and historic sites offer genuine attractions to the visitor, despite the suburban sprawl.

Statue outside the Egyptian Museum and Planetarium

Exploring San Jose

San Jose's colonial pueblo was situated on what is now Plaza Park, off Market Street. During 1849–50, California's first State Capitol was located in a hotel on the east side of the plaza, roughly on the site of the present Fairmont Hotel (see p551).

Other historic sites along Market Street include the San Jose Museum of Art and the birthplace of Amadeo P Giannini (see p315).

The well-known Winchester Mystery House (see pp430–31), is located on the town's outskirts.

🏚 Peralta Adobe

175 W St John St. **Tel** (408) 993-8182. ◯ noon–5pm Sat–Sun. ◯ public hols. 🈂️
🈲 🈳 ♿ first floor only.
One block to the left of Market Street is San Jose's oldest surviving

Mission Santa Clara detail

building, the Peralta Adobe. Built in 1797 it is the sole remnant of the Spanish pueblo. Upscale bars and cafés now surround the area.

⛪ Mission Santa Clara de Asis

500 El Camino Real. **Tel** (408) 554-4023. ◯ daily.
On the campus of the Jesuit University of Santa Clara, 5 miles (8 km) northwest of downtown San Jose, this mission church is a modern replica of the adobe original, first built in 1777 and reconstructed many times thereafter. Relics on display include bells given to the missionaries by the Spanish monarchy. The gardens adjacent to the church are carefully maintained in their original splendor.

🏛 Rosicrucian Egyptian Museum and Planetarium

Naglee & Park Aves. **Tel** (408) 947 3600. ◯ 10am–5pm Tue–Fri, 11am–6pm Sat–Sun. ● Jan 1, Easter Sun, Thanksgiving, Dec 25. 🈂️
This large museum displays the most extensive collection of ancient Egyptian artifacts west of the Mississippi. Housed in a complex of Egyptian- and Moorish-style buildings, each gallery represents a different aspect of Egyptian culture, from mummies, burial tombs, and canopic jars to domestic implements and a variety of children's toys. There are also replicas of the sarcophagus in which Tutankhamen was discovered in 1922, and of the Rosetta Stone.

The museum is operated by a nonsectarian organization known as the Rosicrucian Order, which is dedicated to spiritual development by combining modern science with the ancient wisdoms.

🏛 Tech Museum of Innovation

201 S Market St. **Tel** (408) 795-6100. ◯ 10am–5pm Tue–Sun. ●
Jan 1, Easter, Thanksgiving, Dec 25. 🈂️ **www**.thetech.org
Located in the heart of San Jose, this fascinating science museum has its eyes set on the future. The Tech Museum is crowded with hands-on exhibits, which encourage visitors of all ages to discover how various technological inventions work. Its main focus is on understanding the workings of computer hardware and software. The Imax Dome Theater is also worth a visit.

SILICON VALLEY

The world-famous center of the computer industry, Silicon Valley covers approximately 100 sq miles (260 sq km) from Palo Alto to San Jose. However, the term refers to myriad businesses rather than to a defined geographical location.

The name, based on the material used in the manufacture of semiconductors, was first used in the early 1970s to describe the area's expanding hardware and software industries. The seeds, however, were sown a decade earlier, at Stanford University and the Xerox Palo Alto Research Center, as well as in the garages of computer pioneers William Hewlett, David Packard, and later Steve Jobs and Stephen Wozniak, who invented the Apple personal computer.

Many world-class high-tech firms are based here, including Intel, Silicon Graphics, and Cisco Systems.

Silicon chip circuitry

🏛 San Jose Museum of Art

110 S Market St. ***Tel*** *(408) 271-6840.* 🕐 *Tue–Sun.* ● *Jan 1, Thanksgiving, Dec 25.* ♿ **www**.sjmusart.org

This small but daring art museum is known for some of the Bay Area's most interesting and popular art exhibits. The permanent collection focuses on well-known contemporary California artists.

🏛 Children's Discovery Museum of San Jose

180 Woz Way. ***Tel*** *(408) 298-5437.* 🕐 *10am–5pm Tue–Sat, noon–5pm Sun.* ● *Jan 1, Dec 25.* ♿ **www**.cdm.org

This large purple building, designed by Mexican architect Ricardo Legoretta, has interactive exhibits and programs for all the family. Arts and technology are featured in this warm, inviting space.

🏛 De Saisset Museum

500 El Camino Real. ***Tel*** *(408) 554-4528.* 🕐 *Tue–Sun.* ● *Jan 1, Thanksgiving, Dec 25.* **Donation**.

Next to the Santa Clara Mission, this museum exhibits artifacts from the 18th-century mission and other eras of California history, along with a vast collection of paintings, prints, and photographs.

San Jose
TRANSIT
MALL
129
Trolley car at the San Jose Historical Museum

🏛 San Jose Historical Museum

1650 Senter Rd. ***Tel*** *(408) 287-2290.* 🕐 *noon–4pm Tue–Sun.* ● *Thanksgiving, Dec 25.* ♿ 🛍

One mile (1.5 km) southeast of downtown San Jose, in Kelley Park, more than two dozen historic structures of San Jose have been reassembled into an outdoor museum. Highlights include a trolley car, a gas station from the 1920s, and 19th-century business premises including a doctor's office, a hotel, and the original Bank of Italy.

By 2001 the museum aims to have 75 structures, completing this life-size model of San Jose as it used to be.

VISITORS' CHECKLIST

Road map inset B. 👥 *846,000.* ✈ *San Jose International Airport, 2 miles (3 km) NW of San Jose.* 🚆 *65 Cahill St.* 🚌 *70 Almeden St.* ℹ *180 S Market St (888 726-5673).* 🎉 *Festival of the Arts (Sep).* **www**.sanjose.org

🎢 Paramount's Great America Amusement Park

2401 Agnew Rd. ***Tel*** *(408) 988-1776.* 🕐 *mid-Mar–Jun: Sat & Sun; Jul– mid-Oct: daily.* ♿

The best amusement park in Northern California packs a wide variety of attractions into its 100-acre (40-ha) site.

The park is divided into several different areas, each one designed to evoke various regions of the United States. These include Orleans Place, Yankee Harbor, and the Yukon Territory. Along with high-speed roller coasters, such as the Demon and the Tidal Wave, many rides incorporate themes from films and television shows produced by Paramount Studios, including *Top Gun* and *Star Trek*. Open-air pop concerts are often held on summer evenings in the large amphitheater.

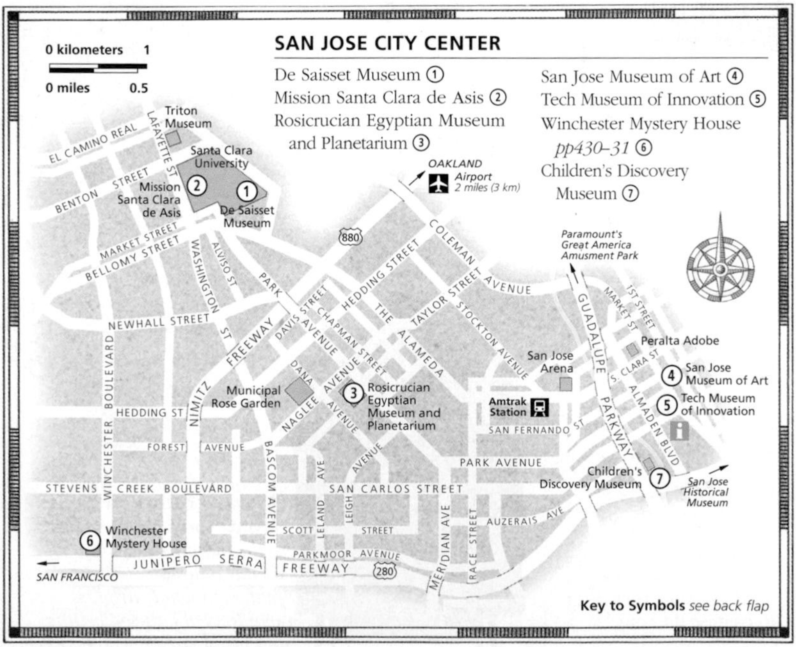
SAN JOSE CITY CENTER
De Saisset Museum [1]
Mission Santa Clara de Asis [2]
Rosicrucian Egyptian Museum and Planetarium [3]
San Jose Museum of Art [4]
Tech Museum of Innovation [5]
Winchester Mystery House pp430–31 [6]
Children's Discovery Museum [7]
0 kilometers 1
0 miles 0.5
Triton Museum
Santa Clara University
Mission Santa Clara de Asis
De Saisset Museum
EL CAMINO REAL
LAFAYETTE ST
BENTON STREET
MARKET STREET
BELLOMY STREET
WASHINGTON ST
ALVISO ST
OAKLAND
Airport 2 miles (3 km)
880
COLEMAN AVENUE
HEDDING STREET
PARK
DAVIS STREET
CHAPMAN STREET
THE ALAMEDA
TAYLOR STREET
STOCKTON AVENUE
Paramount's Great America Amusment Park
GUADALUPE PARKWAY
MARKET ST
1ST STREET
Peralta Adobe
S. CLARA ST
San Jose Arena
San Jose Museum of Art
Tech Museum of Innovation
ALMADEN BLVD
NEWHALL STREET
FREEWAY
AVENUE
NIMITZ
Municipal Rose Garden
DANA AVENUE
NAGLEE AVENUE
Rosicrucian Egyptian Museum and Planetarium
Amtrak Station
SAN FERNANDO ST
WINCHESTER BOULEVARD
HEDDING ST
FOREST AVENUE
BASCOM AVENUE
PARK AVENUE
Children's Discovery Museum
San Jose Historical Museum
STEVENS CREEK BOULEVARD
SAN CARLOS STREET
LELAND AVE
LEIGH
MERIDIAN AVE
RACE STREET
AUZERAIS AVE
SCOTT STREET
Winchester Mystery House
PARKMOOR AVENUE
JUNIPERO SERRA FREEWAY
280
SAN FRANCISCO
Key to Symbols see back flap

San Jose: Winchester Mystery House

Winchester Mystery House is a mansion with a remarkable history. Sarah Winchester, heiress of the Winchester Rifle fortune, moved from Connecticut to San Jose in 1884 and bought a small farmhouse. Convinced by a medium that its expansion would exorcise the spirits of those killed by the rifle, she kept builders laboring on the house 24 hours a day, 7 days a week, for 38 years, until her death in 1922. The result is a bizarre complex of 160 rooms, including stairs that lead nowhere and windows set into floors. The total cost of the construction amounted to $5.5 million. The house has been refurbished with replica 19th-century furniture.

Stone cherub fountain

★ **Main Bedroom**
Sarah Winchester eventually died in her plush bedroom. The flooring is English mitered herringbone. At night she would play the harmonium situated opposite the elaborately carved bed.

Tiffany Stained-Glass Window
The full beauty of the multi-colored Tiffany glass in this window is lost by its placement on an inside wall.

The Greenhouse incorporates 13 glass cupolas.

FACTS AND FIGURES

- The house contains 2,000 doors, 10,000 windows, 47 fireplaces and 17 chimneys.
- The number 13 is used superstitiously throughout – 13 bathrooms, 13 windows in a room, and 13 lights in the chandeliers.
- When the top of the house collapsed during the 1906 earthquake, building continued outward rather than upward.
- Mrs. Winchester's height of 4 ft 10 in (147 cm) explains hallways 2 ft (0.6 m) wide and doors only 5 ft (152 cm) high.
- Mrs. Winchester selected a new bedroom out of the 40 in the house each night, to confuse the spirits.

★ **Grand Ballroom**
This elaborate organ is one of the main features of the Grand Ballroom. Other features include artglass windows, a paneled ceiling, and hand-carved woodwork.

Switchback Stairs
Each of these 44 steps is only 1.5 inches (3.8 cm) high, and the entire stair-case rises only 9 ft (2.7 m) from start to finish. It is thought they were built in this way to ease Sarah Winchester's arthritis.

VISITORS' CHECKLIST

525 S Winchester Blvd.
Road map inset B.
Tel (408) 247-2000.
🚌 25, 60, 85. 🕐 9am–5pm
Sun–Thu; end Apr–mid-Jun
9am–5pm Sun–Thu, 9am–7pm
Fri & Sat . 🔴 Dec 25.
🎥 📷 ♿ gardens only.
🛍 📧 📖 www.
winchestermysteryhouse.com

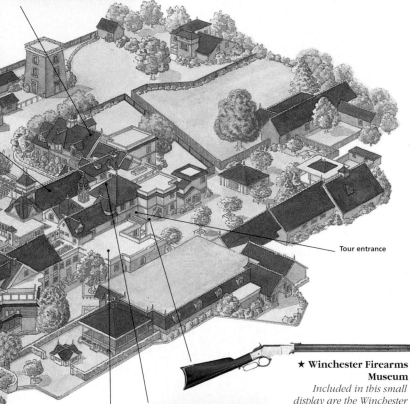

Tour entrance

★ **Winchester Firearms Museum**
Included in this small display are the Winchester Repeating Rifle and the Model 1873, which came to be known as "The Gun that Won the West." Commemorative rifles include the Theodore Roosevelt and the John Wayne.

The Winchester Products Museum contains items, other than rifles, produced by the company, including roller skates, electric irons, and lawn mowers.

STAR FEATURES
★ Grand Ballroom

★ Main Bedroom

★ Winchester Firearms Museum

Stairwell to the Ceiling
This stairway leading nowhere is just one of the many unexplained oddities within the house.

NORTHERN
CALIFORNIA

Northern California at a Glance

Northern California stretches for more than 500 miles (800 km), from the sparsely populated border with Oregon to the high-tech urban civilization that marks the beginning of Southern California. Vast areas of wilderness cover the region, including volcanic landscapes and dense forests, imposing mountain ranges and rugged coastlines, proudly preserved by a series of national parks. Northern California also has a rich history, from the first European settlers in Monterey to the celebrated Gold Rush of 1849. Its natural beauty is enhanced by equally picturesque and significant towns, including the state's capital, Sacramento.

THE NORTH
(see pp442–65)

Redwood National Park (see p450) *is a protected landscape of dense, awe-inspiring redwood forests, including the world's tallest tree, which reaches a height of 368 ft (112 m). The area is perennially popular with anglers, hikers, bird-watchers, and campers.*

WINE COUNTRY
(see pp454–5)

Sonoma (see pp464–5) *was the site of the Bear Flag Revolt in 1846, when Americans rebelled against Mexican rule and tried to turn California into a republic. The vineyards of Sonoma County and the Napa Valley (see pp462–3), benefiting from good soil and an ideal climate, produce world-class wines.*

Carmel Mission (see pp512–13) *was founded in 1770 by Junípero Serra and became the most important of all the 21 Franciscan missions, serving as the administrative center for Northern California. Today, restored to its original splendor, it is considered to be the state's most beautiful church.*

0 kilometers 50

0 miles

Lassen Volcanic National Park (see p453) *was formed in 1914, when more than 300 eruptions resulted in a new landscape of mudflows and sulfurous streams heated by molten lava. Mount Lassen, part of the Cascade Mountain Range, is considered to be still active.*

Sacramento (see pp472–5) *has been the state capital since 1854, and the Capitol is one of California's finest buildings. Old Sacramento preserves its historic structures from the 1860s and 1870s, when the town was the western terminus of the transcontinental railroad.*

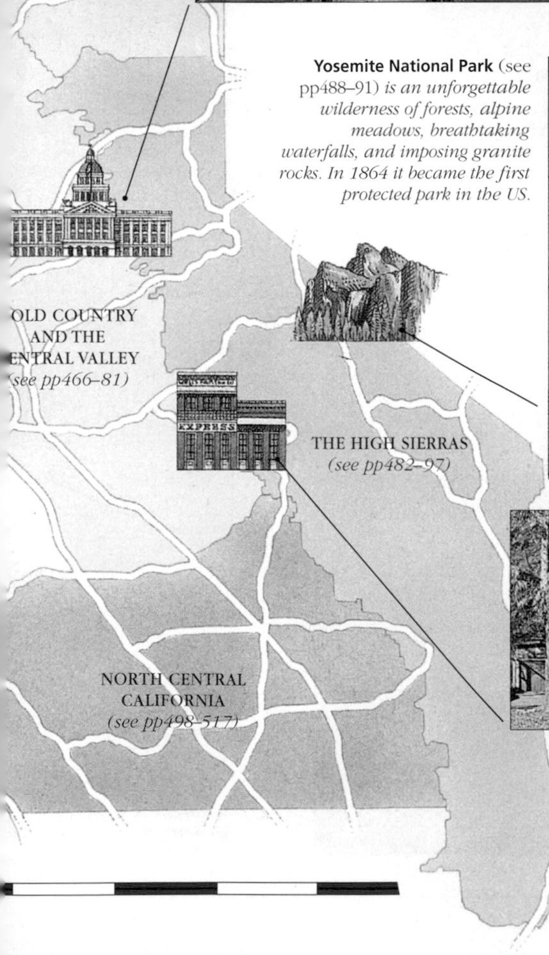

Yosemite National Park (see pp488–91) *is an unforgettable wilderness of forests, alpine meadows, breathtaking waterfalls, and imposing granite rocks. In 1864 it became the first protected park in the US.*

GOLD COUNTRY
AND THE
CENTRAL VALLEY
(see pp466–81)

THE HIGH SIERRAS
(see pp482–97)

NORTH CENTRAL
CALIFORNIA
(see pp498–517)

Columbia State Historic Park (see pp480–81) *was once the second largest town in California and is now the best preserved of the old gold mining centers.*

Wildlife and Wilderness

Eons ago, most of Northern California was under water, until geological forces pushed up the floor of the Central Valley, causing the Pacific Ocean to recede. Diverse terrains and ecosystems then emerged and Northern California is now a land of peaks, canyons, and headlands. Unique flora grows here, such as giant sequoias in the High Sierras *(see pp496– 7)* and Monterey cypress trees *(see p511)*. Black bears roam redwood groves and hawks hover above Yosemite Valley *(see pp488–9)*. Legend has it that Bigfoot, America's version of the Yeti, makes his home in these parts. In order to protect this landscape, the environment-friendly Sierra Club began here in 1892 and is still active today.

Prairie Creek State Park has a herd of protected Roosevelt elk, which roam the dunes of Gold Bluff Beach.

Redwood National Park
(see pp448–9) *contains the world's tallest redwood tree, reaching 368 ft (112 m). These evergreens soak up the winter's heavy rainfall and are kept moist in summer by fogs, which move in from the ocean. Wood-peckers, spotted owls, mule deer, squirrels, and banana slugs frequent the groves.*

The Sacramento National Wildlife Refuges protect the many birds that stop off on the Pacific Flyway.

Point Reyes Peninsula (see pp412–13) *is a small "island," almost separated from the mainland by the San Andreas Fault. Its forested ridges, littoral rocks, and rock pools are a prime habitat for crustaceans such as the Pacific rock crab.*

The Farallon Islands
(see pp412–13) *are an important breeding ground for sea birds, including the puffin, and elephant seals. Visitors are not per-mitted on the islands.*

Año Nuevo State Reserve *(see p504)* is occupied every winter by hundreds of breeding elephant seals.

The Monterey Peninsula *(see pp510–11)* is the winter home of the beautiful migratory monarch butterfly.

KEY

- National Park
- State Park
- National Forest
- Wildlife refuge
- River

Map labels: Six Rivers National Forest · Klamath National Fo... · Trinity National Forest · Shasta National Forest · Clair Engle Lake · Shasta · •Eureka · •Red... · Sacra... · THE NORTH · Klamath River · Black Butte River · Sinkyone Wilderness · Eel River · Mendocino National Forest · Mendocino · Sutter N... Wildlife ... · Clear Lake · Cache C... · WINE COUNTRY · Lake Sonoma · Lake Barrye... · Sonoma · San Francisco • · San Jose • · WIN... BAY A... · Big B... Redw... State... · Point Lo... Res... · Point Lo... Res...

0 kilometers 25

0 miles   25

NORTHERN CALIFORNIA

Northern California at a Glance

Northern California stretches for more than 500 miles (800 km), from the sparsely populated border with Oregon to the high-tech urban civilization that marks the beginning of Southern California. Vast areas of wilderness cover the region, including volcanic landscapes and dense forests, imposing mountain ranges and rugged coastlines, proudly preserved by a series of national parks. Northern California also has a rich history, from the first European settlers in Monterey to the celebrated Gold Rush of 1849. Its natural beauty is enhanced by equally picturesque and significant towns, including the state's capital, Sacramento.

THE NORTH
(see pp442–65)

WINE COUNTRY
(see pp454–5)

Redwood National Park (see p450) *is a protected landscape of dense, awe-inspiring redwood forests, including the world's tallest tree, which reaches a height of 368 ft (112 m). The area is perennially popular with anglers, hikers, bird-watchers, and campers.*

Sonoma (see pp464–5) *was the site of the Bear Flag Revolt in 1846, when Americans rebelled against Mexican rule and tried to turn California into a republic. The vineyards of Sonoma County and the Napa Valley (see pp462–3), benefiting from good soil and an ideal climate, produce world-class wines.*

Carmel Mission (see pp512–13) *was founded in 1770 by Junípero Serra and became the most important of all the 21 Franciscan missions, serving as the administrative center for Northern California. Today, restored to its original splendor, it is considered to be the state's most beautiful church.*

0 kilometers 50

0 miles

Tule Lake Wildlife Refuge
(see p453) *is one of the prime bird-watching areas on the West Coast. It is home to a number of bald eagles.*

The Lava Beds Wilderness
is part of the Lava Beds National Monument (see p452) and is inhabited by rattlesnakes and rodents.

Biscar Wildlife Area, *the desert area of the Great Basin, on the border of Nevada, is populated with bobcats, badgers, and antelope.*

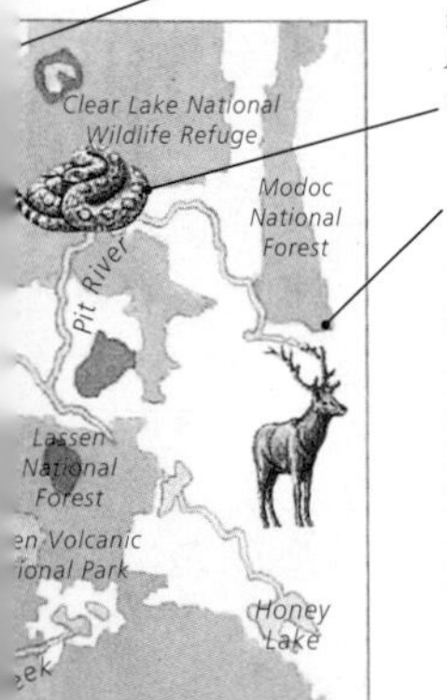

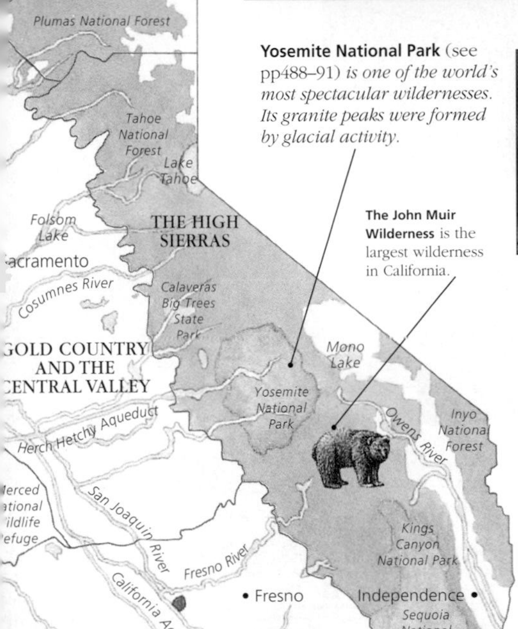

Yosemite National Park (see pp488–91) *is one of the world's most spectacular wildernesses. Its granite peaks were formed by glacial activity.*

The John Muir Wilderness is the largest wilderness in California.

Clear Lake National Wildlife Refuge

Modoc National Forest

Pit River

Lassen National Forest

en Volcanic ional Park

Honey Lake

Plumas National Forest

Tahoe National Forest

Lake Tahoe

Folsom Lake

acramento

THE HIGH SIERRAS

Cosumnes River

Calaveras Big Trees State Park

GOLD COUNTRY AND THE CENTRAL VALLEY

Mono Lake

Hetch Hetchy Aqueduct

Yosemite National Park

Inyo National Forest

Owens River

Merced ational ildlife efuge

San Joaquin River

California Aqueduct

Fresno River

Kings Canyon National Park

• Fresno

Independence •

NORTH CENTRAL

Sequoia National Park

os edres ational orest

Tulare Lake

Sequoia National Forest

Sequoia and Kings Canyon National Parks (see pp496–7) *together contain over 75 groves of the world's largest living tree, the giant sequoia. The tree is unique to California and Oregon.*

The Ventana Wilderness at Big Sur *(see pp514–15)* is chaparral country. The area is home to 900 plant species, coyotes, jack rabbits, and the California quail.

The Wine of Northern California

California is the most important wine-growing area in the United States, producing 90 percent of the nation's wine. More than 327,000 acres (132,000 ha) of the state's land is used for viticulture. Half of the grapes grown here are harvested from the fertile soil of the interior region, particularly the stretch of land bordered by the Sacramento Valley to the north and the San Joaquin Valley to the south. The north coast region accounts for less than a quarter of California's total wine-growing acreage, but many of the country's best Chardonnay, Sauvignon Blanc, Cabernet Sauvignon, and Merlot grapes are grown here. The north coast is also home to most of the state's 800 wineries. Chardonnay and Pinot Noir grapes are the mainstays of the central coast region, which extends from the San Francisco Bay Area to Santa Barbara.

LOCATOR MAP

Northern California wine region

Grape harvest at V. Sattui Winery near St. Helena in Napa Valley

Late Harvest Zinfandel *from the Hop Kiln Winery is a red dessert wine made from grapes left on the vine longer than usual to increase their sweetness. The winery is housed in an historic hop kiln barn.*

THE STORY OF ZINFANDEL

The story of Zinfandel is one of the great success stories of California wine. This versatile grape is thought to have been brought to America from Croatia's Dalmatian coast. Zinfandel arrived in California in the 1850s, but only gained widespread popularity relatively recently. The Zinfandel reds, particularly those from the Dry Creek and Russian River valleys, are now in great demand. Some have oaky flavors while others have strong fruity flavors. The rosé White Zinfandel was created by winemakers to use up their surplus red grapes.

Saintsbury's Vin Gris *is a Burgundy-style rosé wine, which is made from the juice of Pinot Noir grapes.*

• Fort Bragg

Ukiah •

Healdsburg •

• Santa

SAN FRANCISCO

Oakl

KEY

☐ Lake County	☐ Carneros Valley
▨ Anderson Valley	☐ Santa Cruz Mountains
■ Alexander Valley	▨ Livermore Valley
☐ Dry Creek Valley	■ Lodi Valley
▨ Russian River Valley	☐ El Dorado Valley
▨ Napa Valley	☐ Redwood–Ukiah Valley
▨ Sonoma Valley	▨ San Joaquin Valley

KEY FACTS ABOUT CALIFORNIA WINES

Location and Climate

California's latitude, proximity to the ocean, and sheltered valleys create a mild climate. Winters tend to be short and mild, while the growing season is long and hot but cooled by summer fogs. Combined with fertile soil, these factors mean that large areas have ideal grape-growing conditions.

Grape Varieties

California's most widely planted grape variety is **Chardonnay**, used to make a dry wine with a balance of fruit, acidity, and texture. Other popular whites include **Sauvignon Blanc** (also known as **Fumé Blanc**), **Chenin Blanc**, **Pinot Blanc**, **Gewürztraminer**, and **Johannisberg Riesling**. California's red wines are typically dry with some tannic astringency and include the rich, full-bodied **Cabernet Sauvignon**, **Merlot**, **Petite Sirah**, **Pinot Noir**, and **Zinfandel**.

Good Producers

Chardonnay: Acacia, Byron, Château Montelena, Ferrari-Carano, Kendall-Jackson, Kistler, Kunde Estate, Sonoma-Cutrer *Cabernet Sauvignon*: Beaulieu, Beringer, Grgich Hills, Heitz, The Hess Collection, Jordan, Joseph Phelps, Silver Oak, Robert Mondavi, Stag's Leap, Wente, Whitehall Lane. *Merlot*: Clos du Bois, Duckhorn, Frog's Leap, Silverado, Sterling. *Pinot Noir*: Dehlinger, Etude, Gary Farrell, Saintsbury, Sanford. *Sauvignon Blanc:* Duckhorn, Glen Ellen, Kenwood, Matanzas Creek, J Rochioli. *Zinfandel*: Dry Creek, Lake Sonoma, De Loach, Hop Kiln, Ridge, Rosenblum, Sebastiani.

Good Vintages

(*Reds*) 2004, 2003, 2002, 2001, 2000, 1999, 1998, 1997, 1996.
(*Whites*) 2004, 2003, 2002, 2001, 2000, 1999, 1998, 1997, 1996.

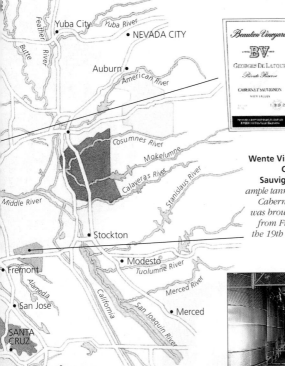

Beaulieu Vineyard's Private Reserve
Cabernet Sauvignon is a medium-bodied red wine with ripe cherry and black-currant aromas. It has been produced since 1936 and was the first wine in the US to be called Private Reserve.

Wente Vineyard's Cabernet Sauvignon *has ample tannins. The Cabernet grape was brought here from France in the 19th century.*

Fermentation tanks *at Sterling Vineyards are typical of the high-tech methods now used.*

The Bohemian North

Perhaps because the region attracted a wide range of people and enjoyed enormous wealth during the Gold Rush *(see pp48–9)*, Northern California has always tended to be nonconformist and somewhat hedonistic. This has caused some anguish over the years, as charlatans and crackpots have taken advantage of the region's broad-mindedness, but it has certainly made the area a colorful place. During the late 19th century San Francisco's Barbary Coast was home to casinos, opium dens, and brothels *(see p314)*. Utopian communities, organized around humanitarian, religious, or dietary principles, have been another facet of Northern California life. In the 1960s, the area's air of liberality made it a haven for members of the "Make Love, Not War" generation *(see p359)*. It has since attracted everybody from nudists and hot-tub lovers, to religious gurus and the latter-day hippies who helped turn marijuana into a chief crop of Humboldt County.

Spiritual guidance *became popular during the 1850s, and 1860s. San Francisco attracted many spiritualist "mediums," who held regular seances. There are still a few spiritualist churches operating in the Bay Area.*

Sally Stanford, *born in 1903, was a virtual pariah in Sausalito when she took over the Valhalla (now the Chart House), the town's oldest restaurant, in 1950. Local citizens didn't approve of her previous occupation as a San Francisco madam. But Sally's personality eventually won the town over, and she served one term as the town's mayor (1976 – 8). She died in 1982.*

UTOPIAN COMMUNITIES

From the 1850s to the 1950s, more Utopian communities were founded in Northern California than in any other place in the nation. William Riker's Holy City was established in 1918 in the Santa Cruz Mountains. Riker, a racist and forecaster of apocalypses, called his totalitarian community the "headquarters for the world's perfect government." It eventually died out because the community was celibate.

Fountain Grove was a Utopian outpost north of Santa Rosa, founded in 1875 by New York mystic Thomas Lake Harris. Harris's theory was that God was bisexual and Christ was the Divine Man-Woman. Under attack for alleged sexual and financial abuses, Harris was forced to close his commune in 1892.

William Riker

Young and old lived and traveled together in communities.

Bright colors and childlike designs were influenced by the lights and patterns experienced during drug-induced hallucinatory "trips."

Psychedelic Pop Art *posters of the 1960s were distinctive for their inflated, crammed typeface, developed by artist Wes Wilson.*

JIM JONES AND THE PEOPLE'S TEMPLE

The Reverend Jim Jones (1931–78) was a popular cult leader in the Bay Area during the 1970s, preaching an amalgam of racial and religious egalitarianism, political empowerment, doomsday visions, and sexual freedom. He was alternately a fundamentalist, supposedly "healing" people through touch, and a modern minister, with his services accompanied by music and dance. But he was also a self-proclaimed messiah. After building up a congregation of some 20,000 at his People's Temple in San Francisco, in 1978 he moved almost 1,000 of them to an isolated agricultural mission in Guyana, South America. After rumors of physical abuse and weapons caches at the colony brought international scrutiny, Jones ordered a mass suicide. Investigators later found hundreds of his followers' corpses in the jungle; they had all drunk a cyanide-laced fruit drink, and the despotic reverend had been shot in the head.

Jim Jones

Hippies from the 1960s

PSYCHEDELIA

The term "psychedelic" originally referred to ideas or approaches that were somehow outrageous, non-conformist, or "mind-expanding." But after San Francisco witnessed the opening of the Psychedelic Shop on Haight Street in 1966 *(see p358)*, the word became associated with the hallucinatory drugs popular among the region's hippie generation.

Psychedelia then turned into a symbol of an entire lifestyle: young hippie communities rejecting conformity and traveling from one gathering to another on brightly painted buses, taking drugs, and preaching peace.

The Esalen Institute (see p515) *became famous in the 1960s as the center of the "human potential movement," a philosophy emphasizing individual responsibility for both the good and bad events in life. Today it is an expensive retreat where former flower children and stressed corporate executives all discuss spiritual insights while reclining in hot springs overlooking the Pacific Ocean.*

THE NORTH

Ranging from deserted beaches strewn with giant driftwood logs to dense forests at the foot of alpine peaks, the far north of California is the state at its most wild and rugged. The landscape is as diverse as any continent – lush redwood groves, the volcanic Cascade Mountains, the arid plains at the edge of the Great Basin – yet all this is confined within one-quarter of the state.

Native Americans settled in extreme Northern California around 10,000 BC. They coexisted peacefully with each other and with the earth, leaving behind few signs of their existence apart from discarded sea shells and pictographs on cave walls. When the Europeans arrived in the area in the 19th century, things changed swiftly.

The first to come were fur trappers, in search of beavers, sea otters, and other pelts. Soon afterward gold seekers descended upon the region's rivers, hoping for similar riches to those found in the Sierra Nevada *(see pp48–9)*. Some gold was found, but the real wealth was made at the end of the century when lumber companies began to harvest the forests of coastal redwoods. These giant redwood trees *(Sequoia sempervirens)* are the region's defining feature. The finest forests have been protected by state and national parks and exude a palpable sense of history.

Inland, an even more ancient sight confronts visitors to the strange volcanic areas of Mount Lassen and the Lava Beds National Monument. Millions of years worth of geological activity has formed a stunning landscape that is devoid of civilization.

Far Northern California is sparsely populated, with a few medium-sized towns, such as Redding and Eureka. The prime attractions are natural, and life here, for visitors and residents, revolves around the great outdoors.

Lost Creek in Redwood National Park

◁ **Imposing snow-capped peak of Mount Shasta**

Exploring the North

Rugged, wild, and sparsely populated, California's northern extremes have more in common with neighboring Oregon and Washington than they do with the rest of the state. Dense forests of pine, fir, and redwood trees cover more than half the landscape, and two parallel mountain ranges, the Coast Range and, farther inland, the Sierra Nevada Mountains, divide the north into three very different sections. Along the coast, Cape Mendocino makes a good base for exploring the often deserted beaches and coastal redwood groves. Inland, the Sacramento Valley provides access to the beautiful snow-capped Mount Shasta, the volcanic spectacles of Lassen Volcanic National Park, and the Lava Beds National Monument.

SIGHTS AT A GLANCE

Patrick's Point State Park in
Humboldt County

GETTING AROUND

A car is essential for visiting northern California. Two north–south routes run parallel up and down the region, but the only comfortable route through the mountains east–west is Hwy 299. Bisecting the north, I-5 runs through the Sacramento Valley, while to the west US Hwy 101 runs through the lush valleys of the Russian and Eel Rivers. Public transportation is limited to Greyhound buses along the two main highways and a midnight train through the Sacramento Valley to Seattle.

KEY

▭	Freeway
▭	Major road
▬	Secondary road
▬	Minor road
▬	Scenic route
⁓	Main railway
─	Minor railway
▭	State border
△	Summit

Impressive peak of Mount Shasta

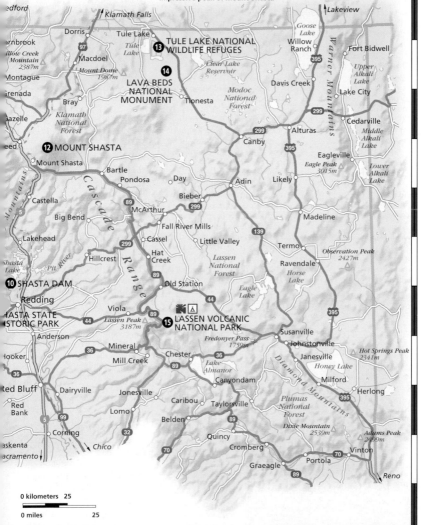

edford

Klamath Falls

Lakeview

Dorris

Tule Lake

Goose
Lake

Willow
Ranch

Fort Bidwell

arnbrook

97

illow Creek
Mountain
2387m

Macdoel

Mount Dome
1987m

13 TULE LAKE NATIONAL
WILDLIFE REFUGES

Clear Lake
Reservoir

395

Upper
Alkali
Lake

Montague

Tule
Lake

14

Davis Creek

Lake City

renada

Bray

LAVA BEDS
NATIONAL
MONUMENT

Tionesta

Modoc
National
Forest

299

Cedarville

azelle

Klamath
National
Forest

Canby

Alturas

Middle
Alkali
Lake

eed

12 MOUNT SHASTA

395

Eagleville

Eagle Peak
3015m

Lower
Alkali
Lake

Mount Shasta

Bartle
Pondosa

Day

Adin

Likely

Castella

Cascade

Bieber

Madeline

Big Bend

McArthur

299

5

Fall River Mills

139

Termo

Observation Peak
2427m

Lakehead

299

Cassel

Little Valley

Pit River

Hillcrest

Range

Hat
Creek

Lassen
National
Forest

Ravendale

Horse
Lake

hasta
Lake

10 SHASTA DAM

89

Old Station

Eagle
Lake

395

Redding

44

HASTA STATE
STORIC PARK

44

Viola

Lassen Peak
3187m

89

15 LASSEN VOLCANIC
NATIONAL PARK

Susanville

Johnstonville

Anderson

Fredonyer Pass
1759m

Hot Springs Peak
2341m

ooker

36

Mineral

Chester

36

Janesville

Honey Lake

36

Mill Creek

89

Lake
Almanor

Milford

Herlong

ed Bluff

Dairyville

Canyondam

Diamond Mountains

395

Red
Bank

Jonesville

Caribou

Taylorsville

Plumas
National
Forest

5

99

Lomo

Belden

89

Dixie Mountain
2539m

Adams Peak
2499m

askenta

32

Quincy

Vinton

acramento

Chico

Cromberg

Portola

70

Graeagle

89

Reno

```
0 kilometers   25
0 miles        25
```

For additional map symbols see back flap

Redwood National Park ❶

See pp448–9.

Arcata ❷

Road map A2. 🚶 *16,400.* 🚌 ✈
Arcata/Eureka Airport, 8 miles (13 km)
N of Arcata. ℹ *62 G St (707 822-3619).* **www**.arcatachamber.com

Arcata is a small town and its life revolves around Humboldt State University, in the hills above. Arcata's main square, with palm trees and a statue of President McKinley (1843–1901), is filled with bookstores and cafés. The town is a pleasant base for exploring the redwood region.

The forests east of Arcata are thought to be the stomping grounds of Bigfoot, the US equivalent to Asia's Yeti. No one has yet proved its existence, but footprints larger than those of the biggest bear have been found.

Eureka ❸

Road map A2. 🚶 *27,600.* 🚌
✈ *Arcata/Eureka Airport, 15 miles (24 km) N of Eureka.* ℹ *2112 Broadway (707 442-3738).*
www.eurekachamber.com

Eureka was founded by gold miners in 1850, who were so excited by their find that they

Ornate Carson Mansion in Eureka

REDWOODS AND THE LUMBER INDUSTRY

The tallest tree on earth, the coniferous coastal redwood *(Sequoia sempervirens)* is unique to northern California and southern Oregon, although it is also related to the giant sequoia *(Sequoiadendron gigantea)* of the High Sierras and the *Metasequoia glyptostrobiodes* species, native to China. Redwoods can live for 2,000 years and reach 350 ft (107 m), despite roots that grow up to 200 ft (61 m) horizontally but only 4–6 ft (1–2 m) deep.

The redwood's fast growth and resistance to disease makes it ideal for commercial use. By the 1920s, logging had destroyed 90 percent of the groves. The Save the Redwoods League was formed, buying land now protected in state parks. However, some groves are still owned by lumber companies, and their future is a major issue on both local and national levels.

Stacked redwood lumber

proudly named it after the state's ancient Greek motto meaning "I have found it." It has since expanded into the northern coast's largest industrial center, with extensive logging and fishing operations surrounding the state protected natural harbor.

West of US 101, between E and M streets along the waterfront, is Eureka's interesting Old Town. Its restored 19th-century buildings, many of them with cast-iron façades, have now been converted into cafés, bars, and restaurants.

Situated at M and Second streets is the extravagant Victorian architecture of Carson Mansion *(see pp30–31)*. It was built in 1885 for millionaire lumber baron William Carson. Its whimsical Gothic design is enhanced by its redwood construction typical of the area, painted to resemble the more expensive medium of stone. Carson Mansion is now a gentlemen's club and is closed to the general public.

Samoa Cookhouse ❹

79 Cookhouse Ln & Samoa Rd, Eureka.
Road map A2. **Tel** *(707) 442-1659.*
◻ *daily.* ● *Thnksg, Dec 25.* ♿

The Samoa Cookhouse was built in 1900 as a dining room for workers at the adjacent Louisiana Pacific pulp mill, one of many lumber mills standing on the narrow Samoa Peninsula. It was opened to the public in the 1960s, when automation in the mills had reduced the size of the workforce and the need for on-site dining facilities. The restaurant has retained its rustic décor and its giant-sized portions of ham and eggs, fried chicken, and other traditional American dishes. Old photographs and antique logging equipment add to the unique ambience.

Ferndale ❺

Road map A2. 🚶 *1,400.*
✈ *Arcata/Eureka Airport, 40 miles (64 km) N of Ferndale.* ℹ *PO Box 325, Ferndale (707 786-4477).*

Located on a flood plain near the mouth of the Eel River, Ferndale is a pastoral respite from the wilderness of California's northern coast. The town was founded in 1852 by Danish, Swiss-Italian, and Portuguese immigrants who together established a lucrative dairy industry here. In 1992, Ferndale was hit by one of the most powerful earthquakes in California's recent history, measuring 7.1 on the Richter scale, but damage was limited. Exhibits of the town's history can be seen in the **Ferndale Museum**.

The town is perhaps best known as the host of the annual Kinetic Sculpture Race, during which contestants ride their self-made vehicles from Arcata to Centerville County Beach, outside Ferndale.

🏛 Ferndale Museum
Shaw & 3rd St. **Tel** (707) 786-4466.
⬤ Feb–Dec: 11am–4pm Wed–Sat,
1–4pm Sun; Jun–Sep: 11am–4pm
Tue–Sat, 1–4pm Sun. ⬤ Jan.
www.ferndalemuseum.org

Gingerbread Mansion, one of Ferndale's Victorian houses

Scotia ❻

Road map A2. 🏔 2,500. 🚌
✈ Arcata/Eureka Airport, 40 miles (64 km) N of Scotia. 🛈 715 Wildwood Ave (707 764-3436).

The town of Scotia was built in 1887 to house the workers from the **Pacific Lumber Company**'s massive redwood mill, which dominates the south end of town. Palco, as the company is better known, was established in 1869 and owns and manages nearly 200,000 acres (80,000 ha) of prime redwood forest along the banks of the Eel River and its tributaries. Incorporating two sawmills, a school, medical clinics, and housing for nearly 300 lumber

Palco's redwood visitors' center in Scotia

employees and their families, Scotia is the only complete lumber community still in existence in California.

Exhibits on the history of Scotia, and on the redwood lumber industry as a whole, are displayed in a small museum in the center of town, which also dispenses passes for self-guided tours of the lumber mill. Here visitors can see each stage of the milling process: huge logs are debarked by powerful jets of water, sliced by laser-guided saws into lumber, then dried and stacked ready for shipping.

🚜 Pacific Lumber Company
125 Main St. **Tel** (707) 764-2222.
⬤ Mon–Fri. 🌐 **www**.palco.com

Avenue of the Giants ❼

🚐 Garberville. 🛈 Weott (Nov–Apr: 10am–4pm daily; May–Oct: 9am–5pm daily (707 946-2263).
www.hrsp@humboldtredwoods.org

The world's tallest redwood trees and the most extensive primeval redwood groves stand along the banks of the

Eel River in the impressive 50,000-acre (20,200-ha) Humboldt Redwoods State Park *(see p448)*. The best overall sense of these trees can be seen by driving along the 33-mile (53-km) Avenue of the Giants, a winding two-lane highway running parallel to US 101 through the park. For the best experience, however, leave your car in one of the many parking areas and walk around the groves, taking in the full immensity and magnificence of the trees.

The tallest individual specimen, the 364-ft (110-m) Dyersville Giant, was blown over during a storm in the winter of 1991, but its size is perhaps even more astounding now, lying on its side in Founder's Grove at the north end of the park. Currently the tallest and largest trees stand within the Rockefeller Forest above the west bank of the river.

The visitors' center, halfway along th e Avenue of the Giants on US 101, exhibits displays on the natural history of these mighty forests. It also supplies maps and detailed information on the many hiking and camping facilities available within the park.

Avenue of the Giants, in Humboldt Redwoods State Park

A Tour of Redwood National Park 1

Redwood National Park protects some of the largest original redwood forests in the world, stretching along the coastline of Northern California. Established by President Johnson in 1968 to promote tourism to the area, the 58,000-acre (23,500-ha) park includes smaller areas that had already been established as state parks. A tour of the area takes one full day, although two days allows time to walk away from the roads and experience the tranquillity of these majestic groves.

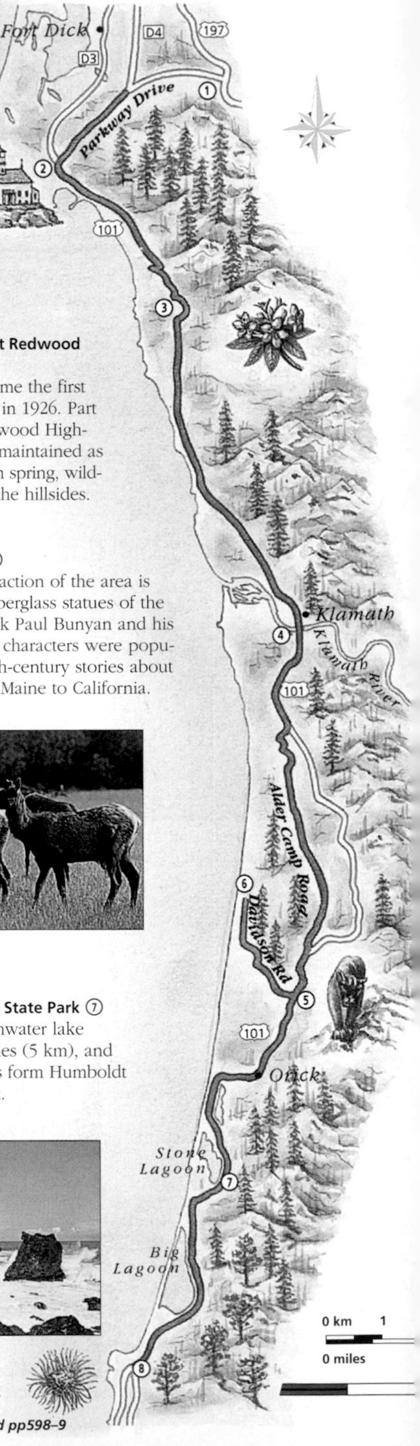

Coastal redwood trees

Del Norte Coast Redwood State Park [3]
This park became the first protected area in 1926. Part of the old Redwood Highway has been maintained as a hiking trail. In spring, wildflowers cover the hillsides.

Trees of Mystery [4]
A major tourist attraction of the area is marked by giant fiberglass statues of the mythical lumberjack Paul Bunyan and his ox, Babe. The two characters were popularized in early 20th-century stories about their journey from Maine to California.

Tall Trees Grove [5]
The world's tallest tree, a 368-ft (112-m) giant, stands in the aptly named Tall Trees Grove, at the southern end of the park. The park provides a habitat for one of the world's last remaining herds of Roosevelt elk.

Gold Bluffs Beach [6]
This 11-mile (18-km) beach is rated by many as the most beautiful in Northern California.

Humboldt Lagoons State Park [7]
Big Lagoon, a freshwater lake stretching for 3 miles (5 km), and two other estuaries form Humboldt Lagoons State Park.

Patrick's Point State Park [8]
In winter, the headlands are a good place to watch for migrating gray whales. Rock pools abound with smaller marine life.

For hotels and restaurants in this region see pp552–4 and pp598–9

Jedediah Smith Redwoods State Park ①

Found among the 9,200 acres (3,720 ha) of this park are the most awe-inspiring coastal redwoods. The park was named after the fur-trapper Jedediah Smith, the first white man to walk across the US. He explored this region in 1828 *(see p46).*

Crescent City ②

This northern town is the site of the headquarters and main information center for Redwood National Park.

KEY

▬▬ Tour route

═══ Other roads

TIPS FOR DRIVERS

Tour length: Arcata to Crescent City is 78 miles (125 km). US 101 is the quickest route.
Duration of trip: One could drive the entire route in under two hours one-way, but to experience a more satisfying and relaxing visit to the Redwood National Park area, allow at least a full day.
When to go: September and October are ideal months to travel. Spring and summer can be foggy, but the best flowering plants are on view during these months. Winter is often rainy but is best for whale-watching. Summer is the prime tourist season, although crowds are rarely a problem in this remote area of the state.
Where to stay and eat: Tourist services are comparatively few and far between in this region. However, there is a limited range of restaurants and motels available in Orick and Klamath, while a much wider range of facilities is available in Crescent City (see pp542 & 598) and Arcata, south of the park (see p446).
Visitor information: Redwood Information Center, Hwy 101, Orick. ○ *9am–5pm daily.* ● *Jan 1, Dec 25, Thanksgiving.* *Tel (707) 464-6101.* www.nationalpark.com/redwood

The Lost Coast, near Crescent City

The Lost Coast ⑧

Road map A2. 🚌 *Garberville.* ℹ️ *Shelter Cove (707 923-2613).* www.*garberville.org*

Covering a small section of coastline so craggy and wild that no road could reasonably be built along it, the so-called Lost Coast is the largest remaining stretch of undeveloped shoreline in California. Protected by the government within the Sinkyone Wilderness State Park and the King Range National Conservation Area, the Lost Coast region stretches for more than 40 miles (64 km).

The salmon-fishing port of Shelter Cove, tucked away within a tiny bay, is at the center of the Lost Coast. Its remote location has kept the village small, but it remains a good base for hikers and wildlife enthusiasts. Sixteen miles (25 km) of hiking trails, inhabited only by fauna such as black bears, deer, mink, and bald eagles, run along the clifftops, interspersed with free camp sites. Shelter Cove is accessible only via a winding but well-maintained road.

A good feel for the Lost Coast can be had by taking Hwy 211 west of US 101 and then following the scenic road between Humboldt Redwoods State Park and Ferndale *(see p446).* This beautiful 50-mile (80-km) road runs to the edge of the Pacific Ocean around Cape Mendocino, the westernmost point on the coast of California.

Weaverville ⑨

Road map A2. 🚶 *3,500.* ✈️ *Redding Municipal Airport, 40 miles (64 km) E of Weaverville.* ℹ️ *317 Main St (530 623-6101).* www.*trinitycounty.com*

The small rural town of Weaverville, set back in the mountains between the coast and the Central Valley, has changed little in the 150 years since it was founded by gold prospectors.

At the heart of the small commercial district, which boasts the state's oldest drugstore, is the **Jake Jackson Museum**. This small museum has displays tracing both the history of Weaverville and its surrounding gold-mining and lumber region. Adjacent to the museum, the Joss House State Historic Site is the oldest and best-preserved Chinese Temple in the country. Built in 1874, it serves as a reminder of the many Chinese immigrants who arrived in the US to mine gold and stayed in the state as cheap labor building the California railroads *(see pp50–51).*

North of Weaverville, the Trinity Alps, part of the Salmon Mountain Range, rise up at the center of a beautiful mountain wilderness. They are popular with hikers and backpackers in the summer and with cross-country skiers during the winter months.

🏛️ **Jake Jackson Museum**
508 Main St. *Tel (530) 623-5211.* ○ *noon–4pm Apr–Nov: daily; Dec–Mar: Tue & Sat only.* **Donation.**

Towering coastal redwood trees in Redwood National Park ▷

Shasta Dam, controlling the North's water supplies

Shasta Dam ⑩

🚌 *Redding.* **Visitors' Center**
Tel (530) 225-4100, (800) 874-7562.
www.visitredding.org

In order to provide a steady
supply of water for agriculture, a cheap source of electricity for manufacturers, prevent flooding in the valley,
and offer jobs for workers who
had been left unemployed by
the downturn in local mining
industries, the US government
funded the Central Valley
Project. This was a network
of dams, canals, and reservoirs,
set up during the Depression
of the 1930s and centered upon
the 602-ft (183-m) high, 3,460-ft
(1,055-m) long Shasta Dam.
With a spillway three times as
high as Niagara Falls, the dam
is one of the most impressive
civil engineering achievements
in the country to this day.

Shasta State Historic Park ⑪

Road map A2. 🚌 *Redding.*
Visitors' Center *Tel (530) 225-2065.*
⬜ *10am– 5pm Wed–Sun.*
www.parks.ca.gov

During the 1850s, Shasta was
one of the largest gold mining
camps in the state and the
base of operations for prospectors working along the Trinity,
Sacramento, McCloud, and Pit
Rivers. As the Gold Rush
faded, the town faded too,
especially after the railroad was
rerouted through the town of
Redding, 5 miles (8 km) east.
 Shasta is now a ghost town,
but in the early 1920s the

state of California, realizing its
historical importance, took
over and began to restore it.
Numerous old brick buildings
are preserved in a state of
arrested decay, and the **Shasta
Courthouse** has been restored
to its original condition.
Exhibits at the small visitors'
center traces the town's history.
 One mile (1.5 km) west of
Shasta town, the land around
Lake Whiskeytown forms the
smallest parcel of the three-part
Shasta-Whiskeytown-Trinity
National Recreation Area, a
forest preserve surrounding the
three reservoirs. Lake Shasta is
the largest of the three. Trinity
Lake is also known as Clair
Engle Lake, in honor of the
local politician who helped
make this ambitious reclamation project a reality. All
three lakes are popular with
fishermen, water- skiers,
houseboat owners, and other
recreational users.

> 🏛 **Shasta Courthouse and
> Visitors' Center**
> Main St. **Tel** (530) 243-8194.
> ⬜ 10am–5pm Wed–Sun.

Mount Shasta ⑫

Road map B1. 🚃 *Dunsmuir.*
🚌 *Siskiyou.* 🚌 *Shasta.*
Visitors' Center Tel (530)
926-4865. ⬜ *daily.*
www.mtshastachamber.com

Mount Shasta reaches a
height of 14,162 ft (4,316 m)
and is the second highest of
the Cascade Mountains, after
Mount Rainier in Washington
State. Visible more than 100
miles (160 km) away and
usually covered with snow,
the summit is a popular destination for mountaineers.

**Mount Shasta, towering over the
town of Shasta below**

Tule Lake National Wildlife Refuges ⑬

Road map B1. 🚌 *Klamath Falls.*
Visitors' Center Tel (530) 667-2231.

Six refuges on both sides of
the California–Oregon border
form one of the most popular
bird-watching spots in the
western United States.

Interior of the preserved Shasta Courthouse

Centering upon Tule Lake and the Lower Klamath River, much of the region has been set aside as wildlife refuges *(see pp436–7)*, popular with bird-watchers. In the autumn the refuges attract hundreds of thousands of wildfowl as they make their migration south, from Canada to the Central Valley and beyond. Tule Lake is also the winter home to as many as 1,000 bald eagles, a comparatively rare species in California.

Lava Beds National Monument ⓮

Road map B1. ▦ *Klamath Falls.*
Visitors' Center *Tel* *(530) 667-2282.*
◯ *daily.* www.nps.gov / labe

The Lava Beds National Monument spreads over 46,500 acres (18,800 ha) of the Modoc Plateau, the volcanic tableland of northeastern California, and preserves an eerie landscape of lava flows and cinder cones. Beneath the lava beds are more than 200 caves and lava tubes – cylindrical tunnels created by exposed lava turning to stone.

The greatest concentration of caves can be visited via the Cave Loop Road, 2 miles (3 km) south of the park's visitors' center. From here, a short trail leads down into Mushpot Cave, the only one with lights and a paved floor. The name derives from splatters of lava found near the entrance.

Other caves along the road are also named for their main feature: Crystal Cave contains sparkling crystals, and Catacombs Cave requires visitors to crawl through its twisting passages. To visit any of the caves, wear sturdy shoes, carry a flashlight, and be sure to check first with the visitors' center.

The park is also notable as the site of the Modoc War of 1872–3, the only major war between the US and the Native Americans in California. After being removed from the area to a reservation in Oregon, a group of Modoc Indians returned under the command of Chief Kientpoos, or "Captain Jack." For six months they evaded the US Cavalry, but

Captain Jack's Stronghold in Lava Beds National Monument

Captain Jack was eventually captured and hanged, and the rest were forced into a reservation in what is now Oklahoma. Captain Jack's Stronghold is along the park's north border.

Lassen Volcanic National Park ⓯

Road map B2.
▦ *Chester, Red Bluff.*
Visitors' Center *Tel* *(530) 595-4444.* ◯ *daily.*

Prior to the eruption of Mount St. Helens in Washington in 1980, the 10,457-ft (3,187-m) high Lassen Peak was the last volcano to erupt on the mainland United States. In a series of nearly 300 eruptions between 1914 and 1917, Lassen Peak laid waste to 100,000 acres (40,500 ha) of the surrounding land. The area was set aside as Lassen Volcanic National Park in 1916.

The volcano is the southernmost in the Cascade Mountain range and is considered to be still active. Numerous areas on its flanks show clear signs of the geological processes. Bumpass Hell was named

after an early tour guide, Kendall Bumpass, who lost his leg in one of the boiling mudpots in 1865. This boardwalk trail leads past a series of steaming, sulfurous pools of boiling water, heated by molten rock deep underground. Bumpass Hell is one of the park's most interesting stops and is located along Hwy 89, 5 miles (8 km) from the Southwest Entrance Station.

In winter, Hwy 89 across the park is closed because of weather conditions. In summer, the road winds through the park, climbing more than 8,500 ft (2,590 m) high, up to Summit Lake. The road continues across to the Devastated Area, a bleak gray landscape of rough volcanic mudflows, ending at Manzanita Lake in the northwest corner of the park. Here the **Loomis Museum** displays a photographic record of Lassen Peak's many eruptions.

The park contains more than 150 miles (240 km) of hiking trails, including a very steep 2.5 mile (4 km) route up the side of Mount Lassen to the ashen gray summit.

血 Loomis Museum
Lassen Park Rd, North Entrance.
Tel *(530) 595-4444.* ◯ *late Jun–mid-Sep: daily.*

Sulfur springs in Lassen Volcanic National Park

THE WINE COUNTRY

Famous throughout the world for its superlative wines, the Wine Country interior has a temperate climate, miles of vine-covered hills, and spectacular architecture. To the west lie the dramatic, rocky landscapes of the Sonoma and Mendocino coastlines. Throughout the region, a wide choice of excellent food and, of course, premium wine is available, making this an ideal place for a relaxing retreat.

California's wine industry was born in the small, crescent-shaped Sonoma Valley, when, in 1823, Franciscan fathers planted grape vines to produce sacramental wines. In 1857, the flamboyant Hungarian Count Agoston Haraszthy brought winemaking in California to a new level: using imported European grape varieties, he planted the state's first major vineyard at Sonoma's revered Buena Vista Winery (see p465). Haraszthy made a name not only for himself (he is known as the "father of California wine") but also for this previously unrecognized wine-producing region.

Over the years, many wine producers have followed in the count's footsteps, most of them favoring the rich, fertile soil of the Napa Valley. Hundreds of wineries now stand side by side along the length of the valley floor. Most of them offer tours of their facilities and wine tastings. Many are also of architectural interest, including such gems as the Mission-style Robert Mondavi Winery and the white Mediterranean-style Sterling Vineyards, which is perched on a volcanic bluff. Nearby, the stunning modern winery of Clos Pegase is distinguished by rows of imposing russet- and earth-colored columns and towers.

Nestled at the northernmost edge of the Napa Valley is the small town of Calistoga, famous for its restorative mud baths, enormous geysers, and hot mineral-water tubs. West of the valley, the Russian River which is bordered by the Sonoma and Mendocino coastal areas flows into the Pacific Ocean. These wild stretches of shoreline provide perfect opportunities for bird-and whale-watching and beachcombing.

Goat Rock Beach at the mouth of the Russian River

◁ Mustard plants growing in a Napa Valley vineyard in the spring

Exploring the Wine Country

The sheltered valleys of the coastal ranges provide the best conditions for planting vines, particularly within the Russian River, Sonoma, and Napa valleys. To the west of these famous wine-producing areas, quaint coastal towns, such as Mendocino, Jenner, and Bodega Bay, are surrounded by pristine, secluded beaches and small rock pools. Inland, visitors can explore the ancient redwood groves on foot, horseback, or by train. For those who prefer to have a bird's-eye view of the region, trips are available in hot-air balloons that soar gracefully above the vineyards. A short drive away are several immense state historic parks, with dense forests and unique architecture. Nearby, a wide variety of watersports is offered at Clear Lake, California's largest freshwater lake, and Lake Berryessa, which is the second largest artificial lake in the state.

Gerstle Cove, site of a marine preserve at Salt Point

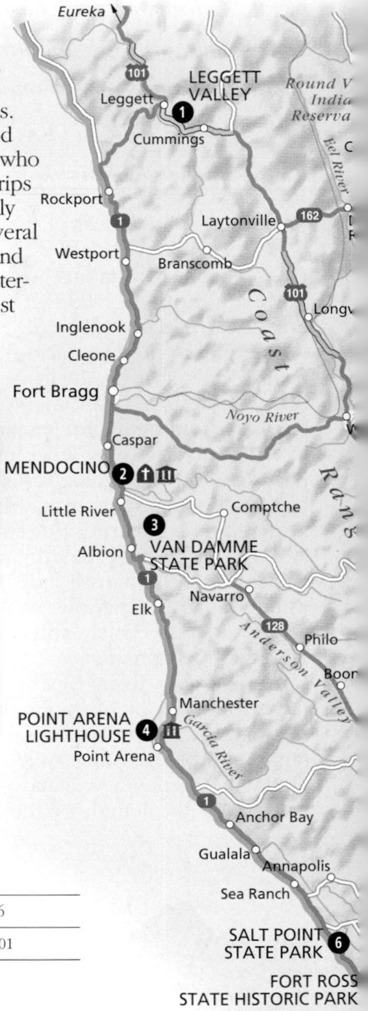

GETTING AROUND

The majority of visitors explore the Wine Country and the scenic areas along the Sonoma and Mendocino coasts by car. From San Francisco, Hwy 1 follows the coast; Hwy 101 runs south–north through the center of the region and into Humboldt County. Route 20 links Nevada City and the Wine Country, joining Hwy 101 north of Lake Mendocino. Public transportation services in the area are limited, although bus tours from San Francisco are available, and train tours of the Napa Valley *(see pp462–3)* and of the northern redwood forests *(see p459)* operate regularly. The closest international airports are in San Francisco and Oakland *(see pp628–9)*.

SEE ALSO

- **Where to Stay** pp554–6
- **Where to Eat** pp599–601

KEY

═══ Freeway

━━━ Major road

━━━ Secondary road

═══ Minor road

━━━ Scenic route

─── Minor railway

△ Summit

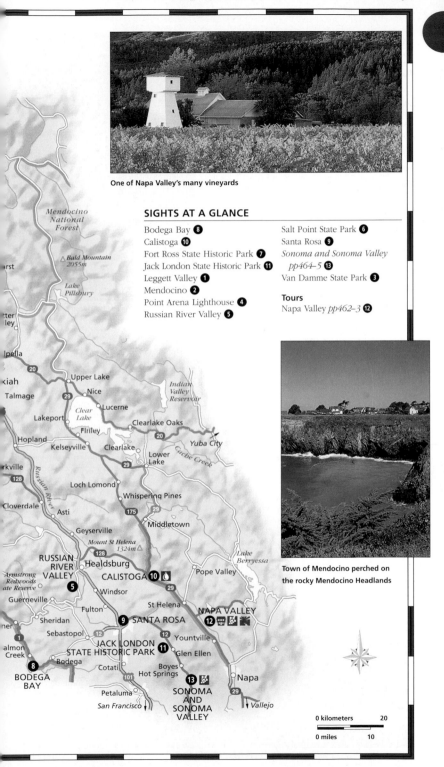

One of Napa Valley's many vineyards

SIGHTS AT A GLANCE

Bodega Bay **8**
Calistoga **10**
Fort Ross State Historic Park **7**
Jack London State Historic Park **11**
Leggett Valley **1**
Mendocino **2**
Point Arena Lighthouse **4**
Russian River Valley **5**

Salt Point State Park **6**
Santa Rosa **9**
Sonoma and Sonoma Valley pp464–5 **13**
Van Damme State Park **3**

Tours
Napa Valley *pp462–3* **12**

Town of Mendocino perched on the rocky Mendocino Headlands

0 kilometers   20
0 miles   10

Leggett Valley ❶

Road map A2. 🚃 *to Leggett.*
ℹ️ *70400 Hwy 101.*

This lush, green valley, separated from the Pacific Ocean by the King Mountain Range, is famous in California for its majestic giant redwoods. In the 1930s a hole was cut in the trunk of one enormous redwood to allow motorists to drive through the tree.

Hikers come to Leggett Valley and the surrounding area to enjoy the atmospheric redwood forest trails (part of the forest here was used to film scenes for George Lucas's science-fiction epic, *Star Wars*). The local wildlife population includes raccoons and deer, and golden eagles can often be seen soaring above the trees, searching the forest floor for unsuspecting prey.

South Fork Eel River, which is rich in salmon and steelhead trout, attracts many birds, including herons. The river is also popular with anglers and, in summer, swimmers.

Mendocino ❷

Road map A3. 🏘️ *1,200.* 🚃
ℹ️ *332 N Main St, Fort Bragg
(707) 961-6300; 800 726-2780).*
www.mendocinocoast.com

The settlers of this fishing village came to California from New England in 1852. They built their new homes to resemble as closely as possible those they had left behind on the East Coast, with pointed gables and decorative wooden trims. As a result, the Mendocino coastline is often referred to as "California's New England Coast." Perched on a rocky promontory high above the Pacific Ocean, Mendocino has retained the picturesque charm of its days as a major fishing and logging center. Although tourism is now its main industry, the town remains virtually untarnished by commercialism. It is a thriving arts center and has a large number of artists and writers. Visitors can stroll around the many boutiques, book-shops, galleries, and cafés. Those who prefer the attractions of nature can admire the beauty of the heather-covered bluffs, the migrating gray whales, and the stunning ocean vistas.

Giant ferns lining the beautiful Fern Canyon Trail in Van Damme State Park

Van Damme State Park ❸

Comptche Ukiah Rd. *Tel* (707) 937-5804. 📠 (707) 937-4016. 🚃 *from Point Arena.* 🕐 *daily; Apr–Oct: reservations needed for camping.* 🏞️ ♿

This beautiful 2,200-acre (890-ha) preserve has some of California's most scenic forest trails, shaded by immense redwoods and giant ferns, and accompanied by meandering creeks. The coastal areas of the park are popular with abalone divers. For visitors who want to enjoy a hike or jog through gorgeous countryside, the lush Fern Canyon Trail is one of the best in the park, which also has several cycle trails.

Visitors also come to Van Damme to contemplate the peculiar Pygmy Forest, an eerie grove of old, stunted trees. Due to a combination of poor soil and bad drainage, these trees grow no taller than about 4 ft (1.2 m). The Pygmy Forest, 3 miles (5 km) north of the park, is accessible on foot or by car.

Point Arena Lighthouse ❹

Road map A3. *Tel* (707) 882-2777.
🚃 *from Point Arena.* **Lighthouse
and Museum** 🕐 *May–Sep: 10am–4:30pm daily; Oct–Apr: 10am–3:30pm daily.* 🏞️ ♿ *museum only.* 🎫
www.pointarenalighthouse.com

One mile (1.5 km) north of the Point Arena fishing village stands this impressive 115-ft (35-m) lighthouse. Erected in 1870, the original brick building was destroyed in the earthquake of 1906 *(see p24)*. The present reinforced concrete structure was produced in San Francisco by the Concrete Chimney Company.

A climb up the 145 steps to the top of the lighthouse provides a stunning view of the coast – the effort is particularly

Mendocino overlooking the ocean from the bay's rocky headlands

For hotels and restaurants in this region see pp554–6 and pp599–601

worthwhile on fog-free days. Tours of the lighthouse (available all year round) offer a chance to see its huge original Fresnel lens close-up. Built in France, it measures over 6 ft (1.8 m) in diameter, weighs more than 2 tons, and floats in a large pool of mercury.

The adjacent fog signal building, which dates from 1869, now houses a museum. Among the exhibits are several compressed-air foghorns and displays on the history of the lighthouse, including some fascinating old photographs.

THE SKUNK TRAIN

Since 1885, the Skunk Train has been running from Fort Bragg, a coastal logging town north of Mendocino, into the heart of the redwood groves. Thanks to the odoriferous mix of diesel and gasoline once used to fuel the locomotive, waiting passengers could always smell the train before they could see it, hence its name. Today, locomotive lovers can ride on one of the steam, diesel, or electric trains for a half- or full-day tour through the forests.

Skunk Train and its smoke cloud

Point Arena Lighthouse overlooking the Pacific Ocean

Russian River Valley ❺

from Healdsburg. 🛈 16209 First St, Guerneville (707 869-9000). www.russianriverchamber.com

Bisected by the Russian River and its tributaries, the area known as the Russian River Valley is so vast that it contains several smaller valleys, some dominated by hillsides planted with grapevines and apple orchards, others by redwood groves, family farms, and sandy river beaches. About 60 wineries, many of which are open for wine tastings, are scattered throughout the valley.

At the hub of the valley is the small town of Healdsburg, where visitors often congregate around the splendid Spanish-style town square, with its shops, cafés, and restaurants.

Southwest of Healdsburg lies the tiny, friendly town of Guerneville, a summertime

haven for San Francisco Bay Area residents, particularly gay men and women. Every year in September, Guerneville plays host to the very popular Russian River Jazz Festival at Johnson's Beach. Johnson's is also a good place from which to take a canoe or rafting trip down the gentle Russian River, where turtles, river otters, and great blue herons are often sighted. Hikers and equestrians flock to Guerneville to visit the 805-acre (330-ha) **Armstrong Redwoods State Reserve**, which is the site of one of the few remaining old-growth redwood forests in California. Among the mighty redwoods in the park is a 308-ft (94-m) giant – a 1,400-year-old tree named Colonel Armstrong.

🌿 Armstrong Redwoods State Preserve
17000 Armstrong Woods Rd, Guerneville. **Tel** (707) 869-2015, 865-2391. ⬭ daily.

Salt Point State Park ❻

Hwy 1. **Tel** (707) 847-3221, 847-3465. 🚌 from Santa Rosa. ⬭ daily. 🏊 ♿

Within this forested 6,000-acre (2,400-ha) seaside park are several rocky coves, frequented by abalone divers and surf fishers. Salt Point also includes Gerstle Cove Marine Reserve, where divers admire protected sea anemones, starfish, and various rock fish.

Numerous bridle paths and hiking trails wind through Salt Point's pines, redwoods, and flower-filled meadows. In April and May, the most popular park attraction is the route that leads through the 317-acre (130-ha) Kruse Rhododendron State Reserve, where rhododendrons with brilliant pink and purple blooms grow up to 30 ft (9 m) tall.

Gerstle Cove in Salt Point State Park

Cannon on display in front of the Russian Orthodox chapel at Fort Ross

Fort Ross State Historic Park ❼

Road map A3. **Tel** (707) 847-3286.
🚌 from Point Arena. 🔅 sunrise–sunset daily. 🍂 Thanksgiving, Dec 25. 🎫 ♿

On a windswept headland, 12 miles (19 km) north of Jenner, stands the grand Fort Ross State Historic Park. A well-restored Russian trading outpost, the fort was founded in 1812 and was occupied until 1841 (the name "Ross" is a derivative of the Russian word "Rossyia", meaning Russia).

The Russians were the first European visitors to the region, serving as representatives of the Russian-American Company, which had been established in 1799. Although it was the presence of Russian fur hunters in the North Pacific that induced Spain to occupy Alta California in 1769, the Russians never tried to expand their territory in California. After 30 years of peaceful trading, they abandoned the fort.

Built in 1836, the original house of the fort's last manager, Alexander Rotchev, is still intact today, and several other buildings have been painstakingly reconstructed within the wooden palisade. The most impressive structure in Fort Ross is the Russian Orthodox chapel, which was constructed from local redwood in 1824.

A small visitors' center offers picnic facilities and maps and booklets about the fort. Every year, a living history day is held on the last Saturday of July. More than 200 costumed participants re-create life at the outpost in the 1800s.

Bodega Bay ❽

Hwy 1. 🏃 1,300. 📧
🛈 850 Hwy 1 (707 875-3866).
www.bodegabay.com

In 1963, the coastal town of Bodega Bay, with its white clapboard houses, appeared in Alfred Hitchcock's classic film, *The Birds*. In the tiny neighboring town of Bodega, visitors can still see the Potter Schoolhouse, which was in the film.

Bodega Head, the small peninsula sheltering Bodega Bay, is one of California's best whale-watching points. Other favorite Bodega Bay pastimes include golfing, bird-watching, digging for clams, and deep-sea fishing. In the evening, visitors can watch the fishing fleets unload their day's catch at Tides Wharf dock on Hwy 1.

The northern end of Bodega Bay marks the beginning of the Sonoma Coast State Beach, a 10-mile (16-km) stretch of ten beaches, separated by rocky bluffs. At the northernmost tip

of this chain of beaches sits the charming little town of Jenner. Here, the wide Russian River spills into the Pacific Ocean, and hundreds of gray harbor seals bask in the sun and breed on Goat Rock Beach. The most rewarding time to watch the seals is during their "pupping season," which begins in March and lasts until late June.

Santa Rosa ❾

Road map A3. 🏃 136,000.
✈ Sonoma County Airport,
6 miles (10 km) N of Santa Rosa.
📧 🛈 9 4th St (707 577-8674;
800 404-7673).
www.visitsantarosa.com

Santa Rosa, which is one of the fastest-growing cities in California, is best known for its past and present residents, most notably the horticulturist Luther Burbank (1849–1926). Burbank lived here for more than 50 years and became world famous for creating 800 new plant varieties, including fruits, vegetables, and ornamental flowers. Self-guided tours explore the one-acre (0.5-ha) site of the **Luther Burbank Home and Gardens**, which includes a rose garden, and an orchard. The Victorian garden features plants often found in domestic gardens in the 1880s.

In a restored historical post office dating from 1909 is the Sonoma County museum. It illustrates the history of

A harbor seal on Goat Rock Beach

Fishing boats at North Beach Jetty Marina in Bodega Bay

Spring flowers in bloom at Luther Burbank Home and Gardens

Sonoma County through rare historical photographs, documents, and artifacts.

The late Charles Schulz, creator of the "Peanuts" series, was a resident of Santa Rosa. Fans of his cartoon characters can visit **Snoopy's Gallery and Gift Shop**, which stocks the widest range of Snoopy, Charlie Brown, and "Peanuts" products in the world.

🌷 **Luther Burbank Home and Gardens**
204 Santa Rosa Ave. **Tel** (707) 524-5445. **Gardens** ☐ daily.
Home ☐ Apr–Oct: Tue–Sun. 🖼
www.lutherburbankhome.org

🏛 **Sonoma County Museum**
415 7th Street. **Tel** (707) 579-1500.
☐ 11am–4pm Wed–Sun.
www.sonomacountymuseum.com

📷 **Snoopy's Gallery and Gift Shop**
1665 Steele Lane. **Tel** (707) 546-3385. ☐ 10am–6pm daily. ⚫ public hols. **www**.snoopydist.com

Calistoga ❿

Road map A3. 👥 4,715. 🚌
ℹ 1458 Lincoln Ave (707) 942-6333).
www.calistogachamber.org

Visitors have had mineral or mud baths here since this little spa town was founded in the mid-19th century by the state's first millionaire, Sam Brannan (1819–89). Today, crowds are still drawn here by its specialized spa treatments and good Wine Country cuisine. The town also has a range of pleasant accommodations and small boutiques selling everything from handmade soaps to European

home furnishings. Two miles (3 km) north of the town, the **Old Faithful Geyser** spouts jets of boiling mineral water 60 ft (18 m) into the sky about once every 40 minutes. To the west lies the **Petrified Forest**. Here hikers can see huge redwoods turned to stone by a volcanic eruption over three million years ago (see p462).

Many visitors who prefer to hike among living redwoods travel east to the Robert Louis Stevenson State Park, where the author of *Treasure Island* and his wife, Fanny Osbourne, spent their honeymoon in 1880 (see p26). Those who climb the 5 miles (8 km) from the park to the summit of the 4,343-ft (1,325-m) Mount St. Helena, the Wine Country's highest peak, are rewarded by a breathtaking view of the vineyards below. To enjoy the view without making the rigorous ascent, it is worth taking a trip in a glider or hot-air balloon. These are available at the gliderport in nearby Calistoga.

🌋 **Old Faithful Geyser**
1299 Tubbs Lane. **Tel** (707) 942-6463. ☐ daily. 🖼 **www**.oldfaithfulgeyser.com

🌋 **Petrified Forest**
4100 Petrified Forest Rd. **Tel** (707) 942-6667. ☐ daily. ⚫ Dec 25. 🖼 🚫 limited. **www**.petrifiedforest.org

Jack London State Historic Park ⓫

London Ranch Rd, Glen Ellen. **Tel** (707) 938-5216. **Park and Museum** ☐ daily. ⚫ Jan 1, Thanksgiving, Dec 25. 🖼 🚫 museum only. 🖼 **www**.jacklondonpark.com

In the early 1900s, the world-famous author of *The Call of the Wild, The Sea Wolf,* and more than 50 other books (see p26) abandoned his hectic lifestyle to live in this tranquil 800-acre (325-ha) expanse of oaks, madrones, California buckeyes, and redwoods. London (1876–1916) aptly named this territory the Beauty Ranch, and it still contains his stables, vineyards, and the cottage where he lived and died. Also here are the eerie ruins of London's dream home, the Wolf House, which was mysteriously destroyed by fire just before its completion. The park is ideal for a quiet picnic and a hike.

After London's death, his widow, Charmian Kittredge (1871–1955), built a magnificent home on the ranch, called the House of Happy Walls. The house is now a museum displaying London memorabilia. The author's writing desk and early copies of his work are exhibited, as well as his collection of South Pacific art objects.

Old Faithful Geyser spurting hot water into the sky

Napa Valley Tour [12]

The sliver of land known as Napa Valley is 35 miles (56 km) long and lies at the heart of Northern California's wine industry. More than 250 wineries are scattered across its rolling hillsides and fertile valley floor, some dating from the early 19th century. Most of the wineries hug the scenic Silverado Trail and Hwy 29, two major arteries that run the length of the valley and through the towns of Yountville, Oakville, Rutherford, St. Helena, and Calistoga *(see p461)*. Many of Napa Valley's popular wineries offer visitors free tours of their facilities, while some charge a small wine-tasting fee.

Statue at Clos Pegase

Sterling Vineyards (7)
An aerial tramway provides access to this large, white, Mediterranean-style winery, which is perched on a hill overlooking the valley and vineyards.

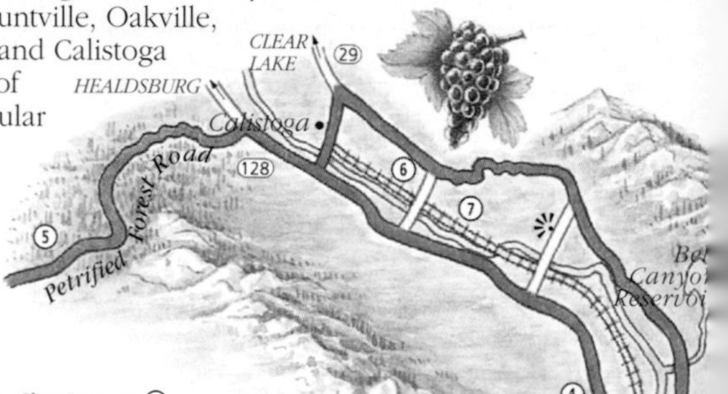

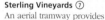

Clos Pegase (6)
Renowned architect Michael Graves designed this Post-Modern winery, which is well known for its distinctive art collection and fine wines.

Petrified Forest (5)
This forest is the home of the largest petrified trees in the world *(see p461)*.

Bale Grist Waterwheel (4)
Built in 1846, this waterwheel still grinds grain into meal and flour on weekends.

FOOD AND WINE IN THE NAPA VALLEY

In addition to a number of superior wines, the Wine Country is well known for its fresh produce and prestigious chefs. Produce stalls and farmers' markets line the valley roads, selling organic vegetables and fruit and freshly squeezed juices. Restaurants in most small towns serve excellent meals, prepared with the freshest ingredients. Classic Wine Country cuisine includes dishes such as Sonoma leg of lamb with fresh mint pesto, creamy risotto with artichoke hearts and sun-dried tomatoes, wild-mushroom sauté in herb-garlic phyllo pastry, and Sterling salmon sautéed and served with a Pinot Noir sauce.

Restaurant terrace at Domaine Chandon in Yountville

Robert Mondavi Winery (3)
Beautiful sculptures and paintings are on display throughout this huge, Mission-style winery. Guided tours are available year round.

KEY

- Tour route
- Other roads
- Viewpoint

Napa Valley vineyard in the late-afternoon sunlight

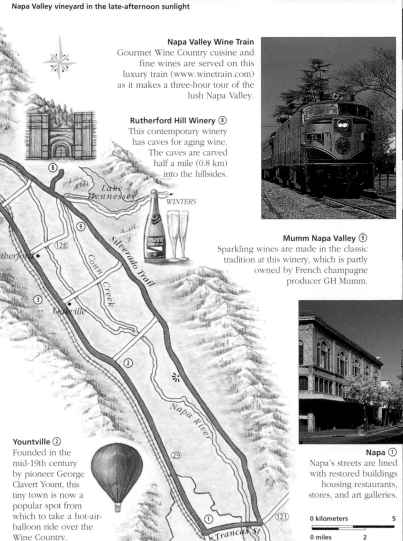

Napa Valley Wine Train
Gourmet Wine Country cuisine and fine wines are served on this luxury train (www.winetrain.com) as it makes a three-hour tour of the lush Napa Valley.

Rutherford Hill Winery ⑧
This contemporary winery has caves for aging wine. The caves are carved half a mile (0.8 km) into the hillsides.

Mumm Napa Valley ⑨
Sparkling wines are made in the classic tradition at this winery, which is partly owned by French champagne producer GH Mumm.

Yountville ②
Founded in the mid-19th century by pioneer George Clavert Yount, this tiny town is now a popular spot from which to take a hot-air-balloon ride over the Wine Country.

Napa ①
Napa's streets are lined with restored buildings housing restaurants, stores, and art galleries.

0 kilometers 5

0 miles 2

Sonoma and Sonoma Valley ⓭

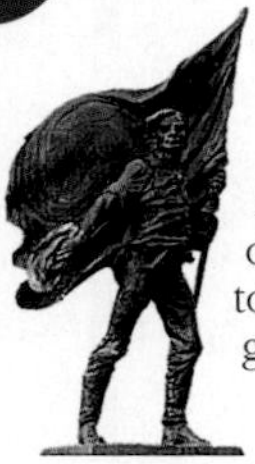

Bear flag monument

Nestling in the narrow, 17-mile (27-km) long Sonoma Valley, cradled by the Mayacama Mountains to the east and by the Sonoma Mountains to the west, are 6,000 acres (2,400 ha) of vineyards. At the foot of the valley lies the tiny town of Sonoma with its 8-acre (3-ha) plaza, a grass-covered town square designed in 1835 by Mexican General Mariano Vallejo (1808–90).

In the early 1840s, American settlers arriving in the area discovered that land ownership was reserved for Mexican citizens. On June 14, 1846, about 30 armed American farmers took General Vallejo and his men prisoner, seized control of Sonoma, and declared California an independent republic. The rebels' flag was adorned with a red star and stripe and a crude drawing of a grizzly bear. Although the republic was abolished 25 days later, when the United States annexed California *(see p47)*, the state legislature adopted the Bear Flag design as the official California flag in 1911.

Exploring Sonoma

Sonoma's main attractions are its internationally renowned wineries and the attractive area immediately surrounding the Spanish-style **Sonoma Plaza**. The well-shaded plaza is lined with dozens of meticulously preserved historical sites. Many of the adobe buildings around the square house wine shops, charming boutiques, and chic restaurants serving excellent California and Wine Country cuisine. At the very center of the town's plaza stands the **Sonoma City Hall**, a stone Mission Revival building *(see p31)* designed in 1908 by the San Francisco architect AC Lutgens. Close to the plaza's northeast corner is the bronze **Bear Flag Monument**, which serves as a memorial to the group of American settlers who rebelled against the ruling Mexican government in 1846.

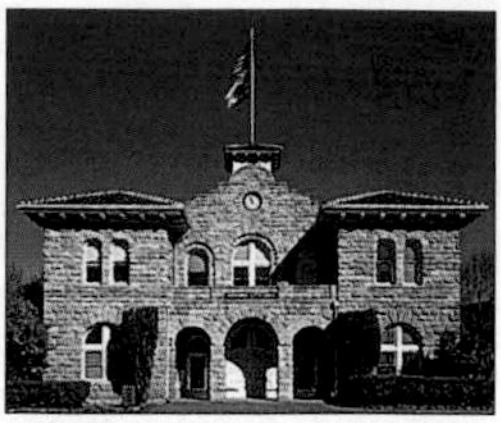

Sonoma City Hall at the center of the historic Sonoma Plaza

🏛 Vasquez House

414 1st St East, El Paseo. ***Tel*** *(707) 938-0510.* 🕒 *Wed–Sun. 1:30–4:30pm.* 💲 ♿

This 1855 gabled house belonged to Civil War hero "Fighting Joe" Hooker, who later sold it to settlers Pedro and Catherine Vasquez. The house is now the headquarters of the Sonoma League for Historic Preservation. Various historical exhibits and information on Sonoma walking tours are available here.

🏛 Toscano Hotel

20 E Spain St. ***Tel*** *(707) 938-0510.* 🕒 *Sat–Mon 1–4pm.* 💲 ♿ *only.*

Located on the north side of the plaza, the restored Toscano Hotel is now a historic monument. The two-story wood-frame building dates from the

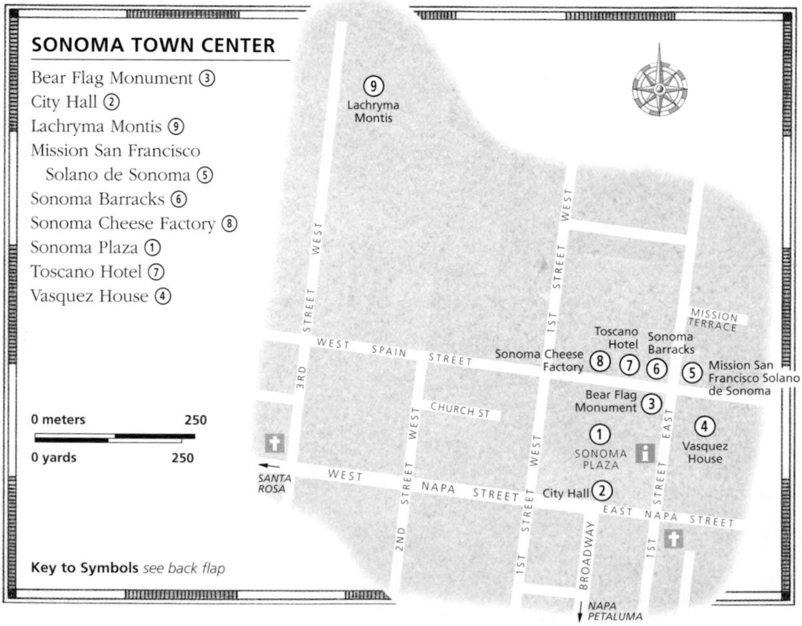
SONOMA TOWN CENTER
Bear Flag Monument ③
City Hall ②
Lachryma Montis ⑨
Mission San Francisco Solano de Sonoma ⑤
Sonoma Barracks ⑥
Sonoma Cheese Factory ⑧
Sonoma Plaza ①
Toscano Hotel ⑦
Vasquez House ④
0 meters 250
0 yards 250
Key to Symbols see back flap
Lachryma Montis
WEST STREET
WEST SPAIN STREET
CHURCH ST
3RD WEST
2ND STREET WEST
1ST STREET WEST
WEST NAPA STREET
EAST NAPA STREET
1ST STREET EAST
BROADWAY
MISSION TERRACE
Toscano Hotel
Sonoma Barracks
Sonoma Cheese Factory
Mission San Francisco Solano de Sonoma
Bear Flag Monument
SONOMA PLAZA
Vasquez House
City Hall
SANTA ROSA
NAPA PETALUMA

1850s, when it was used as a general store and library. It was converted into a hotel for gold miners in 1886 and now belongs to the state.

🔲 Sonoma Cheese Factory
2 W Spain St. **Tel** (707) 996-1931.
⬭ daily. ⬤ Jan 1, Thanksgiving, Dec 25. **www**.sonomajack.com
The famous Sonoma Jack cheese has been produced in the enormous vats in this factory since 1931. Visitors can watch the production process through a large observation window. The finished mild, white cheese can be purchased in the factory shop.

🏛 Lachryma Montis
W Spain & W 3rd Sts. **Tel** (707) 938-9559. ⬭ daily. ⬤ Jan 1, Thanksgiving, Dec 25. 🆔
Visitors can glimpse the lavish lifestyle of Mexican General Vallejo by exploring Lachryma Montis, his former home. This yellow and white Gothic Revival house was built of redwood in 1852. It features an eclectic array of Vallejo memorabilia, which ranges from the general's silver epaulettes and a cattle brand to his favorite books and photographs.

The name of the house is Latin for "tears of the mountain," a reference to a mineral spring on the property.

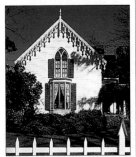

Lachryma Montis, once home to Mexican General Mariano Vallejo

🏛 Mission San Francisco Solano de Sonoma
E Spain St. **Tel** (707) 938-9560.
⬭ daily. ⬤ Jan 1, Thanksgiving, Dec 25. 🆔
Named after a Peruvian saint, this beautifully restored old mission (commonly called the Sonoma Mission) was the last of the historic chain of 21

Façade of the Mission San Francisco Solano de Sonoma

Franciscan missions built in California (*see p46*). Father José Altimira of Spain founded the mission in 1823 at a time when California was under Mexican rule. Today, all that survives of the original building is the corridor of Father Altimira's quarters. The present adobe chapel was built by General Vallejo in 1840 to be used by the town's families and soldiers.

VISITORS' CHECKLIST
Road map A3. 🏘 8,600.
✈ Sonoma County Airport, 6 miles (10 km) N of Santa Rosa.
🚌 90 Broadway & W Napa Sts, Sonoma Plaza. ℹ 453 1st St E (707 996-1090). 🍷 Valley of the Moon Vintage Festival (late Sep).

🏛 Sonoma Barracks
E Spain St. **Tel** (707) 938-1519.
⬭ daily. ⬤ Jan 1, Thanksgiving, Dec 25. 🆔
Native American labor was used to build this two-story adobe structure between 1836 and 1840, when it served as the headquarters for General Vallejo and his troops. After the 1846 Bear Flag Revolt, the barracks became an outpost for the United States Army for about a decade. After being purchased by the state in the late 1950s, the building was restored. It is now a California Historical Landmark.

SONOMA VALLEY WINERIES

The arms of the Sebastiani Vineyards

The Sonoma Valley has a rare perfect combination of soil, sun, and rain for growing superior wine grapes. In 1824, Father José Altimira planted Sonoma's first grapevines, in order to produce sacramental wine for the masses held at the Mission San Francisco Solano de Sonoma. When, in 1834, the ruling Mexican government secularized the mission, General Vallejo replanted grapevines on its land and sold the wine he produced to San Francisco merchants. In 1857, Hungarian Count Agoston Haraszthy (*see p455*) planted the nation's first European varietals at Sonoma's Buena Vista Winery, now the oldest premium winery in the state.

The Sonoma Valley encompasses the Sonoma Valley, Carneros, and Sonoma Mountain wine-growing regions. The climate varies slightly in each region, creating different environments suitable for producing particular grape varieties, including Cabernet Sauvignon and Chardonnay. Today, Sonoma is home to more than 35 wineries, which produce a total of 5.4 million cases of wine a year. Some of the valley's most notable wineries are Sebastiani Vineyards, Sonoma's largest premium-variety winery; Glen Ellen Winery; Gundlach-Bundschu Winery; and Château St. Jean. Most of Sonoma's wineries offer picnic areas and free wine tastings and tours.

Vineyards in the Sonoma Valley

GOLD COUNTRY AND THE CENTRAL VALLEY

L ocated at the geographical heart of California, the Gold Country is also central to the state's allure as the land of overnight success. Long before the gilded world of Hollywood took shape, this was a real life El Dorado, where a thick vein of solid gold, known as the Mother Lode, sat waiting to be discovered.

The Gold Country is largely rural, despite being the birthplace of modern California with the Gold Rush of 1849 and the designation of Sacramento as state capital.

Before the miners arrived, this quiet region, located on the far fringes of the Spanish colonial empire, was sparsely populated by members of the Miwok and Maidu peoples. With the discovery of gold flakes in January 1848, however, the region turned into a lawless jamboree, and by 1852 an estimated 200,000 men from all over the world were working in the mines. But by 1860 most of the region had fallen silent again, as the mining boom went bust *(see pp48–9)*.

A few years after the Gold Rush, the region experienced another short-lived boom. The transcontinental railroad was constructed through the Sierra Nevada Mountains by low-paid laborers, many of whom were Chinese *(see pp50–51)*. In the early 20th century, the Central Valley became the heart of the state's thriving agricultural industry, which today exports fruit and vegetables worldwide.

Stretching for more than 100 miles (160 km) north to south, the region's landscape is ideal for leisurely hikes or afternoon picnics. The Gold Country also offers one of California's best scenic drives along Hwy 49. The route climbs up and down rocky ridges between pastoral ranch lands, lined with oak trees and crossed by fast-flowing rivers. Many of the picturesque towns it passes through, such as Sutter Creek, have survived unchanged since the Gold Rush.

Malakoff Diggins State Park, preserving the heyday of the Gold Rush

◁ California State Capitol in Sacramento

Exploring the Gold Country

The Gold Country ranges from flat delta flood plains to the rugged, river-carved foothills of the Sierra Nevada Mountains. At the heart of the region is Sacramento, the state capital and largest Gold Country city, which has the highest concentration of sights. But the real attraction of this area is in traveling along its many scenic routes. The rural landscape is dotted with small historic towns. Some are still thriving communities, while others are ghostly memorials to their past. The Central Valley, along I-5, is scattered with picturesque farming towns. Larger towns, such as Nevada City and Sutter Creek, make excellent bases for a Gold Country tour, and visitors are welcomed and well taken care of everywhere.

Impressive State Capitol building in Sacramento

Parrots Ferry Bridge over the picturesque New Melones Lake along Hwy 49 in Tuolumne County

SIGHTS AT A GLANCE

Angels Camp **16**

Chaw'se Indian Grinding
   Rock State Park **11**

*Columbia State Historic
   Park pp480–81* **19**

Empire Mine State
   Historic Park **3**

Folsom **7**

Grass Valley **2**

Jackson **12**

Jamestown **20**

Malakoff Diggins State
   Park **1**

Marshall Gold Discovery
   State Park **6**

Moaning Cavern **17**

Mokelumne Hill **13**

Murphys **15**

Nevada City **4**

Placerville **8**

*Sacramento
   pp472–5* **5**

San Andreas **14**

Sonora **18**

Stockton **21**

Sutter Creek **9**

Volcano **10**

Replica dwelling in the Chaw'se Indian Grinding Rock State Park

1 MALAKOFF DIGGINS
   STATE HISTORIC PARK

ADA CITY **20**

4

Reno

2 **3** EMPIRE MINE STATE
   HISTORIC PARK

ASS
LEY

Foresthill

Auburn

6 MARSHALL GOLD
   DISCOVERY STATE PARK

Coloma

50

8 PLACERVILLE

OLSOM

Cosumnes River

Grizzly Flat

Cooks Station

ho
eta

Plymouth

VOLCANO **10** **11** CHAW'SE INDIAN
   GRINDING ROCK
   STATE PARK

88

TER CREEK **9**

JACKSON **12** **13** MOKELUMNE
   HILL

*Camanche
Reservoir*

Arnold

SAN ANDREAS **14**

ckeford

MURPHYS **15** **17** MOANING CAVERN

ANGELS CAMP **16**

aterloo   Copperopolis

19 COLUMBIA STATE
   HISTORIC PARK

JAMESTOWN **20** **18** SONORA

Farmington

4

nteca   Valley Home **108**

120

aus River   Oakdale

*Don Pedro
Reservoir*   Coulterville

120

La Grange   *Yosemite*

Modesto   Waterford **132**

yson   Snelling   *Lake
McClure*   **140** Midpines

Turlock   Hornitos   Mariposa

Patterson   Catheys Valley

Winton   Ahwahnee

Newman   Merced **140**

Gustine   *San Joaquin River*   Le Grand

99

Chowchilla

52   Los Banos **152**

*Luis
rvoir*   Fresno

SEE ALSO

• *Where to Stay* pp556–8

• *Where to Eat* pp601–2

GETTING AROUND

A car is essential for exploring the California Gold Country. Most sights are located along the Gold Rush Highway, Hwy 49. This makes the best and most scenic driving route as it undulates along the foothills through the most interesting Gold Country towns. Public transportation is severely limited, with only two long-distance bus services along the two main highways, I-80 and US 50, and a daily train service over the mountains from Sacramento. The area's main domestic airport is also in Sacramento, while the nearest international airport is San Francisco.

KEY

▬▬	Freeway
▬▬	Major road
▬▬	Secondary road
══	Minor road
▬▬	Scenic route
—	Main railway
—	Minor railway
△	Summit

0 kilometers   25

0 miles   25

The man-made canyon created by hydraulic mining at Malakoff Diggins

Malakoff Diggins State Park ❶

Road map B3. **Tel** (530) 265-2740. 🚌 from Nevada City. ⬜ daily. **Museum:** 10am–4pm, Sat & Sun. ● buildings Oct–Apr: 🎫 ♿ 🏳️

As the original gold mining techniques became less rewarding in the late 1850s, miners turned to increasingly powerful and destructive ways of extracting the valuable ore. When the more easily recoverable surface deposits disappeared, the miners began to strip away the soil with powerful jets of pressurized water. Spraying more than 200,000 gal (115,000 liters) of water per hour, the jets washed away entire mountainsides in search of gold, a process known as hydraulic mining. In 1884 the California legislature forbade the dumping of gravel into streams, but huge swathes of land had already been ruined and the rivers had been clogged up with debris (see pp48–9). One of the largest of these hydraulic mining operations was at Malakoff Diggins, 27 miles (45 km) northeast of Hwy 49, in the mountains above Nevada City. The eroded hillsides created a canyon that now forms an eerily beautiful state park, with several preserved buildings from the 1870s mining town of North Bloomfield.

Grass Valley ❷

Road map B3. 🏛 9,000. 🚉 🛈 248 Mill St (530 273-4667). www.grassvalleychamber.org

Long the largest and busiest town in the northern Gold Country, Grass Valley served the Empire Mine and other nearby hard rock gold mines.

In the 1870s and 1880s Grass Valley welcomed workers from the tin mines of Cornwall, England, who were affectionately known as "Cousin Jacks." Their expertise enabled the local mines to recover underground ore deposits and so remain in business after the rest of the area had fallen quiet (see pp48–9). Grass Valley also has one of California's best mining museums. The **North Star Mining Museum** is situated in the powerhouse of the former North Star Mine. Surrounding the museum's entrance are the giant Pelton wheels that greatly increased production in the region's underground mines. Displays include a stamp mill (a giant pulverizer used to crush ore), a Cornish pump (used to filter out underground water), as well as various artifacts relating to the Cornish background of the local miners.

A nugget of gold set inside quartz crystal

🏛 **North Star Mining Museum**
Mill St at Allison Ranch Rd. **Tel** (530) 273-4255. ⬜ Apr–Oct: daily. **Donation**.

Empire Mine State Historic Park ❸

Tel (530) 273-8522. 🚌 from Nevada City. ⬜ daily. ● Jan 1, Thanksgiving, Dec 25. 🎫 ♿ Grounds & Empire Cottage. 🖥 www.powermine.org

One of the longest surviving and most lucrative gold mining operations in the state, the Empire Mine was in business until 1956. It has now been preserved by the state as a historic park. Starting with surface workings in the 1850s, the Empire Mine grew to include 365 miles (585 km) of underground tunnels, from which pure gold estimated at 5.8 million ounces (16.5 million grams) was recovered.

Head frames, which held the mine's elevator shafts and other mining equipment, are scattered over the park's 785 acres (318 ha), but for a real sense of how much money was made here you should visit Empire Cottage.

Designed by San Franciscan architect Willis Polk in 1897 for the mine's owner, William Bourn, the granite and red-brick exterior resembles an English manor house, while the redwood interior gives an air of casual affluence. The gardens next door to the cottage contain nearly 1,000 rose bushes and a large greenhouse.

More exhibits on the history of the Empire Mine and on hard-rock gold mining are on display in the visitors' center, along with samples of the precious metal.

Original stamp mill used to crush ore at the Empire Mine

Firehouse Number 1's façade, a Nevada City landmark

Nevada City ❹

Road map B3. 🏚 2,855. 🏠 ▦
ℹ *132 Main St (530 265-2692).*
www.*nevadacitychamber.com*

With Victorian houses and commercial buildings lining its steep streets, picturesque Nevada City deserves its reputation as "Queen of the Northern Mines." Located at the northern end of the Mother Lode gold fields,

Nevada City thrived until gold mining peaked in the 1860s, then it faded into oblivion. Nearly a century later, the city was resurrected as a tourist destination, with galleries, restaurants, and inns re-creating Gold Rush themes.

Hwy 49 takes visitors arriving in Nevada City to the foot of Broad Street. Looking up the street, the large building on the left is the **National Hotel**. One of the oldest hotels in California, it first opened in the mid-1850s *(see p557)*.

A block east of the hotel is **Firehouse Number 1 Museum**, one of the region's most photographed façades. Dainty balconies and a white cupola decorate the exterior, and inside, a small museum displays local Maidu Indian artifacts, pioneer relics, including some relating to the tragic Donner Party *(see p486)*, and the altar from a Gold Rush Chinese temple. Antique mining devices are displayed in the park

opposite, and several plaques on the city's walls commemorate events from its past.

Back on Broad Street, the arcaded brick façade marks the historic **Nevada Theater**, which has been in use as a performance venue since 1865. A block to the south is the **Miner's Foundry**, an old metalworks where the innovative Pelton wheel was first developed and produced. A block to the north is the Art Deco façade of the city's **County Courthouse**, one of the city's few 20th-century works of architecture.

🏛 **Firehouse Number 1 Museum**
214 Main St. **Tel** *(530) 265-5468.* ◻
11:30am–4pm Thu–Sun. **Donation.**

Nevada Theater, used as a playhouse since 1865

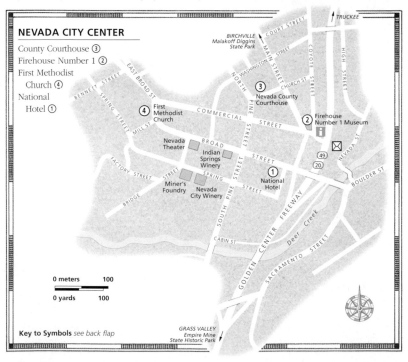

NEVADA CITY CENTER

County Courthouse ③
Firehouse Number 1 ②
First Methodist
  Church ④
National
  Hotel ①

Key to Symbols *see back flap*

Street-by-Street: Old Sacramento ❺

Californian railroad logo

Covering six blocks between the river and the modern city, Old Sacramento preserves many historic buildings within a precinct of shops, restaurants and museums. Some of the structures protected here were built to serve the gold miners of 1849 *(see pp48–9)*, but most date from the 1860s and 1870s, when Sacramento confirmed its position as the link between rural California and the commercial centers along the coast. The Pony Express and transcontinental railroad both had their western terminus here, with paddle-wheel riverboats providing the connection to San Francisco. A handful of museums trace the area's historic importance, and the riverfront location is ideal for walking and cycling.

Delta King Riverboat
One of the last Sacramento Delta riverboats still afloat, this moored paddle-wheel steamer is now a hotel and restaurant.

The former steamboat depot was the embarkation point for freight bound for San Francisco in the 1860s.

Old Schoolhouse
This one-room building is typical of a 19th-century California schoolhouse.

```
0 meters        5
0 yards         5
```

Theodore Judah Monument
This bas-relief commemorates Theodore Judah, the engineer who planned the transcontinental railroad (see pp50–51).

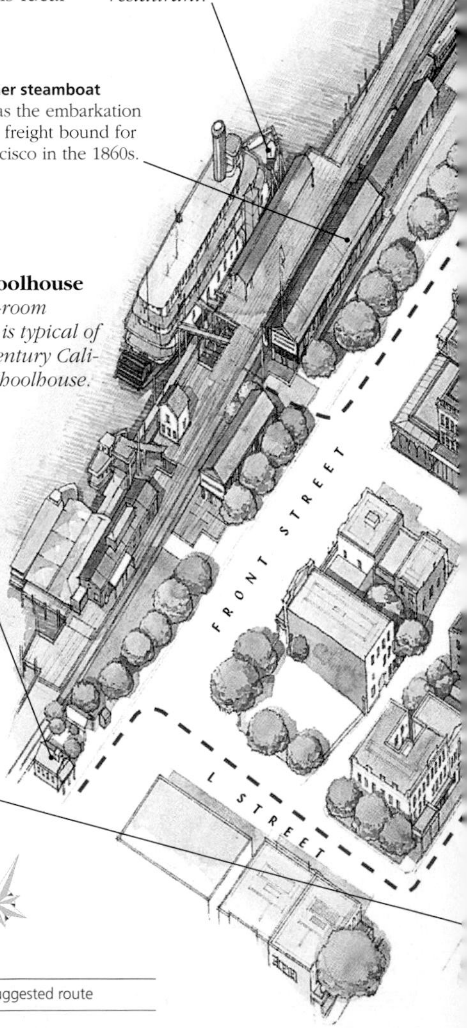

STAR SIGHTS

★ BF Hastings Building

★ California State Railroad Museum

KEY

– – – Suggested route

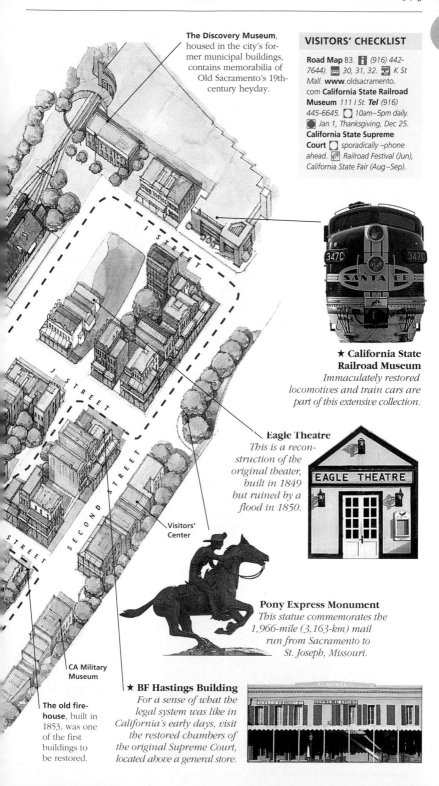

The Discovery Museum, housed in the city's former municipal buildings, contains memorabilia of Old Sacramento's 19th-century heyday.

★ **California State Railroad Museum**
Immaculately restored locomotives and train cars are part of this extensive collection.

Eagle Theatre
This is a reconstruction of the original theater, built in 1849 but ruined by a flood in 1850.

Visitors' Center

Pony Express Monument
This statue commemorates the 1,966-mile (3,163-km) mail run from Sacramento to St. Joseph, Missouri.

CA Military Museum

The old firehouse, built in 1853, was one of the first buildings to be restored.

★ **BF Hastings Building**
For a sense of what the legal system was like in California's early days, visit the restored chambers of the original Supreme Court, located above a general store.

Sacramento: California State Capitol

Standing at the center of a vast, landscaped park, the California State Capitol is Sacramento's primary landmark and one of the state's handsomest buildings. It was designed in 1860 by Miner F Butler in grand Renaissance Revival style, with Corinthian porticos and a tall central dome. The building was completed in 1874 after almost 15 years of construction and expenses totaling $2.5 million. The Capitol was expanded in the 1950s and completely renovated and restored in the 1970s. The Governor of California operates from his Capitol office, but the building also stands as a shining example of the Golden State's proud past.

Along with the chambers of the state legislature, which are open to visitors when they are in session, the Capitol serves as a museum of the state's political and cultural history.

VISITORS' CHECKLIST

10th St & L St., Capitol Mall, Capitol Park. **Road map** B3. **Tel** (916) 324-0333. 🚌 from Los Angeles & San Francisco. 🚏 30, 31, 36, 38, 61, 62. ⏰ 9am–5pm daily. ⬤ Jan 1, Thanksgiving, Dec 25. ☑ 📷 ♿ first floor only. 🏛 🍴 🚻

★ **Capitol Rotunda**
The impressive rotunda was restored to its original 19th-century splendor in 1975. The copper ball on top of the dome is plated in gold.

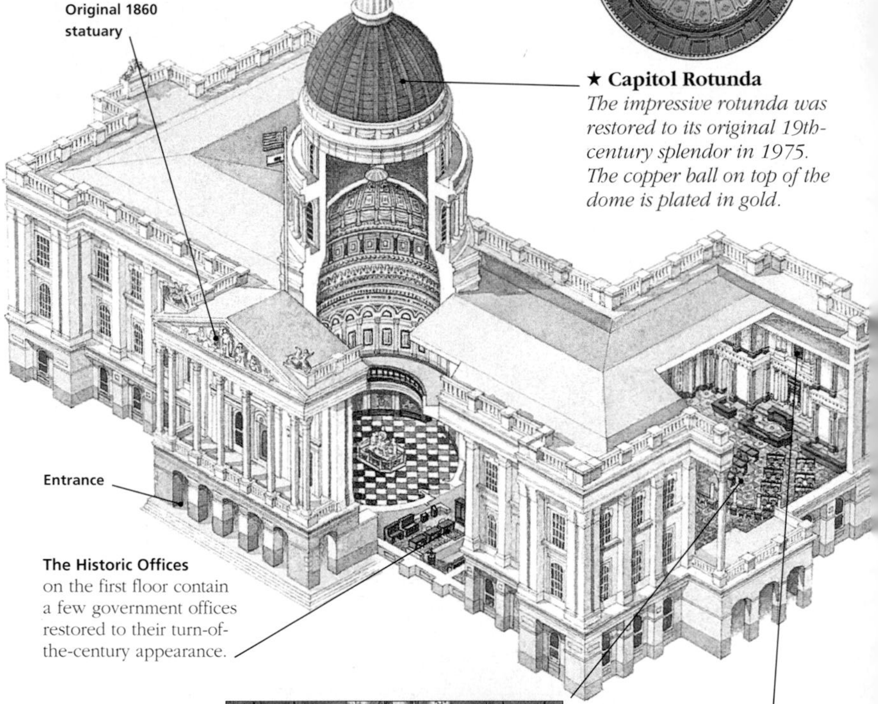

Original 1860 statuary

Entrance

The Historic Offices on the first floor contain a few government offices restored to their turn-of-the-century appearance.

★ **State Senate Chamber**
The mezzanine gallery is open all year, but it is most interesting when the legislature is in session, making speeches and holding votes on issues of importance.

A portrait of George Washington, the first US president, occupies the focal point on the Chamber wall.

STAR FEATURES

★ Capitol Rotunda

★ State Senate Chamber

🏛 Crocker Art Museum

216 O St. **Tel** *(916) 264-5423.* ⬤
10am–5pm Tue–Sun (9pm Thu). ⬤
Jan 1, Jul 4, Thanksgiving, Dec 25. 📷
📷 www.crockerartmuseum.org

Founded in 1873, the Crocker Art Museum is the oldest public art museum west of the Mississippi. The collection includes Victorian painting and sculpture from Europe and the United States, but its real strength is the California art and photography, and the touring shows that the museum exhibits.

Another prime attraction is the Italianate Victorian building itself, designed by the architect Seth Babson. The gallery includes polychrome tile floors, elaborately carved woodwork, and a graceful central staircase. It was built in 1869 as a home for the brother of Charles Crocker, one of the "Big Four" transcontinental railroad barons *(see pp472–3).*

Foyer of the Crocker Art Gallery

🏯 Sutter's Fort

2701 L St. **Tel** *(916) 324-0539.*
⬤ *daily.* ⬤ *Jan 1, Thanksgiving, Dec 25.* 📷

Now somewhat marooned amid the suburban streets of the modern state capital, Sutter's Fort in its heyday was one of the most important and populous sites in early California history.

Established by John Sutter in 1839, the fort became the cultural and economic center of northern California in the years leading up to the Gold Rush. Apart from the 21 Spanish missions along the coast, Sutter's Fort was the only Anglo-European settlement in California. Throughout the 1840s, new immigrants following the rugged overland trails from the eastern states stopped here to avail themselves of the fort's blacksmith shop, grain mill, and its many other facilities.

Reconstructed 19th-century kitchen at Sutter's Fort

The three-story central building is all that survives of the original fort. The rest of the complex has been reconstructed to give a picture of frontier life. A courtyard, surrounded by 18-ft (5.5-m) walls, houses various historical exhibits along a self-guided audio tour. These include a prison, a bakery, and a blacksmith's. This is the one of the few official sites in California where the Mexican flag still flies.

🏛 California State Indian Museum

2618 K St. **Tel** *(916) 324-0539.*
⬤ *daily.* ⬤ *Jan 1, Thanksgiving, Dec 25.* 📷

This area of California was once occupied by the Maidu people. This small but fascinating museum, set in a park adjacent to Sutter's Fort, explores the different Native American cultures that existed in the state before the 16th-century arrival of the first Europeans *(see pp44–5).* Displays of handicrafts focus on the beautiful reed baskets that held both a practical and spiritual value to the Indians, and a series of dioramas recreate the look and feel of tribal reservations. Slide shows, tape recordings, and films document other aspects of tribal culture, from language to agricultural skills.

Special programs, generally held on weekends, celebrate the survival of ancient Native American ways of life into the present day.

JOHN SUTTER

The story of the early California entrepreneur John Sutter is a classic real-life rags to riches to rags adventure. Following bankruptcy in his native Switzerland, Sutter emigrated to California in 1839. Only a year after his arrival, he was granted a 50,000-acre (20,000-ha) tract of land by the Mexican government, which he patriotically named New Helvetia (New Switzerland). In 1843 Sutter went into debt once again in order to buy Fort Ross on the northern coast from its Russian owners *(see p460).* For the next five years his land and wealth made him virtual lord and master over most of northern California.

However, the discovery of gold flakes by his employee James Marshall at his mill in 1848 *(see p470)* spelled the end of his vast empire. Thousands of miners swarmed to the region and almost immediately took over his land. Sutter spent the rest of his life in Washington, DC, hoping for compensation from the US government, but he died almost penniless in 1880.

John Sutter (1802–80)

Reconstructed Sutter's Mill, where gold was first discovered

Marshall Gold Discovery State Park ⑥

Road map B3. **Tel** *(530) 622-3470.* 🚍 *from Placerville.* ⏱ *8am–5pm daily.* ⬤ *Jan 1, Thanksgiving, Dec 25.* 🅿 ♿ 📷 www.parks.ca.gov

Covering some 250 acres (101 ha) along the banks of the American River, this peaceful state park protects and interprets the site where gold was first discovered in January 1848. James Marshall spotted shiny flakes in the water channel of a sawmill he and his fellow workmen were building for John Sutter *(see p475)*, and the rest is history.

Within a year, some 10,000 miners had turned Coloma into a thriving city, but with news of even richer deposits elsewhere the boom went bust as quickly as it began, and nowadays there is little sign of this busy era.

A full-scale reproduction of Sutter's Mill stands on the original site, and a statue of James Marshall can be found on a nearby hill to mark the spot where he is buried. The park's visitors' center includes the small **Gold Country Museum** with Native American artifacts, films, and other displays on the discovery of gold, as well as memorabilia relating to James Marshall.

🏛 **Gold Country Museum**
1273 High St, Auburn. **Tel** *(530) 889-6500.* ⏱ *11am–4pm Tue–Sun.* ⬤ *Jan 1, Thanksgiving, Dec 25.* 🅿

Folsom ⑦

Road map B3. 🏙 *46,000.* 🚍 ℹ *200 Wool St (916 985-2698).* www.folsomchamber.com

Folsom is now a pleasant Sacramento suburb, despite being the site of the state penitentiary made famous by Johnny Cash's 1970s song "Folsom Prison Blues."

It played an important role as the last station on the Pony Express and transcontinental railroad. Folsom is now one of the few remaining transcontinental railroad sites, as documented in the local **Folsom History Museum**. Antique shops line the Wild West-style Sutter Street, set amid boxcars and other railroad memorabilia.

At the foot of Riley Street, behind Folsom Dam, there is also a large lake, which is a popular summer vacation spot with residents and visitors, for boating and fishing.

🏛 **Folsom History Museum**
823 Sutter St. **Tel** *(916) 985-2707.* ⏱ *11am–4pm Wed–Sun.* ⬤ *public hols.* **Donation**.

Placerville ⑧

Road map B3. 🏙 *15,000.* 🚍 ℹ *542 Main St (530 621-5885).* www.eldoradocounty.org

During the Gold Rush, Placerville was a busy supply center for the surrounding mining camps. Still located on one of the main routes to Sacramento, Placerville has retained its importance as a transportation center, although the stagecoaches have long since given way to cars and trucks along US 50.

The downtown business district preserves a handful of historic structures and sites, but the best sense of Placerville's past comes from the **Placerville History Museum** on Main Street and the **El Dorado County Historical Museum**. The displays range from old mining equipment and a replica of a 19th-century general store to artifacts from the Chinese settlement and other local historical exhibits.

🏛 **El Dorado County Historical Museum**
104 Placerville Dr. **Tel** *(530) 621-5865.* ⏱ *10am–4pm Wed–Sat, noon–4pm Sun.* ⬤ *public hols.* **Donation**.

Gold Rush general store in Placerville's El Dorado Museum

Sutter Creek ⑨

Road map B3. 🏙 *2,000.* 🚍 ℹ *125 Peek St, Jackson (209 223-0350).* www.amadorcountychamber.com

Named after John Sutter *(see p475)*, Sutter Creek is one of the prettiest Gold Country towns, full of antique shops and whitewashed country inns. It grew up around 1860 to service the Old Eureka Mine, which was owned by Hetty Green, reputedly the "Richest Woman in the World."

Leland Stanford, one of the "Big Four" railroad barons *(see pp50–51)*, made his fortune in Sutter Creek. He put $5,000 into the town's Lincoln Mine, which turned into a multimillion-dollar investment. He used the money to become a railroad magnate and then, governor of California.

An attractive drive in the region is along Sutter Creek Road to Volcano, past remains of former mining equipment.

Volcano ⑩

Road map B3. 🏠 150. 🚌 🚹 125 Peek St, Jackson (209 223-0350). **www**.amadorcountychamber.com

For a taste of the Gold Rush without the tourist trappings, visit Volcano, a picturesque ghost of a mining town containing a wealth of historic sights.

During the Gold Rush, the town had an unusual reputation for sophistication and culture, creating the state's first library and its first astronomical observatory. The old jail, stagecoach office, brewery, and a cannon dating from the Civil War are among the preserved buildings and artifacts on display around the four-block town. The most attractive Victorian building is the former **St. George Hotel**, covered with Virginia creeper.

Springtime visitors to the region should also follow the signs to Daffodil Hill, 3 miles (5 km) north of Volcano, when more than 300,000 naturalized daffodil bulbs come into full bloom on the hillside.

🏨 **St. George Hotel**
16104 Main St, off Volcano Rd. **Tel** *(209) 296-4458.* ⏰ *mid-Feb–Dec: Wed–Sun.* **www**.stgeorgehotel.com

Chaw'se Indian Grinding Rock State Historic Park ⑪

🚌 *from Sacramento.* 🚃 *from Sacramento.* 🚌 *from Jackson.* **Tel** *(209) 296-7488.* **Jackson Visitors' Center** ⏰ *daily.* **Tel** *(209) 223-0350.*

Tucked away amid the oak trees in the hills above Jackson, this 136-acre (55-ha) park protects one of the largest and most complete Native American sites in the country. The area was once home to the Miwok people and the park is dedicated to their past and future. The aim of this comprehensive museum is to increase understanding of Native American life, centering on the Californian foothill peoples. Exhibits include an array of basketry, dance regalia, and ancient tools.

Hundreds of mortar holes form the main focus of the park. These limestone pockets were formed by generations of Miwok Indians grinding meal from acorns. There are also many rock carvings and replica Miwok dwellings, including a ceremonial roundhouse.

St. Sava's Serbian Orthodox Church outside Jackson

Jackson ⑫

Road map B3. 🏠 3,500. 🚌 🚹 125 Peek St (209 223-0350). **www**.amadorcountychamber.com

Located at the crossroads of two main Gold Rush trails, Jackson was once a bustling gold mining community and has continued to thrive as a commercial center and lumber mill town since 1850.

The town center features a number of old Gold Rush buildings, but the most interesting stop is the **Amador County Museum**, located on a hill above the town. Here visitors can view working models of stamp mills *(see p470)* and a variety of other old mining equipment.

North of the town, in a small park off Hwy 49, are the massive tailing wheels from the Kennedy Mine, one of the deepest in the United States. Reaching 58 ft (18 m) in diameter, these wheels were used to dispose of leftover rocks after the gold had been extracted. St. Sava's Serbian Orthodox Church, built in 1894 with a delicate white steeple, is also in the park. It is a testament to one of many cultures that contributed to the history of the Gold Country.

🏛 **Amador County Museum**
225 Church St, Jackson. **Tel** *(209) 223-6386.* ⏰ *10am–4pm Wed–Sun.* ● *public hols.* **Donation.**

Replica of a Miwok ceremonial roundhouse in Chaw'se State Park

Headstone on "Moke Hill"

Mokelumne Hill ⓭

Road map B3. 🏚 *1,200.*
ℹ️ *1211 S Main St, Angels Camp
(209 736-0049; 800 225-3764).*
www.gocalaveras.com

Bypassed by Highway 49, Mokelumne Hill is one of the most intriguing old Gold Country towns. A handful of old buildings, including the Hotel Leger and the old Wells Fargo stagecoach station, form a one-block business district. But the sleepy ambience of "Moke Hill," as it is commonly known, belies the town's unsavory and violent history.

Although much of the town has fallen into picturesque decay, during the Gold Rush era the hotels and saloons were packed with rowdy miners, whose drunken fights resulted in an average of one killing per week. Many of the victims ended up in the hilltop Protestant Cemetery – a short walk to the west of town. Here the multilingual headstones are now all that remain of the international population who came here in search of gold.

San Andreas ⓮

Road map B3. 🏚 *1,500.* ℹ️ *1211 S Main St, Angels Camp (209 736-0049).* **www**.gocalaveras.com

San Andreas is now a small, bustling city, home to the Calaveras County government. During the Gold Rush era,

however, it was a gritty mining camp, originally built by Mexicans who were later forcibly removed by white Americans after rich deposits of gold were found *(see pp48–9).* In 1883 the legendary outlaw Black Bart was captured here.

Very little now remains from the Gold Rush days, although San Andreas does house one of the Gold Country's best museums, the **Calaveras County Historical Museum**, in the old courthouse just north of Hwy 49. Along with exhibits tracing gold mining history from 1848 to the 1930s, the collection includes Miwok Indian artifacts and the courtroom where Black Bart was tried and convicted. His prison cell during the trial, situated behind the museum, is now surrounded by a pleasant, if somewhat incongruous, garden of indigenous plants and trees.

🏛 **Calaveras County Historical Museum**
30 N Main St. **Tel** *(530) 233-6328.*
⭕ *daily.* ⬤ *Jan 1, Thanksgiving, Dec 25.* 📷

Murphys ⓯

Road map B3. 🏚 *2,000.*
ℹ️ *1211 S Main St, Angels Camp (209 736-0049).*

With mature sycamores, elms, and locust trees lining its quiet streets, Murphys is among the prettiest towns in the southern Gold Country. It offers a quiet break from the frantic tourism of many of the

other Mother Lode towns and sights in the area.

Having played host to such luminaries as Ulysses S Grant, Mark Twain, and Will Rogers, the restored Murphys Hotel, built in 1855, is now the town landmark. Across the street, the **Old-Timers' Museum** houses a quirky collection of Gold Rush memorabilia. The outside wall displays a series of humorous plaques detailing the town's history.

🏛 **Old-Timers' Museum**
450 Main St. **Tel** *(209) 728-1160.*
⭕ *11am–4pm Fri–Sun.* ⬤ *Jan 1, Thanksgiving, Dec 25.* 📷

Angels Camp ⓰

Road map B3. 🏚 *3,000.*
ℹ️ *1211 S Main St (209 736-0049).*

Angels Camp is a former gold mining town what was best known as the real-life location of Mark Twain's classic short story "The Celebrated Jumping Frog of Calaveras County" *(see pp26–7).* Today the town has grown into a commercial center for the surrounding area.

A few historic structures, including the Angels Hotel where Twain heard the story of the jumping frog, still line the steep streets of the compact downtown area, which comes alive every May for a popular reenactment of the frog-jumping competition.

Two huge 19th-century locomotives stand on Hwy 49 in front of the **Angels Camp Museum**, which contains a standard array of old mining

Picturesque main street of the gold mining town, Angels Camp

equipment. There is also a large collection of Indian artifacts and exhibits on Mark Twain and the jumping frog.

🏛 **Angels Camp Museum**
753 S Main St. **Tel** (209) 736-2963.
⬜ Apr–Nov: daily; Mar–Nov: daily,
10am–3pm; Jan–Feb: weekends
only. ⬤ Thanksgiving, Dec. 🈲

Moaning Cavern ⑰

Tel (209) 736-2708. ⬜ daily. 🈲
www.caverntours.com

One of the largest limestone caverns in the area, Moaning Cavern took its name from the groaning sound emitted by the wind flowing out of the entrance. Unfortunately the sound was destroyed when the cavern was enlarged to improve public access. Guided tours, lasting about an hour, focus on the main "room," which is about 165 ft (50 m) high – tall enough to house the Statue of Liberty. Visitors can descend into the caves using the stairs or, if they dare, by rappelling down a rope.

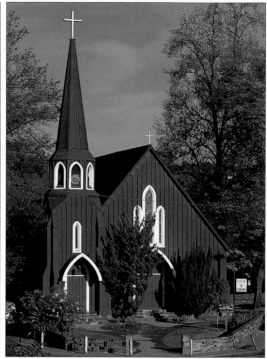
Nineteenth-century St. James Episcopal Church in Sonora

A guided tour of Moaning Cavern

Sonora ⑱

Road map B3. 🏘 5,000. 🚂
ℹ 55 W Stockton St (209 533-
4420). **www.**tcvb.com

Outstripping Columbia (see pp480–81) for the seat of county government during the Gold Rush, Sonora is now the Tuolumne County seat and a busy commercial center and logging town. Its sedate main street shows little sign of the town's once-violent reputation during the second half of the 19th century. Many of its historic buildings have been preserved, including the St. James Episcopal Church on Washington Street. There are also a number of interesting Victorian houses.

Sonora's old jail was built in 1857 and renovated after being destroyed by fire in 1866. It is now home to the **Tuolumne County Museum and History Center**. It houses a collection of Gold Rush artifacts, including gold nuggets and a number of 19th-century photographs.

🏛 **Tuolumne County Museum and History Center**
158 W Bradford St. **Tel** (209) 532-
1317. ⬜ daily. ⬤ Jan 1, Dec 25.

BLACK BART

Famous for his politeness to his victims and his habit of leaving doggerel poetry at the scene of his crimes, the outlaw known affectionately as Black Bart has become one of the state's best-loved legends.

After holding up stagecoaches between 1877 and 1883, he was caught when the laundry mark on his handkerchief was traced to San Francisco. Black Bart turned out to be Charles Boles, a mining engineer.

After being tried and convicted in San Andreas, he spent five years in San Quentin prison. He disappeared from public view after his release in 1888.

The outlaw Black Bart

Street-by-Street: Columbia State Historic Park ⓳

Stagecoach schedule sign

At the height of the Gold Rush, Columbia was one of the largest and most important towns in the Gold Country. Most of California's mining camps were abandoned; they quickly disintegrated and disappeared after the gold ran out in the late 1850s. Unusually, Columbia remained active. It was proudly kept intact by its remaining residents until 1945, when the California government turned the entire town into a state historic park. A few of the buildings have been reconstructed, but the majority of them have been preserved in their original state.

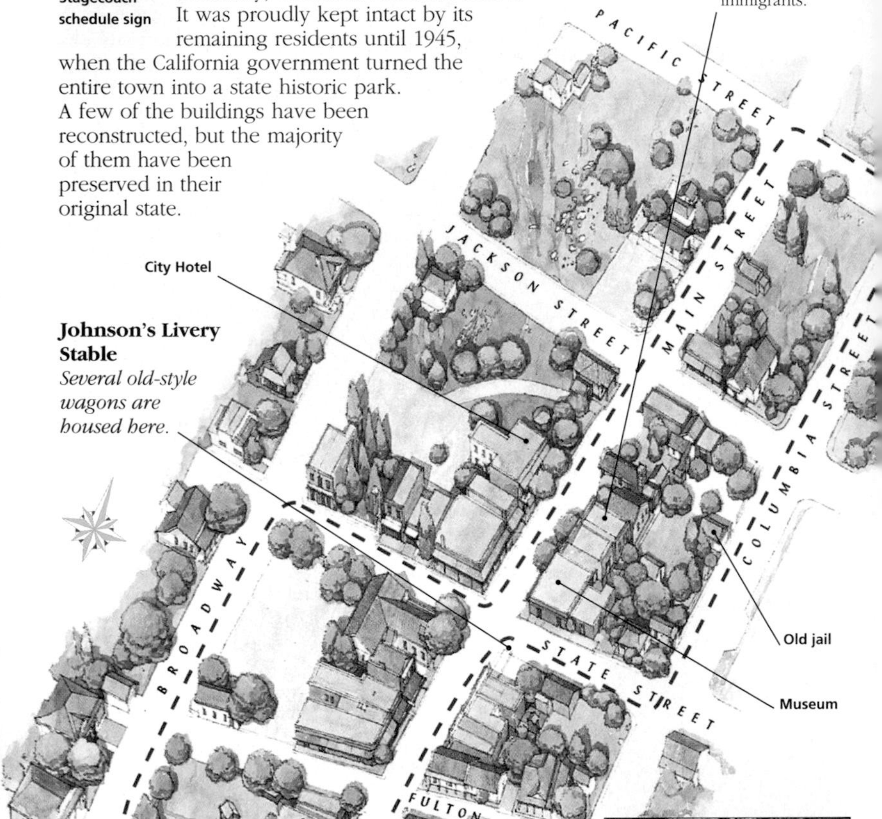

The Chinese Herb Shop contains traditional medicines brought to the state by Chinese immigrants.

City Hotel

Johnson's Livery Stable
Several old-style wagons are housed here.

Old jail

Museum

★ **Wells Fargo Express Office**
This stagecoach office was the center of the town's transportation network.

Matelot Gulch Miners Supply
Visitors are sold pans of sand and gravel here so that they can try panning for gold themselves.

VISITORS' CHECKLIST

Hwy 49. **Road map** B3.
22708 Broadway (209 532-0150).
☐ ☐ ☐ **Wells Fargo Express
Office** ☐ *10am–4pm daily
(Jun–Aug until 6pm).* ● *Thanks-
giving, Dec 25.* ☐ **Columbia
Schoolhouse** ☐ *10am–4pm
daily (Jun–Aug until 6pm).*
● *Thanksgiving, Dec 25.* ☐

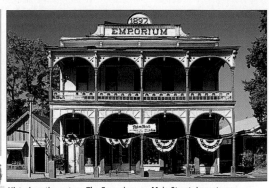

Historic antique store, The Emporium, on Main Street, Jamestown

★ **Columbia Schoolhouse**
*The building was last used
as a school in 1937, but in
1960 it was restored with
the help of funds raised by
California schoolchildren.*

0 meters	100
0 yards	100

KEY

– – – Suggested route

STAR SIGHTS

★ Columbia
  Schoolhouse

★ Wells Fargo
  Express Office

Jamestown ⑳

Road map B3. 🏚 *2,300.* 🚌
🛈 *55 W Stockton St, Sonora (209
532-4212).* **www** pcchamber.com

Jamestown was home to the
largest gold mine in operation
until 1993. The mine is still
visible south of the town along
Hwy 49. Some of the historic
town was destroyed by fire in
1966, but Main Street still has
many picturesque buildings.
  **Railtown 1897 State Historic
Park**, north of downtown,
preserves the steam loco-
motives and historic carriages
of the Sierra Railroad. Rides
are offered on weekends.

**🏛 Railtown 1897 State
Historic Park**
5th Ave & Reservoir Rd. **Tel** *(209)
984-3953.* ☐ *daily.* ● *Jan 1,
Thanksgiving, Dec 25.* **Donation**.

Stockton ㉑

Road map B3. 🏚 *250,000.* 🚌 🛈
*445 W Weber Ave, Suite 220 (209 547-
2770).* **www**.visitstockton.org

Stockton is an inland port
and a transportation hub for
Central Valley farms. It is set
on the eastern edge of the
delta at the confluence of the
Sacramento, American, and
San Joaquin Rivers. Stockton's
history is told at the Haggin
Museum, which includes
Native American crafts, 19th-
century storefronts and works
by Renoir. It also traces the
development by a local inventor of the Caterpillar track, later
adapted for use on army tanks.

🏛 Haggin Museum
1201 N Pershing Ave. **Tel** *(209)
462-4116.* ☐ *Tue–Sun, 1:30–5pm.*
● *Dec 23–25, 30, 31, Jan 1.* 📷

JOAQUIN MURIETA: THE CALIFORNIA BANDIT

Little documentary evidence exists about Joaquin Murieta,
the Gold Country criminal portrayed as everything from a
19th-century Gold Rush Robin Hood to a murderous outlaw.
  His legend can be traced to the writer John Rollins Ridge,
who published a novel called *The Life and Adventures of
Joaquin Murieta, Celebrated
California Bandit* in 1854.
Ridge drew on the criminal
exploits of five outlaws, all
named Joaquin. The Gover-
nor of California offered a
$1,000 reward for the capture
of any of these men. In 1853
a man named Harry Love
delivered the head of one
Joaquin Murieta, which had
been pickled in a glass jar.
Ridge's novel was published
the following year, and the
Murieta legend was born.

THE HIGH SIERRAS

*F*orming a towering wall along the eastern side of central California, the densely forested Sierra Nevada mountains rise to over 14,000 ft (4,270 m) and include many of the most impressive peaks in the mainland United States. Known as the High Sierras, these rugged mountains make up one of the state's most popular recreation areas, preserved by a series of splendid national parks.

The most popular High Sierras destination is Yosemite National Park, one of the world's most spectacular natural sights. Waterfalls, ranging from delicate cascades to raging torrents, drop steeply down the granite walls of this alpine valley.Rock-climbers, photographers, and sightseers come from all over the globe to experience the park first-hand. South of Yosemite, the Sequoia and Kings Canyon National Parks preserve more of the state's high country scenery, including groves of sequoia, the tallest living trees on earth.

To the north, Lake Tahoe has been a year-round recreational haven for over a century. It offers hiking, camping, and water sports on one of the bluest bodies of water in the US. In winter, the region becomes a skier's paradise, with many Olympic-class resorts.

East of the Sierra Nevada's granite spine lies a less-visited but equally compelling region. The ghost town of Bodie is preserved as it was when gold miners abandoned it in 1882. Nearby, Mono Lake is an eerie sight of limestone towers and alkaline water. The eastern slope of the High Sierras merits exploration, including the 14,500-ft (4,420-m) Mount Whitney, the highest peak on the US mainland, and the bristlecone pines of the White Mountains, some of which are more than 4,000 years old.

Bodie State Historic Park, a preserved ghost town to the east of the Sierras

◁ Imposing granite peak of Half Dome in Yosemite National Park

Exploring the High Sierras

The highest peaks, the tallest trees, and some of the most impressive natural scenery in the United States are found in California's Sierra Nevada. This region includes one of the best-known wonders of the world, Yosemite National Park, as well as countless other remarkable examples of nature's prowess. North of Yosemite, the emerald waters of Lake Tahoe are set within an alpine valley at the highest point of the High Sierras, while to the south stand the immense groves of Sequoia and Kings Canyon National Parks.

Other than the resorts encircling Lake Tahoe, there are no real towns in the High Sierras. East of the mountains, however, near the shores of the eerily beautiful Mono Lake, the best ghost town in the state, Bodie, is immaculately preserved.

SIGHTS AT A GLANCE

Bodie State Historic Park **5**
Devil's Postpile National Monument **7**
Donner Memorial State Park **1**
Mono Lake **6**
Mount Whitney **10**
Owens Valley **9**

Sequoia and Kings Canyon National Parks pp496–7 **11**
Truckee **2**
White Mountains **8**
Yosemite National Park pp488–9 **4**

Tour
Lake Tahoe *p487* **3**

HOW THE SIERRAS WERE MADE

The Sierras were formed 3 million years ago when a giant granite batholith (igneous rock), approximately 6 miles (10 km) deep, lifted up the earth's surface and tilted it from a tectonic "hinge" beneath California's Central Valley. The effects of this uplift are most clearly visible on the steep eastern slopes, typical of mountains on the earth's faults. The western slopes are more gradual, made up of sedimentary, volcanic, and metamorphic rock, mixed together over the epochs.

Granite peaks of the High Sierras

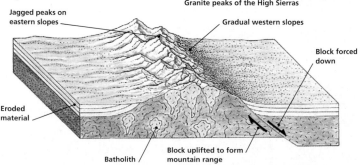

Jagged peaks on eastern slopes

Gradual western slopes

Block forced down

Eroded material

Batholith

Block uplifted to form mountain range

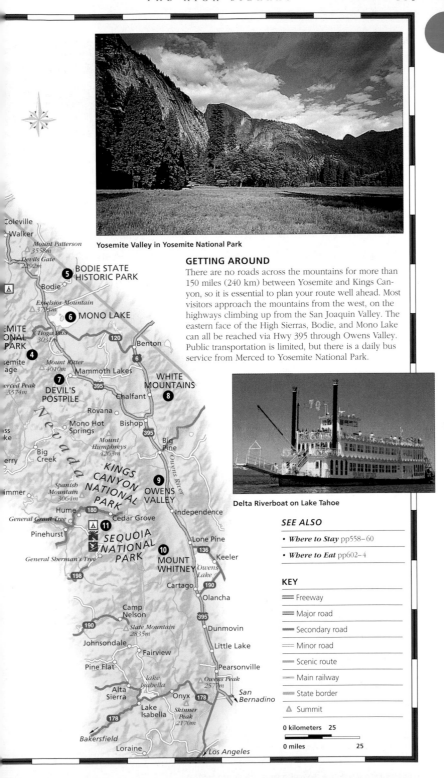

Yosemite Valley in Yosemite National Park

GETTING AROUND

There are no roads across the mountains for more than 150 miles (240 km) between Yosemite and Kings Canyon, so it is essential to plan your route well ahead. Most visitors approach the mountains from the west, on the highways climbing up from the San Joaquin Valley. The eastern face of the High Sierras, Bodie, and Mono Lake can all be reached via Hwy 395 through Owens Valley. Public transportation is limited, but there is a daily bus service from Merced to Yosemite National Park.

Delta Riverboat on Lake Tahoe

SEE ALSO

- *Where to Stay* pp558–60
- *Where to Eat* pp602–4

KEY

═══	Freeway
▬▬▬	Major road
▬▬▬	Secondary road
═══	Minor road
────	Scenic route
▬▬▬	Main railway
▬▬▬	State border
△	Summit

0 kilometers 25

0 miles 25

Coleville
Walker
Mount Patterson 3558m
Devils Gate 2192m
5 BODIE STATE HISTORIC PARK
Bodie
Excelsior Mountain 3795m
6 MONO LAKE
YOSEMITE NATIONAL PARK
Tioga Pass 3031m
120
Benton
6
4
Yosemite Village
Mount Ritter 4010m
Mammoth Lakes
WHITE MOUNTAINS
Merced Peak 3574m
7 DEVIL'S POSTPILE
395
Chalfant
8
Rovana
Mono Hot Springs
Bishop
Big Pine
Mount Humphreys 4263m
395
Big Creek
KINGS CANYON NATIONAL PARK
Owens River
9 OWENS VALLEY
Spanish Mountain 3064m
Hume
180
Cedar Grove
Independence
General Grant Tree
11
Pinehurst
SEQUOIA NATIONAL PARK
Lone Pine
136
General Sherman's Tree
MOUNT WHITNEY
Keeler
Owens Lake
198
Cartago
190
10
Olancha
Camp Nelson
395
Slate Mountain 2835m
Dunmovin
Johnsondale
190
Little Lake
Fairview
Pine Flat
Pearsonville
Owens Peak 2577m
San Bernadino
Alta Sierra
Lake Isabella
Onyx
178
Skinner Peak 2170m
178
Bakersfield
Loraine
Los Angeles

Donner Memorial State Park ❶

Tel *(530) 582-7892.* 🚉 *Truckee.* 🚌 *Truckee.*

This tranquil 350-acre (140-ha) park, to the south of I-80, marks the site of one of the most tragic episodes of the United States frontier era.

In the winter of 1846–7 a group of 89 California-bound emigrants from Independence, Missouri, were trapped by heavy snowfall. Known as the Donner Party because two of the families shared that surname, the group was one of the many wagon trains bound for the West Coast from the Midwest, along the Oregon Trail. Halfway into their journey, the Donner families, and another family headed by James Reed, decided to leave the established trail and try a shortcut recommended by the contemporary adventurer Lansford Hastings. This turned out, however, to be a far more difficult route, and added three weeks to what in the best of circumstances was already an arduous journey. The Donner

Party finally arrived at the eastern foot of the Sierra Nevada Mountains in October 1846, having lost the majority of their cattle and belongings.

After resting for a week they were caught by an early winter storm east of Truckee. A few members decided to struggle on foot across the snowy mountains to seek help from Sutter's Fort *(see p475),* but the rest of the party, now trapped by the heavy snow and with insufficient supplies, were forced to resort to cannibalism in order to survive. By the time rescuers were able to reach them in mid-February 1847, 42 of the 89 pioneers had already died.

A statue of this heroic pioneering family, standing atop a 22-ft (6.7-m) pedestal indicating the depth of the snow they encountered, now marks the site. The park's **Emigrant Trail Museum** details the Donner Party's story, as well as describing the natural history of the High Sierras.

🏛 **Emigrant Trail Museum**
12593 Donner Pass Rd. *Tel (530) 582-7892.* ⭘ 9am–4pm daily. ● Jan 1, Thanksgiving, Dec 25.

SKIING AROUND LAKE TAHOE

The peaks surrounding Lake Tahoe, particularly on the California side, are famous for their ski resorts. The world-class Alpine Meadows and Squaw Valley are where the Winter Olympics were held in 1960. The largest ski area, Heavenly Valley, is above the city of South Lake Tahoe, with many more around the lake and at Donner Pass, west of Truckee, along I-80. There are also cross-country ski areas with groomed trails. The Lake Tahoe area receives more than 10 ft (3 m) of snow each winter and is the state's major center for winter recreation from November to March.

Skiing at Lake Tahoe's Alpine Meadows resort

Façade of the 19th-century Old Truckee Jail, now a museum

Truckee ❷

Road map B3. 🏔 *13,000.* 🚉 🚌
ℹ *10065 Donner Pass Road. Tel (530) 587-2757. Tel (530) 546-5253 winter weather hotline.* **www**.truckee.com

One of the highest and coldest towns in California, Truckee is thought to have gotten its name when a native Paiute greeted the first white Americans with "Trokay," meaning "peace."

Truckee is situated along the main highway (I-80) and rail route across the Sierra Nevada Mountains. Its history as a transportation center goes back to 1863, when it was founded as a changeover point for railroad crews along the transcontinental railroad *(see pp50–51).* The Southern Pacific Depot still serves rail and bus passengers as well as operating as a visitors' center.

Much of the town's Wild West character and history as a lumber center survives, especially along Commercial Row in the heart of town, where a line of old brick and wooden buildings faces the tracks. Many of these have now been converted into atmospheric shops, restaurants, and cafés.

Another evocative survivor of the town's past is the **Old Truckee Jail**, built in 1875. It is a small museum depicting the wilder side of frontier life. Located only 25 miles (40 km) from Lake Tahoe, Truckee is also a popular historical base for winter skiers and summer hikers.

🏛 **Old Truckee Jail**
Jibboom & Spring Sts. *Tel (530) 582-0893.* ⭘ *May–Sep: 11am–4pm Sat & Sun.* ● *public hols.* 🈲

A Tour of Lake Tahoe [3]

The most beautiful body of water in California, Lake Tahoe is 1,645 ft (501 m) at its deepest point and is surrounded by forested peaks. The area began to develop as a tourist resort after the construction of the first road in 1915 made it more accessible. Casinos opening on the Nevada border in the 1930s and the Winter Olympics in 1960 further increased its popularity.

View of Lake Tahoe from Heavenly Valley

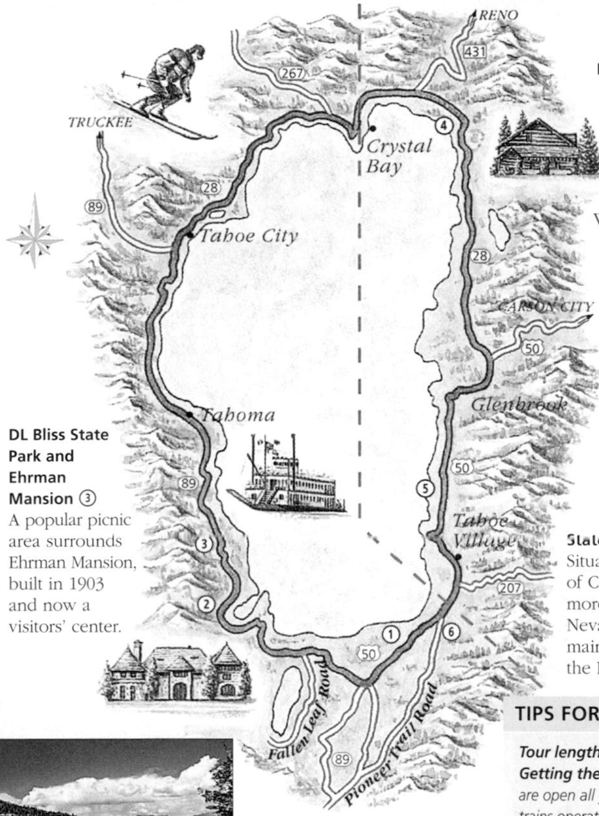

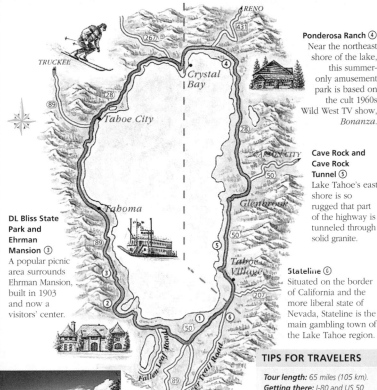

Ponderosa Ranch ④
Near the northeast shore of the lake, this summer-only amusement park is based on the cult 1960s Wild West TV show, *Bonanza*.

Cave Rock and Cave Rock Tunnel ⑤
Lake Tahoe's east shore is so rugged that part of the highway is tunneled through solid granite.

DL Bliss State Park and Ehrman Mansion ③
A popular picnic area surrounds Ehrman Mansion, built in 1903 and now a visitors' center.

Stateline ⑥
Situated on the border of California and the more liberal state of Nevada, Stateline is the main gambling town of the Lake Tahoe region.

Emerald Bay State Park and Vikingsholm ②
The beautiful inlet of Emerald Bay is the most photographed part of the lake. Vikingsholm, built as a summerhouse in the 1920s, is an incongruous reproduction of an old Nordic castle.

South Lake Tahoe ①
The largest town in the area, South Lake Tahoe caters for visitors to Nevada's casinos.

0 kilometers 10

0 miles 10

KEY

Tour route

Other roads

Viewpoint

TIPS FOR TRAVELERS

Tour length: *65 miles (105 km).*
Getting there: *I-80 and US 50 are open all year round. Amtrak trains operate to Truckee. Greyhound buses and limited flights from San Francisco and Oakland serve South Lake Tahoe.*
When to go: *Peak tourist seasons are July, August, and winter, when the ski resorts are open. Spring and autumn are less crowded, but some facilities may be closed.*
Where to stay and eat: *For the best information, contact Lake Tahoe Visitors' Authority.*
Tourist information*: Lake Tahoe Visitors' Authority, South Lake Tahoe.* ***Tel*** *(800) 288-2463.*

Yosemite National Park ❹

A wilderness of evergreen forests, high meadows, and sheer granite walls, much of Yosemite National Park is accessible only to experienced hikers or horseback riders. The spectacular Yosemite Valley, a good base from which to explore the park, is easily reached by car and there are 200 additional miles (320 km) of paved roads providing access to more remote areas. Soaring cliffs, plunging waterfalls, gigantic trees, rugged canyons, mountains, and valleys all combine to lend Yosemite its incomparable beauty.

Yosemite Museum
The history of the Miwok and Paiute people is displayed here, along with works by Yosemite artists.

Lower Yosemite Falls
Yosemite Creek drops 2,425 ft (740 m), to form the highest waterfall in the US (see p490).

Ahwahnee Hotel
Rustic architecture, elegant décor, and beautiful views make this hotel one of the most renowned in the country (see p491).

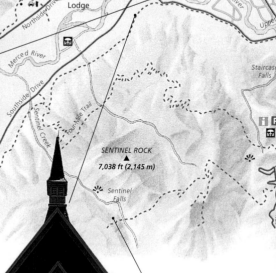

Yosemite Chapel (1879)
This tiny wooden church is all that is left of Yosemite's 19th-century Old Village.

Sentinel Dome can be reached on foot from the valley floor. The trail continues to Glacier Point.

Valley Visitor Center

To Upper Yosemite Falls

Yosemite Creek

Yosemite Falls Trail

Yosemite Village

Sunnyside

Yosemite Lodge

Northside Drive

Merced River

Southside Drive

Sentinel Creek

Four Mile Trail

Lower River

Upper

Staircase Falls

SENTINEL ROCK
▲
7,038 ft (2,145 m)

Sentinel Falls

Mirror Meadow
Park rangers no longer interfere with nature by dredging the lake, so the water at the foot of Half Dome is now silting up and forming a meadow (see p491).

VISITORS' CHECKLIST

Road map C3. **i** *PO Box 577, Yosemite.* **[**(209) 372-0200. **from Merced.** **Yosemite Valley.** **from Merced.** *daily.* **www**.nps.gov/yose

KEY

▬	Major road
═	Minor road
- -	Paths and trails
- -	Shuttle bus
▬	Bike route
➣	Rivers
P	Parking
🚗	Gas station
🔺	Camping
🏠	Picnic area
i	Tourist information
🔆	Viewpoint

Washington Column

NORTH PINES

LOWER PINES

Tenaya Creek

P

urry llage

UPPER PINES

Merced River

Half Dome
A formidable trail climbs to the top of this cliff, which juts above the valley floor (see p490).

Vernal Fall
The Merced River pours into its canyon over the 317-ft (97-m) lip of this fall.

Merced River
This beautiful river can be appreciated along both the Mist Trail and the Panorama Trail. Anglers enjoy fishing for brown trout in its waters.

0 meters   1000

0 yards   1000

Exploring Yosemite National Park

Some of the world's most beautiful mountain terrain is protected within the 1,170 sq miles (3,030 sq km) of Yosemite National Park. Hundreds of thousands of visitors descend upon the park each year to admire its breathtaking views, formed by millions of years of glacial activity. Each season offers a different experience, from the swelling waterfalls of spring to the rustic colors of autumn. The summer months are the most crowded, but during the snowbound winter months several roads are inaccessible. Bus tours and well-maintained cycle paths, hiking trails, and roads are all aimed at leading visitors from one awe-inspiring panoramic scene to another.

Upper Yosemite Falls, swollen with ice-melt in the spring

Half Dome

Eastern end of Yosemite Valley.
○ *daily.*

Standing nearly 1 mile (1.6 km) above the valley floor, the silhouette of Half Dome has become a symbol of Yosemite. Its curved back rises to a wave-like lip, before dropping vertically to the valley below.

Geologists believe that Half Dome is now three-quarters of its original size, rather than a true half. It is thought that as recently as 15,000 years ago, glacial ice floes moved through the valley from the Sierra crest, scything off rock and depositing it downstream.

The 8,840-ft (2,695 m) summit of Half Dome offers an unsurpassed view of the valley. Follow the 9-mile (14-km) trail from Happy Isles trailhead to reach the peak.

Yosemite Falls

North Yosemite Valley. ○ *daily.*
Yosemite Falls are the highest waterfalls in North America and tumble from a height of 2,425 ft (740 m) in two great leaps, Upper Yosemite and Lower Yosemite Falls. One of the most recognizable features of the park, the cascades are visible all over the valley.

The top of Upper Yosemite Falls, by far the longer and more elegant of the pair, can be reached via a strenuous 7-mile (11-km) round-trip trail. The Lower Falls are easier to visit, via a short trail that starts next to Yosemite Lodge and frames an unforgettable view of both falls.

As with all the park's waterfalls, Yosemite Falls are at their peak in May and June, when the winter snows melt and fill the creek to capacity. Conversely, by September the falls often dry up and disappear altogether, their presence marked only by a dark stain on the granite wall.

Vernal and Nevada Falls

Eastern end of Yosemite Valley.
○ *daily.*
A popular half-day hike in Yosemite National Park is the Mist Trail, which visits these two waterfalls.

The first fall visited on this 7-mile (11-km) round-trip is Vernal Fall, which plunges 320 ft (95 m) and spreads its spray across the trail. The trail then continues for 2 miles (3 km) to the top of Nevada Falls, which drops an impressive 595 ft (180 m). At the top of Nevada Falls the Mist Trail joins the John Muir Trail, which runs around the back of Half Dome all the way south to the summit of Mount Whitney (see p495).

Sheer drop of El Capitán

For hotels and restaurants in this region see pp558–60 and pp602–4

🦌 Glacier Point

Glacier Point Rd. ⭘ *May–Oct: daily.*

The great Yosemite panorama can be experienced from Glacier Point, which rests on a rocky ledge 3,215 ft (980 m) above the valley floor. Most of the waterfalls and other features of Yosemite Valley are visible from here, but the dominant feature is Half Dome. The panorama also includes much of the surrounding landscape, a beautiful area of alpine peaks and meadows.

Glacier Point can be reached only during the summer. The road is blocked by snow during winter at Badger Pass, which was developed in 1935 as California's first commercial ski resort. Another summer route is the Four-Mile Trail, which begins at the western side of the valley. Summer bus services also allow hikers to ride up to Glacier Point then hike down to the valley.

🦌 Mariposa Grove

Visitors' Center Hwy 41, South Entrance. ⭘ *mid-May–Oct: daily.*

At the southern end of Yosemite, this beautiful grove was one of the main reasons the park was established. More than 500 giant sequoia trees can be seen here, some of which are more than 3,000 years old, 250 ft (75 m) tall and more than 30 ft (9 m) in diameter at their base. A series of hiking trails winds through

Tunnel View, looking across Yosemite Valley

the grove, and open-air trams make a 5-mile (8-km) circuit along roads constructed during the early years of Yosemite tourism.

🦌 Tunnel View

Hwy 41 overlooking Yosemite Valley. ⭘ *daily.*

One of the most photographed views of Yosemite can be had from this lookout on Hwy 41 at the western end of the valley. Despite the name, which is taken from the highway tunnel that leads to Glacier Point Road, the view is incredible, with El Capitán on the left, Bridalveil Fall on the right and Half Dome at the center.

🦌 El Capitán

Northwestern end of Yosemite Valley. ⭘ *daily.*

Standing guard at the western entrance to Yosemite Valley, the granite wall of El Capitán rises more than 4,500 ft (1,370 m) from the valley floor. The world's largest exposed rock, El Capitán is a magnet to rock-climbers, who spend days on its sheer face to reach the top. Less adventurous visitors congregate in the meadow below, watching the rock-climbers through binoculars.

Named by US soldiers, who in 1851 were the first white Americans to visit the valley, El Capitán is the Spanish phrase for "captain."

🦌 Tuolumne Meadows

Hwy 120, Tioga Rd. ⭘ *Jun–Sep: daily.*

In summer, when the snows have melted and the wild-flowers are in full bloom, the best place to experience the striking beauty of the Yosemite landscape are these sub-alpine meadows along the Tuolumne River. Located 55 miles (88 km) from Yosemite valley via Tioga Pass Road, Tuolumne Meadows are also a base for hikers setting off to explore the area's many granite peaks and trails.

Black-tailed deer roaming Yosemite's meadows

🏨 Ahwahnee Hotel

Yosemite Valley. **Tel** *(209) 372-1407.* ⭘ *daily. See Where to Stay p536.*

A building that comes close to matching Yosemite's natural beauty, the Ahwahnee Hotel was built in 1927 at a cost of $1.5 million.

It was designed by Gilbert Stanley Underwood, who used giant granite boulders and massive wood timbers to create a rustic elegance that is in tune with its surroundings. The interior of the Ahwahnee Hotel also emulates the natural setting, decorated in a Native American style. A few Native American arts and crafts are on display in the lobbies. The hotel is also noted for its high-quality restaurant *(see p604)*.

Giant sequoia trees in Mariposa Grove

Sierra Nevada, near Lone Pine ▷

Ghostly wooden buildings in Bodie State Historic Park

Bodie State Historic Park ❺

Road map C3. 🏃 10. 🚌 *from Bridgeport.* 🏁 *End of Hwy 270 (760 647-6445).* ⭕ *daily.*

High up in the foothills of the eastern Sierra Nevada, Bodie is the largest ghost town in California.

Now protected as a state historic park, Bodie was, during the second half of the 19th century, a bustling gold mining town, with a population that topped 8,000 in 1880. Named after the gold prospector Waterman S Bodey, who first discovered placer deposits (surface gold) here in 1859, Bodie boomed with the discovery of hard rock ore in the mid-1870s. Soon so many different mines had been established in the area, but it all came to an end when the gold ran out in 1882. Later, a series of fires destroyed much of the town. Only the Standard Mine remained in business, but it closed in 1942 because of a wartime ban on mining.

The state acquired the entire town in 1962, and has maintained the 170 buildings in a condition of "arrested decay." The result is an evocative experience of empty streets lined by deserted wooden buildings. The Miners' Union Hall has been converted into a visitors' center and museum, with artifacts from Bodie's early days.

Mono Lake ❻

Road map C3. **Tel** *(760) 647-3044.* 🚉 *Merced.* **www**.monolake.org

One of the strangest looking places in the United States, and possibly one of the oldest lakes in the world, Mono Lake is a 60-sq mile (155-sq km) body of alkaline water at the eastern foot of the Sierra Nevada Mountains, set between two volcanic islands. The lake has no natural outlet, but evaporation in the summer heat combined with water diversion to LA has caused it to shrink to one-fifth of its original size. The result is extremely brackish water, three times saltier than sea water. It has also exposed a number of contorted tufa spires. These were formed when calcium from underground springs came into contact with carbonates in the lake water, forming limestone. The tufa formations once sat under water, but the evaporation has left them arrayed along the lakeside.

In recent years, Mono Lake has also been the subject of a heated political and environmental debate, part of an ongoing battle over water rights. The City of Los Angeles purchased a large amount of land in the eastern Sierras and Owens Valley in 1905, and began diverting the streams and rivers through a system of aqueducts to LA in 1941. This has accelerated the lake's shrinkage and put local wildlife, particularly the state's large seagull population, which breeds on the lake's islands, in danger *(see pp202–3).* In 1994 the California State Government ruled that LA must preserve the lake and its surrounding ecosystem at 6,392 ft (1,950 m) above sea level.

Tufa spires rising out of Mono Lake

Devil's Postpile National Monument ❼

Road map C4. **Tel** (760) 934-2289. 🚍 shuttle from Mammoth Mountain Inn. ◯ mid-Jun–Sep: daily. 🏩 ♿ 🌐 www.nps.gov/depo

On the west of the Sierra Nevada crest, but most easily accessible from the eastern resort of Mammoth Lakes, Devil's Postpile National Monument protects one of the most impressive geological formations in the state.

A wall of basalt columns, in varying geometrical shapes, predominantly pentagons and hexagons, cover a 545 sq yard (652 sq m) area. More than 60 ft (18 m) tall, they rise 7,560 ft (2,320 m) above sea level. The columns were formed around 100,000 years ago, when molten lava cooled and fractured. Set at the heart of an 800-acre (320-ha) park, they resemble a tiled floor seen from above. The monument is covered in snow most of the year and is only accessible in summer via shuttle bus. Rainbow Falls, 2 miles (3 km) from the Postpile, are named after the refraction of sunlight in their spray.

White Mountains ❽

ℹ️ 798 N Main St, Bishop (760 873-2500).

Rising along the eastern side of Owens Valley, the White Mountains, at 12,000 ft (3,660 m), are almost as high but far drier than the 13,000-ft (3,960-m) parallel range of Sierra Nevada. Lack of water has kept the peaks rugged and largely free of vegetation, but the few trees that do survive here, the bristlecone pines *(Pinus aristata)*, are among the oldest living things on earth.

These gnarled pine trees seem to thrive on the adverse conditions, which batter them into strange, contorted shapes. The species is found only on the lower slopes of the White Mountains and on a few of the mountains in neighboring Nevada. Extremely slow

Bristlecone pines on the slopes of the White Mountains

growing, they seldom reach more than 50 ft (15 m) in height, despite living for more than 4,000 years – 1,000 years longer than the oldest sequoia tree *(see pp496–7)*.

Owens Valley ❾

🚂 Lone Pine. ℹ️ 126 S Main St, Lone Pine (760 876-4444). www.lonepinechamber.org

Owens Valley has more in common with Nevada than with the rest of California. It is sparsely populated but ruggedly beautiful, the valley being wedged between the White Mountains and the Sierra Nevada. Once covered with farms and ranches, the land here was bought secretly in 1905 by agents working for the City of Los Angeles. Los Angeles needed to secure a water supply, and the aqueducts still drain the valley, destroying local agriculture.

In 1942 a detention camp was established at Manzanar for 10,000 Japanese-Americans, who were deemed a threat to national security and imprisoned for the duration of World War II. Exhibits on this and other aspects of Owens Valley can be seen at the **Eastern California Museum**, in the town of Independence.

🏛 **Eastern California Museum** 155 Grant St, Independence. **Tel** (760) 878-0364. ◯ 10am–4pm Wed–Mon. ● Jan 1, Easter Sun, Thanksgiving, Dec 25. **Donation**.

Mount Whitney ❿

Tel (760) 876-6200. 🚍 Merced.

The highest peak on the US mainland, Mount Whitney rises to a height of 14,496 ft (4,420 m), forming a sheer wall above the town of Lone Pine. A steep 11-mile (18-km) trail leads from Whitney Portal Road to the summit, offering a panorama over the High Sierras. A permit is required to hike the trail. The mountain, named in honor of the geologist Josiah Whitney, was first climbed in 1873.

Mount Whitney borders the beautiful Sequoia National Park *(see pp496–7)*, and the surrounding alpine meadows are ideal for backpacking in the summer months.

Owens Valley, backed by the White Mountains

Sequoia and Kings Canyon National Parks ⑪

Sequoia National Park sign

These twin national parks preserve lush forests, granite peaks, and glacier-carved canyons. Breathtaking scenery complements a habitat rich with wildlife. The parks embrace 34 separate groves of the giant sequoia tree, the earth's largest living species. America's deepest canyon, the south fork of the Kings River, cuts a depth of 8,200 ft (2,500 m) through Kings Canyon. Along the eastern boundary of Sequoia is Mount Whitney *(see p495)*, the highest summit on the US mainland.

Roads serve the western side of the parks; the rest is accessible only to hikers or with rented pack-trains of horses or mules. Winter visitors can ski cross-country over both marked and unmarked trails.

Road "tunnel" formed by a felled giant sequoia in Sequoia National Park

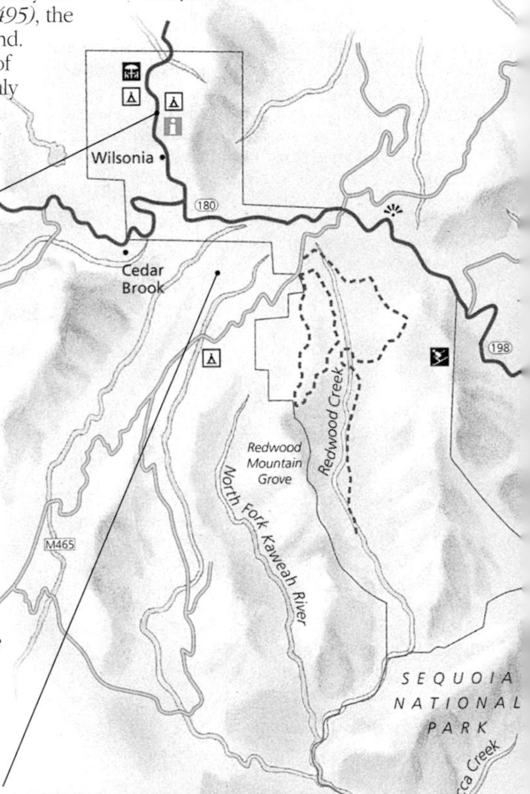

General Grant Tree
The third-largest sequoia is known as the "Nation's Christmas Tree."

Wilsonia

Cedar Brook

Redwood Mountain Grove

North Fork Kaweah River

Redwood Creek

SEQUOIA
NATIONAL
PARK

Yucca Creek

KEY

▬	Major road
▭	Minor road
▪▪▫	Paths and trails
▬	National Park boundary
⌁	River
▨	Skiing
Ⓐ	Camping
⊞	Picnic area
ℹ	Tourist information
⋇	Viewpoint

Big Stumps
The sequoia's unyielding nature makes it uneconomical for lumber, as these tall stumps, left by loggers in the 1880s, prove.

Moro Rock
A staircase carved into the rock takes visitors to the top of this granite monolith and affords a 360° view of the High Sierras and the Central Valley.

VISITORS' CHECKLIST

Ash Mountain, Three Rivers.
Road map C4. **Tel** (559) 565-3341. ◯ *daily.* 🅿️ 📷 ♿ *call ahead.* 📷 📷 *summer only.*
🍴 💻 www.nps.gov/seki

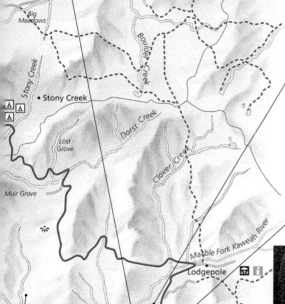

General Sherman's Tree
The world's largest living thing is 275 ft (84 m) tall, with a trunk measuring 36 ft (11 m) around its base. The tree still grows 0.4 inches (1 cm) every ten years.

Tharp's Log, a hollowed-out sequoia, was home to Hale Tharp, a 19th-century farmer who was introduced to the area by Native Americans.

Crescent Meadow
An array of sequoias border this area, which is more of a marsh than a meadow and too wet at its heart for the trees to survive.

Crystal Cavern, one of the few caves open to visitors, is filled with stalagmites and stalactites.

Giant Forest contains one of the largest groves of living sequoias in the world.

0 kilometers 2

0 miles 2

NORTH CENTRAL CALIFORNIA

With a rugged shoreline rising from the Pacific Ocean and dense forests covering coastal mountains, North Central California marks the visual transition between the north and south of the state. The landscape holds an embarrassment of riches, with golden beaches, splendid wilderness, and inland valleys that include some of the world's most productive agricultural regions.

The natural beauty of the area, combined with a wealth of cultural history, makes this one of the state's most engaging regions. Native Americans lived along the coast and in the inland valleys for centuries prior to the arrival of Europeans in the 17th century. More than a century later the first European settlement was established at Monterey on June 3, 1770, marking the beginning of today's California. Monterey remained the capital of Upper California until the United States took formal control in 1848. The city still retains a unique character, with its many historic buildings now protected and restored.

North central California has also inspired some of the state's most significant literature, from the poetry of Robinson Jeffers to the novels of Nobel prize-winner John Steinbeck. Many of the world's best photographers, including Ansel Adams and Edward Weston, have lived and worked here.

For all its culture and history, the region also abounds in recreational activities. Visitors can enjoy the historic amusement park at Santa Cruz, play golf on the world-famous courses at Pebble Beach, or simply walk around the many nature preserves, including the state's most beautiful stretch of coastline, Big Sur.

Writer John Steinbeck's house in Salinas

◁ Bixby Creek Bridge on Coastal Hwy 1 at Big Sur

Exploring North Central California

Monterey, the Spanish colonial capital of California, is at the heart of north central California and the best base from which to explore the region. The wealthy resorts of Pacific Grove and Carmel stand on a rugged peninsula just south of the town. Farther south is the wildest length of coastline in the state, Big Sur, where otters and whales can be spotted offshore. To the north is Santa Cruz, a lively beach town, backed by densely forested mountains. Inland, the Salinas and San Joaquin valleys give a taste of California's productive agricultural areas.

Pfeiffer Burns State Park at Big Sur

San Francisco

1 BIG BASIN REDWOODS STATE PARK

2 AÑO NUEVO STATE RESERVE

Swanton   Felton

3 SANTA CRUZ

Scotts Valley

4

ROARING CAMP AND BIG TREES RAILROAD

Oakland

San Jose

Gilroy

San Luis Reservoir

152

Los Banos

Dos Pal

Sar Rita

Sar

California Aqu

152

Watsonville

Monterey Bay

SAN JUAN BAUTISTA **5** Hollister

Castroville   Prunedale

Tres Pinos

Paicines

Marina

Diablo Range

Pacific Grove

9 SALINAS

MONTEREY **6**   Seaside

Carmel

Chualar

Panoche

Point Lobos State Reserve

7 CARMEL MISSION

Gonzales

10 PINNACLES NATIONAL MONUMENT

Idria

Carmel Valley

Salinas River

Soledad

Bitterwater

San Benito Mountain 1597m

1 Jamesburg

Greenfield

198

Point Sur

BIG SUR

Big Sur

Santa Lucia Range

8 Tassajara Hot Springs

King City

Julia Pfeiffer State Park

Junipero Serra Peak 1787m

San Lucas

Lopez Point

San Ardo

Jolon

Lockwood

101

Jade Cove Cape St Martin   Gorda

Lake San Antonio

Bradley

1

Bryson

San Luis Obispo

GETTING AROUND

Hwy 1, which runs along the coast south from Monterey to Big Sur, is one of the world's most beautiful drives and a must on any tour of California. A car, or a bicycle and strong legs, is the best way to get around, although there is a skeletal network of buses centering upon Monterey. Inland from the coast, Hwy 101 and I-5 run north–south through the predominantly agricultural region, but there are very few roads between the coast and inland valleys.

Looking out across Big Sur along Hwy 1

SIGHTS AT A GLANCE

Elephant seals at the Año Nuevo State Reserve

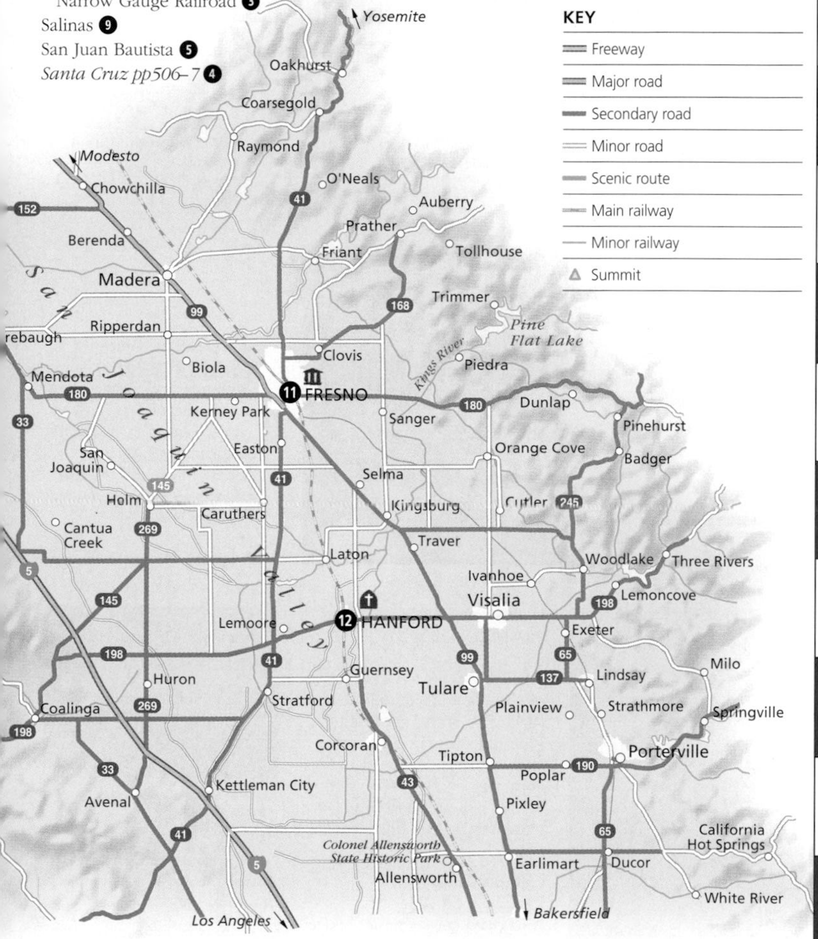

KEY

▬▬	Freeway
▬▬	Major road
▬▬	Secondary road
▬▬	Minor road
▬▬	Scenic route
—	Main railway
—	Minor railway
△	Summit

Map showing locations including Yosemite, Oakhurst, Coarsegold, Raymond, Modesto, Chowchilla, O'Neals, Auberry, Prather, Berenda, Friant, Tollhouse, Madera, Trimmer, Pine Flat Lake, Ripperdan, rebaugh, Mendota, Clovis, Piedra, Biola, FRESNO, Dunlap, Kerney Park, Sanger, Pinehurst, San Joaquin, Easton, Orange Cove, Badger, Holm, Selma, Cutler, Cantua Creek, Caruthers, Kingsburg, Laton, Traver, Woodlake, Three Rivers, Ivanhoe, Visalia, Lemoncove, Lemoore, HANFORD, Exeter, Huron, Guernsey, Tulare, Lindsay, Milo, Coalinga, Stratford, Plainview, Strathmore, Springville, Corcoran, Tipton, Poplar, Porterville, Avenal, Kettleman City, Pixley, California Hot Springs, Colonel Allensworth State Historic Park, Earlimart, Ducor, Allensworth, White River, Los Angeles, Bakersfield

0 kilometers   20

0 miles   20

The North Central Coastline

The beaches of north central California are varied, from long, thin stretches to tiny coves at the foot of coastal bluffs. In summer, sun-worshipers and volleyball players congregate on the sands, and while the water is generally too cold for swimming, surfers don wet suits to brave the chilly waves. With almost no commercial developments along this stretch of coastline, these beaches are also ideal for leisurely walks, searching for driftwood or seashells. You may also catch a glimpse of the area's abundant wildlife, which ranges from shore birds and tidepool-dwellers to elephant seals and migrating gray whales.

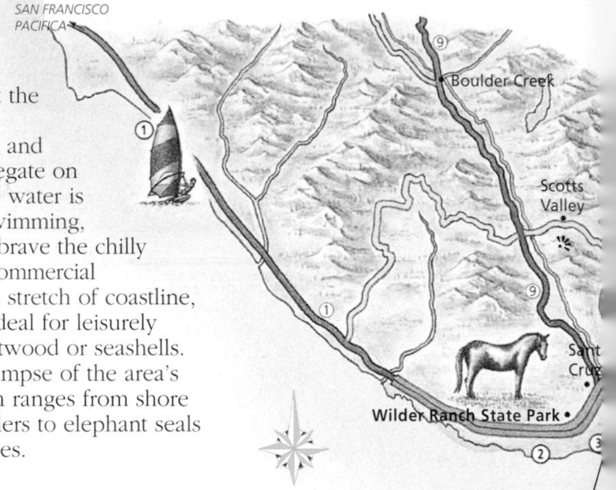

Moss Landing *is a colorful harbor and the home port for most of Monterey Bay's commercial fishing boats. It has many good seafood restaurants along its wharves.*

0 kilometers 5

0 miles 5

★ Santa Cruz Beach ③

🏄 🏊 ⛑ ♿ 🚻

With free volleyball courts and barbecue pits backed by the popular Boardwalk Amusement Park *(see p506)*, this broad golden expanse is the area's most popular beach.

Waddell Creek Beach ①

🏊 ⛑ ♿ 🚻

This golden strand of beach is part of the Big Basin Redwoods State Park *(see p504)* and is a favorite spot for picnickers, anglers, and windsurfers.

Lighthouse Field State Beach ②

🏄

This rugged 36 acres (14 ha) of shoreline is well suited to surfing or simply admiring the sculpted 40-ft (12-m) sandstone headlands. It is also a good place to spot sea otters, brown pelicans, and the occasional whale offshore.

Capitola Beach ④

🏄 🏊 ⛑ ♿ 🚻

A wooden railway trestle bridges the small creek that meets the ocean at this sandy beach. Next to the beach is Capitola Wharf, with restaurants, shops, and observation decks. The Capitola Bluffs are an important paleontological site, and the prehistoric shells can be seen at low tide.

Marina State Beach ⑤

🏄 🏊 ⛑ ♿ 🚻

Backed by sand dunes, this beach was once a part of a US Army base and is now part of a university campus.

KEY

- Freeway
- Major road
- Minor road
- River
- Viewpoint

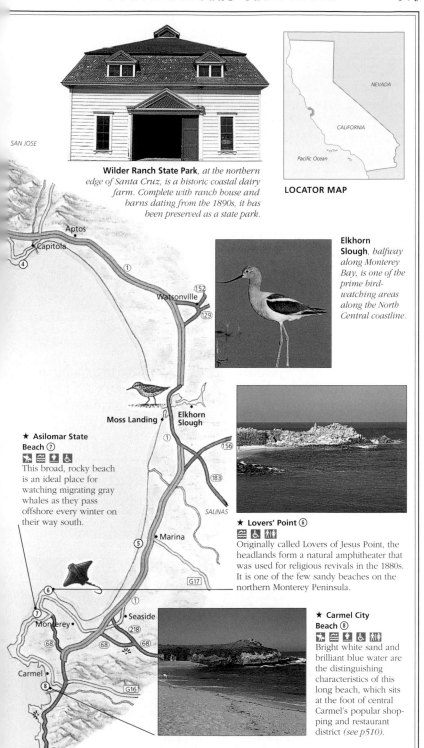

Wilder Ranch State Park, *at the northern edge of Santa Cruz, is a historic coastal dairy farm. Complete with ranch house and barns dating from the 1890s, it has been preserved as a state park.*

NEVADA
CALIFORNIA
Pacific Ocean

LOCATOR MAP

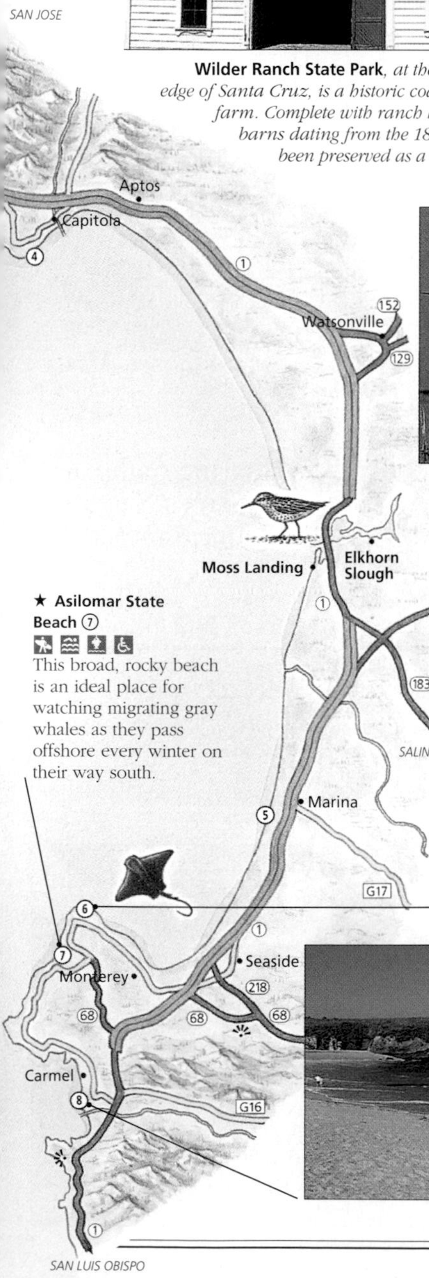
SAN JOSE
Aptos
Capitola
4
1
152
Watsonville
129
Moss Landing
Elkhorn Slough
1
156
183
SALINAS
Marina
5
G17
6
1
7
Seaside
Monterey
218
68
68
68
Carmel
8
G16
1
SAN LUIS OBISPO

Elkhorn Slough, *halfway along Monterey Bay, is one of the prime bird-watching areas along the North Central coastline.*

★ Asilomar State Beach (7)

🏄 🌊 🛟 ♿

This broad, rocky beach is an ideal place for watching migrating gray whales as they pass offshore every winter on their way south.

★ Lovers' Point (6)

🌊 ♿ 🚻

Originally called Lovers of Jesus Point, the headlands form a natural amphitheater that was used for religious revivals in the 1880s. It is one of the few sandy beaches on the northern Monterey Peninsula.

★ Carmel City Beach (8)

🏄 🌊 🛟 ♿ 🚻

Bright white sand and brilliant blue water are the distinguishing characteristics of this long beach, which sits at the foot of central Carmel's popular shopping and restaurant district *(see p510)*.

Elephant seals ashore at Año Nuevo State Reserve

Big Basin Redwoods State Park ❶

🏞 *Santa Cruz, Boulder Creek Golf Course.* **Visitors' Center** *Tel (831) 338-8860.* **www**.bigbasin.org

In 1900 a group of environmentalists formed the Sempervirens Club with the aim of preventing the logging of redwoods. This resulted in Big Basin Redwoods State Park, California's first state park, established in 1902. It covers 16,000 acres (6,475 ha) and protects the southernmost groves of the coastal redwood tree *(see p446)* and forests of Douglas fir and other conifers. It is also home to wildlife such as black-tailed deer and the mountain lion.

Trails lead through redwood groves to the park's many waterfalls, including the popular Berry Creek Falls. There are also more than 100 miles (160 km) of other routes, including the Skyline-to-Sea Trail, which drops down to the Pacific Ocean at Waddell Creek *(see pp502–3)*.

Exhibits detailing the park's history are on display inside the visitor center.

Año Nuevo State Reserve ❷

Road map B4. 🚉 *Santa Cruz, Waddell Creek.* 🛈 *(650) 879-2025.* 🕐 *daily.*

The Año Nuevo State Reserve, 60 miles, (96 km) north of Monterey, has as its main point of interest the breeding grounds of the Northern elephant seal, one of the world's

most fascinating creatures. A short stretch of sandy beach and a small offshore island are populated each winter by hundreds of these giant mammals, which arrive here from all over the Pacific Ocean to mate and give birth.

Elephant seals were hunted almost to extinction in the 19th century because of their valuable oil-bearing blubber. A few survivors found refuge off the coast of Mexico and made their way back to California in the 1950s. The first pups were born at Año Nuevo in 1975. There are now some 120,000 elephant seals off the coast of California.

The seals are named after the dangling proboscis of the male, which can reach 20 ft (6 m) in length and weigh upward of 2 tons. Ungainly on land, elephant seals can perform incredible feats in the sea – remaining under water for up to 20 minutes at a time and diving more than 4,000 ft (1,220 m) beneath the surface. Each December, the male seals arrive here and begin

the battle for dominance, engaging in violent fights. Only a handful of the most powerful males are able to mate, but one male can father pups with as many as 50 different females in one season. After spending most of the year at sea, the females arrive in January to give birth to young conceived the previous winter. Mating follows soon after, although conception is delayed for up to four months while the female recovers from giving birth.

The name Año Nuevo ("New Year") was given to the island by explorer Sebastián Vizcaíno, who sailed past the area on January 1, 1603 *(see pp46–7)*. The park is open all year, but during the winter when the elephant seals are present, visitors are allowed only on guided tours. Tickets are available through the California State Parks reservation service, DestiNet *(see p610)*.

Roaring Camp and Big Trees Narrow-Gauge Railroad ❸

Tel (831) 335-4400. 🚉 *Santa Cruz.* 🕐 *Jan–Mar: Sat & Sun.* ◉ *public hols.* 🅿 ♿ 🎦 *11am, 12:15pm, 2pm.* **Santa Cruz Big Trees Railroad** *Tel (831) 335-4400.* 🕐 *call for times.* 🅿 ♿ 🎦 **www**.roaringcamp.com

High up in the Santa Cruz Mountains, near the town of Felton, a pair of historic logging railroads have been kept in operation as the focus

Roaring Camp and Big Trees Railroad

Façade of Mission San Juan Bautista

of a family-orientated theme park devoted to the late 19th-century and early 20th-century lumber industry. Between December and March, a narrow-gauge train departs on a weekend 6-mile (10-km) round-trip through the adjacent forests of Henry Cowell Redwoods State Park. From April to November, the traditional-gauge Big Trees, Santa Cruz, and Pacific Railroad, sets off from Roaring Camp on an hour-long trip through the mountains and down to Santa Cruz. There is a three-hour stopover, during which passengers can enjoy the beach and Boardwalk Amusement Park before the return journey (see pp506–7). The trip can also be taken as a round-trip from Santa Cruz.

Santa Cruz ❹

See pp506–7.

San Juan Bautista ❺

Road map B4. 🏠 *1,650.* 🚌 *from Hollister.* 🛈 *402 3rd St (831) 623-24 54.* **www**.san-juan-bautista.ca.us

For a quick insight into California's multifaceted history, there is no better place than San Juan Bautista. This small town has retained its rural character, despite being a mere 30 miles (48 km) from the heart of the high-tech Silicon Valley (see p428).

The main attraction of the town is Mission San Juan Bautista, which stands to the west of the central plaza. The

largest of the missions built during Spanish colonial rule, it is also the only one to have aisles along the nave. Alfred Hitchcock used the mission's façade for the final scenes of his film *Vertigo*. The adjacent monastery has been converted into a museum of mission history, displaying mission artifacts and photographs of the town at various stages of development.

El Camino Real sign

On the north side of the church there is a cemetery, next to which a faint trail marks the historic route of El Camino Real. This 650-mile (1,050-km) path linked the 21 California missions, all within a day's journey of their nearest mission (see pp46–7). By coincidence, this trail also follows the San Andreas Fault, the underlying source of all California's earthquakes (see pp24–5). A small seismograph on the edge of the town's plaza monitors tectonic activity along the fault line.

The east and south sides of the plaza are lined by three historic buildings, all of which have been preserved as part of San Juan Bautista State Historic Park. The Plaza Hotel incorporates part of the original barracks built in 1813. The town's stables now house antique carriages and stagecoaches, and Castro House was owned by Patrick Breen, a survivor of the tragic Donner Party (see p486).

THE LOMA PRIETA EARTHQUAKE

The powerful tremor that rocked San Francisco on October 17, 1989 had its epicenter beneath Loma Prieta, a hill between Santa Cruz and San Juan Bautista. Although the international media concentrated on the extensive damage caused in and around San Francisco, the worst damage occurred in Santa Cruz and the surrounding communities, where a number of homes and commercial buildings were destroyed. Approximately 40 businesses were forced to relocate to tentlike temporary buildings occupying three full blocks. The downtown district of Santa Cruz was a vast building site until the end of 1994. The majority of the damaged structures have now been repaired or replaced, but empty lots still remain where buildings once stood.

Destruction caused by the Loma Prieta earthquake

Santa Cruz ❹

Perched at the northern tip of Monterey Bay, Santa Cruz is a composite of small-town California, with an agricultural rather than suburban feel. Its surrounding farmland forms a broad shelf between the bay and the densely forested Santa Cruz Mountains that rise to the east. These mountains separate Santa Cruz from the urban Silicon Valley *(see p428)* and, along with the scenic coastline, provide residents and visitors with an easy access to nature. The city's past is preserved in a replica 18th-century mission and in the excellent local history museum. The large University of California campus in the town, attracting students and professors from all over the world, also gives Santa Cruz a cosmopolitan and erudite character.

Reconstructed façade of Santa Cruz Mission

Exploring Santa Cruz

The downtown, which centers on Pacific Avenue, is 875 yards (800 m) inland. Much of this area was badly damaged by the Loma Prieta earthquake *(see p505)*, but the city has recovered swiftly, with many good bookstores, art galleries, and cafés lining the streets. The historic core of the city, including the remains of the 1791 Mission Santa Cruz, is on a hill to the northeast of the town.

The highlight of Santa Cruz is the waterfront, including the Boardwalk Amusement Park and scenic Cliff Drive that runs along the coast.

Detail of the Giant Dipper

🎡 Santa Cruz Beach Boardwalk

400 Beach St. *Tel (831) 423-5590.* ◯ *call ahead for opening times.*
The last surviving old-style amusement park on the West Coast, the Santa Cruz Beach Boardwalk offers a variety of attractions and games lined up along the beachfront. Visitors can wander freely, deciding which of the rides to try. The main attraction is the Giant Dipper roller coaster, built in 1924 by Arthur Looff and now a National Historic Landmark. The car travels along the 1-mile (1.6-km) wooden track at 55 mph (88 km/h). The carousel nearby features horses and chariots hand-carved by Looff's father, craftsman Charles Looff, in 1911. The ride is accompanied by a 100-year-old pipe organ. The park also has 27 more modern rides and an Art Deco dance hall.

🔒 Mission Santa Cruz

Emmet & High Sts. *Tel (831) 426-5686.* ◯ *10am–4pm Tue–Sat, 10am–2pm Sun.* **Donation.**
On top of a hill overlooking the town, Mission Santa Cruz was founded on September 25, 1791 by Father Lasuén, as the 12th Franciscan mission in California. The buildings were completed three years later. The mission was never a great success, however, due to earthquakes, poor weather, and its isolated location, all of which have eliminated any remains of the original structure. A park outlines the site, and a 1931 replica of the mission has been constructed. This houses a small museum that contains 18th-century relics and displays on mission history.

🏛 Museum of Art and History at the McPherson Center

705 Front St. *Tel (831) 429-1964.* ◯ *11am–5pm Tue–Sun (7pm Thu).* 🔴 *Jan 1, Thanksgiving, Dec 25.* ♿ www.santacruzmah.org
One positive development to arise out of the rubble of the 1989 Loma Prieta earthquake was this 20,000 sq ft (1,858 sq m) cultural center, which opened in 1993 to house the local art and history galleries. The Art Gallery shows works primarily by north central artists depicting the local landscape. The History Gallery includes a series of displays tracing the development of Santa Cruz County, from the pre-colonial and mission eras through to the present day.

Also in the History Gallery are exhibits detailing the region's agricultural and industrial heritage, with photographs of late 19th-century and early 20th-century farms and logging operations. The museum also incorporates the adjacent Octagon Gallery that was completed in 1882 as the County Hall of Records.

Giant Dipper roller coaster in the Boardwalk Amusement Park

For hotels and restaurants in this region see pp560–61 and pp604–5

Eroded archway at the Natural Bridges State Beach

VISITORS' CHECKLIST

Road map B4. 👥 *252,000.* ✈ *San Jose International Airport.* ✈ *Monterey Peninsula Airport.* 🚌 *920 Pacific Ave.* ℹ *701 Front St (831 425-1234).* 🎪 *Santa Cruz Fungus Fair (Jan); Clam Chowder Cook-Off (Feb).*

🏞 Natural Bridges State Beach

2531 W Cliff Dr. ***Tel*** *(831) 423-4609.* ⏰ *daily.* ♿ **Visitors' Center** *end of W Cliff Drive.* ⏰ *10am–4pm daily.*

Natural Bridges State Beach takes its name from the picturesque archways that were carved into the cliffs by the ocean waves. Two of the three original arches collapsed but one still remains, through which waves roll into a small sandy cove. The park also preserves a eucalyptus grove and a nature trail, showing all the stages in the life cycle of the beautiful monarch butterfly *(see p219)*.

🏛 Santa Cruz Surfing Museum

Lighthouse Point, W Cliff Drive ***Tel*** *(831) 420-6289.* ⏰ *noon–4pm Thu–Mon.* ⛔ *Jan 1, Thanksgiving, Dec 25.* **Donation**.

In a lighthouse overlooking the region's main surfing area, this museum has artifacts from every era of Santa Cruz surfing. The sport was brought to the state from Hawaii to promote tourism. It evolved into a truly Californian pursuit with the music of the Beach Boys in the 1960s *(see pp56–7)*. The surfboards range from the redwood planks of the 1930s to today's high-tech laminates.

🏞 Mystery Spot

465 Mystery Spot Rd. ***Tel*** *(831) 423-8897.* ⏰ *daily.* ♿ **www**.mysteryspot.com

Two miles (3 km) east of Santa Cruz, a redwood grove has been drawing visitors for decades due to various strange events. Balls roll uphill, parallel lines converge, and the laws of physics seem to be suspended. Part tourist trap, part genuine oddity, the Mystery Spot has to be seen.

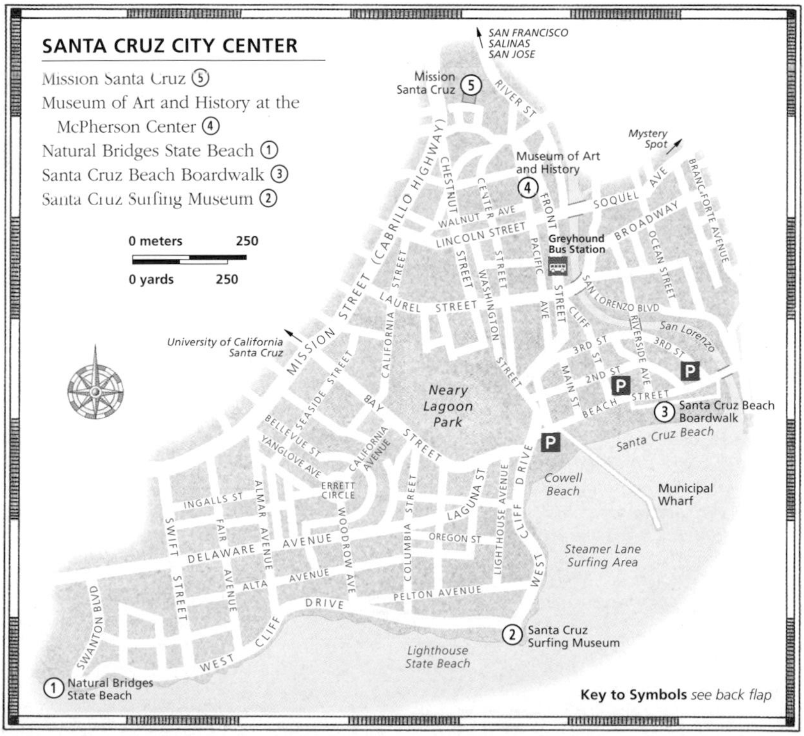
SANTA CRUZ CITY CENTER
Mission Santa Cruz 5
Museum of Art and History at the McPherson Center 4
Natural Bridges State Beach 1
Santa Cruz Beach Boardwalk 3
Santa Cruz Surfing Museum 2
0 meters 250
0 yards 250
SAN FRANCISCO
SALINAS
SAN JOSE
Mission Santa Cruz
RIVER ST
Mystery Spot
Museum of Art and History
CHESTNUT
CENTER
FRONT
SOQUEL AVE
BRANCIFORTE AVENUE
WALNUT AVE
LINCOLN STREET
Greyhound Bus Station
BROADWAY
OCEAN STREET
PACIFIC AVE
MISSION STREET (CABRILLO HIGHWAY)
LAUREL STREET
SAN LORENZO BLVD
San Lorenzo
RIVERSIDE AVE
3RD ST
2ND ST
MAIN ST
BEACH STREET
Santa Cruz Beach Boardwalk
Santa Cruz Beach
University of California Santa Cruz
CALIFORNIA STREET
WASHINGTON STREET
Neary Lagoon Park
BAY STREET
SEASIDE STREET
BELLEVUE ST
YANGLOVE AVE
CALIFORNIA AVENUE
Cowell Beach
Municipal Wharf
ERRETT CIRCLE
INGALLS ST
ALMAR AVENUE
FAIR AVENUE
SWIFT STREET
DELAWARE AVENUE
WOODROW AVE
COLUMBIA STREET
LAGUNA ST
OREGON ST
LIGHTHOUSE AVENUE
WEST CLIFF DRIVE
Steamer Lane Surfing Area
ALTA AVENUE
PELTON AVENUE
SWANTON BLVD
Santa Cruz Surfing Museum
Lighthouse State Beach
Natural Bridges State Beach
Key to Symbols see back flap

Street-by-Street: Monterey ❻

The Spanish explorer, Sebastián Vizcaíno, landed here in 1602 and named the bay after his patron, the Count of Monterrey. But it was not until the Spanish captain Gaspar de Portolá (1717– 1784) and Father Serra *(see pp46–7)* landed here in 1770 and established a church and presidio that the garrison grew into a pueblo. Monterey served as the capital of California until 1848. After the Gold Rush *(see pp48–9)* the city lost its status to San Francisco and settled into the role of a hardworking fishing port, market town, and military base.

Today, visitors come to tour the historic sites, dine on seafood at Fisherman's Wharf, and attend the annual jazz festival.

California's First Theater
Built in 1847 as a boarding house, it became a theater in 1848. Victorian melodramas are still performed here every night.

★ Colton Hall
The California State Constitution was first signed here in 1849. The hall now houses a museum commemorating the event.

Larkin House
Thomas Larkin, an East Coast merchant, built this house in 1832. The architecture has become representative of Monterey style (see pp30–31).

The Sherman Quarters were General Sherman's military base from 1847–1849.

The Cooper-Molera Complex combines a garden, a carriage display and personal mementos of three generations of the Cooper family, who built the house between 1827 and 1900.

FRANKLIN STREET
PIERCE STREET
PACIFIC STREET
CALLE PRINCIPAL
JEFFERSON STREET
MUNRAS AV

STAR SIGHTS
★ Colton Hall
★ Fisherman's Wharf

0 meters   100
0 yards   100

KEY
– – – Suggested route

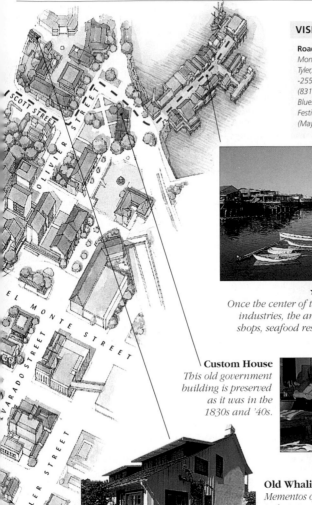

VISITORS' CHECKLIST

Road map B4. 🏠 *35,000.* ✈️ *Monterey Peninsula Airport.* 🚌 *Tyler, Pearl & Munras Sts, (831) 899 -2555.* ℹ️ *401 Camino el Estero (831 648-5350).* 🎭 *Monterey Blues Festival (Jul); Monterey Jazz Festival (Sep); Laguna Seca Races (May–Oct).* **www**.mpcc.com

★ Fisherman's Wharf
Once the center of the fishing and whaling industries, the area is now known for its shops, seafood restaurants, and markets.

Custom House
This old government building is preserved as it was in the 1830s and '40s.

Old Whaling Station
Mementos of the Monterey whaling industry are displayed in the house. The paving outside the building was made using whale bones.

Stevenson House
Robert Louis Stevenson lived here in 1879. The house is now a museum.

The Royal Presidio Chapel, built in 1794, is the town's oldest surviving building.

Exploring Monterey Peninsula

Writers and artists have long extolled the spectacular coastline of the Monterey Peninsula. Its granite rocks have been cut into rugged coves and jutting points by the ocean. Forests of Monterey cypress and pine trees, wintering grounds of the monarch butterfly, cover the inland area. Otters and sea lions swim in the kelp forests beyond the shore. The peninsula is home to three main towns: Monterey, the capital of Spanish California (see pp508–9); the former religious retreat, Pacific Grove; and the picturesque village of Carmel-by-the-Sea.

Marine bird at the Monterey Bay Aquarium

✈ Monterey Bay Aquarium
886 Cannery Row. **Tel** (831) 648-4888. ◯ daily. ● Dec 25. 🖭
www.montereybayaquarium.org
Monterey Bay Aquarium is the largest aquarium in the US., with more than 570 species and 350,000 specimens from the Monterey Bay area. Among the exhibits are an enclosed kelp forest, a rock pool, and a live jellyfish display. Visitors are allowed to touch the specimens, including sea stars and bat rays, relatives of sting rays.

A pool connected to the open bay attracts sea otters. The Outer Bay Wing has a huge tank in which the conditions of the ocean are re-created. It contains yellowfin tuna, ocean sunfish, green sea turtles, and barracuda. The Research Institute offers a chance for visitors to watch the marine scientists at work, and the Splash Zone is a hands-on aquarium/museum for kids.

⚏ Cannery Row
David Ave & Coastguard Pier.
Tel (831) 649-6695. ◯ daily.
www.canneryrow.com
This six-block harbor-front street, celebrated by John Steinbeck in his ribald novels

Cannery Row and Sweet Thursday (see p517), was once the site of more than 20 fish-packing plants that processed sardines from Monterey Bay. The canneries thrived from the early 20th century, reaching their greatest volume of production in the early 1940s. In 1945 the sardines suddenly disappeared, perhaps as a result of overfishing, and most of the canneries were abandoned, later to be demolished or burned down. The buildings that remain today house an eclectic collection of shops and restaurants. One notable historic building that remains, at No. 800, is the old laboratory of "Doc" Ricketts, noted marine biologist, and best friend of Steinbeck. The building is now a private club.

Street sign in Cannery Row

⚏ Pacific Grove
Forest & Central Aves.
Tel (831) 373-3304. ◯ daily.
● Jan 1, Thanksgiving, Dec 25.
www.pacificgrove.org
This sedate town was founded in 1889 as a religious retreat, where alcohol, dancing, and

even the Sunday newspaper were banned. Today it is best known for its wooden houses, many now converted into inns, its beautiful coastal parks, and the monarch butterflies that arrive between October and April (see p219). The annual return of the insects, which are protected by city ordinance, occasions a lively parade.

The Point Pinos Lighthouse was built in 1852 and is now the oldest operating lighthouse in California.

⚏ Carmel-by-the-Sea
San Carlos, 5th & 6th Sts. **Tel** (831) 624-2522. ◯ Mon–Sat. ● Jan 1, Thanksgiving, Dec 25.
The varied array of homes in this picturesque village border the steep hillsides down to the ocean. City ordinances restricting streetlights, mail deliveries, and sidewalks gives the town its quaint atmosphere. Art galleries and shops abound along Ocean Ave, and the town also sponsors an annual playwriting contest, a Bach Festival, and many art exhibitions.

🎋 Carmel River State Beach
Carmelo & Scenic Rds.
This 106-acre (43-ha) state park straddles the mouth of the Carmel River, containing a lagoon and wetland nature preserve for a bountiful population of native and migratory birds. Fishing is permitted on the beach, but swimming is discouraged because of dangerous currents and cold temperatures. The beach is a favorite picnic spot of Carmel residents.

Point Pinos Lighthouse at Pacific Grove

The 17-Mile Drive

Sightseers may tour the Monterey Peninsula via a toll road, the 17-Mile Drive. The road offers spectacular views of what the area has to offer, including crashing surf, coastal flora, and the Del Monte Forest. The extraordinary beauty of the region has also attracted many wealthy people to build imposing estates and mansions in the area. Most celebrated of all its attractions are the country clubs and championship golf courses.

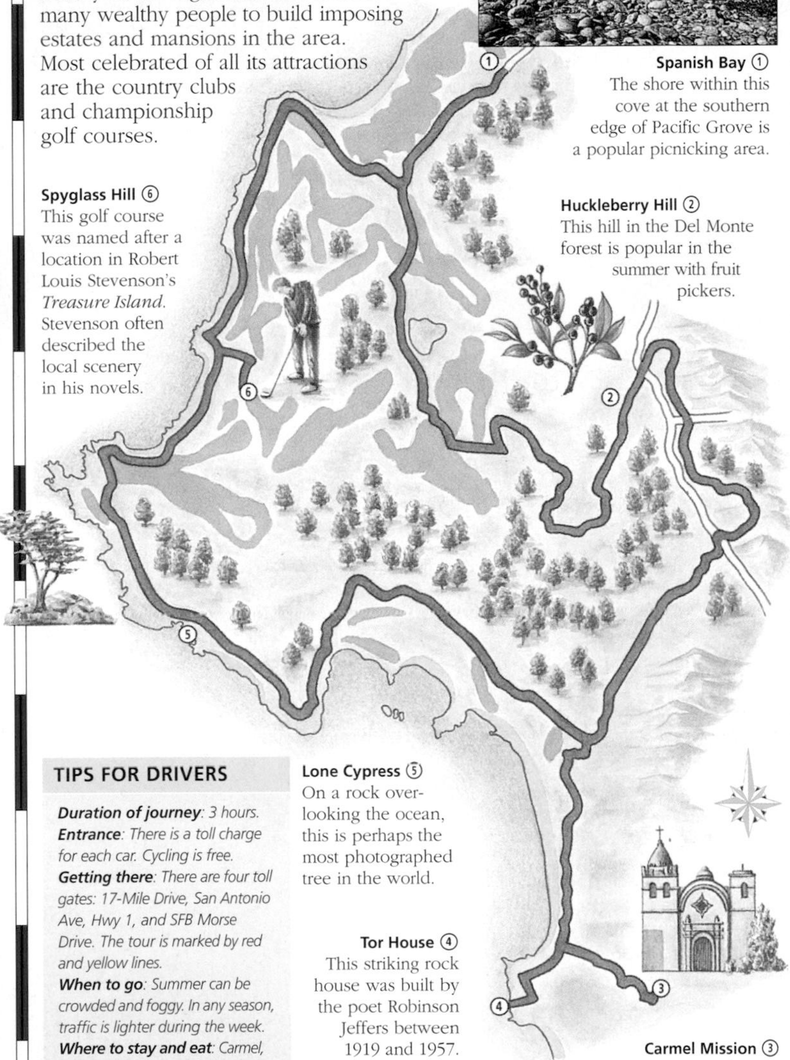

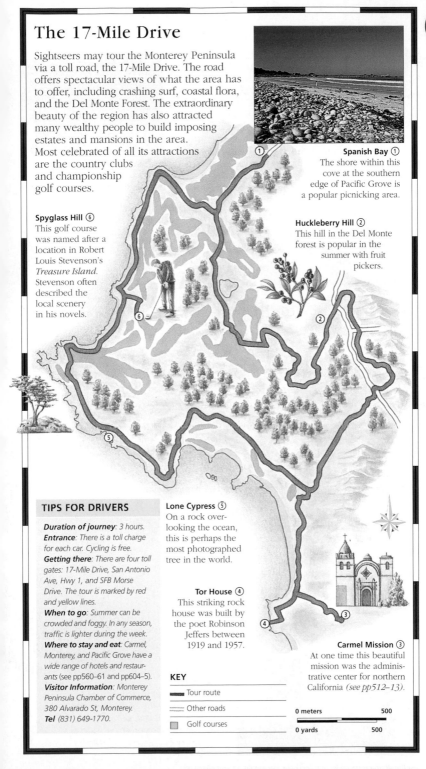

Spanish Bay ①
The shore within this cove at the southern edge of Pacific Grove is a popular picnicking area.

Huckleberry Hill ②
This hill in the Del Monte forest is popular in the summer with fruit pickers.

Carmel Mission ③
At one time this beautiful mission was the administrative center for northern California *(see pp512–13)*.

Tor House ④
This striking rock house was built by the poet Robinson Jeffers between 1919 and 1957.

Lone Cypress ⑤
On a rock overlooking the ocean, this is perhaps the most photographed tree in the world.

Spyglass Hill ⑥
This golf course was named after a location in Robert Louis Stevenson's *Treasure Island*. Stevenson often described the local scenery in his novels.

TIPS FOR DRIVERS

Duration of journey: *3 hours.*
Entrance: *There is a toll charge for each car. Cycling is free.*
Getting there: *There are four toll gates: 17-Mile Drive, San Antonio Ave, Hwy 1, and SFB Morse Drive. The tour is marked by red and yellow lines.*
When to go: *Summer can be crowded and foggy. In any season, traffic is lighter during the week.*
Where to stay and eat: *Carmel, Monterey, and Pacific Grove have a wide range of hotels and restaurants (see pp560–61 and pp604–5).*
Visitor Information: *Monterey Peninsula Chamber of Commerce, 380 Alvarado St, Monterey.*
Tel *(831) 649-1770.*

KEY

Tour route
Other roads
Golf courses

0 meters 500
0 yards 500

Carmel Mission ❼

Founded in 1770 by Father Junípero Serra (1713–84) and built of adobe brick by Native American laborers, Carmel Mission served as the administrative center for all the Northern California missions. Father Serra resided here until his death and is now buried at the foot of the altar. The mission was secularized and abandoned in 1834, quickly falling into disrepair. Restoration work began in 1924, carefully following the plans of the original mission, and replanting the gardens. The reconstructed living quarters detail 18th-century mission life. The mission still functions as a Catholic church.

Decorative wall plaque

The sarcophagus depicts Father Serra recumbent in death, surrounded by three mourning padres. It is among the finest of its type in the United States.

Kitchen
This restored room shows the kitchen as it was in missionary days, including the oven brought from Mexico. A section of the original adobe wall can be seen.

Bell tower

Dining room

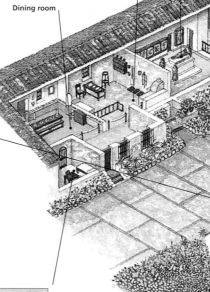

Statue of Junípero Serra
Set within the beautiful front courtyard, a statue of Serra faces the mission church he founded.

★ Serra's Cell
Father Serra's simple way of life is evident in this sparse, restored cell. The wooden bed, chair, desk, and candlestick were the only pieces of furniture he possessed. He died here in 1784.

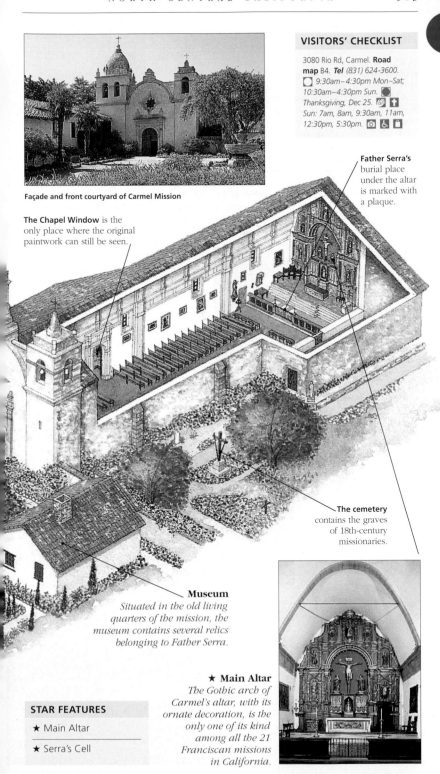

VISITORS' CHECKLIST

3080 Rio Rd, Carmel. **Road map** B4. **Tel** *(831) 624-3600.* ◯ *9:30am–4:30pm Mon–Sat; 10:30am–4:30pm Sun.* ◯ *Thanksgiving, Dec 25.* Sun: 7am, 8am, 9:30am, 11am, 12:30pm, 5:30pm.

Façade and front courtyard of Carmel Mission

Father Serra's burial place under the altar is marked with a plaque.

The Chapel Window is the only place where the original paintwork can still be seen.

The cemetery contains the graves of 18th-century missionaries.

Museum
Situated in the old living quarters of the mission, the museum contains several relics belonging to Father Serra.

★ **Main Altar**
The Gothic arch of Carmel's altar, with its ornate decoration, is the only one of its kind among all the 21 Franciscan missions in California.

STAR FEATURES

★ Main Altar

★ Serra's Cell

Big Sur ❽

In the late 18th century, Spanish colonists at Carmel named this stretch of land *El Pais Grande del Sur*, the "big country to the south," and the coastline of Big Sur has been attracting hyperbole ever since. The novelist Robert Louis Stevenson called it "the greatest meeting of land and sea in the world," and the 100 miles (160 km) of breathtaking mountains, cliffs, and rocky coves still leave visitors grasping for adjectives.

The scenic Hwy 1 was constructed across this rugged landscape during the 1930s, but otherwise Big Sur has been preserved in its natural state. There are no large towns and very few signs of civilization in the area. Most of the shoreline is protected in a series of state parks that offer dense forests, broad rivers, and crashing surf, all easily accessible within a short walk of the road.

Crashing surf and rocky cliffs, typical of the Big Sur coastline

Point Lobos State Reserve
This is the habitat of the Monterey cypress, the only tree to survive the region's mixture of fog and salt spray. Its branches are shaped by the sea winds.

Bixby Creek Bridge
This photogenic arched bridge was built in 1932. For many years it was the world's largest single-arch span, at 260 ft (79 m) tall and 700 ft (213 m) long. Hwy 1 was named the state's first scenic highway here in 1966.

Point Sur Lighthouse sits atop a volcanic cone. It was manned until 1974 but is now automated.

Nepenthe is a lovely resort hidden from the road by oak trees. It has long been frequented by Hollywood movie stars.

KEY

═══	Minor road
━━━	Scenic route
- - -	Hiking trails
───	National park boundaries
〰️	Rivers and lakes
🅰	Camping
☼	Viewpoint

Andrew Molera State Park
Opened in 1972, this park includes 10 miles (16 km) of hiking trails and 2.5 miles (4 km) of quiet, sandy beach.

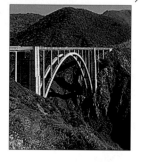

Julia Pfeiffer Burns State Park
A tunnel under Hwy 1, accessible only on foot, leads to the 100-ft (30-m) high bluff from which the McWay Creek waterfall spills into the Pacific Ocean.

VISITORS' CHECKLIST

Road map B4. 🚶 *1,500.* 🚌 *Nepenthe Park.* ☎ *(831) 667-21 00.* **www**.bigsurcalifornia.org

Ventana Wilderness
Part of the Los Padres National Forest, many of the steep ridges of this beautiful wilderness are accessible only to experienced hikers. Camp sites cover the lower reaches.

The Esalen Institute was set up in the 1960s to hold New Age seminars. Its hot springs were first frequented by Native Americans and still attract visitors *(see p441).*

VENTANA WILDERNESS

Tassajara Creek

LOS PADRES NATIONAL FOREST

Big Creek

Lucia

Nacimiento Fergusson Rd

Jade Cove
This beautiful cove can be reached only by way of a steep path down the cliff face. The removal of jade is prohibited above the high tide level.

Plaskett

Los Burros Rd

Antonio River

Lake San Antonio

Plaskett Creek

Nacimiento River

San Simeon Point is a natural harbor that was used by William Randolph Hearst to ship in materials for his estate, Hearst Castle™, on the inland hilltop *(see pp212–13).*

Alder Creek

Lake Nacimiento

| 0 kilometers | 10 |
| 0 miles | 10 |

San Simeon

Nobel prize-winning author John Steinbeck (1902–68)

Salinas **9**

Road map B4. 128,343.
119 E Alisal St (831 424-7611).
www.salinaschamber.com

Situated at the north end of the predominantly agricultural Salinas Valley, which stretches for more than 50 miles (80 km) between San Francisco and San Luis Obispo, Salinas is the region's primary agricultural center. Vegetable-packing plants and canneries line the major highways and railroad tracks. The region is often referred to as the "salad bowl of the nation," its prime produce being lettuce, as well as tomatoes and garlic.

The town is perhaps best known, however, as the birthplace of the Nobel prize-winning author John Steinbeck, who set many of his natural-istic stories here and in the surrounding area. A selection of books, manuscripts, photo-graphs, and personal mem-orabilia relating to the author is on permanent display in a special room of the **John Steinbeck Library**. The library also supplies information on

Steinbeck-related places to visit in the area and on the Steinbeck Festival, held in Salinas every August.

Hat in Three Stages of Land-ing, a large-scale, bright yellow steel sculpture of three cow-boy hats by the acclaimed Pop artist Claes Oldenberg, was erected in the town in the 1970s. It stands, appropriately, in front of the entrance to the California State Rodeo. Each Fourth of July one of the largest rodeos in the world is held here, bringing riders, live-stock and other entertainment from all over the country.

John Steinbeck Library
350 Lincoln Ave. **Tel** (831) 758-7311.
Mon–Sat. public hols.

Pinnacles National Monument **10**

Road map B4. **Tel** (831) 389-4485.
King City & Soledad. daily.
some trails.

High in the hills above the Salinas Valley, 12 miles (20 km) east of the town of Soledad on US101, the Pin-nacles National Monument preserves 16,000 acres (6,500 ha) of a unique volcanic land-scape. A solid ridge of lava flows, eroded over millions of years into oddly contorted crags and spires, runs through the center of the park, in places forming cliffs more than 500 ft (150 m) tall. There are no roads across the park, but there are many carefully-maintained hiking trails.

One of the most popular and accessible spots in the park is the Balconies forma-tion, reached by a 1.5-mile

(2.5 km) leisurely trail. Here beautiful red and gold cliffs rise high above the ground, attracting rock-climbers, photo-graphers, and bird-watchers. At the base of the cliffs, huge boulders caught between the narrow canyons have formed a series of dark talus caves. These were reputedly used in the past as hideouts by robbers and other outlaws.

The park is best visited in spring, when the temperature is cool and the wildflowers are in bloom. Mountain lions, coyotes, and eagles can occa-sionally also be sighted.

Volcanic crags of the Pinnacles National Monument

Fresno **11**

Road map C4. 411,600.
Fresno Air Terminal.
2331 Fresno St (559 495-4800).
www.fresnochamber.com

Fresno is located at approxi-mately the geographical center of the state and is its eighth largest city. It is often referred to as the "Raisin Capital of the World" because of its abundant production of the dried fruit.

Vegetable pickers and packers in the Salinas Valley

Its central position makes a convenient base to make excursions to the High Sierras, Kings Canyon, Sequoia, and Yosemite National Parks *(see pp482–97)*.

⬛ Fresno Metropolitan Museum
1515 Van Ness *Tel (559) 441-1444.* ◯ *11am–5pm Tue–Sun.* 🎫
www.fresnomet.org

Homegrown Fresno raisins

Environs
In Kearney Park, 7 miles (11 km) west of Fresno, is **Kearney Mansion**. This elaborate French Renaissance-style house was erected in 1903 by Theodore Kearney, an agriculturalist who helped establish California's raisin industry. The house is now a period museum.

⬛ Kearney Mansion
7160 W. Kearney Blvd, Hwy 99. *Tel (559) 441-0862.* ◯ *Fri–Sun.* 🎫 🎫

Colonel Allen Allensworth, resident of Hanford

Hanford ⑫

Road map C4. 🏘 *40,000.* 🚌 🚊 ℹ
200 Santa Fe Ave, Suite D (559 582-0483). www.hanfordchamber.com

One of many medium-sized farming communities in the area, Hanford is significant because of its diverse, multiethnic heritage. The China Alley neighborhood was once inhabited by one of the largest Chinese communities in California, many of whom worked on the construction of the transcontinental railroad *(see pp50–51).* Located east of the town center, China Alley

surrounds the historic **Taoist Temple**, built in 1893. The temple operated as a hostel for Chinese immigrants and a Chinese school as well as a religious shrine. Downtown Hanford, around Courthouse Square, has a beautiful antique carousel and a number of elegant buildings dating from the late 19th century, now converted into shops and restaurants.

🏮 Taoist Temple
China Alley. *Tel (559) 582-4508.* ◯ *by appointment only.* 🎫 📷

Environs
The **Colonel Allensworth State Historic Park** is 30 miles (50 km) south of Hanford. Colonel Allen Allensworth believed his fellow African-Americans could combat racism by building their own future. He established a unique farming community in 1908 with a group of African-American families. Memorabilia of this independent community are now on display in the old farmhouses.

⬛ Colonel Allensworth State Historic Park
Off Hwy 99 on County Rd J22, Earlimart. *Tel (661) 849-3433 or 634- 3795.* ◯ *daily.* 🎫

JOHN STEINBECK

One of California's most successful 20th-century writers, John Steinbeck (1902–68) was born in Salinas to an established family of farmers and ranchers. When he dropped out of Stanford University *(see p427)*, Steinbeck moved to the Monterey Peninsula in the late 1920s to write fiction. After several attempts he eventually gained a measure of success with the publication of the novella *Tortilla Flat* in 1935. Steinbeck then began a series of short stories and novels, the majority of them focusing on the people and places he knew well in the Salinas Valley and Monterey area. These included some of his greatest work: *Of Mice and Men* (1937), *Cannery Row* (1945), and *East of Eden* (1952).

His best-known work is *The Grapes of Wrath* (1939). The novel fictionalizes the mass westward migration that took place during the Depression of the 1930s, by documenting the struggles of the Joad family as they fled the dust bowl of Oklahoma for the greener pastures of California. It was an immediate bestseller and earned Steinbeck a Pulitzer Prize, although many Californians took its unhappy ending as an insult to their state, and even as Communist propaganda. Steinbeck reacted to this antipathy in 1943 by going to North Africa and becoming a war correspondent. On his return to the United States in 1945 he settled on Long Island, New York. In 1962, he was awarded the Nobel Prize for Literature. Steinbeck is the only American author to have received both the Pulitzer Prize and the Nobel Prize.

He died in New York City on December 20, 1968, but is buried in his hometown, in the Garden of Memories at No. 768 Abbott Street.

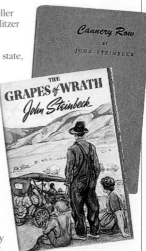

First editions of Steinbeck's most famous works, Cannery Row and The Grapes of Wrath

TRAVELERS' NEEDS

WHERE TO STAY

Framed by rugged coastal mountains, lush wooded hills, sophisticated urban centers, and a long stretch of coastline, California is one of the premier vacation destinations in the world. Whether rustic lodges or five-star resorts suit your budget, there is a wealth of options for travelers to the state.

Top hotels can range from film-star luxury to high-tech business centers. Budget accommodations are widespread, from roadside motels to atmospheric inns that offer an insight into the state's history. All accommodations, are however, likely to

Doorman

offer double beds, bathrooms, and comfortable surroundings. A range of camping facilities is also available for those interested in the great outdoors.

Free magazines containing discount coupons for all sorts of accommodations are available from street distribution bins at freeway rest stops and at car rental centers. Many hotels also offer discounts on reservation during the off season, and it is worth booking ahead to negotiate the rate. The listings on pages 524–66 give full descriptions of quality accommodations throughout the state to suit all budgets.

HOTEL CLASSIFICATIONS

The California tourist industry is recognized for its quality lodgings. A guideline of value to travelers is the diamond rating system of the California State Automobile Association. Every lodging, from the most expensive four-diamond hotel to the budget one-diamond motel, is rated for service, cleanliness, and the range of facilities offered.

Another guideline is *Relais et Châteaux*, an established French organization that rates top holiday destinations worldwide. Only 26 properties in the United States have been invited to join the organization, and seven of these are located in California.

HOTELS

In California, hotels come in every shape and size. There are the historic showplaces such as the Sheraton Palace

in San Francisco *(see p547)*, the Biltmore in Los Angeles *(see p526)*, and the Ahwahnee in Yosemite National Park *(see p560)*. These were originally built to impress East Coast bankers and prove that the West Coast was worth their investment. There are also the trendy, visually stunning urban getaways such as the Hotel Triton in San Francisco *(see p544)* and the Mondrian in West Hollywood *(see p531)*. There are hotels with fashion shops, with corporate conference centers, chandelier ballrooms, or landscaped gardens. There are also small hotels, called "boutique hotels," which have fewer than 100 rooms and the intimate ambience of a bed-and-breakfast.

No matter the size, you can always count on every hotel having a spacious foyer, a restaurant or café, a pool or exercise room, and a range of services such as laundry, iron-

Lounge bar in the exclusive Beverly Wilshire Hotel *(see p525)*

ing, and in-room video movies. If the hotel does not have its own exercise facility on-site, there is often an arrangement with a nearby health club that hotel guests can use for a fee of $8–$12 per day. No-smoking rooms are always available – many hotels have now set aside entire floors for nonsmokers only.

Rates for hotels range from an inexpensive $75 per night to a moderate $175. Rooms at upscale, well-located hotels can range from $175–$275. There are some luxury hotels in California, however, be it in Beverly Hills, Big Sur, or Napa Valley, that charge $185 for the smallest room off season, and in peak season can be as much as $500 a night.

Hotels are also subject to city and state taxes, which

Biltmore Hotel in Los Angeles *(see p526)*

range from 11 percent in San Francisco to 14 percent in Los Angeles. Not included in room rates are additional charges, such as for parking, as well as heavy surcharges

CORPORATE HOTELS

These cater to business travelers by offering weekly and monthly rates. There are also a number of all-suite hotels, with living rooms, in-room computers, and fax connections. Some even have on-site computer centers, providing ample work space for business travelers. Check the hotel listings on pages 524–66 to see where these services are available.

CHAIN HOTELS

You can count on good service, moderate prices, and comfortable surroundings at a chain hotel. The popular chains in California include the **Westin, Hilton, Sheraton, Marriott, Ramada, Hyatt,** and **Holiday Inn**. Some of these chains operate more than one hotel in each city and designate one location as the flagship facility. All chain hotels listed on page 523 have Internet web sites, or you can call the hotel's toll-free number to ask about rates and availability.

Chateau Marmont on Sunset Boulevard *(see p530)*

Sign over small chain hotel

TIPPING

The hotel porter will often carry your bags to your room on arrival and load up your car on departing. A tip of $1–$2 per bag is fair for this service. If the hotel has valet parking, a tip of 15–20 percent of the parking charge should be given to the driver only when you leave. Room service also requires a 15–20 percent tip. A $2–$5 tip for maid service, especially after a long stay, is acceptable.

RESORTS

Whether a resort has less than 100 rooms or close to 300, the cottages, villas, and grounds are always arranged to encourage privacy. Resorts have all the services of a hotel but are spread over larger grounds.

The key to a quality resort is the range of indoor and outdoor facilities that are offered, be it horseback riding, tennis courts, golf courses, Olympic-size swimming pools, yoga instruction, full-service health spa, or a four-star restaurant. A vacation at a resort is a destination in itself – the natural setting and range of on-site activities will more than hold your attention. Stays in resorts are expensive, but for both relaxation and sports they are worth every penny.

You may want to choose a resort based on location – wine country, oceanside, mountain hideaway, or urban retreat. California has many such hidden treasures, and some of the best are listed on pages 524–66.

San Diego Marriott and Marina Hotel, on San Diego Bay *(see p538)*

Historic Mendocino Hotel *(see p555)*

MOTELS

Inexpensive roadside motels sprang up in California in the 1950s, as a product of an increasingly car-oriented lifestyle. Motels offer minimal facilities – double, queen, or king-size beds, television, telephone, tea and coffee, and bathroom facilities. There is always ample parking for cars, and many motels also have outdoor swimming pools – a necessity for travelers in California's summertime heat. Some have kitchen facilities, and most offer non-smoking rooms. Always check with the motel to see if they allow pets.

There are a number of popular motel chains throughout the state that have a reputation for clean rooms and good service at inexpensive prices. These include **Best Western**, **Quality Inn**, **Motel 6**, and **Travelodge**. Rates range from $30–$65 a night.

HISTORIC INNS

Rich in regional history, these inns are often all that remain of late 19th-century buildings in many of California's small towns. As well as reflecting local history, some inns also have their own story to tell, having been, perhaps, a hunting and fishing lodge, a stern-wheeler riverboat, a Victorian mansion, or a hideaway for Hollywood movie stars in earlier times. Whatever their heritage, they all share a unique architecture and ambience. Many such inns, built during the era of railroad expansion in the West,

have achieved protected status and cannot be demolished or architecturally altered.

Similar to bed-and-breakfast hotels in atmosphere, historic inns are larger, with 20–100 rooms. Most serve complimentary continental breakfast and afternoon snacks of cakes or cookies. For more information, contact **California Historic Country Inns**.

Smaller lodgings, many also with a claim to historical significance, may have small, individual cabins with kitchen facilities for efficiency accommodations (self-catering). Rarely do these inns have on-site restaurants, cafés, or room service. The majority of them allow you to bring along pets, many have outdoor swimming pools, and larger ones may also have tennis courts. Check in advance whether smoking is allowed in the cabins – some inns in California now pride themselves on providing guests with a completely smoke-free environment.

BED-AND-BREAKFAST ACCOMMODATIONS

Most bed-and-breakfasts in California were originally private homes built many years ago and which retain the charm of a bygone era. In addition to breakfast, afternoon snacks or evening drinks may also be available. Prices range from $60–$175 a night. Ask whether the room has its own bathroom. There is often a two-night minimum stay, especially in peak season. Libraries, living rooms, landscaped gardens, and swimming pools are common features. The manager is also often the owner and can provide details of local history and sights. See pages 524–66 for a range of bed-and-breakfasts, or contact the **California Association of Bed-and-Breakfast Inns**.

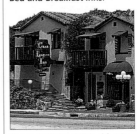

Casa Laguna Bed-and-Breakfast in Laguna Beach *(see p535)*

ROOMS IN PRIVATE HOMES

While many small inns and lodges may offer kitchen facilities, there is nothing like staying in a private home to get the real flavor of a specific

Deetjen's Big Sur Inn *(see p560)*

Big Bear Log Cabin, near Lake Arrowhead

city or town. There are two ways you can arrange this type of accommodation. The first is to rent an apartment or house from a real estate agency. Every city and town in the state has at least one, if not several, estate agencies that specialize in vacation rental property. These agencies will quote rental rates by the night, week, month, or even longer. Prices per week can range anywhere between $300 – $3,000, depending on location and size of the rented property. You will have to pay a cleaning deposit, which is refundable when you leave. For the widest choice of properties, it is best to make reservations at least one month in advance. Contact any town's Chamber of Commerce for details of agencies.

Another option is to arrange a house exchange with a California resident. **Intervac US** is part of a worldwide home exchange network and publishes quarterly directories of people willing to exchange their homes for yours during vacations. Fees to obtain or be listed in this directory range from $65– $85 per year. The network does not match people up; arrangements are made by the individuals.

YOUTH HOSTELS

This is the least expensive accommodation option in California. Hostels offer clean, modern facilities, often in picturesque locations (such as lighthouses, on national parkland, and mountain hideaways). They usually offer dormitory-style, single-sex sleeping arrangements, though some do have one or two private rooms available only to married couples. Most hostels also provide kitchen facilities.

Despite the name, youth hostels in the United States are not only for the young. There are also a number of Elder Hostels, catering to senior citizens who opt for budget travel. Contact **American Youth Hostels** for a full list of accommodations.

CAMPING, TRAILERS, AND RVS

Campers are always welcome in California's national and state park system *(see p610)*. There is also a large network of privately run camp sites with a range of facilities for trailers and RVs, such as electricity hook-up, water supply, disposal stations, picnic areas, and grocery stores.

Camping in Yosemite National Park
(see pp488–9)

(see p610)
(see pp488–9)

DIRECTORY

CHAIN HOTELS

Hilton
Tel (800) 774-1500.
www.hilton.com

Holiday Inn
Tel (800) 465- 4329.
www.ichotelsgroup.com

Hyatt
Tel (888) 591-1234.
www.hyatt.com

ITT Sheraton/Starwood
Tel (888) 625-5144.
www.sheraton.com

Marriott
Tel (888) 236-2427.
www.marriott.com

Ramada
Tel (800) 298-2054.
www.ramada.com

Westin/Starwood
Tel (888) 625-5144.
www.westin.com

CHAIN MOTELS

Best Western
Tel (800) 780-7234.
www.bestwestern.com

Motel 6
Tel (800) 466-8356.
www.motel6.com

Quality Inn
Tel (800) 228-5151.
www.qualityinn.com

Travelodge
Tel (800) 578-7878.
www.travelodge.com

HISTORIC INNS

California Historic Country Inns
www.californiainns.com

BED-AND-BREAKFAST

California Association of Bed-and-Breakfast Inns
Tel (831) 462-9191.
www.cabi.com

ROOMS IN PRIVATE HOMES

Intervac US
30 Corte San Fernando, Tiburon, CA 94920.
www.intervacus.com

YOUTH HOSTELS

American Youth Hostels
312 Mason St, San Francisco, CA 94102.
Tel (415) 788-5604.

Choosing a Hotel

The hotels in this guide have been selected across a wide price range for their good value, facilities, and location. These listings highlight some of the factors that may influence your choice. Entries are listed by region, beginning with Los Angeles. For more details on restaurants see pages 568–605.

PRICE CATEGORIES
For a standard double room per night in high season, including tax and service charges.

[$] under $100
[$][$] $100–$150
[$][$][$] $150–$200
[$][$][$][$] $200–$250
[$][$][$][$][$] over $250

LOS ANGELES

AIRPORT Furama Hotel LAX — [$][$]

8601 Lincoln Blvd, 90045 ***Tel*** *(310) 670-8111* ***Fax*** *(310) 337-1883* ***Rooms*** *773* — ***Road map*** *inset A*

This family-friendly hotel, with an outdoor garden swimming pool, offers great value for budget-minded business travelers. Rooms are equipped with the latest business amenities. Free shuttle services are provided to and from the airport and there is an on-site currency exchange. **www.furamalax.com**

AIRPORT Sheraton Gateway Los Angeles Airport Hotel — [$][$][$]

6101 W Century Blvd, 90045 ***Tel*** *(310) 642-1111* ***Fax*** *(310) 645-1414* ***Rooms*** *802* — ***Road map*** *inset A*

Recently revamped with a resort-style atmosphere, this hotel is close to the airport but has more of a beach ambience. Business facilities feature wireless Internet access. Good family packages are available. The newly added restaurant, Shula's Steakhouse, is worth a visit. **www.sheratonlosangeles.com**

AIRPORT Westin Los Angeles Airport — [$][$][$]

5400 W Century Blvd, 90045 ***Tel*** *(310) 216-5858* ***Fax*** *(310) 417-4545* ***Rooms*** *740* — ***Road map*** *inset A*

Four blocks from the airport, this well-managed hotel offers rooms appointed with the latest business amenities, including high-speed Internet access in all rooms and public spaces. There is a top-notch fitness facility and a good restaurant in the lobby. **www.starwood.com/westin**

AIRPORT Los Angeles Airport Marriott — [$][$][$][$]

5855 W Century Blvd, 90045 ***Tel*** *(310) 641-5700* ***Fax*** *(310) 337-5358* ***Rooms*** *985* — ***Road map*** *inset A*

Situated very close to the airport, this full-service property offers spacious rooms complete with state-of-the-art business facilities, including two-line phones, faxes, and wireless Internet access. The excellent guest service is complemented by an on-site coffeehouse, and a good steakhouse. **www.marriott.com**

BEL AIR Luxe Hotel Sunset Boulevard — [$][$][$]

11461 Sunset Blvd, 90049 ***Tel*** *(310) 476-6571* ***Fax*** *(310) 440-3090* ***Rooms*** *161* — ***Road map*** *inset A*

Secluded and sophisticated, this luxurious hotel features generously proportioned rooms, with high-speed Internet access and spa-like amenities such as plush bathrobes and expensive soaps. There is a free daily shuttle service to the Getty Museum. Tennis lessons from a professional coach are also available. **www.luxehotels.com**

BEL AIR Hotel Bel-Air — [$][$][$][$][$]

701 Stone Canyon Rd, 90077 ***Tel*** *(310) 472 1211* ***Fax*** *(310) 476-5890* ***Rooms*** *92* — ***Map*** *4 A2*

This Los Angeles classic oozes celebrity glamor and high-end luxury at every turn. The secluded rooms feature private entrances surrounded by lush garden landscape, and are appointed with fine Italian linen, fireplaces, and bath amenities. Complimentary transportation to and from shopping districts is provided. **www.hotelbelair.com**

BEVERLY HILLS Maison 140 — [$][$][$]

140 Lasky Dr, 90212 ***Tel*** *(310) 281-4000* ***Fax*** *(310) 281-4001* ***Rooms*** *41* — ***Map*** *5 D2*

This small, stylish hotel offers upscale luxury at a great price. Rooms are sleekly, with touches of Asian flair and retro sophistication. Amenities include high-end linen and bath accessories, as well high-speed Internet access. There is a popular bar and restaurant on site. **www.maison140beverlyhills.com**

BEVERLY HILLS Luxe Hotel Rodeo Drive — [$][$][$][$]

360 N Rodeo Dr, 90210 ***Tel*** *(310) 273-0300* ***Rooms*** *88* — ***Map*** *5 F3*

Central to world-famous shops, this intimate hotel is charming and well appointed. Many rooms have private sun decks. The location is within walking distance from many attractions, but a town car service is also available. Guests can also make use of the facilities at the hotel's sister property, Sunset. **www.luxehotels.com**

BEVERLY HILLS The Crescent — [$][$][$][$]

403 N Crescent Dr, 90210 ***Tel*** *(310) 247-0505* ***Fax*** *(310) 247-9053* ***Rooms*** *35* — ***Map*** *5 E2*

This boutique property exudes understated elegance and contemporary appeal. The gracefully designed rooms are well furnished with flat-screen TVs and wireless Internet access. There is a cozy outdoor fireplace in the lobby, which attracts a handsome group of romantics. **www.crescentbh.com**

Key to Symbols *see back cover flap*

BEVERLY HILLS Beverly Hills Hotel and Bungalows 💳 🍴 🏊 🏋 🍸 $$$$$

9641 Sunset Blvd, 90210 ***Tel*** *(310) 276-2251* ***Fax*** *(310) 887-2887* ***Rooms*** *203* ***Map*** *5 D5*

No detail is too small for the staff at this famed Los Angeles property, set tastefully among lush gardens, and central to all area attractions and several shops. Many rooms have a homey feel, and are spacious with private patios and fully-appointed kitchens. Features include tennis courts and a full-service spa. **www.beverlyhillshotel.com**

BEVERLY HILLS Beverly Hilton 💳 🍴 🏊 🏋 🍸 $$$$$

9876 Wilshire Blvd, 90210 ***Tel*** *(310) 274-7777* ***Fax*** *(310) 285-1313* ***Rooms*** *570* ***Map*** *5 E4*

A recent multi-million-dollar re-modeling injected new life to this stylish LA icon, home to the Golden Globe Awards and Jerry Lewis telethon. The updated rooms feature fine linen as well as state-of-the-art amenities for business travelers. A great spa and top-notch fitness facilities are available. **www.beverlyhilton.com**

BEVERLY HILLS Hotel Avalon 💳 🍴 🏋 🍸 $$$$$

9400 W Olympic Blvd, 90212 ***Tel*** *(310) 277-5221* ***Fax*** *(310) 277-4928* ***Rooms*** *86* ***Map*** *5 F4*

A splendid, mid-20th-century boutique hotel, the Avalon offers friendly service, chic accommodation, and a central location. The atmosphere is calm and serene, and the rooms are equipped with up-to-date features. The restaurant is award winning; dine poolside for a memorable LA experience. **www.avalonbeverlyhills.com**

BEVERLY HILLS Peninsula Beverly Hills 💳 🍴 🏊 🏋 🍸 $$$$$

9882 S Santa Monica Blvd, 90212 ***Tel*** *(310) 551-2888* ***Fax*** *(310) 788-2319* ***Rooms*** *196* ***Map*** *5 E4*

The last word in LA luxury for the rich and the famous, this sleek, elegant hotel pays meticulous attention to detail. Rooms are equipped with every conceivable amenity, including a remote control that operates almost everything. It also has a top-rated spa and restaurant. **www.peninsula.com**

BEVERLY HILLS Regent Beverly Wilshire 💳 🍴 🏊 🏋 🍸 $$$$$

9500 Wilshire Blvd, 90212 ***Tel*** *(310) 275 5200* ***Fax*** *(310) 274-2851* ***Rooms*** *399* ***Map*** *5 F4*

This polished hotel offers European charm and style in the heart of Beverly Hills. Accommodation choices include spacious, well-appointed rooms in the historic Wilshire Wing or the contemporary Beverly Wing, which has a clean, modern look. **www.regenthotels.com**

CENTURY CITY Stars Inn $

10269 Santa Monica Blvd, 90067 ***Tel*** *(310) 556-3076* ***Fax*** *(310) 277-7827* ***Rooms*** *20* ***Map*** *5 E5*

An immaculate, no-frills motel, Stars Inn enjoys a great location across the street from Century City Shopping Center and is within convenient access to the area's major roadways. Some of the well-lit units feature kitchenettes. There are laundry facilities on premises.

CENTURY CITY Park Hyatt 💳 🍴 🏊 🏋 $$$$$

2151 Ave of the Stars, 90067 ***Tel*** *(310) 277-1234* ***Fax*** *(310) 785-9240* ***Rooms*** *367* ***Map*** *5 E5*

Renowned for its business facilities, this modern hotel features spacious and well-connected rooms, all with a balcony or patio, and including fax machines with private numbers. Extras include a great spa and limousine service for shoppers and theatergoers. **www.parklosangeles.hyatt.com**

CENTURY CITY Westin Century Plaza Hotel and Tower 💳 🍴 🏊 🏋 🍸 $$$$$

2025 Ave of the Stars, 90067 ***Tel*** *(310) 277-2000* ***Fax*** *(310) 551-7532* ***Rooms*** *728* ***Map*** *5 D5*

Still enjoying the $70-million upgrade that brought the elegant property to new luxurious standards in 2001, this local icon has hosted heads of state and Hollywood stars for decades. The rooms are large and feature great city or coastal views. The spa and dining facilities are first rate. **www.westincenturyplaza.com**

DOWNTOWN Ramada Wilshire Center 💳 🍴 🏊 🏋 $

3900 Wilshire Blvd, 90010 ***Tel*** *(213) 736-5222* ***Fax*** *(213) 736-5038* ***Rooms*** *86* ***Road map*** *inset A*

Located just outside downtown toward Hollywood, this tidy, reliable hotel offers great-value rooms featuring comfortable beds and linen, as well as high-speed Internet access. There is a restaurant on site serving steaks and sandwiches. Guests enjoy free admission to a nearby gym. **www.ramada.com**

DOWNTOWN Best Western Dragon Gate Inn 💳 🍴 🏋 $$

818 N Hill St, 90012 ***Tel*** *(213) 617-3077* ***Fax*** *(213) 680-3753* ***Rooms*** *52* ***Map*** *11 F2*

You will find little more than the basics at this clean, friendly hotel in Chinatown. Rooms are spacious and have data ports. There is a café and cigar bar on premises, as well as a pharmacy. Its location is convenient to most downtown sights and attractions. **www.dragongateinn.com**

DOWNTOWN Figueroa Hotel 💳 🍴 🏊 🏋 🍸 $$

939 S Figueroa St, 90015 ***Tel*** *(213) 627-8971* ***Fax*** *(213) 628-1201* ***Rooms*** *285* ***Map*** *10 C5*

Quirky and charming, this welcoming hotel, popular for parties and events, blends elements of Southern California, Mexico, and Northern Africa for an eclectic effect. The rooms vary in size and style, but all feature decent amenities and soft linen. The service is excellent. **www.figueroahotel.com**

DOWNTOWN Holiday Inn City Center 💳 🍴 🏊 🏋 $$

750 S Garland Ave, 90012 ***Tel*** *(213) 748-1291* ***Fax*** *(213) 748-6028* ***Rooms*** *195* ***Map*** *10 B4*

Looking good since a major top-to-bottom upgrade, rooms at this well-run hotel offer comfortable beds and separate seating areas, as well as complimentary on-site fitness facilities. Across the street from the Staples Center, it is located close to downtown shops and attractions. **www.hicitycenter.com**

DOWNTOWN Miyako Inn and Spa $$

328 E 1st St, 90012 **Tel** *(213) 617-2000* **Fax** *(213) 617-2700* **Rooms** *174*   **Map** *11 F4*

Japanese-inspired hospitality in Little Tokyo, this pretty hotel is popular for its extensive list of treatments in the health spa as well as for its lively karaoke lounge. Rooms are outfitted in a simple style and feature most essential amenities. Children under 12 stay free. **www.miyakoinn.com**

DOWNTOWN The Inn at 657 $$

657 W 32nd St, 90007 **Tel** *(213) 741-2200* **Rooms** *11*   **Road map** *inset A*

Resembling a cozy LA apartment, this property features one- and two-bedroom suites, with garden entrances and pleasant sitting areas. The rooms are comfortable and modestly appointed, most are sunny and bright. The price includes breakfast and local calls. **www.patsysinn657.com**

DOWNTOWN The Mayfair $$

1256 W 7th St, 90017 **Tel** *(213) 484-9789* **Fax** *(213) 484-2789* **Rooms** *290*   **Map** *10 C4*

This is a popular hotel for business travelers on a budget, who like the clean, comfortably equipped rooms, and excellent luncheon buffet in the Orchid Gardens Restaurant. The location is central to the civic center, the garment district, Chinatown, and Little Tokyo. Secured covered parking is available. **www.mayfairla.com**

DOWNTOWN Los Angeles Athletic Club $$$

431 W 7th St, 90014 **Tel** *(213) 625-2211* **Fax** *(213) 689-1194* **Rooms** *72*   **Map** *11 D5*

Originally a private club, this hotel and recreation facility features oversized Victorian-style rooms and suites, with big tile baths. Rates include the use of the extensive fitness facility and a Continental breakfast. It is situated close to all downtown attractions. **www.laac.com**

DOWNTOWN Millennium Biltmore $$$

506 S Grand Ave, 90071 **Tel** *(213) 624-1011* **Fax** *(213) 612-1545* **Rooms** *683*   **Map** *11 D4*

An LA icon, the Biltmore is tied to local filmmaking lore and has hosted celebrities and royalty through the years. It was also the venue of several early Academy Awards ceremonies. The rooms are tidy, a bit small, but nicely furnished. The ornate lobby is the place to spend time. **www.millenniumhotels.com**

DOWNTOWN New Otani Hotel and Garden $$$

120 S Los Angeles St, 90012 **Tel** *(213) 629-1200* **Fax** *(213) 622-0980* **Rooms** *434*   **Map** *11 E4*

Adjacent to Little Tokyo, this efficient hotel offers Japanese-style graciousness, and several Japanese dining options. A large traditional garden features waterfalls and foot bridges. The New Otani also provides a courtesy mini-bus service within downtown, business support services, a health spa with shiatsu massage, and a fitness center. **www.newotani.com**

DOWNTOWN Hilton Checkers Hotel $$$$

535 S Grand Ave, 90071 **Tel** *(213) 624-0000* **Fax** *(213) 626-9906* **Rooms** *188*   **Map** *11 4D*

Dating from the 1920s, this luxurious hotel provides top-notch service. Large and relaxing rooms come with marble tubs and sumptuous bath amenities. There is a rooftop swimming pool and deck. The location allows an easy walk to the nearby theaters, nightlife, and convention center. **www.hiltoncheckers.com**

DOWNTOWN Omni Los Angeles California Plaza $$$$

51 S Olive St, 90012 **Tel** *(213) 617-3300* **Fax** *(213) 617-3399* **Rooms** *453*   **Map** *11 4D*

This appealing, mid-sized hotel is ideally situated for shopping or visiting museums. Rooms are large, stylish, and cater to the business traveler as well as to the leisure traveler who enjoys comfort. The signature restaurant, Noe, should not be missed. A complimentary car service is available for theatergoers. **www.omnihotels.com**

DOWNTOWN Westin Bonaventure Hotel and Suites $$$$

404 S Figueroa St, 90071 **Tel** *(213) 624-1000* **Fax** *(213) 612-4800* **Rooms** *1364*   **Map** *10 C5*

One of the largest hotels in LA, and a landmark on the downtown terrain, the Westin Bonaventure has circular glass towers that have been featured in films and on TV. The rooms are spacious and well appointed, and most afford great city views. The lobby is like a city unto itself, offering dozens of shops and restaurants. **www.westin.com**

DOWNTOWN Sheraton Los Angeles Downtown $$$$$

711 S Hope St, 90017 **Tel** *(213) 683-1234* **Fax** *(213) 629-3230* **Rooms** *485*   **Map** *11 D4*

Formerly operated by Hyatt, this Financial District hotel was given a new name, along with a complete refurbishment and fresh vibrancy. The rooms are large and appointed with business facilities. The lobby lounge is stylish and relaxing. The hotel is linked to the Macy's Plaza shopping complex. **www.starwoodhotels.com**

GLENDALE Chariot Inn Motel $

1118 E Colorado St, 91205 **Tel** *(818) 507-9600* **Fax** *(818) 507-9774* **Rooms** *31*   **Road map** *inset A*

With quiet and comfortable rooms, this no-frills roadside property is located just outside downtown LA. All rooms are air conditioned and some have whirlpool baths. Amenities include a heated outdoor swimming pool. They serve a decent Continental breakfast.

GLENDALE Hilton Glendale Hotel $$$$

100 W Glenoaks Blvd, 91202 **Tel** *(818) 956-5466* **Fax** *(818) 956-5490* **Rooms** *348*   **Road map** *inset A*

This well-run hotel is conveniently located, with easy highway access to many points of interest in LA. Rooms offer data ports and other business amenities. There is an on-site swimming pool, as well as a spa, and a full-service fitness center. The staff are friendly and efficient. A courtesy car service is available. **www.hilton.com**

Key to Price Guide *see p524* **Key to Symbols** *see back cover flap*

HOLLYWOOD Hollywood Orchid Suites
⊡⊞ $$

1753 Orchid Ave, 90028 **Tel** *(323) 874-9678* **Fax** *(323) 874-9931* **Rooms** *40* **Map** *2 B4*

There are few hotels more central to major Hollywood attractions as this converted apartment-hotel, which stands directly behind the famed Chinese Theater. There are two-bedroom suites as well as tidy, well-appointed rooms, some of which come with kitchenettes. **www.orchidsuites.com**

HOLLYWOOD Ramada Inn Hollywood Near Universal Studios
⊡⊞⊞ $$

1160 N Vermont Ave, 90029 **Tel** *(323) 660-1788* **Fax** *(323) 660-8069* **Rooms** *130* **Road map** *inset A*

This corporate-run hotel has full amenities, including many family-friendly conveniences. Recently refurbished, it offers complete conference facilities. A number of amusement parks are a short drive from the hotel, and a shuttle service to Universal Studios is available. **www.ramada.com**

HOLLYWOOD Beverly Garland's Holiday Inn
⊡⊞⊡⊞ $$$

4222 Vineland Ave, 91602 **Tel** *(818) 980-8000* **Fax** *(818) 766-5230* **Rooms** *255* **Road map** *inset A*

Located in North Hollywood, close to Universal Studios, this quiet, family accommodation features rooms with private balconies or patios, as well as a recently renovated on-site restaurant. Wireless Internet access is available throughout the property. Children under 12 stay and eat free. **www.beverlygarland.com**

HOLLYWOOD Farmer's Daughter Hotel
⊡ $$$

115 S Fairfax Ave, 90036 **Tel** *(323) 937-3930* **Fax** *(323) 932-1608* **Rooms** *66* **Map** *2 B4*

Country charm meets urban sophistication at this stylish, fun hotel across from the famous Farmers Market and CBS Studios. The rooms are spacious and comfortable, and fashioned as "his" or "hers" with gender-oriented touches in each. The service is friendly and welcoming. **www.farmersfdaughterhotel.com**

HOLLYWOOD San Vicente Inn
⊡⊞⊡ $$$

845 San Vicente Blvd, 90069 **Tel** *(310) 845-6915* **Rooms** *26* **Map** *6 B1*

This small-scale men-only, clothing-optional boutique property in West Hollywood is close to the shops and sights of Melrose Avenue and Santa Monica Boulevard. The rooms are clean and contemporary, and feature updated amenities. The well-kept grounds are wonderfully secluded. **www.gayresort.com/sanvicenteinn**

HOLLYWOOD Hollywood Roosevelt Hotel
⊡⊞⊞⊡⊞ $$$$

7000 Hollywood Blvd, 90028 **Tel** *(323) 466-7000* **Fax** *(323) 462-8056* **Rooms** *302* **Map** *2 B4*

The history and glamor of old Hollywood live on at this recently refurbished classic, which is enjoying a renaissance in popularity among the young and hip. The hotel features elegant rooms that include cabana-style suites situated around a courtyard pool. Good for celebrity-spotting. **www.hollywoodroosevelt.com**

HOLLYWOOD Magic Castle Hotel
⊡⊞⊞ $$$$

7025 Franklin Ave, 90028 **Tel** *(323) 851-0800* **Fax** *(323) 851-4926* **Rooms** *40* **Map** *2 B4*

This classic Hollywood hotel and club has been a favorite in the area for decades, renowned for its attentive staff, good value, and whimsical castle-like design. Spacious suites and studios are equipped with comfortable bedding, good bath amenities, and full kitchens. Be sure to catch a magic show. **www.magiccastlehotel.com**

HOLLYWOOD The Standard Hotel Hollywood
⊡⊞⊞⊡ $$$$

8300 Sunset Blvd, 90069 **Tel** *(323) 650-9090* **Fax** *(323) 6650-2820* **Rooms** *163* **Map** *2 B4*

This Sunset Strip hotel oozes hipness and cutting-edge style, but does not break the bank. Rooms are modestly appointed, but have plenty of flair. Book a "budget" room and save for cocktails in the ultra-chic lounge, or keep an eye out for celebrities in the diner-style restaurant. **www.standardhotel.com**

HOLLYWOOD Renaissance Hollywood Hotel
⊡⊞⊞⊞ $$$$$

2619 Wilshire Blvd, 90057 **Tel** *(323) 856-1200* **Fax** *(323) 491-1343* **Rooms** *637* **Map** *2 B4*

This centrally located hotel offers rooms featuring expansive views of surrounding Hollywood. Some have French windows with scenic vistas, a baby grand piano, and a Jacuzzi. Spend an afternoon lounging by the rooftop pool. Close to shopping and many tourist attractions. A friendly, courteous service. **www.renaissancehollywood.com**

LONG BEACH Inn of Long Beach
⊡⊞⊞ $

185 Atlantic Ave, 90802 **Tel** *(562) 435-3791* **Fax** *(562) 436-7510* **Rooms** *150* **Road map** *inset A*

With a convenient downtown location, and within walking distance from the beach, this pleasant motel has large comfortable rooms. The pool and a generously-proportioned enclosed courtyard are great for families. Guests can make free local calls. **www.innoflongbeach.com**

LONG BEACH Super 8 Motel
⊡⊞⊡ $

4201 E Pacific Hwy, 90804 **Tel** *(562) 435-3791* **Fax** *(562) 494-7373* **Rooms** *48* **Road map** *inset A*

A good budget option for individuals and families, this motel provides clean and comfortable rooms; some come with kitchenettes. It is located close to such attractions as the *Queen Mary* and the aquarium. The service is gracious and accommodating. **www.super8motel.com**

LONG BEACH Coast Long Beach Hotel
⊡⊞⊡⊞ $$

700 Queensway Dr, 90802 **Tel** *(562) 435-7676* **Fax** *(562) 437-0866* **Rooms** *31* **Road map** *inset A*

Expect great value for money at this friendly waterfront hotel. The well-appointed rooms provide free high-speed Internet access. Some rooms feature balconies overlooking the garden or with panoramic ocean views. The hotel is close to local attractions. **www.coasthotels.com**

LONG BEACH Hotel Queen Mary $$$

1126 Queen's Hwy, 90802 **Tel** *(562) 435-3511* **Fax** *(562) 437-4531* **Rooms** *365*   **Road map** *inset A*

Guests booking aboard this recently restored historic cruise liner are afforded ship tours and treated to a bit of ocean-going history. Rooms are newly refurbished and equipped with select modern amenities. The restaurant and spa facilities are first-rate. The Ghost Tour is a fun diversion. **www.queenmary.com**

LONG BEACH Renaissance Long Beach Hotel $$$

111 E Ocean Blvd, 90802 **Tel** *(562) 437-5900* **Fax** *(562) 499-2509* **Rooms** *374*   **Road map** *inset A*

This large hotel is central to downtown and close to the harbor attractions. A recent renovation spruced up all guest rooms and public areas, including the installation of high-speed Internet access. On-site amenities include a car reservation desk and two good restaurants. **www.marriott.com**

LONG BEACH Hyatt Regency $$$$$

200 S Pine Ave, 90802 **Tel** *(562) 491-1234* **Fax** *(562) 983-1491* **Rooms** *522*   **Road map** *inset A*

With a great harborside location, this corporate-run hotel is popular with conventioneers and business travelers. The recently updated rooms are brightly decorated and have plenty of amenities. Recreational features include a heated outdoor pool, nearby golf courses, and a full-service gym. **www.longbeach.hyatt.com**

MALIBU Casa Malibu Inn on the Beach $$$$

22752 Pacific Coast Hwy, 90265 **Tel** *(310) 456-2219* **Fax** *(310) 456-5418* **Rooms** *21*   **Road map** *inset A*

This small, friendly beachside inn retains some of the old coastal charm. Rooms have a private feel. A few have fireplaces, while many have been updated with tile tubs. Amenities include high-end linen and bathrobes. The hotel has a secluded sun deck and its own stretch of private beach.

MALIBU Malibu Beach Inn $$$$$

22878 Pacific Coast Hwy, 90265 **Tel** *(310) 456-6444* **Fax** *(310) 456-1999* **Rooms** *47*   **Road map** *inset A*

Intimate, luxurious property overlooking the Pacific, Malibu Beach Inn boasts its own private beach. Each room is bright and outfitted with Mission-style decor and comfortable linen. A cottage-like feel prevails, with decks overlooking the water. **www.malibubeachinn.com**

MARINA DEL REY Foghorn Harbor Inn $$$$

4140 Via Marina, 90292 **Tel** *(310) 823-4626* **Rooms** *40*   **Road map** *inset A*

This modest, low-slung hotel near the beach provides exceptional value for its location. Rooms are spacious and comfortably appointed, all with patios or balconies. Amenities include wireless Internet access and complimentary continental breakfast. The staff are charming and gracious. **www.foghornhotel.com**

MARINA DEL REY Marina del Rey Hotel $$$$

13534 Bali Way, 90292 **Tel** *(310) 301-1000* **Fax** *(310) 301-8167* **Rooms** *157*   **Road map** *inset A*

Enjoying easy access to the beach and the Marina, this comfortable hotel offers well-appointed rooms with many business-traveler amenities. Some of them come with private balconies or patios with water views. There is a relaxing waterfront lounge. A free airport shuttle service is available. **www.marinadelreyhotel.com**

MARINA DEL REY The Inn at Venice Beach $$$$

327 Washington Blvd, 90291 **Tel** *(310) 821-2557* **Fax** *(310) 827-0289* **Rooms** *43*   **Road map** *inset A*

Bright and cheery rooms are provided at this pleasant inn, located just a block from the famed Venice Beach Boardwalk and adjacent to the yacht harbor. Amenities include free high-speed wireless Internet and a tasty Continental breakfast. The staff are welcoming and attentive. **www.innatvenicebeach.com**

MONROVIA Holiday Inn $$

924 W Huntington Dr, 91016 **Tel** *(626) 357-1900* **Fax** *(626) 359-1386* **Rooms** *170*   **Road map** *inset A*

Located near such attractions as Santa Anita Racetrack and Rose Bowl. Rooms are spacious and nicely appointed, with high-speed wireless Internet in some. Guests are offered discounts to select sights, including Universal Studios tours. Free morning coffee and muffins are provided. **www.holiday-inn.com**

NAPLES/SEAL BEACH Seal Beach Inn $$

212 5th St, 90740 **Tel** *(562) 493-2416* **Fax** *(562) 799-0483* **Rooms** *24*   **Road map** *inset A*

Dating from the 1920s, this historic inn retains much of the luxury and charm of its era. Rooms are cozy, intimate, and decorated with antiques and pieces selected from the owner's world travels. Room rates include a large, freshly prepared breakfast each morning. **www.sealbeachinn.com**

PASADENA Comfort Inn Eagle Rock $$

2300 W Colorado Blvd, 90041 **Tel** *(323) 256-1199* **Fax** *(323) 255-7768* **Rooms** *58*   **Road map** *inset A*

Set in scenic surrounding, with convenient access to Rose Bowl, Comfort Inn is a preferred accommodation option in the area. The no-frills rooms come with some creature comforts, including satellite TV. Good value for families on a budget. **www.comfortinn-er.com**

PASADENA Artist's Inn $$$

1038 Magnolia St, 91030 **Tel** *(626) 799-5668* **Fax** *(626) 799-3678* **Rooms** *10*   **Road map** *inset A*

A cozy, comfortable inn in south Pasadena, this hotel is located near the train station and within easy walking distance to Old Pasadena. Each room is decorated in an individual style, inspired by a particular artist from the region. The breakfast is widely acclaimed. **www.artistsinns.com**

Key to Price Guide *see p524* **Key to Symbols** *see back cover flap*

PASADENA Hilton Pasadena

$$$

168 South Los Robles Ave, 91101 **Tel** *(626) 577-1000* **Fax** *(626) 584-3148* **Rooms** *296*　　　**Road map** *inset A*

Within walking distance from the downtown area, this business-friendly hotel was recently renovated, updating rooms and public spaces. Bedrooms are comfortably furnished in a traditional style, and there is a fitness room and pool. The Trevor's restaurant serves excellent California cuisine. Sightseeing can be organized on request. **www.hilton.com**

PASADENA Sheraton Pasadena

$$$

303 E Cordova St, 91101 **Tel** *(626) 449-4000* **Fax** *(626) 584-1390* **Rooms** *317*　　　**Road map** *inset A*

Newly refurbished, this well-run downtown hotel offers many executive-friendly features, including a 24-hour business center. Rooms are spacious and well equipped. Recreational amenities include a complete fitness center and tennis courts. It is connected to the convention center. **www.sheratonpadadena.com**

PASADENA The Bissell House Bed and Breakfast

$$$

201 Orange Grove Ave, 91030 **Tel** *(626) 441-3535* **Fax** *(626) 441-3671* **Rooms** *6*　　　**Road map** *inset A*

Formerly a private mansion in an area of town known as "Millionaire's Row," the Bissell House is an intimate B&B with historic appeal. Each uniquely decorated room is equipped with Internet access and outfitted with period furnishings and sumptuous linen. **www.bissellhouse.com**

PASADENA Ritz Carlton Huntingdon Hotel

$$$$$

1401 S Oak Knoll Ave, 91106 **Tel** *(626) 568-3900* **Fax** *(626) 568-3700* **Rooms** *392*　　　**Road map** *inset A*

With luxury and sophistication at every turn, this hotel offers exemplary service and a secluded location away from the city center. The grounds are quiet and well manicured. The historic building boasts modern amenities in each room, including top-end linen and robes. The full-service spa is a prime attraction. **www.ritzcarlton.com**

SANTA MONICA Best Western Gateway Hotel

$$$

1920 Santa Monica Blvd, 90404 **Tel** *(310) 829-9100* **Fax** *(310) 829-9211* **Rooms** *122*　　　**Road map** *inset A*

Located downtown, this budget-minded hotel has a European atmosphere, enhanced by the multilingual staff. The rooms are basic, yet comfortable, offering few frills. Complimentary services include shuttle transportation to and from the airport, as well as to the beach and Third Street Promenade. **www.gatewayhotels.com**

SANTA MONICA Hotel Carmel by the Sea

$$$

201 Broadway, 90401 **Tel** *(310) 451-2469* **Fax** *(310) 393-4180* **Rooms** *90*　　　**Road map** *inset A*

Formerly one of the first in the area, this classic resort has been restored to its 1920s splendor. The beach-style rooms are generously proportioned, and equipped with many comfortable amenities. The hotel is located close to the ocean and shopping areas. Daily tours of the area depart from the lobby. **www.hotelcarmel.com**

SANTA MONICA Hotel California

$$$$

1670 Ocean Ave, 90401 **Tel** *1-866-269-3662* **Fax** *(310) 393-1063* **Rooms** *20*　　　**Road map** *inset A*

A charming find among the high-end beach resorts in the area, this great-value hotel offers modern comforts and ocean views. Rooms are bright and include elegant linen and upscale bath products. Located close to the Santa Monica Pier, there is an outdoor lap pool and fitness room. **www.hotelca.com**

SANTA MONICA Doubletree Guest Suites

$$$$$

1707 4th St, 90401 **Tel** *(310) 395-3332* **Fax** *(310) 452-7399* **Rooms** *253*　　　**Road map** *inset A*

A large hotel near the beach, the Doubletree offers spacious two-room suites. Among the up-to-date amenities in each room are high-speed Internet access and two-line telephones. Its location provides easy freeway access. An ideal choice for families with children. **www.doubletree.com**

SANTA MONICA Fairmont Miramar Hotel

$$$$$

101 Wilshire Blvd, 90401 **Tel** *(310) 576-7777* **Fax** *(310) 458-7912* **Rooms** *302*　　　**Road map** *inset A*

Luxurious, fully-appointed cliffside hotel, the Fairmont Miramar is a frequent haunt for the rich and famous. The garden bungalows are secluded and private, while there are sweeping ocean views from many rooms. Accommodation amenities are first rate, as are the spa and fitness facilities. **www.fairmont.com**

SANTA MONICA Huntley Santa Monica Beach

$$$$$

1111 2nd St, 90403 **Tel** *(310) 394-5454* **Fax** *(310) 458-9776* **Rooms** *209*　　　**Road map** *inset A*

A recent change of operator and complete remodeling has breathed modern life into this stylish property, located one block from the beach and close to area shops. Each room comes equipped with a high-speed Internet connection, a plasma TV, and a DVD player. **www.preferredhotels.com**

SANTA MONICA Loews Santa Monica Beach Hotel

$$$$$

1700 Ocean Ave, 90401 **Tel** *(310) 458-6700* **Fax** *(310) 458-6761* **Rooms** *342*　　　**Road map** *inset A*

A personalized service by attentive staff at this four-diamond resort-style hotel makes for a memorable stay. The striking lobby is flanked by towering palm trees. Rooms are sumptuously appointed, affording fabulous ocean views and casual beach luxury. There is also a full-service fitness center and spa. **www.santamonicaloewshotel.com**

SANTA MONICA Sheraton Delfina Santa Monica

$$$$$

530 Pico Blvd, 90405 **Tel** *(310) 399-9344* **Fax** *(310) 399-2504* **Rooms** *308*　　　**Road map** *inset A*

Recently remodeled and redesigned, this hotel offers the latest amenities in its contemporary guest rooms, including upscale linen and luxury bath soaps. Many rooms have ocean views. On-site features include a state-of-the-art fitness center and a day spa. **www.sheratonsantamonica.com**

SANTA MONICA Shutters on the Beach $$$$$

1 Pico Blvd, 90405 **Tel** *(310) 458-0030* **Fax** *(310) 458-4589* **Rooms** *198*   **Road map** *inset A*

This superb luxury hotel on the beach is renowned as a haunt for celebrities and the well heeled. A recent renovation has upgraded amenities in the rooms as well as in the excellent restaurant and top-rated spa. Guest rooms offer casual comfort and elegance, plus easy access to the beach. **www.shuttersonthebeach.com**

SANTA MONICA The Georgian Hotel $$$$$

1415 Ocean Ave, 90401 **Tel** *(310) 395-9945* **Fax** *(310) 452-3374* **Rooms** *84*   **Road map** *inset A*

A beautiful bit of seaside luxury can be found at this four-diamond historic property, which features ocean views from most rooms and high-end comfort throughout. The well-preserved property is located close to the beach as well as local restaurants and shops. Pets are welcome. **www.georgianhotel.com**

UNIVERSAL CITY Hilton Los Angeles Universal City $$$

555 Universal Hollywood Dr, 91608 **Tel** *(818) 506-2500* **Fax** *(818) 509-2058* **Rooms** *453*   **Road map** *inset A*

In the heart of the Hollywood entertainment district, this large family-friendly hotel is located directly across from the entrance to Universal CityWalk. Rooms were recently updated and feature such amenities as oversized beds and large closets. There is an on-site fitness and business center. **www.hilton.com**

UNIVERSAL CITY Sheraton Universal $$$$

333 Universal Hollywood Dr, 91608 **Tel** *(818) 980-1212* **Fax** *(818) 985-4980* **Rooms** *436*   **Road map** *inset A*

A Universal City landmark since 1969, the Sheraton stands on the back lot of Universal Studios. Free high-speed Internet access is available in all rooms. Services include laundry and baby-sitting. The on-site restaurant, California's, offers contemporary cuisine. A complimentary shuttle service to the entertainment district. **www.sheraton.com/universal**

VAN NUYS Holiday Inn Express Van Nuys $$

244 Orion Ave, 91406 **Tel** *(818) 989-5010* **Fax** *(818) 909-0408* **Rooms** *132*   **Road map** *inset A*

Located near the Magic Mountain and Universal Studios theme parks, this convenient, good-value hotel offers spacious rooms with work areas and efficient service. High-speed Internet access, a heated pool, and generous breakfasts are some of the amenities provided here. **www.ichotelsgroup.com**

VENICE The Cadillac Hotel $$

8 Dudley Ave, 90291 **Tel** *(310) 399-8876* **Fax** *(310) 399-4536* **Rooms** *41*   **Road map** *inset A*

There are lovely ocean views from each room at this hip, yet affordable, property, located directly on the famed Venice Beach boardwalk. A trendy vibe pervades the historic hotel, from the spa to the sun terrace. Ideal for a comfortable, no-frills accommodation. Close to great restaurants, shops, and nightlife. **www.thecadillachotel.com**

VENICE BEACH The Venice Beach House $$

15 30th Ave, 90291 **Tel** *(310) 823-1966* **Fax** *(310) 823-1842* **Rooms** *9*   **Road map** *inset A*

This charming historic B&B is located close to the beach. The property is secluded and intimate, and set on well-manicured grounds. With a distinct character and definitive style, each room is uniquely themed, such as the Speedway Room and Olympics Suite. The breakfast is first-rate. **www.venicebeachhouse.com**

VENICE BEACH Best Western Marina Pacific $$$

1697 Pacific Ave, 90291 **Tel** *(310) 452-1111* **Fax** *(310) 452-5479* **Rooms** *88*   **Road map** *inset A*

Ideal for long vacations, the Marina Pacific offers attractive extended-stay rates. Well-maintained rooms and thoughtful amenities are provided at this modest hotel on the famed Boardwalk. Suites feature kitchens and fireplaces. Continental breakfast and high-speed Internet access are available. **www.mphotel.com**

WEST HOLLYWOOD Argyle Hotel $$$$

8358 Sunset Blvd, 90069 **Tel** *(323) 654-7100* **Fax** *(323) 654-9287* **Rooms** *64*   **Map** *6 C1*

A beautiful Art Deco hotel, with a rich history in Hollywood, Argyle Hotel has elegant, well-equipped rooms, ranging from standard size to gorgeous home-like suites. The pool deck, though small, is popular for celebrity sightings and lounging in the Southern Californian sun. The restaurant is highly rated. **www.argylehotel.com**

WEST HOLLYWOOD Best Western Sunset Plaza $$$$

8400 Sunset Blvd, 90069 **Tel** *(323) 654-0750* **Fax** *(323) 650-6146* **Rooms** *100*   **Map** *6 C1*

Surprisingly well appointed and elegant for a chain-operated hotel, this property offers attractive guest rooms, with plenty of amenities and a central Sunset Strip location. The pool is set in a pleasing garden patio. An elaborate Continental breakfast is served each morning. **www.sunsetplazahotel.com**

WEST HOLLYWOOD Le Parc Suites $$$$

733 N West Knoll Ave, 90069 **Tel** *(310) 855-8888* **Fax** *(310) 659-7812* **Rooms** *154*   **Map** *4 A4*

This stylish hotel is situated off the beaten path in a residential part of town. Rooms are quiet and cozy, with comfortable linen and modern conveniences, including CD players and free Internet access. The secluded grounds feature a lovely pool as well as a full spa and fitness center. **www.leparcsuites.com**

WEST HOLLYWOOD Chateau Marmont $$$$$

8221 Sunset Blvd, 90046 **Tel** *(323) 656-1010* **Fax** *(323) 655-5311* **Rooms** *63*   **Map** *1 B5*

Enjoying a well-documented reputation as a celebrity hideaway, Chateau Marmont has standard rooms, suites, and private cottages. All offer home-like amenities and top-notch service from the attentive staff. The pool deck has pretty views of the Strip and surrounding valley. **www.chateaumarmont.com**

Key to Price Guide *see p524* **Key to Symbols** *see back cover flap*

WEST HOLLYWOOD Hyatt West Hollywood $$$$$

8401 Sunset Blvd, 90069 **Tel** *(323) 656-1234* **Fax** *(323) 650-7024* **Rooms** *262* **Map** *6 C1*

With a boisterous history during which it was known as the "Riot House" for its celebrity-party reputation, this hotel is still a fun, high-profile option on Sunset Strip, and is partly owned by singer Justin Timberlake. Rooms are spacious and clean. It can be noisy here, depending on who happens to be staying. **www.westhollywood.hyatt.com**

WEST HOLLYWOOD Mondrian Hotel $$$$$

8440 Sunset Blvd, 90069 **Tel** *(323) 650-8999* **Fax** *(323) 650-5215* **Rooms** *237* **Map** *6 C1*

One of the hottest spots on the Strip, stylish Mondrian Hotel features spacious rooms with full kitchens, large work spaces, and dazzling city views. Decor is minimalist, but sleek and classy. The pool and lounge areas are key see-and-be-seen spots. The Asia de Cuba restaurant is wildly popular. **www.mondrianhotel.com**

WESTWOOD Royal Palace Hotel $$

1052 Tiverton Ave, 90024 **Tel** *(310) 208-6677* **Fax** *(310) 824-3732* **Rooms** *36* **Map** *4 A4*

This small hotel is an inexpensive, no-frills option in the heart of Westwood Village, within walking distance of museums, shops, restaurants, and the university campus. Rooms are tidy, some featuring kitchens. The staff are friendly and courteous. A complimentary Continental breakfast is offered. **www.royalpalacewestwood.com**

WESTWOOD Doubletree Hotel Westwood $$$

10740 Wilshire Blvd, 90024 **Tel** *(310) 475-8711* **Fax** *(310) 475-5220* **Rooms** *296* **Road map** *C5*

With a central location, this large, full-service hotel is convenient to many local attractions. The recently updated rooms are well furnished with upscale amenities. Tours and rental car service can be arranged. There is a lively lounge as well as a sundeck. **www.doubletree.com**

WESTWOOD Hilgard House Hotel $$$

927 Hilgard Ave, 90024 **Tel** *(310) 208-3945* **Fax** *(310) 208-1972* **Rooms** *47* **Map** *4 A4*

Affordable and cozy, the Hilgard House is situated near the UCLA campus and within walking distance to the Armand Hammer Museum. Some of the sophisticated European-style rooms have Jacuzzis and kitchenettes. Free wireless Internet access and Continental breakfast are provided. **www.hilgardhouse.com**

WESTWOOD W Los Angeles Westwood $$$$$

930 Hilgard Ave, 90024 **Tel** *(310) 208-8765* **Fax** *(310) 824-0355* **Rooms** *258* **Road map** *C5*

Sleek and stylish, rooms at this hip hotel are large and equipped with every imaginable amenity. Features include a state-of-the-art spa, two outdoor pools, and the famed "whatever-whenever" service from the polished staff. The high-profile lounge and bar areas enhance the vibrant ambience. **www.whotels.com**

SOUTH CENTRAL CALIFORNIA

BAKERSFIELD Courtyard by Marriott $$

3601 Marriott Dr, 93308 **Tel** *(661) 324-6660* **Fax** *(661) 324-1185* **Rooms** *146* **Road map** *C5*

Clean and updated, this chain hotel is situated near the local airport, and features great amenities for the business traveler, including free high-speed Internet access and large work stations in each room. The breakfast buffet is extensive and reasonably priced. **www.marriott.com**

CAMBRIA San Simeon $$

7200 Moonstone Beach Dr, 93428 **Tel** *(805) 927-4648* **Rooms** *58* **Road map** *B5*

A motel-style property close to the beach, San Simeon offers cozy rooms with large beds and upgraded linen, many with wood-burning fireplaces. Select cottages feature landscaped backyards. While some sections of the hotel are adults-only, family-friendly rooms are also available. There is an on-site golf course. **www.sspines.com**

CAMBRIA Burton Drive Inn $$$$

4022 Burton Dr, 93428 **Tel** *(805) 927-5125* **Rooms** *12* **Road map** *B5*

Set among the shops and galleries of downtown Cambria, charming Burton Drive Inn has large suites and a friendly, warm service. The rooms are appointed with period ambience, while bathrooms have spa-like amenities, with luxury soaps and robes. **www.burtoninn.com**

CAMBRIA Best Western Fireside Inn $$$$$

6700 Moonstone Beach Dr, 93428 **Tel** *(805) 927-8661* **Fax** *(805) 927-8584* **Rooms** *45* **Road map** *B5*

This romantic oceanside hotel on Moonstone Beach features generously proportioned rooms that possess the essential comforts, but few other frills. Situated close to the village of Cambria, it is convenient for local attractions, including Hearst Castle. **www.bestwesternfiresideinn.com**

CAMBRIA Blue Whale Inn $$$$$

6736 Moonstone Beach, 93428 **Tel** *(805) 927-4647* **Fax** *(805) 927-3852* **Rooms** *6* **Road map** *B5*

An award-winning gem along the Central Pacific Coast, this luxurious, four-diamond inn stands on a bluff above the shoreline. Every individually decorated room has a romantic fireplace, a canopy bed, a plush private bath, and a scenic sea view. The service is friendly and the breakfast hearty. **www.bluewhaleinn.com**

MONTECITO Montecito Inn $$$$

1295 Coast Village Rd, 93108 **Tel** *(805) 969-7854* **Fax** *(805) 969-0623* **Rooms** *61*   **Road map** *C5*

Built in 1928 by Charlie Chaplin, Montecito Inn features a complete film library of the legendary actor. It is a comfortable Mediterranean-style hotel with luxurious features and easy beach access. Refurbished recently, it is fitted with such accessories as flat-screen TVs and large Jacuzzis. **www.montecitoinn.com**

MONTECITO San Ysidro Ranch $$$$$

900 San Ysidro Lane, 93108 **Tel** *(805) 969-5046* **Fax** *(805) 565-1995* **Rooms** *38*   **Road map** *C5*

Perennially ranked among "most romantic" hotels, this secluded ranch blends nature and luxury seamlessly and stylishly. Each private cottage is intimate and sumptuously arranged, with a wood-burning stove and patio. Spa services available in-room. An excellent restaurant on site. **www.sanysidroranch.com**

MORRO BAY Blue Sail Inn $$

851 Market Ave, 93442 **Tel** *(805) 772-7132* **Fax** *(805) 772-8406* **Rooms** *48*   **Road map** *B5*

A pleasant hotel in the quaint coastal town of Morro Bay, Blue Sail Inn offers great value. Rooms are differently decorated and come in various sizes. Most of them have fireplaces and private balconies, with great views of the bay and its famous rock. Wireless Internet access is available. **www.bluesailinn.com**

MORRO BAY Embarcadero Inn $$$

456 Embarcadero, 93442 **Tel** *(800) 292-7625* **Fax** *(805) 772-6897* **Rooms** *32*   **Road map** *B5*

Situated directly on the working harbor, this friendly inn features rooms facing the water; most have balconies and fireplaces. A new family suite offers groups a chance to stay together. The staff are attentive and efficient, and eager to give advice on recreation choices in the area. **www.embarcaderoinn.com**

MORRO BAY Inn at Morro Bay $$$

60 State Park Rd, 93442 **Tel** *(805) 772-5651* **Fax** *(805) 772-4779* **Rooms** *90*   **Road map** *B5*

Charming and luxurious, this French country-style inn is situated in a state park overlooking the bay. The rooms are cozy and contemporary; most featuring fireplaces and all with featherbeds and patios. A good seafood restaurant and spa are on the premises, and there are several golf courses neaby. **www.innatmorrobay.com**

PASO ROBLES Paso Robles Inn $$$$

1103 Spring St, 93446 **Tel** *(805) 238-2660* **Fax** *(805) 238-4770* **Rooms** *100*   **Road map** *B5*

A popular destination for over a century, Paso Robles Inn is set in lush grounds that feature gardens, a creek, and natural hot springs. Rooms are basic, Mission-style; some featuring a deluxe mineral spa. There is a good steakhouse and a historic ballroom on the property. **www.pasoroblesinn.com**

SAN LUIS OBISPO Apple Farm Inn $$$

2015 Monterey St, 93401 **Tel** *(800) 255-2040* **Fax** *(805) 544-2040* **Rooms** *104*   **Road map** *B5*

This quaint hotel is utterly charming, with Victorian flair, modern conveniences, and an able staff. Family-friendly, yet perfect for couples, the rooms are graciously appointed with sumptuous beds and bath amenities. The grounds feature gardens and large shade trees. Choose the Trellis Court rooms for discounted rates. **www.applefarm.com**

SAN LUIS OBISPO Garden Street inn $$$

1212 Garden St, 93401 **Tel** *(805) 545-9802* **Fax** *(805) 545-9403* **Rooms** *13*   **Road map** *B5*

Built in a restored 1860 Victorian building, this delightful B&B is set in the central section of downtown San Luis Obispo. The rooms are furnished with antiques and each has a fireplace, a private bath, and Jacuzzi. There is an impressive library on the premises. **www.gardenstreetinn.com**

SAN LUIS OBISPO The Madonna Inn $$$

100 Madonna Rd, 93405 **Tel** *(805) 543-3000* **Fax** *(805) 543-1800* **Rooms** *108*   **Road map** *B5*

As much a roadside curiosity as an inn, this landmark property features unique rooms decorated in fantasy themes such as cave, jungle, and Swiss chalet. The on-site restaurants, shops, and novelty stores attract passers-by. The grounds are always bustling, and the service friendly. **www.madonnainn.com**

SAN LUIS OBISPO Comfort Inn & Suites Lamplighter $$$$

1604 Monterey St, 93401 **Tel** *(805) 547-7777* **Fax** *(805) 547-7787* **Rooms** *40*   **Road map** *B5*

Surprising touches at this chain-operated motel include charming ambience, friendly service, and free high-speed Internet access. Some of the otherwise modest rooms have full kitchens. It is close to many local attractions, including the university. **www.lamplighterinn.com**

SAN LUIS OBISPO San Luis Creek Lodge $$$$

1941 Monterey St, 93401 **Tel** *(805) 541-1122* **Fax** *(805) 541-2475* **Rooms** *25*   **Road map** *B5*

This small, chic B&B is one of the newest entries in the area. Luxurious, yet affordable, accommodation is provided in three buildings on a campus, away from the traffic on secluded grounds. Rooms are cozy and well appointed, with upscale bedding and basic amenities. **www.sanluiscreeklodge.com**

SANTA BARBARA Glenborough Inn $$$

1327 Bath St, 93101 **Tel** *(805) 966-0589* **Fax** *(805) 564-8610* **Rooms** *11*   **Road map** *C5*

Romantic and cozy, this B&B provides individually-themed rooms that are situated in three separate houses. Each room features a bedside fireplace, private deck and whirlpool, and a large soaking tub. Breakfast is delivered to the room each morning. **www.glenboroughinn.com**

SANTA BARBARA El Encanto Hotel and Garden Villas 🍴 🏊 $$$$

1900 Lasuen Rd, 93103 ***Tel*** *(805) 687-5000* ***Fax*** *(805) 687-3903* ***Rooms*** *77* ***Road map*** *C5*

Situated in the hills above the ocean and amid eucalyptus trees, this bungalow-style hotel has custom-designed rooms. A celebrity hideaway from Hollywood's golden era, it still attracts couples seeking serenity without remoteness. Rooms are well appointed with modern amenities. **www.elencantohotel.com**

SANTA BARBARA Hotel Santa Barbara ⇅ $$$$

533 State St, 93101 ***Tel*** *(805) 957-9300* ***Fax*** *(805) 962-2412* ***Rooms*** *75* ***Road map*** *C5*

Five blocks from the beach, this 1926 hotel retains some of its historic charm. Tidy and well-equipped rooms offer comfortable bedding and nice bath accessories. A light breakfast is served, which can be enjoyed on a lovely outdoor patio. **www.hotelsantabarbara.com**

SANTA BARBARA Santa Barbara Inn ⇅ 🍴 🏊 👪 $$$$

901 E Cabrillo Blvd, 93103 ***Tel*** *(800) 231-0431* ***Rooms*** *71* ***Road map*** *C5*

This hotel has location in its favor, close to downtown shops and restaurants, and just across the street from the beach. Modestly appointed rooms feature comfortable beds and enough space for families. Suites and a penthouse room are also available. The on-site restaurant is quite good, with fine ocean views. **www.santabarbarainn.com**

SANTA BARBARA Tiffany Inn $$$$

1323 De la Vina St, 93101 ***Tel*** *(805) 963-2283* ***Fax*** *(805) 962-0994* ***Rooms*** *7* ***Road map*** *C5*

Historic charm and familial service set this intimate B&B apart. The house and the rooms are appointed with period antiques, and are meticulously maintained. Guests are served complimentary wine in the garden or by the living room fireplace each evening. **www.tiffanycountryhouse.com**

SANTA BARBARA Upham Hotel & Country House ⇅ $$$$

1404 De la Vina St, 93101 ***Tel*** *(805) 962-0058* ***Fax*** *(805) 963-2825* ***Rooms*** *50* ***Road map*** *C5*

Opened in 1871, the Upham is Southern California's oldest continuously operating hotel. The inn is set on lovely grounds, with a high degree of privacy. Rooms are comfortable and stylishly furnished. Some are cottage-style, and many have fireplaces. **www.uphamhotel.com**

SANTA BARBARA Four Seasons Biltmore ⇅ 🍴 🏊 👪 🏋 $$$$$

1260 Channel Dr, 93108 ***Tel*** *(805) 969-2261* ***Fax*** *(805) 565-8323* ***Rooms*** *213* ***Road map*** *C5*

Exquisite seaside luxury and attention to every detail make this the premier Santa Barbara indulgence. The Spanish Colonial-style property is set elegantly on sprawling grounds, close to the beach and away from town. Rooms are sumptuous and secluded, and come with every amenity. **www.fourseasons.com**

SANTA BARBARA Inn by the Harbor ⇅ 🏊 $$$$$

433 W Montecito St, 93101 ***Tel*** *(805) 963-7851* ***Fax*** *(805) 962-9428* ***Rooms*** ***Road map*** *C5*

Expect affordable grace at this plush hotel located close to the beach. Suites are spacious and have full kitchens; ideal for family stays. Rooms are pleasingly designed in French country decor and feature pine furniture. Amenities include a delicious Continental breakfast, a large sundeck, and heated swimming pool. **www.sbhotels.com**

SANTA BARBARA Simpson House Inn ⇅ $$$$$

121 E Arrellaga, 93101 ***Tel*** *(800) 676-1280* ***Fax*** *(805) 564-4811* ***Rooms*** *15* ***Road map*** *C5*

The only B&B in North America with the five-diamond distinction, this delightful inn offers generous amenities, top-notch service, and a gorgeous garden setting. Rooms and cottages are elegantly appointed and secluded, though the property is a short walk from restaurants and shops. **www.simpsonhouseinn.com**

SANTA PAULA Santa Paula Inn ⇅ 🏊 $

111 N 8th St, 93060 ***Tel*** *(805) 933-0011* ***Fax*** *(805) 497-9211* ***Rooms*** *11* ***Road map*** *C5*

In a pastoral setting, among lemon and avocado groves, this quaint inn is located only a 10-minute drive from the coast. Rooms are snug and well kept, and feature Jacuzzis, and feather beds; some have kitchenettes. The garden patio offers a tranquil setting for an evening glass of wine. **www.santapaulainn.com**

SIMI VALLEY Posada Royale ⇅ 🏊 🏋 $$

1775 Madera Rd, 93065 ***Tel*** *(800) 994-4884* ***Fax*** *(805) 581-5353* ***Rooms*** *120* ***Road map*** *C5*

The staff prides itself on providing personal attention at this comfortable hotel. The recently remodeled guest rooms have upgraded amenities, including two-line telephones and wireless Internet capabilities. Located close to major freeways, there is also has a fitness facility and heated pool. **www.posadaroyale.com**

SIMI VALLEY Simi Valley Holiday Inn ⇅ 🏋 $$

2550 Erringer Rd, 93065 ***Tel*** *(805) 584-6006* ***Fax*** *(805) 527-5629* ***Rooms*** *96* ***Road map*** *C5*

Close to freeway access, this great-value hotel provides comfortable, basic rooms. It was recently renovated and offers many business amenities, including wireless Internet access. There is a sauna and whirlpool on site. A buffet breakfast is served every morning. **www.ichotelsgroup.com**

SOLVANG Royal Copenhagen Inn ⇅ $$$

1579 Mission Dr, 93463 ***Tel*** *(800) 624-6604* ***Fax*** *(805) 688-7029* ***Rooms*** *48* ***Road map*** *C5*

The tradition of an old Danish inn is recalled at this friendly property, which is modeled on an actual street in Denmark. It features rooms with large walk-in showers and generous amenities. Complimentary freshly-made pastries are served each morning and there is a wine service every evening. **www.royalcopenhageninn.com**

SOLVANG Storybook Inn $$$

409 1st St, 93463 **Tel** *(805) 688-1703* **Fax** *(805) 688-0953* **Rooms** *9* **Road map** *C5*

Each unique room at this quiet, family-run B&B is named after a Hans Christian Andersen story, and is decorated with fine antiques and comforts such as featherbeds and upscale linen. Wine and cheese are served each afternoon. The service is friendly and attentive. **www.solvangstorybook.com**

SOLVANG Petersen Village Inn $$$$$

1576 Mission Dr, 93463 **Tel** *(805) 688-3121* **Fax** *(805) 688-5732* **Rooms** *40* **Road map** *C5*

This charming, comfortable inn, in the heart of Santa Barbara wine country, features spacious rooms with canopy beds and modern conveniences. The lovely on-site restaurant is open exclusively to guests, and a morning coffee service is offered in rooms. Mid-week specials are available. **www.peterseninn.com**

ORANGE COUNTY

ANAHEIM Little Boy Blue Motel $

416 W Katella Ave, 92802 **Tel** *(714) 635-2781* **Fax** *(714) 635-4254* **Rooms** *19* **Road map** *D6*

At this bare-bones motel, the rooms are typically clean and comfortable. The property is located within quick walking distance of the Disneyland gates. Amenities include a swimming pool, a light complimentary breakfast, and free parking. **www.anaheim-littleboyblue.com**

ANAHEIM Anaheim Desert Inn & Suites $$

1600 S Harbor Blvd, 92802 **Tel** *(714) 772-5050* **Fax** *(714) 778-2754* **Rooms** *145* **Road map** *D6*

Across from Disneyland's main entrance, this family-friendly hotel offers good value and convenience. Rooms range in size and some sleep eight comfortably. There is a roof deck outfitted for viewing the park's fireworks each night. It is popular with business travelers too. **www.anaheimdesertinn.com**

ANAHEIM Anaheim Marriott Hotel $$$

700 W Convention Way, 92802 **Tel** *(714) 750-8000* **Fax** *(714) 748-2477* **Rooms** *1033* **Road map** *D6*

This huge, convention-style hotel is central to major Anaheim attractions, and features recently renovated rooms and many family-friendly conveniences. Accommodations are spacious and comfortable, and some have views of the Disneyland Park. Amenities include high-speed Internet access. **www.marriottanaheim.com**

ANAHEIM Disneyland's Paradise Pier Hotel $$$$$

1717 S Disneyland Dr, 92802 **Tel** *(714) 999-0990* **Fax** *(714) 776-5763* **Rooms** *489* **Road map** *D6*

A bright, California beach-themed hotel, the Paradise Pier is located inside Disneyland Park. The entire property was recently refurbished, sprucing up the public spaces and recreational amenities. Rooms are contemporary; some have imposing views of the theme park. There is a full business center on site. **www.disneyland.com**

AVALON Hotel Vista del Mar $$$

417 Crescent Ave, 90704 **Tel** *(310) 510-1452* **Fax** *(310) 510-2519* **Rooms** *15* **Road map** *C6*

A small and cozy beach hotel, the Vista del Mar stands in a lovely setting, with a picturesque garden courtyard. The rooms are contemporary and bright, and many have fireplaces and ocean views. Freshly-made cookies and milk are offered each night. **www.hotel-vistadelmar.com**

AVALON Hotel Metropole $$$$

Metropole Market Place, Crescent Ave, 90704 **Tel** *(310) 510-1884* **Fax** *(310) 510-2534* **Rooms** *48* **Road map** *C6*

Experience luxurious comfort in an intimate setting at this chic boutique hotel located near the beach. Rooms are appointed in a modern style, and while most rooms have ocean views, many have fireplaces and Jacuzzis. Ideal for romantic and family getaways. **www.hotel-metropole.com**

COSTA MESA Vagabond Inn $

3205 Harbor Blvd, 92626 **Tel** *(714) 557-8360* **Fax** *(714) 662-7596* **Rooms** *127* **Road map** *D6*

This good-value hotel is near the local airport and many major Orange County attractions, including the South Coast Plaza shopping center. It features spacious family-size rooms and business-ready amenities such as large work desks and high-speed Internet access. A cheerful staff. **www.vagabondinn.com**

COSTA MESA Ayers Hotel & Suites $$

325 Bristol St, 92626 **Tel** *(714) 549-0300* **Fax** *(714) 662-0828* **Rooms** *281* **Road map** *D6*

Rooms at this charming hotel have boutique appeal and are decorated in French country style. The staff are friendly; personal touches include complimentary buffet breakfast and evening treats. The property is conveniently located near several local attractions and shops. **www.ayershotel.com**

COSTA MESA Residence Inn by Marriott $$

881 W Baker St, 92626 **Tel** *(714) 241-8800* **Fax** *(714) 546-4308* **Rooms** *144*

The rooms at this friendly, recently renovated hotel are large suites, and have a residential feel, with kitchenettes and separate living areas. There is a heated pool, whirlpool, and a sports court. A welcoming and efficient staff. The Residence Inn is close to South Coast Plaza shopping district. **www.marriott.com**

Key to Price Guide *see p524* **Key to Symbols** *see back cover flap*

COSTA MESA Wyndham Orange County Airport
$$

3350 Avenue of the Arts, 92626 **Tel** *(714) 751-5100* **Fax** *(949) 751-0129* **Rooms** *238*   **Road map** D6

With spacious and superbly appointed rooms, this well-run, recently renovated hotel is located close to the performing arts center and other major attractions. Features include wireless Internet access and cordless phones in each room. The on-site restaurant offers good Italian fare. **www.wyndham.com**

DANA POINT Blue Lantern Inn
$$$$

34343 Street of the Blue Lantern, 92629 **Tel** *(800)950-1236* **Fax** *(949) 496-1483* **Rooms** *29*   **Road map** D6

Overlooking the harbor, romantic gable-roofed Blue Lantern Inn has luxurious rooms, furnished in country charm, each provided with a fireplace and a jetted tub. The suites offer private decks and spectacular water views. **www.foursisters.com**

DANA POINT Ritz-Carlton Laguna Niguel
$$$$$

1 Ritz-Carlton Dr, 92629 **Tel** *(949) 240-2000* **Fax** *(949) 240-0829* **Rooms** *393*   **Road map** D6

Set on the bluffs above the shore, this elegant resort-style property recently upgraded all guest rooms and public areas. The grounds are spectacular and now have a new spa and fitness center. Rooms feature five-star amenities. The on-site restaurant is worth a visit. **www.ritzcarlton.com**

HUNTINGTON BEACH Best Western Inn
$$

800 Pacific Coast Hwy, 92648 **Tel** *(714) 536-7500* **Fax** *(714) 536-6846* **Rooms** *50*   **Road map** D6

Excellent value for the good view, this no-frills hotel on the Pacific Coast Highway has suites and rooms with fireplaces. The property is well managed and the staff are friendly and helpful. The rooftop spa offers panoramic views of the beach and the mountains. Free high-speed Internet access is available. **www.bestwestern.com**

HUNTINGTON BEACH Waterfront Hilton Beach Resort
$$$$$

21100 Pacific Coast Hwy, 92648 **Tel** *(714) 845-8000* **Fax** *(714) 845-8425* **Rooms** *224*   **Road map** D6

Among the premier places to stay in Huntington, this full-service, four-diamond resort is close to the beach, and features well-appointed guest rooms with upscale bath amenities and plush spa-like robes. The oceanfront suites have wraparound balconies. **www.hilton.com**

LAGUNA BEACH Hotel Laguna
$$

425 S Coast Hwy, 92651 **Tel** *(949) 494-1151* **Fax** *(949) 497-2163* **Rooms** *65*   **Road map** D6

The oldest hotel in town, the Laguna retains its historic ambience, and keeps guests returning with attentive service and good value. The property is secluded and has a private beach for guests only. Complimentary breakfast is served with the newspaper each morning. **www.hotellaguna.com**

LAGUNA BEACH Casa Laguna Inn
$$$$

2510 S Coast Hwy, 92651 **Tel** *(949) 494-2996* **Fax** *(949) 494-5009* **Rooms** *20*   **Road map** D6

Though a small-scale B&B, this utterly charming oceanside inn has Mission-style architectural features. The rooms have pillowtop mattresses and sumptuous bath amenities. The service is exceptional. Full gourmet breakfast and afternoon refreshments are served on secluded patios. **www.casalaguna.com**

LAGUNA BEACH Surf and Sand Resort
$$$$$

1555 S Coast Hwy, 92651 **Tel** *(949) 497-4477* **Fax** *(949) 494-2897* **Rooms** *150*   **Road map** D6

Ranked among top California resorts, this hotel provides contemporary beachfront luxury in each guest room and suite, with large plantation shutters and pleasant views of the water. The property was recently renovated, breathing fresh life into the entire grounds. It has a great location and an excellent restaurant. **www.surfandsandresort.com**

NEWPORT BEACH Fairmont Newport Beach
$$$$

4500 MacArthur Blvd, 92660 **Tel** *(949) 476-2001* **Fax** *(949) 476-0153* **Rooms** *435*   **Road map** D6

Blending European elegance with Californian flair, this large hotel near the beach has a corporate feel, yet maintains friendly service. Rooms are large and well appointed; some have balconies and ocean views. The business center is equipped with the latest features. Just 5 miles (8 km) from the Pacific Ocean. **www.fairmont.com**

NEWPORT BEACH Four Seasons Hotel
$$$$$

690 Newport Center Dr, 92660 **Tel** *(949) 759-0808* **Fax** *(949) 759-0568* **Rooms** *285*   **Road map** D6

A relaxed atmosphere and sophisticated charm are the hallmarks of this high-end resort, one of the top hotels on the coast. While some rooms have great ocean views, all are equipped with luxurious amenities. The staff are polished, attentive, and professional. **www.fourseasons.com/newportbeach**

SUNSET BEACH Harbour Inn & Suites
$

16912 Pacific Coast Hwy, 90742 **Tel** *1-800-546-4770* **Fax** *(562) 592-3547* **Rooms** *25*   **Road map** D6

This affordable, well-run B&B is not far from the beach, and offers spacious rooms and special discounts. Rooms have European-style charm and have large beds, refrigerators, and microwave ovens. It is close to many local attractions. **www.harbourinn.net**

TWO HARBORS Banning House Lodge
$$$$$

1 Banning House Rd, Catalina Island, 90704 **Tel** *(310) 510-2800* **Fax** *(310) 510-0244* **Rooms** *11*   **Road map** C6

Built on the hillside overlooking the village, this former hunting lodge has peaceful, secluded rooms. The property is well manicured, and features a trellised courtyard, ideal for enjoying a quiet cocktail at sunset. They have on-site tennis court and shops. Friendly staff can arrange outdoor activities as well.

SAN DIEGO COUNTY

CARLSBAD Carlsbad
$$$

320 Walnut Ave, 92008 **Tel** *(760) 434-5995* **Fax** *(760) 434-7649* **Rooms** *10* **Road map** *D6*

Each room at this cozy B&B is named after a Southern California beach, and features a fireplace, feather bed, and private entrance. The hotel can arrange activities for guests, including day spa visits and scenic airplane rides. Enjoy the superb full breakfast in the inside parlor or on the pretty garden-patio. **www.pelican-cove.com**

CARLSBAD Best Western Beach Terrace Inn
$$$

2775 Ocean St, 92008 **Tel** *(760) 729-5951* **Fax** *(760) 729-1078* **Rooms** *49* **Road map** *D6*

Basic, yet comfortable, this corporate-run hotel is situated right by the ocean. The appealing, one-bedroom suites feature kitchenettes and fireplaces. All rooms have a private terrace and panoramic ocean views. There are also a few studio units that come without a balcony. **www.beachterraceinn.com**

CORONADO Coronado Island Marriott Resort
$$$$$

2000 Second St, 92118 **Tel** *(619) 435-3000* **Fax** *(619) 435-4183* **Rooms** *300* **Road map** *D6*

Situated on a huge section of beachfront property, this large hotel has expansive bay and downtown San Diego views. Well appointed, the hotel has spacious rooms as well as one- and two-bedroom villas with kitchenettes and whirlpool tubs. A full-service spa is available on site. **www.marriott.com**

CORONADO Hotel Del Coronado
$$$$$

1500 Orange Ave, 92118 **Tel** *(619) 435-6611* **Fax** *(619) 522-8238* **Rooms** *700* **Road map** *D6*

A landmark in San Diego for more than a century, this grand Victorian building is as famous for its accommodations as for its welcoming hospitality. Situated on a stretch of beautiful beach, the hotel offers every amenity. The rooms are modern, comfortable, and well appointed. A spa was added recently. **www.hoteldel.com**

CORONADO Loews Coronado Bay Resort
$$$$$

4000 Coronado Bay Rd, 92118 **Tel** *(619) 424-4000* **Fax** *(619) 424-4400* **Rooms** *430* **Road map** *D6*

This large, well-run resort-style hotel has spacious rooms overlooking the bay from private balconies. On-site amenities include tennis courts and boat rentals from the private 80-slip dock. A sprawling new spa and fitness center is on the premises. **www.loewshotels.com**

DEL MAR Clarion Del Mar Inn
$$

720 Camino Del Mar, 92014 **Tel** *(858) 755-9765* **Fax** *(858) 792-8196* **Rooms** *80* **Road map** *D6*

With quiet rooms set among English-style gardens, this quaint property, with a Tudor look, offers comfortable amenities, including some rooms with kitchenettes. The courteous staff serve a morning breakfast buffet and afternoon tea service. **www.delmarinn.com**

DEL MAR Del Mar Hilton
$$$$

15575 Jimmy Durante Blvd, 92014 **Tel** *(858) 792-5200* **Fax** *(858) 792-9538* **Rooms** *257* **Road map** *D6*

A recent renovation has spruced up the interiors of Del Mar Hilton. The lobby is magnificent, while the guest rooms either have ocean views or overlook the adjacent racetrack. The property is close to the beach, and adjacent to tennis courts and a golf driving range. A free shuttle service to nearby attractions. **www.sandiegodelmarhilton.com**

DEL MAR L'Auberge Del Mar Resort & Spa
$$$$$

1540 Camino Del Mar, 92014 **Tel** *(800) 245-9757* **Fax** *(858) 755-4940* **Rooms** *120* **Road map** *D6*

This elegant, full-service luxury resort offers ample recreational amenities, including golf, tennis, and hiking. Spacious, well-furnished rooms come with marble baths and private balconies. A small pathway leads from the resort to the beach. There is a great spa on site. **www.laubergedelmar.com**

ENCINITAS Encinitas Inn & Suites
$$

85 Encinitas Blvd, 92024 **Tel** *(760) 942-7455* **Fax** *(760) 632-9481* **Rooms** *94* **Road map** *D6*

Set on a hillside, this well-priced, family-friendly hotel offers clean, comfortable, and spacious rooms; many with ocean views overlooking Moonlight Beach. Free wireless Internet access is provided to guests. The service is prompt and immaculate. Encinitas is close to many local attractions. **www.bwencinitas.com**

JULIAN Julian Gold Rush Hotel
$$

2032 Main St, 92036 **Tel** *(800) 734-5854* **Fax** *(760) 765-0327* **Rooms** *15* **Road map** *D6*

A well-run, Victorian-era inn located in a historic mining town, Julian is great for a romantic getaway. The beautifully restored rooms are furnished with antiques and a fireplace. A special suite for honeymooners is also available here. Within walking distance of gift shops, restaurants, museums, and gold mines. **www.julianhotel.com**

LA JOLLA Embassy Suites Hotel
$$

4550 La Jolla Village Dr, 92122 **Tel** *(858) 453-0400* **Fax** *(858) 453-4226* **Rooms** *335* **Road map** *D6*

This mid-size, efficiently run hotel is convenient for families and groups. The property features two-room suites, and is central to freeway access and many San Diego attractions. Full business amenities are also offered, including high-speed Internet access and large work desks. **www.embassysuites.com**

Key to Price Guide *see p524* **Key to Symbols** *see back cover flap*

LA JOLLA La Jolla Beach and Tennis Club
$$$$$

2000 Spindrift Drive, 92037 **Tel** *(858) 454-7126* **Fax** *(858) 456-3805* **Rooms** *90* **Road map** D6

At this classic Californian beach club, rooms are available in one-, two-, and three-bedroom suites; many have balconies and kitchens. The family-friendly club features understated luxury, and offers ready access to golf, tennis, and croquet. The staff are courteous. **www.ljbtc.com**

LA JOLLA Bed and Breakfast Inn at La Jolla
$$$$$

7753 Draper Ave, 92067 **Tel** *(858) 456-2066* **Fax** *(858) 456-1510* **Rooms** *16* **Road map** D6

An elegant and charming B&B, this historic inn retains its old-world charm while offering the latest in guest comfort. All rooms have individual flair, and many have dazzling ocean views. Staff are friendly and helpful. This inn is popular with both business and leisure travelers. **www.innlajolla.com**

LA JOLLA La Valencia Hotel
$$$$$

1132 Prospect St, 92037 **Tel** *(858) 454-0771* **Fax** *(858) 456-3921* **Rooms** *115* **Road map** D6

Affectionately known as the "pink lady," this beautiful luxury hotel is an icon of La Jolla, featuring graciously appointed rooms, with plush bath amenities and sweeping coastal views. The Ocean Villas have private butler service. The entire property was recently updated. **www.lavalencia.com**

LA JOLLA Marriott San Diego/La Jolla
$$$$$

4240 La Jolla Village Dr, 92037 **Tel** *(858) 587-1414* **Fax** *(858) 546-8518* **Rooms** *360*

Close to the beach and nearby restaurants, this large hotel features facilities for the business traveler. The generously proportioned rooms are furnished with upscale linen, and have small private balconies. Some offer views of the village and coastline. Free morning coffee is served here. **www.marriott.com**

RANCHO SANTA FE Rancho Valencia Resort
$$$$$

5921 Valencia Circle, 92067 **Tel** *(858) 756-1123* **Fax** *(858) 756-0165* **Rooms** *49* **Road map** D6

Set on an expanse of rolling hills, this resort-style property features an array of activity options, from golf and tennis to hiking. The hacienda-style rooms are spacious and comfortably furnished, offering peaceful seclusion and an attentive staff. Some suites have a private pool and Jacuzzi. Full spa services are available. **www.ranchovalencia.com**

SAN DIEGO Blom House
$

1372 Minden Dr, 92111 **Tel** **Rooms** *4* **Road map** D6

This intimate B&B comes with surprising personal touches such as fresh homemade cookies offered every afternoon. Rooms are comfortable, with shared and private baths. There are spectacular views of the city from the large deck. A convenient location, with freeway access.

SAN DIEGO Comfort Inn and Suites Hotel Circle
$$

2201 Hotel Circle S, 92108 **Tel** *(619) 881-6800* **Fax** *(619) 542-1227* **Rooms** *216* **Road map** D6

Of the many hotels situated in this section of town, the Comfort Inn is among the most reliably clean and well-run. Located near major sights, this family-friendly hotel has outdoor grills near the pool, a spa, and a children's pool. Complimentary breakfast is provided. **www.comfortinnhotelcircle.com**

SAN DIEGO Holiday Inn Mission Bay
$$

3737 Sports Arena Blvd, 92110 **Tel** *(619) 881-6100* **Fax** *(619) 224-9248* **Rooms** *307* **Road map** D6

Ideal for families as well as large groups, this corporate-run hotel is convenient to the beach and such local attractions as Sea World. Rooms are spacious and immaculately maintained. The staff are friendly and attentive. Great online discounts are offered regularly. **www.himb.com**

SAN DIEGO Beach Haven Inn
$$$

4740 Mission Blvd, 92019 **Tel** *(858) 272-3812* **Fax** *(858) 272-3532* **Rooms** *23* **Road map** D6

Located close to Pacific Beach, a couple of blocks from the Crystal Pier, this modest hotel offers great value and convenient amenities. The rooms are tidy; some have kitchenettes. Large family suites are also available. Facilities include a heated swimming pool with spa and a poolside barbecue. **www.beachhaveninn.com**

SAN DIEGO Heritage Park Inn
$$$

2470 Heritage Park Row, 92110 **Tel** *(619) 299-6832* **Fax** *(619) 299-9465* **Rooms** *10* **Road map** D6

Housed in a Queen Anne Victorian house, this intimate, charming inn is located near the famous zoo. Rooms are cozy and appointed with period furnishing such as clawfoot tubs. Service is friendly and swift. Complimenatry homemade gourmet breakfast is served on the lovely veranda. **www.heritageparkinn.com**

SAN DIEGO Beach Cottages
$$$$$

4255 Ocean Blvd, 92109 **Tel** *(858) 483-7440* **Fax** *(858) 273-9365* **Rooms** *78* **Road map** D6

This family-run hotel on the beach has been a staple in the area for decades. The accommodations range from basic motel rooms to cottages, with complete kitchens ideal for extended family stays. Several recreational choices are on offer, including shuffleboard and beach games. **www.beachcottages.com**

SAN DIEGO Hilton San Diego Mission Valley
$$$$$

901 Camino del Rio S, 92108 **Tel** *(619) 543-9000* **Fax** *(619) 543-9358* **Rooms** *350* **Road map** D6

A comfortable and convenient hotel near downtown and the beach. Rooms were recently renovated and are well appointed, featuring upgraded accessories and many business-friendly amenities. The service here is prompt and courteous. **www.hilton.com**

SAN DIEGO Hotel Solamar

435 6th Ave, 92101 **Tel** *(619) 531-8740* **Fax** *(619) 531-8742* **Rooms** *235* **Road map** *D6*

This stylish new hotel near the ballpark and vibrant Gaslamp neighborhood features rooms with the latest in technology and guest comfort. Furnishings are chic and amenities sumptuous. There is a lively lounge on the rooftop, which is also where the pool is. Jsix and Jbar are the trendy restaurant and bar on site. **www.hotelsolamar.com**

SAN DIEGO Manchester Grand Hyatt

One Market Place, 92101 **Tel** *(619) 232-1234* **Fax** *(619) 233-6464* **Rooms** *1685* **Road map** *D6*

The towers of Manchester Grand Hyatt, the largest hotel in the city, are fixtures on the skyline. The centrally-located downtown property has guest rooms of all sizes, well appointed and comfortable, as well as complete business amenities, a recently renovated restaurant, and a new spa. **www.manchestergrand.hyatt.com**

SAN DIEGO Omni San Diego

75 L St, 92101 **Tel** *(619) 231-6664* **Fax** *(619) 231-8060* **Rooms** *511* **Road map** *D6*

New high-rise hotel near the ballpark and the Gaslamp Quarter, Omni San Diego has sleek rooms featuring top-notch amenities, flat-screen TVs, and spa-quality bath accessories. Most rooms have great views of the bay or downtown. The Omni has first-rate business amenities and professional staff. **www.omnihotels.com**

SAN DIEGO Rancho Bernardo Inn

17550 Bernardo Oaks Dr, 92128 **Tel** *(877) 517-9142* **Fax** *(858) 675-8501* **Rooms** *287* **Road map** *D6*

Enjoying an exclusive atmosphere, this resort property in San Diego North has beautiful grounds, ample recreation, and fine dining. All rooms have a patio or a private balcony, and are equipped with handsome furnishings and upscale amenities. The suites have wood-burning fireplaces. **www.ranchobernardoinn.com**

SAN DIEGO San Diego Marriott and Marina

333 West Harbor Dr, 92101 **Tel** *(619) 234-1500* **Fax** *(619) 234-8678* **Rooms** *1357* **Road map** *D6*

With convenient access to San Diego waterways, this large, business-friendly hotel has a nautical theme and a bustling lobby and public areas. The rooms are spacious and offer lovely views of downtown and the bay. Located within easy walking distance to the Gaslamp Quarter. **www.marriott.com**

SAN DIEGO US Grant

326 Broadway, 92101 **Tel** *(619) 232-3121* **Fax** *(619) 232-3626* **Rooms** *285* **Road map** *D6*

In the heart of downtown, this beautiful historic property features rooms with a period feel, but equipped with modern amenities, including plush bath robes and pillowtop mattresses. The lobby and public areas are opulent and regal. Within walking distance of many shops and restaurants. **www.usgrant.net**

TIJUANA Grand Hotel Tijuana

Blvd Agua Caliente 4500, CP, 22420 **Tel** *(866) 472-6385* **Rooms** *423* **Road map** *D6*

Just south of the United States border in Mexico, this large, modern hotel is part of a complex featuring resort-style amenities, including a swimming pool and recreational facilities. The suites have kitchens and Internet access. Service is helpful and prompt. **www.grandhoteltij.com.mx**

THE INLAND EMPIRE AND LOW DESERT

BIG BEAR LAKE Hillcrest Lodge

40241 Big Bear Blvd, 92315 **Tel** *(909) 866-7330* **Fax** *(909) 866-1171* **Rooms** *12* **Road map** *D5*

Some rooms at this rural mountain resort have a private Jacuzzi, fireplace, and kitchen. Choose from motel rooms, suites, and cabins, all exuding rustic charm and decorated with comfortable furnishings. The Hillcrest is close to summer hiking trails and winter skiing paths. **www.hillcrestlodge.com**

BIG BEAR LAKE Grey Squirrel Resort

39372 Big Bear Blvd, 92315 **Tel** *(909) 866-4335* **Fax** *(909) 866-1171* **Rooms** *17* **Road map** *D5*

From motel rooms to three-bedroom cottages, this year-round mountain resort offers easy access to recreational activities and other amenities. Accommodations are rustic, but all are completely furnished with classy linen and comfortable bedding. **www.greysquirrel.com**

BIG BEAR LAKE Windy Point Inn

39015 N Shore Dr, 92333 **Tel** *(909) 866-2746* **Fax** *(909) 866 1593* **Rooms** *5* **Road map** *D5*

This rustic, intimate, and romantic inn is situated on the lake, and has rooms appointed with feather beds, wood-burning fireplaces, and private decks. There are splendid views of the lake, forest, and mountains from every room. The service is exemplary and has earned the place a loyal following. Breakfast is included. **www.windypointinn.com**

BORREGO SPRINGS Palms at Indian Head

2220 Hoberg Rd, 90024 **Tel** *(760) 767-7788* **Fax** *(760) 767-9717* **Rooms** *12* **Road map** *D6*

Resplendent in mid-20th-century modern style, this California hotel was formerly a getaway for Hollywood celebrities. It still retains its classic charm, with rooms that are chic and well furnished. Krazy Koyote, the on-site restaurant, is good. The newly-built Zen Garden is a beautiful place for yoga and meditation. **www.thepalmsatindianhead.com**

Key to Price Guide *see p524* **Key to Symbols** *see back cover flap*

BORREGO SPRINGS La Casa Del Zorro $$$$$
3845 Yaqui Pass Rd, 92004 **Tel** *(760) 767-5323* **Fax** *(760) 767-5963* **Rooms** *77* **Road map** *D6*

Set on expansive, well-manicured grounds, this romantic desert hotel has a Zen-like atmosphere of wellness and rejuvenation. Rooms are luxuriously appointed and range in size from cozy to spacious; some have fireplaces and patios. As large as four bedrooms, the casitas feature a private pool or spa. **www.lacasadelzorro.com**

DESERT HOT SPRINGS Two Bunch Palms $$$$$
67425 Two Bunch Palms Trail, 92240 **Tel** *(760) 329-8791* **Fax** *(760) 329-1317* **Rooms** *45*

Renowned for its rejuvenating mineral pools, this adults-only oasis getaway offers rooms in casitas, suites, and villas. All rooms are comfortably appointed, while the Casino Dining Room serves good fine dining options. The vast array of spa treatments help the resort maintain a loyal following. Closed in August. **www.twobunchpalms.com**

IDYLLWILD Creekstone Inn $$
54950 Pine Crest Ave, 92549 **Tel** *(951) 659-3342* **Rooms** *9* **Road map** *D6*

This quaint, rustic country inn has had incarnations as a restaurant and a general store. It is set at the edge of town and very close to hiking trails and the local wilderness. Most of the uniquely furnished rooms come with fireplaces, while some have Jacuzzis. **www.creekstoneinn.com**

IDYLLWILD Fern Valley Inn $$
25240 Fern Valley Rd, 92549 **Tel** *(951) 659-2205* **Fax** *(909) 659-2630* **Rooms** *11* **Road map** *D6*

Each cottage at this rustic, family-run hideaway has a fireplace, private bath, and large deck. The no-frills amenities are basic and comfortable. The grounds feature a garden gazebo and a swimming pool. The inn is close to the shops and galleries in town. **www.fernvalleyinn.com**

INDIAN WELLS Hyatt Grand Champions Resort $$$$
44600 Indian Wells Lane, 92210 **Tel** *(760) 341-1000* **Fax** *(760) 568 2236* **Rooms** *336* **Road map** *D6*

Designed for the golf lifestyle, this resort is set on two famous golf courses offering recreation in myriad varieties. The grounds are expansive and well kept. Rooms are spacious and appointed with many modern luxuries. There is a full spa and skin clinic on premises. **www.grandchampions.hyatt.com**

INDIAN WELLS Indian Wells Resort Hotel $$$$
76–661 Hwy 111, 92210 **Tel** *(760) 345-6466* **Fax** *(760) 772-5083* **Rooms** *155* **Road map** *D6*

A luxurious desert resort set on a golf course, the Indian Wells offers an excess of recreational pursuits. Rooms range from small and serviceable to huge and opulent. All feature private balconies or patios and high-speed Internet access. The staff are polished and friendly. **www.indianwellsresort.com**

INDIO Best Western Date Tree Hotel $
81909 Indio Blvd, 92201 **Tel** *(760) 347-3421* **Fax** *(760) 863-1338* **Rooms** *120* **Road map** *D6*

An affordable, well-run hotel situated close to a world-famous golf course, tennis facilities, and local attractions. The immaculate guest rooms are tastefully decorated. The grounds are quiet and feature a full spa and Olympic-size pool. The superb Continental breakfast is complimentary. **www.datetree.com**

PALM DESERT Marriott Desert Springs Resort & Spa $$$$
74855 Country Club Dr, 92260 **Tel** *(760) 341-2211* **Fax** *(760) 341-1872* **Rooms** *844* **Road map** *D6*

This large, corporate-run property is recognized as one of the top destination resorts and spas in the area. The rooms have gorgeous views and are sumptuously appointed, with granite and marble finishes. Recreation includes golf and tennis. The staff are wonderfully attentive. **www.desertspringsresort.com**

PALM DESERT Shadow Mountain Resort $$$$$
45750 San Luis Rey, 92260 **Tel** *(760) 346-6123* **Fax** *(760) 346-6518* **Rooms** *167* **Road map** *D6*

Family-friendly Shadow Mountain Resort is located close to a golf course and area shops. The well-appointed rooms range in size from one-, two-, and three-bedroom condominiums to villas, all featuring kitchenettes and balconies or patios. There are 16 tennis courts on offer. **www.shadow-mountain.com**

PALM SPRINGS Palm Court Inn $
1983 N Palm Canyon Dr, 92262 **Tel** *(760) 416-2333* **Fax** *(760) 416-5425* **Rooms** *107* **Road map** *D6*

Exceptional value in a great central location can be found at this well-manicured hotel, which features attractive grounds, courteous staff, and rooms with balconies and views of the mountains. Select accommodations have Jacuzzis. Complimentary breakfast is served at the on-site restaurant.

PALM SPRINGS Palm Springs Super 8 Lodge $
1900 N Palm Canyon Dr, 92262 **Tel** *(760) 322-3757* **Fax** *(760) 323-5290* **Rooms** *65* **Road map** *D6*

Rooms at this value-minded hotel are sparsely appointed, but comfortable and well maintained. Located near downtown, the property benefits from highway access. The staff are helpful. Children 12 and under stay free. Complimentary breakfast is included in the rate. **www.super8.com**

PALM SPRINGS Spa Resort and Casino $$
100 N Indian Canyon, 92262 **Tel** *(888) 999-1995* **Fax** *(760) 325-3344* **Rooms** *228* **Road map** *D6*

One of the few full-service properties downtown, this hotel and casino were remodeled recently, and have amenities such as an impressive spa and hot springs on premises. The rooms are appointed with upscale linen and bath accessories. The casino features live entertainment regularly. **www.sparesortcasino.com**

PALM SPRINGS Terra Cotta Inn $$
2388 E Racquet Club Rd, 92262-2629 **Tel** *(760) 322-6059* **Fax** *(760) 322-4169* **Rooms** *17*   **Road map** *D6*

This is a clothing-optional resort, which celebrates "naturalism" in an intimate, well-run environment. The rooms are large, basically appointed, and well maintained. On-site amenities include a pool and barbecue facilities. Spa services are available indoors as well as outdoors. **www.sunnyfun.com**

PALM SPRINGS Hyatt Regency $$$
285 N Palm Canyon Dr, 92262 **Tel** *(760) 322-9000* **Fax** *(760) 969-6005* **Rooms** *193*   **Road map** *D6*

This convenient, corporate-run downtown hotel features cozy rooms and a full array of business amenities. The well-appointed one- and two-bedroom suites have balconies affording great desert views. Within walking distance of many shops, galleries, and entertainment venues. **www.palmsprings.hyatt.com**

PALM SPRINGS Villa Royale $$$
1620 Indian Trail, 92264 **Tel** *(760) 327-2314* **Fax** *(760) 322-3794* **Rooms** *31*   **Road map** *D6*

An intimate luxury inn with an adults-only environment, Villa Royale provides romantic rooms, each decorated uniquely in the style of a specific European region. Popular with honeymooners, it is set on lovely grounds and includes a pool and restaurant. A complimentary breakfast is included. **www.villaroyale.com**

PALM SPRINGS Desert Shadows Inn $$$$
1533 Chaparral Rd, 92262 **Tel** *(760) 325-6410* **Fax** *(760) 327-7500* **Rooms** *92*   **Road map** *D6*

A secluded nudist resort with luxury appeal, Desert Shadows Inn is home to the area's largest nudist spa. Comfortable, spacious rooms, ranging to two-level villas, are provided. Amenities include clothing-optional recreation including tennis and croquet. **www.desertshadows.com**

PALM SPRINGS Hilton Palm Springs $$$$$
400 E Tahquitz Canyon Way, 92262 **Tel** *(760) 320-6868* **Fax** *(760) 320-2126* **Rooms** *260*   **Road map** *D6*

A downtown hotel, with rooms situated around a large swimming pool. The rooms are spacious and comfortably appointed; many have mountain views and balconies. Amenities include a full spa and fitness facilities. Plaza Al Fresco is a poolside lounge, while the lovely Terrace Restaurant is an excellent dining choice. **www.hiltonpalmsprings.com**

PALM SPRINGS Le Parker Meridien Palm Springs $$$$$
4200 E Palm Canyon Dr, 92264 **Tel** *(760) 770-5000* **Fax** *(760) 324-2188* **Rooms** *144*   **Road map** *D6*

This sleek-looking desert classic is newly renovated, and features hotel rooms, suites, and villas, each with the latest amenities. The staff are friendly and efficient, and the service is first-rate. There is a new top-of-the-line spa and fitness facility on the premises. **www.lemeridien.com**

RANCHO MIRAGE Rancho Las Palmas Resort $$$$
41000 Bob Hope Dr, 92270 **Tel** *(760) 568-2727* **Fax** *(760) 568-5845* **Rooms** *422*   **Road map** *D6*

Rooms at this large, family-friendly hotel feature good amenities and private balconies or patios. The property is well-run and comfortably appointed. Recreational facilities include tennis and the on-site, 27-hole golf course. Discounts are offered regularly. **www.marriott.com**

RANCHO MIRAGE The Lodge at Rancho Mirage $$$$
68900 Frank Sinatra Dr, 92270 **Tel** *(760) 321-8282* **Fax** *(760) 321-6928* **Rooms** *240*   **Road map** *D6*

Set in the hills above Coachella Valley, this full-service resort offers refined luxury and a casual ambience. The oversized rooms at the recently renovated property have contemporary furnishings and upscale amenities. Most afford excellent views of the city below. **www.ranchomirage.rockresorts.com**

RIVERSIDE 3649 Mission Inn Ave $$$$$
3649 Mission Inn Ave, 92501 **Tel** *(909) 784-0300* **Fax** *(909) 683-1342* **Rooms** *239*   **Road map** *D6*

An icon of the city, this beautiful hotel dates to 1888 and encompasses an entire block. The property is exquisite, with much of its original Spanish Colonial charm intact. The updated rooms are elegant and appointed with every amenity. A full-service spa and five restaurants complete the all-inclusive scene. **www.missioninn.com**

TWENTYNINE PALMS Best Western Garden Inn & Suites $
71487 Twentynine Palms Hwy, 92277 **Tel** *(760) 367-9141* **Fax** *(760) 367-2584* **Rooms** *84*   **Road map** *D5*

Select rooms at this tidy, well-located hotel are beautifully appointed, featuring kitchenettes. Amenities include a pool, hot tub, laundry facilities, and free parking. Guests are offered special admission rates to Joshua Tree National Monument, which is located just 5 miles (8 kms) away. **www.bestwestern.com**

THE MOJAVE DESERT

BARSTOW Barstow Super 8 $
170 Coolwater Lane, 92311 **Tel** *(760) 256-8443* **Fax** *(760) 256-0997* **Rooms** *109*   **Road map** *D5*

Decent rooms and friendly staff make this affordable option in the desert worthwhile. Select business amenities include Internet access, facsimile service, and a copying center. Refrigerator units are available, as is complimentary parking for guests. The Barstow Super is located close to restaurants and shops. **www.super8.com**

Key to Price Guide *see p524* **Key to Symbols** *see back cover flap*

BARSTOW Best Western Desert Villa Motel $

1984 E Main St, 92311 ***Tel*** *(760) 256-1781* ***Fax*** *(760) 256-9265* ***Rooms*** *95* ***Road map*** *D5*

Suites at this comfortable motel have jetted tubs, and all rooms feature complimentary high-speed Internet connections. There is a pool and outdoor whirlpool as well. The intimate lounge, La Sala, is ideal for a quiet cocktail. Free Continental breakfast. It is close to retail factory outlets shops. **www.bestwestern.com**

BARSTOW Comfort Inn $

1431 E Main St, 92311 ***Tel*** *(760) 256-0661* ***Fax*** *(760) 256-8392* ***Rooms*** *64* ***Road map*** *D5*

A popular retreat from the desert heat, this downtown hotel is close to shops and restaurants, and offers good value, but very few extras. Rooms are tidy and the pool area is well kept. The complimentary breakfast goes a little beyond the typical coffee and muffin. The staff are quite friendly. **www.choicehotels.com**

BARSTOW Ramada Inn $

1511 E Main St, 92311 ***Tel*** *(760) 256-5673* ***Fax*** *(760) 256-5917* ***Rooms*** *148* ***Road map*** *D5*

This updated motor inn is designed in the Mission style. The rooms are no-frills, but clean and comfortable, and feature high-speed Internet access as well as premium television channels. Room service can be ordered from the on-site restaurant. **www.ramada.com**

DEATH VALLEY Amargosa Hotel and Opera House $

Death Valley Junction, 92328 ***Tel*** *(760) 852-4441* ***Fax*** *(760) 852-4138* ***Rooms*** *14* ***Road map*** *D4*

A quirky hotel in the desert, the Amargosa is a working theater where cabaret shows are performed. Rooms are comfortable, if a bit eccentric, and decorated with fantastical wall murals painted by the proprietor. In keeping with the historic ambience, telephones and televisions are not available. **www.amargosa-opera-house.com**

DEATH VALLEY Delight's Hot Springs Resort $

368 Tecopa Hot Springs Rd, 92389 ***Tel*** *(800) 928-8808* ***Fax*** *(760) 852-4301* ***Rooms*** *9* ***Road map*** *D4*

Renowned for its natural hot springs, this small hotel is within a short drive of Las Vegas, and features motel rooms and cabins with kitchenettes. The unpretentious decor lays emphasis on retaining the old-world charm. The staff are friendly and attentive. Guests under the age of 21 are not allowed. **www.delightshotspringsresort.com**

DEATH VALLEY Shoshone Inn $

Junction of Hwy 127, Hwy 128, 92384 ***Tel*** *(760) 852-4335* ***Fax*** *(760) 852-4250* ***Rooms*** *16* ***Road map*** *D4*

A pleasant oasis in the expansive Mojave Desert, this rustic inn with sunny rooms is outfitted in a Southwestern motif. Some have kitchenettes, while all have cable TV. Shoshone Inn is located in the village, close to stores, restaurants, and cafés. There is a spring-fed swimming pool nearby. **www.shoshonevillage.com**

DEATH VALLEY Stove Pipe Wells Village $$

Hwy 190, Death Valley, 92328 ***Tel*** *(760) 786-2387* ***Fax*** *(760) 786-2389* ***Rooms*** *83* ***Road map*** *D4*

Though the guest rooms are well appointed and contemporary, this retreat has rustic appeal and is set on a stunning desert landscape. Close to the general store and Big Sand Dunes, local area activities include hiking and golf. The staff are eager to assist. **www.stovepipewells.com**

DEATH VALLEY Furnace Creek Inn and Ranch Resort $$$$$

1 Main St, 92328 ***Tel*** *(760) 786-2345* ***Fax*** *(760) 786-2514* ***Rooms*** *68* ***Road map*** *D4*

A gorgeous oasis in the desert, this historic landmark property has amenities on par with top luxury resorts. Rooms are elegant and sumptuously appointed. Recreational pursuits include swimming in a spring-fed pool, golf, and tennis. Closed in summer. **www.furnacecreekresort.com**

EAST MOJAVE Hotel Nipton $

107355 Nipton Rd, 92364 ***Tel*** *(760) 856-2335* ***Fax*** *(760) 856-2352* ***Rooms*** *4* ***Road map*** *E5*

Like a slice of gold-mining history, this small hotel has rustic charm, but offers updated amenities, including wireless Internet access. Built in the Spanish adobe style, the rooms feature central heating and cooling. Guests share two common bathrooms. Continental breakfast is included. **www.nipton.com**

LAKE HAVASU Hidden Palms Resort Condominiums $

2100 Swanson Ave, 86403 ***Tel*** *(800) 254-5611* ***Fax*** *(928) 855-2620* ***Rooms*** *22* ***Road map*** *E5*

A quiet inn near the lake, the Hidden Palms was recently renovated. The one-bedroom suites have new furniture, custom cabinetry, and upgraded bathroom accessories. Rooms are spacious and appointed with kitchenettes and separate dining areas. Set in a beautiful palm tree setting, the courtyard is relaxing and idyllic. **www.hiddenpalms.com**

LAKE HAVASU The Nautical Inn Resort $$$

1000 McCulloch Blvd, 86403 ***Tel*** *(928) 855-2141* ***Fax*** *(928) 453-5808* ***Rooms*** *139* ***Road map*** *E5*

This resort-style hotel is set on the river, and features large rooms in various sizes. Most have private patios, while the suites feature full kitchens. The location offers easy access to water activities. Dock your boat in front of your suite. The hotel has a private guests-only beach. **www.nauticalinn.com**

LAKE HAVASU London Bridge Resort $$$$

477 Queens Bay, 86403 ***Tel*** *(866) 331-9231* ***Fax*** *(928) 855-5404* ***Rooms*** *150* ***Road map*** *E5*

European charm and contemporary amenities can be found in abundance at this riverfront property. Most rooms offer exceptional views of the relocated London Bridge. Facilities include high-speed Internet access, cordless telephones, and kitchenettes. Full spa services are available. **www.londonbridgeresort.com**

SAN FRANCISCO

PACIFIC HEIGHTS Broadway Manor Inn ⬛⬛   Ⓢ

2201 Van Ness Ave, 94109 **Tel** *(415) 776-7900* **Fax** *(415) 928-7460* **Rooms** *56*   **Map** *4 F3*

Located within walking distance of the Marina District and Fisherman's Wharf, Broadway Manor Inn is great value for tourists on a budget. The rooms are basic, but clean, and some have wireless Internet access, which is also available in the lobby. Guest rooms have microwaves and refrigerators. **www.staysf.com/broadwaymanor**

PACIFIC HEIGHTS Heritage Marina Hotel ⬛⬛⬛⬛⬛   Ⓢ

2550 Van Ness Ave, 94109 **Tel** *(415) 776-7500* **Fax** *(415) 351-1336* **Rooms** *134*   **Map** *4 E2*

Conveniently located near the Marina and all local tourist spots, this hotel was built in the 1950s and remodeled in 2003. It is ideal for the budget traveler looking for no-frills accommodation, and every room has a microwave. Rates include a deluxe Continental breakfast and there is an on-site, Italian-style eatery. **www.heritagemarinahotel.com**

PACIFIC HEIGHTS The Greenwich Inn ⬛   Ⓢ

3201 Steiner, 94123 **Tel** *(415) 921-5162* **Fax** *(415) 921-3602* **Rooms** *32*   **Map** *4 D2*

The Greenwich Inn is a basic inn and affordable option for travelers wishing to stay close to San Francisco's Marina District and Presidio Park. The comfortable rooms have been recently renovated, and the staff are friendly. Countless restaurants and shops are within easy walking distance. **www.greenwichinn.com**

PACIFIC HEIGHTS Cow Hollow Motor Inn ⬛   ⓈⓈ

2190 Lombard St, 94123 **Tel** *(415) 921-5800* **Fax** *(415) 922-8515* **Rooms** *129*   **Map** *4 D2*

This hotel is situated between the fashionable Cow Hollow and Marina Districts of San Francisco, famous for world-class dining and shopping. The rooms here are simple, if not slightly outdated, and families traveling with children may enjoy the option to stay in one of the 12 guest suites. **www.cowhollowmotorinn.com**

PACIFIC HEIGHTS Marina Inn ⬛   ⓈⓈ

3110 Octavia St, 94123 **Tel** *(415) 928-1000* **Fax** *(415) 928-5909* **Rooms** *40*   **Map** *4 E2*

Well located two blocks from Fort Mason and its grassy park, this low-priced Marina District hotel has stunning views of the Bay. It is clean and the staff are friendly, though street noise from Lombard Street can be obtrusive. It is convenient for the Union Street shops and restaurants. **www.marinainn.com**

PACIFIC HEIGHTS Marina Motel ⓈⓈ

2576 Lombard St, 94123 **Tel** *(415) 921-9406* **Fax** *(415) 921-0364* **Rooms** *30*   **Map** *4 D3*

Tucked away in a flower-filled Mediterranean courtyard, Marina Hotel enjoys a quiet and private location, close to the neighborhood market, restaurants, and public transport. The Spanish-style building, built in 1939, has bright, airy, and individually decorated rooms, each with a private bathroom. **www.marinamotel.com**

PACIFIC HEIGHTS Motel Capri ⬛   ⓈⓈ

2015 Greenwich St, 94123 **Tel** *(415) 346-4667* **Fax** *(415) 346-3256* **Rooms** *46*   **Map** *4 D2*

This clean and comfortable, family-owned motel is a good choice for budget-minded travelers. It is situated in a quiet residential street at the center of the Marina District. Two kitchenettes are now available. The hotel is close to public transportation and provides free on-site parking. **www.motelcaprica.com**

PACIFIC HEIGHTS Pacific Heights Inn ⬛   ⓈⓈ

1555 Union St, 94123 **Tel** *(415) 776-3310* **Fax** *(415) 776-8176* **Rooms** *40*   **Map** *4 E2*

This pleasant, 1960s-era motel is on a quiet block of Union Street, just west of Van Ness Avenue. It is convenient for public transportation and has free on-site parking for guests with their own cars. The restaurants, shops, and bars of the energetic Cow Hollow neighborhood are just a few blocks away. **www.pacificheightsinn.com**

PACIFIC HEIGHTS Chateau Tivoli Bed and Breakfast ⓈⓈⓈ

1057 Steiner St, 94115 **Tel** *(415) 776-5462* **Fax** *(415) 776-0505* **Rooms** *9*   **Map** *4 D4*

One of San Francisco's "painted ladies," this 100-year-old Victorian house was the center of the 1970s New Age Movement, marked by rebirthing, Reichian release, and nude communal bathing. It has since been restored to its original splendor, with frescoed ceilings, stained-glass windows, and several antiques. **www.chateautivoli.com**

PACIFIC HEIGHTS Edward II Inn and Suites ⓈⓈⓈ

3155 Scott St, 94123 **Tel** *(415) 922-3000* **Fax** *(415) 931-5784* **Rooms** *32*   **Map** *3 C2*

Edward II Inn and Suites is a real find for those looking for a quiet place in a convenient location. The house, built in 1914, is now a three-story inn, a few blocks from San Francisco's Yacht Harbor. Some of the suites have Jacuzzis, and there are two small meeting rooms available. **www.edwardii.com**

PACIFIC HEIGHTS Hotel del Sol ⬛⬛⬛   ⓈⓈⓈ

3100 Webster St, 94123 **Tel** *(415) 921-5520* **Fax** *(415) 931-4137* **Rooms** *57*   **Map** *4 D2*

Celebrating California's lively culture, this boutique hotel features a playful design with palm trees, hammocks, mosaics, and a pool. The rooms are bright and spacious, with rainbow-colored bedspreads. There are also 10 themed suites. The family suite has bunk beds, board games, toys, and child-friendly furnishings.

Key to Price Guide *see p524* **Key to Symbols** *see back cover flap*

PACIFIC HEIGHTS Laurel Inn ⇅ 🧒 $$$

444 Presidio Ave, 94115 ***Tel*** *(415) 567-8467* ***Fax*** *(415) 928-1866* ***Rooms*** *59* ***Map*** *3 C4*

This quiet, stylish boutique hotel features a hip mid-20th-century style. The comfortable, brightly-colored guest rooms come with CD players, VCRs, and writing desks and tables. Complimentary Continental breakfast and free parking are provided. The hotel's trendy G Bar is great for a pre-dinner drink. **www.thelaurelinn.com**

PACIFIC HEIGHTS Queen Anne Hotel 🍸 $$$

1590 Sutter St, 94109 ***Tel*** *(415) 441-2828* ***Fax*** *(415) 775-5212* ***Rooms*** *48* ***Map*** *4 E4*

The recently-restored Queen Anne is a beautiful Victorian hotel, built in 1890. Each room is done up differently with antique furniture and authentic decorations. Room rates include Continental breakfast, wine in the evenings, and a weekday morning town car airport shuttle. **www.queenanne.com**

PACIFIC HEIGHTS Jackson Court $$$$

2198 Jackson St, 94115 ***Tel*** ***Fax*** *(415) 929-1405* ***Rooms*** *10* ***Map*** *4 E3*

A stay at Jackson Court will make you feel like turn-of-the-19th-century royalty, as this stunning 100-year-old brownstone sits in one of the most beautiful neighborhoods of San Francisco. The rooms are simple and elegant, some with fireplaces, all with TV/VCR combos, hair dryers, and phones.

PACIFIC HEIGHTS The Hotel Majestic ⇅ 🍴 $$$$

1500 Sutter St, 94109 ***Tel*** *(415) 441-1100* ***Fax*** *(415) 673-7331* ***Rooms*** *57* ***Map*** *4 E4*

One of the few top-notch San Francisco hotels to have survived the 1906 earthquake, the Majestic is an exquisite early 20th-century building in a quiet neighborhood between Pacific Heights and San Francisco Bay. Antique furniture graces the rooms, most of which have canopied beds and open fireplaces. **www.thehotelmajestic.com**

PACIFIC HEIGHTS Union Street Inn $$$$

2229 Union St, 94123 ***Tel*** *(415) 346-0424* ***Fax*** *(415) 922-8046* ***Rooms*** *6* ***Map*** *4 D3*

When you check into Union Street Inn, you will wish you lived here. Each of the spacious guest rooms is tastefully decorated, and the idyllic back garden is the perfect setting to enjoy a complimentary glass of wine at the end of a long day of sightseeing. Two-day minimum stays are required on weekends. **www.unionstreetinn.com**

PACIFIC HEIGHTS Hotel Drisco 🍸 $$$$$

2901 Pacific Ave, 94115 ***Tel*** *(415) 346-2880* ***Fax*** *(415) 567-5537* ***Rooms*** *48* ***Map*** *3 C3*

Perched at the top of the glamorous Pacific Heights neighborhood, Hotel Drisco offers stately accommodation, perfect for business travelers and tourists. Many of the guest rooms feature spectacular views of San Francisco Bay and the Golden Gate Bridge. Complimentary nightly wine service and Continental breakfast.

FISHERMAN'S WHARF AND NORTH BEACH San Remo Hotel $

2237 Mason St, 94133 ***Tel*** *(415) 776-8688* ***Fax*** *(415) 776-2811* ***Rooms*** *62* ***Map*** *5 B2*

The only budget hotel in the area, San Remo is a well-maintained Italianate building, and one of the first to be constructed following the earthquake and fire of 1906. All the rooms in this non-smoking hotel share bathrooms, with the exception of the rooftop Honeymoon Suite. **www.sanremohotel.com**

FISHERMAN'S WHARF AND NORTH BEACH Best Inn Fisherman's Wharf ⇅ 🧒 $$

2850 Van Ness Ave, 94109 ***Tel*** *(415) 776-3220* ***Fax*** *(415) 921-7451* ***Rooms*** *42* ***Map*** *4 E2*

This three-story motel, though not an architectural wonder, offers proximity to some of the major sites – Fisherman's Wharf, North Beach, and Chinatown. Clean rooms, equipped with high-speed Internet access, microwaves, and refrigerators make the Best Inn a good choice for budget travelers.

FISHERMAN'S WHARF AND NORTH BEACH Best Western Tuscan Inn ⇅ 🍴 🧒 $$$

425 Northpoint St, 94133 ***Tel*** *(415) 561-1100* ***Fax*** *(415) 561-1199* ***Rooms*** *220* ***Map*** *5 B1*

Tuscan Inn is a spacious and stylish hotel in the middle of Fisherman's Wharf. It is a popular spot for business travelers as well as for visiting film and television crews. Children under 18, accompanied by an adult, stay free of charge. Complimentary wine is served every afternoon. **www.tuscaninn.com**

FISHERMAN'S WHARF AND NORTH BEACH Hotel Boheme ⇅ $$$

444 Columbus Ave, 94133 ***Tel*** *(415) 433-9111* ***Fax*** *(415) 362-6292* ***Rooms*** *15* ***Map*** *5 B3*

The stylish and hip Boheme is a homage to the Beat Generation, in the heart of where it all began. Bold color schemes and whimsical touches enhance the hotel's poetic vibe. The rooms are cozy and the staff are exceptional. Located amid the hustle of North Beach, it is close to many great restaurants and bars. **www.hotelboheme.com**

FISHERMAN'S WHARF AND NORTH BEACH The Wharf Inn 🧒 $$$

2601 Mason St, 94133 ***Tel*** *(877) 786-4721* ***Fax*** *(415) 776-2181* ***Rooms*** *51* ***Map*** *5 B1*

This 1960s-style three-story motel is bright, cheerful, and clean. All the rooms are decorated in bold colors, and many feature couches and small sitting areas. The inn is located directly above the bustling Fisherman's Wharf, and offers complimentary parking – a rarity in San Francisco. **www.wharfinn.com**

FISHERMAN'S WHARF AND NORTH BEACH The Sheraton ⇅ 🍴 🏊 🧒 🍸 $$$$

2500 Mason St, 94133 ***Tel*** *(415) 362-5500* ***Fax*** *(415) 956-5275* ***Rooms*** *525* ***Map*** *5 B1*

Primarily a family-oriented, tourist hotel, the Sheraton is housed in a large, attractive 1970s building, with all the comforts expected by regular travelers. It provides easy access to Fisherman's Wharf and the ferry that goes to Alcatraz Island. It is also popular with business travelers. **www.sheratonatthewharf.com**

FISHERMAN'S WHARF AND NORTH BEACH Suites at Fisherman's Wharf $$$$

2655 Hyde St, 94109 **Tel** *(415) 771-0200* **Fax** *(415) 346-8058* **Rooms** *24*   **Map** *5 A2*

Families and groups tend to stay here, in the city's only all-suite hotel. Business people also come here regularly. Each suite, spacious enough to accommodate four people, has its own kitchen and dining facilities. The hotel is steps away from the Hyde Street cable car. **www.thesuitesatfishermanswharf.com**

FISHERMAN'S WHARF AND NORTH BEACH Washington Square Inn $$$$

1660 Stockton St, 94133 **Tel** *(415) 981-4220* **Fax** *(415) 397-7242* **Rooms** *15*   **Map** *5 B2*

One of the few hotels in the North Beach area, this is the only one facing Washington Square Park, where you can watch people practicing Tai Chi or strolling around the park. Room rates include a complimentary breakfast, though walking to the famous Mamma's Restaurant, just across the street, is a preferred option. **www.wsisf.com**

FISHERMAN'S WHARF AND NORTH BEACH Courtyard by Marriott $$$$$

580 Beach St, 94133 **Tel** *(415) 775-3800* **Fax** *(415) 441-7307* **Rooms** *127*   **Map** *4 F1*

Sitting just one block from Fisherman's Wharf, the Courtyard is great value for its location and amenities. Clean, modern rooms feature high-speed Internet access, and are perfect for both vacationing families and business travelers. On-site business meeting facilities are also available. **www.marriott.com**

FISHERMAN'S WHARF AND NORTH BEACH Hyatt at Fisherman's Wharf $$$$$

555 N Point, 94133 **Tel** *(415) 563-1234* **Fax** *(415) 749-6122* **Rooms** *313*   **Map** *5 A1*

This Hyatt is more family-oriented than the other Hyatt hotels in San Francisco, though it provides service of the same quality. Families are offered a discount on the price of their second room, and there is a heated swimming pool. It is a convenient place for visiting Alcatraz. **www.fishermanswharf.hyatt.com**

CHINATOWN AND NOB HILL Hotel Astoria $$

510 Bush St, 94108 **Tel** *(415) 434-8889* **Fax** *(415) 434-8919* **Rooms** *80*   **Map** *5 C4*

Travelers on their own get a good deal at the modest Hotel Astoria, where reasonably priced single rooms are available. The hotel is conveniently situated between Chinatown and Union Square, very close to the dramatic Chinatown gates. **www.hotelastoria-sf.com**

CHINATOWN AND NOB HILL Hotel Triton $$

342 Grant Ave, 94108 **Tel** *(415) 394-0500* **Fax** *(415) 394-0555* **Rooms** *140*   **Map** *5 C4*

Design and media professionals frequent the small but stylish Triton, with a friendly and cheerful ambience. It is just across the street from Chinatown and in the heart of San Francisco's art gallery district. For overseas travelers, foreign newspapers are normally available at the downstairs Café de la Presse. **www.hoteltriton.com**

CHINATOWN AND NOB HILL Holiday Inn, Financial District/Chinatown $$$$

750 Kearny St, 94108 **Tel** *(415) 433-6600* **Fax** *(415) 765-7891* **Rooms** *565*   **Map** *5 C3*

San Francisco has five Holiday Inns, each a huge concrete tower filled with identical rooms. This one is in a good location near Chinatown and Portsmouth Plaza. There is also a first-class day spa located in the lobby. Cable car lines are just two blocks away. Children under 19, accompanied by an adult, stay free. **www.hiselect.com**

CHINATOWN AND NOB HILL Nob Hill Lambourne $$$$

725 Pine, 94108 **Tel** *(415) 433-2287* **Fax** *(415) 433-0975* **Rooms** *20*   **Map** *5 C4*

The Lambourne is among San Francisco's ritziest hotels. Its stylish interior reflects a contemporary French design. Each room has exquisite furniture, and bathrooms contain king-size tubs into which residents may pour an assortment of luxurious lotions. The suites also offer exercise equipment.

CHINATOWN AND NOB HILL Fairmont Hotel $$$$$

950 Mason St, 94108 **Tel** *(415) 772-5000* **Fax** *(415) 781-3929* **Rooms** *596*   **Map** *5 B4*

Famous for its gorgeous lobby and opulent public rooms, the Fairmont is the grandest of all the grand hotels at the top of Nob Hill. It has been much admired since it reopened in 1907, a year after an earthquake and fire ravaged it. The panoramic views are unbeatable. **www.fairmont.com**

CHINATOWN AND NOB HILL Huntington Hotel and Nob Hill Spa $$$$$

1075 California St, 94108 **Tel** *(415) 474-5400* **Fax** *(415) 474-6227* **Rooms** *140*   **Map** *5 B4*

Built in 1922 as a luxury apartment building, the Huntington was converted into a high-class hotel in 1945. Each of the spacious rooms is individually decorated – many have a wet bar, and some have kitchens. Indulge yourself at the world-famous Nob Hill Spa, located on the upper floors of the hotel. **www.huntingtonhotel.com**

CHINATOWN AND NOB HILL Mark Hopkins Inter-Continental Hotel $$$$$

999 California St, 94108 **Tel** *(415) 392-3434* **Fax** *(415) 421-3302* **Rooms** *380*   **Map** *5 B4*

Located atop Nob Hill, the Mark Hopkins is a 1926 architectural landmark. Completely renovated and refurbished in 2000, it is one of the finest hotels in San Francisco, rich and lavish in style. The Top of the Mark sky lounge, on the 19th floor, offers panoramic views of the city from the peak of Nob Hill. **www.markhopkins.net**

CHINATOWN AND NOB HILL The Ritz-Carlton San Francisco $$$$$

600 Stockton, 94108 **Tel** *(415) 296-7465* **Fax** *(415) 291-0288* **Rooms** *336*   **Map** *5 C4*

Since it opened in 1991, the Ritz-Carlton has been rated one of San Francisco's best hotels. It is housed in an historic Beaux Arts building in an entire block along California Street, near the top of Nob Hill. Service is excellent. There is a four-star dining room, an indoor pool, and a fitness center. **www.ritzcarlton.com**

Key to Price Guide *see p524* **Key to Symbols** *see back cover flap*

FINANCIAL DISTRICT AND UNION SQUARE Taylor Hotel

615 Taylor St, Post St, 94102 **Tel** *(415) 775-0780* **Rooms** *36*

Map 5 B5

A simple, no-frills hotel, ideally located and priced for the budget traveler. The rooms are clean and all have private bathrooms and free wireless Internet access. The staff are always happy to help and advise about any aspect of your stay. A maid service and parking are provided at an extra charge. **www.sanfrancisco-budgethotel.com**

FINANCIAL DISTRICT AND UNION SQUARE Hotel des Arts

447 Bush St, 94108 **Tel** *(415) 956-3232* **Fax** *(415) 956-0399* **Rooms** *51*

Map 5 C4

Hotel des Arts is as much a functioning art gallery as it is a hotel. A portion of the rooms, painted and decorated by a rotating roster of local artists, makes it one of the most unusual places in the city. These rooms may be reserved by phone only. Union Square, Chinatown, and the Financial District are close by. **www.sfhoteldesarts.com**

FINANCIAL DISTRICT AND UNION SQUARE Commodore Hotel

825 Sutter St, 94109 **Tel** *(415) 923-6800* **Fax** *(415) 923-6804* **Rooms** *113*

Map 5 B4

Even on the foggiest San Francisco day, the brightly-hued lobby of the Commodore is sure to make you think of sunshine. Another unique touch is the exclusive, free-of-charge Golden Gate Greeters program that pairs guests with a San Francisco local, who acts as your guide for an afternoon. **www.jdvhospitality.com**

FINANCIAL DISTRICT AND UNION SQUARE Hotel Bijou

111 Mason St, 94102 **Tel** *(415) 771-1200* **Fax** *(415) 346-3196* **Rooms** *62*

Map 5 B5

Movie buffs will love Hotel Bijou, with its decor themed around San Francisco's cinematic history. Even the guest room draperies are a deep and dramatic burgundy-velvet, and a small theater screens double-features daily. The convenient Union Square location and complimentary breakfast round off the charm. **www.hotelbijou.com**

FINANCIAL DISTRICT AND UNION SQUARE The Savoy Hotel

580 Geary St, 94102 **Tel** *(415) 441-2700* **Fax** *(415) 441-0124* **Rooms** *83*

Map 5 B5

Recently refurbished, the Savoy offers elegance, helpful service, and feather beds with goosedown pillows in all rooms. Each guest is offered a free tequila shot on check-in. Or, if you prefer something more mellow, there is a complimentary wine service every evening from 4pm until 6pm in the hotel lobby. **www.thesavoyhotel.com**

FINANCIAL DISTRICT AND UNION SQUARE Touchstone Hotel

480 Geary St, 94102 **Tel** *(415) 771-1600* **Fax** *(415) 931-5442* **Rooms** *62*

Map 5 B5

Just steps from Union Square, Touchstone Hotel is a blend of old-world charm and modern convenience. It is a small, intimate B&B, owned and managed by the same family for over 50 years. Rates include breakfast and there is a complimentary shuttle from the airport to the hotel. **www.thetouchstone.com**

FINANCIAL DISTRICT AND UNION SQUARE Crowne Plaza Union Square

480 Sutter St, 94108 **Tel** *(415) 398-8900* **Fax** *(415) 989-8823* **Rooms** *401*

Map 5 C4

Right on the Powell Street cable car line, the Crowne Plaza has been recently refurbished. In-room amenities include high-speed Internet access and coffee makers. The hotel allows pets, and is extremely convenient for business travelers and families. There are two on-site restaurants and a cocktail lounge. **www.crowneplaza.com**

FINANCIAL DISTRICT AND UNION SQUARE Hotel Diva

440 Geary St, 94102 **Tel** *(415) 202-8787* **Fax** *(415) 346-6613* **Rooms** *114*

Map 5 B5

Stepping into Hotel Diva gives one the impression of having wandered into the Museum of Modern Art. The lobby and rooms are whimsically and colorfully decorated and accented by many architectural touches. The tone is hip luxury and the rooms will not disappoint even the most style-conscious traveler. **www.hoteldiva.com**

FINANCIAL DISTRICT AND UNION SQUARE Hotel Union Square

114 Powell St, 94102 **Tel** *(415) 202-8787* **Fax** *(415) 399-1874* **Rooms** *131*

Map 5 C5

Conveniently located two blocks from Union Square, this hotel is ideal for those looking for good value in the heart of San Francisco's shopping hub. Rooms are small and purpose-built, but amenities include fee-based wireless Internet access in the lobby and on-site currency exchange. **www.hotelunionsquare.com**

FINANCIAL DISTRICT AND UNION SQUARE Maxwell Hotel

386 Geary St, 94102 **Tel** *(415) 986-2000* **Fax** *(415) 397-2447* **Rooms** *153*

Map 5 B5

Built in 1908, the Maxwell is located in the heart of Theater District. The lobby has been recently renovated, and all rooms offer amenities such as data ports and in-room safes. All of the larger suites have free wireless high-speed Internet access and CD players. **www.jdvhospitality.com**

FINANCIAL DISTRICT AND UNION SQUARE White Swan Inn

845 Bush St, 94108 **Tel** *(415) 775-1755* **Fax** *(415) 775-5717* **Rooms** *26*

Map 5 B4

A small, country-style establishment, the White Swan has rooms with bright floral prints and very comfortable beds. There is also a fireplace that holds a convincing, but artificial, gas-powered open fire. A complimentary English breakfast is served each morning, and wine is offered every evening. **www.whiteswaninnsf.com**

FINANCIAL DISTRICT AND UNION SQUARE York Hotel

940 Sutter St, 94109 **Tel** *(415) 885-6800* **Fax** *(415) 885-2115* **Rooms** *96*

Map 5 A4

Comfortable, quiet rooms are available in the York, another central hotel that has had a facelift in recent years. The rooms at the back are particularly quiet. Every evening, a highly-rated cabaret show is performed in Plush Room, off the lobby. Interestingly, the hotel stairs were featured in Alfred Hitchcock's *Vertigo*. **www.yorkhotel.com**

FINANCIAL DISTRICT AND UNION SQUARE Argent Hotel $$$$$

50 3rd St, 94103 **Tel** *(415) 974-6400* **Fax** *(415) 543-8268* **Rooms** *667*   **Map** *5 C5*

Views from the floor-to-ceiling windows of the luxurious Argent are breathtaking, looking down over the Yerba Buena complex and the San Francisco Museum of Modern Art. Only a short walk to the Moscone Convention Center, the hotel's location is ideal for business people. **www.argenthotel.com**

FINANCIAL DISTRICT AND UNION SQUARE Harbor Court Hotel $$$$

165 Steuart St, 94105 **Tel** *(415) 882-1300* **Fax** *(415) 882-1313* **Rooms** *131*   **Map** *6 E4*

Housed in what was originally a YMCA building, Harbor Court is the only hotel in San Francisco with a location right on the waterfront. Rooms are on the small side, though some have good views of the Bay Bridge. Guests have free access to the fitness facilities of the new Y gym next door. **www.harborcourthotel.com**

FINANCIAL DISTRICT AND UNION SQUARE Hotel Rex $$$$

562 Sutter St, 94102 **Tel** *(415) 433-4434* **Fax** *(415) 433-3695* **Rooms** *94*   **Map** *5 B4*

This pleasant hotel has been recently renovated, with rooms painted in rich colors and walls embellished with the works of local artists. A real gem – and the pride of Rex – the downstairs lobby has a dark-hued and cozy library. The lobby bar often hosts literary events and small shows. **www.jdvhospitality.com**

FINANCIAL DISTRICT AND UNION SQUARE Kensington Park Hotel $$$$

450 Post St, 94109 **Tel** *(415) 788-6400* **Fax** *(415) 399-9484* **Rooms** *86*   **Map** *5 B5*

Located in the 1920s Spanish Revivalist-style Elks Lodge building, Kensington Park is a comfortable, medium-sized hotel close to Union Square. The lobby is gorgeous, and the nicely furnished rooms are spacious. The reasonable tariff includes free Continental breakfast and afternoon wine. **www.kensingtonparkhotel.com**

FINANCIAL DISTRICT AND UNION SQUARE Renaissance Parc Fifty Five $$$$

55 Cyril Magnin St, 94102 **Tel** *(415) 392-8000* **Fax** *(415) 403-6002* **Rooms** *1009*   **Map** *5 C5*

The huge Parc Fifty Five, a newly renovated hotel just off Market and Powell Streets, caters to conventions and large groups. There are good views from the upper floors. Tariffs are high, but special B&B and weekend offers make it worth considering. **www.parc55hotel.com**

FINANCIAL DISTRICT AND UNION SQUARE San Francisco Hilton $$$$

333 O'Farrell St, 94102 **Tel** *(415) 771-1400* **Fax** *(415) 771-6807* **Rooms** *2044*   **Map** *5 B5*

Filling an entire block just west of Union Square, the city's largest hotel provides excellent views from its 46-story tower. The service, too, matches the establishment's grand scale. The numerous facilities include an outdoor swimming pool, five restaurants, two bars, a barber shop, and a steam room. **www.hilton.com**

FINANCIAL DISTRICT AND UNION SQUARE The Inn at Union Square $$$$

440 Post St, 94102 **Tel** *(800) 288-4346* **Fax** *(415) 989-0529* **Rooms** *30*   **Map** *5 B5*

In the middle of Union Square, this cozy hotel has the warmth and intimacy of a private apartment. Many rooms have been recently renovated. Complimentary Continental breakfast and a newspaper are delivered to your room. Wine and hors d'oeuvres are served in the lobby every evening by the fireplace. **www.unionsquare.com**

FINANCIAL DISTRICT AND UNION SQUARE Andrews Hotel $$$$$

624 Post St, 94109 **Tel** *(800) 926-3739* **Fax** *(415) 928-6919* **Rooms** *48*   **Map** *5 B5*

Clean and comfortable rooms are offered in this small, family-owned hotel, located just two blocks away from Union Square. The prices are moderate, and include a complimentary Continental breakfast. An Italian restaurant is situated just off the lobby, and guests are offered a free glass of wine every evening. **www.andrewshotel.com**

FINANCIAL DISTRICT AND UNION SQUARE Campton Place Hotel $$$$$

340 Stockton St, 94108 **Tel** *(415) 781-5555* **Fax** *(415) 955-5536* **Rooms** *110*   **Map** *5 C4*

The small and elegant Campton Place is situated just off Union Square. It offers plush, well-appointed rooms, good service, and sumptuous public areas. Particularly appealing is the intimate bar off the lobby. Guests can choose between dinner on the roof terrace, or in the deluxe Campton Place Restaurant. **www.camptonplace.com**

FINANCIAL DISTRICT AND UNION SQUARE Clift Hotel $$$$$

495 Geary St, 94108 **Tel** *(415) 775-4700* **Fax** *(415) 931-7417* **Rooms** *363*   **Map** *5 B5*

The dramatic Clift is a striking example of modern design, with a lobby created by Phillippe Starck. Each room is elegantly furnished, with all the amenities one would expect from a hotel of this caliber. The downstairs Redwood Room and award-winning Asia de Cuba Restaurant are enchanting. **www.morganshotelgroup.com**

FINANCIAL DISTRICT AND UNION SQUARE Four Seasons $$$$$

757 Market St, 94103 **Tel** *(415) 633-3000* **Fax** *(415) 633-3001* **Rooms** *277*   **Map** *5 C5*

Four Seasons is one of San Francisco's classiest hotels. Spacious and understatedly stylish, each room has cozy sitting areas. The ultra-chic Sports Club/LA is available for guest use. This hotel provides easy access to Union Square, the San Francisco Museum of Modern Art, and the Yerba Buena Center. **www.fourseasons.com**

FINANCIAL DISTRICT AND UNION SQUARE Grand Hyatt San Francisco $$$$$

345 Stockton St, 94108 **Tel** *(415) 398-1234* **Fax** *(415) 391-1780* **Rooms** *686*   **Map** *5 C4*

The 36-story Grand Hyatt towers over the north side of Union Square, offering great views from all of its rooms. The rooftop Grand View restaurant has live piano music on Friday and Saturday evenings. The location is handy for the Financial District as well as for Union Square shops and theaters. **www.grandsanfrancisco.hyatt.com**

Key to Price Guide *see p524* **Key to Symbols** *see back cover flap*

FINANCIAL DISTRICT AND UNION SQUARE Hotel Monaco ⬛⬛⬛⬛ $$$$$

501 Geary St, 94102 **Tel** *(866) 622-5284* **Fax** *(415) 292-0111* **Rooms** *201* **Map** *5 B5*

Funky and charming, the Monaco is a few blocks west of Union Square. The guest rooms – a study in pattern and texture – feature many luxurious extras, such as Frette robes, down pillows, and fax machines. The Grand Café is set in a spectacular turn-of-the-19th-century ballroom downstairs. **www.monaco-sf.com**

FINANCIAL DISTRICT AND UNION SQUARE Hotel Nikko ⬛⬛⬛⬛⬛ $$$$$

222 Mason St, 94102 **Tel** *(415) 394-1111* **Fax** *(415) 394-1106* **Rooms** *534* **Map** *5 B5*

The ultra-modern Nikko caters primarily to business travelers, especially those from Japan. The hotel's excellent fitness center, with its glass-enclosed swimming pool and full range of exercise equipment, is among the best in the city. The lobby-level Anzu restaurant is perfect for drinking or dining. **www.hotelnikkosf.com**

FINANCIAL DISTRICT AND UNION SQUARE Hotel Vitale ⬛⬛⬛⬛⬛ $$$$$

8 Mission St, 94105 **Tel** *(888) 890-8688* **Fax** *(415) 278-3150* **Rooms** *199* **Map** *6 E4*

Built in early 2005, the flamboyant Hotel Vitale is the latest and, possibly, the grandest venture from the JDV Hospitality Group. Situated along the Embarcadero, it has all the advantages of a destination resort, in the heart of the city. The guest rooms boast every amenity, and Spa Vitale has stunning views. **www.jdvhospitality.com**

FINANCIAL DISTRICT AND UNION SQUARE Hyatt Regency San Francisco ⬛⬛⬛ $$$$$

5 Embarcadero Center, 94111 **Tel** *(415) 788-1234* **Fax** *(415) 398-2567* **Rooms** *803* **Map** *6 D3*

The Hyatt, built in 1973 around a 15-story atrium lobby, has recently been renovated and its rooms largely upgraded. Designated mainly for business travelers, the Regency Club floor has a full-time attendant, always on call. This hotel is located next to a small shopping center and theater complex. **www.sanfranciscoregency.hyatt.com**

FINANCIAL DISTRICT AND UNION SQUARE Mandarin Oriental ⬛⬛⬛ $$$$$

222 Sansome St, 94104 **Tel** *(415) 276-9888* **Fax** *(415) 433-0289* **Rooms** *158* **Map** *6 D3*

Particularly convenient for business travelers, Mandarin Oriental is first class in every respect. The Mandarin Rooms have floor-to-ceiling windows, offering magnificent views of San Francisco Bay and the Golden Gate Bridge. Another attraction is the excellent restaurant, Silks, located on the second floor. **www.mandarinoriental.com**

FINANCIAL DISTRICT AND UNION SQUARE Pan Pacific ⬛⬛⬛ $$$$$

500 Post St, 94102 **Tel** *(415) 771-8600* **Fax** *(415) 398-0267* **Rooms** *338* **Map** *5 B5*

John Portman was the architect of this beautifully appointed, daringly designed modern hotel, which has an atrium lobby 17 stories high, rising to a rooftop skylight. The public areas are glamorous, and the bedrooms refined and elegant. Business travelers will find the staff extremely helpful. **www.panpacific.com**

FINANCIAL DISTRICT AND UNION SQUARE Park Hyatt San Francisco ⬛⬛⬛ $$$$$

333 Battery St, 94111 **Tel** *(877) 557-5368* **Fax** *(415) 421-2433* **Rooms** *360* **Map** *6 D3*

Of all the Hyatt hotels in San Francisco, the Park is the smallest and most luxurious. Located next to the Embarcadero Center, it is preferred by business travelers. Visitors can benefit from special rates on weekends. There are also good family deals offering discounts on the price of a second room. **www.sanfranciscoparkhyatt.com**

FINANCIAL DISTRICT AND UNION SQUARE Prescott Hotel ⬛⬛⬛ $$$$$

545 Post St, 94102 **Tel** *(415) 563-0303* **Fax** *(415) 563-6831* **Rooms** *166* **Map** *5 B5*

Business travelers predominate at this sumptuous hotel that resembles a gentleman's club, with dark wooden walls and a large fireplace in the entrance lobby. Complimentary drinks are served in the afternoons. Postrio Restaurant is a little past its prime, but still serves consistent food in an elegant ambience. **www.prescotthotel.com**

FINANCIAL DISTRICT AND UNION SQUARE San Francisco Marriott ⬛⬛⬛⬛⬛ $$$$$

55 4th St, 94103 **Tel** *(415) 896-1600* **Fax** *(415) 486-8101* **Rooms** *1500* **Map** *5 C5*

Someone may like the futuristic look of this 39-story tower, but no one in San Francisco has dared to say so. However, the hotel has proved a popular spot for conventions. Families always appreciate the indoor pool and the fact that children under 18, when accompanied by an adult, can stay here free. **www.sfmarriott.com**

FINANCIAL DISTRICT AND UNION SQUARE Serrano Hotel ⬛⬛⬛⬛ $$$$$

405 Taylor St, 94102 **Tel** *(866) 289-6561* **Fax** *(415) 474-4879* **Rooms** *236* **Map** *5 B5*

This 17-story Spanish-Revivalist-style hotel has convenient access to both Union Square and the Theater District. Each guest room features high ceilings and a warm glow, accented by characteristic Spanish and Moroccan-influenced design. The appealing Ponzu restaurant is located on the lobby level. **www.serranohotel.com**

FINANCIAL DISTRICT AND UNION SQUARE Sheraton Palace Hotel ⬛⬛⬛⬛⬛ $$$$$

2 New Montgomery St, 94105 **Tel** *(415) 512-1111* **Fax** *(415) 543-0671* **Rooms** *550* **Map** *5 C4*

Early in the 20th century, the Palace was one of the most famous hotels in the world, hosting royalty and heads of state, including President Harding, who died here in his sleep in 1923. Renovated in the late 1980s, it is now known for its glamorous Garden Court, where afternoon tea is served. **www.sfpalace.com**

FINANCIAL DISTRICT AND UNION SQUARE Sir Francis Drake Hotel ⬛⬛⬛⬛ $$$$$

450 Powell St, 94102 **Tel** *(800) 795-7129* **Fax** *(415) 392-8559* **Rooms** *417* **Map** *5 B4*

A long-established Union Square hotel, the Sir Francis Drake glows in Art Deco splendor. It is famed for its Beefeater-uniformed doormen and Harry Denton's Starlight Room, a beautiful rooftop bar. The location on the Powell Street cable car line is unbeatable for access to the Financial District and North Beach. **www.sirfrancisdrake.com**

FINANCIAL DISTRICT AND UNION SQUARE Westin St. Francis 🛗 🍴 👪 🍸 $$$$$

335 Powell St, 94102 ***Tel*** *(415) 397-7000* ***Fax*** *(415) 774-0124* ***Rooms*** *1200* ***Map*** *5 B4*

Since 1904, Union Square's skyline has been defined by the triple towers of Westin St. Francis. Following damage in the earthquake and fire of 1906, the hotel was restored and enlarged. In the 1970s, a 32-story tower, complete with glass elevators, was added onto the back. The best rooms have views of Union Square. **www.westinstfrancis.com**

CIVIC CENTER Best Western Miyako Inn 🛗 👪 $$

1800 Sutter St, 94115 ***Tel*** *(415) 921-4000* ***Fax*** *(415) 923-1064* ***Rooms*** *125* ***Map*** *4 E4*

The fully-renovated Hotel Miyako is perfect for travelers in search of good value, above-average accommodation, and world-class dining just steps from the front door. Located in the heart of Japan Town and close to many good sushi restaurants, it has perfectly acceptable guest rooms. **www.bestwestern.com**

CIVIC CENTER Grove Inn $$

890 Grove St, 94117 ***Tel*** *(415) 929-0780* ***Fax*** *(415) 929-1037* ***Rooms*** *18* ***Map*** *4 E5*

Grove Inn, an Italianate-Victorian B&B, with a good location near San Francisco, dates to the late 1800s. The multilingual hosts have been running the place for over 20 years. The sunny rooms come with a queen-sized bed and direct dial phone. Rates include a complimentary Continental breakfast. **www.grovinn.com**

CIVIC CENTER Hotel Metropolis 🛗 👪 🍸 $$

25 Mason St, 94102 ***Tel*** *(415) 775-4600* ***Fax*** *(415) 775-7606* ***Rooms*** *110* ***Map*** *5 B5*

A funky boutique hotel, the Metropolis has a nature theme throughout, with each floor reflecting the elements. The Holistic room is perfect for escaping the hustle of nearby Union Square. All rooms offer amenities, including bars, two-line phones and data ports with voicemail, and Nintendo. **www.hotelmetropolis.com**

CIVIC CENTER Monarch Hotel $$

1015 Geary St, 94109 ***Tel*** *(415) 673-5232* ***Fax*** *(415) 885-2802* ***Rooms*** *101* ***Map*** *4 F4*

The Monarch is preferred by budget travelers looking for basic amenities and a central San Francisco location. All rooms have cable TV and safe-deposit boxes. Coffee is served throughout the day in the lobby, and parking is available at an additional cost. **www.themonarchhotel.com**

CIVIC CENTER Phoenix Hotel 🍴 🏊 👪 $$

601 Eddy St, 94109 ***Tel*** *(415) 776-1380* ***Fax*** *(415) 885-3109* ***Rooms*** *44* ***Map*** *4 F4*

This funky two-story motel, in the heart of the Tenderloin District, conjures up images of old Route 66. Grab a drink at the house bar, Bambuddah, and head out to the courtyard pool to spot celebrities (past guests include Dave Navarro and Linda Ronstadt). The rooms are basic, but great value for a central location. **www.jdvhospitality.com**

CIVIC CENTER Radisson Miyako Hotel 🛗 🍴 👪 $$

1625 Post St, 94115 ***Tel*** *(415) 922-3200* ***Fax*** *(415) 921-0417* ***Rooms*** *218* ***Map*** *4 E4*

Located within the Japan Center complex, the stylish Miyako Inn appeals to business travelers as well as regular tourists. Ask for one of the rooms featuring a Japanese steam bath. Japanese rooms with *tatami* mats are also available. The Dot restaurant is just downstairs. Children under 12 stay free. **www.miyakohotel.com**

CIVIC CENTER Alamo Square Inn 👪 $$$

719 Scott St, 94117 ***Tel*** *(415) 315-0123* ***Fax*** *(415) 931-1304* ***Rooms*** *15* ***Map*** *4 D5*

Alamo Square Inn consists of two, beautifully restored historic buildings overlooking Alamo Square at the center of San Francisco. One of the pair is blue and white, built in 1895 in Queen Anne style; the other is from 1896, in mock-Tudor style. A complimentary full breakfast is served daily in the sunny conservatory. **www.alamoinn.com**

CIVIC CENTER Best Western Americania 🛗 🏊 👪 🍸 $$$

121 7th St, 94105 ***Tel*** *(415) 626-0200* ***Fax*** *(415) 863-2529* ***Rooms*** *143* ***Map*** *11 A1*

Though technically in the trendy South of Market neighborhood of San Francisco, the Americania is a short walk from Union Square. The modern, spacious, and comfortable facilities are a refreshing contrast to the buzz of the city. Free Internet access is available, and the parking is free of charge. **www.theamericania.com**

CIVIC CENTER Archbishop's Mansion Inn 🛗 👪 $$$$

1000 Fulton St, 94117 ***Tel*** *(415) 563-7872* ***Fax*** *(415) 885-3193* ***Rooms*** *15* ***Map*** *4 D5*

This imposing building, in the style of the Second French Empire, was built in 1904, but has recently been carefully restored. Inside there is an elaborate three-story open staircase, topped by a stained-glass skylight. All rooms are luxuriously decorated and designed around operatic themes. **www.jdvhospitality.com**

HAIGHT ASHBURY AND THE MISSION 24 Henry $

24 Henry St, 94114 ***Tel*** *(415) 864-5686* ***Fax*** *(415) 864-0406* ***Rooms*** *5* ***Map*** *9 D2*

In the heart of the Castro District, 24 Henry is a charming B&B that caters to a primarily gay clientele. It enjoys a serene ambience on a quiet, tree-lined street. Facilities include free wireless DSL, complimentary breakfast, and private phones in all rooms. Rates are reasonable. **www.24henry.com**

HAIGHT ASHBURY AND THE MISSION Element's Hostel 🛗 🍴 $

2524 Mission St, 94110 ***Tel*** *(415) 647-4100* ***Fax*** *(415) 550-9005* ***Rooms*** *26* ***Map*** *9 F3*

This sparkling new, European-style hostel offers both dormitories and private rooms, right in the heart of San Francisco's Mission District. There is a restaurant and bar downstairs, but perhaps the most enticing aspect of Elements is the roof deck – complete with sun chairs and a telescope. **www.elementssf.com**

Key to Price Guide *see p524* **Key to Symbols** *see back cover flap*

HAIGHT ASHBURY AND THE MISSION Beck's Motor Lodge $$

2222 Market St, 94114 **Tel** *(415) 621-8212* **Fax** *(415) 241-0435* **Rooms** *57* **Map** *10 E1*

Beck's is a standard 1960s motel, convenient for the restaurants and nightlife of the Castro, Lower Haight and Mission Districts. Free parking, cable TV, and a quiet location are its main attractions. There is also a sunny roof deck, a perfect setting for a glass of wine before heading out for the night.

HAIGHT ASHBURY AND THE MISSION Inn 1890 $$

1890 Page St, 94117 **Tel** *(415) 386-0486* **Fax** *(415) 386-3626* **Rooms** *17* **Map** *9 B1*

One of the many imposing mansions built along the Panhandle of Golden Gate Park, this 1897 Queen Anne-style building was converted in 1984 into a comfortable and stylish B&B. The guest rooms are decorated with wallpaper designed by William Morris. A good Continental breakfast is served daily. **www.inn1890.com**

HAIGHT ASHBURY AND THE MISSION Red Victorian Bed and Breakfast $$

1665 Haight St, 94117 **Tel** *(415) 864-1978* **Fax** *(415) 863-3293* **Rooms** *18* **Map** *9 B1*

The Red Victorian is the ubiquitous Haight Street accommodation, perfect for travelers who want to channel San Francisco in the "Summer of Love." All the rooms are individually themed, with names such as Redwood Forest and Flower Child. No radios or TVs are available, but there is a meditation room. **www.redvic.com**

HAIGHT ASHBURY AND THE MISSION Tenth Avenue Inn $$

579 10th Ave, 94118 **Tel** *(415) 751-6220* **Fax** *(415) 751-6220* **Rooms** *3* **Map** *8 F1*

Tenth Avenue Inn is located just two blocks from the Golden Gate Park. There are only two guest rooms and one guest apartment, but the intimate setting is warm and inviting to a tourist in a strange city. Breakfast is served daily, as is nightly wine and cheese. A minimum two-night stay is required. **www.tenthaveinn.com**

HAIGHT ASHBURY AND THE MISSION Village House $$

4080 18th St, 94114 **Tel** *(415) 864-0994* **Fax** *(415) 864-0406* **Rooms** *5* **Map** *9 D3*

The sister guesthouse to the nearby 24 Henry, the quiet Village House has cheerful and bright rooms with a private phone line, just a half block away from the throbbing Castro nightlife. A TV/VCR and piano are available for guests to use in the community parlor. **www.24henry.com**

HAIGHT ASHBURY AND THE MISSION Willows Bed and Breakfast $$

710 14th St, 94114 **Tel** *(415) 431-4770* **Fax** *(415) 431-5295* **Rooms** *12* **Map** *10 E2*

Built in 1903, the Willows is a European-style B&B in the Castro District. Each room comes with a sink, kimono bathrobes, and luxury soaps, as well as a TV, VCR, and wireless Internet access. Eight private water closets are situated adjacent to the rooms. The staff are extremely friendly. **www.willowssf.com**

HAIGHT ASHBURY AND THE MISSION Stanyan Park Hotel $$$

750 Stanyan St, 94117 **Tel** *(415) 751-1000* **Fax** *(415) 668-5454* **Rooms** *36* **Map** *9 B2*

Doctors, patients, and patients' families often stay in this lovely Queen Anne-style hotel that enjoys a proximity to the San Francisco Medical Center. Opened in 1983 after extensive renovation, the hotel overlooks Golden Gate Park. The rooms are cozy, with fireplaces in many of them. **www.stanyanpark.com**

SAN FRANCISCO Inn on Castro $$$

321 Castro St, 94114 **Tel** *(415) 861-0321* **Rooms** *12* **Map** *10 D2*

The Inn on Castro, a fully-restored Edwardian building, blends old and modern, with eclectic flower bouquets and modern art adorning the traditional interiors. It is perfectly poised in the heart of the Castro District, and offers guest suites and self-service apartments. A free Continental breakfast is served daily. **www.innoncastro2.com**

THE BAY AREA

BENICIA Union Hotel $$

401 1st St, 94510 **Tel** *(707) 746-0110* **Fax** *(707) 745-3032* **Rooms** *22* **Road map** *inset B*

A charming inn on the Bay offering nicely appointed rooms, each with private baths and Jacuzzis. Furnished with period pieces, the inn recalls a slice of old California. Select suites have spectacular water views. Breakfast is included. They also offer special rates to corporate travelers. **www.unionhotelbenicia.com**

BENICIA Jeffersen Street Mansion $$$$$

1063 Jefferson St, 94510 **Tel** *(707) 746-0684* **Fax** *(707) 746-1639* **Rooms** *5* **Road map** *inset B*

This Civil War-era military mansion was graciously restored, and serves as an elegant B&B with comfortable accommodations and great food. The rooms are luxurious and appointed with period antiques and upscale bath amenities. The service is also exceptional. **www.jeffersonstreetmansion.com**

BERKELEY Bancroft Hotel $$

2680 Bancroft Way, 94704 **Tel** *(510) 549-1000* **Fax** *(510) 549-1070* **Rooms** *22* **Road map** *inset B*

Located across from the UC Berkeley campus *(see p418)*, this former women's club was designed in the Arts and Crafts style. Beautifully maintained rooms feature all the latest amenities, and many have large balconies or decks. The property is adjacent to a popular outdoor café, Caffè Strada. **www.bancrofthotel.com**

BERKELEY Rose Garden Inn $$

2740 Telegraph Ave, 94705 **Tel** *(510) 549-2145* **Fax** *(510) 549-1085* **Rooms** *49*   **Road map** *inset B*

A beautiful Victorian inn set in five buildings surrounded by pretty gardens and within walking distance of the campus. Rooms are decorated in a variety of motifs, but all feature comfortable amenities and plenty of space. Complimentary wireless Internet access and breakfast included. **www.rosegardeninn.com**

BERKELEY Hotel Durant $$$

2600 Durant Ave, 94704 **Tel** *(510) 845-8981* **Fax** *(510) 486-8336* **Rooms** *140*   **Road map** *inset B*

Situated near the campus, this friendly hotel has European charm and well-appointed rooms, outfitted with linen and such amenities as a business center, high-speed Internet access, and disabled access. The lobby-level restaurant, Henry's, is a local institution and gets very crowded on sporting-event days. **www.hoteldurant.com**

BERKELEY Claremont Resort & Spa $$$$$

41 Tunnel Rd, 94705 **Tel** *(510) 843-3000* **Fax** *(510) 843-3229* **Rooms** *279*   **Road map** *inset B*

A large, historic retreat set in the hills above Berkeley, near the border with Oakland. Facilities include comfortable guest rooms, appointed with all the modern amenities, a large spa, meeting rooms, and children's programs. There are also tennis courts and a good restaurant on the premises. **www.claremontresort.com**

BOLINAS Smiley's Schooner Saloon and Hotel $

41 Wharf Rd, 94924 **Tel** *(415) 868-1311* **Fax** *(415) 868-0502* **Rooms** *5*   **Road map** *inset B*

Set in the charming coastal town of Bolinas, this intimate hotel has Western character and a noisy neighbor in the bar downstairs. Rooms are utterly basic, with no phones or TVs, but the beds are comfortable. The ambience is the main attraction here. They also have a beautiful outdoor sitting area.

HALF MOON BAY Zaballa House $$

324 Main St, 94019 **Tel** *(650) 726-9123* **Fax** *(650) 726-3921* **Rooms** *20*   **Road map** *inset B*

A charming B&B that moves at an easy pace, as is the case with this coastal town. Set in the oldest still-standing house in the city, the structure is completely restored and updated to modern standards. The rooms are neat and comfortable, all have private bathrooms and some have a fireplace. **www.zaballahouse.net**

HALF MOON BAY Mill Rose Inn $$$

615 Mill St, 94019 **Tel** *(650) 726-8750* **Fax** *(650) 726-3031* **Rooms** *6*   **Road map** *inset B*

A friendly, English country-style inn situated near shops and galleries. The rooms are cozy, with fireplaces, period furnishings, and original watercolors. The grounds are delightful, filled with trellised rose bushes. They also offer business facilities. Very popular for weddings and romantic getaways. **www.millroseinn.com**

HALF MOON BAY Ritz Carlton Half Moon Bay $$$$$

1 Miramontes Point Rd, 94019 **Tel** *(650) 712-7000* **Fax** *(650) 712-7070* **Rooms** *261*   **Road map** *inset B*

Nestled majestically on a bluff overlooking the ocean, this elegant and relaxing resort is one of the top destinations on the North Coast. Rooms are opulently furnished and appointed with luxurious linen and bath amenities. Many have amazing ocean views. They also have a spa, a golf course, and an excellent restaurant. **www.ritzcarlton.com**

INVERNESS Manka's Inverness Lodge $$$$$

Argyle at Callendar, 94937 **Tel** *(415) 669-1034* **Fax** *(415) 669-1598* **Rooms** *14*   **Road map** *A3*

Supremely alluring, this rustic and secluded inn offers cabin-style accommodation with luxurious beds and stone fireplaces. The property is a former hunting lodge and retains remnants of its history. You can also opt for the boathouse or the annexe. The award-winning restaurant is worth a visit. **www.mankas.com**

LAFAYETTE Lafayette Park Hotel and Spa $$$$$

3287 Mount Diablo Blvd, 94549 **Tel** *(925) 283-3700* **Fax** *(925) 284-1621* **Rooms** *139*   **Road map** *inset B*

This top-rated East Bay property, central to freeway access, features well-appointed rooms, a spa, a fitness center, meeting rooms, and two excellent restaurants. Personal touches here include a complimentary wine hour each weekday evening, great service, and helpful staff. **www.lafayetteparkhotel.com**

MENLO PARK Mermaid Inn $

727 El Camino Real, 94025 **Tel** *(650) 323-9481* **Fax** *(650) 323-0662* **Rooms** *36*   **Road map** *inset B*

Mermaid Inn is a friendly, well-run hotel near the Stanford University and other Silicon Valley attractions. The property provides basic rooms, with private baths, cable TV, high-speed Internet access; some have kitchenettes. Also offers a heated swimming pool, free parking, and complimentary breakfast. **www.mermaid-inn.com**

MENLO PARK Stanford Park Hotel $$$$$

100 El Camino Real, 94025 **Tel** *(650) 322-1234* **Fax** *(650) 322-0975* **Rooms** *165*   **Road map** *inset B*

This elegant, European-style hotel is Silicon Valley's only five-star property. Features include well-appointed guest rooms, with top-grade linens and fine furnishings, as well as free coffee and newspaper each morning. There is a pool and fitness center on site. Also offers conference facilities. **www.stanfordparkhotel.com**

MILL VALLEY 707 Redwood Hwy $

707 Redwood Hwy, 94941 **Tel** *(415) 383-0340* **Fax** *(415) 381-2132* **Rooms** *52*   **Road map** *inset B*

An efficient, well-operated motor inn near San Francisco, Muir Woods, and Tiburon. The rooms are basic, with facilities such as air conditioning, phones, and TVs, but only some have Jacuzzis. There is an on-site restaurant, and the staff are friendly and attentive. Free parking is also available. **www.travelodge.com**

MILL VALLEY Acqua Hotel ⇅ 🏋 🍸 [$][$][$]

555 Redwood Hwy, 94941 ***Tel*** *(415) 380-0400* ***Fax*** *(415) 380-9696* ***Rooms*** *50* ***Road map*** *inset B*

Tucked away off the edge of the highway and in the shadows of Mount Tamalpais, this chic hotel is close to San Francisco. Acqua Hotel has an air-and-water theme, and provides modern conveniences with ample style. Rooms are simply appointed without any fuss. The staff are courteous and attentive. **www.acquahotel.com**

MOSS BEACH Seal Cove Inn ⇅ [$][$][$][$]

221 Cypress Ave, 94038 ***Tel*** *(650) 728-4114* ***Fax*** *(650) 728-9116* ***Rooms*** *10* ***Road map*** *inset B*

Each room at this charming, award-winning country inn has a fireplace and a private balcony with spectacular views of the ocean. The grounds are secluded and well maintained, close to the beach and tide pools. Additionals include complimentary breakfast and an evening wine service. **www.sealcoveinn.com**

MUIR BEACH The Pelican Inn 🍴 [$][$][$][$]

10 Pacifica Way, 94965 ***Tel*** *(415) 383-6000* ***Fax*** *(415) 383-3424* ***Rooms*** *7* ***Road map*** *inset B*

Tucked away in the hills above the ocean, this English-style inn has cozy rooms and a delightful pub, perfect for fog-shrouded afternoons. Each room is uniquely furnished with period accessories and such flourishes as four-poster beds. Some have pleasant views, and all have a private bath or shower. **www.pelicaninn.com**

OAKLAND Waterfront Plaza Hotel ⇅ 🍴 ≋ 🏋 🍸 [$][$][$][$][$]

10 Washington St, 94607 ***Tel*** *(510) 836-3800* ***Fax*** *(510) 832-5659* ***Rooms*** *144* ***Road map*** *inset B*

Situated among the shops and restaurants of Jack London Square, this full-service hotel has well-appointed rooms, some with balconies and views across the Bay toward San Francisco. Amenities include high-speed Internet access, a fitness center, a heated pool, and sauna. The staff are multi-lingual and attentive. **www.waterfrontplaza.com**

PRINCETON-BY-THE-SEA Pillar Point Inn ⇅ [$][$][$]

380 Capistrano Rd, 94018 ***Tel*** *(650) 728-7377* ***Fax*** *(650) 728-8345* ***Rooms*** *11* ***Road map*** *inset B*

A quaint, comfortable B&B in a charming seaside village. All the rooms are uniquely decorated and feature such comforts as pillowtop beds and fireplaces; most overlook the harbor. A hearty, country-style breakfast is included. They also have on-site parking. **www.pillarpointinn.com**

SAN JOSE Fairmont San Jose ⇅ 🍴 ≋ 🏋 🍸 [$][$][$]

170 S Market St, 95113 ***Tel*** *(408) 998-1900* ***Fax*** *(408) 287-1648* ***Rooms*** *808* ***Road map*** *inset B*

This full-service hotel is located in the heart of San Jose's downtown convention and entertainment district. The rooms are spacious and have all the latest amenities, especially catering to business travelers. A rooftop pool and a fully-equipped heath center are add-ons. Also has a good lobby-level restaurant. **www.fairmont.com/sanjose**

SAN JOSE Hotel De Anza ⇅ 🍴 🏋 [$][$][$]

233 W Santa Clara St, 95113 ***Tel*** *(408) 286-1000* ***Fax*** *(408) 286-0500* ***Rooms*** *101* ***Road map*** *inset B*

Located downtown near the convention center, this plush boutique hotel has beautifully appointed rooms and exemplary customer care. Rooms range from standard size to large suites, and all feature upscale amenities, including a wet bar, Jacuzzi, and a steam room. The on-site Italian restaurant is quite good. **www.hoteldeanza.com**

SAN JOSE San Jose Marriott ⇅ 🍴 ≋ 🏋 🍸 [$][$][$][$]

301 S Market St, 95113 ***Tel*** *(408) 280-1300* ***Fax*** *(408) 278-4444* ***Rooms*** *506* ***Road map*** *inset B*

Recently opened, this sleek business-friendly, high-rise hotel is located next to the convention center and within walking distance to downtown restaurants and attractions. The rooms are fully equipped with the latest technology, and many have excellent cityscape views. The street-level restaurant is exceptional. **www.sanjosemarriott.com**

SAN RAFAEL Panama Hotel ⇅ 🍴 [$][$]

4 Bayview St, 94901 ***Tel*** *(415) 457-3993* ***Fax*** *(415) 457-6240* ***Rooms*** *14* ***Road map*** *inset B*

Reminiscent of the inns of New Orleans or Key West, this charming hotel in the downtown district has well-furnished rooms decorated in different styles, some featuring clawfoot tubs and canopy beds. The staff are friendly and attentive. The restaurant features live jazz on occasion. **www.panamahotel.com**

SAUSALITO Casa Madrona Hotel ⇅ 🍴 [$][$][$][$]

801 Bridgeway, 94965 ***Tel*** *(415) 332-0502* ***Fax*** *(415) 332-2537* ***Rooms*** *34* ***Road map*** *inset B*

Built on a hillside, this elegant hotel features a mix of rooms, from historic and eclectically decorated, to modern and sleekly furnished. Casa Madrona has a top-notch spa offering various body and holistic treatments, and an excellent Italian restaurant at the lobby level. **www.casamadrona.com**

SAUSALITO Hotel Alta Mira 🍴 [$][$][$][$]

125 Bulkley Ave, 94965 ***Tel*** *(415) 332-1350* ***Fax*** *(415) 331-3862* ***Rooms*** *27* ***Road map*** *inset B*

Nestled on a hill above the town, rooms at this enchanting hotel are intimate, sunny, comfortably furnished, and command exceptional Bay views. The dining room and public area offer sweeping vistas. Accommodation is available in the main house or the cottages. The service is prompt and friendly. **www.sausalitoaltamira.com**

SAUSALITO The Inn Above Tide ⇅ [$][$][$][$][$]

30 El Portal, 94965 ***Tel*** *(415) 332-9535* ***Fax*** *(415) 332-6714* ***Rooms*** *29* ***Road map*** *inset B*

Set in an out-of-the-way corner of town, this boutique property is nonetheless centrally located to all of the shops and galleries. The inn is perched directly above the water, and each stylish room features balconies with great views of the Bay and San Francisco. Well suited to business travelers. **www.innabovetide.com**

WALNUT CREEK Marriott Hotel $$$$$

2355 N Main St, 94596 **Tel** *(925) 934-2000* **Fax** *(925) 934-6374* **Rooms** *338* **Road map** *inset B*

Situated close to the area freeways and public transit, this full-service hotel is well equipped for the business traveler. Rooms are spacious and nicely appointed, with large work desks. Hotel amenities include an outdoor pool and a complete fitness center. Also has a games room for children. **www.marriott.com**

THE NORTH

ARCATA Best Western Arcata Inn $

4827 Valley W Blvd, 95521 **Tel** *(707) 826-0313* **Fax** *(707) 826-0365* **Rooms** *62* **Road map** *A2*

A well-operated hotel situated close to many shops and restaurants and several landmarks, including the university. The rooms are clean, and a few guest comforts are offered, including laundry, free high-speed Internet access, and Continental breakfast. The grounds feature a heated indoor pool and a hot tub. **www.bestwestern.com**

ARCATA Fairwinds Motel $

1674 G St, 95521 **Tel** *(707) 822-4824* **Fax** *(707) 822-0569* **Rooms** *27* **Road map** *A2*

A tidy, family-run hotel across from Humboldt State University, that provides basic amenities at very reasonable prices. They also have wireless Internet access. The staff are friendly and accommodating. Fairwinds Motel is close to various eateries, boutiques, business centers, the beach, and Arcata Marsh. **www.fairwindsmotelarcata.com**

ARCATA Hotel Arcata $$

708 9th St, 95521 **Tel** *(707) 826-0217* **Fax** *(707) 826-1737* **Rooms** *32* **Road map** *A2*

Situated on the town's central square, this friendly historic hotel features comfortable rooms, furnished with clawfoot tubs and period antiques, as well as many modern amenities. The suites are spacious and overlook the square. They also have conference rooms. The staff are friendly. **www.hotelarcata.com**

CRESCENT CITY Curly Redwood Lodge $

701 Redwood Hwy S, 95531 **Tel** *(707) 464-2137* **Fax** *(707) 464-1655* **Rooms** *36* **Road map** *A1*

This rustic hotel earned its name from the distinctive curled grain of the redwood tree, polished remnents of which are visible throughout. The rooms are spacious, with cable TV and phones. It is close to the area's many restaurants. Activities such as surfing and river rafting can also be arranged here. **www.curlyredwoodlodge.com**

CRESCENT CITY Hampton Inn & Suites $$$

100 A St, 95531 **Tel** *(707) 465-5400* **Fax** *(707) 465-0962* **Rooms** *53* **Road map** *A1*

This clean and efficiently run property enjoys an incredible location right at the beach, and many of its rooms enjoy similar views from balconies overlooking the rugged surf. Spacious rooms include comfortable beds, free movies, and complimentary breakfast. The staff are swift and amicable. **www.hamptoninn.com**

DUNSMUIR Caboose Motel $$

100 Railroad Park Rd, 96025 **Tel** *(530) 235-4440* **Fax** *(530) 235-4470* **Rooms** *27* **Road map** *B2*

Caboose Motel offers lodging that is decidedly unique and quirky. The comfy rooms are built into renovated railroad cabooses, arranged in a circle around a central swimming pool. The restaurant displays an impressive collection of railroad memorabilia. **www.rrpark.com**

EUREKA Quality Inn $

1209 4th St, 95501 **Tel** *(707) 443-1601* **Fax** *(707) 444-8365* **Rooms** *60* **Road map** *A2*

A chain hotel in the heart of old town Eureka, providing basic amenities such as a swimming pool and sauna. Some rooms have whirlpool baths. The hotel offers special rates and upgrade considerations for business travelers. They also serve an elaborate Continental breakfast. **www.qualityinneureka.com**

EUREKA Abigail's "Elegant Victorian Mansion" $$

1406 C St, 95501 **Tel** *(707) 444-3144* **Rooms** *958* **Road map** *A2*

This elegant B&B is situated in a historic Victorian gem – a landmark 1888 structure that has been lovingly preserved and restored. Operated with a friendly touch, the inn has comfortable rooms appointed with period furnishings. Rates include a hearty breakfast. Grounds feature lovely gardens and a croquet lawn. **www.eureka-california.com**

EUREKA Best Western Humboldt Bay Inn $$

232 W 5th St, 95501 **Tel** *(707) 443-2234* **Fax** *(707) 443-3489* **Rooms** *114* **Road map** *A2*

The rooms at this chain hotel, located close to the coast and near redwood forests, are clean and comfortable. On-site amenities include indoor and outdoor heated swimming pools, a business center, a spa, and a nice garden atrium. A complimentary limo service to local restaurants is available on select nights. **www.bestwestern.com**

EUREKA Clarion Resort $$

2223 4th St, 95501 **Tel** *(707) 442-3261* **Fax** *(707) 442-2317* **Rooms** *68* **Road map** *A2*

Efficiently run, Clarion Resort is close to the downtown area and within easy driving distance to many beaches. Rooms are spacious and well appointed, with microwaves and refrigerators. Geared towards business travelers, they offer large work desks and free Internet access. Breakfast is included. **www.choicehotels.com**

Key to Price Guide *see p524* **Key to Symbols** *see back cover flap*

EUREKA Carter House Inns

301 L St, 95501 **Tel** *(707) 444-8062* **Fax** *(707) 444-8067* **Rooms** *24*   **Road map** *A2*

Rooms at this gracious hotel are in four different Victorian-era buildings, including cozy cottages and a renovated historic house. All rooms are well appointed and come with breakfast and evening wine service. The restaurant is memorable, the wine shop boasts an excellent collection, and the service is friendly. **www.carterhouse.com**

FERNDALE Gingerbread Mansion

400 Berding St, 95536 **Tel** *(707) 786-4000* **Fax** *(707) 786-4381* **Rooms** *11*   **Road map** *A2*

The rooms at this historic fairytale-like inn range from small and intimate to grand and opulent, with period furnishings and clawfoot tubs. The grounds feature lovely English gardens, and the staff are prompt and attentive. Many special rates and packages are offered online. **www.gingerbread-mansion.com**

GARBERVILLE Best Western Humboldt House Inn

701 Redwood Dr, 95542 **Tel** *(707) 923-2771* **Fax** *(707) 923-4259* **Rooms** *76*   **Road map** *A2*

This clean and well-kept motel is near the entrance to Redwoods State Park, and features spacious, nicely appointed rooms. Additionals at the property include meeting facilities, high-speed Internet access, a spa, and a heated swimming pool. Complimentary breakfast and wine and cheese service in the evening are available. **www.bestwestern.com**

GARBERVILLE Benbow Inn

445 Lake Benbow Dr, 95542 **Tel** *(707) 923-2124* **Fax** *(707) 923-2897* **Rooms** *55*   **Road map** *A2*

A gorgeously preserved historic, Tudor-style inn featuring beautiful rooms of all sizes. All the rooms are furnished with handsome accessories and relaxing beddings. The property has an excellent restaurant and lounge; live entertainment is featured on occasion. Guests are also provided use of bicycles. **www.benbowinn.com**

MCCLOUD McCloud Guest House

606 W Colombero Dr, 96057 **Tel** *(530) 964-3160* **Fax** *(530) 964-3202* **Rooms** *5*   **Road map** *B1*

McCloud Guest House is a stately former private home, built by a lumber baron, set among towering trees. Each room is cozy and well appointed with fine antiques. Stay includes a hearty breakfast, which can be enjoyed on the large wraparound porch. **www.themccloudguesthouse.com**

MOUNT LASSEN Mineral Lodge

PO Box 160 Mineral, 96063 **Tel** *(530) 595-4422* **Fax** *(530) 595-4452* **Rooms** *20*   **Road map** *B2*

A great rest stop for hikers in Lassen Volcanic National Park *(see p453)*. This modest hotel has a Western ambience, and features recently updated rooms as well as a friendly general store and a saloon. The owners also offer rentals of outdoor recreation equipment. **www.minerallodge.com**

MOUNT SHASTA Best Western Tree House Inn

111 Morgan Way, 96067 **Tel** *(530) 926-3101* **Fax** *(530) 926-3542* **Rooms** *95*   **Road map** *A2*

Part of the Best Western chain, this comfy hotel is outfitted with redwood furniture, and has nice rooms as well as a welcoming lounge with a fireplace. Tree House Inn has a fully equipped business center, a swimming pool, non-smoking rooms, and a restaurant on the premises. Also caters to disabled guests. **www.bestwestern.com**

MOUNT SHASTA Mount Shasta Ranch Bed & Breakfast

1008 W A Barr Rd, 96067 **Tel** *(530) 926-3870* **Fax** *(530) 926-6882* **Rooms** *8*   **Road map** *A2*

The rooms at this B&B are spacious and well equipped with minimalist facilities. Most have views of the mountain, and are decorated with antiques and queen size beds. The main house features rooms with huge baths. They also have a games room with a pool table. **www.stayinshasta.com**

MOUNT SHASTA Mount Shasta Resort

1000 Siskiyou Lake Blvd, 96067 **Tel** *(530) 926-3030* **Fax** *(530) 926-0333* **Rooms** *64*   **Road map** *A2*

Set below the towering Mount Shasta, this tranquil recreational resort offers rooms in private chalets, as well as more basic woodland accommodation. Rooms are decently furnished and equipped with all the necessary amenities. They also have a spa and an 18-hole golf course on the premises. **www.mountshastaresort.com**

MOUNT SHASTA Cold Creek Inn

724 N Mount Shasta Blvd, 96067 **Tel** *(800) 292-9421* **Fax** *(530) 926-9852* **Rooms** *18*   **Road map** *A2*

Rooms at this friendly hotel are simple, but offer such facilities as pillowtop beds, cable TV, air conditioning, and high-speed data ports. Most rooms have great views of the mountain. A new suite with a kitchenette was recently added. Non-smoking, and pets are not allowed. **www.coldcreekinn.com**

WEAVERVILLE Motel Trinity

1112 Main St, 96093 **Tel** *(530) 623-2129* **Fax** *(530) 623-6007* **Rooms** *25*   **Road map** *A2*

Rooms in this mountain hotel have pine-paneled walls, and some feature whirlpool tubs and kitchenettes. They also have a heated swimming pool and a shady lawn area. The property is close to many outdoor recreational pursuits, including hiking and stream fishing. **http://moteltrinity.shasta-trinity.com/**

WEAVERVILLE Best Western Victorian Inn

1709 Main St, 96093 **Tel** *(530) 623-4432* **Fax** *(530) 623-4264* **Rooms** *65*   **Road map** *A2*

This clean, well-run hotel is outfitted in a Victorian motif. The rooms are tidy, comfortable, and nicely appointed. On-site amenities include meeting rooms, an outdoor pool, free Continental breakfast, and parking. Friendly staff can arrange activities such as golfing, fishing, boating, jet skiing, and much more. **www.bestwestern.com**

WEAVERVILLE Weaverville Hotel ⓢⓢⓢⓢ
203 Main St, 96093 **Tel** *(530) 623-2222* **Rooms** *8* **Road map** *A2*

Set in the upper floors of a historic building in the heart of town, this old-fashioned hotel names its cozy rooms after the county's former gold mines. Some rooms have charming four-poster beds and clawfoot tubs. The Victorian-style parlor has an attractive fireplace where you can relax with a book from their library. **www.weavervillehotel.com**

WINE COUNTRY

BODEGA BAY Bodega Coast Inn 🔲🔳 ⓢⓢⓢⓢ
521 Coast Hwy 1, 94923 **Tel** *(707) 875-2217* **Fax** *(707) 875-2964* **Rooms** *44* **Road map** *A3*

A recently remodeled property on the coast, and surrounded by cypress trees. All the rooms are bright, spacious, and well appointed. Suites have color TVs, coffee makers, refrigerators, fireplaces, and whirlpool tubs. Close to a golf course and other recreation areas. Also suited to business travelers. **www.bodegacoastinn.com**

BOYES HOT SPRINGS Fairmont Sonoma Mission Inn & Spa 🔲🔟🔳🔳🔳 ⓢⓢⓢⓢⓢ
18140 Sonoma Hwy, 95476 **Tel** *(707) 938-9000* **Fax** *(707) 938-4250* **Rooms** *250* **Road map** *A3*

A beautiful hotel set on secluded grounds close to a golf course and many local wineries. A recent renovation added updated amenities such as a minibar and air conditioning in each luxurious room, and spruced up the grounds, including the top-rated spa and an excellent restaurant. **www.fairmont.com/sonoma**

CALISTOGA Dr Wilkinson's Hot Springs Resort 🔲🔳🔳🔳 ⓢⓢ
1507 Lincoln Ave, 94515 **Tel** *(707) 942-4102* **Fax** *(707) 942-4412* **Rooms** *42* **Road map** *A3*

Since 1952 this modest hotel has placed Calistoga on the map with its hot springs and rejuvenating mud baths. Still family run, the property was recently renovated, and features the latest facilities in each room, as well as an enhanced menu of spa services. The front veranda is perfect for people watching. **www.drwilkinson.com**

CALISTOGA Calistoga Hot Springs Resort Motel 🔲🔳🔳🔳 ⓢⓢⓢ
1006 Washington St, 94515 **Tel** *(707) 942-6269* **Fax** *(707) 942-4212* **Rooms** *57* **Road map** *A3*

This modest hotel offers good value with its comfortable rooms, all with kitchenettes. There are four, naturally heated pools on the property. They also have a meeting room with a wet bar and an outdoor deck offering panoramic views. The staff are friendly, and the property is close to town. **www.calistogaspa.com**

CALISTOGA Comfort Inn Napa Valley North 🔲🔳🔳 ⓢⓢⓢ
1865 Lincoln Ave, 94515 **Tel** *(707) 942-9400* **Fax** *(707) 942-5262* **Rooms** *54* **Road map** *A3*

Rooms are bare bones but decent at this budget property located within walking distance of the town center and within close proximity to many wineries. Amenities include a swimming pool, sauna, spa, and tennis courts. The staff are courteous and attentive. They also have a few rooms for disabled guests. **www.comfortinn.com**

CALISTOGA Indian Springs 🔳🔳🔳 ⓢⓢⓢⓢ
1712 Lincoln Ave, 94515 **Tel** *(707) 942-4913* **Fax** *(707) 942-4919* **Rooms** *17* **Road map** *A3*

A classic spa resort that helped start the mud bath trend, this friendly hotel sits on thermal geysers and volcanic ash, and uses both for relaxing and rejuvenating its guests. The rooms and bungalows are well appointed, situated around a central courtyard. The historic mineral water pool is the best in town. **www.indianspringscalistoga.com**

GEYSERVILLE Geyserville Inn 🔲🔟🔳 ⓢⓢ
21714 Geyserville Ave, 95441 **Tel** *(707) 857-4343* **Fax** *(707) 857-4411* **Rooms** *38* **Road map** *A3*

A great location as there are more than 70 wineries within a 15-mile (24-km) radius of this friendly, family-run hotel. Rooms are spacious and have been designed on various wine themes. Some feature fireplaces and balconies. Geyserville Inn also has a swimming pool, spa, and a good restaurant. **www.geyservilleinn.com**

GUALALA Whale Watch Inn 🔲🔟 ⓢⓢⓢⓢ
35100 Hwy 1, 95445 **Tel** *(800) 942-5342* **Fax** *(707) 884-4815* **Rooms** *18* **Road map** *A3*

If the time of year is right, you might actually see a whale from your room at this intimate, secluded inn perched above the shore on a cliff. Accommodation ranges from luxurious suites to cozy, inn-style rooms, with no phone or TV. Fireplaces, refrigerators, and private baths are a plus. **www.whalewatchinn.com**

HEALDSBURG Best Western Dry Creek Inn 🔲🔟🔳🔳🔳 ⓢⓢ
198 Dry Creek Rd, 95448 **Tel** *(707) 433-0300* **Fax** *(707) 433-1129* **Rooms** *103* **Road map** *A3*

A budget-conscious hotel near the town plaza and many wineries, this Spanish-motif inn has spacious rooms with comfortable amenities, including cable TV, refrigerators, and free high-speed Internet access. Complimentary breakfast and a bottle of wine at check-in. There is also a fitness center and a pool. **www.drycreekinn.com**

HEALDSBURG Camellia Inn 🔲🔳 ⓢⓢⓢⓢ
211 N St, 95448 **Tel** *(707) 433-8182* **Fax** *(707) 433-8130* **Rooms** *9* **Road map** *A3*

A romantic inn near the town center, occupying a Victorian house dating to 1869. The hotel is set among gardens of the namesake flower, and features comfortably appointed guest rooms, with fireplaces and whirlpool tubs. Service is exceptional. Staff can arrange activities such as fishing, boating, waterskiing, and more. **www.camelliainn.com**

Key to Price Guide *see p524* **Key to Symbols** *see back cover flap*

HEALDSBURG Hotel Healdsburg ⬚⏹⛆🏃📺 $$$$$

*25 Matheson St, 95448 **Tel** (707) 431-2800 **Fax** (707) 431-0414 **Rooms** 55* **Road map** *A3*

Located in the heart of town, this sleek, stylish hotel features extravagant guest rooms, many with huge soak tubs and private balconies, as well as every conceivable amenity. The atmosphere is completed by an on-site spa and restaurant, both outstanding. They have live jazz on Friday and Saturday evenings. **www.hotelhealdsburg.com**

MENDOCINO Mendocino Hotel ⬚⏹⛆ $$

*45080 Main St, 95460 **Tel** (707) 937-0511 **Fax** (707) 937-0513 **Rooms** 51* **Road map** *A3*

A Victorian-era hotel overlooking the coast, featuring period furnishing in its well-kept guest rooms. Some rooms have commanding ocean views. The garden suites are a contemporary alternative to the historic original house. It also caters to business travelers. **www.mendocinohotel.com**

MENDOCINO MacCallum House ⬚⏹⛆🏃📺 $$$

*45020 Albion St, 95460 **Tel** (707) 937-0289 **Fax** (707) 937-2243 **Rooms** 19* **Road map** *A3*

Rooms at this charming coastal inn are set in various historic structures, and range from the antiques-filled main house to private cottages with fireplaces and decks. The landscaped gardens are lovely. Within walking distance to various shops and galleries in town. **www.maccallumhouse.com**

NAPA The Chateau Hotel ⛆🏃📺 $$

*195 Solano Ave, 94558 **Tel** (707) 253-9300 **Fax** (707) 253-0906 **Rooms** 115* **Road map** *A3*

A good choice for the budget-minded business traveler in the Wine Country. Located near downtown, the hotel has large and simple rooms, with basic facilities such as private baths, color TV, and air conditioning. They also have a swimming pool and a spa. The staff are courteous and helpful. **www.thechateauhotel.com**

NAPA Best Western Elm House Inn ⬚⏹ $$$$

*800 California Blvd, 94559 **Tel** (707) 255-1831 **Fax** (707) 255-8609 **Rooms** 22* **Road map** *A3*

Surprising charm and value are in equal measure at this small property, which has some fireplace rooms, as well as a spa and lovely gardens. They also have conference facilities, and a wine tasting service. A complimentary breakfast buffet is offered. Elm House Inn is near downtown and close to shops and restaurants. **www.bestwestern.com**

NAPA Embassy Suites Napa Valley ⬚⏹⛆🏃📺 $$$$

*1075 California Blvd, 94559 **Tel** (707) 253-9540 **Fax** (707) 253-9202 **Rooms** 205* **Road map** *B3*

Centrally located with easy access to downtown shops and restaurants and to the area's wineries, this well-run hotel has surprising charm and comfortable amenities. Rooms are suite size and feature wet bars, ovens, and refrigerators. The grounds have two swimming pools, a cocktail lounge, and a spa. Free breakfast. **www.embassynapa.com**

NAPA Carneros Inn ⬚⏹⛆🏃📺 $$$$$

*4048 Sonoma Hwy, 94559 **Tel** (707) 299-4900 **Fax** (707) 299-4950 **Rooms** 86* **Road map** *B3*

Operated by the owners of a popular Napa winery, this inn makes an effortless blend of Wine Country charm and urban sophistication. Situated on a sprawling vineyard, the luxurious property features stylish rooms designed to reflect the bucolic surroundings. Also has an excellent restaurant and a serene pool. **www.thecarnerosinn.com**

NAPA Poetry Inn ⛆ $$$$$

*6380 Silverado Trail, 94558 **Tel** (707) 944-0646 **Fax** (707) 945-0766 **Rooms** 5* **Road map** *A3*

Set on a hillside overlooking the Stags Leap district vineyards, this wonderful new inn offers casual ambience and exceptional luxury in each of its spacious rooms. Every amenity is present, from soft linen and huge tubs to outdoor showers. A gourmet breakfast is offered each morning. The balloon flights are an attraction. **www.poetryinn.com**

NAPA Silverado Country Club Resort ⬚⏹⛆🏃📺 $$$$$

*1600 Atlas Peak Rd, 94558 **Tel** (707) 257-0200 **Fax** (707) 257-2867 **Rooms** 260* **Road map** *A3*

This popular Wine Country resort is renowned for its golf course and casual sophistication. The rooms are spacious and well appointed, set in bungalows among beautiful grounds. Additional amenities include indoor and outdoor swimming pools, a top-rated spa, fitness center, tennis, and golf. **www.silveradoresort.com**

RUTHERFORD Auberge du Soleil ⬚⏹⛆🏃📺 $$$$$

*180 Rutherford Hill Rd, 94573 **Tel** (707) 963-1211 **Fax** (707) 963-8764 **Rooms** 50* **Road map** *A3*

Among the top destination spa resorts in the Wine Country, this newly renovated property has stylish, comfortable rooms with fireplaces, Italian linen, flat-screen TVs, coffee makers, and Internet access. Rooms offer spectacular views of the valley. They also have an exceptional restaurant. **www.aubergedusoleil.com**

SANTA ROSA Hotel La Rose ⬚⏹🏃 $$

*308 Wilson St, 95401 **Tel** (707) 579-3200 **Fax** (707) 579-3247 **Rooms** 49* **Road map** *A3*

A friendly hotel in the heart of the historic downtown district, with simple rooms and country ambience. Rooms are well appointed and offer some updated features. Well suited to business travelers as they also have conference rooms. Complimentary breakfast is served, and there is a popular restaurant at lobby level. **www.hotellarose.com**

SANTA ROSA Vintners Inn ⬚⏹🏃 $$$$

*4350 Barnes Rd, 95403 **Tel** (707) 575-7350 **Fax** (707) 575-1426 **Rooms** 44* **Road map** *A3*

With European style and country charm, this inn offers a quintessential Wine Country experience. The hotel is set amid working vineyards, and provides luxuriously appointed rooms and suites arranged around a central fountain. Top-notch bath accessories are a plus. The restaurant is one of the region's best dining spots. **www.vintnersinn.com**

SONOMA El Pueblo Inn

⬜🔟🏊♿🔟 $$$$

896 W Napa St, 95476 **Tel** *(707) 996-3651* **Fax** *(707) 935-5988* **Rooms** *53*   **Road map** *A3*

Located close to the town's plaza, this charming, family-run inn has lovely grounds and rooms appointed with modest style and casual comfort. Most rooms face the garden and offer privacy. The Sonoma rooms' facilities include DVD players and private patios. Spa treatments and a whirlpool are add-ons. **www.elpuebloinn.com**

SONOMA Lodge at Sonoma

⬜🔟🏊♿🔟 $$$$$

1325 Broadway, 95476 **Tel** *(707) 935-6600* **Fax** *(707) 935-6829* **Rooms** *182*   **Road map** *A3*

This large, family-friendly hotel is located near the historic plaza, and offers comfortable, luxurious rooms arranged around a swimming pool and deck. The service is top quality and there is a fine spa and restaurant on premises. Guests can also rent bikes or enjoy golf nearby. **www.thelodgeatsonoma.com**

SONOMA MacArthur Place

⬜🔟🏊♿🔟 $$$$$

29 E MacArthur St, 95476 **Tel** *(707) 938-2929* **Fax** *(707) 933-9833* **Rooms** *64*   **Road map** *A3*

This historic inn near the town's central plaza has recently added cottages, wonderfully appointed with overstuffed beds, fireplaces, and DVD players. A state-of-the-art fitness center, spa, and pool are add-ons. The grounds are well manicured and private. There is an excellent steak house on site. **www.macarthurplace.com**

ST. HELENA White Sulphur Springs Resort

🏊 $$$

3100 White Sulphur Springs Rd, 94574 **Tel** *(707) 963-8588* **Fax** *(707) 963-2890* **Rooms** *37*   **Road map** *A3*

A true Wine Country retreat, with simple cabin-style rooms set on secluded grounds, and luxuries such as hammocks, lounge chairs, and shaded picnic tables. There are no televisions or phones in the rooms. The spa treatments and sulfur springs are the attraction here. **www.whitesulphursprings.com**

ST. HELENA Harvest Inn

🏊🔟 $$$$$

One Main St, 94574 **Tel** *(707) 963-9463* **Fax** *(707) 963-4402* **Rooms** *54*   **Road map** *A3*

Though it is just off the highway, this cozy inn feels a world away. Rooms are rustic, but perfectly appointed; most have fireplaces and private decks overlooking vineyards. Leisure facilities include a swimming pool, massage and spa treatments, or mountain biking. Close to various shops and restaurants in town. **www.harvestinn.com**

ST. HELENA Meadowood Resort Hotel

⬜🔟🏊♿🔟 $$$$$

900 Meadowood Lane, 94574 **Tel** *(707) 963-3646* **Fax** *(707) 963-3532* **Rooms** *99*   **Road map** *A3*

Tucked in the hills of the Stags Leap district, this intimate retreat features simply elegant rooms, appointed with casual sophistication. The resort presents a lifestyle of health and recreation; the grounds feature tennis courts, a croquet lawn, and a golf course. The restaurant serves delicious cuisine. **www.meadowood.com**

YOUNTVILLE Napa Valley Lodge

⬜🏊♿🔟 $$$$$

2230 Madison St, 94599 **Tel** *(707) 944-2468* **Fax** *(707) 944-9362* **Rooms** *55*   **Road map** *A3*

Situated at the edge of town, this friendly hotel has simple, but spacious rooms; some with fireplaces and balconies. A complimentary breakfast buffet is offered each morning. Complete business amenities are available as well. The pool, spa, sauna, and fitness center are a plus. **www.napavalleylodge.com**

YOUNTVILLE Villagio Inn & Spa

⬜🔟🏊♿🔟 $$$$$

6481 Washington St, 94599 **Tel** *(707) 944-8877* **Rooms** *55*   **Road map** *A3*

At once casual and elegant, this centrally located inn features guest rooms with large baths, luxurious robes, balconies, and fireplaces. Other amenities include a business center, a swimming pool with a trellis-covered deck, and Jacuzzi. Complimentary champagne breakfast. Staff can arrange outdoor activities as well. **www.villagio.com**

GOLD COUNTRY AND THE CENTRAL VALLEY

AMADOR CITY Imperial Hotel

🔟 $$

14202 Hwy 49, 95601 **Tel** *(209) 267-9172* **Fax** *(209) 267-9249* **Rooms** *6*   **Road map** *B3*

Set in a restored brick structure dating to 1879, this charming little hotel offers comfortable guest rooms decorated in whimsical Victorian-era style. Service is friendly, and the location offers convenient access to the region's vineyards. Good restaurant on site, and the bar has fine Californian and imported wines and beers. **www.imperialamador.com**

AUBURN Best Western Golden Key

⬜🏊♿🔟 $

13450 Lincoln Way, 95603 **Tel** *(530) 885-8611* **Fax** *(530) 888-0319* **Rooms** *68*   **Road map** *B3*

Rooms are comfortable at this no-frills hotel, which has a rustic appeal, and features a swimming pool, spa, and a lovely rose garden. Complimentary breakfast and high-speed Internet access are included. A few rooms are especially adapted for disabled guests. Children 17 and below are free. **www.bestwestern.com**

GRASS VALLEY Best Western Gold Country

⬜🏊♿ $

11972 Sutton Way, 95945 **Tel** *(530) 273-1393* **Fax** *(530) 273-4229* **Rooms** *84*   **Road map** *B3*

The rooms at this friendly hotel are situated in five buildings on pine tree-covered grounds. Amenities include a swimming pool, spa, high-speed Internet access, and complimentary tea and coffee all day. Continental breakfast is served on the patio. **www.bestwestern.com**

Key to Price Guide *see p524* **Key to Symbols** *see back cover flap*

GRASS VALLEY Holbrooke Hotel and Restaurant

212 W Main St, 95945 **Tel** *(530) 273-1353* **Fax** *(530) 273-0434* **Rooms** *27*   **Road map** *B3*

Established in 1851, this historic landmark property is still a standard of hospitality in the Gold Country. The hotel retains its Old West charm, but at the same time offers many modern conveniences. Rooms have exposed brick walls, private baths, and clawfoot tubs. They also have a library. **www.holbrooke.com**

MURPHYS Murphys Historic Hotel and Lodge

457 Main St, 95247 **Tel** *(209) 728-3444* **Fax** *(209) 728-1590* **Rooms** *35*   **Road map** *B3*

Like a story from California's Wild West, this historic stone-made hotel has old-time charm and a lively saloon. Most rooms are decorated in period style, but there are some updated rooms available in the "modern" wing. Free Continental breakfast. It is also close to wineries, galleries, and recreational centers. **www.murphyshotel.com**

MURPHYS Murphys Suites

134 Hwy 4, 95247 **Tel** *(209) 728-2121* **Fax** *(209) 728-9442* **Rooms** *70*   **Road map** *B3*

This friendly inn is close to the Ironstone winery, and is among the more popular in the area, beloved for its value and attention to guest comfort. It has spacious rooms and suites, all with refrigerators and microwaves. Luxurious bed linen and bath accessories are provided, and free espresso and juice delivered to your room. **www.centralsierralodging.com**

NEVADA CITY National Hotel

211 Broad St, 95959 **Tel** *(530) 265-4551* **Fax** *(530) 265-2445* **Rooms** *42*   **Road map** *B3*

This Victorian-style hotel has been in operation since 1855 and still recalls the thriving Gold Rush era, from the friendly staff to the covered sidewalk. The rooms are quaint and outfitted in period decorations; most have private baths. The swimming pool is perfect for sunny afternoons. **www.thenationalhotel.com**

NEVADA CITY The Parsonage Bed and Breakfast

427 Broad St, 95959 **Tel** *(530) 265-9478* **Fax** *(530) 265-8147* **Rooms** *6*   **Road map** *B3*

This Victorian-era B&B is quiet and romantic, and offers an excellent country-style breakfast, which is included in the room rate. The rooms are comfortable, each with a private bath, and most are furnished in period detail. Conveniently located close to Sacramento and Reno. **www.theparsonage.net**

NEVADA CITY Emma Nevada House

528 E Broad St, 95959 **Tel** *(530) 265-4415* **Fax** *(530) 265-4416* **Rooms** *6*   **Road map** *B3*

A charming B&B furnished with beautiful antiques, featuring a relaxing sunroom for afternoon reading. The rooms are tidy and comfortably appointed with Jacuzzis or walk-in showers. The inn has been completely restored and given modern amenities. **www.emmanevadahouse.com**

SACRAMENTO Embassy Suites Hotel

100 Capitol Mall, 95814 **Tel** *(916) 326-5000* **Fax** *(916) 326-5001* **Rooms** *242*   **Road map** *B3*

This contemporary hotel is situated between the old town and the business district. It has spacious two-room suites offering facilities such as TVs, coffee makers, microwaves, and refrigerators. The property boasts many works by local artists; there is a lively lounge in the lobby. Complimentary breakfast is included. **www.embassysuites.com**

SACRAMENTO River Boat Delta King Hotel

1000 Front St, 95814 **Tel** *(800) 825-5464* **Fax** *(916) 444-5314* **Rooms** *44*   **Road map** *B3*

Set in a permanently docked historic paddle wheeler, this charming hotel features comfortable rooms with period furnishings, many with superb river views. The boat also has a theater and a restaurant that is quite good. It holds regular wine classes, and hosts a business center as well. **www.deltaking.com**

SACRAMENTO Sterling Hotel

1300 H St, 95814 **Tel** *(800) 365-7660* **Fax** *(916) 448-8066* **Rooms** *17*   **Road map** *B3*

This elegant inn, set in a beautifully restored Victorian mansion, has period furnishings in its rooms, as well as select Asian pieces. Accommodations are large, and feature marble baths, Jacuzzis, and lavish linen. The staff are helpful and chivalrous. It is close to the Sacramento convention center. **www.sterlinghotel.com**

SACRAMENTO Hyatt Regency

1209 L St, 95814 **Tel** *(916) 443-1234* **Fax** *(916) 321-3099* **Rooms** *503*   **Road map** *B3*

This smoothly operated hotel is central to downtown and directly across from the Capitol building. The rooms are spacious and well appointed with cable TV, full bath amenities, and Wi-Fi access. There is a good lobby-level lounge near the pool and a fitness center. The IMAX theater is just behind the hotel. **www.sacramento.hyatt.com**

SOMERSET Fitzpatrick Winery and Lodge

7740 Fair Play Rd, 95684 **Tel** *(800) 6245-9166* **Fax** *(530) 620-6838* **Rooms** *5*   **Road map** *B3*

This quaint B&B is set in the hills above El Dorado wine country. Rooms are rustic and comfortably appointed, and the inn is run with family-like zeal. Features include a lap pool and an outdoor hot tub. A hearty breakfast is included. They also have a wine cellar where wine tasting is held. **www.fitzpatrickwinery.com**

SONORA Gunn House Hotel

286 S Washington St, 95370 **Tel** *(209) 532-3421* **Rooms** *20*   **Road map** *B3*

Quaint, with a rich history, this eclectic inn dates to 1850, and has the distinction of being the first two-story structure in town. The meticulously restored property is now a well-run hotel, appointed with period antiques and mementos. Rooms are cozy and quiet. Grounds feature lovely gardens, a nice pool, and a patio. **www.gunnhousehotel.com**

SONORA Lavendar Hill $$

683 Barretta St, 95370 **Tel** *(209) 532-9024* **Rooms** *4*   **Road map** *B3*

An old-fashioned Victorian inn set among beautiful flower gardens and overlooking the town. Rooms are intimate and romantic and all feature private baths. The building has a pleasant sitting room and a library. The friendly staff can arrange outdoor activities such as biking, hiking, fishing, and horse riding. **www.lavenderhill.com**

SONORA Sonora Days Inn & Café $$

160 S Washington St, 95370 **Tel** *(209) 532-2400* **Fax** *(209) 532-4542* **Rooms** *64*   **Road map** *B3*

Set in a historic Spanish-style structure, this friendly hotel has hosted the likes of Grace Kelly and Drew Barrymore. The facility was recently remodeled, and has well-furnished rooms and an annexe with microwaves and refrigerators. They also have conference facilities and a rooftop swimming pool. **www.sonoradaysinn.com**

SUTTER CREEK Grey Gables Inn $$$

161 Hanford St, 95685 **Tel** *(209) 267-1039* **Fax** *(800) 267-0998* **Rooms** *24*   **Road map** *B3*

There is a fireplace in every room at this historic inn, which has English-like country charm and friendly staff. Features include individually air-conditioned rooms, free wireless Internet access, and a full breakfast, as well as tea service in the afternoon. Ideally suited for water sports. Children under 10 are not allowed. **www.greygables.com**

SUTTER CREEK Sutter Creek Inn $$$

75 Main St, 95685 **Tel** *(209) 267-5606* **Fax** *(209) 267-9287* **Rooms** *17*   **Road map** *B3*

Built in 1859, this country-style inn has private cottages with wood-burning fireplaces, and is surrounded by shady gardens laced with walkways and hammocks. Some rooms have beds that swing from the ceiling. Sutter Creek Inn is a good base for exploring the Amador County wineries and other historic sites. **www.suttercreekinn.com**

SUTTER CREEK Foxes Inn $$$$

77 Main St, 95685 **Tel** *(209) 267-5882* **Fax** *(209) 267-0712* **Rooms** *7*   **Road map** *B3*

Well-run, Victorian-era property in the heart of the town offering cozy, individually furnished rooms; most have private entrances and such details as clawfoot tubs and fireplaces. Guests are provided with personalized breakfast times and can select anything from the menu. Breakfast is included in the price. **www.foxesinn.com**

THE HIGH SIERRAS

BISHOP Best Western Bishop Holiday Spa Lodge $

1025 N Main St, 93514 **Tel** *(760) 873-3543* **Fax** *(760) 872-4777* **Rooms** *50*   **Road map** *C4*

Rooms at this recreation hotel are spacious and available at bargain prices. Amenities include a business center, Internet access, an indoor barbecue room, a picnic area, and free parking. The beautifully manicured grounds have a hot tub and a heated swimming pool. Complimentary breakfast is offered. **www.bestwestern.com**

BISHOP Best Western Creekside Inn $$

725 N Main St, 93514 **Tel** *(760) 872-3044* **Fax** *(760) 872-1300* **Rooms** *89*   **Road map** *C4*

A comfortable, chain-run inn set on landscaped grounds alongside a stream. Rooms are spacious and comfortably appointed; all have a patio overlooking the creek. Only a few rooms have air conditioning, private baths, and kitchenettes. Amenities include a pool and Jacuzzi. **www.bestwestern.com**

EL PORTAL Cedar Lodge $$

9966 Hwy 140, 95318 **Tel** *(209) 379-2612* **Fax** *(209) 379-2712* **Rooms** *206*   **Road map** *C3*

Rooms at this family-friendly hotel range from standard size to a suite that sleeps 14. Facilities include two pools, a spa, and private river access. Some rooms have kitchenettes. Grounds feature two restaurants, a cocktail lounge, and a gift shop. Cedar Lodge is located close to the entrance of Yosemite National Park *(see pp488–91).*

FISH CAMP Narrow Gauge Inn $$

48571 Hwy 41, 93623 **Tel** *(559) 683-7720* **Fax** *(559) 683-2139* **Rooms** *26*   **Road map** *C4*

This romantic gem is located at the southern end of Yosemite, and features quaint, comfortable rooms, some with private decks. Amenities include a swimming pool and a fabulous restaurant. The staff are attentive, friendly, and can arrange outdoor activities for guests. **www.narrowgaugeinn.com**

FISH CAMP Tenaya Lodge $$

1122 Hwy 41, 93623 **Tel** *(559) 253-2005* **Rooms** *240*   **Road map** *C4*

This well-known lodge offers creature comforts and rustic appeal. Rooms are appointed with plush amenities, and some have fantastic views of the wilderness. There are nice business facilities as well. The spa and restaurant are first-rate. Tenaya Lodge also has a fitness center, indoor and outdoor pools, and retail stores. **www.tenayalodge.com**

JUNE LAKE Boulder Lodge $

2282 Hwy 158, 93529 **Tel** *(760) 648-7533* **Fax** *(760) 648-7330* **Rooms** *60*   **Road map** *C3*

This remote, year-round lodge is quiet and rustic, and close to ample outdoor recreation. The rooms are comfortable and basically appointed, with color TV, direct phone lines, and microwaves; some have kitchenettes. There is an indoor heated pool, a large whirlpool, a tennis court, and a children's playground as well. **www.boulderlodge.net**

Key to Price Guide *see p524* **Key to Symbols** *see back cover flap*

KINGS CANYON NATIONAL PARK Montecito Lodge

8000 Generals Hwy, 93633 **Tel** *(559) 565-3388* **Fax** *(559) 565-3223* **Rooms** *52*   **Road map** *C3*

With ample activity options, this mountain lodge appeals to families and large groups year-round. Rooms are lodge-style or in cabins, and feature large beds, deluxe bunks, and complete bath amenities. Camp-style activities are planned regularly for guests. Meals are included in the price. **www.mslodge.com**

KIRKWOOD Kirkwood Resort

1501 Kirkwood Meadows Dr, 95646 **Tel** *(209) 258-7000* **Fax** *(209) 258-7400* **Rooms** *120*   **Road map** *C3*

Kirkwood is a popular year-round resort featuring well-appointed rooms and suites, many with fireplaces and balconies. There are numerous activities readily available, from fishing and golf to snow skiing. The grounds host live performances and other events. The Bub's Sports Bar is lively and has huge TV screens. **www.kirkwood.com**

LEE VINING Best Western Lake View Lodge

30 Main St, 93541 **Tel** *(760) 647-6543* **Fax** *(760) 647-6325* **Rooms** *46*   **Road map** *C3*

The clean, simple rooms at this friendly hotel on the western edge of Mono Lake make a nice overnight rest spot between Southern California and Tahoe. Some rooms have kitchens. Lake-view cottages with full amenities are available as well. There are a few especially adapted rooms for disabled guests. **www.bestwestern.com**

LONE PINE Frontier Motel

1008 S Main St, 93545 **Tel** *(760) 876-5571* **Fax** *(760) 876-5357* **Rooms** *73*   **Road map** *C3*

A modest motor inn with rustic accommodations, close to many outdoor recreational activities including hiking, fishing, and golf. Rooms are basic with few frills, and some have mountain views. A large Continental breakfast and free high-speed Internet access is included. Business facilities and an outdoor pool are add-ons. **www.bestwestern.com**

MAMMOTH LAKES Shilo Inn Suites

2963 Main St, 93546 **Tel** *(760) 934-4500* **Fax** *(760) 934-7594* **Rooms** *70*   **Road map** *C4*

Conveniently located close to ski areas and other outdoor recreation, Shilo Inn offers updated amenities in suite-size rooms, with free Internet access. There is an indoor pool, spa, steam room, and a fitness center as well. The staff are friendly and helpful. It also provides a free shuttle to the airport. **www.shiloinns.com**

MAMMOTH LAKES Austria Hof Lodge

924 Canyon Blvd, 93546 **Tel** *(760) 934-2764* **Fax** *(760) 934-1880* **Rooms** *22*   **Road map** *C4*

Rooms at this charming mountain lodge were recently refurbished, and now feature facilities such as marble bathroom fixtures, DVD players, and free wireless Internet access. Some rooms have fireplaces, Jacuzzis, and kitchenettes. The staff are friendly and accommodating. **www.austriahof.com**

SOUTH LAKE TAHOE Best Western Timber Cove Inn

3411 Lake Tahoe Blvd, 96150 **Tel** *(530) 541-6722* **Fax** *(530) 541-7959* **Rooms** *262*   **Road map** *C3*

This full-service establishment offers great value for its lakeside location. Rooms are spacious and well appointed, with fireplaces and balconies overlooking the beach. Added attractions include in-room movies and Nintendo games. Close to many winter and summer recreational opportunities. **www.timbercovetahoe.com**

SOUTH LAKE TAHOE Marriott Timber Lodge

4100 Lake Tahoe Blvd, 96150 **Tel** *(530) 542-6600* **Fax** *(530) 542-6610* **Rooms** *369*   **Road map** *C3*

This large, full-service hotel is located close to both winter- and water-skiing areas, and near the casinos of Stateline. Master suites have king-size beds, full kitchens, fireplaces, optional whirlpool tubs, separate living areas, and a breakfast bar. Special online reservation rates are available as well. **www.marriott.com**

SQUAW VALLEY Resort at Squaw Creek

400 Squaw Creek Rd, 96146 **Tel** *(530) 583-6300* **Fax** *(530) 581-6632* **Rooms** *404*   **Road map** *B3*

This beautiful, luxuriously appointed resort recently underwent a complete renovation, and features top-notch rooms with plush beds, nice bath supplies, and full amenities. It also provides spa services and abundant recreation options to choose from, including golf and skiing. It offers free transportation to Squaw Valley. **www.squawcreek.com**

TAHOE CITY Tahoe City Travelodge

455 N Lake Blvd, 96146 **Tel** *(530) 583-3766* **Fax** *(530) 581-6632* **Rooms** *47*   **Road map** *B3*

This modest hotel offers good value and a central location, and is close to ample year-round outdoor recreation such as fishing, rafting, horse riding, and much more. The rooms are clean and simple, and the staff are friendly and attentive. Amenities include a Continental breakfast and an outdoor spa tub. **www.travelodge.com**

TAHOE CITY Chaney House

4725 W Lake Blvd, 96145 **Tel** *(530) 525-7333* **Fax** *(530) 525-4413* **Rooms** *4*   **Road map** *B3*

Chaney House is a charming, traditional stone and timber lodge recalling Lake Tahoe the way it used to be. It has cozy, romantic rooms, and features a large fireplace in the main room and private beach access. A good breakfast is offered each morning. Nearby activities include biking, fishing, hiking, and rafting. **www.chaneyhouse.com**

TRUCKEE Donner Lake Village Resort

15695 Donner Pass Rd, 96161 **Tel** *(530) 587-6081* **Fax** *(530) 587-8782* **Rooms** *64*   **Road map** *B3*

Set on the shore of crystal blue Donner Lake and featuring its own marina, this rustic-style lodge offers condominium-style accommodations. Fully-equipped kitchens come with two-bedroom suites and two-bath town homes. Reno's nightlife is only a 45-minute drive from this resort. **www.donnerlakevillage.com**

YOSEMITE NATIONAL PARK Wawona Hotel $$$

State Hwy 41, 95389   **Tel** *(559) 253-5635*   **Fax** *(209) 375-6601*   **Rooms** *104*   **Road map** *C3*

A landmark of the High Sierras, this charming hotel is straight out of the Old West, and is popular for its historic ambience, comfortable rooms, and its location near meadows and streams. Well suited for adventure activities, and an on-site, nine-hole golf course is available as well. Book well in advance for summer. **www.yosemitepark.com**

YOSEMITE NATIONAL PARK Yosemite Lodge $$$

Yosemite Valley, 95389   **Tel** *(559) 253-5635*   **Fax** *(209) 372-1444*   **Rooms** *245*   **Road map** *C3*

This large and popular lodge is situated on the valley floor close to the village. It offers a wide selection of accommodation, from cabins to modern-style lodge rooms with patios or balconies. Attractions include an amphitheater, food court, shops, and a post office. Internet access is available. **www.yosemitepark.com**

YOSEMITE NATIONAL PARK Ahwahnee Hotel $$$$$

Yosemite Valley, 95389   **Tel** *(559) 253-5635*   **Fax** *(209) 372-1403*   **Rooms** *123*   **Road map** *C3*

This famed historic hotel is synonymous with the valley. Opened in 1927, it is elegant and rustic, built of stone and timber, with a Native American ambience. The lodge features a soaring lobby, well-appointed rooms, and an excellent restaurant. The solarium and winter club room are great. **www.yosemitepark.com**

NORTH CENTRAL CALIFORNIA

APTOS Best Western Seacliff Inn $$$

7500 Old Dominion Court, 95003   **Tel** *(831) 688-7300*   **Fax** *(831) 685-3603*   **Rooms** *149*   **Road map** *B4*

Located close to Seacliff State Beach, this modest hotel features friendly service and surprisingly comfortable rooms, complete with upscale bath amenities, high-speed Internet access, and video games. The suites are large and have a Jacuzzi. There is also a full-service restaurant available. **www.seacliffinn.com**

APTOS Rio Sands Motel $$$

116 Aptos Beach Dr, 95003   **Tel** *(831) 688-3207*   **Fax** *(831) 688-6107*   **Rooms** *50*   **Road map** *B4*

A well-operated motel near the beach, with rooms ranging from standard to suites with kitchenettes; many feature balconies overlooking the gardens. Amenities include a swimming pool, spa, and barbecue and picnic areas. A complimentary Continental breakfast is included. Check for special off-season weekly rates. **www.riosands.com**

BIG SUR Big Sur River Inn $$$

Hwy 1, Pheneger Creek, 93920   **Tel** *(831) 667-2700*   **Fax** *(831) 667-2743*   **Rooms** *20*   **Road map** *B4*

A quaint, historic inn set on secluded grounds among massive redwoods along the river. Rooms are intimate, well appointed, and many have balconies overlooking the water. Big Sur River Inn also has a heated outdoor pool, an on-site general store, and a gift shop. **www.bigsurriverinn.com**

BIG SUR Deetjen's Big Sur Inn $$$

48865 Hwy 1, 93920   **Tel** *(831) 667-2377*   **Fax** *(831) 667-0466*   **Rooms** *20*   **Road map** *B4*

Known as much for its restaurant as its cozy, eclectic rooms, this popular inn has a personality of its own. Rooms are private and quiet, and each is furnished with a whimsical artistic touch. Guests can choose rooms with private or shared bathrooms. The staff are friendly and attentive. **www.deetjens.com**

BIG SUR Post Ranch Inn $$$$$

PO Box 219, Hwy 1, 93920   **Tel** *(831) 667-2200*   **Fax** *(831) 667-2512*   **Rooms** *30*   **Road map** *B4*

Architecturally stunning, this away-from-it-all resort features sumptuously appointed rooms, with dazzling ocean views and romantic seclusion – an unforgettable experience. Morning yoga is offered. They also have a spa, pool, and fitness center. The restaurant is exceptional. **www.postranchinn.com**

BIG SUR The Ventana Inn $$$$$

Hwy 1, 93920   **Tel** *(831) 667-2331*   **Fax** *(831) 667-2419*   **Rooms** *63*   **Road map** *B4*

This gorgeous cliffside property is one of the most stunning inns on the coast. It has rooms with romantic charm, as well as fireplaces, luxurious bath areas, and redwood decks; some have spectacular ocean views. The restaurant and spa are top-notch. They also have a spa boutique that sells unique items. **www.ventanainn.com**

CARMEL Los Laureles Lodge $$

313 W Carmel Valley Rd, 93924   **Tel** *(831) 659-2233*   **Fax** *(831) 659-0481*   **Rooms** *31*   **Road map** *B4*

Rooms at this eclectic, relaxed inn are built into former horse stables. The hotel features generous amenities in each of its rooms. The grounds boast a patio, a lovely garden, and a good restaurant and bar. Nearby recreational activities include hiking, fishing, horse riding, and tennis. **www.loslaureles.com**

CARMEL Pine Inn $$

Ocean Ave & Monte Verde, 93921   **Tel** *(831) 624-3851*   **Fax** *(831) 624-3030*   **Rooms** *47*   **Road map** *B4*

Iconic and regaled, this charming inn is the oldest in town, and still sets the tone for Carmel hospitality with its gracious rooms and friendly service. The rooms have been updated over the years to offer modern comforts to guests. The restaurant, Il Fornaio, serves excellent authentic Italian cuisine. **www.pine-inn.com**

Key to Price Guide *see p524* **Key to Symbols** *see back cover flap*

CARMEL Crystal Terrace Inn $$$

24815 Carpenter St, 93921 **Tel** *(831) 624-6000* **Fax** *(831) 624-5111* **Rooms** *17* **Road map** *B4*

Located in a wooded area outside downtown Carmel, this cozy and romantic inn is secluded, but within an easy walk to the shops, galleries, and restaurants. Rooms are well appointed, some with kitchenettes, microwaves, and wet bars. Breakfast is included. **www.crystalterraceinn.com**

CARMEL La Playa Hotel $$$

Camino Real at Eighth, 93921 **Tel** *(831) 624-6476* **Fax** *(831) 624-7966* **Rooms** *75* **Road map** *B4*

This Mediterranean-style hotel has comfortable rooms offering friendly service along with all the latest facilities. A variety of room types are available, including cottages that feel like a private vacation home. La Playa has a full spa on the premises, and is close to Monterey Bay Aquarium, Pebble Beach, and Big Sur. **www.laplayahotel.com**

CARMEL Cypress Inn $$$$

Lincoln & 7th, 93921 **Tel** *(831) 624-3871* **Fax** *(831) 624-8216* **Rooms** *52* **Road map** *B4*

An elegant inn with Spanish-style architecture, located just a few blocks from the beach. The property has well-furnished rooms with basic facilities; some have ocean views and fireplaces. Pets are welcome. Personal service is provided by the attentive staff. Actress Doris Day is the owner of this inn. **www.cypress-inn.com**

CARMEL Carmel Valley Ranch $$$$$

1 Old Ranch Rd, 93923 **Tel** *(831) 625-9500* **Fax** *(831) 624-2858* **Rooms** *144* **Road map** *B4*

This luxurious resort set on a 400-acre (121-ha) estate has a peaceful and relaxing atmosphere that makes for a memorable stay. The hotel offers oversized suites, with fireplaces and plush bath amenities. Additionals include a golf course and a spa among its facilities. Suits business travelers as well. **www.wyndham.com**

CARMEL Highlands Inn & Restaurant $$$$$

120 Highlands Dr, 93923 **Tel** *(831) 620-1234* **Fax** *(831) 626-1574* **Rooms** *142* **Road map** *B4*

Long a Carmel favorite, this splendidly rustic inn is set on an ocean bluff among coastal pines offering fabulous views. Rooms have all the modern facilities such as CD players, coffee makers, full bath amenities, refrigerators, and data ports. The restaurant is a destination unto itself. **www.highlandsinn.hyatt.com**

CARMEL Quail Lodge $$$$$

8205 Valley Greens Dr, 93923 **Tel** *(888) 828-8787* **Fax** *(831) 624-3726* **Rooms** *97* **Road map** *B4*

This wonderful, self-contained retreat features super-luxury in its guest rooms, a spa, fitness center, and restaurant. The grounds are beautiful and provide easy access to outdoor recreation. There is a top-rated golf course on the premises, with a professional trainer to assist you. **www.quaillodge.com**

MONTEREY Casa Munras Garden Hotel $$$

700 Munras Ave, 93940 **Tel** *(831) 375-2411* **Fax** *(831) 375-1365* **Rooms** *166* **Road map** *B4*

Settled on wonderfully manicured gardens, this charming hotel has cozy rooms of all sizes located in structures throughout the property. The property is close to many major local attractions such as Colton Hall Museum, California's First Theater, Fisherman's Wharf, and downtown Monterey *(see pp508-11)*. **www.casamunras-hotel.com**

MONTEREY Monterey Bay Lodge $$$

55 Camino Aguajito, 93940 **Tel** *(831) 372-8057* **Fax** *(831) 655-2933* **Rooms** *46* **Road map** *B4*

Great value and friendly service are the hallmarks of this tidy hotel situated near the Wharf and other popular attractions. Surrounded by nice gardens, the recently remodeled rooms feature comfortable bedding and the latest conveniences. It also has family suites and deluxe rooms with a fireplace and spa. **www.montereybaylodge.com**

MONTEREY Monterey Bay Inn $$$$$

242 Cannery Row, 93940 **Tel** *(831) 373-6242* **Fax** *(831) 373-7603* **Rooms** *47* **Road map** *B4*

This friendly, centrally located inn recently underwent a complete remodeling, and features modern, comfortable rooms, with excellent bath and business amenities. Many have spectacular bay views. In-room delivery of a complimentary breakfast is provided. They also have various massage treatments. **www.montereybayinn.com**

MONTEREY Monterey Plaza Hotel & Spa $$$$$

400 Cannery Row, 93940 **Tel** *(831) 646-1700* **Fax** *(831) 646-5937* **Rooms** *291* **Road map** *B4*

One of the best-known hotels in the area, this well-run establishment has European styling and is situated centrally on the bay. Spacious rooms have all the facilities, including fantastic bath accessories and high-speed Internet connections. There is a notable restaurant on the premises. **www.montereyplazahotel.com**

SANTA CRUZ Terrace Court $$$

125 Beach St, 95060 **Tel** *(831) 423-3031* **Fax** *(831) 423-2607* **Rooms** *40* **Road map** *B4*

A popular, great value motel-style hotel located within easy walking distance to the beach and Boardwalk. Terrace Court features comfortably appointed rooms and suites, ranging in size from standard to three-room family suites, many with commanding ocean views. It has an on-site surf shop, market, and deli. **www.terracecourt.com**

SANTA CRUZ Coast Santa Cruz Hotel $$$$$

175 W Cliff Dr, 95060 **Tel** *(800) 716-6199* **Fax** *(831) 427-2025* **Rooms** *163* **Road map** *B4*

Located two blocks from Boardwalk, this chain hotel offers exceptional value for its beachfront location. The rooms have been recently renovated and now offer all the comfortable amenities such as refrigerators, coffee makers, and air conditioning. Many have balconies and splendid views of the ocean. **www.coasthotels.com**

WHERE TO EAT

Of all the states in the US, California has perhaps the widest variety of places to eat. "California cuisine" – light food prepared in a range of international styles using locally grown ingredients – was pioneered by chefs such as Jeremiah Towers, Wolfgang Puck, and Alice Waters and is now internationally recognized. There is an ample number of Italian and French restaurants, but many other international cuisines are also available. In every town you can eat Japanese sushi, Thai noodles, Chinese dim sum, Mexican burritos, Middle Eastern falafel, or Indian tandoori. While ethnic cooking reflects the state's many cultures, there is also no shortage of that classic all-American meal: hamburger, French fries, and cola. The restaurants listed on pages 568–605 have been selected for their variety, service, and good value. Some typical meals served in California are shown on pages 564–5.

California diner sign

CALIFORNIA EATING PATTERNS

Some say Americans make the best breakfast in the world, and this is evident in California. From diners to top restaurants, the breakfast menu is vast. Omelettes with fries and toast, pancakes or waffles topped with fruit and syrup, and eggs, bacon, or sausage served with toast or a muffin are popular options. Less filling choices are coffee with a bagel or pastry, or cereal topped with raisins or bananas. Breakfast is served from 6:30am to 11am. Brunch extends the breakfast menu with grilled meats. It is always available on Sundays, and in selected restaurants on Saturdays, from 9am to 2pm.

California lunch is light – soup and salad or a sandwich. Dinner is the main meal of the day for Americans. Many restaurants make dinner a special occasion by setting out candles and tablecloths, and presenting the chef's specialties as creatively as possible. Dinner is served from 5:30pm to 10:30pm.

PRICES AND TIPPING

Eating out in California is very reasonable. A snack in a café should cost no more than $5 per person. A main meal in a diner will set you back up to $15. A three-course meal in a good restaurant, excluding wine, will cost $25–$30, but gourmet meals can begin at $40. Fixed-price menus are rare, but lunch menus are much cheaper and are generally very similar to the dinner menu.

Tipping should be based on service: if satisfactory, leave 15 percent; if superlative, leave 20 percent. Make sure the tip is calculated on the net cost of the meal and does not include the tax. Restaurant tax in California is up to 8.5 percent.

FAST FOOD

A ubiquitous feature of the California landscape, fast-food outlets are rarely more than five minutes away. They offer filling, inexpensive food, which stretches the travel budget for families. Chain-owned diners include Denny's, Sizzlers, and Marie Callendar's. While the seating areas are large and the selections on the menu are extensive, the food is prepared in bulk and may therefore be a little bland.

Planet Hollywood

HEALTHY EATING

A number of restaurants in California now follow the American Heart Association's guidelines for reducing cholesterol and dietary fat. A red heart beside a dish denotes an AHA-approved "Healthy Heart" meal, low in calories and cholesterol. If a restaurant does not offer such meals, you can ask your waiter to omit certain ingredients where appropriate.

Vegetarian cuisine is not a strong feature in California restaurants, but they all offer salads and many of them will make up meat-free meals for customers if requested.

Rex Restaurant in the Oviatt Building, LA

COFFEE HOUSES, TEA HOUSES, AND CAFES

Coffee houses exist all over California. At "internet" coffee houses, patrons plug into computers as they eat and drink. Other coffee houses are attached to bookstores, where customers can drink and read. Coffee houses do not offer a full menu, but specialize in drinks (coffees, sodas, juices, and wine) and cakes.

Tea houses are also popular, particularly in LA, for their elegant and subdued atmosphere.

Cafés usually have only one or two tables for outside dining, but the atmosphere inside is usually informal and long stays are encouraged.

El Paseo Restaurant, Santa Barbara *(see p577)*

Ratto's Italian delicatessen in Oakland

PICNICS AND TAKEOUTS

Delicatessens and supermarkets with deli counters stock cold meats, cheeses, pickles, and salads. They will also make up fresh sandwiches to your personal order to take-out and enjoy in one of the parks or open areas that abound in California.

You can also order takeouts from any restaurant, although the prices for this are the same as eating in the restaurant itself.

MICROBREWERY BARS

In the world of beer, micro-breweries are big news. In every city there is a healthy number of on-site brewmasters with bars serving a selection of national and international beers, but also brewing their own specials, such as Anchor Steam in San Francisco and Karl Straus Amber Lager in San Diego *(see pp566–7)*. If a beer proves successful locally, it can then go on to earn national and sometimes international recognition.

A variety of snack foods is also served at microbrewery bars to soak up the beer.

SMOKING

California is an antismoking state, and the California State Legislature has banned smoking in all restaurants and public places unless there is a separate air circulation system. Some restaurants with outdoor tables may have a separate section reserved for smokers, and sometimes the bar area will allow smokers in a separate section. Cigars are rarely allowed.

Elegant and leisurely Craviotto's Café in Santa Barbara

WHEELCHAIR ACCESS

All new restaurants in California, and old restaurants undergoing renovation, must make their site accessible to wheelchair users. This means that there should be no steps into the restaurant or to the tables, and that there should be wide bathroom doors.

CHILDREN'S FACILITIES

Most restaurants are children-friendly and offer a children's menu and high chairs or booster seats. However, in the quieter, upscale restaurants, parents are expected to keep children seated at the table, and take noisy or upset children outside until they calm down.

DRESS CODES

With California's leisurely lifestyle, many gourmet restaurants do not require men to wear jackets and ties or women to wear dresses, although jeans, shorts, sneakers, and T-shirts are definitely not allowed.

BOOKING AHEAD

It is always best to make a reservation in advance to avoid disappointment. City restaurants, in particular, are often very busy, and established or fashionable spots are sometimes booked up more than a month in advance. If you make a reservation that you later cannot keep, call the restaurant and cancel.

The Flavors of California

One heady whiff of a California farmer's market and you'll understand how California cuisine – rooted in the simple concept that ingredients should be fresh, healthful, and homegrown – developed in the sun-kissed Golden State. Ethnic cuisine, too, especially sizzling Mexican but also Mediterranean and spicy Chinese and Thai, makes a bold appearance across the state. And, of course, traditionalists can indulge in the all-American burger and fries at a classic diner. Better yet, for a quintessential California car culture moment, pull into a drive-in for a burger-on-the-dash meal.

Coriander and bay leaves

Stalls at a Californian market, laden with local produce

A birds-eye view of the state reveals verdant herb gardens unfolding from one end to the other; wild mustard fields giving way to scented swathes of cilantro (coriander), bay, and basil, to be used in everything from sauces to salads.

FRESH FRUITS AND NUTS

Fruits and nuts flourish in California's year-round sunny climate. The healthy soil, fed by an abundance of fresh water, yields downy-skinned peaches, caramel-sweet dates, and the state's famed avocados. The world's most popular avocado is the rough-skinned Haas variety, a California native, prized for its silky texture and mild, nutty flavor and used extensively in salads and sandwiches and to concoct velvety dips. The thin-skinned, green Fuerte

LOCALLY GROWN VEGETABLES AND HERBS

The seasons reign supreme in California cuisine and chefs develop their menus around what's fresh at the market. The summer warmth brings forth heavy vine tomatoes and a rainbow of peppers, while the autumnal cool reaps lush broccoli, artichokes and acorn squash.

Dates • White peaches • Persimmons • Papaya • Mango • Kumquats • Fresh figs
Mouthwatering selection of ripe Calfornian fruits

CALIFORNIAN DISHES AND SPECIALTIES

Food in California reflects the ethnic diversity of the state's population as well as the natural bounty of produce available year-round. Due to similarities in climate, Californian cooking is also strongly influenced by Mediterranean cuisine. However, traditional Italian or Provençal recipes are often given a twist with the addition of New World ingredients, resulting in innovative pizzas and pasta dishes and exotic, colorful salads. Sauces and salad dressings tend to be light and fresh, designed to enhance and complement the key ingredients of the dish. Locally produced goat cheese is used liberally, its tangy flavor pairing beautifully with vegetables and meat. Desserts make the most of local fruits, and will often be as simple as a mixed-fruit platter with a passion-fruit sauce or home-made ice cream.

Jalapeño chilis

Mesclun salad with dates and goat cheese *Mixed baby greens mingle with sweet dates and crumbled cheese.*

A bustling Mexican snack bar in the lively Haight neighborhood

MEXICAN CUISINE

There's no need to head south of the border for *comida Mexicana*. Nearly every town has its share of casual, colorful *taquerias* where you can dig into Mexican fare at a price that's easy on the wallet. At less than $10 for a blimp-sized burrito or platter overflowing with seasoned rice, beans and chicken, a Mexican meal remains one of the best bargains in the state.

THE MEXICAN MENU

Tortilla A Mexican staple, this is a round, flat unleavened corn- or wheat-flour bread.

Burrito Warmed tortilla, filled with *arroz* (rice), *frijoles* (beans), and *pollo* (chicken), *carne* (meat) or veggies.

Quesadilla Tortilla stuffed with *queso* (cheese) and other fillings, then grilled or pan-fried to melt the cheese.

Taco A crisp tortilla, usually deep-fried, folded, and stuffed with a savory filling.

Chile Relleno Stuffed green chili pepper fried in batter.

Salsas Spicy fresh sauces, from traditional chunky tomato to trendy slivers of papaya, mango or peach to vegetable salsas with corn and black beans.

Mole This rich, dark sauce is an aromatic blend of bitter chocolate, spices, and chilis, often drizzled over chicken.

avocado is another creamy favorite, as are California black walnuts, whose rock-hard shells hide an intensely flavorful meat used by chefs as a nutty seasoning.

FISH AND SEAFOOD

California's seas and rivers abound with fish and shellfish, from delicate Dungeness crab to meaty swordfish and albacore tuna, and many waterfront restaurants serve up fish so fresh it's practically flopping on your plate. Petrale sole, found everywhere from Fort Bragg to Monterey, is the premium flatfish at the market, with a fine-textured, low-fat flesh that grills to perfection. Named after their rock-hard shell, Ridgeback Santa Barbara shrimp can be tough little guys to peel but boast the sweetest tasting meat in the Pacific. The best freshwater fish is the state's king salmon, which spawns in the Sacramento and San Joaquin rivers and is prized for its delicate, velvety meat that melts on the tongue.

Succulent crabs plucked straight from the Pacific ocean

Salmon on watercress with citrus vinaigrette *Local fish and peppery leaves are offset by a piquant vinaigrette.*

Grilled chicken breasts with tomato salsa *Whole black beans and guacamole complement this healthy dish.*

Poached fresh persimmons *A luscious concoction of silky persimmons are draped over vanilla ice cream.*

What to Drink in California

Beer label

Californians are devoted to the consumption of beverages, partly because they tend to do so much outdoor exercise in the heat and partly as a social activity. Soft drinks, or "sodas," play the largest role in the state's beverage culture, although alcohol is also important. Many restaurants tempt weekend customers with champagne brunches. Beer can be enjoyed on the beach or while watching a game of baseball. Wine, particularly local California wine *(see pp438–9)*, is popular with dinner.

Sign in the Napa Valley wine-producing region in Northern California

Tequila bottle **Colorful Sunset Strip** **Strawberry Daiquiri** **Margarita with slice of lime**

COCKTAILS

Sipping cocktails beside the ocean at sunset is part of the popular image of the "California dream." The margarita cocktail still ranks as the firm favorite throughout the state. Served in ever-wider glasses, margaritas are a blend of tequila, lime juice, and an orange-flavored liqueur, with the rim of the glass dipped in salt.

The Sunset Strip, named after the infamous section of Sunset Boulevard *(see pp102–7)*, consists of equal parts of gin, rum, triple sec, vodka, pineapple juice, and lemonade.

Another cocktail popular in the state is the piña colada. This is a blend of fresh pineapple, cream of coconut, and equal parts of papaya juice, lime mix, orange juice, and pineapple juice. A shot of rum is added, and the finished drink is served over ice in tall, elegant glasses.

SOFT DRINKS

Californians are generally very health-conscious, and they consume a lot of fruit juice. Staff at juice stalls in shopping centers or on the street will squeeze juice from almost any kind of fruit, or a mixture of fruit and vegetables, while you wait. Also available on the street, as well as in most hotel lobbies, are machines supplying soft drinks and free cold water and crushed ice. Most fast-food outlets offer a range of soft drinks in three sizes, although the same products can usually be purchased much less expensively from supermarkets.

Iced cola

The most popular nonalcoholic drink in the state remains the all-American cola. However, health awareness has led to a growth in the consumption of diet and caffeine-free versions of colas and other carbonated soft drinks.

Sports-loving Californians often carry flexible thermos flasks filled with drinks chilled overnight in the refrigerator.

Freshly squeezed strawberry juice

TEA AND COFFEE

People in California consume large quantities of "designer" coffee. Café latte, café au lait, cappuccino, frappuccino (iced coffee), and flavored brews, such as almond and mocha, are on hand at coffee houses and street stalls. Tea is also becoming increasingly popular, and imported teas come in every imaginable flavor.

Cappuccino

Café latte

Frappuccino

Lemon tea

WINE

Grape vines thrive in the mild climate of Northern California, where cooling fogs help the fruit to reach perfection. The main red wine varieties grown in the region are Cabernet Sauvignon, Pinot Noir, Merlot, and Zinfandel (see pp438–9). White wines are also classified by grape variety, with Chardonnay by far the most popular of recent years. Grown throughout the West Coast region, this prestige grape produces wines varying in character from dry, light, lemon, and vanilla-scented to the more headstrong and oaky.

California has acquired an international reputation for excellent champagne-style wines at the right price, reflected in the fact that the finest French producers have huge investments in the state. Moët & Chandon and Mumm, among others, have set up wineries in the Napa Valley and elsewhere.

Wine is much cheaper in supermarkets or liquor stores than in restaurants. State law allows customers to take their own bottles into restaurants, where the corkage fee is generally $5–10.

Sparkling Cuvée Napa by Mumm

Rosé or blush wine

Napa Chardonnay

Cabernet Sauvignon

WATER

A variety of mineral waters is produced in the state, the best of which comes from the spa town of Calistoga in the Napa Valley (see p461). Many mineral waters are flavored with fresh fruit and most are carbonated. Most public places, including office buildings, have water dispensers. California tap water is fresh, clean, and safe to drink.

Calistoga mineral water

ALCOHOLIC DRINKS

Alcohol cannot be purchased or consumed in California by anyone under the age of 21. It is not uncommon for shops and bars to refuse service or admittance to anyone not carrying documents proving that they are at least 21 years old. Licensing hours, however, are relaxed; those old enough to drink legally can buy or consume alcohol from 6am until 2am, seven days a week.

Busy bar in Santa Barbara

BEER

Anchor Steam Beer **Red Tail Ale** **Liberty Ale**

Beers of every variety – foreign, American, even homemade – have become highly desirable. The recent resurgence in small breweries across the United States can be credited to the success of San Francisco's Anchor Brewery, whose Steam Beer, Liberty Ale, and other products show that American beer need not be bland and tasteless. Other excellent local brews to look out for include Mendocino County's rich Boont Amber and Red Tail Ale.

Copying the self-brewing concept that began in Canada, many Californians are now opening do-it-yourself breweries. Experts are on hand to assist with malting, boiling, carbonating, hopping, fermenting, and bottling. A personal-label brew takes two to six weeks to ferment. Microbrewery beers, brewed on the premises of a bar (see p563), are also extremely popular.

Choosing a Restaurant

The restaurants in this guide have been selected across a wide range of price categories for their exceptional food, good value, and interesting location. These listings highlight some of the factors that may influence your choice. Entries are listed by region, beginning with Los Angeles.

PRICE CATEGORIES
For a three-course meal for one, a glass of house wine, and all unavoidable extra charges, including tax.

$ under $25
$$ $25–$35
$$$ $35–$50
$$$$ $50–$70
$$$$$ over $70

LOS ANGELES

BEL AIR Hotel Bel-Air $$$$$
701 Stone Canyon Rd, 90077 **Tel** *(310) 472-1211*   **Map** *4 A2*

Dining on the terrace of this exclusive retreat, overlooking the swan pond, is relaxing and romantic – a quintessential LA experience. Inside, it is posh and conservative. The menu, which incorporates ingredients from local farmers, features a California-French style that ranges from the traditional to the avant-garde. A favorite celebrity haunt.

BEVERLY HILLS Barney Greengrass $$
Barneys New York, 9570 Wilshire Blvd, 90212 **Tel** *(310) 777-5877*   **Map** *5 F4*

Tucked into the swanky Barneys department store, this is not your average kosher deli, but you can still find your familiar corned beef or pastrami sandwich and a tremendous selection of smoked fish. The terrace provides a great view of downtown Beverly Hills, and lunch is popular with both celebrities and transplanted New Yorkers.

BEVERLY HILLS Nate 'n Al's $$
414 N Beverly Dr, 90210 **Tel** *(310) 274-0101*   **Map** *5 F3*

It may be in one of the fanciest neighborhoods in town, but this unassuming traditional deli could just as easily be found on a Brooklyn side street – and that is the beauty of it. Homesick New Yorkers or anyone looking for simple treats such as pastrami on rye or potato knishes head to Nate 'n Al's, where the Beverly Hills glitz is left at the door.

BEVERLY HILLS Da Pasquale $$$
9749 Little Santa Monica Blvd, 90210 **Tel** *(310) 859-3884*   **Map** *5 E3*

In the midst of ritzy Beverly Hills, Da Pasquale is a friendly, family-operated restaurant that celebrates the cuisine of Naples. Decorated with murals and vintage photos of Old Napoli, this place is famous for its thin-crusted pizzas and excellent pastas. While it may attract movie industry folks from nearby offices, this is still a "regular" joint.

BEVERLY HILLS Enoteca Drago $$$
410 N Cañon Dr, 90210 **Tel** *(310) 786-8236*   **Map** *5 F3*

An *enoteca* is an Italian wine bar serving tapas-like snack foods, and this casual but sophisticated eatery, sheathed in rich wood, offers an abundance of interesting delicacies. Items such as deep-fried olives and grilled octopus are paired with a glass of wine from one of the most interesting lists in town. Full-sized entrées are also available.

BEVERLY HILLS Kate Mantilini $$$
9101 Wilshire Blvd, 90210 **Tel** *(310) 278-3699*   **Map** *6 F4*

With its casual but clubby ambience, endless menu, and convenient late hours, this cavernous eatery is a great place to visit. The fare is primarily American comfort food, and the kitchen does a fine job with dishes such as chicken potpie, mac and cheese, and meatloaf. It is a good spot to go after a movie or simply grab a martini after shopping.

BEVERLY HILLS The Farm of Beverly Hills $$$
439 N Beverly Dr, 90210 **Tel** *(310) 273-5578*   **Map** *5 F3*

Bringing a refreshing bit of the Heartland to downtown Beverly Hills, the Farm provides a wide array of classic American foods, such as meatloaf and fried chicken, along with new twists on old favorites. It is an airy, unpretentious setting, with a great sidewalk patio for viewing the street scene. The brownies are great.

BEVERLY HILLS Lawry's Prime Rib $$$$
100 N La Cienega Blvd, 90211 **Tel** *(310) 652-2827*   **Map** *6 C4*

A beloved LA dining tradition since 1938, this is the place to go for classic prime rib with all the trimmings. The dining room is grand, but the service is humble. After a signature Spinning Bowl Salad, guests tuck into perfectly cooked prime rib, expertly carved at the table from a massive stainless steel cart. The creamed corn is delicious.

BEVERLY HILLS Matsuhisa $$$$$
129 N La Cienega Blvd, 90211 **Tel** *(310) 659-9639*   **Map** *6 B4*

This flagship restaurant in sushi chef Nobu Matsushisa's worldwide empire is one of LA's most influential eateries. Attracting lots of celebrities despite its ordinary decor, Matsuhisa specializes in modern sushi, incorporating diverse ethnic influences (the chef lived in Peru and uses many Latin ingredients). Ask for the *omakase* (chef's choice).

Key to Symbols *see back cover flap*

BEVERLY HILLS The Grill on the Alley ♿ $$$$

9560 Dayton Way, 90210 ***Tel*** *(310) 276-0615* ***Map*** *5 F3*

One of Beverly Hills' premier power-lunching scenes, this is where studio heads hold court to discuss their next mega-deal over Cobb salads, perfectly grilled steaks, and pastas. The room reflects the traditional sensibilities of a classic chophouse, with high-backed leather booths and lots of polished wood. The service is among the best in the city.

BEVERLY HILLS Crustacean 👶 ♿ ♫ 🌳 $$$$$

9646 Little Santa Monica Blvd, 90210 ***Tel*** *(310) 205-8990* ***Map*** *5 E3*

A modern LA interpretation of colonial Saigon, the decor at this trendsetting venue includes a floor-to-ceiling aquarium and a meandering glass-topped "stream" embedded into the marble floor. From the owners' "secret kitchen" comes addictive garlic noodles, massive prawns, and crab simmered in Chardonnay, sake, and cognac.

BEVERLY HILLS Spago 👶 ♿ 🌳 $$$$$

176 N Cañon Dr, 90210 ***Tel*** *(310) 385-0880* ***Map*** *5 F3*

The flagship restaurant of celebrity chef Wolfgang Puck remains one of the most entertaining places in LA to dine. The stylish, contemporary dining room is always filled with recognizable faces, but the average suburban couple is not snubbed. The menu offers modern French specialties, plus some traditional Austrian dishes.

CENTURY CITY Clementine 👶 ♿ 🌳 $

1751 Ensley Ave, 90024 ***Tel*** *(310) 552-1080* ***Map*** *5 D4*

Clementine, one of LA's best kept secrets, is a sensational little Parisian-style café, with colorfully-draped tables spilling onto the sidewalk. In the morning, it is perfect for breakfast or simply a cup of cappuccino or hot chocolate. Lunch means delicious soups, salads, and sandwiches on freshly-baked breads. It closes early in the evening.

CENTURY CITY La Cachette 👶 ♿ $$$$$

10506 Santa Monica Blvd, 90025 ***Tel*** *(310) 470-4992* ***Map*** *4 C5*

This lovely, flower-laden venue – the name means "the hideaway" – is an ideal choice for an updated brand of French cooking that is elegant and delicious, but without the burden of heavy, cream-based sauces. Some vegetarian and vegan dishes, prepared with classic French technique, are also offered. One of the best-looking restaurants in the city.

CULVER CITY Beacon 👶 ♿ 🌳 $$$

3280 Helms Ave, 90034 ***Tel*** *(310) 838-7500* ***Road map*** *inset A*

Beacon's diverse Pacific Rim-inspired menu features innovative dishes, ideal for sharing in a casual, contemporary setting carved out of an old industrial bakery. Items such as deep-fried oysters with yuzu tartar sauce, ahi pizza, and miso-glazed black cod are deftly prepared, moderately priced, and beautifully presented. Extremely popular.

DOWNTOWN Philippe The Original 💳 👶 ♿ $

1001 N Alameda St, 90012 ***Tel*** *(213) 628-3781* ***Map*** *11 F3*

One of the city's oldest restaurants (founded in 1908) and claiming to be the originator of the French dip sandwich, this downtown landmark serves beef, lamb, pork, and turkey versions of the sandwich. Settle into one of the communal tables and slather on some of the eatery's legendary hot mustard.

DOWNTOWN Ciudad 👶 ♿ ♫ 🌳 $$$

445 S Figueroa St, 90071 ***Tel*** *(213) 486-5171* ***Map*** *11 D4*

Celebrity chefs Mary Sue Milliken and Susan Feniger, of Border Grill fame, have created this venue that celebrates the many diverse cuisines of the Americas. Traditional cocktails and dishes from Mexico, Cuba, Central America, Brazil, Argentina, and Peru are offered in a dining room that is stylish and cool, with bold colors and modern art.

DOWNTOWN Traxx ♿ 🌳 $$$

Union Station, 800 N Alameda St, 90012 ***Tel*** *(213) 625-1999* ***Map*** *11 F3*

Tucked into the historic Union Station – one of downtown's landmarks – this Art Deco restaurant is located just off the bustling concourse, but has a hidden outdoor courtyard in the rear. The dishes coming out of the open kitchen possess classic American themes, but are infused with modern touches that always keep the menu interesting.

DOWNTOWN Cicada 👶 ♿ $$$$

617 S Olive St, 90014 ***Tel*** *(213) 488-9488* ***Map*** *11 D4*

Possibly the grandest dining room in LA, Cicada is housed in the historic Oviatt Hotel, and its dramatic Art Deco design features soaring maple columns, lots of gold leaf, and Lalique glass. The cuisine is a blend between modern Italian and progressive American, with everything from foie gras to risotto turning up on the intriguing menu.

DOWNTOWN Patina ♿ 🌳 $$$$$

Walt Disney Concert Hall, 141 S Grand Ave, 90012 ***Tel*** *(213) 972-3331* ***Map*** *11 D3*

After many years on Melrose Avenue, this temple of gastronomy moved into the stunning Disney Hall. In a room wrapped in a "curtain" of rich wood, one can expect the highest standards in LA dining: an indulgent caviar cart, major league wine list, and a menu laced with luxurious items. Dishes such as *côte de boeuf* for two are also served.

DOWNTOWN Water Grill ♿ $$$$$

544 S Grand Ave, 90071 ***Tel*** *(213) 891-0900* ***Map*** *11 D4*

Considered by many the city's premier seafood restaurant, this is a hybrid between an old-fashioned oyster bar and sophisticated dining room. The raw bar offers a bounty of wonderfully fresh shellfish, and entrées include marvelous dishes such as peeky toe crab salad and slow poached loup de mer that showcase the freshest ingredients.

GLENDALE La Cabañita

3447 N Verdugo Rd, 91208 **Tel** (818) 957-2711   **Road map** inset A

Most Mexican restaurants in LA offer virtually interchangeable menus of tired dishes that are not particularly authentic. La Cabañita is different, serving classics such as *chilies en nogada* (chilies stuffed with meat, fruit, and nuts, finished with a walnut-pomegranate sauce). The small, festive-looking restaurant has a strong local following.

HOLLYWOOD Canter's Fairfax

419 N Fairfax Ave, 90036 **Tel** (323) 651-2030   **Map** 7 D2

Nobody claims Canter's is the best deli in the world, but its attributes are aplenty; it is open 24 hours, which is rare in LA; it offers big portions of classic kosher deli fare; it has a respectable bakery on the premises; and even has an adjacent lounge with live music.

HOLLYWOOD El Cholo

1121 S Western Ave, 90006 **Tel** (323) 734-2773   **Road map** inset A

One of the city's most legendary Mexican restaurants, El Cholo has been around since 1927, serving what many Angelenos believe is the best margarita in town. Also famous at this always-mobbed eatery are the fresh-made guacamole, crabmeat enchiladas, and blue corn tamales. The place has the warm, worn look of a true classic.

HOLLYWOOD Fred 62

1850 N Vermont Ave, 90027 **Tel** (323) 667-0062   **Road map** inset A

An institution on hip Vermont Avenue, Fred 62 has much of what you expect in a traditional American diner, right down to the toasters on the tables. Much of the food is predictable, but some dishes on the pun-filled menu are sophisticated. A diverse crowd, from young rockers to button-down businessmen.

HOLLYWOOD Pink's Famous Chili Dogs

709 N La Brea Ave, 90038 **Tel** (323) 931-4223   **Map** 7 F1

Folks line up in the middle of the night at this legendary Hollywood hot dog stand, where Orson Welles once ate 18 frankfurters. The classic chili dog is the favorite, but the menu now includes many specialty hot dogs, such as an Ozzy Osbourne (spicy Polish with the works), and bacon burrito hot dog wrapped in a tortilla.

HOLLYWOOD Roscoe's House of Chicken 'n Waffles

1514 N Gower St, 90028 **Tel** (323) 466-7453   **Map** 3 D5

Southern-style fried chicken is accompanied by a stack of very tasty waffles; an unlikely combination that proves to be a winner. The menu also features "smothered" or deep-fried chicken livers, chicken sandwiches, collard greens, mac and cheese, and sweet potato pie.

HOLLYWOOD The Gumbo Pot

Farmers Market, 6333 W 3rd St, 90036 **Tel** (323) 933-0358   **Map** 7 D3

Finding an authentic taste of the Big Easy in LA is not a simple matter, but this little operation, hidden in the historic Farmers Market, is the genuine article. This casual, order-at-the-counter eatery is one of the few places to find authentic beignets and *muffaletta* or po'boy sandwiches, not to mention solid jambalaya and, of course, gumbo.

HOLLYWOOD Cha Cha Cha

656 N Virgil Ave, 90004 **Tel** (323) 664-7723   **Map** 9 F1

The bold flavors of the Caribbean are showcased at this colorful, quirky little restaurant that provides a unique experience from the moment you enter. Specialties include jerk chicken or pork, Spanish paella, Argentine-style steak, curried shrimp, and many multi-cultural dishes. Cha Cha Cha offers a refreshing change for breakfast too.

HOLLYWOOD Chan Dara

310 N Larchmont Blvd, 90004 **Tel** (323) 467-1052   **Map** 8 B2

Known in some circles for its head-turning waitresses, the food here is also well worth commenting on. Housed in a little bungalow just north of Larchmont Village, Chan Dara is a charming, tastefully appointed restaurant where good Thai noodles, soups, satays, and curries can be enjoyed at prices that are every bit as agreeable.

HOLLYWOOD Cheebo

7533 Sunset Blvd, 90046 **Tel** (323) 850-7070   **Map** 1 C5

A splash of bright paint, reasonable prices, and a terrific rectangular pizza "slab" ordered by the foot makes this a quintessential Hollywood hangout. But Cheebo is no ordinary pizza joint. It also has sandwiches, a signature mesquite-grilled burger with applewood-smoked bacon, and dinner entrées such as rack of lamb and osso buco.

HOLLYWOOD Cobras & Matadors

7615 W Beverly Blvd, 90036 **Tel** (323) 932-6178   **Map** 7 E2

A very earnest attempt at creating an authentic Spanish tapas bar in LA. This is a popular spot, thanks to its moderate prices, lively atmosphere, and wide-ranging menu of small plates that allows for plenty of variety. There is no wine list here, but next door the owner operates a wine store that boasts an almost exclusively Spanish inventory.

HOLLYWOOD A.O.C.

8022 W 3rd St, 90048 **Tel** (323) 653-6359   **Map** 7 D3

The acronym for Appellation d'Origine Contrôlée (the French regulatory system for wines), A.O.C. offers over 50 wines by the glass and a compendium of tapas-like small bites from around the Mediterranean. It also serves pâtés and sausages from the restaurant's own charcuterie bar, duck confit, fresh fish, salads, and unusual seasonal veggies.

Key to Price Guide see p568 **Key to Symbols** see back cover flap

HOLLYWOOD Ca' Brea
♿ $$$$

346 S La Brea Ave, 90036 **Tel** *(323) 938-2863*   **Map** *7 F3*

Sharing a street with some of the city's top restaurants and art galleries, Ca' Brea is an appealing Italian restaurant. The multi-tiered, art-filled place is stylish and hip, but not at the expense of comfort. The menu offers some unique items such as a big hall of goat cheese wrapped in pancetta. For dessert, go for the velvety Italian custard.

HOLLYWOOD Tantra
♿ $$$$

3705 Sunset Blvd, 90026 **Tel** *(323) 663-8268*   **Road map** *inset A*

Tantra is one of the sensuous Indian restaurants you are likely to encounter. On one side is a sleek, attractive bar, on the other a dining room featuring bold colors, interesting lighting fixtures, and a dramatic use of contemporary and traditional themes. The modern Indian cuisine, such as green chicken tikka and salmon kebab, is addictive.

HOLLYWOOD Angelini Osteria
$$$$$

7313 Beverly Blvd, 90036 **Tel** *(323) 297-0070*   **Map** *7 F2*

Gino Angelini has proven himself to be one of LA's top Italian chefs, turning out a combination of rustic dishes – his grandmother's lasagna with herb sauce is simply marvelous – plus fresher, newer creations. Daily specials run the gamut from veal kidneys to wood-roasted leg of pork. Unfortunately, the dining room is often crowded and noisy.

HOLLYWOOD Campanile
$$$$$

624 S La Brea Ave, 90036 **Tel** *(323) 938-1447*   **Map** *7 F4*

Housed in a Mediterranean-style structure built by Charlie Chaplin, Campanile is a revered restaurant in Los Angeles. The open, airy design, with a fountain-laden courtyard, perfectly complements the simple yet stylish Mediterranean cooking. Thursday's grilled cheese sandwich night – with sophisticated renditions – is a favorite event.

HOLLYWOOD Musso & Frank Grill
$$$$$

6667 Hollywood Blvd, 90028 **Tel** *(323) 467-7788*   **Map** *2 B4*

Hollywood's oldest restaurant never seems to go out of style. It is a classic chophouse – mahogany and red leather – with good martinis and a menu of old school favorites such as chicken pot pie, Welsh rarebit, liver and onions, and steaks. The flannel cakes, served until 3pm, are legendary. It draws a diverse crowd of tourists and locals alike.

HOLLYWOOD Table 8
$$$$$

7661 Melrose Ave, 90046 **Tel** *(323) 782-8258*   **Map** *7 E1*

Although it shares a façade with the upstairs tattoo parlor, Table 8 is one of the hottest restaurants in LA. The cuisine is New American, which means you will find lots of familiar themes accented with elegant touches inspired by the Mediterranean and occasionally Asia. The bar is a great place for a watermelon martini and a gourmet snack.

HOLLYWOOD Geisha House
$$$$$

6633 Hollywood Blvd, 90028 **Tel** *(323) 460-6300*   **Map** *2 B4*

In a city filled with trendy sushi bars, this is among the hottest, attracting a clientele that includes celebrities. A sake lounge (complete with sake sommeliers), sushi bar, and dining room are filled with patrons enjoying sushi, sashimi, and tempura, or larger plates such as Kobe beef steaks. A hip, dramatic design harmonizes the vibrant scene.

HOLLYWOOD Providence
$$$$$

5955 Melrose Ave, 90038 **Tel** *(323) 460-4170*   **Map** *8 B1*

Chef/owner Michael Cimarusti offers a sophisticated dining experience at this stylish seafood restaurant, where American classics share a menu with dishes heavy in French and Japanese influences. Purveyors in Maine call the chef every day to report on the catch – that is how dedicated he is to premium ingredients.

LONG BEACH Parkers' Lighthouse
$$$$

435 Shoreline Village Dr, 90802 **Tel** *(562) 432-6500*   **Road map** *inset A*

With a real working lighthouse, this Long Beach landmark has great views of the harbor and the *Queen Mary (see pp134–5)*. The menu showcases mesquite-grilled seafood, including salmon, swordfish, mahi mahi, and halibut. Nothing too fancy or cutting-edge here, but a bucket of steamed clams on the patio is a great way to spend a summer evening.

LONG BEACH Sir Winston's
$$$$

Queen Mary, 1126 Queen's Hwy, 90801 **Tel** *(562) 435-3511*   **Road map** *inset A*

A grand dining venue on the *Queen Mary*, this is one of Long Beach's most elegant and romantic restaurants. The menu continues the theme, offering caviar service, foie gras and lobster bisque, followed by rack of lamb and, finally, a chocolate soufflé. The Continental fare is traditional.

MALIBU Gladstone's Malibu
$$$

17300 Pacific Coast Hwy, 90272 **Tel** *(310) 573-0212*   **Road map** *inset A*

One of the top-grossing restaurants in the nation, this monster-sized beachfront seafood house is famous for its sprawling patio overlooking the Pacific. Big portions of chowder, grilled fish, lobster, *cioppino*, and Cajun-style blackened salmon may not be the world's finest, but most folks are thrilled with its quintessential LA feel.

MALIBU Granita
$$$$

23725 Malibu Rd, 90265 **Tel** *(310) 456-0488*   **Road map** *inset A*

This Wolfgang Puck outpost specializes in California seafood. Its design features a whimsical nautical motif, resulting in a casual elegance that suits posh yet laid-back Malibu. Items of interest on the frequently changing menu might include grilled bigeye tuna with shiitake-plum wine glaze, or crispy Cantonese duck.

MALIBU Geoffrey's 👶 ♿ ☀ [$][$][$][$][$]
27400 Pacific Coast Hwy, 90265 ***Tel*** *(310) 457-1519* ***Road map*** *inset A*

There is virtually no interior at this stunning restaurant perched high on a cliff above the Malibu coast. It is casual but high-end, with umbrella-laden tables and fire pits to keep its customers cozy. The California-American menu starts with crab cakes and ahi tartare, continuing with porcini-dusted salmon and a two-pound Maine lobster.

MALIBU Saddle Peak Lodge 👶 ♿ ☀ [$][$][$][$][$]
419 Cold Canyon Rd, 91302 ***Tel*** *(818) 222-3888* ***Road map*** *inset A*

Tucked into the Santa Monica Mountains, this old hunting lodge feels a million miles from chaotic LA. The rustic, multi-tiered restaurant is filled with wall-mounted stag and moose heads, yet an air of elegance permeates the scene with romantic, candlelit tables dressed in white linen. There is no better game – elk, buffalo, or venison – in town.

MARINA DEL REY Killer Shrimp 👶 ☀ [$]
523 Washington Blvd, 90292 ***Tel*** *(310) 578-2293* ***Road map*** *inset A*

The choices are not particularly plentiful at this place, but to its admirers, that's the beauty of it. Its loyal patrons return again and again for the same dish served three ways: a big bowl of Louisiana shrimp with rice, bread, or pasta. Whichever you choose, these crustaceans come swimming in a garlicky broth fired-up with chili sauce.

MARINA DEL REY The Cheesecake Factory 👶 ♿ ☀ [$][$]
4142 Via Marina, 90292 ***Tel*** *(310) 306-3344* ***Road map*** *inset A*

This chain is now found everywhere, but one of its most pleasant branches is the one right on the marina, where the outdoor terrace is a delight. One can always expect massive portions of well-prepared food from a menu featuring everything from Thai chicken pasta to meatloaf to jambalaya, not to mention a dizzying array of superb cheesecakes.

MARINA DEL REY Café Del Rey 👶 ♿ ♫ ☀ [$][$][$][$]
4451 Admiralty Way, 90292 ***Tel*** *(310) 823-6395* ***Road map*** *inset A*

With its dockside location and expansive windows providing panoramic views of the marina, this is no casual chowder shack, but a sophisticated dining venue. Eclectic but largely Pacific Rim-inspired, the menu ranges from Cuban black bean soup to Kung Pao and shellfish sausage to steak. Weekend brunch on the patio is an LA tradition.

MARINA DEL REY Jer-Ne 👶 ♿ ☀ [$][$][$][$][$]
Ritz–Carlton Hotel, 4375 Admiralty Way, 90292 ***Tel*** *(310) 574-4333* ***Road map*** *inset A*

Jer-Ne is not what you might expect a Ritz–Carlton dining room to be. Its design is not traditional but cutting-edge, and its menu imports flavors from throughout the Pacific Rim to arrive at imaginative flavor combinations. A bento box of appetizers showcases the chef's innovation, and cherry blossoms or chrysanthemums are used as accents.

PASADENA Saladang Song 👶 ♿ ☀ [$]
383 S Fair Oaks Ave, 91105 ***Tel*** *(626) 793-5200* ***Road map*** *inset A*

Next door to its sister restaurant, Saladang, this establishment is architecturally acclaimed, as high walls with laser-cut ironwork enclose a sprawling patio. Here you can forgo the standard Thai fare, indulging instead in unique breakfasts, spicy fish cakes, and salmon with curry sauce. Desserts are made from the exotic rambutan fruit.

PASADENA Yujean Kang's 👶 ♿ [$][$]
67 N Raymond Ave, 91103 ***Tel*** *(626) 585-0855* ***Road map*** *inset A*

This is not your typical neighborhood Chinese restaurant. The dining room is elegant and tasteful, the service polished, and the menu unique. Innovative chef/owner Kang incorporates non-traditional ingredients, such as Parma ham and salmon, into unique dishes prepared with classic Chinese technique. Delicious desserts and good wines.

PASADENA Mi Piace 👶 ♿ ☀ [$][$][$]
25 E Colorado Blvd, 91105 ***Tel*** *(626) 795-3131* ***Road map*** *inset A*

Mi Piace was one of the first restaurants to take a chance on the redevelopment of the Old Pasadena commercial district, and the gamble paid off. Always packed with a youthful crowd, this trattoria offers traditional pastas and pizzas, plus a few more innovative dishes. The desserts are famous and an adjoining lounge is a popular hangout.

PASADENA Shiro ♿ [$][$][$]
1505 Mission St, South Pasadena, 91030 ***Tel*** *(626) 799-4774* ***Road map*** *inset A*

This pioneering Asian-French restaurant is not as cutting-edge as it once was as it no longer draws big crowds from across town, but it remains very good indeed. The digs are modern and cool, more Westside than sleepy South Pasadena. The sophisticated California-Asian cuisine includes a signature whole deep-fried catfish with ponzu sauce.

PASADENA Parkway Grill 👶 ♿ ♫ [$][$][$][$]
510 S Arroyo Pkwy, 91105 ***Tel*** *(626) 795-1001* ***Road map*** *inset A*

A favorite since 1985, this place is nicknamed "Spago of Pasadena", thanks to its exhibition kitchen, wood-fired pizzas, and creative California cuisine. Southwestern influences abound, an adjacent organic garden ensures great salads, and wild game is a specialty. The wine list is solid and the garden-like setting is casually elegant.

PASADENA The Dining Room 👶 ♿ ♫ [$][$][$][$][$]
Ritz–Carlton Huntington Hotel & Spa, 1401 S Oak Knoll Ave, 91106 ***Tel*** *(626) 577-2867* ***Road map*** *inset A*

For many years a stodgy hotel dining room, the restaurant at this historic hotel has upgraded its cuisine to the ranks of LA's finest. Luxury ingredients from around the world are flown in to benefit lucky diners selecting elegant renditions of California-French cuisine or opting for memorable multicourse tasting menus paired with fine wines.

Key to Price Guide *see p568* **Key to Symbols** *see back cover flap*

PLAYA DEL REY Chloe

333 Culver Blvd, 90293 **Tel** *(310) 305-4505*   **Road map** *inset A*

Chloe put Playa del Rey on the dining map. The cozy dining room may feel like a neighborhood hangout, but the kitchen's exquisite California-French menu, laced with diverse ethnic influences, draws diners from the metropolitan area. The menu changes monthly to keep things fresh and exciting. The rear garden room is very appealing.

REDONDO BEACH Chez Mélange

Palos Verdes Inn, 1716 Pacific Coast Hwy, 90277 **Tel** *(310) 540-1222*   **Road map** *inset A*

Pioneering a sophisticated modern cuisine in the South Bay, this restaurant remains one of the area's most popular. The airy dining room, adjoining a modest inn, is relaxed and comfortable. The cuisine is eclectic, with inspirations ranging from Louisiana to Thailand to Italy. Recent updates include a sushi bar.

SAN PEDRO Papadakis Taverna

301 W 6th St, 90731 **Tel** *(310) 548-1186*   **Road map** *inset A*

Papadakis has become the most famous Greek restaurant in town, not only for its extensive menu of top-drawer Greek specialties, such as *spanakopita*, moussaka, pastitsio, and lamb, but also for its lively music and dancing in which both waiters and patrons participate. A true institution in the harbor community of San Pedro.

SANTA MONICA Broadway Deli

1457 3rd St Promenade, 90401 **Tel** *(310) 451-0616*   **Road map** *inset A*

This massive, bustling restaurant offers a wide range of traditional deli specialties, and the menu goes way beyond corned beef or pastrami sandwiches. Here you will find everything from pizzas to ostrich burgers to duck enchiladas. There is also a wine shop on the premises and a gourmet market for picnickers.

SANTA MONICA Border Grill

1445 4th St, 90401 **Tel** *(310) 451-1655*   **Road map** *inset A*

A local institution founded by TV chefs Mary Sue Milliken and Susan Feniger, the Border Grill presents an alternative to the stale pseudo-Mexican cuisine common in LA. While they may have incorporated some of their own ideas, their inspiration is derived from authentic recipes gathered throughout Mexico. The results are memorable.

SANTA MONICA Chinois on Main

2709 Main St, 90405 **Tel** *(310) 392-9025*   **Road map** *inset A*

Despite the wild, wacky design of this pioneering Wolfgang Puck restaurant, the Asian-French fusion cuisine served here is serious stuff. The menu remains fresh and exciting after many years, and items such as Chinois Chinese chicken salad, Mongolian lamb chops, and Shanghai lobster with ginger-curry sauce have become cult classics.

SANTA MONICA Drago

2628 Wilshire Blvd, 90403 **Tel** *(310) 828-1585*   **Road map** *inset A*

Superchef Celestino Drago's flagship restaurant offers a sleek, whitewashed decor that is customary of trendy LA, but much of his menu reverts to his rustic Sicilian roots. This is the kind of place you might order spaghetti with *bottarga* (pressed tuna roe) or *pappardelle* with pheasant and morel ragu. For dessert, try the panna cotta pudding.

SANTA MONICA JiRaffe

502 Santa Monica Blvd, 90401 **Tel** *(310) 917-6671*   **Road map** *inset A*

More stylish than a bistro but without much pretension, this two-story restaurant's California cooking is among the best in town. Starters include items such as a roasted tomato tart or beet salad, while entrées involve items such as crispy-skinned salmon with parsnip purée and balsamic nage. Produce comes directly from the Farmers Market.

SANTA MONICA Ocean Avenue Seafood

1401 Ocean Ave, 90401 **Tel** *(310) 394-5669*   **Road map** *inset A*

With a view of the ocean and an elegant atmosphere that suits virtually any occasion, Ocean Avenue's diverse menu offers a solid selection of multicultural seafood specialties from tuna tartare to lobster taquitos to paella. The raw bar always has a wide selection of oysters on hand, which seem to taste best on the patio.

SANTA MONICA The Lobster

1602 Ocean Ave, 90401 **Tel** *(310) 458-9294*   **Road map** *inset A*

Built on the site of an old-time lobster shack, this slick reincarnation is lively and fun, with a wraparound terrace that provides wonderful sunset views. Naturally, lobster shows up in a variety of wonderful forms: lobster cocktail, lobster salad, classic live Maine, or the alternative Pacific spiny lobster. Other seafood and meats are also well prepared.

SANTA MONICA Mélisse

1104 Wilshire Blvd, 90401 **Tel** *(310) 395-0881*   **Road map** *inset A*

One of the city's most glamorous and serious restaurants, Mélisse specializes in modern French cuisine fueled by market-fresh California ingredients. For a true gastronomic experience, consider a multicourse tasting menu paired with wines from a world-class cellar. Diners can also indulge in one of the best cheese boards in Los Angeles.

SANTA MONICA Valentino

3115 Pico Blvd, 90405 **Tel** *(310) 829-4313*   **Road map** *inset A*

Suave, sophisticated owner Piero Selvaggio has built his flagship restaurant into one of the finest Italian restaurants in the nation. Regulars do not even look at the menu, but defer to Selvaggio or his staff to create a memorable tasting experience. The wine list, literally the size of a phone book, is backed by a cellar of 200,000 bottles.

SHERMAN OAKS Café Bizou   ⛷&🛏 $$

14016 Ventura Blvd, 91423 **Tel** *(818) 788-3536*   **Road map** *inset A*

Housed in an inviting old bungalow, Bizou is very popular thanks to its solid California-French cooking and extremely reasonable prices. Soup or salad can be added for just a dollar and the corkage fee is only $2, encouraging guests to raid their own cellars. The menu offers everything from salmon to sweetbreads to short ribs. Reserve in advance.

STUDIO CITY Art's Deli   ⛷&🛏 $

12224 Ventura Blvd, 91604 **Tel** *(818) 762-1221*   **Road map** *inset A*

Art's is a bit more expensive than many delis, but its affluent Valley clientele and patrons from nearby studios do not mind. The sandwiches, which are "works of art" according to the proprietor, are nearly too large for the average person to handle alone. In addition to the pastrami sandwiches, smoked fish and big breakfasts are favored here.

STUDIO CITY Pinot Bistro   ⛷&🛏 $$$$

12969 Ventura Blvd, 91604 **Tel** *(818) 990-0500*   **Road map** *inset A*

The first, and arguably the best, of a local chain of upscale bistros, this is an attractive restaurant offering good-value food. The varied menu includes fancy fare such as foie gras and lobster, but also plenty of bistro favorites such as steak frites and lamb shank. The staff are friendly, and the charming bar area is reminiscent of a true Parisian bistro.

UNIVERSAL CITY Ca' del Sole   ⛷&🛏 $$$

4100 Cahuenga Blvd, 91602 **Tel** *(818) 985-4669*   **Road map** *inset A*

The dining room here resembles an old home, with a fireplace, hanging copper pots, and cozy booths. The patio, despite being separated from the heavy LA traffic by a single wall, feels like a Tuscan garden. The salads are fresh, pastas, such as ravioli stuffed with lobster or pumpkin, are first-rate, and the main courses are attractively priced.

VENICE Jody Maroni's Sausage Kingdom   🍽⛷&🛏 $

2011 Ocean Front Walk, 90291 **Tel** *(310) 822-5639*   **Road map** *inset A*

Although there are now franchises around town, this original venue is a true Venice Beach landmark. Jody's offers stellar sausages, served on freshly baked rolls like hot dogs. Among the dozen-plus varieties are innovations such as tequila-chicken or Bombay curried lamb. The boardwalk setting provides great people-watching opportunities.

VENICE Rose Café   ⛷&🎵🛏 $

220 Rose Ave, 90291 **Tel** *(310) 399-0711*   **Road map** *inset A*

Representative of the old bohemian Venice that is gradually disappearing in favor of rapid gentrification, the Rose Café has a roomy interior and a pleasant, sunny patio. An assortment of pastries, quiches, and salads are what the regulars return for. A cappuccino and a croissant, with a book on the patio, is a good way to spend time here.

VENICE Joe's   &🛏 $$$$$

1023 Abbot Kinney Blvd, 90291 **Tel** *(310) 399-5811*   **Road map** *inset A*

Chef/owner Joe Miller has more competition these days, but this Venice pioneer is still one of the neighborhood's favorites. His California cuisine has subtle French and Mediterranean themes, reflected in items such as potato-scaled red snapper with red wine sauce. Desserts are recommended at this sophisticated but laid-back eatery.

WEST HOLLYWOOD Mandarette   ⛷& $

8386 Beverly Blvd, 90048 **Tel** *(323) 655-6115*   **Map** *6 C2*

A casual spin-off of a fancy Beverly Hills restaurant, this cozy Chinese café has lots of character and good taste, not to mention a value-oriented menu of intriguing items. Noodle dishes, fresh salads, curried chicken dumplings, and entrées such as Kung Pao chicken or unusual strawberry shrimp make a visit to Mandarette a rewarding experience.

WEST HOLLYWOOD The Spanish Kitchen   &🎵🛏 $$$

826 N La Cienega Blvd, 90069 **Tel** *(310) 659-4794*   **Map** *6 C1*

This handsome hacienda-style restaurant, inspired by the diverse cooking methods of the southern regions of Mexico (Chiapas, Yucatan, and Oaxaca), turns out many intriguing dishes. A lively cocktail bar dispensing flavored margaritas and the *mariscos y mescal* bar, are part of the festive atmosphere. This is not your typical Mexican eatery.

WEST HOLLYWOOD Ago   &🛏 $$$$

8478 Melrose Ave, 90069 **Tel** *(323) 655-6333*   **Map** *6 C1*

Backed by Robert De Niro and film directors Tony and Ridley Scott, this celebrity-driven restaurant is packed all the time. Its fans suggest it serves some of the best Italian cuisine in the city, while its detractors complain about the service (if you are not a celebrity) and the high prices for average quality food. Great for stargazers and wine lovers.

WEST HOLLYWOOD Dolce   &🛏 $$$$

8284 Melrose Ave, 90046 **Tel** *(323) 852-7174*   **Map** *6 C1*

Celebrity-owned and frequented, Dolce is a bit self-consciously hip, but delivers some quality food along the way, as well as a major league wine list. In addition to regular-sized portions of traditional and modern Italian cooking, there is a more affordable *enoteca* (vintage wines) menu featuring small tapas-sized plates ideal for sharing.

WEST HOLLYWOOD EM Bistro   &🎵 $$$$

8256 Beverly Blvd, 90048 **Tel** *(323) 658-6004*   **Map** *6 C2*

With the ambience of an old-fashioned supper club, this stylish place draws a wide cross-section of guests to its tables with oversized club chairs. The menu offers modern interpretations of American food such as homemade potato chips with onion crème fraîche, short ribs, and Boston cream pie. A jazz lounge adjoins the dining room.

Key to Price Guide *see p568* **Key to Symbols** *see back cover flap*

WEST HOLLYWOOD Mimosa Restaurant 🧒 ♿ ⛱ $$$$

8009 Beverly Blvd, 90048 ***Tel*** *(323) 655-8895* **Map** 7 D2

With its mustard-colored walls, cozy tables, and lack of pretension, Mimosa is a genuine bistro. The menu reinforces the authenticity, with a perfect *salade Lyonnaise*, entrecôte, lamb shank, bouillabaisse, and tarte Tatin. Everything is beautifully prepared, service is friendly and crisp, and the restaurant never deviates from its simple but noble mission.

WEST HOLLYWOOD Wa Sushi & Bistro ♿ $$$$

1106 N La Cienega Blvd, 90069 ***Tel*** *(310) 854-7285* **Map** 6 C1

A trio of chefs from the renowned Matsuhisa *(see p568)* opened this little spot with a hillside view of the city. In addition to superb sushi and sashimi, these chefs use an old range behind the sushi bar to prepare some classic French-inspired sauces to go into their intricately cooked dishes.

WEST HOLLYWOOD Bastide ♿ ⛱ $$$$$

8475 Melrose Pl, 90069 ***Tel*** *(323) 651-5950* **Map** 6 C1

This bastion of haute cuisine is either loved or hated, but always delivers a unique experience. The design of Bastide – the name refers to a Provençal farmhouse – includes intimate dining rooms and a lovely olive-shaded patio. Here you can indulge in some classic French dishes as well as many avant-garde creations that would shock traditionalists.

WEST HOLLYWOOD BOA Steakhouse ♿ $$$$$

Grafton Hotel, 8462 Sunset Blvd, 90069 ***Tel*** *(323) 650-8383* **Map** 6 C1

BOA Steakhouse serves delicious aged USDA Prime beef. With its trendy modern design as a backdrop, this restaurant offers great steaks complemented by an assortment of unusual rubs, sauces, and condiments. Excellent seafood is on offer here, too.

WEST HOLLYWOOD Jar 🧒 ♿ $$$$$

8225 Beverly Blvd, 90048 ***Tel*** *(323) 655-6566* **Map** 6 C2

This restaurant takes the comfort foods of our youth – familiar items such as deviled eggs and pot roast – and presents them with a polished, sophisticated spin. Sauces like lobster Bearnaise enhance the steaks. With its zinc bar, deep wood tones, club chairs, and cork floor, Jar has a stylish retro feel to it.

WEST HOLLYWOOD L'Orangerie ♿ ♫ ⛱ $$$$$

903 N La Cienega Blvd, 90069 ***Tel*** *(310) 652-9770* **Map** 6 C1

In casual, laid-back LA, L'Orangerie is a welcome anomaly. The closest thing the city has to a three-star Michelin restaurant, it is opulent and relatively formal. Chefs tend to come and go, but the dedicated owners have maintained very high standards in service and cuisine for over 25 years. A true special occasion restaurant.

WEST HOLLYWOOD Lucques ♿ ⛱ $$$$$

8474 Melrose Ave, 90069 ***Tel*** *(323) 655-6277* **Map** 6 C2

Chef/owner Suzanne Goin is one of the city's top chefs, and her menu is both contemporary and traditional. Every dish is filled with interesting and delicious organic produce, making vegetables fun for all. The stylish dining room is carved out of the former carriage house of silent star Harold Lloyd.

WEST HOLLYWOOD Sona ♿ $$$$$

401 N La Cienega Blvd, 90048 ***Tel*** *(310) 659-7708* **Map** 6 C2

Ambitious owners/chefs David and Michelle Myers have created a striking modern dining room as a backdrop to their progressive French cuisine incorporating frequent Asian influences. Dishes such as seared foie gras with nectarine sorbet, Indonesian-inspired chicken, and bento box desserts make this a memorable culinary journey.

WEST HOLLYWOOD The Palm ♿ $$$$$

9001 Santa Monica Blvd, 90069 ***Tel*** *(310) 550-8811* **Map** 6 A2

A branch of the famous Manhattan eatery, The Palm is a serious steakhouse, and its dark wood and brass help it look the part. Caricatures of celebrities clutter the walls around diners tucking into pricy steaks and even pricier gargantuan lobsters. Cheesecake is flown in from New York. The service here sometimes feels rushed.

WESTWOOD/WEST LA Apple Pan 💳 🧒 $

10801 W Pico Blvd, 90064 ***Tel*** *(310) 475-3585* **Road map** *inset A*

One of the city's most endearing places, this diner consists solely of a horseshoe-shaped counter, and you usually have to patiently wait for your turn. But the wait is worth it, particularly for the legendary burgers topped with Tillamook cheddar or the barbecue burger. For dessert, go for the apple pie or the delicious banana cream pie.

WESTWOOD/WEST LA Guelaguetza 🧒 ♿ $

11127 Palms Blvd, 90034 ***Tel*** *(310) 837-1153* **Road map** *inset A*

One of the few places in LA that celebrates the cooking of Oaxaca, the city often considered the culinary capital of Mexico. As in all Oaxacan restaurants, the mole (a complex sauce made from ground spices, chilies, seeds, and often a touch of unsweetened chocolate) takes center stage. Several versions of mole – in different colors – are offered.

WESTWOOD/WEST LA John O'Groats 🧒 ♿ $

10516 Pico Blvd, 90064 ***Tel*** *(310) 204-0692* **Road map** *inset A*

This old-fashioned little coffee shop serves some of the best breakfasts in LA, complete with perfect homemade biscuits. Popular items include pumpkin or blueberry pancakes and their own rendition of *huevos rancheros*. Fish and chips are a midday favorite at this friendly place named after a town in Scotland. Expect a wait in the morning.

WESTWOOD/WEST LA Versailles

10319 Venice Blvd, 90034 **Tel** *(310) 558-3168*   **Road map** *inset A*

The most popular spot for Cuban cooking in LA, this no-frills eatery has a big menu of Cuban specialties. Among the favorite dishes are the shredded pork, *ropa vieja*, paella, and a garlic chicken dish that has diners literally lining up. Accompanied by black beans, rice, and plantains, these are filling meals often concluded with flan or bread pudding.

WESTWOOD/WEST LA Bombay Café

12021 W Pico Blvd, 90064 **Tel** *(310) 473-3388*   **Road map** *inset A*

There are some dishes on the menu of this Indian restaurant that are fiercely authentic, including some hard-to-find snack food. You may order the tandoori thali or South Indian thali for a complete meal. There are also some lighter, more refined creations that appeal to health-conscious Angelenos. They have a wonderful selection of chutneys.

WESTWOOD/WEST LA La Serenata Gourmet

10924 Pico Blvd, 90064 **Tel** *(310) 441-9667*   **Road map** *inset A*

A casual spin-off of a venerable East LA restaurant, this place is always packed with loyal customers getting their fix of outstanding Mexican seafood. Dishes include ceviche, mahi mahi tacos, *gorditas* (thick cornmeal griddle cakes) stuffed with shrimp, or salmon in fresh spinach sauce. This kind of authentic Mexican cooking is rare in LA.

WESTWOOD/WEST LA Tanino

1043 Westwood Blvd, 90024 **Tel** *(310) 208-0444*   **Map** *4 A4*

Housed in a splendid building designed by legendary architect Paul Williams, Tanino's ornate dining room is filled with rich handcrafted wood, marble, and glass. But the architecture is not the only reason to dine here, as the menu features excellent risotto and pasta dishes, osso buco, and seafood. This is one of Westwood's best dining options.

WESTWOOD/WEST LA Mori Sushi

11500 W Pico Blvd, 90064 **Tel** *(310) 479-3939*   **Road map** *inset A*

This spare, unassuming establishment is among the most elite purveyors of sushi in LA. The chef is a master at refined, highly aesthetic creations presented on unique plates fired in his own kiln. Rare species of fish, hand-picked at the fish market, are crafted into delicious, edible works of art. The personalized service is extremely gracious.

SOUTH CENTRAL CALIFORNIA

BAKERSFIELD Wool Growers

620 E 19th St, 93305 **Tel** *(661) 327-9584*   **Road map** *C5*

One of the most prominent restaurants in a region with a strong Basque heritage, Wool Growers serves plenty of side dishes – soup, beans, pasta, potatoes, and veggies – with every family-style meal. Choices for the main course include everything from lamb chops to oxtail stew to fried chicken. Portions are substantial and reasonably priced.

BUELLTON The Hitching Post II

406 E Hwy 246, 93427 **Tel** *(805) 688-0676*   **Road map** *B5*

Prominently featured in the movie *Sideways*, this place is famous for its oak wood-grilled steaks. At this Wine Country favorite, rustic charm is enhanced with a touch of elegance. Appetizers and sides are included, and the steaks and chops are complemented by a good selection of local wines (including their own).

CAMBRIA The Brambles Dinner House

4005 Burton Dr, 93428 **Tel** *(805) 927-4716*   **Road map** *B5*

Occupying an old home, the Brambles offers an old-fashioned but endearing English-style dining room and a patio. The menu is somewhat predictable, with old favorites such as oysters Rockefeller, steaks, and beef Stroganoff. But there is also bouillabaisse and, thanks to the owners' Greek heritage, moussaka and pastitsio.

CAYUCOS Hoppe's Garden Bistro

78 N Ocean Ave, 93430 **Tel** *(805) 995-1006*   **Road map** *C5*

Possibly the busiest spot in the sleepy beach town of Cayucos, this acclaimed Central Coast eatery is famous for the chef/owner's signature dish: Cayucos red abalone in hazelnut-mango butter. The extensive menu also offers everything from prime rib to local lobster to salmon glazed with honey and sesame. It also has lovely gardens.

LOS OLIVOS Los Olivos Café

2879 Grand Ave, 93441 **Tel** *(805) 688-7265*   **Road map** *C5*

Located in the heart of quaint Los Olivos, this is an ideal spot to recharge after a day of wine tasting. A rustic little dining room is paired with a charming wisteria-covered sidewalk patio. For nibbling, there are pizzas, olives, and artisan cheeses, and for serious appetites order pastas, lamb shank, or pot roast. There is also a wine shop and wine bar.

MONTECITO Montecito Café

Montecito Inn, 1295 Coast Village Rd, 93108 **Tel** *(805) 969-3392*   **Road map** *C5*

The charming Montecito Inn, reputed to have been a venture of Charlie Chaplin, houses this unpretentious little restaurant. The open, airy space is simple yet substantial, and the food is equally appealing. Leg of lamb is scented with garlic and rosemary, while a simple herb cream enhances the filet mignon.

Key to Price Guide *see p568* **Key to Symbols** *see back cover flap*

MORRO BAY Windows on the Water
699 Embarcadero, 93442 **Tel** *(805) 772-0677*   **Road map** B5

The inviting name says it all, as generous windows provide striking views of the water from every table of this big, airy restaurant. People love the crab cakes with jalapeño aïoli, and a prawn martini is accompanied by an inventive cocktail sauce sorbet. Cedar-planked salmon, Pacific bouillabaisse, and steaks complete the menu.

OJAI The Ranch House
500 S Lomita Ave, 93024 **Tel** *(805) 646-2360*   **Road map** C5

When dining here amidst herb gardens and burbling fountains, it is hard to believe this idyllic setting is a short drive from congested LA. The kitchen buys its ingredients from local farmers and ranchers, so the seasonal dishes evoke the essence of unspoiled California. The incredible 50-page wine list is one of the best found outside of a major city.

PASO ROBLES Bistro Laurent
1202 Pine St, 93446 **Tel** *(805) 226-8191*   **Road map** B5

Bistros and the Wine Country go together marvelously as is the case with this place. The modern mustard-colored dining room with white linen-topped tables is tucked into an old brick structure and the patio is a good place for sipping local wines. The menu offers bistro favorites such as *cassoulet* and roasted chicken, as well as California dishes.

PISMO BEACH Spyglass Inn Restaurant
Spyglass Inn, 2703 Spyglass Dr, 93449 **Tel** *(805) 773-1222*

Every table at this restaurant, perched on a bluff above the ocean, offers dramatic views of the crashing waves along a rugged stretch of the Pacific coast. On the menu, you will find an abundance of fresh seafood from local waters, plus steaks. A Mexican influence also appears with dishes such as lobster and shrimp tacos and tequila shrimp.

SAN LUIS OBISPO Buona Tavola
1037 Monterey St, 93401 **Tel** *(805) 545-8000*   **Road map** B5

Next to the historic Fremont Theatre, this is a cosmopolitan, art-filled trattoria with a lovely garden patio that is more serene than the bustling interior. The moderately priced menu offers a wide choice of antipasti, pastas such as agnolotti stuffed with scampi in saffron sauce, steaks, and chicken. A good wine list is featured here as well.

SAN LUIS OBISPO Café Roma
1020 Railroad Ave, 93401 **Tel** *(805) 541-6800*   **Road map** B5

This charming Northern Italian eatery has been a local favorite since 1980, with its rustic, homey surroundings, linen-dressed tables, and mural of the Tuscan countryside. A respectable wine list complements pastas, Tuscan chicken, osso buco, and fresh fish, plus a delicious caramelized onion-Gorgonzola pizza.

SANTA BARBARA La Super-Rica
622 N Milpas St, 93103 **Tel** *(805) 963-4940*   **Road map** C5

The devoted locals who patiently stand in line at this little roadside shack can tell you it is one of their city's true culinary treasures. The blackboard menu features simple Mexican street vendor fare. Tacos, made from freshly-grilled tortillas, are filled with marinated pork, beef, chicken, or chorizo. Even super-chef Julia Child loves this place.

SANTA BARBARA Brophy Bros. Clam Bar & Restaurant
119 Harbor Way, 93109 **Tel** *(805) 966-4418*   **Road map** C5

This dockside eatery with great harbor views is where big groups of locals gather for well-prepared fresh fish from a daily-changing menu. Solo diners cozy up to the clam bar for raw shellfish, bowls of legendary chowder, or *cioppino*. Drawing a diverse crowd, fishermen and office workers alike are found waiting for tables.

SANTA BARBARA Cold Spring Tavern
5995 Stagecoach Rd, 93105 **Tel** *(805) 967-0066*   **Road map** C5

The interior of this ivy-covered, 1860s former stagecoach stop is like an intimate hunting lodge, complete with mounted stag heads, but with elegant table settings for dinner. A diverse crowd of bikers and yuppies tucks into wild game specialties, steaks, chili, and ribs. For dessert order Jack Daniel's pecan pie. There is also a lively bar next door.

SANTA BARBARA El Paseo
10 El Paseo, 93101 **Tel** *(805) 962-6050*   **Road map** C5

With its hacienda-style courtyard, this historic restaurant provides wonderful local flavor. The building dates back to 1827 and has been used as a restaurant since 1922. Ask for a table by the fountain, start off with a margarita made from one of the 100 plus tequilas, and fill your freshly made tortillas with fajitas, fresh seafood, or *carne asada*.

SANTA BARBARA Emilio's Ristorante & Bar
324 W Cabrillo Blvd, 93101 **Tel** *(805) 966-4426*   **Road map** C5

One of the area's more romantic restaurants, Emilio's is noted for its charming patio, friendly staff, and very own organic farm. The menu features many Italian specialties but is eclectic enough to include seared ahi with wasabi-mashed potatoes and paella. Portions are generous and the candlelit, art-filled dining room is delightful.

SANTA BARBARA Louie's at the Upham
Upham Hotel, 1404 de la Vina St, 93101 **Tel** *(805) 963-7003*   **Road map** C5

A charming, unfussy restaurant tucked into a historic boutique hotel (founded in 1871), this is a place to score some exceptional California cuisine at reasonable prices. At night it turns quietly romantic, and the patio is lovely on a summer evening. Gourmet pizzas and pastas share a menu with regional American classics.

SANTA BARBARA Pascucci 🧒 ♿ ⛱ $$$

729 State St, 93101 ***Tel*** *(805) 963-8123* ***Road map*** *C5*

Just outside the busy Nuevo Paseo shopping center, some of Pascucci's tables spill out onto the sidewalk for diners interested in being part of the lively State Street scene. Inside, the neo-rustic setting suits the familiar, casual trattoria fare. The menu offers a wide selection of salads, pizzas, pastas, and main courses at fair prices.

SANTA BARBARA The Palace Grill 🧒 ♿ ♫ $$$

8 E Cota St, 93101 ***Tel*** *(805) 963-5000* ***Road map*** *C5*

If you fancy a traditional New Orleans-style good time, there is no better place to be. Start with a Cajun martini or Dixie beer with your crawfish popcorn or gumbo, move on to étouffée or blackened redfish flown in from the Big Easy, and finish with Banana Foster. The Palace Grill also has zydeco music.

SANTA BARBARA Bouchon ♿ ⛱ $$$$

9 W Victoria St, 93101 ***Tel*** *(805) 730-1160* ***Road map*** *C5*

A classy, inviting bistro that exudes a warm, comfortable aura, Bouchon offers a terrific array of French classics. Favorites include seared foie gras, fresh terrines, and braised lamb shank along with some contemporary dishes utilizing the area's seafood and farms. On weekends, an adjoining wine bar offers local wines and cheeses.

SANTA BARBARA Citronelle 🧒 ♿ ⛱ $$$$

Santa Barbara Inn, 901 E Cabrillo Blvd, 93103 ***Tel*** *(805) 963-0111* ***Road map*** *C5*

This modern French restaurant offers striking ocean views from its third-story resort perch. The airy but sophisticated dining room is favored for items such as ahi steak *au poivre*, crispy red snapper in lobster coral sauce, and beef with Bearnaise sauce. The prices are quite reasonable for a big-name spot and kids are welcome.

SANTA BARBARA Downey's ♿ $$$$

1305 State St, 93101 ***Tel*** *(805) 966-5006* ***Road map*** *C5*

More restrained than many State Street eateries, Downey's represents a classic California cuisine experience in a simply elegant, unstuffy dining room. Crab, lobster, and mussels from local waters often appear on the daily-changing menu, and meats are finished with uncomplicated but perfect sauces.

SANTA BARBARA El Encanto Restaurant 🧒 ♿ ⛱ $$$$

El Encanto Hotel, 1900 Lasuen Rd, 93103 ***Tel*** *(805) 687-5000* ***Road map*** *C5*

Hidden in a historic hotel with spectacular views of the area, El Encanto is one of the city's most romantic restaurants. The sophisticated California-French cuisine showcases a bounty of produce from neighboring farms and the kitchen buys fresh seafood direct from local fishermen.

SANTA BARBARA The Wine Cask 🧒 ♿ ⛱ $$$$

813 Anacapa St, 93101 ***Tel*** *(805) 966-9463* ***Road map*** *C5*

With an adjoining wine shop, this restaurant features inventive California cuisine reflected by nuanced dishes such as venison rack with blueberry risotto and duck with smoked Mission fig nage. The bustling room, complete with handcrafted beamed ceilings and a stately fireplace, is casually elegant. The stellar wine list fills 60 pages.

SANTA BARBARA La Marina 🧒 ♿ ♫ $$$$$

Four Seasons Biltmore Hotel, 1260 Channel Dr, 93108 ***Tel*** *(805) 969-2261* ***Road map*** *C5*

With the refined elegance of a country auberge and breathtaking views of the ocean, this is one of the most acclaimed dining rooms in the region. The California cuisine has a strong French foundation, with dishes such as foie gras-truffle terrine and rack of veal with lavender honey. The menu also offers vegetarian and heart-healthy dishes.

SANTA BARBARA Olio e Limone 🧒 ♿ ⛱ $$$$$

11 W Victoria St, 93101 ***Tel*** *(805) 899-2699* ***Road map*** *C5*

This intimate, sparingly appointed dining room is one of the city's favorite trattorias. Some authentic Sicilian specialties are offered here, such as spaghetti with *bottarga* (pressed tuna roe), while other pastas are more familiar, and the veal and chicken dishes are good bets. The Italian staff are gracious and the wine list is very respectable.

SANTA YNEZ Trattoria Grappolo 🧒 ♿ ⛱ $$$

3687 Sagunto St, 93460 ***Tel*** *(805) 688-6899* ***Road map*** *C5*

A bustling mural-laden trattoria with good service, a wide selection of pizzas, generously plated pastas, and hearty main courses, too. The wine list, with moderate prices, honors both local wineries and esteemed vintages from the Tuscan countryside. Ricotta cheesecake and tiramisu are among the desserts.

SHELL BEACH Sea Cliffs Restaurant 🧒 ♿ ♫ ⛱ $$$$

The Cliffs Resort, 2757 Shell Beach Rd, 93449 ***Tel*** *(805) 773-3555* ***Road map*** *B5*

Located on a bluff overlooking Shell and Pismo Beaches, this restaurant is particularly popular for its laid-back Sunday brunch. At dinner, guests typically begin with oysters Rockefeller or a sashimi plate and move on to surf and turf, an Asian-inspired *cioppino* or cilantro-crusted salmon. The patio takes full advantage of the ocean views.

SOLVANG Bit o' Denmark 🧒 ♿ $$$

473 Alisal Rd, 93463 ***Tel*** *(805) 688-5426* ***Road map*** *C5*

Housed in an early 20th-century building, this former church is now the best place to experience the Danish culture for which this city is famous. Traditional blue and white china adorns the walls while guests saddle up to the smorgasbord. The regular menu offers classic Scandinavian fare and the desserts are worth saving room for.

ORANGE COUNTY

ANAHEIM Cuban Pete's
$$$

*1050 W Ball Rd, 92801 **Tel** (714) 490-2020*

Road map D6

A festive, colorful restaurant/nightclub that attempts to recreate 1950s Havana, this place features many authentic Cuban dishes. Specialties include croquetas, *ropa vieja*, and *bistec empanizado* served with plantains and black beans. It is lively enough to rival Old Havana, with a variety of entertainment, from salsa to merengue to hip-hop.

ANAHEIM Goofy's Kitchen
$$$

*Disneyland Hotel, 1150 Magic Way, 92803 **Tel** (714) 778-6600*

Road map D6

A popular attraction for children at the Disneyland Hotel, Goofy's Kitchen offers a kid-friendly buffet, with items such as Mickey Mouse-shaped waffles, peanut butter and jelly pizza, and chocolate cake. Naturally, Goofy and all his friends are present to keep the kids busy. This place provides a taste of Disneyland even before entering the park.

ANAHEIM Anaheim White House
$$$$

*887 S Anaheim Blvd, 92805 **Tel** (714) 772-1381*

Road map D6

The grand façade of this old home, with colonial columns and a sprawling veranda for after-dinner drinks and cigars, hints at the elegant, romantic interior. A refined Northern Italian cuisine with indulgent French influences and occasional Asian accents is artfully presented, from soup to soufflés. Intimate rooms are named after presidents.

ANAHEIM Mr. Stox
$$$$$

*1105 E Katella Ave, 92805 **Tel** 714 634-2994*

Road map D6

One of Orange County's top tables, its polished wood-clad dining rooms have been drawing gourmands since 1968. The menu is filled with familiar dishes such as lobster bisque, grilled salmon, and filet mignon, all prepared with subtle modern twists. The wine list, supported by a 25,000-bottle cellar, is nationally recognized.

BUENA PARK Mrs. Knott's Chicken Dinner
$

*8039 Beach Blvd, 90620 **Tel** (714) 220-5080*

Road map D6

For natives of Southern California, this place is a part of growing up. In fact, Mrs. Knott started serving her chicken in 1934 and millions of people have been lining up ever since. Biscuits, mashed potatoes, gravy, and veggies come with the chicken, which is best followed by Knott's signature boysenberry pie. Non-chicken dishes are served, too.

CATALINA ISLAND The Landing Bar & Grill
$$

*El Encanto Market Place, Avalon, 90704 **Tel** (310) 510-1474*

Road map C6

Sitting on the patio with a cold drink overlooking the blue Pacific is what being on Catalina Island is all about. Sandwiches and quesadillas are offered at lunch, while dinner is geared more to pastas, steaks, and grilled fish. A big selection of international beers and microbrews, including a local Catalina one, is available, along with stronger potions.

CORONA DEL MAR Five Crowns
$$$$

*3801 E Coast Hwy, 92965 **Tel** (949) 760-0331*

Road map D6

Old fashioned but timeless, this Tudor-style dining house is homey but elegant, with rich wood, crackling fireplaces, and crisp white linen. Beef is the specialty of the house, particularly prime rib, but you will also find rack of lamb, duck, and seafood. Locals enjoy Sunday brunch and the garden is particularly appealing when the weather permits.

COSTA MESA Memphis
$$

*2920 Bristol St, 92626 **Tel** (714) 432-7685*

Road map D6

The spare decor is straight out of the 1960s, and this is a favored spot of the young, hip crowd. The cuisine is surely inspired by the jazz-crazed city for which it is named, but most dishes are updated versions of traditional soul food favorites. Pulled pork sandwiches, jambalaya, gumbo, and catfish omelets (for breakfast) are menu highlights.

COSTA MESA Chat Noir Bistro & Jazz Lounge
$$$$

*655 Anton Blvd, 92626 **Tel** (714) 557-6647*

Road map D6

Evoking the feel of an Art Nouveau Parisian bistro, the beamed ceiling, banquettes, fireplaces, and adjoining jazz lounge make this a lovely spot. Big shellfish platters, *moules marinières*, and steak frites comprise the authentic bistro fare. Diverse arrays of musical acts take the stage in the lounge. This venue is coveted for both food and music.

COSTA MESA Scott's
$$$$$

*3000 Bristol St, 92626 **Tel** (714) 979-2400*

Road map D6

A San Francisco import, this seafood house offers a warm, inviting dining room with a big central chandelier and prominent fireplace. Mostly old school, the kitchen turns out classics such as oysters Rockefeller, lobster bisque, and *cioppino*, along with USDA Prime steaks with optional blue cheese on top. Finish with bread pudding or cheesecake.

HUNTINGTON BEACH Red Pearl Kitchen
$$$

*412 Walnut Ave, 92648 **Tel** (714) 969-0224*

Road map D6

A stylish combination of quaint and hip, Red Pearl Kitchen is a charming Asian café. Starters include a wide variety of Chinese dim sum, Thai satays, and Japanese tempura. Varied national cuisines show up in the entrée selection as well, which offers Peking duck, Malaysian *mee goreng*, and whole deep-fried catfish.

IRVINE Bistango

19100 Von Karman Ave, 92612 **Tel** *(949) 752-5222*   **Road map** *D6*

Irvine's most prominent restaurant, Bistango is tucked into the stylish Atrium Building, where rotating modern art, a lively bar scene, and nightly live jazz are part of the vibe. Befitting the environment, the cuisine is contemporary California, including pizzas, ahi tuna, and rack of lamb. It has a winning wine list, too.

LAGUNA BEACH Café Zinc & Market

350 Ocean Ave, 92651 **Tel** *(949) 494-6302*   **Road map** *D6*

This combination café and market is open for breakfast and lunch. Locals and visiting picnickers stock up on salads, soups, and gourmet items. Specialties include Tuscan white bean soup, vegetarian chili, and personal-size pizzas. An umbrella-laden garden patio makes this an ideal place to recharge before hitting the beach or the boutiques.

LAGUNA BEACH Five Feet

328 Glenneyre St, 92651 **Tel** *(949) 497-4955*   **Road map** *D6*

A truly groundbreaking restaurant, particularly for Orange County, Five Feet features a progressive Pacific Rim cuisine that incorporates classic French technique in its sauces. Flash-fried whole catfish is accompanied by a tomato-peanut-citrus sauce, and Hawaiian *opakapaka* arrives in a soy-balsamic reduction. The restaurant can be congested.

LAGUNA BEACH Javier's Cantina & Grill

480 S Coast Hwy, 92651 **Tel** *(949) 494-1239*   **Road map** *D6*

A great place to hang out, party, or people-watch, this Mexican restaurant has a nice patio, ocean view, and hip vibe. Favorites here include Dungeness crab enchiladas in tomatillo sauce, tamales, and carnitas. The bar, boasting a huge selection of tequilas and dispensing potent margaritas to a hip, good-looking crowd, is always packed.

LAGUNA BEACH Las Brisas

361 Cliff Dr, 92652 **Tel** *(949) 497-5434*   **Road map** *D6*

A popular place to get married, this sprawling coastal restaurant offers spectacular ocean views. The cuisine is upscale Mexican, including specialties such as ceviche, red snapper stuffed with shrimp, and a bouillabaisse-like seafood stew. A wide array of tequilas is offered and the bar is adept at potent margaritas, ensuring a festive vibe.

LAGUNA BEACH Ti Amo

31727 S Coast Hwy, 92651 **Tel** *(949) 499-5350*   **Road map** *D6*

Ti Amo is pure romance, thanks to a roaring fire, flattering candlelight, copious flowers, and classical guitar music. Beyond the Tuscan villa atmosphere, the menu delivers high-quality Northern Italian fare such as rigatoni with porcini cream sauce and grilled ahi with sun-dried tomato risotto. Also try dishes such as the honey-and-chili-glazed scallops.

LAGUNA BEACH Sorrento Grille

370 Glenneyre St, 92651 **Tel** *(949) 494-8686*   **Road map** *D6*

A rustic Mediterranean villa ambience – complete with aged stucco, a fireplace, and wrought-iron chandeliers – is the setting for a wine-friendly California menu. Dishes such as filet mignon with cognac-peppercorn sauce and salmon with spiced pecan-mustard crust make a visit to this handsome restaurant a rewarding experience.

LAGUNA BEACH Splashes

Surf & Sand Resort, 1555 S Coast Hwy, 92651 **Tel** *(949) 497-4477*   **Road map** *D6*

Tucked into one of Orange County's top resorts, this restaurant offers dramatic ocean views from virtually every table, but the best seating is on the palm-shaded terrace overlooking the crashing waves. The California menu is innovative, seasonal, market-driven, and sometimes daring, such as roasted chestnut soup with truffle ice cream.

LAGUNA BEACH Studio

Montage Resort & Spa, 30801 S Coast Hwy, 92651 **Tel** *(949) 715-6420*   **Road map** *D6*

Housed in a freestanding building on the grounds of the exclusive Montage Resort, Studio is coveted for its sensational ocean views and exquisite cuisine. It feels like an elegant beachfront home and the menu, eschewing heavy sauces, reflects a modern French approach with imaginative uses of artisanal California ingredients.

NEWPORT BEACH Pascal Restaurant

1000 N Bristol St, 92660 **Tel** *(949) 263-9400*   **Road map** *D6*

Chef/owner Pascal Olhats prepares some of the finest French cuisine in Orange County. Specialties such as sautéed foie gras, rabbit in mustard sauce, and steak in peppercorn sauce are served in an elegant, yet welcoming dining room. An adjoining gourmet shop offers a selection of cheeses, pâtés, and other picnic items.

NEWPORT BEACH The Ritz Restaurant & Garden

880 Newport Center Dr, 92660 **Tel** *(949) 720-1800*   **Road map** *D6*

For two decades, this restaurant has been a favorite of well-heeled, middle-aged Orange County residents. The signature "carousel" is a Lazy Susan for the table, loaded with smoked fish, pâtés, steak tartare, and more. Entrées include rack of lamb, steak Diane, and other Continental dishes finished with a soufflé. All graciously served.

ORANGE The Hobbit

2932 E Chapman Ave, 92669 **Tel** *(714) 997-1972*   **Road map** *D6*

This is one of Southern California's most unique restaurants. This place specializes in seven-course prix-fixe feasts, which begin with hors d'oeuvres and champagne in the wine cellar before moving upstairs for heavy French-Continental dishes. An intermission involves a tour of the kitchen, making this a memorable dining experience.

Key to Price Guide *see p568* **Key to Symbols** *see back cover flap*

SAN CLEMENTE Iva Lee's 🧒 ♿ 🎵 ☀ [$][$][$]

555 N El Camino Real, 92672 ***Tel*** *(949) 361-2855* ***Road map*** *D6*

Iva Lee's celebrates the cooking of the South, with beautiful presentations of dishes such as fried green tomatoes layered with goat's cheese and grilled pork chop with a brown sugar-pecan glaze. The setting, enhanced by live blues and jazz acts, possesses the warmth of the jambalaya and sweetness of the bourbon-pecan pie.

SAN JUAN CAPISTRANO Cedar Creek Inn 🧒 ♿ ☀ [$][$][$]

26860 Ortega Hwy, 92675 ***Tel*** *(949) 240-2229* ***Road map*** *D6*

A good looking Spanish mission-inspired design contributes to the inviting, casually elegant location. The extensive menu is straightforward and moderately priced, with everything from pastas to fish and chips and rack of lamb to prime rib. Extremely versatile, you can come here on a date or with your kids. The patio is lovely.

SANTA ANA Antonello Ristorante ♿ ☀ [$][$][$][$]

3800 Plaza Dr, 92704 ***Tel*** *(714) 751-7153* ***Road map*** *D6*

From businessmen power-lunching to couples dining under the stars, this is a highly revered restaurant. A very impressive wine list accompanies a menu that boasts mostly traditional dishes such as spaghetti alla puttanesca, *cioppino*, scampi, and risotto laced with Gorgonzola. The ambience, like the menu, is Old World.

SUNSET BEACH Harbor House Café 🧒 ♿ ☀ [$]

16341 Pacific Coast Hwy, 90742 ***Tel*** *(562) 592-5404* ***Road map*** *D6*

This roadside café is decorated with surfing and nautical gear, movie posters, and other collectables. The cluttered decor gives the place an inviting, lived-in look. Slide into a cozy booth and enjoy one of nearly 30 omelets, great burgers, malts, and other all-American food from the extensive, modestly priced menu. Open 24 hours.

TUSTIN Zov's Bistro 🧒 ♿ ☀ [$][$][$]

17440 E 17th St, 92680 ***Tel*** *(714) 838-8855* ***Road map*** *D6*

A beloved local favorite bistro, café, and bakery in a contemporary setting. The Mediterranean menu features influences from Greece, Italy, Lebanon, Morocco, and beyond. Prices are reasonable, a versatile wine list is provided, and the on-site bakery turns out an impressive array of cakes, tarts, cookies, and breads.

SAN DIEGO COUNTY

CORONADO Azzura Point ♿ 🎵 [$][$][$][$]

Loews Coronado Bay Resort, 4000 Coronado Bay Rd, 92118 ***Tel*** *(619) 424-4477* ***Road map*** *D6*

With panoramic views of the Coronado Bay bridge and the glistening city skyline, Azzura Point is a dazzling contemporary room that is not overly formal. The diverse Californian-Mediterranean menu includes foie gras, lobster risotto, and healthful ahi tuna. Linger over the view with fine wine, cheeses, and winning desserts.

CORONADO Prince of Wales ♿ 🎵 ☀ [$][$][$][$][$]

Hotel Del Coronado, 1500 Orange Ave, 92118 ***Tel*** *(619) 522-8490* ***Road map*** *D6*

No visit to the historic Hotel Del Coronado is complete without a memorable feast at its grand restaurant. The terraces of Prince Charles deliver majestic views and a heavy dose of romance. Superb seafood, prepared with intriguing California accents, and meats dressed in light, nuanced sauces enhance the magic.

DEL MAR J. Taylor's 🧒 ♿ 🎵 ☀ [$][$][$][$][$]

L'Auberge Del Mar Resort & Spa, 1540 Camino Del Mar, 92014 ***Tel*** *(858) 793-6460* ***Road map*** *D6*

Truly romantic, but exuding a relaxed attitude, this dining room boasts a roaring fireplace, elegantly appointed tables, and French doors leading to a delightful terrace amidst gurgling waterfalls and a herb garden. A New American menu of Pacific bouillabaisse, molasses-seared elk, and pan-roasted salmon are accompanied by fine wines.

LA JOLLA Alfonso's of La Jolla 🧒 ♿ ☀ [$][$][$]

1251 Prospect St, 92037 ***Tel*** *(858) 454-2232* ***Road map*** *D6*

A La Jolla institution, this family-operated eatery brings together a fresh Pacific catch and the spices of Mexican cooking in a casual, festive setting. Shrimp ceviche, lobster fajitas, and lobster burritos join familiar chicken and beef dishes on the menu. Sitting on the patio, people-watching over a margarita, is a long-standing tradition.

LA JOLLA French Pastry Shop 🧒 ♿ ☀ [$][$][$]

5550 La Jolla Blvd, 92037 ***Tel*** *(858) 454-9094* ***Road map*** *D6*

This local shop has been dispensing delicious French pastries, fresh breads, and cakes for over two decades. In addition to enjoying its famous breakfasts, regulars stop in at lunch for soups, baguette sandwiches, salads, and pâtés. At dinner, this simple, no-frills establishment specializes in pastas and simple seafood dishes.

LA JOLLA Tapenade ♿ ☀ [$][$][$]

7612 Fay Ave, 92037 ***Tel*** *(858) 551-7500* ***Road map*** *D6*

A bit of Nice in the heart of La Jolla, this casually elegant restaurant derives its cuisine from the south of France. Escargots, duck, and steak *au poivre* are offered. The Maine lobster here comes in many forms, such as salad, soup, and risotto. Desserts are decadent, and a fine plate of cheeses is also available.

LA JOLLA Fresh Seafood Restaurant
1044 Wall St, 92037 **Tel** *(858) 551-7575*   **$$$$**

    Road map *D6*

This stylish retaurant offers an eclectic array of seafood specialties, featuring sesame-crusted ahi tuna and traditional fish and chips. Everything is prepared with classic technique, imaginative flair, and a strong sense of seasonality. A wide selection of small tapas-sized plates and seasonal cocktails make it ideal for an upscale happy hour.

LA JOLLA George's at the Cove
1250 Prospect St, 92037 **Tel** *(858) 454-4244*   **$$$$**

    Road map *D6*

With scenic views of La Jolla Cove, this popular three-tiered restaurant can be a bit hectic. Nonetheless, the casually elegant settings and consistently good seafood make battling the crowds worth it. The compelling menu prominently features prosciutto-wrapped halibut in orange-fennel emulsion and sesame-crusted tuna. There is a great wine list, too.

LA JOLLA Roppongi
875 Prospect St, 92037 **Tel** *(858) 551-5252*   **$$$$**

    Road map *D6*

With a huge list of Pacific Rim-style tapas, sushi, and sashimi, as well as innovative specialties inspired by every corner of Asia, Roppongi's menu is one of the most intriguing in San Diego. For lunch, cross-cultural bento boxes are offered. Asian antiques fill a stylish dining room, while a sleek lounge and fountain-laden patio draw a diverse crowd.

LA JOLLA The Marine Room
2000 Spindrift Dr, 92037 **Tel** *(858) 459-7222*   **$$$$$**

    Road map *D6*

Of the many venerable La Jolla oceanfront restaurants, The Marine Room arguably has the most dramatic views, with waves crashing just outside its reinforced windows. A pricy bastion of innovative California cuisine, this place harmonizes Asian twists and French influences on a menu laced with foie gras, truffles, and caviar.

LA JOLLA The Sky Room
La Valencia Hotel, 1132 Prospect St, 92037 **Tel** *(858) 454-0771*   **$$$$$**

    Road map *D6*

Perched atop the historic La Valencia Hotel, this exclusive room with only a dozen tables, offers unobstructed ocean views. In this strictly romantic, special-occasion territory, big money can buy you luxury items such as Kobe beef carpaccio, foie gras in fig-balsamic sauce, or abalone stacked with turbot and white truffles.

PACIFIC BEACH Nick's at the Beach
809 Thomas Ave, 92109 **Tel** *(858) 270-1730*   **$$$**

    Road map *D6*

A wide selection of dishes is available at this casual oceanfront restaurant. The diverse menu includes oyster shooters, crab cake sandwiches, Louisiana-style blackened catfish, Jamaican-inspired salmon, and jalapeño chicken pasta. Happy hour, offering good finger foods, draws a lively crowd to the upstairs bar. This is a Pacific Beach favorite.

RANCHO SANTA FE Mille Fleurs
6009 Paseo Delicias, 92067 **Tel** *(858) 756-3085*   **$$$$$**

    Road map *D6*

Hidden away in an exclusive suburb, Mille Fleurs is one of the most romantic restaurants in the area. The brilliant cooking is a worthy complement to the lovely surroundings and impeccable service. Superb ingredients, flown in from around the world or plucked from nearby farms, enhance the creative modern French cuisine served here.

SAN DIEGO The Big Kitchen
3003 Grape St, 92102 **Tel** *(619) 234-5789*   **$**

    Road map *D6*

Located behind Balboa Park, this little gem of a diner, which now boasts a nice little patio, is extremely popular for its huge breakfasts. The omelets, pancakes, and *huevos rancheros* are quite good. Its owner has a strong personal following and artistic and cultural groups often convene meetings over coffee at this quirky, but endearing, eatery.

SAN DIEGO The Little Fish Market
2401 Fenton Pkwy, 92108 **Tel** *(619) 280-2277*   **$**

    Road map *D6*

Ideal for those looking for a quality, value-oriented lunch in a hurry, this place has an order counter, though limited table service is provided. Fish and chips, charbroiled salmon, mahi mahi, and chowder in a hollowed-out loaf of bread, all feature at this fish market-cum-café. The location, close to Qualcomm Stadium, is perfect for sports fans.

SAN DIEGO Karl Strauss Brewing Company
1157 Columbia St, 92101 **Tel** *(619) 234-2739*   **$$**

    Road map *D6*

Now part of a burgeoning chain, this downtown microbrewery is a great place for a casual but compelling menu of comfort foods featuring blackened salmon, steaks, and meatloaf. The sausage platter is an ideal complement to the wide assortment of handcrafted beers on tap. Many seasonal beers are offered.

SAN DIEGO Café Eleven
1440 University Ave, 92103 **Tel** *(619) 260-8023*   **$$$**

    Road map *D6*

A charming, casual bistro with a delightful garden patio, this wonderful Hillcrest neighborhood gem is truly one of San Diego's best-kept secrets. The reasonably priced French-Continental menu offers deftly prepared crêpes, roast duckling, rack of lamb, and beef Wellington. The attractive prices and well-cooked food draw a regular clientele.

SAN DIEGO Candelas
416 3rd Ave, 92101 **Tel** *(619) 702-4455*   **$$$**

    Road map *D6*

Mexican cooking is raised to new heights, well beyond the ubiquitous burrito, at this lovely Gaslamp Quarter-adjacent restaurant. Innovatively prepared food is served in the stylish, candlelit dining hall. Try the stuffed calamari with tomato and blue cheese sauce, the creamed black bean soup, or the mushroom- and jalapeño-stuffed lobster.

Key to Price Guide *see p568* **Key to Symbols** *see back cover flap*

SAN DIEGO Indigo Grill 👪 ♿ [$][$][$]

1536 India St, 92101 ***Tel*** *(619) 234-6802* ***Road map*** *D6*

Indigo Grill is a popular spot to explore an innovative "New Western" cuisine. The totem poles and Latin artifacts, decorating the contemporary dining room, signal a celebration of all indigenous cultures in the Americas. The bold, intense at times, hot menu follows through with modern twists on cooking, from the Pacific Northwest to Mexico.

SAN DIEGO Sevilla ♿ ♫ [$][$][$]

555 4th Ave, 92101 ***Tel*** *(619) 233-5979* ***Road map*** *D6*

With its rustic decor, complete with aged brick arches, a wooden bar, and bullfighting murals, this restaurant transports you to the Iberian peninsula. The authentic tapas, paella, and free-flowing sangría reinforce the colorful flavor. Live flamenco provides the perfect accompaniment to the authentic Spanish cuisine at this popular local spot.

SAN DIEGO Trattoria Fantastica 👪 ♿ ☀ [$][$][$]

1735 India St, 92101 ***Tel*** *(619) 234-1735* ***Road map*** *D6*

At this homey spot in Little Italy, rustic Sicilian flavors are featured on the extensive, traditional menu. Regulars tuck into wonderful pizzas from a wood-burning oven, hearty pastas, gnocchi, veal, and chicken. The family-operated restaurant offers a casual dining room with muraled walls and a charming courtyard patio that is recommended.

SAN DIEGO Chive ♿ ☀ [$][$][$][$]

558 4th Ave, 92101 ***Tel*** *(619) 232-4483* ***Road map*** *D6*

Chic and modern, this Gaslamp Quarter standout is accented with green neon. Red Sea salt-dusted escolar with sweet pea hummus, and mustard-rubbed lamb with leek-chanterelle ragout represent the updated American menu. A globetrotting wine list is offered and the bar dispenses mojitos and designer martinis to a hip, stylish crowd.

SAN DIEGO Dobson's 👪 ♿ [$][$][$][$]

956 Broadway Circle, 92101 ***Tel*** *(619) 231-6771* ***Road map*** *D6*

Serving a California cuisine laced with ethnic influences, Dobson's always comes through with beautifully presented items, such as the impressive mussel bisque *en croûte*, ginger-lime salmon with wasabi aïoli, rack of lamb, and pastas. At lunch, politicians crowd the old-fashioned dining room with a nice mezzanine level above the antique bar.

SAN DIEGO El Agave 👪 ♿ ☀ [$][$][$][$]

2304 San Diego Ave, 92110 ***Tel*** *(619) 220-0692* ***Road map*** *D6*

The tequila is reason enough to visit this Old Town favorite that boasts one of the nation's largest selections. The hacienda-style dining room, sunny patio, and shady deck are attractive features. The kitchen turns out gorgeous presentations of ancient Aztec recipes with sophisticated European influences. Do not pass on the mole.

SAN DIEGO Laurel Restaurant & Bar [$][$][$][$]

505 Laurel St, 92101 ***Tel*** *(619) 239-2222* ***Road map*** *D6*

With a distinctly East Coast air about it, Laurel is one of the city's most cosmopolitan dining spots. Some are drawn by the incredible wine list, others by a modern French menu exhibiting flavors from throughout the Mediterranean. Whether a dish is infused with a touch of Provence or an exotic taste of Morocco, Laurel rarely disappoints.

SAN DIEGO Star of the Sea 👪 ♿ ☀ [$][$][$][$]

1360 N Harbor Dr, 92101 ***Tel*** *(619) 232-7408* ***Road map*** *D6*

With a sunny patio, views of the harbor, and the historic sailing ship, *Star of India*, this classy diner is one of the city's most popular restaurants. The menu is upscale, with foie gras, caviar, lobster, and Kobe beef playing prominent roles. The decor is contemporary, dishes are artfully presented, and the soufflés make worthy finalés.

SAN DIEGO Sushi Ota 👪 ♿ [$][$][$][$]

4529 Mission Bay Dr, 92109 ***Tel*** *(858) 270-5670* ***Road map*** *D6*

The modest, minimal location may not look promising, but Sushi Ota is among the area's best purveyors of sushi. The ubiquitous California and other popular rolls are dispensed in large numbers. The skilled chefs are also capable of more traditional, serious sushi crafted from impeccable ingredients. Expect a wait.

SAN DIEGO The Prado 👪 ♿ ☀ [$][$][$][$]

House of Hospitality, 1549 El Prado, Balboa Park, 92101 ***Tel*** *(619) 557-9441* ***Road map*** *D6*

In Balboa Park's ornate House of Hospitality, this restaurant takes full advantage of its majestic architecture in the interior and patio areas. The fusion menu is laced with Italian, Latin, and Asian influences, reflected by dishes like ahi tuna served over black licorice risotto with a plum wine reduction, or rack of lamb with anise-black olive demi-glace.

SAN DIEGO Trattoria La Strada 👪 ♿ ♫ ☀ [$][$][$][$]

702 5th Ave, 92101 ***Tel*** *(619) 239-3400* ***Road map*** *D6*

A favored option for Italian cuisine in the Gaslamp Quarter, both the patio and coveted window tables provide a great view of the lively street scene. To start, several carpaccios are among the house specialties, and pastas exceed the usual trattoria fare. Prices are high for this neighborhood, but dishes are deftly prepared and presented.

SAN DIEGO Bertrand at Mr. A's ♿ ☀ [$][$][$][$][$]

2550 5th Ave, 92103 ***Tel*** *(619) 239-1377* ***Road map*** *D6*

On the 12th floor of a downtown office building, this posh restaurant has spectacular views of the skyline and incoming jetliners. The food is delicious, with the likes of Maine lobster strudel and foie gras burger in brioche. In a city filled with ocean vistas, here is a delightful, breathtaking alternative that pampers its guests.

SAN DIEGO El Bizcocho   ⚄⚄⚄⚄⚄

Rancho Bernardo Inn, 17550 Bernardo Oaks Dr, 92128 **Tel** *858 675-8500*   **Road map** *D6*

Hidden in the exclusive Rancho Bernardo Inn, this understated dining room is one of the area's most honored restaurants. The elegant interior features warm earth tones, a fireplace, a view of the golf course, and finely appointed tables. Modern French cooking is artistically presented by a polished staff. This place is great for a special occasion.

SAN DIEGO Le Fontainebleau   ⚄⚄⚄⚄⚄

Westgate Hotel, 1055 2nd Ave, 92101 **Tel** *(619) 557-3655*   **Road map** *D6*

Despite its modern façade, the interior of the Westgate has a distinct hint of Versailles, and this striking restaurant is ideal for perfect occasions. The menu, consisting of caviar service, Châteaubriand and lobster, is rather traditional but perfectly executed and formally presented in a glamorous, opulent setting. The Sunday buffet brunch is awesome.

SAN DIEGO Rainwater's on Kettner   ⚄⚄⚄⚄⚄

1202 Kettner Blvd, 92101 **Tel** *(619) 233-5757*   **Road map** *D6*

With a menu offering all the steakhouse classics, this homegrown establishment has been drawing hordes of locals for years. The three-cheese meatloaf, osso buco, and a variety of fresh seafood are as popular. The dining room has the requisites of a traditional steakhouse. It is a hub of power-lunching politicians.

SAN DIEGO WineSellar & Brasserie   ⚄⚄⚄⚄⚄

9550 Waples St, 92121 **Tel** *(858) 450-9557*   **Road map** *D6*

Off the beaten path but worth the trip, this acclaimed restaurant began as a modest complement to the downstairs wine shop, whose inventory now supports one of the nation's most honored wine lists. The California-French cuisine, creative but built on a strong classic foundation, is served in a lovely room that is charming and unpretentious.

THE INLAND EMPIRE AND LOW DESERT

BIG BEAR CITY Old Country Inn   ⚄⚄⚄

41126 Big Bear Blvd, 92315 **Tel** *(909) 866-5600*   **Road map** *D6*

Breakfasts are elaborate in the mountains, and this place offers hearty options to start your day with. Salads and sandwiches are offered at midday, and for dinner there is everything from prime rib to seafood. A selection of authentic German specialties sets this homey place apart. There are some good German beers to go with your schnitzel.

BIG BEAR CITY The Iron Squirrel   ⚄⚄⚄

646 Pine Knot Blvd, 92314 **Tel** *(909) 866-9121*   **Road map** *D6*

With its rustic wood-clad dining room and French country cuisine, The Iron Squirrel has become a favorite dining place in Big Bear. Ideal for a romantic interlude or family gathering, it offers classic dishes such as garlicky escargots, country pâtés, and duck *à l'orange* that prove to be an irresistible combination with the mountain air.

BORREGO SPRINGS Borrego Springs Resort   ⚄⚄

1112 Tilting T Dr, 92004 **Tel** *(760) 767-5700*   **Road map** *D6*

This quiet desert resort enjoys a view of the Santa Rosa mountains. The ornate but informal dining room features an all-American menu at linen-clad tables. Items such as Southwest chicken, filet mignon, salmon, and sea bass reflect the varied but straightforward fare. it is immensely popular for happy hour and Sunday brunch. Check timings.

CHINO Centro Basco   ⚄⚄

13432 Central Ave, 91710 **Tel** *(909) 628-9014*   **Road map** *D6*

Formerly part of an old lodging house for Basque sheep herders, this sprawling dining room provides big hearty meals. An extensive menu offers a massive tureen of soup, salad, delicious pickled beef tongue, and pasta. Main dishes include rotisserie chicken, rack of lamb, trout, or prime rib. Considering the generous helpings, it is a bargain.

CORONA Napa 29   ⚄⚄⚄⚄

280 Teller St, 92879 **Tel** *(951) 273-0529*   **Road map** *D6*

Named after the highway running through Napa Valley, this sleek, wood-clad restaurant offers a sophisticated Wine Country cuisine. Reminiscent of a trendy Northern California eatery, it has cozy booths to enjoy innovative meat and seafood dishes embellished with skillful reduction sauces. The wines are moderately priced.

IDYLLWILD Gastrognome   ⚄⚄⚄

54381 Ridgeview Dr, 92549 **Tel** *(951) 659-5055*   **Road map** *D6*

The "Gnome", as the locals call it, boasts a delightfully rustic, timbered dining room with a prominent stone fireplace. A perfect mountain retreat, the hearty fare includes crab cakes, orange-glazed roast duck, salmon with Hollandaise, and lobster tacos. At lunch, you can enjoy a burger on the deck and admire forest.

LA QUINTA La Quinta Cliffhouse   ⚄⚄⚄⚄

78250 Hwy 111, 92253 **Tel** *(760) 360-5991*   **Road map** *D6*

Set in a historic ranch house with a rustic beamed ceiling, stone fireplace, and a terrace carved out of rock, La Quinta Cliffhouse is one of the desert's most popular dining venues. The menu features crab-crusted mahi mahi with red pepper aïoli, lobster, USDA Prime steaks, and a legendary burger. With a loyal following, the place can get crowded.

Key to Price Guide *see p568* **Key to Symbols** *see back cover flap*

LA QUINTA Azur by Le Bernardin 🚸 ♿ ♫ ⛱ $$$$$

La Quinta Resort & Club, 49499 Eisenhower Dr, 92253 ***Tel*** *(760) 777-4835* ***Road map*** *D6*

Tucked into an exclusive resort, this is a venture of the owners of Le Bernardin, New York's most celebrated seafood restaurant. No detail has been overlooked and no cost spared to ensure that the same standards are established here. The globe's freshest seafood is prepared with a Mediterranean style and formally presented. Check timings.

PALM DESERT Louise's Pantry 🚸 ♿ $

44491 Town Center Way, 92260 ***Tel*** *(760) 346-9320* ***Road map*** *D6*

Originally founded down the road in 1945, this old-style diner still offers familiar all-American foods. Locals seem happy to stand in line for specialties such as big old-fashioned breakfasts, chicken dumplings, grilled cheese sandwiches, and apple pie that come fresh from the oven. The Reuben sandwich is a particular favorite.

PALM DESERT Ristorante Tuscany 🚸 ♿ $$$$

Marriott Desert Springs Resort & Spa, 74855 Country Club Dr, 92260 ***Tel*** *(760) 341-2211* ***Road map*** *D6*

Better than most hotel dining rooms, this place is one of the desert's preferred northern Italian restaurants. The main room is a soaring space with floor-to-ceiling murals and elegantly appointed tables. The diverse menu features fresh seasonal ingredients and a superb selection of seafood. Try the Parmesan-crusted scallops and Tuscan shellfish stew.

PALM DESERT Cuistot 🚸 ♿ ⛱ $$$$$

73111 El Paseo, 92260 ***Tel*** *(760) 340-1000* ***Road map*** *D6*

The chef/owner worked with the great Paul Bocuse in France and his modern French cuisine has long been one of the desert's premier culinary attractions. Inspired by a French country farmhouse, the restaurant features a beamed ceiling, a stone fireplace, and a patio. From the exhibition kitchen come spectacular looking and tasting creations.

PALM DESERT Jillian's ♿ ⛱ $$$$$

74155 El Paseo, 92260 ***Tel*** *(760) 776-8242* ***Road map*** *D6*

Intimate rooms face a charming courtyard at this rustically elegant, romantic venue. The menu provides familiar American themes, dressed up with subtle innovative twists, complemented by an award-winning wine list. Start with a spicy corn chowder, move on to roasted rack of lamb with rosemary jus, and finish with an upscale bread pudding.

PALM SPRINGS Europa ♿ ⛱ $$$$

Villa Royale Inn, 1620 Indian Trail, 92264 ***Tel*** *(760) 327-2314* ***Road map*** *D6*

Europa is one of Coachella Valley's most romantic restaurants, tucked into a charming little inn. Guests can enjoy classic Continental cuisine either in the intimate dining room by the fireplace, or out on the poolside patio. Menu highlights include rack of lamb, salmon *en papillote*, and duck in Grand Marnier-honey sauce.

PALM SPRINGS St. James at the Vineyard 🚸 ♿ ♫ ⛱ $$$$

265 S Palm Canyon Dr, 92262 ***Tel*** *(760) 320-8041* ***Road map*** *D6*

The dining room at this restaurant is filled with artifacts – Buddhas from Asia, masks from Africa – from the journeys of the globetrotting owners. The equally eclectic menu features Burmese-style bouillabaisse, tamarind-glazed salmon with wasabi cream, and a variety of curries. The wine list is predominantly Californian.

PALM SPRINGS Le Vallauris ♿ ⛱ $$$$$

385 W Tahquitz Canyon Way, 92262 ***Tel*** *(760) 325-5059* ***Road map*** *D6*

Regarded by some as the grande dame of the Palm Springs dining scene, this restaurant is still going strong. The main dining room is a study in refined elegance, while the garden patio is shaded by ficus trees. French items, such as escargots and foie gras, share a menu with spicy ahi tuna tartare and lobster ravioli. Impressive list of Bordeaux.

RANCHO MIRAGE Las Casuelas Nuevas 🚸 ♿ ♫ ⛱ $$

70050 Hwy 111, 92270 ***Tel*** *(760) 328-8844* ***Road map*** *D6*

This handsome hacienda-style restaurant specializes in familiar Mexican dishes such as enchiladas, fajitas, tostadas, and carnitas. There is live entertainment nightly and potent margaritas can be chosen from over a dozen varieties. The busy bar also stocks an endless list of premium tequilas. A favored destination for Sunday brunch.

RANCHO MIRAGE Roy's 🚸 ♿ ⛱ $$$

71959 Hwy 111, 92270 ***Tel*** *(760) 340-9044* ***Road map*** *D6*

Celebrity chef Roy Yamaguchi brings his acclaimed regional Hawaiian cuisine to this sprawling, bustling restaurant. The food is consistently well prepared and beautifully presented. Seared ahi tuna, with a sweet and a hot sauce, is a specialty, and so is the macadamia-crusted mahi mahi in a lobster butter sauce.

RANCHO MIRAGE Prime 10 Steakhouse ♿ $$$$$

Agua Caliente Casino, 32250 Bob Hope Line, 92270 ***Tel*** *(760) 202-6063* ***Road map*** *D6*

Although it is located just steps from the endless clatter of slot machines, this casino restaurant proves to be a stylish, soothing setting, with rich wood accents and linen-clad tables. The menu showcases USDA Prime beef, as well as plenty of seafood. Steakhouse classics share the menu with Asian influences, and the wine list is solid.

RANCHO MIRAGE Wally's Desert Turtle ♿ ♫ ⛱ $$$$$

71775 Hwy 111, 92270 ***Tel*** *(760) 568-9321* ***Road map*** *D6*

One of the grand dining rooms of the desert, Wally's is the kind of place guests come dressed to the nines. Mirrored ceilings, Peruvian artifacts, and elegant murals contribute to the dramatic decor. Prices are high, but top-drawer ingredients go into the rack of lamb, sautéed ostrich, and filet of beef with a peppercorn or Bearnaise sauce.

REDLANDS Joe Greensleeves   🏃♿ $$$$

220 N Orange St, 92374 **Tel** *(909) 792-6969*   **Road map** *D6*

This endearing restaurant inhabits an old building in downtown Redlands. A fireplace, cozy booths, and flattering lighting create a subtly romantic ambience. However, the prime attraction comes out of the glass-enclosed kitchen: wild game, whole-baked branzino (sea bass), osso buco, pastas, and steaks cooked over a wood grill.

RIVERSIDE Las Campanas   🏃♿♪🚗 $$$

Mission Inn, 3649 Mission Inn Ave, 92501 **Tel** *(951) 341-6767*   **Road map** *D6*

This charming courtyard is shaded by towering palms, fountains and flowering cacti, and candles reinforce a romantic ambiance. Start with ceviche spiked with a splash of tequila, before moving on to grilled salmon with an orange-tequila reduction or lobster tail in tomatillo sauce. Finish with flan or coconut sorbet served in a coconut shell.

RIVERSIDE Mario's Place   🏃♿♪🚗 $$$$

3646 Mission Inn Ave, 92501 **Tel** *(951) 684-7755*   **Road map** *D6*

Just across from the historic Mission Inn, Mario's is a sleek, cosmopolitan restaurant with sensuous Art Deco touches. The kitchen skillfully plays with both Asian and French technique, as well as serving up traditional Italian specialties such as carpaccio, risotto with squab and mushrooms, veal chop, and pizza from a wood-burning oven.

RIVERSIDE Duane's Prime Steak & Seafood   🏃♿ $$$$$

Mission Inn, 3649 Mission Inn Ave, 92501 **Tel** *(951) 341-6767*   **Road map** *D6*

By the time you sit down at your table, you will have already had the pleasure of walking through the magnificent Mission Inn, one of California's most historic hotels. Wood-clad Duane's is dignified and stately, with splendid art and elegant table settings. The USDA Prime steaks are superb and the elaborate Sunday brunch is an experience.

TEMECULA Café Champagne   🏃♿♪🚗 $$$$

Thornton Winery, 32575 Rancho California Rd, 92589 **Tel** *(951) 699-0088*   **Road map** *D6*

Diners have sweepiing views of the nearby rolling vineyards from Café Champagne, you will nearly be fooled. Freshness is a priority here, evidenced by the restaurant's own herb garden. Try the ahi-avocado Napoleon or crispy roasted duck with lavender honey sauce. The delightful patio is an occasional live jazz venue.

UPLAND Café Provençal   🏃♿🚗 $$$

967 W Foothill Blvd, 91784 **Tel** *(909) 608-7100*   **Road map** *D5*

In the suburb of Upland, Café Provençal is run by a delightful couple from Marseilles. An authentic place to find traditional bouillabaisse, this rustic dining room with a stone fireplace is also favored for crêpes, steak *au poivre*, and rack of lamb. Desserts excel and a blackboard lists nightly specials.

THE MOJAVE DESERT

BAKER The Mad Greek's Diner   🏃♿🚗 $

72112 Baker Blvd, 92309 **Tel** *(760) 733-4354*   **Road map** *D5*

Whether headed to Vegas or Death Valley, weary drivers are advised to skip the big national chains and stop instead at the Mad Greek's. Besides the usual burgers, tasty gyros, hummus, kebabs, and other Mediterranean fare are on offer. The strawberry shakes are famous, and tourist assistance is offered in several languages.

BARSTOW Idle Spurs Steak House   🏃♿🚗 $$$

690 Old Hwy 58, 92311 **Tel** *(760) 256-8888*   **Road map** *D5*

This traditional, Western-style steakhouse is a good, relaxing place to recharge after a long day of driving. The jalapeño poppers and chicken wings are popular starters, followed by tender aged steaks. The old school bar is a popular watering hole for locals. The attractive patio, dominated by a massive tree, offers a pleasant alfresco option.

DEATH VALLEY Wrangler Steakhouse   🏃♿ $$

Furnace Creek Ranch, Hwy 190, 92328 **Tel** *(760) 786-2345*   **Road map** *D4*

Not as formal as the dining room at the adjoining Furnace Creek Inn, this restaurant is housed in a former working ranch, beautifully preserved to reflect the mystique of this desert oasis. The restaurant features an all-you-can-eat buffet for breakfast and lunch. In the evening, it operates as a traditional steakhouse.

DEATH VALLEY Inn Dining Room   🏃♿♪ $$$$

Furnace Creek Inn, Hwy 190, 92328 **Tel** *(760) 786-2345*   **Road map** *D4*

Housed in a historic adobe and stone resort, which closes every summer, this rather upscale dining room is noted for its Sunday brunch and afternoon tea. The sophisticated dinner menu, with Southwestern and Asian accents, reflects the desert environment in its cactus salad and rattlesnake empanadas. The steaks are also popular.

LAKE HAVASU Barley Brothers Brewery & Grill   🏃♿ $$

1425 McCulloch Blvd, 86403 **Tel** *(928) 505-7837*   **Road map** *E5*

Offering a view of London Bridge, this versatile place is great for families, yet can also be somewhat romantic, given the view, soft lighting, and conversation-conducive atmosphere. Wood-fired pizzas complement a choice of handcrafted beers, and entrées include Jamaican salmon, pastas, ribs, and steaks.

Key to Price Guide *see p568* **Key to Symbols** *see back cover flap*

LAKE HAVASU Shugrue's Restaurant 👪 ♿ $$

1425 McCulloch Blvd, 86403 ***Tel*** *(928) 453-1400* ***Road map*** *E5*

With a next-door brewpub catering to a livelier crowd, this quiet family restaurant offers a fine view of London Bridge and its distinctive library setting makes for a pleasant respite. Steaks, seafood, burgers, and pastas are the main attractions. Excellent desserts are made on the premises. Bargain-priced early bird dinners are also available.

LAS VEGAS Sam Woo BBQ 👪 ♿ $

4215 Spring Mountain Rd, NV 89102 ***Tel*** *(702) 368-7628* ***Road map*** *E4*

In a developing Chinatown of Las Vegas, this bargain-priced eatery specializes in traditional Chinese barbecue, prominently announced by whole pigs, chickens, and ducks hanging in the window. Even after the casinos have bankrupted you, you can afford a big portion of delicious barbecued meat, from the familiar to the exotic.

LAS VEGAS Top of the World 👪 ♿ $$$$

Stratosphere Hotel, 2000 Las Vegas Blvd S, NV 89104 ***Tel*** *(702) 380-7777* ***Road map*** *E4*

This restaurant does not boast a world-famous celebrity chef, but there is no place in town that can match its 360-degree panoramic view from 800 ft (244 m). The food is surprisingly good for a view restaurant, with fresh seafood, steaks, pasta, and rack of lamb getting rave reviews. Fine desserts and an impressive wine list keep diners lingering.

LAS VEGAS Andrés French Restaurant ♿ 🍴 $$$$$

401 S 6th St, NV 89101 ***Tel*** *(702) 385-5016* ***Road map*** *E4*

Long before the big-name restauranteurs arrived on the Strip, André Rochat was turning out superb French cuisine at this homey freestanding restaurant in downtown Vegas. With the aura of a rustic country auberge, it specializes in dishes such as *vichyssoise*, foie gras terrine, Dover sole Véronique, and beef with peppercorn sauce. Extraordinary wine list.

LAUGHLIN The Deli 👪 ♿ $

Golden Nugget, 2300 S Casino Dr, NV 89029 ***Tel*** *(702) 298-7222* ***Road map*** *E5*

Though not particularly quiet or comfortable, this popular riverside gambling town eatery is ideal for a quick bite or late night snack after hitting the tables. Traditional New York deli items feature overstuffed pastrami and corned beef sandwiches on quality rye bread. Pizzas, hot dogs, and other budget-friendly options can also be found here.

SAN FRANCISCO

GOLDEN GATE PARK AND THE PRESIDIO Angkor Wat 👪 ♿ $

4217 Geary, 94118 ***Tel*** *(415) 221-7887* ***Map*** *3 5A*

Authentic, beautifully presented East Asian cuisine, candlelight, and a friendly staff have made Angkor Wat a special occasion destination. The authentic cooking is reflected in its delicious curries, especially the duck curry. Diners are encouraged to join in the dancing on weekends, and will feel most comfortable in dressy casual attire.

GOLDEN GATE PARK AND THE PRESIDIO Ebisu 👪 ♿ $

1283 9th Ave, 94122 ***Tel*** *(415) 566-1770* ***Map*** *8 F3*

Often crowded, this sushi restaurant has visitors lined up to sample what some say is the best and freshest sushi in town, served by laughing, cleaver-flashing chefs at the bar. Try the house specialty, Ebisu maki, featuring salmon and vegetables. Ebisu is seafood-as-entertainment, and queues for table space are not uncommon.

GOLDEN GATE PARK AND THE PRESIDIO Good Luck Dim Sum 👪 ♿ $

736 Clement St, 94118 ***Tel*** *(415) 386-3388* ***Map*** *3 5A*

A local favorite, this joint is known to serve the freshest dim sum at rock-bottom prices. Those joining the long queues usually come for take-out. The Formica tables in the back provide a steady surface to eat from if not much else. Good Luck always sells out by early afternoon, so get there in the morning for the best selection.

GOLDEN GATE PARK AND THE PRESIDIO Khan Toke 👪 ♿ $

5937 Geary Blvd, 94118 ***Tel*** *(415) 668-6654* ***Map*** *8 E1*

A temple-like interior and colorfully dressed staff transports diners to Thailand. Featuring both floor- and Western-style seating, this long-established restaurant serves Thai standards such as spicy, lemon calamari salad and grilled satay with peanut sauce. Reservations are recommended.

GOLDEN GATE PARK AND THE PRESIDIO King of Thai 👪 ♿ $

639 Clement St, 94118 ***Tel*** *(415) 752-5198* ***Map*** *3 A5*

The late-night hours and extremely inexpensive steaming noodle dishes make King of Thai a great hit. Many branches of this citywide chain are open late, and none take credit cards or checks. Spiciness can be adjusted according to each diner's preference. Vegetarian entrées are available.

GOLDEN GATE PARK AND THE PRESIDIO Marnee Thai 👪 ♿ $

2225 Irving St, 94122 ***Tel*** *(415) 665-9500* ***Map*** *8 E3*

Large servings of consistently good Thai food have made this cozy, friendly restaurant a dependable choice. Marnee Thai's green curries are quite good. The tight seating and sometimes long waits for a table do not deter loyal fans. Another location at 1243 Ninth Avenue expands diners' choices.

GOLDEN GATE PARK AND THE PRESIDIO La Vie

5830 Geary Blvd, 94121 **Tel** (415) 668-8080 · **Map** 8 E1

A wonderful neighborhood find in the outer Richmond area – a good stop before or after a visit to Golden Gate Park – La Vie gets consistently good reviews for its Vietnamese menu prepared and served with a French flair. The flaming beef and prawns are a favorite.

GOLDEN GATE PARK AND THE PRESIDIO Park Chalet

1000 Great Hwy, 94122 **Tel** (415) 386-8439 · **Map** 7 A1

The view is of a garden rather than the ocean, but the big stone fireplace and retractable glass walls of this Beach Chalet addition make dining here an alfresco experience even on chilly days. Serves great beers from the Beach Chalet brewery, plus *cioppino* and fancified pub specialties.

GOLDEN GATE PARK AND THE PRESIDIO Ton Kiang

5821 Geary Blvd, 94121 **Tel** (415) 387-8273 · **Map** 8 E1

Ton Kiang is one of the best and most popular dim sum restaurants in town – beware of the queues down the block on weekends. The huge variety of dishes is always fresh, and always rolling your way on cart after cart. Full plate dishes are also served. Do not miss the minced squab with lettuce leaves.

GOLDEN GATE PARK AND THE PRESIDIO Aziza

5800 Geary Blvd, 94121 **Tel** (415) 752-2222 · **Map** 8 E1

At Aziza, guests are welcomed by sprinkling rosewater over their hands. Exotic Moroccan specialties are brought to the table, as diners lounge on luxurious cushioned seats. Moroccan classics are prepared with a modern twist. The meal is finished with sweet mint tea. On weekends, belly dancers perform while you dine.

GOLDEN GATE PARK AND THE PRESIDIO Beach Chalet Brewery

1000 Great Hwy, 94122 **Tel** (415) 386-8439 · **Map** 7 A2

Craft brews, big hamburgers with side dishes of crispy fries, and a spectacular view of the Pacific make Beach Chalet Brewery a promising destination after a day in Golden Gate Park. The WPA murals on the first floor and carved stone stair-rails are a must-see. An excellent brunch is served at weekends and there is live music on Tuesdays and Fridays.

GOLDEN GATE PARK AND THE PRESIDIO Cliff House

1090 Point Lobos Ave, 94121 **Tel** (415) 386-3330 · **Map** 7 A1

The original Cliff House, built in 1863, was where rich San Franciscans brunched. Twice destroyed by fire, the renovated fresh seafood place has the best views of the barking seals below on Seal Rocks. Enjoy cocktails at Zinc Bar. The formal restaurant is open for lunch and dinner, and the informal bistro for all meals daily.

GOLDEN GATE PARK AND THE PRESIDIO Pacific Café

7000 Geary Blvd, 94121 **Tel** (415) 387-7091 · **Map** 7 C1

Opened in the 1970s, Pacific Café is redolent of the era, down to the stained-glass windows. Good, reliable seafood is served to one's liking. Diners who have to wait for a table are often treated to a glass of wine. There are branches all over the Bay area; this was the original location.

PACIFIC HEIGHTS Fresca

2114 Fillmore, 94115 **Tel** (415) 447-2668 · **Map** 4 D4

This Peruvian restaurant has a country-feel interior with an open kitchen. There are plenty of great home-style meat and seafood dishes. Specialties include the ceviche dishes, based on halibut with ginger and *amarillo aji* (yellow Peruvian chili), and seabass with lime and cilantro. The casual ambience adds to its appeal.

PACIFIC HEIGHTS La Mediterranee

2210 Fillmore St, 94115 **Tel** (415) 921-2956 · **Map** 4 D4

Taking up only a narrow space, La Mediterranée serves delicious Mediterranean specialties, such as hummus and falafel, with the reasonably-priced house wine. For dessert, try the tasty baklava. This old neighborhood haunt still displays a flying dove and the name of the former tenants on the stained glass over the door.

PACIFIC HEIGHTS Zao Noodle Bar

2406 California St, 94115 **Tel** (415) 345-8088 · **Map** 4 D4

Reliable, quick, cheap, and healthy noodle dishes, served up in large bowls, are the perfect alternative to greasy fast food. Though the preparation style is more home-cooking than *haute cuisine*, it is still one of the best deals in town. There are several branches in the city and beyond.

PACIFIC HEIGHTS Elite Café

2049 Fillmore St, 94115 **Tel** (415) 346-8668 · **Map** 4 D4

In the middle of the Fillmore shopping area, Elite Café is an institution, with intimate booths and a hopping bar that serves fresh oysters along with stiff drinks. The New Orleans-style gumbos and jambalayas also feature on the weekend brunch menu. Service is warm and attentive.

PACIFIC HEIGHTS Rica

1838 Union St, 94123 **Tel** (415) 474-3773 · **Map** 4 E2

A place to see and be seen, Rica is a stylish addition to the Union Street scene. It has plasma screens displaying a constantly-changing vista of Spanish artworks, while diners sip fresh-fruit cocktails from the sleek bar, and sample a variety of tapas served on small plates. The cheery ambience attracts a young, trendy clientele.

Key to Price Guide see p568 **Key to Symbols** see back cover flap

PACIFIC HEIGHTS Balboa Café

319 Fillmore St, 94123 **Tel** *(415) 921-3944*

Map *4 D2*

Dependable lunches and brunches are the mainstay of Balboa Café, the elder statesman of the area known as "the Triangle" for its trendy bars. A must-try are the hamburgers here. After dinner, this restaurant with an elegant decor becomes a meet-and-greet hotspot for 30-somethings.

PACIFIC HEIGHTS Brazen Head

3166 Buchanan St, 94123 **Tel** *(415) 921-7600*

Map *4 D2*

This cash-only, dark, pub-like hideaway is the favored destination for those craving a traditional grilled steak, a scotch on the rocks, and quiet conversation late at night after the other local restaurants have closed. The extensive wine list is well chosen. Visitors know the location by the address – there is no sign.

PACIFIC HEIGHTS Clementine

126 Clement St, 94118 **Tel** *(415) 387-0408*

Map *3 A5*

It is best to arrive early at Clementine, a softly-lit corner of Paris in the inner Richmond area. The bargain prix-fixe menu fills up the small space quickly, especially on the weekends. French bistro classics, such as *cassoulet* and lamb shank with white beans are some of the consistent favorites.

PACIFIC HEIGHTS Greens

Building A, Fort Mason Center, 94123 **Tel** *(415) 771-6222*

Map *4 E1*

Greens is considered by many as the city's most famous vegetarian restaurant. Its elegant, pale walls and views of the Golden Gate Bridge are the perfect setting for the imaginative meat-free delicacies that even a carnivore would love. The bread basket is always heaped with exceptional offerings from the in-house bakery.

PACIFIC HEIGHTS PlumpJack Café

3127 Fillmore St, 94123 **Tel** *(415) 563-4755*

Map *4 D2*

PlumpJack Café, a tiny, ultra-hip eatery, has remained a top destination since it opened in 1993. The innovative Mediterranean menu is enhanced by fresh local produce and meats, and the wine list is well-chosen and reasonably priced. An intimate atmosphere prevails throughout. Reservations are a must.

PACIFIC HEIGHTS Rose's Café

2298 Union St, 94123 **Tel** *(415) 775-2200*

Map *4 D3*

At Rose's Café, the tables set outside look over the quiet end of Union Street, while the interior features a cheery yellow space with big windows. The restaurant's main draws are the weekday lunches, with good salads and pastas, as well as weekend brunches. Specialties include French toast and breakfast pizzas. Live music on Monday nights.

FISHERMAN'S WHARF AND NORTH BEACH Brandy Hos

217 Columbus Ave, 94133 **Tel** *(415) 788-7527*

Map *5 C3*

Renowned for its hot and sour curries, this hole-in-the-wall restaurant earned a fiery reputation for delicious, authentic Hunan dishes. Be forewarned – "medium spicy" means hot, while "hot" is alarming. Savvy diners know to quell the fire with rice, not water. Order a "mild" plate and enjoy.

FISHERMAN'S WHARF AND NORTH BEACH Capp's Corner

1600 Powell St, 94133 **Tel** *(415) 989-2589*

Map *5 B3*

A lower-cost option popular with families, Capp's Corner serves up an Americanized version of Italian cooking. Do not expect fine cuisine, but generous portions of all the traditional favorites. Opened in 1960, the restaurant features a photographic gallery of famous former diners.

FISHERMAN'S WHARF AND NORTH BEACH Gira Polli

659 Union St, 94133 **Tel** *(415) 434-4472*

Map *6 B2*

Wonderful rotisserie-roasted chicken with a choice of side dishes is the specialty of this small, unassuming spot. The decor is uninspired, but the food and the prices in this part of North Beach are unbeatable. There is a good range of pasta, salads, and desserts. The restaurant is usually filled with locals.

FISHERMAN'S WHARF AND NORTH BEACH Caffe Macaroni

59 Columbus, 94111 **Tel** *(415) 956-9737*

Map *5 C3*

This densely packed, two-story eatery serves reliably good pastas (the creamy Alfredo is a favorite) and meat dishes to tourists and locals alike. The bustling café is known for its friendly, enthusiastic waiters, and generous portions that satisfy the biggest appetite. The antipasti is exceptionally good.

FISHERMAN'S WHARF AND NORTH BEACH Caffe Sport

574 Green St, 94133 **Tel** *(415) 981-1251*

Map *5 C3*

Big, family-style platters of garlic-infused vegetables, spaghetti Bolognese, and other Italian favorites, such as the superb *ziti* pasta in marinara sauce, are served by waiters known for their bossy attitude in this loud, busy eatery. They are happy to tell diners what to order – just ask.

FISHERMAN'S WHARF AND NORTH BEACH Enrico's Sidewalk Café

504 Broadway St, 94133 **Tel** *(415) 982-6223*

Map *5 C3*

The Beat Generation put Enrico's Sidewalk Café on the map, and nowadays the sidewalk scene, live jazz, bar drinks, and espresso keep it going. The Italian-inspired cuisine is not memorable, but the European café-style ambience is quite charming. A neighborhood – and San Francisco – institution.

FISHERMAN'S WHARF AND NORTH BEACH Fog City Diner

1300 Battery St, 94111 **Tel** *(415) 982-2000* **Map** *5 C2* ⑤⑤

Glorified comfort foods, such as garlic, leek, and basil loaves, Cheddar biscuits, and mu shu pork burritos are on the menu, alongside burgers and fries at this chrome-trimmed diner lookalike. Weekend brunch features new twists on old favorites such as smoked chicken hash and eggs.

FISHERMAN'S WHARF AND NORTH BEACH Helmand

430 Broadway St, 94133 **Tel** *(415) 362-0641* **Map** *5 C3* ⑤⑤

The chefs at Helmand are masters with pumpkin, spinach, and coriander. The unusual combinations of spices and simple ingredients have made this Afghan restaurant an all-time favorite. A decent range of vegetarian and non-vegetarian items are on the menu. Here, even the rice has a unique flavor. The lunch buffets are a bargain.

FISHERMAN'S WHARF AND NORTH BEACH Il Fornaio

1265 Battery St, 94111 **Tel** *(415) 986-0100* **Map** *5 C2* ⑤⑤

A chain that built its reputation on outstanding baked goods, Il Fornaio continues to attract diners with fresh breads, delicious pastas, and grilled meats and fish. The superb butternut squash ravioli in butter sauce is served as both an appetizer and entrée. The well-chosen wine list represents small, regional wineries.

FISHERMAN'S WHARF AND NORTH BEACH The Stinking Rose

325 Columbus Ave, 94133 **Tel** *(415) 781-7673* **Map** *5 C3* ⑤⑤

True to its name, The Stinking Rose uses garlic in every dish – including dessert. This Californian-Italian-style pasta and pizza restaurant is often crowded with those curious about the unusual name, though service and quality can be uneven at times. Be adventurous and try their garlic ice cream.

FISHERMAN'S WHARF AND NORTH BEACH Tre Fratelli

2801 Leavenworth St, 94133 **Tel** *(415) 474-8240* **Map** *5 A2* ⑤⑤

Since the move from its former Hyde Street location, this long-standing restaurant, opened in 1980, has added fresh fish to its excellent pastas and meat dishes. The Alfredo (white-sauce pasta) is particularly creamy and delicious, and the service is friendly and efficient.

FISHERMAN'S WHARF AND NORTH BEACH Zarzuela

2000 Hyde St, 94109 **Tel** *(415) 346-0800* **Map** *5 A3* ⑤⑤

A variety of tasty tapas and strong, fruity sangria combined with a caring staff and charming dining room make Zarzuela a favorite for an authentic light meal or more. The best Spanish food in the city according to those who swear by its paella. There may be a wait for a table in the evenings.

FISHERMAN'S WHARF AND NORTH BEACH Alioto's

8 Fisherman's Wharf, 94133 **Tel** *(415) 673-0183* **Map** *5 A1* ⑤⑤⑤

Lit by spectacular sunsets filtered through the Golden Gate, Alioto's has been serving well-prepared Sicilian-style seafood since 1925. The food is good, especially the bountiful shrimp or crab Louies (juicy seafood on a bed of crisp romaine lettuce). The kitchen uses fresh seasonal ingredients, sourced locally.

FISHERMAN'S WHARF AND NORTH BEACH Moose's

1652 Stockton St, 94133 **Tel** *(415) 989-7800* **Map** *5 B2* ⑤⑤⑤

Perennially popular, Moose's is crowded with fashionable people around the bar, listening to live jazz in the evenings, and enjoying hearty plates of tasty grilled salmon, meatloaf, and other favorites. Regulars call it "style without attitude." Wine lovers can choose from a well-represented, extensive wine list.

FISHERMAN'S WHARF AND NORTH BEACH Scoma's

Pier 47, 1 Al Scoma Way, 94133 **Tel** *(415) 771-4383* **Map** *5 A1* ⑤⑤⑤⑤

To have a street named after you means you've been here awhile, and critically-acclaimed Scoma's started out in 1965 as a coffee shop for local fishermen. A standard-bearer for well-cooked, big portions of fresh fish, this restaurant features an impressive menu of over 90 dishes. Pretty views of the bay enhance the dining experience.

FISHERMAN'S WHARF AND NORTH BEACH Gary Danko

800 North Point St, 94109 **Tel** *(415) 749-2060* **Map** *5 1A* ⑤⑤⑤⑤⑤

In spite of the exorbitant prices, Gary Danko has remained one of the favored restaurants in the city for its New American prix-fixes. Three-, four-, or five-course dinners provide hours of carefully choreographed courses, efficient service, and elegant surroundings. The selection of cheeses is a must-sample.

FISHERMAN'S WHARF AND NORTH BEACH Julius' Castle

1541 Montgomery St, 94133 **Tel** *(415) 392-2222* **Map** *5 C2* ⑤⑤⑤⑤⑤

In a romantic setting, with lovely views of Alcatraz and the Bay Bridge, Julius' Castle is housed in a 1922 San Francisco landmark building. Seared tuna and rack of lamb are stalwarts on the menu of this restaurant. The service is old-fashioned. The wine cellar has an excellent wine list on offer.

CHINATOWN AND NOB HILL Golden Star Vietnamese Restaurant

11 Walter U Lum Place, 94108 **Tel** *(415) 398-1215* **Map** *5 C3* ⑤

Situated across from the Transamerica Pyramid, the Golden Star is narrow and crowded, and the decor is as plain as a school cafeteria. Nonetheless, this little gem serves up big rice dishes and meat portions for very little money. The lunch specials are of exceptional value.

Key to Price Guide *see p568* **Key to Symbols** *see back cover flap*

CHINATOWN AND NOB HILL House of Nanking Ⓢ

919 Kearny, 94133 **Tel** *(415) 421-1429*　　　　　　　　　　**Map** *5 C3*

The good, traditional menu at the tiny House of Nanking attracts a loyal clientele. Even though the waiters here are a little unfriendly, food comes in generous portions and the prices are reasonably low. The menu offers a good selection of vegetarian options. Service is amazingly brisk.

CHINATOWN AND NOB HILL Yuet Lee Ⓢ

1300 Stockton St, 94133 **Tel** *(415) 982-6020*　　　　　　　　　　**Map** *5 B3*

Yuet Lee's excellent fresh seafood menu and low prices are the reasons locals flock here. There is a live fish tank and the chef will cook a whole fish or crab to order. Specialties include steamed fish and seafood; salt-and-pepper squid; and an array of vegetables such as long bean, bok choy, and asparagus. It is open until 3am.

CHINATOWN AND NOB HILL Great Eastern ⓈⓈ

649 Jackson St, 94133 **Tel** *(415) 986-2500*　　　　　　　　　　**Map** *5 C3*

A longtime favorite in Chinatown, Great Eastern has a menu featuring reliable, if not inspired, Mandarin dishes. The real draw here is the fresh seafood swimming in the tanks – make sure to ask the waiter for the day's specials to sample the best that the restaurant has to offer.

CHINATOWN AND NOB HILL Nob Hill Café ⓈⓈ

1152 Taylor St, 94108 **Tel** *(415) 776-6500*　　　　　　　　　　**Map** *5 B4*

Nob Hill Café is a local favorite, frequently crowded to the rafters, as diners enjoy home-style Italian dishes. The bistro type decor is matched by an easy-going ambience. Visitors often spot "The Twins" – the delightful Brown sisters – here. The similarly dressed duo is as much a San Francisco institution as Nob Hill itself.

CHINATOWN AND NOB HILL Street ⓈⓈ

2141 Polk St, 94109 **Tel** *(415) 775-1055*　　　　　　　　　　**Map** *5 A3*

Comfort food at its finest makes this neighborhood restaurant a favorite. Street is noisy and crowded, but the platters are ample. Try one of the best seafood entrées – big, juicy Gulf prawns served in a saffron-laced lobster broth over buttery homemade pasta. Finish with the not-too-sweet pecan bread pudding.

CHINATOWN AND NOB HILL Jai Yun ⓈⓈⓈ

923 Pacific Ave, 94133 **Tel** *(415) 981-7438*　　　　　　　　　　**Map** *5 B3*

Set in a small space and simply decorated, Jai Yun is full of surprises. The daily prix-fixe includes a series of constantly-changing, small dishes containing fresh ingredients purchased the same morning from the markets. The excellent seafood menu features abalone, squid, and shrimp dishes.

CHINATOWN AND NOB HILL Venticello ⓈⓈⓈ

1257 Taylor St, 94108 **Tel** *(415) 922-2545*　　　　　　　　　　**Map** *5 B3*

At Venticello, a trattoria serving fine Northern Italian cuisine, romance is not about holding hands by the fireplace – it is on the menu. The laid-back ambience encourages one to linger with a decaffeinated espresso and port after enjoying a perfectly seasoned plate of scampi. There is an impressive wine list.

CHINATOWN AND NOB HILL Acquerello ⓈⓈⓈⓈ

1722 Sacramento St, 94109 **Tel** *(415) 567-5432*　　　　　　　　　　**Map** *5 A4*

An exquisite wine list, knowledgable waiters who are happy to recommend food-and-wine pairings, carved glass decanters, and fine linen set the stage for a truly memorable experience in this former chapel. A rich, Venetian-themed menu makes for sumptuous dining. There is a unique collection of Italian cheeses.

CHINATOWN AND NOB HILL Big Four ⓈⓈⓈⓈ

1075 California St, 94108 **Tel** *(415) 771-1140*　　　　　　　　　　**Map** *5 B4*

Named after the enormously wealthy railroad barons, Big Four is the chosen place for the Nob Hill elite to hobnob. The dark polished-wood paneling and formal service are an appropriate setting for businesspeople and financiers in particular. The contemporary menu is traditional, and top quality.

CHINATOWN AND NOB HILL Ritz-Carlton Terrace ⓈⓈⓈⓈ

600 Stockton St, 94108 **Tel** *(415) 773-6198*　　　　　　　　　　**Map** *5 C4*

The garden of the Ritz-Carlton Terrace – the so-called poor sister to the Dining Room – bulges with the rich and beautiful at lunchtime. Equally popular, the Sunday jazz brunches require reservations. Good food, prepared in the Ritz's great kitchen, is served by a professional waitstaff. There is live music on Sundays.

CHINATOWN AND NOB HILL Fleur de Lys ⓈⓈⓈⓈⓈ

777 Sutter St, 94109 **Tel** *(415) 673-7779*　　　　　　　　　　**Map** *5 B4*

The prix-fixes on the French *nouvelle cuisine* menu at Fleur de Lys are the ultimate in gourmet dining, and the waiters flawlessly guide diners from one dish to the next in a lovely tented room. The restaurant also serves a superb vegetarian prix-fixe dinner. Try the oven-roasted yellow and red beet salad and artisanal French cheeses.

CHINATOWN AND NOB HILL Masa's ⓈⓈⓈⓈⓈ

648 Bush St, 94108 **Tel** *(415) 989-7154*　　　　　　　　　　**Map** *5 B4*

In Masa's stylish, urbane setting, diners are treated like royalty as they sample exquisite *nouvelle cuisine*. Benefitting from a celebrated local chef for several years, this well-renowned restaurant continues to beguile diners by changing much of the menu every day, based on fresh market buys.

CHINATOWN AND NOB HILL Ritz-Carlton Dining Room 👶 ♿ $$$$$

600 Stockton St, 94108 ***Tel*** *(415) 773-6198* ***Map*** *5 C4*

Ranked number one in many city and travel magazine surveys, the elegant Dining Room is a perfect example of premium service in the grand European tradition. The highly praised menu exhibits an Asian influence, introducing ingredients found in local markets. The cheese board features a wide variety of artisanal cheeses.

DOWNTOWN Café Bastille 👶 ♿ 🎵 ⛱ $$

22 Belden Place, 94104 ***Tel*** *(415) 986-5673* ***Map*** *5 C4*

Tucked away in a traffic-free alley, this mini-Paris is often crowded with diners enjoying the fine weather at the outside tables during the day or jazz in the evenings. Basic bistro soups, salads, beer and wine are served along with French specialties such as *moules marinières* with *harissa* (red chili) sauce and tripe sausage with caramelized onions.

DOWNTOWN Delancey Street Restaurant 👶 ♿ ⛱ $$

600 Embarcadero, 94107 ***Tel*** *(415) 512-5179* ***Map*** *6 E5*

A wonderful place for dining, Delancey Street Restaurant serves delicious comfort food, including the excellent meatloaf and ribs, and other American dishes. The service is beyond good. The restaurant supports a respected substance-abuse recovery program. Reservations are recommended.

DOWNTOWN Gaylord India 👶 ♿ $$

1 Embarcadero Center, 94111 ***Tel*** *(415) 397-7775* ***Map*** *6 D3*

Gaylord turns out Indian standards – lamb curry, biriyanis, and vegetarian dishes – in pleasant surroundings. One of two branches in the city, this is the better of the two, and often crowded at lunchtime with local businesspeople. The other branch has relocated from 900 Northpoint to Sausalito.

DOWNTOWN Harbor Village Restaurant 👶 ♿ $$

4 Embarcado Center, 94111 ***Tel*** *(415) 781-8833* ***Map*** *6 D3*

Dozens of varieties of dim sum, served during the lunch hour, is the big draw at Harbor Village Restaurant, a spacious and noisy dining room. The kitchen also turns out reliable Cantonese entrées at night. The wait can be very long on weekends, but the view is worth it. The staff are prompt and efficient.

DOWNTOWN Sanraku at Metreon 👶 ♿ $$

101 4th St, 94103 ***Tel*** *(415) 369-6166* ***Map*** *5 C5*

Set amidst the noisy whirl of the Metreon, with its multiple theaters, children's attractions, and a video-game floor, Sanraku serves a dependable lunch and dinner. Japanese fare, such as crispy *gyoza* and wet and dry noodles, is served at good prices. They also also offer a superb sushi menu.

DOWNTOWN Yank Sing 👶 ♿ $$

101 Spear St, 94105 ***Tel*** *(415) 957-9300* ***Map*** *6 E4*

Much loved for its exquisite dim sum, Yank Sing allows diners to choose from over 100 different items, displayed on the constantly circulating carts. The upscale surroundings make this a cut above most dim sum parlors. Abuzz with a business clientele on weekdays, the restaurant turns into a family affair on the weekends.

DOWNTOWN Kuleto's 👶 ♿ $$$

221 Powell St, 94102 ***Tel*** *(415) 397-7720* ***Map*** *5 B5*

The exceptionally pretty Kuleto's is primarily frequented by those looking for a people-watching spot. It has an interior salvaged from an elegant old San Francisco hotel. Standard, if not spectacular North Italian dishes make up the menu. Enjoy appetizers at the bar for the best view.

DOWNTOWN La Scene Café & Bar 👶 ♿ $$$

490 Geary St, 94102 ***Tel*** *(415) 292-6430* ***Map*** *5 B5*

Simple French bistro-style food such as *cassoulet* and lamb shank makes this unpretentious restaurant a favorite with theatergoers. The prix-fixe menu is a bargain. The service is prompt, and the waitstaff are guaranteed to get you out of the door on time. Tasty weekend brunches are offered.

DOWNTOWN MacArthur Park 👶 ♿ $$$

607 Front St, 94111 ***Tel*** *(415) 398-5700* ***Map*** *6 D3*

Large and warm, with an updated-clubhouse feel, this downtown restaurant serves large portions of standard American favorites. The smoked baby back ribs with a side dish of garlic mashed potato get top honors. The service can be a little stiff, but the food is consistently good.

DOWNTOWN Palio d'Asti ♿ $$$

640 Sacramento St, 94111 ***Tel*** *(415) 395-9800* ***Map*** *5 C4*

Palio d'Asti is another favorite of the midday lunch crowd looking for authentic North Italian pastas and veal. The evening happy hours bring them all back with a free wood-fired pizza for a two-drink minimum. Murals of the medieval Palio horse race decorate the walls. Service is smooth in this ever-bustling place.

DOWNTOWN Palomino 👶 ♿ ⛱ $$$

345 Spear St, 94105 ***Tel*** *(415) 512-7400* ***Map*** *6 E4*

Palomino is a business-lunch favorite. Though part of a chain, it offers an extremely broad menu that features Italian, French, and American favorites. The convenient location features a gorgeous view of the Bay Bridge from the outdoor tables. The atmosphere is pleasantly upbeat in this classy restaurant.

Key to Price Guide *see p568* **Key to Symbols** *see back cover flap*

DOWNTOWN Sam's Grill and Seafood Restaurant   ♿ $$$

374 Bush St, 94104 **Tel** *(415) 421-0594*   **Map** 5 C4

Founded in 1866, Sam's Grill is the oldest seafood restaurant in the city. It has been serving outstanding sand dabs and other fresh fish to generations of visitors. At midday, one can can hear the murmur of businesspeople closing deals in the high-backed booths. It is closed on weekends.

DOWNTOWN Tadich Grill   🚹♿ $$$

240 California St, 94111 **Tel** *(415) 391-1849*   **Map** 6 D4

Founded during the Gold Rush, Tadich Grill is the oldest continuously operating restaurant in the state. It serves excellent *cioppino* and the fresh grilled fish is a tradition among seafood lovers. The wait for a table can be long in the evenings, but lunch is always a good bet. The old-fashioned waiters serve with great style.

DOWNTOWN Bix   ♿🎵 $$$$

56 Gold St, 94133 **Tel** *(415) 433 6300*   **Map** 5 C3

The slick Art-Deco interior in this swanky supper club, named after jazz great Bix Beiderbecke, is a sophisticated setting for French-American dishes impeccably served with a tinkling jazz piano. Locally produced ingredients are used in the cooking. Bix has great martinis and a see-and-be-seen afterwork crowd.

DOWNTOWN Kokkari Estiatorio   🚹♿ $$$$

200 Jackson St, 94111 **Tel** *(415) 981-0983*   **Map** 6 D3

The Kokkari serves stylish Greek food in a large, comfortable dining area with darkwood floors and a big, cozy fireplace. The signature moussaka and perfectly grilled lamb are top picks. The restaurant features an extensive list of Greek wines. The staff can guide your choices.

DOWNTOWN Rubicon   ♿ $$$$

558 Sacramento St, 94111 **Tel** *(415) 434-4100*   **Map** 5 C4

An impressive selection of 1,400 wines, paired with excellent French *nouvelle cuisine*, keeps diners coming back to Rubicon for more. Update your wine knowledge from the well-informed sommelier. The exposed brick wall, earth tones, and the use of wood and stone, lend the decor a craftsman feel.

DOWNTOWN Tommy Toy's   ♿ $$$$

655 Montgomery St, 94111 **Tel** *(415) 397-4888*   **Map** 5 C3

The tasting menu at Tommy Toy's is a great way to enjoy the elegant four-star Chinese cuisine served here. There are also sophisticated dishes made with the freshest ingredients, inspired by *nouvelle cuisine*. The dining room is softened with tapestries, etched-glass, antique mirrors, and lamplight.

DOWNTOWN Aqua   🚹♿ $$$$$

252 California St, 94111 **Tel** *(415) 956-9662*   **Map** 6 D4

Chic, airy, and decorated with gorgeous floral displays, Aqua is said by many to be the best seafood restaurant in the city. Its preparation of seafood with a French touch, such as fresh salmon with foie gras, has forged its reputation. The smoked swordfish is also exceptional. The pleasant ambience is perfect for a relaxed meal.

DOWNTOWN Boulevard   🚹♿ $$$$$

1 Mission St, 94105 **Tel** *(415) 543-6084*   **Map** 6 E4

The artistic creations of chef Nancy Oakes have earned fame for Boulevard, a Bay Area icon. The menu is a cross between American comfort food and French favorites. The interior is elegant and welcoming. Try to be seated in the back section to take advantage of the wonderful Bay Bridge views.

DOWNTOWN Campton Place   ♿ $$$$$

340 Stockton St, 94108 **Tel** *(415) 955-5555*   **Map** 5 C4

A serene room classically styled in the subtle colors of an Italian villa, Campton Place exudes elegance. The kitchen creates some of the best Provençal-Mediterranean fusion food in the area, accompanied by a top-notch wine list. This and the smooth service makes for a special night out. A good brunch menu is offered on Sunday.

DOWNTOWN Michael Minna   ♿ $$$$$

335 Powell St, 94102 **Tel** *(415) 397-9222*   **Map** 5 B4

Replacing the venerable Oak Room at St. Francis Hotel, this restaurant serves a new American prix-fixe menu built around a single ingredient prepared in three different styles. The eponymous chef, who was formerly at Aqua, also offers American classics along with 2,000 wines. The surroundings are ultra luxurious.

DOWNTOWN Silks   ♿ $$$$$

222 Sansome St, 94104 **Tel** *(415) 986-2020*   **Map** 5 C4

Dazzling with silken wall-hangings, floor coverings, and hand-painted silk chandeliers, Silks is a good spot for an intimate conversation and celebrity spotting. The efficient service underscores imaginative New Asian cuisine such as chicken and enoki mushroom spring rolls and spicy grilled shrimp.

CIVIC CENTER Mifune   🚹♿ $$

1737 Post St, 94115 **Tel** *(415) 922-0337*   **Map** 4 E4

Big steaming bowls of Japanese-style noodle soups delivered to your table within minutes of ordering, make this Japantown hub a favorite for fans of fresh food and those with limited time. Mifune also serves bento boxes and other non-soup items. There is also a good selection of vegetarian choices.

CIVIC CENTER Hayes St. Grill

320 Hayes St, 94102 **Tel** *(415) 863-5545*

$$$

Map *4 F5*

A reliable favorite for diners attending the nearby symphony, opera or ballet, Hayes St. Grill pairs your choice of fresh-caught fish and accompanying sauce with crispy french fries, among other dishes. The service is efficient and will get you to your seat in time for the start of the show.

CIVIC CENTER Indigo

687 McAllister St, 94102 **Tel** *(415) 673-9353*

$$$

Map *4 F5*

With its cool, blue-themed interior, Indigo lives up to its name. The restaurant is celebrated for its phenomenal wine list and new American menu. The best bargain offered is the Wine Dinner after 8pm, with specially chosen wines and champagnes to accompany and enhance the chef's specialties.

CIVIC CENTER Straits Café

3300 Geary Blvd, 94118 **Tel** *(415) 668-1783*

$$$

Map *3 B5*

Pan-Asian – a blend of Singaporean, Indonesian, Indian, and other flavors and styles of preparation – makes up the menu at this popular fusion restaurant. The beautiful presentation and delicate flavors have won exceptional praise from gourmets. Diners may sample a variety of flavorful, spicy or mild dishes while enjoying drinks from the full bar.

CIVIC CENTER Absinthe Brasserie and Bar

398 Hayes St, 94102 **Tel** *(415) 551-1590*

$$$$

Map *3 B5*

Recreating the 1940s era, this dark romantic setting is among the best European-style brasseries in town. Vintage cabaret music and cocktails are on the menu, along with an array of oysters, the best French onion soup, and hearty bistro food such as *cassoulet*, smoked salmon, and rib eye steak. The wine list is excellent.

CIVIC CENTER Jardinière

300 Grove St, 94102 **Tel** *(415) 861-5555*

$$$$

Map *4 F5*

Thoughtful, efficient service, an elegant atmosphere, and sumptuous California-inspired French food make the popular Jardinière a top choice for special occasions. The jazz duo plays quietly in the background while diners enjoy onion *tarte* and a Dubonnet from the mahogany and marble bar.

HAIGHT ASHBURY AND THE MISSION DISTRICT Axum Café

698 Haight St, 94117 **Tel** *(415) 252-7912*

$

Map *10 D1*

Considered to be the best place in the city to sample Ethiopian food, Axum Café is also popular for its rock-bottom prices. Primarily a hole-in-the-wall, it serves spicy and abundant portions of meat and vegetable stews and pancake-like bread, *injera*. Weekends are usually bustling, with a local clientele. Beer on tap is available.

HAIGHT ASHBURY AND THE MISSION DISTRICT Cha Cha Cha

2727 Mission St, 94110 **Tel** *(415) 648-0504*

$

Map *10 F3*

As much a lively nightlife scene as it is a restaurant, Cha Cha Cha serves small tapas plates and excellent sangria against a background of foot-tapping Latin music. Ever buzzing with an upbeat crowd, this place is not meant for a romantic dinner. Be prepared for an hour's wait, as it gets crowded on Friday and Saturday nights.

HAIGHT ASHBURY AND THE MISSION DISTRICT La Taqueria

2889 Mission St, 94110 **Tel** *(415) 285-7117*

$

Map *10 F4*

Flavorful marinated beef, pork or chicken layered with firm, tasty beans or rice, fresh lettuce, and tomato make for perfect burritos, at great prices. Another specialty here is the guacamole. The cafeteria-style line moves quickly. Table seating is often filled during lunch, but the turnover is quick.

HAIGHT ASHBURY AND THE MISSION DISTRICT Memphis Minnie's BBQ Joint

576 Haight St, 94117 **Tel** *(415) 864-7675*

$

Map *10 E1*

A takeout place and a sit-down restaurant, the Memphis Minnie is all about the slow-smoked Southern-style fork-tender sausage, chicken, beef, ribs, and pork, dripping with barbecue sauce. Order a combo, and do not leave out the handcut fries and barbecued brisket chili. In true San-Francisco style, sake is served here.

HAIGHT ASHBURY AND THE MISSION DISTRICT Pomelo

1793 Church St, 94131 **Tel** *(415) 285-2257*

$

Map *10 E5*

Noodles and rice plates from around the world – Chinese, Japanese, Indian, African, and European – are on the everchanging menu of Pomelo, a restaurant frequented by locals. Visitors will find good prices and an interesting mix of flavors here. Another location, with indoor seating only, is situated at 92 Judah Street.

HAIGHT ASHBURY AND THE MISSION DISTRICT Rosamunde Sausage Grill

545 Haight St, 94117 **Tel** *(415) 437-6851*

$

Map *10 E1*

The menu at Rosamunde's specializes in one dish, and excels in it. Order a sausage – in the German, Italian, or California style – and layer on the condiments. Eat at the eight-stool counter, take your order to the bar next door, or have Rosamunde's deliver it there for you.

HAIGHT ASHBURY AND THE MISSION DISTRICT Ti Couz

3108 16th St, 94103 **Tel** *(415) 252-7373*

$

Map *10 F2*

One of the oldest crêperies in the city, Ti Couz gives you the option of designing your own crêpes, stuffed with a variety of meat and/or vegetable fillings or sweet dessert sauces. If crêpes are not of interest to you, try the large, crispy salads accompanied by one of the hearty Celtic beers from the extensive list.

Key to Price Guide *see p568* **Key to Symbols** *see back cover flap*

HAIGHT ASHBURY AND THE MISSION DISTRICT Zazie

941 Cole St, 94117 **Tel** *(415) 564-5332*

Map *9 B2*

The neighborhood's most popular brunch spot on the weekends, Zazie also serves bistro-style lunches and dinners daily. The bountiful plates are brought by an attentive staff, and the outdoor patio is a lovely place to enjoy a quiet conversation. Zuzie is ideal for a romantic meal.

HAIGHT ASHBURY AND THE MISSION DISTRICT Andalu

3198 16th St, 94103 **Tel** *(415) 621-2211*

Map *10 E2*

An international version of "small plates" (the Spanish tapas concept) using local, Asian-influenced ingredients is served at this popular restaurant. Andalu also boasts excellent sangria and an expansive wine list. A festive, informal atmosphere prevails throughout. Public transport is the best way to get here.

HAIGHT ASHBURY AND THE MISSION DISTRICT Indian Oven

233 Fillmore, 94117 **Tel** *(415) 626-1628*

Map *10 E1*

An upscale option in an area full of Indian eateries, Indian Oven is notable for its exceptional red and yellow curries, fresh-made *naan*, and flavorful vegetarian dishes. Do not forget to try their homemade desserts. Attentive service performed by costumed waiters enhances the experience.

HAIGHT ASHBURY AND THE MISSION DISTRICT Thep Phanom Thai Cuisine

400 Waller St, 94117 **Tel** *(415) 431-2526*

Map *10 E1*

Dinner reservations are a must at this popular Thai restaurant, though lunch is more flexible. An accommodating staff serves well-seasoned Thai favorites, such as *yum pla muk* (spicy, crisp, cold calamari salad), in a comfortable, homey setting. The two-course special menu is outstanding.

HAIGHT ASHBURY AND THE MISSION DISTRICT Delfina

3621 18th St, 94110 **Tel** *(415) 552-4055*

Map *10 E3*

Validated parking in a tough-to-park area makes this restaurant's simple, impeccably seasoned Northern Italian cuisine even better. Ingredients are ultra-fresh, from the morning markets. The wine list is excellent. Delfina is popular, and dining space is at a premium, so get there early.

HAIGHT ASHBURY AND THE MISSION DISTRICT Zuni Café

1658 Market St, 94102 **Tel** *(415) 552-2522*

Map *10 F1*

Perfect burgers and juicy roasted chicken, cooked over an open fire, complement a menu offering a variety of Mediterranean dishes. The all-time favorites include roast chicken and Tuscan bread salad. The glass walls overlook Market Street, giving a great view of the city's action until it slows down late at night.

THE BAY AREA

BERKELEY Bangkok Thai Cuisine

1459 University Ave, 94702 **Tel** *(510) 848-6483*

Road map *inset B*

A clean, bright atmosphere and good food make this a popular spot for Thai cuisine. The fare is well priced and served quickly, especially at lunchtime, when the restaurant can get crowded. It offers meat, chicken, and seafood dishes along with rice and noodles. Favorites include vegetarian spring rolls and beef with broccoli.

BERKELEY Bette's Ocean View Diner

1807 4th St, 94710 **Tel** *(510) 644-3230*

Road map *inset B*

A local classic in the city's famous shopping block, this 1940s-style eatery features traditional, hearty American food. Patrons line up for hours at the weekend for their share of classic comfort food, prepared straightforwardly, and served with a smile. The pancakes, waffles, and scones are a must-try. The noise level can be deafening at times.

BERKELEY Celia's Mexican Restaurant

2040 4th St, 94710 **Tel** *(510) 549-1460*

Road map *inset B*

This casual, often noisy restaurant in the heart of Berkeley's popular shopping district serves top-notch, platter-style Mexican fare, traditionally prepared. Nachos, fajitas, burritos, and enchiladas are on offer along with a nice selection of seafood and vegetarian dishes. The margaritas are well worth trying, too.

BERKELEY Plearn Thai Cuisine

2050 University Ave, 94707 **Tel** *(510) 841-2148*

Road map *inset B*

Having stood the test of time, and the test of the fickle local public, this no-frills Thai house has become a local favorite; no small feat in a city overrun with Thai restaurants. *Pad thai* (a noodle dish with tofu, shrimp, and peanuts) is one of the house specialties. The service is amicable, and the food is reasonably priced.

BERKELEY Chez Panisse Restaurant

1517 Shattuck Ave, 94709 **Tel** *(510) 548-5525*

Road map *inset B*

Proprietor and chef Alice Waters is famed as the innovator of California cuisine, which is on offer in this simple wood-framed restaurant where it all began. Dishes are prepared simply with the freshest ingredients. Book well in advance or opt for the more affordable café upstairs.

BOLINAS Blue Heron Inn

11 Wharf Rd, 94924 **Tel** *(415) 868-0243*   **Road map** *inset B*

Located within a B&B, occupying a Victorian house, this acclaimed restaurant presents a menu of seasonal dishes made with local ingredients. The fresh fish dishes are excellent. Outdoor seating on a shaded patio, overlooking lush foliage and an attractive garden, is also available. It is closed on Tuesday.

BOLINAS Coast Café

46 Wharf Rd, 94924 **Tel** *(415) 868-2298*   **Road map** *inset B*

This fun, friendly restaurant, set in a historic location, has a surfing decor. Coast Café offers well-prepared classic seafood, Cailfornia cuisine, and occasional theme-style menus. Fresh seasonal produce is used to create innovative dishes. Oysters are barbecued on the deck during summer.

BURLINGAME Kuleto's

1095 Rollins Rd, 94010 **Tel** *(650) 342-4922*   **Road map** *inset B*

An offshoot of a San Francisco favorite, this handsome, well-run restaurant features rustic Italian fare. Many dishes are prepared in the huge wood-burning oven that dominates the open kitchen. The dining room is inviting and boisterous, and the waiters are efficient. The place is ideal for a family outing with kids.

HALF MOON BAY Moss Beach Distillery

140 Beach Way, 94038 **Tel** *(650) 728-5595*   **Road map** *inset B*

This is a favorite with locals and visitors alike. The menu serves hearty American and Italian fare and a few good seafood choices. An ever-crowded outdoor deck offers striking views of the ocean, and guests can enjoy a cocktail or sip cocoa while watching the sunset. Moss Beach also features an elaborate brunch on Sunday.

HALF MOON BAY Cetrella

845 Main St, 94019 **Tel** *(650) 726-4090*   **Road map** *inset B*

This top-rated restaurant is at once casual and sophisticated, with Mediterranean touches in the decor and on the menu, which employs the freshest ingredients from the area. Highlights include an impressive assortment of cheeses and an award-winning wine list. Live jazz can be enjoyed from Thursday to Saturday. Cetrella is closed on Mondays.

LAFAYETTE Postino

3565 Mount Diablo Blvd, 94549 **Tel** *(925) 284-3565*   **Road map** *inset B*

Serving faithful preparations of Italian cuisine, this lively, family-type restaurant attracts visitors from all around the Bay area. Specialties include homemade pastas and cheeses, house-cured meats, and oven-roasted dishes. There is also an array of excellent seafood. The rustic decor adds to the charm.

LARKSPUR Lark Creek Inn

234 Magnolia Ave, 94939 **Tel** *(415) 924-7766*   **Road map** *inset B*

Set in a shaded grove among towering trees, this comfortable, home-like restaurant is famous for chef Bradley Ogden's award-winning and often very inventive American country-style fare. There are delicious meat and poultry dishes, as well as a popular Sunday brunch. It is closed for lunch on Saturdays.

MILL VALLEY Samurai

425 Miller Ave, 94941 **Tel** *(415) 381-3680*   **Road map** *inset B*

Highly renowned, this boisterous Japanese restaurant often has a line lasting as long as an hour or more. However, most diners feel the appetizing fare is well worth the wait. Fried tempura, succulent seafood, and absolutely-fresh sushi are some of the house specialties. Closed at lunchtime and on Sundays.

MILL VALLEY Buckeye Roadhouse

15 Shoreline Hwy, 94941 **Tel** *(415) 331-2600*   **Road map** *inset B*

Located conspicuously along the freeway, this friendly restaurant is a staple among the area's comfort-food eateries. The atmosphere is neighborly, with a welcoming, roaring fire, and the menu features simple American cooking, including tasty steaks and seafood dishes. The Sunday brunch is worth trying.

MILL VALLEY Frantoio

152 Shoreline Hwy, 94941 **Tel** *(415) 289-5777*   **Road map** *inset B*

Renowned for its homemade olive oil – made by the only on-site olive press in the US – this bright, cheery eatery offers delicious Italian and Mediterranean cuisine, much of it employing its signature ingredient in abundance. Choose from a variety of pizzas, pastas, and seafood, meat, and poultry dishes.

MILL VALLEY Piazza D'Angelo

22 Miller Ave, 94941 **Tel** *(415) 388-2000*   **Road map** *inset B*

A lively atmosphere and well-prepared Italian menu have made this restaurant, set in the downtown plaza, a longtime favorite. The dining room is open and inviting, and the wood-fired pizzas are outstanding, as are the freshly-made pastas and seafood dishes. Piazza D'Angelo attracts a mixed crowd, from locals to celebrities.

OAKLAND Rockridge Café

5492 College Ave, 94618 **Tel** *(510) 653-1567*   **Road map** *inset B*

Styled to resemble a 1940s diner, this casual restaurant is set in the city's busy shopping district. It is extremely popular with students and families, who flock to the eatery on weekend afternoons for a good burger or a rib-sticking breakfast. The atmosphere here is friendly and unpretentious.

Key to Price Guide *see p568* **Key to Symbols** *see back cover flap*

OAKLAND Bay Wolf
 🏃♿ $$$

3853 Piedmont Ave, 94611 **Tel** *(510) 655-6004* **Road map** *inset B*

With a reputation for excellence, this long-established, elegant restaurant is set in an old Victorian house, and features dishes inspired by Tuscany and the Basque country. The highly acclaimed menu changes each month to represent a different Mediterranean region. It is closed for lunch on Saturdays and Sundays.

OAKLAND Oliveto
 🏃♿ $$$$

5655 College Ave, 94618 **Tel** *(510) 547-5356* **Road map** *inset B*

A local favorite, this welcoming restaurant has a casual café and a full-service restaurant, where the masterful chef prepares appetizing Italian cuisine using the freshest possible ingredients. The menu changes slightly each day to reflect the fancy of the chef's visit to the market. Oliveto is closed for lunch on Saturdays and Sundays.

ORINDA Siam Orchid Thai
 🏃♿ $

23–H Orinda Way, 94563 **Tel** *(925) 253-1975* **Road map** *inset B*

Located in a small village 4 miles (6 km) east of Berkeley, this unassuming, yet pleasant restaurant serves up some of the best Thai cuisine in the area, all with friendly service and at bargain prices. The *pad thai* is outstanding as are the daily specials. Expect a brief wait on weekend evenings.

PALO ALTO Gordon Biersch
 🏃♿🎵 $$$

640 Emerson St, 94301 **Tel** *(650) 323-7723* **Road map** *inset B*

Part of a well-known chain of brewery restaurants, this lively, brightly polished eatery features great food that goes well beyond typical pub-grub. The menu is rounded off by hearty American and Italian classics. The freshly-made pizzas are a good choice to complement the house-made beers.

PESCADERO Duarte's Tavern
 🏃♿ $

202 Stage Rd, 94060 **Tel** *(650) 879-0464* **Road map** *inset B*

Operated by the same family for more than a century, this unpretentious roadside landmark has a cult-like following for its amiable service and homemade pies. The menu is full of innovative creations, including artichoke omelets, and such standards as pork chops and apple sauce.

POINT REYES STATION Station House Café
 🏃♿🎵📶 $

11180 Main St, 94956 **Tel** *(415) 663-1515* **Road map** *A3*

This unassuming, clapboard-style structure painted fire-engine red houses a friendly restaurant, with surprisingly excellent fare and the freshest seafood. Do not miss the barbecued oysters, which are available in season. The atmosphere here is casual and relaxing. It is closed on Wednesdays.

SAN JOSE Tied House Café and Brewery
 🏃♿🎵📶 $$

65 N San Pedro St, 95112 **Tel** *(408) 295-2739* **Road map** *B4*

Lively and sometimes raucous, this microbrewery and pub-style restaurant has an amazing selection of homemade beers on tap to complement the better-than-average seafood dishes and other American fare. The menu is extensive, ranging from Mexican-inspired, to New Orleans-style and Italian classics, and is sure to please even fussy diners.

SAN JOSE Yankee Pier
 🏃♿📶 $$

378 Santana Row, 95128 **Tel** *(408) 244-1244* **Road map** *B4*

Set among the fancy shops and restaurants of Santana Row, this family-style, low-key restaurant is a nice respite, and offers delicious seafood. The menu is prepared with a gourmet touch, and includes top-notch clam chowder. The fare is reasonably priced, and the service is fast and friendly.

SAUSALITO Fish
 🏃♿📶 $$

350 Harbor Dr, 94965 **Tel** *(415) 331-3474* **Road map** *A3*

This small, high-ceiling restaurant at the shoreline has a few tables, and offers its menu by counter service. The specialty here is fresh seafood, simply prepared, and sold at affordable prices. Excellent fish-and-chips and clam chowder. It is extremely busy at lunchtime, and closed on Mondays and Tuesdays.

SAUSALITO Poggio Italian Restaurant
 🏃♿📶 $$

777 Bridgeway, 94965 **Tel** *(415) 332-7771* **Road map** *A3*

Situated in the heart of Sausalito village, this comfortable and friendly restaurant serves hearty and appetizing Italian dishes; many are fired in the large wood-burning oven that anchors the space. The chef pays special homage to Italian classics of Tuscany. The service here is impeccable.

TIBURON Guaymas
 🏃♿🎵📶 $$$

27 Main St, 94920 **Tel** *(415) 435-6300* **Road map** *A3*

With sweeping views of the Bay area from its dining room, this stylish restaurant serves high-end Mexican and Latin American fare, prepared with a gourmet twist and fresh ingredients. The bar mixes excellent margaritas; guests can enjoy them on the pleasant deck. The food is reasonably priced and the service is efficient.

TIBURON Sam's Anchor Café
 🏃♿📶 $$$

27 Main St, 94920 **Tel** *(415) 435-4527* **Road map** *A3*

Thanks to its location on the docks of San Francisco Bay, this fun and casual restaurant and cocktail bar attracts visitors from all around the area. The food is serviceable, with tasty fried calamari, some nice seafood dishes, hearty burgers, and Italian-influenced dishes. Sam's draws a lively crowd, especially on summer weekends.

THE NORTH

ARCATA Arcata Pizza and Deli
1057 H St, 95521 **Tel** *(707) 822-4650*   **Road map** *B2*

This no-frills restaurant is clean and friendly, and serves reliable American and Italian fare such as sandwiches, hamburgers, soups, calzones, and pizzas at great prices. The salads are enormous. It is open until 3am on weekends, and draws an after-party crowd, which makes for an interesting atmosphere.

ARCATA Crosswinds Vegan Restaurant
860 10th St, 95501 **Tel** *(707) 826-2133*   **Road map** *B2*

Set in a historic Victorian mansion, this friendly restaurant has a comfortable dining room with large windows and lots of natural light. The menu comprises vegetarian preparations of American classics. There are also some traditional items on the menu and a popular weekend brunch, which sometimes requires a brief wait for a table.

CRESCENT CITY Ship Ashore
12370 Hwy 101 N, 95531 **Tel** *(707) 487-3141*   **Road map** *A1*

Part of a resort with the same name, this family-friendly restaurant is set near a permanently docked historic ship. The menu presents straightforward American fare, as well as generous helpings of tasty and fresh seafood dishes. The service is amicable, and the atmosphere congenial.

EUREKA Lost Coast Brewery & Café
617 4th St, 95501 **Tel** *(707) 445-4480*   **Road map** *A2*

This fun and funky brewpub, situated in an old stand-alone building, has an unassuming atmosphere and lively ambience provided by the chatting clientele at its collection of wood tables. The food is cheap, the portions are plentiful, and some selections venture well beyond the typical pub grub. The homemade beers are exceptional.

EUREKA Somoa Cookhouse
59 Cookhouse Lane, 95501 **Tel** *(707) 442-1659*   **Road map** *A2*

Begun as a dining hall for hungry North Coast lumberjacks, this friendly, rustic restaurant still serves huge portions of hearty American fare, including ham and eggs, fried chicken, and such homey touches as fresh-baked bread. The staff are efficient, and there is a logging museum on site.

EUREKA Restaurant 301
301 L St, 95501 **Tel** *(707) 444-8062*   **Road map** *A2*

The beautiful, historic Hotel Carter is renowned for its restaurant, 301, which offers gourmet preparations of American and Mediterranean dishes, made with fresh seasonal ingredients. The dining room is handsome and romantic, and the wine list is award winning. It is closed for lunch.

GARBERVILLE Woodrose Café
911 Redwood Dr, 95442 **Tel** *(707) 923-3191*   **Road map** *A2*

Located in the heart of redwood country, this casual café is a mainstay among locals, especially for breakfast. It offers traditional American cuisine, but also has many vegetarian-friendly options, including tofu burgers and sandwiches, as well as a range of organic meals. It is closed on Saturdays and Sundays, and for dinner from Monday to Friday.

LEWISTON Mama's Place
Trinity Dam Blvd, 96052 **Tel** *(530) 778-3177*   **Road map** *A2*

This friendly diner dishes up enormous portions of typical American food at affordable prices. The menu offers the usual favorites such as burgers, steaks, fried chicken, and salads. The bacon burger is a must-try. This is also a great spot for hearty breakfasts, with plate-size pancakes and huge omelets.

MOUNT SHASTA Lily's
1013 S Mount Shasta Blvd, 96067 **Tel** *(530) 926-3372*   **Road map** *B1*

This charming restaurant, set in a modest structure surrounded by a white picket fence, offers a little bit of everything on the diverse menu. It features seasonal dishes, a few American classics, and some Mexican and Indian fare. Advance reservations are highly recommended.

MOUNT SHASTA Michael's
313 N Mount Shasta Blvd, 96067 **Tel** *(530) 926-5288*   **Road map** *B1*

Quite popular among locals, this welcoming, intimate restaurant serves mostly Italian cuisine, including such staples as linguine and spaghetti. A good selection of salads and sandwiches is also available for lunch. The efficient service and relaxing ambience add to the charm. Michael's is closed on Sundays.

ORICK Rolf's Park Café
Hwy 101 at Davidson Rd, 95555 **Tel** *(707) 488-3841*   **Road map** *A1*

Operated by a German-born chef, this rustic restaurant serves favorites from his homeland, including large portions of sauerbraten and a range of Bavarian specialties. There are also many seafood, game, and meat dishes on offer, as well as hearty breakfasts. It is closed in winter.

Key to Price Guide *see p568* **Key to Symbols** *see back cover flap*

REDDING Jack's Grill 👪 ♿ $$

1743 California St, 96002 ***Tel*** *(530) 241-9705* ***Road map*** *B2*

A well-run steakhouse serving top-grade meats and poultry to a loyal following since 1940. The fried chicken and huge beef dinners are fantastic. The place is friendly and accommodating, but the lines can be long and reservations are not accepted. It is closed on Sunday, and for lunch from Monday to Saturday.

REDWAY Mateel Café 👪 ♿ ☀ $$

3342 Redwood Dr, 95560 ***Tel*** *(707) 923-2030* ***Road map*** *A2*

Serving health-conscious meals, from fresh fish and hearty salads and pizzas to Mideast-inspired dishes, this casual, out-of-the-way café also doubles as a regional cultural center and a gathering spot for locals sharing news of the day. The freshly-baked bread and desserts are delicious. It is closed on Sunday.

SUSANVILLE Black Bear Diner 👪 ♿ $

2795 Main St, 96130 ***Tel*** *(530) 257-4447* ***Road map*** *B2*

Although part of a chain of restaurants in the West, this friendly, casual inn has the feel of a one-off diner, with comfortable booths and familiar service. The classic American fare is hearty and well prepared, including excellent burgers and sandwiches, steaks, chops, and huge salads. Breakfasts are very popular here.

TRINIDAD Larrupin Café ♿ $$$

1658 Patrick's Point Dr, 95570 ***Tel*** *(707) 677-0230* ***Road map*** *A2*

A favorite among locals, and with views of the Pacific Ocean, this warm little restaurant, just north of Arcata, has a homely ambience and is known for its fresh seafood and gracious hospitality. The barbecued oysters are a popular choice as appetizers. Larrupin's is closed on Tuesdays, and for lunch from Wednesday to Sunday.

UKIAH Ukiah Brewing Company 👪 ♿ ♫ ☀ $$

102 State St, 95482 ***Tel*** *(707) 468-5898* ***Road map*** *A3*

Everything in this bright, lively pub is organically produced, from the wide selection of home-brewed beers, to the complete menu, which features updated American classics. Burgers, hot curries, salads, nachos, pizzas, burritos, sandwiches, filets, and a few vegetarian specials are on offer here.

WEAVERVILLE La Grange Café 👪 ♿ ☀ $

226 N Main St, 96093 ***Tel*** *(530) 623-5325* ***Road map*** *A2*

This cheery café, set in a historic building, serves health-conscious cuisine, from generous portions of organic salads to large sandwiches and a range of vegetarian meals, all offered at affordable prices. La Grange also has an extensive selection of micro-brewed beers on tap. It often attracts a hungry, post river-rafting crowd.

WINE COUNTRY

BOONVILLE Boonville Hotel 👪 ♿ ☀ $$$$

Hwy 128 by Lambert Lane, 95415 ***Tel*** *(707) 895-2210* ***Road map*** *A3*

Acclaimed chef Johnny Schmitt is highly regarded for his well-prepared California cuisine, with Mexican and Italian influences. Organic meats and locally grown produce are used at this approachable gourmet dining room. The menu changes often, and there is an excellent wine list. It is closed on Tuesdays, and for lunch from Wednesday to Monday.

CALISTOGA All Season's Café ♿ $$$

1400 Lincoln Ave, 94515 ***Tel*** *(707) 942-9111* ***Road map*** *A3*

One of the most popular spots in town, this charming restaurant is renowned for its extensive wine list and frequently changing menu of seasonal classics. Do not miss the homemade breads and freshly-made pastas. A wine shop and tasting area are also featured on the premises. The service here is impeccable.

CALISTOGA Brannan's Grill 👪 ♿ $$$

1374 Lincoln Ave, 94515 ***Tel*** *(707) 942-2233* ***Road map*** *A3*

Occupying a historic structure in the heart of town, this handsome restaurant has a thoughtful menu of American grilled cuisine and some Mediterranean-inspired classics. It offers a wide range of gnocchi, steaks, salads, and filet mignons, and boasts an award-winning wine list. The service is friendly and the ambience impressive.

FORESTVILLE Farmhouse Inn & Restaurant 👪 ♿ ☀ $$

7871 River Rd, 95436 ***Tel*** *(707) 887-3300* ***Road map*** *A3*

This charming restaurant is situated in a quaint yellow farmhouse and offers a refined, relaxed atmosphere along with top-notch French country-style cuisine. The menu features local and seasonal ingredients and changes often. Meals are accented with a wonderful selection of cheeses and an exceptional wine list.

NAPA Downtown Joe's Restaurant and Brewery 👪 ♿ ♫ ☀ $

902 Main St, 94558 ***Tel*** *(707) 258-2337* ***Road map*** *A3*

Among the most popular watering holes in town, this lively pub and microbrewery has many beers on tap and an extensive menu of burgers, salads, and pizzas. It serves a great breakfast selection, too. At weekends, the dining room can be overrun by a partying crowd. This is a good place to just hang out and relax.

NAPA Bistro Don Giovanni 👪 ♿ 🍴 $$$$

4110 Howard Lane, 94558 ***Tel*** *(707) 224-3300* ***Road map*** *A3*

This inviting dining room of this extremely popular Napa Valley restaurant has a large wood-burning fireplace and a lovely outdoor terrace. The menu has a delicious offering of rustic Italian fare, with French influence, and an excellent wine list. It presents striking views of magnificent mountains and extensive, well-kept gardens.

NAPA Cole's Chop House 👪 ♿ $$$$

1122 Main St, 94559 ***Tel*** *(707) 224-6328* ***Road map*** *A3*

The dining room, with stone walls and wood beams, creates a causal, yet elegant setting for the signature dry-aged steaks and chops on offer here. Start with a martini, then select something from the extensive Cabernet Sauvignon-oriented wine list. The service is exemplary and knowledgeable. Cole's is closed for lunch.

RUTHERFORD Auberge du Soleil 👪 ♿ 🍴 $$$$$

180 Rutherford Hill Rd, 94573 ***Tel*** *(707) 967-3111* ***Road map*** *A3*

This handsome, elegant restaurant is a must for any serious food lover with time and disposable income. The cuisine, made with fresh regional products, is inventive and appetizing, and the service is polished and deft. The views from the terrace are second-to-none. A truly memorable dining experience.

SANTA ROSA Mixx Restaurant & Bar 👪 ♿ ♫ $$$

135 4th St, 95401 ***Tel*** *(707) 573-1344* ***Road map*** *A3*

This well-known supper club-style restaurant is located in a historic building, and features reliable regional Italian and American fare and some occasional good specials. The service is amiable and gracious. The live jazz playing in the background provides a nice ambience. It is closed on Sundays.

SANTA ROSA Dry Creek Kitchen 👪 ♿ 🍴 $$$$

317 Healdsburg Ave, 95448 ***Tel*** *(707) 431-0330* ***Road map*** *A3*

This sleek restaurant in the equally stylish Hotel Healdsburg is run by famed chef Charlie Palmer, who writes a frequently changing menu of seasonal dishes inspired by local ingredients. The ambience is big-city cachet, with small-town charm. There is a great wine list, exclusively from the area. It is closed for lunch from Monday to Thursday.

SONOMA Maya Restaurant ♿ 🍴 $$

101 E Napa St, 95476 ***Tel*** *(707) 935-3500* ***Road map*** *A3*

Casual and fun, this bright restaurant is located right on the downtown plaza, and features Latin American specialties, prepared with a gourmet twist and using the freshest ingredients. The carnitas are the best around. There are good margaritas, as well as a lengthy list of specialty tequilas. It is closed for Sunday lunch.

SONOMA The Swiss Hotel 👪 ♿ 🍴 $$

18 W Spain St, 94576 ***Tel*** *(707) 938-2884* ***Road map*** *A3*

One of the best meals in town can be found at this historic restaurant on the plaza, with an appetizing menu of rustic Italian classics and pizzas from a wood-burning oven. The atmosphere is convivial and welcoming, and the clientele consists of tourists and locals alike.

ST. HELENA Taylor's Refresher 💳 ♿ $

933 Main St, 94574 ***Tel*** *707-963-3486* ***Road map*** *A3*

A classic roadside drive-in and a local favorite, Taylor's Refresher is renowned for serving incredible burgers, tasty fries, and big, thick milkshakes since 1949. The service is quick, so guests need not be intimidated by the enormous lines that invariably form at the weekends. This is an ideal stop for families and kids.

ST. HELENA Market Restaurant 👪 ♿ $$

1347 Main St, 94574 ***Tel*** *(707) 963-3799* ***Road map*** *A3*

This comfortable restaurant provides an experience of fine dining without fuss. The service is top-notch and the food excellent. It offers traditional American fare, from steaks and poultry dishes to seafood and pasta, prepared with fresh seasonal ingredients and gourmet touches.

ST. HELENA Meadowood Restaurant 👪 ♿ 🍴 $$$

900 Meadowood Lane, 94574 ***Tel*** *(707) 963-3646* ***Road map*** *A3*

This elegant restaurant at the famed Meadowood Napa Valley resort features fresh inventions of Provençal cuisine, served in a serene environment with white table cloths and large windows. There is also a less formal grill on the premises. The atmosphere is bright and inviting.

ST. HELENA Press Restaurant 👪 ♿ $$$$

587 St. Helena Hwy, 94574 ***Tel*** *(707) 967-0550* ***Road map*** *A3*

In the heart of St. Helena, the sophisticated Press Restaurant serves skillfully prepared dry-aged beef, whole roasted chicken, and other specialties from the wood-burning grill and rotisserie. The atmosphere is casual, yet elegant. The service is exceptional. It is open for dinner only.

ST. HELENA Tra Vigne 👪 ♿ 🍴 $$$$

1050 Charter Oak, 94574 ***Tel*** *(707) 963-4444* ***Road map*** *A3*

One of the best-loved restaurants in the region, this lively spot is set among trees and foliage and vine-covered stone walls. The menu offers rustic Italian specialties as well as fresh treats from its on-site bakery. Request a table on the secluded courtyard for a complete Wine Country experience.

Key to Price Guide *see p568* **Key to Symbols** *see back cover flap*

YOUNTVILLE Mustards Grill

7399 St. Helena Hwy, 94558 **Tel** *(707) 944-2424*   **Road map** *B3*

A Napa Valley staple, this roadside restaurant has a lovely setting among vineyards. Well-prepared California cuisine is served in a vibrant atmosphere. Try the famed Mongolian pork chop with homemade mustard sauce. The lemon-lime pie with brown sugar merringue is renowned. Book dinner early, or drop in for a seat at the bar during lunch.

YOUNTVILLE Napa Valley Grille

6795 Washington St, 94599 **Tel** *(707) 944-8686*   **Road map** *B3*

This restaurant's meticulous emphasis on freshness has been imitated in versions around the country to much acclaim. Fresh local ingredients are prepared in Wine Country style and paired with great wines. The specialty here is the Sonoma duck duo. Service is typically swift and reliable.

YOUNTVILLE Bouchon

6534 Washington St, 94599 **Tel** *(707) 944-8037*   **Road map** *B3*

Sample the skill of critically-acclaimed chef Thomas Keller at this excellent bistro. Every dish on the menu is exquisite, especially the steak frites. For starters, choose from the extensive raw bar. Mouthwatering fresh breads and pastries are available from the bakery next door.

YOUNTVILLE The French Laundry

6640 Washington St, 94599 **Tel** *(707) 944-2380*   **Road map** *B3*

This is the famed little house in which chef Thomas Keller built his reputation, and it offers dining at its very best. Book a month in advance, and once you get a reservation, expect to spend a few hours enjoying a monumental dining experience. It is open all days for dinner, with lunch only served on Fridays, Saturdays, and Sundays.

GOLD COUNTRY AND THE CENTRAL VALLEY

AMADOR CITY Imperial Hotel and Restaurant

14202 Hwy 49, 955601 **Tel** *(209) 267-9172*   **Road map** *B3*

Housed in historic Imperial Hotel, this popular restaurant is charming and bright, with a dining room overlooking flower gardens. The seasonal menu features Continental cuisine and many Italian-inspired dishes. Fresh fish specialties and grilled steaks make a regular appearance. It is open for dinner only, and closed on Mondays and Tuesdays.

CHICO Sierra Nevada Brewing Company Restaurant and Tap Room

1075 E 20th St, 95928 **Tel** *(530) 345-2739*   **Road map** *B2*

Wildly popular for its microbrewed beer, the restaurant at this working brewery serves up such memorable fare as apple-malt pork loin and delicious pizzas from a wood-burning oven. Frequented by a young crowd, the place is upbeat and lively, especially on weekend nights. It is closed on Mondays.

GRASS VALLEY Swiss House Restaurant

535 Mill St, 95945 **Tel** *(530) 273-8272*   **Road map** *B3*

This family-friendly restaurant is popular for its Swiss and German specialties, which coexist on an eclectic menu alongside a few Chinese and Asian dishes. The soups are homemade, as is such traditional fare as sauerbraten, Jaeger schnitzel, and bratwurst. Service is prompt and amicable. It is closed on Mondays, Tuesdays, and for lunch.

GRASS VALLEY Holbrooke Hotel and Restaurant

212 W Main St, 95945 **Tel** *(530) 273-1353*   **Road map** *B3*

This charming restaurant in the historic Holbrooke Hotel has a handsome dining room that overlooks Main Street. The menu features American fare with seasonal accents. Choose a seat on the tree-covered patio. It is popular with locals, especially on weekends.

JAMESTOWN National Hotel Restaurant

18183 Main St, 95327 **Tel** *(209) 984-3446*   **Road map** *B3*

Set in a historic Gold Rush-era structure, this cheery restaurant offers a long, impressive menu that stresses mainly Mediterranean fare. Create a light meal from the extensive appetizer menu. Homemade desserts, particularly the crème brûlée, are superb. There is an excellent wine list on offer at the saloon here.

NEVADA CITY Country Rose Café

300 Commercial St, 95959 **Tel** *(530) 265-6248*   **Road map** *B3*

With a bustling atmosphere and casual decor, this restaurant is among the most prolific in the area. The food is French country-inspired, skillfully prepared and presented artistically by the inventive kitchen staff. Service is friendly and spirited. There is occasional live music played in the dining room.

NEVADA CITY Citronée Bistro

320 Broad St, 95959 **Tel** *(530) 265-5697*   **Road map** *B3*

This popular spot has a casual café in front and a more formal restaurant at the rear, each with its own menu. Top-notch bistro-style fare is prepared with the best ingredients and herbs grown on premises. For the adventurous, chef Robèrt creates surprise menus featuring the best of the day's offering. A great wine list. Closed on Sunday.

SACRAMENTO Centro Cocina Mexicana   ⬥⬥   ⑤
2730 J St, 95816   **Tel** *(916) 442-2552*   **Road map** *B3*

The cuisine of regional Mexico and Central America inspires the fresh menu at this bustling midtown eatery. The tempting guacamole, a house specialty, is a good starter. Dishes are prepared with a light touch. The bar scene is energetic on weekend evenings. It is closed for lunch on Saturdays and Sundays.

SACRAMENTO Tower Café   ⬥⬥⬥   ⑤
1518 Broadway, 95818   **Tel** *(916) 441-0222*   **Road map** *B3*

Immensely popular Tower Café is ideal for sitting in the palm-shrouded courtyard on long evenings and sipping imported beers or teas. The menu is casual and eclectic, influenced by regions from Asia to Africa. Service is informal. The interesting beer and wine list features remote global regions.

SACRAMENTO 33rd St Bistro   ⬥⬥⬥   ⑤⑤
3301 Folsom Blvd, 95816   **Tel** *(916) 455-2233*   **Road map** *B3*

This casual, stylish café in the hip midtown area offers good Mediterranean-style fare, including light salads and pastas, served promptly by courteous staff. There are some well-selected wines from under-appreciated regions available at great prices. The leisurely weekend breakfasts are popular with the locals.

SACRAMENTO Dragonfly   ⬥⬥   ⑤⑤⑤
1809 Capitol Ave, 95814   **Tel** *(916) 498-9200*   **Road map** *B3*

With rich red walls and a lively clientele, this good restaurant near the Capitol has an inventive Asian menu. Wide-ranging dishes, including sushi and grilled chicken, are served tapas-style, on small beautifully presented plates. There is a sushi menu as well. Dragonfly is closed for lunch on Sundays.

SACRAMENTO Fat City Bar & Café   ⬥⬥   ⑤⑤⑤
1001 Front St, 95814   **Tel** *(916) 446-6768*   **Road map** *B3*

Built in a historic brick building in Old Sacramento, this friendly restaurant has long been a regular haunt for politicos and local families. The lively atmosphere is perfect for enjoying the hearty American- and Asian-inspired dishes. The dining room gets quite crowded on weekend nights, so book in advance.

SACRAMENTO Esquire Grill   ⬥⬥   ⑤⑤⑤⑤
1213 K St, 95816   **Tel** *(916) 448-8900*   **Road map** *B3*

A New York-style American bistro, Esquire Grill draws a good-looking downtown crowd and the occasional minor celebrity. The menu features well-executed steaks and chops as well as a few seafood highlights. There is a good bar scene on weekends. Closed for lunch on Saturdays and Sundays.

SACRAMENTO Rio City Café   ⬥⬥⬥   ⑤⑤⑤⑤
1110 Front St, 95814   **Tel** *(916) 442-8226*   **Road map** *B3*

There is a warm and inviting atmosphere at Rio City Café, a riverside restaurant, set with high wood-beamed ceilings and huge windows. The menu features light, California cuisine with Asian influences. The weekend brunch is very popular. Reservations are recommended.

SONORA Banny's Café   ⬥⬥   ⑤⑤
83 S Stewart St, Suite 100, 95370   **Tel** *(209) 533-4709*   **Road map** *B3*

Amicable service and a bustling atmosphere set this otherwise nondescript café apart. The menu features an interesting mix of regional styles, including Californian, European, and Asian, though some are better executed than others. There is also a wine bar, with an extensive list of local vintages.

SONORA Gus's Steakhouse   ⬥⬥   ⑤⑤⑤
1183 Mono Way, 95370   **Tel** *(209) 532-5190*   **Road map** *B3*

Set in a Gold Rush-era building, this handsome restaurant resembles a club. The friendly staff serve succulent ribs and steaks, ideally suited to the welcoming surroundings. There are good pasta and seafood choices, too. Expect a wait on weekend nights. Reservations are not accepted. It is closed for lunch on Saturdays and Sundays.

THE HIGH SIERRAS

BIG PINE Rossi's   ⬥⬥   ⑤⑤
100 N Main St, 95313   **Tel** *(760) 938-2254*   **Road map** *C4*

This cheerful family-run restaurant, with a long history in the area, sits in an unassuming corner building. The menu is simple, with many steaks, chops, and pasta specialties, but the dishes are perfect every time. The big steaks and huge bowls of spaghetti are well renowned. Service is amicable and intimate.

BISHOP Whiskey Creek   ⬥⬥⬥   ⑤
524 N Main St, 93514   **Tel** *(760) 873-7174*   **Road map** *C4*

An old standby in the region, this informal neighborhood restaurant has long been a welcoming sight to travelers in the area. There is a huge menu of American classics, most of which are very well prepared. The freshly-made breads, soups, and large salads are also heartwarming on cool evenings.

Key to Price Guide *see p568* **Key to Symbols** *see back cover flap*

FISH CAMP Narrow Gauge Inn

48571 Highway 41, 93623 **Tel** *(559) 683-7720*   **Road map** *C4*

This restaurant in the historic Narrow Gauge Inn is renowned in the region for its high-quality rustic American cuisine. The steaks, fresh fish, and poultry are not to be missed. The lodge-style dining rooms are very romantic, with large stone fireplaces and antique appointments. It is closed on Mondays and Tuesdays, and in winter.

MAMMOTH LAKES Old Mammoth Grill & Bar

452 Old Mammoth Rd, 93546 **Tel** *(760) 924-2003*   **Road map** *C4*

Set inconspicuously in a small shopping mall, this well-priced grill has a lively bar atmosphere and an eclectic menu. Selections range from large burgers and sandwiches to ribs, steaks, fish kebabs, and burritos. Mammoth Club, a house speciality, features roast beef, ham, turkey, and Cheddar cheese with an ortega chili strip on sourdough bread.

MAMMOTH LAKES Whiskey Creek Mountain Bistro

24 Lake Mary Rd, 93541 **Tel** *(760) 934-2555*   **Road map** *C4*

Part popular nightclub, part restaurant, this long-standing local favorite has a lively atosphere, with occasional live music or DJ-spun sounds. The restaurant offers a changing menu of seasonal selections, as well as a list of reliable favorites, including grilled steaks, ribs, and prime rib. It is closed for lunch.

NORTH LAKE TAHOE Bridgetender Tavern and Grill

50 Westlake Blvd, 96145 **Tel** *(530) 583-3342*   **Road map** *C3*

A long-time popular gathering spot for locals and visitors alike, this casual tavern has a great outdoor seating area overlooking Lake Tahoe and the Truckee River inlet. The kitchen is known for its delicious burgers and fries, but also offers some good grilled seafood choices.

NORTH LAKE TAHOE Gar Woods Grill & Pier

5000 North Lake Blvd, 96140 **Tel** *(530) 546-3366*   **Road map** *C3*

Friendly and fun, this restaurant and bar is known for its signature drinks and its hearty American fare as much as for its post-boating cocktail culture. Specialties include grilled seafood and great burgers. Amenities include free boat valet parking. It is open daily for lunch and dinner. There is also an attractive buffet brunch.

NORTH LAKE TAHOE Sunnyside Restaurant

1860 Westlake Blvd, 96145 **Tel** *(800) 822-2754*   **Road map** *C3*

This popular restaurant at a lakeside lodge has a spacious dining room with large wooden beams and huge windows, as well as a sizable deck that gets packed on pleasant afternoons. The menu features good American fare and some lovely seafood dishes. Sunday brunch is a summertime ritual.

SOUTH LAKE TAHOE Lake Tahoe Pizza Company

1168 Emerald Bay Rd, 96150 **Tel** *(530) 544-1919*   **Road map** *C3*

Well-cooked food and excellent prices is the key at this friendly, family-style pizza parlor that uses a special brick oven to make pizzas. The menu mainly features traditional Italian favorites, including barbecued chicken pizza, salads, sandwiches, and pasta. There is also a lean-calorie menu for weight-watchers and a good beer selection.

SOUTH LAKE TAHOE Fresh Ketch

2435 Venice Dr, 96150 **Tel** *(530) 541-5683*   **Road map** *C3*

Impressive cooking, attentive service, and lovely views make a winning combination at this casual restaurant in the Tahoe Keys area. The menu features mostly seafood, with preparations influenced by the Pacific Rim. There is casual dining downstairs and on the lawn, while fine dining is in an intimate upstairs dining room.

STATELINE Sage Room

Hwy 50, NV 89449 **Tel** *(775) 588-2411*   **Road map** *C3*

This fine-dining restaurant at Harvey's Casino has been open since 1947 and has amassed a loyal following. The menu includes standards such as great steaks and chops served in a Western-themed setting. There are also select wild game dishes available on occasion. Bananas Foster is a dessert specialty. It is closed for lunch.

TAHOE CITY Tahoe House

625 Westlake Blvd, 96145 **Tel** *(530) 583-1377*   **Road map** *B3*

There is a great full-service bakery at this interesting restaurant that attracts many people in the morning hours. The Swiss-themed restaurant is also a takeaway deli where picnickers stock up on fresh breads, cheeses, and cakes. There is also an interesting, but approachable, menu of traditional Swiss dishes.

TAHOE CITY Jake's on the Lake

780 North Lake Blvd, 96145 **Tel** *(530) 583-0188*   **Road map** *C3*

Overlooking a large marina, this wood-framed restaurant is popular with locals for afternoon cocktails. The ambience is casual, service attentive, and the innovative Californian cooking excellent. The menu features an extensive list of seafood specialties, including some rare Hawaiian varieties. The bar attracts a boisterous crowd in the evenings.

TAHOE VISTA Le Petit Pier

7238 North Lake Blvd, 96148 **Tel** *(530) 546-4464*   **Road map** *B3*

An elegant dining option on Lake Tahoe's North Shore, this romantic French-inspired restaurant offers such hallmarks as braised lamb, New Zealand vension, and fresh lobster. There are also a few top-notch seafood specialties on offer as well as an interesting wine list. Enjoy panoramic views of the lake. Le Petit Pier is closed on Tuesdays.

TRUCKEE Pianeta   ⊛⊛⊛

10096 Donner Pass Rd, 96161 **Tel** *(530) 587-4694*   **Road map** *B3*

Located in downtown Truckee, this neighborly restaurant offers a reliable menu of rustic Italian fare served in a room with a welcoming mountain ambience. The comfortable booths are the prime seating choice. The service is well-honed and amicable. A full bar and wine list are on offer. It is open for dinner daily.

YOSEMITE NATIONAL PARK Wawona Dining Room   ⊛⊛

State Hwy 41, 95389 **Tel** *(559) 252-4848*   **Road map** *C3*

This restaurant in the historic Yosemite Park hotel is popular for its friendly ambience and service. The basic American fare, prepared without much discipline, features flavorful steaks and trouts. The Victorian dining room, with a delightful rustic flair, can get crowded and noisy, which is all part of the charm. Closed November to March.

YOSEMITE NATIONAL PARK Ahwahnee Dining Room   ⊛⊛⊛⊛

Yosemite Valley, 95389 **Tel** *(559) 252-4848*   **Road map** *C3*

The highlight of dining here is the beautiful setting, although the food has improved recently to match the memorable atmosphere. Mostly American standards find a place on the menu here; the best choices are the grilled steaks and chops. Save some room for the delectable desserts.

NORTH CENTRAL CALIFORNIA

APTOS Bittersweet Bistro   ⊛⊛⊛⊛

787 Rio Del Mar Blvd, 95003 **Tel** *(831) 662-9799*   **Road map** *B4*

One of the best gourmet dining options in the area, this inviting restaurant offers excellent food at great prices. The menu is American bistro with Mediterranean influences, but the quality lies in the fine execution and artful presentation. Premium ingredients are used, with an emphasis on local produce. An impressive wine list is on offer.

BIG SUR Deetjen's   ⊛⊛⊛

48865 Hwy 1, 93920 **Tel** *(831) 667-2378*   **Road map** *B4*

The secluded setting is wonderful at this hotel-restaurant as is the amicable service. The dining room is divided into four eclectically decorated spaces. The menu features interesting dishes in the California cuisine style. The colorful breakfast menu of sweets and savories is hugely popular. Reservations are recommended. Deetjen's is closed for lunch.

BIG SUR Nepenthe   ⊛⊛⊛

Hwy 1 CA, 93920 **Tel** *(831) 667-2345*   **Road map** *B4*

This restaurant, with its stunning coastside setting, has a cult-like following, though the food is not quite as dazzling. The simple preparations of American fare are comforting, as are the freshly-made breads and desserts. The ambrosia burger, a ground steak sandwich with the house-made ambrosia sauce, is a favorite.

BIG SUR Sierra Mar   ⊛⊛⊛⊛⊛

Hwy 1, 93920 **Tel** *(831) 667-2800*   **Road map** *B4*

Part of an inn, this award-winning restaurant has magnificent views from its dining room. The innovative menu of seasonally inspired fare changes daily and is presented prix fixe, however it can be ordered à la carte. Sierra Mar has one of North America's most extensive wine cellars.

CARMEL Hog's Breath Inn   ⊛⊛

Corner of San Carlos Ave & 5th St, 93921 **Tel** *(831) 625-1044*   **Road map** *B4*

With a famous owner – Clint Eastwood – this rustic, cozy bar and restaurant has a great patio upon which to enjoy the hearty California and American cuisine. The ribs are a specialty as is the extensive list of appetizers, which many diners choose to graze their way through on foggy afternoons by the fire.

CARMEL Anton and Michel   ⊛⊛⊛

Corner of Mission Ave & 7th St, 93921 **Tel** *(831) 624-2406*   **Road map** *B4*

A Carmel landmark, this downtown restaurant is popular for its contemporary French-inspired cuisine, sophisticated ambience, and attentive service. The fare is reliably prepared using seasonal ingredients. The pan-roasted duck breast is an all-time favorite. The dining room tends to get a bit touristy. Book in advance, and request a patio seat.

CARMEL The Terrace Grill, La Playa Hotel   ⊛⊛⊛

Corner of 8th Ave & Camino Real, 93920 **Tel** *(831) 624-6476*   **Road map** *B4*

One of the best hotel restaurants in the area, this open-air terrace dining room offers splendid ocean views. The menu here is comprised of fresh California cuisine dishes made with local ingredients artfully presented. There is a great wine selection at the wood-paneled lounge.

CARMEL Grasing's Coastal Cuisine   ⊛⊛⊛⊛

NW Corner of 6th & Mission Ave, 93921 **Tel** *(831) 624-6562*   **Road map** *B4*

This charming chef-owned and operated restaurant has earned many accolades for superb cuisine. The menu features seasonal selections and excellent seafood dishes. Specialities include roast rack of lamb, seared duck, and pork medallions. The top-rated wine list offers a wide range of choices by the glass. A delightful ambience and service.

CARMEL Rio Grill

101 Crossroads Blvd, 93924 **Tel** *(831) 625-5436*

Road map *B4*

The Southwestern-style cuisine at this energetic restaurant ranges from traditional Mexican to American and Mediterranean-style inventions. Showcasing local ingredients, the food is cooked on a wood-burning grill. Fresh fish and pasta are also on offer, along with a wide selection of cocktails.

CARMEL The Covey at Quail Lodge

8205 Valley Greens Dr, 93923 **Tel** *(831) 624-1581*

Road map *B4*

Part of a well-known hotel, this elegant signature restaurant has a loyal following and an ever-changing menu of seasonal California cuisine. Popular delicacies, such as roasted wild-striped bass and slow-cooked salmon, are served in a contemporary setting overlooking a lake and lovely gardens. The service is polished without being fussy.

CASTROVILLE The Franco Restaurant

10639 Merrit St, 95012 **Tel** *(831) 633-2090*

Road map *B4*

A local favorite, with a bright, kitsch decor, this gay bar is part of a well-known hotel, set in a historic building. The eclectic menu features a selection of good diner-style American fare along with some well-prepared Mexican dishes that have amassed a loyal following in the area.

MONTEREY Tarpy's Roadhouse

2999 Monterey-Salinas Hwy, 93940 **Tel** *(831) 647-1444*

Road map *B4*

Built in an old ranch house, this rustic and appealing restaurant has friendly service and a devoted following. The wide-ranging menu includes wood-fired wild game, great steaks, fresh seafood, salads, and burgers. Select a seat on the patio on warm evenings. There is a full bar and a critically-acclaimed wine list. Service is professional.

MONTEREY Domenico's on the Wharf

50 Fisherman's Wharf, 93940 **Tel** *(831) 372-3655*

Road map *B4*

Domenico's is a good wharfside choice for its laid-back atmosphere and scenic views. The Northern Italian-inspired menu predominantly features seafood, and has some standouts. The *cioppino*, a locally beloved seafood and shellfish stew, is a star attraction. The oyster bar is worth a visit, and the wine selection is quite good.

MONTEREY Stokes Restaurant

500 Hartnell St, 93940 **Tel** *(831) 373-1110*

Road map *B4*

Built into a 200-year-old adobe structure, this handsome restaurant is renowned for its expertly cooked Mediterranean cuisine. The menu uses ingredients from local producers, from meats and cheeses to wild mushrooms, prepared with a deft touch. The wine list is excellent. It is closed for lunch on Saturdays and Sundays.

PACIFIC GROVE Fandango

223 17th St, 93950 **Tel** *(831) 372-3456*

Road map *B4*

A long-standing neighborhood spot, this cheery restaurant serves reliable preparations of seafood and steak in different dining rooms. The colorful upstairs room, alcove, cellar, and main dining room all have individual character. The rack of lamb, scampi and bouillabaisse are highly regarded. A full-service bar is located on site.

SANTA CRUZ The Crêpe Place

1134 Soquel Ave, 95062 **Tel** *(831) 429-6994*

Road map *B4*

This quirky, friendly crêperie is a long-time local favorite, with a wide array of crêpes. Create your own variety, choosing from seafood, meat, or vegetarian options. Additional menu items include soups, salads, and freshly-baked bread. The dimly-lit indoor dining room is ideal for couples. For families and large groups, there is a bright patio area.

SANTA CRUZ Crow's Nest

2218 E Cliff Dr, 95062 **Tel** *(831) 476-4560*

Road map *B4*

An icon of the harbor since 1969, this simple, friendly, and entertaining restaurant serves great seafood specialties as well as pasta, steaks, and chops. The upstairs bar, Breakwater, has a more casual atmosphere, serving a selection of sandwiches, burgers, and small seafood plates. There is live music on select nights.

SANTA CRUZ Gabriella Café

910 Cedar St, 95060 **Tel** *(831) 457-1677*

Road map *B4*

Charming and romantic, Gabriella Café uses locally grown organic produce in all its dishes. Specialties include seafood and pasta, all wonderfully fresh and full of flavor, presented artistically in the Tuscan-style dining room. Service is swift and courteous and the ambience upbeat. There is an excellent wine list as well.

SANTA CRUZ Hollins House Restaurant

20 Clubhouse Rd, 95060 **Tel** *(831) 459-9177*

Road map *B4*

Set on the famed Pasatiempo golf course, Hollins House was built in 1929 and offers mesmerizing views of Monterey Bay. The atmosphere is country-clubbish, yet elegant. The menu features great steaks and seafood as well as a few "comfort" items such as macaroni and cheese. The wine list is outstanding.

SEASIDE El Migueleno

1066 Broadway Ave, 93955 **Tel** *(831) 899-2199*

Road map *B4*

One of only a handful of Salvadoran restaurants in Northern California, this modest-looking dining room is worth a stop. Thoughtfully blending the culinary traditions of Mexico and El Salvador, the menu features some interesting dishes. The seafood stew is made with fresh locally-caught fish. The service is efficient and the prices are attractive.

SHOPPING IN CALIFORNIA

California is a manufacturing giant and a major player in the global economy. It is the largest producer of children's clothing in the US, and is equally famous for its sportswear and swimwear. Produce from the San Joaquin Valley, including fruit, nuts, and vegetables, feeds the nation. Aside from the shopping districts of LA *(see pp166 – 7)* and San Francisco *(see*

Antique Dealers' Association sign

pp382–3), the state's smaller towns and countryside offer a wide range of merchandise and local produce. Roadside food stands, wineries, antique shops, and crafts by local artisans are some of the attractions of California's backroads. Prices tend to be cheaper than in the cities, and in some places, such as flea markets, you will be expected to barter and negotiate.

Window-shopping along Ocean Avenue, Carmel *(see p510)*

SHOPPING HOURS

Since the local population tends to view shopping as a recreational activity, most major stores in California are open for business seven days a week. Typical business hours are 10am – 6pm, Monday to Saturday, and noon–5pm on Sundays. In smaller communities, stores may be closed on Sunday or Monday. Opening hours for these stores are sometimes 11am–7pm.

HOW TO PAY

Most stores accept credit cards, including MasterCard, American Express and Visa, and traveler's checks. Paying by traveler's checks requires some form of identification, such as a passport or driver's license. Few stores will accept checks drawn on foreign banks. Cash is the best way to pay for any small purchases *(see pp624 – 5)*.

SALES TAX

Sales tax (VAT) in California ranges from 7.25 to 8.5 percent. All items except groceries and prescription drugs are taxed. In general, tax is not included in the advertised price but is added separately at the cash register.

RIGHTS AND REFUNDS

Merchants are not required by law to give a cash refund or credit for returned goods, although most do so. All stores will refund the cost of a defective item, if it is not marked "flawed" or "sold as is." Inspect the item before you buy it and keep all receipts. If an item is faulty, go back to the store with the receipt and original packaging. Many stores will refund your money up to 30 days after purchase.

SHIPPING PACKAGES

For a charge, most stores ship goods worldwide, or send your items home by Federal Express or US Express Mail Service *(see pp626 – 7)*. You will be asked to fill out a form giving a short description of the goods and stating their monetary value. Keep receipts of the transaction in case the items should get lost in transit.

WHERE TO SHOP

A number of coastal towns noted for their locally owned shops can be found along Hwy 1 or US 101. These include Santa Barbara *(see pp220 –21)*, Big Sur *(see pp514–15)*, Carmel *(see p510)*, Santa Cruz *(see pp506 – 7)*, and Sausalito *(see pp414 – 15)*.

On Hwy 99 and other roads that cross the San Joaquin Valley, many farms sell locally grown fruit and vegetables. Palm Springs *(see pp274 – 5)* is known for its fashion shops. Antique dealers are plentiful in towns in the Sierra foothills, such as Sutter Creek *(see p476)*.

FASHION

California is known for its casual clothing – the dressdown Friday business look was invented here. However,

San Franciscan original, The Gap

the East Coast also looks to California for the very best of cutting-edge fashion. Seventy percent of all swimwear designed in the US is designed here, by names such as

California Wave, and can be found at chainstores like **Diane's Swimwear**. Sixty-five percent of the country's younger female fashion is also produced here. Children's wear is a specialty of the state. **Sara's Prints**, **Gymboree**, and **Levi Strauss** are some of the best.

Other local heroes include designer **Jessica McClintock Inc**, known for her ballgowns and bridal wear, as well as the teen chainstore **Forever 21**. **The Gap**, now an international retail giant, originated in San Francisco in 1969 and was the first store to mass-market denim jeans.

FLEA MARKETS

Flea markets (also called swap meets) are held on weekends, usually on Sundays. Vendors set up booths within a vast parking lot, football stadium, or even in the grounds of one of the famous missions. Just about everything imaginable is for sale. It is often possible to find a one-of-a-kind treasure at a good price, but don't accept the quoted price – bargaining is *de rigueur*. Be sure to bring cash with you because most vendors will not accept credit cards or traveler's checks.

Notable flea markets include the **Berkeley Flea Market**, the **San Jose Flea Market**, the **Rose Bowl Flea Market** in Pasadena, and **San Juan Bautista Peddlars Fair**. Flea markets may charge a nominal entrance fee of 75 cents or $1.

Browsers at an open-air flea market in Sausalito

Cover of a vintage Hollywood magazine from the 1950s

POP CULTURE ANTIQUES

Memorabilia stores are a California specialty. Sun Valley's **The Game Doc** sells a variety of old games for all ages. **Hello Central** sells all kinds of antique telephones, from early models to the 1940s black rotary dial telephones. **Hillcrest Vintage Paper Collectables** and **Sarah Stocking Fine Vintage Posters** specialize in old movie

posters. A range of Hollywood memorabilia is easily found in LA *(see pp166 – 7)*. Other stores, such as **Camperos Collectables** in Sutter Creek, also sell such items.

OUTLET CENTERS

One of the state's most popular retail trends is factory outlet malls. These sell off-season or surplus goods, such as clothing and household items, directly to consumers at prices lower than those in department stores.

Outlet centers usually have around 20 shops, but the **Factory Stores of America at Nut Tree** has more than 100 stores. Other popular centers include the **American Tin Cannery Factory Outlets** in Monterey, **Napa Factory Stores**, **Desert Hills Factory Stores**, **Citadel**, **Pismo Beach Outlet Center**, and the **San Diego Factory Outlet Center**. For special outlet center tours contact **Shopper Stopper Tours**.

SIZE CHART

For Australian sizes follow the British and American conversions.

Children's clothing

American	2	3	4	5	6	6x	7	8	10	12	14	16 (size)
British	2–3		4–5		6–7		8–9		10–11	12	14	14+ (years)
Continental	2–3		4–5		6–7		8–9		10–11	12	14	14+ (years)

Children's shoes

American	7½	8½	9½	10½	11½	12½	13½	1½	2½
British	7	8	9	10	11	12	13	1	2
Continental	24	25½	27	28	29	30	32	33	34

Women's dresses, coats and skirts

American	4	6	8	10	12	14	16	18
British	6	8	10	12	14	16	18	20
Continental	38	40	42	44	46	48	50	52

Women's blouses and sweaters

American	6	8	10	12	14	16	18
British	30	32	34	36	38	40	42
Continental	40	42	44	46	48	50	52

Women's shoes

American	5	6	7	8	9	10	11
British	3	4	5	6	7	8	9
Continental	36	37	38	39	40	41	44

Men's suits

American	34	36	38	40	42	44	46	48
British	34	36	38	40	42	44	46	48
Continental	44	46	48	50	52	54	56	58

Men's shirts

American	14	15	15½	16	16½	17	17½	18
British	14	15	15½	16	16½	17	17½	18
Continental	36	38	39	41	42	43	44	45

Men's shoes

American	7	7½	8	8½	9½	10½	11	11½
British	6	7	7½	8	9	10	11	12
Continental	39	40	41	42	43	44	45	46

Antique shops in Temecula, near Palm Springs

BOOKS, MUSIC, AND CRAFTS

Bookstores, whether part of a large chain or independent, are a feature of even the smallest California town.

The best selection of music is generally available only in major cities, in chains such as **Tower Records**, **Virgin Megastore**, and **Wherehouse**. If a town has a university, head toward the student district where new and used record stores thrive.

Native American and Mexican arts and crafts are available in this state. Contact the **California Indian Museum and Cultural Arts Center** and the Mexican Museum *(see p265)* for more information.

ANTIQUES

California's small towns are awash with traditional antiques such as fine gold and silver jewelry, Native American Indian artifacts, textiles, antique clothing, Bakelite jewelry, and period furniture dating back to the 18th and 19th centuries.

The West Coast is the port of entry to the US for many Pacific Rim countries and, as a result, many antique porcelain sculptures from Japan and China, and antique Asian furniture are available. Twentieth-century collectables include Arts and Crafts and Art Deco furniture, clothing, posters, prewar tin toys, blown glass, and pottery.

Antique dealers often rent space together in one large mall, barn, or warehouse building that is open to the public. The largest antique mall is **Antique Plaza**, just east of Sacramento. Almost 300 dealers trade here. There is also a café serving coffee and sandwiches.

FOOD

Many of California's farms, particularly in Sonoma or Fresno counties, sell their produce to visitors on self-guided farm trails. In Sonoma, contact the **Sonoma County Farm Trails** or the **Sonoma Valley Chamber of Commerce.** The Fresno County Blossom Trail is a 62-mile (100-km) trail passing through groves, orchards, and vineyards. It begins at **Simonian Farms,** which sells local fruits, honey, and mustards. Contact the **Fresno County Farm Bureau** for information.

California has a number of unique food shops scattered around the state. In Napa's Anderson Valley, the **Apple Farm** is a year-round fruit

Fresh local produce at a farmers' market

stand selling locally grown apples and pears. Also in Napa, the **Jimtown Store** sells local jams, honey, olives, mustards, vinegars, and salad dressings. On Hwy 152, east of Gilroy, **Casa de Fruta**, which began as a simple cherry stand in the 1940s, has grown into a vast complex with a fruit stand, coffee shop (Casa de Coffee), restaurant (Casa de Burger), and gift shop (Casa de Gift).

Harris Ranch, almost midway between LA and San Francisco on I-5, is a vast complex set amid a working cattle ranch. The Spanish-style hacienda has a gift shop featuring Harris Ranch produce and fresh meat, as well as a restaurant, coffee shop, and overnight lodging.

Italian Marketplace at the Viansa Winery

WINERIES

In addition to the fine wine of Napa and Sonoma counties, wineries are known for the shops located inside their tasting rooms. A range of merchandise related to wine is for sale. For a list of California's wineries, contact the **Wine Institute of San Francisco**.

The Italian Marketplace at the **Viansa Winery** sells Italian cheeses and breads, cookbooks, and kitchenware. The **Sebastiani Vineyards** sell a variety of wine-related souvenirs. The gift shop in the **Sterling Vineyards** offers silk scarves, silver jewelry, and regional history books.

Family-owned **V. Sattui Winery** has a gourmet deli, as well as a shaded picnic area to eat your purchases.

DIRECTORY

FASHION

California Wave
1250 E Slausen Ave
Los Angeles, CA 90001.
Tel (323) 233-0077.

Diane's Swimwear
116 Main St, Huntington
Beach, CA 92648.
Tel (714) 536-7803.

Forever 21
Beverly Center, 8500
Beverly Blvd #849 & #852,
Los Angeles, CA 90048.
Tel (310) 659-9611.

The Gap
1 Harrison St,
San Francisco,
CA 94105.
Tel (800) 333-7899.

Gymboree
421 N Beverly Hills Dr,
Beverly Hills, CA 90210.
Tel (310) 278-0312.

Jessica McClintock Inc
1400 16th St,
San Francisco, CA 94103.
Tel (415) 553-8200.

Original Levi's Store
Union Square,
San Francisco,
CA 94111.
Tel (415) 501-0100.

Sara's Prints
3018-A Alvarado St,
San Leandro, CA 94577.
Tel (510) 352 - 6060.

FLEA MARKETS

Berkeley Flea Market
1937 Ashby Ave,
Berkeley, CA 94703.
Tel (510) 644-0744.

Pasadena's Rose Bowl
1001 Rose Bowl Drive,
Pasadena, CA 91103.
Tel (626) 577-3100.

San Jose Flea Market
1590 Berryessa Road,
San Jose,
CA 95133.
Tel (408) 453- 1110.

San Juan Bautista Peddlars Fair
Mission San Juan Bautista,
San Juan Bautista,
CA 95023.
Tel (831) 623-2454.

POP CULTURE ANTIQUES

Camperos Collectables
PO Box 1629,
Sutter Creek,
CA 95685.
Tel (209) 245-3725.

The Game Doc
8000 Wheatland Ave,
Sun Valley, CA 91352.
Tel (818) 504 -0440.

Hello Central
2463 Ladera Court,
San Luis Obispo,
CA 93401.
Tel (805) 541 -9123.

Hillcrest Vintage Paper Collectables
3412 W MacArthur Blvd,
Unit G, Santa Ana,
CA 92704.
Tel (714) 751 - 4030.

Sarah Stocking Fine Vintage Posters
472 Jackson St,
San Francisco, CA 94111.
Tel (415) 984-0700.

OUTLET CENTERS

American Tin Cannery Factory Outlets
125 Ocean View Blvd,
Monterey, CA 93942.
Tel (831) 372- 1442.

Camarillo
740 Ventura Blvd,
Camarillo,
CA 93010.
Tel (805) 445- 8520.

Citadel
100-150 Citadel Drive,
Commerce,
CA 90040.
Tel (323) 888- 1724.
www.citadeloutlets.com

Desert Hills Premium Outlets
48400 Seminole Rd,
Cabazon, CA 92230.
Tel (951) 849-5018.

Factory Stores of America at Nut Tree
321–2 Nut Tree Rd,
Vacaville, CA 95687.
Tel (707) 447-5755.

Napa Premium Outlets
629 Factory Stores Drive,
Napa, CA 94558.
Tel (707) 226-9876.

Pismo Beach Outlet Center
Pismo Beach,
CA 93449.
Tel (805) 773- 4661

Shopper Stopper Tours
PO Box 535,
Sebastopol,
CA 95473.
Tel (707) 829- 1597.

BOOKS, MUSIC, AND CRAFTS

California Indian Museum and Cultural Center
5250 Aero Dr,
San Rosa, CA 95403.
Tel (707) 579-3004.
www.cimcc.indian.com

Tower Records
2500 Del Monte St,
Sacramento,
CA 95691.
Tel (916) 373-2500.

Virgin Megastore
8000 W Sunset Blvd,
Hollywood,
CA 90046.
Tel (323) 650-8666.

Wherehouse
17542 Hawthorne Blvd,
Torrance, CA 90504.
Tel (310) 371-0994.

ANTIQUES

Antique Plaza
11395 Folsom Blvd,
Rancho Cordova,
CA 95742.
Tel (916) 852 - 8517.

FOOD

Apple Farm
18501 Greenwood Rd,
Philo, CA 95466.
Tel (707) 895-2333.

Casa de Fruta
10021 Pacheco Pass Hwy,
Hollister, CA 95023.
Tel (408) 842-7282.

Fresno County Farm Bureau
1274 West Hedges,
Fresno, CA 93728.
Tel (559) 237 - 0263.

Harris Ranch
24505 West Dorris Ave,
Coalinga, CA 93210.
Tel (800) 942-2333.
www.harrisranch.com

Jimtown Store
6706 Hwy 128,
Healdsburg,
CA 95448.
Tel (707) 433- 1212.

Simonian Farm
2629 S Clovis Ave,
Fresno, CA 93725.
Tel (559) 237 -2294.

Sonoma County Farm Trails
PO Box 6032,
Santa Rosa, CA 95606.
Tel (707) 571-8288.

Sonoma Valley Chamber of Commerce
651-A Broadway,
Sonoma, CA 95476.
Tel (707) 996- 1033.

WINERIES

Sebastiani Vineyards
389 Fourth St East,
Sonoma, CA 95476.
Tel (707) 938-5532.

Sterling Vineyards
1111 Dunaweal Loane,
Calistoga, CA 94515.
Tel (707) 942-3300.

Viansa Winery
25200 Arnold Drive,
Sonoma, CA 95476.
Tel (707) 935- 4700.

V. Sattui Winery
11 White Lane,
St Helena, CA 94574.
Tel (707) 963-7774.

Wine Institute of San Francisco
425 Market St, Suite
1000, San Francisco, CA
94105.
Tel (415) 512- 0151.

SPECIAL INTEREST VACATIONS AND ACTIVITIES IN CALIFORNIA

California is practically synonymous with the great outdoors. The state has protected its landscape so that future generations can visit places of beauty. The deserts, redwood forests, alpine meadows, granite mountains, lakes, and white beaches all welcome visitors. California

Whitewater rafting on the Merced River (see p612)

has a culture rich with physical activity, and wilderness is never far from any city. Golfers are well provided for around the Monterey Peninsula (see p511) and winter skiers flock to Lake Tahoe (see p487). For details of main events in the sports calendar, see pages 36–7.

Tahquitz Golf Course, Palm Springs

SPECIAL INTEREST VACATIONS

Details of special interest vacations are available from the **California Office of Tourism**. One of the most popular of these are tours of California's missions along El Camino Real (see pp46–7).

Writers who make California their home often give readings at local writers' workshops. The best of these are the **Santa Barbara Writers' Conference** and the **Squaw Valley Community of Writers.**

Artists can take advantage of the state's various craft centers. Nationally renowned artists hold painting courses at the **Crescent Harbor Art Gallery** in Crescent City and at the **Mendocino Arts Center.**

Institutes such as **Gourmet Retreats** at Casa Lana in the Napa Valley and **Tante Marie's Cooking School** provide accommodations, cooking classes, shopping tours, visits to the Wine Country, and fine meals during week-long intensive courses in the summer.

CAMPING

California has always valued its wilderness: Yosemite Valley (see pp488–9) and the Mariposa Grove of giant redwoods were protected parkland as early as 1864. Today there are more than 250 places classified as either state parks, wilderness areas, historic sites, or recreation areas.

At every site, there are hiking trails and parking lots. Many also provide bathrooms and camp sites. All state and federal parks allow day-use visitors, charging a small parking fee. For camping, reserve a site with **State Park Reservations** or **Yosemite Reservations**. Most camp sites accept reservations eight weeks in advance.

Camping trips into the state's desert are organized by **Desert Survivors.** They include environmental information.

HIKING

Day hikes and longer trips in the country are popular with both residents and visitors. There are more than 1 million miles (1.6 million km) of trails in California, the longest being the Pacific Crest Trail. The 2,640-mile (4,245-km) route stretches from Canada to Mexico. One of its highlights is the 200-mile (320-km) John Muir Trail, from Yosemite's high country to Mount Whitney (see pp488–95). The **Sierra Club** organizes guided outings and provides detailed maps.

Hiking along the John Muir Trail at Mount Whitney

HORSEBACK RIDING

Equestrians will find a wide variety of riding trails in California, across all types of landscape – pine-covered mountains, lush meadows, chaparral hills, and dry valleys. Many state and national parks allow horses and pack mules on their trails.

Traditional cowboy life can still be found at privately owned ranches. These are working ranches, and guests can ride with the ranch hands and herd animals, or simply ride for pleasure on their extensive network of trails. **El Alisal Guest Ranch and Resort** holds annual roundups and cattle drives or just let **Hidden Trails** organize a ranch holiday for you.

Horseback riding in Ventura County

MOUNTAIN BIKING

Many state parks allow cyclists on their hiking trails. One spectacular trail for cyclists begins at High Camp in Squaw Valley, Lake Tahoe *(see p487)*. A 2,000-ft (610-m) ascent via an aerial tram is followed by a heart-stopping downhill ride to Shirley Lake. Contact the **Bicycle Trails Council** to find out where mountain bikes are welcome.

Outfitters such as **Backroads** also lead groups of cyclists on tours of the state's abundant rolling countryside, often with stops for leisurely gourmet lunches. Transport vans accompany the cyclists, carrying heavy equipment and camping gear for week-long trips. Popular destinations

Mountain biking in Marin County

include the Napa Valley *(see pp462–3)* and the country lanes of Sonoma, Monterey, and Santa Barbara Counties.

BEACHES

Beaches along California's 900-mile (1,450-km) coastline vary considerably. Some have rough waves and rocky beaches, ideal for rock pool exploration and quiet reflection. Others have the white sand, arching waves, and warm water that attract the surfers of California legend.

Whether you want to surf or simply watch the golden boys of summer, the best beaches include the Leo Carrillo State Beach in Orange County *(see pp230–31)*, Windansea Beach in La Jolla *(see pp248–9)*, and Corona del Mar in Newport Beach *(see pp230–31)*. The **Club Ed Surf School** offers a 7-day surfing camp for beginners to the sport held between April and October.

Many spots along the coast are good diving areas, including Scripps Shoreline Underwater Preserve in La Jolla *(see p249)*, the coves of Laguna Beach *(see p231)*, and Monterey Bay *(see p511)*. Equipment can be rented from the **Aquarius Dive Shop**. The **Underwater Schools of America** in Oceanside also offers diving lessons for beginners.

Natural Bridges State Park in Santa Cruz *(see pp506–7)* and Pfeiffer State Beach in Big Sur *(see pp414–15)* are good sites for rock pool exploration, where the ocean has eroded the rock in unusual formations. Torrey Pines State Beach *(see p248)* offers forests and dramatic white-capped swells. Pismo Beach is famous for its sand dunes, surfing, and clam digging *(see p208)*.

Southern California's water is warm enough for swimming from April to November. In the sea north of San Francisco a wet suit should be worn at all times of the year.

Golden beaches of La Jolla cove

WHITEWATER RAFTING AND KAYAKING

Whitewater rafting is like a thrilling roller coaster ride combined with stunning scenic views. Specialty out-fitters such as **Mariah Wilderness Expeditions**, **Outdoor Unlimited**, and **Whitewater Voyages** provide rafts, paddles, and life jackets. They take groups of six to eight people, accompanied by a guide, down a tributary of one of California's major rivers. Trips may last one day only or include an overnight stay.

The rafting season lasts from April to September. Trips are graded by their level of difficulty: Classes I and II are relatively safe, with a few exciting twists and turns. Beginners wanting a safe but slightly more exciting ride should book a trip on a Class III river. Only experienced rafters should go on a Class IV, or higher, trip.

Most organizations that offer river rafting also provide kayak and canoe trips. For more information, contact **Friends of the River** or the **American River Touring Association**.

Waterskiing in San Diego

WATER SPORTS

The lakes and beaches in California offer a variety of activities. Houseboats are available to rent for a slow cruise through the maze of inlets in the Sacramento Delta. Speedboats are available at Lake Tahoe *(see p487)*, Lake Shasta *(see p452)*, and the man-made lakes that are part of the state recreation system.

One of the newest sports is parasailing. With water skis and a parachute, participants are harnessed to a speedboat and launched into the air for an exhilarating ride. It's a safe sport, but life jackets should be worn. Contact **Parasailing Catalina** for details.

BIRD-WATCHING

California's coastline and rivers are feeding grounds for migrating birds. In autumn, ducks, geese, and other shorebirds leave Canada to winter in South America, stopping in California along the way. The Point Reyes National Seashore *(see pp412–13)* supports at least 45 percent of US bird species. More than 425 species have been sighted here.

Just south of San Diego, the **Tijuana Slough National Estuarine Research Reserve** hosts 400 species, best seen in spring and autumn.

Bird-watching in La Jolla *(see p261)*

FISHING

California is an angler's paradise. From the end of April through to the middle of November, anglers head to the rivers and streams of the Sierra Nevada Mountains for trout fishing. Bass fishing in California's multitude of lakes and reservoirs is plentiful throughout the year. During the autumn and winter months, schools of salmon and steelhead make their way upriver, with especially good fishing in the Klamath, American, Eel, and Sacramento rivers. Sturgeon and striped bass can also readily be caught in the Sacramento River Delta.

Almost every coastal city in the state offers charter boats for deep-sea ocean fishing. In Northern California, the summer months are particularly good for halibut and ocean salmon, but throughout the Pacific, from autumn to early spring, 40–50-lb (18–23-kg) hauls of cod and rock fish are not unusual. In the warmer waters off Southern California, blue fin, yellow fin, and

Rafting at Yosemite National Park *(see pp488–91)*

Fishing on Lake Molena in San Diego

skipjack tuna, as well as barracuda are particularly plentiful during the summer. To rent a charter boat for fishing contact **Helgren's Sportfishing Trips**, or **Anchor Charters**. For organized trips try **Stagnaro's Sport Fishing**.

To find out which fish are in season, contact the **State Department of Fish and Game**. Information on fly fishing, another popular California sport, is available from the **Troutfitter Guide Service** at Mammoth Lakes.

ROCK CLIMBING AND CAVING

Rock climbing combines the dexterity of gymnastics with the grace of dance, as individuals scale vertical rock walls using only their hands and high-friction shoes. The

Rock climbing at Joshua Tree National Park

sport can be practiced throughout the year in rock-climbing gyms in major cities. Other places to learn how to rock climb or simply to watch others in action are the Joshua Tree National Park *(see pp278–9)*, the alpine village of Idyllwild, near Palm Springs *(see p276)*, and Squaw Valley in Lake Tahoe *(see p487)*. Contact the **American Mountain Guides Association** or **Mission Cliffs Climbing School** for information.

Spelunkers (cave explorers) should head for the Pinnacles National Monument *(see p517)* or Lassen Volcanic National Park *(see p453)*, where volcanoes have created unusual caves and rock formations.

HANG GLIDING

If you've ever wanted to ride the thermal air currents at speeds of 25–50 mph (40–80 km/h), this is the sport for you. A hang glider is a kite-shaped, plastic-covered light metal frame. The harnessed rider hangs onto a triangular control bar, jumps from the top of a cliff or hill, and, supported by air currents, glides to the ground. For beginners, flights can be made in tandem with a qualified pilot, equipped with a safety parachute.

The main hang-gliding areas, for both participants and spectators, are

Fort Funston off the Bay Area coastline *(see pp412–13)*, **Torrey Pines Glider Port** in San Diego, or Vista Point in Palm Desert *(see p274)*. If you want to learn the sport, they will recommend instructors. They also sell and rent gliding equipment.

GARDENS

The warm, sunny climate of California has inspired numerous skilled and amateur gardeners to experiment with horticulture. The result is a rich variety of arboretums, botanical gardens, city parks, and private estates all over the state that are now open to the public.

Huntington Library Art Collections and Botanical Gardens are Henry Huntington's idealistic monument to art and culture. Work began on the gardens in 1904. They cover three-quarters of the 200-acre (80-ha) estate and are among the finest of their kind in California *(see pp158–61)*.

The **Descanso Gardens** in La Cañada offer 4 acres (1.6 ha) of roses, an impressive 30-acre (12-ha) grove of live oaks, and a protected forest of camellia trees. William Bourn's landscaped grounds and elegant estate of Filoli in the Bay Area town of Woodside *(see p427)* and **Villa Montalvo Arboretum** in Saratoga are both carefully tended so that their flowers are in bloom all year long. Weekend jazz concerts are held at Saratoga during the summer months, adding to the cultured environment.

Hot air ballooning over California's landscape

HOT AIR BALLOONING

Hot air ballooning is a popular excursion in the Napa Valley *(see pp462–3)*, Monterey *(see pp510–11)*, and Temecula County. The rides are taken at sunrise or sunset when there is the least wind and are quiet and gentle, offering incomparable panoramic views of the countryside. Outfitters such as **Adventures Aloft** and **Napa Valley Balloons** provide private and group outings, which are then followed by a picnic.

WHALE WATCHING

From December through to April, gray whales journey 7,000 miles (11,260 km) along the California coast, having left Alaska's Bering Strait for the warmer climate of Mexico's Baja Peninsula. Ocean cruises offer views of these impressive mammals. Humpback, killer whales, pilot, and blue whales also frequent the coast between San Francisco and Monterey in late summer. Charter operators such as **Shearwater Journeys** provide a glimpse of the gray whales, as well as the dolphins and porpoises that accompany them on their trips. For more information, contact **Oceanic Society Expeditions**.

HOT SPRINGS

A long soak in a hot spring (a bubbling tributary of an underground river, heated by the earth) is said to be very good for one's health. Calistoga in Northern California *(see p461)* has numerous spas, offering everything from heated pools with mineral water to mud baths, steam baths, and massages. Contact the **Calistoga Chamber of Commerce** for a full list of area resorts.

ISLAND HOPPING

Five volcanic islands off the coast of Southern California make up the Channel Islands National Park *(see p224)*. This stark nature preserve is ideal for hiking, viewing wildlife, and exploring rock pools. It is also an excellent spot to see whales and dolphins, as well as many species of shore birds. Ferries depart from Ventura and Santa Barbara harbors. Reserve your trip with **Island Packers**.

The Wrigley Memorial Garden on Catalina Island is accessible by ferry from San Pedro, Long Beach, Redondo Beach, and Balboa. It is more developed than the Channel Islands National Park, with shops, restaurants, and accommodations. Developed as a summer resort in the 1920s by chewing-gum magnate William Wrigley, Jr, the island offers trails for cycling, hiking, and opportunities for diving and snorkeling *(see pp242–3)*.

Farther north, **Angel Island**, in San Francisco Bay, is a 740-acre (300-ha) marine sanctuary, reached by ferry from Fisherman's Wharf. Extensive hiking trails, picnic areas, and camp sites are available to visitors. Gray whales and a wide range of shore birds can be observed.

Two Harbors at Ismus Cove on Catalina Island

DIRECTORY

SPECIAL INTEREST VACATIONS

California Office of Tourism
PO Box 9278,
Van Nuys, CA 91409.
Tel (800) 862-2543.

Gourmet Retreats
Casa Lana, 1316 S Oak St,
Calistoga, CA 94515.
*Tel (707) 942-0615;
(877) 968-2665.*

Mendocino Arts Center
PO Box 765,
Mendocino, CA 95460.
Tel (707) 937-5818.

Crescent Harbor Art Gallery
200 Marine Way,
Crescent City, CA 95531.
Tel (707) 464-9133.

Santa Barbara Writers' Conference
PO Box 304,
Carpinteria, CA 93014.
Tel (805) 684-2250.

Squaw Valley Community of Writers
PO Box 2352,
Olympic Valley, CA 96146.
*Tel (530) 583-5200;
(530) 470-8440.*

Tante Marie's Cooking School
271 Francisco St,
San Francisco, CA 94133.
Tel (415) 788-6699.
www.tantemaries.com

CAMPING

Desert Survivors
PO Box 20991,
Oakland, CA 94620-0991.
Tel (510) 769-1706.

Sequoia National Park Reservations
Tel (888) 252-5757.
www.visitsequoia.com

State Park Reservations
Tel (800) 444-7275.
www.parks.ca.gov

Yosemite Reservations
Tel (559) 252-4848.
www.yosemitepark.com

HIKING

Sierra Club
730 Polk St, San Francisco,
CA 94109.
Tel (415) 977-5500.

HORSEBACK RIDING

El Alisal Guest Ranch and Resort
1054 Alisal Rd, Solvang,
CA 93463. *Tel (805) 688-6411.* www.alisals.com

Hidden Trails
202–380 West 1st Ave
Vancouver, BC V5Y3T7.
Tel (604) 323-1141.
www.hiddentrails.com

MOUNTAIN BIKING

Backroads
801 Cedar St, Berkeley,
CA 94710. *Tel (510)
5271555.*www.backroads
.com

Bicycle Trails Council
PO Box 494,
Fairfax, CA 94978.
Tel (415) 488-1443.

BEACHES

Aquarius Dive Shop
32 Cannery Row,
Monterey, CA 93940.
Tel (831) 375-6605.

Club Ed Surf School
2350 Paul Minnie Ave,
Santa Cruz, CA 95062.
Tel (831) 464-0177.
www.club-ed.com

Underwater Schools of America
225 Brooks St,
Oceanside, CA 92054.
Tel (760) 722-7826.

WHITEWATER RAFTING AND KAYAKING

American River Touring Association
24000 Casa Loma Rd,
Groveland, CA 95321.
Tel (209) 962-7873.
www.arta.org

Outdoor Unlimited
500 Parnassus Ave,
San Francisco, CA 94117.
Tel (415) 476-2078.

Whitewater Voyages
PO Box 20400, El
Sobrante, CA 94820. *Tel
(510) 222-5994.* www.
whitewatervoyages.com

WATER SPORTS

Parasailing Catalina
PO Box 2275,
Avalon, CA 90704.
Tel (310) 510-1777.

BIRD-WATCHING

Tijuana Slough National Estuarine Research Reserve
301 Caspian Way,
Imperial Beach, CA
91932.*Tel (619) 575-3613.*

FISHING

Anchor Charters
PO Box 103,
Fort Bragg, CA 95437.
Tel (707) 964-4550.

Stagnaro's Sport Fishing
PO Box 1340,
Santa Cruz, CA 95061.
Tel (831) 427-2334.

State Department of Fish and Game
1416 9th St,12th Floor,
Sacramento, CA 95814.
Tel (916) 653-7664.

Troutfitter Guide Service
PO Box 1734, Mammoth
Lakes, CA 93546.
Tel (760) 924-3676.
www.troutfitter.com

ROCK CLIMBING AND CAVING

American Mountain Guides Association
710 10th St, Golden
Colorado 80401.
Tel (303) 271-0984.

Mission Cliffs
2295 Harrison St,
San Francisco, CA 94116.
Tel (415) 550-0515.
www.mission-cliffs.com

HANG GLIDING

Torrey Pines Glider Port
2800 Torrey Pines Scenic
Drive, La Jolla,CA 92037.
Tel (858) 452-9858.

GARDENS

Descanso Gardens
1418 Descanso Drive,
La Canada-Flintridge,
CA 91011. *Tel (818) 949-4200.* www.descanso
gardens.com

Villa Montalvo Arboretum
15400 Montalvo Rd,
Saratoga, CA 95071.
Tel (408) 741-3421.

HOT AIR BALLOONING

Adventures Aloft
6525 Washington St,
Yountville, CA 94599.
Tel (707) 944-4408.

Napa Valley Balloons
6795 Washington St,
Yountville, CA 94599.
Tel (707) 253-2224.

WHALE WATCHING

Oceanic Society Expeditions
Fort Mason Center,
San Francisco, CA 94123.
Tel (415) 441-1106.

Shearwater Journeys
PO Box 190,
Hollister, CA 95024.
Tel (831) 637-8527.

HOT SPRINGS

Calistoga Chamber of Commerce
1458 Lincoln Ave, No. 9,
Calistoga, CA 94515.
Tel (707) 942-6333.

ISLAND HOPPING

Angel Island Ferry
Tel (415) 435-2131

Island Packers
1867 Spinnaker Dr,
Ventura, CA 93001.
Tel (805) 642-1393.

SURVIVAL
GUIDE

PRACTICAL INFORMATION

Calfornia is a vibrant and diverse vacation destination. The spirit of the state can be felt in the busy cities of San Francisco, LA, and San Diego as much as in the quiet wilderness of the Sierra Nevada Mountains; and all over the state the needs of visitors are generally well tended. Even so, it is advisable to plan ahead, especially outside the main cities. Most places have visitors' centers providing local information for the

UNITED STATES POSTAL SERVICE®

United States Postal Service logo

surrounding areas. The Survival Guide that follows contains valuable information that will help in every aspect of a visit. Personal Security and Health *(pp622–3)* outlines some recommended precautions. Banking and Currency *(pp624–5)* answers the essential financial questions faced by visitors. There are also sections on how to use the California telephone system and the US postal service *(pp626–7)*.

Skiing on the slopes of Alpine Meadows in Lake Tahoe *(see p486)*

WHEN TO GO

Tourist season, from mid-April to September, sees a rush of visitors to the state's major tourist destinations. The winter months are also very popular with visitors, either for the warm climate of the south or the ski slopes of Lake Tahoe. During the quieter off-season it is sometimes possible to visit many of the tourist attractions at lower admission prices and without the usual crowds.

ADMISSION CHARGES

Major museums, theme parks, art galleries, and other tourist attractions generally charge an admission fee. Entry fees range from $5 to $8, with discounts for the disabled *(see p620)*, students, senior citizens, and children. Smaller tourist attractions are

either free or request a small donation. At most larger institutions entrance is free on one day a month (telephone for details). Free guided tours, demonstrations, and lectures are frequently offered.

OPENING HOURS

Most businesses are open on weekdays from 9am to 5pm and do not close for lunch. Many are also open on Sundays. In addition, some groceries, drugstores, and gas stations in the larger towns and cities are open 24 hours a day.

Most museums are closed on Mondays and/or Tuesdays and on major public holidays, but occasionally stay open until early evening.

Many Californians eat early in the evenings, and restaurants often have their last sitting at about 10pm. Most bars are open until 2am, particularly on Fridays and Saturdays.

TOURIST INFORMATION

Advance information can be obtained from the **California Division of Tourism** or the nearest US Consulate. Maps, guides, event listings, and discount passes for public transportation and tourist attractions are available at local Visitors' and Convention Bureaus. These offices are usually open from Monday to Friday, 9am to 5:30pm.

This guide provides the address and telephone number of the tourist information office in each town or city.

SIGHTSEEING TIPS

To avoid the crowds, visit the region's major sights in the morning and leave unstructured visits and tours until after lunch. Visit a group of sights in the same vicinity on the same day to save time and transportation costs. In general sights are more

Spanish colonial façade of the San Diego Museum of Art *(see p257)*

crowded on weekends. Rush hours are Monday to Friday, 7am to 9am and 4pm to 6:30pm, when transportation and city streets are crowded.

VISAS

Visitors holding an EU or Canadian passport and planning to stay less than 90 days do not require a visa. However, it is necessary to fill out a visa waiver form at the airport check-in desk or on the airplane. Visitors from all other parts of the world need a valid passport and a non-immigrant visitor's visa. This can be obtained from a US Embassy or Consulate.

TAX AND TIPPING

The California State Government levies a 7.25 percent general sales and use tax. In major cities, an additional 1–1.25 percent tax is added to all bought items except those for out-of-state delivery and food for preparation (see p602).

Visitor Information Center in Hallidie Plaza, San Francisco

There are no sales tax charges on hotel rooms, but a 12–14 percent transient occupancy tax is generally incurred.

In restaurants, it is normal to tip 15–20 percent of the total bill. Allow for a tip of 15 percent for taxi drivers, bar staff, and hairdressers. Porters at hotels and airports expect $1–1.50 per bag. It is also usual to leave hotel chambermaids $1–2 for each day of your stay.

SMOKING

It is illegal to smoke in any public building throughout the entire state of California. Ask about smoking policies when reserving a restaurant or hotel room. Remember that in California smoking is banned in restaurants, bars, and in all public places unless there is a separate air-circulation system.

TOURIST INFORMATION

STATEWIDE

California Division of Tourism
102 Q St, Suite 6000, Sacramento, CA 95814.
Tel (800) 862-2543.
Fax (916) 322-2881.
www.gocalif.ca.gov

SAN FRANCISCO

San Francisco
Lower Level Hallidie Plaza, Powell and Market Sts.
Tel (415) 391-2000, (415) 974-6900. www.sfgov.org

THE NORTH

Redding
777 Auditorium Drive.
Tel (800) 874- 7562.
Fax (530) 225-4354.
www.visitredding.org

Eureka
2112 Broadway.
Tel (707) 442-3738,
(800) 356-6381.

WINE COUNTRY

Mendocino County
239 S Main St, Willits.
Tel (707) 459-7910.
www.gomendo.com

Napa Valley
1310 Napa Town Center.
Tel (707) 226-7459.
www.napavalley.com

GOLD COUNTRY

Sacramento
1608 I Street. **Tel** (916) 264-7777, (800) 292-2334.

Tuolumne County
55 W Stockton St, PO Box 4020, Sonora. **Tel** (209) 533-4420, (800) 446-1333. www.tcvb.com

HIGH SIERRAS

Tahoe North
950 N Lake Blvd, Suite 3, Tahoe City.
Tel (800) 824-6348.

Bishop
690 N Main St.
Tel (760) 873-8405.
www.bishopvisitor.com

NORTH CENTRAL

Fresno City/County
808 M St.
Tel (559) 233-0836.
www.fresnocvb.org

Monterey County
380 Alvarado St.
Tel (831) 649-1770.
www.montereyinfo.org

LOS ANGELES

Downtown
685 S Figueroa St.
Tel (213) 689-8822.

Hollywood
6801 Hollywood Blvd.
Tel (323) 467-4270.
www.lacity.com

SOUTH CENTRAL

Santa Barbara
510 State St, Suite 1.
Tel (805) 966-9222.
www.santabarbaraCA.com

San Luis Obispo County
1041 Chorro St. **Tel** (805) 541-8000. www.san luisobispocounty.com

ORANGE COUNTY

Anaheim/Orange County
800 W Katella Ave.
Tel (714) 758-0222.

SAN DIEGO

San Diego
11 Horton Plaza.
Tel (619) 236-1212.
www.sandiego.org

Escondido
720 N Broadway.
Tel (760) 745-2125.

PALM SPRINGS

Riverside
3443 Orange St.
Tel (951) 787-7950.

Palm Springs
69 Hwy 111, Suite 201, Rancho Mirage.
Tel (760) 770-9000.

MOJAVE DESERT

Death Valley
118 Hwy 127, Shoshone.
Tel (760) 852-4524.

Selection of newspapers
available in California

Street distribution bin
for newspapers

local visitors' center. These should give all the up-to-date information on local entertainment and festivals, and details of popular bars and restaurants. In the major cities there is a variety of listings sources, including the *Bay Guardian* in San Francisco, *LA Weekly* and *Los Angeles Reader*, and the *San Diego Reader*.

NEWSPAPERS, TELEVISION, AND RADIO

It is possible to buy the *New York Times* and the *Wall Street Journal* throughout most of California, and the *Los Angeles Times* is read all over the state. There is a selection of local daily papers available, many of which can be purchased from street distribution bins or in bookshops.

Television in California is similar to that all over the US. Much of it is supplied by cable or satellite systems. Most hotel rooms have a television, and bars frequently have screens showing sports. There is a wide selection of national and local channels, most of them showing sitcoms, magazine programs, children's cartoons, and talk shows. There are also Spanish and Asian foreign-language channels and news and music channels. Most newspapers cover program times, and hotel rooms often supply local television schedules.

Similarly, there are numerous commercial radio stations. They cover many subject matters, languages, and music styles. Listings of stations can be found in the local newspapers mentioned above.

ENTERTAINMENT LISTINGS

Most sizable communities have free newspapers that can be found in street distribution bins or at the

DISABLED TRAVELERS

California law requires that every public building is accessible to travelers with disabilities. Direction signs, toilets, and entrances are specially adapted for blind and disabled visitors. Disabled people also receive privileges such as free parking and admission reductions to many national and state parks. It is advisable to notify sights and hotels in advance, so that they can prepare for special needs. The Society for the Advancement of Travel for the Handicapped (SATH) uses a blue H sign to symbolize special facilities in restaurants, hotels, and tourist sights. For information contact the **Disability Rights, Education, and Defense Fund**. Travel for the disabled can be arranged by the **California Relay Service**.

Parking bay for the disabled

GAY AND LESBIAN TRAVELERS

California's large gay community is mainly focused in the major cities, particularly in the Castro District of San Francisco *(see p360)*, Hillcrest in San Diego, and the West Hollywood area of LA *(see pp110–19)*. Free newspapers and magazines that contain gay listings include *The Edge* in Los Angeles; *Frontier,* which covers the whole of Southern California; and the many magazines in San Francisco, such as *Gay Times*. Listings of gay events in San Francisco and the Bay Area can also be obtained from the **Gay and Lesbian Hotline**. The **LA Gay and Lesbian Center** is a referral service in the Los Angeles area that provides crisis support and legal help.

STUDENT TRAVELERS

There are few reductions for students in California. The ISIC (International Student Identity Card) is often not accepted, and it is advisable for the young to carry a passport for entry into bars, as the under-21 ban is strictly enforced. Working vacations for students from other countries can be arranged through the **Student Travel Association**. STA Travel has two offices in the Bay Area and three in LA. There are many youth hostels in the state. For handbooks, listings, and advance information contact **Hosteling International-American Youth Hostels**.

Hitchhiking should be avoided. Check noticeboards at hostels or universities for safe car-sharing opportunities.

CONSULATES

Most countries have consulates in both San Francisco and Los Angeles. They are usually open from 9am to 5pm, Monday to Friday. Although they are not expressly concerned with visitors' problems, it is very important to contact them in times of emergency. Consulates will not lend money, but they can help with lost passports and give advice on legal matters in emergencies. The address of the nearest office in each city can be found in the local telephone directory.

ELECTRICAL APPLIANCES

In the United States all electrical current flows at a standard 110–120 volts AC (alternating current). To operate 220-volt appliances requires a voltage converter and an adapter plug with two flat parallel prongs to fit US outlets. The same applies to battery pack rechargers. Many hotels have hair dryers mounted on the bathroom wall and special plugs for electric shavers that carry 110- or 220-volt current.

Standard plug

CONVERSION CHART

Bear in mind that 1 US pint (0.5 liter) is a smaller measure than 1 UK pint (0.6 liter).

US Standard to Metric
1 inch = 2.54 centimeters
1 foot = 30 centimeters
1 mile = 1.6 kilometers
1 ounce = 28 grams
1 pound = 454 grams
1 US quart = 0.947 liter
1 US gallon = 3.8 liters

Metric to US Standard
1 centimeter = 0.4 inch
1 meter = 3 feet 3 inches
1 kilometer = 0.6 miles
1 gram = 0.04 ounce
1 kilogram = 2.2 pounds
1 liter = 1.1 US quarts

RELIGIOUS ORGANIZATIONS

California, and particularly Northern California, has the reputation of attracting unconventional forms of worship (see pp440–41). Sects, cults, and alternative religions seem to thrive in the state as much as the more conventional churches and temples.

The Catholic Church has the largest following, with nearly a quarter of its number of Hispanic origin. Los Angeles has the second largest Jewish community in the US, and there are many beautiful synagogues. Hindu temples, Islamic mosques, and a range of more unusual shrines abound throughout the state. Details of places for every type of worshiper can be found in the telephone book under "Churches."

Self-realization church, an alternative place of worship

CALIFORNIA TIME

California is in the Pacific Time Zone. Daylight Saving Time begins on the last Sunday in April (at 2am) when clocks are set ahead one hour. It ends on the last Sunday in October (at 2am) when clocks are set back one hour.

City and Country	Hours + or - PT	City and Country	Hours + or - PT
Athens (Greece)	+10	Moscow (Russia)	+11
Auckland (New Zealand)	+20	New York (US)	+3
Beijing (China)	+16	Paris (France)	+9
Berlin (Germany)	+9	Perth (Australia)	+16
Chicago (US)	+2	Sydney (Australia)	+18
Kowloon (Hong Kong)	+16	Tokyo (Japan)	+17
London (UK)	+8	Toronto (Canada)	+3
Madrid (Spain)	+9	Washington, DC (US)	+3

DIRECTORY

DISABLED VISITORS' INFORMATION

California Relay Service
Tel (800) 735-2929 tty.
Tel (800) 735-2922 voice.

Disability Rights, Education, and Defense Fund
2212 6th St, Berkeley, CA 94710.
Tel (510) 644-2555.

STUDENT INFORMATION

Hosteling International-American Youth Hostels
733 15th St NW, Suite 840, Washington, DC 20005.
Tel (800) 909- 4776, (202) 783-6161. www.hiusa.org

Student Travel Association
32 Geary St, San Francisco.
Tel (415) 391-8407.
920 Westwood Blvd, Los Angeles.
Tel (800) 777-0112.
www.statravel.com

GAY AND LESBIAN

Gay and Lesbian Hotline
Tel (415) 355-0999;
(888) THE-GLNH.

LA Gay and Lesbian Center
Tel (323) 993-7400.

CONSULATES

Australian Consulate
625 Market, Suite 200, San Francisco. *Tel* (415) 536-1970.

British Consulate General
1 Sansome St, San Francisco.
Tel (415) 617-1300.

Canadian Consulate
550 S Hope St, 9th floor, Los Angeles.
Tel (213) 346 -2700.

French Consulate
540 Bush St, San Francisco.
Tel (415) 397- 4330.

German Consulate
1960 Jackson St, San Francisco.
Tel (415) 775-1061.

Japanese Consulate
50 Fremont, 23rd Floor, San Francisco.
Tel (415) 777-3533.

Personal Security and Health

WARNING
YOU ARE ENTERING BEAR COUNTRY
BEARS ARE ACTIVE DAY AND NIGHT.
PROPER FOOD STORAGE REQUIRED BY STATE LAW.
PROTECT YOUR PROPERTY AND YOURSELF

violators will be subject to a $500 fine

**Bear warning sign in
Northern California**

Like most major cities, the cities of
California have some dangerous
neighborhoods. Check with friends
or hotel staff which parts of town
are considered unwise to visit, either
alone or at night. San Francisco is
considered one of the safest large
cities in the US; unfortunately,
problems are more visible in some
areas of LA. When traveling in the countryside, always
take a good local map, particularly in the deserts and the
mountains. It is important to take the advice of the local
authorities seriously and in cases of all outdoor pursuits,
normal safety procedures should be observed.

GUIDELINES ON SAFETY

The notorious gangs of
California, particularly in Los
Angeles, are rarely seen
outside their own areas and
are not necessarily interested
in visitors. Visitors are more
likely to be the target of theft
or car crime. Police officers
regularly patrol most of the
tourist areas, but it is still
advisable to prepare the day's
itinerary in advance and to
use common sense. Do not
allow strangers into your hotel
room or give them details of
where you are staying.

Lock any valuables away in
the hotel safe – do not carry
them around with you. Most
hotels will not guarantee the
security of any belongings
kept in your room.

Road safety for pedestrians
is also observed by law: jaywalking, or crossing
the road anywhere
except at an
intersection, can
result in a fine.

**San Francisco
police officer**

LOST PROPERTY

Although the chances of
retrieving property lost in the
street are very slim, telephone the **Police Non-
Emergency Line**. It is
important to report all
lost or stolen items to
the police. If you
want to make an
insurance claim on
your return home,
you will need to
obtain a copy of
the police report to
send to the insur-
ance company. In
case of loss, it is useful
to have a list of serial
numbers or a photo-
copy of all documents
kept separately as proof
of possession.

If your passport is
lost or stolen, get in
contact with your
embassy or consulate
immediately *(see p621)*.
For lost or stolen traveler's
checks or credit cards, you
should contact the near-
est issuing company's
office *(see p623)*.

TRAVEL INSURANCE

Travel insurance is not
compulsory, but strongly
recommended. You should
take out coverage for emergency medical and dental care
while also insuring your
personal property. It is also
advisable to buy insurance
coverage for lost or stolen
baggage and travel documents,
accidental death or injury, trip
cancellation, and legal advice.

SAFETY OUTDOORS

The Pacific Ocean is rarely
warm, even in summer. The
ocean can also be rough,
more suited to surfers than
swimmers, with a strong
undertow. On the beach,
thefts can occur, so
always look after your
valuables. Take full
suntanning precautions.
It is important to
prepare equipment
before hiking in the
wilderness. Notify
someone of your
plans before setting
off. Leave the coun-
tryside as you found it,
and be wary of the
occasionally dangerous
wildlife in many of the
parks. As firewood is
scarce and forest fires can
start quickly, check with
the park ranger whether
camp fires are allowed.

**National park
ranger**

Local maps are available
from the Chamber of
Commerce in the near-
est town. **The Sierra Club** can
advise about excursions.
Rock climbing and moun-
taineering are becoming
increasingly popular
in California. In
many parks there
are services for
climbers *(see
p613)*. Contact local
ranger services for

Patrol motorcycle

Police car

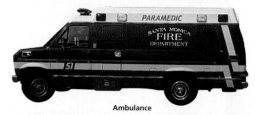

Ambulance

Fire engine

advice on instructors, specific equipment required, and current weather conditions.

Be careful in the desert. At lower levels, it is usually hot and dry; at high elevations, temperatures often drop below freezing at night. Carry extra gas and water. If your car overheats, do not leave it to go for help. Turn it off; check to see if the radiator hoses are broken. If they're not, fill the overflow tank with water and restart the car. For further information contact the Death Valley Visitors' Center (see p290).

MEDICAL MATTERS

To visit a doctor's office, hospital, or pharmacy in the US, it is important to have medical insurance. Even with medical coverage you may have to pay for the services, then claim reimbursement from your insurance company. If you take medication, bring a back-up prescription with you.

EMERGENCIES

For emergencies that require medical, police, or fire services, call 911. Hospital casualty departments are

called emergency rooms; city-owned hospitals, found in the Blue Pages of the telephone book, are often crowded. Private hospitals can be found in the Yellow Pages of the telephone book. Hotels will often call a doctor or dentist to visit you in your room. The national organization **Travelers' Aid Society** can also provide assistance in many kinds of emergency.

EARTHQUAKES

The expectation and fear of earthquakes should not get in the way of everyday activities. You may experience a tremor, but the most important thing is not to panic. Precautions are important, such as keeping shoes and a flashlight by the bed when asleep, in case of power cuts or broken glass. Most injuries occur from falling material. If inside, stand in a doorway or crouch under a table. In a car, decrease speed, pull to the side of the road, and stop. When outside, avoid being near trees, power lines, or bridges. For further information on earthquake precautions, contact **The United States Geological Survey.**

DIRECTORY

CRISIS INFORMATION

All Emergencies
Tel 911 and alert police, fire, or medical services.

Crime Victims' Hotline
Tel (800) 842- 8467.

Police Non-Emergency Line
San Francisco
Tel (415) 553- 0123.
Los Angeles
Tel (877) 275-5273.

Travelers' Aid Society
San Diego
Tel (619) 295-8393.

LOST OR STOLEN CREDIT CARDS AND CHECKS

American Express
Tel (800) 528-4800.

Diners Club
Tel (800) 234 - 6377.

MasterCard
Tel (800) 826 - 2181.

VISA
Tel (800) 336 - 8472.

OUTDOOR RECREATION

California State Department of Parks and Recreation
PO Box 942896,
Sacramento, CA 94296-0001.
Tel (916) 653 - 6995.
www.parkga.gov

National Park Service
Western Region Information Service, 201 Bay & Franklin Sts, San Francisco, CA 94102.
Tel (415) 561-4700.

The Sierra Club
85 Second St, San Francisco, CA 94105. *Tel* (415) 977- 5500.
www.sierraclub.org

EARTHQUAKE INFORMATION

The US Geological Survey
Earth Science Information Centers, 345 Middlefield Rd, Menlo Park, CA 94025.
Tel (650) 329 - 4390

Banking and Currency

San Francisco and LA are major West Coast financial centers – the fine buildings in their financial districts are reflective of their prestige. For the convenience of residents and visitors alike, there are numerous automated teller machines (ATMs) that operate 24 hours a day. In smaller towns, some banks may not exchange foreign currency or traveler's checks, so it is best to note the bank opening times in advance. Credit cards are very useful, and many situations, such as booking hotels or renting a car, require them as a form of security.

Bank in San Francisco

for a credit card imprint on check-in. The majority of car rental companies often penalize patrons without credit cards by asking for a large cash deposit. Hospitals will accept most credit cards in payment.

BANKING

Bank opening times vary throughout the state. They are generally open between 10am and 3pm. Banking hours within major cities may be longer: some open as early as 7:30am and close at 6pm, and are often open on Saturday mornings. Credit Unions serve only their own members, so look for banks that offer services to the general public. Always ask about commissions before making a transaction. US dollar traveler's checks can usually be cashed with a recognized form of photographic identification, such as a passport or an ISIC card. Foreign currency exchange is available in main branches of the larger banks.

CREDIT CARDS

American Express, Diners Club, JCB, MasterCard (Access), and VISA are widely accepted throughout California. As well as the convenience of not carrying cash on your person, credit cards also occasionally offer insurance on bought merchandise or other benefits. They can be used all over the state to book hotel rooms or rent a car *(see p632)*. Most hotels will ask

AUTOMATED TELLER MACHINES

Automated teller machines (ATMs) can be found in most bank foyers or on the outside wall near the bank's entrance. They are in operation day and night, so that cash can be accessed outside normal banking hours. US currency, usually in $20 notes, can be withdrawn electronically from your bank or credit card account within seconds. Ask your own bank which ATM system your card can access in California and how much each transaction will cost. The more popular systems are **Cirrus** and **Plus**. ATMs also accept various US bank cards, in addition to MasterCard (Access), VISA, and other credit cards.

Robberies can occur at ATMs, so it is advisable to use them in the daytime or when there are plenty of people nearby. Withdrawals from ATMs may provide a better foreign currency exchange rate than cash transactions.

TRAVELER'S CHECKS

Traveler's checks issued by American Express and Thomas Cook in US dollars are accepted at most hotels, restaurants, and shops without a fee. It is necessary to show a passport as identification. If you lose your checks, contact **Thomas Cook Refund Assistance** or the **American Express Helpline**.

Foreign currency traveler's checks may be cashed at a large bank or at major hotels. Rates of exchange are printed in the newspapers and posted up at banks where exchange services are offered. Personal checks drawn on foreign banks are rarely accepted.

CURRENCY EXCHANGE

Fees and commissions are charged at currency exchanges. They are usually open on weekdays from 9am to 5pm. The best-known firms are **Thomas Cook Currency Services** and **American Express Travel Service**. Both of these companies have offices throughout California. Alternatively, try a city's main branch of a major bank or look in the Yellow Pages of the telephone directory.

Foreign currency exchange sign

Automated teller machine (ATM)

Coins

American coins come in 1-dollar, 50-, 25-, 10-, 5-, and 1-cent pieces (actual size shown). The new goldtone $1 coins are in circulation, as are the State quarters, which feature an historical scene on one side. Each coin has a popular name: 1-cent pieces are called pennies, 5-cent pieces are nickels, 10-cent pieces are dimes and 25-cent pieces are quarters.

**25-cent coin
(a quarter)**

**10-cent coin
(a dime)**

**5-cent coin
(a nickel)**

**1-cent coin
(a penny)**

Bank Notes

Units of currency in the United States are dollars and cents. There are 100 cents in a dollar. Notes (bills) come in $1, $5, $10, $20, $50, and $100s. $2 bills are rarely circulated. All bills are the same color, so check the amount carefully. The new $20 and $50 bills with extra security features are now in circulation, and there are plans for new $5 and $10 notes.

**1-dollar coin
(a buck)**

DIRECTORY

FINANCIAL SERVICES

Thomas Cook Currency Services
75 Geary St, San Francisco.
Map 5 C4.
Tel (415) 362-3452.

Thomas Cook Refund Assistance
Tel (800) 223-7373.

American Express Travel Service
455 Market St, San Francisco.
Map 6 D4.
Tel (415) 536-2600.
8493 W 3rd St,
Los Angeles.
Map 6 C3.
Tel (310) 659-1682.

American Express Helpline
Tel (800) 221-7282.

Cirrus
Tel (800) 424-7787.

Plus
Tel (800) 843-7587.

1- dollar bill ($1)

5- dollar bill ($5)

10- dollar bill ($50)

20- dollar bill ($20)

50- dollar bill ($50)

100- dollar bill ($100)

Using California's Telephones

Public telephones can be found on many street corners, in hotels, restaurants, bars, theaters and department stores. Most are either coin-operated, using 5-, 10-, and 25-cent pieces, or take phonecards. There are now several, however, that take credit cards.

PUBLIC TELEPHONES

Modern pay phones have a hand receiver and a 12-button key pad. Pacific Bell (PacBell) operates the majority of public pay phones. These are marked by a blue and white receiver sign with a bell in a circle. They are mounted on walls, posts, or in a booth. Some independent companies also operate pay phones, but generally these are not as reliable, and can be more expensive. All charges must be indicated by law. Telephone directories are supplied at most public phones. If there are any complaints about a service, call the operator by dialing 0, the phone company's business office, or the **California Public Utilities Commission.**

PAY PHONE CHARGES

The cost of a local call within the same area code varies with the length of the call, but it is usually a minimum of 50 cents. After three minutes the operator may interrupt the call to request more money. When calling a number outside the town or city you are in but within the same area code, a recorded message will tell you how much more money to add. Long-distance calls are to numbers with a different area code. These can be

Souvenir phonecards

expensive, but will be less so when dialed direct, without the help of the operator.

Local and long-distance calls are cheaper between 6pm and 8am weekdays and on weekends. Hotels charge all calls at premium rate. Telephone numbers that begin with 800, 888, or 877 are free. To make a collect call, you will need to contact the operator.

Phonecards are available from post offices, drugstores, or convenience stores. They are issued by major telephone companies such as AT&T. The cards are convenient if you need to make a call and do not have the correct change; they can be used on any phone by calling the free number on the back of the card and quoting its PIN (personal identification number). The PIN can also be used to receive instructions in your preferred language. To recharge the card, call the recharge number on the back and quote both the PIN and your credit card number.

FAX SERVICE

Worldwide fax services are readily available in post offices, hotels, and copying-service shops. Fax charges

Airport fax machine

USING A COIN-OPERATED PHONE

1 Lift the receiver and listen for the dial tone.

3 Dial or press the number.a

Coins
Make sure you have plenty of these coins available.

5 cents

10 cents

25 cents

2 Insert the required coin or coins. The coin drops as soon as you insert it.

4 If you want to cancel the call before it is answered, or if the call does not connect, press the coin release lever and take your coins from the coin return.

5 If the call is answered and you talk longer than three minutes, the operator will interrupt and tell you how much more money to deposit. Payphones do not give change.

are usually based on the time of day of the transmission, the destination, and the number of pages faxed. Incoming faxes can also be received and will be charged by the page. Look under *Facsimile Transmission Services* in the Yellow Pages of the telephone directory for further details. For telegrams, telexes, faxes, and electronic mail, you can also contact **Western Union**.

REACHING THE RIGHT NUMBER

- Direct-dial call outside the local area code, but within the US and Canada: dial **1**.
- International direct-dial call: dial **011** followed by country code (UK: **44**; Australia: **61**; New Zealand: **64**), then the city or area code (omit the first 0) and then the local number.
- International call via the operator: dial **01**, followed by the country code, then the city code (without the first 0), and then the local number.
- International directory inquiries: dial **00**.
- International operator assistance: dial **01**.
- A **1- 800**, **866**, **888**, or **877** prefix indicates a free call.
- Local directory inquiries: dial **411**.
- There have been changes to some California area codes over the last few years. If you experience difficulties reaching any number, call directory inquiries.
- **For emergency police, fire, or ambulance services, dial 911.**

USEFUL NUMBERS

California Public Utilities Commission
Tel (800) 649 -7570.

Western Union
Tel (800) 325- 6000.

Directory Inquires within the US
Tel 1- (area code) 555-1212.

Sending a Letter

Apart from post offices, letters can be sent from hotel reception desks or mailed in letter slots in office reception areas and at air, rail, and bus terminals. Street mailboxes are painted either blue, or red, white, and blue. Weekend mail delivery is limited. Stamps can be purchased at post offices, hotel reception desks, or from vending machines in convenience stores and supermarkets. Check international and domestic postal rates.

POSTAL SERVICE

All domestic mail is first class and will usually arrive within 1 to 5 days. Letters without the zip (or postal) code will take longer. International airmail to New Zealand, Australia, Canada, Ireland, and the United Kingdom takes 5–10 working days. Packages sent overseas by surface parcel rate may take 4–6 weeks for delivery. The federal post office offers two special services. Priority Mail promises delivery faster than first class mail. The more expensive Express Mail delivers next day within the United States, and within 72 hours to many international destinations. Private express mail can be arranged through the delivery services listed in the Yellow Pages of the telephone directory. The two main international express mail companies are **DHL** and **Federal Express**.

US commemorative stamps

GENERAL DELIVERY

Larger city post offices have a general delivery service where letters sent c/o General Delivery will be held for 30 days before being returned to the sender. The zip code of the post office and the address of the sender should be clearly marked. The recipient's last name should be underlined so that the letter is filed correctly at the receiving office.

US mail van

San Francisco
c/o General Delivery,
Civic Center, 101 Hyde St,
San Francisco, CA 94142.

Los Angeles
c/o General Delivery,
Los Angeles Main Post Office,
900 N Alameda,
Los Angeles, CA 90086.

San Diego
c/o General Delivery,
San Diego Main Post Office,
San Diego, CA 92110.

POSTAL SERVICES

DHL
Tel (800) 225-5345.

Federal Express
Tel (800) 463-3339.

United States Postal Service
Tel (800) 275-8777.

Standard US mailbox

TRAVEL INFORMATION

San Francisco and LA are the two main gateways for visitors traveling to California by air. You can also get there by car, Amtrak train, long-distance bus, or by ocean liner. Despite continuing problems with traffic congestion and environmental pollution, Californians remain devoted to driving.

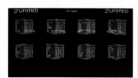

A passenger jet

Large, comfortable cars, cheap gas, and a comprehensive network of roads make this an efficient and pleasurable way to tour the state. Public transportation is a viable and inexpensive option in the major cities, where historic cable cars and ferries work alongside modern buses and mass transit systems.

Airport arrivals board

TRAVELING BY AIR

Air travel is an integral part of the American lifestyle, and California is no exception. Airports are efficiently designed, with computerized ticketing systems. Competition between airlines has led to a high level of service.

Frequent and reliable connections are offered all over the state. Los Angeles (LAX) and San Francisco (SFO) are the two main airports used by visitors to California. International flights also land at San Diego (SAN), Oakland (OAK), and San Jose (SJC). The state has more than 30 airports handling domestic flights. The major domestic airports include Sacramento and Palm Springs, as well as Santa Barbara, John Wayne/Orange County, and Fresno.

AIR FARES

Fare structures are complex, with a variety of passes and bonus systems offered by the numerous airlines flying to and within California. Prices also vary according to season, with the most expensive tickets coinciding with summer months and the holiday periods, such as Christmas and Thanksgiving *(see p39)*. It is always cheaper to travel to or from California on weekdays rather than on weekends. The lowest regular offer

is the APEX (Advanced Purchase Excursion Fare), which should be purchased two to three weeks before departure and is nonrefundable. A reputable travel agent will be able to supply details on all the latest offers and promotions. They will also be able to point out the advantages

and restrictions that accompany the fares and routes available, and tell you whether a visa is required to enter the US.

Most travelers from Europe choose nonstop flights to California, but fares are often cheaper if you fly via another American "hub" city such as Newark or Houston. The

The Encounters Restaurant, Los Angeles Airport

AIRPORT	INFORMATION
Los Angeles (LAX)	*Tel (310) 646-5252*
San Francisco (SFO)	*Tel (650) 761-0800*
Oakland (OAK)	*Tel (510) 577-4000*
San Diego (SAN)	*Tel (619) 231-2100*
San Jose (SJC)	*Tel (408) 277-4759*
Sacramento (SMF)	*Tel (916) 929-5411*
Palm Springs (PSP)	*Tel (760) 318-3800*

volume of passengers flying, particularly in peak season, is so high that it is best to book as early as possible. If you are touring, a fly-drive package booked before you leave will generally be cheaper than making car rental arrangements in California (see p632).

AT THE AIRPORT

With a vast number of passengers arriving and departing at one time, huge international airports such as Los Angeles and San Fran- cisco can seem bewildering to the jet-lagged, first-time visitor. Lines at immigration and customs points are inevitable at peak times. Dispose of any fresh fruit you may be carry- ing (a strictly enforced customs regulation) and plan transportation from the airport to your destination in advance.

All the major airports have multilingual information booths for the newly arrived. These help with inquiries about the airport and also give information on the vari- ous forms of transportation into the city. Car rental desks (see p632), currency exchange facilities (see pp624–5), and shuttle bus services can also be found in the airports.

Most car rental companies supply a shuttle bus to the car pick-up points, usually locat- ed on the outskirts of the air- port. Shuttle buses can also be chartered for a door-to-door service to and from the airport

Baggage check-in desk

and a specific city address. One-way fares vary in price, depending on the distance covered. Journey times given below also vary, according to the number of passengers and their required stops.

All airports have facilities for assisting disabled passengers, although it is advisable to prearrange this through your airline. Smoking is not permit- ted in any of California's airport terminals.

Rental car shuttle

Door-to-door shuttle bus

CUSTOMS AND DUTY FREE

Visitors arriving in the US by air and sea are issued with customs declaration forms that must be filled in completely. Adult nonresidents are permitted to bring in a limited amount of duty-free items. These include 0.2 gals (1 liter) of alcoholic beverages (beer, wine, or spirits), 200 cigarettes, 50 cigars (but not Cuban) or 4.4 lbs (2 kg) of smoking tobacco, and $100 worth of gifts for other people.

AIRLINE CARRIERS (US CONTACT NUMBERS)

All Nippon Airlines
Tel (800) 2359262. www.ana.co.jp

American *Tel* (800) 433- 7300 www.aa.com

British Airways
Tel (800) 247-9297.
www.britishairways.com

Continental *Tel* (800) 525- 0280.www.continental.com

Delta *Tel* (800) 221 - 1212. www.delta–air.com

Southwest *Tel* (800) 435- 9792. www.southwest.com

United *Tel* (800) 241 - 6522. www.ual.com

USAirways *Tel* (800) 428- 4322. www.usairways.com

TWA *Tel* (800) 433-7300. www.twa.com

Virgin Atlantic
Tel (800) 862-8621.
www.virgin–atlantic.com

DISTANCE FROM CITY	TAXI FARE TO CITY	SHUTTLE BUS
15 miles (24 km) from Downtown	approx $40 to Downtown approx $42 to Beverly Hills	30 mins to Downtown
14 miles (22 km) from city center	approx $35 to Downtown	25 mins to city center
8 miles (12 km) from city center	approx $25–28 to Oakland	20 mins to city center
3 miles (5 km) from city center	approx $10–12 to San Diego	10–15 mins to city center
8 miles (12 km) from city center	approx $8–10 to San Jose	15 mins to city center
12 miles (19 km) from city center	approx $30 to Sacramento	20 mins to city center
2 miles (3 km) from city center	approx $10 to Palm Springs	5–8 mins to city center

Getting Around California

Authorized taxi license

Although often more time-consuming, traveling by train, bus, and ferry can be an inexpensive and rewarding way of getting around California. Within the major cities of San Francisco *(see pp396–7)*, Los Angeles *(see pp178–9)*, and San Diego *(see pp266–7)*, there are adequate public transportation networks, offering buses, trams, Metro trains, ferries, and cable cars. They are very busy during the rush hour periods. Taxis and shuttle buses are also useful in the cities. The network of Amtrak railroad lines and connecting bus services serves the state's most populous areas and offers some scenic journeys. It is also possible to travel within the state by bus.

Taxi cabs in San Francisco

Coaster train ticket machine

TRAVELING BY RAIL

The use of railroads in the US is dwindling, yet there are still connections between major cities. **Amtrak** runs direct, long-distance routes from LA to Chicago, Seattle, Albuquerque, and San Antonio, but no longer offers a direct service to the East Coast.

In California, the rail network is divided into three sections: the San Diegan (linking Santa Barbara and San Diego), the Capitol (between San Jose and Sacramento), and the San Joaquin (connecting Emeryville and Bakersfield). A bus service heads out in many directions from stops along these lines. Local commuter lines include **Caltrain** (linking San Jose and San Francisco); the Coast Starlight Connection (between San Luis Obispo and Santa Barbara); LA Metrolink; and the Coaster (connecting San Diego and Oceanside).

LONG-DISTANCE BUSES

The network of bus routes operated by **Greyhound Lines** reaches all parts of the US. In California, services include scenic coastal connections as well as frequent express routes linking major cities such as San Francisco, Sacramento, San Jose, LA, and San Diego. Guided tours provide a leisurely way of sightseeing. Several companies offer short package trips in deluxe buses visiting sights such as Hearst Castle *(see pp212–15)*, Yosemite National Park *(see pp488–91)*, and Monterey *(see pp508–11)*. Information about these services can be found in the Yellow Pages of the telephone book.

For travelers with more time to spare and who wish to get a real feel for the state, the alternative-minded **Green Tortoise** offers leisurely journeys between the major cities of the Pacific Coast. Passengers can break their trip to camp, prepare meals, and explore the countryside.

TAXIS

Taxis (often called "cabs") can usually be found outside main transportation terminals and major hotels. Elsewhere it is best to order one by telephone – numbers can be found in the Yellow Pages of the telephone directory. Never stand in a street at night expecting one to pass.

Not all drivers know their way around, so it will help to have your destination marked on a map if it is off the beaten track. All taxi fares are metered according to the distance traveled. Some taxis take credit cards, but it is best to inquire in advance. A tip of 15 percent is generally expected.

SHUTTLE VANS

Cheaper than taxis and quicker than buses, shuttle vans are a secure and reliable way of traveling within and around California's cities. They provide an efficient travel network, especially between hotels and airports.

Greyhound bus parked along a California highway

When calculating your trip time, bear in mind that other passengers will be picked up and dropped off en route. Competition between shuttle bus companies has led to a high standard of service. Their details can be found in the telephone directory. Call several companies to obtain the best quote before booking a long journey. Bus drivers will expect a tip of at least $1.

BOATS AND FERRIES

Express boat services provide a fast link from Los Angeles to Santa Catalina Island *(see pp242–3)*, while others sail more leisurely across San Francisco Bay *(see pp298–9)*. Most ferries carry foot passengers and bicycles, but not motor vehicles.

Despite the building of new bridges, several commuter ferries survive to offer their customers a breezy alternative to the smog of the rush hour traffic. Routes, such as those connecting Oakland, Sausalito, and Tiburon with San Francisco, and the San Diego–Coronado ferry, provide a pleasant and reasonably priced way to enjoy a city. To find out about ferry timetables, prices, and locations in San Francisco and the Bay Area see page 399, and in San Diego see page 267.

DIRECTORY

TRAIN INFORMATION

Amtrak
Tel (800) 872-7245.
www.amtrak.com

Caltrain
Tel (800) 660-4287.
www.transitinfo.org

BUS AND COACH INFORMATION

Greyhound Lines
Tel (800) 231-2222.
www.greyhound.com

The Green Tortoise
494 Broadway, San Francisco,
CA 94133.*Tel* (415) 956-7500.
www.greentortoise.com

AMTRAK ROUTES

This map shows the main Amtrak routes within California, as well as the bus feeder services to the main stations. Amtrak also has several interstate services to other major cities in the US; the route to Las Vegas is shown below.

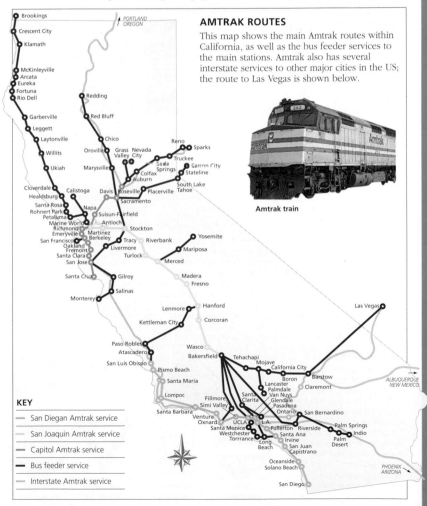

Amtrak train

KEY

— San Diegan Amtrak service

— San Joaquin Amtrak service

— Capitol Amtrak service

— Bus feeder service

— Interstate Amtrak service

Traveling by Car

Driving is an essential part of the California way of life, and for both residents and visitors it is the most convenient way to travel around the state. Roads are well maintained so that they are able to cope with the great volume of rush hour traffic that pours in and out of the main cities every weekday. The state has an efficient network of major roads linking the cities and towns. In remote areas, such as in the deserts and mountains, it is sometimes necessary to use a four-wheel-drive vehicle.

Traffic on the Harbor Freeway, Los Angeles

RENTING A CAR

It is best to arrange a fly-drive package before leaving for California. Take note of exactly what is included in the deal, and find out whether any extra payments may arise when the car is returned. These additions – which can include optional fuel purchase, extended insurance cover, collision damage waiver, delivery or drop-off charges, and vehicle rental tax (a daily city vehicle rental tax) – can double the original prepaid fee. It is particularly important to find out exactly what is included in the insurance policy offered by the rental company. Drivers should remember that in California, where litigation is an everyday occurrence, it is sensible to be fully insured.

To rent a car, the driver must be over 25 and have a US or internationally valid driver's license. A major credit card is also important, if not vital, as a guarantee. Some companies may rent to younger drivers or accept a cash deposit in lieu of a credit card number, but expect higher charges in return. Taking a rented car across the border into Mexico is not permitted without prior arrangement. The gas tank should be full when you return the vehicle, and you should allow sufficient time to process and check your final bill.

Car rental is generally least expensive at airports *(see p629)*, but call the free numbers advertised by rental companies to find out about discounts.

Rental cars generally have automatic transmission. If necessary, spend some time getting familiar with this system. Some companies supply cars with manual transmission ("stick-shift") on request. Classic cars, Harley-Davidson motorcycles, and RVs (motor homes) can also be rented from specialty companies.

RULES OF THE ROAD

Californians drive on the right. Seat belts are compulsory for both driver and passengers. In the US, speed limits are individually set by each state. In California, the maximum speed limit is generally 65 mph (104 km/h) but on selected freeways, 70 mph (110 km/h) limits have now been introduced. In cities, the speed limits are restricted as marked. These controls are rigorously enforced by the Highway Patrol. Drunk driving is a serious offense and carries very heavy penalties.

Highways are known as Freeways or Interstates. Bicycles are not permitted on these roads. In rush hours, carpool or diamond lanes, which can only be used by cars carrying more than one passenger, come into force on

TRAFFIC SIGNS

A range of different signs offer warnings and instructions for drivers. Speed limits may vary every few miles, depending on the conditions of the road and the amount of traffic, and should be adhered to. In more remote areas, drivers must be wary of wildlife that may occasionally stray onto the roads. Disregarding traffic signs will result in fines from the Highway Patrol.

Wildlife warning

Traffic flows in a single direction

Entry prohibited

Maximum speed

Give way to all vehicles

Stop at intersection

Curbing wheels in San Francisco – the curb acts as a block

PREVENT RUNAWAYS CURB WHEELS PARK IN GEAR SET BRAKE

PARK AT 90 DEGREES

Curbside parking signs in San Francisco to prevent cars rolling downhill

Time elapsed shown here

Insert coins here

Turn handle to register coins

some roads. It is permissible to turn right on red at traffic lights if there is nothing coming the other way. The first vehicle to reach a stop sign junction has the right of way.

The **Automobile Association of America** (AAA) offers maps, emergency road service, and discounts at many hotels and restaurants. The AAA is linked with many automobile clubs abroad, so inquire ahead whether they will honor your membership. If not, the annual fee is about $60.

AAA sign

GASOLINE

Gas, or gasoline, is either unleaded or diesel quality. It is sold in gallons rather than liters. Inexpensive by European standards, the price includes a small gasoline tax. Gas stations are not as widespread as many visitors expect, so be sure to fill up the tank before driving into the mountains, desert, or through other remote areas. Many gas stations have pump attendants. Some pumps take credit cards, and in self-service stations it is common to pay for your gas prior to putting it into the car.

PARKING

Parking in California cities is strictly controlled and can be expensive. Valet parking is obligatory if you pull up outside many hotels and restaurants. Hand the keys to the attendant and pay on departure. Most parking meters accept quarters, but some systems require dollars to be "posted" into the slot relating to the parking space. Parking lots have their own set prices. Parking is free outside at shopping malls or, if parking inside, you can have your ticket validated at any store where you've made a purchase to reduce the parking fee.

Parking restrictions are indicated by curb colors. If the curb is painted red, parking is prohibited; yellow indicates a loading zone; green allows parking for up to ten minutes; white five minutes only during business hours. Blue curbs are for disabled parking only. If parking on the steep hills in San Francisco, you must curb your wheels into the road if facing uphill and toward the curb if facing downhill. If your vehicle is booted or towed, contact the local **Police Department Towed Vehicle Information Center**.

DIRECTORY

CAR RENTAL AGENCIES

Alamo *Tel* (800) 327-9633. www.alamo.com

Avis *Tel* (800) 331-1212. www.avis.com

Budget *Tel* (800) 527-7000. www.drivebudget.com

Hertz *Tel* (800) 654-3131. www.hertz.com

Cruise America Motorhome Rental *Tel* (800) 327-7799.

Dubbelju Motorcycle Services *Tel* (415) 495-2774. www.dubbleju.com

ROAD CONDITIONS INFORMATION

Statewide *Tel* (800) 427-7623.

Northern California *Tel* (916) 445-7623.

Southern California *Tel* (213) 897-3656.

AUTOMOBILE ASSOCIATIONS

Automobile Association of America 1000 AAA Drive, Heathrow, FL 32746. *Tel* (800) 222-4357.

California State Automobile Association 150 Van Ness Ave, San Francisco, CA 94102. *Tel* (415) 565-2012.

Automobile Association of Southern California 2601 S Figueroa St, Los Angeles, CA 90007. *Tel* (213) 741-3111.

POLICE DEPARTMENT TOWED VEHICLE INFORMATION

San Francisco *Tel* (415) 553-1235.

Los Angeles *Tel* (323) 913-4460.

San Diego *Tel* (619) 531-2844.

General Index

Acknowledgments

Dorling Kindersley would like to thank the following people whose contributions and assistance have made the preparation of this book possible.

Main Contributor
Jamie Jensen grew up in LA and now lives in Northern California. He contributed to *San Francisco* in the DK Guides series, and his most recent book is *Road Trip USA: Cross-Country Adventures on America's Two-Lane Highways*.
Ellen Payne is Managing Editor of *Los Angeles Magazine* and has worked on numerous travel publications.
J Kingston Pierce is a Seattle writer specializing in West Coast history. He is a contributing editor of *San Francisco Focus* and *Seattle* magazines and his book credits include *San Francisco, You're History!*
Rebecca Poole Forée is Editor-in-Chief at Foghorn Press, San Francisco. She has written many travel books, including *Northern California Best Places*.
Nigel Tisdall is the author of several travel guides. He has contributed to *France, Seville and Andalusia* and *Portugal* in the DK series.
Stanley Young lives in LA. He has written several books including *The Missions of California* and *Paradise Found: The Beautiful Retreats and Sanctuaries of California and the Southwest*.

Contributors and Consultants
Virginia Butterfield, Dawn Douglas, Rebecca Renner, Tessa Souter, Shirley Streshinsky, Barbara Tannenbaum, Michael Webb, John Wilcock.

Additional Photography
Demetrio Carassco, Steve Gorton, Gary Grimaud, Bonita Halm, Trevor Hill, Kirk Irwin, Neil Lukas, Neil Mersh, Ian O'Leary, David Peevers, Erhard Pfeiffer, Robert Vente.

Additional Illustrators
James A Allington, Arcana Studios, Hugh Dixon, Richard Draper, Dean Entwhistle, Eugene Fleury, Chris Forsey, Andrew Green, Steve Gyapay, Toni Hargreaves, Philip Hockey, John Lawrence, Nick Lipscombe, Mel Pickering, Sallie Alane Reason, Peter Ross, Simon Roulston, John See, Tristan Spaargaren, Ed Stuart, Paul Williams.

Cartography
Lovell Johns Ltd, Oxford, UK; ERA-Maptec Ltd, Dublin, Ireland; Alok Pathak, Kunal Singh. Street Finder Maps based upon digital data, adapted with permission from original survey by ETAK INC 1984–1994.
MAP CO-ORDINATORS Emily Green, David Pugh

Design and Editorial
MANAGING EDITORS Vivien Crump, Helen Partington
DEPUTY ART DIRECTOR Gillian Allan
DEPUTY EDITORIAL DIRECTOR Douglas Amrine
SENIOR EDITOR Fay Franklin
REVISIONS EDITOR Mani Ramaswamy
Shahnaaz Bakshi, Peter Bennett, Vandana Bhagra, Hilary Bird, Sophie Boyak, Sherry Collins, Joanna Craig, Cullen Curtiss, Donna Dailey, Stephanie Driver, Michael Ellis, Rob Farmer, Jo Gardner, William Gordon, Emily Green, Roger Grody, Bonita Halm, Vinod Harish, Paul Hines, Thomas A Knight, Esther Labi, Kathy McDonald, Ciaran McIntyre,

Annie McQuitty, Sam Merrell, Ella Milroy, Mary Ormandy, Ellen Root, Shailesh Sharma, Jonathan Schultz, Azeem Siddiqui, Asavari Singh, Alka Thakur, Ingrid Vienings, Marek Walisiewicz.

Special Assistance
Marianne Babel, Wells Fargo History Museum, San Francisco; Liz Badras, LA Convention and Visitors' Bureau; Craig Bates, Yosemite Museum; Joyce Bimbo, Hearst Castle, San Simeon; Elizabeth A Borsting and Ron Smith, the *Queen Mary*, Long Beach; Jean Bruce-Poole, El Pueblo de Los Angeles National Monument; Carolyn Cassady; Covent Garden Stamp Shop; Marcia Eymann and Joy Tahan, Oakland Museum of California; Donna Galassi; Mary Jean S Gamble, Salinas Public Library; Mary Haas, California Palace of the Legion of Honor; Nancy Masten, Photophile; Miguel Millar, US National Weather Service, Monterey; Warren Morse, LA County Metropolitan Transportation Authority; Anne North, San Diego Visitors' and Convention Bureau; Donald Schmidt, San Diego Zoo; Vito Sgromo, Sacramento State Capitol Museum; Dawn Stranne and Helen Chang, San Francisco Visitors' and Convention Bureau; Cherise Sun and Richard Ogar, Bancroft Library; Gaynell V Wald, Mission San Juan Capistrano; Chris Wirth, Wine Institute, San Francisco; Cynthia J Wornham and Lori Star, the J Paul Getty Trust.

Photography Permissions
Dorling Kindersley would like to thank the following for their assistance and kind permission to photograph at their establishments: Balboa Park, San Diego; Columbia State Historic Park; Disney Enterprises, Inc.; J Paul Getty Museum, LA; Hearst Castle, San Simeon; Huntington Library, San Marino; Knotts Berry Farm, Buena Park; Los Angeles Children's Museum; Los Angeles County Museum of Art; Museum of Contemporary Art, LA; Museum of Miniatures, LA; Museum of Television and Radio, LA; Museum of Tolerance, LA; Norton Simon Museum, Pasadena; Petersen Automotive Museum, LA; *Queen Mary*, Long Beach; Sacramento State Capitol; San Diego Aerospace Museum; San Diego Automotive Museum; San Diego Museum of Art; San Diego Wild Animal Park; San Diego Zoological Society; Santa Barbara Mission; Southwest Museum, LA; John Steinbeck Library, Salinas; Tao House, Danville; Timken Museum of Art, San Diego; Universal Studios, LA; University of California, Berkeley; University of California, LA; University of Southern California, LA; Wells Fargo History Room, San Francisco; Winchester Mystery House, San Jose; and all other churches, missions, museums, parks, wineries, hotels, restaurants, and sights too numerous to thank individually.

Picture Credits
t = top; tl = top left; tc = top center; tr = top right; cla = center left above; ca = center above; cra = center right above; cl = center left; c = center; cr = center right; clb = center left below; cb = center below; crb = center right below; bl = bottom left; b = bottom; bc = bottom center; br = bottom right; bla = bottom left above; bca = bottom center above; bra = bottom right above; blb = bottom left below; bcb = bottom center below; brb = bottom right below; d = detail.

blown calcedonio glass, 12.5 x 19.5 cm, 85c; Gospels (Helmarshausen, c.1120–40), tempera colours, gold and silver on vellum bound between paper boards covered with brown calf, 22.8 x 16.4 cm, 85b; GOLDEN GATE BRIDGE HIGHWAY AND TRANSPORTATION DISTRICT: 55t, 380tl, 380c, 380b, 380–1t, 381c, 381cb; Charles M Hiller 55tl; GOLDEN GATE NATIONAL RECREATION AREA, NATIONAL PARK SERVICE: 339blb, 339bc; RONALD GRANT ARCHIVE: 52tl, 102cr, 105cl, 107cl, 607t; Capitol 198tr; *LA Story*, Warner Bros 20t; *Rebel Without A Cause*, Warner Bros 68cra; *The Last Action Hero* Columbia Pictures 68crb; *E.T., The Extra-Terrestrial*, Spielberg/ Universal Studios, 69br; *Gidget*, Columbia Pictures 198c. ROBERT HARDING PICTURE LIBRARY: 196t, 203c, 298c, 608t; Bildagentur/Schuster 198b; FPG 24cl, 52cla, 53clb, 55cra; Jon Gardey 497t; Tony Gervis 483; Michael J Howell 23tr; Dave Jacobs 437b, 497c; Robert Landau 73crb; Westlight/Bill Ross 14b, 150tr, Steve Smith 23br 33t; HEARST CASTLE/HEARST SAN SIMEON STATE HISTORICAL MONUMENT: Z Baron 212br; John Blades 212tr, 212clb, 213b, 214c, 215c; V Garagliano 212bc; Ken Raveill 212ca, 213t, 213cra, 214b; Amber Wisdom 213crb; PHOEBE HEARST MUSEUM OF ANTHROPOLOGY: 45crb; HOLLYWOOD ENTERTAINMENT MUSEUM: 108cla; ROBERT HOLMES PHTOGRAPHY: Markham Johnson 305bl; HOTEL CASA DEL MAR: 174b; HULTON GETTY: 57cr, 105t; HUNTINGDON LIBRARY, ART COLLECTIONS, AND BOTANIC GARDENS: 29b, 158b, 159cr, 160b; *Madonna and Child*, Roger van der Weyden 71crb; *Breakfast in Bed*, Mary Cassatt 158c; Gutenberg Bible 159t; *Blue Boy*, Thomas Gainsborough 159crb; *Diana the Huntress*, Houdon 160t; The Wife of Bath from *The Canterbury Tales*, Chaucer (Ellesmere MS), 160c; HUTCHISON LIBRARY: Robert Francis 289t; B Regent 166cl. IMAGE BANK: David Hamilton 23tl; Marvin E Newman 324; Charles C Place 451t; 202clb; Paul Slaughter 512tl; Weinberg-Clark 438tl; IMAGE WORKS: Lisa Law 440–1c; IMPACT: Mike McQueen 203t; KIRK IRWIN: 20b, 197t, 218c, 218b, 291b, 445, 616–17. CATHERINE KARNOW: 200br; KATZ PICTURES: Lamoine 166cr; SABA/Steve Starr 25tl, Lara Jo Regan 69bl; ROBERT E KENNEDY LIBRARY: Special Collections, California Polytechnic State University 215t; KNOTT'S BERRY FARM: 236-237c, 236br, 237br; KOBAL COLLECTION: *Sabrina*, © 1995 Paramount/Brian Hamill 69tr; *LA Story*, Guild Film Distribution 69cla, *The Big Sleep*, Warner Bros 79b; *The Wild One*, Columbia Pictures 200bl. LA CONVENTION AND VISITORS' BUREAU: Michele & Tom Grimm 179; LA COUNTY MUSEUM OF ART: *La Trahison des Images (Ceci n'est pas une pipe)*, René Magritte, purchased with funds provided by the Mr & Mrs William Preston Harrison Collection, 70t; *In the Woods at Giverny: Blanche Hoschedé at Her Easel with Suzanne Hoschedé Reading*, Claude Monet, Mr & Mrs George Gard De Sylva Collection 114t; *Mother About to Wash Her Sleepy Child*, Mary Cassatt, Mrs Fred Hathaway Bixby Bequest 114cla; *Flower Day*, Diego Rivera, LA County Fund 114c; *Mulholland Drive: The Road to the Studio*, David Hockney, purchased with funds provided by the F Patrick Burnes Bequest 115t; Plate, purchased with funds provided by the Art Museum Council

115cr; Standing Warrior (The King), The Proctor Stafford Collection, purchased with funds provided by Mr and Mrs Allen C Balch 116tl; *Magdalen with the Smoking Flame*, Georges de La Tour, gift of The Ahmanson Foundation 116tr; *Monument to Honoré de Balzac*, Auguste Rodin, gift of B Gerald Cantor; 116c; *The Cotton Pickers*, Winslow Homer, Acquisition made possible by museum trustees 116b; Pair of Officials, China, 618–907, Gift of Leon Lidow 117t; Dunes, *Oceano*, Edward Weston, © 1981 Center for Creative Photography, Arizona Board of Regents 117b; LA DEPARTMENT OF WATER AND POWER: 52clb, 202b; LA DODGERS INC: 152b; Los Angeles Philharmonic: Tom Bonner 125br; JACK LONDON COLLECTION: California State Parks 26b.
MAGNES MUSEUM PERMANENT COLLECTIONS: 19th-century blue velvet embroidery brocade robe, 419t; MAGNUM PHOTOS: Michael Nichols 57bl; MARINE WORLD AFRICA USA: Charlotte Fiorito 298tr; ANDREW MCKINNEY PHOTOGRAPHY: 47cl, 300tl, 300tr, 301cr, 302tr, 303tr, 303br, 307cr, 307bc, 313crb, 331t, 346c, 369b, 381bl, 414t; METROPOLITAN TRANSIT DEVELOPMENT BOARD, SAN DIEGO: Stephen Simpson 266cla; METROPOLITAN WATER DISTRICT OF SOUTHERN CALIFORNIA: 202c; ROBERT MONDAVI WINERY: 464br; JOHN MUIR NATIONAL HISTORIC SITE: National Park Service 414b; MUNI 397t, 397cl, 397b; MUSEUM OF TELEVISION AND RADIO: Grant Mudford 90t. THE NAMES PROJECT: AIDS Memorial Quilt © 1988 Matt Herron 57cl; THE NATIONAL MOTOR MUSEUM, BEAULIEU: 201bl; PETER NEWARK'S AMERICAN PICTURES: 47br, 48br, 201tl, 303crb; PETER NEWARK'S WESTERN AMERICANA: 48cla, 48bl, 48–9c, 195 (inset), 253br, 295 (inset), 433 (inset), 519 (inset), 617 (inset); NHPA: Joe Blossom 81tr; Rich Kirchner 39t, 460c; Stephen Krasemann 503cra; P McDonald 242b; David Middleton 436t, 448t; Kevin Schafer 436b; John Shaw 219b, 230b, 279t, 436cl, 491c; Roger Tidman 241b; NEW YORK PUBLIC LIBRARY: I N Phelps Stokes Collection, Miriam and Ira D Wallach Division of Art, Prints and Photographs, The New York Public Library, Astor, Lenox and Tilden Foundations 44clb; THE NORTON SIMON FOUNDATION, PASADENA: *Still Life with Lemons, Oranges and a Rose*, Francisco de Zurbaran (1633) 156b; Buddha Enthroned, Kashmir, India (8th century) 157b; *Woman with a Book*, Pablo Picasso (1832), Estate of Robert Ellis Simon, 1969, 156t; *Saints Paul and Frediano*, Filippino Lippi (1483) 157t; *Self-Portrait*, Rembrandt van Rijn (c.1636–38) 156c; *The Little Fourteen-Year-Old Dancer*, Edgar Degas (1878–81) 157bc. COURTESY OF THE OAKLAND MUSEUM OF CALIFORNIA: *Yosemite Valley*, Albert Bierstadt (1868) 8–9; *Figure on a Porch*, Richard Diebenkorn (1959) 28cl; *Ocean Park 107* Richard Diebenkorn (1958) 424c; *Afternoon in Piedmont*, Xavier Tizoc Martinez (c.1911) 28br; *California Venus*, Rupert Schmid (c.1895) 29c; The Oakland Museum History Department: 24bl, 43b, 44cla, 44–5cb (2), 45cla, 47cr, 49ca, 49crb, 50tl, 52tr, 53cb, 56cla, 56bl, 379br, 424tl, 424tr, 424b, 425t, 441t; The Oakland Museum Kahn Collection 475b; The Oakland Tribune Collection, Gift of Alameda Newspaper Group 54b, 440cl, 440b; OXFORD SCIENTIFIC FILMS:

Daniel J Cox 437ca; Michael Fogden 496c; Stan Osolinski 437cr. PASADENA CONVENTION AND VISITORS' BUREAU: 154b; ERHARD PFEIFFER: 25tr, 30t, 30b, 31b, 63bl, 72t, 73tl, 88, 89, 90b, 91c, 120, 122cl, 132cla, 132b, 133t, 133c, 133b, 140, 141, 149t, 563b; PHOTO NETWORK: Mary Messenger 608b; Phyllis Picardi 201br; Woodard 36b; PHOTO-PHILE: 34b, 61t, 196c, 244; Jose Carrillo 37b; Scott Crain 18c; Arthur Fox 612t; Mark Gibson 607b; Jim Gray 197b; Michael Hall 68tr, 172t; Matt Lindsay 21b, 37c, 266b, 267b, 630c; Sal Maimone 127bl, 167, 196b, 252br, 434b, 522c; LLT Rhodes 46tl; PHOTO TREK INC: M J Wickham 434cb; PICTOR INTERNATIONAL–LONDON: 58–9, 62t, 62bl, 62br, 200tr, 236bl; 286–7, 292b, 299tl, 466, 498, 513t; PICTORIAL PRESS LTD: J Cummings 359b; PICTURES COLOUR LIBRARY: 22t, 39bl, 74, 123t; Leo de Wys 611c; POPPERFOTO: 516t. PRESIDIO OF SAN FRANCISCO: NPS staff photos 377tl, 377cra, 377br; RETNA PICTURES LTD: LGI Photo Agency/Marco Shark 27br; Steve Granite 69t; REUTERS: Kimberley White 57tr; REX FEATURES: 360b; RIVERSIDE MUNICIPAL MUSEUM: Chris Moser 44cr. SALINAS PUBLIC LIBRARY: Courtesy of the Steinbeck Archives, 27t, 517b; SAN FRANCISCO ART INSTITUTE: D Wakely 306c (d), 341t; SAN FRANCISCO CABLE CAR MUSEUM: 303tl, 303bl; SAN FRANCISCO CONVENTION AND VISITORS' BUREAU: 39br, Mark Gibson 302c; Courtesy of Brown, Zukov & Associates 382t; SAN FRANCISCO MUSEUM OF MODERN ART: *Back View*, 1977, Philip Guston, oil on canvas, gift of the artist, 305cr; *Zip-Light*, 1990, Sigmar Willnauer, leather, polyester, zipper, SFMOMA purchase, 318tl; *Les Valeurs Personnelles*, 1952, by Rene Magritte, purchased through a gift of Phyllis Wattis 318tr; No. 14, 1960 by Mark Rothko 318c; *Melodious Double Stops*, 1980, Richard Shaw, porcelain with decal overglaze, purchased with funds from the National Endowment for the Arts and Frank O Hamilton, Byron Meyer and Mrs Peter Schlesinger, 319tl; *The Nest*, 1994, by Louis Bourgeois, steel; Points of Departure; Connecting with Contemporary Art, March 23-August 7, 2001 318bl; *The Flower Carrier*, 1935, by Diego Rivera, oil and tempera on masonite, Albert M Bender Collection, gift of Albert M Bender in memory of Caroline Walter, 319cra; *Country Dog Gentlemen*, 1972, by Roy De Forest, polymer on canvas, gift of the Hamilton-Wells Collection, 319b; *Orange Sweater*, 1955, by Elmer Bischoff, oil on canvas, gift of Mr and Mrs Mark Schorer, 323cr; SAN FRANCISCO PUBLIC LIBRARY HISTORY ROOM: 54cla, 339bla, 369c; SAN MATEO COUNTY HISTORICAL ASSOCIATION: 412t; SANTA BARBARA MISSION ARCHIVE LIBRARY: 46cl, 47tl; SANTA BARBARA MUSEUM OF ART: *The Ripened Wheat*,

Jules Bastien-Lepage (1884), Museum purchase with funds provided by Suzette and Eugene Davidson and the Davidson Endowment Fund 220cl; SCIENCE PHOTO LIBRARY: NASA 284c; George Bernard 428b; Simon Fraser 18t; David Parker 24t; Peter Menzel 24cr, 505b; SONOMA VALLEY VISITORS' BUREAU: Bob Nixon 465b; SOUTHWEST MUSEUM: ID CT.122, Photo by Don Meyer (491.G.802) 71tr; SPECTRUM COLOUR LIBRARY: 2–3, 200tl, 265tl, 472tr, 509t, 610b; D&J Heaton 344, 562t; THE STANDARD, DOWNTOWN LA: Martin Kunz 174t; STANFORD UNIVERSITY ARCHIVES: Department of Special Collections, 51b; STEVENSON HOUSE COLLECTION, MONTEREY STATE HISTORIC PARK: Sharon Fong 508t, 509cr, 509b TONY STONE IMAGES: 38b, 413crb, 434t, 484; Jerry Alexander 463t; Glen Allison 364; Ken Biggs 36t, 63tl, 178c; James Blank 149; David Carriere 612b; Jim Corwin 310; Chad Ehlers 63tr; Johan Elzenga 280, 283, 290t, 292t; David R Frazier 442; Roy Giles, 334cla; Lorentz Gullachsen 19t; Gavin Hellier 494t; John Lamb 332; D C Lowe 487t; David Madison 611t; David Maisel 298b; Ed Pritchard 294–5; A&L Sinibaldi 19br, 435cr; Alan Smith 215b; Larry Ulrich 443; John Warden 450–1; LEVI STRAUSS & CO: 343cr, 343b; TIM STREET-PORTER: 32b, 33b, 72bl. TATE GALLERY LONDON: *It's a Psych-ological Fact that Pleasure helps your Disposition*, 1948, Eduardo Paolozzi 54–5c; TELEGRAPH COLOUR LIBRARY: 15, 18b; EDWARD THOMAS PHOTOGRAPHY: 32t. TRAVELPIX: Robert Holmes 630tr; ULSTER MUSEUM, BELFAST: By kind permission of the Trustees 45cl; © 2000 UNIVERSAL STUDIOS INC All Rights Res-erved 147b, 148tl, 148cr, 148cl, 148br, 149tr, 149bl; BY COURTESY OF THE US POSTAL SERVICE: 618t; Stamp Designs © 1995, 317c, 627t. WELLS FARGO BANK:49bl, 312b, 314b, 479b; WILLIAMS-SONOMA, INC.: 384cr; WORLD PICTURES: 16, 17b, 21t, 34c, 68tl, 136–7, 147c, 166b, 175, 199t, 226, 410, 606c, 631. YOSEMITE MUSEUM: National Park Service 44tl, 44cra, Craig & Jennifer Bates 44cl; Michael Dixon 44clb; YOSEMITE NATIONAL PARK RESEARCH LIBRARY: 51ca. ©ZEFA: 1, 39c, 438cla, 492–3; Damm 632t; K. Hackenberg 12b; BILL ZELDIS PHOTOGRAPHY: 42; ZEUM: 322clb; ZOOLOGICAL SOCIETY OF SAN DIEGO: 259b.

All other images © Dorling Kindersley. See www.DKimages.com for more information.

JACKET
Front - DK PICTURE LIBRARY: Trevor Hill cb; Neil Lukas clb; Neil Setchfield bl; GETTY IMAGES: Richard Price main image. Back - DK PICTURE LIBRARY: Max Alexander t; WORLD PICTURES: Stuart Pearce b. Spine - GETTY IMAGES: Richard Price.

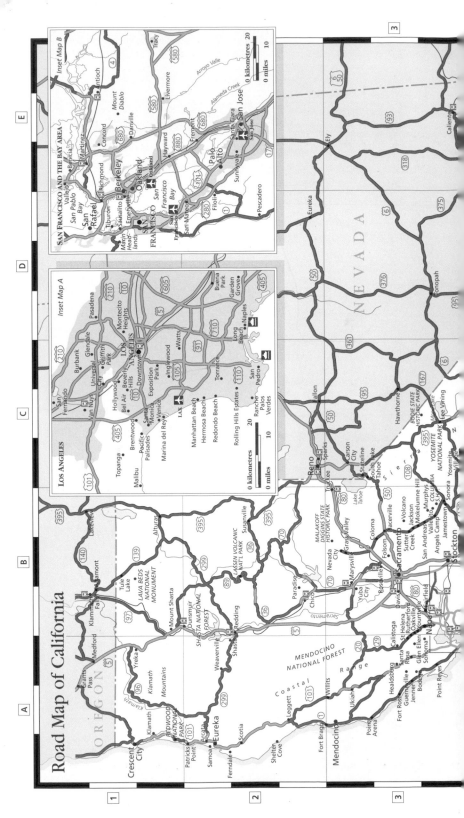

Road Map of California

Inset Map A

LOS ANGELES

Inset Map B

SAN FRANCISCO AND THE BAY AREA